MW00559398

SPARKLING GEMS FROM THE GREEK 2

SPARKLING GEMS FROM THE GREEK 2

365 New Gems To Equip and Empower You for Victory Every Day of the Year

Rick Renner

Sparkling Gems From the Greek 2
ISBN 978-0-9903247-4-4

8316 E. 73rd St.
Tulsa, OK 74133

Published by Harrison House Publishers
Shippensburg, PA 17257
www.harrisonhouse.com

4 5 6 7 8 / 23 22 21

Editorial Consultant: Cynthia D. Hansen
Text Design: Lisa Simpson, www.SimpsonProductions.net
Cover and Graphic Design: Debbie Pullman, Zoe Life Creative Media
Design@ZoeLifeCreative.com, www.ZoeLifeCreative.com

DEDICATION

I dedicate this second volume of *Sparkling Gems From the Greek*
to my dear mother, Erlita Renner.

To Mother —

From the time I was a child,
you have influenced me in the things that matter most.
You taught me the importance of loving Jesus
more than anything else in the world.
You taught me to love the Bible
and to let it be the guiding light of my life.
You demonstrated a life of service to others,
and thereby showed me how to serve.
You encouraged me to use the gifts
that God placed in my life.

Mother, I am eternally thankful for you —
for your love, for your prayers,
and for serving alongside Denise and me
all these many years.
You are an example to me in every way,
and I thank God for you.

For all these reasons and many more,
it is my joy to dedicate *Sparkling Gems 2* to you.

TABLE OF CONTENTS

ACKNOWLEDGMENTS

I would be remiss if I did not acknowledge those people whose time, talent, and effort helped to produce *Sparkling Gems From the Greek, Volume 2*. As you read and learn from this book, you will be receiving not only from the teaching God has entrusted to me, but also from the labors of others who worked with me to produce these life-changing pages.

First, I would like to thank Denise, our three sons, Paul, Philip, and Joel, and their wives, for their encouragement to me to keep writing on this enormous project. I am also thankful to my "A-Team" who regularly exhorted me to stay on track with my writing. Those who read and reap the benefits of this second volume will be eternally grateful to you.

Second, I wish to thank the staff of Rick Renner Ministries, Renner Institute, and the Moscow Good News Church pastoral team for your prayers and for your excellent attitude as I was writing for thousands of hours to produce this book. You will reap a reward in Heaven for what you are doing for the Kingdom of God and for the excellent attitude with which you are doing it. I am so thankful for you and that we serve together in the Kingdom of God.

Third, I wish to thank my editor, Cindy Hansen. As I've said before, I believe you are without a doubt the finest editor I've ever worked with, and you are tremendously loved and appreciated by Denise and me. Your touch is throughout this book, and for this I am very thankful. Not only are your editorial suggestions appreciated, but your spiritual insights are also a blessing to me. Together, as writer and editor, we are growing in the grace of God.

In addition, I wish to thank Dougal Hansen and Becky Gilbert for their help in editing and in proofreading this huge project. I'm grateful for their diligence in helping to make the many pages of this devotional easy to read and error-free. My thanks to Beth Parker and Ingrid Williams as well for adding their skill and attention to detail to the proofreading process — assistance that proved to be a great help in getting the book ready for the printer on time. I also want to acknowledge my gratitude to Andrell Corbin for her editorial contributions to this book. I am thankful for her creative and skilled assistance in bringing this volume to the level of excellence it should be.

Fourth, I want to thank Lisa Simpson for her diligence and excellence in producing the text design of *Sparkling Gems 2*. Her willingness to work long hours to help produce a book of such quality speaks volumes, and I'm grateful.

Fifth, I want to thank Cullen Swanson, Joel Renner, and Lori Stout for handling all the negotiations and logistics regarding the publishing of this book in order to get it into the readers' hands. This part of the project is huge by any definition. I'm also thankful for our Renner Institute assistant, Pam Grosse, for her help in facilitating the multifaceted process of producing this book. All of your dedication to produce this book on time and with excellence means so much to me and to our faithful family of readers. Multiplied thousands of readers will be affected because of the time and effort you have placed into this project.

Sixth, I want to express my profound gratitude to Debbie Pullman for the cover design and for being patient to work with me until we found a cover that we deemed appropriate for this second volume. You are a blessing to me in so many ways. I am thankful for you.

Last and foremost, I want to thank the Holy Spirit for empowering me to write consistently day after day, month after month, until we reached the final day of this completed devotional. Psalm 119:18 says, "Open thou mine eyes, that I may behold wondrous things out of thy law." I thank You for opening my eyes to behold wondrous truths and for showing me how to write them in a way that will be a benefit to our family of readers. I am so thankful to You, Holy Spirit, for Your work in my life!

Rick Renner
Moscow, Russia

FOREWORD

The peerless mind of God pours itself unreservedly, relentlessly, and eternally into the container of language. When conveying the glorious truths of the New Testament, the Author of Life and Sustainer of history's march chose *Koine* Greek above all the languages of earth. The Lord employed this particular tongue to articulate the fulfillment of what the Law masterfully projected and that for which the prophets longingly wept.

Although the Word translated into any language contains more than enough power to forgive, heal, and deliver to the utmost, it finds its purest expression in its original language. There is a barrier both unintentionally and unavoidably erected by layers of language between *Koine* Greek and modern vernaculars.

Although that barrier obscures the clarity of truth contained in Scripture, believers placing an appropriate value on God's Word gladly roll up their sleeves and dig through these layers to reach theological gold. They seek first to know what Scripture means in its purest form and then to accurately apply it to daily life. Those bent on such a holy endeavor will thank God for Rick Renner's work displayed in *Sparkling Gems From the Greek 2.*

I have said before that Rick Renner stands as a competent scholar, an exceptional theologian, and a brilliant author. I can attest that his language studies, exegesis, and application all prove to be rock solid. Nevertheless, the veracity of his giftings is most powerfully displayed *in the changed lives of his readers.*

The first volume of *Sparkling Gems From the Greek* has left in its wake both an endless parade of positive testimonies and incalculable destruction to the kingdom of darkness. It also sparked within the Body of Christ a desire for *more* of the rich spiritual fare that the first volume of *Sparkling Gems* offers.

Thankfully, *Sparkling Gems 2* answers that desire with more wealth than the reader could have conceived.

Rick skillfully takes away the opaque glass separating the First Century from today. He walks through the house of wisdom with its multiple storerooms, each containing massive piles of treasure, surveys what the Church needs most, and employs the key of language to unlock various doors. The result is an immense download of wisdom and truth treasures spilling forth for the discerning reader to reach out and boldly seize.

Occasionally, books have been written promising similar results. However, readers disappointedly discover that the treasure received only works in the ambiguous land of theory. This is never the case with Rick Renner. The gems of wisdom he both mines and offers freely never fade. They increase their value over time, and, most importantly, actually spend in the economy comprised of real-life challenges.

Readers applying these insights will consistently experience drastic, lasting, character-transforming results. These gems sparkle, not for show but for the illumination of truth, allowing believers to walk God's path that grows brighter and brighter until the brilliant light of the noonday sun (*see* Proverbs 4:18).

Keith Trump
BA degrees in Biblical Studies and Missions, Evangel University
Master of Divinity, Assemblies of God Theological Seminary
Recipient of American Bible Society Scholar Award
Recipient of Zondervan Medal of Achievement
for Outstanding Greek Studies

PREFACE

As I write this Preface, I am sitting in the living room of my Moscow home. I am seated in the chair that has become my meeting place with God every morning. I sensed that it was most appropriate to write these words here in this room and in this chair, where I experience God's presence every morning and where so much of *Volume 2* has been written.

I started writing *Volume 2* not long after I completed the first *Sparkling Gems From the Greek*. However, as time passed, the ministry grew, my responsibilities increased, building programs commenced, and there were other books I also needed to write. As a result, it took me nearly a decade to complete this volume that you now hold in your hands.

Yet I am certain that the time that has lapsed between *Sparkling Gems 1* and *2* will turn out to be to your advantage. During these years, I have grown both in my walk with the Lord and in my knowledge of God's Word. I believe this deeper walk is reflected in *Sparkling Gems From the Greek 2* — and I pray that you will profit from the work God has wrought in my own life over these years that have passed since the first volume was published.

Often in studying a particular verse in the New Testament, I come to a place where I think I have unearthed every gem that can possibly be found in that verse. But then the next time I study that same verse, the Holy Spirit wonderfully opens my eyes and illuminates my mind to show me "wondrous things" that I previously had not seen (*see* Psalm 119:18).

I have invested thousands of hours of prayer and study into the writing of this second volume. It is my deep desire that God will use this book and all the time invested in it to take you to a deeper, higher, and broader place in your relationship with Jesus Christ.

Although this book is designed as a daily devotional, it can also be used as a Greek reference tool for your own personal study with the help of the Greek, English, and Scripture indices in the back of the book. I ask that as you read this book, you will call upon the Holy Spirit to assist you in comprehending the truths contained in these pages. Although you utilize your mind to search and study facts, history, and language, only the Holy Spirit can illuminate your heart and impart divine revelation.

In the pages to follow, you will occasionally see a paraphrased, interpretive version of the specific New Testament verse or verses being discussed in a particular *Sparkling Gem*. These are not intended to be word-for-word translations; rather, they are designed to give you a fuller and expanded understanding of the meaning behind the scripture under discussion. I endeavored to carry that picture into a contemporary, interpretive version in order to give you a broader comprehension of what God is trying to say to you through that particular scripture.

There are approximately 1,000 Greek word studies in *Volume 2*. With the Holy Spirit as my Helper and Guide, I believe that these have been "mined" from the treasure trove of God's Word to help enrich your spiritual understanding. Each Greek word study has been written in a way that offers a practical application to your own walk with God.

As you embark on your yearlong journey with this book, I pray that the Holy Spirit will open your eyes to see "wondrous" truths you've never seen before — and that as a result, your relationship with Jesus Christ will become your dearest prize and most cherished pursuit along the road to fulfilling His good will for your life.

Rick Renner
Moscow, Russia

All scripture is given by inspiration of God,
and is profitable for doctrine,
for reproof, for correction,
for instruction in righteousness:
that the man of God may be perfect,
throughly furnished unto all good works.
— 2 Timothy 3:16,17

Open thou mine eyes,
that I may behold wondrous things
out of thy law.
— Psalm 119:18

SPARKLING GEMS FROM THE GREEK 2

365 New Gems To Equip and Empower You for Victory Every Day of the Year

Rick Renner

JANUARY 1

Say Goodbye to the Past and Hello to the Future!

Brethren, I count not myself to have apprehended:
but this one thing I do, forgetting those things
which are behind, and reaching forth
unto those things which are before.
— Philippians 3:13

On this first day of the year, family and friends are gathered together around the world to celebrate the New Year holiday. Millions of people are thinking and even talking about changes they need to make in their lives as they get started in a brand-new year. Unfortunately, this is also a day when people experience deep regret for what they didn't accomplish in the previous year, such as commitments they made to themselves that they didn't keep, promises they made to others that they left unfulfilled, or goals they set that they didn't attain. Some are disappointed in themselves for a lack of spiritual progress.

I have a suggestion for you: Rather than live in regret about what you didn't do last year, make this a day to spend some quality time with the Lord and repent for not doing what you should have done. Then make the decision to *stop wallowing in regret* about something that's in the past and that you can't do anything about now. It's time for you to shake off that negative focus of what you didn't do right last year and to start thanking God that today offers a new opportunity to do better! Think about it — *this new year presents you with a golden opportunity to make some serious changes in your life!*

That's why I love to meditate on Philippians 3:13 every year on January 1. The apostle Paul gave us sound advice for leaving the past behind and focusing on the future before us! He said, "Brethren, I count not myself to have apprehended: but this one thing I do, forgetting those things which are behind, and reaching forth unto those things which are before."

Today I want you to focus on the part of this verse that says, "...forgetting those things which are behind...." The word "forgetting" is taken from the Greek word *epilanthano*, which is a compound of the words *epi* and *lanthano*. When these two words are compounded into one word, as they are in this verse, it forms the Greek word *epilanthano*, which the *King James Version* translates as "forgetting" in Philippians 3:13. However, the first part of this Greek compound word is *epi*, which in this context denotes *a turning*, as in *turning from one thing to focus on something else*. The second part of this compound word is the word *lanthano*, which comes from a root that describes *something that is finished, done with, or obsolete.*

When these two words are joined together, they form the word *epilanthano*, which portrays the idea of something you should *turn away from* and *forget*. When used in a passive sense, it pictures something to be *put aside, deliberately ignored, purposefully disregarded,* and *completely forgotten.* It denotes something that may have really been true in the past, but is *no longer applicable.* If you were to paraphrase this word in today's language, you could say: *"Stop thinking about it! Put it out of your mind. Put it behind you, wipe it out, and erase it from your memory. Get it out of your system; quit paying attention to it; get your eyes off of it; be oblivious to it; and forget about it!"*

But wait — what was Paul telling you and me to forget about? He said we must forget "those things which are *behind*." Pay close attention to this, because what you are about to read is *really* powerful! The word "behind" is the Greek word *opiso*, which categorically describes something so obsolete that it should be permanently *relegated to the back or to the past, abandoned*, or *left behind.* This is something in your past that should be *left in the past.* It is behind you, and you are never to turn around to look at and focus on it again. In other words, the Greek word *opiso* means, *"Leave it behind and never revisit it!"*

It is *very* interesting that this word *opiso* is the same word used in Matthew 16:23 when Peter tried to interfere with the plan of God. After listening to Peter protest His impending death, Jesus spoke up with great authority and said, "...Get thee behind me, Satan...." Of course, Peter was not Satan, but the devil was speaking through Peter, as he has done with people so often throughout history — and still does today. But rather than listen to those words, Jesus spoke with firmness and rebuked the devil-inspired insinuations and ideas that were being spoken through Peter's lips.

When Jesus said, "Get thee *behind* me," the word "behind" is this same Greek word *opiso* that Paul used in Philippians 3:13 when he told us to forget the past. This means when you are hassled, harassed, or tormented about past failures, it may not be just your memories speaking to you — it could be Satan trying to harass you! This is especially true if you have already sought forgiveness and this mental onslaught continues. The devil could be trying to drag you back into regret over past things that are done with, over, and not changeable.

In such moments, you must do as Jesus did when He rebuked the devil. You must speak with *bold authority* in Jesus' name! *Speak* to those thoughts like they are enemies sent from the devil to drag you down into depression and defeat. Don't listen to them! If you do, the devil will hound you relentlessly with thoughts of failure — and little by little, you'll find yourself becoming trapped in the memories of past disappointments. Don't let that happen! It's time for you to *speak out loud* and remind the devil that those failures and negative memories are in the *past.* They are under the blood of Jesus and therefore no longer applicable! Resist those thoughts of failure just like you would resist the devil. *Command them to get behind you and to stay away forever in Jesus' name!*

Make the decision today that you're *finished* with fixing your mind on things that are in the past — things that you have repented about, that have been erased by the blood of Jesus, and that you can't do anything about now. You have the power right now to *turn away* from yesterday and start focusing on what is in front of you. Yesterday is a done deal! The clock cannot be turned back. Living in regret will only keep you from moving forward into the future.

- Maybe you made a commitment to lose weight last year, and now you're upset because you failed to do it. If so, it's time to stop moaning about the weight you *didn't* lose last year and to become willing to do whatever you must do to lose weight *this* year.
- Maybe you promised yourself that you were going to start exercising regularly and get in better shape last year, but you didn't do it. What does it profit you to sit around and condemn yourself about what you didn't do? Shake off that condemnation! *This is a new year and a new opportunity!*
- Perhaps you didn't exercise enough discipline to get your finances into better shape last year. If so, repent for being irresponsible and then stop fretting about last year's failures! Today represents a new opportunity! This is a new year and a new opportunity to get *victory* in this area of your life.
- If all you've been thinking about are the promises you made to yourself that you've broken, it's time for you to say goodbye to the failed commitments and personal disappointments in your past. Leave all those things behind you, and say *hello* to the fabulous future that lies before you!

Today is the first day of a new year — a brand-new start and a new opportunity for you to repent for past failures. *This is your opportunity to say goodbye to the past and hello to the future.* This is your golden moment to begin reaching forth to the wonderful possibilities that lie before you!

An interpretive translation of Philippians 3:13 could read:

> *"It's time for you to turn loose of the past! You need to put it aside, deliberately ignoring and purposefully disregarding what happened yesterday. The past is old and obsolete, so why fixate on it any longer? Stop turning around to reflect on the past. You need to get it out of your system, put it behind you forever, and purposefully forget about it…"*

If you've repented for past failures, it's time for you to turn them loose and let them go! Since Jesus has forgiven you, you should quit looking backward. That's right — you can put the past behind you and never revisit it again!

If you need to repent for past failures, then *repent.* But after you sincerely repent, it's time for you to quit fixating on what you failed to do last year. Thank God for *repentance* and *cleansing.* Now it's time for you to start thanking God that He has given you a new year filled with new opportunities to do better than you've done in the past 12 months! He has given you the gift of a new year, so reach forward to achieve those dreams and longings that you've put off again and again. Throw open your arms of faith, and embrace the rich future Jesus has waiting for you as you follow Him step by step in the days ahead!

MY PRAYER FOR TODAY

Father, I repent for not doing what I should have done last year, and I receive Your forgiveness. I thank You for this new year and for the new opportunity it presents for me to make serious changes in my life. You are the God who makes all things new. I yield to Your power at work in me as I deliberately choose to do Your will and to walk in Your ways with diligent obedience. Holy Spirit, I ask for and receive Your help to fulfill the will of God for my life. My past is not a prophecy of my future! Today I make the decision to put aside memories of past failures, and by faith I reach out to the future You have planned for me.

I pray this in Jesus' name!

MY CONFESSION FOR TODAY

I confess that I am not a failure and that my past is not a prophecy of my future! Even though I have not done as well as I should have in the past, God's Spirit in me will enable me to do better from this point forward. I am willing to make whatever changes I must make. I will alter my lifestyle. I will fix things in my life that are messed up. I will do whatever is required to move forward into the fabulous future God has waiting for me! From this moment on, I will run this race with my eyes fixed on the goal before me. I am committed, determined, and willing to pay any price to obtain full and complete victory in my life!

I declare this by faith in Jesus' name!

QUESTIONS FOR YOU TO CONSIDER

1. As you begin this new year, have you taken time yet to make a list of the things you would like to accomplish in the next 12 months? If not, I recommend that you take some time to pray and seek the Lord regarding what He wants you to achieve in your life this year. Afterward, write down those goals, and keep the list in a place where you can read and regularly pray over it.
2. If you failed to accomplish important tasks or goals due to a lack of commitment last year, have you taken time to repent before the Lord? It's important for you to do this so you can "clean the slate" and start this new year with a right heart before God. Why not take the time today to get honest before the Lord and ask Him to forgive you for any past failures?
3. Are there any changes you need to make — such as toxic relationships or environments you need to remove from your life — so you can fulfill what God has given you as goals for this new year? What are those changes?

JANUARY 2

It Takes Determination To Follow Through on New Year's Resolutions!

Brethren, I count not myself to have apprehended:
but this one thing I do, forgetting those things
which are behind, and reaching forth
unto those things which are before.
— Philippians 3:13

Today is the second day of the new year. If you are like many other believers, you have mentally made a list of things you'd like to change or accomplish in your life and in your walk with God this year. We often call them "New Year's resolutions" — but for us as Christians, that list should actually consist of Spirit-led commitments before the Lord concerning areas of our lives we need to focus on to further our own personal growth in the months ahead.

So if you haven't actually taken time to write down the goals God has put on your heart, it would be good for you to do that today. Writing down your vision on paper often helps you nail down what you really want to do. Keep that paper as a reminder to help you stay on track and to gauge your progress throughout the year.

As I have talked to people over the years, I have found that New Year's resolutions can often be summarized into the following categories. Of course, people make *countless* resolutions at the beginning of a new year, but the most common commitments they make are to:

- Lose weight.
- Start exercising.
- Get finances in shape.
- Work on marriage and family relationships.
- Make a deeper commitment to the Lord.

These are noble and admirable resolutions. However, for you to reach any of these goals will require a fierce determination on your part to be a *finisher* and not just a *starter*! The truth is, most people have made some of these same commitments in the past and didn't achieve them. However, as we saw in yesterday's *Sparkling Gem*, if you have already repented for past failures, you are not to live in the regret of what you didn't do yesterday. Now it's time to focus on the future. With the help of the Holy Spirit, this year you can gain victories you've never gained before! But to reach these goals, you must be very determined and committed.

This is why the apostle Paul continued to tell us in Philippians 3:13 that we must persistently be "...reaching forth unto those things which are before." This statement is packed with divine insight, so let's take a few minutes on this second day of the new year to examine the words in this verse and see how they will help us achieve our goals in the months to come.

When Paul wrote that we must be "reaching forth" to the things before us, he used the Greek word *epekteino* — an old word that was used to picture *runners in a foot race.* It is a triple compound of the words *epi*, *ek*, and *teino.* The word *epi* means *upon*; the word *ek* means *out*; and the word *teino* means *to stretch out* or *to strain forward.*

When these three words are compounded into one word as they are in Philippians 3:13, where Paul urged us to be "reaching forth" to the things before us, it portrays the mental image of *a runner who is running with all his might toward the finish line before him.* As he approaches the goal in front of him, he reaches out (*ek*) toward the goal before him. Straining with every ounce of his being (*teino*), he stretches out and *presses* toward the finish line. At long last, he leans forward to lay hold upon (*epi*) the goal — the finish line. If the runner is to reach that goal and receive the cherished prize, he must give his very best effort to the race. He can reach the finish line and win the prize, but it will not happen without a firm commitment to be the best — nor will it occur unless he possesses a willingness to push harder than any of the other runners. *This prize will go only to those who are the most determined and who have pushed the hardest!*

This lets us know that if we are to accomplish our Holy Spirit-inspired goals and win the prize, we're going to have to focus on those goals — and on God and His Word — as we commit to giving 100 percent of our efforts to achieving the desired result. Therefore:

- If you are to lose weight this year;
- If you are to establish that long-talked-about exercise regimen to get into physical shape;
- If you are to get your finances in shape the way you want to;
- If you are to enhance your marriage relationship;
- If you are to grow in your relationship with the Lord — you are going to have to run your race *to win*!

These goals are noble, but such aspirations are not attained accidentally. Success doesn't come without *sustained commitment.* If you are going to do better this year than you did last year, you must make a decision that by God's grace, you're going to *maintain* your commitment until you reach the finish line and you can say, "I achieved my goal through Christ who strengthened me!" A haphazard, "take-it-easy-and-don't-be-too-hard-on-yourself" approach will *not* cause any significant changes to take place in your life. If you are really committed to fulfilling these objectives, you must ask the Holy Spirit for His help and then start reaching forward toward these goals with every ounce of your heart, mind, soul, body, and strength.

This is precisely why I encourage you to write down your goals! When a runner runs, he keeps his eye focused on the finish line before him. That finish line is always in his sight and gives him direction as he runs. As longs as he keeps his gaze fixed on the goal before him, he runs in a straight line. But even the best runner with the best intentions will wander off course if he has no visible goal to keep him on track.

Similarly, you need clearly stated goals. So I must ask you: Can you articulate your goals? Have you written them down for this year? Today is your golden moment to begin "reaching forth" to the wonderful possibilities that God has in store for you! If you'll determine to focus on Him and on *His* plan for your new year, the Holy Spirit will empower you to make it all the way to the finish line as a winner!

The second part of Philippians 3:13 could be interpreted:

> *"You need to keep your eyes on the goal before you — straining with every ounce of your being to reach that goal, even if your success demands that you push harder than you've ever pushed before. This prize will go only to those who push the hardest. So give it your best shot!"*

This new year is your gift from God to achieve those dreams and longings you've put off again and again. Now is the time for you to commit yourself to the race and start running forward with the power of the Spirit to lay hold of the goals you and God have set for your life this year!

MY PRAYER FOR TODAY

Father, I am so grateful that You have gifted me with this new year and this new opportunity. I thank You for a fresh start to be more fruitful and to accomplish more for Your glory this year than I did last year. Help me set goals that are realistic and attainable so I can reach them by the power of the Holy Spirit assisting me. I ask You to strengthen me with might in my inner man to apply the determination and commitment to reach these goals. I praise You for the supernatural ability at my disposal according to the power that is already at work in me through Christ. I look to You to empower me as I press forward toward the finish line before me.

I pray this in Jesus' name!

MY CONFESSION FOR TODAY

I confess that I can do all things through Christ who empowers me! I finish what I start, and I accomplish whatever I set my heart to do. I do not set goals based merely on my desire, but I listen to the direction of the Holy Spirit as He guides me in setting goals for this year. He knows me better than I know myself, and He knows what I should achieve this year and where I should apply my efforts. I run my race this year with commitment, determination, and diligence. At the end of this year, I will say with a satisfied heart: "With God's help, I have achieved each goal I set out to accomplish!"

I declare this by faith in Jesus' name!

QUESTIONS FOR YOU TO CONSIDER

1. What goals have you set for this year? Do you know your goals so well that you could articulate them to someone else if that person asked you what they are? As an experiment, why don't you sit down with someone you trust and see how well you can articulate what is on your heart to achieve before the year's end?
2. Have you written your goals down where you can read them, review them, and gauge how well you are doing in achieving them? If you know your goals, write them down and put them in a visible place — such as on your refrigerator or on the mirror you use every morning — so you can be reminded of the commitments you have made for this year.
3. I assure you that you'll do better at achieving your goals if you make them a part of your daily prayer life. How can you help yourself remember to do that? Perhaps you could write down those goals and place them on your refrigerator or on a mirror you use each morning. It might also be good for you to write them on a piece of paper that you keep in your Bible or prayer journal so your goals are easily accessible for you to pray over each day.

JANUARY 3

Is It Time for You To Shed a Few Extra Pounds?

Let not sin therefore reign in your mortal body,
that ye should obey it in the lusts thereof.
— Romans 6:12

Since this is a week when you're thinking about New Year's resolutions, I want to go ahead and hit hard on the subject of losing those *extra pounds* you might think about all the time!

Have you stood in front of the mirror and lamented about the double chin that has appeared under your face in the past few years? Perhaps you spend time each morning despairing over the roll around your waist that bulges over your belt. Instead of enjoying your clothes as you once did, you may find yourself turning this way and that way as you look in the mirror to see if the bulge shows through your clothes. Or you may be one who has shifted to wearing dark colors because you're trying to hide your real size. How many times have you asked your spouse or someone else whether you look too fat in the outfit you're wearing?

It is amazing how long human beings will tolerate something before they finally decide to take action. I can personally vouch for what I am writing because I struggled with my weight for many years. Day after day, I'd look in the mirror, feel disgusted with myself, and then ask Denise how I looked — expecting her to confirm how terrible I felt about my appearance. When I got out of bed in the mornings, I'd run to the bathroom to step on the scales to see if I was bigger or smaller than the day before.

This fixation on weight completely controlled me. I felt trapped. Instead of exercising restraint, I felt hopeless to overcome. So when it was time to eat, I'd eat anything I wanted, which resulted in gaining *more* weight and feeling even more down in the dumps about my physical appearance. The truth is, I was in a prison in this area of my weight, like so many others are in today, and I didn't know how to get out.

Instead of accepting responsibility for my condition, I'd blame my weight gain on pastors who wanted to take me out to eat and enjoy a time of fellowship after evening church services. Night after night, I would find myself eating in restaurants late in the evening. But instead of exercising self-control, I'd order hamburgers with extra mayonnaise, French fries with "tons" of ketchup, and a large-size Coke, topped off with a dessert — and then I'd head to my hotel to go to bed. Then before I fell asleep, I'd mentally beat myself up for eating so badly and would swear before God that I was going to start doing better and losing weight the next day.

But time after time and year after year, I kept struggling with my weight. It was up and down, up and down! And when people would see me for the first time in a few years, I'd think they were looking me over to see if I was bigger or smaller than the last time they had seen me. It was a tormenting thought that deeply bothered me.

I was totally disgusted with myself regarding this area of my life. I was exhausted with fretting about how my clothes fit or what others thought of my size But at long last, I came to a place where I decided *enough was enough*!

The big change in me started one day as I was looking in the mirror and thinking about how terrible I looked and how food had been ruling my life. Suddenly the Holy Spirit quickened Romans 6:12 to my heart: "Let not sin therefore reign in your mortal body, that ye should obey it in the lusts thereof."

It was like a bolt of divine revelation shot through me — and in that split second, I *knew* that my allowing food to control me and to lord itself over my life was a sin. Until that day, I had called it a personal problem, a hang-up, and a struggle. But in that moment, I saw it as *God* saw it. It was much more than a personal hang-up — it was *sin* calling the shots in my life. The day I recognized this truth was a landmark day in my spiritual walk, for I realized God was calling me to repent and to change. He didn't want me to feel badly about myself — but, most importantly, He didn't want *anything* ruling my life other than the Lord Jesus Christ. That day I repented — and when I did, those wrong eating habits immediately began to lose lordship over my life.

I'm so thankful the Holy Spirit reminded me of Romans 6:12, where it says, "Let not sin therefore reign in your mortal body, that ye should obey it in the lusts thereof," the word "reign" is the Greek word *basileuo,* which is the very old Greek word for *a king* or *one who rules supreme.* It is the picture of a mighty ruler who makes all the decisions, calls all the shots, and controls and completely governs his subjects. This verse described my situation well, for I was definitely being *ruled* by food. Even though I loved Jesus with all my heart, it was simply a fact that He was not Lord over my eating habits!

But in Romans 6:12, God tells us, "*Let not* sin therefore reign in your mortal body...." Notice it says, "Let not...." The Greek tense used for "Let not" is an *authoritative prohibition* ordering us to put an end to something *immediately.* A correct interpretive translation could read, *"I want you to stop this and stop it right now!"*

When I understood that God was saying, *"Stop it and stop it right now,"* I knew I had the power to change my behavior. *God wouldn't tell me to stop something if I didn't have the power to stop it.* Therefore, He was making *me* responsible to do something about food ruling as a king in my life. It was time for me to quit complaining, moaning, fretting, and condemning myself about how I looked and to finally take action.

Instead of listening to the commands of my flesh to overeat and to eat the wrong types of food, it was time for my flesh to listen to *me*! It was up to me to make a firm, heartfelt decision to repent from this wrong lordship in my life and allow Jesus to step back on the throne of my life to rule my flesh in the area of food. As I did my part, the Holy Spirit would rise up inside me, and His grace would enable me to make sure this sin never ruled me or called the shots in my life again!

How about you? Does this discussion sound personally familiar to you? If it does, I'm wondering if you are weary of feeling badly about yourself or being constantly fixated on your weight. If so, it's time to ask yourself, *Am I ready to put an end to the way food has ruled me physically and emotionally?*

"Yes, that's me! I'm ready for a real change!" If that's your answer, today Jesus wants to assume His position over your appetite and physique. He wants to be Lord in this area of your life. If you'll confess that you've allowed this sin to rule your flesh — and then genuinely repent of it — I assure you that the Holy Spirit will help you carry out that decision. And as Jesus takes control, it won't be long until your body will begin to return to its God-ordained size and you'll begin to feel good about yourself again. *It makes such a huge difference in our lives when we allow Jesus to rule our mortal flesh!*

I shared my personal experience with you today because I know many people are making New Year's resolutions at this time of year about losing weight. *Jesus can give you the same victory He has given to so many others.* All it takes is a decision to turn from what you have been doing and let Jesus be Lord in this area of your life. You may have to follow a diet or learn to eat the right kinds of foods, but it all starts with a decision.

Just determine today that you are going to willingly obey, step by step, whatever Jesus asks you to do to get your appetite and your physical condition back under His control. If you'll make that heartfelt, sincere, and firm decision today, the Holy Spirit will empower you to eat right and to take the right steps on the road to a healthier lifestyle in your walk with God!

MY PRAYER FOR TODAY

Father, today I repent for allowing food to control so much of my life. It really has affected me in so many ways — in my thinking, my self-image, my appearance, and even my self-respect. I have lived in condemnation for too long, and I'm ready for a real change in my life. Forgive me for tolerating gluttony and calling it everything else except sin. Today I confess that I have permitted sin to rule in my mortal flesh, and I ask You to forgive me and cleanse me from this unrighteousness. Holy Spirit, I am depending on You to help me walk free of this wrong habit and make Jesus the Lord of my appetite.

I pray this in Jesus' name!

MY CONFESSION FOR TODAY

I boldly declare that Jesus is the Lord of my life and that nothing else may rule over me! My appetite for food does not lord itself over me any longer. Overeating is sin and a tool that Satan wants to use to hurt my health, my self-image, and my self-respect. I have lived in this mental prison long enough, and I refuse to live there any longer. From this day forward, I am giving Jesus the throne in every part of my life — and that includes my physical appetite and my eating habits!

I declare this by faith in Jesus' name!

QUESTIONS FOR YOU TO CONSIDER

1. Has it been a struggle for you to maintain a healthy weight over the years? What has been the main cause of weight gain in your life? How does being overweight affect your life and your self-image?
2. Have you made New Year's resolutions in the past to exercise control over your eating habits and to lose weight? Did you follow through on your past commitment? If not, why didn't you? Is it possible that your appetite has been giving the ultimate orders in your life?
3. Have you ever taken time to let the Holy Spirit show you that overeating is not just a personal hang-up or a health risk, but rather *sin* ruling in your mortal flesh? Have you ever seen it the way that *God* sees it? Don't you think it would be wise to let the Holy Spirit open your eyes to help you see that your desire for food — more than Jesus — is ruling this area of your life? If you'll let the Holy Spirit speak to your heart and if you'll truly repent of letting your flesh rule in this area, Jesus will take His place on the throne of your appetite and set you free from this prison you've been incarcerated in and held captive by for so long!

JANUARY 4

Is It Time for You To Start Exercising?

Now no chastening for the present seemeth to be joyous,
but grievous; nevertheless afterward it yieldeth the peaceable fruit
of righteousness unto them which are exercised thereby.
— Hebrews 12:11

In yesterday's *Sparkling Gem,* I encouraged you to be faithful to your commitment to lose weight this year. Today I want to take it one step further and exhort you to stick with your commitment to start exercising!

If one of your New Year's resolutions was to begin an exercise program, I want to ask you:

- Have you begun to exercise regularly as you pledged to do in this new year?
- Do you find that you are already making excuses for not getting started?
- Are you already saying, "Tomorrow I'll get started," but tomorrow keeps getting further and further away? Do you find yourself already procrastinating in this area?
- The Lord is watching as you read this, so you might as well be honest about it. How are you doing at keeping this new commitment so far this year?

It is day four of this new year. If you're still on track with your commitment to regularly exercise, well done! If you're already faltering in that commitment after just four days, you need help getting started and maintaining that heartfelt commitment to the Lord.

You may tell yourself, *Well, I'll start tomorrow.* But the world is filled with people who put things off again and again! Are you going to let that be *your* story this year as well? Are you going to take your place among world-class procrastinators who never do what they promise about getting in shape and who therefore deteriorate physically year by year because they won't take care of themselves? Remember, you need to stay strong physically not just for your own sake, but to be able to finish your spiritual race strong for Him!

So let me ask you: If you haven't done anything yet to prove that you're really serious about starting an exercise program, what are you going to do *now* to get back on track with your original commitment?

Many years ago, Denise and I decided we would start exercising regularly. Instead of purchasing Christmas gifts for one another as we normally did each year, we decided to put our money together to buy a computerized treadmill that could read blood pressure, heartbeat, and even tell us how many calories we were burning as we huffed and puffed each morning during our exercise regimen. But we felt that a treadmill was not enough, so we also purchased a stationary bicycle to be a part of our exercise equipment. The treadmill and bicycle were top-notch and cost a lot of money. Denise also wanted to work on her circulation, so we added a mini-trampoline to our collection of home equipment so she could jump up and down every morning to increase her blood circulation.

At first, we were faithful — walking, bicycling, and jumping every morning. But after a while, it got more and more difficult to get on that treadmill, bicycle, and mini-trampoline. Soon I found myself using only the treadmill — and for fewer and fewer minutes each day. It wasn't long until all that equipment became silent pieces of unused machinery in our Moscow apartment.

One day I was sitting in my easy chair, thinking about how I needed to exercise, when I looked over at the treadmill and realized it had become a platform for boxes! Clothes on hangers were now hanging from the handlebars we used to hold on to so tightly as we briskly walked! I turned to the exercise bike just behind the comfortable chair where I was sitting. The seat we once sat on while we exercised was now piled high with stacks of study books. The mini-trampoline that Denise previously jumped on each morning to get her blood circulating was sitting upright on its side against the wall, collecting dust.

As I looked at it all from my big comfortable chair where I was sitting, I remembered how noble our intentions were when we spent the money to purchase all that equipment. But Denise and I had fallen into the same trap so many people fall into when they start exercising. The biggest part of our commitment was spending money to buy the equipment, but we had not been committed enough to consistently get on the equipment and exercise. Our good intentions were not enough. The only way we would ever take control of our flesh and submit it to this discipline of exercise was if we were committed and determined to do it, *regardless* of the cost.

I pondered all the exercise equipment Denise and I had purchased and how much I *despised* exercise, despite the fact that I so wanted to be in better physical shape. Then the Holy Spirit brought Hebrews 12:11,12 to my mind, and I began to feel very uncomfortable because it brought such conviction to my heart! The passage says, "Now no chastening for the present seemeth to be joyful, but grievous; nevertheless it yieldeth the peaceable fruit of righteousness to them which are exercised thereby. Wherefore, lift up the hands that hang down, and the feeble knees."

Although this passage is actually talking about the chastening of the Lord, the fact remains that the principle is applicable to the subject of exercise or *any* form of discipline. The word "chastening" in verse 11 is actually the Greek word *paideia*, which is taken from the Greek word *pais*, the word for *a child*. However, when it becomes the word *paideia*, it refers to *child-rearing*; *child discipline*; or *the process of transforming an undisciplined child into a disciplined child*. Eventually it became a word that referred to *all* forms of discipline. Therefore, it could refer to *budgetary discipline*, *mental discipline*, *spiritual discipline*, or *physical discipline*, such as *exercise*. Therefore, the verse actually could be translated, "Now no *discipline* for the present seemeth joyful…"

Notice this verse says no discipline for the "present" seems joyful. The word "present" in Greek is the word *paron*, which literally means *at this very moment*. Let's talk about this word before we proceed any further in the study of this verse.

Isn't it true that when you're trying to teach a child discipline, this is often the moment when wills collide and that innocent-looking little child can put up the fight of a lifetime! *Isn't it amazing to see how strongly a child can resist your instructions!* At that moment, the conflict between parent and child may seem unending, but the truth is, it is *fleeting* and *temporary*. As tough as it can be to win the battle of wills and teach a child who's in authority, it is necessary for the parent to endure that moment in order to establish who's in charge and teach that child the need to obey and submit to parental authority.

However, this enduring of unpleasant moments isn't only true of dealing with children; it can be applied to any area of flesh where discipline is needed. For instance, flesh despises and resists *financial* discipline because it has to say no to things it wants to purchase. Flesh hates *dietary* discipline because it has to push away the plate when it wants to overeat. And flesh loathes the *physical* discipline of exercise because it doesn't want to be subjected to the "hardness" of such rigorous activity. It abhors the inconvenience of getting out of bed early, walking down the hallway to the exercise equipment, and feeling forced to do something physical. Flesh doesn't want *anyone* forcing discipline on it. *It's like a child who must be taught to obey!*

So as you begin the exercise program you pledged to do as a part of your New Year's resolutions, know in advance that when it's time to start exercising, your flesh will probably rant, rave, scream, resist, and recall everything you could be doing at that moment instead of exercising. It will try to escape by reminding you of other things that you need to do, people you need to call, other places you need to be, things you need to fix, and so on. The pain of discipline isn't attractive to the flesh, so it may look for a way out of that momentary discomfort.

This is exactly why Hebrews 12:11 goes on to say, "...No chastening for the present seemeth joyous...." The word "seemeth" is the Greek word *dokeo*, and in this verse, it could be translated as *feels*. The word "joyful" is the Greek word *chara*, and it means *enjoyable*, *pleasant*, or *joyful* in this context. Thus, the verse could be translated, *"No discipline feels pleasant or enjoyable at the moment it is happening...."*

This verse goes on to say that, far from enjoyable, discipline at first feels "grievous." In Greek, the word "grievous" is *lupe*, which depicts something *painful*, *sorrowful*, or something that is filled with *anguish*, *torment*, or *agony*. What a description of what I felt every time I walked to my own treadmill! My flesh did everything it could to resist it — and at times, forcing myself to get on that machine was *pure agony*! However, if I wanted to get in shape, I had to speak to my flesh and tell it to obey, whether it wanted to or not!

I have a suggestion for those moments when you fantasize about physical development and weight loss that requires no effort — or on those mornings when your flesh tries to escape exercise. It would be good for you to have a photograph placed in a visible place, such as on your refrigerator or the mirror you use each morning, that reminds you of what you'd like to look like as a result of dieting and exercising. It may be painful to get through the process of achieving that goal or vision, but the fruit of experiencing your desired outcome is worth it all!

That's why the remainder of the verse says, "...Nevertheless afterward it yieldeth the peaceable fruit of righteousness unto them which are exercised thereby." The fruit of discipline and exercise is available to anyone who is willing to pay the price to obtain it. If you and I will be willing to endure the momentary *pain, anguish, agony,* and *inconvenience* of regularly exercising, it will pay off big time when you begin to *look sharper* and actually *feel physically stronger.*

Hebrews 12:11 could be interpreted:

"No discipline feels pleasant or enjoyable at the time it is happening. But later on, it produces long-awaited righteous fruit in the lives of those who are willing to undergo the discipline required to attain it."

So when it's time for you to head to the gym or get on your home exercise equipment, expect your flesh to put up a fight and look for an escape. But just determine beforehand that you're going to steadfastly *subdue* and *conquer* that fleshly "pull" to give up on your commitment. You have to let the flesh know that it is *your* servant and *you* are the boss!

There is a price to pay for any success. You must decide how far you are willing to go to win the victory in the physical realm. What price are you willing to pay to look better and finish your race *strong*?

MY PRAYER FOR TODAY

Father, I made a commitment to begin an exercise program. It is my will to keep this promise that I made both to myself and to You. I have been convicted for a long time that I need to take better care of myself, to get into good physical shape, and to honor this body that is the temple of the Holy Spirit. I thank You for the indwelling power of the Holy Spirit who will help me take charge of my flesh in order to carry out this commitment. I receive Your grace and mercies that are new every morning to help me to exercise control over my flesh. I yield to Your quickening power that will help me maintain this position of victory. Thank You for strengthening me to remain steadfast in this area of my life, each day from this day forward.

I pray this in Jesus' name!

MY CONFESSION FOR TODAY

I confess that I am in charge of my flesh and my flesh is not in charge of me. It has ruled and dominated me long enough! So starting today, with God's help, I am taking charge and submitting my fleshly desires to the sanctifying power of the Spirit of God. My body is His temple, and I will treat it with respect. I will care for it; I will discipline and exercise it. I will do everything I can to make sure it looks good, feels strong, and is equipped to live a long and healthy life. God has a lot for me to do in this world! Therefore, I will get my body in shape so

I can run this race and have a long and blessed life with a physical body that is free from the adverse effects of physical inactivity and lack of discipline.

I declare this by faith in Jesus' name!

QUESTIONS FOR YOU TO CONSIDER

1. If one of your New Year's resolutions was to start exercising this year, how are you doing so far? Are you on track with your exercise program, or are you already losing ground in this commitment you made to yourself and to the Lord?
2. What are you going to do to change your present course of action? What is your exercise program? Exactly what kind of plan have you developed to get moving toward your goal? Can you articulate what you want to achieve and the specific goals you've set for yourself, as well as the plan to attain them?
3. If you have struggled in the past with self-discipline in this area of your life, is there someone who can exercise with you or at least check in with you every day so you can be held accountable in your new exercise regimen? Who can you bring into the process to help you stay on track in this way?

JANUARY 5

Do You Really Want To Get Your Finances in Shape?

If therefore ye have not been faithful
in the unrighteous mammon, who
will commit to your trust the true riches?
— Luke 16:11

Was getting your finances in shape one of your New Year's resolutions? Do you wish you had more money available to give to the Gospel? Do you long to be free of the credit-card debt that has a hold on your life? Do you allow debt to keep you from being obedient to God in the area of tithes and offerings?

If you answered *yes* to any of these questions, I want you to know you shouldn't feel alone, because most of the world, including the Christian community, longs for more financial freedom and less debt.

The fact is, most of the world is in financial debt. Nations are in debt; families are in debt; churches are in debt. But *you* don't have to fall into this pattern of slavery and bondage. You can be financially free if you really want freedom in this area. You just have to realize that to get free and *stay* free will require a firm commitment on your part to make some tough decisions regarding your spending habits.

Many people declare they want to be financially free. But when it's time to say no to something they really want to buy and to wait until later when they can pay cash for it, their flesh cries out to have it *now*!

But that is when the true level of your commitment becomes evident. At that time, you must decide: Will you stick with your commitment to exercise discipline and self-control and thereby stay debt-free or avoid incurring new debt? Or will you succumb to the flesh and make that purchase using your credit card, thereby adding to your debt load? It may be difficult to stick with your commitment to do what it takes to become free of debt. But if you'll exercise discipline and self-control in these types of decisions, afterward you'll be happy you did when you're on a solid foundation in your finances! And you'll never stop thanking God for helping you do what you committed to do until you reached your goal — *financial freedom for life*!

For most people, credit is easy to get; all they need to do is apply for a credit card. It's also easy to use! But it *isn't* so easy to get free from the debt that builds up from using it. It's all so convenient and so deceiving as the message is hurled at people, "Why delay purchasing what you want now when you can charge it, enjoy it, and pay for it later?" But the reality is that debt is a destroyer if not properly managed, as is evidenced by the nearly two million credit-card holders who declare bankruptcy each year in the United States. And one of the largest contributors to these bankruptcies is last-minute, emotional spending on credit cards.

So — do you *really* wish you had more available money to give to the Gospel or to meet the needs of others? Do you long to be free from the load of debt that has a hold on your life? Are you burdened by the struggle to pay your tithe?

If your answer is *yes*, it's time to ask God for specific wisdom regarding what needs to be adjusted in your life. For instance, do you owe too much money to creditors because you didn't exercise discipline and wait to make certain purchases? Do you carry a balance on your credit card and pay a large amount of monthly interest to your creditors?

If you were free of credit debt, you would have more money to give to the Gospel and to meet the needs of others. And if you weren't paying so much interest to your creditors, it would be much easier for you to obey God with your tithes and offerings — which would remove any guilt you carry in your soul from feeling like you're robbing Him and His Kingdom.

You probably don't have a real picture of how much you're paying in interest each month, so it would be good for you to take a look at your monthly bills, add up how much you're paying in interest, and see how much money you're throwing away each month on those interest payments. This situation of compounded interest is so serious in the United States that the total amount of finance charges paid annually is astronomical! At the time I am writing this book, consumer debt is completely out of control! European debt is growing at a similar pace. *This means there are very few people in this world who are financially free.*

But just because the rest of the world has fallen into this trap and so many people live like this doesn't mean *you* have to remain trapped in the prison of debt. The truth is, how you handle your finances is a very spiritual issue. According to Luke 16:11, your finances — how you manage and respect them — is a test God uses to assess whether or not you are ready for higher levels of blessing, prosperity, responsibility, and authority. Jesus clearly taught that God watches how you manage your money and that this helps Him determine if you are ready for promotion. This is precisely what Jesus meant in Luke 16:11 when He said, "If therefore ye have not been faithful in the unrighteous mammon, who will commit to your trust the true riches?"

Pay attention, because it is very important for you to understand what Jesus was telling us in this verse. In the Greek New Testament, the word "faithful" used in this verse is the word *pistoi*, which paints a picture of someone who is known to be *faithful, responsible, conscientious*, and *trustworthy* — in contrast to a person who is *impetuous, thoughtless, rash, irresponsible*, and therefore *not trustworthy*. This verse could be interpreted to mean: *"If you are impetuous, thoughtless, rash, irresponsible, and untrustworthy with unrighteous mammon, who will commit to your trust the true riches?"*

The word "unrighteous" is from the Greek word *adikia*, which in this verse is used to convey the idea of something *unspiritual, common, worldly*, or *something that belongs to the realm of human beings*. The word "mammon" is the word *mamonas*, a very old Greek word that denotes *money* or *wealth*. When these words "unrighteous mammon" are used together as they are in this verse, it means *common, worldly money*. It refers to money with all of its buying power in this earthly sphere. In this verse it means, *"If you are impetuous, thoughtless, rash, irresponsible, and untrustworthy with money and all of its buying power in this earthly realm, who will commit to your trust the TRUE riches?"*

When Jesus refers to "true riches," the word "true" is the Greek word *alethinos*, which means *true, real, bona fide, genuine, indisputable*, or *authentic*. You see, money seems so powerful in this earthly realm with all of its buying power, but it's *nothing* compared to the power of God! Heavenly power and heavenly riches far surpass the power and authority of money. For those who have proven themselves faithful and reliable, God will upgrade the level of spiritual power and authority that operates through them. But according to Jesus' words in Luke 16:11, before God upgrades this level of spiritual power and authority in a person's life, first He watches to see how the person manages money. That's the *big* test!

If you aren't faithful, responsible, and trustworthy with money, which is the lowest form of power in this earthly realm, why would God promote you into greater levels of spiritual power, responsibility, and authority?

Your money — how you handle it, how you manage it, and what you do with it — is far more important than you've ever realized. It's good that you want to get your finances in shape this year and get out of debt, but you need to know that *what you do with your money is a big test*. God is watching to see how you are managing it, and what you are doing with it. If He finds you faithful with money, He will know you can be trusted with real spiritual riches that are unequaled in power.

So determine to listen to the Spirit of God, use common sense, exercise self-control, and plan your purchases in advance. As you do, you will begin to live a life that becomes freer and freer of debt — until the day arrives when you are out from under that burden *completely*! It will take determination to do it, but if you really want to become debt-free and *remain* free, there *is* a way for you to achieve it!

MY PRAYER FOR TODAY

Lord, I am so thankful that You have spoken to my heart today about my finances. The Holy Spirit has been speaking to my heart about getting my finances into better shape, and I now see how crucial it is that I pass this very important test. I want You to trust me with promotion to higher levels of responsibility, authority, and spiritual power. Therefore, I ask You to help me prove myself trustworthy by demonstrating my readiness for promotion by the way I handle my finances. Thank You for granting me divine wisdom, strategies, and strength to help me stay the course until I am finally debt-free!

I pray this in Jesus' name!

MY CONFESSION FOR TODAY

I confess that I listen to the Spirit of God. I have the mind of Christ, and I walk in divine wisdom concerning finances in my life. I will exercise self-control, and I am disciplined in all things. I plan my purchases in advance and practice restraint so I can live a debt-free life. I am determined to remain free with the Holy Spirit's help. I make the decision to get my finances in order. Therefore, I diligently manage my money, and I spend it with prudence. As a result, I pass this test that is so important in the eyes of God.

I declare this by faith in Jesus' name!

QUESTIONS FOR YOU TO CONSIDER

1. Do you know how much money you are spending on interest every month? Have you ever taken a look at all your credit cards, lines of credit, and other forms of debt to see how much money you are "throwing away" each month that could be used in other ways if you were *not* in debt?
2. Do you pay your tithe on your income? Are you able to support other ministries as the Holy Spirit leads you, or does your debt burden keep you from being the blessing you really want to be?
3. What specific steps come to mind that you could start taking *today* to get on the path that leads to financial freedom? Write those steps down, and then continue to add to the list as God gives you wisdom. Trust Him to help you develop a "getting out of debt" plan that works as you focus on reaching this all-important goal this year. Then determine to *stick to the plan*!

JANUARY 6

Do You Really Want To Improve Your Relationships This Year?

And the things that thou hast heard of me
among many witnesses, the same commit thou
to faithful men, who shall be able to teach others also.
— 2 Timothy 2:2

The holiday season is a time when family and friends gather to celebrate — but it is also a time when some experience profound loneliness, heaviness, depression, and feelings of isolation. This is especially true if a loved one has died or if a person has suffered the loss of a relationship in the previous year. You may have experienced some of these emotions yourself this past holiday season.

If people have deficiencies in their relationships, the holiday season has a way of bringing them face to face with that deficit. Frequently that deficit becomes visible *because* they are with family and friends with whom they have had past personality conflicts, struggles, or disagreements. As a result, holidays can be times when old wounds are reopened, and emotions that a person thought were dealt with and dead start screaming again. Personalities collide. Feelings are hurt. People get rubbed the wrong way. Regretful words are spoken. And what *should* have been a wonderful time together degenerates into another hurtful event.

It is a statistical fact that the holiday season is among the most emotionally charged times of the year. This is one reason why we who are mature in the Lord must be a source of peace in potentially difficult situations, and we must keep a watchful eye on those who struggle with personal loss and loneliness. We also need to stay sensitive to the Holy Spirit, who frequently uses this time of year to confront us with the status of our relationships — and awaken us to our need to improve them.

So let me ask you — as you gathered with family and friends over the holidays, did the Holy Spirit make you aware of relationships that needed your attention and improvement? Did you experience loneliness or become conscious of your need to reach out to make new friends in order to fill a void in your life? Do you presently feel satisfied with the condition of your relationships, or are you aware of your need to put forth extra effort in order to take them to a higher level?

Relationships are like savings accounts; you have to put something *into* them if you expect to get something *out of* them. If all you do is *take*, eventually you will drain that relationship, like a bank account that gets drained and has nothing left in it. For your relationships to remain healthy and vibrant, you need to make many deposits into them. As you invest in the people in your life, they will grow. But if you put nothing *into* a relationship and keep expecting to take *from* that other person, you will eventually come to a point where that relationship will be drained and nothing will be left for you to draw upon. That's when you'll regret that you didn't make better choices and invest more into that relationship to make it the long-lasting blessing God intended it to be in both your lives.

But you don't have to live with that kind of regret. If you'll make the proper investments into your relationships today, it will pay off tomorrow. Even if you've made mistakes in past relationships and you are facing the consequences of that now, there is no need to despair. The Holy Spirit is present to restore your soul and help you start making right investments into the people God has brought into your life. You can enjoy healthy, fulfilling relationships to the very end of your life. *It's never too late to start!*

When Timothy was presiding as senior pastor of the church of Ephesus, he came face to face with a deficit in his own relationships. Those leaders he thought were his friends — those he assumed would be with him to the end — were the very ones who walked out and deserted him during the worst moments of persecution he and his church had ever faced. Timothy thought he would be able to lean on these coworkers in the Kingdom during difficult and challenging times, yet they abandoned him in his hour of need.

I can't even begin to imagine the feelings of hurt, loneliness, and isolation Timothy must have felt at that time. He was, in fact, so hurt by this experience that he wrote to the apostle Paul and asked for spiritual help. Paul wrote back to the younger minister, and the letter Paul wrote to him became the book of Second Timothy in the New Testament.

In Second Timothy 2:2, Paul wrote to his young disciple and told him, "...The things that thou has heard of me among many witnesses, the same *commit* thou to faithful men, who shall be able to teach others also." The word "commit" in this verse is a powerful key to building strong and lasting relationships. It is the Greek word *parathou*, which is a compound of the words, *para* and *thou*, the latter being a form of the word *tithemi*. The word *para* means *alongside* and carries the idea of a close relationship. This word *para* emphatically pictures two or more people who *stand side by side* or *are mentally, spiritually, or physically in close proximity to each other*. The word *thou*, a form of the Greek word *tithemi*, means *to place, to put*, or *to deposit*. When the words *para* and *tithemi* are compounded into one word, the new word is *parathou*, which means *to come closely alongside someone else in order to put, place, or deposit a part of oneself into that person.*

Paul was telling Timothy that he couldn't afford to sit in despair and loneliness over the loss and disappointment of close relationships. It was time for Timothy to start all over again and "commit" himself to a new group of people and friends. As difficult as it was for Timothy to do this, he had to push beyond his hurt, reach out to strengthen the relationships that remained, and choose new people to draw close to and build a future with. It *wasn't* time for him to "tuck his tail and run." It was time for him to *parathou* — *to come closely alongside others in order to put, place, or deposit a part of himself into them.*

So Paul instructed Timothy to commit himself to "faithful men." Although it isn't stated emphatically, it is implied that the group who disappointed Timothy were not faithful people.

Perhaps they were talented, bright, and full of potential, but they lacked the most important quality in relationships: *faithfulness*. As Timothy got ready to start all over again, Paul counseled him, "This time, make sure you invest yourself into people who are faithful." The good news was that all the unfaithful people were gone already. Only faithful people remained, making it easier for Timothy to select people he could depend on even in difficult times of challenge and pressure.

The same may be true in your life. If you have felt forsaken, abandoned, or disappointed by certain people you thought were trustworthy, at least you now know who is faithful, for they are the ones who are still standing alongside you. They may not shine as brilliantly as the others who have disappeared from your life, but at least you can easily identify the people who will stick with you through difficult times. Those who have faithfully stayed with you through all your difficulties are exactly the kind of people who are worthy of your personal investment into them.

You may be at a similar crossroads moment to Timothy's. It may be time for *you* to shake off a spirit of despair that has tried to attach itself to you. If that describes your situation, you can decide today to stop wallowing in discouragement concerning things that are in the past and are unfixable. If you made a mistake, learn from it and let the Holy Spirit lead you into the wonderful life that lies directly ahead of you. As you reach out to build new and better relationships, any feelings of loneliness, heaviness, or depression will go.

This week, if you have become aware of a relationship that needs attention or if you have come face to face with mistakes you have made in past relationships, determine to learn from the experience and then get over it as quickly as possible so you can move forward in life. As you allow the Holy Spirit to help you, He will show you how to make solid investments into your new relationships. He'll also guide you in making fresh deposits into the lives of those who have been close to you for many years.

So I encourage you to let this be your commitment: "I will do all I know to do to keep the relationships God has brought into my life healthy and long-lasting — starting today!"

MY PRAYER FOR TODAY

Lord, I realize that I've made some mistakes in my relationships in the past. I know I got too busy at times and quit making deposits into the people I loved and needed. I expected them to perform for me, but I didn't put enough good back into them, and now I'm experiencing the consequences both of my actions and my inaction. Please forgive me for not showing appreciation to the people who are so precious to me. I repent for misplacing my priorities. I ask You to please help me restore the relationships that are restorable and to strengthen the relationships that remain in my life right now. Help me make solid investments into the people who are close to me so I can be a real blessing to them and so these relationships will stay strong and close till the very end of my life.

I pray this in Jesus' name!

MY CONFESSION FOR TODAY

Today I shake off the spirit of despair that has tried to attach itself to me. I refuse to wallow in discouragement about things that are over and unfixable. I have repented and received forgiveness for my mistakes, so I will learn from them and let the Holy Spirit lead me into the wonderful future that lies directly ahead of me. Feelings of loneliness and isolation are lying emotions that must go in Jesus' name! The Lord surrounds me with people who stick with me through times of difficulty. These faithful people are worthy of my time, attention, and personal investments. Therefore, I forget the past and its pain, and by faith in God I allow myself to build new relationships and to trust again.

I declare this by faith in Jesus' name!

QUESTIONS FOR YOU TO CONSIDER

1. How has your first week of the new year been so far? As you gathered with family and friends, has the Holy Spirit made you aware of relationships that need your attention and improvement?
2. Have you experienced loneliness and become conscious of your need to reach out to and make new friends to fill the void that currently exists in your life? Have you felt satisfied with the condition of your relationships, or are you aware of your need to put forth extra effort in order to take your relationships to a higher level?
3. What do you need to do to make your relationships stronger? What is the Holy Spirit saying to your heart about the deposits you need to make into your present and even your future relationships so that those relationships will remain vibrant and long-lasting?

JANUARY 7

The Power of a Daily Habit: Reading Your Bible

All scripture is given by inspiration of God,
and is profitable for doctrine, for reproof, for correction,
for instruction in righteousness.
— 2 Timothy 3:16

When I was a small boy, every summer I attended the Vacation Bible School that was conducted at our church. I loved it so much! It was one of the highlights of my summertime.

What wonderful memories I have of those times in my childhood! I'm so thankful that my parents loved me enough to make sure I took advantage of every opportunity to learn the Bible. That Vacation Bible School was a magnificent tool to help place God's Word into the tender hearts of every child who participated each summer.

One of my favorite memories from Vacation Bible School was the moment when all of us children marched like soldiers into the main church auditorium and took our seats for the opening morning session each day. Once we were all in our places, the pastor stood in the pulpit, commanded us to stand, and led us in the morning Bible pledge. Every year at the beginning of each day of Vacation Bible School, we all lifted our voices and boldly proclaimed:

I pledge allegiance to the Bible, God's Holy Word.
I will make it a lamp unto my feet,
a light unto my path,
and I will hide its words in my heart
that I might not sin against God.

Since that time, I admit that I've had to regularly renew my commitment to make God's Word the center of my life. Although I am a pastor, Christian educator, author of Christian books, and a visible Christian leader, I must conquer the same struggles that others face, including the temptation to get so busy that I unintentionally neglect the daily reading of my Bible. Time and again, I've spoken to my flesh, commanding it to get back in line, and I've deliberately renewed my commitment to make God's Word the center of my existence.

I even find myself inwardly repeating the simple pledge I made as a child at Vacation Bible School. That pledge made such an impact on my soul as a child that I still repeat it as I once again commit myself to the daily reading of the Bible. The words of that pledge remain deep inside me and continue to impact me even to this day.

What about you? Have you made a commitment to God to read your Bible every day? Is this an area in which you've been on again, off again? Would you like to become consistent and regular in reading God's Word? If you'll allow the Holy Spirit to help you, you can win this victory in your life. And even if you unintentionally skip your reading of the Bible for a few days, don't let the devil condemn you. Ask for forgiveness and get back on schedule.

The truth is, there is nothing more powerful than the Word of God! It has the answer to every question you will ever ask, and it contains the power to meet every need in your life. The Word promises that if you will obey it, it will produce health for your body. In essence, it is the answer to every human need.

Conversely, when you neglect God's Word and fail to include it in your daily life, that neglect will eventually affect every part of your life. The regular absence of God's Word from your life will jeopardize your faith, steal your joy, produce an intolerance of others, and create putrid attitudes that disgust not only God and others, but *you* as well! In fact, ignoring the daily reading of your Bible will affect your ability to be spiritually productive and eventually make you *spiritually infertile.*

Paul wrote, "All scripture is given by inspiration of God, and is profitable for doctrine, for reproof, for correction, for instruction in righteousness" (2 Timothy 3:16). In the May 2 *Gem* of *Sparkling Gems 1*, I share extensive insight about the word "inspiration" in this verse. If you have not read it, I strongly encourage you to study those pages because I believe it will richly bless you. But today let's look at the benefits of God's Word that the apostle Paul listed in Second Timothy 3:16. Once you really understand what the Word of God does for you every day when you take time to read it, you will find yourself getting more and more passionate about protecting your Bible reading time!

Paul wrote that the Bible is "...profitable for doctrine, for reproof, for correction, for instruction in righteousness." Let's look at each part of this verse so we can get the full benefit of what Paul was telling us. First, he stated that the Bible is "profitable for doctrine." The word "profitable" is the Greek word *opheilo*. The meaning of this word includes the idea of something that is *needful* or *obligatory*, like a *debt* that is owed. It can be translated as the word *indebted*, and it refers to something that is *mandatory*, *essential*, or *an absolute requirement*. By using this word, Paul was telling us that God's Word is not optional in our lives; it is *mandatory*, *essential*, and *an absolute requirement* for us.

Paul connected the word "profitable" to the word "doctrine," which is the Greek word *didaskalia*, the word for *doctrine* used in the New Testament to denote *those things that we affirm and believe to be true*. Some Christians sneer at the mention of "doctrine," thinking it to be stuffy or unimportant. But that kind of attitude reveals their ignorance regarding the importance of doctrine.

Doctrine is the foundation of what we believe. It impacts what we think. It affects our worldview. It determines what we believe is right and wrong. It guides us in life, determines our convictions and standards, and affects all of our actions and activities in life.

In short, we are the product of our doctrine. Therefore, it is *mandatory, essential, obligatory,* and *an absolute requirement* that our lives be based and built on the Bible and that we must see ourselves as indebted to it. It is also very important to point out that the word "profitable," the Greek word *opheilo*, was originally a word used in connection with *law*. Just as laws must be obeyed and we are obligated to live by them, we as believers must live our lives with the Bible as our guidebook and our law for life, obeying it absolutely to the best of our ability. If we take this approach, the power of God's Word will be released in our lives, causing us to profit in every realm of our existence!

Next, Paul wrote that the Word of God produces "reproof" in our lives. The word "reproof" in Greek is *elegmos* and is found nowhere else in the New Testament. In the Septuagint version of the Old Testament, the word *elegmos* is used for *conviction*. When God's Word shines into our lives, its glorious and brilliant light is so strong that it exposes every dark area that remains in our souls and minds. As the light of the Word shines on our darkness and works in our hearts and minds, we are *reproved*, *convicted*, or *censured* by the Holy Spirit. As a result, we don't remain in darkness! We are *changed* as our minds are renewed to think correctly. *What a benefit the Word of God is to us!*

Paul went on to write that the Word of God brings "correction" into our lives. But wait — isn't the word "reproof" that is mentioned above the same as "correction"? What is the difference between these two words?

The word "correction" is actually very different from the word "reproof." One reason it doesn't seem so is that "correction" is a poor translation of the Greek word *epanorthosis*. This word is very difficult to translate, but the following is a serious attempt to convey its meaning. The word *epanorthosis* is actually a Greek triple compound composed of the words *epei*, *an*, and *orthos*. When *epei* and *an* are compounded, the new word means *whenever*, *at any moment*, or *at any time*. The third Greek word in this compound is *orthos*, which means *straight*, *erect*, *upright*, or *level*.

So let's see what this triple compound word *epanorthosis* — "correction" — means in Second Timothy 3:16, where Paul used it in connection with the power of the Bible. The apostle was declaring that *whenever*, *wherever*, *at any moment*, or *at any time* a person makes the decision to build his life on the Word of God — and to allow its light to shine into the deepest parts of his being to expose the dark areas that need to be changed — that Word will release the power required for the necessary change. God's Word will lift that person, even if he has been knocked flat on his back in life, and will *set him back up on his feet again*. This "correction" that comes from God's Word will cause him once again to *stand erect* and *upright*, regardless of how long he has been down and out. The Word of God will release so much power in that person's life that it will *put him back on level ground*!

Once it has put that person back on his feet, the Word of God will then become his "instruction in righteousness." The word "instruction" in Greek is *paideia*, from the word *pais*, which is the Greek word for a *child*. The word *paideia* used in this verse means *to train a child*. In New Testament times, it simply meant *to educate a child* or *to give a child everything necessary to prepare him for life*. Hence, this word simply refers to *child training* or *the process of getting a child ready for life so afterward he can be sent out fully equipped and successfully live as he was taught and trained to do*. It was believed by the ancients that such child training was essential for success in life.

The word "righteousness" is *dikaiosune*, from the root word *dikaios*, which is the Greek word for *that which is right or just*. Although this word has a wide range of meanings in the New Testament, the form *dikaiosune* in this verse refers to *right living* or *just living*, and it epitomizes those who live by a *righteous standard* that results in *upright living*. When used in connection with the word "instruction," the Greek word *paideia*, it tells us that when God's Word is taken into our hearts and applied to our lives, it fully equips us *to successfully live by a higher standard* that leads to *upright, godly, clean living*.

When you put all of these word meanings together,
an interpretive translation
of Second Timothy 3:16 could read:

"All Scripture is given by inspiration of God and is a mandatory, essential, and absolute requirement for those things we affirm and believe to be true. It brings reproof, conviction, and censure into our lives. It can take anyone — including those who have been knocked flat on their backs in life — and it can set them back up on their feet again, regardless of how long

they have been down and out. The Word of God will make them once again stand erect and upright. It will put them back on level ground, fully equipping them to successfully live life by a higher standard that leads to upright, godly, clean living."

When you see all the benefits of God's Word, it is amazing that you would ever skip a day of reading the Bible! There is no other book in the world like the Bible. It literally has the power to change your life and put you on a path for success.

As you start this new year, let me encourage you to renew your commitment to read your Bible every day. With all the benefits you've read about today, why would you not include God's Word in your daily schedule? Yes, I know that life gets busy, but it should never get too busy to exclude this wonderful Book that has the power to put you back on your feet and keep you on level ground!

If you've been on again, off again in reading the Bible every day, this year is your opportunity to break this sporadic pattern and become *consistent* in reading God's Word every day. The Holy Spirit is your Helper, so ask Him to help you develop a daily habit of reading the Bible. It would be a good idea to make plans to read the entire Bible this year. I promise you that by the time you've completed that goal, the power in God's Word will have made a huge change in how you think, in how you behave, and in the way you see life. *You'll be a much better person because you decided to make God's Word a central part of your existence.*

MY PRAYER FOR TODAY

Lord, I am amazed at the power of Your Word and what it can do in the life of anyone who will read it, believe it, and apply it to his or her life. Every answer I need for life is in the Bible, whether it be for healing, deliverance, marriage, children, health, business, or success. Heavenly Father, thank You for giving us the Word of God. Please forgive me for the times I've let it sit on my shelf instead of reading it, meditating on it, and incorporating it into my life. This year I ask You to help me break the pattern of being on again, off again in reading my Bible. I thank You that by Your grace, I will become a consistent reader and applier of God's Word to every part of my life!

I pray this in Jesus' name!

MY CONFESSION FOR TODAY

I confess that I read my Bible every day. I do not skip days, forgetting to read it. God's words are the very center of my existence, and I draw my strength from what I read in my Bible every day. It shines its glorious light into every dark part of my soul and renews my thinking to what God thinks. I receive the conviction God's Word brings to areas of my life that are wrong. It picks me up, sets me back up on my feet, and keeps me on level ground. The Word of God prepares and equips me with everything I need to live a successful and godly life in this world.

I declare this by faith in Jesus' name!

QUESTIONS FOR YOU TO CONSIDER

1. Do you have a habit of reading your Bible every day? If yes, do you really ponder the truths you are reading so you can apply them to your life?
2. If you were advising others about how to start reading their Bible every day, what advice would you give them? Do you have a specific plan to help you read through the Bible every year?
3. Can you think of ways that your life has been changed because of God's Word affecting the way you think? Take a few minutes and write down ten ways that your life has been changed or strengthened as a result of making God's Word a daily part of your life.

JANUARY 8

Kick Back and Take a Breather Every Once in a While!

And to you who are troubled rest with us,
when the Lord Jesus shall be revealed
from heaven with his mighty angels.
— 2 Thessalonians 1:7

Whether we like it or not, there are moments when we run into troubling times in our lives. The trouble may arise in our job, our marriage, our children, our finances, or some other area of our lives. It can feel like there is no let-up from the constant, never-ending grind of what is happening to us. Although we can take this kind of nonstop pressure for a while, eventually it becomes too much if there is no let-up from it, and we begin to feel like we're going to collapse from the burden we're carrying.

If we walk in the Spirit, we can avoid many pitfalls that the devil and life try to throw our way. But the truth is, as long as we are in the world — where the devil actively seeks to kill, steal, and destroy — there will be troubles from time to time in our lives. Therefore, we need to know how to respond when we feel like we are being assaulted by nonstop problems and there seems to be no let-up or relief from the stress we're experiencing.

I remember a time in Moscow when I was battling enemies on every front. Because our church was rapidly growing, we were in perpetual need of more finances. In addition, we had been kicked out of several auditoriums by local authorities and were about to be kicked out again. I felt like we were spending our lives searching high and low for an auditorium that would accommodate our growing church, but to no avail. We couldn't seem to find another auditorium for our church meetings, and time was running out. *I felt like I was at the end of my rope!*

I lay in my bed night after night, asking God to help us find a solution to these problems. Finally, Denise said to me, "Rick, you need to get away and take a break from all this!"

I asked her, "How can I take a break when we are in such a tight jam? How can I get away right now when we're facing so many challenges?"

She answered, "If you'll get away and rest a little — if you'll step back from these all-consuming problems — your thoughts will clear up. It will be easier to see the situation from *God's* perspective so you can receive the wisdom you need from Him."

I remember thinking how irresponsible it would be for me to get away during such a time of difficulty. But I was studying my Bible at that moment, and just then I saw something in Second Thessalonians 1:7 I had never seen before. Paul told the Thessalonians, "And to you who are troubled *rest* with us...." When I saw that word "rest," I reached for my Greek New Testament to look it up — and was I ever blessed when I saw what it meant!

Before I tell you what I discovered that day, let me first give you a little bit of background about what was happening to the Thessalonian church at the time the apostle Paul wrote this verse to them.

Paul and his apostolic team first preached the Gospel in Thessalonica and subsequently established the church there (*see* Acts 17:1-9). It was during this time that he and his team laid the first foundations for a church that would eventually challenge the forces of paganism and the hatred of the Jews. The opposition from the Jews became so intense and violent that they were driven from the city and fled to Berea (*see* Acts 17:10).

Because of the spiritual, religious, and political environment in Thessalonica, the intensity of persecution there was terrific — among the most outrageous demonstrations of persecution that occurred while the New Testament Church was being established. Although these believers were submitted to pounding pressures from outside forces, they refused to surrender to defeat. Day after day, they lived, breathed, and functioned without relief within this climate of extreme persecution and pressure. That is why Paul told them, "And to you who are *troubled* rest with us...."

The word "troubled" in this verse was a favorite word with Paul when he described the difficult events he and his team encountered in ministry. It is the Greek word *thlipsis* — a word so *strong* that it leaves no room for the *intensity* of these persecutions to be misunderstood. It conveys the idea of a *heavy-pressure situation.* One scholar says it was first used to describe *the specific act of tying a victim with a rope, laying him on his back, and then placing a huge boulder on top of him until his body was crushed.* Paul used this word to alert us to moments when he or others went through *grueling, crushing situations* that would have been *unbearable, intolerable,* and *impossible to survive* if it had not been for the help of the Holy Spirit.

Then Paul went on to say, "To those of you who are troubled *rest* with us...." The word "rest" is the Greek word *anesis*, which means *to let up, to relax, to stop being stressed,* or *to find relief.* One scholar notes that it was used in the secular Greek world to denote *the release of a bowstring that has been under great pressure.* It was also used figuratively to mean *relaxation from the stresses of life* or *freedom to have a little recreation.* In this case, Paul was urging the Thessalonians to find *relief* from the constant stress they were undergoing as a result of opposition to their faith. Paul exhorted them *to let it go, shake it off,* and learn how to find *relief,* even in the midst of difficult circumstances.

An interpretive translation of Second Thessalonians 1:7 could read:

> *"To you who are going through difficulties right now, it's time for you to let up, take a breather, and relax. We know what it's like to be under constant pressure, but no one can stay under that kind of stress continuously. So join us in learning how to loosen up a bit. Shake off your troubles, and allow yourself a little relaxation and time for recreation."*

When I saw these Greek words in this verse, I told my wife, "You're right! I need a break from all these troubles — and here's a scripture that confirms it! It tells me I need to loosen up and allow myself a little time for relaxation and recreation."

So I took time away from the office, refused to talk about work, and simply allowed myself to enjoy a few days with no pressure. And when I returned to work, I found that I could clearly see the answer I had been struggling to find.

If you feel depleted and fatigued, is it possible that you need to get away for a little while? Could it be that the Lord is urging you to take a breather from the constant pace you're maintaining so you can shake off the problems and relax a little bit? Don't you agree that when you're under constant pressure, it affects your ability to think right and see things clearly? Now you have a scripture to back you up when you need to get alone with the Lord to pray and worship Him — or simply allow yourself some time for recreation. And don't feel guilty about it — *it's the recommendation of the apostle Paul himself*!

We live in a world that is spinning faster and faster, so we have to learn how to keep our lives in balance so we can keep our focus clear. *So why don't you start putting a little time aside for yourself so you can shake off the problems that are trying to steal your joy today!*

MY PRAYER FOR TODAY

Lord, I ask for wisdom to know how to balance my life and work with times of relaxation and recreation. I am tempted to work nonstop and never take a break, and as a result, I get tired and worn out. Forgive me for not taking better care of myself. I yield to Your peace, and I resist the feelings of guilt that try to overwhelm me when I am away from my work and responsibilities. I now know that You want me to take a break from this constant pace and learn to relax a little. Holy Spirit, I thank You for helping me make this change in my life.

I pray this in Jesus' name!

MY CONFESSION FOR TODAY

I confess that I live my life in balance! I work hard, but I also set aside time for my mind and my body to be refreshed. God's Word declares that I need to take a breather from time to time, so I do it obediently and joyfully with no feelings of guilt or condemnation. God expects me to work hard, but He also expects me to be recharged and refilled! I am making a change in my life so I can include time to be revitalized and refreshed!

I declare this by faith in Jesus' name!

QUESTIONS FOR YOU TO CONSIDER

1. Do you give yourself a little time for rest and relaxation, or do you feel guilty when you are not always working?
2. Can you think of a time when you worked so hard that you nearly depleted yourself of strength, and when you took a little time off and rested, you came back to work refreshed, refilled, and recharged?
3. When you are tired and need a break from your regular schedule, what do you do for that scheduled time of rest? What are some things you could do to make sure you have your needed time of refreshment?

JANUARY 9

The Life-Changing Impact of God's Power!

That your faith should not stand in the wisdom of men,
but in the power of God.
— 1 Corinthians 2:5

I was *speechless* the first time I attended a meeting where I saw the power of God in demonstration! The reason I was so shocked was that from childhood, my denomination had taught me the age of miracles had passed. We had been indoctrinated that miracles such as the ones we read about in the New Testament had ceased and passed away with the death of the apostles. "Miracles were part of the apostolic age," we were told, "and they no longer occur in today's world."

So you can imagine how *stunned* I was when I saw miracles happening right before my eyes! At that service I was attending, I remember feeling like a whirlwind of power passed through that auditorium — and with my own eyes, I saw miracles happening all around me! A miracle of healing happened here, there, and everywhere. Soon people were lining up near the stage to testify about what had happened in their bodies. Wheelchairs were emptied; paralyzed people got up from their stretchers and walked; blind eyes were opened; deaf ears were unstopped; and the mute were starting to speak!

All my doubts about God's miracle-working power still being in operation on the earth today were eradicated that day as I watched those wheelchairs being emptied and people who had been brought in on stretchers walking and even *running* from one end of the stage to the other. Soon the entire front of the auditorium and the aisles were jammed with people who had come forward to give their lives to Christ.

In a matter of hours, all my denominational teaching about the lack of miracles in this present age melted away. As much as I loved my denomination, I could see with my own eyes that I had been wrongly informed my entire life. After that experience with the power of God, I was changed, altered, and forever impacted because of what I witnessed. When I went back to my church and told them what I had experienced, they tried to talk me out of it. But all of their talking was a lost cause! It was too late, because I had personally seen and experienced the power of God!

There is nothing like an encounter with the power of God to alter one's way of thinking and believing. Often we preach and appeal to people with all the right words, but we stop short of the one thing that will put an end to all doubts: *one outstanding demonstration of God's power.* A real miracle or healing demonstrated right before the eyes of doubters can have a greater impact than years of coaxing and begging. *The fact is, there is NOTHING more gripping than an actual, personal encounter with the power of God!* When we allow God to "show off," that supernatural manifestation drives the message deeper into people's hearts and makes a far greater impact than we could ever achieve with mere words.

When the apostle Paul first started preaching to the Corinthians, who were deeply pagan and immersed in gross darkness, he knew words alone would never do the job. To reach them, he would need a demonstration of God's power. In First Corinthians 2:4, he reminded them about the manner in which he first preached to them. He said, "And my speech and my preaching was not with enticing words of man's wisdom, but in demonstration of the Spirit and of power."

In the next verse, Paul continued to tell them the reason he wanted them to see a demonstration of God's power. He wrote, "That your faith should not stand in the wisdom of men, but in the power of God" (1 Corinthians 2:5).

Just as I was so deeply impacted by the miracles I saw in that meeting many years ago, the apostle Paul knew that miracles, healings, and other displays of power would have a great impact on his listeners. If all he offered them were "enticing words of man's wisdom," they could argue, disagree, or debate with him. But if an unquestionable miracle happened right before their eyes — *a demonstration of supernatural power that literally knocked them off their feet* — they would know that God Almighty was behind the message Paul was preaching!

I'll never forget what one great man once told me about the power of God. He said, "You can't win an argument with a man who has had a supernatural experience." This is true! When people have an encounter with the power of God, it puts an end to all speculation and all arguments.

Paul knew that a display of God's power would have a great influence on his audience, so in addition to carefully crafting a message that would touch their hearts, he took it one step further and made the choice to allow the power of God to do its unparalleled work. Paul knew the power of God would melt away every doubt and put an end to all debate, so he stepped aside and allowed God's power to show off and thus confirm that the message he preached was indeed the truth!

Paul later told the Corinthians the reason he took this approach: "That your faith should not *stand* in the wisdom of men, but in the power of God." The word "stand" in this verse is the little Greek word *en,* which simply means *in.* As used here, this word describes the medium in which faith is *rooted.* It could be translated, "I took this approach so your faith would not be rooted in the wisdom of men...." Then he continued to write, "...but *in* the power of God."

The word *en* is used again when Paul referred to the power of God, which lets us know that Paul wanted his listeners' faith to be rooted deeply *in* the power of God. The word "power" in this verse is the Greek word *dunamis.* This well-known, often-used word denotes the *mighty power of God.* In this verse, it denotes not merely power, but *tremendous power.* This word *dunamis* denotes God's supernatural power, which is *explosive, mighty,* and *awe-inspiring* to those who see it or experience it.

Paul's words in First Corinthians 2:5 could thus be paraphrased:

"I took this approach so your faith would not be rooted in the wisdom of men, but so your faith would be steadfastly rooted in the power of God."

Don't make the mistake of taking only a mental approach when you preach the Gospel or share the Word with people who are less informed than you are. Of course, you must use your mind to its maximum capacity. God gave you your mind and expects you to use it as you share Christ and His Word with others. But you should always get quiet in your heart first and ask the Holy Spirit what *He* would like to do in those moments. What needs in the lives of your listeners would He like to step in and meet supernaturally to reveal His great love for them? He'll lead you each step of the way if you'll stay sensitive to Him.

And if you ever come to a standstill in a conversation — when it is your word against another person's — that may be the golden moment when you need to step aside and allow God to step in and do what only *He* can do! Give His supernatural power an opportunity to intervene and *confirm* the truth you are attempting to drive into that person's heart.

When you come to one of those moments when the greatest efforts of your mind seem futile, yield to the power of God that resides within you and allow the Holy Spirit to do what you could never do by yourself. *When the Spirit of God is finished confirming the Word with supernatural demonstrations of power, all arguments will cease, the case will be closed, and the person you are trying to reach will be convinced!*

MY PRAYER FOR TODAY

Lord, I ask You to teach me when to step aside so that You can step in to do what I cannot do. Help me to speak the right words, to say those words with the right attitude, and to speak them under the anointing of the Holy Spirit. But also help me to know when words are not enough. Help me stay sensitive to You and to be bold to allow You to move through me in supernatural ways to confirm that the message is accurate and true.

I pray this in Jesus' name!

MY CONFESSION FOR TODAY

I confess that God is my Partner! It is His work to step in and do what I cannot do when I am presenting truth to people who are in darkness. The Holy Spirit's power is always available to confirm His truth, and it is the Father's desire to demonstrate His supernatural ability to people in order to bring them out of the darkness and into the light. So starting today, I will always ask the Holy Spirit to demonstrate His power as He desires through me. From this moment onward, I will look to Him as my Partner to flow through me with His power to fulfill His purpose in every situation and to meet the need of the moment in convincing unbelievers and doubters about the truth of God's Word.

I declare this by faith in Jesus' name!

QUESTIONS FOR YOU TO CONSIDER

1. Can you think of a time when you were trying to share God or impart truth from the Word and you felt crippled or impaired to fully make the point? Did you say everything you knew to say, and still the listener did not agree with your point?
2. Have you ever had a moment when you stepped back and let the power of God do the convincing work for you as you allowed His power to flow *through* you? What happened when you allowed that opportunity for the Spirit of God to work? What did God do that utterly convinced that person of the truth you were trying to impart?
3. After reading today's *Sparkling Gem,* what changes do you need to make in the way you share Christ and the Word with others? Why don't you take a few minutes to pray over what you have read today and let the Holy Spirit sink this message deep into your own heart.

JANUARY 10

Do Your Best To Be at Peace With Everyone

If it be possible, as much as lieth in you,
live peaceably with all men.
— Romans 12:18

Do you know anyone who rubs you the wrong way so badly that when you walk away from that person you feel like you're about to explode? Does it seem like that person always says something so rude, unkind, impolite, or derogatory that it nearly makes your blood boil when you are with him or her? Well, consider this: Have you ever had the thought that *you* may be rubbing that person the wrong way as well?

As I relate the following story to you, I am obligated by God to begin by telling you that, over the course of many years, the enemy I am about to describe became a friend. In fact, he is so dear to me today that I cherish every time I get to see and spend time with him. So I testify to you from the onset that the majority of horrible relational situations *can* be turned around *if* you will obey what Romans 12:18 tells you to do. That is what I want to talk to you about today.

Many years ago, I had to regularly deal with a pastor who was one of the rudest and most belittling people I had ever met in my life. But the man lived in the same city as I did, so I couldn't avoid seeing him from time to time. Whenever he and I found ourselves in the same room, I was nearly always shocked at what came out of his mouth. He freely gossiped and spoke malicious things about other pastors and churches. Everyone was his target — *including me*!

Because he was a pastor in our same city, I tried very hard to get along with him. But he was one of those people who simply rubbed me the wrong way, and I just didn't like him. And I definitely didn't like being near him! I repeatedly asked the Lord to help me forgive the callous words he had spoken about me to other pastors and leaders. Because he and I were pastors of the two largest churches in that particular nation, I knew I had to get along with this man. Nevertheless, trying to draw close to him was like trying to hug a cactus. I got jabbed and stabbed every time I came close!

I tried to convince myself that my inner conflict with this pastor was the result of a wrong mix of personalities. But if that were the case, this man had a wrong personality mix with every pastor in our city! The truth was that he was simply an offensive person. He knew he was offensive; he enjoyed it; and he had no intention of changing. And the way he affected me was exactly the way every other pastor I knew felt as well.

After many years of struggling in my relationship with this man, I finally came to realize that although this man was mightily gifted as a *public* communicator, he had no people skills on a *personal* level. He really was ill-mannered. The problem truly was *him*. Because this pastor respected no one but himself and was not submitted to any spiritual authority, no one could find a way to speak into his life to help him.

So what was I to do in this situation? As I said, he and I were each pastors of the two largest churches in our city, so we were continually attending meetings in which both of us were expected to participate. Like it or not, I was going to regularly be in this man's company. It was impossible for me to avoid the man, so I began to ask the Lord to help me know how to get along with him so I didn't leave upset every time the two of us had to be at the same place.

The Holy Spirit led me to Romans 12:18. It says, "If it be possible, as much as lieth in you, live peaceably with all men." This verse gave me direction. It provided helpful answers that enabled me to deal successfully with this difficult situation. And I believe these answers will also help you know how to deal with that person who constantly rubs *you* the wrong way!

Notice that the apostle Paul began this verse by saying, "If it be possible...." The fact that he began with the word "if" — the Greek word *ei*, which is like an open question mark with no definitive answer — means there may be times when we run into a case where it is *not* possible to have peace with all men. As we are all well aware, it can be very difficult to be at peace with some people — not necessarily because *we* are so difficult, but because *they* are hard to get along with. But remember, they may think the same of us! But regardless of the difficulty of the task or the ugly behavior of those we encounter along the way in life, the command of God remains: To the best of our ability, we must give our best efforts to be at peace with all men.

The word "possible" comes from the Greek word *dunaton*. In this verse, it expresses the idea of *something that is potentially difficult but nonetheless doable*. But because this phrase begins with the word "if," it casts a shadow on whether or not it is truly doable. Maybe peace is attainable; maybe it isn't. But if it *is* doable, you are to give it your best shot. For this reason, this phrase could be translated: "If it is doable..."; "If it is feasible..."; or as the *King James Version* translates it, "If it is possible...."

Paul continued to say, "...As much as lieth in you, live peaceably with all men." The words "as much as lieth in you" come from a mixture of Greek words that means "as far as it depends on you." This phrase points toward you and me, placing the responsibility of maintaining peace and a good attitude on us, *not* on the person we find to be so offensive. This clearly means that God is expecting us to do everything we can from our perspective and to give it our best to "live peaceably with all men."

The words "live peaceably" are from the word *eireneuo*, a form of the word *eirene*, which means to *to live in peace* or *to possess peace*. In Romans 12:18, it carries this idea: *"Once you've finally obtained peace, you must determine that you are going to do your best to make sure it is maintained and kept."* In other words, instead of being a contributor to the problem, you are to do all you can to be a *facilitator* of peace!

And notice that Paul said we are to do this with "all men." In my case, these words "all men" meant I had to live peaceably with the ill-mannered pastor who continually upset me with his offensive behavior. But the words the Holy Spirit used in this verse are unquestionable. The words "all men" is a translation of the words *panton anthropon*. The word *panton* is an all-encompassing word that means *everyone*. The word *anthropon* comes from *anthropos*, the Greek word that describes *all* of *mankind*, including every male and female of every race, nationality, language, religion, and skin color — no one excluded. There is no phrase in Greek that could be more all encompassing than *panton anthropon*. It literally embraces the entire human race. It does not say we have to agree with all people or condone their behavior — but as much as it depends on us, we are to be at peace with them.

At the very moment Paul wrote this verse, he and other Christians were facing horrible pagan and religious opposition from those who had no tolerance for "narrow-minded" believers. Yet it was at this same time that the Holy Spirit commanded them through this verse to do everything they could to get along with everyone.

And this same divine command is directed toward *us*. It doesn't say to live peaceably only with friends, family, peers, or those who agree with us. It says that if it's possible, we are to live at peace "with *all* men." An interpretive version of Romans 12:18 could be rendered: *"If it's doable at all, then as much as depends on you, be at peace with everyone, no one excluded."*

This verse was so helpful to me when I was learning how to get along with that ill-mannered pastor. I understood that Jesus did not expect me to be his best friend, but Jesus *did* expect me to give it my best effort to live peacefully in that situation. If being at peace with him meant perhaps not engaging in a lengthy conversation with him, then whatever I had to do, I was determined not to live upset with this man who had been such a source of pain and irritation to me. I had to let it go, let God deal with him, and walk away from my hankering to fix or correct him. As much as it depended on me, from my side, I was going to do whatever was necessary to be at peace with him.

I know that you have relationships that trouble you, as this is true of everyone. If you're tired of getting upset or being irritated or unsuccessfully trying to correct those individuals, perhaps you should choose the route of simply seeking to be at peace. Negotiation with a difficult person is not always possible, so sometimes the best option is simply doing whatever is necessary to be at peace. This was the message the Holy Spirit spoke to me, and I believe it is the message the Holy Spirit may be speaking to you right now as well.

So if you're exhausted from trying to fix an unfixable relationship, and yet your contact with that person is inescapable, ask the Holy Spirit to help you deal with your own heart so that you can be at peace *even with that person*. That difficult relationship is part of the "all men" with whom the Holy Spirit commanded you to be at peace. As stated before, it doesn't mean that you have to agree with that person, condone what he or she does, or discard your beliefs to obtain peace. It simply means you choose not to enter into the fray with that person any longer. You'll be more at peace as a result, and you will be unmoved by the difficult people in your life because you have set yourself to be at peace with *all* men, regardless of what anyone says or does.

MY PRAYER FOR TODAY

Lord, I thank You for speaking to my heart today. I repent for my carnal response toward certain people in my life. I confess that I have allowed myself to become irritated with them, and at times I have even been judgmental of them. Today I release forgiveness toward them, and I choose from this point onward to see myself as a force for peace. I purpose in my heart to exercise the patience that is a quality of Your love within me. I ask You for wisdom to know what to say and do and what not to say and do when I am in the presence of these individuals. Thank You for leading and guiding me in each contact I make with them.

I pray this in Jesus' name!

MY CONFESSION FOR TODAY

I let the peace of God act as umpire continually in my heart, deciding and settling with finality all questions or concerns that arise in my mind. I refuse to be ruled by my emotions, and I am not moved by what I see, feel, or hear. I have the mind of Christ, and I hold the thoughts, feelings, and purposes of His heart. The wisdom of God determines my responses and reactions to those I consider ill-mannered or badly behaved who are not within my realm of authority to correct. I boldly declare that I will not live my life upset or bothered by something I cannot fix. Whatever is necessary to be at peace and to remain at peace is what I will do, as I have been commanded in Romans 12:18.

I declare this by faith in Jesus' name!

QUESTIONS FOR YOU TO CONSIDER

1. Have you ever considered that you may affect someone who rubs you the wrong way the same way that he or she affects you? Are you sure that you are not somehow contributing to the atmosphere you experience when you are with that person?
2. What do you need to do to eliminate the conflict between yourself and that individual? Since Romans 12:18 commands you to do everything from your side to be at peace, what steps do you need to take to obey that verse? Wouldn't it be worth your time to think this through and perhaps write down a few thoughts about what you could change or do differently to have peace with that individual?
3. Is it possible that the person who irritates you is ignorant of his insensitivity or has just never awakened to the impact he is having on others? Why don't you take a prayerful position for him and leave him in the hands of Jesus?

JANUARY 11

The Holy Spirit — The Great Revealer!

But as it is written, Eye hath not seen, nor ear heard, neither
have entered into the heart of man, the things which
God hath prepared for them that love him.
But God hath revealed them unto us by His Spirit....
— 1 Corinthians 2:9,10

Over the years, we have received millions of letters from viewers who have written in response to our TV programs. If I were to amass all of those letters and analyze the number-one need that people write to us about, I would have to say it is their desperate desire to know God's will for their lives.

People struggle to know what is right or wrong, what jobs they should or shouldn't take, what school they should attend for higher education, whom they should or should not marry, whether or not to go full time into the ministry — and on, on, and on. Often well-meaning, misinformed people have told them, "Well, you can't always know God's plan." These misled people even quote First Corinthians 2:9 and use it as an excuse for ignorance. They say, "You know what the Bible says: 'Eye hath not seen, nor ear heard, neither have entered into the heart of man, the things that God hath prepared for them that love him.' You see, even the Bible tells us we can't always know what God has planned for us!"

However, that was *not* the point the apostle Paul was trying to make when he wrote this verse! We cannot use First Corinthians 2:9 as an excuse for *ignorance*. It's true that there was a time long ago under the Old Covenant when it wasn't possible to fully know God's plan as we can know it today. Paul paraphrased from the Old Testament when he said, "...As it is written, Eye hath not seen, nor ear heard, neither have entered into the heart of man, the things which God hath prepared for them..." (*see* Isaiah 64:4). Isaiah was bemoaning the perplexing problem of man's inability to know what God has planned for him. At that time, before the Holy Spirit came to indwell the hearts of people, it was difficult and often impossible to fully discern the things God had planned for each of His children.

Think about how perplexing this problem must have been! God meticulously prepared wonderful, prearranged blessings for His people, but they weren't able to discern these things in advance! The word "prepared" is important in this text, for it is the Greek word *etoimadzo*, which carries the idea of a *readiness* or something that has been *fully prepared*. The use of this word in this verse alerts us to the fact that God has a divine plan for each of our lives and is ready to reveal it! How wonderful to realize that God's plan for us is not happenstance, accidental, or a product of last-minute planning. He has been meticulously working out a plan for our lives since before the foundation of the world. He is the *Great Planner*!

Under the Old Covenant, however, the Holy Spirit didn't reside in the human heart, so people struggled tremendously to find God's predetermined plan for their lives. In their efforts to uncover His will, they sought special, divine signs and even visited prophets of the region in an attempt to find answers and gain God's guidance and direction. Although God had prepared so much for His people, they were blind to much of what had been provided for them because they didn't have the Great Revealer living in their hearts.

How I wish I could say that it was different today, but most modern Christians live their lives as if they were still living under the Old Covenant! This is especially sad when you consider that Christians have the Holy Spirit living inside their hearts and therefore have access to all the answers they could ever need. But because they have never developed a spiritual sensitivity or learned to recognize the voice of the Holy Spirit, they still live like Old Testament people, depending on special signs, divine signals, or advice from others.

This shouldn't be the case! *The Holy Spirit has come to tell you and me everything we need to know to walk in the fullness of God's plan for our lives.*

Because the Holy Spirit has come, the ignorance that once existed among God's people has permanently been *eliminated*. No one can rightfully use First Corinthians 2:9 as an excuse for ignorance or for not knowing the will of God. People who use this verse in this way are sadly misinformed about its purpose. Taken in context with the following verse, this verse clearly reveals that God does *not* want His people to be ignorant about His purposes, blessings, promises, and provisions that He has so meticulously planned for their lives.

First Corinthians 2:10 continues to tell us, "But God hath revealed them unto us by His Spirit…." What does the word "them" refer to? It refers to all the things that used to be hidden! The word "revealed" is the Greek word *apokalupsis*, a compound of the words *apo* and *kalupsis*. The word *apo* means *away*, and the word *kalupsis* is the Greek word for *a veil*, *a curtain*, or some type of *covering*. When compounded into the word *apokalupsis*, which is normally translated as the word "revelation," it literally means *to remove the veil* or *to remove the curtain* so you can see what is on the other side.

This word *apokalupsis* plainly refers to *something that was veiled or hidden for a long time and suddenly becomes clear and visible to the mind or eye*. It is like pulling the curtains out of the way so you can see the scene outside your window. The view was always there for you to enjoy, but the curtains blocked your ability to see the real picture. Once the curtains are drawn apart, you suddenly behold what was previously hidden from your view. The moment you see beyond the curtain for the first time and observe what has been there all along but wasn't evident to you — *that* is what the Bible calls a "revelation."

Now apply this to First Corinthians 2:9,10. In verse 9, Paul indeed said that there was a time in the past when the eye could not see, the ear could not hear, nor could the heart begin to imagine all the amazing, wonderful things God had prepared for those who love Him. God had prepared those benefits according to His prearranged plan, but they were veiled — *hidden* to us, obscured from our sight. But when Jesus ascended, the Holy Spirit came, and one of His major works in our lives is to remove the veil that once obstructed our view so our eyes can see, our ears can hear, and our hearts can fully comprehend the specific, special plans that God has meticulously prepared for each of us!

So I want to tell you, if you've been using this verse to claim ignorance of God's ways, it's time for you to change your thinking and speaking about it! This verse doesn't give us an excuse for ignorance. In fact, it says just the opposite! This verse declares *the day of not knowing what God has prepared for us is gone forever*! The Holy Spirit — the *Great Revealer* — now lives inside our hearts, and He wants to reveal God's blessings, promises, provisions, and plans to you and to me!

Thank God, you no longer have to seek special signs or divine signals. You don't have to seek out prophets as they did in the Old Testament. Right inside your heart is the greatest Source of revelation on planet earth — the Holy Spirit! *If you'll develop a spiritual sensitivity and learn to listen to His voice, He will reveal everything that God has meticulously planned for you so you can be all God has destined you to be.*

MY PRAYER FOR TODAY

Lord, I thank You for the presence and the ministry of the Holy Spirit in my life. Forgive me for the times I've ignored this precious Partner whom You have sent to instruct and lead me in all the affairs of life. I repent for trying to find my way in life without His counsel and assistance. I confess that I've often sought the advice of family, friends, counselors, pastors, books, and other sources more than I've sought the counsel of the Holy Spirit — yet He is the One who knows the end from the beginning. Father, I thank You for providing the greatest source of revelation inside my own heart through His presence within me. Starting today, I seek the guidance of the Holy Spirit for each and every decision I make in life. Father, since You have meticulously planned my life and have sent the Holy Spirit to reveal that plan to me, from this day onward I want to let the Holy Spirit provide the revelation I need to fulfill that plan!

I pray this in Jesus' name!

MY CONFESSION FOR TODAY

I declare that I am led by the Holy Spirit and that He reveals to me the will of God for my life. I am not ignorant, and I am not left to find my way on my own. God loves me so much that He sent the Holy Spirit to dwell within me and to provide me with all the details of God's awesome plan for my life. As I develop my spiritual sensitivity and listen to the Holy Spirit's voice, I am enlightened step by step to what He wants me to do with every part of my life. Because the Holy Spirit dwells in me, my eyes see, my ears hear, and my heart is able to comprehend the things God has planned for me!

I declare this by faith in Jesus' name!

QUESTIONS FOR YOU TO CONSIDER

1. Do you know the overall framework of God's plan for your life? If so, what is it? Could you clearly state God's will and plan for your life if someone asked you to do it?
2. Are you spiritually developing so you can more and more easily perceive the voice of the Holy Spirit in your heart? What steps can you start taking to increase your level of spiritual sensitivity?
3. If someone were to ask you for help in determining God's will for his life, what would you tell him to do?

JANUARY 12

Abstain From All Appearance of Evil

Abstain from all appearance of evil.
— 1 Thessalonians 5:22

When I was getting started in the ministry, God blessed me with an opportunity to serve as associate pastor to an older man of God who taught me many important principles for my life and ministry. One of the most important principles he taught me — one that I now require of every leader who works in our ministry — is the necessity of abstaining from all appearance of evil.

When I first heard this pastor's rules, I thought they were a little overboard. For instance, men on the pastoral staff could not meet alone with members of the opposite sex, counsel a woman alone behind closed doors, or ride alone in a car with a woman other than one's wife. I thought these types of rules made life very inconvenient. But the pastor was very strong on never doing anything that gave a wrong impression or that opened a door for criticism or accusation.

I've been in the ministry many years and know of numerous times when pastors were accused of inappropriate behavior. The behavior was sometimes real and at other times imagined, but the opportunity for accusation was almost always the result of carelessness in keeping certain boundaries. So I now agree wholeheartedly that there is great wisdom in adhering to restrictions like the ones my senior pastor required in my early days of ministry. By taking this cautious approach, men and women of God are able to steer clear of insinuations and accusations. This, however, should apply not only to ministers of the Gospel, but to every believer who cares about the integrity of his or her witness.

The verse that my senior pastor used as the basis for his rules, and the verse I use in my own ministry to provide guidance to our team on such issues, was First Thessalonians 5:22. In this verse, the apostle Paul wrote, "Abstain from all appearance of evil." Today I would like for us to take a deeper look to see what we can learn from this key verse in the Word of God.

Paul began by saying, "*Abstain....*" The word "abstain" is from the Greek word *apecho*. This word means *to deliberately withdraw from*; *to stay away from*; *to put distance between oneself and something else*; or *to intentionally abstain*. The word *apecho* is also used in First Peter 2:11, where Peter wrote, "Dearly beloved, I beseech you as strangers and pilgrims, *abstain* from fleshly lusts, which war against the soul." In this case, the word "abstain" — *apecho* — means *to deliberately refrain from something*; hence, it could be translated, "...I urge you *to refrain from* fleshly lusts, which war against the soul." The implication is that believers should put distance between themselves and temptations of the flesh and soul.

There are other examples of the word *apecho* in the New Testament that also demonstrate how this word depicts some type of *distance* between objects. For example:

- In Luke 7:6, the word *apecho* is used to describe *the physical distance* between Jesus and the house of the centurion.
- In Matthew 15:8 and Mark 7:6, the word *apecho* is used to describe human hearts that are hardened and therefore *distant* and *far* from God.
- In Acts 15:20, the word *apecho* is used when James, the leader of the Jerusalem church, gave instructions that the new Gentile believers should *abstain* from food offered to idols, from sexual immorality, from the meat of strangled animals, and from the consumption of raw blood. In that verse, the word *apecho* is so strong that it makes a *demand* on the new Gentile believers *to withdraw from* and *permanently terminate* their contact with these things. It is actually a command *to refrain, to desist, to discontinue*, and *to terminate* any further contact with them, and it calls for *a permanent halt* to the practice of allowing such contact.

Keeping this in mind, we know that when Paul told us, "Abstain from all appearance of evil," he was strongly urging you and me to *put distance between* ourselves and any appearance of evil. This Greek word *apecho* demands that we do not allow even the smallest hint of inappropriate behavior or any act that could be misinterpreted or viewed as being immoral or unethical. There is no doubt about it — the word *apecho* calls for extreme caution and vigilance.

The word "from" is the Greek word *apo*, which means *away*. However, because the word *apecho* had already been used, meaning *to put distance between yourself and some other thing*, it means the word *apo* was really not needed — *unless* Paul intended to place *very strong emphasis* on this point. By adding the word *apo*, it makes the point abundantly clear that believers should not only put distance between themselves and what is obviously evil, but they must also put *a great deal* of distance between themselves and whatever fits this description, even in appearance.

The word "appearance" in the Greek is *eidos*, a word that is only used five times in the New Testament, but depicts an *outward form, visible appearance, a likeness*, or *a resemblance* of something. Therefore, Paul was telling us, "It doesn't matter what *you* think or what *you* know to be true; what matters is what *appears* to be true in the eyes of others." Even if there is a small chance that someone may mistake your actions as evil or if what you do even *resembles* something evil or wrong, you need to stay as far away from it as you possibly can.

What makes this even more serious is the fact that this word "evil," the Greek word *poneros,* is often used in the Greek Septuagint version of the Old Testament to describe *actions that are ultimately damaging to a person's testimony and reputation* (*see* Deuteronomy 22:14). There is no doubt that Paul was telling us that we must do everything in our ability to *put a lot of distance between ourselves and anything that would bring harm or injury to our reputation or to our godly witness in front of other people.*

Think about it! How many people do you know who did something that they "thought" was all right to do — but other people saw their action and misinterpreted it, and as a result, it stained their reputation? I'm talking about situations like pastors being accused of immoral behavior because they had close contact with a member of the opposite sex who wasn't their spouse. Maybe nothing wrong occurred, but what people saw *resembled* something bad, and the pastor was therefore falsely accused. This is why it is a good rule never to counsel a member of the opposite sex alone! By using common sense and refraining from ever being in such a situation where you could be accused, you have put *distance* between yourself and potential accusations.

Have you ever heard a rumor about a preacher who wrongly used money that was intended for the work of the ministry? The truth may be that the minister never did anything wrong at all with those funds, but because his actions gave a wrong impression to people who were watching, what he did resulted in a damaged testimony. Preachers can avoid these types of accusations by determining never to touch ministry funds personally and by establishing a bookkeeping system that demands accountability. Just by using common sense and choosing to refrain from activities that might give a mistaken impression, those in the ministry can put great *distance* between themselves and suspicious-looking situations. In so doing, there will never be room for accusation that they misuse ministry funds or participate in *any* questionable activity or behavior.

As I said, this principle of refraining from every appearance of evil isn't pertinent only to ministers. It applies to every believer who wants to maintain a godly reputation. The fact is, if your testimony in the eyes of others is important to you, you must make the decision to withdraw from, refrain from, desist from, discontinue, and permanently terminate any action that gives the appearance of evil. Although this may require a new set of rules for your life, you will be taking vital steps toward preserving your testimony and godly reputation.

How much is your reputation — and the reputation of the Holy One you represent — worth to you? If you want to maintain a good name and testimony in front of others, you must refrain from any action, language, or contact that gives the appearance of evil. And this is not just my suggestion — it is the commandment of God found in First Thessalonians 5:22.

By understanding the Greek words in this verse, we can interpret First Thessalonians 5:22 to read:

"You need to terminate contact with any place, action, language, or relationship that gives people the impression that you are doing something wrong. It doesn't matter what you think is acceptable; what matters is what other people perceive. So put a great deal of distance between yourself and anything you are doing that people could misinterpret and that could thereby stain your reputation."

So many people have forfeited their testimony because they didn't use their heads and think about how their actions might be perceived by others! Perception is often reality in the eye of the beholder.

Even if you know that you're doing nothing wrong at all, the fact remains that people don't see your heart — they see your actions. If they see you do something that appears immoral or unethical, you will likely be judged by what they perceive.

If you're like me, your highest desire is to glorify Jesus in this life in all you say and do. That's why our hearts can agree with what Paul says in this verse — that it's always best to "abstain from all appearance of evil" because we are His representatives on this earth!

MY PRAYER FOR TODAY

Lord, I understand that Your Word commands me to break off and desist from doing anything that would give the impression of evil to people who are looking at my life from the outside. Today I have a new and a fuller realization of the great impact my actions can have on my reputation and on other people. Please forgive me for doing things that could be misconstrued, misunderstood, or misinterpreted. I am truly sorry. Help me today to put safeguards in my life that will help me to abstain from all appearances of evil from this point forward.

I pray this in Jesus' name!

MY CONFESSION FOR TODAY

I confess that I use common sense in the way that I conduct my life. I am thoughtful about my actions; I am careful to remember that people are watching me; and I am led by the Holy Spirit in how I conduct my life. Because I want to maintain a godly reputation, I care about what people think of me. I will not do anything that would cast a shadow on Jesus' name, my name, or my testimony as a child of God. With God's help, I will live a life that is free of accusation!

I declare this by faith in Jesus' name!

QUESTIONS FOR YOU TO CONSIDER

1. Have you ever known someone who stained his testimony because contact with a place, action, language, or relationship gave people the impression that he or she was doing something inappropriate?

2. As you look back on that particular situation now, what steps could that person have taken to circumvent the accusations and charges that were brought against him or her?
3. Are there any areas or actions in *your* life right now that others might perceive to be questionable? Be honest with yourself! What are those areas, and what steps should you begin to take to put distance between yourself and future accusation?

JANUARY 13

Don't Give Up on Your Seed!

And let us not be weary in well doing:
for in due season we shall reap, if we faint not.
— Galatians 6:9

Today I am thinking about people who have sown their financial seed into the soil of their churches or of their good ministries. Or perhaps they have sown love, kindness, forgiveness, and patience into their relationships, and now they are waiting for a return or a harvest on what they have sown.

Maybe *you* have been trusting God for a desire of your heart to burst forth in your life, but have gotten discouraged during the time of waiting between the *seed sown* and the *harvest reaped.* I want to encourage you not to quit before you've received what you've been expecting. You can rest assured that if you won't give up, God *certainly* won't fail to perform His Word for you! In fact, Galatians 6:9 promises: "And let us not be weary in well doing: for in due season we shall reap, if we faint not."

I want to talk to you about *not* being discouraged while you wait for your seed to grow and your harvest to be reaped. First I'll tell you a story from my childhood. When I was a boy, I decided to grow corn, so I carefully measured the rows along the backside of my father's garage, prepared the ground, and then meticulously planted the seeds. What a beautiful little garden it was, and I was so proud of it!

Every day before school, I'd run to that little patch to see if anything had pierced the soil during the night. When I got home from school, I'd run back to that garden to see if anything became visible while I was away for the day. Before I'd go to bed at night, I'd return to see if my seeds were producing anything I could visibly see. Finally, I got so impatient waiting to see results that I told myself, *Nothing is happening with my seeds. I need to dig them up and see if they are defective.*

So just as meticulously as I had planted the seeds, I began to dig them up one at a time to see if anything was happening below the surface. By the time I was done, there before my eyes, cupped in my hands, were *all* the seeds I'd planted, uprooted by my own doing. The little pile of seeds had a tangled mass of roots and little shoots that had begun to grow upward toward the surface of the soil. But because I became impatient waiting for the "due season" of my corn, I completely ruined my harvest. After all the hard work I'd done, I had dug up my seeds and ruined them.

The next year I decided to return to the patch behind the garage to do it again. But this time, I was determined that I would wait for those seeds to produce. I had learned not to dig up my seeds. Finally, the day came when I saw tiny green shoots pierce through the soil. *Whew* — I was so excited! Day after day I watched as the little shoots grew taller and taller. Everything was going great — *until* little Ricky Renner once again became impatient.

The cornstalks were tall, and ears of corn were already on the stalks. But it seemed like the ears of corn were taking too long to get bigger and to mature. I began to wonder, *Is something wrong with this corn? Shouldn't it be growing faster?* I inwardly argued, *Maybe insects are eating it below the husks, or maybe this corn is simply defective.*

So instead of staying on track and being patient, I pulled every ear of corn off the stalks and peeled back the husks to see what was happening inside. There in front of my eyes were perfectly formed ears of corn with everything intact. But because I pulled them off the stalks too early, I destroyed my harvest again. If I had not given in to impatience, it wouldn't have been much longer before I would have been eating fresh corn. It wasn't insects, weather, or the devil that destroyed my harvest — it was *me*!

The seeds were working perfectly both times I ruined my harvest. With this thought in mind, let's return to Paul's admonition in Galatians 6:9 that says, "And let us not be weary in well doing: for in due season we shall reap, if we faint not." *None of us wants to lose our harvest*, so I want to look at seven key words today: 1) "weary," 2) "well," 3) "doing," 4) "due season," 5) "reap," 6) "if," and 7) "faint."

1. The word "weary" is the word *egkakeo*, a compound of the Greek words *en* and *kakos*. The word *en* in this case means *to give in*, and the word *kakeo* is a form of *kakos*, a word frequently used to denote something that is *evil, destructive*, or even *unjust*. But when these words are compounded, the new word depicts *one who is tempted to give up because he feels accosted by an evil, destructive, or unjust person or circumstance.*

   Have you ever tried hard to do what is right, but felt crushed or continually resisted by some circumstance or person? Has that opposition caused you to feel tempted to throw in the towel? In spite of the destructive forces that may have tried to rail against you or loom over your life, even if a truly unjust situation has reared its ugly head against you, God commands you to *not* surrender to the temptation to become weary and give up. He is the One who says, "Let us *not* be weary in well doing…."

2. The word "well" is the Greek word *kalos*, which means *good* but would be better translated here as *useful*. The word "good" itself is too broad a term and leaves one wondering what is included. But when it is more accurately translated as the word "useful," it gives clarity that a "good" work is a "useful" work. This suggests that there are "*un*useful" works. Indeed, there is a lot of energy and time expended on things that have no benefit to anyone. But Paul's use of the word *kalos* tells us that we must focus on those works that are "useful" with some type of measurable results. This tells us that what is sown is not only financial *seeds*, but also good *deeds*.

3. The word "doing" is from the Greek word *poieo* and refers to any type of *activity*. It can even carry the idea of *creative doing* when the action doesn't come easily or naturally. In other words, if we can't easily see a way to do something that is beneficial, it's time for us to get creative! God is looking for us to be consistent and productive with *useful* works. It must be noted that this word, as used here, is also a participle. This means it is ongoing, uninterrupted action. In other words, the type of "well doing" that Paul described is not a one-time event, but an *ongoing action*. It is a *lifestyle* of sowing *seeds* and *deeds*.

4. Paul promised that "in due season," we shall reap a harvest for our efforts. The words "due season" are *idios* and *kairos*. The word *idios* means *its own*. The word *kairos* refers to *a set season*. Thus, each seed has *its own set season* — a specific, individual time when it will produce a harvest. Even if many multiple seeds of different kinds are all planted at one time, each has *its own season* to be reaped, depending on the nature of the seed. One seed produces during one set season, while another seed is reaped during a different season. Thus, it is a mistake to judge our seed and *its* time of harvest by the harvest time of other seeds, because each seed has its unique set season to mature. We just need to remember God's promise: If we are consistent — if we steadfastly keep sowing our seed into the ground and refuse to allow weariness to derail us — a time will come when we *shall* reap.

5. The words "shall reap" are from the word *therismos*, a word that describes the *reaping or harvesting of crops*. What is important to note is that the Greek tense describes a future, fixed event. Hence, the harvest is in the future, but it is *fixed* and guaranteed to happen — *if* we will do our part and stay on course. This is why Paul continued by saying, "...if we faint not."

6. The word "if" tells us that *our actions have the power to disrupt a harvest* — just as I twice disrupted the reaping of my corn crop! Paul added the word "if" to help us understand that our consistency and refusal to surrender for *any* reason

is vital in reaching the set season of our seed. If we "faint" at any point along the way, we can jeopardize the long-term harvest of what we have sown.

7. The word "faint" is the Greek word *ekluo*, a compound of the words *ek* and *luo*. The word *ek* means *out*, and the word *luo* means *to loosen* or *to relax*. When compounded, the new word means *to loosen out*. It is *a relaxed mental state that results in loss*. It pictures *a person who has become so weary that he gives up and forfeits what he had long awaited and was so close to reaping*. As a result, the person *loses* the desired outcome that was so near. Pressures applied against this person have unraveled him, causing his grip to slacken until the answer he was holding on to slips from his hands. The result is *loss*. In the case of Galatians 6:9, he has lost *a harvest*.

The most common factor that causes us to loosen our grip is when we become "weary." Thus, Paul urges us not to give in and quit in times of spiritual, physical, or mental exhaustion.

It's exciting to plant seeds of faith, and it's *really* exciting when the harvest comes — that moment when your faith finally turns into sight! But in order to reach that point, you must hold tight to what God has told you and remember that your seed — whether it's financial seed or seeds of uninterrupted, useful deeds toward others — has a set season when it will produce, *if* you do not disrupt the process. As long as you *stay the course*, it is guaranteed that you will reap what you have planted.

Many people have consistently sowed their finances or kind actions toward others. Often they are tempted to quit just because they become tired. Although they are trying to be obedient, they may feel unappreciated. Perhaps circumstances out of their control are coming against them, or someone is treating them unjustly.

Maybe *you* have experienced the temptation to give up. But Galatians 6:9 urges you not to loosen your grip on your *future, fixed harvest*! If you will remain steadfast, the time of waiting will eventually end and your harvest will come! It may not come at the time you were hoping it would — but regardless, don't dig up your seed or pull the ears of corn off the stalks too early! The seeds you have sown have a set season, and God promises they *will* produce — if you don't do something to disrupt the process!

I don't know what you're trusting God for in this present season of your life. We are all believing for something and sowing seeds toward it. Perhaps no one knows but you because you've kept it between you and the Lord. Maybe it's a financial harvest, a breakthrough in a relationship, a physical healing, or a restoration in some other area. Maybe this harvest is taking longer than you had anticipated.

But I want to reassure you that God's Word and His promises are eternal, and if you *just won't quit*, it's only a matter of time until your long-awaited blessing arrives. God's Word is absolutely true, so I encourage you to remain steadfast and keep thanking Him for the harvest He has in store that's been tailor-made just for you!

MY PRAYER FOR TODAY

Lord, I ask You to help me be patient as I wait for the seeds I've sown to grow and be multiplied back into my life. It seems like it has taken a long time, but I will not loosen my grip on the fixed, future harvest You have planned for me. You are the Lord of the harvest, so I fix my eyes on You and trust that You have set a season for my seeds and deeds to reach their full growth so I can enjoy the harvest of my endeavors. You are faithful; Your Word is true; and today I rest in those truths!

I pray this in Jesus' name!

MY CONFESSION FOR TODAY

I boldly declare that I will continue to release my faith and believe for God to multiply the seeds and deeds I have sown in the past. At times, weariness has tried to attack me, injustice has been done to me, and other outside pressures have made me feel tempted to throw in the towel. But I will not surrender to any pressure to bend, break, or give up on God's promise that I will enter a season of reaping a harvest from the good seed I have sown. The Holy Spirit will empower me to hold tight, hang on, and remain steady and steadfast until I reap my harvest and enjoy the fruit of my faith and labor!

I declare this by faith in Jesus' name!

QUESTIONS FOR YOU TO CONSIDER

1. Have you been tempted to become impatient as you wait for your seed to be multiplied back to you? Take the time to make a list of the ways you have already received a harvest on past seeds and deeds that you have sown. It will both surprise and encourage you to see how much of a harvest you have already reaped in your life from the seed you have sown in the past!
2. Seeds mature at varying speeds. Think about the fact that it just may not be time yet for some of the seeds you've sown to mature. If they've been in the soil a long time, it's likely that your harvest is not far away.
3. Have you ever dug up your deeds and seeds sown and ruined a harvest? Have you ever been so impatient that you "pulled your ears of corn off the stalk, peeled back the husk," and ruined a harvest all by yourself? What did you learn from that experience, and how did it affect your waiting for a harvest afterward?

Your seed has a set season when it will produce,
IF you do not disrupt the process.
As long as you STAY THE COURSE,
it is guaranteed that you will reap what you have planted.

JANUARY 14

When God Hooked My Heart!

But when it pleased God, who separated
me from my mother's womb, and called
me by his grace, to reveal his Son in me, that
I might preach him among the heathen; immediately
I conferred not with flesh and blood.
— Galatians 1:15,16

I know it sounds fantastic to believe, but the first time I ever saw a Russian Bible, I was *instantly* able to *phonetically* read it. I didn't understand what I was reading, but phonetically, I could pronounce the words and read them out loud. As you may already know, I had studied classical Greek at the university level, but I didn't realize the vast similarities between Greek and Russian. The two written languages are so close that I could phonetically read Russian the first time I picked up a Russian Bible.

I'll never forget that moment. I was a speaker at a missions' conference, and as I waited for my turn to speak, I noticed a Bible sitting on the pew next to me. I wondered whose it was, so I picked it up — and when I began flipping through its pages, I understood it was a Russian Bible. But as I looked at it, I realized that I could *phonetically* read the words. I was literally mesmerized by the fact that I was reading Russian! When the service was over and my time of ministering was finished, I quickly rushed to the front row, picked up that Russian Bible and "borrowed" it for a night so I could keep looking at it. I didn't know to whom it belonged, but I took it home and read it for hours, planning to return it to the exact same spot where I had "borrowed" it that morning.

That night in my hotel room, I spent hours flipping through the pages of that Russian Bible. Slowly, I pronounced the words, fairly certain that I was accurately pronouncing what I was looking at. God knows I have a love for languages — and that night, God hooked my heart with the Russian language in a Russian Bible. The next morning, I returned that Russian Bible to the exact place where I had found it. But that experience ignited a desire in me to learn the Russian language — and that is really what started my love for the Russian language and people!

I searched for a system of learning the Russian language, and I found one that suited me very well. Every night before I went to bed, I began to memorize Russian words and study Russian grammar. I would practice my new words and phrases on Denise — all the while not understanding why I was so driven to learn this language. In just a short time, I had committed to memory 800 Russian words and could speak key phrases and sentences. Something inside me was calling out for me to learn this language.

Not long after I started studying Russian, I received a phone call from a dear friend, who invited me to join him and a few other men who were going to teach in the first aboveground Bible school established in the Soviet Union for more than 70 years. At first I didn't want to go, but the idea of practicing Russian in real life had *hooked* my heart, and I found myself agreeing to join them on the trip. Within a matter of weeks, I was in the USSR, and to my delight, I spoke and understood some Russian without mistakes. That stoked the coals of the fire ignited in my heart on the night I started flipping through that Russian Bible, making me want to understand and speak the Russian language even better.

In Russia, I found myself in a land completely different from our own in the United States, but I supernaturally fell in love with the people, the culture, and even the inconveniences that existed at that time. It was like a spirit of adventure had been loosed inside me. It was, without question, a life-transforming moment in my life. But this divine adventure all started the night I "borrowed" the Russian Bible at the mission conference some months before. That I could immediately *phonetically* read the Russian language was a miracle to me!

Prior to this revelation, I had always assumed that my life and ministry would be based in the United States, and I never dreamed of ministering in Russia. But I learned that God has deep-laid plans for our lives that are usually revealed to us one step at a time.

This experience makes me think of the apostle Paul, who was perfectly trained to minister to Hebrew-speaking people, yet God sovereignly called him and separated him to minister to the heathen nations of the world. Although he was unaware of it, it had always been a part of the plan of God for his life.

Paul referred to this in Galatians 1:15 and 16, where he said, "But when it pleased God, who separated me from my mother's womb, and called me by his grace, to reveal his Son in me, that I might preach him among the heathen; immediately I conferred not with flesh and blood."

According to Paul, God had a plan for him from his birth, and that grace carried him toward his life call even when he was unaware of it. God "separated" him from his mother's womb for a purpose. The word "separated" is from the Greek word *aphoridzo*, which means *to mark off, to set boundaries around*, or *to specifically set aside and thus dedicate for a special purpose*. Although Paul was ignorant of it, God had already marked his life and dedicated it for a ministry to the Gentiles. Heaven's plan was set in motion by grace and ultimately led him to his place of divine destination.

Paul went on to say in verse 16, "To reveal his Son in me, that I might preach him among the heathen; immediately I conferred not with flesh and blood." Paul uniquely understood that although his entire life had trained him to minister to Hebrew-speaking people, God's hand was on his life to point him in a different direction: to minister the Gospel of Jesus Christ to the heathen. The Gentile world was totally different from the world Paul knew and felt comfortable in, yet it was his place of divine purpose. When he realized it, Paul said that he "immediately did not confer with flesh and blood...."

The word "immediately" is important, because it tells us that when Paul first realized God's call on his life, he didn't confer with flesh and blood. A time came later when he sought the counsel and friendship of Jewish leaders who would affirm his ministry. But initially he simply embraced the call before the Lord with all of his heart. The word "conferred" is the Greek word *prosanatithimi*, and it refers to *obtaining favor or approval from others to endorse one's activities.* Paul knew so strongly that he was called to the Gentile world that he didn't need or seek the approval of others. *This calling was seared into his soul.*

Likewise, when I knew that God was calling me to the Russian-speaking people, I *really* knew it. I did seek the counsel of others out of respect for them. However, their answers wouldn't have swayed me from my decision, because I inwardly knew that God was moving our family to the former USSR to impart the teaching of God's Word at a crucial moment in the history of Christianity in that part of the world. I heard God's call, and I accepted it. I knew that He had marked my life off, set His boundaries around me, and specifically dedicated me for this place of service.

For me, it all started with my picking up that Russian Bible — God used that incident to hook my heart with a love for the Russian language. As I think about my journey from that moment to this present day, I am in awe of God and His ways. How lovingly He works to hook our hearts and get us on the right path for our lives!

In what ways has God hooked *your* heart to get you pointed in the right direction for your life? You are not here by accident. God has a plan for your life. He separated you from your mother's womb to fulfill that assignment. If you don't know that yet, ask the Holy Spirit to begin to open your eyes to see why you are here and what you are to do with your life. Your life will begin to take on real purpose only when you know what you are supposed to do and you begin to follow that plan.

Like the apostle Paul, God's plan may be different from what you had anticipated. But keep your heart open to Him, knowing that God only has *good* plans in store for you and that He wants your life to make an impact for eternity!

MY PRAYER FOR TODAY

Father, I thank You for the plan for my life that is already written by Your hand deep within me. Father, I realize that Your plan may be different from what I've previously assumed. So I choose now, as an act of my will, to lay aside my own preferences. I make a conscious decision right now that my will is to do Your will. Set my feet upon the path of Your perfect plan for me. Holy Spirit, help me not to frustrate the grace of God, but to be open-minded so I can hear You speak to me. And give me the courage to obey what I hear. I know that You have marked off my life and set boundaries around me, preparing me for a special purpose. Help me have open ears and an open heart so I can hear and understand and follow exactly what Your plan is for me.

I pray this in Jesus' name!

MY CONFESSION FOR TODAY

I confess that according to Ephesians 2:10, Jesus Christ has a predetermined purpose for my life, and His grace is carrying me toward that divine destination. I will not follow the voice of a stranger, but I will follow the voice of my Shepherd as He leads and guides me on the path to the center of His will for my life. I am so thankful that God's grace is at work in me. I fully trust in this work of grace, and I declare that because of it, I will always be right on time and right where God wants me to be — doing precisely what He has asked me to do and thus fulfilling His will for my life.

I declare this by faith in Jesus' name!

QUESTIONS FOR YOU TO CONSIDER

1. Can you think of other Bible characters who were called out of their comfort zones to minister to people who were different from them? Who are some of those people? What can you learn by meditating on their lives and experiences as they followed God's plan?
2. Do you personally know people, like myself, who thought they knew the will of God, only to find out later that He had a different plan? Who are some of those people? What happened as a result of their redirecting the course of their lives to follow God's plan?
3. What do you believe God is calling you to do right now? Is there anything that has hooked your heart and God has used as a "lure" to lead you in a new direction? Pay attention when God hooks your heart, for this may be the way He is revealing the correct path for your life to you.

JANUARY 15

Don't Render Evil for Evil

See that none render evil for evil unto any man;
but ever follow that which is good,
both among yourselves, and to all men.
— 1 Thessalonians 5:15

I'll never forget the day when a man who had been recently saved in our church came to me and said, "Pastor, just say the word, and I'll send someone across town to eliminate the man who has tried to hurt you and our church."

Before coming to Christ, this man had been heavily involved in the Russian mafia, and in that capacity, he had done a lot of dark deeds in the name of loyalty for his former boss. Still newly saved, the only kind of loyalty he understood at this point was retribution — and he viewed me, his pastor, as his new "boss." So when he heard that a man had deliberately abused the church and tried to harm our reputation, he responded the only way he knew to respond. He was so incensed with anger that he was ready to "get" the guy and thereby send a loud signal that no one dare touch his pastor and his church — or they would pay for it!

"Pastor," this man told me, "I have connections. Just say the word, and I'll make sure that person never bothers you or anyone else ever again!"

I had to explain to this man that retribution is not the way we do business in the Kingdom of God. "If there is any retribution," I said, "that is something *God* would deal with, not *us*." I continued by telling him that we are in the business of *redeeming* lost men, not killing them when we get angry!

Nevertheless, when this newly saved man presented me with his sincere offer, I inwardly chuckled because I had never heard anyone be so blatant about his desire to "get" someone. But as I thought about it, I wondered how many times Christians have wished they *could* render some form of justice against someone they were upset with because of something that person had done or failed to do.

Any of us can be tempted to be vindictive from time to time — especially if someone has seriously disappointed us, harmed us or our families or friends, or tried to hurt our personal reputation. But no matter what evil others have done to us, we must remember what the apostle Paul wrote in First Thessalonians 5:15: "See that none render evil for evil unto any man; but ever follow that which is good, both among yourselves, and to all men."

The Greek tense in this verse is not a suggestion but the *strongest* form of a command. When Paul wrote, "See that none render evil for evil," it could be translated, "I am unquestionably commanding that none of you renders evil for evil...." It is absolutely clear that Christians are commanded to abstain from all acts of retaliation and self-vindication. The word "none" is all-inclusive, letting us know that this order is categorically directed to every single person. This means that regardless of the circumstance, no one who calls Jesus his Lord should be involved in the practice of rendering evil for evil.

The word "render" in this verse is from the word *apodidomi*, a compound of the words *apo* and *didomi*. The word *apo* means *back*, as *to return* something back to its original owner or to send something *back* to someone. The word *didomi* simply means *to give*. When these two words are compounded into the word *apodidomi*, as we find it in this verse, the new word means *to send back*, *to return*, or *to pay back*. In other words, it is never our task *to retaliate*, *to get even*, *to get revenge*, *to make someone pay for what he did*, or *to settle the score* with someone we think did evil against us.

The word "evil" is the Greek word *kakos*. It describes *an action that is harmful, hurtful, or injurious* or *something done with an evil intent*. These are the actions of a person who intentionally acts to cause some kind of damage or ruin in someone else's life. But this verse talks about "evil for evil" — the Greek phrase *kakon anti kakou* — which carries the idea of a person who thinks, *You did wrong to me, so now I'm going to do wrong to you. I'm going to do to you exactly what you did to me!* In God's view, such vindictive behavior is completely unacceptable for committed Christians, even if someone has grievously wronged them.

Instead, Paul wrote that we must "...ever follow that which is good, both among yourselves, and to all men." The word "ever" is *pantote*, a word that means *always, at all times*, or *constantly*. The word "follow" is the word *dioko*, which in historic Greek literature meant *to hunt, to pursue, to chase*, or *to track down and kill*. It is the picture of an outdoorsman who is so determined to hunt down an animal that he will stop at nothing to pursue, chase, track down, and ultimately get his game!

Do hunters accidentally bag their game, or do they strategize and plan to get a good kill shot each hunting season? *Hunters strategize!* They talk to other hunters about the best places to hunt. They dress in camouflaged clothes. They often perch themselves high up on tree branches and wait for hours upon hours for an unlucky deer to walk into their path. Once the deer comes in range, *they shoot to kill!* They hunt, hound, and stalk that animal until they finally get their game. Then they throw the big catch in the back of their truck and head home with their trophy — and the prospect of many good venison meals in their future! That is exactly what Paul meant when he told us to ever "follow" that which is good.

The fact that what is good must be pursued means doing the right thing does not always come easy! But regardless of how hard it is to do it, you and I must *always* be committed to doing what is good and right. The word "good" in this verse is the word *agathos*, the Greek word that means *anything that is good, beneficial, or profitable*.

You may be tempted to resist being a blessing or to do nothing for someone you feel has done wrong to you. But as I've noted, it is *never* your job to pay someone back for what he or she did to you, or to withhold a blessing when you are able to give it.

Paul plainly taught that it is God's will that we "ever follow that which is good." That means we must be dedicated to pursuing that which is good, beneficial, and profitable. But must we really do good to *all* men? Must we seek to do good even to those who have done wrong to us?

Paul answered that question when he wrote that we must behave like this "both among yourselves, and to all men." The phrase "among yourselves" in Greek is *eis allelous* and it unquestionably refers to the relationships that existed between the brethren in church. But we are not to be in the occupation of doing good only to our fellow brethren. Paul also went on to say "to all men." This phrase "all men" would include those outside the Church, or those who are outside of Christ and therefore non-Christian.

If you feel that someone has committed an injustice against you or simply treated you badly, and you find yourself wishing you could "get back" at that person for what he or she did, that is a moment when you must take charge of your emotions and remind yourself that vindictive behavior is *never* God's will. Regardless of the evil others have committed against you, it is imperative that you remember what the apostle Paul wrote to the Thessalonians in First Thessalonians 5:15: "See that none render evil for evil unto any man; but ever follow that which is good, both among yourselves, and to all men."

An interpretive translation of First Thessalonians 5:15 could read:

"I am commanding you that not a single one among you should be involved in the business of retribution or revenge. It is not your task to retaliate, to get even, to take revenge, to make someone pay for what he did, or to settle the score. Your assignment is not only to pursue anything that will be beneficial and good for your Christian friends, but also for people who are outside of Christ."

Never forget that retribution is not the way we do business in the Kingdom of God. If there is any retribution, let it be something taken care of by God and not by you or me. Let's remember that we are in the business of redeeming the lost, *not* taking revenge or getting even with people when they upset us!

To consistently do good to others who haven't treated you right will require your commitment and dedication to obey Jesus. Achieving this will take your utmost concentration, undivided attention, and empowerment by the Holy Spirit. Commit yourself to following God's command not to render evil for evil, but to ever follow that which is good. As you do, the Holy Spirit will stand right alongside you to help you carry out this act of obedience. *Leave retribution in God's hands, and make it your business to do good to all men.*

MY PRAYER FOR TODAY

Father, I ask You to help me have a right attitude and heart toward people, including those who have hurt me and let me down. You know how deeply disappointed I have been in people that I expected to behave on a much higher level. Help me recall the many times I've let You down, yet You have never forsaken me, rejected me, or cast me aside. In spite of my personal failings, You continue to show Your love, mercy, and forgiveness to me — and Your blessings continue to abound in my life. Just as You have been steadfast in Your love for me, I ask You to help me have a steadfast heart filled with love, mercy, and goodwill for others.

I pray this in Jesus' name!

MY CONFESSION FOR TODAY

I declare that I am filled with the love of God and never want to do harm to anyone. God wants me to be a blessing to everyone I know and meet. Therefore, I am determined that strife, vengeance, and retribution toward others are not, and will not be, a part of my life. Jesus has called me to walk the high road, and I am committed to getting on the road of love and forgiveness. I will be a blessing to my Christian brethren and even to those who are without

Christ. I will obey God's Word and always seek to do good to people I know and meet. Other people's lives will be more richly blessed as a result of being around me and knowing me.

I declare this by faith in Jesus' name!

QUESTIONS FOR YOU TO CONSIDER

1. In this *Sparkling Gem*, I related the story of a man who wanted to "get" someone who had wronged us and our church. Did you identify with that story? Have you ever secretly wished you could pay someone back for the wrong you perceived he or she did to you?
2. Have you ever felt like the brunt of someone's efforts to "get back" at you for some wrong he perceived you did to them? When that happened, were you shocked to find that this person thought *you* had deliberately tried to mistreat *him*?
3. If you look at the people in or near your life right now, in what ways can you begin to reach out to benefit and bless them?

JANUARY 16

What Kind of a Special Vessel Are You?

But in a great house there are not only vessels of gold and silver,
but also of wood and earth....
— 2 Timothy 2:20

There are many different roles in God's Kingdom, and each role is significant and important. The devil often tells people that their role is not important because it is less visible than the role of others. Let me address that misconception by first telling you about an experience I had many years ago in an antique store that specialized in ancient relics.

When I looked at the shelves of the antique store, I was amazed at the many antiquities that appeared to have been sitting there for decades and were covered with a thick film of dust. An archeologist's treasure trove, this shop was also a housekeeper's nightmare because it hadn't been cleaned in years! I sneezed as I accidentally breathed in dust while rubbing my hand across the front of a beautiful vase I had taken from a high shelf.

From where I was standing, it appeared to me that the higher shelves were loaded with interesting historical items, such as vases of marble, jasper, and alabaster. I grabbed a stepladder and stretched upward on my toes so I could peer deeper into the cache of relics on that top shelf — and there I discovered genuine Roman antiquities made of silver and gold. Astonishment is the only word I know to describe the intense emotion that rushed through me as I reached out to take hold of those precious artifacts.

The lower shelves were also filled with memories from the ancient world, but these were primarily items made from stone and clay. I saw pottery from the Iron Age, oil lamps from the Byzantine period that had been dug from the soil of Israel, and authentic pottery from the ancient city of Corinth that was still completely intact.

As I stood back and looked at the floor all around me, I could see that I was surrounded by less expensive ancient items that were primarily made from wood, such an ancient harness used for oxen, feeding troughs, and Egyptian baskets of woven ancient reeds from the Nile River. The thought hit me strongly that whether these different objects were made of superior or relatively inferior material, they had all successfully endured the test of time and survived thousands of years.

I pondered all these objects for a moment, wondering:

- *Who had owned these objects?*
- *How had they been originally used?*
- *Who were the wealthy people who owned the gold and silver objects?*
- *How had the precious items been originally displayed in the palaces of the rich?*

When I picked up the items made of wood and clay, I could still see stains that remained from ancient times. I wondered:

- *Who had used these wooden and clay utensils?*
- *Had they been a part of a kitchen?*
- *Were they originally used in some type of workroom?*
- *Were some of these ancient items once used in someone's barn?*

Before me were vessels of gold, silver, stone, wood, and clay, all of which had survived the test of time and now sat in that shop as a reminder of a people from the ancient past. The rich, the poor, the upper class, the lower class, the educated, the uneducated, old and young — all the various classes of society were represented in the array of utensils and articles before me that day.

When I saw this amazing mixture of gold, silver, wood, and earthen vessels, my thoughts went to Paul's words to Timothy, where he told the younger minister, "But in a great house there are not only vessels of gold and silver, but also of wood and earth: and some to honor, and some to dishonor" (2 Timothy 2:20).

I want you to notice that Paul began this verse by writing about "a great house." At this point, Paul reached into the secular world and borrowed an example to make his point. In his mind, he recalled the magnificent homes that belonged to the rich upper class. When he wrote about a "great" house, he used the word *megale*. The word *megale* depicts something *very large*. The word "house" is *oikos*, the regular word for *a house*. But when the words *oikos megale* are used together, it no longer refers to just a regular residence or house like any citizen would live in. Now it paints the picture of *a very large house*.

Remnants of large, elegant residences from Paul's day are still evident today in cities like Rome, Athens, Pompeii, and ancient Ephesus. Such homes belonged to the wealthy upper class and were both splendid and grandiose. Paul used the illustration of these impressive houses to depict the majesty of *God's* house, which is the grandest and greatest of them all.

Paul went on to say that just as in the large homes of the wealthy, in God's house, "…There are not only vessels of gold and silver, but also of wood and earth…."

The word "vessels" is the Greek word *skeuos*. It refers to a *vessel, container*, or *utensil*. In ancient times, there was a wide array of *skeuos*, and each had a specific and designated purpose. The word *skeuos* could be used to depict utensils, agricultural instruments, baggage, equipment of various sorts, vases used in worship, kitchen items, and elegant articles of gold and silver put on public display.

Vessels made from "wood and earth" were usually functional items used for everyday household chores. The wooden items were also used as containers for water, flour, oil, or wine. Vessels fashioned from "gold and silver" were evidently intended for exhibition and therefore displayed in visible places in the homes of the rich. Gold and silver objects were meant to be seen and appreciated rather than serve a practical function.

There is no doubt that Paul was describing real gold and silver vessels, because he used the word *chrusos*, the Greek word for *gold*, and the word *arguros*, the Greek word for *silver*. The Greek word for "wood" is *zulina*, which describes any vessel made of *wood*. The word "earth" is the Greek word *ostrakinos*, which refers to *pottery*. (For a deeper study of the word *ostrakinos*, *see* the February 13 *Gem* in *Sparkling Gems 1*.) What a variety of vessels we see in this verse!

With this example, Paul teaches us that all kinds of vessels and people are needed in God's house. Imagine how dysfunctional a house would be if all the vessels in it were made of gold, silver, precious stones, or highly priced porcelain. You couldn't function in such a house! In fact, you would probably be afraid to even move about in a house where everything was made of precious materials. For a house to function normally, it needs regular pots and pans. The utensils in the kitchen may not receive the same adulation as the more elegant objects displayed in the living room showcase, but kitchen utensils are indispensable for the proper functioning of a household. Just try cooking bacon and eggs in porcelain vases or with utensils made of gold and silver, and you'll be quickly reminded how important regular ol' pots and pans are!

By using such imagery, Paul let us know that all kinds of vessels — people with different functions and roles — are needed in God's house. Although they are different from each other, each is important and special. Each serves a specific purpose. Just as was true with the vessels of the fabulous ancient homes, in God's house there must be many different kinds of people with different positions, functions, and purposes. In fact, His house is filled to overflowing with human vessels whose various gifts and talents are essential to the effective functioning of God's house. Some people have visible positions; other people have less visible positions. But each person is vital to the operations of God's house.

As you ponder your own role in God's house, it is important for you to remember that some people's roles are more visible, while others have a less visible part to play. Yet *everyone's* role is vital and of great consequence. If those working behind the scenes didn't do their part, those with more visible roles wouldn't be able to do *their* parts.

Human beings tend to glamorize people who perform on the stage, but entertainers wouldn't seem so glamorous if they had no makeup artists to prepare them. They wouldn't shine so brightly if there were no lighting specialists to light up the stage. Their voices would be unheard if there were no sound technicians. The makeup artists, lighting specialists, and sound technicians are unseen, but I guarantee you that their absence would be noticed if they didn't do their jobs! *They are all vital for the show to go on!*

So don't let the devil badger you into thinking your role is not important because it is less visible than others. Your part is very important in God's house!

There are many different roles in God's Kingdom, and each role is significant and important. Maybe your role is visible, or maybe yours is behind the scenes. Regardless of the role you have right now, consider it an honor that God would use you in His house! I encourage you to say *yes* to the role God has given you at this time. Throw open your arms, embrace it, and hold it close. Take deep into your heart the place of service to which God has assigned you for this season. Master that position — fulfilling its responsibilities with an excellent attitude — and then watch Him move you to higher levels of responsibility according to His will and His purposes for your life!

MY PRAYER FOR TODAY

Father, I thank You for speaking to me so strongly today about my role in Your House. I admit that in the past, there have been times when I was tempted to think that I was less important than others because my role wasn't as visible as theirs. But now I understand that my part in Your house is just as vital as those who are more public, for without my role, it would be much harder for them to do what You have called them to do. I ask You to give me grace to embrace, hold close, and take deep into my heart the position You have given me at this time in my life. Help me master it and fulfill my part in a way that is helpful to others and that honors and glorifies You.

I pray this in Jesus' name!

MY CONFESSION FOR TODAY

I confess that I am thankful for the role I have in God's house. I am not a complainer or one who bemoans the task that has been given to me. I fulfill my role with a happy heart, as unto the Lord, knowing that I will answer to Him for the assignment He has given me. Because I do my part, others are able to do their part. We are a team, and each of us is very important to the proper functioning of God's household. I appreciate my role; I value those who have different roles than mine; and I am known as a person who expresses my gratitude to others for what they do in God's house.

I declare this by faith in Jesus' name!

QUESTIONS FOR YOU TO CONSIDER

1. Have you ever been frustrated with the task that has been given to you in God's house? Did you think your role was less important than others' tasks because yours was *only* a supportive role? After reading today's *Sparkling Gem*, how has your attitude changed toward the supportive role you have been given?
2. Can you think of someone you know who is infected with "star sickness" and who treats others badly if they don't hold a prominent position? What have you learned by observing this person's inappropriate treatment of other people? Through observation, what have you learned that you never want to do to other people who have less visible roles than yourself?
3. Has the Holy Spirit spoken to you today about embracing your place in God's house? What changes do you need to make in your attitude to be successful in your present role in His Kingdom?

JANUARY 17

It's Time for You To Quit Comparing Yourself to Others!

...But they measuring themselves by themselves,
and comparing themselves
among themselves, are not wise.
— 2 Corinthians 10:12

Earlier in life, I struggled terribly with an inferiority complex. Inadequacy, insufficiency, incompetence, and deficiency are just a few words to express the feelings that tried to master my self-image. Today I want to share what I learned from that experience, as well as a great truth I found in my studies of Second Corinthians 10:12, which says, "...They measuring themselves by themselves, and comparing themselves among themselves, are not wise." I believe that the principle I discovered in this verse will help you if you've faced a similar struggle and you long to be free.

When our teaching ministry was first getting started, I wondered, *Who will ever want to have us minister in their church or conference?* Denise and I had been living in a small city and had very few contacts beyond our little circle, so it seemed like a logical question. On one hand, I knew that God had called us to teach His Word across the earth, but on the other hand, I questioned that call — how it would be fulfilled. No one knew who we were. No one had ever heard us teach the Bible. There was simply no logical reason for anyone to invite us to teach the Word in their churches or conferences.

We began to schedule meetings in small churches all across the United States. We joyfully walked through every door and took every opportunity that opened for us, even accepting invitations to speak in home Bible studies. But frequently the enemy would bombard my mind with tormenting thoughts to inflame old feelings of insecurity: *You'll never do anything on a large or significant scale. Your entire ministry will be to small groups of people!* When we got in the car to leave those meetings, I shared my struggling thoughts with Denise, and she'd try to encourage me. But the devil was hounding me with accusing thoughts of impending failure, telling me that I would be insignificant for the rest of my life.

I especially felt assaulted when we attended conferences or seminars to hear other speakers. Rather than be blessed, I vividly recall the devil telling me:

- *"You don't measure up to other speakers."*
- *"You are nothing in comparison to them."*
- *"Your style isn't like theirs."*
- *"You'll live and die a failure because you are too different from everyone else and you'll never be accepted."*
- *"You ARE nothing and HAVE nothing to offer in comparison to others."*

I fell into the trap of measuring and comparing myself against others, with the end result of always feeling like I fell hopelessly short. The devil literally tried to devastate me with feelings of inadequacy, deficiency, and inferiority. The more I compared myself to others, the more I felt "less than" — that is, until God's Spirit reached into my heart and set me free!

The reason I share this intimate struggle from my past is that I know there are many who compare themselves to others as I once did. That may be *your* struggle. If it is, today I want to share what I found in this scripture that helped set me free. I believe the principle I discovered in this verse will help set *you* free as well!

When the apostle Paul wrote to the Corinthians, he explained an important principle along this line: "...But they measuring themselves by themselves, and comparing themselves among themselves, are not wise" (2 Corinthians 10:12). The word "wise" is the Greek word *sophos*, which means *specially enlightened*, *wise*, *sharp*, or *bright*. This means the verse could be interpreted: *"Comparing yourselves among yourselves is not the sharpest or brightest thing to do!"*

I can attest from personal experience that habitually comparing yourself to others is not the brightest thing to do. It can be a fruitless endeavor that makes you feel worse and even more inferior. The word "comparing" is the Greek word *sunkrino*, and it is the picture of *two or more who stand side by side to thoroughly examine themselves in comparison to each other and then to critically judge who is superior among the candidates.* One group is classified as superior, and the other is classified as inferior. It is a fleshly endeavor that produces no spiritual fruit. It elevates one and puts another down, and it fails to recognize the many diverse graces of God that exist within the Christian community.

The Corinthian believers were fighting among themselves to prove who was the greatest among them. When Paul wrote this verse, he wrote it to rebuke them for making such comparisons. They didn't have a problem with inferiority, as I had struggled with earlier in life. They had an issue with feelings of *superiority* and were in fierce competition with each other. Paul wrote this verse to rebuke the Corinthian believers for making comparisons, exhorting them to stop their infighting as they tried to prove who was the most spiritual among them.

In the March 4 *Sparkling Gem*, we will address the ugly spirit of superiority that should never be permitted in a believer's life. However, there is a principle in this verse that the Holy Spirit used to help set me free from a spirit of inferiority. So here is the point I want to get across to you today: God intentionally made you different from others. You are actually a result of His divine design. Your mannerisms, insights, and style that are different from others may be the very qualities that make you uniquely positioned to fulfill a specific need.

Of course, we all have areas in our lives that need to be changed, and God will show these to you one at a time. But if you will quit comparing yourself to others — if you will stop disparaging the very qualities that cause you to stand out from those around you — you'll open the door to freedom from a spirit of inferiority so your unique gifts can begin to shine brightly as God intended.

The thing that personally bothered me most was that I felt so *different* from other people. In fact, the issue of feeling strange or "less than" others began when I was a child. Even when I was very young, I felt that I was *different* in comparison to others. While all the other boys were playing football, I was visiting museums. While other boys were talking about and watching baseball games, I was taking art lessons and visiting the symphony. Although it's true I was different in many ways from my peers, that difference *didn't* mean I was inferior to them. However, at that young moment in my life, the devil used those differences to sow harmful thoughts into my soul that something had to be wrong with me because I was different than others. Years later when I was an adult, this root was still affecting me as I fell into the trap of comparing myself to others and constantly feeling that I was too different to be accepted by them.

What I thought was a negative trait — being "different" from others — was the very thing that made me uniquely qualified to fulfill my call. When I finally understood that *God* was the One who made me different, I began to see that I could shine His light in ways that others could not. What I thought would hold me back is actually what gave me my place in His plan! When I began to accept who God made me to be, I was freed from the devil's mental assault and began to step out of the shadows so God could begin to use me in a greater way. I was finally able to *embrace* my uniqueness that made me shine differently from others.

That can be your story too! You can make the decision *today* that you're never going to go down that bumpy, twisted road of comparing yourself to others and always coming up short. Today you're going to start *celebrating* the differences that make you uniquely *you*!

MY PRAYER FOR TODAY

Father, I thank You for the ways in which You made ME unique and different from others. Forgive me for the times I've struggled with being different. Now I understand that my differences distinguish me from others. You specially made me to fulfill a role no one else can fulfill. I accept what You have made me to be, and, Holy Spirit, I surrender my life to You. I ask You to help me present all that I am to the Father, changing what needs to be changed, so that my life will bring glory to Jesus Christ.

I pray this in Jesus' name!

MY CONFESSION FOR TODAY

I declare that what I am, I am by the grace of God and that He didn't make any mistakes in the way He made me! He gifted me with talents, emotions, humor, insights, perspectives, and unique qualities that set me apart from others. My differences are some of the most positive attributes in my life, and I will not reject myself anymore simply because I am different. Being different puts me in a special category that I will no longer despise, but will use for the glory of God!

I declare this by faith in Jesus' name!

QUESTIONS FOR YOU TO CONSIDER

1. Have you struggled with being "different" from others? In what ways do you think you are different from other people?
2. After reading today's *Sparkling Gem*, can you see how being unique puts you in a category of your own? Why not take a few minutes to write down the ways that being unique is a positive factor in your life?
3. How can you maximize your uniqueness? Every product is known because it has something to offer that other products do not offer. What do *you* have to offer that distinguishes you from other people?

You are actually a result of God's divine design.
Your mannerisms, insights, and style
that are different from others may be the very qualities
that make you uniquely positioned
to fulfill a specific need.

JANUARY 18

Gold, Silver, Precious Stones, Wood, Hay, or Stubble

Now if any man build upon this foundation gold,
silver, precious stones, wood, hay, stubble.
— 1 Corinthians 3:12

If you are ever fortunate to visit the city of Rome, you will be *amazed* to see how much of that ancient city has survived the past 2,000 years. Right in the heart of Italy's modern capital, you can almost take a peek into ancient Rome as you gaze upon ruins from the time of the Roman Empire, such as the Coliseum, Pantheon, Roman Forum, and so much more. It is truly *remarkable.*

The reason so much of ancient Rome can still be seen today is that most of its buildings were constructed of stone. Romans wanted their greatness to be etched into human history forever. Therefore, when they built the city, they constructed buildings designed to declare the Caesar's glory for millennia. Government buildings, palaces, streets, monuments, columns, and statues — all of these were intended to tell future generations how great the Romans were. Although the *gold, silver,* and *precious stones* that once adorned these buildings have since been stripped away, scores of these structures remain intact. And just as the original builders intended, they tell us about the glory of the Romans.

However, not all of Rome was made of stone, gold, silver, and precious stones. There was another side of Rome, where the flimsy, poorly made wooden dwellings of the poor were located.

Because wealthy Romans didn't like to do manual labor, they imported foreigners from across the great Roman Empire and forced them into slavery. As a result of this massive importation of slaves, each year the slave population grew larger and larger until it became the largest sector of Rome. Some estimate that the slave population outnumbered the free population of the city by three to one! In effect, the city of Rome had become a city of slaves who lived to serve the needs, whims, and desires of their masters.

As large as this slave sector was, the ancient dwellings of the slaves did not survive the past 2,000 years. Over the centuries, the weather, decay, and fire that ravaged Rome also ravaged those flimsy wooden structures. The homes of the slaves, who had no personal funds and were generally poorly treated by the rich Romans, were constructed quickly and cheaply using wood, hay, and stubble as building materials. That's why almost nothing remains of these shabby dwellings today. They could not pass the test of time and were never intended to survive like the massive stone structures that tell about the greatness of the Romans.

Because the apostle Paul traveled throughout the Roman Empire, he witnessed the disparity between the rich and the poor. He'd gaze upon the massive stone structures of the rich. Then right next to those impressive buildings, he'd see the flimsy homes where slaves were forced to live. What a comparison! One type of structure was built to last *forever*, whereas the other type was so rickety that it wouldn't even last a *lifetime*.

As Paul wrote to the Corinthians and urged them to be careful about how they lived and built their lives, he used this comparison as an illustration. His point was this: Although all believers have the solid Rock of Jesus Christ under their lives, what they build on top of that foundation is so very important.

Hence, Paul wrote, "Now if any man build upon this foundation gold, silver, precious stones, wood, hay, stubble." In this statement, Paul was asking us:

- *Are you building your life with eternity in mind?*
- *Are you using materials that will stand the test of time — or that will produce a structure that won't last long?*
- *Are you building your life hastily and cheaply for today — or in a way that will count forever?*

Let's look at the building materials Paul listed in this verse. First, he mentioned "gold." This word "gold" is the Greek word *chrusos*, which means *gold* and describes the most valuable material that existed in the Roman Empire. Nothing was more expensive or costly than gold. Gold was extremely *rare* — especially before the time of Alexander the Great — and was therefore *highly prized*. Gold wasn't strong enough to be an actual building material. But if a building was extremely important, gold was used ornamentally on the outside relief of buildings and in the decor of its interiors. When gold was used, either on the exterior or inside décor of a building, it indicated that this building was a structure of great significance.

The word "silver" is the Greek word *arguros*, which often referred to *silver money* because silver was the primary metal used for coins. For example, the Bible tells us that Judas Iscariot betrayed Jesus for "thirty pieces of silver" (*see* Matthew 26:15). The word "silver" is this Greek word *arguros* and conveys the idea of *money*.

However, silver was also used inside special buildings for ornamentation and decoration, similar to the way gold was used, and items for worship or prestige were often fashioned of silver. In Acts 19:24, we read that idols depicting the goddess Artemis in Ephesus were made of silver. Anything in the ancient world that was made of silver was considered *expensive* and *precious*.

The phrase "precious stones" in Greek is *lithous timious*, from the word *lithos*, the Greek word for *stone*, and the word *timao*, a Greek word meaning *honorable*, *costly*, or *precious*. When Paul mentioned "precious stones," he was not alluding to diamonds, rubies, emeralds, sapphires, or other gemstones. Paul was referring to expensive building materials, such as *marble* or *granite*. These materials were considered top-of-the-line building materials because they could endure *weather*, *fire*, and *time*. Any building made to last was fashioned of marble or granite.

Gold, silver, and precious stones (marble and granite) were the most expensive and the highest quality materials used in the construction of a building in Paul's day. *These were durable, long-lasting, resilient materials!* That's why buildings made of these materials are still standing today.

But Paul went on to describe another category of building materials: *wood, hay,* and *stubble.* Let's also look at these words for just a moment to see why he mentioned them in this verse. You are about to see that Paul was making a very dramatic comparison!

First, the word "wood" is the Greek word *zulos*, and it means *wood, wooden timbers, branches of a tree, boards*, or *anything made of wood.* It primarily denoted *building materials.* However, this word was also frequently used to depict *fuel for a fire.* This word *zulos* describes a building composed of *cheap, temporary, perishable, burnable materials.* You can quickly build such a building, but a house of wood is never built to last for the ages. This was the primary material used in construction of slave dwellings in Rome. These wooden houses were homes that could go up in smoke very easily.

Second, Paul mentioned "hay," which was another material used in the construction of slave dwellings. The word "hay" is the word *chortos*, and it means *grass* or *hay.* This "hay" should never have been used as a construction material, for it was meant to be the food that was fed to animals; in fact, it was often used to mean *fodder.* In other words, this "hay" was meant to be *eaten*, not used for *construction.* Because of its fragile, transitory nature, hay was considered to be *the poorest material* to use in construction. Yet in the slave homes of Rome, it was commonly used for the *roof.*

Third, Paul mentioned "stubble." This is the Greek word *kalame*, which simply means *straw* or *stubble.* This material was so inferior that even animals wouldn't eat it. Yet in the homes of slaves, it was used as a *floor covering*, as *insulation*, and as *stuffing for beds.* It was cheap, disposable, and replaceable. Think of it! These slave dwellings were made of wood and sticks; the roofs were made of grass; and the walls were insulated with straw. *No wonder these dwellings didn't last!*

As I've stated, one type of building was built to last *forever*, whereas the other was so rickety that it wouldn't even last a *lifetime.*

By using this illustration, Paul was confronting us with the question: *How are you building your life?* Are you building hastily and with perishable materials? Or are you taking your life seriously, building carefully with materials that will last throughout your life and are strong enough to impact not only this present generation, but also the generations to come?

This is precisely what Paul was saying when he wrote, "Now if any man build upon the foundation gold, silver, precious stones, wood, hay, stubble."

The Foundation under our lives is Jesus, but what we build on top of that Foundation depends on our personal commitment and the level of excellence we demand of ourselves in every area of our lives. So I ask you: Are you building something with your life that will be enduring — or are you building so hastily and poorly that everything you've built could go up suddenly in a puff of smoke?

Look at your life and ask yourself:

- **How am I building my marriage?**

  Based on what I am doing today, will my marriage flourish or perish?

- **How am I building my children?**

  Will my children pass the tests of life because of what I am putting into them?

- **How am I building my relationships?**

  Am I building my relationships so they can stand up against any storm?

- **How am I building my ministry?**

  Am I doing a lot of "quick fixes" that aren't real solutions to problems in my ministry, or am I taking time to build my ministry right so it will last a lifetime?

- **How am I building my business?**

  Will the steps I am taking today build a long-term business, or will I later regret that I didn't make longer-lasting decisions?

- **How am I building my finances?**

  Am I using money in a way to build my future, or am I throwing away my future by being reckless today?

- **How am I building my health?**

  If I keep doing what I am doing right now, will I be healthy later in life, or is my present lifestyle jeopardizing my future physical health?

Yes, Jesus is the Foundation under your life. Thank God for this awesome truth! But what you build on top of that foundation depends upon *you.* I advise you to ponder the questions I've posed to you in this *Sparkling Gem* and to spend some time talking to the Lord about how you answer them. This is such an important issue, because the ultimate outcome of your life depends on your getting those answers right.

MY PRAYER FOR TODAY

Lord, as I start my day today, I ask You to help me seriously consider the way I've been building my life, my finances, my business, my ministry, my relationships, and my family. Forgive me for getting in a hurry and for doing things too hastily at times when I need to be concentrating on doing things right. Help me build my life in such a way that it will survive the test of time. Give me the insight I need to know when I am building correctly and when I am building too quickly. I know that my life is important and that You have trusted me as a steward over everything I have. So today I confess that I need Your help to build with the right materials and to build in such a way that what I do for You impacts future generations and passes the test of time.

I pray this in Jesus' name!

MY CONFESSION FOR TODAY

I confess that with God's help, I am building my life wisely and with materials that will pass the test of time. My life is a gift from God, and I am a careful steward over this wonderful gift. Instead of being too hasty, I am carefully taking one step at a time, building my life, vision, business, and family so they will be strong for years to come. I would never be smart enough to build a life that lasts in my own strength, but with the assistance of the Holy Spirit, I am learning to build my life wisely, carefully, and for longevity!

I declare this by faith in Jesus' name!

QUESTIONS FOR YOU TO CONSIDER

1. Can you think of areas of your life that were built incorrectly and therefore didn't last the way you had wished? What were those areas, and what did you learn from these experiences?
2. Are you presently building certain parts of your life with shaky, flimsy materials? If so, what steps are you going to take to change this?
3. Take a few minutes today to let the Lord help you review your life so you can honestly ascertain if you are building your life correctly or incorrectly. Never forget that your life is a gift from God and that you are called to be a wise steward of that gift by building your spiritual house with gold and silver and precious stones!

JANUARY 19

Could You Survive a Fire?

Every man's work shall be made manifest:
for the day shall declare it,
because it shall be revealed by fire;
and the fire shall try every man's work
of what sort it is.
— 1 Corinthians 3:13

I will never forget the sound of the fire engines one night several years ago. We lived in a high-rise building in central Moscow, so when those fire trucks came speeding through the city with their horns blaring, the sound reverberated between the buildings on either side of the street as sound might ricochet off the walls in a great cavern.

I saw the lights flashing from the back side of our apartment, so Denise and I stepped out onto the balcony to see what was happening. The building directly behind us was on fire — and the flames were literally piercing the top of the roof and ferociously crackling upward into the smoke-filled air. The heat was so intense that the firemen were unable to get very close to the building. They had to stand back and watch the fire do its worst work before they could begin pumping water close enough to put out the burning timbers on the roof.

After the fire finally subsided, the only part of the building that remained was the part made of stone and mortar. Everything composed of burnable material was gone — *reduced to ashes and burned to a crisp*!

With today's sophisticated technology and machinery, fires are usually extinguished quickly, thus reducing the amount of damage done. But in the apostle Paul's day, there was no such equipment. Fires were a huge problem in large ancient cities. In fact, when a fire began, it often raged out of control for many days.

What made this even worse was the fact that the slave population in large cities lived in dwellings made of *wood, hay,* and *stubble.* As we saw in yesterday's *Sparkling Gem*, this was exactly the picture Paul had in his mind when he wrote, "Now if any man build upon this foundation gold, silver, precious stones, *wood, hay, stubble*" (1 Corinthians 3:12).

To review, the word "wood" in this verse is the Greek word *zulos*, and it means *wood, wooden timbers, branches of a tree, boards*, or *anything made of wood.* However, this word was also frequently used to depict *fuel for a fire.* Thus, this word *zulos* can describe a building composed of *cheap, temporary, perishable, burnable materials.*

The word "hay" in the same verse is the Greek word *chortos*, and it means *grass* or *hay.* This "hay" should never have been used as a construction material, for it ignited very easily. It was meant to be the food that was fed to animals and is often translated as "fodder."

The word "stubble" in First Corinthians 3:12 is the Greek word *kalame*, which means *straw* or *stubble.* This material was so inferior that even animals wouldn't eat it. Yet in the homes of slaves, it was used as a *floor covering, insulation*, and *stuffing for beds.* It was cheap, disposable, and replaceable.

Think of it! Those slave dwellings were made of wood and sticks, covered with a roof of grass, and insulated with straw. *Imagine how quickly these flimsy structures went up in smoke when a fire touched them!* When a fire struck one of those little houses, it ignited like a box of matches and started a chain reaction. Pieces of burning wood, grass, and straw whirled upward into the air as hot embers and fell on the surrounding slave dwellings. One after another, every little house made of wood, hay, and stubble burst into flames and began to burn like an inferno. Wood, hay, and stubble fueled the fire!

When these fires ran their course and died out, everything that *could* be burned *was* burned. Everything made of wood, hay, and stubble was *gone*!

This is one reason important buildings were made of stone. The builders knew that if a fire ever raged through the city, a stone building might get scorched but would still survive. Although it might be stained with smoke, the building would endure the worst of a fire and be fixable!

Living in the First Century AD and ministering in large cities, Paul had no doubt seen the effects of fire. Knowing that hardships, tests, and trials eventually come to every person's life, he used this example as a backdrop when he said, "Every man's work shall be made manifest: for the day shall declare it, because it shall be revealed by fire; and the fire shall try every man's work of what sort it is" (1 Corinthians 3:13).

Paul began this verse by saying, "Every man's work shall be made manifest…." By using the words "every man," the apostle informed us that eventually a time comes to *every person* when he will be tested. The words "every man" are from the Greek word *hekastos*, an all-encompassing word that means *everyone, no one excluded.* Hence, Paul was telling us that no one in this world is completely exempt from fiery situations that arise to test him and thus reveal the true quality of what he is doing and building with his life.

By using our faith and yielding to the leading of the Holy Spirit, we can avoid many catastrophes and demonic attacks in life. But as long as we are in this world where the devil operates, there will be moments when fire comes to test our *works*. When these fires come, that is the golden moment when we discover if our works are made of *gold, silver*, and *precious stones* — or if we have been building our lives with *wood, hay*, and *stubble.*

The word "work" in First Corinthians 3:13 informs us of *what* will be tested. The Greek word is *ergos*, which refers to *the work* or *the output* of one's life. It signifies *some kind of action, deed, or activity*. Very often it referred to *a person's occupation, a person's labor*, or *the things produced by a person's effort or life*. Thus, it could describe *a person's line of work, his career, his acts of labor*, or even *his profession.*

Paul warned us that a day will come when our works will be tested. On that day, the true quality of our works and the real motive, intention, and reason behind our works will become evident. That is why he said, "Every man's work shall be made *manifest….*"

The word "manifest" is the Greek word *phaneros*. It describes something that is *visible, observable, obvious, clear, open, apparent*, or *evident*. In fact, our works will become so evident that, as Paul said, "Every man's work shall be made manifest: for the day shall declare it, because it shall be *revealed* by fire…" (1 Corinthians 3:13).

That word "revealed" is the Greek word *apokalupto*. It is a compound of two Greek words, *apo* and *kalupsis*. The word *apo* means *away*. The word *kalupsis* means *a curtain* or *a veil*. When these two words are compounded, the new word describes *something that has been veiled or hidden for a long time, but is now clear and visible because the veil has been removed.*

It is like pulling the curtains out of the way so you can see what has always been just outside your window. The scene was always there for you to see, but the curtains blocked your ability to see the real picture. However, when the curtains were drawn apart, you could suddenly see what had been hidden from your view. In that moment, you saw beyond the curtain for the first time and observed what was there all along but had not been visible to you.

Often we see things on the surface, but we don't know the real motivations of a person's heart or the hidden reason why people do what they do. However, a day is coming when our works and the works of others will suddenly come into view. On that day, the curtains will be drawn apart, and the picture will become clear both to ourselves and to others. On that day, Paul said *fire* will pull the curtains apart so that the real picture becomes clear.

Paul went on to say, "Every man's work shall be made manifest: for the day shall declare it, because it shall be revealed *by fire*...." The words "by fire" can either be translated *by fire* or *in the midst of fire*. The language makes it 100-percent clear that *fire* is the medium that will expose the truth about what we have done and what we are doing with our lives. We are tested *by* fiery situations or *in the midst of* fiery situations.

Paul goes on to say, "...And the fire shall *try* every man's work of what sort it is." The Greek word translated "try" is the word *dokimadzo*. It means *to test, to try*, or *to scrutinize*. It was used to describe the testing of metals or other materials to see if they could stand up under pressure. If these materials had a flaw of any kind, the pressure of this test was so intense that it would cause that object to crack or to break into pieces.

The purpose of the test was not to hurt the object, but to expose flaws that could later do greater damage to many people. Putting materials through such *dokimadzo* tests was intended to point out the weak, dangerous, hidden flaws before these materials were used. It was simply a fact that later when these materials were used, they would be put under tremendous stress. If hidden flaws remained undiscovered, it could prove disastrous. Moving too quickly or using materials that were improperly made could result in the loss of an entire project, in the loss of money, and even in the loss of life.

Like it or not, it's just a fact that tests come to us all in life. So rather than shut our eyes to this reality, we must allow the Holy Spirit to expose the hidden flaws in our souls, our character, and our work that would later break us when even more fiery trials come our way. It is up to us to make sure that we are building our lives with materials that will pass the test and won't crumble under pressure!

Can you think of a time when you, your work, your job, or your ministry was tested? I can think of several times when our own ministry experienced hardships that revealed hidden flaws in our organization. I didn't relish the experience, but afterward I was thankful that the fire had revealed weaknesses that we were unaware of but really needed to deal with. As difficult as those situations were, I was grateful I saw the defects and the areas where we had incorrectly built our ministry. Those fiery situations exposed the truth that we *needed* to see!

That is why Paul concludes this verse by saying, "Every man's work shall be made manifest: for the day shall declare it, because it shall be revealed by fire; and the fire shall try every man's work of *what sort* it is" (1 Corinthians 3:13).

As we have seen, in the ancient world, fires occasionally consumed everything that was made of wood, hay, and stubble. However, everything made of gold, silver, and precious stone survived. When the fire was done, it revealed what had been built cheaply, hastily, and with perishable materials, and it also revealed what had been built with right materials and by right methods. As Paul says in First Corinthians 3:13, fire tells us *what sort* of thing we've been building with our lives!

An interpretive paraphrase of First Corinthians 3:13 could read as follows:

"Regardless of you who are, it is just a fact that a day will eventually come when the true nature of what you have built with your life will be exposed by fiery situations. When the fire comes, you'll be so thoroughly tested that you'll have a clearer picture afterward of what you have been building right and what you have been building wrong."

I don't know how our discussion today has affected you, but it makes *me* want to seek the face of God to make sure I am building my life, my marriage, my children, my finances, my household, my ministry, my organization, and every other part of my life in a way that will pass every test of life.

It is just a fact that if you and I build our lives hastily, cheaply, or with the wrong motives, a situation will eventually arise that will reveal the truth. When that day comes, everything we've done wrong will be burned and will go up in smoke, just like a fire consumes wood, hay, and stubble.

So rather than waste our precious time on works that have no eternal value, let's choose to be wise by getting before God so He can speak to our hearts. God is more than willing to show us what we need to correct *before* a fire comes to teach us the hard way!

MY PRAYER FOR TODAY

Father, help me take a good look at my life to see if I am building it correctly with the kind of materials that will last through any difficult time. I do not want to be irresponsible in the way I build my life, my family, my business, or my calling, so please help me be very attentive to what I am doing and how I am doing it. I realize that tests eventually come to everyone, and I know that if I am diligent with my life right now, I will stand up stronger and last longer when the storms of life try to assail me. So help me today, Holy Spirit, to start seriously pondering my life to see how I can be building better.

I pray this in Jesus' name!

MY CONFESSION FOR TODAY

I confess that with the help of the Holy Spirit, I am building my life in such a way that I will be able to survive any attack! Because I am building wisely — with the right materials and the right methods — my life is becoming so strong that it will be capable of passing every test. I forsake hasty, irresponsible living, and I press forward with purpose to make a difference in this world. Therefore, I am giving my best efforts to build something that is excellent, respectable, and will bring glory to Jesus.

I declare this by faith in Jesus' name!

QUESTIONS FOR YOU TO CONSIDER

1. Can you think of any areas of your life that "went up in smoke" because you moved too hastily, built with the wrong materials, or used the wrong methods? What were those areas, and what did you learn from those experiences?
2. What have you done differently since you experienced this loss in your personal life? Take a few minutes to write down your thoughts about what you should do differently in order to build your life so it can withstand even the worst fire.
3. Do you know anyone going through tests and trials right now who could use some encouragement? If you remember what it was like to go through hard times, why not look for ways to comfort those who are hurting with the same comfort you received from God?

JANUARY 20

Do You Follow the Rules?

Moreover it is required in stewards
that a man be found faithful.
— 1 Corinthians 4:2

When we were growing up, my father often reminded me and my siblings, "As long as you live under my roof, you are going to abide by my rules!"

My parents were wonderful examples and godly leaders in our home. They loved us deeply. However, my father made it very clear who was in charge. We understood that Dad was the head of the home — and, as such, he made the rules. When wills collided and we wanted to do something contrary to his way of doing things, we were reminded that he was the one in charge, *not* us. Resisting Dad's rules in one of those moments was like running into a wall of solid concrete. If anyone was going to bend, it wasn't going to be him — it was going to be *us*.

I am so thankful for this lesson that my father taught me when I was young. I feel sorry for children today who are not taught to respect authority at home, because they're not being adequately prepared for the realities of life they will later face. Because they were permitted to bend the rules or, even worse, to manipulate their way around the rules, they will be in for a big shock when they enter the work world and discover that their boss is *not* going to bend for them or allow their manipulation. If we love our children, we must teach them that living by the rules is a part of life.

Because my father made the rules very plain, we knew what was expected in our home and we knew the kinds of behavior that would never be tolerated. This knowledge created stability and taught responsibility to me and my siblings. I am so thankful that my parents taught us that we must live by the rules. When my own sons were growing up, I told them the same thing my father had told me: "As long as you live in our house, you are going to abide by my rules." Today as I look at our sons, I can see the great fruit this firmness produced in their lives. They are authority-honoring, law-abiding, responsible men.

Living by the rules is a necessary part of every realm of life. In the natural, it's true that your habitual violation of the rules will eventually result in negative consequences or punishment. On the other hand, if you abide by the rules, you position yourself for a life of order, stability, and freedom from enforced restriction. In the same way, God has rules — and if you are a son or daughter in His house, He expects you to live by the rules. In fact, if you refuse to abide by His rules, you will probably never be greatly used by God. He looks for the obedient — those who respect Him, honor His Word, and follow His instructions.

Paul told the Corinthians, "Moreover it is required in stewards that a man be found faithful" (1 Corinthians 4:2). This verse is filled with lots of important teaching, but today I want us to look carefully at the word "steward," which is so important to understand if you want God to use you significantly in this life. However, first I want to draw your attention to the word "required."

The word "required" is actually translated improperly in the *King James Version*. It is the Greek word *zeteo*, and it means *to seek*, *to search*, or *to look very intensively* for something. It was used as a legal term to denote *a judicial investigation*, and it could even refer to *a scientific investigation*. It denotes an intense and thorough searching for accurate, concrete facts, *not* a mere surface investigation. The *King James Version* says, "Moreover it is required in stewards that a man be found faithful," but the Greek could be interpreted, *"Moreover, God is making a concentrated, exhaustive, and thorough search in pursuit of stewards who are faithful."*

Because the word *zeteo* is used, we know that the high caliber of stewards God is *seeking* is not abundant in His house. Such "stewards" are so uncommon that God must *search thoroughly* and *exhaustively* to find those who respect, honor, and abide by the rules of His house. Just consider what it means, then, when God does find the rare treasure called a faithful steward. No wonder "...the eyes of the Lord move to and fro throughout the whole earth to show Himself strong in behalf of those whose hearts are blameless toward Him" (2 Chronicles 16:9 *AMPC*)!

Now let's focus on the word "steward." This word in Greek is *oikonomos*, which is a compound of the words *oikos* and *nemoo*. The first part of the word, *oikos*, is the word for a *house*. It expresses the idea of a real physical residence where a family resides, including the residents, furniture, finances, property, and household items connected to that particular family and home. Because the word *oikos* is all-inclusive not only of the *house*, but also of its residents and their possessions, finances, affairs, and everything else in or connected to that particular house — it is often translated *household*, which correctly conveys the idea of this Greek word.

The second part of the word *oikonomos* is the word *nemoo*, which means *to dispense* or *to administrate*. It is derived from the word *nomos*, which is the Greek word for *law* and refers to anything *laid down, ordered, established*, or *made into law*. It depicts *standards, norms, or laws that are firmly established, publicly accepted, and categorically expected*. These rules are to be respected and followed. Violating such a rule of law would result in penalty.

When the word *oikos* and *nomos* are compounded into one word, as in First Corinthians 4:2, the new word formed is *oikonomos*, which means *the rule or management of a house*. In the Old Testament Greek Septuagint, the word *oikonomos* depicted leaders so trusted by the king or state that they were appointed to administrate entire departments or nations. In secular documents of that time, the word *oikonomos* is translated *court officials* or *palace officials*, and it described *anyone entrusted with a public office*. As public officials, they were to set the supreme example of honoring the law in their private lives, households, and personal affairs.

Over time, the word *oikonomos* was applied to *household stewards*. Household stewards were individuals entrusted with managerial responsibility in wealthy homes. It was their job to *run the household in an orderly fashion and according to the rules* set forth by the owner or *to administer the rules* of the house. The word "steward" could designate *the gatekeeper, the chief concierge, the head janitor, the head cook*, or *the chief accountant*. These were not mere laborers, but directors of departments who had oversight, responsibility, and who were therefore *accountable* for areas entrusted to their care. Most importantly, they knew, respected, and followed the rules set forth by the one in authority over them, and they made sure others in the household followed the rules as the head of the household expected.

In the New Testament, the word *oikonomos* appears only ten times. A key example is Romans 16:23, where it is used to describe a brother in Corinth named Erastus. In that verse, Paul referred to a brother he called "Erastus the chamberlain of the city." For historical purposes, I want to note that a marble slab with an inscription identifying Erastus as the chamberlain of Corinth was discovered buried in the remains of ancient Corinth.

The word "chamberlain" that described this brother and leader in Corinth is the word *oikonomos*, which clearly tells us that Erastus was the *chief administrator* of the city. For a Christian to hold such a title in the pagan world of Paul's time was very rare, but this shows that the Christian influence was beginning to be felt on every level of life. As the *chamberlain, manager*, or *administrator* of the city, Erastus was responsible to *know* the law, *live by* the law, *enforce* the law, and *apply* the law to others. If you take this meaning into First Corinthians 4:2, where Paul discusses "stewards" in God's house, it unmistakably means that God is seeking leaders who know His rules and live by them, who set themselves as an example for others by applying His rules in every situation, and who therefore teach others how to live by those rules as well.

The word "required" precedes the word "stewards," and it comes from the Greek word *zeteo*, which implies *a thorough search*. This emphatically means God is ardently seeking people who are committed to His Word. When He finds a man or woman who knows the Word, honors the

Word, and follows the Word in every situation, He has found the type of person to whom He will give authority and responsibility. The fact that this individual knows the rules and lives by them demonstrates to God that he or she can be trusted with greater responsibility.

Just as my father reminded me that as long as I lived under his roof, I was going to live by his rules, God also expects us to live by the rules of *His* house. We must remember that we are His sons and daughters in the household of faith. It is our obligation and responsibility to live under God's roof according to His rules. I assure you that if we are out of sync with God's Word, He isn't going to bend to accommodate *us. We* are the ones who must change and conform to *Him.*

Especially if you are a leader or if you desire to be a leader who has influence on others, it is imperative for you to know and to live by God's rules and to ensure that these rules are honored by all under your charge. If you are a person who already does this, throw up your arms and rejoice, because God is searching for you and is about to tap you on the shoulder to do something marvelous! I assure you that God is listening to your prayers — and He is watching to see if He can trust you with a bigger assignment. If He finds you faithful, a new assignment will soon arrive at your door.

However, if you are sloppy about how you apply God's rules to your life, you need to be honest with yourself and realize that the big break you've been hoping for may still be very far away. *For God to give you a big assignment, He needs to know that He can trust you to live according to the rules of His house!*

I encourage you to take an honest survey of your life and examine every detail to see if you have been honoring God's Word and obeying it as strictly as you should. If not, then make this your opportunity to repent. Follow your repentance with change, and know that God will watch to see if your repentance is genuine. Once your heart is set to do your best to keep His rules, a new assignment will soon be on the way. But never forget that before God gives a big assignment to someone, He carefully observes his actions to see if he is living according to the rules of His house.

Since this is true, wouldn't it be wise for you to examine your life before the Lord to determine what HE sees as He watches you?

MY PRAYER FOR TODAY

Father, I thank You for making me Your child — and today I am renewing my commitment to live according to the rules of Your house. It is a great honor to be Your child. I want to honor You by being obedient to You. I want to understand Your rules — what they mean, why You require them, and how to apply them to every situation in my life. When You look at me, I want You to see me as a child of God who is ardently doing all I can to honor Your rules, to live by Your rules, and to help others honor and obey them too. In my own flesh, it is impossible to do it all, but with the help of Your Spirit who dwells inside me, I can do what You expect and live in a way that brings glory to Your name. Holy Spirit, today I am turning to You for help as I endeavor to honor God in the way that I live under His roof.

I pray this in Jesus' name!

MY CONFESSION FOR TODAY

I confess that I am Christ-honoring and Word-keeping in the way I live and conduct my life. The Holy Spirit empowers me to think right, to do right, and to order my life according to the law of God. I am not a law-breaker — I am a law-abiding child of God. When God sees me, He finds me to be faithful and honoring of the rules that are so very important to Him. I am thankful to be saved and honored to be called a child of God. Therefore, I will do everything in my power to honor God in the way I live in His house and under His roof.

I declare this by faith in Jesus' name!

QUESTIONS FOR YOU TO CONSIDER

1. Can you think of areas in your life where you are sloppy in your obedience to the Word of God? Have you been cutting yourself too much slack in areas that God doesn't take lightly? What are those areas, and how long have you been sloppy in your obedience to these important issues?
2. If you were God and you were looking at your life, would you consider yourself to be a law-keeper or one who tries to bend or get around the rules?
3. For you to genuinely repent, what necessary changes do you need to make in your life? God already knows the truth about you, so why don't you take a few minutes today to be honest with God and with yourself so you can begin to make the changes He wants to see in your life.

JANUARY 21

The Most Important Requirement!

Moreover it is required in stewards,
that a man be found faithful.
— 1 Corinthians 4:2

People frequently ask, "How does God choose whom He wants to use?" This is an important question to ask, and one that you *should* ask if you desire to be used by the Lord. As you look at those whom God uses in a significant way, it will quickly become obvious to you that God doesn't choose people simply because of raw talent or gifts. So there must be another, higher reason that causes Him to reach out and lay His hand on an individual to use him or her in a special way. What is that reason?

There are several answers to this question. In my book *Say Yes*, I discuss the reasons why God chooses some people and not others. Certainly God loves everyone, but God is not obligated to use everyone He loves. There are certain qualities that cause God to reach out and use some more than others. You need to know those reasons.

In First Corinthians 4:2, the apostle Paul gave us *one answer* to this question. Paul stated this so categorically that it seems this quality is at the top of God's list of requirements for those who will do His work. Paul wrote, "Moreover it is required in stewards that a man be found faithful."

I want to draw your attention to the word "faithful" in this verse. This word "faithful" comes from the Greek word *pistos*, which is derived from the word *pistis*, the Greek word *faith*. However, in First Corinthians 4:2, the word *pistos* doesn't refer to faith as a spiritual force; rather, it denotes a person who is *faithful*. This is a person whom God has found to be *faithful, trustworthy, reliable, dependable, true*, and *unfailing*.

But how does God know if a person is faithful, trustworthy, reliable, dependable, true, and unfailing? Paul answered this question when he wrote, "Moreover it is required in stewards that a man be *found* faithful." There is no second-guessing with God about this question. The word "found" emphatically means that God watches us over a long period of time and in many different circumstances to see if we are faithful, trustworthy, reliable, dependable, true, and unfailing.

If you were God looking for someone to use in a mighty way, wouldn't you first watch a person's character and actions to see if he or she was someone on whom you could depend for a big assignment? *Even secular employers inspect employees to see who is trustworthy of a big promotion!*

The word "found" is the Greek word *eurisko*, which means *to find* or *to discover*. It is a discovery made as a result of careful observance. It tells us that God is carefully watching us to see our actions and reactions. He is watching to see how we treat people, how we respond to pressure, and whether or not we have the tenacity to stay on track when distractions try to thwart our obedience. Before He taps us on the shoulder to give us a new assignment, He carefully observes to see how well we have done with the last assignment. Did we do it as He expected? Did we finish it completely, or did we leave parts of the assignment incomplete? Did we do it in a way that glorified the name of Jesus?

God wants to know if we are faithful, trustworthy, reliable, dependable, true, and unfailing. Rather than take a shot in the dark and simply hope for the best, He bases His decision on *discovery*. That means that God is watching *you* today. He watches your actions and reactions. He observes how you treat people and how you respond to pressure. He looks to see if you have the tenacity to keep going, even in the face of opposition.

So what has God *found* about you?

If you were an employer, before you promoted someone into a position of great authority, wouldn't you watch that person first to see if he or she would be found faithful? Since this is true of humans when they look for someone to oversee short-lived, temporal responsibilities, how much more is this true of God, who entrusts people with matters that impact people's lives for all eternity? There is nothing more serious than eternal business. That's why before God promotes someone over greater spiritual matters, He watches to see if they are *found* faithful.

Once God knows a person can be trusted with more, it isn't long before a new assignment comes their way. In First Corinthians 4:2, Paul said, "Moreover it is required in stewards that a man be found faithful." As noted in yesterday's *Sparkling Gem*, the word "required" is the Greek word *zeteo*, which means *to seek, to search*, or *to look very intensively* for something. It was a legal term to denote *a judicial investigation* and could even refer to *a scientific investigation*. It describes an *intense* and *thorough searching*. It could be interpreted, *"Moreover, God is making a concentrated, exhaustive, and thorough search in pursuit of stewards who are found faithful."*

This means that the people who possess the necessary qualities that God wants in order to use them are not abundant in the Christian community. Faithful, trustworthy, reliable, dependable, true, and unfailing people are so rare that God must *thoroughly* and *exhaustively search* to find them. But once He finds through observation that a particular believer is committed to do His will and to do it with excellence, God has made a valuable *discovery*. He has found a faithful person He can depend on to lead and carry out a new and important assignment.

Over the years, I've worked with thousands of people, and it is very rare to find people who are completely reliable. Most are distracted by other things. They start out with a desire to be faithful, but the affairs of life pull them away. Any pastor could testify of the myriads of people who started projects but didn't finish them. But when a person is discovered who is faithful, trustworthy, reliable, true, and unfailing in keeping his or her word, it is a rare find — a real gem!

When God looks at you, what does He see? Do all you possibly can do to make it easy for Him to say, "Now, *that* person is a real treasure whom I can trust with the next big assignment!" Don't let His answer be, "Not yet!" because you refused to make the necessary changes.

Since God is watching, don't you agree that it is vital that we take a serious look at ourselves to see what He is finding as He watches what we do, the promises we make, and the seriousness with which we obey Him and His Word? Has God found that He can trust us, or would He be wiser to choose someone else?

So if you want to move into a higher realm of responsibility that holds more exciting and significant assignments in life, do everything you can to be found faithful in what you are doing right now. *When God has found you faithful in your present project, you have your best guarantee that a door will soon open for you to step through so you can walk out the dream He placed in your heart.*

MY PRAYER FOR TODAY

Father, I admit that I've often been slack in the way that I've carried out the assignments You have given to me. I haven't always been diligent in many things You have expected of me, and yet I've somehow thought that You would promote me anyway. Now I understand that You are watching and waiting for me to be found faithful. Only then will You be assured that I can be trusted with something bigger than what I am doing right now. Forgive me for my faulty thinking in the past. I ask You to make my thoughts agreeable to Your will, as You create in me both the desire and the ability to do what pleases You. I thank You, Lord, for helping me do Your will Your way. From this moment onward, I will do my best to be faithful at the tasks in my life right now. Even if I don't relish what I am being asked to do, I will do it with all of my heart until You and I both know that I can be trusted with something bigger and better.

I pray this in Jesus' name!

MY CONFESSION FOR TODAY

I confess that I am committed to doing my present job with joy and excellence. I do not complain; I do not drag my feet; and I do not behave lazily or half-heartedly. I am completely committed to doing this job with excellence and in a manner that brings praise to the name of Jesus Christ. When God looks at me, He smiles because He sees me giving 100 percent of everything I am to the task of doing this the best that it can be done. With the help of the Holy Spirit, I am a faithful steward over all that God has entrusted to my care and oversight. Because I am completing my assignment with my whole heart and with the highest level of excellence I'm capable of, God finds me faithful and will promote me to a higher level and a bigger assignment.

I declare this by faith in Jesus' name!

QUESTIONS FOR YOU TO CONSIDER

1. What is the major assignment God has asked you to deal with in your life right now? Maybe it is a work assignment, a relationship assignment, or an assignment to deal with a specific personal issue in your life. Can you name the most significant assignment God has given you — the one you know He is watching most closely to see how you are doing in completing that assignment?
2. If you were to rate your performance on a scale of 1 to 10 (10 being the best and 1 being the worst), how would you rate your present performance with the main assignment that God is watching in your life? *Be honest!*
3. Why did you rate yourself the way you did? What are you doing that causes you to think you rate so low or so high? Now ask the Holy Spirit to give you *God's* rating of your present performance!

When God has found you faithful in your present project,
you have your best guarantee
that a door will soon open for you to step through
so you can walk out the dream He placed in your heart.

JANUARY 22

Be Specific When You Pray!

And if we know that he hear us, whatsoever
we ask, we know that we have the petitions
that we desired of him.
— 1 John 5:15

When our youngest son Joel was first learning how to pray, he always prayed the same exact prayer every time he bowed his head. When we got on our knees alongside his bed at night, he repeated the same prayer. If we asked him to pray over the meal at breakfast, lunch, or dinner, we already knew exactly what he was going to say. If we were taking a trip in the car and wanted to pray for safety, we knew we'd never get to the prayer for safety if Joel prayed because he would pray the same prayer he had prayed the night before when he went to bed. It was always word for word the same prayer.

Regardless of the place, event, or time of the day, Joel prayed: *"Heavenly Father, please bless my parents, bless my brothers, bless my grandparents, bless the whole world, and please give us a good day. I pray this in Jesus' name!"* The only variation that ever occurred in his prayers was when he occasionally threw in a request for God to bless our family dog!

When Joel was only five years old, we thought this was cute, and we enjoyed his amusing regularity in prayer. But a time came when it wasn't cute anymore! He was getting older — and Denise and I knew our youngest son needed to step forward in his relationship with God and in his ability to pray more effectively. I remember the day I looked into his little blue eyes and told him, "Joel, you need to be more *specific* when you pray. It's all right to ask for God's blessing every time you pray, but if you'll get specific with God when you pray, He will answer your specific prayer requests."

Just as is true for all of us as we walk with God, there came a time for Joel when he was asked to take a step higher in prayer. He needed to learn to be specific when he prayed and not just ask for a general, sweeping bestowal of blessing on our family and the earth's population.

Unfortunately, there are many people — even older adults who have known the Lord for many years and are well advanced in terms of age — who still sound like small children when they pray. They've never grown in their prayer life, and therefore they still pray only general, childlike prayers that beseech God to bestow His blessings on them and those they love. Of course, it's good to ask for God's blessing and to be childlike in our faith, but God pleads with His people to get specific with Him when they pray!

In First John 5:14, the Bible tells us that if we ask anything according to His will, God hears us. Then in the next verse, it continues: "And if we know that he hear us, whatsoever we ask, we know that we have the petitions that we desired of him" (1 John 5:15).

First, I want to point out that this verse says we are to "ask" when we pray. This means there is nothing wrong with asking if we are doing it according to the will of God! But wait — before we go any further, let's stop and look at this word "ask." In this word, we find a treasure trove that will help us know what kind of attitude we must have when we make our requests known to God.

In First John 5:15, the word "ask" in Greek is the word *aiteo*. This Greek word eliminates any religious suggestion that we are "lowly worms" who have no right to come into the presence of God to make a request. It also destroys the picture that we must pitifully beg and plead for the things we need from the Lord. The word *aiteo* means to be *adamant* in requesting and even demanding assistance in meeting tangible needs, such as food, shelter, money, and so forth.

Of course, we don't want to be disrespectful when we pray, so for those who are concerned about sounding rude, let me assure you that the Greek word *aiteo* does not give us license to be arrogant or rude in this approach to God. In fact, in the New Testament and in other secular literature from New Testament times, the word *aiteo* is often used to portray a person addressing a superior. The person may insist or demand that a need be met, but he approaches and speaks to his superior with *respect* and a sense of *honor*. However, the petitioner is so sure that his request is correct that he asks boldly with a firm expectation that he will receive the desired outcome.

This word *aiteo* describes a person who speaks out and prays boldly and authoritatively. This person knows specifically what he needs and isn't afraid to boldly come into God's Presence to ask and expect to receive what he has requested.

As we have stated, the previous verse (*see* 1 John 5:14) states that you must know you are praying according to the will of God if you want Him to hear and answer you. So since you are praying in line with God's will, you don't have to sheepishly mumble your requests. You are praying precisely according to what God wants to do, so you can boldly assert your faith and expect Him to move on your behalf. He *wants* you to act boldly and courageously in prayer! He wants you to seize His will for your life and demand that it come into manifestation! He's just waiting for you to ask.

Furthermore, don't think that you can come to God only for spiritual blessings. As noted earlier, the word *aiteo* most often has to do with requesting *things of a physical and material nature*, such as food, clothes, shelter, money, and so forth. So find out what God promises you in His Word regarding such provision, and then boldly ask Him to meet your needs!

John went on to say, "And if we know that he hear us, whatsoever we ask, we know that we have the petitions that we desired of him" (1 John 5:15). Let's look next at the word "petitions," because the form used in the original text emphatically informs us that God wants us to get *very specific* when we pray!

The word "petition" is the Greek word *aitema*, which is a form of the word *aiteo* that we discussed above, but now it denotes *a specific, exact, explicit, precise, detailed request*. This request is so in-depth, thorough, and comprehensive that there is no room for misunderstanding exactly what has been asked. This is why the *King James* translators translated it as the word "petition." It paints the picture of a prayer so detailed and explicit that it is like a bona fide "petition" that has been prepared and submitted.

With the meanings of these Greek words in mind,
First John 5:15 could be interpreted:

"And if we can be confident that God hears us, regardless of what we ask or what physical or tangible need we may want Him to meet for us, we can be sure that we will have a 'yes' to the specific, exact, explicit, detailed requests that we desired of Him."

So let me ask you this: When you pray, do you pray general, sweeping prayers for blessings, or have you learned the secret of getting specific with God when you pray? That kind of vague, general prayer may be cute for a little child, but as you grow in your walk with God, He expects you to get bold, courageous, and very specific about the things you request of Him. We know this very clearly because of the Greek words *aiteo* and *aitema* that are used in First John 5:15.

So let me encourage you today to open your Bible and explore its pages until you find *specifically* what the will of God is for your situation. Once you know it, be assured that you have the right as a child of God to go straight into His presence and, with honor and respect, *insist* that His will be done in this matter! In fact, God *wants* you to come to Him boldly like that!

So when you make your requests known to Him, get as specific and detailed as you can. I suggest that you even think it through, write it down on a piece of paper, and then submit it as your "petition" to God.

If you have a specific request, you need to be *specific* when you ask God to bring about His will in the matter you're bringing before Him. You'll only experience discernible answers to prayer if you get specific when you pray. *So make this the day you decide you are stepping up higher in your prayer life! It's time to become very specific when you come boldly before the Father's throne of grace to receive mercy and grace to help in your time of need (Hebrews 4:16)!*

MY PRAYER FOR TODAY

Heavenly Father, today I come to You in Jesus' name, thanking You for the Holy Spirit who leads me and guides me into all truth. Your Word is filled with promises that meet every need in my life. Thank You for directing me to find Your promises that apply to the specific situations in my life right now. Holy Spirit, once You have enabled me to find those promises, I purpose in my heart to come to the Father in confidence and assurance as I submit specific, detailed requests to the concrete needs I am facing in my life. You have commanded me to ask that I might receive and that my joy would be made full. From this point onward, I commit myself to honor You with specific requests when I pray! And I will be faithful to glorify Your Name when the answers are granted!

I pray this in Jesus' name!

MY CONFESSION FOR TODAY

I confess that I am finished with praying only general, sweeping prayers for God's blessings. From this moment forward, I intend to be very specific when I pray. God's Word holds answers and promises that He wants to bring to pass in my life. With the help of the Holy Spirit, I will find those answers, discover those promises, and then be very concrete about the things for which I release my faith to receive from God. This is the confidence that I have in my Heavenly Father: If I ask anything according to His will — and His Word is His will — He hears me. And according to First John 5:14, since I know that He hears me, I know that I have the petition I have desired from Him. Therefore, I am now stepping up to the next level of maturity in prayer, where I speak up, speak out, and pray with authority every time I make my requests known to God.

I declare this by faith in Jesus' name!

QUESTIONS FOR YOU TO CONSIDER

1. When you pray, are you specific about what you want God to do, or do you pray mostly general, sweeping prayers that are not detailed or explicit? If someone else asked you to do the exact same thing you've been asking God to do, would you understand what that person wanted you to do?
2. What do you want God to do for you? Can you express it in clear and unambiguous terms? Are you so clear on the subject that you could write it on a piece of paper and submit it to God as an official "petition"?
3. Why don't you take a few minutes today to write down the requests you want to present to God. You may discover that you aren't clear about what you want God to do for you. This exercise may help you attain a better understanding of *exactly* what you want God to do for you based on His Word.

JANUARY 23

Use What Influence You Have!

But sanctify the Lord God in your hearts:
and be ready always to give an answer to every man
that asketh you a reason of the hope that is in you
with meekness and fear.
— 1 Peter 3:15

Several years ago my heart was stirred to pray for a method to reach the elderly population in the city of Moscow. The majority of them grew up under Communism and therefore lived a life devoid of God. Although the rule of Communism is gone, that ideological system still pervades much of the thinking of the older generation. This makes them one of the most difficult groups to reach with the Gospel.

My heart has been burdened for this older segment of Russian society for several reasons, but the most important reason is that multitudes of these senior citizens will soon leave this world and pass into eternity without Christ unless we first reach them with the Good News of Jesus Christ. As I prayed for these seniors, I wanted to know how to have *influence* with this group of people so I could make a positive impact on them.

Suddenly one day, an idea dropped into my heart about how to reach the elderly community in the city of Moscow. It was an idea right from the throne of Heaven — an idea so brilliant and different that I could have never come up with it on my own. It was an idea that came from the Spirit of God in answer to my prayers for a method to reach these precious people. Years have passed since that idea first came into my heart — and with God's help, we have built what may possibly be the single largest outreach to senior citizens in the world. In all of our research, we've never been able to find anything to compare to this massive outreach to the elderly.

Awhile back during one of these monthly events, a member of our staff — one of our drivers — was sitting in the back of the auditorium, waiting to watch the program that had been designed specifically for this senior audience. One of the elderly people sitting next to him — an old, hard-hearted, dedicated Communist and atheist — skeptically commented, "I don't understand why Rick Renner does all these things for us. No one else seems to care about us anymore. So why would he and his team spend all this time and money on us? There must be some hidden agenda. I just don't get it. Why would they do so much for us? What is the *real* reason behind all of this?"

The elderly man didn't realize he was speaking to a member of our team. But God had carefully orchestrated that moment, ensuring that one of our drivers — a very sensitive man who compassionately cares especially for hurting people — would sit next to the elderly man and hear his skeptical comment. In response, the driver reached over to put his arm around that old Communist and answered, "What kind of price tag can be put on a person's soul? There's nothing in the world more precious or eternal than your soul, my friend. That is why this kind of love and attention is shown to you every month. It's all about your soul and your eternal destiny. That's why this is done for you."

With that answer, that old Communist's skepticism melted away and he replied, "Thank you so much for your kindness to help me understand what this demonstration of love and attention is all about." On that day, God used the influence of a driver from our ministry to soften the hardened heart of that lost soul for whom Jesus died.

People frequently make a wrong assumption that they must have a seminary degree or a Bible school diploma before they can be used by God. But in New Testament times, there were no seminaries or Bible schools to attend because the Church was new and was still being established. But because the Christian faith was still in its infancy and was so different from the pagan religions of the Roman Empire, people were skeptical of Christianity and didn't understand its message.

In fact, many were even afraid of Christians! Pagans had many questions about what Christians really believed, and false rumors about followers of Christ abounded.

In the midst of this situation, the apostle Peter told the early believers, "But sanctify the Lord God in your hearts: and be ready always to give an answer to every man that asketh you a reason of the hope that is in you with meekness and fear..." (1 Peter 3:15). Remember, when Peter wrote this verse, he was *not* writing to a classroom filled with theologians; he was writing to believers — many of them *new* believers — to encourage them to use whatever *influence* they had to bring people to Jesus Christ.

Peter exhorted believers, "...Be ready always to give an answer to every man that asketh a reason of the hope that is in you...." The phrase "be ready always" is a translation of the Greek words *etoimoi aei*. The word *etoimoi* is a form of the word *etoimos,* which means *to be ready* or *to be prepared.* It is an attitude that is always *set to go, eager, prompt*, and *raring to get started.* It is a perpetual mindset of being *ready* to get started on a project, to take on a challenge, or to take initiative of some sort. To have such a *readiness* also implies *preparation.* Inherent in this command to be *ready* is the idea that one must do everything in his power to equip himself for that moment when he is to be called to action.

In fact, this perpetual mindset to "be ready always" is made abundantly clear in Greek by the use of the word *aei*, which can be translated *always, at all times, constantly*, or *perpetually.* In First Peter 3:15, the apostle Peter was urging his readers (and us as well), *"...Be constantly and perpetually ready, set to go and prompt to act...."*

Then Paul went on to write what you must be "ready" to do! He said you must "...Be ready always to give an answer to every man that asketh a reason of the hope that is in you...."

The word "answer" is the Greek word *apologia,* a compound of the word *apo* and *logos.* In this case, the word *apo* means *back*, and the word *logia*, from *logos*, is the Greek word for *words*. But when they are compounded, the new word *apologia* means *to answer back, to reply, to respond, to explain*, or *to defend.* It is the same word that the apostle Paul used in Philippians 1:16 when he wrote that he had been "...set for the *defense* of the gospel." In using this word, Paul acknowledged that part of his God-given task was to *answer* questions put to him by unbelievers about the Gospel.

There is no doubt about it. Because Peter used the word *apologia*, he unmistakably was telling you that, as a Christian, you must *"...Be constantly and perpetually ready, be set to go, and be prompt to answer every man that asks a reason of the hope that is in you...."*

Peter says we are be fully prepared to answer "every man" who inquires about what we believe — explaining the nature of the hope that resides in our hearts and why we believe it. The words "every man" in Greek is *panti*, which is an all-encompassing word that literally means *every man, every individual*, and *every person* — with no exceptions! This one statement affirms that the Gospel is for *every man* on the face of the earth, regardless of race, class, or color. Peter told us not to be surprised if people "ask" about our faith. In fact, we should anticipate that they *will* ask. This is the reason Peter urged us to be *prepared* and *ready* to answer!

When Peter says non-Christians will "ask" about the hope that is in us, the word "ask" is the Greek word *aiteo.* The word *aiteo* means *to be adamant in requesting and demanding something*. In other words, this is not a mere wish, but a *demand for an answer to an insatiable longing either to have something or know something*. In fact, the word *aiteo* is the very word used in Mark 15:43, where the Bible tells us that Joseph of Arimathea "craved" the body of Jesus after the crucifixion. The word "craved" is a great translation of the word *aiteo*, for that night an all-consuming desire drove Joseph of Arimathea to go to Pilate to *strongly demand* and *adamantly insist* that Jesus' body be released to him. (For more on this word, *see Sparkling Gems 1*, April 10.)

Peter used this same strong word — *aiteo* — to alert us to the fact that when non-Christians finally work up the nerve to "ask" us questions or to inquire about the faith and hope they see in us, we need to be quick to answer, because they *really* want to know — or they wouldn't be asking! It's just like the old Communist who inquired why we were doing so much for the elderly population of Moscow. Although his question seemed skeptical, the truth was that this elderly man *really* wanted to know why we were doing what we did. He longed to know the answer; that's why he asked. *Thank God, there was a "regular ol' believer" sitting next to him who was ready to give him the answer!*

- ➤ How ready were you to give an answer the last time someone asked you about your faith?
- ➤ If you found yourself sitting next to a non-Christian who asked you about what you believe, why you believe it, and how your faith affects your life, how would you answer these questions?
- ➤ How prepared are you today to give an answer to those who ask a reason for the hope that is in you?

Don't make the mistake of thinking you aren't adequate to answer such questions because you haven't been to seminary or Bible school. I remind you again that when Peter wrote this verse, there were no seminary or Bible school graduates with diplomas. All that was there at that time were simple, everyday Christians — *just like you.* They went to work and conducted their normal affairs every day. And in the process of it all, they were constantly rubbing elbows with non-Christians from every walk of life, every class of society, and every ethnic group, who asked: "What is your faith all about?" "Why do you believe what you believe?" "Can you give me the reason for the hope that is in you?"

God uses people, and you may find that He orchestrates a meeting between you and a person who ends up sitting next to you. You don't have to be a theologian to tell someone why you love Jesus and what He has done in your life. But it would be wise for you to ponder what you would say if someone asked you a reason for the hope that is in you. In doing so, you're taking heed to Peter's admonition to the early Christians when he wrote: "*...Be constantly and perpetually ready, be set to go, and be prompt to answer every man that asks a reason of the hope that is in you....*"

Today God is calling out to you and me, urging us to be available and always ready to give an answer to those who crave to know more about Jesus and what He has done in our lives. We are spiritually obligated to answer to those who want to know. So let me ask you: Are you available to share your testimony or to use your influence to help someone come to a personal knowledge of Jesus Christ? *Are you ready to give an answer to every person who asks a reason for the hope that is in you?*

MY PRAYER FOR TODAY

Lord, I am deeply convicted that I need to be more open about sharing my faith with non-Christians I see and talk to every day. I know they feel empty and are searching for the real reason for life. I remember how lost I felt before You came into my life and gave me a new purpose. I thank You for giving me Your compassion for those who are without Christ. Let me speak words so filled with wisdom and grace that they will minister grace and clearly explain the hope I have in Christ — a hope that they, too, can share. Thank You for causing a burning passion to grow within me to see people saved. I don't ever want to be so busy in my own affairs that I forget people need to be saved. I don't want to be hardhearted or uncaring about people's eternal status. So I stir up a strong desire deep inside me to see people saved and delivered by Your power!

I pray this in Jesus' name!

MY CONFESSION FOR TODAY

I confess that I am deeply concerned for unsaved people — especially those that I rub elbows with every day. I accept my God-given responsibility to share Jesus with those who are lost — especially to those who appeal to me for answers regarding the reason for the hope that is in me. When people ask me, I am not ashamed of the Gospel, for it is the power of God that leads to salvation; rather, I am bold, eager to answer, and ready to tell them the Good News about Jesus Christ. He has changed my life! Therefore, I am prepared at any moment to introduce others to the same saving and life-changing message that has revolutionized my life and given me a relationship with God Almighty.

I declare this by faith in Jesus' name!

QUESTIONS FOR YOU TO CONSIDER

1. Can you think of one person you are acquainted with who needs to know Jesus Christ? *Who is that person?*
2. Be honest — what steps have you taken to help that one person personally know Jesus Christ? Can you truthfully tell God that you have done your part to share the truth about Jesus and of His power to save him or her?
3. If First Peter 3:15 commands us to be ready to answer every man that asks a question about the hope that is in us, what are you doing to prepare yourself so that you can answer questions about your faith, why you believe what you believe, what your faith does for you, or what the Bible teaches about Jesus Christ? *What are you doing to get yourself ready to answer the questions any non-Christian may ask?*

JANUARY 24

An Overflowing and Thankful Heart

We give thanks to God always for you all,
making mention of you in our prayers;
— 1 Thessalonians 1:2

So often in this age, people face disappointments in life — and one of the most difficult things to face is disappointment in *relationships*. Think of how often people get their feelings hurt for real or imagined reasons or feel like their trust has been violated. Think of how many marriages end in divorce. Such hurts occur so frequently and can be so painful that people often end up entirely focusing on their hurts and disappointments and forget about all the wonderful people who have been and remain a blessing to them. Satan uses hurt, pain, and personal let-downs to get people so side-tracked by what one person or a small group of people did that they forget about all the good and kind things that others have done for them.

There are no words to express the emotion and love my wife and I feel for the people who support our ministry with their finances and prayers. As far as we're concerned, they are the real heroes responsible for the mighty things God has done through our ministry over the years. Yes, God has used Denise and me; we know that very well. But the fact remains that He has equally used our partners who have given and given time and again to assist Denise and me as we obey the call God placed on our lives to reach the people of the former Soviet Union.

It's never a burden to continually pray and thank God for our partners. I think of how faithfully they have given over the years. I ponder the fact that they often could have used those funds elsewhere to meet needs and desires in their own lives, yet they opted to sacrifice and to give to the work of the Gospel instead of meeting their own needs. As I consider all of this, my heart literally overflows with thanksgiving for our partners and for what they do for the work of the Gospel.

Every morning when I wake up, one of the first things I do is pray for our partners because of this deep gratitude I feel for them. It is no struggle to pray for them! As I begin to call out their names to God, thankfulness flows up from the deepest parts of my being. And as I begin to pray for our partners, I can hardly stop! I pray for them to be blessed in their families, jobs, finances, children, health, and relationships. I cry out in faith for them to grow in their relationship with God. Before I close my time of prayer, I always confidently make my request to God for Him to richly multiply the financial seed they have sown into our work. My heart's cry is for our partners to be blessed in every way, including financially and materially. We are so spiritually connected to our partners that it is a great joy to pray for them!

When the apostle Paul thought about the believers in Thessalonica, he must have felt the same way about them. They had endured such difficult times of persecution and had faced nearly unbearable pressure, yet they had never given way to fear or relinquished their stance of faith. The experience Paul and his apostolic team had enjoyed with them had been such a pleasure, and they had seized such a big part of his heart that he told them, "We give thanks to God always for you, making mention of you in my prayers" (1 Thessalonians 1:2).

The word "we" in Greek is plural and refers to the heartfelt thanks shared by Paul, Silas, and Timothy. The Thessalonians were a great source of blessing, and it wasn't just Paul who abounded with a sense of thanksgiving for them. Paul's entire team was impacted and encouraged by the faith and example of the Thessalonian believers. They were *all* filled with thankfulness for this church!

The word "thanks" comes from the Greek word *eucharistos*, a compound of the words *eu* and *charis*. The word *eu* means *good* or depicts something *extremely pleasant* or *gratifying*. The word *charis* is the Greek word for *grace*. When these two words are compounded, the new word portrays *a person who is so satisfied and full of deep pleasure and gratitude that it pours forth from his heart*. Just as God freely and liberally bestows His grace upon us, this deep thanksgiving liberally abounds and pours forth to God from our heart with no effort. This depicts a sense of thankfulness so strongly felt that it would be difficult to hold it back or restrain it.

And Paul wasn't just *occasionally* thankful for them either! He said, "We give thanks to God *always* for you...." The word "always" is the Greek word *pantote*, which carries the idea of *every moment*, *every opportunity*, or *every time we get the opportunity*. It tells us that every time the believers in Thessalonica came to Paul's mind, his heart was instantly filled with warm memories and gratitude for them. It was truly effortless for Paul to thank God for the Thessalonians.

The verse continues, "We give thanks to God always *for* you...." The word "for" in this verse is derived from the word *peri*. In this case, the word *peri* means *about*. Every time Paul thought *about* the Thessalonian believers, he was thankful. When considering everything about them, he couldn't help but stop what he was doing to express to God the deep gratitude he felt for them.

Then Paul continued, "We give thanks to God always for you *all*...." The word "all" is the Greek word *panton*. It is an all-encompassing term that means this heartfelt gratitude was not directed toward just a few of the Thessalonians, but toward *all* of them. In contrast to all the problems and opposition Paul had encountered in his ministry and all the people who had disappointed him through the years, the believers in Thessalonica were a bright, shining source of joy, and he literally thanked God for *every single one* of them and for *all* that pertained to them.

When you put all these words together,
First Thessalonians 1:2 could be translated:

"We thank God for you! We are simply so full of gratitude for everything connected to you that we just can't hold it back! In fact, thanking God for you is one of the easiest and most effortless things we do — it just flows out of our hearts. We find ourselves thanking Him for you all the

time. What a joy it is that our attitude of thankfulness is not just for a few of you, but it really is something we feel about every last one of you!"

Whom do you have in your life today that makes your heart overflow with thanksgiving? Can you think of someone, or perhaps a group of people, who are such a blessing to you that when you think about them, your heart immediately begins to fill up with tender thoughts of gratitude?

In this day we live in, we all experience many disappointments with people, and relationships often don't seem to last very long. People move from place to place; some break commitments; and often people make wrong choices that can wrench your heart. But when you have a friend or a group of people who faithfully follow the Lord and who remain steadfast year after year, it truly is a delight. Such relationships are a special treasure from God that should be cherished and deeply appreciated.

Paul set a good example for you and me that we must follow in our own lives. He wrote and told the Thessalonians how deeply he felt about them. He cherished his relationship with this body of believers, and he wanted them to know how he felt about them.

Likewise, if we have such treasured relationships in our lives, we must take the time to express how deeply grateful we are for what these people mean to us. Don't assume that they already know how you feel. Take the time to write them a note, call them, or take them to dinner so you can make sure they know how much you appreciate them.

Wouldn't it bless you if someone did this for you today? Why don't you take a few minutes right now to make a list of those people who are special, shining sources of joy in your life and begin to thank God for them as Paul did for the Thessalonians? Then do something special for them to demonstrate how much you appreciate them. It takes only a few minutes of your day to do it, yet it will communicate so much to the hearts of those who have been such a blessing to you!

MY PRAYER FOR TODAY

Lord, I thank You for the people You have placed in my life who are a special blessing to me. In this world today, where disappointments and letdowns are so common, it is rare to find good friends and coworkers in Your Kingdom who are faithful, consistent, and truly genuine in their commitment to me. I am so sorry that I haven't previously made enough of an effort to let them know how grateful I am for them. Starting right now, I ask You to help me learn how to better communicate to these special people how thankful I am to God for them!

I pray this in Jesus' name!

MY CONFESSION FOR TODAY

I confess that I am careful to let people know how grateful I am for them and for all they do. I am not negligent to say thank you, I don't take people and their kindness for granted. I express my heartfelt thanks to people who mean a lot to my life. I am blessed to have such friends, and the Holy Spirit is teaching me to convey my gratitude for all they do and for the valuable place they hold in my life. Every day I will spend a few minutes thanking God for them, and every day I will go out of my way to let someone know how thankful I am for the blessing he or she is in my life!

I declare this by faith in Jesus' name!

QUESTIONS FOR YOU TO CONSIDER

1. Who can you think of today in your life for whom you are especially thankful? Why are you so grateful to have these individuals in your life? What have they done that has affected you so positively and makes your heart overflow with thankfulness to God for them?
2. Have you taken time to let that person or persons know how much they have meant to you? If not, what has stopped you from articulating how you feel about them? Wouldn't it mean a lot to you if someone expressed such heartfelt thanks for the blessing you are in his or her life?
3. Before you get too busy today, write down the names of some of the main people who have been a special blessing to your life. Once you have written down the names of those special people, take a few minutes to pray for them. Ask the Holy Spirit to give you creative ideas about how to express your appreciation for who they are and what they have meant to you in your life.

JANUARY 25

'Welcome to Your New Home!'

As they ministered to the Lord, and fasted,
the Holy Ghost said, Separate me Barnabas and Saul
for the work whereunto I have called them.
— Acts 13:2

When I made my first missions trip to the USSR, it was in the spring of 1991, just months before the Soviet Union finally dissolved. I was shocked by how dilapidated everything seemed to be. From what I observed, the mighty USSR was worn out and falling apart. The streets, sidewalks, cars, shops, people's clothing — everything I saw — simply looked either broken, exhausted, or worn out.

I checked into my hotel, and when I pulled the curtains back to give me a view of the street below, they were so rotten that they ripped right off the curtain rod into my hands. For the rest of my stay there, I had no curtains. There was a dead mouse in one corner of the room, and the shower looked like it hadn't been cleaned in decades. I was simply stunned that a global superpower that had kept the rest of the world in fear for so many years was so utterly dilapidated.

The next morning after our arrival, my teammates and I walked to the building where the first aboveground Bible school was being conducted — the first in more than 70 years. Two hundred and twenty students had gathered from every republic of the USSR to attend the school, and I wept when I realized this was a dream come true for them. They lifted their hands to worship, and the Spirit of God moved across the large classroom in a powerful manner. His presence was so strong.

When I stood in front of that room full of young people from all over the Soviet Union to teach them for the first time, I approached the lectern to begin my first teaching session, opened my Bible, took a step back, and looked up at the room full of students eagerly looking back at me. And at that moment, I vividly heard the Holy Spirit speak loudly to my heart and say, *"WELCOME TO YOUR NEW HOME!"*

I know the voice of the Holy Spirit, and there was no doubt in my heart or mind that it was the Spirit who had spoken these words to me. Feeling shocked by what I'd just heard, I choked up and stumbled with my words a bit. Then the Holy Spirit spoke it a second time: *"WELCOME TO YOUR NEW HOME!"*

With that, I *knew* God was calling me to relocate my family to the Soviet Union. As I looked at those 220 students and the dilapidated surroundings all around me, I kept thinking, *God is calling me to make THIS my home and to embrace these students and the USSR for me and my family's future.*

Later that day in prayer, the Lord continued speaking to my spirit. He explained, *"There are many good Bible teachers in the United States, but I need skilled Bible teachers HERE to undergird the massive move of My Spirit that is happening. That is why I am calling you to move here and to do it as quickly as possible."*

This was completely contrary to the plans I had made for my life and ministry. Back in those days, we were receiving 900 invitations a year to come and hold seminars in churches and speak in conferences. The growth of our ministry was literally exploding in the United States — and my books were becoming bestsellers. I had never dreamed of moving away from America and leaving that life behind. But that was exactly what God was calling us to do. That week as I ministered every day to the students, the love of God in me connected me to them, and I could begin to visually see our family living in the USSR.

When I came back to Tulsa after that missions trip, I knew I needed to break the news to Denise. I didn't know how she would respond, but the Lord had prepared her heart before I ever said a word, and the same grace that was upon me was upon Denise. She said, "I'm not excited yet, but when we step onto that plane to move, I'll be filled with faith and anticipation." Our sons were too young to understand what the Soviet Union was, so they just exploded with glee that we were going to be doing something adventurous as we followed the will of God.

Finally, the morning came when Denise and I and our three small sons gathered at the airport with family and friends. We hugged and kissed everyone and told them all farewell; then we stepped onto the plane that would carry us to our new home in the former Soviet Union. As we sat down in those seats on the plane, Denise and I looked at each other with jubilation, because we knew we had passed a major test. We had said *yes* to the Lord, surrendering to His revealed will for us, and we were on our way to the greatest adventure of our lives.

Saying *yes* to the Lord requires surrender. I'm talking about that moment when you are willing to lay down all your own plans and yield to what the Holy Spirit has revealed to you about God's will for your life. Some people pass this test, whereas others do not. However, those who surrender, yield, and obey experience the joy, power, and victory of the Spirit. They live an enriched life filled both with opportunities to be seized and obstacles to be overcome in order to attain victory and to complete the assignment.

I want to tell you how I felt that day when the Holy Spirit said, *"WELCOME TO YOUR NEW HOME!"* It immediately reminded me of Acts 13:2, which says, "As they [the elders in Antioch] ministered to the Lord, and fasted, the Holy Ghost said, Separate me Barnabas and Saul for the work whereunto I have called them."

Barnabas and Saul had been serving in the church of Antioch for several years when suddenly during a time of prayer and fasting, the Holy Spirit said, *"Separate me Barnabas and Saul for the work whereunto I have called them."* The word "separate" is the Greek word *asphortidzo*, and it means *to mark off, to set boundaries around*, or *to set apart for a special purpose.* The verse continues to say that they were to be set apart "...for the work whereunto I have called them." Apparently, God had a "work" for these two men that exceeded what they had done in Antioch.

Serving in Antioch was an honor, but it was not the ultimate goal of God's call on their lives. Way beyond Antioch, Barnabas and Saul [Paul] would be used by God to touch and revolutionize the Gentile world. Had they stayed in Antioch, they would have missed the adventuresome apostolic life that God had designed for them. Accepting and obeying God's call thrust them forward into a life and ministry of divine purpose that radically affected the development and growth of the Church of Jesus Christ all over the Roman Empire.

Everything Paul and Barnabas had done in ministry until that time had been nothing more than preparation for what lay ahead. Although they had spent several serious years in ministry, it was simply "getting-ready time" for the ultimate call that was before them.

This is precisely how I felt when the Holy Spirit spoke to me about my new home. God has blessed our ministry immensely, but I was suddenly aware that everything that had occurred until that moment was preparation for what was about to follow. And what was about to transpire was so immense that it made everything up to that moment look minuscule. Those previous days were days of proving to learn how to be faithful. God was watching — and now that He was satisfied, He was ready to launch us into the calling He had for our lives, which was far larger than anything that Denise or I had imagined or anticipated.

Barnabas and Saul were immediately sent forth to begin their apostolic ministries, but it took me several months to really embrace what God had said. However, I did come around, and our family entered the greatest phase of our lives as a result. We have never had any regrets about leaving America behind and moving to the former USSR.

Today I want to encourage you to let the Lord reveal to you His plan for your life. It may be different from what you had previously thought. It is possible that everything you have done up until now has merely been preparation for a greater call before you. So open your heart and be careful to pay heed if the Holy Spirit affirms that He's leading you to take a new direction. It could add more fruitfulness and adventure to your life than you ever dreamed possible!

MY PRAYER FOR TODAY

Father, I thank You for Your predetermined plan for my life — and that You want to launch me into it as soon as I'm ready. I ask You to help me prove myself faithful where I am, so I will be prepared for the call that lies ahead of me. Help me not to be stuck in my thinking — assuming that where I am is the ultimate end of what I am called to do. I ask You to open my eyes to see that great and wonderful things lie ahead of me if I will fully surrender to You!

I pray this in Jesus' name!

MY CONFESSION FOR TODAY

I confess that God knows the good plans He has for me. He is ordering my steps along His ordained path, and I am following the Holy Spirit's direction to do all He is leading me to do in preparation for God's next phase of my life. I recognize now that all I have done thus far has been preparation for the next part of His call on my life. Jesus, You said if a man is faithful in little, You will put him over much. So I declare that I will be faithful in every assignment You've given to me now, and I believe that You will promote me to the next phase when You have found me proven and ready.

I declare this by faith in Jesus' name!

QUESTIONS FOR YOU TO CONSIDER

1. What are you doing right now to give yourself fully to the tasks at hand, so God will know that you are proven and ready for the job ahead of you?
2. Has God ever told you something that caught you off-guard and by surprise? If so, when was that, and what did He say? Have you followed through on what He spoke to your heart?
3. Are you doing what God has told you to do right now? Are you being faithful with the call that He's given you? If God were asked this question, how would He answer about you?

JANUARY 26

It's Time for You To Stop Wrestling and Start Resting!

There remaineth therefore a rest to the people of God.
For he that is entered into his rest, he also hath ceased
from his own works, as God did from his.
— Hebrews 4:9,10

When I was a young boy, I was *terrified* that I wasn't really saved. A powerful revivalist visited our church and preached a message that became etched into my mind about people who *thought* they were saved but weren't — people who died thinking they were going to *Heaven* but whose final destination was *hell.* That sermon *terrified* me!

Every night I went to bed troubled, thinking that if I died during the night, I would end up in hell. I had asked Jesus into my heart when I was five years old and had understood what I was doing. But after hearing that man's bloodcurdling sermon, I was gripped with fear that I might be among those who *thought* they were saved but were in fact lost.

Every night my mother would lie by my side and listen as I told her how frightened I was that I wasn't saved. She would hold me — her little six-year-old boy — and pray with me until I fell asleep each night.

That dread lingered in my life for many years. I can't count the times I prayed: "Dear Lord Jesus, I know I've asked You into my heart so many times before, but just in case I didn't really mean it all those other times, I am asking You to come into my heart again right now." *I must have prayed that prayer 10,000 times.*

Each time I felt a sigh of relief for a couple of hours — and then the panicky thought would hit me again: *Maybe YOU are among those who just think they are saved but have never really been sincere! Maybe you are one of those who think they're going to Heaven but are going to end up in hell!* This fear overwhelmed me. I found myself obsessed with the need to be saved, yet incapable of feeling secure that I *was* saved.

I silently cried out for inner peace as I dedicated and rededicated my life to the Lord. Over and over again at church, I'd lay before the altar and plead with God for peace of mind. Privately — at home, on the street, wherever I was — I'd beg God to reach down and rescue me. Every Sunday when the pastor gave the invitation at the end of the service, he would ask the congregation to search their hearts to see if they were genuinely saved. Each week that question initiated the whole painful process all over again for me. *I was living in torment.*

If I called home as a teenager and no one answered the telephone, my heart would sink with the thought that the Rapture had occurred and I had been left behind. I'd begin frantically calling members of our church, hoping someone would pick up the telephone. If a church member answered, it meant I had *not* been left behind!

When I was 24 and newly married, I was still intermittently struggling with this issue about my salvation. One day I fell on my knees at the altar of the large Baptist church where I worked as an associate pastor and cried out to the Lord: *"This is it! I've spent most of my life trying to get saved. I've prayed 10,000 times for you to save me, and I'm finished asking! If I'm not saved, there is nothing more I can do to be saved, so I'm not asking again!"*

The moment I prayed that prayer, the monstrous fear that had engulfed me for so many years of my life simply evaporated. For the first time in my life, I had the *assurance* that I was saved. The truth is, I'd been saved many years earlier at the age of five. But because a seed of fear had been sown into my heart by the preaching of that revivalist so many years earlier, I had never been able to "rest" in my salvation.

But on that day at that altar, I gave up my struggle of *trying* to be saved, and I made the decision to simply *rest* in God's grace. I realized that if His grace wasn't enough to do the work, all my asking and begging wasn't going to make a difference anyway. At that moment, I quit *wrestling* and started *resting*. And that was the moment I finally began to enjoy my salvation!

When I read Hebrews 4:9 and 10, I always think of the rest that came to my soul when I finally accepted the fact that I was saved by grace. Oh, what a blessed day that was! I finally gave up my fight and *accepted* the salvation I had already received many years earlier as a young child. For so many years I'd been driven by fear — constantly asking, pleading, and begging, trying to prove my sincerity to the Lord. But all it took for me to be saved was to turn my heart to Jesus and receive Him as my Savior — and that's what I had done as a young child. I had been saved all along, but I had never learned to "rest" in my salvation.

Hebrews 4:9 says, "There remaineth therefore a rest to the people of God." Today I want us to look at several words in this verse. Let's begin with the word "rest."

The word "rest" in this verse comes from the Greek word *sabbatismos*, which is used in the Greek Septuagint version of the Old Testament to refer to the *Sabbath day*. This means Hebrews 4:9 should really be translated, "There remaineth therefore *a Sabbath rest* to the people of God."

What does "Sabbath rest" mean in the context of this verse? Let's go back to the book of Genesis just for a moment. God worked for six days when He created the heavens and earth. At the end of those six days, the Bible tells us that when God looked at everything He had made, it was *so perfect, complete, finished*, and *flawless*, He knew there was nothing else that could be added to it. It was a complete, finished work that required nothing more. Since this masterpiece of creation was completely finished, the biblical record tells us that God "rested" from his labor on the seventh day and simply enjoyed creation.

In Genesis 2:2 and 3, we read, "And on the seventh day God ended his work which he had made; and he rested on the seventh day from all his work which he had made. And God blessed the seventh day, and sanctified it: because that in it he had rested from all his work which God created and made."

This day when God "rested" was the first official *Sabbath day* — the day when God rested from all His work. Later when Moses received the Ten Commandments, God explicitly ordered the children of Israel to remember the Sabbath day and to keep it holy. So every week on the Sabbath day, the children of Israel ceased from all labor and rested as a way of honoring the day when God rested from His own works. Therefore, the Sabbath was a day of unbroken rest and cessation from work.

By telling us, "There remaineth therefore *a Sabbath rest* to the people of God," the Bible declares that the people of God can rest in their salvation once they have given their lives to Jesus Christ. His work on the Cross was so complete, perfect, finished, and flawless that there is nothing anyone can do to add to it. A person isn't brought any closer to salvation by asking, begging, pleading, and imploring God to be saved or from trying to prove his sincerity so he can be worthy of salvation. If a person has given his life to Christ, he can "rest" in the fact that it is a done deal. Instead of struggling the way I did as a young man, every person who has trusted in Christ can *relax*, *unwind*, *calm down*, *lighten up*, and *rest* in the completed work of God that was purchased on the Cross of Jesus Christ!

Just as I did years ago, you must also make a decision to give up your struggle of *trying* to be saved and make the decision to simply *rest* in God's grace. If God's grace isn't enough to do the job, all of your asking and begging isn't going to make a difference anyway. It's time for you to quit *wrestling* and started *resting* so you can begin to enjoy your salvation!

Hebrews 4:10 continues to tell us, "For he that is entered into his rest, he also hath ceased from his own works, as God did from his."

The word "entered" is the Greek word *eiserchomai.* It is a compound of the words *eis* and *erchomai.* The first part of the word means *into.* The second part of the word *erchomai* means *to go.* It gives the idea of a person who is *traveling* or *journeying* to some destination. When these words are compounded into one, as they are in this verse, it forms the word *eiserchomai*, which expresses the idea of a person who *enters into* a certain place. He doesn't just come near to this location; he actually *enters into* that location.

This means that those who have given their lives to Jesus Christ have *entered into* the completed work of God that occurred on the Cross of Jesus Christ.

Yes, the moment Jesus became Lord of *your* life was the exact split second you *entered into* God's completed work of salvation. Regardless of what the devil may try to whisper to make you think that you must do more to *really* be saved, the fact remains that if your life has been given to Jesus Christ, you have already entered into the perfect, complete, finished, and flawless work of God. There is nothing you can add to it, so instead of allowing tormenting fear to steal your joy, it's time for you to quit struggling and start resting in what Jesus has done for you. You can calm down, relax, and be at peace!

The rest of the verse says, "For he that is entered into his rest, he also hath ceased from his own works, as God did from his." This verse says it's time for you to rest in this perfect, complete, finished, flawless work, just as God did on the seventh day when He was assured that His work of creation was done.

If you are resting in Christ's work, then you can rest from *your* work! That's why this verse continues to say, "For he that is entered into his rest, he also hath *ceased* from his own works, as God did from his."

This word "cease" is the word *katapauo* — a compound of the words *kata* and *pauo*. The word *kata* means *down*, and the word is *pauo* means *to pause*. When these words are compounded, the new word gives the idea of *someone who has worked hard, but now has sat down, settled down, and has ceased from his labor*. This is the picture of a person who has thrown off his work clothes and is now reclining in a restful position! You might say that he has finished his work and entered into retirement! The work is behind him, and that phase of his life is done and over. He is entering into a lasting and permanent rest.

So I want to encourage you today: If you struggle with your salvation, wondering whether or not you are *really* saved, nail it down forever by praying one last prayer of repentance and surrendering your life to Jesus Christ. Then walk away from that place of commitment and *never* revisit it again. Instead of habitually asking over and over to be saved, just pray in faith that God's Word is true, quit struggling, and start resting in what Jesus has done for you!

There is a "Sabbath rest" for the people of God, and it belongs to every person who simply comes in faith to Jesus Christ. If you belong to Him, it is high time for you to kick back and *rest* in the fact that Jesus saved you and that this work of redemption is utterly complete. *Just make the decision today that from this day forward, you are going to enjoy the benefits of this wonderful salvation that Jesus purchased for you on the Cross!*

MY PRAYER FOR TODAY

Lord, I thank You that You died on the Cross for me and purchased my salvation. Thank You for saving me from sin and its penalty. Thank You that there is nothing I can do to add to Your work on the Cross. Today I am making the decision to quit struggling about my salvation and to simply rest in the salvation You have provided for me. I asked You to save me, and You saved me. I asked You to forgive me, and You forgave me. From this day forward, I will rest in the complete work of redemption that You purchased for me with Your precious blood. Thank You, Jesus, for saving me!

I pray this in Jesus' name!

MY CONFESSION FOR TODAY

I confess that I am saved, forgiven, and born again by the Spirit of God. I asked Jesus to save me, and He saved me. I asked Jesus to forgive me, and He forgave me. I asked Jesus to come into my life, and now He lives in me by His Spirit. In Him I have redemption, deliverance, and salvation through His blood. In Christ I have the complete removal and forgiveness of sin in accordance with the generosity of God's great goodness and favor toward me (see Ephesians 1:7). I am as saved as a person can be! I refuse to let the devil torment me, steal my joy, or make me think that I haven't done enough to be saved. There is nothing I can add to the work of the Cross, so I am simply going to rest in what Jesus has already done for me!

I declare this by faith in Jesus' name!

QUESTIONS FOR YOU TO CONSIDER

1. What was the actual time in your life when you repented, asked Jesus Christ into your heart, and gave Him control of your life? Can you actually refer to the moment this happened?
2. Have you ever struggled with your salvation and wondered if you were really saved? How did you end this personal struggle and find peace of mind?
3. What would you say to someone else who is struggling with the question of whether or not he is really saved? What advice would you give that person, and what would you tell him or her to do to permanently find peace of mind?

JANUARY 27

Golden Candlesticks!

And I turned to see the voice that spake with me.
And being turned, I saw seven golden candlesticks;
and in the midst of the seven candlesticks,
one like unto the Son of man....
— Revelation 1:12,13

When the apostle John was exiled on a barren stretch of rock called the Isle of Patmos, Jesus appeared to him without warning and began to reveal mysteries concerning the role of the Church in these end times. Today and tomorrow, I want to focus on one feature about this divinely granted appearance: What were the "golden candlesticks" that Jesus spoke about? The answer to that question is not just an intellectual exercise. It's a very important truth to grasp in order to better understand Jesus' heart and to grow in your ability to see as He sees and to love what He loves.

In Revelation 1:10, John stated that *suddenly* he heard a great voice speaking to him. Captivated, John quickly turned to see its source. He wrote, "And I turned to see the voice that spake with me. And being turned, I saw seven golden candlesticks; and in the midst of the seven candlesticks, one like unto the Son of man..." (Revelation 1:12,13).

Notice that John said Jesus was standing "...in the midst of seven golden candlesticks...." Revelation 1:20 reveals what this symbolism was supposed to convey: "...The seven candlesticks which thou sawest are the seven churches." According to this verse, the seven golden candlesticks that John saw in verse 12 and 13 specifically represented seven functioning churches that existed in the Roman province of Asia during the time the apostle John was prisoner on the Isle of Patmos. Yet the message Jesus was about to deliver to John not only was intended for these specific congregations, but also to the Church as a whole in every age.

The word "golden" in Revelation 1:12 is the Greek word *chrusos*. This Greek word was used throughout Scripture and other ancient literature to denote the precious metal *gold*. It described *gold, gold coins, gold jewelry, gold fabric*, and other items that were fashioned of *pure gold*.

In the ancient world, there were two kinds of gold — gold that was absolutely pure and gold that was an alloy, meaning it had been mixed with other metals such as silver. Pure gold was considered to be the highest quality and most desirable form of the metal. Varieties that had been mixed with other metals were considered to be less valuable and of a lower grade. The Greek word *chrusos* — the same word John used in Revelation 1:12 to describe the "golden candlesticks" — referred to *pure gold of the highest quality*.

Raw gold is typically discovered encased in rock. Once the gold-bearing rock is removed from the earth, it must be crushed in order for the gold to be extracted. After the rock is crushed, water is forced over the broken fragments to wash away everything except the raw gold itself. With the rubble removed, the gold is exposed and then placed into a fiery furnace. There the blazing hot temperatures melt the gold into liquid form and bring all the impurities hidden in the metal to the surface where they can be scraped off by a refiner who oversees the whole process. The heat is turned up again and again, and with each increase in temperature, more impurities are brought to the surface where they can be scraped away.

If the impurities in the metal are not removed, they will become a defect that decreases the strength of that batch of gold. Intense fire is necessary to remove these impurities, and the refining process requires time, patience, and many degrees of blazing hot temperatures. If the process is carried through to completion, however, the result is a soft, pliable pure gold that a gold worker can beat and shape into an exquisite object. From beginning to end, this is a lengthy, tedious, expensive, and complicated process.

Because of the great cost in producing refined gold, it was associated with kings and royalty. Even the cups, bowls, and plates used on a king's table were frequently made of the pure gold. Today in the Moscow Kremlin Palace Museum, not far from where my family lives, there is a vast collection of cups, bowls, plates, saucers, and platters made of pure gold that were once used to serve food and drink to the Russian royal family. Only *pure gold* would do for magnificent kings and their royal families.

When ambassadors or heads of state came to visit mighty kings in ancient times, they always came with a gift to present to the king. Of all possible gifts, the greatest honor was to bring a gift made of *pure gold.* Giving a gift of pure gold demonstrated honor and respect and showed one's appreciation of the ruler's great worth.

Unlike silver, gold does not tarnish, rust, corrode, or corrupt with time. Gold coins might lie buried in the earth or at the bottom of the sea for hundreds or even thousands of years, but when they are discovered, they appear as brilliant as the day they were lost. Thus, because of its incorruptible nature, pure gold became a symbol of *enduring value.*

In both Old and New Testament times, there was nothing more valuable than *pure gold.* Therefore, God's use of the word "golden" (*chrusos*) to describe the Church conveys a very important message about what He thinks about the Church of Jesus Christ — and, therefore, what He thinks about *you* and every one of your brothers and sisters in Christ!

First, because the word *chrusos* describes *gold of the highest purity*, we see that the Church is *pure gold* in the eyes of Jesus Christ! Like a miner who goes deep into the earth to extract rock that contains gold, Jesus stepped into the darkness of sin in the human race to extract the Church from this lost world. The Gospel was preached; the lost were convicted of sin, and the Word of God, like rushing water, poured over the souls of the redeemed to remove rubble, wreckage, and waste from their lives. Since the birth of the Church 2,000 years ago, Jesus, our Great Refiner, has been washing the Body of Christ with His Word and overseeing the purifying and refining of His precious Church!

The specific seven churches in the book of Revelation that Jesus referred to had some *very* serious problems, many of which are the very same problems we see in the Church today. In fact, the book of Revelation tells us:

- They left their first love (Revelation 2:4).
- They were spiritually fallen (Revelation 2:5).
- They had false doctrine (Revelation 2:14 and 2:20).
- They had the compromise of the Nicolaitans in their midst (Revelation 2:6 and 2:15). (For more information on the Nicolaitans, *see* page 631 in *Sparkling Gems 1.*)
- They had works that were weak and ready to die (Revelation 3:2).
- They had works that were incomplete (Revelation 3:2).
- They struggled with staying on fire for the Lord (Revelation 3:15).
- They were lukewarm (Revelation 3:16).
- They were strongly rebuked by the Lord (Revelation 3:19).
- They were told to repent of wrong attitudes and actions (Revelation 2:5; 2:16; 3:3; 3:19).
- They were *far* from perfect!

You may feel disheartened by what you see or know about the church where you attend or some of the people who attend with you. Perhaps your emotions are trying to convince you that the situation is hopeless and your church family will never turn around for the better. Or perhaps the devil is attempting to dissuade you from further involvement by whispering negative thoughts in your ear about the sad condition of your church. Although it's true that there is room for change in any church, you must never forget that Jesus died for His Church and there is nothing in the world more precious to Him than the Body of Christ — *including your local congregation*. You may see problems, but Jesus sees the Church only as pure gold.

The Church has always had imperfections; this is nothing new, for only God is perfect. When we finally see Jesus face to face, we will be transformed into His image and become just like Him with no imperfections. However, until that time, Jesus will keep working as our Great Refiner — washing us with the water of His Word and putting us through His purification process to make us pliable and usable in His hands! *The work of purification and refinement goes on!*

Peter was referring to this very same principle when he wrote, "Forasmuch as ye know that ye were not redeemed with corruptible things, as silver or gold, from your vain conversation received by tradition from your fathers; but with the precious blood of Christ, as of a lamb without blemish and without spot" (1 Peter 1:18,19). This verse emphatically tells us that Jesus gave His own blood to purchase the Church. The Church may still be in the process of purification and refinement, but we must never forget that Jesus gave His life for it. He loves His Church, and we must love it too. To Him, it is *pure gold* — worth more than anything else in the whole world — and we must also learn to see it as *pure gold* and *precious*.

Therefore, whenever you are tempted to be discouraged about the state of the Church at large or about certain things that bother you in your own local church, proclaim to yourself: *Regardless of what I see, feel, or know, Jesus died for the Church, and it is golden to Him. Therefore, the Church at large, and my local church in particular, are golden to me — and NOTHING is going to tarnish my view of it!*

Make that confession the next time you feel tempted to speak negatively about a fellow believer or the Body of Christ. Always remember: *Our Great Refiner is still continually in the process of purifying His Church — so just make sure your focus is always on loving the Body and allowing Him to purify YOU.*

MY PRAYER FOR TODAY

Lord, I am so thankful that You saved me and made me part of Your Church. I now realize that even with all of our imperfections and weaknesses, You see us as golden and precious. Help me to treasure Your Church and Your people just as You do. Help me to truly love the Church, to serve Your people from my heart, and to give my time, talents, and gifts for the benefit of my brothers and sisters in Christ. From this moment forward, help me refrain my tongue when I am tempted to criticize the Church. And help me to become more and more aware that there is nothing in the world more precious to You, Father, than the Body of Christ! You died on Calvary for the Church, and I know I can't grasp how deeply You love those whom You have redeemed with Your own precious blood. But I ask You to help me see Your Church through Your eyes and to love Your people with Your love more and more in the days to come.

I pray this in Jesus' name!

MY CONFESSION FOR TODAY

I confess that I love and cherish the Church of Jesus Christ with all of my heart! Jesus died for her; He sent His Spirit to indwell her; and there is nothing in the world more precious to Jesus than the Church. Rather than criticize or judge others, I will seek to undergird and strengthen those who may be weakened from attacks by the enemy. Instead of judging others, I will inspect my own heart to see how I may become a purer example of Jesus Christ. I will no longer dwell on the imperfections that I see; instead, I choose to focus on the unchanging truth that the Church of Jesus Christ is golden to God and therefore golden to me!

I declare this by faith in Jesus' name!

QUESTIONS FOR YOU TO CONSIDER

1. Have you ever been tempted to be negative and critical of the church you attend? Do you ever hear yourself speaking negatively about the Church at large?
2. When you spoke negatively about the Church, did you ever notice that your heart was grieved by what you were saying? Were you ever aware that you were grieving the Holy Spirit by being so negative about the Church that Jesus loves so much?
3. Now that you've gained a better understanding about how precious the Church is to Jesus, how will your attitude and conversation about your own local church and the Church at large be affected?

JANUARY 28

But Why Candlesticks?

And I turned to see the voice that spake with me.
And being turned, I saw seven golden candlesticks.
— Revelation 1:12

As we saw in yesterday's *Sparkling Gem*, there was no commodity in the ancient world more valuable than *pure gold*. In fact, the desire to obtain hoards of gold was the root of countless wars and brought ruin upon many civilizations because it fueled man's lust for wealth and power. Therefore, it is very significant that gold would be used to symbolize the Church in Revelation 1:12, when John witnessed "seven golden candlesticks" in his vision of the exalted Christ. *This was God's way of conveying the immense value He places upon the Church of Jesus Christ!*

However, there is another very important element of symbolism in Revelation 1:12 — it is the identification of the Church as a "*candlestick*." Today I want focus on this word to see why the Holy Spirit chose it to depict the Church.

The word "candlesticks" in this verse is the Greek word *luchnos*, which refers to *an oil-burning lamp* rather than a wax candle as are commonly found in homes today. Such lamps were fashioned of earthen clay with a reservoir to hold oil and a wick that gave light in darkness once it was lighted.

Once when I was traveling in Israel, I came across a store that was filled with wonderful antiquities — rare archeological pieces that had been unearthed from locations across the Middle East. In that store, I saw pristine coins from the Roman Empire, small statuettes from Persia, aqua-green colored effigies from tombs in Egypt, and broken fragments of Greek and Roman idols, among numerous other treasures. In one large glass case, I noticed a large collection of ancient *oil-burning lamps* that had been discovered in archeological excavations across Israel.

In today's world, we are fortunate to have electricity and lights nearly everywhere, but in the ancient world, *oil-burning lamps* were a very important part of life. From the smallest house to the greatest palace, every residence depended on oil-burning lamps for light at night. Every house, apartment, store, and place of business in the ancient world had at least one and often many small oil-burning lamps to give light in darkness. Oil-burning lamps were also used in certain religious rituals, such as the seven-branched golden candelabra used in the Jewish temple, which was a fabulous creation of seven oil-burning lamps.

Because the ancient world depended on oil-burning lamps to illuminate darkness, the image of the Church as an oil-burning lamp (*luchnos*) in Revelation 1:12 is especially significant. Jesus was making an important declaration about the Church and its role in this world. Let's take a moment to study the characteristics of these lamps in order to fully appreciate this powerful message about the Body of Christ.

The first fact to note is that oil-burning lamps during New Testament times were made from fragile, brittle earthen clay. Paul referenced this material in Second Corinthians 4:7 when he wrote, "But we have this treasure in earthen vessels, that the excellency of the power may be of God, and not of us." The phrase "earthen vessels" in this verse is a translation of the Greek word *ostrakinos*, which was used to describe *small, cheap, easily broken pottery that was crafted from inferior materials*.

This kind of pottery was *weak, fragile*, and *valueless*, and it often had noticeable defects. Because of the cheap, disposable nature of this "bargain-basement" pottery, it was rarely if ever found in wealthy homes. Rather, it was purchased by people in lower-class neighborhoods who couldn't afford to buy better merchandise. Over time, this word *ostrakinos* eventually came to represent *anything inferior, low-grade, mediocre, shoddy, second-rate*, or *substandard*. This is exactly the type of shoddy, fragile clay that Paul was referring to in Second Corinthians 4:7. Therefore, since the oil-burning lamps (*luchnos*) in New Testament times were made from this same material, we see that the Church is made of people who tend to be fragile, frail, and imperfect. However, this is not the full story!

The second key point to note about oil-burning lamps is that they contained oil. This is important because it reveals that the Church of Jesus Christ is the container of the Holy Spirit on planet earth! Even though we may be fragile and seem inferior or imperfect, the fact remains that God has deposited His Spirit inside the Church! *We contain an endless supply of the oil of the Holy Spirit!*

Furthermore, these oil-burning lamps also had wicks that ran deep into the oil reservoir and soaked up oil until they were completely saturated. These saturated wicks could then be ignited to burn and give light. In the Church today, each of us is like one of those wicks! We as believers are permanently placed in the Body of Christ, where we soak up the oil of the Holy Spirit. God's plan is for every believer to be so saturated with the Spirit that we can be set ablaze to shed light into the darkness of a lost and dying world, just as a lamp lights up a room. And the amazing news is that the Church has a whole reservoir of the Spirit, so it's possible for every believer to be drenched with the oil of the Holy Spirit!

It is a fact that God has fashioned the Church to shine His light into darkness, and that is what we must do regardless of where we live or work. If we succumb to the devil's attacks in our Church — allowing Him to trample on the lamp, drain the oil, and put out the fire of the Spirit — it will snuff out God's light in our world! *That is why the devil hates the Church and wants to extinguish its flame!*

As we blaze with the Spirit's fire and preach the uncompromising Word of God, a piercing light shines forth into the darkness that surrounds us. Imagine how dark the world would be if there were no Church, no preaching, no declaration of the Bible, and no movement of the Spirit. *It is no wonder why the devil hates the Church! We are his greatest threat!*

In Second Corinthians 4:4, Paul spoke of the Church shining light into the lives of unbelievers, saying, "In whom the god of this world hath blinded the minds of them which believe not, lest the light of the glorious gospel of Christ, who is the image of God, should shine unto them." By burning with the oil of the Spirit and shining light in the world, we can hinder the work of Satan in this world and cause men who are blinded by darkness to see the light that can set them free!

The Church is the "oil-burning lamp" of God in the world. Therefore, don't let the devil extinguish your light or talk you into giving up on the Church! Satan is terrified of the Body of Christ because he knows it is his greatest enemy in the world. Don't ever forget this, regardless of what you see, hear, or feel about the Church. And remember — you are a member of the Body, and the devil is terrified of *you*! So make the decision today to let the Holy Spirit set your heart afire. Then guard that flame and don't let *anything* snuff it out, so that you and the local body of believers God has placed you in can keep shining the light of the Gospel to those who are lost in darkness!

MY PRAYER FOR TODAY

Father, I thank You for sending Jesus to give His life and His blood to purchase the Church! You have graciously filled me with the oil of the Holy Spirit so I can bring the saving light of the Gospel to those who sit in darkness. Set me ablaze with the fire of the Holy Spirit so those who are blinded by Satan can also come to know the boundless love and power of Jesus Christ!

I pray this in Jesus' name!

MY CONFESSION FOR TODAY

I confess that as a believer, I am permanently placed in the Body of Christ, which is the Church. God's plan for me is to be saturated with the Holy Spirit, just as a wick would soak up oil, so that I can be set ablaze to shed light into the darkness of a lost and dying world. Even though I may seem fragile or imperfect, God has chosen to deposit the power and preciousness of His Holy Spirit within my earthen vessel so I can shine brightly to the glory of God! Therefore, I walk with confidence in life, knowing that the devil is terrified and Jesus Christ is glorified as I shine bright with the power and the presence of the Holy Spirit within me!

I declare this by faith in Jesus' name!

QUESTIONS FOR YOU TO CONSIDER

1. Are you burning with the fire of the Holy Spirit as God intends? What evidence lets you know that you are alight with the Spirit's flame?
2. Was there a time in your life when you burned with the Spirit more brightly than you do now? If you answered yes, when was that time, and what caused your fire to dim over the years?
3. If you met someone who no longer burns with the Spirit's fire as he or she once did, what steps would you recommend that person take in order to reignite that lost fire?

JANUARY 29

Out-of-the-Ordinary Miracles!

And God wrought special miracles
by the hands of Paul....
— Acts 19:11

All miracles are extraordinary, but every once in a while, God performs miracles that are truly out of the ordinary. A great example of these exceptional miracles is found in Acts 19:11, where the Bible says, "And God wrought special miracles by the hands of Paul." This verse provides great insight into the subject of miracles, but in order to grasp its full significance, it is important to understand the historical context in which these miracles occurred.

At the time these miracles took place, the apostle Paul was ministering in the city of Ephesus in the Roman province of Asia. This major metropolis was famous throughout the ancient world as a center of paganism and was home to approximately 250,000 people who were consumed with paganism, idolatry, and witchcraft. In fact, the cults in this city were so renowned that people journeyed from every corner of the Roman Empire to experience the dark supernatural forces in the city's temples.

For example, on the outskirts of Ephesus stood the great Temple of Artemis, a structure so magnificent that it was listed as one of the seven wonders of the ancient world. At the center of this enormous complex stood a gargantuan statue of Artemis, the Ephesian goddess of fertility, and behind these temple walls, her worshipers engaged in dark, perverse rituals.

Other prominent pagan religions existed in Ephesus as well. The temples of *Gaius Julius Caesar* and *Dea Roma* sat side by side on a high point in the city. These twin structures were constructed at the order of the Emperor Augustus and served as a hub for emperor worship in Ephesus during the First Century AD. Pagan priests swarmed these temple grounds, offering sacrifices to the gods and serving as chosen vehicles of mystical power — those who uttered dark secrets and spoke prophetic declarations as mediums between the spirit world and man.

The massive Temple of Serapis — the Egyptian god of the heavens, the underworld, and medicine — was another center of pagan worship in Ephesus. Even in the spiritually charged atmosphere of Ephesus, the cult of Serapis was famous for its supernatural activity. It attracted people who were especially driven to know the dark secrets of the underworld and participate in the rituals that transpired in this temple around the clock.

However, it was in this wicked, spiritually charged city that the apostle Paul experienced some of the most extraordinary miracles of his ministry. If he was to capture the attention of the Ephesians so they would open their hearts to the message of the Gospel, a special miracle-working power would be required. That is why Acts 19:11 tells us that "...God wrought special miracles by the hands of Paul."

I want to draw your attention to the word "wrought" in this verse. It is from the Greek word *poieo,* which denotes *creativity.* Because the word *poieo* is used in this context, we know that the miracles taking place in Ephesus were *miracles of a creative nature.* Furthermore, the tense of this Greek word conveys the idea of *continuous action.* This means that when this unique demonstration of miracles began, it was not just one or two miracles that occurred at the hands of the apostle Paul, but rather *a practically unending flow of miracles.*

In the Greek text, two words are used to express the type of miracles that were being wrought at the hands of Paul. First, the word "miracles" is the Greek word *dunamis,* which refers to *explosive, dynamic power.* This tells us that explosive, phenomenal power was flowing through Paul's hands. In fact, this power was so out of the ordinary that the Bible describes it as "special," which is a translation of the Greek word *tugchano.* This Greek word means *to hit upon, to happen upon,* or *to fall upon.* It implies *something unique that overtakes someone* or *a power that falls on someone as if to take him or her by surprise.*

Paul literally *hit upon, happened upon,* or *fell into* a level of power that was without equal in his experience. He found himself suddenly operating in a realm of miracles that was extraordinary and powerful beyond his wildest expectations. Of course, all miracles are uncommon, but there was something about these miracles in particular that transcended every miracle that Paul had previously experienced during his ministry. From the usage of this Greek word *tugchano*, it seems that Paul himself was *surprised* by the *exceptional assortment of miracles* that were occurring at his own hands.

This is the only record we have in the book of Acts where "special miracles" occurred at the hands of the apostle Paul. Certainly miracles occurred frequently throughout his ministry, but not miracles of *this* magnitude and quality. In fact, a better rendering of the phrase "special miracles" would be *"mighty, exceptional, out-of-the-ordinary deeds."* These were acts of a supernatural phenomenon of the highest order! Although God performed many miracles through Paul at different times in his ministry, it seems that these particular manifestations of His power may have occurred only in one particular season of Paul's ministry, as it is recorded in Acts 19:11.

God knows how to reach people in every unique situation. In Ephesus — a city obsessed with supernatural activity — normal miracles would never have been enough to hold the attention of the local population. Therefore, God unleashed His power and performed special miracles at the hands of Paul that were truly out of the ordinary. These were rare, unusual, unique, extraordinary, incomparable works of God. Because the word *poieo* ("wrought") is used in this verse, it suggests these were creative miracles — such as the sudden, miraculous replacement of limbs or body parts. Certainly that kind of supernatural demonstration is above and beyond normal healing power and would fall into the category of "special miracles"!

The supernatural power operating through Paul was so great that it caused a multitude of Ephesians to turn to the Lord. Acts 19:18,19 tells us that those who had previously been involved in occult practices repented before Christ and burned their books of sorcery and witchcraft. As a result of God working "special miracles" through the hands of Paul, one of the most powerful churches of the New Testament was established in the city of Ephesus.

Never forget that God knows how to reach every group of people. He knows exactly what kind of power you need to fulfill your assignment and what kind of powerful demonstrations are needed to reach the unique group of people you are called to influence in your life. If you will allow the Lord to have His way and to use you as He wishes, you may find yourself surprised at the level of power He allows to flow through you!

Rather than say, "Oh, this person is hard to reach," or, "This city is dark and very hard to penetrate with the Gospel," why don't you open up your heart and let the Holy Spirit unleash His powerful, creative abilities to work through you? If He did it through Paul, He can do it through you! *If you'll just open up your heart and become a willing vessel, you may be surprised to see a special, out-of-the-ordinary kind of power begin to flow through you!*

MY PRAYER FOR TODAY

Lord, I make myself available for You to unleash Your power through me! You are not a respecter of persons, so I know that if You did it through Paul, You can do it through me. Forgive me for thinking that some of the people in my life are too difficult to reach with the Gospel. Help me remember that You are acquainted with those I'm trying to reach and You know exactly what needs to be done to reach them and to keep them. I open my heart to You today with confident expectation that out-of-the-ordinary power will begin to flow through me for the glory of God and the benefit and blessing of others. So today I make myself available to You, Father, in a fresh way. Be glorified through my body as You stretch forth Your hand. I am Yours.

I pray this in Jesus' name!

MY CONFESSION FOR TODAY

I confess that God wants to manifest Himself through me! From this day forward, I choose to live conscious of God's mighty power that is already at work within me. The same Spirit who raised Christ from the dead dwells in me. Therefore, I know that God wants to reveal Himself. The eyes of the Lord are searching throughout the earth, looking for someone through whom He can work and show Himself strong. That someone might as well be me! Starting today, I am opening my heart and mind to the possibility that God will reveal His amazing power through me! I believe it; I expect it; and I now anticipate the moment when this divine power starts operating in me!

I declare this by faith in Jesus' name!

QUESTIONS FOR YOU TO CONSIDER

1. What is the most remarkable miracle you have ever witnessed firsthand?
2. Can you remember the first miracle you ever saw? Can you recall where you were and what happened when you witnessed your first miracle?
3. Have you ever entered into a place and time, just as the apostle Paul did, when God was doing miracles through you that were beyond your wildest dreams? If not, do you desire to experience this kind of miracle-working power of God?

JANUARY 30

Ministry to the Sick, the Diseased, and Those With Evil Spirits

So that from his [Paul's] body were brought
unto the sick handkerchiefs or aprons,
and the diseases departed from them,
and the evil spirits went out of them.
— Acts 19:12

We saw in yesterday's *Sparkling Gem* that the Bible explicitly tells us that Paul experienced a level of God's power that had been previously unknown to him when he came to the city of Ephesus, resulting in dramatic healings and deliverances of all sorts. Today we're going to examine the types of supernatural occurrences that accompanied that flow of supernatural power.

In Acts 19:12, there is a specific list regarding the various categories of people who were healed and delivered as a result of the divine invasion of power that accompanied Paul's ministry in Ephesus. It says, "So that from his body were brought unto the *sick* handkerchiefs or aprons, and the *diseases* departed from them, and the *evil spirits* went out of them."

To gain a better understanding of these three categories of people, let's consider the Greek words in this verse for "sick," "diseases," and "evil spirits." In the Greek text, these are three very different words that tell very different stories about the various categories of infirmed people that were changed as a result of the Holy Spirit's manifested power.

First, Acts 19:12 refers to the "sick." This is the Greek word *astheneo*, which is a word that generally describes *a person who is frail in health*. This word *astheneo* commonly referred to *people who were so physically weak that they were unable to travel* — in this case, to the location where Paul was teaching the Word of God. It carried the idea of those who were *feeble*, *fragile*, *faint*, *incapacitated*, *disabled*, or simply in such *poor health* that it would be unthinkable to transport them. Their condition was so delicate that they would most likely be *shut-ins* or *homebound*.

Second, the word "diseases" is used, translated from a Greek word that has a very different meaning than the one translated "sick." Actually, the word translated "diseases" can actually be considered an amplification of the word "sick" (*astheneo*), providing even greater insight into the frail condition of these people who were homebound because of their conditions. That Greek word translated "diseases" is *nosos*, an old word with a long and interesting history.

In ancient Greek literature, the word *nosos* was specifically used to describe *illnesses caused by invisible entities*, such as *demons*. In fact, nearly every time the word *nosos* was used in connection with illness, it was understood that the sickness was *spirit-inflicted*. The word portrayed *people who were tormented physically or mentally*; *people who were afflicted by an unseen entity*; or *those who were vexed with lunacy or madness*. The ancient view was that these individuals had been ruthlessly subjected to cruel treatment by spirits and were therefore "*dis*-eased" people.

The word *nosos* was also used to describe *plagues* that were attributed to demonically inspired disasters or *physical terminal illnesses* for which medical science had no known remedy. If it was a *nosos* plague sent to an entire city or region, the ancients believed it was a scourge of demon spirits that simply had to run its course because none of their natural efforts could stop it. Medical attempts to treat a *nosos* illness were considered futile because *nosos* was a type of sickness or demonic attack beyond help and recovery.

Whether the manifestation of *nosos* was terminal cancer, some other deadly illness, or a spirit-inflicted mental madness, people of that day assumed that someone with a *nosos* disease had no hope of recuperation. Every time the word *nosos* was used, it described what the ancient Greeks believed to be *an unalterable, irreversible, incurable, permanent condition*.

Due to the multiplicity of dark pagan religions that flourished in Ephesus, the city was a fertile breeding ground for demonic activity. The religion of Artemis, the supreme goddess of the city, as well as the many other alternative forms of pagan worship, all involved worshipers in occult rituals and supernatural activities that could have caused people to fall under the influence of evil spirits. It should therefore come as no surprise that many people in this city were tormented with untreatable, spirit-inflicted sickness that came upon them as a result of curses, spells, and magic.

However, as we read in Acts 19:12, when Paul's garments were laid on them, "...The diseases departed from them, and the evil spirits went out of them." The wording in Acts 19:12 makes it clear that the elimination of these diseases was linked to the departure of evil spirits. The moment victims were freed of evil spirits, they were freed of the sicknesses the evil spirits had caused, confirming that the diseases were spirit-induced. The verse says that the diseases "departed" — translated from the Greek word *apallasso*, which means *to be set free, to be changed, to be radically transformed*, or *to be liberated or unfettered from something.*

It is significant that the word *apallasso* is used in this verse, because it was actually a First Century medical term that described people who had been *completely cured of a disease.* This term never denoted a temporary cure — only a permanent one. Thus, we know that when the divine power that operated in Paul's ministry touched these afflicted people, they were permanently freed of the sickness and oppression that had relentlessly tormented them.

Acts 19:12 also states that the diseases left when "the evil spirits went out" of them. To understand the significance of this statement, we must first take a closer look at the word "evil" in connection with "evil spirits." The word "evil" is the word *poneros*, a well-known word that describes something that is *foul, vile, malicious, malevolent, malignant, hostile*, and *vicious*. In the Bible, it is often used to depict actions, laws, or people whose behavior is opposed to the righteous nature of God. For example, God's nature is *righteous, good, holy*, and *pure*, but the word *poneros* would depict something that is *unrighteous, wicked, unholy*, and *impure*.

When the Greek word *poneros* is used in connection with *animals*, it often depicts animals that are *savage, wild, vicious*, and *dangerous*. Such beasts are so dangerous that they pose a risk of death to those near them. Similarly, when the word *poneros* is connected to the word *spirits* to form the phrase "evil spirits," as is found in Acts 19:12, we know that these spirits created *havoc* and *destruction*, were *malicious* to those in whom they dwelt, and brought *harm* and *danger* to anyone nearby. This may explain why severe demoniacs lived far from population centers, such as the two demon-possessed men in Matthew 8:28 who lived in a remote region of the Gadarenes.

Acts 19:12 goes on to say that when the power operating through Paul's clothing or hands touched the diseased, the evil spirits "went out" of them. The phrase "went out" comes from the Greek word *ekporeuomai*, a compound of the words *ek* and *poreuomai*. The word *ek* means *out*, as in *to go out, to leave*, or *to go away*. The word *poreuomai* means *to journey*, as in *to leave one place and go to another*. When the two words are compounded, the new word *ekporeuomai* implies an even stronger meaning. It gives the impression that when Paul's garments touched those who had "evil spirits," the anointing transmitted from his garments to them caused the evil spirits so much anguish and torment that they swiftly *went out* of the afflicted like those who are *evicted, ousted, thrown out*, or *forcibly removed.*

God's power came in and the evil spirits swiftly went out — and when they departed, the physical and mental afflictions caused by those spirits left with them. The evil spirits were literally *ejected* or *evicted*, just as an unwanted person would be ejected or evicted from a house. One expositor states that the word *ekporeuomai* actually gives the impression that these evil spirits *escaped* from the anointing operating through Paul. And when they left, the cure was permanent. Once touched by Paul or his clothes, the sick and diseased were *liberated* and *set free.*

One may *not* conclude from this text that all sickness and disease are spirit-induced. However, it leaves open the possibility that some who are tormented with agonizing physical and mental conditions that medical science cannot help may be suffering from afflictions that are not natural but rather are the result of an evil spiritual entity. At least we should be open to consider that if medical treatment does not help, there may be a spiritual root to the physical problem.

In this case, not only is a good doctor needed, but also an experienced pastor or minister who knows how to administer the power of God to those who cannot get relief by medical means. Jesus Christ is the same yesterday, today, and forever — and since He healed those in Acts 19:12, He is more than willing to help those who come to Him for help today. The power of God has never changed — it is still operating and flowing from Heaven; it is still healing the sick; and it is still evicting evil entities from human beings. We must learn to be increasingly sensitive to the Holy Spirit's leading so we can know what ailments are simply physical problems and which are spirit-inflicted. Then once we know, we can deal with the situation by the Spirit and take the actions *He* leads us to take to help bring healing and freedom!

MY PRAYER FOR TODAY

Father, I thank You for opening the eyes of my understanding today as I've read about the various types of sicknesses and diseases that were healed during Paul's ministry in Ephesus. I think I've made the mistake of thinking everything could be treated with medicine, but it is clear from this Sparkling Gem that some afflictions are spirit-induced and therefore can only be cured with the power of God. I ask You to teach me more about the gifts of the Holy Spirit — particularly the gift of healing. I ask also that You make me an instrument through which Your supernatural power flows to heal those who will never be healed in any other way.

I pray this in Jesus' name!

MY CONFESSION FOR TODAY

I boldly confess that God uses me as an instrument of healing, deliverance, and freedom for the sick whom medical science has been unable to help. The Holy Spirit resides in me — and with Him are all of His gifts, including the gift of healing and the working of miracles. Father, I embrace the truth that You want Your power to operate in me and through me — and that I should be an extension of Jesus' ministry to bring healing and freedom to those who need relief. Therefore, I declare that I will yield to You and lay my hands on the sick, expecting You to cause them to recover. I will use my voice to release Your authority and command spirit-inflicted illnesses to go. In Jesus' name, I will see results and people will be made free, for the glory of God the Father!

I declare this by faith in Jesus' name!

QUESTIONS FOR YOU TO CONSIDER

1. Have you ever personally witnessed a healing, miracle or deliverance from a spirit-inflicted illness? When was that and what did you observe? How would you describe it to someone else?
2. Although these instances are very rare, have you ever encountered a person whom you thought was controlled by evil spirits? When was that? What led you to believe that evil spirits controlled them?
3. Have you ever been in an atmosphere so charged with God's power that you personally witnessed the sick, the diseased, and those with evil spirits be set free? Do you ever witness such demonstrations of power at your church? If not, why not?

JANUARY 31

The Great Refiner!

But as we were allowed of God
to be put in trust with the gospel,
even so we speak: not as pleasing men,
but God, which trieth our hearts.
— 1 Thessalonians 2:4

Have you ever felt like God was putting you through a test in order to prepare you for the next step in your life? These experiences can be trying, but they are necessary for your spiritual growth. Even the apostle Paul wrote that God tested him, and the language he chose clearly conveys that sometimes those tests felt like fiery experiences indeed. In First Thessalonians 2:4, he wrote, "But as we were allowed of God to be put in trust with the gospel, even so we speak: not as pleasing men, but God, which trieth our hearts." Today I want to examine this word "tried" and its application in our lives. If you've been through a trial or are currently in the middle of one right now, I believe you will be encouraged by what you are about to read!

The word "trieth" is translated from the Greek word *dokimadzo*. This word was used to describe any kind of *intense test that was intended to prove the quality and trustworthiness of a product*. For instance, it was often used to denote an *intense examination* of individuals who were running for public office to determine if their character was fit for the job.

The Greek word *dokimadzo* also described the process of purifying and refining metal. In the ancient world, metal was put through multiple degrees of fire and heat to expose any impurities. Such flaws could significantly weaken a piece of metal; therefore, testing it to prove its purity and trustworthiness was very important. This refining process is referenced in Malachi 3:2 and 3, which states, "…For he is like a refiner's fire, and like a fuller's soap; and he shall sit as a refiner and purifier of silver: and he shall purify the sons of Levi, and purge them as gold and silver, that they may offer unto the Lord an offering in righteousness." This passage clearly states that God — our Great Refiner — used fire to purify His people so they might offer up a righteous offering to Him.

Another application of the Greek word *dokimadzo* that is particularly relevant in the context of this verse is its use to describe the process of firing ceramic pottery in a kiln. This process is an essential step in the creation of pottery because it exposes defects within a piece that can then be corrected. My sister, Ronda Roush, an expert ceramic and porcelain maker, whose pottery and fine china grace the shelves of numerous statesmen and movie stars, provided the following insight concerning the inescapable need for fire when crafting a superior product:

> The beautiful, artistic design that is enjoyed on a piece of porcelain or pottery is not a permanent part of the piece until the piece has been *fired at the highest temperatures in the oven*. Before fire is applied to the piece, the design is merely superficial and easily erasable. It is not an actual part of the piece until the piece has been placed into the oven at a very high temperature. The *heat of the fire* is what permanently fuses the design into the piece, causing the design to become a part of the permanent glaze.
>
> The most desirable colors, such as deep, rich jewel tones, contain gold in their chemical makeup. However, the gold in the porcelain paint powder that makes these rich jewel tones so beautiful isn't visible at first. It takes *intense fire* to cause the gold in those colors to really shine and make those tones deep and rich. Gold must be fired at a *hotter temperature*. At a normal firing temperature, these colors will turn out dull and lifeless, but *hotter firing* brings out the richness, which can't be seen any other way. When working with pure gold, it is black and ugly when it is first applied to a piece. It is not until it comes out of the oven that it turns to rich patina, which is the crowning glory to most beautiful porcelain pieces.
>
> *Invisible flaws in the porcelain only become visible in the firing process*. As a piece is being fired, one can look into the oven and see all kinds of things during the firing process that were formerly invisible to the naked eye. This process purifies in ways that we don't even know are needed. But at the end of the firing, *the flaws are gone*, and a perfect, mirror-like finish shines back at us from the bottom of the kiln.

The firing process is necessary, and it has to be done a certain way. *There are no short-cuts.* It has to go all the way through the cycle. Trying to circumvent is risky business. Removing a piece from the oven before it has gone the full circle can cause the piece to crack, or even break apart. This process is so important that when the piece is finished being fired, it has to completely cool down before it is removed from the oven. *Rushing the process can ruin the piece.*

What looks like a mistake may end up being the greatest part of the design. Early in my career, a porcelain painter explained to me, "Once when I was working on an exquisite piece, a hairline crack developed. I painted vines and flowers over that crack and added another dimension to the piece, which totally changed it, and made it so much more beautiful. Some of the most beautiful elements to a design are discovered due to flaws that show up in the firing process.

One firing is not enough with the most exquisite and intricate pieces. *Designs are layered, one upon the other, and they must be fired again and again, sometimes up to 20 times for a very valuable piece.* When I take a finished piece out of the kiln that I am pleased with, I know it will find a special place in someone's home, where it will be enjoyed or used to serve some kind of purpose. Firing kilns every day serves as a constant illustrative reminder to me that refinement is vital if I want God to use me, to take me off the shelf and do something with me. God isn't finished with me yet, nor will He ever be! To understand that truth is both humbling and thrilling at the same time. What a relief to know that if the needed changes are not quite there yet, God can take us back into the kiln to refire us and fix the flaws.

It is important to note that when the apostle Paul wrote, "God...tried (*dokimadzo*) our hearts," the verb tense used here indicates the testing was ongoing. Even after Paul's many years in the ministry, God still regularly put him through the fires in order to test his heart.

Tests are a necessary part of life that allow you to move onward and upward in your spiritual walk. The finest porcelain product must be fired to bring out its richest colors and prove its trust-worthiness before it is put on display or sent out to serve. If this is how a human artist tenderly works to create a high-quality product, think of how wonderful Jesus, *your Great Refiner*, is! He doesn't test you to hurt you; rather, He wants to glaze truth onto your heart and bring out a richness of color that you otherwise would not know.

Our God is indeed a consuming fire (*see* Hebrews 12:29)! The refining fires of testing actually clear away debris within us so the fire of the Holy Spirit can perform a deep and lasting work of transformation from the inside out. Then He sets us ablaze with His glory so we can obey what He asks us to do and reveal His nature and power to others through our lives!

So as you move forward in your spiritual walk, realize that Jesus' fires *will* continue to test you. But I want to encourage you to decide today that you're going to be receptive to His purifying process. Let Him expose and remove your defects. Allow Him to teach you what aspects of your life need to change. As you do, those refining fires will make you spiritually richer, stronger, and more qualified to be used by the Lord for His glory!

MY PRAYER FOR TODAY

Father, instead of resisting the changes You are trying to make in my life, I choose to willfully surrender to Your holy fire that exposes my flaws and brings correction. It is clear that Your refining fire is for my good. I know that You would never send a test that is abusive or hurtful. Your work in me produces strength, even as You guide me through situations designed to reveal and remove the flaws that need to be purged from my life. Therefore, Holy Spirit, I ask You to help me understand what You are teaching me. I choose to cooperate with the process so I can get out of the kiln and be placed in Your service!

I pray this prayer in Jesus' name!

MY CONFESSION FOR TODAY

I confess that the Lord is the Potter, and I am the clay. Jesus is molding me into the vessel that He wants me to be. He has every right to expose and remold what needs to be corrected and then put me in the kiln and turn up the heat. And when He brings me out, I know I will be freer than I've ever been before because the flaws that once hindered my walk with Him will be removed!

I declare this by faith in Jesus' name!

QUESTIONS FOR YOU TO CONSIDER

1. Is God currently putting you through a test to see if you are ready to move forward in your life?
2. Are you cooperating with Him or prolonging the process by resisting?
3. Why don't you take a few minutes and write down several things you learned about yourself during the times God has tested you that you needed to change so you could expedite that testing process?

Refining fires of testing
actually clear away debris within us
so the fire of the Holy Spirit can perform
a deep and lasting work of transformation
from the inside out.
Then He sets us ablaze with His glory
so we can obey what He asks us to do
and reveal His nature and power
to others through our lives!

FEBRUARY 1

What To Do When Someone Deliberately Tries To Malign Your Integrity, Character, or Name

Being defamed, we intreat....
— 1 Corinthians 4:13

When we were first starting our work in the former Soviet Union in the city of Riga, Latvia, Denise and I labored around the clock to teach people the Bible and get newly saved people established in the truths of the New Testament. We were working harder than we had ever worked in our lives!

However, as we poured our energy into seeing the Church established in this spiritually barren land, hostile forces began to resist our message of truth with insidious tactics. We were constantly engaged in intense spiritual warfare as we proclaimed the message of the Gospel to the people of Latvia. Those early years were a time of both great triumph and great struggle. Yet despite the best efforts of the enemy to thwart our ministry, we kept seeing the powers of darkness pushed back and the glorious light of the Gospel shine into broken lives that had long been held in the darkness of Communist atheism.

The church in Riga grew rapidly, and every week we witnessed numerous people give their lives to Christ. Once held in bondage, their lives were being made whole by God's grace. It was a thrill to see families restored, sick people healed, and addicts set free from debilitating drug and alcohol addictions. Watching the work God was doing in this region was absolutely precious, and Denise and I were so thankful that He had called us to minister to this part of the world.

However, one day when I went to the store to buy a few groceries, I noticed a strange-looking article on the front page of a national newspaper that was displayed on a rack by the door. The artwork that accompanied the article looked so unique that I reached over, picked it up, and started to read to see what it was about. To my utter shock, *the article was about me*! Sadly, it was an article designed to attack, defame, and vilify the work that God was doing through our ministry in that city.

The artwork was an artist's rendering of a man with a dazed, stupefied look on his face, mindlessly staring off into space with empty eyes. A massive hand rested atop his head with elongated fingers that curled over the front of his forehead and gripped his flesh like a giant claw. It looked *awful*. The bold words of the headline said: "DO WHAT I TELL YOU TO DO!" It was so compelling that I picked it up to see what the article was about. It was only as I began to read the article that I realized the claw-like hand was supposed to be *my* hand!

The article stated that I used hypnotism to control people who were coming to Christ, and that I even used hypnotism to control people *through the television* as they watched our TV programs. When I looked to see who wrote the article, it was one of our fiercest adversaries — a journalist and committed atheist who fought to resist us with every ounce of his being. This man despised Christianity and was even trying to make a name for himself by defaming us and our ministry. He was doing everything he could to smear our reputation and besmirch the Gospel. Once I had encountered this journalist on an airplane, where he approached me and in a condescending voice asked, "Are you still preaching those 'fairy tales' from the Bible?"

When I read what had been written about me in this national newspaper, I wasn't thrilled, of course. It's never pleasant to think that people all over a nation are reading derogatory, false, and hateful words about you. But on the other hand, I rejoiced because it put me in good company with countless other believers who have been attacked for doing the Lord's work. My mind went to First Corinthians 4:13, where Paul wrote, "Being defamed, we intreat; we are made as the filth of the world, and are the offscouring of all things unto this day."

As believers, we live in a world today that is filled with scoffers who are becoming increasingly aggressive in their stance against those who preach the Gospel. More and more, we find our message and ourselves at conflict with the world around us when we espouse the principles of the Bible. In fact, if we take a stand that's biblically right but not politically correct, we almost certainly will find ourselves on the receiving end of a vitriolic attack. Because this hostility is becoming ever more blatant, it is imperative that we as believers know how to respond when we are lambasted by attacks from the enemy.

Paul addressed this very issue in First Corinthians 4:13, saying, "Being defamed, we intreat: we are made as the filth of the world, and are the offscouring of all things unto this day." When he wrote these words, Paul was speaking from his own personal experience.

Throughout his missionary travels, Paul had to contend with principalities and powers that constantly tried to thwart his ministry at every turn. Commonly, these attacks took the form of vicious smear campaigns that sought to destroy his name through false accusations. These malignant character attacks were a regular occurrence in the lives of Paul and his apostolic team. Therefore, we should pay close attention to Paul's words in First Corinthians 4:13, for he told us not only how he responded to these attacks, but how we as Christians should respond as well.

Paul began by saying, "Being *defamed*, we intreat...." This word "defamed" is crucial to our understanding of Paul's message because he carefully chose it to let us know what he had endured from his critics. It is the Greek word *dusphemeo*, which means *to slander*, *to slur*, *to smear*, or *to vilify*. It literally means *to maliciously malign someone's good name*. In today's language, we would say the Greek word *dusphemeo* depicts someone who deliberately *does a hatchet job on someone's integrity, character, or name*. This attack is done with the purposeful intention of damaging someone's reputation in the eyes of others.

By using the particular Greek word *dusphemeo* ("defamed"), Paul confirmed that he and his traveling companions had been victims of malicious and nasty character attacks on numerous occasions. But how did he respond when this occurred? Did he become bitter and wounded?

Did he become angry and react aggressively against his attackers? Did he respond by waging a counter attack?

We find insight into how Paul carried himself in these situations in what he wrote next in First Corinthians 4:13: "Being defamed, we *intreat....*" The word "entreat" is from the Greek word *parakaleo*, a compound of the Greek words *para* and *kaleo*. The word *para* means *alongside*, as in *one who comes up close alongside of another person*. The word *kaleo* means *to call, to beckon*, or *to beseech*. But when these two words are joined to form the word *parakaleo*, it presents the picture of *one who has something so important to say that he pulls right up alongside his listener, getting as close to him as possible, and then begins to plead with him to take some course of action*. This person urgently calls out, pleading with his listener to hear what he has to say and to do what he is suggesting.

Because the word "entreat" — the Greek word *parakaleo* — is *plural* in this particular verse, we know that when these kinds of attacks occurred against Paul's ministry, he and his team pulled together to "entreat" each other. That means they looked each other in the eyes and spoke words of strength and encouragement to each other. The word *parakaleo* in this context can even mean they *consoled* one another.

Carefully consider this fact: The caliber of people who surround you is *especially* important when you are under attack. The people you confide in during these moments will have great impact on how you respond. They will affect your emotions, your thinking, and your resolve.

- ➢ If you are surrounded by people who are angry and retaliatory, their words and reactions may incite you to react in anger or with other negative and non-productive emotions. Stomping, screaming, and making threats won't help you. In fact, that kind of behavior always just makes situations worse!
- ➢ On the other hand, if you are surrounded by people who encourage you, saying, *"Let it go! God will vindicate you. Forgive these people who are being used by the devil to assault you"* — this will help you trust God and forgive the wrongdoing of your attackers.

Thus, the character of those you have around you is *very* important when you are under attack. That's why you must take care to surround yourself with patient, steadfast, forgiving men and women of God.

There was another military usage of the Greek word *parakaleo* ("entreat"), which conveys a powerful message in the context of Paul's message. In the ancient Greek world, before military leaders sent their soldiers into battle, they called the troops together in order to address them. Rather than hide from the painful reality of war, the leaders would speak straightforwardly with the soldiers about the potential dangers of the battlefield and the glories of winning a major victory. They came right alongside their troops and urged, exhorted, beseeched, and pleaded with them to stand tall; throw back their shoulders; look the enemy straight on, eyeball to eyeball; and face their battles with courage. This is the essence of the word *parakaleo*.

Because Paul used the word *parakaleo* ("entreat"), we know that when he and his team were assaulted with false accusations and vicious slander, they quickly began to encourage one another to be strong in the middle of the fight. Like fellow soldiers, they looked into each other's eyes and exhorted and encouraged one another to remain faithful, regardless of the war raging around them. They knew that discipline and a steadfast, committed warfare mentality was required for them to come through the battle they were facing victoriously!

I can almost hear Paul and his team proclaim to each other, *"This is warfare! We must be good soldiers and be faithful to the end regardless of what people say or do to us! Let's not get bogged down with hurt feelings. We have to trust God, forgive these people, and let it go!"*

Paul's words in First Corinthians 4:13 could be interpreted:

"When people assault our integrity, our character, or our name, we begin to exhort and encourage one another...."

When this horrible article about me appeared in the newspaper many years ago, I was surrounded with the right team! Just as Paul's team did with him, the members of my own team exhorted and encouraged me to let it go, overlook it, forgive the man who wrote the horrible article about me, and trust God to vindicate my name and character.

As a result of this God-honoring response, the article had little impact. But had I taken a different approach and retaliated against the journalist who wrote the piece, it probably would have stirred the waters and made the situation much more turbulent. Going through that experience helped put steel in my spiritual backbone. It was the first major attack, but certainly not the last! Taking this approach helped me stay on track regardless of what people said, did, or wrote about us. As a result, we were unhindered in taking the vision God had given us to the next level, again and again, no matter what opposition we faced in the following years.

It's never comfortable to know that people are saying untrue or unfair things about you. If you are currently in this situation or have been in this situation before, you know how badly the flesh wants to rise up in defensiveness and fight back. But it's your responsibility to respond according to God's ways and His love. You must keep your heart free from anger so the devil cannot bog you down in an emotional battle.

If you are being attacked by what people are saying or doing to you, allow your friends or team members to exhort and encourage you to be faithful. When you are defamed, it is time for you and those around you to remind one another, *"This is warfare! We must be good soldiers and be faithful to the end regardless of what people say or do to us! Let's not get bogged down with hurt feelings. We have to trust God, forgive these people, and let it go!"*

MY PRAYER FOR TODAY

Father, I receive Your grace to help me mature to the point where I trust You to protect my name and vindicate who I really am when people say things about me that are untrue or unjust. I refuse to react emotionally with retaliation because of my hurt. Instead, I choose to obey Your Word by keeping myself in the love of God so my faith will not fail. You've promised me that no weapon formed against me shall prosper, and every tongue that rises against me in judgment or false accusation, I will prove or demonstrate to be in the wrong (Isaiah 54:17). Lord, You have assured me that if my ways are pleasing to You, Lord, You will cause my enemies to be at peace with me (Proverbs 16:7). So, I thank You, Father, for helping me to remember that this is warfare with Satan's unseen forces. I will never forget that You are ultimately in control and that if I respond in a Christ-like manner when facing an attack, it will smother the fires and give You the freedom to bring about the outcome You desire in my life.

I pray this in Jesus' name!

MY CONFESSION FOR TODAY

I confess that when the devil uses people to falsely accuse me, malign my name, or to do injury to my integrity, character, or name, I will respond as Jesus did and pray: Father, forgive them for they don't know what they are doing. Just because others act like the devil doesn't give me the right to react like the devil. I choose to yield to the spirit of life in Christ Jesus that keeps me free from sin. Therefore, I make up my mind that I will walk in love and forgiveness, regardless of what people do to me or say about me. I will be a faithful soldier, and I will stay in the fight regardless of any attack that comes to assault who I am. Jesus is in me, and He is greater than anything that could ever come against me!

I declare this by faith in Jesus' name!

QUESTIONS FOR YOU TO CONSIDER

1. Can you think of a time in your own life when your integrity, character, or name was purposely and maliciously attacked by someone who wanted to hurt your reputation?
2. If this has happened to you, how did you respond to that attack? Did you trust God and let it go, or did you allow the devil to drag you into a war of words? If you fell into a war of words, what was the result?
3. Now that this situation is behind you, evaluate your reaction. What did you learn from your response to this situation? Did your reaction make it better, or did it make the situation worse?

The caliber of people who surround you
is especially important when you are under attack.
The people you confide in during these moments
will have great impact on how you respond.

FEBRUARY 2

What To Do When Your Spirit Is Inwardly Disturbed

I had no rest in my spirit,
because I found not Titus my brother:
but taking my leave of them,
I went from thence into Macedonia.
— 2 Corinthians 2:13

Many years ago, I developed an uneasy feeling about a longtime member of our team who worked in a leadership position in our ministry. However, because this person had always been faithful during his years with our organization, I tried to shrug off this uneasiness and ignore what I was feeling. Naturally speaking, there was no reason for me to be suspicious of him or to question his activities. All outward signs said he was doing an excellent job; yet I kept getting a gnawing feeling in my spirit that I should no longer trust him. To put it simply, I was *deeply troubled* on the inside and knew something was *wrong.*

When an occasion would arise for this man and me to be together, I'd look deeply into his eyes when he spoke to see if I could detect whether there was something he was trying to hide. When he spoke, I'd listen carefully to his words to see if there was anything misleading in what he told me. I took notice of his gestures, trying to ascertain whether or not he was acting nervous in my presence because he had something to hide. From all outward signs, everything seemed normal — yet *inwardly* I was still extremely disturbed.

I would tell Denise, "I don't know what it is, but I sense that something is wrong with that person. Is God speaking to my spirit, or am I just being suspicious and untrusting of someone who has been faithful for a long time?" Because I could never put my finger on anything this man had done wrong, I decided that *I* was the problem — that I was being overly suspicious and needed to stop being so skeptical and wary of this devoted employee.

For the next year, I tried hard to shake off those uneasy feelings, but I just couldn't do it. Even though I couldn't identify a specific problem, I *inwardly* knew that things on the surface were not as they really seemed concerning this employee.

After a year of struggling with this issue, I discovered that this man had been acting fraudulently on many fronts. It wasn't just a case of someone doing something wrong by accident; this was purposeful wrongdoing and manipulation of the truth for his own advantage. He had been conniving and deliberately misleading. I was *shocked* when I discovered the length and breadth he had gone to deceive me and our other leaders.

By the time I made my discovery of what this employee had been doing, severe damage had already been done in that department of our organization. But the truth is, the Holy Spirit had been warning me of the problem for a very long time. That inward uneasiness I had experienced was His warning to me to back away from this man!

God's Spirit was trying to save me from the troubles produced by this employee who was conspiring against the work of the Gospel. If I had listened to my heart and followed what I sensed on the inside, I could have avoided the pain this man tried to bring about in our lives. I praise God that when I finally made this discovery, I had the courage to take fast action and terminate this attack!

From this experience that took place so many years ago, I learned the important lesson of paying attention when my spirit is inwardly disturbed. Very often this is God's way of giving us an *alert signal* that something is not right or that something is not as it seems on the surface.

That's why you must learn to pay attention when your spirit is inwardly troubled. Set aside some time to spend with the Lord, and ask the Holy Spirit to help you quiet your mind and emotions so He can reveal to you anything you need to know about the situation. Back up and take a good look at what is happening around you, and be willing to see the truth — even if it is something you'd rather not acknowledge! If you find that everything is fine, you can then move forward with the confidence that you did your homework. But if you find out that something is wrong, you'll be thankful you listened to your spirit and slowed down so you could make this discovery in order to deal with it — for your sake and the sake of others who may be adversely affected by it!

So ask yourself these questions:

- ➢ Have you ever had an inward uneasiness or a lack of peace that you later wished you hadn't ignored?
- ➢ Can you think of a time when the Holy Spirit tried to warn you of a problem, but you didn't listen to your heart and therefore ended up with a problem that could have been avoided?
- ➢ Have you discovered that God is often speaking to you when you have a lack of peace in your heart — and that He is trying to tell you to back up and slow down, to take a more cautious approach to what you are doing?

This kind of *inward disturbance* must be what Paul experienced when he came to the city of Troas and didn't find Titus waiting for him there. Although this exact event isn't recorded in the book of Acts, Paul mentioned it in his second letter to the Corinthian church. On one of his missionary journeys, Paul came to Troas, expecting to find Titus waiting for him. Paul was so taken aback that Titus wasn't there that he wrote, "I had no rest in my spirit, because I found not Titus my brother: but taking my leave of them, I went from thence into Macedonia" (2 Corinthians 2:13).

The word "rest" that Paul used in this verse comes from the Greek word *anesis*, which means *to let up*, *to relax*, *to stop being stressed*, or *to find relief.* In the Greek world, this word *anesis* could denote *the release of a bowstring that had been under great pressure*. Hence, it suggests the idea of *relief.* When used on a personal level, the word *anesis* depicts a person who has been under some type of pressure for a long time but has suddenly found a *release* from that pressure. You could say that this person has decided he is going to *shake off* and *let go of* whatever that has been bothering him or the pressure he has been under.

However, Paul told us he could *not* shake off what he was inwardly feeling in his spirit. He was so *restless* or *inwardly disturbed* that he immediately left Troas and went on to Macedonia to search for his dear friend Titus. The phrase "taking my leave of them" is very strong in the Greek. It lets us know that Paul didn't take a long time to respond to this inward disturbance in his spirit; rather, he took it as a God-given signal that something wasn't right. Hence, Paul bade the believers in Troas farewell and quickly traveled into Macedonia to seek out his missing ministry friend.

Unlike my own scenario that I just related to you, the apostle Paul *listened* to his spirit. He knew that if he was *inwardly disturbed*, it could be a warning sign that something was wrong. Thus, he responded with urgency and took appropriate action when he had this kind of inner witness. How I wish I had done the same thing years ago! If I had listened to what my spirit was telling me, I could have avoided the many troubles that leader tried to create for me and for our ministry.

In light of all this,
Second Corinthians 2:13 could be paraphrased:

"Regardless of how hard I tried to shake off a sense of inward disturbance, in my spirit I knew something was wrong. I tried to shake it off and let it go, but inwardly, I knew things were not right."

As believers, we must learn to pay attention to the lack of peace we feel in our spirits. Sometimes that lack of peace or inward disturbance is God's way of alerting us to something important or of telling us that something isn't right. God lovingly tries to spare us from problems and catastrophes. However, if we don't pay attention to the still, small voice in our hearts when the Holy Spirit tenderly speaks to us, we will end up with troubles that could have been altogether avoided or corrected before they got out of hand.

God is faithful to speak to you — but His voice can often be heard only by what you sense in your own heart. If you sense peace in your heart, it could be the Holy Spirit telling you, *"You have a green light, so you can proceed."* But if you have a lack of peace or an inward disturbance, never forget that it could be God's way of saying *"Yellow light, so proceed with caution."* Or He may even be telling you, *"Red alert! Stop! Something is wrong!"*

Don't make the mistake I made many years ago by ignoring that lack of peace in your heart. It will be far better for you if you take a little time to back up, slow down, and find out why you're feeling uneasy on the inside. If you find that everything is all right, you will then be able to move forward with assurance. But if you learn that something is *not* right, you'll be so thankful that you listened to your heart and got things in order before you proceeded any further and damage was done!

MY PRAYER FOR TODAY

Father, I thank You for Your Spirit, who is so faithful to alert me when things are not right. Please forgive me for the many times You tried to warn and help me, but I ignored Your voice and found myself in a mess I could have avoided. From this day forward, I am asking You to help me become more sensitive to my spirit. Help me pay attention to the peace or the lack of peace I inwardly sense so I can respond appropriately when You are trying to warn me that something isn't the way it should be.

I pray this in Jesus' name!

MY CONFESSION FOR TODAY

I confess that I am sensitive to the Spirit of God. When He speaks to my heart, I quickly respond to Him and obey His instructions. I hear His voice indicating when I have God's green light to move ahead; therefore, I step out in faith. When I sense God's yellow light to move slowly and with caution, I am careful and cautious. When my spirit is inwardly disturbed and I have no peace, I know that this is God's red light — one of the ways He alerts me that something is not right. Because I am sensitive to what God is telling me in my spirit, I am able to move forward with confidence that I am not going to make a mistake!

I declare this by faith in Jesus' name!

QUESTIONS FOR YOU TO CONSIDER

1. Can you think of a time when you were inwardly disturbed but you ignored it — and then later found out it was God trying to warn you about something? When was that, and what happened?
2. What did you learn from that experience when you ignored what you sensed in your spirit?
3. When you sense an inward disturbance, a lack of peace, or a restlessness in your spirit, how should you respond to it?

If we don't pay attention to the still, small voice
in our hearts when the Holy Spirit tenderly speaks to us,
we will end up with troubles
that could have been altogether avoided
or corrected before they got out of hand.

FEBRUARY 3

What Is Godly Sorrow, and What Is Its Purpose?

For godly sorrow worketh repentance
to salvation not to be repented of: but the sorrow
of the world worketh death.
— 2 Corinthians 7:10

When Paul wrote his first letter to the Corinthians, he addressed many problems that existed in the congregation at Corinth, including strife, ambition, and drunkenness. However, the most notorious problem was an act of immorality by a brother in the church who was committing fornication with his father's wife (*see* 1 Corinthians 5:1).

Paul was so stunned by this blatant act of immorality that he told the Corinthians that this kind of immorality didn't even exist among unbelievers — an amazing statement considering he was writing to the church located in Corinth, a city that was known worldwide as a citadel of some of the most vile sexual perversions in human history. In this city, the goddess Aphrodite was worshiped, and moral decadence was widespread. Yet inside the Corinthian congregation was a type of fornication so revolting that it couldn't even be found on the sex-laden streets of Corinth!

When Paul wrote his first letter to the Corinthians, he rebuked them for various acts of carnality that were raging in their midst. In fact, out of all Paul's epistles, his first letter to the Corinthians was the harshest, sternest, and most severe. The Corinthian church also had many wonderful attributes, including a great number of spiritual gifts that were in manifestation. Paul himself had started this church, and from its inception, God's grace had been poured out on these believers in a powerful way. Paul loved this congregation, and he didn't want to see his work in Corinth jeopardized. Therefore, he adamantly urged these believers to take immediate action against these spiritually poisonous activities before the whole church was contaminated.

It is clear in reading Paul's second letter to the Corinthians that this congregation took Paul's orders very seriously. They must have been embarrassed and saddened by the fact that Paul had to rebuke them, because the apostle told them, "...I made you sorry with a letter..." (2 Corinthians 7:8).

The word "sorry" is from the Greek word *lupeo*, which describes *pain* or *grief.* Apparently Paul's first letter caused the Corinthian congregation to feel deeply *pained* and *grieved.* Paul knew this had been their response so he went on to tell them, "...I perceive that the same epistle hath made you sorry...." Twice in Second Corinthians 7:8, Paul acknowledged that they had been embarrassed and pained by the previous letter he sent them.

However, Paul continued in Second Corinthians 7:9 by saying, "Now I rejoice, not that ye were made sorry, but that ye sorrowed to repentance: for ye were made sorry after a godly manner...." When Paul said, "Now I rejoice, not that ye were made sorry...," the word "sorry" is again from *lupeo.* Therefore, an interpretative translation of the first part of this verse could read, *"I don't rejoice because I caused you to feel pain and grief...."*

Paul went on to say that he was glad they "...sorrowed to repentance...." The word "sorrowed" is once again from the same Greek word *lupeo,* denoting *pain* or *grief.* The word "repentance," however, is *metanoeo,* the word for "repentance" that refers to *a complete, radical, total change.* It is *a decision to completely change or to entirely turn around in the way that one is thinking, believing, or living.* By using this word *metanoeo,* Paul revealed that the Corinthians didn't just listen to his earlier message — they heeded it completely and made the decision to change. In fact, they had obeyed him so entirely that they had experienced a total transformation, making them unrecognizable from the sinful condition for which Paul rebuked them in a previous epistle. Thus, the entire phrase in Second Corinthians 7:9 could be interpreted, *"I don't rejoice that I caused you to feel pain and grief, but I do rejoice that my letter made you want to change...."*

Paul went on to elaborate: "...For ye were made sorry after a godly manner...." This phrase "godly manner" in Greek is *kata theon.* In the context of this verse, it could be translated *"your pain was in response to God's dealing with you."* The Holy Spirit had used Paul's eariler epistle to prick their hearts, and Paul was quick to acknowledge this. Although the sorrow the Corinthian believers felt may have been initiated by his letter, the truth was that their hearts felt pained because *God's Spirit* was dealing with them about the sinful activities going on in their midst. Thus, the verse could be rendered, *"I don't rejoice that I caused you to feel pain and grief, but I rejoice that my letter made you want to change. Your pain was your response to God's dealing with you...."*

Paul continued in Second Corinthians 7:10 by saying, "For godly sorrow worketh repentance to salvation not to be repented of: but the sorrow of the world worketh death." When Paul wrote about "godly sorrow" in this verse, the Greek actually reads *he gar kata theon lupe,* which could be translated: *"...the pain you feel in response to God dealing with you...."* The word "worketh" is from the Greek word *ergadzomai,* meaning *to work* or *to produce,* and as we saw earlier, the word "repentance" comes from the word *metanoeo.* Finally, the word "salvation" is a translation of the Greek word *soterion,* which can mean *salvation* in the eternal sense, but in this context refers to *deliverance* from their past carnality.

When all these words are taken together as one complete phrase, the first part of Second Corinthians 7:10 could be interpreted:

"The pain you feel in response to God dealing with you has produced a real change and deliverance...."

The Corinthian believers were prompt to respond to God's dealings with them. In fact, they acted so swiftly and seriously to obey Paul's instruction that in his next letter to them, the apostle declared, "For behold this selfsame thing, that ye sorrowed after a godly sort, what carefulness it wrought in you, yea, what clearing of yourselves, yea, what indignation, yea, what fear, yea, what vehement desire, yea, what zeal, yea, what revenge! In all things ye have approved yourselves to be clear in this matter" (v. 11).

Not wanting to grieve the Holy Spirit any longer, the believers in Corinth had moved with indignation and fear to purge themselves of sin and carnality. This was *proof* that genuine repentance had occurred in their lives, for as we have seen, true repentance produces an indisputable transformation of one's behavior. The change in the Corinthian church was evidence enough for Paul to say they were now completely "clear" in the matters where they had previously been wrong! They had been completely exonerated!

Have you ever felt sorrow because of a sin you committed that grieved the heart of God? Did you allow that sorrow to do its full work in you and produce a desire to change within your heart? Or did you merely brush it off and thereby resist God's dealings with you?

If we will be sensitive to the Holy Spirit and listen to His voice, we will hear Him speak to us when we do something that grieves the heart of God. In that moment, we have a choice: We can harden our hearts and turn a deaf ear to God's Spirit, or we can allow the Holy Spirit to deal deeply with us and produce a desire in us to never transgress in that particular way again. God is willing to work in us and with us, but we must have hearts that want to positively respond to His dealings, as the Corinthians exhibited so well.

If God's Spirit has been trying to deal with you, can you honestly say that you've allowed a godly sorrow to have its full effect in you, thereby producing a strong desire to change and to never fail in the same way again? Regardless of what you have done, God offers you forgiveness, and He will give you the strength needed to enact powerful, permanent change in your life if your heart is truly repentant. *It's up to you!*

MY PRAYER FOR TODAY

Father, I ask You to please forgive me for the things I've done or tolerated that are offensive to You. I know that when I willfully sin or tolerate attitudes that are wrong, it grieves the Holy Spirit. I ask You to help me feel the pain of my sin so deeply that I will never want to cross that line again. I never want to be hardhearted or stubborn toward You when Your Spirit speaks to me, so please help me keep my heart soft and pliable and remain tenderhearted to the dealings of the Spirit.

I pray this in Jesus' name!

MY CONFESSION FOR TODAY

I confess that my heart is soft and pliable in the hands of God. I want to please the Lord, and I never want to grieve the Holy Spirit. I receive the empowerment of the Holy Spirit to strengthen me with His might and to guide me in life, because He is the last Person I would ever want to offend! The Lord creates in me the desire and the ability to do His will and good pleasure, as He conforms my thoughts to be in agreement with His will. When the Father's heart is grieved, my heart is grieved too. From this day forward, I will be quick to hear and to obey the Lord's voice, and as a result, I expect it to go well with me in all the affairs of life.

I declare this by faith in Jesus' name!

QUESTIONS FOR YOU TO CONSIDER

1. Can you think of an exact moment in your life when you knew inwardly that you had grieved the Holy Spirit? Did that realization bring great pain to your own heart? When was that moment? When that happened to you, how did you respond?
2. Can you recall a time when the Holy Spirit tried to deal with you about something that was grievous to Him, but you didn't listen? What was the result of not listening and paying heed to His voice?
3. What area is the Holy Spirit trying to deal with you about right now? Are you responding to His counsel and direction, or are you ignoring His tender work in your heart? Based on your past experience, is your present response leading you on a path that will end well?

FEBRUARY 4

Flee Fornication!

Flee fornication....
— 1 Corinthians 6:18

In the early years of our marriage, my wife Denise and I pastored an adult singles ministry, and one of my responsibilities in this role was to regularly meet with people who needed counseling. During one session, a distraught young man began to pour out his heart to me about how he kept habitually falling into sexual sin. As he sat before me, I could see that he was disappointed in himself, spiritually broken, and feeling like a miserable failure. With tears streaming down his face, he told me, "Before I know what is happening, I find myself in the middle of a sexual sin. I just can't seem to control myself."

I asked him, "Where are you when this sin usually takes place?"

He told me, "It usually happens at my house or at my girlfriend's house."

I looked into his eyes and asked, "Don't you think it would be wise for the two of you never to be alone together at your house or her house so you don't put yourself in a position where it's easy for you to fall into sin? If that's the place where you keep falling into sin, I strongly recommend that you don't spend time alone in her house or yours!"

He responded, "Are you suggesting that I run away from my problem and my weaknesses? *No way!* I am not going to run away from my weaknesses! I intend to prove that I can overcome these temptations. I don't believe I need to change my environment. I just need to be stronger!"

As the years passed, I watched this man continue to struggle with sin. His plan wasn't working! He was sincere, but the approach he was taking was not wise. Not only was he not conquering his temptations, but he was being conquered by them! It was time for him to use his brain to *get up* and *get out* of those places where he had habitually fallen into sin. He needed to heed the words of the apostle Paul to the Corinthian believers when Paul urged them to "flee fornication…" (1 Corinthians 6:18). If this man would have just obeyed the wise counsel of the Word, he could have escaped those years of misery, feeling like a spiritual failure.

"Fleeing fornication" would have been very hard to do in a city like Corinth! Corinth was known for its perversion and twisted sinful activities, as well as for its drunkenness. In short, it had a worldwide reputation for being a "party city" and a center for "sexual freedom," where one could avail himself to the vilest of human instincts without any fear of others' disapproval. The entire city was devoted to the sex industry; therefore, any kind of sex was considered acceptable and fair. Some have speculated that after Sodom and Gomorrah, Corinth may have been one of the most perverted cities in human history.

The city had a constant flow of sailors who came to town to party, and this fed the prostitution business — the largest source of revenue in the city of Corinth. Furthermore, the city abounded with idolatry, which frequently incorporated sexually immoral behavior into their rituals, and the Corinthian bathhouses brimmed with homosexual activity.

In addition to all these excesses, wine was integrally tied into nearly every aspect of the city's culture. It was used in idol worship as a sacrament and a tool to commune with the spirit realm; it was commonly imbibed by prostitutes and their customers; and it was readily available in the city's bathhouses to loosen people's inhibitions so they would more readily participate in homosexual activities. Basically, all these factors combined meant the alcohol business in Corinth was booming! So not only was Corinth rife with idolatry and all manners of gross sexual perversion, but the city also struggled with serious alcohol abuse and addiction.

In fact, the city of Corinth became so synonymous with perversion and drunkenness that the term "to Corinthianize," first coined by the Greek author Aristophanes (450-385 BC), became a common term used in other cities of the Roman Empire to describe *drunken or immoral debauchery.*[1] Regardless of where you lived, if you knew a person who was given to excess and drunkenness, that person was referred to as "a Corinthianizer." Corinth's reputation was so stained that if an actor in any city of the Roman Empire was required to play the role of a drunkard on stage, he was always depicted as a drunk Corinthian.

[1]William Barclay, *The Letters to the Corinthians* (Philadelphia: Westminster Press, 1975), pp. 2-3.

This was the environment the Corinthian believers faced every day, and because they were so new in their faith, the lure of the world and the flesh still had a strong hold on them. Paul knew they needed to use their minds to think carefully about where they went and what situations they should avoid. Even today, we know it's just common sense that if a person struggles with alcohol, he needs to stay out of bars! Likewise, Paul knew that these Corinthian believers needed to avoid environments where they might be tempted to fall back into sin. *Fleeing from sinful environments was the smartest thing they could do if they really wanted to stay free from sin!*

This meant the newly saved Corinthian believers had to avoid *a lot* of places in Corinth! It meant they had to reassess how to maneuver in the city in order to avoid all the places where sin tried to call out to them. Because there were so many sinful places in Corinth, it took concentration and serious planning for them to obey Paul's exhortation to "flee fornication." However, because Paul admonished them to stay away from these cesspools of sin and perversion, the committed believers in Corinth learned to move as quickly as possible to "flee" from these establishments.

The word "flee" that Paul used in First Corinthians 6:18 is the Greek word *pheugo*, which means *to run, to flee*, or even *to take flight*. Making this word even stronger is the fact that the tense used in this verse conveys the idea of a *habitual fleeing* or *a continuous escaping*. This plainly means Paul is telling believers that they need to make a habit of *running* from sin!

The Greek word *pheugo* is used throughout Scripture to depict the act of:

- *Fleeing* from evil influences.
- *Fleeing* from youthful lusts.
- *Fleeing* from morally bad friends.
- *Fleeing* from a corrupt stimulus.
- *Fleeing* from wrongdoing and sin.

In short, the word *pheugo* means *to run like crazy*!

Sometimes the smartest thing you can do is *get up* and *get out* of a situation as fast as you can. Just as Joseph fled with haste to escape the seductive advances from Potiphar's wife (*see* Genesis 39:11,12), if you're in a setting where you're being tempted or you feel yourself being lured to do something contrary to the Word of God — *get out of there*! Rather than stick around to prove you can resist, it's time for you to get your feet moving and resist sin by saying *goodbye* as you walk out and let the door slam behind you! A weak person won't have the strength to say *no* and walk away — but a person who is strong will say, *"Enough is enough!"* and walk away.

Paul's order to the Corinthian congregation was to "flee fornication." In order for them to obey Paul's command, these believers had to make drastic changes in their routines. They had to change the places they frequented, the activities they participated in, and the people who surrounded them. If they were going to walk away from sin and stay free from it, they would have to deliberately avoid the situations that previously made it so easy for them to fall into sin.

How does Paul's message apply to you?

For you to stay free, it may be necessary for you to choose new friends. You may need to make a break from the places where you used to spend your free time. You may need to quit watching the TV programs or movies that once were a big part of your life. It is possible that you may need to stop reading the material you once read. It may even mean that you need to discontinue your Internet service so you won't gravitate to pornographic sites that keep luring you into their seductive, entangling web.

Is it possible that you've been praying for strength to resist sin, when actually all you simply need to do is to stay away from the things that encourage you to sin? If you're tempted to overeat, stay out of the kitchen! If you're lured to pornographic websites, then add filters to block those sites, or, if necessary, discontinue your Internet service. Permanently fix your situation by removing yourself from the things and the places that have a negative influence on you. *Taking this commonsense approach may be the answer to the prayers you've been praying to be free!*

If you are serious about your walk with God, you need to make every change necessary to stay both spiritually strong and free from guilt and condemnation. I admonish you to take Paul's words deep into your heart and "flee" from those things that have an adverse effect on your soul and on your spiritual life. It's what you would tell someone else to do if you were giving them counsel about how to stay free from alcohol or drugs, *so don't you think it would be wise for you to start applying the same advice to your own life?*

MY PRAYER FOR TODAY

Lord, I thank You for speaking to my heart today about making a break with my past and with the places that tend to pull me down. I admit that I've allowed my flesh to lead me, and I have been wrong for not making better choices for my life. I've tried to blame the devil and others for my failure, but today I am taking personal responsibility for the control and direction of my life — and I am walking away from those places, people, and deeds that negatively affect me. Holy Spirit, I tap into Your mighty power already at work within me to strengthen me with might in my inward man as I make these right choices. With Your help and by Your grace, I can and I will walk free and STAY free!

I pray this in Jesus' name!

MY CONFESSION FOR TODAY

I confess that I do not linger in compromising situations where I am tempted to think wrong, speak wrong, and do wrong with my mind, mouth, or body. I am the temple of the Holy Spirit, and I honor the Holy Spirit's presence in me. I never want to grieve the Spirit by slipping back into those sins from which I've been delivered. Therefore, I am making every effort to stay away from people, places, and deeds that have a negative impact on me!

I declare this by faith in Jesus' name!

QUESTIONS FOR YOU TO CONSIDER

1. Can you think of people, places, or deeds that you need to make a break from in your life? Make note of them, and then determine a plan of action you can take to avoid them so you can remain free from sin.
2. Was there a time in your life when you felt seduced by sin, yet you stayed in that bad environment? Did you falsely think that you could overcome it, but instead succumbed to sin over and over again? When and where was that time in your life? What did you learn as a result of that experience?
3. If you were counseling individuals who were struggling with an addiction or some habitual sin, what would you say in counsel to them to help them stay free? Do you apply this same counsel to your own life?

FEBRUARY 5

What Does Patience Look Like?

For ye have need of patience,
that, after ye have done the will of God,
ye might receive the promise.
— Hebrews 10:36

People often throw in the towel and quit when they don't see results as quickly as they want. I am amazed at how short-lived some people's faith really is. If their prayers for healing aren't answered immediately, they allow their flesh to convince them, for example, that it is God's will for them to be sick. Or if they sow their finances and believe for a financial harvest but don't see that harvest in a matter of months, they are tempted to think that everything they have been taught concerning prosperity must be a lie. The problem is that these Christians want quick "microwave answers" to problems that probably took some time to develop. *They need to give their faith time to work!*

Most people quit before their faith has time to fully work. These folks need a good dose of patience to go along with their faith! You see, faith and patience are *partners*. You need both to receive the promises of God. Hebrews 10:36 says, "For ye have need of patience, that, after ye have done the will of God, ye might receive the promise."

The word "patience" comes from the word *hupomene*, which is a compound of the words *hupo* and *meno*. The word *hupo* at the beginning means *under*, and *meno* means *to stay* or *to remain*. When you put these two words together, the Greek word means *endurance* or *to stay under*. It is the picture of a person who is under a heavy load but has resolved that to stay put in that one spot, regardless of how hard or heavy that load gets.

This person is *thoroughly committed* to maintaining his position. He will stay in that spot as long as it's necessary for him to achieve victory. He is intent on standing by his commitment, regardless of the cost he must pay. Nothing can sway or move him to change his mind. He is not going to relinquish his territory! I call this "bulldog faith." It is a faith that manifests as a tough, resistant, persistent, obstinate, stubborn, tenacious spirit that refuses to let go of what it wants or believes.

If you haven't done well in the past at standing firm in your faith against the pressure of the enemy, don't feel condemned. Just receive this as an encouragement from the Lord to get back up and go for it again! To experience a breakthrough regarding a difficult situation or trap that you've struggled with for too long, you must take a bold stance of faith and then *stand still*.

Yes, it may take time for your answer to manifest. Just because your request is in accordance with God's will, the answer doesn't always quickly come to pass without a hitch. There's a devil out there that doesn't want you to experience God's will for your life. You also have your own flesh to deal with, and flesh loves comfort — it does *not* like a challenge. Your faith may need to grow. God wants you to come to a higher level in the process of receiving the answer to your prayer. You need to renew your mind so you can "…ask in faith, nothing wavering..." (James 1:6).

Faith has focused desire. It knows what it wants. It doesn't vacillate. It never moves. *Faith stands still in one spot.* So make your bold confession of faith: "God, this is what I want. This is Your revealed will for my life, and I'm not moving until I receive the fulfillment of it!" You must have this type of patience if you intend to beat the devil at his game and successfully do what God has called you to do. Endurance is absolutely essential if you intend to stay in the fight until your enemies are under your feet and you emerge victorious.

Believe me, friend, when this kind of patience is working in your life, it's not a matter of *if* you'll win — it's just a matter of *when* you will win. So keep your arms of faith wrapped around that promise, dig in your heels, and refuse to be moved!

MY PRAYER FOR TODAY

Father, I repent for each time I have fallen short of Your promises simply because I gave up before my faith had time to fully work. I neglected to feed my faith on the Word of God. As a result, I began to give place to the fleshly tendency to become impatient when what I really needed to do was to persevere in faith and be strong. I receive Your forgiveness and cleansing, and I ask You to strengthen me with might in my inner man so I can let patience have its perfect work in me.

I pray this in Jesus' Name!

MY CONFESSION FOR TODAY

I let patience have its perfect work in me (James 1:4). Through faith and patience, I inherit the promises of God for my life. Having done all to stand, I stand with bulldog faith and tenacity, committed to seeing the will of God for my life fulfilled!

I declare this by faith in Jesus' name!

QUESTIONS FOR YOU TO CONSIDER

1. Can you think of a time when you were tempted to throw in the towel and give up on what you were believing to come to pass, but because you decided to hold your ground and stay in the fight, you saw your victory manifest just a short time later? What if you had quit just before you won your victory? Aren't you glad you didn't quit?
2. Everyone faces struggles like I've described in today's *Sparkling Gem*. Do you know people who are facing a battle right now and could use an encouraging phone call from you to cheer them up in their fight of faith? Wouldn't it have blessed you if someone had done that for you when you were in the middle of *your* fight?
3. What are you believing God to see manifested in your life? Maybe it's more than one thing. Are you being steadfast and immovable until you see the answer to your prayer? I urge you to dig in your heels and *refuse* to be moved by *anything* until you see God's promise come to pass!

FEBRUARY 6

Do You Know the Role You're Supposed to Play?

I have planted, Apollos watered;
but God gave the increase.
So then neither is he that planteth any thing,
neither he that watereth;
but God that giveth the increase.
— 1 Corinthians 3:6,7

When I was growing up, my pastor, Brother Post, was like a hero to me. He was a master Bible teacher who taught the Word of God with intelligence, conviction, and passion.

His intense enthusiasm for the Bible deeply affected me, and I am certain that my love for the Word of God today and my desire to mine the Greek New Testament for these *Sparkling Gems* is directly connected to the way he taught me the Bible.

Wednesday night church services were my favorite because that was when Brother Post would dig deep into the Word and feed us richly! However, I must admit that I also loved Wednesday nights because our church hosted a supper for the entire congregation each week before the service began — and at those dinners, we got to eat Bobbie Jo's awesome shiny, butter-covered rolls! Bobbie Jo was our church cook, and no one made bigger, better, or more delicious rolls than Bobbie Jo!

Each week as Wednesday drew near, I grew so excited to think I would soon be eating those big fluffy rolls! I'd consume as many as I could before my parents would rebuke me for eating too much. Then I'd head across the street with a full stomach to the church building for the Wednesday night service where Brother Post would fill my spiritual stomach with masterful, thoughtful, in-depth teaching from the Word of God.

Brother Post was the only Bible teacher I personally knew until I attended college as a young man. There is no way to exaggerate the biblical foundation that he laid in my life. During my college years, I was exposed to other wonderful Bible teachers, and not long after I left the university, I took a position as an associate pastor in a large Baptist church under a godly pastor named Dr. Bill Bennett. This man was as knowledgeable as any person I've ever met in my life. He read Greek; he knew history; he had a doctorate of theology. In my opinion, he was and remains one of the most brilliant Bible teachers I've ever met anywhere in the world.

For several years during my earliest period of ministry, my chief role was to serve my senior pastor. I carried his books and traveled with him as his assistant. I relished every minute of this season because Dr. Bennett spent time speaking to me from the Word of God and helping me establish my thinking in sound doctrine. I tremendously respected his knowledge, his teaching ability, and the godly life he led. Working at his side and serving him as I did was one of the greatest honors that God ever gave to Denise and me. God used that man to set me on a solid biblical foundation.

When I look back at the roles Brother Post and Dr. Bennett played in my life, I can see that *both* were vital to my spiritual development. One planted and another watered my spiritual development — just as the apostle Paul told the Corinthians, "I have planted, Apollos watered…" (1 Corinthians 3:6).

As an apostle called to the city of Corinth, Paul was responsible for starting the church in that city. However, he also served as their first pastor until God raised up another pastor to take his place. This replacement was a well-respected, highly educated man from Alexandria in Egypt named Apollos — and soon after Paul's departure, he became the senior pastor of the Corinthian church. History tells us that Apollos was a gifted orator who was renowned for his eloquence.

In Paul's absence, the Corinthian believers naturally began to compare the different speaking styles of Paul and Apollos. Some who had been in the church from the beginning and were extremely affectionate toward Paul apparently didn't like the style of the new pastor. There were others in the church who loved Apollos and asserted that his preaching was superior to Paul's. Yet the message Paul and Apollos preached was the same — *they just had different styles.*

When Paul heard of divisions forming in the church of Corinth over the issue of his and Apollos' different styles of ministry he wrote to them and said, "I have planted, Apollos watered…" (1 Corinthians 3:6). Let's take a closer look at the Greek in this statement to see exactly what Paul meant.

The word "planted" in this verse is translated from the Greek word *phuteuo*, which is a form of *phuton*, the Greek word for *a plant*, and it simply refers to *the act of planting a plant.* By using this word, Paul was metaphorically describing *his role* in Corinth. He was *a planter.* His task was to penetrate the darkness of the city and plant a church there. There is no doubt that this city had some of the toughest spiritual ground he had ever encountered. It was surely one of the most difficult places to minister in the ancient world.

Like a neglected garden overrun with pests and weeds, Corinth was infested with demonic powers. In order to plant the Gospel in people's hearts and firmly establish the Church in that tough environment, he had to press forward and till the ground with the power of God; then he had to get on his hands and knees and *pull* the weeds. *This was hard work!* Yet for one and a half years, Paul poured his life into this pioneering job. When he finally left Corinth to pursue his apostolic call in another city, the Corinthian church had not only been planted — it was *deeply rooted* and *producing good fruit*!

Paul described his role in Corinth as a planter; however, he was fully aware where his responsibility ended and another equally important responsibility began. That is why he continued in First Corinthians 3:6, "I have planted, *Apollos watered….*" The word "watered" here is from the Greek word *potidzo*, which most often means *to water* or *to irrigate.* It is the very word that would have been used to depict a farmer watering his garden to provide nourishment to his plants so they could grow. It can also be translated *to imbibe*, which in this context would convey the act of a field becoming *soaked* or *saturated* in water.

By describing Apollos' role in Corinth with the Greek word *potidzo*, Paul actually gave Apollos *a great compliment.* It is as if Paul said, "*Apollos didn't just water you; he saturated you….*" In other words, Paul acknowledged what a wonderful, vitally important job Apollos played in the Corinthian church! Paul had pulled the weeds, chased away the pests, planted the seed, and established the new growth of the young plant. Apollos then nurtured that plant, watering it regularly with the Word of God and thus contributing equally to the great increase that happened in that church. The roles of both ministers were absolutely vital. One was not better than the other; rather, each played a significant role in the spiritual development of that church.

Paul continued in First Corinthians 3:6 by saying, "I have planted, Apollos watered; but God gave the increase." This word "increase" is the Greek word *auxano*, which means *to cause to grow, to cause to increase*, or *to cause to become enlarged.* By using this word, Paul was teaching us that we are always dependent upon God to provide growth and increase — even if we do everything right as we plant and water our crop. Or to put it another way: We can carry out our different roles of planting and watering, but only God can provide the sunshine and weather that allows it to grow. If God doesn't intervene and provide His part, all of our planting and watering will be in vain. Therefore, as we carry out our roles as effectively and efficiently as we can, we must always be conscious of the fact that we're not responsible for growth and success. If growth comes, ultimately it is God who gives the increase.

I am thankful for my first pastor, Brother Post, and for Dr. Bennett, the pastor whom I later served. One firmly planted the seed in my life, and the other watered that seed until I was saturated with the Word of God. Both of these men were vital to my early growth as a man of God — but, ultimately, it was *God* who made me grow. These two men were part of the process, and I'm so thankful to Him for what they invested in my life. But the One who caused me to grow was *God Himself*.

It's right for you to acknowledge and thank the people who have played a major role in your life. But don't make the mistake the Corinthians made and get so fixated on personalities that you forget that God is the One who really makes seed grow!

Also, as you play a God-given role in someone else's life, let me encourage you to do the very best with what He has entrusted to you. Till the ground, plant the seed, and pour on the nourishment required to make the seed grow. God expects you to do your part. But never forget that He is your greatest Partner. You are completely dependent on Him to do the part you cannot do for yourself — *increase* and *growth*!

MY PRAYER FOR TODAY

Lord, I sincerely want to take just a moment to say thank You for the people who have played such an important role in my spiritual development. So many people have helped me, corrected me, assisted me, and taught me. When I think of how many people have made investments into my life, I am amazed and grateful that You would love me so much. Holy Spirit, help me express my gratitude to these people whom You have used to develop me. Most of all, I want to thank You for providing all the other ingredients that no one else could provide. Even though others invested so much in me, I know that You are the One who is responsible for the growth, increase, and success I am experiencing in my life. Without You, none of this would be happening today, so I want to say thank You!

I pray this in Jesus' name!

MY CONFESSION FOR TODAY

I confess that God is using me to play a significant role in other people's lives. Just as others loved me and invested in my spiritual development, God is now using me to help others. I consider it a privilege to plant spiritual seed into other people's lives. It is an honor to tend that seed with love and care and to nourish it with the water of the Word of God. All around me are people with great potential who need someone to help them. Because the Holy Spirit is working in my life and making me more like Jesus Christ, I am willing, ready, and desirous to be a blessing, just as key people have been to me. God has given me a role to play in the spiritual development of others, and I will faithfully do exactly what He has asked me to do.

I declare this by faith in Jesus' name!

QUESTIONS FOR YOU TO CONSIDER

1. Who are the people who have played the most important role in your spiritual development? In what ways did they affect your spiritual growth?
2. Have you ever taken the time to call, write, or make a personal visit to those people who helped you along the way in your walk with God? Have you expressed how profoundly thankful you are for the role they played in your life? If you haven't done this, why not? Don't you think it is right to go out of your way to say thank you to someone who had such a dramatic influence in your life?
3. Who are you helping spiritually develop right now? Are you planting seed in someone's life? Are you watering seed that has already been sown in another's life? God has a role for you to play in helping others, so take a good look at your life and ask, *"In whose life am I making a difference today?"*

FEBRUARY 7

Early Beginnings

Moreover it is required in stewards,
that a man be found faithful.
— 1 Corinthians 4:2

When the Holy Spirit first told us to begin our TV ministry in the former USSR, Denise and I had no idea what we were doing. We had never done a TV ministry before, and television equipment was not available to purchase in the Soviet Union. But with a small staff and a tiny budget — and a single home-video camera — we began to film the first programs of *Good News With Rick Renner.*

At that time, television programming on Soviet television was dark and bleak. Some of it was still broadcast in black and white. So even though we were filming with a home-video camera, the low-budget programs we produced looked at least as good as the other programs being broadcast on the Soviet stations. Although we started in such a primitive fashion, I had great expectations for what God was going to do through this new television outreach.

Adding interest to the program was the fact that there were *no* Americans broadcasting on Soviet television at the time. When our faces appeared on TV sets across the huge region where we first broadcast, it was a breakthrough that had never occurred before. People were mesmerized that Americans were on their televisions, and people began to tune in to hear what we had to say. Most often, I was the only one on the program, but from time to time, Denise joined me as well.

At first, we began to notice that people recognized us when we went to the open market to purchase groceries for our house. They thanked us for our programs and reached out to touch us in a tender way, trying to express their thanksgiving for what we brought into their homes. Then the letters started to pour in, taking us completely off-guard. We had not anticipated such a huge mail response! The first book we printed and offered as a free gift on television was *Dream Thieves* — and when we made that offer, boxes upon boxes of mail poured into our offices. It was the beginning of a TV ministry that has continued for decades uninterrupted, right up to the present day.

My team and I had little knowledge of what we were doing. Our equipment was just an old, used home-video camera, and the lights we used to light up the "set" (our living room) were the lamps from our house. Yet God used the simplicity of it all and began the process of opening entire nations to the teaching of God's Word via television! It was a small beginning, *but it was a beginning*. Today this outreach has blossomed into a TV ministry that reaches not only the Russian-speaking nations of the former USSR, but people all over the world through satellite and the Internet.

When you start out with a new assignment from Heaven, you have to start with what you have and with what you know. Whether it is a business, a church, a ministry, or some other pursuit — you can only start at the level where you are and with the amount of money you have at your disposal. You must measure where you are, what stage you are in, and move cautiously and smartly as you proceed to obey and fulfill the call of God on your life. Denise and I weren't thrilled about starting our TV ministry with an old home-video camera and living-room lamps, but that is what we had and what we could afford. And because we were faithful with what we had, God blessed it and increased us over time.

In First Corinthians 4:2, Paul talked about faithfulness and people who are charged with overseeing projects, saying, "Moreover it is required in *stewards*, that a man be found faithful." As we were slowly building our TV ministry, my mind often went to this verse, because it clearly teaches that God watches to see if we are faithful with what has been entrusted to us. Being faithful wouldn't have been demonstrated by complaining that we had to use a home-video camera. Being faithful was making the decision that we'd cheerfully use that camera to its maximum potential! Faithfulness has a lot to do with attitude — it is *not* based only on performance.

Notice that Paul spoke of "stewards" in this verse. It comes from the Greek word *oikonomos*, which is a compound of the word *oikos* and *nomos*. The word *oikos* means *house*, and *nomos* means *law*. When compounded, the new word means *the rule or administration of a house*. It could also be used to denote the *administrator* of any project.

Such "stewards" had control of household finances and personal information about their employers; therefore, they had to be highly trusted individuals. Many "stewards" were highly educated and trained for years to attain such positions. However, most started as lowly servants and advanced to higher ranks over a period of time as they proved themselves faithful. Their superiors learned to trust them immensely because they had proven themselves faithful time and time and time again. Thus, a valued steward was generally thoroughly vetted and time-tested.

But First Corinthians 4:2 says, "…It is required in stewards that, a man be *found* faithful." The word "found" is the word *eurisko*, and it depicts *a discovery* that is made after a long period of study and investigation. The idea this word carries is that of a *successful conclusion* to a diligent search. After performing a long and arduous study of a person, carefully examining his behavior and ability to work and fulfill responsibilities, at last one determines that this person is "faithful."

The word "faithful" is the Greek word *pistos*, which in this particular case denotes one who is *utterly reliable*. It is one who shows unchanging affection or support in the face of difficulty. It is allegiance to a superior or employer. It is *unwavering support* to a cause, person, or assignment. This is a person whom an employer can depend on — and a person God can count on to carry through an assignment to the end.

So if you are starting a project on a small level, as Denise and I did with the beginning of our TV ministry, I urge you to be faithful to the core. Be utterly reliable with what God has entrusted into your hands. What you demonstrate to God will determine whether He finds you prepared for advancement or deems it necessary to keep you at your current level.

Today I see the vast impact our TV ministry is having, especially in the Russian-speaking nations of the world. But I have not forgotten that we started with a home-video camera and house lamps in our living room. Rather than complain, we used what God provided and made the most of it. God saw our efforts — and *eureka!* — by His grace, He found us faithful, advanced our TV ministry, and gave us better equipment to reach a larger audience. *We give all the praise and glory to Him, because it was His grace that even enabled us to be faithful!*

What is the task before you today? Are you starting small, as Denise and I did when we started our TV ministry in the former USSR? Never forget that Zechariah 4:10 admonishes us not to despise the day of small beginnings! So start where you are, use what you have, and be faithful to the task the Lord has given you. And as God watches you over a period of time and sees that you are utterly reliable to complete with excellence the tasks He gives, He will advance you; He will entrust more to you; and He will promote you! That is a biblical principle found throughout the Word of God — *and you can be guaranteed that it's true for you!*

MY PRAYER FOR TODAY

Father, help me to keep my eyes fixed on the task You have assigned to me. Help me to not complain that my beginning is so small, and teach me how to use this opportunity to learn everything I can before my venture grows larger. I know that You are with me — and You are watching to see what kind of steward I will be. So Holy Spirit, I draw upon Your mighty strength within me to rise up and help me be the best I can be. Most of all, I want to be found pleasing to the Lord and be one whom He can trust with much!

I pray this in Jesus' name!

MY CONFESSION FOR TODAY

I confess that I am committed to be utterly reliable in every task that Heaven entrusts to my care. I will be faithful to use what I have to the best of my ability and to demonstrate to the Father that I do not despise the day of small beginnings. I take this beginning time as an opportunity to learn, to excel, and to prove to God that I am a man or woman He can trust!

I declare this by faith in Jesus' name!

QUESTIONS FOR YOU TO CONSIDER

1. What is the task before you right now? You can only start out at the level where you are and with the cash that is available to you. Be faithful with what you have — stretch it as far as you can make it go, do excellently with what is entrusted into your hands, and believe that God will see it and give you an upgrade!
2. What Bible character had a small beginning but ultimately made a huge impact with his life? If you have time to do it, it would be good for you to make a list, because there are quite a few of them. This would be quite an encouraging assignment for your heart and soul!
3. Can you think of someone you personally know who started a dream on a small level, but worked and *worked* at it until it grew and became significant? Who is that person? What character traits does that person demonstrate that added to his or her success and that you would like to see added to your life?

FEBRUARY 8

God's Spirit Dwells in You!

Know ye not that ye are the temple of God,
and that the Spirit of God dwelleth in you?
— 1 Corinthians 3:16

When we first started our church in Moscow in the year 2000, God moved supernaturally in our church's midst, and our congregation miraculously began to grow by leaps and bounds. It wasn't long before the auditorium we had rented was filled to maximum capacity, and we still needed room for more people. So we rented a bigger auditorium — but once again, soon we were at capacity. This happened again and again over the years.

In addition, because our church membership was growing so rapidly, it soon meant we needed a larger office to accommodate the business end of things, and so the search began. After a period of looking, we finally secured an office in an ideal location. It was directly in the center of downtown Moscow — a two-minute walk from the *Bolshoi Theatre* and a short seven-minute walk from *Red Square*. You couldn't get any closer to the heart of the city than this location. It was *ideal* in every way!

Because of the building's prime location, I knew that many high-ranking visitors would come to this office to meet with our ministry. Therefore, our space needed to be decorated professionally and beautifully to make a first-class impression of the Gospel on every person who entered that office. To this end, Denise and I worked hard to choose the perfect wallpaper, carpet, and furniture to adorn our church office. Finally, the day came when the interior decorating work was to commence on the new office. The first work to be done that day was to hang the wallpaper Denise and I had so carefully chosen. We were so excited to see how it would transform the "look" of that office!

The reception area was the first room in our office to be wallpapered. This was the most important part of our office because it was where people's first impressions of our ministry would be made. Many people in this region of the world have historically ridiculed people of faith, so it was essential to us that our guests associate excellence with the name of Jesus Christ as they entered our reception area. Therefore, we chose an elegant, intricate, floral-patterned wall covering for that space, and we knew it would take a real master to hang it correctly.

The person we chose to hang the wallpaper was a woman from our congregation who maintained that she was such a master at the craft. She had even volunteered to do the job and to do it for free as a gift to the church, and we were delighted. I met her at the office and showed her the wallpaper, and she got started. I left the site because I had a meeting in another part of the city, assuming this "master" would do a beautiful job. However, when I returned to see what she had done, I was *shocked*!

She had hung a lot of paper and had done it very quickly, but none of the patterns from strip to strip matched each other. I was so stunned that for a few moments, I was literally *speechless.*

She asked me, "How do you like my job?"

I regained my composure and replied, "Do you realize none of the patterns match?"

She said, "Oh, you wanted the patterns to match? Why didn't you tell me?"

I told her, "When I heard you were a professional paper hanger, I assumed you would know to match the patterns of each strip. I'm sorry, but you'll have to take it down and start all over again."

On her second attempt, she matched the patterns, but this time the wallpaper was very visibly *crooked.* As I explained to her that this room would be a reception for very important guests and the wallpaper couldn't be crooked, she said, "But if you look at it like *this*, it doesn't look crooked." With that, she tilted her head sideways and framed the crooked wallpaper between her hands. She said, "If you tilt your head and look at it like this, it looks normal. See?"

I was astounded that she would try to tell me that it would look normal if I would just cock my head to the left. I replied, "People won't walk into this office and cock their heads sideways so the wallpaper will look normal. People will walk in here standing upright, as people do, and they will think this wallpaper looks crooked and crazy. Please tear it down, and I'll find someone else to properly hang the paper."

When I instructed this woman to rip the paper off the walls, I heard people gasping. A staff member privately suggested, "Pastor, this wallpaper is expensive. What if we just paint it and forget about it? Does it really have to be torn off the walls a second time? Do you really think anyone will notice that it's crooked? Can't we just leave it the way it is instead of losing money?"

I finally had to walk over to the wall and begin tearing the paper off myself — as everyone around me gazed in shock. The sound of expensive paper being ripped from the walls filled the ears of all who stood by. Piece by piece, the wallpaper fell to the ground. When I saw people staring in disbelief at what I was doing, I turned and explained to them, "This room is designed for guests. Nothing less than our best is acceptable. I want every person who enters this room to sense that we care about them and have prepared a place for them that is special and shows them respect."

That day my staff finally realized how important it was to me that we do our best to make guests feels honored and welcomed. But as important as it was for me to treat the guests of our ministry with respect, it is far more important that we do our very best to make *God* welcome in our lives.

In First Corinthians 3:16, the apostle Paul wrote, "Know ye not that ye are the temple of God, and that the Spirit of God dwelleth in you?" This word "dwelleth" is the Greek word *oikeo*, which denotes a *house*. However, the word *oikeo* as used by Paul in this verse means *to dwell in* or *to take up residency in a house*. This means God is not like a guest who comes and goes. Rather, when a person repents and comes to Christ, God's Spirit moves in and takes up residence. In other words, that newly saved believer's heart becomes the Holy Spirit's *permanent home*.

When a believer first accepts Christ as his Lord and Savior, there are areas in his life that need to be healed, restored, and changed. By walking in obedience to the Word of God and learning to serve in the local church, a person's mind can become conformed to the mind of Christ, and his life can gradually become transformed to reflect the excellence of Jesus Christ. However, for these changes to occur in a person's life, it requires his complete participation. These kinds of changes don't occur without hard work, commitment, and determination to make one's heart a place where God feels honored.

Never forget that God's Spirit — *the Spirit of holiness* — now lives inside you. What are you doing to make Him feel welcome? Are you allowing the crooked and mismatched places of your life to remain unchecked, or are you doing your best to rip them away, one piece at a time, so you can make your heart a place that shows God honor and respect?

It's great that we do so much to make guests feel welcomed in our homes, churches, or offices. But think about how much more important it is that we build our lives in such a way that conveys to God just how thankful we are that He dwells in our hearts!

God has moved into your heart and made it His permanent home. Don't you think you should "hang the wallpaper" in your heart in such a way that it shows Him how happy and honored you are that He is there?

MY PRAYER FOR TODAY

Lord, I thank You for coming to live permanently in my heart. What a miracle it is that You would want to live in someone like me. I am amazed and dumbfounded by this great act of grace — and my heart is overwhelmed with thankfulness that You have chosen to make my heart Your home. I know that I have a lot of areas in my life that need attention, and I'm asking You to give me the grace and power to deal with each of these areas one step at a time. Without Your help, I can't change myself. But with Your grace working inside me, I can be conformed to think with the mind of Christ, and my behavior can be transformed to reflect the character of Christ. I thank You in advance for helping me get rid of all the crooked and mismatched places in my soul so I can become a dwelling place where You are comfortable to abide.

I pray this in Jesus' name!

MY CONFESSION FOR TODAY

I confess that I obey the instructions of the Holy Spirit as He guides me to correct all the crooked and mismatched places in my mind, my soul, and my character. God's Spirit lives in me, and He is giving me the insight, wisdom, and strength to peel flawed areas away from my life so I can become a shining example of what Jesus desires His people to be. By myself I cannot change. But thank God, the Holy Spirit who lives within gives me the power to confront every area of my life that needs to be brought into alignment with His perfect will. His strength is MY strength to make wrong things right. I can do all things through Christ who strengthens me, as He continually helps me become all that He wants me to be!

I declare this by faith in Jesus' name!

QUESTIONS FOR YOU TO CONSIDER

1. Can you think of specific parts of your life that are intolerable and hurtful to God's Spirit, but that you have allowed to continue in your life? What are the areas in your life that you know are wrong and God is asking you to change? Why don't you make a list of these areas and keep it nearby so you can be reminded of the changes you need to implement as you pray each day?
2. What do you do in your life that especially makes God feel welcomed, honored, and respected?
3. If you were God and were looking for a heart that made you feel welcomed, honored, and respected, what qualities would you be looking for that let you know you were truly wanted?

FEBRUARY 9

God's Payback System for Those Who Trouble You

Seeing it is a righteous thing with God
to recompense tribulation to them that trouble you.
— 2 Thessalonians 1:6

We once had an employee whom we "thought" was the cream of the crop. He had come to one of my meetings to tell us that he believed God was calling him to be a leader in our ministry. Although I knew he had been in the ministry a long time, I didn't know him very well personally, so I felt the need to dig deep to verify information about him. Everything I checked out confirmed this man would be a splendid addition to our team. At that time we needed a man with his skills, so we hired him to work in the office in a lower position to observe how he worked and performed with other people.

Over a period of several years, my top leadership team was very impressed with this man's style of work and his commitment to get tasks done on time. He was professional and eager to learn, and he showed himself faithful in many respects. When the position of office manager opened up in that nation, we felt it right to move this man into that position. But once he had been entrusted with the oversight of money, serious problems started showing up. At first, the financial discrepancies were small, and we thought they were simply mistakes. But over time, it became apparent that there was a serious problem. This man was stealing money in very devious ways.

I loved this man, so when I finally discovered that he was secretly robbing us of money, I personally traveled hundreds of miles to give him an opportunity to be honest about what he had been doing. When I walked into our ministry office to meet with him, and he realized we knew about what he had been doing, he *erupted* in anger!

I suddenly saw a man I had never seen or known before! He screamed, yelled, and commanded that we get out of *his* office, which in fact was *our* office! It was the official headquarters for our ministry in that particular nation. When I reminded him it was *our* office and he had no right to tell us to leave, he shouted, "So you think this is your office? Who signed the contract? *I* did! I signed it! It's in my name — and legally that makes it *my* office! So I am ordering you to move off the premises immediately, or I'll call the police to have you arrested for trespassing."

My team and I were shocked at his behavior. We had known him a long time, and I'd anticipated that he would admit what he had done and ask for forgiveness. My goal was not only to confront the problem, but also to see how I could help restore this man. But suddenly the mask he had donned for years fell off, and when it did, it revealed a face red with anger! His eyes looked like a demon peering at us, and he screamed with a complete lack of restraint. He was a man out of control and wholly given to anger. He got so close to my face as he screamed that at one point, I actually thought his nose would touch my face.

But no matter how loud the man turned up the volume, I remained calm and told him that I wasn't leaving until he was honest with me about the discrepancies we had found. The next thing I knew, he was picking up the telephone to call the police to have us evicted from our own office. Rather than allow this to escalate into a worse situation, my team and I walked out the door and left. *That was the last time I ever saw that man.*

Because we had operated our ministry in that location for years, I turned around to see it for the last time as we walked down the corridor. There on the door was the name of our ministry boldly printed for all those who visited. Behind those doors were nearly 100,000 letters addressed to Denise and me from our TV viewers. The shelves and the basement were filled with 250,000 copies of my books that we sent free of charge to people who wrote in response to our TV program. Eighty full-time employees paid by our ministry were working on desks, computers, typewriters, copy machines, fax machines, and tape duplicators that were purchased by our ministry.

The next day, we discovered that not only had this man robbed us of ministry funds, but secretly he had also legally registered everything in *his* name. This meant we had no legal claim to anything in that office. He had even registered the ministry automobile in his name! It was the slickest, most polished case of professional thievery I had ever personally witnessed.

One of my leaders suggested I take the man to court to reclaim what belonged to us. But because we were so well known in that region of the world, I knew that such an action would end up on the front page of the newspapers, and it would be talked about from one end of that nation to the other end. In that former Communist nation where faith had historically been persecuted, I knew that a story like this hitting the newspapers would "load the gun" of every atheist and Communist who hated the Gospel. The newspapers would surely report this as the "war of the preachers," and it would have profoundly negative consequences on the work of God in that country.

I knew that the reputation of the Gospel — and the impact it was having on countless precious souls — was worth far more than our loss. So instead of getting into a legal quandary that we couldn't win, we made the choice to leave it all behind. We only asked that he give us the letters addressed to us, the 250,000 books that had our names on them, and the sign on the door. It was hard to refuse the letters, books, and sign, because our name was written on them and we could prove ownership of these things. But everything else was lost as we relocated to another city and reopened our office with directors who had been with Denise and me for more than a decade. After that experience, we fixed things *tight* legally so this kind of situation could never occur again.

At the time these events transpired, staff members were amazed at how peaceful I was throughout the entire ordeal. They asked, "How can you just walk away so peacefully from this situation with no bitterness or contempt for this man?" But the truth was, I felt sorry for him, and I was more concerned about his soul than our loss. For him to do such a thing, I knew he had to be extremely deceived. I also knew that if he didn't repent and make it right, God would hold him accountable and would avenge this situation. I really didn't want him to reap something terrible, but there is a universal law involved here — the law of sowing and reaping — and a harvest *will* come from seed sown, whether people have sown good or bad seed. This man had planted terrible seed in the ground, and if he didn't repent for his actions, that seed would take root and grow in his life as deadly fruit.

In Romans 12:19, Paul told believers who had suffered injustice, "Dearly beloved, avenge not yourselves, but rather give place unto wrath: for it is written, Vengeance is mine; I will repay, saith the Lord." According to this verse, it was time for me in *my* situation to peacefully move out of the way and leave it all to be settled by God. I told our staff how thankful I was that I was *not* in the vengeance business! However, I knew that if this man didn't repent, he would eventually reap the terrible fruit of his actions.

When Paul wrote to the Thessalonian believers, they were suffering severe persecution and horrific abuse at the hands of Jewish unbelievers and pagans. That's when he told them, "Seeing it is a righteous thing with God to recompense tribulation to them that trouble you..." (2 Thessalonians 1:6).

Let's take a little time today to dig into this verse to see what powerful truths we can extract that pertain to our daily lives.

In this verse, the word "righteous" is the word *dikaios*, which portrays something that is *just*, *fair*, or *right*. In the phrase "with God," the word "with" is a translation of the Greek word *para*, which normally means *alongside*. However, this word *para* means *with God* or refers to *God's way* of doing things.

For example, if you heard someone refer to me and say, "That's the way it is with Rick Renner," you would understand they were referring to my behavior, my habits, or my way of doing things. In this verse, the word *para* is used in this same way to tell us the way things are "with God." It is used to describe the manner in which God behaves — I'm talking about His behavior, His habits, or His style. Thus, the first part of this verse could be paraphrased, *"Being just and fair is the way it is with God! It's His behavior, His habit, and His way of doing things...."*

Paul continued by telling us about a specific behavior of God we need to know about. The apostle wrote, "Seeing it is a righteous thing with God to recompense tribulation to them that trouble you."

Now let's look at the word "recompense." It is the Greek word *antapodidomi*, which is a compound of the words *anti*, *apo*, and *didomi*. The word *anti* means *against*; the word *apo* means *to return*; and *didomi* mean *to give*. When these three words are compounded as they are in Second Thessalonians 1:6, it means *to pay back*, *to repay*, *to give someone exactly what is due them*, *to give someone exactly what they deserve*, or *to settle the score*. It is *a full and complete requital of what is due*. This means the verse could be paraphrased, *"Being just and fair is the way it is with God! Making sure people get exactly what they deserve is His behavior, habit, and way of doing things...."*

God doesn't have to actually get involved in this "divine payback system" because it works like a law. The law states, "Be not deceived; God is not mocked: for whatsoever a man soweth, that shall be also reap" (Galatians 6:7). This means if you do good for others, this spiritual law will make sure that others do good for *you.* If you wrong others, this spiritual law will see to it that others wrong you. *Whatever you do is precisely what will come back to you.* (For more in-depth study on the law of sowing and reaping, *see Sparkling Gems 1*, August 2).

How others have treated you is what they will experience from others. Likewise, how you have treated others is the way you will be treated by others. This is a spiritual law that cannot be broken or violated.

Now, that's *not* to say that if you've ever been mistreated, it *necessarily* means you have mistreated someone else in the same way. But when it comes to what you dole out in negative attitudes or negative treatment toward others, without repentance *from your heart,* that harvest will most certainly find its way back to you.

On the other hand, if you have been a source of blessing to someone else, this spiritual law will see to it that a blessing comes back to you. And if a person has deliberately done wrong or intentionally tried to hurt you, this spiritual law will see to it that they are paid back for what they did to you.

This is a fixed spiritual law that always works, so we must be careful in our treatment of others, for what we do to others is precisely what will be done to us. *Only repentance has the power to eradicate bad seed from the ground and thereby stop it from producing fruit.*

Paul said that God will recompense "tribulation" to them that trouble you. So what does the word "tribulation" mean? It is the Greek word *thlipsis,* a word so strong that it leaves no room for misunderstanding. It conveys the idea of a *heavy-pressure situation.* In his epistles, Paul often used this word to describe *grueling, crushing situations* that are *unbearable*, *intolerable*, and *impossible to survive.* The word *thlipsis* is often translated as the word "affliction," which means the verse could be translated, *"God will give a full measure of affliction to those who have afflicted you."*

By using this word, Paul was telling us that when God recompenses people for the evil they have done, it is a *full requital.* Those who deliberately trouble us will receive a full measure of what they dished out.

The law of sowing and reaping is activated even in this sphere of life, and the way a person does or does not treat others is part of the process that determines the type of justice he receives from the Lord. God's payback system is just, fair, and equitable.

An interpretive translation of Second Thessalonians 1:6 could read:

"It's God's habitual practice and normal behavior to be just and fair, so you can be sure people who have wronged you will get exactly what they deserve. He will see to it that they are reimbursed and that they receive a full settlement of trouble for the traumatic circumstances they

have put you through. Those who have afflicted you will receive a full measure of affliction in return."

I can personally think of no better illustration for the way God's payback system works than the man I told you about at the beginning of today's *Sparkling Gem.* He had an opportunity to repent and get his heart right with God and with me. Instead, he rejected this divinely granted opportunity. I'm so sorry to say that today he is a totally discredited individual. His loss of reputation had nothing to do with our response to his misdeeds, for Denise and I made the decision that we would never tell what he had done. We left it silently in the hands of God, but over time we watched the truth of Second Thessalonians 1:6 come to pass in this man's life. *What he did to others is exactly what was done to him.*

In light of this, I encourage you to keep your heart free of bitterness when someone has wronged you, abused you, or falsely accused you. Vengeance is God's business, and you must not enter this realm that belongs only to Him. Make it your aim to forgive those who have wronged you, and leave the rest in God's hands. And if you have done wrong to others, I strongly advise you to repent and make that relationship right today. The law of sowing and reaping is actively working, so if you're wise, you'll do everything you can to stay on the good side of the law!

MY PRAYER FOR TODAY

Father, after reading today's Sparkling Gem, I want to make sure that my own heart is right with You and others. I know I haven't always done right, so if there is anyone to whom I need to go and make it right, please bring it to my memory so I can take care of it today. I want to stay on the good side of the law of sowing and reaping. If I've ever sown bad seed, I want to rip it up through the act of repentance. And when I am tempted to be upset with others who have done wrong to me, please help me remember that my focus must be to keep my heart free, and it is Your responsibility to give people what is due them. Help me, Lord, to stay out of the vengeance business and to focus on keeping my own heart pure and clean!

I pray this in Jesus' name!

MY CONFESSION FOR TODAY

I confess that I keep my heart free of judgment and I do not venture into the realm of revenge. God sees what is happening to me, and I can silently trust that He will be faithful to take care of me and to deal with those who have tried to harm or hinder me. That is His business, not mine, and I refuse to allow my emotions or anyone else to drag me into the ring to fight it out. I will focus on my own heart to make sure that I am inwardly clean. As the Holy Spirit reveals people I've hurt or wronged in the past, I will quickly go to them to ask forgiveness because I want to stay on the good side of the law of sowing and reaping!

I declare this by faith in Jesus' name!

QUESTIONS FOR YOU TO CONSIDER

1. As you read the story of the man who robbed our ministry many years ago, did you think of people who wronged you, your family, or your business in the past? Who was the person who wronged you? Have you really forgiven that person for what he or she did?
2. When you look at what happened to that person's life since the time he or she wronged you, what do you see has happened? Has the law of sowing and reaping produced its results in that individual's life?
3. Is there anyone you've wronged in the past with whom you have yet to make it right? Now that you understand you need to communicate with that person and ask for forgiveness, what steps do you need to take? Is it possible that some of the trouble you've experienced in life is a result of the law of sowing and reaping bringing a negative harvest back to you because of what you did to someone else?

FEBRUARY 10

Continue in Watchful Prayer

Continue in prayer,
and watch in the same with thanksgiving….
— Colossians 4:2

Have you ever gone through a period in your life when you were tempted to give up on something you were praying for because the answer seemed too long in coming?

The truth is, we've all experienced times when we prayed in faith, but the answer to our prayers seemed to come far too slowly. In fact, this situation is so common that my wife and I receive thousands of letters from our television viewers, who ask questions such as:

- How long should I continue believing God for the answer to my prayer to come to pass in my life?
- Should I just give up hope that my answer will ever come?
- Is there anything special I should be doing while I am waiting for God to answer my prayer request?
- What attitude should I maintain while I continue to wait for my answer?

These questions are all very applicable to our spiritual walk, so let's see what the Bible has to say about how we should respond when the answers to our prayers are delayed. In Colossians 4:2, the apostle Paul outlined the kind of attitude we must maintain as we wait for the answers to our prayers. He wrote, "Continue in prayer, and watch in the same with thanksgiving...."

Let's examine several key words in this very important verse. First, Paul began by saying, "*Continue* in prayer...." This word "continue" is translated from the Greek word *proskartereo*, which is a compound of the words *pros* and *kartereo*. The word *pros* is the preposition *to* or *toward*, and it carries the idea of *close, up-front, intimate contact* with someone else. A good example of this word *pros* is found in Ephesians 6:12, where it is used to describe our *close contact* with unseen, demonic spirits that have been marshaled against us. The second word *kartereo* means *to be strong, to be stout, to bear up, to have fortitude*, or *to be steadfast*. Typically, it carries the idea of something that is *strong, robust, tough, solid*, or *heavy duty*.

When these two words are compounded, as they are in Colossians 4:2, the new word depicts *a strong, solid, "never-give-up type" of leaning toward an object*. It pictures a person who wants something so fiercely that he is leaning forward toward that object — *pressing toward it, devoted to the goal of obtaining it, and busily engaged in activities that will bring the object of his desire to him.*

Thus, by using the word *proskartereo*, Paul was emphatically urging us to do three things as we wait for God to answer our prayers:

- Stay forward-directed and focused in prayer.
- Keep *pressing* into the Spirit.
- Resolutely refuse to give up until we have obtained that for which we are praying.

There will undoubtedly be times in your life when the answers to your prayers won't come quickly. However, God requires you to stay spiritually strong — pushing forward and continuously engaging in robust prayer until you see what you are believing Him for come to fruition. If you are tenaciously determined to *continue* in prayer, you will receive the answers you seek.

The Greek word translated "prayer" in this verse is also very important. It is the word *proseuche*, a compound of the Greek words *pros* and *euche*, and it is used 127 times in the New Testament. As we saw earlier, the word *pros* is the preposition *to* or *toward*, and it carries the idea of *closeness*. The word *euche* is an old Greek term that describes *a wish, a desire, a prayer*, or a *vow*. This word was originally used in Scripture to depict a person who makes a vow to God because of a *need* or *desire* in his life. This person is so desperate for an answer that he promises to give something of great value to God in exchange for a favorable answer to his prayer. When these two words are compounded, the new word conveys a multifaceted and powerful meaning.

The first part of the word *proseuche* — *pros* — tells us that prayer should bring us face to face with God. Prayer is more than a mechanical act or a formula to follow; it is a vehicle through which you can enjoy a close, intimate relationship with God, especially when you are trying to break through spiritual barriers or press deep into the Spirit.

Secondly, the word *euche* conveys that *sacrifice* is a vital component of prayer. When you come before the Lord, you must be willing to surrender yourself and make any changes in your life that God might require of you, because there are potential areas in your life that can block His ability to bless you. As you draw near to God, the Holy Spirit will convict your heart of any areas that need to be surrendered to Him. If you respond to His conviction and repent, the obstacles in your life that were hindering your prayers will be removed, and the answers to your prayers can come quickly.

God wants you to meet Him face to face and surrender every area of your life to Him. In return, He promises that you will receive the answers you seek.

Paul continued in Colossians 4:2 by saying, "Continue in prayer, and *watch*...." The word "watch" is the word *gregoreo*, meaning *to be awake, to be watchful*, or *to be vigilant*. It refers to *a spiritual, watchful attitude* and can be translated, *"Be wide awake...."* Rather than go to sleep on the job after spending time praying, pressing, and interceding, you need to *keep your eyes wide open* so you can watch for the answer you are requesting!

Remember, the word "continue" (*proskartereo*) refers to someone who wants something so fiercely that he is leaning forward and pressing toward it, busily engaged in activities that will bring the object of his desire to fruition. He is forward-directed, *focused* in prayer, *pressing into* the Spirit, and *resolute* in his determination not to give up until he has received the answer to his prayers. It is the picture of a believer who has prayed long and hard and is now becoming weary from constant prayer. Therefore, Paul exhorted us, *"Stay awake! Stay on your guard! Keep your eyes open!"*

Once you pray in faith and begin to make the changes God requires of you, you need to stay vigilant and watch for the answers to your prayers to show up!

The final point Paul made in this verse is that you must "...watch in the same with *thanksgiving*...." The word "thanksgiving" is the Greek word *eucharistia*, which is a compound of the words *eu* and *charis*. The word *eu* means *good* or *well*, and it always denotes *a good disposition* or *a good feeling about something*. The word *charis* is the Greek word for *grace*. When these two words are compounded, the new word describes *an outpouring of grace and wonderful feelings that freely flow from the heart in response to someone or something.*

By using this word, Paul taught that you must persistently engage in aggressive prayer — heartily seeking a specific answer from God as you keep your attitude vigilant and your eyes watchful for the soon-to-be-manifested answer. As you take that stance of faith, lift your voice to thank God *in advance* for the answer you are seeking! *Thanksgiving is the voice of faith that thanks God for the answer before it comes!* It is hard to be discouraged or defeated when you are continually thankful, so be sure to maintain a thankful, faith-filled heart as you watch for your answer to arrive!

Given what we have learned,
Colossians 4:2 could be paraphrased:

"Be committed to ongoing and relentless prayer! You have to press toward that answer you are seeking. You have to be devoted to the goal of obtaining it as you stay engaged in the robust, strong, stout, never-give-up kind of prayer that brings you straight into the presence of God! While you are persistently and aggressively praying, you also need to stay wide awake,

constantly keeping your eyes open as you look for and expect your answer. And while you are doing all of this, don't forget to stay in an attitude of thankfulness that gives thanks to God in advance for the answers you are seeking...."

So what should you do if you are praying in faith and the answer still hasn't come? It's time for you to *dig in* and *press* in the Spirit toward the answer. Be willing to make whatever changes God may require of you, and keep your eyes open for the answer. Finally, lift up your voice, and start thanking Him now for the answer even *before* it comes!

Are you going through one of those trying times right now? Have you been tempted to give up on something you've been praying for because the answer isn't coming as quickly as you wish? If so, don't throw up your hands in exasperation and walk away! *Stay in faith and stay alert, because you may be on the very brink of receiving your long-awaited answer!*

MY PRAYER FOR TODAY

Lord, I am making the decision to turn up my fervency in prayer! You are telling me to pray consistently and persistently and to press in harder than ever before, so that is what I am going to do. If there are issues in my life that are blocking the answers to my prayers, please reveal them to me, and I will surrender them to You. With the help of Your Spirit, I will stay in faith with a watchful eye for the answer I have sought from You. Right now by faith, I thank You in advance for the answer I am seeking.

I pray this in Jesus' name!

MY CONFESSION FOR TODAY

I confess that I press forward in the Spirit, persisting in prayer until I get a breakthrough from the Lord. As God's Word instructs me, I will be committed and unrelenting in prayer until every blockage is removed and the answer manifests in my life. By faith I keep a watchful eye for the answer I have requested from the Lord. Right now I lift my voice in faith and begin to consistently thank Him in advance for those things I have asked of Him.

I declare this by faith in Jesus' name!

QUESTIONS FOR YOU TO CONSIDER

1. Can you say that you've been unrelentingly committed to continuing in your prayers until you receive the answers you have sought from the Lord?
2. Have you maintained an attitude of thankfulness while you've waited for your request to be manifested? *Be honest!* Have you lifted your voice by faith to thank Him in advance for the answer even though you haven't seen it yet?
3. Before you do anything else, why don't you begin taking a few minutes, starting today, to get into an attitude of thanksgiving and verbally praise and worship God for hearing and answering your prayer?

FEBRUARY 11

What Does It Mean To Be Blameless?

A bishop then must be blameless....
— 1 Timothy 3:2

Many Christians who are called to a leadership position in the Church feel excited about their new role until they read First Timothy 3:2, which says, "A bishop then must be blameless...." The moment their eyes fall on the word "blameless," they feel disqualified because it seems to imply that they must be "perfect." However, this is a misinterpretation of that scripture. No man or woman is perfect except for Jesus; therefore, no one would qualify to be a spiritual leader if that were really God's requirement to be called and to function in ministry. *So what then does the word "blameless" mean?*

The word "blameless" in this verse is the Greek word *anepilemptos,* which is a combination of the Greek prefix *a* and the words *epi* and *lambano*. In the context of this verse, the word *epi* means *against*, and the word *lambano* means *to receive* or *to take something into one's possession*. Finally, the addition of the prefix *a* to the beginning of the word has a canceling effect that essentially gives the word the *opposite* meaning.

To better understand this word *anepilemptos*, we must first look at its meaning without the prefix *a*. If only the words *epi* and *lambano* are compounded to form the word *epilemptos*, the new word describes *a person whose character is so wrong that others have lodged a charge or accusation against him*. Because of that person's nefarious behavior, other people have a legitimate complaint against him and cannot *receive* him as a leader. Perhaps it was a past crime, a sin, or bad behavior that tarnished his reputation. Whatever the case may be, in the minds of those who know him, that person is guilty. In fact, the word *epilemptos* can describe a person who has so much wrong in his life that others can reach out, take hold of it, and use it to accuse him. The obvious sin in that person's life disqualifies him from leadership.

It is simply a fact that if a person is living a blatant life of sin or disobedience to the Word of God and the Christian community knows about it, that behavior will disqualify him from leadership in the Church. Or if an individual's actions don't correspond with the Bible's requirements for spiritual leadership and he does nothing to self-correct, he shouldn't be considered for a leadership position. The Word of God makes this perfectly clear.

However, what if an individual who was once living in sin repents and experiences a genuine transformation of character? Is he forever disqualified from leadership in the Church because of actions in his past that in no way reflect on his character today? The answer to these questions is found in the prefix *a* in the Greek word *anepilemptos* used in First Timothy 3:2. That little *a* totally reverses the meaning of this word, and it is *good news* for the person who has brought correction to his or her life!

When the prefix *a* is added to the front of the Greek word *epilemptos*, it has a canceling effect. The resultant word carries the idea that if a person truly repents and undergoes a transformation of character, his old sins are irrelevant — *regardless* of how reproachable or shameful that person once was. Because time has passed, corrective action was taken, and his reputation was restored, this individual can be viewed as "blameless." There is nothing active in his life that would disqualify him from serving in a higher capacity in the Church. He can therefore now be viewed as a candidate for leadership.

You may have sins in your past that make you feel unworthy to be called "blameless." But have you repented and reestablished your testimony? If your answer is yes and you are now walking right with God, your blame has been removed and you are eligible for leadership. Although you were once guilty, God's forgiveness, along with your commitment to live a holy life, has freed you from any charges that people may have once legitimately held against you.

Remember that it was the apostle Paul who wrote the word "blameless" in First Timothy 3:2. Before he came to Christ, he had watched Stephen's murder (*see* Acts 7:58), and he had personally overseen the arrest, imprisonment, and even execution of numerous believers (*see* Acts 26:10). If God judged people by their past actions, Paul would have never qualified for leadership or apostleship. But Christ's forgiveness, coupled with Paul's obedience to the Word of God, transformed his lurid reputation into a glorious testimony!

Paul referred to this dramatic change in his own life when he wrote, "And I thank Christ Jesus our Lord, who hath enabled me, for that he counted me faithful, putting me into the ministry; who was before a blasphemer, and a persecutor, and injurious..." (1 Timothy 1:12,13). By the grace and love of Jesus Christ, Paul was forgiven and restored, and the person he used to be was no longer relevant. He met God's requirement of "blameless" and went on to serve the Body of Christ as the most famous apostle who ever lived.

Today I encourage you to review your life and see if there are any areas that require attention. And if you desire to be a leader but the devil keeps reminding you of past failures for which you've already sought forgiveness and experienced restoration, tell him to shut up and get behind you in Jesus' name! If you have dealt with your past sins and failures before God — and, if necessary, before anyone you may have hurt or offended — that means you, too, can qualify for leadership!

MY PRAYER FOR TODAY

Lord, I thank You for speaking to my heart today through this Sparkling Gem. I ask You to help me make a thorough inventory of my life to see if I have truly repented for past wrongs. If there is any area in me that requires attention, please show me so I can bring it to Your Cross and allow Your Spirit's sanctifying power to purify my life and conscience. I want to be used by You, so I ask You to delve into the deepest parts of my being and expose anything in me that would discredit me from being used. If you show me something that still needs to be changed, please give me the courage to do what is needed to bring correction to that area of my life.

I pray this in Jesus' Name!

MY CONFESSION FOR TODAY

I declare that I am not a prisoner to my past and that God has a good plan for me, regardless of my former mistakes. I confess those things as sin, and I do everything within my power to clear the slate. I declare that the blood of Jesus has left me blameless of the things that others once held against me. I pursue a life that is blameless; I seek to be an example of Christ; I endeavor to serve with a pure heart; and I know that Jesus Christ wants to use me more than ever before. Therefore, I am a candidate to be used by God in a powerful way to effect change in my generation!

I declare this by faith in Jesus' name!

QUESTIONS FOR YOU TO CONSIDER

1. Can you think of areas in your life that would hinder others from following you as a leader? If so, what do you believe the Holy Spirit would have you to do to correct that wrong and make it right with those individuals?
2. Can you think of people you personally held a grudge against because of their past actions even though they have since put forth their best efforts to bring correction to themselves or to the situation? Do you continue to hold them as prisoners to their past behavior or have you released them from that judgment?
3. Now that you have read today's *Sparkling Gem* about the word "blameless," how would you describe the meaning of the word "blameless" to someone else?

FEBRUARY 12

Presenting Every Man Perfect in Christ

Whom we preach, warning every man, and teaching every man in all wisdom;
that we may present every man perfect in Christ Jesus.
— Colossians 1:28

After reading a book on the subject of church leadership and the need for every organization to have a "purpose statement," I realized that the purpose statement for our church and ministry was too long for anyone to remember it, and it was certainly too long to be able to repeat it to someone else. So I started praying for a short, concise way to state the purpose of our ministry.

After a lot of prayer, my heart kept going back to the simple statement the apostle Paul made in Colossians 1:28, a verse that has been the theme of our ministry since its earliest inception and remains the purpose of our ministry after decades of service. However, I had never thought of a way to present it to people as a purpose statement until I was challenged by that book. Colossians 1:28 speaks of Christ's glorious presence in each of us and of our need to declare truth in various ways to others with the ultimate goal of presenting every person perfect in Christ. It says, "Whom we preach, warning every man, and teaching every man in all wisdom; that we may present every man perfect in Christ Jesus."

I can emphatically say that our ministry has always been, is, and will always be a preaching, warning, and teaching ministry — just as Paul described in Colossians 1:28. And like Paul, we have an audience of "every man." The word "every" is the Greek word *panta*, an all-encompassing word that embraces all people with no exceptions. To the lost, we *preach.* To those who are saved, we *warn* and *teach.* But Paul said the ultimate goal is *to present every man perfect in Christ.* "Perfect" sounds very hard to attain, if not almost unreachable, so what was Paul really referring to when he spoke of presenting people "perfect" in Christ?

The word "perfect" in this verse is the Greek word *telios.* Paul used this word only five times in the New Testament — each time to describe *full-grown adults* (*see* 1 Corinthians 2:6; 14:20; Ephesians 4:13; Philippians 3:15; and Colossians 1:28). It describes how, as a person develops, he or she transitions from being youthful and immature to an individual who is *full-grown* and *mature.*

In addition, Paul used *telios* twice (*see* Romans 12:2; Colossians 4:12) to denote *spiritually mature individuals who are living in accordance with the will of God.* For this reason, the more recent translation of *The Amplified Bible* states, "…that we may present every person mature (full-grown, fully initiated, complete, and perfect) in Christ…." Thus, we see the word "perfect" that Paul referred to in Colossians 1:28 as one who is spiritually mature and endeavoring to live out his or her life in accordance to God's perfect will.

In the context of discerning our ministry purpose, this verse gives very clear direction. It tells us that we are not called just to win masses to Christ and then leave them behind as spiritual infants. Rather, our God-given task is to help people walk out of immaturity while leading them onward into spiritual maturity. Bringing people up to this level of maturity is an undertaking so huge that Paul acknowledged it could only be done with the power of God. He said, "Whereunto I also labour, striving according to his working, which worketh in me mightily" (Colossians 1:29).

The word "labour" in Colossians 1:29 is the Greek word *kopos,* which describes *the most physically and mentally exhausting type of labor.* By using this word, Paul reminded us of the *extremely hard work* that is required to help a person attain spiritual maturity. According to this, Paul worked very hard to bring people from spiritual infancy into spiritual adulthood. In fact, the next word he chose, the word "striving," drives this point home. It comes from the Greek word *agonidzo*, from which we get the word *agony*.

The use of these two words "labour" (*kopos*) and "striving" (*agonidzo*) tells us that the task of helping individuals move from spiritual infancy to spiritual adulthood requires focus, effort, and hard work — and that it can often be as agonizing as raising a natural child to become a level-headed adult. And we're not just spiritually raising one person, but *many* people at one time. This would be humanly impossible if it were not for "his working," which, as Paul said, works in us *mightily*.

The word "working" here is the Greek word *energeo*, which, of course, is where we get the word for *energy*. Furthermore, the word "mightily" is the word *dunamis*, which Paul used to describe Christ's *divine ability* that resides in each true believer. So Paul was acknowledging that it is only possible to present every man "perfect" in Christ because of His divine, supernatural energy that works mightily in us. We are insufficient in ourselves for such a task. We can only accomplish it because of the infusion of Christ's mighty *dunamis* power that works in us. Hence, the task of helping someone grow from spiritual infancy into spiritual adulthood is a supernatural feat that can only be accomplished in cooperation with Christ's mighty power that works in us and through us.

If you feel that you have failed to stick it out to the end with the individuals you've been called to help mature, take heart! Yield to the Holy Spirit's presence in your heart, for you are only up to the task *if* the Holy Spirit's power is working in you and through you. And should *you* be looking for a purpose statement for your church, your ministry, or your personal walk with God, consider Colossians 1:28: "...that we may present every man perfect in Christ Jesus...."

As believers, this should always be our purpose. We must not only win people to Jesus but also disciple them to maturity so they can live the balance of their lives as fully grown spiritual adults who live to do the will of God.

MY PRAYER FOR TODAY

Father, I have long sought a purpose statement for my life. Today I align myself with the purpose that the apostle Paul wrote of in Colossians 1:28. I ask You to help me know with whom to share the Gospel, how to warn other believers who need to be warned, what ways I should teach believers, and how to let the power of the Holy Spirit flow through me. Shape me into an instrument to help bring other Christians to a place of spiritual maturity to do the will of God. I can do this consistently only if Your power is released consistently in me, so today I yield to the power of the Holy Spirit and commit myself to this great endeavor.

I pray this in Jesus' name!

MY CONFESSION FOR TODAY

I confess that God uses me to preach Christ to the lost, to warn and teach believers the truths of God's Word, and to help bring others into spiritual adulthood where they are no longer tossed to and fro as young spiritual infants. God wants all believers to reach spiritual maturity — including me — and He desires to use me to help others attain it as well. Although this is a huge task, I yield to the power of the Holy Spirit in me according to Colossians 1:28, and the Spirit works with me and through me to fulfill this God-given purpose.

I declare this by faith in Jesus' name!

QUESTIONS FOR YOU TO CONSIDER

1. What is the purpose statement for your life? Can you summarize it and easily repeat it to someone else? Do you know it well by memory, and are you able to write it down on a piece of paper?
2. If you know the purpose of your life, what are you doing to fulfill it? Doing what God has asked you to do will require resolve, determination, and supernatural power. Is His power actively flowing through you? Is it time for you to have a new experience with the Holy Spirit so that you are refreshed for the task?
3. Has God used you to help someone grow spiritually? Who is that person? Whom did God use in *your* life to help you grow spiritually? When you think of the time and effort these individuals spent to help you grow from spiritual infancy to spiritual adulthood, doesn't it make you so thankful for them? Why not take the time to call or write these important people in your life and express your gratitude to them today?

FEBRUARY 13

Coming Into Compliance With God's Will

And he took with him Peter and the two sons of Zebedee,
And began to be sorrowful and very heavy.
Then saith he unto them, My soul is exceedingly sorrowful,
even unto death: tarry ye here, and watch with me.
And he went a little further and fell on his face, and prayed,
saying, O my Father, if it be possible, let this cup pass from me:
nevertheless not as I will, but as thou wilt.
— Matthew 26:37-39

When God asks you to strike out into uncharted territory and accomplish something new and difficult, it can be challenging to bring your will into compliance with what He is asking you to do. Your mind will try to argue as if it knows best, and your flesh will try to drag its feet every step of the way. In these moments, you are faced with a defining moment in your life when you must place your trust in God's plan for your life and obey Him unconditionally.

I know this struggle intimately from experiences in my own life. When God first asked our family to move to the USSR, I knew He had something truly wonderful in store for us, but my flesh didn't relish the idea. Each night as I lay in bed, my mind would bombard me with a stream of negative thoughts of doubt and unbelief. My flesh would tell me, *Rick, this is the stupidest thing you could ever do in your life. If you really go through with this absurd notion, you will lose everything you have and never recover.* I remember asking God, *"Are You really asking me to do this?"*

At the time God called our family to the Soviet Union, our ministry in the United States was growing by leaps and bounds, and we were finally experiencing stability and success after many years of sacrifice. However, as good as our lives seemed at the time, God had something far bigger and more wonderful planned for our ministry, so He asked us to lay down our dream and trust in Him. As we entered this new, unfamiliar phase, we didn't understand His full design, but we chose to defer to His voice and trust that He knew what He was doing with our lives. And because we placed our trust in His divine plan and obeyed His call to move, our ministry exploded in ways that we could never have dreamed!

If you haven't yet run into one of these moments in your life, there *will* come a time in your future when you'll have to step out and do what God is saying, even though you don't relish the idea of what He is asking you to do. In that moment, it is vital that you follow the guidance of the Holy Spirit so He can lead you into new realms of wonder and possibility.

In fact, the Bible tells us that Jesus Himself faced one of those moments in the Garden of Gethsemane. Matthew 26:37 and 38 relates, "And he took with him Peter and the two sons of Zebedee, and began to be sorrowful and very heavy. Then saith he unto them, My soul is exceedingly sorrowful, even unto death: tarry ye here, and watch with me." This verse reveals what took place as Jesus faced the horror of the Cross and all that He would have to endure in the atonement of mankind's sin. The reality of what the Father was asking Him to do was being brought to bear on Jesus, and it says He "...began to be sorrowful and very heavy" (v. 37). This word "sorrowful" is derived from the Greek word *lupeo*, which denotes *physical pain* or *emotional suffering*. It can also be translated as *broken-hearted, in despair, displeasure, downcast, grief, mournful, in pain, sorrowful,* or *wounded*. It describes the intense grief of someone who has been wounded emotionally by a person or a situation.

Furthermore, the phrase "very heavy" in Matthew 26:37 is a translation of the Greek word *ademoneo*, which depicts *anguish, depression,* or *dejection*. The word "sorrowful" and the phrase "very heavy" are each sufficient on their own to convey the deep emotions Jesus was feeling in this moment of anguish. However, because they are used together, it is unmistakably clear that Jesus was tempted to be overwhelmed by the unimaginably hellish ordeal He was about to face. Although He had always known that the Cross was an integral part of His destiny on earth, it appears that the reality of His assignment weighed heavily upon His mind and body, and He was tempted to sway under the weight of it all.

In the following verse, Matthew wrote, "Then saith he unto them, My soul is exceedingly sorrowful, even unto death: tarry ye here, and watch with me" (Matthew 26:38). The word "soul" is the Greek word *psyche*, which denotes the *inner life*, *mental makeup*, or *emotions* of an individual. The phrase "exceedingly sorrowful" is a translation of the Greek word *perilupeo*, which is a compound of the words *peri* and *lupeo*. The word *peri* means *around* or *to be surrounded*, and *lupeo* is the same word we saw above that describes *intense grief*. When they are compounded in the context of this verse to form the word *perilupeo*, it tells us that Jesus was feeling nearly emotionally suffocated with despair as He faced the painful reality of God's plan for Him.

Then Matthew 26:39 continues, "And he went a little further, and fell on his face...." The stress and pressure Jesus was under was so heavy that He was able to go only "a little further" before He collapsed and "fell on his face." The force of the Greek language here indicates that Jesus literally collapsed under the weight of what He was experiencing. And as He fell, He fervently prayed, "...O my Father, if it be possible, let this cup pass from me: nevertheless not as I will, but as thou wilt" (v. 39).

However, in this intense moment as Jesus' soul was bombarded with mental and emotional anguish, He did not succumb to the will of His flesh. Rather, Jesus pushed through to embrace the will of God that He knew was His divine destiny. He surrendered and complied with the path the Father had set before Him, saying, "...Nevertheless, not as I will, but as thou wilt." Jesus was resolved to do the Father's will rather than seek a way out of the situation.

The Father's plan for Jesus included His trials before the Sanhedrin, Herod Antipas, and Pontus Pilate, as well as Jesus being mocked, spit upon, scourged, and crucified. Although Jesus knew that the Father was faithful to Him and a glorious resurrection shortly awaited Him, this was the defining moment in His earthly life when *trust* and *obedience* were required in a measure greater than ever before. He had to "commit himself" to God and trust that His Heavenly Father would raise Him from the dead and deliver Him from the unspeakable horrors of spiritual darkness. Jesus could have rejected God's plan at this point, but He chose instead to bring His mind into compliance with the will of God. As a result of His obedience, He brought salvation to mankind through His sacrifice, and He was raised from the dead to sit at the Father's right hand as the Head of the Church and our eternal High Priest.

If Jesus Himself agonized over doing the will of the Father, then it should come as no surprise that we will wrestle with God's plan for our lives from time to time. Like Jesus, we must choose to push aside our reservations and commit to doing whatever God asks of us. We must learn to trust and obey.

If you follow your Heavenly Father's plan, you'll overcome any obstacle that tries to trip you up, and you'll find yourself seated in a place of victory that you will never regret. It may be uncomfortable right now, but those emotions and struggles are temporary. They will pass, and when it's all said and done, you will be glad that you came into compliance with the will of God!

As I look back at the moment when God asked me to move my family to the former USSR, I have no regrets. It was hard for my soul at the moment, but the victories won over many years make it clear that God only had good plans in store for us, even though it was difficult to understand that when it all began. Likewise, God has a good plan in store for you. He simply needs your compliance, trust, and obedience.

MY PRAYER FOR TODAY

Father, I ask You to help me push beyond my inward struggles concerning what You are asking me to do. Your requests have exposed my need to come up higher in my level of trust. This has revealed an area where I need to grow spiritually. Learning where I need to improve is good for me, so I thank You for leading me to this place where You can show me where I need to change and grow. Just as Jesus surrendered to Your will, I place my trust in You, and I will comply with Your plan regardless of how difficult it may be for me to understand in the moment. With the help of Your Spirit, I will trust and obey.

I pray this prayer in Jesus' name!

MY CONFESSION FOR TODAY

I confess that God is faithful. If He is asking me to do something I don't completely understand, I can trust Him to have my best interest at heart. I don't need to be fearful of what He is telling me to do. I refuse to let my emotions get the best of me, and I choose to follow God's will for my life. I declare that I will not shrink back from the assignment God has given me, and I am determined that I will comply with His plan for my life!

I declare this by faith in Jesus' name!

QUESTIONS FOR YOU TO CONSIDER

1. Can you think of an area of your life where God is asking you to comply with His plan and you're having a tough time obeying? What is that area, and what is specifically making it difficult for you to comply?
2. Do you know someone today who is struggling to do the will of God? What can you do to encourage that person? What personal experience of obeying God can you share in order to provoke that person to follow God's plan for his or her life?
3. What stands out in your mind regarding what you just read in this *Sparkling Gem*? What did you learn about Jesus and His time in the Garden of Gethsemane that you've never considered before?

Like Jesus, we must choose
to push aside our reservations
and commit to doing whatever God asks of us.
We must learn to trust and obey.

FEBRUARY 14

Escorted Into the Love of God

And the Lord direct your hearts into the love of God,
and into the patient waiting for Christ.
— 2 Thessalonians 3:5

Often I am invited to attend meetings with other ministers in Moscow who gather to discuss spiritual leadership issues. These meetings take place in a different location each time in order to maintain a sense of neutrality, and they are often held in places that are completely unknown to me. In fact, trying to find the exact meeting room for these events can be difficult because the buildings are often expansive and the layouts unfamiliar.

Because of this potential difficulty, individuals are appointed to help guide leaders like me to the new meeting room. They meet each of us outside where our cars drop us off, and they escort us to the room where the event is to be held. If these individuals were not present to help us find the meeting room, we would all eventually find our way to the place where we were supposed to be, but the experience would take longer and potentially create needless confusion. Believe me when I tell you that we all greatly appreciate the service that these people graciously provide as they escort us right to where we need to be so expeditiously.

Similarly, Paul taught that the Lord Himself wants to be our Escort to lead us directly into the love of God with no distractions along the way. In Second Thessalonians 3:5, he wrote, "And the Lord direct your hearts into the love of God...."

Today I want you to particularly notice the word "direct" in this verse, as it reveals so much about God's great desire to guide us directly into His divine love. The word "direct" is translated from the Greek word *kateuthuno*, which is a compound of the words *kata* and *euthus*. The word *kata* gives a sense of *force* or *direction*, and the word *euthus* describes *a straight path* as opposed to a path that is *wandering* or a route that is *indirect*. Although an indirect route may eventually get you to the same location, it takes longer; it involves unnecessary expense of energy; and it is more time-consuming. A direct path will get you to your destination more quickly and less expensively, and you will expend less energy. However, if you've never made the journey before, finding the shortest route may be difficult unless you have a guide who will direct and escort you along the way.

This leads us back to Paul's teaching in Second Thessalonians 3:5, where he wrote, "And the Lord direct your hearts into the love of God...." The word "hearts" is the Greek word *kardias*, the plural form of *kardia*, which describes the *heart*. Although this word was sometimes used to denote the heart as a physical organ, it was regularly employed throughout the Old Testament, Classical Greek literature, and the New Testament to describe *emotions*, *instincts*, and *passions*. In Second Thessalonians 3:5, Paul used it to portray the inner aspects of a person's life — intellectually, psychologically, and spiritually. Paul was literally praying for a person's inner being to be directed into the love of God, as opposed to contrary paths that would lead elsewhere.

Furthermore, because the Greek word translated "direct" (*kateuthuno*) in this verse begins with the prefix *kata*, we see that God does more than merely guide and escort us. He wants to meet us and lead us so our hearts don't wander aimlessly on the way to completion in His love. In the context of Second Thessalonians 3:5, it tells us that God Himself wants to put us on a straight path and steer us right into His love. In fact, the word *steer* is exactly how the word *kateuthuno* ("direct") could be translated in James 3:4. God doesn't want us to waste time and energy or to take too long to get into His love. He wants to steer us right into His love. The Lord desires to put us on a straight path and be our personal Guide, escorting us into His love with no distractions or unneeded detours along the way.

An interpretative translation of the first part of Second Thessalonians 3:5 could read:

"May the Lord steer your hearts and put you on the path that leads you directly into divine love itself. We pray that you encounter no rough roads on this journey but rather that your heart reaches its ultimate destination — the love of God."

As you grow in your relationship with God, remember that He wants to meet you and escort you along every step of the journey. He doesn't just say, *"Here is what I want for you — now figure out how to get there by yourself."* God wants to step in front of you and lead you! If you'll listen, you'll hear Him say, "I'm here to lead you, so follow Me, and I'll lead your heart to the place where I want you to be — right into the center of My love!"

MY PRAYER FOR TODAY

I prayerfully admit that so often I have tried to figure out my route in life on my own, even though God has desired to lead me each step of the way. My heart moves out of peace when I struggle to figure out what steps to take, which way to go, or what to do. Since the Holy Spirit wants to be my Guide to personally escort me into His perfect plan for my life, I surrender to His leadership today and yield to Him as my Escort. Father, thank You for meeting me where I am and leading my heart on the most direct route into Your plan and Your love.

I pray this prayer in Jesus' name!

MY CONFESSION FOR TODAY

Today I declare that I am sensitive to the leadership of the Lord in my life; therefore, I no longer wander aimlessly about as I attempt to fulfill God's will for my life. I want to do God's will, and He wants to lead me so I can get into the center of His plan more quickly, less expensively, and without wasting needless energy. Instead of trying to figure it all out by myself, I will heed God's Word; I will carefully listen to the voice of the Holy Spirit; and I will let the Lord be my personal Guide to escort me along the path of His love and into His plan for my life.

I declare this by faith in Jesus' name!

QUESTIONS FOR YOU TO CONSIDER

1. Can you think of a time when God wanted to lead you on a short route to His destination, but you didn't listen? Did it end up costing you more time and energy than was necessary for you to get into His will for your life?
2. How do you know when God is leading you? What are the signals you sense when the Holy Spirit is saying, "Follow Me, and I'll get you there more quickly and less expensively?" Could you describe to someone else what it's like for the Lord to lead you on a straight path?
3. Can you remember a moment when you didn't listen to the leading of the Lord and ended up way off-track? What did it cost you? How would things have been different if you had listened? What did you learn from that experience that you would want someone else to learn so he or she could avoid your mistakes?

FEBRUARY 15

A Demonstration of the Power of God!

And my speech and my preaching
was not with enticing words of man's wisdom,
but in demonstration of the Spirit and of power:
that your faith should not stand in the wisdom of men,
but in the power of God.
— 1 Corinthians 2:4,5

When Paul first came to the city of Corinth, it was in the wake of his experience in the illustrious Greek city of Athens. During his stint in Athens, he had marvelously presented the Gospel message, yet his teaching did not produce outstanding results. As Paul left Athens and began traveling toward Corinth — *a city rife with demonic activity and wholly given over to idolatry and extreme sexual perversion* — he must have pondered his performance in Athens. He probably thought about what he had done right, what he done wrong, and why his results weren't as outstanding there as they had been in other cities.

However, when you study Paul's ministry in the cities where he had his most dramatic results, you find that he did something in those places that he did not do in Athens. In Athens, he labored to preach a brilliant, intellectual, culturally relevant message to the Greek judges on Mars Hill. But when you look at how he ministered in other cities, you find that in addition to preaching brilliant messages, he also *demonstrated* the miraculous power of God. That demonstration of God's power was very important in pagan communities where the occult was pervasive and supernatural manifestations were commonplace. For example:

- In Acts 13:6-12, Paul had a face-to-face confrontation with a local sorcerer. The power that Paul demonstrated as he rebuked this sorcerer was so dramatic that city authorities were *stunned.* Verse 12 tells us, "Then the deputy, when he saw what was done, believed...." This demonstration of God's power threw open the door for the Gospel in this region.

- In Acts 14:8-18, Paul again demonstrated supernatural power. Seeing a crippled man who had never walked in his life, Paul told him, "Stand upright on thy feet. And he leaped and walked" (v. 10). This event had such great impact that verse 11 says, "And when the people saw what Paul had done, they lifted up their voices, saying in the speech of Lycaonia, The gods are come down to us in the likeness of men." As a consequence of this wonderful miracle, people turned their attention to the Gospel message with outstanding results.

- In Acts 16:16-18, Paul encountered "a certain damsel possessed with a spirit of divination." After this girl harassed Paul and his associates for a number of days, Paul turned to her and addressed the spirit of divination. In verse 18, he said, "...I command thee in the name of Jesus Christ to come out of her. And he [the spirit of divination] came out the same hour." When the demon exited that damsel, it created such a mighty stir with the local people that the apostolic team was thrown into prison for doing damage to the fortune-telling business of the city.

  That night Paul and Silas were praying and singing songs when another act of power occurred. Acts 16:26 says, "And suddenly there was a great earthquake, so that the foundations of the prison were shaken: and immediately all the doors were opened, and every one's bands were loosed." This act of power was so colossal in its impact that the keeper of the prison cried out, "Sirs, what must I do to be saved?" (v. 30).

  These combined acts of power led to the salvation of this man's family. History tells us this keeper of the prison eventually became one of the chief leaders in the church of Philippi.

- In Acts 19, when Paul found himself in the midst of Ephesus — *the world center of Artemis worship and a city filled to the brim with demonic supernatural activity* — it was a moment when a demonstration of God's power was desperately needed. Acts 19:11,12 tells us that in Ephesus, "And God wrought special miracles by the hands of Paul: so that from his body were brought unto the sick handkerchiefs or aprons, and the diseases departed from them, and the evil spirits went out of them."

When the Ephesians saw this demonstration of power, verses 18 and 19 tells us that "...many that believed came, and confessed, and shewed their deeds. Many of them also which used curious arts [occult activities] brought their books together, and burned them before all men: and they counted the price of them, and found it fifty thousand pieces of silver." As a result of these combined manifestations of God's power, verse 20 tells us, "So mightily grew the word of God and prevailed."

➢ In Acts 28:6, Paul was shipwrecked on an island that was filled with barbarians. When he was helping the shipwrecked sailors gather wood to build a fire, a venomous snake latched hold of Paul's hand. Instead of dying from the bite, he simply shook it into the fire with no physical harm to himself. When the local barbaric people saw the snakebite had no effect, they were so taken aback that they said he was a god.

  Because of this miraculous event, the door to this island was thrown wide open for Paul to boldly preach the Gospel to them! When Publius, the chief man of the island, saw that his own father was critically ill, he knew whom to call for help! He called upon Paul to come pray for his father, and Acts 28:8 says, "And it came to pass, that the father of Publius lay sick of a fever and of a bloody flux: to whom Paul entered in, and prayed, and laid his hands on him, and healed him." Because of this miraculous demonstration of power, verse 9 says, "So when this was done, others also, which had diseases in the island, came, and were healed."

When Paul came into new and dark territories to bring the light of the Gospel, the book of Acts shows us that he repeatedly came with a demonstration of God's power that had a powerful effect upon his audience.

Is it possible that in Athens Paul was so gripped with the need to present the Gospel in an intellectual, culturally relevant way to the judges on Mars Hill that he overlooked the need to accompany his message with a demonstration of the power of God as he had done in so many other cities? *Did he become mesmerized by the intellectual tone of the environment and leave the Holy Spirit and the power of God out of the equation of his preaching and teaching?*

Because Athens was a world center of idolatry, it was overflowing with demonic, supernatural activity, and if a demonstration of God's power was needed anywhere, it was certainly in the city of Athens. Just for a moment, ponder what could have happened if Paul had allowed the gifts of the Spirit to operate in front of those judges so they witnessed phenomenal manifestations of God's power far superior to anything they had ever seen in their pagan temples? *Is it possible that such a demonstration of power may have shaken those listening judges and that the results that day would have been different?*

It seems that as Paul approached the city of Corinth, he was reviewing his performance in Athens. By his own testimony in First Corinthians 2:1, he wrote, "And I, brethren, when I came to you, came not with excellency of speech or of wisdom, declaring unto you the testimony of God." In Athens, he had brilliantly used "words of man's wisdom" as he quoted their poets and their Greek philosophers — a message that, no doubt, could be included in the most exceptional messages ever recorded.

But when Paul later recalled his first ministry in the city of Corinth, he said, "And my speech and my preaching was not with enticing words of man's wisdom, but in demonstration of the Spirit and of power: that your faith should not stand in the wisdom of men, but in the power of God" (1 Corinthians 2:4,5).

It is clear from his own testimony that when Paul preached the powerful message of the Gospel to the Corinthians, he had determined to go one step further than simply preaching an intellectually and culturally relevant sermon. *This time* he had made up his mind to also come with the "demonstration of the Spirit and of power," as he had done so many times in other pagan cities where he was the first person to penetrate the darkness with the preaching of the Gospel.

The word "demonstration" is translated from the Greek word *apodeixsis*, and it means *to display, to show off,* or *to demonstrate*. Paul knew that to reach the pagans in Corinth, it would require a demonstration of power so outstanding that it would convince the unbelieving audience that his preaching was more than mere words — it was a message backed up by Almighty God Himself! He knew it would take an awe-inspiring demonstration of power to get their attention and to persuade them that his Gospel message was true. Thus, Paul started his ministry in Corinth not only with words, but also with a "demonstration of the Spirit and of power."

The word "power" is *dunamis*. This Greek word and its various forms are used 119 times in the New Testament, and it denotes the *mighty power of God*. As used in this verse, the word denotes not merely power, but *tremendous power*. In fact, the word *dunamis* is where we get the word *dynamite*. I believe this is an important fact to point out, for the word *dynamite* — denoting *an explosive power* — very well expresses the type of power Paul is describing in this verse. This word *dunamis* denotes God's supernatural power, which when released on a human level, is *explosive*, *mighty*, and *awe-inspiring* to those who see it or experience it.

An interpretive translation of these words
in First Corinthians 2:4 and 5 could be taken to mean:

"And my speech and my preaching was not with enticing words of man's wisdom, but I came with a display of power so outstanding that it really showed off the power of God."

There is no concrete record in the book of Acts about Paul's earliest preaching in Corinth. But from his own memory recorded in First Corinthians 2:4 and 5, we know that Paul's objective was to bring such a mighty display of power with his preaching that the unbelieving Corinthians would be taken aback by the power of God and forever changed.

I feel compelled to ask you: *What kind of power do you demonstrate with your life and your message as you share Christ with your friends, family, or acquaintances?*

So often we preach the right words to people, but they are constantly hearing words — words from other people, from all forms of media — television, Internet, advertisements — and from all kinds of other sources. This constant stream of words that is trying to get people's attention or to lure them to spend money or to make some kind of decision. People are *inundated* with words and messages in our world today.

But when they are confronted with a bona fide manifestation of God's power so outstanding that they cannot debate its reality, they are forever impacted and changed by it. Certainly we must be wise in the way we preach and present the Gospel, but we must never forget the importance of preaching the Gospel with a "demonstration of the Spirit and of power." *Nothing impacts an unbelieving crowd more than the power of God!* The need for divine power is just as important today as it was 2,000 years ago when Paul wrote these words to the Corinthian believers.

After reading today's *Sparkling Gem,* what do you need to do differently in the way that you present Christ to people who are lost and unsaved? Are you making room for God's power to operate and show off in front of the unsaved or unbelieving? Today I want to encourage you to open your heart to the possibility that God may want to demonstrate His power to those people you are trying to reach.

Instead of relying only on your own careful selection of words, why don't you start seeking the Lord with greater fervency than ever before for His divine power and articulation as you present the Gospel to people who are in darkness? The impact of His words spoken with His power behind them through your mouth will leave your listeners inwardly reeling — and those words will hang in the air and rest in their hearts, not to be easily forgotten by them.

Remember, Romans 1:16 says that the Gospel is the power of God, and I assure you that He is just as willing today to back up His Word with a supernatural display of power as He was 2,000 years ago!

MY PRAYER FOR TODAY

Lord, I ask You to help me surrender myself to the power and working of the Holy Spirit as I present the Gospel to people in darkness. Yes, I need to speak the right words and to speak it in a way that is relevant to those who are listening to me, but I also need to come with a demonstration of the power of God. Holy Spirit, I am looking to You to help me find the right words, to empower me and flow through me, and to do Your mighty work as I share Christ with people who are lost and in darkness. Today I ask You to release Your great power through me and to help me surrender when it's time to allow that power to operate!

I pray this in Jesus' name!

MY CONFESSION FOR TODAY

I confess that I am an instrument through which the power of the Holy Spirit can flow to touch other people. I am not afraid of the power of God, nor do I hinder the operation of the gifts of the Holy Spirit. When it is time for God to show up in all of His marvelous supernatural ability, I move out of the way and make room so that God can do exactly what He wants to do. Rather than hinder or thwart the power of God, I am a facilitator that creates environments and provides time for God to show up and show off so that people will see and know His mighty strength!

I declare this by faith in Jesus' name!

QUESTIONS FOR YOU TO CONSIDER

1. Can you think of a time when you seemed to have said all the right words, but because you didn't allow the Holy Spirit's supernatural power to operate in conjunction with your message, the results weren't so outstanding?
2. Can you think of a time when you *did* allow the Holy Spirit to move, and you watched in amazement as people's hearts were softened and touched — and afterward they wanted to know more about the Lord?
3. What are you going to do differently when you present the Gospel to lost people as a result of today's *Sparkling Gem?* Is the Holy Spirit speaking to your heart, providing you with direction? *If so, what is He saying to you?*

FEBRUARY 16

Does the Mention of Someone's Name Put a Smile on Your Face?

But we are bound to give thanks
always to God for you....
— 2 Thessalonians 2:13

One day Denise and I were talking about different things we had survived throughout our many years of ministry together. It started out as a positive conversation, but before I realized what was happening, I had slipped into thinking of all the people who had wronged us over the years. Soon I felt myself sinking mentally and emotionally into the sticky mire of those negative thoughts.

Finally, I realized my thoughts were going in the wrong direction and swiftly put on the brakes. I shifted into reverse to get out of that mode of thinking and began to mentally compile a list of everyone who had been a *blessing* to us over the years. The number of individuals who had been a blessing to us was so long that I couldn't stop listing them! In comparison, the sheer number of these blessed connections *swallowed* the names of those who had become negative memories in our lives.

One brother's name in particular literally made me smile. Just the mention of his name put a smile on my face. I decided I would say his name to several other people who knew him to see how his name affected them — and every person, without exception, smiled when I mentioned his name. I thought, *What a blessing that the mere mention of a person's name would make people smile!*

This must have been how Paul felt about the Thessalonian believers, because when he wrote to them, he said, "But we are bound to give thanks always to God for you…" (2 Thessalonians 2:13).

The word "bound" is the Greek word *opheilo*, which describes *an obligation.* Whenever Paul began to ponder the great things God had done in the lives of the Thessalonian congregation, he felt *obligated* to stop what he was doing and give thanks to God for that group of believers. The mere thought of the Thessalonians put a smile on his face! They had been such a blessing to Paul that he literally felt an *obligation* to stop whatever he was doing to thank God for them.

Likewise, we, too, must learn to stop and thank God for what He has done in the lives of those around us — especially those who have been a blessing to us and who cause us to smile at the mere thought of them! We have an *obligation* to stop and remember all that God has done and to give Him thanks.

The phrase "to give thanks" in this verse is the Greek word *eucharistos.* The first part of the word is *eu.* This word means *good* and implies *a good feeling* or a *pleasant, inner warmth.* The second word is *charis*, which is the Greek word for *grace*. By compounding these two words, Paul revealed that when he thought of the Thessalonians, the feelings he had for them were so rich, warm, pleasant, and gratifying that thanksgiving flowed effortlessly out of his heart like a river of divine grace. Thanking God for these believers wasn't hard for Paul; on the contrary, *restraining* his thanksgiving for them would have been much more difficult. It was *easy* for Paul to thank God for this particular group of believers.

The word "always" is the Greek word *pantote*. In this context, it means *every time we think of you* or *at each and every opportunity*. Paul's memory of the Thessalonians was so sweet that *whenever* he thought of them, thanksgiving arose in his heart.

**This part of Second Thessalonians 2:13
could be interpreted to mean:**

"Every time we think about you, thanksgiving floods out of our hearts! We are so overwhelmed with thanksgiving that we actually feel obligated to stop whatever we are doing to take a few minutes to express to God how much we appreciate you…."

I don't know if you've ever slipped into the mode of remembering everyone who has ever done something wrong to you. If you have, you know what a negative experience that can be. But today I want to urge you to do the opposite — make a list of those who have been a blessing in your life! I believe you'll find that your heart begins to overflow with thanksgiving to the Lord, just as was true for the apostle Paul concerning the Thessalonians. The mere thought of certain people He has brought into your life to bless you will probably put a big smile on your face!

MY PRAYER FOR TODAY

Lord, I want to say thank You for the people who are so faithful, kind, and encouraging that the mere mention of their names makes me want to smile. I am grateful for such people. Forgive me for focusing on the negative experiences I've had with people when the actual list of people who have been a blessing to me is so large. I ask You to help me remember those who put a smile on my face when I am attacked, hurt, or offended by others. Help me quickly remember that bad experiences with people are in the minor category, and that most people have been a blessing to me. As I make a list of those who have been true blessings in my life, show me how to express my gratitude to You and to them for the blessing they have been in my life.

I pray this in Jesus' name!

MY CONFESSION FOR TODAY

I boldly and easily declare that my life has been blessed with people who have loved me, cared for me, and have been a blessing to me. When I am tempted to drag up the names and memories of those who have hurt me in some way, I will refuse to dwell on those memories but will put on the brakes and act in reverse, compiling a list of the people who have been a blessing. The truth is, there are more who have been for me than those who have been against me. When I think of all the longstanding relationships with people who have loved and forgiven me in spite of myself and are still being kind to me even today, it would be ungrateful for me to dwell on negative people. So with the help of the Holy Spirit, I am reversing my mental focus! I'm going to thank God for the people He has used to put a smile on my face.

I declare this by faith in Jesus' name!

QUESTIONS FOR YOU TO CONSIDER

1. Have you ever made a list of people who have been a blessing to you over the course of your lifetime? It may be easier for you to think of people who have wronged you, since human nature has an easier time remembering negative experiences. But why don't you set aside some time to write down the names of those people who have been a blessing to you? I think you'll be surprised to see how long your list becomes!
2. Do certain individuals come to mind when you ask yourself who always puts a smile on your face? Have you ever stopped to tell them what they mean to you? Put yourself in their shoes, and think how much it would mean to you if someone told *you* how much you had been a blessing to him or her. It doesn't take long to write a note, make a call, or send a text message. *Why not do this for someone today?*
3. Are you the kind of person that the mere mention of your name or the mere thought of you makes someone else want to smile? Does the thought of you uplift others and put a smile on their faces, or does your name evoke a sense of heaviness and negative memories? If the answer is the latter, what areas might need to change in your behavior to reverse that negative testimony with other people?

FEBRUARY 17

Should You Ever Ask God for an Explanation?

If any of you lack wisdom, let him ask of God,
that giveth to all men liberally,
and upbraideth not; and it shall be given him.
— James 1:5

When our sons were younger, I often asked them to take on certain chores or responsibilities that they didn't really want to do. Nonetheless, I expected them to obey me. However, I was never offended if they asked me *why* I wanted them to do those things.

Whether or not I could answer my sons to their satisfaction — or whether or not they were sufficiently experienced in life to understand the reason behind my request — I still expected them to trust me enough to obey what I'd asked of them. They knew that I loved them and that I had more years of experience than they did, and that knowledge warranted their complete trust in me. My children understood as they were growing up that I'd only demand of them what I knew was ultimately good for them. Their close relationship with me caused them to know that they could trust me implicitly, even when they didn't understand what I was telling them.

Likewise, God is never offended when you ask Him for an explanation. You may not understand His answer; you may not like it; or you may not be mature enough to understand it. But as your Father, He is not offended by your asking for clarification. This is why James 1:5 says, "If any of you lack wisdom, let him ask of God...."

The word "if" assumes that there *are* times when you need an answer from God. The word "lacks" is a form of the Greek word *leipo* and describes a *deficiency*. In the Old Testament Septuagint, it describes possessing something *only* in a measure — which, of course, means you were *lacking* the rest. Maybe you possessed a little bit of something, but it was just a *remnant* of what you really needed.

Later this word *leipo* came to depict a *deficit, insufficiency, shortage,* or *undersupply*. As used in James 1:5, it meant *to be without, to have want of, to be in need of, to be lacking, to be short of, to be low on, to not have enough of,* or something that exists in *an insufficient amount*. All of these meanings correctly convey the idea in the Greek text. But for our purposes, we will say it could be interpreted, *"If you are short on wisdom..."* or *"If you find yourself to be lacking wisdom...."*

But what did James mean by "wisdom"? The word "wisdom" is a form of the Greek word *sophos*, which describes *special insight* or *special understanding*. Hence, this verse could be interpreted, "If any one among you lacks special understanding [regarding an issue]...." This word denoted *special insight and understanding that could be worked out in real-life practice.* It was *an answer, an insight,* or *an enlightenment that had some type of practical application.* Thus, the verse could be interpreted to mean: *"If any of you are short on knowing what to do…"*; *"If any one of you is experiencing a deficit regarding what action to take…"*; or *"If any one of you is in need of special answers regarding what to do…."*

Next, James told us what to do. He wrote, "If any of you lacks wisdom, let him *ask*…." The word "ask" is from the Greek word *aiteo*, a word that primarily means *to be adamant in requesting and demanding assistance to meet tangible needs, such as food, shelter, money, and so forth.* Additionally, it expresses the idea that one can possess a *full expectation* to receive what has been *firmly requested.*

This means you shouldn't go to God *only* for spiritual blessings. The use of the word *aiteo* tells us that most questions about which you seek His wisdom will involve practical answers as well as spiritual — pertaining to tangible needs such as food, shelter, money, etc.

But God gives us one condition that we must fulfill before He will answer our petitions for wisdom. Verse 5 continues, "If any of you lacks wisdom, let him ask *of* God…." The word "of" in Greek is *para*, which means *close, side by side*, or *alongside.* As used in this verse, this word provides the condition we must meet in order for God to answer us. To qualify for God's answer, we must be in a close, side-by-side position with Him.

God our Father truly desires to clearly and abundantly answer our questions. He will not refrain from answering us — as long as *we* get in the right position to ask Him. You see, God doesn't want to just answer our request for wisdom. He wants us to come alongside Him, close to His heart. In that position, He will not only answer us, but He will *embrace* us, *cleanse* us, and *change* us.

Hence, the Father first beckons us to draw as near to Him as possible. Then once we are in that close, side-by-side position, God opens His hand to show us the wisdom we lack and are seeking to gain.

Think of it! You are just a prayer away from assuming that close, side-by-side position with God!

With these thoughts in mind,
we can read this verse as follows:

"If you are short on answers you need, ask God to give you those answers. But the one request He makes first before He will provide the answers you are asking Him for is that you come alongside Him…."

Tomorrow I will show you what God promises will happen when you put yourself in that close, side-by-side position alongside Him. But for today, I want you to see the point that if you are experiencing a shortfall of wisdom, God invites you to ask Him for insight. Your asking for an explanation does not offend God. In fact, in James 1:5, He *encourages* you to ask!

When God answers, you may not enjoy what He tells you or you may not be mature enough to truly understand it, but one thing is clear: He wants you to ask for clarification if you need it. So draw near to the Lord, and ask Him for the wisdom you lack. He is utterly faithful to His promises — and He promises that He *will* give you what you ask for, liberally and without reproach!

MY PRAYER FOR TODAY

Father, You said if any man lacks wisdom, he is to ask of You, and wisdom will be granted liberally. I thank You for Your willingness to give me answers, understanding, and clarification about my life and the situations I am facing right now. If I don't enjoy the answer or have the maturity to completely understand, I ask You for the grace to obey You regardless, as I know that You only have the best in mind for me and my family.

I pray this in Jesus' name!

MY CONFESSION FOR TODAY

I confess that God is not offended by my questions for explanation and clarification. He invites me – and even encourages me – to seek Him for answers. Whenever I am in need of understanding about what He is asking me to do. I declare that I know the Voice of the Holy Spirit and that He will not led me astray or misguide me. I can trust what He tells me, even if I don't fully understand it. God has the best in mind for me; so regardless of how He answers, I will accept it and trust Him to be Lord and God of my life.

I declare this by faith in Jesus' name!

QUESTIONS FOR YOU TO CONSIDER

1. Can you think of a time that you lacked wisdom about a specific issue, and when you asked God for an explanation, He answered you? Or can you think of a time that He answered you, but you didn't like the answer or weren't mature enough to understand it?
2. What issues in your life are you facing right now in which you really need some clarification or guidance from the Lord? Have you asked Him for wisdom, and do you firmly believe you're going to receive what you asked of Him?
3. If drawing near to the Lord is His condition you must meet before He answers you, can you say that you meet His requirement? Are you staying close to His heart, or are you living far from the heart of God?

God wants you to ask for clarification if you need it.
So draw near to the Lord, and ask Him
for the wisdom you lack.

FEBRUARY 18

God's Five Guarantees!

If any of you lack wisdom, let him ask of God,
that giveth to all men liberally,
and upbraideth not; and it shall be given him.
— James 1:5

Have you ever asked someone a question that you knew he or she could answer, but instead of being helpful with a clear response, that person skirted the issue and answered indirectly? In these situations, it may have appeared that the person was hiding his knowledge to retain a sense of control by keeping you in the dark. What an unpleasant experience, especially when you know that the person could just simply answer you!

This is the way many people wrongly perceive God. They know that He has the answers to their questions, but often they don't believe He will actually answer them. In their minds, He dangles the answer before them and then jerks it back out of reach just as they attempt to take hold of it. They think this is the way God keeps people on their knees in a humbled position of supplication. But in fact, James 1:5 gives us five guarantees that God does *not* act like this at all!

As we saw yesterday, God isn't offended or upset when you ask Him for clarification on the issues you're facing in life. In fact, He encourages you to come alongside Him and ask for the answers you lack. If you meet this requirement of drawing near to Him, pulling right up alongside His heart, James 1:5 says that God will answer you liberally. He'll play no games with you once you meet this one condition when you ask.

James wrote that God "…giveth to all men liberally, and upbraideth not; and it shall be given him." In this verse, we find *five guarantees* that God makes to those who seek answers to their questions.

1. We are *guaranteed* that God "giveth."
2. We are *guaranteed* that God gives "to all men."
3. We are *guaranteed* that God gives "liberally."
4. We are *guaranteed* that God "upbraideth not."
5. We are *guaranteed* that answers "shall be given" to the one asking.

Let's look at each one of these five guarantees.

1) James 1:5 guarantees that when we ask for wisdom and we meet God's condition of drawing close to Him, God will "give" us the answers we are falling short of. The Greek word used for "giveth" is *didontos*, a form of *didomi*, which means *I give*. But in this Greek case, the grammar does

not describe the random, occasional act of God, but rather the *regular behavior* of God. In fact, the entire Greek phrase is *tou didontos theou* and is literally translated *the giving God.* Hence, God is not one who holds out on us when we need wisdom or information. He is, in fact, the giving God — one who is reputed for habitually giving answers to those who meet His conditions.

2) James 1:5 guarantees that God gives "to all men." This removes the uncertainty that God may answer some and not others. If God's condition has been met — that is, if we have drawn near to His heart and come closely alongside Him — He will answer us, because each of us fits into that phrase "all men"!

3) James 1:5 guarantees that God gives to all men "liberally." This is the Greek word *haplos*. It denotes something that is *bountiful*. It actually portrays one who gives *copiously*, *amply*, *extravagantly*, *generously*, *lavishly*, *liberally*, *plentifully*, or *richly*. This is a person who has an *open hand*, as opposed to one who keeps a closed fist. Hence, God doesn't dangle the bait before us and then quickly jerk it out of our reach. If we have met His conditions and pulled up alongside His heart, He reaches down with an open hand to give the answer we seek — and He gives us the answer *bountifully*.

4) James 1:5 guarantees that God "upbraideth not." This is a translation of the Greek phrase *me oneididzontos*. The word *me* is emphatic for *not*, while the word *oneidodzontos* is a form of the word *oneinidzo*, which means *to berate*, *to censure*, *to correct*, *to rebuke*, or *to scorn*. In other words, God is *not* going to get upset with you if you ask Him for answers. He will never berate, censure, correct, rebuke, or scorn you when you come alongside Him to receive wisdom.

5) James 1:5 guarantees that answers "shall be given" to the one who is seeking them and who has fulfilled God's conditions. The Greek tense used for "shall be given" makes this verse a promise. Even if you don't know the answer right now, the answer that you seek will be given to you!

James 1:5 conveys this idea in the Greek:

"If you are short on the answers you need, insistently ask God for them. But God first requests that you come alongside Him. That is the one request He makes before He will provide the answers you seek Him for. God is the giving God. He is known for habitually answering those who seek answers from Him, and when He answers, He does so lavishly and with an open hand. He never berates, scolds, or scorns you for asking. One thing is for sure — answers will be given to you when you ask God's way!"

Remember, God isn't offended when you ask Him for clarification. He *encourages* you to ask! When He answers, you may not enjoy what He has to tell you, or you may not be mature enough to really understand it yet. But one thing is very clear: God *likes* it when you ask Him for His wisdom! So as you draw near to Him and ask in faith today, you better get ready to receive a *bountiful, liberal, extravagant* dose of *divine insight and guidance* for the path right up ahead!

MY PRAYER FOR TODAY

According to James 1:5, I should ask God for the answers I need for my life. So in agreement with this verse, today I asking for Your wisdom and guidance in every area of my life. Father, in Jesus' name, I specifically ask You for answers. to my questions involving ______ (fill in the blank). I receive Your grace to understand what You're saying to me and to accept and apply Your wisdom to my life!

I pray this in Jesus' name!

MY CONFESSION FOR TODAY

I declare that God has thrown open the doors and has invited me to come boldly to ask Him for the wisdom and answers I need for my life. There is no need for me to be embarrassed or to fear that God will get upset with me for asking. He wants me to be informed, and He asks me to ask! So today I ask in faith and I declare that I receive answers to the questions I have posed to the Lord!

I declare this by faith in Jesus' name!

QUESTIONS FOR YOU TO CONSIDER

1. When you've prayed in the past, were you able to come boldly and unashamedly to God, or did you feel too unworthy to approach Him like that? Did you wonder if you'd be reprimanded for getting too specific in asking for the answers you needed?
2. Can you recall a time when you asked God for a specific, concrete answer, and He gave it to you? How did it affect you when you realized that God really answered you with the wisdom you needed for that moment?
3. What do you need to know from the Lord right now? Have you gone to Him in prayer and confidently asked Him to direct you? Why don't you make a list of things you need to know from the Lord and officially present it to Him in Jesus' name?

FEBRUARY 19

Fight the Good Fight of Faith!

Fight the good fight of faith....
— 1 Timothy 6:12

Many believers have the misconception that walking *by faith* means they should be able to effortlessly glide all the way to God's destination for their lives with no hiccups or struggles along the way. But the Bible teaches quite the opposite in First Timothy 6:12. In that verse, the apostle Paul wrote, "Fight the good faith of faith...." According to this verse, the path of faith often requires a fight to see it through to completion.

The word "fight" is the Greek word *agonidzo*, which refers to *a struggle, a fight, great exertion*, or *effort*. It is where we get the word *agony* — a word often used in the New Testament to convey the ideas of *anguish, pain, distress*, and *conflict*. The word *agonidzo* itself comes from the word *agon*, which is the word that depicted the *athletic conflicts and competitions* that were so famous in the ancient world. It frequently pictured wrestlers in a wrestling match, with each wrestler struggling with all his might to overcome his opponent in an effort to hurl him to the ground in a fight to the finish.

The very fact that Paul would use *this* word, a word that was very well known in the world of his time, alerts us emphatically that when we step out to do something by faith, it often pushes us into a previously unknown fight. It throws us into some type of *agony — anguish, conflict, pain, distress*, or *a struggle*. It isn't that God wants us to struggle. Instead, this is a fight that results from:

- The flesh that resists the will of God.
- The mind that struggles to understand what God has told us to do.
- Circumstances that seem to stand in the way.
- People who oppose us.
- The devil himself who throws his weight against each step of faith we take.

The point you must see is that Paul recognized when we step out in faith, we don't just effortlessly glide to the destination God is directing us toward. We must fight the good fight of faith to reach the victorious position that allows us to one day hear those cherished words, "Well done!" from our Commander-in-Chief. But rather than shrink from the match that is before us, the apostle Paul urges us to give this fight our best effort! He tells us, "Fight the *good* fight of faith..." The word "good" is from the Greek word *kalos*, which denotes something *exceptional, of the highest quality, outstanding*, or *superb*. In the context of a *fight*, it pictures one who has given his *best effort* to the struggle in which he is engaged; hence, he is one who is doing a *first-rate* or *first-class* job at resisting his opponents.

Then Paul repeated the word "fight" a second time in this verse. He wrote, "Fight the good *fight* of faith...." This second usage of the word "fight" is also from the Greek word *agon* — the same word he used when he referred to a "fight" at the first of the verse. It conveys the idea of one who is giving his *complete concentration* to the conflict and is *totally focused* on *engaging the conflict* at hand and achieving victory, regardless how long it takes or how much *agonizing effort* is required. It is the picture of *total commitment to victory*.

This is a far cry from simply *gliding* to God's destination for your life with no hiccups or headaches along the way! As Paul told us in this verse, anything that is done by faith will require a fight of some sort in order to win. So if you are experiencing a struggle along the path to your personal victory — if you've been fighting off some very real mental or spiritual assaults along the way — don't be taken off guard or by surprise. The Holy Spirit warned in advance through the apostle Paul that you must commit yourself to giving the pursuit of God's will for your life your very best effort and to doing whatever is necessary to finish the goal set before you!

God is calling upon you to stand up and *fight* — giving your concentrated efforts to stand *firm* for what you believe. Fight in a manner that is noble, admirable, and worthy of the reward that awaits you. *And remember — the greater reward usually requires a greater fight.* Keep this in mind as you press forward to be first-class in your determination to overcome every obstacle and resistance along the way. Stay in the fight until you can shout, *"The fight is finished and victory obtained!"*

MY PRAYER FOR TODAY

Father, I admit that I'm in a fight. I need grace and strength to stay in this match and finish it to completion. I didn't realize how much would be required of me. But I am determined and committed to keep up the good fight of faith until I can say the fight is finished and victory is accomplished. Holy Spirit, I ask You to fill me with a fresh supply of Your power, strength, and resolve — a supernatural level of commitment — so I will stay in the fight till my assignment is fulfilled.

I pray this in Jesus' name!

MY CONFESSION FOR TODAY

I boldly declare that God knows exactly what I am facing. I am not fighting this good fight of faith by myself! The Holy Spirit lives in me and fills me with His power — enough power to resist any opponent that would try to stop me from fulfilling God's plan. Today I yield to the Holy Spirit and allow Him to fill me to the brim with His power that resists every opposing force and endures strong to the end so I can stay in this fight until it is over and I've won the victory.

I declare this by faith in Jesus' name!

QUESTIONS FOR YOU TO CONSIDER

1. Think of a biblical example of someone who fought a good fight of faith and stayed in the battle until his fight was complete and his victory was attained. Can you name more than one?
2. Can you call to mind some contemporary examples of individuals who fought a good fight of faith? What did they achieve by staying in the battle? How long did it take them to attain victory? What would have happened if they had given up and not followed through to completion?
3. How long have you been fighting your good fight of faith? What is in jeopardy if you give up your fight and throw in the towel?

FEBRUARY 20

Set Your Affection on Things Above

Set your affection on things above,
not on things on the earth.
— Colossians 3:2

When Denise and I attended the annual International Antique Exposition in Moscow, I was stunned by the vast amount of wealth that was on display. There were acres and acres of antique furniture, bronze and marble sculptures, marvelous gold-gilded clocks veneered in rich malachite, jewelry, paintings by world-class artists, and rare porcelain objects of all shapes and sizes. Denise and I walked down row after row and floor after floor of what seemed like an endless tour of rare treasures that were available for those with enough cash to purchase them. The brand-new, sparkling white Rolls Royce that sat at the main entry should have signaled what lay before us — but the extensive number of treasures on exhibition was simply more than we could have ever anticipated.

What was equally amazing was the number of people who seemed to have sufficient resources to take some of those treasures home with them. I stood back and watched the potential buyers in amazement. It was obvious that many of them were of the richer Russian upper class and knew what they were looking for and were obviously experts on the subject of rare art and treasures as they negotiated their purchases. It seemed like Denise and I were the only ones there just to roam as onlookers and enjoy an afternoon outing. But even though these objects were beyond our financial reach and we had no need of them, I could feel their lure reaching out to grab hold of me.

After strolling through acres of treasures, Denise and I took a seat on a padded bench to give our feet a break from the hard surface of the exhibition hall. As we sat there, I realized that I had pondered on these material objects too long. So I began to reflect on eternal treasures instead — those things that are in Heaven and that never fade with the passing of time. Specifically, my mind went to Colossians 3:1 and 2, which says, "If ye then be risen with Christ, seek those things which are above, where Christ sitteth on the right hand of God. Set your affection on things above, not on things on the earth." Based on this scriptural command, I knew it was time for me to make a deliberate decision to *refocus* my mind on eternal things.

We finished our afternoon stroll and returned home, where I opened my Greek New Testament to look up this passage in Colossians 3. When I turned to these verses in the Greek text, I discovered that the word "seek" in verse 1 is the Greek word *zeteo*. This word means *to earnestly seek*. It doesn't depict a casual seeker, but rather one who makes an *earnest inquiry* for something so *intense* that it causes one to put his whole effort forward in *search* of it. So when Paul told us to "seek" those things that are above — namely, the things where Christ is — he was urging us to put forward our most earnest efforts. This is precisely what I had chosen to do that afternoon at the exhibition! I had chosen to *refocus* my thoughts from those material objects and to put my mind on "things above."

Then in verse 2, Paul wrote, "Set your affection on things above...." The words "set your affection" are a very poor translation of the Greek text, where Paul used the word *phroneo*. This word is derived from the Greek word *phren* — a word that describes one's *mind* or *intellect*. As Paul used this word in Colossians 3:2, it could be interpreted as *to focus one's thoughts*. Thus, it could be translated, "Fix your *thoughts* on things above..."; "Make the decision to *focus* on things above..."; or "Deliberately *think* on things above...." It depicts *a choice* or *a decision* made with a person's *mind* that is independent of his or her emotions.

Paul then plainly told us again that we are to put our focus on "...things above, not on things on the earth." In Greek, the words "things above" is *ta ano*. In this case, *ta* means *things*, as in *many* things, and the Greek word *ano* means *above*, as opposed to the many things that are *below*. What multitude of *things* do you and I possess that are "above"? Well, from verse 1, we know first of all that *Christ Himself* is above, seated at the right hand of the Father. And as we focus our thoughts on Jesus, we are putting ourselves in remembrance of all He has provided for us in Him. Of course, there is a rich inheritance of blessings He has supplied for us to enjoy in *this* life on the earth, but Paul says there are *many* things above that we are to set our attention on! Today I want us to focus on this question: What are some of the "things above" we should set our thoughts on that will be ours to enjoy once we get to Heaven?

- A reunion with our family members, friends, and acquaintances who have preceded us (*see* Hebrews 12:1)
- Rewards earned as a result of our obedience (*see* 1 Corinthians 3:8; Revelation 22:12)
- No more tears, no death, no pain, no sickness, no past, no curse, no darkness, no night (*see* Revelation 21:4, 21:25; 22:3,5)
- Eternal life (*see* Romans 2:7)

There are so *many* eternal treasures that have been laid up for us in Jesus Christ that it is impossible to compile a complete list. Truly, piles upon *piles* of divine blessings and rewards "above" await us. There just isn't enough time or space for any of us to make a list that encompasses all God has freely bestowed upon us through His Son Jesus!

That's why "things below," or *on the earth*, are low-level compared to the treasure trove of "things above" that God has provided us. When we are tempted to feel that we aren't blessed or that we've suffered too much or that we lack what others possess, it's time for us to obey Paul's command to refocus our attention on eternal things and not on things on the earth. The word "on" in Greek is *epi*, which depicts something that is just sitting "on" the earth and is therefore movable and temporary, such as antiques and heirlooms that are passed from one generation to the next. No one takes these things with them when they die because they are all earth-connected.

**With this in mind,
Colossians 3:1,2 could be paraphrased:**

"Since then you are raised together with Christ, earnestly and intensely seek the things that are above, where Christ is seated at the right hand of God. Focus your mind on the many things that are above, and don't get stuck in low-level thinking about temporary things here on the earth."

Today I want to encourage you to refocus your thoughts — and not to depend on your emotions to do it. Your emotions aren't needed for what I'm describing. Whether or not you feel like it, deliberately put your mind on things above — on *all* that God has prepared for you to share with Him in the eternity to come! If needed, go ahead and make a list. Do whatever you must do, but move your thoughts from low-level thinking to high-level thinking, and focus on those things above that really matter.

You really are the one who decides what you *set* your thoughts on. It's up to you to maintain your focus on Jesus and the "things above" that He has waiting for you to enjoy. So today and every day, no matter what's going on around you, keep your eyes fixed on Jesus and your heart open to receive the victory and blessing He's provided for you, both in *this* life and in the life to come!

MY PRAYER FOR TODAY

Father, I thank You for the many blessings laid up for me in Christ to partake of here on this earth. And many more blessings and rewards are waiting for me when I reach Heaven. Please forgive me for getting stuck in low-level thinking about all the things it seems I lack right now. Instead of focusing on what I don't have right now here on earth, please help me reset my thoughts and begin focusing on things above.

I pray this in Jesus' name!

MY CONFESSION FOR TODAY

I confess that Heaven is loaded with spiritual blessings and treasures that are waiting for me! Only that which pertains to eternal life awaits me! There will be no more tears, sickness, pain, or death. So I choose to refocus my thoughts and I declare that I will not dwell on low-level thinking about the earthly possessions I do not have. And I will receive by faith and enjoy all the blessings God has for me here on earth as well. These are all just a taste of the treasure trove of blessings that are waiting for me!

I declare this by faith in Jesus' name!

QUESTIONS FOR YOU TO CONSIDER

1. Can you think of some awards that await you in Heaven because of your obedience to do what God has asked you to do here on earth? Why not encourage yourself by making a list?
2. You will see again one day your loved ones, who preceded you to Heaven. In what way does that thought encourage you?

3. What treasures are yours as a child of God in *this* life? I encourage you to make a list, and then begin today to claim those treasures as *yours* in the Name of Jesus!

FEBRUARY 21

Possessing a Trouble-Free Heart

...Let not your heart be troubled,
neither let it be afraid.
— John 14:27

I'll never forget the day waves of panic rolled through me as we were reconstructing a big building as a permanent home for our church in Moscow. Paying for the building had itself already required the most miraculous level of faith I had ever experienced. When we started the project, we estimated what it would cost to reconstruct the facility. However, we didn't know in the beginning of the process that the floors and columns of the entire building would have to be reinforced to hold the weight of the balcony we were adding to the building.

When I learned of the additional costs associated with reinforcing the floors and columns, a sense of panic surged through my whole being. Alarm, dread, horror — all these words could describe the emotions that tried to grip my soul. Within seconds, I felt cold sweat and heat simultaneously flushing across my face, neck, ears, and upper chest. It felt like I had to somehow get hold of myself or I would fall to pieces.

There was one thing I knew in that moment: allowing panic to get hold of me was not going to change the situation! So I politely excused myself from the meeting where the facts and figures were being presented to me, and I took a walk by myself to catch my breath and bring my soul into submission before fearful emotions could wreak havoc with my peace.

As we proceeded to move forward on that building project, I had to face those same tumultuous emotions more than once. Taking a walk by myself to bring my soul into submission became a very familiar practice en route to completing that project. During those times, I learned to turn to Jesus' words in John 14:27, where He said, "...Let not your heart be troubled, neither let it be afraid." These words proved to be of great comfort to me in those times when my soul was tempted to give way to fear and trepidation.

As I'm sure you personally know, there is perhaps nothing more tormenting than to go through your daily life with a troubled heart. It can make you wallow in tumultuous feelings of worry, inadequacy, or regret. It can tear you up emotionally and steal your joy. And when fear is added to the mix, it can escalate your troubled state to an even higher level of anxiety. That's why it's so important that you take Jesus' words deep into your heart that you do not *ever* have to live with a troubled and fearful heart.

Jesus said, "...Let not your heart be troubled, neither let it be afraid" (John 14:27). The word "troubled" is the Greek word *taresso*, which is used in various places in the New Testament to mean *to shake, to trouble, to disquiet, to unsettle, to perplex, to cause anxiety,* or even *to cause feelings of grief.* It is the picture of *someone feeling inwardly shaken, unsettled, confused, and upset.* If you've felt that way, you know exactly I mean!

Often when these troubling emotions begin to work in the soul, they open the door to other negative emotions and eventually pull you over into the realm of fear. That's why it is so important to bring the soul into submission *before* this happens. This is precisely why Jesus continued to say, "Let not your heart be troubled, neither let it be afraid."

The word "afraid" is from the word *deilos*, and depicts *a gripping fear or dread that produces a shrinking back or cowardice.* In essence, it saps your ability to look at the problem head-on and causes you to retreat into your own mode of self-preservation — which, in effect, is *cowardice* or the lack of courage to face what is before you.

This word *deilos* is the same Greek word that Paul used in Second Timothy 1:7 when he told Timothy, "God has not given us the spirit of fear; but of power, and of love, and of a sound mind." Timothy was facing real problems at the time Paul wrote this verse to him. His problems were *not* imaginary. Nevertheless, Paul didn't want Timothy's emotions to be in bondage to a spirit of fear that would turn him into a coward. Shrinking back from reality wouldn't help the younger minister or anyone else involved in the situation. So Paul told Timothy that his being subject to a sense of fear or panic was *not* the will of God, for the Lord had given him spiritual equipment of an entirely different nature — *a spirit of power, love,* and *a sound mind!*

With this in mind, look again at the words of Jesus in John 14:27, which can convey this idea:

"Don't let your heart be torn up by things that unsettle you, neither let it be taken with fear that causes you to shrink back into cowardice."

How well Jesus understands what you and I are facing! We were not created to be torn up in our emotions! That's why we must quickly learn to grab hold of our emotions and tell ourselves, *I wasn't made for this! I refuse to allow this sense of panic and fear to get hold of me! Jesus is Lord over every situation I commit to Him, and that includes the one I'm looking at right now!*

In moments when fear has tried to grip me, and I admit it has happened multiple times over the years, I've learned to run to John 14:27 and to rehearse the words of Jesus to myself over and over again. Jesus knows us. He knew what we'd be facing in life, so He instructed us in advance on how to deal with it!

Allowing yourself to stay in a state of feeling troubled, upset, and fearful won't help you in life. In fact, it will hinder you in running the race God has set before you! So take Jesus' words very seriously and *refuse to let* your heart be troubled. Jesus wouldn't tell you to do something you couldn't do, so you can know that you are well able to make that choice!

Don't allow yourself to yield to fear in any form. You have the spirit of power and love and a sound mind working in you. That means you are well able to grab hold of any negative emotions and *pull* them in line with God's Word, even in a situation that challenges you to the core. You can just settle it for yourself today: You are *not* of those who shrink back (*see* Hebrews 10:39). No, you're among those who bring their souls into submission to God's Word and live as *overcomers* in this life!

MY PRAYER FOR TODAY

Father, I acknowledge that I've allowed myself to get into a troubled state of heart and soul. Circumstances have left me feeling shaken and upset, and I haven't dealt with those feelings according to the Word. As a result, a door was opened to a spirit of fear that is now trying to call the shots in my life. I repent, because it is sin for me not to trust You, and I ask You to please forgive me for allowing these negative emotions to find a place to take up residence in my life. So now I open my heart for the Holy Spirit to infuse me with the power I need to take authority over the spirit of fear and tell it to leave me once and for all.

I pray this in Jesus' name!

MY CONFESSION FOR TODAY

I confess that my heart, mind, and emotions are not made to be a refuge for fear and intimidation to take up residence in me and torment me. I refuse to nurse these negative emotions any longer or to let them operate inside my soul! I have tolerated fear too long! I refuse to retreat into a toxic state of isolation and self-preservation. God has too many things for me to do in this life to waste a moment in torment and fear, so I'm moving forward by faith to defeat the enemy's strategy against me today. I do it in the power of the Holy Spirit and with the name of Jesus!

I declare this by faith in Jesus' name!

QUESTIONS FOR YOU TO CONSIDER

1. Can you think of an experience when a spirit of fear tried to grab hold of you? What did you do to break its grip on your soul?
2. If you had a friend who was being torn up emotionally and mentally by a spirit of fear, what would you advise that friend to do? Have you taken this advice for yourself?
3. Do you know someone who is dealing with a troubled heart or being tormented by thoughts of fear right now? What should you do to help that person get victory over that situation?

FEBRUARY 22

Praying With Boldness and Confidence!

In whom we have boldness and access
with confidence by the faith of him.
— Ephesians 3:12

I'm so grateful for all the truths and godly qualities that my pastor and church family planted in me during my growing-up years. But I have to say, in all the years I attended that church, I personally can't remember a time when I heard anyone pray boldly or confidently. I simply had no idea what bold, confident praying sounded like until I attended a seminar at another church where a special speaker was teaching on the subject of faith.

At that seminar, I could hardly believe my ears! The man prayed like he actually believed what he was praying would come to pass! At first I was offended, because I mistook his confidence for arrogance. But the longer I listened, the more I realized this man *really* believed that God was listening to him and that God would do what he had asked of Him. With all the years of sincere praying I had heard in my life, I had never heard such *confidence* in prayer. That day changed my life as I realized for the first time this truth: If we really know the will of God, we can approach God *boldly* and *confidently*!

One of the scriptures that came alive to me at that time of my life was Ephesians 3:12, which says, "In whom we have boldness and access with confidence by the faith of him." The words "in whom" tell us that our confidence is not based on ourselves, but on our relationship with Jesus Christ. And when you really know that you are in Christ, there is no longer a need to be sheepish about asking for what God has already promised you in His Word. Ephesians 3:12 tells us that we can come to God with *boldness* and *confidence*!

The word "boldness" in this verse is from the Greek word *parresia*, which describes *a frankness of speech* that is often viewed as *unflinching authority* — even in the face of opposition. It presents a picture of *unashamed boldness*. It also is associated with *joy* and *courage*. But in addition, Paul goes on to tell us that we can have "confidence" in Christ as we pray.

The word "confidence" is a derivative of the Greek word *peitho*, which, in most cases, means *persuasion*. However, in this verse, the word *persuasion* isn't enough. The Greek form used here depicts *absolute confidence* — that is, one who is *doubly persuaded*. You could say that this person is *convinced to the core* — rock-solid *certain* about what he believes or feels. He is so *completely persuaded* and *trustful* of what he believes that no element of doubt remains.

These words describe exactly what I heard so long ago in that seminar when I first heard someone pray with utter boldness. It caught me off-guard because I'd never heard such bold praying. But as I listened, I understood that the man prayed with such confidence because he *knew* he was standing firm on promises in God's Word. His boldness was based in his assurance of God's faithfulness to perform what He had promised. This man was *thoroughly convinced* that God's promises were *trustworthy* and *true*, and that *confidence* caused him to pray with bold authority.

When you are certain of your rightstanding in Christ, it provides you with a foundation on which to stand. You are convinced of what God has promised you. You have a certainty that when you pray, God hears you and will do as you have asked. This means you don't need to feel sheepish or embarrassed when you come to Jesus' throne of grace. You can come boldly to seek mercy in your time of need.

So use your God-given authority without flinching as you boldly and unashamedly put God in remembrance of His promises. *He is waiting to hear your voice of authority!*

MY PRAYER FOR TODAY

Father, thank You for inviting me to come boldly and confidently to You in prayer. I'm so thankful I don't need to feel embarrassed or sheepish when I come to You with vital needs in my life. As I stand on the promises of Your Word, I will lift my voice in humility and confidence, believing that You hear me and knowing that if I ask anything according to Your will, I will receive it.

I pray this in Jesus' name!

MY CONFESSION FOR TODAY

I declare that I have no need to be embarrassed or ashamed when I come to God in prayer. The blood of Jesus has purchased me, cleansed me, and given me rightstanding with God. On that principle, I come before Him convinced to the core that His promises are alive, active, and at work in my life. When I pray, I pray like God really hears me, because I am absolutely convinced that He does! It's not arrogance; it's divinely inspired confidence. And when I pray like this, Heaven and earth move out of the way for God to activate His power and manifest His blessings on my behalf!

I declare this by faith in Jesus' name!

QUESTIONS FOR YOU TO CONSIDER

1. Have you ever heard a person pray with great boldness in prayer? How did it impact you when you first heard it? Have you ever experienced a moment when utter boldness came out of *your* spirit as you prayed?
2. Can you think of an area of your life in which you are so convinced about something that no room is left for any element of doubt? If so, what is that area in which you feel such confidence?
3. In what area are you lacking confidence when you pray? What do you need to do to reassure yourself so you can pray confidently?

FEBRUARY 23

Corrupt Communication

Let no corrupt communication
proceed out of your mouth,
but that which is good to the use of edifying,
that it may minister grace unto the hearers.
— Ephesians 4:29

Some of the "dirtiest talk" I've ever heard used to happen almost every week at the end of our living room couch as I was growing up. About once a week, a certain member of our church would drop by to visit with my parents. She was the church gossip, and she always came loaded with the "latest scoop" on people's personal matters that were absolutely none of her business to know or to discuss. Although my parents loved her, I can still see my dad rolling his eyes when he realized it was her ringing the doorbell of our house. She'd plop down on the end of the couch and within seconds, the verbal garbage would begin to flow about everyone and everything — absolutely no one's personal business was off-limits! If a person attended our church, then like it or not, that person was a potential victim of this woman's tongue.

This woman's fairly regular visits to our house represented some of the ugliest moments of socializing I've ever witnessed in my life. Outright cursing would have been totally inappropriate for any believer, much less for a leading church member. Yet what this woman did in our living room almost every week was as distasteful to God as cursing — *if not more so.*

Talking badly about others behind their backs, such as the outpouring of gossip that proceeded from this woman's mouth, is a type of nasty conversation too often tolerated in the Church. The apostle Paul called this kind of talk "corrupt communication" — and he strictly forbade it when he said to let *no* talk of this type proceed out of our mouths!

In the Greek text, the word "corrupt" is the *sapros*, a word that depicts something that is *putrid* or *rotten.* The word "putrid" describes meat that has gone so bad that it emits a foul smell. The decomposing meat reeks of a noxious and rancid smell that nearly makes a person sick to his stomach. The word "rotten" describes fruit that is spoiled, decayed, and sickening to the taste. It can also be described as putrid. Either way, whether meat or fruit, if something is putrid, it is disgusting to taste or smell. So when the Holy Spirit inspired the apostle Paul to use the word *sapros* to describe "corrupt communication," he was describing communication that is really *nasty.*

The word "communication" is the Greek word *logos*, which simply means *words.* But when it is used in conjunction with the word "corrupt," the Greek phrase describes *words or forms of communication that are putrid or disgusting to the recipient.* As far as God is concerned, this type of communication *reeks.* And those who consume this type of talk find it to be so putrid that it sickens them, just as spoiled meat would do. And just as a rotten apple must be removed from a bucket of apples or it will eventually spread and ruin the entire batch of good apples, this is how ruinous "corrupt communication" can be to those who listen to it, as far as God is concerned. Everything about corrupt communication has a *putrefying effect* on others.

Paul says instead of spreading corrupt communication to others, we must learn to speak that which is "edifying" to hearers (*see* Ephesians 4:29). The word "edifying" is the Greek word *oikodomeo* and, as used here, means to *build others up*. These words never result in tearing someone down, but rather cause others to be left in an *improved state* after we are done talking to or about them.

Have you ever known a person who always had something good to say about someone else? Doesn't that person leave a sweet taste in your mouth? You feel good about the time you spend with such a positive, sweet-speaking individual. In fact, you feel challenged to rise higher and be better every time you leave that person's presence! What a difference that experience is from an encounter with a person who tears others down and leaves a bitter taste in people's mouths!

The Holy Spirit is urging us to become a wellspring of good words when we talk to and about others. Rather than have the putrefying effect that a gossiper has on his or her listeners, we must determine that our words build others up and leave them in a much-improved state of being! *That is the Holy Spirit's message in Ephesians 4:29.*

The woman I told you about earlier was someone who never missed church and served faithfully, but she had never learned to control her tongue. Had she really understood the stench her words were releasing into the atmosphere and into the ears of her listeners, I'm sure she would have asked the Holy Spirit to help her change.

I believe that today the Holy Spirit is speaking to you about *your* tongue and *your* words. Ask yourself this: *Does God commend me for leaving others in better shape because of my words, or is He saying that I need to get a grip on my tongue and stop talking in a way that puts others down and harms their reputations?* Only you know the answer to these questions!

Why don't you make the determined decision that from this day forward, when you leave a room or a conversation, you leave it with the sweet fragrance of Jesus lingering behind you? Let people remember you for the kind words you left behind. You can be known as one who leaves a sweet taste in people's mouth every time you leave a conversation or walk out of a room!

MY PRAYER FOR TODAY

Father, I ask You to forgive me for allowing myself to get involved in conversations that were unfruitful and hurtful to those who were listening. Out of the abundance of the heart, the mouth speaks. Gossip is a form of putrid communication that defiles both the speaker and the hearer. I realize that I have been guilty of gossiping and discussing things that are none of my business, and I sincerely repent for these actions. I ask You to set a guard over my mouth so I no longer do this. I want to be only a river of life to others who are near me. Let my words be of benefit to others to build them up so that after I leave them, they are in better shape than they were before they talked to me.

I pray this in Jesus' name!

MY CONFESSION FOR TODAY

I confess that my mouth speaks good things about others. I do not gossip about others, nor do I tear others down with my words. The Holy Spirit is inside me, and I do not grieve Him by foul talk. I yield to the Spirit, and as a result, I speak words that minister grace to those who hear me. After spending time conversing with people, I leave a sweet taste in their mouths and they are blessed by the fellowship they shared with me.

I declare this by faith in Jesus' name!

QUESTIONS FOR YOU TO CONSIDER

1. Have you ever known someone whose mouth was like an open sewer because that person's conversation was so often full of gossip about others? What kind of effect did his or her "gossipy" attitude have on you and others?
2. If you find yourself in a situation where a gossip is spewing out putrid information about others, what is your responsibility? Should you simply be silent and let it go on uninterrupted, or would the Holy Spirit want you to take some other action?
3. Are you guilty of speaking about matters that are none of your business and that don't edify those who are listening? If you've been guilty of gossiping and disseminating information about others that is none of your business, what is the Holy Spirit expecting you to do about it?
4. Can you think of a person whose words always build you up and leave you glad that you had the opportunity to talk to him or her? Who is that person?

FEBRUARY 24

Run!

…And let us run with patience
the race that is set before us.
— Hebrews 12:1

When I was a younger man, I had a friend who would meet me each evening, and we'd jog together for about an hour. I had never been a runner, so when we first started jogging, it was very difficult for me and I'd get easily discouraged. My friend was a little younger than I and definitely in better shape, so he'd say, "Come on, Rick, you can do it! Keep going!" What was at first a very difficult jog eventually became a regular and fairly easy daily event. In fact,

I looked forward to the doorbell ringing each evening so I could meet my friend and run our course together.

The neighborhood Denise and I lived in wasn't exactly pristine; in fact, it was not a good area of town. So if I ran a little too long and came in a little later than expected, it would bother her. To alleviate Denise's concerns, my jogging buddy decided he would drive through the neighborhood, chart a course, and measure it in miles so we'd know the exact distance that course included. I never had to think about where we were going to run, and Denise would know where to look for me if I didn't come home on time. Running that predetermined course not only gave Denise a greater measure of peace, but it also helped me because I had a prearranged race set before me that helped me pace myself for the run. My friend chose the route, the length, and the amount of time it would take us to run. All that was required of me was to run the race he had set for me.

Often as I ran that course, I thought of Hebrews 12:1, which urges us, "...Let us run with patience the race that is set before us." Today I want to talk to you about running the race Jesus has set before *you*. Just as my buddy set a prearranged course for me, this verse declares that Jesus has set a pre-appointed course for *your* race in this life. And believe me when I say that you're not smart enough to figure out your own course by yourself! But Jesus has gone ahead of you; He has prearranged the course; and now He pleads with you to *run* the race He has set before you.

Let's begin by looking at the word "run." It is a translation of the Greek word *trechos*, which means *to run*. This is not fast walking — this is *running*. This is a picture of a person who has jumped into the race and is pressing ahead with all his might to reach a goal set before him. He is running at such a pace that both feet never hit the ground at the same time. With his eyes fixed on the finish line, he makes a run for it, steadily moving forward toward the goal. The fact that it requires such effort tells us that this race may not always be easy. That's why the verse goes on to tell us that we must run it with "patience."

The word "patience" is the Greek word *hupomeno*, a word that is used over and over in the New Testament to describe *endurance*. It is a compound of the words *hupo*, meaning *to be under*, and the word *meno*, which means *to abide* or *to stay in one spot*. When these two words are compounded, it forms the word *hupomeno*, which pictures *the attitude of a person who is under a very heavy load but has decided to stay put and stand firm*. He refuses to move from his commitment, regardless how difficult the challenges that are placed upon him.

Starting anything is always the fun, easy part of a project, whereas finishing requires a commitment to endure until it is completed. This process can be so challenging that Hebrews 12:1 calls it a "race" — the Greek word *agona*, which is most often translated *to struggle* or *to wrestle*. A form of this word is where we get the word "agony."

How is wrestling connected to a race? It does seem like a mixed picture, doesn't it? But you have to remember that in order to stay in a race, especially a long one, a *wrestling* in your emotions may be involved as your mind screams at you to throw in the towel and *quit*. The soul can begin to wrestle with you when weariness sets in — screaming that the race is too difficult, that it's taking longer than you expected, or that it's requiring more effort than you originally bargained for. Thus, the use of this Greek word *agona* really makes the point regarding how intense our struggle with the mind and emotions can be.

But you can rejoice that just as my jogging buddy charted a course for me, you don't have to figure out on your own the path that will lead you to your destination! Jesus has chosen your route for you. What is required of you is to jump in the race and run with all your might — *fixing* your eyes on Jesus and the goal He has set before you. That's why the verse says we must run with patience the race that was "set before" us.

The words "set before" are a translation of the Greek word *prokeimenon*, which is a compound of the words *pro*, meaning *before*, and the word *keimai*, which means *to be set, to be appointed*, or *to be established*. Compounded into one word, as used here in Hebrews 12:1, the new word describes a race course that has been predetermined for you by someone else. That "Someone" is Jesus, who has *appointed* a goal for your life and who has even *pre-established* the course you need to run to get there! Just as my jogging buddy charted the course for me, Jesus has gone before us and has established the race for us. We're not smart enough to figure out how to reach God's goal for our lives, so Jesus has taken care of that part for us. He just needs our willingness to jump into the race and run with all our might — keeping our eyes on the goal!

I want to encourage you that Jesus has already gone before you, and He is beckoning you to run your race with all your might. It's very possible that weariness will try to set in at times and that your mind and emotions will wrestle with you, telling you to quit. Your emotions may even tell you that the entire endeavor is just not worth it because it's so much more than you bargained for when you began.

But quitting is *not* the answer. Jesus didn't give you a goal you cannot reach! Just shove your negative emotions out of the way by setting the focus of your mind and heart on *Him*. Make a determined decision that you *are* going to stay put in the race, and *then make a run for it!* Once you get moving, the Holy Spirit will give you supernatural momentum. You'll find yourself speeding down the track toward your goal, getting closer and closer all the time!

MY PRAYER FOR TODAY

Father, I thank You for the Person of the Holy Spirit, who positioned me in this race and who now empowers me to stay in the race until I reach completion. You are fair, Father, and You wouldn't give me a goal I couldn't reach. So when my mind and emotions argue with me, telling me that the finish line is too difficult to reach, I thank You that You've given me the mind of Christ that enables me to rule over my emotions. For the joy set before Him, Jesus endured in His race, and I thank You that I can do the same thing! I receive Your precious gift of divine strength that empowers me so that nothing moves me. I set my focus on Jesus and strive for the mastery, running according to Your ways so I can reach my goal. I can achieve whatever You have told me to do, Father, because Jesus has gone before me and prepared the way!

I pray this in Jesus' name!

MY CONFESSION FOR TODAY

I confess that God's plan for my life holds only victory. He has made total provision for me to fulfill what He has called me to do through Jesus Christ. God has not called me to quit; therefore, I will not quit this race that I am running right now. He has already prepared me for this task. I will run my race; I will stay in the fight; and I will reach the finish line that Jesus has prearranged for me. I take the path He prepared ahead of time, and I will live the life He has made ready for me to live. Quitting is not an option. Therefore, I will say no to my flesh. I say no to the devil's attempts to insert thoughts of doubt that defy the word of the Lord for my life. I can and I will do what God has asked me to do. I will run this race to completion and finish my course with joy!

I declare this by faith in Jesus' name!

QUESTIONS FOR YOU TO CONSIDER

1. What is the goal that Jesus Christ has set before your life? Can you write it out on a piece of paper well enough that you could communicate it clearly to someone else?
2. Do you have intermediate goals on the way to your final goal? Thinking of the intermediate goals you have already met along the way may encourage you to keep going, so which of these goals have you already reached on the way to completing your course?
3. How do you encourage yourself when you grow weary or when the devil tries to attack you mentally or emotionally? What do you say or do to stir yourself up to stay in the race?
4. Can you think of a specific person you know who needs your encouragement right now so he or she is strengthened to keep pressing forward in the race of faith?

FEBRUARY 25

The Unseen Power Behind the Throne

...take ye no thought how or what thing ye shall answer,
or what ye shall say: for the Holy Spirit shall teach you
in the same hour what ye ought to say.
— Luke 12:11,12

In Moscow stands the Kremlin — an architectural wonder that is simply breathtaking in terms of beauty. Within this great walled city are palaces, ancient churches, governmental buildings, and the State Armory Museum, a fabulous structure that holds treasures, crowns, diamonds, carriages, and thrones of the Russian state. One throne in particular has captured my attention every time I visit the Armory. It is a gigantic, double-seated throne with a strange opening just behind the seat to the right side.

In 1676, Tsar Alexis Romanov died, leaving his sickly son, Ivan, to inherit the throne. As a result of a number of political manipulations, it was decided that Ivan would be proclaimed Tsar jointly with his ten-year-old brother, Peter. For a brief period of time, both brothers ruled Russia, sitting together on the gigantic, double-seated throne that is now on display in the Armory. Young Ivan sat on the left side of the throne, and his brother Peter sat on the seat to the right. Eventually Ivan proved to be too physically and mentally feeble to rule, so he resigned his position. His brother Peter remained as Tsar and ruled Russia until his death in 1725. Today he is respectfully referred to as *Peter the Great* because of the great accomplishments and lasting impressions he made during his reign.

But why was there an opening behind the seat where Peter sat upon the throne? That opening was made so Peter's sister, Sophia, could sit behind the young Tsar and privately provide him with correct responses to questions and comments made to him by visiting dignitaries. As the young Tsar listened to his sister's words spoken quietly to him through a veil, and as he in turn communicated what he heard to those who approached him, an impression was made that he was intellectually powerful, even at an early age. The truth was, young Peter *was* brilliant, but his sister, although unseen, was the *real* power behind the throne.

When I've visited the State Armory Museum and looked at that strange opening in the double-seated throne, I've pondered the words of Jesus in Luke 12:11,12. Jesus told His disciples what to do when they faced difficult circumstances in which they didn't know what to say or how to respond: "...Take ye no thought how or what thing ye shall answer, or what ye shall say: for the Holy Spirit shall teach you in the same hour what ye ought to say."

Notice Jesus said, "...Take ye *no thought* how or what thing ye shall answer...." That doesn't mean Jesus was advocating mindlessness. Rather, He was saying that there is no need for us to be *anxious* or *worried* in those moments because the Holy Spirit will be the unseen Presence, advising us what to say.

It would be easy in the natural for us to feel fretful, uneasy, upset, or distraught in those moments of not knowing how to answer. That's why it's important to understand that the Greek word for "thought" in this verse is actually Jesus' prohibition *against* our being fretful in such moments. We may not always know how to respond to every question put before us or every situation we face. But Jesus is telling us that we have no need to be ill at ease because His Spirit will teach us "in that hour" — that is, in our specific moment of need — *exactly* what we need to say.

The sister of Peter the Great was an invisible advisor to her brother as she sat behind the strange opening in that double-seated throne. But the Holy Spirit wants to be an infinitely more effective unseen Advisor to *you*. If you will allow Him to take that position in your life, and if you will determine to learn how to hear and trust His voice, the Holy Spirit will give you answers to the questions and situations you encounter that you're unable to answer or solve on your own.

So open your heart to the Holy Spirit today, and receive Him as your personal Advisor. As you train your heart to hear what He's saying to you more and more accurately, He will help you respond with His insight and wisdom to every situation you could ever face in this life!

MY PRAYER FOR TODAY

Father, I thank You for the wonderful ministry of the Holy Spirit. I repent for the times I've allowed myself to become fretful and upset because I didn't know what to do or say. Holy Spirit, I receive and give place to Your ministry as my personal, private, invisible Advisor. I allow You to take this position in my life, and I purpose in my heart to learn to hear and trust Your voice. Thank You for giving me answers to questions and situations that I would be unable to answer or to solve on my own.

I pray this in Jesus' name!

MY CONFESSION FOR TODAY

I confess that the Holy Spirit is my personal Counselor. In every situation of life, I listen to the voice of the Spirit. He speaks to my heart and mind, and He tells me precisely what I am to say and what I am to do. I am not helpless, confused, or caught off-guard because the Holy Spirit lives within me as my ever-present Helper. With Him inside me to guide me, I am never at a loss for wisdom in critical moments. He is my Helper, my Teacher, my Comforter, and my Advisor!

I declare this by faith in Jesus' name!

QUESTIONS FOR YOU TO CONSIDER

1. Can you recall a moment when you had no answer for a question being put before you — and then suddenly the Holy Spirit showed you what to say and what to do? When was that experience? Is it something you could share with others to encourage them in similar moments?
2. What questions or situations are you facing right now that you do not naturally know how to answer or how to solve? Have you asked the Holy Spirit to help you?

If you will determine to learn how to hear and trust the Holy Spirit's voice, He will give you answers to the questions and situations you encounter that you're unable to answer or solve on your own.

FEBRUARY 26

A Family Mystery

In whom we have redemption through his blood,
the forgiveness of sins, according to the riches of his grace.
— Ephesians 1:7

My father's father, who is known to me as Grandpa Renner, immigrated to the United States from Germany in 1927. When he left Germany, he left *everything* behind — his family, his history, and literally any knowledge of his past.

As an immigrant in 1927, Grandpa worked hard to make a new life as a good, godly man. But his previous life in Germany was a subject that was *not* discussed. Even my father didn't know much about his father's previous life in Germany, as it was considered an off-limit conversation. It seemed there was something about his past that he did not want known.

Approximately ten years after Grandpa and Grandma Renner passed away, an elderly friend of Grandma Renner called my mother and said, "I want to tell you something about Mr. Renner that you have a right to know. It's something confidential that no one has ever told any of you about his life in Germany before he came to America. Please meet me, so I can tell you something secret that you need to know."

But before my mother could meet this elderly friend of the family, this friend unexpectedly passed away — and when she died, she took to the grave whatever it was that she knew and wanted to tell my mother about my Grandpa Renner. Now many years have passed, and I still know almost nothing of the history of our Renner ancestors or what happened in my grandfather's previous life in Germany.

Over the years, I've wondered what it was about my grandfather's past that he so meticulously hid. I even tried to unearth information about his life in Germany. But no matter how hard I tried to find information about a "secret" that may have occurred in his earlier life, this information is simply not available. I even hired genealogists who could provide me with legal information from Germany, but their efforts didn't yield even one clue. Whatever the big secret was — and for whatever reason my Grandpa refused to acknowledge his past — it is something that my family will never know. The last possible link to that knowledge was Grandma Renner's friend who took that secret information with her to the grave. When her grave was closed, the case was closed forever.

After years of frustration in trying to dig up whatever I could about our family's secret past and hitting wall after wall, I realized one day that God didn't *intend* for us to know that hidden information from the past. Why should I be seeking it out, anyway, since Grandpa didn't want us to know it? Besides, he had become a blood-cleansed believer, and God didn't hold it against him, anyway, whatever "it" may have been!

Jesus' blood utterly wipes away the past. Whatever we did before Christ is buried by God forever. As far as God is concerned, the past is irretrievably gone and forgotten!

In Ephesians 1:7, the apostle Paul stated this glorious truth of forgiveness when he wrote, "In whom we have redemption through his blood, the forgiveness of sins, according to the riches of his grace." The word "forgive" is the Greek word *aphiemi*, which means *to permanently dismiss, to liberate completely, to discharge, to send away*, or *to release*. It was used in New Testament times to mean *to cancel a debt* or *to release someone from an obligation of a contract, a commitment, or a promise*. It means to *forfeit any right to hold a person captive to a previous commitment or a wrong he has committed*.

So when Paul used this word in Ephesians 1:7 to describe the forgiveness of sins, he was saying that God has permanently *dismissed* our past sins from us. We are *liberated completely* from them. He has *discharged* them from us; He has *sent them away*; and He has *released us* from them. The debt we once owed due to past transgressions is *canceled*, and God has *freed* us from the guilt of those previous actions. Because the blood of Jesus was shed for the payment of our sin, God has *forfeited* any right to hold us captive for that which we have already received forgiveness.

Isn't this what we're told in Psalm 103:12? It says, "As far as the east is from the west, so far hath he removed our transgressions from us."

If God said He removed our sins from us as far as the north is from the south, we would eventually meet our sins again, because there is a north pole and a south pole. However, if you go east and you never change direction, you'll never meet west because you'll always be going east. Likewise, if you travel west and never change direction, you'll never meet east because you'll always be traveling west. East never meets west, and west never meets east — and that's how far God has removed our sins from us! He has removed your past sins from you forever. In fact, Micah 7:19 declares that once God has dealt with your sins, He throws them into a sea of forgetfulness.

God has put your sins behind His back forever, never to look at them again. He has chosen to release you from those sins completely — *as if you never did it.* God doesn't have a poor memory. He could remember if He chose to, but He has *chosen* to never remember them again. *He has thrown them into the depths of the sea, where He will never retrieve them to bring them up to you again.*

The "sea of forgetfulness" is clearly where Grandpa Renner's past ended up. Whatever it was that he wanted forgotten, it was *irretrievably removed* from memory and from any existing records. And finally I came to understand the power of redemption reflected in our inability to find out anything about my grandfather's past. If God had put it away, I needed to put it away, too, just as I would want my own past regrets put away and forgotten. So I chose to close the book on that question about Grandpa's secret past and to never try to reopen it again.

What about you? Since you are in Christ and therefore have received forgiveness from God by the shed blood of Jesus, why do you keep dragging up your past again and again, as if God were reminding you of it? If He has placed your past actions into the sea of forgetfulness, shouldn't you leave all that past mess where *He* has left it? Why don't you make the decision today to leave *your* past messes in the depths of the sea and allow yourself to be released from them once and for all by the power in the blood of Jesus? *That is exactly what God wants you to do!*

MY PRAYER FOR TODAY

Lord Jesus, words fail to express the depth of my gratitude for Your precious blood and for the price You willingly and completely paid to cancel all the debt from my past sin and actions. Your grace toward me is more than I can comprehend, but today I must stop to say THANK YOU for displaying Your amazing grace toward me!

I pray this in Jesus' name!

MY CONFESSION FOR TODAY

I confess that I am completely forgiven. God has liberated me completely, discharged, sent away, and released me from all of my sin, which He has forgiven. By the blood of Jesus, my debt has been cancelled and I have been released from it. Neither the devil, others, nor I have the right to hold me captive to a previous wrong. I am totally and completely forgiven!

I declare this by faith in Jesus' name!

QUESTIONS FOR YOU TO CONSIDER

1. Do you beat yourself over things you said or did in the past? What good has it profited you to bring up a sad reminder over and over again?
2. Consider what would change in your life if you chose to accept total forgiveness and walk away from your past, to never bring it up to again. How would this type of freedom affect the way you think and the way you are living?
3. Have you ever thought about how far the east is from the west and what that tells you about how far God has removed your sins from you?

FEBRUARY 27

My Job at the Cemetery

Likewise, reckon ye also yourself to be dead indeed unto sin,
but alive unto God through Jesus Christ our Lord.
— Romans 6:11

When I received my Social Security card as a young boy, my father said, "Rick, it's time for you to get a job and learn what it's like to earn a living." Like other boys, I had mowed lawns to earn a little money on the side. I had even helped clean the church building on Saturdays for a whopping salary of 25 cents a week! But now that I was 12 years old, it was time for me to get a "real" job. Since I wasn't old enough to drive, I had to look for some place to work that was close enough for me to walk there every day, and the only possibility that fit that description was the local cemetery.

So at my father's urging, I walked to the cemetery to ask the grounds director — a gruff, old man who had run the cemetery for years — if there was any job available for a 12-year-old boy. After interviewing me, he hired me as a lawn boy to mow the graves, edge the tombstones, oversee the flowerbeds, and remove wilted flowers from the graves. Every weekday after school, I walked down the street and through the huge arched entry to the cemetery, pulled the giant industrial lawnmower out of the shed, and went to work mowing graves or trimming the grass that grew up around the tombstones.

Thus, for my first fully paid job — every day after school, five days a week — I found myself working among the dead. And in all the time I worked there, I can't recall a single instance when I discovered a corpse that had crawled out of his grave because he was tired of being dead! Once the person was dead, it was permanent. When goodbyes were spoken at gravesite rites, they were always final farewells, with everyone present being well aware that the person would never be seen alive again.

I've often thought of that when reading Romans 6:11, which says, "Likewise reckon ye also yourselves to be dead indeed unto sin, but alive unto God through Jesus Christ our Lord." The word "reckon" is the Greek word *logidzomai*, and in this verse, it means *to count a deed already done*; hence, it simply means that something is *reckoned* to be so or to be a *fact*. Thus, the verse carries the idea, *"Consider yourself to already be dead to sin — a deed that has already been accomplished, a fact that has already been established, which simply needs your affirmation and recognition."* This is important because it tells us that in the mind of God, whoever you were in the past no longer has any claim to who you are now in Christ. Sin and its stimulating power has been slain by the power of the Cross. In Christ, that old person is absolutely *dead*.

The word "dead" in Romans 6:11 is the Greek word *nekros*, which describes *a corpse* just as real as any corpse in a morgue or a dead body being buried in a cemetery. Its life is gone, and it is nothing more than a hull. Nothing can resuscitate it; no one can breathe life back into it; and there is nothing that can stimulate it back into action again, because it's *dead* and its life has been *permanently terminated*. Hence, this word "dead," the Greek word *nekros*, pictures a body that is *permanently disconnected* to life. Making this even stronger is the fact that Paul said we are dead "indeed" unto sin. The word "indeed" means *unquestionably*, *undeniably*, or *as a matter of fact*. Paul declares this to be an immitigable truth!

Paul continued that we are "dead indeed unto sin." The word "sin" describes our identities and activities that existed before we surrendered to the Lordship of Jesus Christ. It involves the sinful nature we were born with, including all of its actions and behaviors that were contrary to God (*see* Colossians 1:21).

But in Christ, all of "that" has been made dead. In God's mind, this is not a mere theoretical death. When we came into Christ, God deemed that old identity dead and powerless over us. Now in Him, there is a permanent disconnection to the old person we used to be and to the things we once did. Christ rendered the old man dead and gave us new life!

That is why Paul went on to say, "Likewise reckon ye also yourselves to be dead indeed unto sin, but alive unto God through Jesus Christ our Lord." My friend, you are not a resuscitated, newly improved version of the person you used to be. That old man is dead, buried, and permanently gone. *Who you are right now in Christ is completely brand-new!*

So if those old things from your past or former ways of thinking attempt to express themselves again, speak to those voices and remind them that they have lost their power over your life. If they try to wake up and act like they still have life, your task is to reckon them lifeless — that is, keep them buried, "six feet under," locked away in a casket that is covered with the grace of God. Never — *not for a second* — allow your old memories to tell you they have the right to live. Christ has rendered them powerless, and you never have to return to who you were or to what you did.

So remember —
Romans 6:11 could actually be interpreted:

"Consider yourself to already be dead to sin. It's a deed that has already been accomplished and a fact that has already been established and simply needs your affirmation and recognition."

Don't argue with what the Holy Spirit is teaching you about this glorious truth. Throw your arms open, accept it, declare it, and walk free from those things that Christ has utterly and permanently disconnected from you!

MY PRAYER FOR TODAY

Father, I sincerely ask You to help me embrace the truth that I've been set free from the past and from past behaviors. I am so thankful that Jesus has become the Lord of my life and that He has rendered my old personality, my old character, my old life, to be terminated. I likewise thank You that Christ didn't just slay my old man, but He has given me a new identity in Christ! Today I declare that I will step forward to embrace who Christ has made me to be and that I am free!

I pray this in Jesus' name!

MY CONFESSION FOR TODAY

I declare that the past has no power over me. In Christ, I have been made free from the power of sin and its impulses to do wrong. The law of the Spirit of life in Christ Jesus has set me free from the law of sin and death; therefore, sin shall not have any dominion over me. I reckon the fleshly nature dead. Therefore, I refuse to allow its impulses to find expression through my body. If the past tries to raise its voice and speak to me, calling out to beckon me to let it assert itself, I will silence it forcefully and vocally by declaring my allegiance to obey Romans 6:11. Christ has set me free, and I declare that I am free indeed! My freedom is not a feeling — it is a reality! I embrace and enforce the truth of the liberty Jesus died to provide for me!

I declare this by faith in Jesus' name!

QUESTIONS FOR YOU TO CONSIDER

1. Have you ever really deeply embraced the fact that Christ has liberated you completely from who you used to be? If you really believed that you were free from your past identity and old behaviors, how would that belief affect the way you are living right now?
2. Do you know any individuals who have recently come to the Lord, but they do not understand that they are new creatures in Christ? Have you taken the time to help them understand that Christ no longer recognizes who they used to be and that they are truly new in Jesus? If you were in their place, wouldn't you be grateful if someone took the time to explain that Good News to you?

FEBRUARY 28

Hoodwinked in the Last Days!

...Take heed that no man deceive you.
— Matthew 24:4

For those who have a listening ear to the Spirit of God, it is clear that we have entered into the very last part of the last days. As a result, recent decades have brought us face to face with difficult issues, whether we wanted to be confronted with them or not. According to Bible prophecy, things are only going to get more intense as the days pass, because we are living at the end of the age when Jesus, Paul, and Peter all prophesied that society as a whole would be deceived on a massive scale.

Jesus' disciples had specifically asked Him, "...What shall be the sign of thy coming, and of the end of the world?" (Matthew 24:3). In response to that specific question, Jesus identified a list of exact signs that would indicate the very end of the age and His imminent return. Jesus gave many signs, but the first sign Jesus told them about contained a clear warning of a *wide-scale deception* that would emerge in the last part of the last days — and the need for people to prepare and guard against it. Jesus said, "...Take heed that no man deceive you" (v. 4).

In the original Greek, the words "take heed" were intended to *jar* and *jolt* the disciples to get their attention. As they perked up to really listen to what Jesus was telling them, they heard Him warn that as the present age came to a conclusion, an unprecedented deception would attempt to encompass every part of society.

In Matthew 24:4, the word "deceive" is used to depict this period when it will look as if delusion is taking over the world. It is the Greek word *planao*, which means *to lead astray* or *to wander off course*. This word "deceive" could depict a *single individual* who has wandered far off-course, or it could describe a *whole nation* or *nations* that have morally veered from the position once held to be true.

Planao depicts a person (or nation) who, although once established on solid ground, is now morally drifting and teetering on the edge of a crooked, dangerous path. This individual has lost his bearings and has drifted off-track. He had already departed, or was in the process of departing, from what he once morally believed. He has begun going cross-grain against all that was once a part of his belief system.

In the years that lapsed between the Old and New Testaments, this same word "deceive" was often used to forecast a wide-scale deception that would one day envelope the earth. It was believed by scholars of that time that this deception would be a precursor to the glorious coming of the Messiah. Furthermore, it was widely held that a deception of this order could occur only as a result of the activity of evil spirits that would work intensely in the earth at the very end of the age. Scholars believed these dark powers would lead the world into deception *en masse*.

The apostle Paul also confirmed this long-forecasted deception. In Second Thessalonians 2, he described distinct events that would occur on the planet at the very end of the age and continue with greater aggression and intensity. He stated that the world's population would become so ensnared in deception that they would be controlled by a strong "delusion" (v. 11). The word "delusion" in Greek is *plane*, a form of *planao*, the same word used in Matthew 24:4. However, in Second Thessalonians 2:11, the Greek word was translated "delusion" instead of "deception." But the word *planao* nonetheless depicts a culture that has strayed so far that it has become *beguiled*, *bewitched*, *duped*, and *seduced* into believing a lie in place of the truth.

In Second Thessalonians 2:11, the Holy Spirit prophesied through Paul that society in the last days will become supernaturally *hoodwinked* — that is, it will be ensnared by an unparalleled period of deception on every front. This period of deceitfulness will be so intense that people will believe what is false over what is obviously true, even denying facts and truths that are common sense and that nature itself teaches (*see* Romans 1:20). This era of worldwide falsehood and deception will occur at the very end of this age and will continue into the time of the Great Tribulation. It will mark a time when wrong belief and delusion will pervade every realm of society. This is the clear teaching of prophetic Scripture about developments that will occur at the conclusion of this age.

Just look at the world around you today. Can you see deception at work? Watch the developments in the news. In a culture where moral standards bend so easily with the times, can you sense we have reached the tipping point where many are being deceived even now, not only in the United States, but also around the globe?

In Matthew 24:4, Jesus accurately foretold this worldwide deception on the earth in the last days and alerted His disciples that it would be a sign that His return was nigh. As we come closer and closer to the very last days of this age, we need to remember Christ's forewarning of a season in time in which deception would grip the entire world. From all the signs around us, it appears that we are *already there.*

This is why it is so important that we keep our minds soaked with the Word of God, which renews us to right thinking in a world that has morally slipped in a wrong direction. It is imperative that we put the Word into our hearts — keeping it before our eyes and hearing it with our ears. It's equally important to verbalize the truth of God's Word to ourselves and to other believers, thus strengthening the truth *in us* and *between us* in a day when truth is slipping away.

Today I sense it's my responsibility to ask you — what is your level of commitment to your Bible? Is it a lamp unto your feet and a light unto your path (Psalm 119:105)? Is it the joy and rejoicing of your heart (Jeremiah 15:16)?

Rather than become victims of the age and spiritual casualties in the Body of Christ, we can hold our Bibles dearer and closer to our hearts and minds than ever before. We can reinforce ourselves against the days in which we live *and* the days that are forecast as yet to come. So let's grab hold of the unalterable truths of God's Word, dig our heels deep into it, and decide that we will stand *firm* on the truth that never changes, regardless of how society around us changes in the days to come!

MY PRAYER FOR TODAY

Father, I see that the world is slipping into falsehood and delusion on so many fronts, just as You said it would in Matthew 24:4,5. Long-held moral truths are being reconsidered and changed; truths of the Bible are being discounted and laid aside; and it seems that this process is occurring at a faster and faster pace as we come to the close of this age. I ask You to give me the inner courage to stand fast on the Word of God — to embrace it, dig my heels into it, and not sway from the unalterable truths of Scripture, even if the world around me is slipping away from it. Help me to embrace the Bible tighter than ever before and to keep my thoughts in agreement with Your will, regardless of what is happening in the world around me.

I pray this in Jesus' name!

MY CONFESSION FOR TODAY

I declare that I am committed to the eternal, unchangeable truths of God's Word, regardless of what is happening in society all around me. The world may change what it believes and endorses, but not one word of God's truth ever changes. I declare that I will wrap my arms around the Word of God, embrace it, and dig my heels into it. I will never surrender my conviction to the truths of the Bible. Holy Spirit, I need Your power and inner fortitude to do this, so I am asking You to reinforce me, along with my other close Christian friends, so we stand by the truth and refuse to be bullied into lowering our standards of believing the deception that is at work in the world in these last days!

I declare this by faith in Jesus' name!

QUESTIONS FOR YOU TO CONSIDER

1. Do you know any believers who have slipped from their firm commitment to the eternal truths taught by the Bible? What has been your response to this slipping away? Have you prayed for them? Have you lovingly spoken to them about the direction they are taking?
2. Can you think of ways that the moral foundation in the world is changing — and how society is trying to push these changing morals on everyone? What would be one example that stands out in your mind?
3. What is your personal response to all of this? This is a question that you will definitely have to face in the days to come, so what is your answer right now? Are you going to be bullied or hoodwinked to change your view along with the rest of the world, or are you going to stand on the truth that never changes?

FEBRUARY 29

Be Thou Faithful Unto Death (Leap Year)

Fear none of those things which thou shalt suffer:
behold, the devil shall cast some of you into prison,
that ye may be tried; and ye shall have tribulation ten days:
be thou faithful unto death, and I will give thee a crown of life.
— Revelation 2:10

Today I want to speak to people who feel that they are facing circumstances that are beyond their control. That may even be *you*. If you are in the midst of a very difficult situation, hopelessness and fear may have tried to wrap its tentacles around you and drain you of the personal fortitude you need to stay in the battle. But I want to tell you the truth: Every person has faced something fearful at some point in his or her life. If you are feeling this way, I want to encourage you to stay faithful to the very end, because victory lies at the end of the battle you are facing right now.

It's so important to learn how to respond to a crisis, because the one you're facing right now is *not* the last one you're going to face in life. It's naïve to think that the devil is just going to lie down and watch you flow from one victory to the next. He does *not* want you to succeed at fulfilling the will of God for your life. You will always have another opportunity to be tested. That's why you have to make the decision before it happens that you are never going to quit, throw in the towel, or bend to circumstances. You are required to have a determined mindset that says, *It doesn't matter what happens to me or what the devil says. I am going to do what God called me to do.*

To be victorious we must *decide* that we will not budge in our commitment, regardless of the price that is to be paid. Any other attitude will lead to compromise, and compromise leads to failure, and failure leads to defeat. We must decide that we are committed to the end — even if, as Revelation 2:10 says, "the end" means that we must be "faithful unto death"!

We must not forget that many people in previous generations, as well as many people right now on this earth, are facing crushing circumstances every day that seem to be beyond their control. That was true of the believers in the church at Smyrna, one of the seven churches that Jesus addressed in Revelation 2 and 3. They were under a constant onslaught of persecution, and Christ was aware of the situation they were facing — just as He is aware of what *you* are facing today.

Jesus knew that the believers in Smyrna refused to throw in the towel and to surrender to the hostile forces that were arrayed against them. Aware of their steadfastness and the possible troubles that still awaited them, Christ urged them, "Fear none of those things which thou shalt suffer: behold, the devil shall cast some of you into prison, that ye may be tried; and ye shall have tribulation ten days: *be thou faithful unto death....*"

Christ did not give them a false hope. He saw what lay before them and warned them honestly that pressures against them were far from over. But in spite of the fact that they were facing more persecution, imprisonment, and possible death, Christ said, "Be thou faithful unto death...." Let's examine those words today and see what we can extract from them that will encourage us in our own challenging situations.

The words "be thou" are a translation of the Greek word *ginou*, a form of the word *ginomai*, which describes *a process of becoming*. Thus, the phrase "be thou faithful" could literally be interpreted *"become faithful"* or "*keep on becoming faithful.*" Thus, the idea conveyed in this verse could read, *"...Give it your best effort, putting all your energies into the goal of progressively becoming more and more faithful...."*

The word "faithful" is the Greek word *pistos*, which is the most common New Testament word for *faith*. It conveys the idea of people who are *faithful*, *reliable*, *loyal*, and *steadfast*. No matter what assails them or how hot the fires of persecution blaze, these believers were to remain unwavering in their commitment to Jesus Christ. Thus, Jesus was requiring His people to remain *devoted*, *trustworthy*, *dependable*, *dedicated*, *constant*, and *unwavering*, even in the face of the worst circumstances imaginable. Breaking their commitment to Him under the weight of external pressures, no matter how extreme, was not an acceptable option.

The word "unto" is *archi*, which means *unto, up to*, or *including*. In other words, these believers were *never* to renege on their commitment to Christ. This divine call to commitment — regardless of the price that had to be paid — was so serious that, if necessary, Christ expected them to be faithful *unto, up to*, or even *including* death itself.

A faith that remains steadfast only when times are good is unacceptable.

The Savior endured the Cross in order to experience His resurrection and exaltation — and now He calls on you and me to endure to the end. Just as the Holy Spirit enabled Jesus to run His race to the end, the Spirit of God will enable us to endure any affliction, hardship, pressure, problem, trial, or tribulation we encounter as we prove the authenticity and sincerity of our faith. When the battle is finished, like Christ, we will experience resurrection and exaltation!

We are called to pick up our cross and follow Jesus, regardless of the price we are required to pay. That may not be pleasant to consider, but it is a fact nonetheless. Scripture never teaches that we are to draw back from our faith when hardships approach. Rather, Jesus asks for our commitment and faithfulness, even unto the point of death, if that's what is required as a part of our journey in Him.

Believers who live in parts of the world that are hostile to the Christian faith understand this type of commitment very well. Those who have come to Christ in a non-hostile environment often don't comprehend the life-and-death type of commitment others have been required to make. Yet throughout the centuries of Church history, Christians have often given their very lives for what they believed. And this isn't just a past reality. It is a statistical fact that in the past century, more believers died for their faith than in all the previous centuries of accumulated Christian history combined. Believers have suffered "unto death" for Jesus' sake in the past, and they still are doing so today.

The word "death" in this verse is the Greek word *thanatos*, which is a word that is used more than 120 times in the New Testament. It describes *the physical state of death* or *extinction of life*. But in the New Testament, it also depicts *a mortal danger, a dangerous circumstance*, or *something that is fatal*. In the Roman legal system, it described *the death penalty*.

Jesus had already foretold the church of Smyrna that they would be falsely accused, thrown into prison, and intensely tested by the devil. In addition, He forewarned them in a most straightforward manner that mortal dangers were coming — and that for many who faithfully followed Christ, the danger would prove to be fatal. For these believers, a death penalty would be issued against them and carried out with great cruelty. Yet regardless of what they might have to endure, Christ urged them to "be faithful unto death."

Very few, if any, of those who ever read this *Sparkling Gem* will be required to make a commitment that requires their death. But regardless, that is the level of the actual commitment that

Jesus Christ is asking each one of us to make. If we make the commitment to be faithful to the end — regardless of the price that must be paid — being defeated will simply not be an option.

Oh, my friend, I want to remind you that God has great plans for you. So rather than look at your dire situation today and think that there is no way out, ask God to open your eyes to see the opportunity in the midst of the crisis. Every crisis holds opportunity. When the world screams and rails against you, it is temporary. If you push it all aside and endure to the end, you will receive the ultimate reward.

You and I must ask the Lord to help us see each situation as *He* sees it. When Jesus died, God didn't accept the thinking of the vast majority who said, "Jesus is dead. It's over. It's finished." Instead, God saw an opportunity for *resurrection*! Oh, that He would give us His eyes so we can see how He sees!

Your best days are not behind you — they are before you! But for you to reach a glorious conclusion, it requires a rock-solid decision on your part. From this moment on and for the rest of your life, you must choose to be "faithful unto death" to the One you call your Lord and Savior. You must set your eyes on Jesus, the Author and Finisher of your faith, and determine that you will never look back again. Every moment that you live and breathe is all for Him — to the very end of this life and on into the ages to come!

MY PRAYER FOR TODAY

Father, You are asking every believer for a higher level of commitment than we've ever made before. Today I understand that You are asking me personally for commitment of the highest magnitude — just as Jesus displayed a commitment of the highest magnitude to You, Father, in my behalf. Through that great sacrifice of Himself, I am now more than a conqueror through Him who loved me and washed me from sin in His own blood. Therefore, I do not fear death, but I joyfully commit my life unto You, Lord, knowing that I will not be able to be defeated because resurrection and exaltation await those who are faithful even unto death. So today I ask You to help me rise to a higher place of commitment so I can be faithful to the very end.

I pray this in Jesus' name!

MY CONFESSION FOR TODAY

I confess that I am committed to do what God has called me to do. Regardless of the forces that are arrayed against me, I will endure to the end and receive an eternal reward — a crown of life presented to the faithful who stand before the Lord on that day when we give an account of what we've done. I will not only be rewarded in Heaven so I can have a crown to lay at Christ's feet on that day, but also I will taste victory here on earth. My best days are not behind me — they are before me! I declare that I am committed to the very end.

Therefore, I reach a glorious conclusion because faith, confidence, and boldness arise in me! I fear no evil because the love of God in me and toward me drives out all fear!

I declare this by faith in Jesus' name!

QUESTIONS FOR YOU TO CONSIDER

1. Are you feeling tempted to fear right now? What are you doing to combat that spirit of fear and to command it to leave you? I encourage you to open your heart to someone who knows how to pray and to ask them to pray with you for courage and confidence.
2. What does remaining faithful "until the end" mean to you personally? Can you recall past experiences where you thought you wouldn't make it, but because you were committed to do what God asked you to do, you ended up seeing great victory in your life? What is the last time you experienced this? How many times have you seen obstacles move out of the way and victory move into place in your life?

MARCH 1

No Other Foundation!

For other foundation can no man lay
than that is laid, which is Jesus Christ.
— 1 Corinthians 3:11

In the late 1990s, our ministry set out to construct a large church building for our congregation in Riga, Latvia. One of the most important steps in this complex process was creating a foundation that could support the church building, and since the planned structure was massive, the foundation would have to be *immense.* This also meant it would be *very expensive*!

The land that our ministry had purchased for this church building was ideal in terms of its location, but the ground itself was composed of *peat moss*! Peat moss is a beautiful, rich, dark soil, but structurally, it is very unsound. In fact, if we had built on top of it, our building would have sunk down into the soil! So before we could start building our foundation, bulldozers had to come and remove that rich, dark soil.

Day after day, I watched as the crew dug deeper and deeper, trying to find hard ground beneath all that peat moss — until at long last they found hard soil *12 feet deep* in the earth! When it was all said and done, 12 feet of peat moss had to be removed from an area the size of a football field. Every day I went to the site to watch as dump trucks loaded with rich, dark peat moss drove away to dump that soil into the river!

When the huge depression for the foundation was finally dug, I climbed down into it and walked from one end to the other. I was so proud of that big hole in the ground! It alone had cost more money than any other project I had ever taken on in my life. However, once the soil was excavated, it was then time to fill the hole with copious amounts of sand and gravel so the concrete foundation could be poured.

Over the course of the next few months, the same dump trucks that had previously carried soil away returned to pour layers upon layers of sand and gravel into that big, expensive hole. Before long, that hole was history! By the time the hole was refilled with rock and sand, our church building had already cost a fortune!

The next step was to build the foundation for our church building. The workers built a wood frame around the perimeter of the building site and then laid steel to reinforce the concrete once it was poured. Once the frame was secure, the concrete trucks arrived and began pouring concrete. *That was such an exciting day!*

For weeks cement trucks churned sand, water, and cement into concrete, and the workers poured it onto the site. Because there wasn't a lot of sophisticated construction equipment in the former USSR at that time, everything had to be done by hand. The newly poured concrete had to be carefully smoothed by hand before it dried, and the laborers worked quickly and efficiently to complete each new section before moving on to the next. Everyone involved worked meticulously with an observant eye to ensure no mistakes were made in this important process.

Finally, the day came when all the trucks left, and I could examine our new foundation. At 306 feet long and 108 feet wide, that slab was *huge*! In fact, it was so big that it took several minutes for me to walk from one end to the other! Soon after, the crew arrived with their noisy grinding machines and literally ground the surface of that foundation until it was nearly as smooth as silk. Then it was time for the next phase — the construction of the building's steel frame!

However, before they put that steel frame in place, I would drive out to the site early each morning, walk around the foundation, and look at it in wonder. I would think about how it began as an abandoned field of peat moss, and then through a lengthy, elaborate, *expensive* process, it became our rock-solid foundation.

I loved that foundation! When we started to build it, our ministry didn't have the money needed to complete it. Day by day, I prayed and believed God for the money to dig that hole, buy the sand and rock, and purchase and pour the concrete. No one appreciated that foundation as much as I did because no one else knew what a miracle it was that we had been able to pay for it. That foundation had been built by faith. *It was my miracle foundation!*

When the church building was completed, it almost broke my heart when the carpet was laid over that foundation! So much work had gone into building that foundation, and the carpet would completely hide it. In fact, no one would ever even think of the foundation as they walked over it. Everyone who came into that building to worship God would never realize the fortune of sand, rock, and concrete that was beneath their feet, yet it was there whether or not they realized it. Although that foundation was no longer visible to anyone's sight, it was *essential* to keeping that building standing strong for many years to come.

Think about it — how often do you walk into a gorgeous building and say, "Wow, what an awesome foundation this building has!" *NEVER!* When you walk into a new building, you see carpet, tile, wallpaper, light fixtures, and other beautiful cosmetic work, but you don't see the foundation. You probably don't even think about the foundation! However, if the foundation isn't properly put in place, that building won't last very long. *The longevity of the whole building depends on the foundation.*

Building a foundation is a hard, elaborate, lengthy, expensive process, but it is *extremely important.* In First Corinthians 3:11, the apostle Paul wrote about the spiritual foundation he had laid in the church of Corinth. He said, "For other foundation can no man lay than that is laid, which is Jesus Christ."

The word "foundation" that Paul used in this verse is the Greek word *themelios,* a compound of the words *lithos* and *tithemi.* The word *lithos* is Greek for *stone,* and *tithemi* means *to lay something down.* When these words are compounded, they form the word *themelios,* which describes *a foundation set in stone that is strong, stable, and enduring.*

In addition to describing a physical foundation, the word *themelios* was also used metaphorically to denote the *laying of a moral, theological, or educational foundation in a person's life.* These figurative foundations, just like an actual physical foundation of a building, are all built with enormous effort, intense concentration, and great expense.

When the apostle Paul first entered Corinth, the city was utterly consumed with idolatry and heathenism. In fact, it is no exaggeration to say that Corinth was one of the most wicked, perverted cities on the face of the earth at that time. Therefore, for Paul to establish a church in that evil environment, he had to push like a spiritual bulldozer in the Spirit to shove those demonic powers out of the way. Once the spiritual rubbish had been cleared from his path, he then preached the Word in order to establish a firm foundation under the feet of these newly saved Corinthians. Paul' s enormous effort and intense focus produced a foundation under them that would withstand any attack of the enemy — including horrific persecution — and would last for generations!

Whenever Paul left a congregation to establish a church in a new region, a new pastor would follow in his stead to build on top of his work. However, every spiritual foundation that the apostle set beneath a church was rock-solid and needed no improvements. That is why he confidently stated to the Corinthians, "For other foundation can no man lay than that is laid, which is Jesus Christ" (1 Corinthians 3:11).

Because of Paul's hard work, the church in Corinth was set on a firm spiritual foundation that enabled it to become one of the most influential congregations of the Early Church. Although other spiritual leaders followed Paul and contributed their part, a large part of the fruit produced in the Corinthian church can be directly attributed to the talents, energy, and gifts Paul used to establish the foundation for that congregation.

With this in mind, first take a moment to evaluate your own spiritual foundation with the help of the Holy Spirit. Are there any gaps that need to be filled in? Are there "swampy" areas in your mindsets and beliefs that need to be dug out and filled in with solid, Word-based soil? Ask the Lord for wisdom, and the Spirit of God will be faithful to give you all that you need to make sure your foundation is deep, wide, and bedrock-solid so you can build your life high and wide and strong in Him!

Then as you reflect on your life, see if you can think of a person or people who helped build a godly foundation in your life, such as a family member, a friend, a teacher, or a pastor. At the time these individuals were pouring themselves into your life, you might not have even realized the significance of their actions. However, as you look back on all they did, aren't you grateful for the time and energy they invested in you in order to build a firm foundation in your life?

When I think back on all the people Denise and I have poured ourselves into over the years, it makes me realize how much it means to us when they come back to say thank you for what we did for them. Those expressions of thanks mean so much! Although it is not demanded or expected, it is a wonderful reward to hear that we have touched people's lives and that our actions helped them get established on a firm foundation.

Have you taken time to thank people for the sacrifices they made to do this very thing for you? For those who invested themselves in you, I recommend that you take time to do something special to express your heartfelt thanksgiving for how they helped you in a pivotal moment of your life.

Never forget that the longevity of a building greatly depends on the foundation. Although laying a spiritual foundation is a hard, elaborate, lengthy process that can come at great cost, it is nevertheless *extremely important.* If a godly foundation is laid correctly, a person's life will be well supported, and he will be able to pass the test of time. On the other hand, if a foundation under a person's life is built too hastily or on shifting soil, that person will not have a firm footing as he proceeds forward in his spiritual walk.

As a closing thought, I encourage you to remember Jesus' exhortation: "Freely ye have received, freely give" (Matthew 10:8). This means that you should actively seek to build up the spiritual foundation of other people, just as others took the time to help strengthen *your* foundation. Do everything you can to help build strong foundations in the lives of those around you, even as you ensure that your own foundation is built strong and sure to hold the full weight of all that God has destined you to be!

MY PRAYER FOR TODAY

Lord, I want to thank You for loving me so much that You placed people in my life to help build a solid foundation underneath me. Because of what they invested in me, my life is set on a firm foundation. I am so thankful for everything that was graciously done on my behalf! Please help me fortify my own foundation in every area that might need shoring up or strengthening. And I ask that You open my eyes to people around me who need the same kindness and care shown to them. Your Word says "freely ye have received, freely give," so I know I have a responsibility to give of myself as others gave to me. I want to be a positive influence in someone else's life, so I ask You, Holy Spirit, to show me how to be the same kind of blessing that others have been to me.

I pray this in Jesus' name!

MY CONFESSION FOR TODAY

I confess that I have a strong foundation in God, firmly based on the truth of His Word. And I allow Him to use me to positively influence other people's lives. I have gifts, talents, abilities, and experience that will help put others on a firm foundation for life. Rather than keep those gifts, talents, abilities and life experiences to myself, I allow God to use these to help other people get started on a firm foundation. Because I allow the Holy Spirit to use me, I am a great blessing to people who are around me. God works through me, and other people's lives are benefited because I am willing to invest myself in them and in their future.

I declare this by faith in Jesus' name!

QUESTIONS FOR YOU TO CONSIDER

1. Who helped establish a foundation underneath your life? As you look back on your life and recall all that those individuals did to help you in your life and career, are you deeply thankful for their great investment of time and energy to ensure that your life or career was established on a firm foundation?
2. Have you taken time to thank those people for the sacrifices they made for you? I recommend that you take a few minutes today to write them, to call them, or to do something special to express a heart-felt thanksgiving for what they invested in you at a pivotal moment in life!
3. Who are you investing yourself in today? If God cared enough for you to send a person into your life that would help you get a firm footing in life, then don't you think it is right that you should do this for someone else? *Who are you helping in life?*

Never forget that the longevity of a building greatly depends on the foundation.

MARCH 2

On What Basis Will You Be Rewarded?

If any man's work abide which he hath built thereupon,
he shall receive a reward.
— 1 Corinthians 3:14

It is a fact that one day we will all stand before Jesus. On that day, each of us will give account for what we did with our lives. We'll answer to Him for what we did, what we didn't do, and what we should have done with our lives. On that day, there will be no hiding or twisting of facts. Hebrews 4:13 (*NIV*) says, "Nothing in all creation is hidden from God's sight. Everything is uncovered and laid bare before the eyes of him to whom we must give account." Make no mistake — Jesus sees it all! One day He will deal with us, and we will give an account. So if we're smart, we will ask and discover the answer to the question: *On what basis will you and I be rewarded when we get to Heaven?*

Today I want us to look at a very important verse in which the apostle Paul answered that question for us. In First Corinthians 3:14, Paul wrote, "If any man's work abides which he hath built thereupon, he shall receive a reward."

Notice that Paul said, "If any man's work *abide*...." What does the word "abide" mean? It comes from the Greek word *meno*, which means *to stay*, *to remain*, *to continue*, or *to permanently abide*. It gives the idea of something that *lasts, remains, persists*, or *endures*. It speaks of something that has *lasting power*. Implied in this word "abide" is the idea that tests will come in life that will try our works.

It is just a fact that tests come in life. Many wrongly assume that God is the source of all such tests, but I assure you that life by itself will send many tests your way. Your relationships, your job, your finances — all of these will be *tested* along the path of life, and God's participation is not needed to make these tests happen. They are just part of the package of life. But in addition to this, the devil will try to test your works. If he can find a way to do it, the enemy will pry his way into as many of your affairs as possible. He would love to set fire to your relationships, your job, your finances, or anything else that you hold dear.

So be assured that between life and the devil, you *will* encounter fiery tests in the course of your life. I'm not prophesying bad news to you; rather, I'm endeavoring to equip you to build your life right so you can withstand every test, regardless of its source. If you have built your works right, you and your works will pass the test. But if you have built works made of *wood*, *hay*, or *stubble* (*see* 1 Corinthians 3:12), one of these tests will ignite them like a match set to hay!

The good news is that even if your works fail and are consumed before your eyes, underneath you is a foundation that is *immovable*! In First Corinthians 3:11, Paul said, "For other foundation can no man lay than that is laid, which is Jesus Christ." Jesus is your Foundation! As we saw in yesterday's *Sparkling Gem*, the word "foundation" in this verse is from the Greek word *themelios*. It is a compound of the words *lithos*, the Greek word for *stone*, and the word *tithemi*, which means *to lay something down*, like the laying of a foundation. This describes *a foundation set in stone* and thus a foundation that is *strong*, *stable*, and *enduring*. Even if everything else burns, your foundation will remain intact!

But who wants to lose everything in the end? There will be no special rewards for works that burn! In fact, Paul says we will only be rewarded for works that "abide." If only works that survive will merit a reward, we must be very careful in the way we build our works.

So let me ask you: How are you building your life, your relationships, your children, your job, your ministry, and so on? Paul says, "If any man's work abides which he hath *built thereupon*...." The words "built thereupon" are from the Greek word *epoikodomeo*, which is a compound of the words *epi* and *oikodomeo*. The word *epi* means *upon*, and the word *oikodomeo* is a word borrowed from the world of construction. It means *to build* or *to construct*. When these two words are compounded as in this verse, the new word means *to build on top* of something.

The apostle Paul was alerting us to the fact that once the foundation of Jesus Christ is laid in our lives, it is our responsibility *to build on top* of that foundation. This foundation cannot be improved upon, but what is built on top of it depends on *us*. We can build *marvelous structures* that endure the test of time, or we can build *shacks* that crumble and eventually go up in a puff of smoke. What is built on top of the foundation depends on *us*.

When the fires of life come — and they *will* come — those fires will reveal the quality of what we have built. Works that were built wrong will burn, and works that were built right will endure. And Paul assured us that we will be rewarded only for the works that abide. Man measures man's success by activity and earthly achievement, but God measures success by how well we built our works and by the longevity of our works. As impressive as works may be at the moment, if they don't pass the test of time, they will not merit a reward. That is why the Bible declares, "If any man's work *abides* which he hath built thereupon, he shall receive a reward."

The words "shall receive" point to a *future moment* when each of us will stand before Jesus. At that moment, the books will be opened, and Jesus will carefully examine our lives. He will look to see if our works survived or if they failed in the fires of life. By looking at His ledger, He will know if we built our lives thoughtfully in a manner that brought honor to His name or if we built shacks on top of the glorious foundation He established under us through the riches of our spiritual inheritance in Him.

If our works were built right and endured the tests of life, Paul says we will receive a "reward." The word "reward" is the Greek word *misthos*, an old Greek word that denotes *pay, salary*, or *reward*. In other words, Jesus will make sure you are *well-compensated* and *rewarded* for all of your works that were built right! When you stand before Him and He sees that your life and works survived every test, you will receive *full remuneration* for every sacrifice you made. Because you built your life and works correctly, you'll get a *bonus* that will last for all of eternity!

This verse could be taken to mean:

> *"Every person is set on a rock-solid foundation, but what he builds on top of it is his responsibility. If he has constructed his life and works so well that they remain after all the fires of life have come and gone, this is what will merit him a reward in the future."*

What a shocking insight this is! It means that as important as we think our activities are, God's measuring stick by which He determines rewards is not determined by how busy or active we are in life. His measuring stick is how well we accomplished our activities according to His instruction and whether or not our actions were built to survive the fires of life. Why would God reward us for anything we built that ultimately went up in a puff of smoke because of our shoddy workmanship or because our building materials were mixed with wrong motives and "good ideas" that were not "*God's* ideas"? He is looking for *obedience, excellence, permanence,* and *durability*. These are the qualities that give Him glory.

Take a moment to look at your life today. What can you ascertain about your future reward based on the character of your actions? Have you built your life and works in a way that gives glory to Jesus? Jesus Christ is your glorious Foundation, but what have you built on top of that foundation? Have you constructed something marvelous that honors Him and gives Him glory, or have you built your life and works so fast and cheap that they can't endure the many tests of life?

Since we will be rewarded only for what "abides," we must ask the Holy Spirit to help us take an honest look at our lives to see what has been built right and what has been built wrong. It's never too late to start doing it right. If you've built your life and works on such a solid foundation that it can pass any test, then rejoice! But if you know that your works aren't built to survive, now is the time for you to let the Spirit of God help you start all over again!

If your works have already burned, this is very regretful. But the good news is your foundation is still in place. The foundation of Jesus Christ in your life is immovable! Because you still have Him as your Foundation in your life, with God's help you can start building your life and works again. *Ask the Holy Spirit to help you, and He'll show you how to build better this time!*

MY PRAYER FOR TODAY

Father, I thank You for speaking to me today through what I just read. Now I understand that You are looking for excellence, permanence, and durability in my life. Forgive me for thinking that You would reward me only for being active and busy. Now I understand that You want quality from my life, not just quantity. You are looking for more than a lot of works – You are looking for works that remain! From this moment onward, I ask You to help me constantly take an honest appraisal of what I am doing and what I am building to make sure that I am investing myself wisely into works that will endure the tests of life. I want You to be pleased the day I look into Your eyes, so I am asking You to help me carefully measure my works and to make sure that I am living and building my life in a way that will merit a reward.

I pray this in Jesus' name!

MY CONFESSION FOR TODAY

I confess that the Holy Spirit is helping me to build my life and works so strong that they will resist any test that comes in life. I am living by the Word of God, listening to the voice of the Holy Spirit and obeying God's commands. As I walk in obedience to the Word of God and build my life on this solid foundation, I can rest assured that what I am building will pass the test of time. I am committed to living a life of excellence, to building my life for permanence, and to bringing glory to the name of Jesus Christ in all that I do.

I declare this by faith in Jesus' name!

QUESTIONS FOR YOU TO CONSIDER

1. As you look at your life, can you see areas of your life that because you built too quickly and too cheaply, they therefore didn't last very long? What were those areas, and what did you learn from these experiences?
2. As you look forward to the rest of your life, how are you constructing your life and works right now? What steps and actions are you taking now that are different from what you did in the past to assure that your works will abide?
3. If you saw someone else building their works in a way that wouldn't resist a fiery test, what would you tell them to do differently in order to prevent a painful loss? Can you think of such a person that you know right now? Pray that you or someone else will have an opportunity to speak the truth to them in order to help them avoid a catastrophe later in life.

MARCH 3

The Smell of Smoke!

If any man's work shall be burned, he shall suffer loss:
but he himself shall be saved; yet so as by fire.
— 1 Corinthians 3:15

I'll never forget the day as a boy that I accidentally set our kitchen *on fire*! I had wanted to surprise my parents by cooking a wonderful meal for our family. I'd planned to set it on the table and have it ready for them when they arrived home from work. I cooked the corn, the green beans, and the biscuits — and, finally, it was time to fry the hamburger meat.

Because time was running out, I decided to turn up the fire so the meat would cook faster. The oil in the bottom of the pan grew so hot that it began to spit into the air. I jumped back to avoid being struck by it, but knew I had to do something quick because that hot oil was splattering all over the stove top and creating a huge mess. I reached to turn the fire down, but just as I did, the hamburger meat in the frying pan burst into flames! And when the fire on the meat burned down to the oil in the pan, the oil *exploded* into fire. My well-prepared hamburger patties were being *cremated* right before my eyes!

I reached for a pitcher of water and threw it on the flames to put the fire out. When I did, the hot, burning oil *detonated* like a bomb! An explosion of fire surged into the air. Red-hot embers of flaming hamburger exploded in front of me like lava spewing forth from a volcanic eruption. I watched as those burning embers sailed into my mother's beautiful curtains that hung above the kitchen sink and engulfed them in flames. I was so completely stunned by what was happening that I stood motionless. I watched in shock as the fire *consumed* my mother's delicate curtains.

Soon the tips of the flames reached upward and curled around the kitchen ceiling and cabinets. Smoke began to fill the room. The air became so smoke-filled that it began to hurt my eyes. That is when it dawned on me that I better act fast because I had a serious situation on my hands. So much happened so quickly that I don't recall how the fire was extinguished. By the time my parents arrived home, the fire was gone. But instead of surprising them with a wonderful meal, they came home to a kitchen that was severely burned by a fire started with *hamburgers*!

The fire was gone, but the smell of smoke lingered for days. That acrid smell was in our clothes; it was in the walls; and it hung in the air. However, as bad as those cabinets looked, the damage was primarily cosmetic. With the aid of sandpaper, an electric sander, and a lot of hard work, my father put those burnt cabinets back in shape again. When he finished, no one could ever tell that there had been an inferno of flaming hamburger in our kitchen!

In First Corinthians 3:15, the apostle Paul wrote about the loss that can be created by fire. He wrote, "If any man's work shall be burned, he shall suffer loss: but he himself shall be saved; yet so as by fire."

The word "burned" in Greek is *katakaio* — a compound of *kata*, meaning *down*, and *kaio*, meaning *to burn*. When compounded, the resulting word means *to burn down*, such as a building that burns all the way to the ground. In other words, this is no small fire. This is a fire that completely devours a building so that nothing remains but the foundation. Normally we would say a building *burned up*, but in actuality the word *katakaio* in this verse means *to burn down* until nothing remains *but the foundation*.

Such a consuming fire would be a great loss! That is why Paul went on to say, "If any man's work shall be burned, he shall suffer loss…." The word "loss" is from the word *zemia,* which means *to suffer loss*, *to experience damage*, or *to forfeit one's reward*. This word pictures great injury, harm, and loss of property. It is the sad image of a man standing in the burned-down, charred remains of his house or building — but in this case, he is standing in the midst of his works that are now *burnt to a crisp*! Now nothing remains but a pile of rubble. After all his years of living and doing, everything went up in smoke, and now he has nothing to show for his life or works!

But Paul gave us this good news: "...But he himself shall be saved; yet so as by fire." Even though this person's works have burned, he is still saved himself. His works have been lost, but not his salvation.

Although it's good news that this person is still saved and headed to Heaven, Paul tells us that he is saved "yet so as by fire." The phrase "yet so as by fire" comes from the Greek words *dia puri*. The word *dia* means *through*, and the word *puri* is the word for *fire*. When these words are used together as in this verse, most commentators agree that the Greek phrase means, "...He shall be saved, but like one who is escaping through the flames." Or it could even be translated, *"...He is saved, but he has the smell of smoke on his clothes."*

We should always be so thankful that God's grace covers our sin, our mistakes, and the things we have built wrongly in our lives. But who wants to look into the face of Jesus and say, "Lord, I made it, but everything I did in my life went up in a puff of smoke"?

God has so much planned for us, and if we will listen to the Holy Spirit and build our lives and works wisely, our works will endure any fire that comes to test them. Then when we stand before Jesus, we will joyfully look into His eyes! Isn't that better than having the smell of smoke on your clothes because your works were built so shabbily that they were burned in the fire and lost?

At the beginning of this *Sparkling Gem*, I gave the example of the kitchen I nearly burned to the ground. When the fire went out, there was smoke in the walls and the carpet, and the smell of smoke hung in the air for days and weeks. But rather than gaze on the mess in a state of despair, my father took his sandpaper and sander and went to work to put those kitchen cabinets back into good shape again.

If you can see that much of what you have built in the past has already burned up, of course you should *repent* for building your works wrongly in the first place. But wallowing in unending remorse won't help you make any changes in your life. Never forget that God is on your side and He is just as sorry about your losses as you are!

Today I urge you to grab hold of the Holy Spirit's power and begin to rebuild your works — and build them correctly this time. There is nothing you can do about the past except repent for what you did wrong. However, you *can* do something about the present and the future! Make the decision that from this moment onward, you are going to build your works right. *I know that you don't want to show up in Heaven with only the smell of smoke to show for your life. So ask the Holy Spirit to help you begin building works that will survive every test and bring a testimony of Jesus for eternity to the glory of God!*

MY PRAYER FOR TODAY

Lord, I thank You for speaking to my heart today about what I am building with my life. I must admit that a lot of what I've done has already gone up in smoke. Yes, I know that I'm saved and headed to Heaven one day when I die, but when I see You face to face, I want to have something to show for my life. I don't want to have only the smell of smoke to show for the years You have given me here on planet earth. I repent and ask You to please forgive me for what I've built too hastily and wrongly in the past. Holy Spirit, I ask You to help me build my works correctly this time!

I pray this in Jesus' name!

MY CONFESSION FOR TODAY

I declare by faith that I am cautious in the way that I build my life, my works, my relationships, my business, my ministry, and my family. One day I will stand before Jesus, and on that day I will give account for my life. Because I am aware of that day, I live my life circumspectly and am very thoughtful and careful in the way I construct my life. Because the Holy Spirit guides me and I listen to Him, I build works that abide!

I declare this by faith in Jesus' name!

QUESTIONS FOR YOU TO CONSIDER

1. Can you think of past areas in your life that went up in a puff of smoke because you didn't build them right in the right place? What were those areas of your life?
2. What did you learn from that experience? Did you just feel sorry and regretful that you lost so much, or did you allow the Holy Spirit to teach you from that experience?
3. Are there areas of your life that the Holy Spirit is trying to correct right now so that they will not go up in a puff of smoke later in life? Are you listening to the pleading of the Spirit? What areas are you most concerned about right now?

MARCH 4

There's No Excuse for an Attitude of Spiritual Superiority!

For who maketh thee to differ from another? and what has thou
that thou didst not receive? now if thou didst receive it,
why dost thou glory, as if thou hadst not received it?
— 1 Corinthians 4:7

In the January 17 *Sparkling Gem*, I wrote about the feeling of inferiority that once tried to rule my life. If you are struggling with inferiority, I encourage you to go back and read that teaching again. However, today I want to address an issue at the opposite end of the spectrum — a spirit of *superiority*. When a person has this attitude, he feels he is spiritually superior to other people because of giftings, experience, social or economic status, or position in the church. But regardless of the reason a person feels superior to others, make no mistake — this attitude is absolutely unacceptable for a Christian.

In First Corinthians 4:7, we find that an attitude of spiritual snobbery was beginning to surface in the church of Corinth. This spirit of superiority was so prevalent that it had begun to permeate the entire Corinthian congregation. Paul responded with a sharp rebuke, saying, "For who maketh thee to differ from another? and what has thou that thou didst not receive? Now if thou didst receive it, why dost thou glory, as if thou hadst not received it?"

From its very beginnings, the church at Corinth had experienced an amazing amount of supernatural grace, which had manifested in a variety of ways. However, one way it had *especially* manifested was in the gifts of the Spirit that operated in their congregation. In fact, Paul even told them, "So that ye come behind in no spiritual gift..." (1 Corinthians 1:7), implying that the Corinthians had a greater measure of spiritual gifts operating in their midst than any other New Testament church. The phrase "come behind" is a translation of the Greek word *hustereo*, which means *to be behind, to fall short of,* or *to be inferior*. Thus, this verse could be translated, *"You fall behind no one else in respect to spiritual gifts..."* or *"You are not inferior to anyone when it comes to spiritual gifts...."* In modern language, it could read, *"When it comes to the gifts of the Spirit, you are second to none!"*

The Corinthian believers were aware of their unique status as a congregation, and they allowed it to go to their heads. Essentially, they developed a superiority complex and a snobbish attitude concerning their spirituality as compared to other churches. That is why Paul reminded them in First Corinthians 4:7, "...What hast thou that thou didst not receive? Now if thou didst receive it, why dost thou glory, as if thou hadst not received it?"

When Paul wrote "...why dost thou glory...," he was referring to believers in Corinth who were boasting of themselves and putting others down who didn't share their same spiritual experiences. In Greek, this word "glory" is *kauchaomai*, which means *to boast of oneself, to uplift yourself, to imply that you are better than others*, or *to speak so highly of yourself that you derogatorily imply others are less than you.* It can simply be translated *to vaunt*, and it conveys a *pride* that says, "I am better than you." It is the very word that Paul used in First Corinthians 13:4 when he said, "Charity [that is, *agape* love] *vaunteth* not itself..." (*see* September 11 in *Sparkling Gems 1*). In other words, people who are motivated by love do *not* go around boasting about themselves in a way that leaves others feeling inferior!

It is important to note that the problem in the church of Corinth did not stem from the gifts of the Spirit. The gifts of the Spirit don't foster pride. The problem was the character of the Corinthian believers, which needed to be dealt with by God!

Paul's rebuke to the Corinthian believers tells us that we have no right to be prideful about our spiritual experiences. When you and I have been blessed by God with an extraordinary supernatural experience or knowledge of spiritual matters that exceeds that of many others, we should strive to demonstrate humility. We must not carry ourselves with an air of superiority, thinking we are better than others because they haven't had our experience or attained to our level of knowledge. We must remember that everything we have, we received from God. We did nothing on our own, so we really have no reason to gloat about it as though we did! If we've really received something special from God, we need to show only humble gratitude for His gift.

Have you ever known a person who was snobbish toward other believers because of his great spiritual experiences or spiritual knowledge? To me personally, it's a huge turn-off. The root of that superior attitude isn't what the Holy Spirit has done in him; rather, it's just a sign that He needs to do *more* in him!

So don't get offended if you know someone like this. Just pray for that person — and pray for yourself, too, so that you never fall into the trap of acting like you're better than others!

MY PRAYER FOR TODAY

Father, spiritual snobbery is a big turn-off. I ask You to help me look inward to discern if I have even the smallest hint of this in me. Lord, if anything like that exists in me, please show me, and begin the process to remove it from me! You resist the proud but give grace to the humble. Right now I humble my heart before You and I thank You for doing a work in my heart to remove any thought or attitude that does not please You or reflect Your holy ways.

I pray this in Jesus' name!

MY CONFESSION FOR TODAY

I confess that I am thankful for every spiritual experience I've had with the Lord. I am grateful for the knowledge God has blessed me to attain. But I realize that I have so much further to go and so much more to learn. I don't think I've arrived, and I know there is so much more to reach for in God. Therefore, I choose to put my eyes on the adjustments I need to make, and I embrace God's grace to change me. And if I've carried bad attitudes about spiritually snobbish people, today I release those attitudes and those people from my judgment. They belong to the Lord, and they are not mine to judge!

I declare this by faith in Jesus' name!

QUESTIONS FOR YOU TO CONSIDER

1. Can you think of a person who was spiritually snobbish toward you? How did it affect you and others?
2. Have you ever been guilty of thinking of yourself as better than people who haven't had your same experience? When you talk to others, do you make them desire your experience, or do you put them off because they feel put down by the way you talk to them?
3. As a thought exercise, why don't you take a moment to think about the people you've thought were spiritually snooty and try to figure out what it is they do

that makes you feel uncomfortable in their presence? Once you think it through, ask yourself if there is anyone to whom you've acted in a similar manner, and if so, ascertain what you need to correct so that people never feel that way in your presence again.

MARCH 5

You Are Salt!

Ye are the salt of the earth....
— Matthew 5:13

In the verse above, Jesus taught that we are to be *the salt of the earth.* Considering the various uses of salt in the ancient world and how important salt was in that time, this statement carried great weight. When He likened His listeners to salt, all kinds of images flashed through their minds, and they understood the many connotations that salt carried with it. By using this illustration of salt, Jesus was teaching about the *influence* that we are supposed to have upon the world in which we live.

The word "salt" in Greek is the word *halas*, and it describes *salt* exactly like the salt we use in our homes and kitchens today. Today salt is so common that it can easily be purchased in any grocery store. But in New Testament times, salt was an expensive and treasured commodity that was crucial and needed in many spheres of life, as you will see in today's *Sparkling Gem.*

High-quality salt could only be found in a few places in Israel. One location was the Hill of Salt, a seven-mile stretch located on the southwest coast of the Dead Sea. Salt could also be collected from the marshes situated along the embankment of the Dead Sea, or it could be gathered from salt pits near the Dead Sea. In each of these locations, the gathering of salt was an expensive process, which made the salt very costly. It was a commodity so rare that it was seldom wasted, sparingly used, and highly valued.

Salt was used as a preservative.

Especially in the warm temperatures of Israel, meat would quickly rot, spoil, and decay. But when salt was added, it acted as a *preservative.* Therefore, salt was very important in the preservation of meats and other kinds of perishable foods.

Those who heard Jesus' teaching that we are to be "the salt of the earth" therefore understood that He meant that through our *influence*, we should be a *preserving force* in a world that is filled with rot, spoil, and decay. God's Word working in our lives causes us to be like salt, and our very presence helps abate the corruption that is eating away at the world.

Salt was used as a flavor enhancer.

Salt is one of the most profound enhancers of taste that exists in the culinary world. An eater quickly becomes aware of how powerful this flavor enhancer is when he eats food that contains no salt. Unsalted food is often monotonous, bland, and uninteresting, but when salt is added, the flavor is ignited. Just like today, salt was used in the ancient world to give food a stronger and richer flavor. It was considered *essential* for the long-term preservation of food and for the enhancement of taste. Therefore, it was vital in every kitchen.

This tells us that not only should our presence abate the evil in the world, but our presence should also *change the flavor* of society as we bring the savor of Christ to our surroundings wherever we go.

In light of this, let me ask you: In what ways does your personal presence make a difference in your world? *Are you doing your job as the salt of the earth?*

Salt was used as an antiseptic.

In the ancient world where dirt and disease were common enemies to health, salt was used as an *antiseptic.* Especially in areas considered unclean, tainted, or contaminated — areas so filthy that it could potentially become hazardous to one's health — it was believed that salt would work like a disinfectant. If properly applied in heavy doses, salt sanitized, hygienically cleansed, and made a location relatively germ-free. The application of salt in such circumstances was considered to be enormously advantageous because people believed such an application of salt sterilized non-sterile environments.

If a rapidly spreading disease was known to exist in a village, the sick people were cleared out and relocated, and salt was immediately spread to disinfect the contaminated area and to prevent the further spread of disease. Salt was such a powerful cleansing force that the ancient world believed it would assist in freeing the environment of infection.

As an antiseptic, salt was used in the fodder of barns and barnyards — places where sickness and disease could swiftly spread among animals. A small dose of salt scattered on the fodder of a barn or barnyard served as a deterrent to the proliferation of sickness and disease among animals.

Therefore, when Jesus said we are to be "the salt of the earth," those who heard Him understood that through our *influence*, we are called to be a kind of *spiritual antiseptic* to a world that is diseased with sin. Even a small dose of the spiritual salt we carry within ourselves is such a powerful disinfecting agent that if scattered in society, it will help deter the spread of sin and moral decay.

You see, if you are doing your job as "the salt of the earth," your very presence can hinder the proliferation of sin and its effects. So when you look at your life and the things that surround you, do you see any evidence that your personal presence is making a difference and that you are helping to promote a more spiritually sanitized environment? *Are you doing your job as the salt of the earth?*

Salt was used as a medicinal and healing agent.

Salt was also a very important ingredient for physicians and those employed in the field of medicine, for they used salt as a *healing agent.* For instance, if a person was severely wounded, salt was poured into the wound to sanitize the wound from germs, to stop the spread of infection, to stop the bleeding, and to speed up the healing of the wound. It is a fact that salt has healing properties that cause wounds to heal more readily.

In the ancient world where medications were rare, salt was an indispensable product in every doctor's medical bag, and it was especially valuable in cases where there was an open wound. In every home, business, and public place, salt was kept close at hand in case it was needed for the treatment of an open wound or sore. It was always kept nearby for emergency treatments.

When Jesus said that His people were to be "the salt of the earth," those who heard Him understood that through our *influence*, we should be *carriers of physical healing* to a world that is suffering with all manner of sickness and ailments. Through the preaching of God's Word and personal ministry to those who are physically ill, we are supposed to be "the salt of the earth" that brings healing to those who are physically suffering. The fact is, the power of the Holy Spirit that we carry within ourselves is fully sufficient to administer physical healing to those afflicted with sickness and disease — always, of course, in the authority given to us in the Name of Jesus!

As "the salt of the earth," you are a vehicle God has chosen to carry healing power to those who are struggling physically. When you look around you, is there evidence to show that you are carrying this power to those who are physically infirm or challenged in some way, just as Jesus has asked you to do? *Are you doing your job as the salt of the earth?*

Salt was used to give protection from and to drive away evil spirits.

In the ancient world, salt was also a very important ingredient used in pagan religious rituals *to give protection from and to drive away evil spirits.* At the time Jesus said we are to be "the salt of the earth," Israel was subject to Rome, and because of this, they regularly witnessed the pagan practices of Roman religions. One practice of the Romans and other pagan religions of the time was rubbing salt over a newborn baby in order to protect that child from evil spirits or to drive evil spirits away from that child. It was commonly believed in many pagan nations that salt had magical powers to protect one from evil and to drive away evil spirits.

The Romans and other pagans believed so wholeheartedly in the magical, protective powers of salt that they regularly administered heavy quantities of salt to the thresholds of their homes and businesses, believing it would create a strong barrier that evil spirits could not cross. They also spread salt on their windowsills, believing that salt could keep evil spirits from entering their homes or places of business through the windows.

So those who heard Jesus say that Christians were to be "the salt of the earth" understood that through our *influence*, we are to be *a source of spiritual protection, deliverance, safety, and freedom* to people who have been assaulted by demonic powers. By using Jesus' name and spreading God's

Word, we can create spiritual barriers so strong that Satan is unable to successfully attack those standing on God's promises. *We are to be carriers of protection, safety, and deliverance!*

When you look around at the people who are near you, do you see that they are spiritually protected, experiencing deliverance, safety, and freedom from the attacks of the enemy? *Are their lives different, safer, and better because of you?*

Salt was used as a fertilizer.

Salt was also a very important ingredient used by farmers to enrich and fertilize their soil in order to produce larger crops of a higher quality. Even a small amount of salt scattered sparingly on the ground could improve the quality of the soil and result in bigger harvests and healthier crops. Therefore, it was viewed as an essential ingredient in the farming industry. The best salt nourished and stimulated the earth to produce better crops.

When Jesus said we were to be "the salt of the earth," it could actually be translated "the salt of the soil." The implication is that through our *influence*, we should affect the world in which we live. In other words, our very presence should enhance life and make this world a better place to live. The world we touch should become productive and our godly presence should positively impact the quality of life for those around us. *That is how much power we have as believers!*

So as the "salt of the earth," we are to enrich the atmosphere wherever we go through our *influence*, simply because we carry the life of God within us. As carriers of His presence, we make life better for those around us. When we walk into a situation, the environment surrounding us is filled with more peace, joy, and hope than it was before we arrived! As the salt of the earth, we have the power to make a difference everywhere we are scattered.

Are you making a difference in every place where you find yourself?

In Colossians 4:6, the apostle Paul also used the word "salt" to tell us that our conversation should be "seasoned with salt." In light of what you have read today, this means that instead of speaking complaining, critical, negative words with the rest of the world, you can exert a spiritually positive *influence* on your environment. When you're seasoned with salt, you will speak:

- Words that bring preservation.
- Words that flavor life and make it "taste" better.
- Words that bring healing to the sick.
- Words that "disinfect" and free those who were once were contaminated.
- Words that are filled with protection, safety, and deliverance.
- Words that are so faith-filled, they create a blessed environment around us.

Jesus plainly taught that we are supposed to be the salt of the earth! Considering the various ways salt was used in the ancient world, can you see how powerful Jesus' point is?

If you are doing your job as "the salt of the earth," there should be fruit all around you to show that God's "salt" in you is doing its job. As you take a look around your life, can you see visible proofs of your "salty" influence?

Before you do anything else today, why don't you take a few minutes to reflect on your life to see if you are having the kind of influence on your world that Jesus wants you to have. The Holy Spirit will help you honestly assess your fruit so you can see if you are doing your job as "the salt of the earth" the way God has called and equipped you to do!

MY PRAYER FOR TODAY

Lord, I am so thankful that You called me to be "the salt of the earth." Today I want to step forward and surrender to be the salt of the earth that You intended me to be. Help me guard my mouth so that I speak words that bring preservation; words that make life better; words that bring healing to the sick; words that disinfect and free people who were once contaminated by evil; words that are filled with protection, safety, and deliverance; and words so faith-filled they create a blessed environment everywhere I go. Jesus has called me to be the salt of the earth, and that is exactly what I am going to be!

I pray this in Jesus' name!

MY CONFESSION FOR TODAY

I declare that I am what God's Word says I am — and Jesus called me the salt of the earth, so that is exactly what I am. Because of who He is in me, I am a preserving, healing, delivering, life-enhancing force that positively affects every person every place I go. It isn't me, but it's the Greater One who lives in me that makes such a powerful difference in my environment. Because He lives in me, I am able to positively influence everyone my life touches. I am the salt of the earth!

I declare this by faith in Jesus' name!

QUESTIONS FOR YOU TO CONSIDER

1. What did you learn new from today's *Sparkling Gem?* What made the greatest impact on you about what it means to be the salt of the earth?
2. Can you think of ways you are acting like "salt" in the lives of other people in the lives of others in your family, church, community, or workplace? How have others changed in those environments because of your presence?
3. When you listen to the words that come out of your mouth, can you honestly say that your words are "seasoned with salt"? Is your mouth regularly filled with words of preservation, healing, freedom, cleansing, protection, safety, deliverance, and faith? Do your words create a changed, positive environment, or do your words have a contrary effect?

MARCH 6

A Magic Marker and a Map

He [Abraham] staggered not
at the promise of God through unbelief:
but was strong in faith, giving glory to God.
— Romans 4:20

When we first began our TV ministry in the former USSR, I traveled long distances to reach cities where I could become personally acquainted with the directors of massive TV stations and begin a relationship with them that would enable me to negotiate for time on their stations. I always traveled with my associate — and in the early days, I often took my eldest son Paul along with me so he could see and experience the miracles God performed to open doors for our TV ministry.

On one such trip, late at night, faith erupted in my heart for the expansion of our TV ministry across *all* the former USSR. I'll never forget that moment! Prior to that revelation, we had begun to broadcast the message of the Gospel through our TV program, but I never realized until that night how vast our TV outreach was destined to become.

After a full day of exhausting travel and meetings with TV station managers — just when I thought I was about to go to bed for the night — a "spark" of faith suddenly ignited in my heart. It was like dynamite had been detonated in my spirit, and I *knew* that something massive had been moved in the spirit realm. My spiritual eyes were opened in an instant, and I supernaturally knew that this TV outreach was to be far larger than I had ever dreamed.

I asked my associate for a large folded map of the USSR that we carried with us, and I found myself unfolding it and laying it out on the floor of my hotel room. I asked for a magic marker. As if a divine hand was guiding me, I took that magic marker and begin to circle huge geographic areas where the Holy Spirit drew my attention. I knew the Spirit of God was instructing me to take the teaching of the Bible to these vast territories through our television ministry.

There had never been Christian TV in the Soviet Union, so we were breaking brand-new ground. Hence, I knew that *all* the areas where the Spirit led me to circle were virgin territory for the broadcasting of the Word of God. It wasn't long before the entire divine strategy was laid out on the map before me.

My associate and son watched as the Holy Spirit guided my hand and the magic marker. I circled one region, then another, and another, until a massive chain of connecting circles covered one side of the map all the way to the other far extreme. It reached all the way from Riga in the west, across the cities nestled in the Ural Mountains, all the way to Siberia, and over to Vladivostok in the Far East. Also circled were Estonia, Latvia, Lithuania, Belarus, Ukraine, Moldova,

Georgia, Azerbaijan, Armenia, and all the southern Muslim Republics. To top it off, I even sensed the Holy Spirit leading me to circle vast territories in Russia's northwest lands.

When I finished, I looked at my associate and Paul, and they were astonished. They had witnessed an entire vision supernaturally manifested right before their eyes as I moved that magic marker! That night we laid our hands all over those circled areas and claimed them for the Kingdom of God. I even laid my whole body across that circled map and prayed for the anointing of God to open doors we didn't know how to open. There was no doubt that a major event had been supernaturally birthed by the Spirit of God at that late hour in that hotel room. By midnight, it was conceived, put on paper, and already committed to the hands of God in prayer.

When we returned to our office, which was at that time in Jelgava, Latvia (where we also lived in those early years), I took that large map, framed it, and hung it in the hallway of our offices. It became a reminder of the vision God had supernaturally given us — a reminder of where we were to go and what areas we were to tackle to get our programs on the air. At the time I didn't realize that to broadcast in all those areas would make our TV ministry the largest Christian broadcast in that part of the world — over a network of stations that would reach millions upon millions of TV viewers.

But that was just the beginning. Once the vision was conceived and put to pen and paper so others could see it, the work had to begin. That meant I would have to travel intensively to all those regions. But first, God would have to open the doors for me to meet with the top TV directors of the largest stations in all those areas. Since most of them were Communists and atheists who were opposed to the Gospel, this would take a miracle.

Step by step, God gave us appointments with powerful TV directors — and we watched as those huge, circled areas were seized by the Spirit of God for the broadcasting of our programs. In a relatively brief period of time, doors began to open; agreements were signed; and our TV programs were broadcasted all over the former USSR. It was a *first* for Christian broadcasting in the former Soviet Union.

Naturally speaking, this all seemed impossible. But exactly at that time, God quickened my heart to the story of Abraham and Sarah. Although they were too old to produce children, God made a promise to them — a promise and vision that seemed too fantastic to believe: that they would give birth to a child in their old ages. Romans 4:20 tells us that in spite of the overwhelming odds that seemed to be stacked against them, Abraham believed what God had told him. It says, "He [Abraham] staggered not at the promise of God through unbelief: but was strong in faith, giving glory to God."

Abraham could have doubted the possibility of having a child, or he could have easily convinced himself that this dream was impossible. But the Bible says that Abraham "...staggered not at the promise of God..." (Romans 4:20).

That is exactly how I felt about the vision God had put before me. I knew that God had spoken to me, and as impossible as that vision seemed in the natural, a faith was ignited in my heart that pushed me into the realm of supernatural possibilities. Just as Abraham "staggered not" at the promise of God, I found myself standing in faith, *confidently assured*, that I had heard from God. Although this vision seemed bigger than anything I could ever accomplish, it was one that had been birthed by the Spirit of God — and I knew in my heart that I could not "stagger" at what God had shown me.

Abraham was a man who made many mistakes along his walk of faith, but Romans 4:20 says one thing he did right is that he did not "stagger" at what God had promised him. Regardless of his humanity and blemishes in his character, Abraham knew that God had spoken to him, and he held tightly to what God had promised.

The word "stagger" in Romans 4:20 is derived from the Greek word *diakrino*, which means *to waver*. It pictures one who is doubtful, constantly changing his mind about what he believes, *wobbling* in his faith, and *vacillating* back and forth. In other words, this person is *unstable* in what he believes.

James 1:7 declares that a man who *wavers* cannot receive what God has promised: "For let not that man [a wavering man] think that he shall receive any thing of the Lord." And then in verse 8, James likens a wavering man to a "double-minded" man. In Greek, the word "double-minded" is *dipsychos*, and it pictures *a man with two minds*. One mind directs one way, and the other mind directs another way. As a result, he is pulled in two directions, constantly fluctuating in what he believes. One day he believes; the next day he doesn't believe. Thus, even if God has made a promise to such an individual, this constant vacillation will keep him from receiving it. Being "double-minded" is serious business — so don't be double-minded!

Those who do not stagger are *single-minded* about what God has told them. They stand in a solid, convinced position, and they hold tightly to what God has told them. Heart, soul, and mouth — all are in agreement with that which God has promised. Although they may have imperfections that seem glaring to them personally, this one quality of being *single-minded* and *unwavering* is enough to bring the manifestation of what God has promised them, regardless of their other flaws.

Abraham took such a position of faith. He was single-minded about what God had promised, and he did not *move*, *budge*, or *waver*. The vision he saw went directly into his heart, and he did not vacillate on believing God would fulfill His promise. That confident foundation of faith carried Abraham through many years of waiting — and because of this non-negotiable stance, he and Sarah received the son God had promised.

That is what happened to me in the early days of our ministry in the former USSR. God *spoke*. I *believed*. And a sure confidence came into my heart that carried Denise and me through numerous battles and challenges until, *finally*, we began to see our TV program spread far and wide across the former Soviet Union. Because we did not stagger at the vision God had revealed, the Gospel ended up being broadcasted into millions of homes across the 11 time zones of the former USSR. It may have seemed far-fetched when God first revealed His plan, but God delights in making the "impossible" possible for those who do not waver in their faith!

What are you believing for in your life right now?

Has God shown you a vision for your life that you know you are supposed to accomplish? *God wants to do the far-fetched for you!* But like Abraham and others who have seen the impossible come to pass, you must be steadfast and stable in your stance of faith — not moving, not budging, and not wavering. You must resolve to stand in faith and give glory to God that what is impossible with men is possible with God.

Today I encourage you to pray the prayer below and speak out from your heart the following confession. Ask God to ignite faith in your heart that will cause you to become *immovable* in your stance of faith regarding what God has promised you. Never let the devil convince you that your dream is too far-fetched, because with God, *all* things are possible!

MY PRAYER FOR TODAY

Father, I thank You for revealing Your plan for my life. When I first understood the greatness of what You wanted to do through me, it boggled my mind. But now I understand that all things are possible to those who believe. Like Abraham and others who have seen You do the impossible in their lives, I believe that I will see my seemingly impossible dream come to pass in my life. You will always do exactly what You have promised to do. Ignite faith in my heart to believe, and help me stand firm, stable, and unwavering in my faith. Help me stay focused until I receive the manifestation of what You have revealed to me about my life!

I pray this in Jesus' name!

MY CONFESSION FOR TODAY

I boldly confess that I will see the manifestation of what God has revealed to me about my life. Naturally speaking, it seems grandiose and far-fetched, but God delights in doing what seems impossible for those who believe, and I am among those who believe. I declare that my faith is confident and solid — that I do not waver or wobble in my faith! And I do not doubt the vision that God has shown me concerning my life. It's not a question of "if" it will happen, but merely a question of "when" it will come to pass. Until then, I will remain spiritually strong and stable, not staggering at the promise of God!

I declare this by faith in Jesus' name!

QUESTIONS FOR YOU TO CONSIDER

1. Can you think of other men and women of God in the Bible who received a grand vision and stood in faith until they saw it manifested? Why not make a list and encourage yourself by the examples of others who believed and received the manifestation of their promise from the Lord?
2. How would you describe the vision that God has shown you for your life? Do you understand in detail what God wants to do through you and for you? Have you really meditated on it to the point where it has percolated deep in your spirit and you know that you have it by faith? Are you ready to take action through preparation for that vision to come to pass?

3. What impossible things have you already seen God do in your life? It would be very healthy for you to meditate on those things and strengthen your faith by remembering them.

MARCH 7

Bobbie Jo's Biscuits

And let us consider one another
to provoke unto love and to good works:
not forsaking the assembling of ourselves together,
as the manner of some is; but exhorting one another:
and so much the more as ye see the day approaching.
— Hebrews 10:24,25

When I was growing up, every time the door was open for a church event, the Renner clan was there. But my all-time favorite event of the week involved eating *Bobbie Jo's biscuits*. I'm talking about the large, fluffy, butter-covered biscuits that were baked and then served by the church cook each week at our church's Wednesday night supper before the midweek service.

To a young Rick Renner, there was just nothing in the world to compare to Bobbie Jo's golden, fluffy biscuits. Although it's been many decades since I've eaten one of them, I can still hear her yelling, "RICKY RENNER — get out of this kitchen and keep your hands off the biscuits!" I was always trying to sneak an extra biscuit before or after dinner was served!

The Wednesday night church meal included regular servings of ketchup-covered meatloaf, creamy mashed potatoes with heavy brown gravy, and cherry or apple pie. But for me, Bobbie Jo's biscuits were the "grand slam" of everything on the menu. However, what really *indelibly* marked my life, more than those biscuits, was the *rich fellowship* that transpired around those tables each Wednesday night among the people who ate together at our church supper. Those people were pillars in our church — people we knew would always be there; those on whom we could depend; people we knew really loved us. They were such consistent examples to me as a young boy. Around those tables of fellowship, these men and women spoke *strength* into each other's lives. Much of what I believe about church fellowship was formed in those Wednesday night suppers. *Fellowship* — what a gift from God it is to you and me and to our local churches!

The Bible tells us in Hebrews 10:25, "Not forsaking the assembling of ourselves together, as the manner of some is; but exhorting one another: and so much the more, as ye see the day approaching."

Apparently there were already some believers in the First Century who were skipping church. People tend to stay away from church and other believers when they get discouraged. Perhaps these Christians are embarrassed that their faith isn't working as well as they think it should. Perhaps they're ashamed that they're still struggling with problems that they believe should have been conquered long ago. They don't want anyone to know they're still wrestling with the same old issues, so they disappear from sight.

The writer of Hebrews used a Greek word that tells us why most Christians start "forsaking" the assembling of themselves together. In Greek, the word "forsaking" is *egkataleipontes,* which is a compound of three different Greek words: *ek, kata,* and *leipo*. The word *ek* means *out*; the word *kata* means *down*; and the word *leipo* means *behind* or *to be lacking*. When these three words are compounded, the new word pictures a person who feels *out, down,* and *behind.* In other words, he feels like he's *outside the circle of his group*; he feels *discouraged* or *depressed*; and he feels like everyone else has *surpassed* him. This word describes *someone who feels extremely left out and defeated.* He feels like he's *trailing far behind everyone else* in his spiritual life or in his life in general. To him, it seems like everyone is succeeding but him. Yet rather than go to church to be encouraged and strengthened, this person allows his emotions to control him and he starts missing church meetings. In other words, he "forsakes" the assembly of believers.

Have you noticed that when Christians need encouragement the most, it's often the time they start running from church? They decide to skip church, stay home, and do something else instead. *They isolate themselves when they're in their greatest need of encouragement!*

Hebrews 10:25 says it's important that we meet because we need "exhorting" from one another. The word "exhorting" in Greek is *parakaleo*, a compound of the words *para* and *kaleo. Para* means *alongside*, and *kaleo* means *to call, to beckon*, or *to speak to someone.* When these two words are compounded, the new word depicts *someone who comes right alongside a person, urging him, beseeching him, and begging him to make some kind of correct decision.*

In the ancient Greek world, the word *parakaleo* was often used by military leaders before they sent their troops into battle. Rather than hide from the painful reality of war, the leaders would summon their troops together and speak straightforwardly with them about the potential dangers of the battlefield. The leaders would also tell their troops about the glories of winning a major victory.

Instead of ignoring these clear-cut dangers of battle, these officers came right alongside their troops and urged, exhorted, beseeched, begged, and pleaded with them *to stand tall, throw back their shoulders, look the enemy straight on, eyeball to eyeball, and face their battles bravely.* All these ideas are contained in the word "exhort" in Hebrews 10:25.

If you know someone who is discouraged because his fight isn't won yet, speak to that person truthfully and forthrightly, the way a commanding officer would speak to his troops. Remind that person of others who have stood the test of time and won their battles. Be sure to remind him of the sweetness of victory when the battle is over. He needs to hear a passionate, heartfelt word of exhortation from you!

I think that *this* is the real reason I loved Wednesday night suppers at our church when I was growing up. Sure, Bobbie Jo's biscuits were terrific. But even those big fluffy, buttery biscuits could not compare to the fellowship, encouragement, and love that was exchanged across those tables as people ate together. *It was truly a weekly love feast.*

Although decades have passed and people have moved away to various places, most of these church members still stay in touch and deeply love one another. They were real troops who encouraged each other — and if someone disappeared, we looked until we found them! We weren't going to let them fall out of fellowship simply because they were discouraged! *That's when they needed us the most!*

Maybe you know someone who has forsaken the assembling of himself with other believers in church. Maybe you've even done it. I want to encourage *you* today: Stay in fellowship, and don't forsake the assembling of yourself together with other believers. If you're feeling "out, down, and behind," confess that to someone you trust spiritually and let that person pray with you. And if you notice that someone has recently been missing from church, realize that the devil may be assaulting his mind. Or perhaps his faith feels a little tired, and that person needs some strengthening from someone like you. So make it your aim today to find that individual and speak words of encouragement to him to get him back to the table of rich fellowship with the brethren!

MY PRAYER FOR TODAY

Father, I thank You for my church family and for the encouragement I receive from other church members. You have called us to be a body. I don't want to allow myself to be disconnected when discouragement tries to wage war against my mind and emotions. Help me run to fellowship in times like that instead of letting the devil talk me into staying away. The devil knows that fellowship will strengthen me and others. That is why he tries to keep us apart from each other during the times when we need each other the most. So today I take a firm stand against this diabolical strategy and declare that I will stay connected to my church family and other believers — and I will do all I can to keep others connected as well because we are stronger together!

I pray this in Jesus' name!

MY CONFESSION FOR TODAY

I confess that the enemy's plan to separate me from others will not work! God's Word plainly says that I am not to forsake the assembling of myself with other believers, and I will obey what the Word tells me to do. Even if I am under assault emotionally, assembling to fellowship with others is one thing I simply will not negotiate. Nothing will keep me from gathering with other believers to receive and to give supernatural strength. Furthermore, I choose to be a voice that speaks encouragement to others who are feeling outside, let down, or left behind. Rather than focus on myself and my own needs, I will focus on how to become a source of strength to others who are around me!

I declare this by faith in Jesus' name!

QUESTIONS FOR YOU TO CONSIDER

1. Have there been moments in your life when you ran from Christian fellowship because you were discouraged? What happened in your thinking to convince you that you should stay away from other believers in such a moment?
2. Do you know anyone right now who has disappeared from church? Have you wondered where that person is? Do you know if anyone has checked on him or her? Is the Holy Spirit speaking to you today, encouraging *you* to seek out that person?
3. Most churches don't have Wednesday night suppers anymore. What other avenues of fellowship — Sunday school, small-group studies, etc. — does your church offer that you can take advantage of? Have you looked to see what is available for you to attend in order to receive and give strength to others?

MARCH 8

Indicators of Nicolaitanism in the Church Today

But this thou hast, that thou hatest the deeds
of the Nicolaitans, which I also *hate*.
— Revelation 2:6

So hast thou also them that hold to the doctrine
of the Nicolaitans, which thing I *hate*.
— Revelation 2:15

I personally think the word "hate" should rarely be used. But in Revelation 2:6 and 15, Jesus used the word "hate" twice when He referred to the teachings and deeds of a group of erring spiritual leaders that were finding some success in the churches at Ephesus and Pergamum. He referred to these erring leaders as Nicolaitans. (I suggest you read pages 631-635 in *Sparkling Gems 1*, to learn more about the Nicolaitans and their origins.)

The word "hate" in these verses is from the Greek word *miseo*, which means *to hate, to abhor*, or *to find utterly repulsive*. It describes a *deep-seated animosity* to something that one finds to be *completely objectionable*. A person experiencing this level of *miseo* not only *loathes* the object of his animosity, but he *rejects* it entirely. This is not just a dislike; it is a case of *actual hatred*.

Christ didn't hate these individuals whom He called Nicolaitans, but He certainly *hated* what they were teaching — which was a doctrine of *inclusiveness* and *compromise* to the Church. Unfortunately, this doctrine has reemerged in recent years. In the Christian world today, there are some spiritual leaders who, like the Nicolaitans of the past, seek a dangerous truce with the world under the guise of *inclusiveness* and *compromise.* Many of these emerging spiritual leaders once held strong doctrinal positions, upholding the Bible as true and absolute — but over time, they have shaped their beliefs to meld with the changing moral climate of society, and in the process, they have produced a Gospel very different from the one presented in the Bible.

Although the world may change, Hebrews 13:8 teaches that Christ is the same yesterday, today, and forever — and truth does not change based on societal trends. Truth is truth, regardless of the particular brand of immorality society has labeled "acceptable." Today, just as before, whenever believers take a firm stand on absolute truth, they are viewed by the world as intolerant. But when it comes to the eternal truth of God's Word, there is no room to mitigate or adapt one's beliefs.

Those who practice spiritual compromise generally believe that Christ is just one of many acceptable types of faith. The big issue to them is not truth, but *respect.* As such, truth takes a second seat to equally honoring the beliefs of other people, even if those beliefs are diametrically opposed to the doctrines of the Bible. Ultimately, Christ is demoted in their minds, viewed as just one option among many. According to this inclusive mindset, everyone is right and no one is wrong. This modern belief system harbors dangerous similarities with both the pagan mindset of the Roman Empire and the doctrine of the Nicolaitans that Christ "hated."

As the problem of worldly compromise continues to spread in the Church and to be promoted by some of today's most visible Christian leaders, it is vital for believers to be able to recognize the modern signs that point to a rise of Nicolaitanism in the Church today. The following list doesn't necessarily represent every indicator of modern Nicolaitanism. However, it provides sufficient evidence to prove a direct parallel in modern times to the spiritual error that was developing in congregations in the latter years of the First Century.

- **No emphasis on living holy and separated from the world.**

  Modern Nicolaitanism dresses itself in the guise of *inclusivity.* Rather than living separately from the world, those who espouse this view reason, "Since everyone is right and no one wrong both spiritually and morally, why should there be a need for separation?" Leading denominational churches have taken the position that the time has come to help lesbians and homosexuals blend into the church community and lead "holy" lives along with other church members. This sentiment mirrors the teaching of the Nicolaitans of the First Century, for these modern-day church leaders promote a message that will make them more acceptable with the multitude instead of one that will put them in opposition with the expectations of modern society.

➢ **No emphasis on the doctrinal teaching of the Bible.**

Modern Nicolaitanism dresses itself in the guise of *progressiveness*, dismissing much of the Bible as being too restrictive or exclusive of other people's beliefs. Instead of being a guide to absolute truth, the Bible is used merely as a reference for illustrations, motivational sermons, inspirational ideas, principles to build a marriage or business, and so on.

Today this trend is so rampant in the Church that the basic tenets of the Christian faith are largely not known by most churchgoers, especially by those who are younger. Basic Bible doctrines such as the virgin birth, the sinlessness of Christ, sin, salvation, holiness, and eternal judgment are often unknown, inadequately taught, or considered optional. Where modern Nicolaitanism prevails, sound doctrine is replaced with social action, social justice, and an attempt to appeal to mass audiences by making people feel better about themselves. Thus, true doctrinal teaching of the Bible is diminished, replaced by different variants of watered-down, "politically correct" instruction.

➢ **No emphasis on absolute truth or absolute biblical morality.**

Modern Nicolaitanism dresses itself in the guise of being *open-minded*. It cries that it is unfair and unjust to assert that beliefs alone are the absolute foundation for truth. Even if we believe what we believe, it makes allowances that we may be wrong or that others are equally right but with a different approach. To demonstrate how deeply this damaging influence has already permeated the Church, it is a statistical fact that more than *half* of evangelical Christians do *not* believe in absolute truth. These statistics — which reflect a general change in society and in the Church — are growing at such an alarming rate that they will no doubt be out of date by the time the first issue of this book is published. To understand where this trend is headed, just hold an honest conversation with young people under the age of 25, and you will learn firsthand that *many* young people, even young Christian men and women, hold a negative view of people who adhere to absolute truth or absolute morality.

➢ **No exclusionary belief that Christ alone is the Way to Heaven.**

Modern Nicolaitanism dresses itself in the guise of *tolerance*, asserting that everyone has a piece of the truth. It ultimately levels the playing field and makes Christianity simply "*a* truth" among other truths. If the doctrine of Nicolaitanism is followed to its logical conclusion, it eventually leads to *universalism*, which is the belief that everyone and everything — even Satan and hell — will ultimately be reconciled to God. In fact, it is a pagan premise that there are many roads leading to the same eventual destination in the afterlife and that every person should therefore be able to find his own way.

According to this mindset, to categorically declare that Christ alone is the way to Heaven to be nonsensical and intolerant. Christians who adhere to some Nicolaitan principles have not usually followed this teaching to its ultimate conclusion and

> would be shocked if they did. Yet the doctrine of universalism is the inevitable destination at which this doctrine must eventually arrive. A recent survey conducted among one of the most Bible-based groups reveals that more than one-third of young Christians in America believe that adherence to the teachings of Jesus, Mohammed, Buddha, and other religious leaders all lead to Heaven. We are often reminded that young people are the leaders of the next generation. If this is so, what then are the implications of these statistics for the next generation of the Church?

There are many other indicators of modern Nicolaitanism, but these are the primary signs. These faulty beliefs reveal doctrinal ignorance and result in a powerless, weakened version of Christianity where sin is tolerated, separation is ignored, and the need for ongoing repentance is disregarded.

Jesus was *repulsed* by the teachings of the Nicolaitans and loathed their presence in the churches at Ephesus and Pergamum. While He loved them as individuals, He found their teachings to be *utterly objectionable.*

Although the Bible instructs us to love everyone, we must think like Jesus thinks when it comes to any teachings that result in a diluted, powerless, compromised version of Christianity. If we are to be like Jesus, we must think like Jesus — and what Jesus hates, we also must hate. *Now, that's something for you to think about today.*

MY PRAYER FOR TODAY

Father, I know that we are living in the last times, and during these days, false teachers will arise that will lure many people into compromise with the world. I ask You to heighten my spiritual discernment, make me sensitive to what I see and hear, and keep my spirit alert so that I will not consume strange doctrines that can only produce powerlessness and weaken my spiritual life. Help me love what You love and loathe what You loathe. As You do, I choose to have a loving attitude toward every person, and I draw on Your love in me to love people even if I loathe what they represent and teach.

I pray this in Jesus' name!

MY CONFESSION FOR TODAY

I confess that I have nothing to do with teachings that will lure people into a powerless, weakened version of Christianity where sin is tolerated, separation is ignored, and the need for ongoing repentance is disregarded. I love everyone, but like Jesus, I do not appreciate or tolerate teachings that suggest there is no need for repentance or that we never need to change or be transformed. Holy Spirit, I know that You are calling us to be different from the world, and I declare my intention to You to cooperate with Your sanctifying work of holiness inside me. My deepest desire is to be like Jesus and not to tolerate the things of the world in my life.

I declare this by faith in Jesus' name!

QUESTIONS FOR YOU TO CONSIDER

1. Based on what you have read in today's *Sparkling Gem*, do you recognize anyone who is teaching and leading others in the error of the Nicolaitanism?
2. How will you pray for those you think may be teaching or following this error?
3. Think of those whom you allow to influence you. Do they encourage you to live a life of holiness, separation from worldly attitudes and actions, and repentance? Or do they suggest that these qualities are unnecessary? Your answer to this question is very important, so think deeply about it.

MARCH 9

Keeping the Fire Burning!

Wherefore I put thee in remembrance
that thou stir up the gift of God,
which is in thee
by the putting on of my hands.
— 2 Timothy 1:6

Do you ever struggle to keep the fire of the Holy Spirit burning in your heart? Perhaps it sometimes feels like all that is left burning are a few small embers — or perhaps even the embers are starting to die out and become cold! How do you stoke that fire inside you so that it begins burning in your heart again? That's what I want to talk to you about today. But let me begin by turning to a story from our family's earliest days in the former USSR and what we learned about *keeping the fire burning*.

We had purchased an abandoned apartment in the heart of our city. It was in miserable condition — so ruined that it should have been condemned. But after restoration work was complete, the apartment was just as elegant as it had been in the years before the Soviet occupation. Before restoration, the apartment was a morass of mold, collapsed ceilings, and plaster falling off the walls. But when the work was complete, the walls were covered with fine wallpaper, and magnificent chandeliers hung once again from giant, hand-carved medallions in the center of the ceilings. The giant crown molding that wrapped around the ceilings of each room had been meticulously restored. Every room had beautiful, new parquet floors to match those that had existed before the Revolution. And the nine fireplaces — one for each big room and in each bedroom — were the most magnificent features of all. Once restored, they looked like something that belonged in a museum! Meanwhile, every other apartment in the building still remained in a state of devastation and abandonment.

Eventually the whole building would be beautifully restored, but when we moved into our apartment, the other apartments and the central staircase of the building looked like something that had been bombed in World War II. It looked so abandoned that derelicts slept in our entry way. We were told by city authorities that the city-wide heating system would be connected to the building before winter, so we installed new pipes to carry the heat to every room in preparation of wonderful heat. But as the weather turned cold and winter approached, it was apparent that heat was not coming that year and our family would be living in freezing temperatures inside our apartment. This was a serious problem, because that city got *very* cold in the winter.

Suddenly those museum-quality fireplaces became necessities — and we started using those lavish fireplaces to provide heat for our home. Transporting wood was difficult because we lived downtown and there was no nearby source of wood. But in that desperate situation, our young sons — Paul, Philip, and Joel — came up with an idea about where we could get wood so our family would have heat for the winter. When it's really cold, that's a good time to get creative! So our sons, out of their desire not to feel cold, thought of something Denise and I would have never thought of in a million years.

The apartment directly below us was in such a horrible condition and it was owned by no one. When we first purchased our own apartment, it was so ruined that the bathroom had a hole next to the toilet. Men had "missed" the toilet for so many years that the urine had eaten a hole through the floor! That apartment under us was so unkempt and so destroyed that *nothing* could be salvaged. Walls were half gone; fireplaces were destroyed; and there was no glass in the windows! That latter feature was especially bad for us because our apartment, located directly above, felt the effect of the freezing winter wind blowing through the apartment beneath our floor.

The floors of that lower apartment had once been splendid parquet with all types of inlaid exotic woods and designs. But those same floors had become ruined from water leaks, and the parquet tiles were half ripped up and lying all over the apartment in irreparable, shattered pieces.

One morning when Denise and I were pondering what to do with the cold temperatures that were getting worse by the day and hour, our three sons disappeared — but they soon reappeared, walking through the front door of our apartment with armloads of 100-year-old parquet flooring that they had gathered from the devastated apartment below. Denise and I watched as the two older boys shoved that old parquet into the doors of our fireplaces and then lit each fire. They worked on them until a blaze was going strong in each of those old museum pieces all over the apartment. The wood was so old and dry that it began quickly popping and burning. Soon our apartment was warming up in every room, fueled by the wood from the apartment below that our sons had collected and put on the fire.

When it started to get cold again, we'd throw open the door to the fireplaces to see if the fire was going out, and if we saw that there was nothing left but embers, our sons would throw on their jackets, rush down two flights of steps to the abandoned apartment below, and rip up more flooring (which any eventual buyer would have had to replace anyway). Soon they'd be back with armloads of antique parquet flooring. First, the boys would break it into smaller pieces; then they would shove it through the fireplace doors into the fire, and almost immediately the house would start warming up again.

As long as wood was on the fire, we could be assured that we would have heat. But if there was no wood left to burn or if only embers were left, it was certain that the fire would go out unless we took action. *Fuel was essential to keep those fireplaces going*, for when fuel of any sort is depleted, the fire eventually goes out.

Often there was enough wood to keep the fire burning, but it needed to be stoked — moved around and repositioned with a long poker. We'd insert that long iron rod into the wood and embers; then we'd rigorously rake them back and forth and side to side to provide more oxygen for the embers so the fire would keep burning longer. In fact, if we didn't regularly stoke those embers and fan the flames, we discovered that the fire could go out even if there *was* enough wood to keep it burning. Those embers had to be tended to regularly to keep the fire going.

As I personally took my turn to stoke the embers, I regularly meditated on Paul's words to Timothy in Second Timothy 1:6. In that verse, Paul wrote, "Wherefore I put thee in remembrance that thou *stir up* the gift of God, which is in thee by the putting on of my hands."

The words "stir up" are from the Greek word *anadzoopureoo*, a triple compound of the Greek words, *ana*, *zoos*, and *pur*. The word *ana* carries the idea of *repeating an earlier action* or *doing something again*. The word *zoos* is from the word *zao*, which means *to be enthusiastic*, *to be fervent*, *to be passionate*, *to be vigorous*, *to be wholehearted*, or *to be zealous*. The word *pur* is the Greek word for *fire* — but it must be noted that in Classical Greek, fire was *a life-giving force*. Fire was used on the hearths of every ancient home to keep people warm; it was used in matters related to the divine and supernatural; and it was used as a force to defeat enemies. Fire was central to life and considered both practically and spiritually essential for one's existence.

When these three words are compounded, they form the Greek word *anadzoopureoo* — which is the very word Paul used in Second Timothy 1:6 when he told the younger minister to "stir up" the gift of God that was in him. It implies that the fire in Timothy's heart had ebbed to embers on a low burn. Hence, Paul told the younger minister to passionately and rigorously begin again to *stoke* and *stir up* the gift of God in his life, just as one would stoke the embers of a fire in a hearth or fireplace. Paul was not just kindly suggesting that Timothy take action; the apostle was commanding Timothy to spiritually reach within and begin *to rekindle* the fire in his heart.

At the time Paul wrote this epistle to Timothy, this young man was surrounded by confusion resulting from the intense persecution that was taking place. Is it possible that he was exhausted and that his own fire was beginning to wane? Most likely the answer is yes. But regardless of Timothy's current state, Paul told him to take action before the fire went out. Timothy was to open the door to his heart, look inside to determine the condition of his inward fire, and then take action to "put more wood on the fire" and stir up the gift of God inside him. This would not occur accidentally but would require a proactive response. If Timothy would obey Paul's command, that inward fire would blaze again and Timothy would once again have fire burning in the center of his being. The younger minister would be reconnected to the supernatural power of God and provided with a weapon that would consume his spiritual adversaries. *Wow!*

In those early days of living in the former Soviet Union, the Renner family learned that if we intended to have heat in our freezing apartment, we would have to become proactive to make it happen. We had to find fuel; we had to carry it upstairs; we had to open the door to the fireplaces; we had to put the fuel into the fire; and we had to stoke the fuel regularly throughout the day to keep it burning. *And* if we started to hit a low burn, it meant we had to begin the process all over. Our choices were to be proactive and do what was required or *to freeze.*

It is the same for you. If your "fire" is at a low burn or close to going out, it's time for you to take Paul's words to heart "to stir up" the gift of God that is inside you. You cannot depend on someone else to do something so vital for you. So ask the Holy Spirit how to do it — how to open the door to your heart and take an honest look on the inside to assess your need. Then let Him show you how to proceed in fueling your fire and stirring up those embers so that you will once again become a bright blazing inferno for Jesus Christ!

MY PRAYER FOR TODAY

Lord, I confess that I need to stir up the gift of God that is in me. There was a time when it seemed the fires burned much brighter, but for one reason or another, I've allowed the flame in my spirit to grow colder. I take responsibility for this, as it is my heart, and I ask You to forgive me for letting my condition go this far. Today I am accepting responsibility, and I will look at my heart and determine the truth. And with the help of the Holy Spirit, I will begin to actively and vigorously rekindle that glorious spiritual fire that You intended to burn inside me. Help me, Holy Spirit, to do this not just once, but to continually put spiritual fuel into my heart and stoke the embers.

I pray this in Jesus' name!

MY CONFESSION FOR TODAY

I confess that my heart is a hearth for the fire of the Holy Spirit. It is God's will for my heart to be spiritually ablaze, and today I will begin to do what I must do to rekindle the flame to burn as it once did and to blaze even brighter. I will not allow distractions — whether they come from my own busy schedule, from others, or even from myself — to take my attention off my spiritual condition ever again. I recognize my failure to tend to the fire has affected me, and I declare that from this moment onward, I will dutifully stoke the fire and the gifts of God that have been placed inside me. I will find fuel for the fire and I will take responsibility to make certain it is placed on the hearth of my heart regularly so that the fire burns bright continuously.

I declare this by faith in Jesus' name!

QUESTIONS FOR YOU TO CONSIDER

1. Can you remember a time when your heart was literally "ablaze" with the things of God? What happened along the way to affect that fire? Have you ever stopped

to ponder what you could have done differently to keep it burning regardless of the events that occurred around you?

2. What is your source of spiritual fuel? What feeds you? What keeps your heart on track and ablaze? It would be good for you to take a few minutes to write down the sources that regularly feed your heart and keep you stirred up as you serve Jesus.
3. How long has it been since you paused long enough to really look inside the door of your heart to see how much fuel is still there? Do you spend time with God daily and allow the Holy Spirit to do an inventory of your spiritual condition? If not, why not? This is important enough that you should start doing it every day.

MARCH 10

First Things First!

Now he which established us with you in Christ,
and hath anointed us, is God.
— 2 Corinthians 1:21

We once found a building that had great potential to become the headquarters for our ministry in Russia. The size was perfect; the location was ideal; and the price was remarkably low. We knew a deal like this didn't come along very often, so we quickly moved to contact the seller. When we met him to discuss the building and its legal status, it sounded like everything was in order, so we requested that all the official documents concerning the building be delivered to our office for review.

Soon a huge pile of documents was delivered to our office so we could begin the difficult and laborious process of validating that everything was legally in order. When I saw the stack of documents on the table, I knew the task before us was immense, so we hired a lawyer to immediately get to work on this project. She estimated it could take up to two months to verify the legal status of this building. However, when we were only a few days into the process, we discovered there were serious complications with this property. Everything was *not* as it first seemed! Day by day, we dug up evidence of a mountain of problems associated with this property.

First things first! Before I am going to sign a contract and put my reputation on the line, I want to know that the paperwork is in order and be assured there is no risk to the ministry. *Then and only then will I sign a deal!* In the case of the documents concerning this prospective new building, I had adamantly refused to proceed until all the paperwork was in order — *and I'm so glad I did*!

Doing "due diligence" is always smart before we finalize a deal and sign our name on a contract that legally binds us. But consider this: God also does "due diligence" before He decides whom He will and will not use. If it is logical to do research before signing a contract involving a large sum of money, think how much more logical it is for God to *validate*, *confirm*, and *certify* that we are ready for a big task before He promotes us into a visible position where we will represent Him before many people.

Let's apply this to you for a moment. Perhaps you have a big dream in your heart and a desire for God to use you in a significant way. You may feel eager to get started and wish things would start moving faster. But you need to know that God is not focused on the clock as we usually are. He is more concerned about character, integrity, faithfulness, and purity of heart than about the calendar. These deeper issues are the things God focuses on to see if you and I are ready for a new assignment.

Perhaps you've heard the old phrase, "Don't get the cart before the horse." Nothing could be more applicable to what I am saying right now. *God isn't going to get the cart before the horse.* He isn't going to promote you until He *confirms* that you are ready and have the inward makings for greater responsibility. This principle is clear in Second Corinthians 1:21, where the apostle Paul wrote, "Now he which established us with you in Christ, and hath anointed us, is God."

Today I want to draw your attention to the word "established" in the first part of this verse. It is the old Greek word *bebaios*, a word that means *firm*, *durable*, *dependable*, or *reliable*. By using this word, Paul affirmed that God wants to "establish" us — that is, to make us *firm* in faith, *durable* to withstand any spiritual condition, and *steadfast, trustworthy*, *dependable*, or *reliable.* These are traits He wants to produce in every child of God. Aren't you glad He is steadfastly working to establish you and to make you strong?

You may not feel that you have reached this goal yet, but be assured that God is working deep inside to bring you to this place of *firmness*, *durability*, and *reliability*. Especially if you want God to use you in a mighty way, you must possess these vital character traits. It takes *firmness* to stand for God. Anyone who is a leader must have *durability* to resist difficult, painful, awkward, or uncomfortable times. For you to represent God, He must be assured that you are the kind of person on whom He may *rely*.

But there is another insight regarding the word *bebaios* that is very significant in the context of this verse. This is extremely important for you to understand because it demonstrates that God doesn't lay His hand on someone in a mighty way until He has first done "due diligence" to make sure that person is ready for a greater task.

The word *bebaios* was also a legal term used to depict the lengthy and intensive investigative process involved to validate if a document was *trustworthy*.

In the ancient world, documents were written by hand. If those writing or copying the documents were not careful, mistakes could be made of great legal consequence. Because these often-occurring mistakes made documents flawed, it was not considered wise to give one's final approval to a document until it was tested and proven trustworthy. So before a deal was finalized, it was prudent to test the document to validate its reliability. If the document was found to be valid, the contract could be quickly concluded. If the document had errors in it, those errors had to be corrected *before* the papers were signed and the seal of approval pressed into the hot wax. To sign a document and put one's seal of approval upon it without first validating it would have been an act of foolishness. *You will understand in just a moment why this concept is so important in the study of this verse.*

Let's go further into the verse and look at the word "anointed." The word "anointed" comes from the Greek word *chrio*, which means *to rub, to bathe*, and, in certain contexts, *to massage*. This word depicted the *application* of various substances, such as *oil, medicine*, and *water* — and in some ancient texts, it even depicted the application of *poison*. In most cases, however, the word *chrio* was used to depict the anointing of *oil*. In the Old and New Testament, the word "anoint" is primarily used to depict a person who is anointed by God with the Holy Spirit.

To get the full grasp of the word "anointing" and how it was used in connection with the application of oil, we must stop and ponder the manner in which oil was applied to a recipient. When a person was anointed with oil in ancient times, a prophet, priest, doctor, or therapist would pour oil into his own hands. Once his hands were doused with oil, he would then place his hands on the subject and begin to massage or press the oil into the person's head, hair, or flesh. So the word "anoint" didn't just describe the pouring of oil from an upside-down bottle to drain every drop onto a person. The word depicts the generous application of the oil on a beneficiary by the hands of a master. Oil was very expensive and not to be wasted, so the notion of simply turning a bottle upside down and pouring its contents on a person was almost non-existent. Oil was far too precious to be applied in such a manner.

For a person to be anointed with oil, it required the anointer to put his hands on the anointed. In the truest sense, the word "anoint" describes a "hands-on" experience, for it was nearly impossible to be anointed without someone putting his hands on the recipient in order to apply the oil.

In a religious and political context, the laying on of hands was very important. The moment hands were publicly laid on someone, it was viewed as *endorsement* or *approval*. For example, when elected officials were installed into office, the senior body of politicians publicly laid hands on him as a way of declaring that he was *officially endorsed* and therefore *empowered* to do his job. In both Old and New Testament writings, we find that the laying on of hands was similarly used to declare support and endorsement of an individual. Especially in the early New Testament, the laying on of hands was so significant that it became an official ordinance of the church that was used when a person was promoted into a public position of leadership. When hands were laid on a person, it was also *a public pronouncement of approval.*

Now let's take this truth and apply it to the principle we're studying in Second Corinthians 1:21. In this verse, we find that God does not lay His hands on a person and thereby endorse him or her until He has first validated that the person is *trustworthy* of such an anointing. God does not quickly lay hands on anyone in this way. Furthermore, the moment God lays His hands on someone is the moment the oil of the Holy Spirit is imparted in a greater way. That oil is applied to a person's life with God's very own hands. This act is so holy that God does not carry it out before doing "due diligence" to validate that a person is *trustworthy* of a greater anointing.

The apostle Paul wrote that we are "epistles" that are read and known of all men (*see* 2 Corinthians 3:2). That means you are a living document — and God is reading the pages of your life to observe how you live, how you speak, how you treat others, and so on. He is doing investigative research to determine if you are ready for a promotion or a greater anointing. Don't be too surprised if God finds a few errors that need correction, for none of us is perfect. If there are issues that need correcting — and I'm *certain* there are — you must allow the Holy Spirit to put you through a process to correct those flaws *before* you get the big break you've been dreaming of or before God promotes you to a higher level of responsibility. Remember, God is more concerned about character, integrity, faithfulness, morality, and purity of heart than He is about meeting your schedule requirements! God needs leaders who are *firm*, *durable*, *reliable*, *sound*, and *trustworthy*.

Rather than get in too big of a hurry and rush forward to seize positions you're not ready for, it would be wise for you to take time to get established and work on eradicating errors in your life that would later discredit you, weaken you, or put your ministry, business, or dream at risk. Make it your goal to let God establish you and work these ingredients into your life so He can afterward put His hand on you and thereby anoint you for greater assignments.

First things first! Never forget that the anointing is serious to God — and before He gives you more, He first wants to validate that you are ready for a new dose of the Holy Spirit!

MY PRAYER FOR TODAY

Father, I ask You to work deeply in my life to make me the kind of person I need to be. You know how I desire for You to use me. Your Spirit has filled my heart with dreams of greatness, and I long for the day when You trust me enough to give me a bigger assignment in life. For now, I ask You to delve deep into my life — into my character, my level of integrity, my faithfulness, and my personal purity — to show me any areas that are weak and deficient. Rather than complain that it's taking too long to get started at fulfilling my dream, help me realize that this is a God-given time to strengthen my foundation and to make sure I am ready for the big assignment when it finally comes along!

I pray this in Jesus' name!

MY CONFESSION FOR TODAY

I confess that I am allowing God's Spirit to examine my heart in order to find any areas that could potentially discredit me, weaken me, or spoil my God-given dream. It is good that God has given me this time to look at my heart and to prepare myself. It is an opportunity to strengthen my foundation so that in the future, my life can support the great work that God will entrust to me. I don't complain that it is taking too long or grumble that this time of waiting is difficult. Instead, I embrace this season of preparation as a gift from God to make sure that I am right, that my foundation is right, and that I am ready for the long-awaited assignments that He will give to me.

I declare this by faith in Jesus' name!

QUESTIONS FOR YOU TO CONSIDER

1. Can you think of any areas in your life right now that could potentially weaken you or even "take you down" later in life if you don't deal with it and correct it immediately?
2. Have you ever made a list of the areas in your life that you need to be improving and changing? Before you get too busy today, I recommend you take a few minutes to pray and make a list of those areas that need your attention. It won't take too long to do it, but it will help you focus on areas where you need to change.
3. Can you think of a person who was promoted too high or too quickly, and he came tumbling down because of flaws in his life that had never been corrected? Who was that person, and what can you learn by contemplating what he experienced?

MARCH 11

It's Time for You To Rise and Shine!

Ye are the light of the world.
A city that is set on a hill cannot be hid.
— Matthew 5:14

Just a three-mile walk from the town of Nazareth is an ancient city called *Sepphoris* — a city so elegant in ancient times that it was known as *the ornament of Galilee.* Although it dates to Greek times, the city of Sepphoris was enhanced at the orders of Herod Antipas concurrent to the time Jesus was growing up three miles away in Nazareth. Many people from Nazareth were engaged in rebuilding this fabulous, wealthy city that was the northern home and administrative center for Herod Antipas.

The remarkable city of Sepphoris also became the center of trade and commerce in the northern region of Israel, and it was one of the largest banking centers of the Middle East. Because of the extreme wealth of this city, it had facilities that would normally be associated only with larger cities, such as a huge theater that had a constant array of dramatic presentations. The city had scores of beautiful upper-class villas to accommodate the wealthy people who lived there, and it was adorned with some of the finest mosaics that existed in the First Century. In fact, even today one can see some of the finest examples of early mosaics lying in the ancient ruins of Sepphoris.

This city was exquisite in every way. Sophisticated and wealthy, it attracted visitors from around the world. Every day one could experience a wide range of different cultures, ethnic groups, and customs. People could be heard speaking Greek, Hebrew, and Aramaic in the streets. It was a tri-lingual city known for being open-minded and for having an emphasis on learning, education, and business. This city was so splendid that it influenced the entire region of Galilee.

Three miles away was Nazareth, a small village occupied mostly by workers who were employed in the enhancement of Sepphoris. It was here that Jesus grew up with His parents. Jesus' father was a carpenter, from the Greek word *teknos* — a term that describes not a carpenter as we think of that profession, but *a highly skilled craftsman who works in stone*. Or it could even be used to depict *a construction-site supervisor*. Considering the likelihood that a little town such as Nazareth would not have much work available for a man with these skills, it is likely that Joseph was involved in the high level of construction taking place in nearby Sepphoris.

Growing up next door to such a splendid city, there is little doubt that young Jesus stood in Nazareth and gazed upon "the city set on a hill" that was just a short distance away. From that viewpoint, and especially at night, the city of Sepphoris would have been a spectacular sight. The gleaming lights of countless torches and oil lamps would have shone forth from the city. It must have looked splendid as the lights sparkled and glistened from the majestic buildings in the distance.

Everyone who lived in Galilee also fell under the *influence* of Sepphoris. Its style, its learned culture, its banking system, its mixture of languages — all of these factors had an influence on Galilee. And by reading Jesus' words in the Gospels, it is clear that this "city set on a hill" had an influence on Jesus too. Although He actually grew up in Nazareth, a small and obscure village, He was familiar and comfortable with words, phrases, and knowledge that would not be customary for a boy from a village.

For example, when Jesus told stories, He used illustrations that included vivid descriptions concerning the lifestyles of the wealthy, including the kind of clothes they wore and the luxury they possessed in their daily lives. He spoke of governmental authorities as if He had personal knowledge of the subject — a level of knowledge He could have attained by observation at nearby Sepphoris. When Jesus spoke about money, He used massive amounts of money in His examples — something a village boy would know nothing about unless he had seen it somewhere. And at times, Jesus even used banking terms when He related His stories.

Where did a boy from Nazareth learn about all of these things?

This "city set on a hill" almost certainly had a great *influence* on the life of Jesus from His early childhood, during the time He was growing up as a small boy. Living under the influence of that city helped to form His worldview and His appreciation of different cultures. It gave Jesus experience broad enough to enable Him to venture far beyond Nazareth and speak authoritatively to people on every level of life.

In Matthew 5:14, Jesus was speaking to His disciples about being an influence in the world. He told them, "Ye are the light of the world. A city set on a hill cannot be hid." When Jesus spoke these words, His childhood view of Sepphoris in all likelihood stood out in His mind — the image of a city that shone so brightly that its light could not be hidden. The lights of the city penetrated the darkness and gave light to the night.

In Matthew 5:16, Jesus continued to exhort His disciples, saying, "Let your light so shine before men, that they may see your good works, and glorify your Father which is in heaven."

My friend, let me remind you that God saved you, redeemed you, delivered you, and filled you with the light of His Word. Don't be ashamed of what God has done in you. It's time for you to let that light shine brightly so it can penetrate the darkness in the lives of others and give light to guide them through the night they are experiencing right now in their lives.

If you're like a majority of people, you have probably spent a lot of time putting yourself down and badgering yourself about your failures — and you've been tempted to largely forget about the great work God has done in your life. But it's time for you to put an end to that downward spiral. Stop berating yourself over your missteps, and start thanking God for the progress you've already made! Then reach out to someone else in need so you can become a godly influence to benefit another. That person can be touched, changed, and shaped by the light in your life.

I promise you there are people observing you and taking note of the light that is shining in your life. You may not be aware of it, but that person or group of people are witnessing the way you live, how you act, what you do, and what kind of excellence and attitude you demonstrate in your life. They are watching you — and you are making an impact on their lives.

What an opportunity you have to become a godly influence on someone else who really needs your example. As you lean on the Holy Spirit and do your best to obey Him, that light will begin to shine into someone else's darkness. As you walk in obedience, the Holy Spirit will use you to demonstrate God's Word to someone who really needs your influence. *You, my friend, are a city on a hill, so let your light shine!*

MY PRAYER FOR TODAY

Lord, I am thankful that You believe I can be a light in someone else's life! So often I am overly aware of my weaknesses and shortcomings, and I forget what a great work You have already done in me. Forgive me for not expressing my gratitude to You more frequently for the precious changes You have already brought about in my life. Many people sit in darkness and struggle to find their way in life, and today I hear Your Spirit beckoning me to let my light shine before men that they may glorify You and so that I might have a godly influence on someone else's life.

I accept the call of the Spirit, and I will do my best to let Your light in me shine forth to people who are seeking direction for their lives!

I pray this in Jesus' name!

MY CONFESSION FOR TODAY

I confess that God has done a great work in my life and that I have something I can share and impart to others who are seeking direction for their lives. I am finished with berating myself about what I've done wrong. God has done such a precious work in my life. From this moment onward, I will throw back my shoulders, hold my head high, acknowledge the good work that God has done in my life, and let His light in my life shine before all men!

I declare this by faith in Jesus' name!

QUESTIONS FOR YOU TO CONSIDER

1. Can you think of individuals with whom you hold special influence right now? Who are those individuals and in what ways do you think you are influencing their lives?
2. Can you think of someone who is struggling in life right now and needs a good example to follow? Who is that person? How can you help him or her?
3. Can you think of people who influenced you in the past with their godly example? Aren't you grateful that they allowed God to use them in your life? Who were those individuals? Have you ever taken time to express your gratitude to them? If you haven't already thanked them, what is stopping you from taking a few minutes to express your appreciation to them today?

MARCH 12

You've Got What It Takes!

Neither do men light a candle, and put it
under a bushel, but on a candlestick;
and it giveth light unto all that are in the house.
— Matthew 5:15

Once while in Israel, I took a break from the speaking schedule at a conference we were conducting to enjoy a quick visit to a local archeologist's office and take a look at ancient oil lamps he had collected throughout the years. I eagerly waited for him to pull those rare lamps out of a box so I could examine them, but I had no idea how many of them he had collected.

There were scores of them — and he let me know that this was just the tip of the iceberg compared to the large collection he had put away in storage.

When he saw the surprised look on my face, he immediately began to explain how the soil of Israel is loaded with archeological relics, including ancient oil lamps. "There are so many of these in the ground that you can just about dig anywhere and find an oil lamp," he said.

I asked, "After thousands of years have passed, I thought these would be pretty rare, so why are there still so many of them still being found?"

He answered, "These lamps were the only source of light in the ancient world. As you can see, these lamps aren't very large. If a person really wanted to light his house or building, he had to use a lot of these lamps. That's why there are still so many of them scattered in the dirt throughout the land of Israel."

I reached out to take one of the lamps in my hand. The archeologist told me, "That's a Herodian lamp that dates to the time of Jesus." It was small, formed of clay, shaped to hold oil, and had a small opening at the end of the spout where a wick could be inserted into the base of the lamp to soak up oil. In ancient days when it was time to light the lamp, fire was put to the wick. As long as oil was supplied to the base of the lamp, it would keep burning and giving light.

Today that Herodian lamp sits on my desk in Moscow — and every time I stop to look at it, my mind goes to Jesus' words in Matthew 5:15. He said, "Neither do men light a candle, and put it under a bushel, but on a candlestick; and it giveth light unto all that are in the house."

The word "candle" in this verse gives the impression of a wax candle like we use today, but during the days when Jesus walked the earth, there were no wax candles such as the ones we use. This word "candle" is an unfortunate translation of the Greek word *luchnos*, a word that refers to an *oil lamp* exactly like the ones I just described. A literal translation of this verse should read, *"Neither do men light an oil lamp and put it under a bushel…. "*

In this text, Jesus was exhorting the disciples — *and us* — to let our light shine before men so we can *influence* the world around us. He used the example of an *oil lamp* to make His point, so before we proceed any further, I believe we should delve deeper to see why Jesus used an oil lamp and why this imagery is such a perfect illustration of us!

Oil lamps were made of clay and were very fragile. In fact, they were so fragile that they could be broken by a mere squeeze of the hand holding them. Even in Jesus' day, these oil lamps had to be handled carefully lest they break, the oil spill out, and the light be lost.

Now do you see why Jesus used oil lamps to depict you and me? Although our bodies are a miracle created by God, like the oil lamps in this illustration, we are made from the clay of the earth and we are very fragile. The real miracle is that God would choose to put His Spirit inside us. That is why the apostle Paul wrote about it with such wonder in Second Corinthians 4:7. In that verse, he said, "But we have this treasure in earthen vessels…"

The example Paul gave in this verse is not exactly the same as the oil lamps in Jesus' illustration, but the point is precisely the same. In this verse, Paul used the Greek word *ostrakinos* when he referred to us as being "earthen vessels." The word *ostrakinos* describes *easily broken pottery made of inferior materials.* Shoddy, deficient, substandard pottery is exactly the kind of "earthen vessels" Paul had in mind when he wrote Second Corinthians 4:7. He used the illustration of cheaply made pottery to epitomize us. That explains his amazement that God would place His Spirit in us! *Think of what a miracle it is that God would place His Spirit inside you and me!*

The lamps in Jesus' illustration were fragile oil lamps, yet they contained *oil* that empowered the light. In the Old and New Testaments, *oil* is the symbol of the Holy Spirit. Just like the oil in the lamps to which Jesus referred, God has placed His Spirit in us. Although at times we feel fragile, as long as we yield to the Lord, He continually resupplies us with enough of the Holy Spirit's oil to keep us burning through the night so we can give light to those who are in darkness around us. *We have a continual supply of the oil and the fire of the Holy Spirit!*

But in Matthew 5:15, Jesus told us, "Neither do men light a candle [i.e., an oil lamp], and put it under a bushel...." What did He mean when He spoke about putting a lamp under a "bushel," and what is a "bushel"?

The word "bushel" is the Greek word *modios.* It refers to a jar or container that was used to measure grain. To put a lamp under a jar or container where there is no oxygen would obviously put out the light. Do you see what a powerful statement Jesus was making? He was driving the point home that it makes no sense to light a lamp and then put it under a bushel where no one can see it. Why would anyone want to do that? Furthermore, putting a lamp under a bushel where there is no oxygen would be sure to smother the light.

By using this example, Jesus strongly admonished us to keep our gifts, talents, and influence out in the open where they can be seen, where they can grow, and where they can provide light to other people.

Why would God give you gifts to benefit others and then have you hide them where no one can see them or appreciate them? God never intended for you to conceal your gifts or to hide your influence. *He wants your light to shine brightly!*

Maybe you've seen yourself as being inferior, or maybe the devil has assaulted your self-image and tempted you to wrongly believe that you have nothing to offer. Perhaps you have felt that you fall short in comparison to others whose gifts and talents shine especially bright. But if you've kept your gifts and talents under wraps, you may be shocked to discover how gifted and talented you really are and how much potential influence is inside you just waiting to be tapped. You just have to give yourself the opportunity to shine!

It's time for you to quit hiding in the shadows! God put His Spirit and supernatural abilities inside you — and that truth alone should bring you out into the open! His Spirit in you is a rich reservoir of oil that will burn long and burn brightly. *You have what it takes to be a success!*

But for you to be the phenomenal success and influence God knows that you can be, you have to be willing to quit putting yourself down. And then you have to choose to step out of the shadows! It's time for you to come out from under that bushel where you've been hiding and let the Holy Spirit light your wick with a fire that will make you shine for Him! As long as you are willing to keep yielding to the Holy Spirit, He will keep filling and supplying you with enough oil to burn long and burn strong so you can be a source of light and illumination to many people all the days of your life on this earth.

What a waste of time it is for you to buy into the devil's lies and badger yourself with thoughts that you have nothing to offer! God's Spirit lives in you, and if you'll dare to let Him do it, He will burn so brightly in your life that you will become an illuminating force to people all around you. But if you refuse to bring your gifts and talents out from under wraps, no one will ever know what God has put in you. And if you neglect those God-given endowments too long, eventually they will begin to diminish, just like a fire that eventually goes out for lack of oxygen.

So why don't you make the decision today to get out of the box of insecurity and complacency that has contained you? Stop telling yourself you're not as good or talented as others, and start using what God has given you for His glory! As you press into Him and put your wick down deep into the oil of the Holy Spirit, you'll become so saturated with His presence that you'll begin to burn brighter and brighter for Jesus. Just let your gifts flow, and become the influence He intended you to be! *Believe me, friend, you've got everything it takes!*

MY PRAYER FOR TODAY

Father, my heart is filled with gratitude today for Your Spirit inside me. What a miracle it is that You would place Your richest treasure in me! Today I want to surrender to You anew, and I ask You to refill me with a full supply of the Holy Spirit's oil so I may burn long and bright in this life. You have called me, equipped me, and anointed me to do great things in this life. I know I have been guilty of putting my light under a bushel, but I'll do it no more! I'm making the decision to step out of the shadows and allow God to release my gifts and talents when and how He desires. I choose to shine my light where it will be a benefit to someone else. Jesus, I thank You for helping me realize that it's time for me to step up and step out so that I can be the godly influence You want me to be in someone else's life.

I pray this in Jesus' name!

MY CONFESSION FOR TODAY

I confess that I am stepping out of the shadows. I am releasing my gifts, and I am making the decision to let my light shine so I can be the blessing to others God intends me to be. I am finished badgering myself and putting myself down. I will no longer hide my light and life under a bushel. I am filled to the brim with the Holy Spirit's oil. His fire is burning brightly in me, and very soon it will be evident for all to see!

I declare this by faith in Jesus' name!

QUESTIONS FOR YOU TO CONSIDER

1. Can you truthfully say that you are using all the gifts and talents that God has given you, or have you been reluctant to step out in faith and let those gifts and talents work? What is stopping you from being all that God has planned for you to be?
2. Think just for a moment about your life, and assess the various ways you are using the gifts and talents God gave you. Where are you using them, how are you using them, and are you using them to your maximum potential? Have you ever considered how your life would change if you actually let God's gifts *fully* operate in you?
3. Have you sought the Lord to discover where He might want to position you so your gifts can operate for His purposes? What is the lampstand where your gifts could be best utilized for His glory in this season of your life?

MARCH 13

Guts and Gumption!

Neither do men light a candle, and put it under a bushel,
but on a candlestick; and it giveth light
unto all that are in the house.
— Matthew 5:15

In yesterday's *Sparkling Gem*, we looked at different ways to shine our light into the darkness and positively influence the world around us. God wants you to be a positive influence in *all* areas of your life. However, to have the kind of colossal effect that God wants you to have on other people, you cannot hide your God-given gifts, talents, and abilities. Instead you must put them on full display so you can be the blessing God intends for you to be!

With this truth in mind, I want us to look at Matthew 5:15 where Jesus said, "Neither do men light a candle, and put it under a bushel, but on a candlestick…." At first glance, the word "candlestick" in this verse might give the impression of a candle or candlestick like we use today, but these kinds of candles and candlesticks didn't exist in New Testament times. Rather, the word "candlestick" in Matthew 5:15 is the Greek word *luchnia*, which refers to *an elevated stand on which an oil lamp is placed*. These oil lamps were exactly the kind of lamps described in yesterday's *Sparkling Gem.*

The word *luchnia*, or "candlestick" is used 12 times in the New Testament to depict this kind of elevated lamp stand. In fact, it is precisely the word John used in Revelation 1:12 and 13 to describe the "seven golden candlesticks" he saw during his vision of Jesus. When John recorded that he saw Jesus standing in the "midst of the seven golden candlesticks" (v. 13), it meant that Jesus was standing in the middle of *seven golden elevated stands* that had *oil lamps* resting on top of them. Some scholars suggest that these seven golden lamps may be a reference to a Jewish menorah. Whether this is true or not is not verifiable by Scripture, but one thing is sure — the Greek word *luchnia* means these oil-burning lamps were sitting on some kind of *elevated stand* so they could give maximum light.

During the time of the New Testament, it was customary for homes, palaces, businesses, and public buildings to place brightly burning lamps on pedestals because a higher position provided superior light that could illuminate the entire environment. The higher the lamp, the less darkness in a room. Thus, when Jesus said, "Neither do men light a candle, and put it under a bushel, but on a candlestick...," He was telling us that we must lift our lamps — *our gifts, talents, and personal influence* — as high as possible. When they are elevated in a highly visible position, God can use us to "give light unto all that are in the house."

If you keep your light at table level, you'll illuminate the people around the table. If you keep it in the corner, you'll illuminate people who are in the corner. But if you lift that same light high, elevate it, put it on a pedestal, and make it visible, it will illuminate *everyone* in the room where it previously touched only a handful. The amount of light given is the same, but the elevated position of the light makes the light much more effective.

Allow me to share an example from my own life that is integrally tied to the very book you are reading right now. Years ago, I knew God wanted me to write books that would be read around the world. I thought and dreamt about it constantly, but I would also second-guess myself. I would think, *Who am I to think people would read something I wrote?* Instead of developing my gift and writing books that would shine light into the lives of other people, I only dreamt about it. But one day the Holy Spirit spoke to my heart and told me that it was time to quit dreaming and to start actually using my gifts — *elevating them and believing in them* — so they could become a blessing to people.

If I had never dared to write or to *elevate* and *promote* what I had written, it is doubtful that you would have ever discovered the book you are holding in your hands right now. For my dream to come to pass, I had to accept that my light was needed in the lives of other people, and then I had to elevate it out of the shadows and allow God to use it in His perfect timing to edify and bless others.

The truth is that there are many people who are more talented writers than I, but they're not known because their gifts are still hidden under a bushel and they therefore have not reached a larger audience. Although their skills are tremendous and loaded with power, they remain unknown and will remain unknown until they are willing to do whatever is required according to the Lord's instruction to elevate those gifts and put them on a lamp stand where they will be seen and appreciated. Only then will they begin to affect more than the small handful gathered around the table or the few who are sitting in their corner, metaphorically speaking.

If your light is going to be a blessing to the world, then you must dare to lift your light high and put in on a pedestal where people will see it and be affected by it. Once you've silenced intimidation and made that bold decision, you begin to fulfill your dream of reaching and illuminating a larger audience.

The believers who have influence in the world — such as those who write the songs you sing, the books you read, or the sermons you hear preached on TV — are not necessarily the most gifted, talented, or anointed people. The truth is that they had the nerve to step out by faith to elevate their abilities, regardless of how good or inferior their abilities were, and today they are renowned and influential. They had the guts and gumption to get their light out from under a bushel and let it shine — and that's why *they* have influence and not someone else. A great part of their success is due to their willingness to step out from obscurity to let their light begin to shine.

Jesus said, "Neither do men light a candle, and put it under a bushel, but on a candlestick; and it giveth light unto all that are in the house" (Matthew 5:15). Are your gifts, talents, abilities, and influence giving light to the people around you in all spheres of your life, such as your home, your work, your school, or your church? Think of how deeply satisfying it would be for you to know that people were blessed because you let your light shine!

God has given you everything you need to make that kind of difference in the lives of other people. He has given you the oil and the fire of the Spirit, but *you* are the only one who can decide to put that light out on a lamp stand where it will be a blessing to others. No one can make that decision for you.

So what are you going to do — keep your gifts, talents, and potential influence a secret, or put your light on a pedestal so it can give light to everyone in the house? There's one thing for sure — a part of the success in God that you dream about will come as a result of your willingness to step out from obscurity and *let your light begin to shine*!

MY PRAYER FOR TODAY

Father, I know it's time for me to quit thinking about what I'm going to do and to start doing it. I've prayed, dreamed, talked, and thought about stepping out in faith — and now You are telling me that it's my time to step up and get started. Your Spirit has been tugging at my heart, trying to get me to come out of hiding and into the light, but I've been afraid of what would happen if I took a step of faith. It's time for me to put my fear aside, put my trust in You, and begin to let my light shine. Holy Spirit, help me have the guts and gumption I need to bring my light out from under the bushel so I can begin to shine brighter and further for You!

I pray this in Jesus' name!

MY CONFESSION FOR TODAY

I confess that I will no longer hide in the shadows and conceal the gifts, talents, and abilities that God has given to me. I've hidden them for too long — and now I am willingly making the decision to step out of the shadows and put my light in a place where it will be the blessing God intended it to be. God has gifted me and anointed me, and the Holy Spirit is now telling me that it is my time to rise up and shine. The day of timidity and complacency has passed! I now have the guts, gumption, and boldness needed to use my gifts and abilities to God's glory and to let them illuminate and influence the largest audience possible!

I declare this by faith in Jesus' name!

QUESTIONS FOR YOU TO CONSIDER

1. What are the unique gifts, talents, and special abilities God has given you? What kind of positive impact have you seen when you've been bold enough to allow these gifts, talents, and abilities to freely operate?
2. Can you think of any individuals whose gifts and talents are not as great as some other people you might know, but because they were daring and bold, they became well-known and influential? What attitudes do they possess that caused them to rise to the top while others remain in obscurity?
3. If you keep doing exactly what you're doing right now, where will you be one year from now? Will your progress be any different? Will your influence have grown if you keep doing exactly what you are doing right now? What do you need to do differently in order to gain more ground?

MARCH 14

The Smallest Verse in the Bible

Jesus wept.
— John 11:35

When I was a teenager, we played games in our youth group that helped us memorize Bible verses. Often our Sunday school teacher or youth leader would ask us Bible questions to see how well we really knew God's Word. A question often asked, and one that nearly everyone in the group could answer, was this: *"What is the shortest verse in the Bible?"*

Everyone in the group would simultaneously yell out, "I know, I know!" So the teacher would ask, "All right, what is it?" Almost in chorus, the teenagers would shout, *"Jesus wept!"* Everyone in the group knew the answer to that one!

This little verse is found in John 11, where Jesus had just received information that Lazarus, one of His dearest friends, had died. Several days later, Jesus arrived in Bethany, the city where Lazarus lived with his two sisters, Mary and Martha. As Jesus approached the city, Mary and other friends who had gathered met Him. John 11:33 tells us, "When Jesus therefore saw her weeping, and the Jews also weeping which came with her, he groaned in the spirit, and was troubled."

The Greek New Testament makes it clear that Jesus was *deeply troubled* when He arrived in Bethany. Perhaps He was troubled because of the disbelief of those who were present or because of what Satan had attempted to do to His dear friend. But one thing is sure: What Jesus was experiencing wasn't just a matter of human emotions, for the Bible says He "groaned *in the spirit*, and was *troubled.*"

The word "troubled" comes from the Greek word *taresso*, which depicts one who is *deeply stirred*. This describes a deep, inward form of prayer when Jesus' spirit hooked up with the Holy Spirit in a powerful, supernatural expression of the Father's will and released the anointing required to meet the need of that moment. I understand this type of deep stirring even from my own prayer life. There are times when prayer is too deep for words, and it may be expressed as groanings or with tears as the Holy Spirit takes hold together with me and helps me pray from my spirit what my mind cannot articulate (*see* Romans 8:26). It was in this state of being that Jesus said, "...Where have ye laid him? They said unto him, Lord, come and see."

Immediately John 11:35 states: "Jesus wept."

The word "wept" is the Greek word *dakruo*, which refers to *an abrupt release of tears*. So when the Bible says Jesus *wept*, it means He actually *burst* into tears and *sobbed*. It was *a torrent of tears*. His emotions were gripped by the moment as He looked upon the unbelief of attenders and realized that death that seized His friend. But in that moment, Jesus pushed beyond it all, lifted His voice, and declared, "Lazarus, come forth" (v. 43)!

The Greek here is a command with no hint of a suggestion or any option. What He was commanding, He *expected* to take place. An interpretive translation of this verse could read: *"Lazarus, come out — now!"* And just as Jesus had commanded, it came to pass. John 11:44 tells us, "And he that was dead came forth...."

That day was quite revealing about Jesus. It let us know that Jesus was not always stoic about the issues that He faced in His earthly ministry. There were several episodes in the four gospels where Jesus demonstrated *emotion: anger* with merchants in the temple (*see* John 2:14-16), *sadness* that His disciples did not believe (*see* Matthew 8:26), and *joy* when His disciples got it right (*see* Matthew 16:17). We also see that Jesus experienced fleeting moments when He was tempted to be *troubled*. But rather than give in to that unproductive moment of emotion, Jesus rose above it, took authority over the situation, and turned the moment around for the glory of God. *What could have ended in tears ended in victory because Jesus lifted His voice and gave a command!*

What are *you* facing right now? Do you feel the temptation to be gripped with paralyzing emotions? *This story lets us know that Jesus was tempted with that too.* Do you feel tugged by tears? *Tears tugged Jesus' emotions too.* Is your voice of authority needed to bring a change to the situation you have found yourself in right now? *Jesus' voice was needed too.* He understands completely when you cry, and He knows what it means when you need to push beyond the emotion in order to release faith into a situation.

If you have been gripped by emotion in a particular challenge you're currently facing, I urge you to spend some time today with the Lord and pour out your heart to Him. Once you've worked that emotion out of your soul, it will be time for you to lift your voice and take action. Let the authority embedded in your spirit speak! And when your voice releases that authority that is yours by right as a child of God, don't budge an inch! Speak, as Christ spoke, giving no hint of suggestion or a different option. Command in the name of Jesus what you expect to take place! Just as Jesus rose to the moment, took authority over the situation, and turned it around for the glory of God, this can become *your* moment to rise to victory. *What could have ended in tears can end in victory!*

MY PRAYER FOR TODAY

Father, today I give You my emotions. I confess that at times they have tried to dominate me and steal my joy. I've allowed others to affect me, and I've permitted bad situations to impact me. I'm tired of living the way I've lived, Father. You have called me to live above defeat, and today I am making the choice to let the power of the Holy Spirit within lift me to a new place of victory I've never known before. Rather than just throw in the towel and quit in defeat, I will lift my voice and speak to the need, and I will see the power of God work on my behalf!

I pray this in Jesus' name!

MY CONFESSION FOR TODAY

I confess that I'm not conquered by my emotions or by the situations I am facing in life right now. Jesus is Lord of all in my life! He is Lord over me, my family, my health, my business, my money, my relationships — absolutely everything. I refuse to allow my emotions to dominate my faith and my responses to life. With the Holy Spirit reigning in my spirit, I rise to the moment by the power of God! I speak powerful words of victory that turn potentially bad situations into glorious moments.

I declare this by faith in Jesus' name!

QUESTIONS FOR YOU TO CONSIDER

1. I'm sure you've had moments when you felt your emotions trying to take over. How does it affect you to know that Jesus had to face and overcome those same types of challenges with *His* emotions?
2. After reading today's *Sparkling Gem,* what new insights did you gain from John 11 and the words "Jesus wept"?
3. What would you say to someone who is caught in a maze of emotions and needs to rise to a moment of decision?

MARCH 15

Slow-Moving Judgment

And his feet like unto fine brass [bronze]...
— Revelation 1:15

In our TV room, we have a large coffee table that sits in the middle of the room. It is covered with large coffee-table-sized books, and right on top of them is a rather large-sized bronze statue of a Russian bear, which, of course, is the symbol of Russia. Often when we are watching television, Denise will ask, "Rick, will you move that bear so I can see the TV screen?" I'm happy to move it, but moving it is a task because it's *bronze* — and that means it's *very* heavy. Moving an item made of bronze doesn't happen quickly because of the weight of the object. It takes all my strength to pick it up and move it.

When Denise asks me to move that bronze bear, it often makes me think of Jesus, because Revelation 1:15 says that Jesus' feet are "like unto fine brass" — actually it's the Greek word *chalkolibanos* — a strange word for "bronze." We'll look at why it's a strange word in just a minute. But moving that bronze bear in our TV room, and how much energy and strength it takes to move it, always makes me think how *slowly* Jesus moves when He takes actions toward judgment.

Bronze in Scripture represents *judgment*. This image of Jesus with feet "like unto fine brass [bronze]" tells us that those who resist Jesus' commands will discover that He will ultimately trample down every plan and purpose of man that stands against the character of God.

However, bronze is heavy, and it is difficult to quickly move an object made of this metal. The fact that Jesus' feet were like bronze sends the message that when Christ does move to bring judgment, He does so *slowly*. Even in Revelation 2:21, where Christ is threatening judgment to a woman named Jezebel, He moves *slowly* because he wants to give her "space to repent." Christ always prefers repentance to judgment. But if repentance does not occur, He moves in the direction of the offender to bring correction and judgment where it is needed — yet He moves *slowly* with the hope that repentance will occur before He has to apply his bronze feet of judgment. This is why the symbolism of *bronze feet* is so important in this vision.

But when John wrote about Jesus' feet, he further noted that they looked "as if they burned in a furnace." This tells us the metal had not yet set; in other words, the decision-making process was still being "forged in the crucible." The metal had been heated and poured forth, but because it still glowed brightly, we know that the hardening process was not yet complete. Lifting one foot at a time, Jesus was moving slowly enough to give each person an opportunity to avoid judgment by repenting before suffering the consequences of continued error or sin.

Let's consider why *chalkolibanos* is such a strange word for "bronze." The first part of the word *chalkos* means *bronze*. But it's the second part of the word that is so unusual, for it is the word *libanos* — the word for *frankincense*. It tells us that Christ's feet carry the golden hue of frankincense because He lives in the atmosphere of prayer, where He intercedes as the Great High Priest for every person He has ever washed in His blood. Although He is poised with potential correction and judgment *if* necessary, Jesus *is*, *has been*, and *always will be* interceding for the Church — pleading for His people to hear Him and repent *before* He arrives with judgment.

Just think for a moment of Christians you know who lived wrong for a long time before correction was brought into their lives. Christ did not rush to judge them; rather, He gave them a lot of time to repent and self-correct before He had to do something more radical about it. Jesus always prefers repentance to judgment. That's why His feet are like *bronze* — slow-moving. That's also the reason they are covered in *frankincense*, because He has prayed for every person to respond to His pleadings so He doesn't have to bring a stricter form of correction.

Are you a witness to the longsuffering of God in your own life?

If you know someone who is a Christian but is deliberately living in sin, pray for that person to respond to Jesus' tender mercies that are giving him or her time to self-correct and repent. The fact that Jesus' bronze feet are covered with the hue of intercessory prayer means He doesn't want to carry out stronger action. He is therefore moving slowly enough to give him or her time to self-correct *before* He arrives to apply stronger action. If you know believers who are in this situation, join in prayer for them to hear and repent before stronger action is needed to bring them back to where they ought to be in their walk with God.

That's what I think of every time Denise asks me to pick up the bronze bear and move it from the top of our coffee-table books. It is a reminder of the tender patience of Jesus — but it is also a stern reminder that a day eventually comes when He arrives to deal with the issues that we haven't dealt with on our own initiative!

MY PRAYER FOR TODAY

Father, I am deeply moved by what I have read today, and I know that it is the truth. I know that what I have read today is absolutely the way You deal with those whom You love. Today I pray for my Christian friends who are living wrong and just assume that You don't notice. Now I understand that in Your mercy, You are giving them time to self-correct. Please speak to their hearts and bring them to a place of self-correction and repentance before they must be dealt with in another way. I pray this for myself as well today.

I pray this in Jesus' name!

MY CONFESSION FOR TODAY

I confess that I am quick to respond when the Holy Spirit corrects me. I serve God faithfully. I do those things that please Him. When I am inwardly made to know that I am doing something wrong — or if I have intentionally or unintentionally done something that requires correction — I am quick to admit it and to repent. If I must repent to someone else for something I have done wrong to them, I am also quick to do that. The Holy Spirit makes me sensitive to sin and gives me the desire to live a life of holiness.

I declare this by faith in Jesus' name!

QUESTIONS FOR YOU TO CONSIDER

1. Can you think of any Christians who lived in flagrant sin for a long time, and it seemed like it took forever before God arrived on the scene to deal with it? Do you now understand that Christ prefers repentance to judgment and that He was giving them time to self-correct so that a strong form of discipline wouldn't have to be used?
2. What examples can you think of in the Old or New Testament where God gave someone time to repent *before* He had to deal with him or her more strongly?
3. Have you been a recipient of God's longsuffering as He waited for you to make a change in your life? Are you in that situation right now? What is God giving you time to change *before* He has to take stronger measures to help you? Why are you waiting to make the change He requires of you?

MARCH 16

Convicted!

And when he is come,
he will reprove the world of sin....
— John 16:8

Do you remember the first time you were convicted that you were a sinner? The first time I *really* knew I was a sinner is etched in my mind forever. For me, it was when a guest evangelist came to preach a week of meetings at our church. On one of those nights, he delivered a riveting message about hell. Although I was only five years old at the time, it shook me to my bones. By the time he finished preaching, the Holy Spirit had caused me to know that I was born a sinner and that if I didn't receive Christ, I would spend an eternity in hell.

My five young years had been spent largely in the church. From the time I was eight days old, I was in church. I remember the church nursery, graduating to the next little Sunday school room, and so on. From the earliest age, my parents were teaching me that Jesus and church should be the center of my life — and for that, I am forever thankful.

Although I attended Sunday school where my teachers taught me about Jesus, it was when that guest evangelist delivered his message about hell that the Holy Spirit reached deep into my five-year-old heart and convicted me that I was born a sinner and that I would spend an eternity in hell if I didn't repent and commit my life to Christ. I occasionally hear people say children are too young to comprehend such things. But I assure you that at the age of five, I knew I was a sinner and that if I didn't repent and make Jesus the Lord of my life, I would be eternally lost. It wasn't the horrible sins I had committed that condemned me; I was too young to have committed horrible sins. Nevertheless, I understood that I was born a sinner and my condition separated me from God.

I wanted to walk the aisle to repent, but my parents were concerned that I was too young to really understand what I was doing. They didn't want me to simply fill out a card at the altar without *truly* coming to Christ. But from that day on, every night when it was time to go to bed, I would tremble with fear that if I died in the middle of my sleep, I would slip into an eternity without God. Each night as I fell asleep, my mother would lay at my side and speak to me about salvation to determine if I really understood sin, its consequences, and repentance. But the Holy Spirit had used that evangelist's message to drive truth into my heart, and I was utterly convicted that I was lost. Although I was young, I understood, and therefore I became accountable to God for that knowledge.

In John 16:8, Jesus explained that one of the works of the Holy Spirit is to convict the lost of sin. Jesus said, "And when he is come, he will reprove the world of sin…." According to Jesus, a significant part of the Holy Spirit's work is to reprove the world of sin. That *reproving* work is what I experienced at the age of five when I heard that evangelist preach about hell. In that moment, my eyes were supernaturally opened and I *knew* I was lost.

If you know Jesus Christ, I am certain you can also remember a time in your life when you experienced this *reproving* work of the Holy Spirit and you *knew* that you were a sinner. The word "reprove" used in John 16:8 is from the Greek word *elegcho.* It means *to expose* or *to convict*, such as *to convict someone of a crime or a sin.* This word was used technically in a court of law to describe legal proceedings during which a person was examined and cross-examined by a prosecuting attorney. After a thorough examination, if the person was found guilty of the accusations brought against him, the court *convicted* him of the crime and issued a corresponding judgment. It was a conviction that led to condemnation.

Jesus used this word *elegcho* to describe the work of the Holy Spirit in John 16:8, when He said that the Spirit would "reprove" the world of sin. This means one of the significant works of the Holy Spirit is to cross-examine a sinner's heart until that sinner is utterly convicted that he is lost. But unlike a prosecuting attorney and court judge in the example given above, the Holy Spirit's goal is *not* to condemn a person, but to escort that person from his sin to the forgiveness, freedom, and life offered to him in Jesus Christ.

When a sinner's eyes are opened and he *really* grasps the fact that he is spiritually lost and therefore deserving of judgment, it triggers that moment when from his heart, he cries out to God for salvation. *This is precisely the purpose of conviction!* In Romans 2:4, Paul told us that it is "the goodness of God that leads us to salvation."

The word "leads" is the Greek word *ago*, which gives the picture of God graciously leading us where we could never go by ourselves. Because we are lost, we could never find the way on our own, so God lovingly steps in to escort us to a crucial point of knowledge — where we understand that we are sinners in need of salvation and that we need His help.

This is the reason the Holy Spirit brings conviction of sin! It is not to make a person feel badly, but to help each person become aware of his or her profound need. His purpose is to cause the sinner's heart to cry out for God and to steer that sinner to the Cross of Jesus Christ, where forgiveness and release from judgment is available.

That awakening moment came for me when I heard an evangelist preach about hell. But by studying the different scriptures where the word *elegcho* is used in the New Testament, it is clear that the conviction of sin comes to people in a variety of ways. For example:

- In Matthew 18:15, the word *elegcho* is used to depict the *personal witness* of a friend, family member, or acquaintance, and how that personal witness can bring a person to a point of *conviction* about his sinful condition. We must never forget that we are anointed to take the Good News to people who are unsaved. When we speak to them, it triggers that divine moment when they really see and understand their need for Jesus. *It brings conviction that leads them to repentance.*
- In Luke 3:19, the word *elegcho* is used to illustrate how the *preaching* of John the Baptist brought Herod to a point of conviction about his sinful lifestyle. Herod refused to repent, but because of John's bold and straightforward preaching, Herod could not escape *knowing* that he was a sinner. This is an example of how *Holy Spirit-anointed preaching* can bring a person to a place of *conviction* about his sinful condition.
- In John 3:20, the word *elegcho* is used to demonstrate how the Light — the truth of God's Word — produces *conviction* in people who are in darkness and sin. When the Holy Spirit shines His truth into unbelievers' darkness through one of His many amazing avenues — such as through preaching, a believer's personal witness, the printed page, or a television broadcast — it brings unbelievers to a place of conviction about their sin. At that moment, they have a choice: to run *to* the light and be changed or to run *from* the light and continue in darkness. Those who run to the light are gloriously saved, whereas others knowledgeably run from the light because they do not want to change. However, although they try to escape the light, it is too late, for the light of *truth* has already shone into their darkness and convicted them that their deeds are wrong. *Truth brings conviction of sin!*
- In First Corinthians 14:24, the word *elegcho* is used in the context of a sinner who comes into a church service where the presence of God is so strong that he is stricken with his *unholiness* in light of the *holiness* of God. The result is that he becomes convicted of sin and falls on his face in repentance. Here we find a reason why we should make every effort and do our part to build a strong presence of God in our church services. This environment unleashes His power to convict the sinner of his need to be saved, and it convicts the saint of his need for sanctification and surrender. *A strong presence of God brings conviction of sin!*

- In James 2:9, the word *elegcho* is used to denote how knowing God's law makes a sinner conscious of the fact that he is a sinner and a lawbreaker. Romans 3:20 tells us that "by the law is the knowledge of sin." When people have a knowledge of God's law, such as the Ten Commandments, that knowledge makes them aware that they have fallen short of the glory of God and are therefore lawbreakers and sinners. The law of God is a major instrument by which the Holy Spirit convicts people of sin. Could this be the reason why the devil has worked so hard to remove the Ten Commandments from today's society?

The fact is, if the Holy Spirit doesn't direct a person's eyes to see the truth about his sinful condition, he will never see it. It is a miracle when a man or woman sees that he is lost — and only the Holy Spirit can reveal this to a lost man (*see Sparkling Gems 1*, February 20, for more on this subject).

The wonderful news is that the Holy Spirit has come "to reprove the world of sin...." He knows exactly how to bring every person to a point of conviction. He has the key to every person's heart. He longs to lovingly escort every lost sinner to repentance and to a new life in Jesus Christ — which is precisely what happened to me at the age of five when I heard that evangelist preach his fiery message about hell. There was no escaping from the truth — the Holy Spirit made me to know that I was a sinner. The only remedy was to repent and commit my life to Jesus Christ.

So today I ask you: *Are you available for the Holy Spirit to use you to shine His light into the hearts of spiritually lost people you know?* The Holy Spirit knows how to reach them, but He needs someone like you through whom He can work. *Are you available to Him?* You may hesitate at first, but think how thankful you are that others allowed God to use them to reach you. Now it's your time to let the Holy Spirit work through you to help lost people find their way to the truth that will turn their lives around and change their eternal destiny!

MY PRAYER FOR TODAY

Lord, I am thankful for the work of the Holy Spirit to produce conviction and change in our hearts and lives. I remember when I first became convicted of my own sin, and it eventually led me to salvation. Now I know that You want to use me to shine the Light of Your Word to others who are in darkness as I used to be in darkness. Forgive me for hesitating and being fearful to take this bold step of faith to act on the love of God in my heart for those who need You. Today I am rejecting that spirit of fear, and I am asking You to release Your power in me so I can help lead others to a place of repentance and lasting change. Help me do this for others just as others once helped me!

I pray this in Jesus' name!

MY CONFESSION FOR TODAY

I confess that I am a bold witness for Jesus Christ. There are people I know — friends, relatives, acquaintances, and coworkers — who need to know Jesus Christ. I declare by faith that I am not selfishly holding back what I know to be life-giving truth. I will lovingly tell others the

Good News that Jesus can save them and change their lives. I am a mighty vessel that the Holy Spirit can work through. Because I am available for His use, people in my life who need Jesus are coming to know Him and the freedom He brings!

I declare this by faith in Jesus' name!

QUESTIONS FOR YOU TO CONSIDER

1. Can you remember when you first became aware that you were a sinner and you needed to repent? What were the circumstances, and what exactly happened to you to let you know you were lost and without God?
2. Can you think of specific individuals in your life who you know are lost and you have sensed the Holy Spirit tugging on your heart to speak to them about Jesus? Have you been resisting this tug of the Spirit in your heart? If so, what is stopping you from telling them the most important news in the universe?
3. How long has it been since you've reached out to someone who is lost to tell that person about Jesus? A year from now when you look back, will you have a better answer to that question because of the decision you made today to be a bold witness for Him?

MARCH 17

The Right Kind of Pain

Now when they heard this, they were pricked in their heart,
and said unto Peter and to the rest of the apostles, Men and brethren,
what shall we do? Then Peter said unto them, Repent....
— Acts 2:37,38

None of us likes pain. Yet pain is very important because it is a signal designed to alert us when something is wrong in our bodies. Our response to pain may be to determine the root of the problem or to simply numb the discomfort with painkillers. The painkillers may work for a while, but when the numbing effect wears off, the pain often reemerges because its source was never identified and corrected.

Generally speaking, the only way to permanently get rid of pain is to go to the root of the problem. Once the source is identified and the correct treatment is applied, the pain can usually be eliminated.

This principle is also true spiritually, especially for people who are unsaved or are out of fellowship with God. For example, a sermon about the coming of Jesus that simply thrills my heart and fills me with joy can create great pain in the heart of an unsaved person or a Christian who isn't walking with God. When they hear that Jesus will soon return, it scares them and causes them inner pain and discomfort because they know they're not right with God. That unsettled feeling in the pit of their stomachs — that *pain* — is a signal to let them know things are not well in their souls. Otherwise, they'd be rejoicing!

We live in an age when people want to be comforted and told everything is going to be all right. The truth is, some things are *not* going to be all right unless a change is made. We must love people enough to be graciously honest with them, regardless of how painful it is for them to hear the truth. Especially regarding people's salvation, we must speak the truth and not be fearful of their response. If we are not forthright with unbelievers regarding their spiritual condition, they could spend an eternity separated from God.

It's good to preach positive, uplifting messages. In fact, this is something we *need* to do in a world where there is so much hurt, depression, difficulty, and disappointment. Certainly we need to be a source of encouragement to fellow church members and other people who feel put down by life. But when unbelievers are in our midst, we are obligated to make sure they understand that sin separates them from God. As much as we may like them and enjoy their company, the unsaved are *not* all right with God. It may be painful for them to hear the reality of their situation, but we must not merely toss "painkillers" at them to numb them and keep them ignorant of the truth. We must open their eyes to the root of the problem in their lives — their spiritually lost condition.

Especially when we are talking about reaching unbelievers or the subject of sin, we must address the root. All the motivational and "how-to" sermons in the world cannot cure a sinner's heart. The sin nature cannot be changed by a pat on the back or a hug around the neck. We must come to grips with our responsibility to allow the Holy Spirit to help us be lovingly candid with unsaved people about their spiritual status. If they are lost, there is only one remedy: repentance and faith in Jesus Christ. It may be difficult at first for them to hear the truth, but it's good for them to experience that kind of pain. It will make them inwardly aware that things are not right between them and God.

In Acts 2:37, we see how God used the apostle Peter to address unbelievers on the Day of Pentecost. With a no-nonsense, unapologetic, and direct approach, Peter preached the Gospel with power. He didn't attack his listeners, and neither should we attack those we are trying to reach. There is never a reason to attack or to speak disparagingly to our audience. Even if people are dead in sin, they were made in the image of God, and they deserve to be spoken to with dignity and respect. Peter was respectful, yet he was forthright and honest as he went straight for the root of his listeners' problem, preaching a message that made them so extremely uncomfortable and inwardly pained that they cried out to learn how to be saved!

Let's look at the effect Peter's message had on his listeners and see what we can learn from this New Testament example. Acts 2:37 tells us, "Now when they [the unsaved crowd] heard this, they were pricked in their heart, and unto Peter and to the rest of the apostles, Men and brethren, what shall we do?" I want you to especially notice that this verse says, "They were pricked in their heart." Let's look at the word "pricked" in this verse, which is the Greek word *katanusso*, a compound of the words *kata* and *nusso*.

The word *kata* means *down*. However, used in the word "pricked," it gives the idea of something that is *deep* or something that is *deep down*. The second part of the word *katanusso* is *nusso*, a Greek word that means *to prick, to puncture, to stab, to sting, to stun*, or *to pierce*.

The only other time the word *katanusso* is found in the New Testament is in John 19:34 where John writes about Jesus: "But one of the soldiers with a spear *pierced* his side, and forthwith came there out blood and water." The word "pierced" in this verse is from this same root word *nusso*. It tells how the soldiers with a spear *pierced, punctured, stabbed*, and *sliced open* Jesus' side. It was a *deep puncturing* of His side that pierced even His lungs.

This same root word *nusso* that describes such a deep puncturing is used in Acts 2:37, where it is translated as "pricked." This alone tells us that the unsaved people in the crowd that day were *deeply affected* by Peter's words. In fact, it means that his words had the spiritual effect of *puncturing* their hearts and that they felt *sliced wide open* by his message.

However, when the words *kata* and *nusso* are compounded to become *katanusso*, the new word is even more profound, for it describes not just *a piercing* but *an extremely deep piercing that would produce enormous pain and discomfort*.

The word *katanusso* in Acts 2:37 emphatically means that Peter's listeners were *deeply disturbed* when they heard his message. That message gave them such an intense *stab* to their hearts that it *penetrated* their conscience, *sliced open* their souls, *punctured* their hearts, and *cut* them so deeply on the inside that they cried out for help. The message *stung* their hearts and minds as they became aware of their sin. Suddenly their souls felt an *ache*, and their hearts were filled with *anguish*.

When Peter stood before that lost crowd on the Day of Pentecost, he was standing before sinners in dire need of repentance. They needed truth that would change them, not a painkiller that would make them feel good while failing to remedy their problem. The root of the problem had to be identified so it could be dealt with and eliminated. For those unbelievers to have a supernatural change of nature, it would require repentance, so Peter presented the truth boldly, plainly, and with no apologies.

That day the Holy Spirit reached deep into those people's hearts and convicted them of their sinful condition. The crowd wasn't offended by Peter's message at all. Acts 2:41 tells us that the unbelieving crowd "gladly received his word." The words "gladly received" are from the Greek word *apodechomai*, which means *to take quickly, to take readily*, or *to take with a welcoming attitude*.

People are thankful when someone tells them the truth, even if it is painful to hear at first. They appreciate an honest approach. That day more than 3,000 souls came into the Kingdom of God as a result of the *katanusso* produced in people's hearts by Peter's honest preaching of the Word. Those are very impressive results!

As we present truth to people — especially to unbelievers — we don't need to be ugly or harsh, but neither do we need to water down the truth or act apologetic for what the Bible teaches. When truth is presented clearly and powerfully, it puts a sharp, doubled-edged sword into the hands of the Holy Spirit, which He uses to penetrate the hearts of the unsaved. When the message is watered down, it dulls the edge of the blade and makes it more difficult for the Holy Spirit to slice through the demonic strongholds created in people's minds by sinful habits, bondages, and general spiritual darkness.

Of course, we should always allow the Holy Spirit to lead us in knowing how and when to present the truth to someone who doesn't know the Lord. Then as we speak in a spirit of compassion — and as we do it boldly, straightforwardly, and with no apologies — the root of the listener's problem will be identified and eliminated.

We must never forget that the *Gospel* is the *power of God* that leads to salvation (Romans 1:16). There is never a reason for us to be ashamed of the Gospel or to apologize for the requirements God has set forth for all who would come to Him.

When the unsaved crowd heard Peter preach that day, their hearts were sliced so wide open by the truth Peter preached that they cried out, "Men and brethren, what shall we do?" (*see* Acts 2:37). The people asked Peter and the other apostles to tell them what steps were required for them to be made right with God. That's when Peter boldly told them: *"Repent."*

Think about the way you address unbelievers, and ask yourself the following:

- *When I share truth with unsaved people, do I present it compellingly, compassionately, and clearly enough for them understand the real root of their problem?*
- *Do I comfort the lost and leave them feeling like they're all right in their sin, or do I help them understand their need to be saved?*
- *If I were unsaved, would I feel the urgent need to repent and to give my life to Christ as a result of what I've been telling unbelievers?*
- *Have I been tossing "painkillers" at unbelievers instead of lovingly identifying the root of the problem in their lives and thereby leading them to Christ?*

When we speak to unsaved people, we must not jeopardize their opportunity to receive salvation by watering down the message. To refuse to speak the truth because we feel embarrassed or don't want to be rejected by others is actually selfish because we're placing our desire to be accepted above their need to hear truth that has eternal implications for them. To restrain ourselves in fear that we'll hurt their feelings or offend them isn't justified either.

The truth is, people may feel stung by what we tell them, but that sting may be the very thing that brings them to Jesus Christ. Truth is truth — and we must stand on the side of truth and make it clear that God is calling unbelievers to *repent.* Sin and its consequences are eternal and unchangeable after death. Before lost people leave the sound of our voices, we must make sure they understand the consequences of sin and God's requirement to repent.

Can you think of people you know who need Jesus Christ? Do you love them enough to sit down with them and lovingly tell them the truth, explaining how serious their spiritual condition is according to the Word of God? If you were unsaved, wouldn't you hope someone would love you enough to tell you the truth? Is the Holy Spirit directing you to go to those individuals, share the truth of the Gospel with them, and lead them to Christ?

MY PRAYER FOR TODAY

Lord, I ask You to help me be bold when I speak the truth to people who desperately need Your gift of salvation. In the past, I've been timid and shy about telling the truth, and I ask Your forgiveness for it. At times I've even backed away from witnessing to lost friends and family and failed to tell them about their need to repent. I know I shouldn't be embarrassed about my faith. You said whoever is ashamed of You and Your words, You will be ashamed of them before the Father (see Mark 8:38; Luke 9:26). The truth is still the truth. Many people are lost and headed for hell, and they need to know You in order to be saved. Father, I ask You to give me a heart of love for the lost and the boldness of the Spirit so I may unashamedly proclaim the truth to them and give them the opportunity to escape future judgment and to secure a home in Heaven. Teach me to understand that there is nothing in this world more precious than a soul, and help me reach out to souls in love with the saving message of Jesus Christ.

I pray this in Jesus' name!

MY CONFESSION FOR TODAY

I confess that I make myself available for God to use me to share the truth with people who are lost and who are headed to an eternity in hell. Hell is a very unpleasant thought. However, the Bible teaches that it is a very real place of suffering and that those who die without Christ will inevitably go there. Starting right now, I make the decision to let God's Spirit put a new love for the lost in my heart. I repent for being calloused and insensitive to the spiritual needs of the lost, and from this moment forward, I will allow the Holy Spirit to release His love for them through me. I am yielding my life to God so He can use me as a vessel to reach into the fires of judgment to pull people out before it is too late. Christ died for the unsaved, and I confess that I will be His vessel to proclaim the Good News that Jesus saves!

I declare this by faith in Jesus' name!

QUESTIONS FOR YOU TO CONSIDER

1. Can you remember the specific moment in your life when you came to a place of true repentance and asked Jesus to be the Lord of your life? Did someone reach out to you to help you come to that moment when you received Jesus? How was your life different from that day forward?

2. If you were sharing the Good News with an unbeliever, how would you explain the Gospel to him? How would you explain his spiritually lost condition? Would you tell him about the eternal ramifications of hell? How would you walk him through the process of becoming a child of God?
3. How long has it been since you've reached out to someone who was lost to tell him or her about Jesus? If it's been awhile since that has happened, what's the reason you haven't done it?

MARCH 18

REPENTANCE:
God's Requirement

Then Peter said unto them, *Repent….*
— Acts 2:38

In a recent survey, people who regularly attend church were asked to articulate what the word "repentance" meant to them. The survey resulted in an intriguing and interesting assortment of answers. The majority of those who participated in the survey stated that they believed the word "repentance" meant one or more of the following:

1. To feel sorry about something one did or failed to do.
2. To feel remorseful about some act and to ask for forgiveness for it.
3. To walk forward in a church service to formally ask Jesus into one's heart.

Although these answers are interesting, *none* of them is correct! What's most shocking about this survey is that it was given to people who regularly attend church yet who could not accurately articulate what it means to "repent."

Before we go any further, let's include *you* in the survey. How would you define the meaning of the word "repent"? Try to answer that question before reading on.

The word "repent" is a very important New Testament word. The first time it is chronologically used in the New Testament is in Matthew 3:2, Mark 1:4, and Luke 3:3, where we are told that John the Baptist preached, "…*Repent* ye: for the kingdom of heaven is at hand" (Matthew 3:2). John's ministry was literally launched with that one word "repent." According to the preaching of John the Baptist, the only way to enter into the Kingdom of Heaven was through repentance.

Jesus, too, began His public ministry by beckoning His listeners to repent. In Matthew 4:17, Jesus commenced His preaching ministry when He said, "...*Repent:* for the kingdom of heaven is at hand." Like John the Baptist, Jesus knew that the only way to enter the Kingdom of God was through repentance.

Then in Acts 2:38, we read that Peter launched his preaching ministry on the Day of Pentecost with the same requirement of repentance. Just as John the Baptist and Jesus had called on men to repent, so Peter told his audience in Acts 2:38, "*Repent.*" Peter understood that repentance is the "birth canal" through which people enter the Kingdom of God. In other words, it is the only way to truly be delivered from the kingdom of darkness and to emerge spiritually reborn and filled with the God-kind of life.

Real repentance is very different from remorse. Yet *feelings of remorse for a past action* was one of the most frequent definitions given by people who participated in the aforementioned church survey.

The Greek word for "remorse" in the New Testament is *metamelomai*, which is very different from the Greek word for "repent," the word *metanoeo*. *Metamelomai* expresses *sorrow*, *mourning*, or *grief*. It seldom refers to someone moved to change; rather, it gives a picture of a person consumed with *remorse*, *guilt*, or *regret*.

For example, the word *metamelomai* is used in the gospels to describe the *remorse*, *guilt*, and *regret* that seized the heart and mind of Judas Iscariot after he betrayed Jesus. What Judas experienced was not true repentance, which brings personal change and transformation. Because the Greek word *metamelomai* is used to describe the emotions that captured him, it tells us that Judas was inundated with *distressed*, *regretful* emotions. Such sorrow should not be confused with repentance, for there are many who undergo a flood of regret and sorrow for something they have done, yet they don't truly repent.

Personal change and transformation — NOT remorse, regret, and sorrow — are the true proof of repentance.

The word "repent" that was used by John the Baptist, Jesus, and Peter, is the Greek word *metanoeo*. This is very different from the word *metamelomai*. The word *metanoeo* — "repent" — means *a change of mind*, *repentance*, or *conversion*. In Old Testament and Classical Greek language, *metanoeo* first and foremost meant *a change of mind*. Thus, the use of *metanoeo* is the call *to turn* or *to change one's attitudes and ways*. As used in the New Testament, it demands *a complete, radical, and total change*. It is a decision *to completely change* or *to entirely turn around in the way one is thinking, believing, or living*. The word "repent" in the New Testament gives the image of a person changing from top to bottom — a total transformation wholly affecting every part of a person's life.

The Greek word *metanoeo* is a compound of the words *meta* and *nous*. The word *meta* in this context refers to *a turn* or *a change*. The word *nous* is the word for the *mind*, *intellect*, *will*, *frame of thinking*, *opinion*, or *general view of life*. When the words *meta* and *nous* are compounded, as in the word "repent," it portrays *a decision to completely change the way one thinks, lives, or behaves.*

Metanoeo reflects *a turn, a change, a change of direction, a new course,* and *a completely altered view of life and behavior.* This is not the same as a fleeting sorrow for past actions, but a solid, intellectual decision to take a new direction, to turn about-face, and to revise the pattern of one's life.

I must point out the importance of the word *nous* contained in this definition of repentance. The word *nous,* as previously noted, is the Greek word for *the mind.* This means that the decision to repent lies in the mind, not in the emotions. Emotions may *accompany* repentance, but they are not *required* to repent. Real repentance is *a mental choice to leave a life of sin, flesh, and selfishness, and to turn toward God with all of one's heart and mind in order to follow Jesus.*

A prime example of such a *turning* can be seen in Paul's first letter to the Thessalonian believers when he commended them for the way in which they had "…turned to God from idols to serve the living and true God" (1 Thessalonians 1:9). The word "turned" in this verse is the Greek word *epistrepho,* which means *to be completely turned around.*

Note that Paul said the Thessalonian believers turned from idols "to serve the living and true God." The word "serve" is important, for it tells us that the turn they made produced a life change with visible fruit that reflected the change. The word "serve" is the word *douleuo,* the word for *a servant,* implying that the Thessalonian believers had fully left behind idolatry and had completely dedicated their lives to serving Jesus.

By using this word *douleuo,* Paul informed us that the Thessalonians didn't just claim to have repented; they showed it by changing the way they *thought* and *lived* and *served.* Their dramatically different outward behavior was *guaranteed proof* that real repentance had occurred.

Repentance is not the mere acceptance of a new philosophy or new idea. *It is a conversion to truth so deep that it results in a total life change.* The idea of an across-the-board transformation is intrinsic to the word "repent." In fact, if there is no transformation, change of behavior, or change of desire in a person who claims to have repented, it is doubtful that true repentance ever occurred, no matter what the person claims. Real repentance begins with a decision to make an about-face and to change, but its *proof* can be witnessed as one's outward conduct complies with that decision.

Repentance is God's requirement as presented by John the Baptist, Jesus, and Peter, as well as in other places in Scripture too numerous to count. This means that a person cannot come to God and continue to live as he did before he received the Lord.

We sing the old song, "Just as I Am, Without One Plea"[2] — and certainly we do come to God "just as we are" to receive God's gracious gift of salvation. However, God does not expect us to *remain* the way we are. He expects change, and that is what repentance is all about. With godly repentance, there must be an abandonment of our past and a complete and absolute surrender to the Lordship of Jesus Christ, evidenced by our living according to God's righteous standard.

---

[2] Charlotte Elliott, "Just As I Am," *The Christian Remembrancer Pocket Book* (Poetry, 1835).

As you grow in your walk with God, the Holy Spirit will continue to reveal things in your life that need to change. When He opens your eyes to those things that are displeasing to Him, you must be willing to repent — to make an intelligent, intellectual decision to adjust your thinking and behavior to conform to God's ways. It's a conscious choice. Will you remain belligerent in your attitude and thus defy God's requirement to change — or humbly bow before His holiness and adjust your thinking and behavior to get in agreement with Him and His Word?

More than 2,000 years ago, Jesus began His earthly ministry by preaching, "…Repent: for the kingdom of heaven is at hand" (Matthew 4:17). He is the same yesterday, today, and forever (*see* Hebrews 13:8). Today He is still speaking to people's hearts, telling them to turn from wrong ways that are detrimental to living a life that is holy and pleasing to God. So ask yourself if your ministry to other people reflects that same priority. But first and foremost — what is the Holy Spirit saying to *you*, and how should you respond today?

MY PRAYER FOR TODAY

Father, I am deeply convicted by Your Spirit about areas of my life that need to change. I admit that I've been tolerating things that are unacceptable for a child of God. I have been living far below what You expect of me. I see areas where I have fallen short of Your glory in my thoughts and attitudes, and it has negatively affected my life, my relationships, and my conduct. But starting today, I am choosing to repent. I make up my mind that my life is going to change. I've been wrong to think the way I have thought, and I've been wrong in the way I've behaved. I am no longer ignorant because You have spoken to my heart about these things. Since I am accountable for my attitudes and my actions, I am making the choice to repent and to change — and it starts today!

I pray this in Jesus' name!

MY CONFESSION FOR TODAY

I confess that I am unwilling to tolerate sin in any area of my life. I submit myself to the Holy Spirit and allow the Word of God to cause my thoughts and desires to become conformed to the mind of Christ and agreeable to His will. I align my thoughts and imaginations with the Lord so I can stay in step with His Spirit and in sync with His Word. I am obedient to the Lord, and I live a life that brings glory to His name. I do not just talk about making changes in my life — I prove my repentance is genuine by demonstrating the fruit of a transformed heart.

I declare this by faith in Jesus' name!

QUESTIONS FOR YOU TO CONSIDER

1. Can you think of areas in your own life that are not pleasing to God? If you've given yourself too much latitude and have allowed yourself to hold on to unacceptable attitudes, habits, grudges, and so forth, make it right with the Lord today by deciding to repent and change.

2. As you've ministered to people through the years, have you ever seen someone walk the aisle to give his or her heart to Jesus and yet never really change? What adjustments can you make in the way you preach about repentance to make sure people don't take God's requirements lightly?
3. In what ways did the Holy Spirit help you walk away from who you used to be before you received Christ so you could embrace the new person God created you to be? What habits did you turn away from, and what attitudes and actions did you replace them with in Christ? How can you become more effective in helping others through this same dramatic transformation process?

MARCH 19

The Difference Between Remorse, Guilt, Regret, and Repentance

Then Judas, which had betrayed him, when he saw
that he was condemned, repented himself, and brought again
the thirty pieces of silver to the chief priests and elders,
Saying, I have sinned in that I have betrayed the innocent blood.
And they said, What is that to us? See thou to that.
And he cast down the pieces of silver in the temple,
and departed, and went and hanged himself.
— Matthew 27:3-5

In yesterday's *Sparkling* Gem, I started talking about the subject *repentance*. Over the next few days, I'd like to continue to explore this all-important subject further with you, because so many don't really understand what true repentance is or why it's so foundational and necessary to the Christian walk.

I remember an experience as a young boy growing up in church that made a huge impact on my life and helped me understand the vast difference between two words: *remorse* and true *repentance*. Each year we had annual revival meetings in our church. It was at one of these revival meetings that I heard an evangelist preach about hell, and I became so convicted of my sin that I committed my life to Jesus. However, not long after I walked the aisle and received Christ, I began to seriously doubt whether I had really been saved. This doubt stemmed from watching what happened when others got saved, which was entirely different from my own personal experience. Adults often wept and wept when they bowed at the altar, but I didn't shed a tear the day I got saved. Preying on my insecurity and fears, the devil began to torment me every day with thoughts, such as:

- *Why didn't you cry when you came forward to give your heart to Christ?*
- *Maybe you're not really saved!*
- *If you were really sincere, shouldn't you have cried like all the others did when they repented and got saved?*

As time passed, I began to notice a very important trend. Frequently the people who cried buckets of tears at the altar were the same people who came forward in the altar calls each year during revival meetings. Growing up in church gives a person time to watch people and learn — and I began to recognize that many of these criers were the same people each year. I noticed that after they walked out the back door of the church, many of them didn't show their faces in church again until the next year's revival meeting. Then once again, they ended up back on their knees at the altar — crying buckets of tears and profusely sobbing. Finally, it dawned on me what was happening!

Many of those who cried profusely never changed. Although they nearly used a whole box of tissues sobbing at the altar, it appeared that nothing much deeper occurred than the shedding of tears. I began to realize that a show of emotion isn't always a sign of repentance; sometimes it's only evidence of *remorse.*

Repentance produces *change*, whereas remorse merely produces *sorrow*, which is often confused with repentance. But there is an enormous difference between repentance and remorse. A perfect New Testament example of remorse is found in Matthew 27:3-5, where the Bible tells us about Judas Iscariot. It says, "Then Judas, which had betrayed him, when he saw that he was condemned, repented himself, and brought again the thirty pieces of silver to the chief priests and elders, Saying, I have sinned in that I have betrayed the innocent blood. And they said, What is that to us? See thou to that. And he cast down the pieces of silver in the temple, and departed, and went and hanged himself."

Notice the Bible says that Judas "repented" himself. Usually a person who repents doesn't go out and hang himself afterward, so what really happened in this verse? The answer lies in the word "repented" that is used in this verse. This is not the word *metanoeo*, the word most often used meaning "repent" in the New Testament. Instead, this particular word for "repent" is the Greek word *metamelomai*, which portrays a person who is completely overwhelmed with emotions. This word is used five times in the New Testament, and in each instance, it expresses *sorrow*, *mourning*, or *grief.* The word *metamelomai* rarely gives the picture of someone moved to change, but rather depicts a person who is seized with *remorse*, *guilt*, or *regret.*

1. *Metamelomai* can depict *remorse* that grips a person because of an act he committed that he knows is wrong. If he were willing to repent, he could change and be forgiven. But because he has no plans to repent, stop his sinful activities, and rectify what he has done, he is therefore gripped with remorse. Consequently, this emotion produces *no change* in a person's life.
2. *Metamelomai* can also express the *guilt* a person feels because he knows that he has done wrong, that he will continue to do wrong, and that he has no plans to change

his course of action. He feels shameful about what he is doing but continues to do it anyway, which results in a state of ongoing guilt. This guilt produces *no change* in a person's life or behavior. Yet genuine repentance would fix this feeling of guilt and remove it completely.

3. *Metamelomai* best denotes the *regret* a person feels because he was caught doing something wrong. He isn't repentant for committing the sin; instead, he is sorrowful only because he got *caught*. Now he's in trouble. Rather than being repentant, this person is *regretful* that he got caught and must now pay the consequences. Chances are that if he'd never been caught, he would have continued his activities. This kind of regret likewise produces *no change* in a person's conduct.

Because the word *metamelomai* is used in Matthew 27:3, it means Judas Iscariot did not "repent" in the sense that he was sorry for what he did and wanted to make it right with God. Rather, it confirms that he was *remorseful*, seized with *guilt*, and filled with *regret*. Because of his actions, Judas blew his opportunity to be a high-ranking member of Jesus' inner circle. Judas was more sorrowful for himself than he was for his participation in Jesus' betrayal. This wasn't a demonstration of repentance that leads to salvation, but of sorrow, guilt, and a deep-seated remorse that ultimately led to death. This is precisely what the apostle Paul meant when he wrote in Second Corinthians 7:10 about "the sorrow of the world that worketh death."

Don't misunderstand me — emotion and tears *may* accompany repentance. If we have sinned against the Holy Spirit, it is normal for us to experience godly sorrow for our actions. In Second Corinthians 7:10, Paul wrote about "godly sorrow." Unlike the sorrow of the world that produces death, he wrote that "godly sorrow worketh repentance to salvation." But godly sorrow produces more than tears; it produces a desire to change that leads us to deliverance, freedom, and salvation. *What a contrast to the sorrow of the world that produces hopelessness, defeat, and despair.*

When I was a child and Satan tormented me because I didn't cry at the altar when I got saved, I *was* as saved as it was possible to be saved. I had no tears to cry about my horrid sins because I was five years old when I committed my life to Christ. Even though I didn't cry, my *decision* to serve Him was firm and therefore absolutely real. As a result of this experience, I learned not to confuse sobbing with repentance, for although tears and emotions may accompany this act, they're not requirements, nor are they necessarily evidence that repentance has occurred.

Remember, the word "repent" is *metanoeo* — referring to *a complete turn in the way one thinks, lives, or acts.* For a person to repent, he must simply make up his mind *to change*.

So what is the difference between guilt, remorse, regret, and repentance?

- Guilt is a prison that will keep you perpetually bound and *unchanged.*
- Remorse enslaves you in sorrow that engulfs you emotionally and leaves you feeling sad, depressed, hopeless, and *unchanged.*
- Regret is self-pity that is focused more on your own personal loss than on the pain or loss you caused to others or to the heart of God, and it leaves you *unchanged.*

- Repentance is a quality decision *to change* — and when genuine repentance occurs in a person's heart and mind, you can be sure the Holy Spirit will release His power to effect change in that person's life and lead him to *freedom*!

So in light of what you have read today, are there any areas in your life in which you have felt guilty, remorseful, or regretful — but unchanged? Could it be that you've never really made a firm decision to change, and that's why you've had no enduring victory in these areas of your life?

If you've confused tears with repentance, now you know that you don't have to depend on your emotions to repent. If God is dealing with you about something that needs to change in your life, you can repent right now at this very moment, regardless of what you do or do not feel. *God is waiting for you to make a decision!*

MY PRAYER FOR TODAY

Heavenly Father, I thank You that You have given me the power to choose life. Today I make the decision to turn away from those actions and thought processes that are negative, detrimental, and destructive to my life. I don't want to grieve Your heart in any way. What a joy to know I don't have to wait for emotions to repent! I made the mistake of thinking I had to "feel" something in order to repent, but now I realize that feelings and tears are not requirements for repentance. Therefore, I am responding to the Word of God and to the voice of the Spirit who is speaking to me about making concrete changes in certain areas of my life. Right now I choose to repent of those things that I know are wrong. I make the decision to walk free of them and to stay free of them for the rest of my life. This is my point of no return.

I pray this in Jesus' name!

MY CONFESSION FOR TODAY

I joyfully declare that I walk free of things that have long bound me. God is on my side! He sent His Son to die for my freedom and deliverance; He sent His Spirit to empower me; and I do not have to sit in a spiritual prison any longer. I proclaim that today is the day of deliverance for me! I permanently walk free of those things that have been a hindrance to me. Jesus died so I can be free, and I am free! Today is the day that I begin walking in my victory!

I declare this by faith in Jesus' name!

QUESTIONS FOR YOU TO CONSIDER

1. Can you think of a time when you were so engulfed in sorrow and remorse about something you had done that you were unable to really repent? How did your emotions get in the way of your repentance?
2. When you think back on your life to times when the Holy Spirit required you to repent about some attitude, action, or habit in your life, was your repentance more effective when it was dominated by emotions or when it was purely a

decision of your will to obey? It's different for everyone, so there isn't a right or wrong answer. Which was most effective in your life?

3. What are the areas of your life right now that you need to turn from and leave behind? As you read this *Sparkling Gem*, did the Holy Spirit speak to you about specific areas in your present life? If yes, what were those areas, and what do you intend to do about it?

MARCH 20

Repentance — An Elementary Principle

Therefore leaving the principles of the doctrine of Christ,
let us go on unto perfection;
not laying again the foundation of repentance
from dead works, and of faith toward God,
of the doctrine of baptisms, and of laying on of hands,
and of resurrection of the dead,
and of eternal judgment.
— Hebrews 6:1,2

What would you think of a full-grown adult who never got serious about learning his ABCs and therefore had to keep repeating the first grade over and over again? Imagine 50 or so years passing since that person first entered grade school. As he nears his sixtieth birthday, there he still sits at a tiny little desk in a room full of first-graders.

Would you find that situation normal, or would you find it strange? It would be especially bizarre if that old man was mentally sound, yet found himself still sitting at a tiny desk in a room full of first-graders because he'd been too slothful to apply himself to learn.

Strange as that scenario may seem, it happens all the time in the Christian community. Many believers who have known the Lord for years have remained at the same level of spiritual immaturity ever since they were baby Christians. They never applied themselves or got serious about their spiritual growth, and thus, they perpetually remain spiritually immature. Although they've been saved for many years, they are still sitting in "beginners' class" in Sunday school with children, figuratively speaking. They should be much further along in their spiritual growth, but because they were never diligent about their walk with God, they just keep repeating the basics over and over again.

In Hebrews 6:1, the writer of Hebrews listed what he referred to as "the principles of the doctrine of Christ." The word "principles" is the Greek word *arches*, which denotes something that is *original, early*, or *from the beginning*. In Hebrews 6:1, this word *arches* specifically refers to the *elementary principles* of Christ. These elementary principles comprise the fundamental doctrine for *beginners*. They encompass the basic spiritual principles that every new believer should know, as well as the first steps of faith that every baby Christian should be able to take. In other words, these are the *ABCs of the Christian faith*.

The problem is, most Christians aren't very familiar with these elementary principles. In fact, some don't even know them at all! Furthermore, this failure to know the fundamental truths of the Christian faith causes them to struggle in life. Had they applied themselves at an earlier age, they would be much further along in their walk with God and therefore able to overcome the difficulties that confront them in life. But because they never took time to learn the basics, they are still sitting in a spiritual "beginners' class"!

The first vital, elementary principle that the writer of Hebrews listed was "...the foundation of repentance from dead works...." This word "foundation" is the Greek word *themelios*. It is an early combination of the Greek word *lithos*, which means *stone*, and the word *tithemi*, which means *to place*. When these roots are combined, the new compound word denotes *something that is set in stone*; *a foundation that cannot be easily moved or shaken*; or *something so solid that it will endure the test of time*. Taken together, these different nuances of meaning are the reason the word *themelios* came to be translated as the word "foundation."

By using the Greek word *themelios*, the writer of Hebrews was teaching us that if we are serious about our walk with God, our understanding of repentance should be *set in stone*. This truth should be so rock solid in our lives that we are *immovable* and *unshakable* when it comes to the subject of repentance!

However, this is sadly not the case for many believers in the modern Church. In fact, the survey results we read earlier found that a majority of regular churchgoing Christians could not provide an accurate definition of the word *repentance*! This is very alarming to me because it reveals that most believers are in a stunted state of spiritual maturity. Regardless of their age or how many years they've been saved, most of them are still in "Beginners' Class" spiritually. If they still can't articulate an answer to such a simple question, they are still in *spiritual kindergarten*!

Furthermore, Hebrews 6:1 clearly states that our knowledge concerning repentance should be so set in stone that it should never have to be repeated or taught to us again. It reads, "...*not laying again* the foundation of repentance from dead works...." The words "not laying again" are derived from the Greek word *kataballo*, which is a compound of the words *kata* and *ballo*. The word *kata* means *down*, and the word *ballo* means *to throw*. When these two words are joined together, the new word means *to throw something down* or *to lay something down*.

The use of the word *kataballo* in Hebrews 6:1 tells us something very important: The elementary principles of the Christian faith should be laid down in our lives like a strong foundation as soon as we come to Christ — and once this foundation is set in place, there should never be any need for it to be laid down again.

In fact, Hebrews 6:1 says that seasoned believers should be able to leave the fundamental truths behind and "go on unto perfection." The word "leaving" in this verse is from the Greek word *aphiemi*, which means *to leave it* or *to let it go*. It does not refer to the abandonment of truth, but rather the realization that maturity requires pressing upward to the next level.

The beginning is not a stopping point — it is only a beginning!

This is the reason the writer of Hebrews continued by saying we must "...go on unto perfection...." The words "go on" are derived from the word *phero*, which means *to carry* or *to bear.* However, the tense used in this verse paints the picture of *a force that carries one onward* or *a force that bears one further.* It could literally be translated *let us be carried*, and it conveys the idea that as we grow spiritually, the Holy Spirit picks us up and personally carries us forward in our knowledge and understanding of God.

Where is the Holy Spirit carrying us? Hebrews 6:1 tells us that He is carrying us toward "perfection." The word "perfection" is the Greek word *teleiotes*, which refers to *a child graduating from one class to the next until he finally reaches maturity.* This means that until we meet Jesus face to face in Heaven, there is no end to our spiritual growth. That's why it is so very serious when an older Christian who has been saved for many years can't even articulate the meaning of the word "repentance." He should be much further along in his spiritual growth, but instead of reaching maturity, he has been content to remain in spiritual kindergarten.

Why is it so essential and elementary that we know and understand the doctrine of repentance? As we have already seen in the March 18 *Sparkling Gem,* the word "repentance" in the New Testament depicts *a complete, radical, total change*. It is *a decision to completely change* or *a decision to entirely turn around in the way that one is thinking, believing, and living.* It describes a person who is undergoing a complete and radical transformation that literally affects every part of his or her life.

Repentance is not a fleeting, temporary sorrow for past actions. Rather, it is a solid, intellectual decision to turn around and take a new direction in order to completely change the patterns of one's life on every level. It is a mental choice to turn toward God with all of one's heart in order to follow Jesus. *It is the birth canal through which we are born into the Kingdom of God.*

Repentance is the starting place for all believers, and that is why Hebrews 6:1 lists it as an elementary principle of the doctrines of Christ. It is the place where our turning away from sin begins, and it is the point from which we submit our lives to the Lordship of Jesus Christ.

Repentance is your starting place — so make sure that your understanding of it is laid down like a strong, immovable foundation in your life. Then once you know you are well established in your own personal act of repentance, let the Holy Spirit carry you onward and upward as you reach toward spiritual maturity.

MY PRAYER FOR TODAY

Lord, I want to thank You for helping me understand the importance of repentance and the need to establish this truth as a strong foundation in my life. Please help me meticulously examine my life to see if there are any areas in which I have never fully surrendered to your Lordship. I make the decision now to turn those areas over to You, starting today. I have made my choice that I will no longer live for myself. I purpose to live the remainder of my life to please and serve You with all of my heart. By the help of the Holy Spirit, I move onward and upward in my spiritual growth and press on toward spiritual maturity!

I pray this in Jesus' name!

MY CONFESSION FOR TODAY

I confess that Christ set me free and I have turned from the past sins, habits, and bondages that once held me captive. Those chains may no longer lord themselves over my life. Since I came to Jesus, I have renounced my past ways of thinking and living. Now I live to please Jesus. To serve Him with all of my heart and strength is my highest priority. Jesus is Lord of my life! I live to satisfy Him, and I am being carried onward and upward by the Holy Spirit to new levels of spiritual growth and maturity!

I declare this by faith in Jesus' name!

QUESTIONS FOR YOU TO CONSIDER

1. Have you ever known a Christian who never seemed to grow in his or her walk with the Lord and kept repeating the same basic lessons over and over again? What qualities did you observe in that person's life that hindered him or her from graduating from "spiritual kindergarten"? If that person is you, what steps do you plan to take to move forward and to grow spiritually?
2. Are you growing in your walk with the Lord? Can you say that you are well-established in all the elementary principles of the doctrines of Christ listed in Hebrews 6:1,2?
3. What elementary doctrines listed in Hebrews 6:1,2 are you *not* well-versed in right now? If there are principles in these verses in which your knowledge is deficient, what are you going to do to get established in those principles in order to further your spiritual growth?

Repentance is a solid, intellectual decision to turn around and take a new direction in order to completely change the patterns of one's life on every level.

MARCH 21

It's Not Cool To Be Stupid!

And the times of this ignorance God winked at;
but now God commandeth all men everywhere to repent.
— Acts 17:30

"I'm an agnostic," the man seated next to me on the plane answered proudly after I asked him about his religious affiliation. The two of us had been seated by each other for hours during that flight, talking openly about our political views, our different professions, and our educational backgrounds when suddenly the conversation shifted to the subject of religion.

This successful, wealthy man smugly told me about his impressive educational achievements, which were many. I listened carefully, and honestly, I was very impressed with his level of education. He then asked me about my own educational background and listened with great interest when he learned that I was an author and had knowledge of Classical and New Testament Greek. After hearing this, he wanted to talk in greater depth about history and the influence of Greek culture on today's world.

It was just before the plane landed that the conversation moved to the subject of religion. That is when I asked him about his faith, and he proudly answered, "I'm an agnostic."

I sat back, looked at him, and exclaimed, "Really, an agnostic!"

He asked, "Why is it so amazing to you that I'm an agnostic?"

Since he opened the door, I decided to walk through it, and I answered him, "Do you know what it means to be an agnostic?"

"It means I'm not interested in religion!" he told me.

I responded, "I'm really shocked that a man as educated as you does not *really* know what it means to be an agnostic. You ought to know what you're talking about if you're going to use a term like that."

He answered, "All right, tell me what *you* think it means to be an agnostic."

Since the man was impressed with the fact that I knew Greek, I reached into my arsenal and pulled out a word that would help me reach this man's heart. I said, "The word 'agnostic' is derived from a specific Greek word, and if you really knew what that Greek word meant, I don't think you would want to use it to describe yourself."

He pleaded, "*Please* tell me what the word 'agnostic' means!"

So I looked him in the eyes and said, "In Greek, the word *gnosis* is the word for *knowledge.* When you put an *a* on the front of it, it turns it into the word *agnosis,* from which we derive the word *agnostic.* That little *a* on the front of the word *dramatically* changes the meaning. It no longer means *knowledge*; rather, it means *stupid, unintelligent,* or *unknowledgeable.*" He looked at me in shock as I told him, "To be honest, every time you call yourself an agnostic, you're actually claiming to be stupid."

His mouth fell open and he said, "You've got to be kidding!"

I looked at him and said, "Nope, that's exactly what you're saying every time you claim to be an agnostic. You might as well just say, '*I'm stupid*' because that's what the word means."

He said, "Well, I'm not stupid, and if that's what the word 'agnostic' means, I'm not going to claim to be an agnostic again. *I'm not stupid!* In fact, after this conversation, I think I'm going to start studying so I can find out what I should believe about God. I refuse to be stupid about anything!"

Before we left the plane, I recommended reading material to help him start his spiritual search. The books I recommended would lead him directly to *Jesus.*

In Acts 17:30, the apostle Paul found himself with a group of intellectuals who wanted to hear about his faith. As he stood before them, Paul knew that God had opened a great door for him to share the truth with these learned men. Paul fearlessly told them, "And the times of ignorance God winked at; but now God commandeth all men everywhere to repent...."

When Paul began to speak to these Greek intellectuals about *ignorance,* it must have been quite a shock to them because these men were venerated scholars. Paul freely communicated in Hebrew, Latin, and Greek, but because he was standing before the greatest living minds in Greece, he communicated with them in the Greek language. Just as I had delved into my verbal arsenal and extracted the word *agnosis* in order to reach the heart of this highly educated man sitting next me on the plane, Paul used the word *agnosis* to appeal to the minds of the Athenian judges and scholars who were seated before him.

Paul told them, "...The times of ignorance God winked at...." The word "ignorance" in this verse is the word *agnosis,* which, as we saw, is the same word from which we derive the word "agnostic." Again, the root of this word is the Greek word *gnosis,* which simply means *knowledge.* But just as I related in the story about the man sitting next to me on the plane, the meaning of this word is reversed when an *a* is attached to the front of it. Therefore, *agnosis* doesn't mean *knowledge,* but rather refers to *a lack of knowledge, a lack of intelligence, ignorance,* or even *stupidity.* Think about how bold it was for Paul to talk to these brilliant and educated scholars about *ignorance* and *stupidity*!

Paul went on to say that there was a time in the past when God "winked" at stupidity and ignorance, but now that day was over. The word "winked" is the Greek word *hupereidon,* which is a compound of the words *huper* and *orao.* The word *huper* means *over,* and the word *orao* means *to see.* When these two words are compounded, they form the word *hupereidon,* which means *to overlook, to disregard, to discount, to ignore,* or *to take no notice of a thing.* In fact, an accurate rendering of the word *hupereidon* could be *to deliberately shut one's eyes or turn one's face to avoid seeing something.* By using this word, Paul was plainly telling his listeners that the days of God closing His eyes and overlooking the ignorance of men is long past.

After Paul told his educated audience that God no longer ignored ignorance, he continued by courageously declaring, "...Now God commandeth all men everywhere to repent." This word "command" would have been a difficult word for the Greek intellectuals to accept because they didn't want anyone forcing a new religion upon them. It is the Greek word *parangello,* which means *to instruct, to command,* or *to order.* What was the order that God now gives to every man? As Paul unashamedly told those learned scholars, God commands all men — including *them* — to "repent."

As we discussed in the last few days of *Sparkling Gems,* the Greek word for "repent" is *metanoeo,* which is a compound of the words *meta* and *nous.* The word *meta* means *to turn,* and the word *nous* refers to *the mind.* When these two words are compounded, the new word describes in its most basic sense *a change of mind* or *a complete conversion.* In the New Testament, *metanoeo* is used to denote *a decision to completely change one's thoughts, behavior, and actions.*

Since *metanoeo* is a Greek word and Paul was addressing Greek intellectuals, the notion of *a change of mind* must have been very interesting to them. Paul was appealing to their intellect and reasoning with them to make *a complete turnaround* from the worship of idols to the Lordship of Jesus Christ. He boldly told them this was God's order and made no apology for the truth.

Acts 17:30 concludes by saying that repentance is God's requirement for "all men everywhere." This phrase is all-inclusive, which means there are no exceptions to God's commandment. *All men are commanded to repent!* The word "everywhere" in this verse makes this point even stronger because it is the Greek word *pantachou.* This Greek word literally means *every place* and excludes no person, ethnic group, skin color, or nationality. The message of the Cross and God's command to repent is for mankind in *every* part of the earth!

There was a time when God winked at people's ignorance, but that time has long past. Jesus paid the ultimate penalty for our forgiveness with His own blood on the Cross, and on that day, the time of ignorance came to a grinding halt. Today God no longer winks at or overlooks stupidity. Instead He commands men everywhere to repent — regardless of their nationality, background, social status, educational degrees, or skin color. There is no option or way out from this command! *This is God's requirement for every person on planet earth if he intends to enter the Kingdom of Heaven.*

If you consider yourself a committed Christian, it is needful for you to recognize that you have a God-given responsibility to present the truth to people who are without Christ. Just as I shared the truth with the man on the plane, and Paul fearlessly presented the truth to the scholars in Athens, the Holy Spirit wants to use *you* to reach into your sphere of influence and bring the light of the Gospel to people who are still uninformed and sitting in darkness.

If you'll let the Holy Spirit use you, He will speak through you to bring salvation to your family, friends, and acquaintances. It may be difficult to get started, but the Holy Spirit knows exactly how to appeal to every person's heart. If you'll listen to the Spirit and follow His directions, He will use you to put the key into every man's heart to unlock it for Jesus Christ.

So ask the Lord today: *Whom do You want me to reach in my sphere of influence with the good news of the Gospel?*

MY PRAYER FOR TODAY

Lord, please help me remember that there are people in my sphere of influence who need to be washed in the blood of the Lamb. I ask You to help me love them enough to tell them the truth. I know that You have the key to every person's heart, so please give me the key to unlock people's hearts with Your words of truth so Jesus can come into their lives. I am so thankful that someone was loving and bold enough to tell me the truth so I could repent. Now it is my turn to do it for someone else. I ask You to help me get started reaching people today.

I pray this in Jesus' name!

MY CONFESSION FOR TODAY

I confess that the power of the Holy Spirit is working mightily in me and that I am a bold witness for Jesus Christ. I walk in His wisdom, and I am not afraid to open my mouth to proclaim the truth because it has the power to set men free from the darkness that binds their souls. When I speak the truth in love, people open their hearts and listen to me. Because they see Jesus in me, they readily want to know how to come to God and commit their lives to the Lordship of Jesus Christ.

I declare this by faith in Jesus' name!

QUESTIONS FOR YOU TO CONSIDER

1. What person in your sphere of influence does the Holy Spirit want you to personally share the Gospel with in order to bring him or her to Jesus Christ?
2. When you pray, how often do you pray for unsaved people? Do you feel a sense of urgency for people who are unsaved, or do you forget that they are in need of salvation?
3. If you were an unsaved person, how would you want someone to approach you about Jesus Christ? Why don't you take a few minutes to write down some ideas about effective ways to share the Gospel with someone who doesn't know Jesus?

Today God no longer winks at or overlooks stupidity. Instead, He commands men everywhere to repent.

MARCH 22

Jesus Understands Your Struggles

For we have not an high priest which cannot be touched
with the feeling of our infirmities; but was in all points
tempted like as we are, yet without sin.
— Hebrews 4:15

If you've ever been controlled by hurt feelings and offenses, you know it's a miserable state to be in. Everyone has opportunities to get offended, upset, or "ticked off" at someone. Take a moment to think about a time when a friend or family member did something disappointing to *you.* How successful were you at dealing with it? *Be honest!*

It can often be very difficult to rein in your emotions when you've been hurt, but the good news is that Jesus understands. Hebrews 4:15 says, "For we have not an high priest which cannot be touched with the feeling of our infirmities; but was in all points tempted like as we are, yet without sin." This verse emphatically declares that although Jesus was God in the flesh when He walked on this earth, He still faced *every* temptation you and I face in life. As a result, this verse says that Jesus is "…*touched* with the feeling of our infirmities…."

That phrase "be touched with" comes from the Greek word *sumpatheo,* which means *to share an experience with someone* or *to sympathize with and have compassion for someone.* What a comforting thought! Jesus empathizes with every temptation and struggle you face in this life. He *identifies* and *sympathizes* with you, and He has *compassion* for you regarding what you're feeling and the situation you're facing.

Jesus has been where you are. He has felt what you feel. He has overcome the temptations you are now trying to overcome. And because of His experiences, He understands the emotions, frustrations, and temptations you face in life. There is no need to feel too embarrassed to go to the Savior. If anyone can understand what you are going through right now, *it's Jesus*! He has been tempted in all points just like you, yet He never succumbed to temptation. As a result:

- *He understands your dilemma.*
- *He has experienced your problem.*
- *He is familiar with disappointment.*
- *He knows the temptation to get frustrated.*
- *He sympathizes when you get upset.*

Jesus never fell into one of Satan's traps, but He definitely faced the same frustrations we do in life. In fact, if Jesus *hadn't* been tempted in every realm that we are tempted, He wouldn't be able to understand us and serve as our great High Priest!

For instance, I can only imagine the frustration Jesus must have felt in the Garden of Gethsemane. He had invested three and a half years of His life into His disciples, and for the first time, Jesus needed *them*. Jesus asked three of His disciples to pray for Him during His hour of temptation (*see* Matthew 26:37-45). He asked them for only one hour of prayer, but instead of praying, they fell asleep. He came and pleaded with them a second time to pray with Him, but once more they fell asleep. For a third time, Jesus came and besought His disciples to pray, but again they fell asleep on the job.

What if you had been in Jesus' position that night? What if you had given three years of your life to these disciples — but when you asked them to help you for the first time, *they failed you again and again*?

It would be normal for a person in this situation to be tempted to become resentful, upset, or even offended. Anyone in that position would be tempted to think, *How dare you sleep on the job after all I've done for you! I'm sorry I ever did anything for you bunch of ingrates!* However, Jesus never fell into the trap of *bitterness*, *resentment*, and *unforgiveness*. In fact, even as He hung on the Cross, He prayed for those who had perpetrated this evil on Him, "...Father, forgive them..." (Luke 23:34).

Jesus is on your side! Hebrews 4:16 goes on to promise that when you go to Him for help, you *will* obtain mercy and find grace to help in time of need. So the next time you feel tempted to get upset or frustrated with someone, run to Jesus! He's your faithful High Priest, inviting you to come boldly to Him to receive the grace you need to resist that temptation. Remember, Jesus understands precisely what you're going through because He experienced that same temptation when He walked on this earth. But He also knows how to help you walk in love and forgiveness — just as He did in every situation, without fail!

MY PRAYER FOR TODAY

Father, I am so thankful that Jesus is my Great High Priest and that He understands everything that I face and feel in life. I can come confidently before You in His Name to obtain mercy and find grace to help in time of need. The next time I feel tempted to get upset or frustrated with someone, Father, I make the decision now that I will walk in love and forgiveness just as Jesus did. I am so thankful that as my faithful High Priest, Jesus invites me to come boldly to Him to receive the grace I need to yield to His love and wisdom in me and to resist any temptation that comes against me!

I pray this in Jesus' name!

MY CONFESSION FOR TODAY

I declare that Jesus understands precisely what I'm going through because He experienced that same temptation when He walked on this earth. He knows how to help me walk in love and forgiveness. Jesus has been where I am. He has felt what I feel. He has overcome the temptations arrayed against me. Therefore, I hold fast to my victory in Him. Because of Jesus' experiences as He walked on this earth, He understands the emotions, frustrations, and temptations that I face in life. There is no need for me to feel embarrassed to go to the Savior. If anyone can understand what I am going through right now, it's Jesus. And because of His blood and by the power of His Name, I am more than a conqueror through Him!

I declare this by faith in Jesus' name!

QUESTIONS FOR YOU TO CONSIDER

1. Have you ever thought of the fact that Jesus faced every single temptation that you've ever faced? Of course, He never yielded to the temptation, but what does it mean to you to know that He faced exactly what you face and was tempted to feel exactly what you feel?
2. Are you embarrassed to be totally honest with Jesus about the temptations you are facing, or do you feel you can be straight with the Lord about it? If you feel embarrassed, why do you feel this, especially since you now know Jesus faced every temptation you face?
3. Take a moment to think about a time when a friend or family member did something disappointing to *you.* How successful were you at dealing with it? How does Jesus respond when we disappoint Him?

MARCH 23

Blind to the Truth

In whom the god of this world
hath blinded the minds of them which believe not,
lest the light of the glorious gospel of Christ,
who is the image of God, should shine unto them.
— 2 Corinthians 4:4

I once watched a television interview with a very famous, wealthy businessman who is well known for his public opposition of biblical teaching. During the conversation, the interviewer asked this famously rich unbeliever for his opinion about the state of the world today. I was shocked to hear how he answered!

The man replied that the world in general had never been in better shape than it is in right now. As evidence to support his claim, he specifically mentioned the shift of morality away from traditional values, the widespread acceptance of same-sex marriage, and the emergence on the political and economic scene of a one-world system that he believed will turn the planet into an altogether better place. I was stunned at his answers. I wondered, *How can anyone be so blind to the reality of what is taking place in the world today?*

There does seem to be a very real form of blindness that causes a person not to see what is happening in this modern age. What really amazes me is that often the people who make these comments are actually intellectually brilliant! As I listened to this man speak, I wondered, *How can people be so smart and yet so blind to the truth?* But then the Holy Spirit reminded me of Paul's words in Second Corinthians 4:4, where he wrote, "In whom the god of this world hath blinded the minds of them which believe not lest the light of the glorious gospel of Christ, who is the image of God, should shine unto them." *According to Paul, unbelievers really are blind to the truth!*

When Paul wrote that Satan has "blinded" the minds of unbelievers, he chose the Greek word *tuphloo* for the word "blinded." This is very important because the word *tuphloo* doesn't just depict a person who is unable to see; rather, it vividly portrays a person who has been *intentionally blinded* by someone else. Someone has deliberately removed that individual's eyes and permanently blinded him. This person hasn't just lost his sight; *he has no eyes to see.*

Paul continued by saying that Satan "...blinded the *minds* of them which believe not…." This word "minds" is the Greek word *noema*, which is a form of the word *nous*. The word *nous* simply means *mind*. However, as the word *noema*, it no longer refers to the physical mind, but rather denotes the *thoughts, reasoning, opinions, feelings, beliefs*, or *views* that a person holds. Thus, Paul's words in Second Corinthians 4:4 explicitly state that Satan has "gouged out" the spiritual eyes of skeptics and unbelievers to such a degree that *it has affected their ability to see things correctly.* Their *thoughts, reasoning, opinions, feelings, beliefs*, and *views* of what they experience and perceive are obstructed, hindered, and impeded. As a result, they are *blinded* from a correct *view* of the way things really are.

If you have any unsaved friends or relatives who seem "blind" to the truth, this verse may explain why they can't seem to see the true state of things. Pray for the Holy Spirit to open their spiritual eyes so they can see the truth. The fact is that we are living in the last of the last days, and the world around us is changing very quickly. Events that were long ago prophesied in Scripture are unfolding before our very eyes. We have crossed the line and entered into the final chapter of history as we know it.

Thank God that by studying the Scriptures we can identify the time and exact age in which we live. With this knowledge before us, we can live soberly with eternity in view. Time is short, so we must wisely use the time that remains and shine the light of the Gospel into the lives of those whom Satan has blinded. The moment they believe, the Holy Spirit creates eyes for them to see. That is why it is so important that we don't stop preaching the Gospel — even if people act like they don't want to hear it.

As committed Christians, it is time for us to live with our eyes wide open to the times and to the events that are occurring around us. If we have friends or family who are unsaved and therefore blind to the truth, it is more urgent than ever that we fervently pray for God to give them eyes so they can see the truth that will save and deliver them.

Soon Jesus will come, and everything will change forever. Until then we have time to pray for those whom Satan has blinded. It isn't that they are naive — they are *blind*. Satan has gouged out their eyes, blocked their view, and affected their minds. They have no eyes to see. Spiritual eyes are created for them to see only as the Gospel is preached and the Holy Spirit touches their minds.

Are you someone God wants to use so people's eyes will be opened to see the truth? Maybe it's time for you to quit praying for others to fill that role and recognize that God is asking *you* to be the one to share the Gospel with those who don't know Him and bring them to a saving knowledge of Jesus Christ! Keep your eyes open for opportunities to help the spiritually blind see, and the Lord will accommodate you with people who are hungry to listen and ready to *see*!

MY PRAYER FOR TODAY

Father, I pray for my family, friends, loved ones, and even my enemies as You told me to do. I ask in the name of Jesus that You would open up the eyes of their understanding to Your truth and to the reality of what is taking place in the world around them. Holy Spirit, I ask You to help them turn from darkness to light so that they would abandon what's worthless and come to know and serve You, the Living God. Holy Spirit, I also ask You to help me recognize and respond to the opportunities you bring across my path for me to be a witness for Your glory. I am not ashamed of the Gospel, and I receive Your wisdom to win souls with the right words at the right time.

I pray this in Jesus' Name!

MY CONFESSION FOR TODAY

I confess that I am aware I'm living in the last of the last days. Prophecy is unfolding before my eyes. The world has entered into the final chapter of history as we know it. I exalt You, Father God, and I thank You that Your Holy Word equips me with the strength and wisdom I need for the time and the age I'm living in. I choose to live soberly with eternity constantly in my view. I make the most of every opportunity to let my light shine for Christ brightly and without compromise. My lifelong desire is that others who sit in darkness will be drawn to a saving knowledge of the Lord Jesus Christ through the light they see in me!

I declare this by faith in Jesus' name!

QUESTIONS FOR YOU TO CONSIDER

1. Do you know an unbeliever who is simply going with the whims of the times and who believes that things are getting better in this world system?
2. Are you concerned about unbelieving friends who seem to have no ability to discern the times in which we live? Regardless of what you express to them, does it seem they just can't see the truth?
3. What would the Holy Spirit have you do to bring the people who fit that description to a powerful encounter with God that opens their spiritual eyes to see the truth? In what way could you share Christ with them that could help them see things differently?

MARCH 24

Opportunities and Adversaries!

For a great and effectual door is opened unto me,
and there are many adversaries.
— 1 Corinthians 16:9

Over the course of my ministry, I've had many great, effectual doors open for me to do the work of the Gospel. I'll never forget when I received an opportunity to minister on television in the former Soviet Union. It was as if a great door had suddenly swung open to an entire nation — a door that had never before been opened for anyone else. I knew that I was experiencing something miraculous!

By faith, my wife Denise and I stepped through that door and began to preach the Word of God on television in this spiritually starved corner of the world. Given the former Communist regime's violent campaigns against the Gospel in this region, this opportunity was as miraculous as was the Jordan River dividing for Joshua and the children of Israel! However, with this great open door also came a slew of adversaries, specifically dispatched by Satan to instill fear and doubt into my heart. The devil desperately wanted to prevent me from touching the lives of this spiritually oppressed people, so he positioned evil people with insidious plans to block my view from what God had in store for our ministry.

It was like the children of Israel looking at the Promised Land from the far side of the Jordan River. From that perspective, they saw only the fruitful land of blessing that lay before them. But once in the Promised Land, they had to fight giants of every kind before they could possess that land and enjoy the blessing. In the same way, if Denise and I had taken our eyes off the Lord during this tumultuous period — or if we had focused only on the problems and forgotten about the fruit we were pursuing for God's Kingdom — I'm sure we would have backpedaled to get out of the situation.

However, we knew this opportunity was worth the fight, so we fixed our gaze squarely on the Lord. Girded with the armor of God and the power of the Spirit, we pushed through every obstacle and possessed the ground that God called us to take, and as a result, millions of souls began to hear the Gospel for the first time. *We knew that only God could have opened this door!*

In First Corinthians 16:9, the apostle Paul wrote about the strategic doors of opportunity that open for the Gospel and the adversaries that usually accompany them. He said, "For a great and effectual door has been opened unto me, and there are many adversaries." Notice that Paul uses the words "great," "effectual," "door," and "has been opened" to describe the opportunity that had been set before him.

The word "great" in this verse is translated from the Greek word *megale*, which means *gigantic*. The word "effectual" is the Greek word *energes*, and it depicts something that is *powerful and ready to be set into motion*. The word "door" is the Greek word *thura*, which typically refers to *a door* but in this context denotes *a rare opportunity*. Finally, the phrase "has been opened" is the Greek word *anoigo*, which describes something *standing wide open*. In other words, the door in question couldn't be any *more* open! Thus, an alternate translation of Paul's words in First Corinthians 16:9 could be rendered, *"A gigantic, powerful opportunity is already set in motion and standing wide open...."*

Furthermore, Paul continued by saying, "For a great and effectual door has been opened *unto me*...." You see, Paul *knew* that the particular door he was referring to had never been opened to anyone else, and he stood in awe of the unprecedented opportunity. Walking through these kinds of doors is impossible without divine assistance, and Paul was fully aware of God's role in the matter. That is why he specified that this door had been opened "unto me."

Paul's prayer request in First Corinthians 16:9 was *not* for a door to open because it had *already* opened. His prayer request was to receive God's wisdom to deal with the numerous adversaries who were attempting to come against him. Paul used the Greek word *antikeimenoi* to describe the vast number of "adversaries" that were sent to attack him. This Greek word described something *set against* Paul that was *piled high* and *lying all around* him. In other words, he was dealing with more than a few minor opponents; opposition was stacked high on every side!

The enemy will try his best to keep you from stepping through the gigantic doors of opportunity God desires to open for you. Satan is afraid of what will happen when "his" territory is invaded by someone fully equipped with a full arsenal of spiritual weapons! So know this: God *will* open doors for you — but He needs you to make a determined decision that you *will* walk through them, no matter the opposition, with the help of His Spirit. By opening the door, God has already done His part, which would have been impossible without His assistance. Now He beckons you to come dressed in the whole armor of God and in the power of His Word — and then proceed through that effectual door into new territory. It may look like enemies are everywhere, but it is simply a fact that the devil and his forces flee and collapse when they are subjected to a show of strong faith!

As I mentioned earlier, many great and effectual doors have been opened to me over the years to do the work of the Gospel. In each case, I knew that these doors were unique to me and had never before been opened for anyone else. And just as Paul experienced opposition, there were plenty of enemies that came against me with each opportunity. However, because I obeyed God, the devil was forced to move out of the way, and I walked right into the virgin territory that God had opened to me.

My friend, your situation may look frightful, but think about this: If God has supernaturally opened a new door for you — a door that's never before been opened — He is not beckoning you to walk through it so you can fail. He is with you every step of the way, and He will empower you to defeat every foe and bring Him glory in that new territory that is yours to possess in Jesus' name!

MY PRAYER FOR TODAY

Heavenly Father, You have set before me a rare opportunity for the sake of the Gospel. You have not opened this door for me to fail or to fall short. You opened this opportunity specifically for me; therefore, I know that You have equipped me precisely with all I need to succeed. Your plan for my life and for this opportunity is one of victory. Thank You for the supernatural weapons You have given me through Christ. I ask for and gratefully receive Your wisdom to know what to do and how to do it. By the wisdom and the power of the Holy Spirit, I put on Your mighty strength to exercise the courage and perseverance I need to obey You and to force hell to move out of the way!

I pray this in Jesus' name!

MY CONFESSION FOR TODAY

I confess that I do not draw back, but I move forward in the power of the Spirit to walk through the open door the Lord has set before me! I acknowledge that through Christ, I have wisdom for this task. Dressed in the whole armor of God and in the power of God's Word, I can run through a troop and leap over a wall (see Psalm 18:29)! I will not be deterred, distracted, frightened, or intimidated. Greater is He that is within me than any adversary that seeks to oppose me. The Lord has gone before me to prepare the way; therefore, I follow Him confidently through this new door so I can carve a path for the Gospel and prepare the way for others to enter and follow afterward.

I declare this by faith in Jesus' name!

QUESTIONS FOR YOU TO CONSIDER

1. What miraculous opportunities has God set before you in your life?

2. Do you remember times when God gave you new opportunities, but you paused — perhaps because you were concerned whether you had the guts and gumption to really do it — and as a result, the opportunity passed you by?
3. What did you learn from that experience? If God opens another miraculous door in front of you, what would you do different now?

MARCH 25

Your Life Is Your Pulpit!

Walk in wisdom toward them
that are without, redeeming the time.
— Colossians 4:5

One day as my wife and I were eating out, we discovered that the woman who served our table was a committed Christian. Since it was a slow day at the restaurant, we took a few minutes to talk to her. During our conversation, I happened to ask her what was the best and worst day of the week for a server in terms of tips. Without hesitation, she answered, "Sundays are the worst days. In fact, none of the servers in this restaurant want to work on Sundays. It's the worst day of the week for a waiter."

Fascinated by her answer, I asked her why no one wanted to work on Sundays. She told me, "As a Christian, I am embarrassed to say it, but the most demanding customers — those who are the hardest to please and leave the smallest tips — are usually Christians. In fact, when people come into the restaurant carrying their Bibles, the waiters and waitresses immediately start fighting about who *has* to serve that table because we know it's going to take a lot of work and they won't leave much of a tip."

She continued, "Isn't it sad that a Bible in a person's hands is the warning sign that trouble lies ahead?"

Hearing about this negative influence that Christians had exerted on the employees in that place of business, I decided to delve deeper and ask how this had affected those who worked with her. She categorically told me, "The people who work in this restaurant just can't understand how Christians can go to church on Sunday and then come into this restaurant and treat the servers so badly. Most of the servers here would rather serve unbelievers because they treat them nicer and leave bigger tips."

It is unfortunate — but *true* — that often Christians unintentionally do or say things that leave unbelievers with a sour taste in their mouths. These believers forget that their life is their pulpit and the strongest message they will ever preach.

It is a fact that many believers have lost their Christian *influence* because of things they do or say that reflect a wrong image of Jesus Christ. If we are honest, I think we all probably regret something we did or said in front of unbelievers at some point in our lives. We all have made comments or acted in ways that we later regretted.

For example, has there ever been a time when you listened to someone tell crude jokes, and later learned that the unbelievers who were present couldn't understand how a Christian could laugh at such jokes? Have you ever acted so selfishly that you totally turned off the unbelievers you were trying to win for Christ? Or have you lost your temper, exploded in anger, or uttered words that were not fitting for a child of God — and unbelievers saw you do it?

If you have done any of these things, I don't mean to make you feel guilty or condemned, but as Christians, we must always be aware that a lost world is watching. We can never forget that we may be the only Jesus some people will ever see. This is why we must constantly ask ourselves, "What kind of Jesus do people see as they watch my life?"

In New Testament times, most of society was spiritually lost. As in today's world, the Christians of that time found themselves in a world that was hostile to the Gospel. Because they were a minority in their world and the rest of society didn't understand them or their faith, they were constantly "watched" by the unbelieving world. The apostle Paul knew that if Christians would live uprightly, it would demonstrate their faith. Therefore, their lives were really the strongest message they could preach. In light of this, Paul wrote to the Colossians, "Walk in wisdom toward them that are without, redeeming the time" (Colossians 4:5).

First, I want you to notice the phrase "to them that are without." This phrase is based on the Greek word *exo*, a word that means *without* or *outside*. It depicts those who are *outside*, like someone who is standing *outside* of a circle. You are either *in* the circle, or you are *out* of the circle. In this verse, the word *exo* describes people who are *outside of Christ*. The Jews used this Greek expression when they spoke of people who were *outside the Jewish faith* or were *non-Jews*. The apostle Paul used this identical phrase to portray people who are *outside of Christ* or who are *non-Christian*.

Hence, this part of the verse could be interpreted:

"Walk in wisdom toward those who are non-Christians...."

The word "walk" is the often-used Greek word, *peripateo*. It is a compound of the words *peri* and *pateo*. The first part of the word is *peri*, which simply means *around*. The second part of the word is *pateo*. Typically, the word *pateo* means *to walk*, but it can be translated in a variety of ways, such as *to walk*, *to step*, *to stride*, or *to tread*. When the word *peri* and *pateo* are compounded into one word to form the word *peripateo*, the new word means *to walk around*, or *to walk in one general area as a habit,* or it describes a person's *lifestyle.* It was often used to depict a constant and consistent way of life.

Therefore, when Paul told us to "walk in wisdom toward them that are without," he was telling us that walking in wisdom in the presence of unbelievers should be a way of life for us. The use of the word *peripateo* ("walk") clearly means we must *constantly walk* in wisdom when we are in the presence of people who are non-Christians.

The word "wisdom" is the Greek word *sophia,* a very old word that denotes *wisdom* but which also expresses the idea of *discernment.* In other words, you and I must use *judgment* about the things we do or say in the presence of unbelievers. We must be *sensitive* to the fact that they are monitoring our words and actions. We must use *prudence, caution, good sense, carefulness,* and *good ol' common sense* in the way we conduct ourselves before non-Christians. We should be *distinguishably different* from them and the lost world around us. Unbelievers are watching and are monitoring our actions. By living upright lives before them, we can make a godly impact on them.

In light of these Greek words, the first part of Colossians 4:5 could be interpreted:

"Habitually walk in wisdom — live according to its dictates and let it set you apart from the world around you. You have a responsibility to walk prudently and to use discernment and common sense when you are in the presence of non-Christians who are observing how you live and what you do...."

In tomorrow's *Sparkling Gem,* I want to talk to you about what to do if you have done something that has given a wrong impression of Jesus Christ to non-Christians who are watching you. You may have to swallow your pride, but it is vital that you make things right with those individuals. If you don't present the right image of Christ to them, your bad example could be the very thing that causes them to reject Christ and suffer an eternity without God.

MY PRAYER FOR TODAY

Lord, I ask You to help me be more aware of the unbelievers who are watching my life. Forgive me for the times I've been preoccupied and forgotten that my life is my pulpit and the strongest message I will ever preach. Holy Spirit, help me to stay mindful that non-Christians watch how I live, what I do, and how I treat others. Help me to constantly be aware that my life may be the only sermon some people will ever hear. Help me live my life wisely and in such a godly manner that others will see a contrast between me and the dark world around them. Help me take advantage of every opportunity to shine the light of God's love and His Word to those who sit in darkness.

I pray this in Jesus' name!

MY CONFESSION FOR TODAY

I confess that I am a good witness for Jesus Christ! When people see me — how I live, how I talk, how I act, and how I treat others — they are left with a good impression of Jesus Christ. The Holy Spirit is teaching me how to shine like a light in darkness to those without Christ who are around me. Because of my Christ-like example, many people without Jesus will come into the Kingdom of God. Since my life is the only sermon some people will ever hear, I will live my life each day in a way that accurately reflects the Person of Jesus Christ!

I declare this by faith in Jesus' name!

QUESTIONS FOR YOU TO CONSIDER

1. Have you ever known a person who claimed to be a Christian but who had unethical practices in his life that horribly conflicted with his claims of Christianity? How did this hypocrisy affect unbelievers who were watching his life?
2. Is there anything you are doing right now that would give a wrong impression of Jesus to non-Christians who are watching? Why don't you take a few minutes to ask the Holy Spirit to speak to your heart so He can show you areas in your life where your testimony could be better?
3. Write down those areas the Holy Spirit has shown you where you could improve your Christian testimony. Once you make this list, put it in a visible place where you can be reminded to pray about it daily.

MARCH 26

Is It Time for You To Swallow Your Pride?

Walk in wisdom toward them
that are without, redeeming the time.
— Colossians 4:5

When a Christian has done something so unethical or revolting that it discredits the testimony of Jesus Christ in front of unbelievers who are watching, that Christian has a responsibility to do what is necessary to "redeem the time" and consequently regain his testimony. It is absolutely vital that he make things right with those individuals. It may be necessary for that Christian to swallow his pride, admit he did something wrong, and apologize so that he can restore his testimony.

If you are the one who has done something wrong and have thereby marred your testimony, it's not too late for you to turn your testimony around! Thank God, the apostle Paul told us that we can "walk in wisdom toward them that are without, *redeeming the time*" (Colossians 4:5).

The word "redeem" is from the Greek word *exagoridzo*, and it is the old Greek word used to depict *someone purchasing a slave out of the slave market*. The word *exagoridzo* is a compound of the words *ex* and *agoridzo*. The word *ex* is a preposition that means *out*, and *agoridzo* is the Greek word most notably used to describe *the slave market* — a disgusting place where human beings were bought, sold, and traded like animals. This market was officially called *the agora*, and from this, we get this Greek word *agoridzo*.

When these words *ex* and *agoridzo* are compounded to form the word *exagoridzo*, it pictures a *buyer* who has gone to the market to purchase a slave so he can be set free and restore him to the freedom he formerly possessed. Therefore, the word *exagoridzo* — translated as the word "redemption" in the *King James Version* — actually pictures permanently removing a slave from slavery in order to *return* him to the status of freedom he enjoyed *before* he was enslaved.

But in Colossians 4:5, the word *exagoridzo* isn't used in its normal sense to describe redemption from sin. Instead, the apostle Paul used it in the phrase "redeeming the time." This means time that is lost can be *redeemed*! If you are willing to do whatever is needed to make it happen, God will enable you to regain and recoup time that was previously squandered. He can give you another opportunity that is so wonderful that it makes up for what you previously lost!

In fact, when Paul wrote of "redeeming the time," the word "time" is the Greek word *kairos*, which would be better translated as the word *opportunity*. This means God will help you recoup, recover, regain, and retrieve lost time *and* opportunities!

One way that this phrase could be paraphrased is *to buy back time*. Considering that the word "redemption" (*exagoridzo*) is used here, an expanded interpretation of this phrase "redeeming the time" could read: "*Do everything you can to make up for lost territory! Buy up all the time you can and make the most of every opportunity.*"

- Can you think of opportunities you have lost along the way in life?
- Have you ever squandered an opportunity that God tried to set before you?
- Did God try to increase you, but as a result of negligence on your part, the increase went to someone else?
- Can you think of a possibility that God designed to be yours, but it never happened because you were too lazy to put forth the effort to make it happen?
- Did you lose opportunities to enjoy your children when they were younger because you didn't take advantage of the time you were given to be with them?
- Have you forfeited your testimony in front of non-Christians because you did something unethical or ugly in front of them?

The truth is, we've all lost opportunities along the way in life for various reasons. Some of it was due to our own stupidity or ignorance. Some of it was due to hardships or difficulties in life that prevented us from doing what we wanted to do. But regardless of the reason, Paul told us that if we're willing to go the distance to do whatever is necessary to "redeem time," we can turn things around and end up with a lot of brand-new, wonderful opportunities that make up for any lost or wasted time in your past. I can hear the Holy Spirit crying out to us, *"Do everything you can to make up for lost territory! I'll enable you to buy up all the time you can and make the most of every opportunity."*

This brings us back to the subject of your influence on non-Christians. If you have damaged your testimony for some reason in front of non-Christians, that is truly unfortunate. Losing influence as a result of a lack of integrity or bad behavior will hinder your ability to represent Christ to the people around you. However, with God's grace, even this can be changed and turned around. If you are willing to do whatever is necessary to achieve it, He will help you redeem that lost time and damaged testimony.

For you to redeem the time and recover your testimony, God may require that you apologize to someone, admit you were wrong, or perhaps make a correction in some area of your life. If you are willing to swallow your pride and to do what is right, God will miraculously enable you to buy back a lot of missed opportunities and recover a testimony that had been lost.

Time is precious — and it is a fact that you cannot turn the clock back. Time, once you spend it, is gone. But if you are willing to repent and put forth the effort to correct your mistakes, God's grace will go a long way in enabling you to *buy back* a lot of time, opportunity, territory, or testimony that you previously lost. The Holy Spirit can, and will, help you "redeem the time."

The last part of Colossians 4:5 could read:

> *"Do everything you can to make up for lost territory! Make the most of every moment you have right now, and do everything you can to recover those precious moments and opportunities that you thought were lost forever."*

By choosing to repent, we are able to *buy back* our testimony and once again begin to make a right impression on the non-Christians we may have negatively influenced with our wrong actions in the past.

We must never forget that people are watching us! They see our walk; they hear our talk; and they notice what we say and what we do. We must live our lives wisely and prudently, especially for the sake of the non-Christians who are observing what we say and how we act. Time is a sacred and precious commodity that we must use carefully and not waste.

If you have damaged your witness, now is the time to let the Holy Spirit help you turn your testimony around so you can represent Jesus with honor before the unbelievers who are watching you!

MY PRAYER FOR TODAY

Lord, I ask You to help me make up for time and opportunities I lost or wasted along the way in my life. You have been so good to give me many possibilities for success, to witness, and to advance in life, but I have not taken advantage of everything You have tried to give me. Please forgive me for not being more serious or thoughtful in the past. I ask You for wisdom to know what I need to do to regain the things I've lost. Without You, I know that lost opportunities are gone forever; but with Your grace helping me, I can regain the things I lost and buy back the time I squandered. Thank You for helping me as I set my heart to do the things that will enable me to recoup what I lost earlier in my life.

I pray this in Jesus' name!

MY CONFESSION FOR TODAY

I confess that God can miraculously help me regain time and opportunities that I lost or squandered in the past. Because I am repentant and willing to do whatever I must to make it happen, God is helping me recapture moments, open doors, possibilities, and relationships that seemed forever lost. Time is spent and the clock cannot be turned back, but God's grace is so powerful that it will give me a new opportunity to do what is right. This time, I'll not fail, for I am determined to please Jesus Christ with my life!

I declare this by faith in Jesus' name!

QUESTIONS FOR YOU TO CONSIDER

1. Can you think of opportunities that God planned just for you, but for some reason, you forfeited those opportunities and they passed to someone else?
2. It may be painful to remember, but can you think of a time when you should have been a beacon of light to a non-Christian, but because you did something that was wrong, you lost your witness with that person?
3. To recapture those lost opportunities, what do you need to do? What correction do you need to make? What apology do you need to make to someone? What changes are required for you to recover your testimony and regain an opportunity to be an example of Jesus Christ to those who are watching you?

We must live our lives wisely and prudently,
especially for the sake of the non-Christians
who are observing what we say and how we act.
Time is a sacred and precious commodity
that we must use carefully and not waste.

MARCH 27

How Will You Respond to Negative Situations?

There hath no temptation taken you
but such as is common to man....
— 1 Corinthians 10:13

Have you ever noticed that the more you focus on a problem, the bigger and more intense it seems to become? In fact, if you don't get a grip on your emotions in these situations, your mind will try to blow that problem far out of proportion. Even if you're facing a real crisis, you have the power to get your mind under control with help from the Holy Spirit. However, if you let your emotions have their way, they will play the worst-case scenario over and over in your mind until it finally manifests as a reality in your life.

That's why it is so important to *decide beforehand* how you're going to respond to negative situations! Instead of blowing them out of proportion, you can make the decision before anything bad even happens that you and the Holy Spirit are bigger and stronger than any problem that will ever come your way. The two of you together, armed with the all-powerful name of Jesus, can tackle and overcome anything that ever comes against you! Plus, if you are blessed to have one or two friends who can encourage you in the Word or with agreement in prayer, you have everything to shout about!

The principle is precisely the same when dealing with temptations. All temptations begin as thoughts in the mind. They might appeal to your flesh, but each one of them first takes form in the mind and emotions. In the beginning, those thoughts are manageable, conquerable, and even rejectable. If you'll just change your focus, get out of the situation, and minimize it in your mind by refusing to focus on it, you can leave that temptation in the dust.

Or if you feel that you're losing the battle alone, you can open your heart to a faithful friend and ask for help. With the power of the Holy Spirit and a dear friend at your side, every temptation can really be downplayed, minimized, and conquered!

I like how the apostle Paul taught about this in First Corinthians 10:13. He said, "There hath no temptation taken you but such as is common to man...." The word "temptation" is very fierce in the Greek language. It's the word *peirasmos*, and it depicts *that moment when we feel seized and squeezed by eternal or internal forces that are designed to take us down*. But these feelings are momentary and relatively powerless according to Paul. It's all a masquerade of flesh merely trying to act powerful. Paul described these as being "common to man."

The phrase "common to man" is a translation of the Greek word *anthropinos*, which describes *things that are normally experienced by human beings and are therefore not exceptional.* Rather than blow these temptations out of proportion, Paul downplayed them as being commonplace. Furthermore, he continued by saying that God "…with the temptation will make a way to escape..." (1 Corinthians 10:13). If these temptations were truly overpowering, they would be inescapable. However, Paul clearly stated that we can easily escape them.

The word "escape" is the Greek word *ekbasis*, which is a compound of the words *ek* and *basis.* The word *ek* simply means *out*, and the word *basis* means *to step*. When these two words are compounded, the new word *ekbasis* means *to step out*. In other words, you can *walk away from* or *step out of* a temptation just as easily as you walked into one.

It's all a matter of what you believe.

The devil will always try to convince you that you are a tiny, powerless being with no authority to withstand his lies. If you take his bait, you'll have a very difficult time walking away from the temptations that assail your mind. Instead, you can choose to think like Paul and say, "These silly temptations are nothing special that human beings haven't faced many times. There is nothing powerful or special about them, and I will walk away from these emotions." As you do, you'll find your stance of authority in Christ has increased in strength, and the mental drama you used to experience from those negative thoughts will become negligible!

Decide beforehand how you're going to respond to negative thoughts! You have to make the decision to believe that you and the Holy Spirit are bigger and stronger than any problem that will ever come your way. With Jesus on your side, you can look at those temptations and declare, "You do not have authority over me! You are nothing more than a simple human temptation that has affected millions of people through history before me, and there are legions of people who have resisted and defeated you. And today I am being added to the number of those who say NO to you! I refuse to let this temptation become a drama! I am picking up my feet and walking away from your voice. *In the name of Jesus, you have no more authority over me!*"

MY PRAYER FOR TODAY

Father, I thank You for the truth of Your Word. I allow it to transform me into a new person by changing the way I think. Anytime I feel seized and squeezed by eternal or internal forces designed to take me down, help me remember that there is no temptation that is not common to man. With every temptation that presents itself, You also present the way of escape from it.

I pray this in Jesus' name!

MY CONFESSION FOR TODAY

I declare that I make the decision to leave temptation in the dust. I choose to magnify the Lord and minimize every attempt to lure and appeal to my flesh through temptation in any form. I am not powerless or without authority and strength. I stand strong in the boldness, authority, and strength of God by the power of His Spirit within me. Because I am born of God, I am an overcomer in this life! Knowing that Jesus Christ Himself and countless others have resisted and defeated the very same temptation, I choose to walk away from these silly temptations and the emotions that surround them! The Holy Spirit in me is bigger than any temptation that tries to come against me — I can simply walk away from it!

I declare this by faith in Jesus' name!

QUESTIONS FOR YOU TO CONSIDER

1. Can you think of a temptation or thought that has tried to habitually keep you down and depressed? What do you think about it now after reading today's *Sparkling Gem*? Do you still think this thought or temptation holds power over you, or do you think that you've just been hoodwinked by the devil in this respect?
2. You've said no to many things in the past — what is keeping you from lifting your voice and exercising your authority right now? Is it that you enjoy the sin? *Be honest!*
3. Can you honestly say you're facing something more insurmountable than the power of God can overcome? Why don't you dig your heels in the ground, tell the devil to hit the road, throw up your arms, and start rejoicing that this particular temptation has no right to exercise itself over you any longer?

MARCH 28

Do You Understand How Important It Is That You Build Your Life Correctly?

Know ye not that ye are the temple of God,
and that the Spirit of God dwelleth in you?
— 1 Corinthians 3:16

In the final days of the Soviet Union, the leaders of one prominent city decided they would build a spectacular hotel to impress the many foreign guests who had begun to visit. The site for the hotel was chosen in the most prime and visible location in the city, and the architects finalized their plans for what they declared would be an outstanding architectural wonder.

The city was soon filled with people's continual chatter about the many benefits this new building project would attract to the city. Eager to have the project finished, the city leaders announced an opening date for the hotel that was unrealistic, considering the amount of work that had to be done. Bulldozers began to move dirt, and concrete trucks began to pour concrete in great volumes. Yet it was soon apparent that the project was taking longer than expected.

Impatient and fearful that they wouldn't meet their own self-imposed deadline, city leaders urged the architects and builders to go faster and faster, even though rushing the construction could jeopardize the integrity of the structure.

Before long, a huge, magnificent building was erected on the site — so tall that it could be seen from a great distance. You can imagine what a horror it was to the city leaders and to the entire city when they realized the building was starting to dangerously lean to the side! The foundation had been poured so quickly and with such inferior materials that it wasn't able to hold up the weight of the structure. Eventually the building leaned so much that the entire project had to be abandoned. What had originally been intended as a great architectural achievement became the city's greatest public embarrassment. Today that enormous building still stands leaning and abandoned in the very spot where it had been hastily built by leaders who refused to take the necessary time to ensure it was built properly. Instead of becoming the pride of the city as they had hoped, today it is a permanent reminder of how buildings should *not* be built.

In the apostle Paul's first epistle to the Corinthians, he used the illustration of buildings and building materials to urge his readers to build their lives carefully and with materials of character that were long-lasting. He explicitly pointed out the need to construct their lives in such a way that they could survive the fires and tests that come with life. After speaking to them passionately on this subject, Paul asked them, "Know ye not that ye are the temple of God, and that the Spirit of God dwelleth in you?" (1 Corinthians 3:16).

Notice that Paul said, "Know ye not...." The word "know" in Greek is *oida*, which carries the idea of *perception, understanding,* or *comprehension.* By using the word *oida* at this juncture, Paul was asking his readers:

- "Don't you understand what I am telling you?"
- "Don't you grasp what I am trying to say to you?"
- "Don't you get the picture I am trying to get across to you?"
- "Don't you comprehend what I am saying?"

However, the word "know" — the Greek word *oida* — is preceded by the word *ouk*, which is the strongest *negative* in the Greek language. This means that after everything Paul had told the Corinthian believers thus far, he was still concerned that they weren't getting the full impact of what he was trying to tell them. So in conclusion, he pleaded with them, *"Don't you get it? Don't you understand?"*

As a Christian leader, I have counseled vast numbers of people throughout the years of my ministry, and I can confidently tell you that most people do not think on a long-term basis about their lives. Most live for today with no long-range planning for tomorrow. A simple proof of this is the large number of people who spend every dollar they make and put no money in the bank or invest nothing for retirement. When the age of retirement comes, they have nothing more than their Social Security pay to live on, and they struggle financially. Their claim that there was never enough extra money to save is usually not true. There was extra money, but it was spent on "other things" that brought fleeting, temporary pleasure. Now those "other things" are gone; the bank account is empty; and there is not enough money to live life normally. Although it's not always true, a person's experience of lack at retirement age is often a matter of shortsightedness and lack of long-term planning.

Let me bring this point right to your home in order to make it clearer. What are your financial plans for your future? Are you building a financial base with savings or investments that will help you live a normal life after you retire and you no longer have a monthly paycheck coming to you? What about your children or grandchildren? When you look at the way they're living their lives and spending their money, do you see that they're living only for the present, or are they thinking about their future?

I know I'm hitting a sensitive issue, but addressing people's personal finances makes the point very clear that the majority do *not* think long-term about what they are doing with their lives. For example, think how many people decide they *must* buy a new TV set because they saw one they like better than the one they already have, even though their current one works fine. To satisfy that fleeting "want," they quickly run to the store to purchase that new TV — and if they don't have the money, they charge it on their credit cards. Now they have a new TV sitting in their living room, but that money could have been invested in their future if they had opted to put it into a savings account or investment plan. *This is all the result of short-term thinking.*

Living for today with no thought for tomorrow is a flaw in human nature. In 2,000 years, people haven't made much progress in this area. Just as I am pleading with you today to assess your life and the way you are building it, Paul pleaded with the Corinthian believers when he asked them: *"Don't you know? Don't you get what I'm trying to tell you? How could it be possible that you still don't understand what I'm trying to tell you?"*

Building your life is very similar to constructing a big building. A building must be constructed correctly and with good materials. It can't be built too quickly, or the integrity of the structure might be compromised. Likewise, to build your life, your family, your business, your education, your church, your ministry, or anything else that is precious to you — and to build it wisely and strong enough to endure the tests of time — requires time, energy, patience, and careful planning. Remember, you are building your life and your future, and what you do today *will* have a direct impact on your tomorrow. Mistakes made today will show up tomorrow, so it is wise to move slowly and deliberately and to think before you act. *Never forget that hasty decisions are usually wrong decisions.*

Paul told the Corinthians, "Know ye not that ye are the temple of God...." This statement is so very important, because it tells us that we are not only building our personal lives and things that personally affect our future, but we — that is, our lives, our bodies, and everything that we are — are in fact the "temple" where God resides in this earth. This word translated "temple" that Paul used in this verse is the Greek word *naos*. It is a word used 46 times in the New Testament, so its meaning is very clear. It denotes *a temple* or *a highly decorated shrine*. (For a deeper study on this word *naos*, *see Sparkling Gems 1*, February 25.)

When we hear the word "shrine," our minds immediately evoke images of a building with arched, vaulted ceilings; marble, granite, gold, and silver; hand-carved etchings; and lots and lots of smoke from incense being burned as a part of worship. Shrines are impressive with all their ornamentation. In Russia where my family lives, there are many huge cathedrals that fit this description — and they are *very* impressive. However, in the New Testament, the word *naos* doesn't describe only shrines such as these. It is also the word most often used to depict *the Holy of Holies*, that special room in the Jerusalem temple where God's glory dwelt.

Please take heed to what I am about to tell you. Life is busy, and there are many things that occupy our thoughts and schedules. In the rush of it all, we are tempted to forget who we are and who lives inside us. We tend to think of ourselves as mere human beings, but the Bible plainly teaches that we are much more than that. According to Paul's words in First Corinthians 3:16, you and I are the "temple" of the Spirit of God. Let the realization sink into your heart that *God's Spirit actually lives in us*. This means we are His dwelling place, His residence — the place where He continually abides.

God lives in you! That's why as you build your life and future, you must be careful to build it gloriously and not shabbily, for it is the place where God lives. That's also why it's good to regularly evaluate yourself. Are you building your life wisely so that you survive every season of life, every attack of the devil, every period of hardship, and every fire that comes to you in life? Are you building your life in a way that demonstrates your respect for the One who lives inside you? Are you building your life so carefully, wisely, and honorably that the Spirit of God who dwells inside you is honored that you are His place of residence? *If you were God, would you want to live inside you?*

I realize that time is precious and that we are all tempted to do things as fast as possible. But some things are worthy of taking extra time to make sure they are done correctly. You don't want to build so quickly that you build incorrectly, in a way that ultimately forces you to abandon the project or to tear down what you've built and start all over again. I promise you that it will cost you more than it would have if you had done it right in the first place. Building correctly from the beginning usually takes more time, but it pays off in the end.

As you make your plans for today, seriously consider how your actions may affect your tomorrow. You may be tempted to take shortcuts to speed things up, but do all you can to resist that temptation so you can be sure you're not adversely affecting the quality of what you are building with your life. And as you examine what you have already built, ask yourself:

- Have I built my life strong enough to survive every test? Or have I built it so shabbily that much of what I have achieved will have to be torn down and started all over again, ultimately costing me much more than if I had done it right from the start?
- Will my current decisions and actions make a dwelling place for the Holy Spirit that is glorious, or will my actions create a place unbefitting of His residence in my life?

These are important questions to ask as you consider what you've already done with your life and the future actions you're about to take. Don't forget that what you do today will affect your life tomorrow, so determine to build carefully and wisely. Never forget that you are the temple of the Holy Spirit and that what you do with your life brings Him either honor or disrespect.

In light of what you've read in this *Sparkling Gem,* do you hear the Holy Spirit pleading with you to make a change in the way you are building your life, your family, your business, your education, your church, your ministry, or anything else that is precious to you? Do you hear Him saying:

- "Don't you know?"
- "Don't you get what I'm trying to tell you?"
- "How could it be possible that you still don't understand what I'm trying to tell you?"

Before you do anything else, why don't you take few minutes today to get on your knees and ask the Spirit of God to help you assess what you are constructing with your life? It is far better to ask now and let Him tell you what you could be doing better than to never ask and later regret that you didn't. James 1:5 promises that if you ask God for wisdom, He will answer you. If you'll take time to ask, He will take time to help you see everything that is needed to build your life so well that it can pass all the tests of time.

MY PRAYER FOR TODAY

Father, I want to thank You for speaking to my heart today about the things I am building both correctly and incorrectly in my life. In retrospect, I realize that I have built many things in my life that I now wish I had done differently. I no longer want to live my life in regret for making wrong decisions. I confess that much of what I have built, I have built hastily and with no regard for the wisdom of long-term thinking. As a result, I am reaping the consequences of my past decisions. I ask You to forgive me for not thinking more soundly in the past, and by faith I receive Your forgiveness. Now as I look to the future, I ask You to speak to my heart and show me how to bring correction to what I have done so that I will not repeat the same mistakes. Holy Spirit, I look to You for counsel and direction. I thank You in advance for Your help as I begin to build a life that will bring honor to You and that will gloriously survive all the tests that come in life.

I pray this in Jesus' name!

MY CONFESSION FOR TODAY

I declare by faith that I build my life according to the wisdom of God, with forethought and sound planning. God lives in me — and because I respect His presence in my life, I build my life in a way that brings honor and glory to Him. I give place to the counsel of the Holy Spirit who helps and directs me in such a way that I build orderly, not hastily. I am the temple of the Holy Spirit. Therefore, I carefully build my life in a way that honors His presence in me. I repent for my carelessness in the past. Today I choose to be careful, thoughtful, and prayerful about building my life and my future. I ask for wisdom from above and God answers me — providing me with all the answers I need to build a life that lasts and a life that brings glory to His name.

I declare this by faith in Jesus' name!

QUESTIONS FOR YOU TO CONSIDER

1. When you look at your life and the things you have built with it, are you satisfied that you have built your life correctly, or do you see areas where you know you could have done better? What are those areas that you wish you had built more wisely? Can you correct them? If so, how will you go about that task?
2. What has been the long-term effect on your life from building too hastily and without thought of tomorrow? If you had it to do all over again, what types of changes would you make in the way you have built your life?
3. In order for you to build the rest of your life wisely and strongly, what changes do you need to make in the way that you think? What habits do you need to change? What plans do you need to incorporate concerning your family, your relationships, your job, your education, your finances, and the way you spend your time?
4. As you assess what it's going to take for you to make these significant changes, can you honestly say you're willing to do what is required? If not, are you willing to ask the Holy Spirit to give you the desire to change?

MARCH 29

Rejoicing in Heaven Over One Sinner Who Repents!

I say unto you, that likewise joy shall be in heaven
over one sinner that repenteth, more than over
ninety-nine just persons, which need no repentance.
— Luke 15:7

The Bible tells us much about angels. It gives us different categories of angels and describes how they look, how they fly, what they do in the presence of God, their role in the earth today, and much more. By studying the Scriptures, it is easy to get an accurate perspective of what angels do both on earth and in Heaven. But today I want us to see the one unique thing that causes angels in Heaven to erupt in joy. *What is this solitary act that triggers such a mighty angelic celebration?*

With all the information about angels recorded in the Bible, there are only two verses — a total of 49 words in the *King James Version* — that implicitly describe an event that causes angels to stop what they're doing and throw a celebration that is different from those they regularly experience in the worshipful atmosphere of Heaven. Both of these references are found in Luke 15, where Jesus gives the parable of a shepherd who found one of his sheep that had been lost.

In Luke 15:4-6, Jesus said, "What man of you, having an hundred sheep, if he lose one of them, doth not leave the ninety and nine in the wilderness, and go after that which is lost, until he find it. And when he hath found it, he layeth it on his shoulders, rejoicing. And when he cometh home, he calleth together his friends and neighbors, saying unto them, Rejoice with me; for I have found my sheep that was lost."

The Early Church believed this parable was a reference to Jesus Himself. Jesus left Heaven and, like the shepherd in the parable, came to earth to seek and to save that which was lost. The early Christians of the First and Second Centuries were so convinced this parable was about Jesus that they often used the image of a shepherd carrying a lamb across his shoulders as the graphic to depict Him. In ancient catacombs in Rome where early Christians once gathered to worship and pray, painted images of a shepherd carrying a lamb, representing Jesus, are still visible on the walls.

The Early Church saw Jesus as the Shepherd who left home and came to earth, found them lost in sin, and then lovingly redeemed them and brought them back into right relationship with God. And like the shepherd in the parable, after Jesus accomplished this awesome task, He returned home *rejoicing.*

According to the parable — if we believe that it represents Jesus, as the Early Church believed — when Jesus returned to Heaven, He invited all of Heaven to *rejoice with Him* because man, once lost, was now redeemed. From Jesus' words in His parable, we assume that when He crossed the threshold of Heaven, He called out to the heavenly inhabitants and told them, "Rejoice with Me, for I have found My sheep that was lost!" (*see* Luke 15:6).

The words "rejoice with me" are a compound of the words *sun* and *chairo*. The word *sun* depicts *something that is done in conjunction with someone else*, while the word *chairo* means *to be glad, to rejoice, to exult, to celebrate*, or *to express great joy*. When they are compounded, the new word means *to celebrate in conjunction with someone else* or *to greatly rejoice with other companions*. This particular word is found only seven times in the New Testament, and one of them is here in Luke 15:6 where the shepherd calls on his friends to *rejoice with him* over the lost sheep that was found. It literally means *rejoice with me, celebrate with me*, or *exult with me!*

The finding of lost sheep was such a cause for rejoicing that Jesus called for all of Heaven to celebrate with Him! Just think how serious a man's lost condition must be in order for Jesus to see it as a time to stop and throw a party whenever a sinner repents!

Jesus comprehends the great cost of a person's redemption, for He paid for each soul with His own precious blood. So when a sinner repents, Jesus sees this as a time for Heaven *to celebrate*! He calls on all of Heaven's inhabitants to celebrate every time a sinner is saved! Consider the profound miracle that transpires when a soul doomed to eternal destruction is redeemed by the blood of the Lamb. *It's no wonder that Jesus wants all of Heaven to join with Him in throwing a celebration!*

In Luke 15:7, Jesus continued, "I say unto you, that likewise joy shall be in heaven over one sinner that repenteth...." Some allege that the word "sinner" is too harsh, but it is the word Jesus used to characterize people without God. It is the old Greek word *hamartolos*, a word that has various possible renderings, but the basic meaning is *an offender, a lawbreaker, one who is guilty of missing the mark*, or *a sinner.*

The lost man has failed to meet the requirements of the righteous law of God and is therefore *a lawbreaker* or *a sinner.* If he doesn't repent and receive Christ before he breathes his last breath, the penalty for dying in this lost state is eternal separation from God (*see* Romans 6:23).

You can see why there is such eruptive joy in Heaven when a sinner repents! The word translated "repent" in this verse is the word *metanoeo* (*see* also March 18 and 19 *Gems*). It is the picture of a person who hears the truth, realizes the life he has lived has broken God's laws, and therefore makes up his mind that he will leave that old life and live for God according to His Word. The act of repentance and faith in Christ gives the lost person new birth and entrance into the Kingdom of God.

This is a huge happening! Luke 15:10 tells us, "...There is joy in the presence of the angels of God over one sinner that repenteth." Why is this a cause for rejoicing? Because when a man is saved, his sins are removed, and he is washed in the blood of Jesus — in that moment, his nature is changed and his name is written in the Lamb's book of life. That is an event the entire spirit realm recognizes, including mighty angels who stand in the very presence of God. They get so excited when this mightiest miracle of all takes place in the life of a human that they stop everything to take note of it and to celebrate!

I don't know about you, but I am personally convicted by the lack of excitement I see in church when a sinner gets saved. People yawn and cover their mouth, as if it is just routine activity — when, in fact, it is the greatest miracle that can occur on planet earth! It is worth our shouting, yelling, and jumping up and down in joy, for there is no greater miracle than the new birth!

Angels live in the breathtaking presence of God and regularly see His wonders that are beyond our imagination. Yet they are so thrilled about a person who repents that they rejoice with great joy.

Maybe it's time for us to revisit the subject of our salvation and relearn what great a miracle it is when a lost man is redeemed and quickened to spiritual life by the Holy Spirit. *Since angels get excited about this, isn't it time that we start appreciating it too?*

I pray that your understanding has increased and that this study of Luke 15 has affected you in a meaningful way. Don't let the devil steal these truths from your heart. Remember, God is always calling you higher. Make sure your heart is closely connected to Jesus' heart. Rejoice *greatly* with Heaven the next time you witness someone repenting and becoming a new creation in Christ!

And if there's anything that holds you back from your *own* forward progress in Him, it's time for you to make up your mind to turn from it and adjust your life to show that you are serious about making new gains in God. Your redemption was worth the highest price, Jesus' own precious blood — so live *every* day like you esteem the treasure of your salvation more than all the riches this world could ever offer you!

MY PRAYER FOR TODAY

Lord, I repent for my own apathy concerning the miracle that takes place when a lost man is saved. I was one of those who has yawned and said, "Oh, that's nice." But in truth, there is no greater miracle than a man whose nature is changed. Nothing is more wondrous than the moment a sinner's heart is changed and he is adopted as a child of God! Please forgive me for being so lackadaisical about this marvelous miracle that only You can perform in the heart of a human being. Help me never forget the price that You paid for my salvation — and to never forget how my life has changed since the day I repented. Even more, I ask for Your fire to burn in my heart in a fresh way for those who are still unrepentant. I ask You for open doors for me to tell others about the love of Jesus Christ so their hearts can be changed and they can be spiritually awakened by the Spirit of God.

I pray this in Jesus' name!

MY CONFESSION FOR TODAY

I confess that I will never take my salvation for granted. It is the greatest gift of God in my life, and my salvation is so precious to God that He gave His own Son that I might know Him today. I am thankful and so grateful for the privilege of being a child of God — a child of the Light. I recommit myself to serve Jesus with a passionate heart and a single mind all of my days. Just as Jesus' blood saved and changed me, it is still saving and changing people's lives all over the world. When people come to Christ in repentance, I join the throng of the heavenly host to celebrate this great victory. It is a commemoration of a human nature supernaturally changed, a spot in hell that has been vacated, and a place in the Father's house that will now be filled! This is worthy of my greatest joy and exultation.

I declare this by faith in Jesus' name!

QUESTIONS FOR YOU TO CONSIDER

1. How do people in your church respond when a sinner walks the aisle to repent and commit his or her life to Jesus Christ? Is it a time of real rejoicing or just another part of the program?
2. How long has it been since you took time to deeply ponder the miracle of your salvation? Why don't you consecrate a few minutes of your time to do it today?
3. Let your imagination soar as you consider what it may be like in Heaven when it is announced that a sinner has repented.

MARCH 30

A Rescue Operation!

For the Son of Man is come to seek
and to save what had been lost.
— Luke 19:10

Denise and I had decided to relocate from the small Latvian city of Jelgava to the very heart of the capital city, Riga, which was closer to our ministry offices. After searching a long time for a residence large enough to suit our family, we found an old apartment in a building constructed in 1898 that would meet our needs. This apartment was located in a once-elegant building in Riga's most prestigious neighborhood — that is, a building that was elegant *before* the Bolshevik Revolution.

In the earlier Soviet years, apartments like this one were confiscated and converted into communal flats. In the case of our apartment, this once majestic space had been divided into eight tiny apartments for eight families that shared *one kitchen* and *one toilet*! The people who lived there over a period of nearly 55 years had *no respect whatsoever* for this architectural treasure. Their total lack of care was most obvious in the bathroom. As men used the bathroom over the years, they had missed the toilet so many thousands of times that the acidic effect of the urine had literally burned a hole through the heavy flooring big enough to see straight through it into the apartment below! It was shameful to see what had happened to this once-luxurious apartment where an elite class of people had formerly lived.

As I walked through that horribly deteriorated apartment, I was stunned by the hints of old beauty that somehow still remained. I could see that under years of botched paint jobs, each room was adorned with massive moldings that went all the way around the ceilings. Several of the rooms contained lavish fireplaces so spectacular that they should have been on display in a museum — but the condition of these fireplaces left me aghast. This once-grandiose residence now only boasted of collapsed ceilings, crumbling plaster, and mold that had spread over large sections of the walls. To top it off, hooligans had painted derogatory words and nasty phrases all over the walls throughout the apartment.

Because the apartment was so trashed, it was available for an unbelievably low price. Actually, no one else wanted it! But we knew this was our apartment, so we purchased it and went to work restoring it. Although dirt, grime, filth, and trash were heaped in huge piles in every room, we knew that this place was restorable if we would be willing to do what was necessary to bring it back to its former glory.

So many times when I looked at the work involved of restoring that dwelling place, I thought of how that apartment was like a human life. It often made me reflect on the words of John

10:10, where Jesus told us that Satan always attempts to take what is good and ruin it. But whatever Satan has tried to spoil, *Jesus has the power to reverse*!

As the restoration process took place in our apartment in Riga, we began to peel 55 years of Soviet wallpaper from the walls. One layer at a time, we peeled back decades of history — until finally we came to a discovery that took us completely off guard. When all the Soviet wallpaper was removed, we came upon nearly perfectly preserved Yiddish newspapers that were plastered over every inch of those walls. The papers had been used to level the surface before the next layer of exquisite wallpaper could be hung. When I saw those Yiddish papers, I understood that the original owners of the apartment had been Jewish — and the reason no original owners had ever been located is that they'd been exterminated in the Holocaust. Such history was emerging in that place!

The molding in one room was so intricate that it required one man four months to clean it, and because the details were so sophisticated and multifaceted, dental instruments had to be used to scrape away the ugly paint that had covered it. But finally, after almost one year of nonstop work, that dilapidated apartment was amazingly restored to its original glory. The process was long and painful, but the results were breathtaking, and Denise and I were thrilled that we had invested the time and energy to undertake this effort.

It was almost impossible to believe that this formerly neglected, run-down, decrepit, decayed apartment had become our lovely home — a home we would live in for years before we finally moved to Moscow. But because we were willing to accept the challenge of the task and painstakingly undertake the process of restoring this property, we were rewarded with something very glorious and magnificent that eventually emerged from a ravaged, wasted, and devastated state.

When I sat surrounded by the restored version of this habitation, I often wondered, "How could something so beautiful have become so devastated?" We so quickly adjusted to the restored version that we often "forgot" how horrible it had been just a short time earlier. When people came to visit us, they often commented that it was like a historic treasure — but they had no idea of the hard work, time, effort, and prayer required to transform it and bring it to its new splendor. They only saw the results.

My view was very different. Almost every day of living in and looking at that apartment made me think of Luke 19:10. That verse says, "For the Son of man is come to seek and to save that which was *lost*." That word "lost" always grabs my attention. It's the Greek word *appololos*, derived from the word *appolumi*, and it conveys the idea of *something ruined, wasted, trashed, devastated, or destroyed*. By the way, it's also the same word used for the *Destroyer* — one of the New Testament names to describe Satan's demented nature.

The words "to seek" are a translation of the Greek word *zeteo*, which depicts *a search so intense that it could be likened to an investigation for something*. It tells us that Jesus *has put forth* and *is putting forth* His best efforts to actively seek to save and restore whatever Satan has tried to steal, kill, or destroy. What does "save" mean in this case? It is translated from the Greek word *sodzo*, which mainly implies *rescue*, such as a *rescue* from a raging sea, *rescue* from an illness, *rescue* from immediate danger, and so forth. Inherent in this type of "rescue" is one's return to *safety* and *soundness.*

Just as our 1898 apartment was rescued from destruction and returned to a normal state, Jesus wants to rescue and return *us* to a state of normalcy, safety, and recovery. This isn't just a *salvage operation* I'm talking about — it's a full-scale *rescue* that results in a *redemptive* and *fully restorative operation.*

Someone might say, "Yes, but even if Jesus works mightily in my life, some things will probably never be like they were before this destruction occurred." I, too, know very well what it is to suffer loss on different levels. I know that who you and I are today is not who we used to be. Yet who we are is *not* a second-rate, dumbed-down version of something that used to be better! We may be *different* than we used to be, but memories of the past are not always realistic. Those memories are usually tainted to look better than they really were. In Christ, we are filled with the potential of the Holy Spirit inside us, and the *truth* is that you and I are *not* a weaker, substandard version of what we were before. We're stronger, better, and improved because of what Jesus has done to *rescue* us and to *redeem* and *restore* our hearts and lives to a state of wholeness in Him!

For example, I never saw the original apartment we lived in that was built in 1898 — and, indeed, the original version *may* have been more beautiful than the version that became our home after Denise and I restored it. But if I compare what we restored to what we first found when we began looking at it as a place to live, it's absolutely amazing that a horrible place with a "urine hole" that went right through the floor could once again be beautiful and whole. To accomplish that task required faith, imagination, hard work, and a lot of prayer. It didn't happen overnight. It was a daily effort. But with all that combined effort, faith, prayer, and the help of others, the results were breathtaking! I'm sure that if the original owners in 1898 had seen what we restored from such a decrepit, fallen state — *even if it was different* from the original version — they wouldn't have thought it was a second-rate version. It may have been different, but what came out of that restoration process was still a home of great beauty and value, as was the home that had been exquisitely created in the beginning.

Likewise, Jesus is earnestly seeking to perform a rescue operation in every area of your life where Satan has attempted to bring devastation and ruin. It doesn't matter how the destruction occurred — whether it was due to your own neglect, to the actions of others, to circumstances, or to an attack of Satan himself — Jesus is *still* pursuing you for your *rescue*, your *safety*, and your *recovery*! And if you will participate with Jesus' *active hunt* for you and your good, it will speed up the restoration process in your life. This doesn't apply just to you. Jesus is seeking to rescue those around you who desperately need rescuing. Don't give up on them, because rescue operations are Jesus' specialty!

It took hard work, imagination, and a lot of committed time to restore that old apartment in Riga, and it would never have happened if we had just "hoped" it would get better. Denise and I were the initiators of that renovation process — just as Jesus was the One who initiated His recovery operation in *our* lives. But our ongoing participation was also required. And if we will participate with Jesus in what He is trying to restore in our lives, it is simply a fact that the process will be speeded up as He restores us to the wholeness He originally intended for our lives.

And keep this in mind regarding your own personal renovation process: Although things really may be a little different than they were originally, it doesn't mean they are "less than" they used to be — they may, in fact, actually be better! Let that process continue as you yield to the Holy Spirit's work in you to will and to do His good pleasure (*see* Philippians 2:13).

MY PRAYER FOR TODAY

Father, I thank You that Jesus initiated a rescue operation in my life. He isn't merely salvaging me; He has put forth His best efforts to restore the ruined places of my life to a new splendor that brings glory to His name. Holy Spirit, today I surrender my life into Your power. Please take me and carry out the instructions of Jesus to rescue and restore me as He sees fit. I promise that I will not look at myself as a second-rate version of something that used to be better. Release Your power in me, let it transform me, and I will praise You for what You make me to be for Your glory!

I pray this in Jesus' name!

MY CONFESSION FOR TODAY

I confess that in Christ, I am filled with the potential of the Holy Spirit, and I am not a weak, substandard version of God's original intent for my life. Because Jesus has released the Holy Spirit in me, I am stronger, better, and improved version that far exceeds anything I used to be. I refuse to believe the devil's lies suggesting that I am less than who God made me to be in Jesus Christ. Because I am a partaker of the divine nature, the ideal image of Christ is being reproduced in me by His Spirit!

I declare this by faith in Jesus' name!

QUESTIONS FOR YOU TO CONSIDER

1. What condition were you in when you surrendered your life to the Lordship of Jesus Christ? It is good to remember what Jesus has done in your life. Write down your testimony and keep it for your own personal memory's sake. It will make you thankful for the new version you are today!
2. Would you have wanted to take you on as a transformational restoration project? How often do you take a pause to recognize the new you and to thank Jesus for what He has done in your life?
3. Although you have already been restored to a state far better than you used to be, what areas in your life do you recognize still need to be surrendered to Christ's transforming power? Why do you think you haven't made the decision to surrender them to Him yet?

MARCH 31

Sword Power!

And take...the sword of the Spirit,
which is the word of God.
— Ephesians 6:17

How would you like to deal a debilitating blow to the devil when he tries to attack your life and mind?

Today I want to talk to you about what Ephesians 6:17 calls the "sword of the Spirit" — a *supernatural sword* that has the power to drive back the enemy and deal a blow to his attacks against your life. When you have what I'm about to describe, it gives you *supernatural sword power* against the devil!

In Ephesians 6:17, Paul wrote, "And take...the *sword* of the Spirit, which is the word of God." In order to fully understand Paul's message regarding the sword of the Spirit, let's look at what the apostle had in his mind when he used the word translated "sword." It's the Greek word *machaira*, which is the very word used to describe the type of *sword* that Roman soldiers used in battle.

Because the Roman army was so committed to warfare, Roman soldiers continually practiced the arts of warfare. One daily exercise was sword practice, which they undertook both in the morning and the afternoon. Every soldier practiced sword fighting by striking a six-foot-high wooden post that was firmly fixed in the ground. This post became the soldier's "enemy" during practice. Just as he would if he were fighting a real enemy, the soldier would advance upon his target, strike hard with his sword, and then retreat.

The soldier's job in practice was to learn how to take advantage of his enemy, hit him at his weakest point, and strike him so he could not respond. His aim was nearly always directed toward the area of the post that represented the head or face, the thighs and legs, or occasionally the sides of the target.

The ancient Roman writer Vegetius described Roman sword-fighting tactics in his book *Concerning Military Matters*, saying, "They were likewise taught not to cut, but to thrust with their swords. For the Romans not only made jest of those who fought with the edge of that weapon, but always found them an easy conquest. A stroke with the edges, though, made with ever so much force, seldom kills, as the vital parts of the body are defended both by the bones and armor. *On the contrary, a stab, though it penetrates but two inches, is generally fatal.*"[3]

[3] Publius Flavius Vegetius Renatus, *Concerning Military Matters* (De Re Militari), Book I.

The practices I just described are exactly what Paul had in mind when he wrote, "And take... the *sword* of the Spirit, which is the word of God" (Ephesians 6:17). How vital it is that we *understand* the sword of the Spirit!

Notice particularly where Paul said, "...the sword of the Spirit, which is *the word of God.*" This word "word" is the Greek word *rhema*, which refers to a *specific, quickened word.* In order to have a sword that penetrates a blow to the enemy, we need a *rhema* — a *specific, quickened word* from the Scriptures — placed into our hearts and mouths by the Holy Spirit. With a *rhema* from God placed in our hearts and mouths, we have "*sword power*"!

Remember, all a Roman soldier had to do in order to eradicate his enemies was make a well-placed, two-inch-deep stab wound. Likewise, one *rhema* from the Lord has the power to eliminate the enemy's attacks! *Thank God for the sword of the Spirit!*

The best example of this powerful sword of the Spirit is found in Luke 4:3-13. In this passage, Satan is repeatedly and aggressively attacking Jesus. But Jesus answered him repeatedly with a specific quickened *rhema* from the Holy Spirit. For example, after the devil tempted Jesus with food, Jesus drew the sword of the Spirit and rebuked Satan, saying, "...It is written, That man shall not live by bread alone, but by every word of God" (v. 4). *The enemy could not respond to this sword of the Spirit.*

When Satan offered Jesus all the kingdoms of the world in exchange for worship, Jesus drew another *rhema* and wounded him deeply yet again. Jesus said, "...it is written, Thou shalt worship the Lord thy God, and him only shalt thou serve" (v. 8). *To this sword of the Spirit, Satan had no answer.*

Finally, when Satan tempted Jesus to prove His deity, Jesus answered him again with *a sword*! He said, "It is said, Thou shalt not tempt the Lord thy God" (v. 12). With this *rhema*, Jesus penetrated Satan's armor with one final stab and dealt his enemy a devastating blow. Luke 4:13 tells us that *after* Jesus responded multiple times with a *rhema* — a specific, quickened word that dealt exactly with the type of attack Jesus was facing — the devil "departed" from him. Satan was nullified by these *rhema* words that Jesus drew and used like a spiritual sword against him.

Like the Lord Jesus, when the Holy Spirit quickens a scripture to you and you use it against the enemy, he will eventually "depart" from you because he has no answer with which to engage you in further combat. The sword of the Spirit is a supernatural spiritual weapon that renders the devil powerless. So today I want to urge you to open your heart to let the Holy Spirit reveal the exact scriptures you need to withstand the devil's attacks and to deal him a "fatal" blow. *With those scriptures in your heart and mouth, God will have given you a spiritual sword that the devil cannot resist!*

MY PRAYER FOR TODAY

Father, I am thankful for the ministry of the Holy Spirit. When I need sword power to stand against the enemy, the Holy Spirit quickens Scripture to my heart. When those verses are supernaturally revealed to me, please help me recognize and not forget or underestimate what is happening. Help me realize that the Spirit of God is placing a supernatural sword in my heart and that my job is to put it in my mouth and to wield it against the enemy. And, Father, just as the devil eventually "departed" from Jesus, at least for a season, I know that the devil will depart from me too. Thank You so much for the sword power that You give to me by the Spirit, quickening those verses to me at just the right time!

I pray this in Jesus' name!

MY CONFESSION FOR TODAY

I confess that I have sword power to stand against the devil's attacks because the Holy Spirit quickens Scripture to my heart. When those verses are supernaturally quickened to me, the Spirit places a supernatural sword in my heart. As I release those words like a sword from my mouth, I wield a debilitating blow against the enemy. As I submit myself to God, I resist the devil and he must flee from me (James 4:7). I am thankful for the sword power that the Spirit gives to me and for quickening verses to me just in the right time!

I declare this by faith in Jesus' name!

QUESTIONS FOR YOU TO CONSIDER

1. Can you think of a time when the Holy Spirit "quickened" a verse to you, and that verse gave you instant power to stand against the attacks that were being waged against you? What was the scripture that gave you *sword power* against the enemy? Have you continued to wield it against the enemy as part of your customized arsenal?
2. If you are being attacked in your life or mind right now, have you asked the Holy Spirit to quicken a specific verse to you that will give you *sword power* against the devil's attacks?
3. Do you know of any testimonies of someone who received a *rhema* word that suddenly gave that person direction and power for what he or she was doing or facing? What is that testimony?

Open your heart to let the Holy Spirit quicken
the exact scriptures you need
to withstand the devil's attacks
and to deal him a "fatal" blow.
With those scriptures in your heart and mouth,
God will have given you a spiritual sword
that the devil cannot resist!

APRIL 1

Copy Every Stroke of the Master

For even hereunto were ye called:
because Christ also suffered for us,
leaving us an example, that we should follow his steps....
— 1 Peter 2:21

Can you remember first learning to write as a young child? Oh, how well I remember those early days in the first grade when I carefully studied how my teacher wrote the letters of the alphabet on the blackboard. When she was done, it was our turn to take our lead pencils in hand and copy what she had written.

With all my might, I pressed my pencil onto the paper of my Indian Chief tablet. In fact, I pushed so hard writing those letters that I formed a callous on my finger that I still have to this day! I gave 100 percent of my concentration to exactly duplicate every letter my teacher had written on that blackboard. Day after day and hour after hour, I would write those letters over and over again. I filled my tablet with pages of writing until I finally mastered each letter of the alphabet. It took concentration and commitment, but in time, I learned to write exactly as my teacher had shown me.

I'm sure you, too, can remember when you first learned to write. But did you know that this is precisely the idea Peter had in mind when he told the early believers, "For even hereunto were ye called: because Christ also suffered for us, leaving us an example, that we should follow in his steps" (1 Peter 2:21)?

Let me explain what I mean. When Peter wrote these words to early believers, they were suffering terribly for their faith at the hands of the Roman government. They were suffering unjustly, and there was nothing they could do legally to defend themselves. God's Word commanded them to respect, submit to, and pray for the very government that was harassing and killing them. To the believers who were facing this plight of unjust treatment, Peter said this: "For even hereunto were ye called: because Christ also suffered for us, leaving us an example, that we should follow his steps" (1 Peter 2:21).

The word "suffered" in this verse is from the Greek word *pascho*, meaning *to suffer.* It's the word used to describe the *passion* or *suffering* of Jesus when He died on the Cross. However, there are many examples of the word *pascho* in the New Testament, all of which carry the idea of *suffering, undergoing hardships, being ill-treated*, or *experiencing adversity.*

The truth is, Jesus experienced a measure of suffering throughout His entire life on this earth. When He was a Child, His family suffered as they fled from the murderous plots of King Herod. Later Jesus suffered at the hands of religious leaders who hated Him and continually leveled false accusations against Him. Jesus had to constantly put up with the immature behavior of His disciples as He tried to teach them and set an example for them. He suffered betrayal at the hands of one of His associates, Judas Iscariot. His suffering in the Garden of Gethsemane was so intense that His sweat was as great drops of blood falling down to the ground. And in the end, Jesus suffered the worst suffering of all — death on the Cross. Yet through it all, Jesus lived above the suffering and maintained an attitude of love for those who treated Him unjustly.

Peter reminded his readers of Jesus' suffering, hardship, and ill treatment in order to draw the early believers closer to the Lord in the midst of what they were experiencing themselves. At that time, they desperately needed to know how to respond to unjust situations they could not change. Since no one was better at dealing with such challenges than Jesus, Peter reminded his readers (and us) that "...Christ also suffered for us, leaving us an *example*...."

Now we return to the illustration of a child learning the letters of the alphabet! When Peter chose to use the word "example" in this verse, he reached into the world of early education and borrowed the Greek word *hupogrammos*. This word precisely depicts a schoolchild who carefully watches his teacher write the letters of the alphabet. Then that child painstakingly and carefully copies each letter, matching it as closely as possible to the original letters written by his teacher.

This is exactly the picture Peter had in mind when he told you to follow the "example" of Jesus. Since Jesus is your Teacher and Master, you must focus on your spiritual blackboard — the Word of God — to learn from Him and then reproduce His example in your own life.

You must learn:

- How the Master dealt with unfair criticism, so you can respond like Him when you are unfairly criticized.
- How Jesus responded to attacks that were waged against Him, so you can know how to respond in His strength to attacks that come against you.
- How He responded to people when they failed or betrayed Him, so you can respond the same way when people disappoint or hurt you.
- How Jesus carried Himself with grace and dignity even in the midst of unspeakable abuse, so you can then draw on His strength to walk through difficult situations with the same grace and dignity.
- How He forgave His accusers every step of the way, so you can freely forgive those who mistreat or malign you.

You cannot avoid the fact that you will sometimes face unpleasant situations in which you feel mistreated, abused, or discriminated against. As long as you live in a world where the devil operates and unsaved people have their way, evil and injustice will touch your life from time to time. So when you find yourself subjected to a situation that seems unfair and unjust, you must ask, *How does God expect me to respond?*

Of course, you should pray for God to change a difficult situation. Prayer can make a huge difference in any circumstance. But what if the situation doesn't change as quickly as you wish? How should you respond? For example:

- If your employer treats you badly for no obvious reason and the situation goes on for a long time, what should you do? Of course, you could go find another job. But what if you know that your current job is where God wants you and that you're not supposed to leave it? How should you respond to the foul treatment you are receiving from your superior?
- If fellow employees are out to hurt you, to undercut you, or to see you demoted, what course of action should you take? Perhaps you've taken steps to befriend them, but nothing seems to improve the situation. How should you respond to the unfair treatment you're experiencing?
- Maybe you feel persecuted by fellow students who don't share your faith in Christ and who dislike your personal convictions. You know you can't quit school as a reaction to this difficult situation. But exactly how does God expect you to respond?
- Perhaps your family members are hostile to you because they don't understand your faith or they don't agree with the direction you're taking in life. How should you respond to your loved ones? It's so very important that you know how to respond when your family doesn't agree or support what you are doing — especially when you know the Holy Spirit is the One leading you to take that course of direction.

Certainly you must do everything possible to resolve conflicts with friends and family and to protect yourself and your reputation. Yet sometimes things happen that are beyond your control, that are not so easily resolved, and for which there is no easy recourse. Whenever you're feeling maligned and mistreated, remember that it's a prime opportunity for the devil to tempt you to become bitter, angry, hard-hearted, and resentful of those who have treated you unjustly. If you yield to that temptation, your wrong response won't do anything to improve your situation, but it will produce negative consequences in your own life.

That's why you must absolutely refuse to allow the devil to sow those negative emotions into your heart, which only bear bad fruit. Harboring such emotions is never the answer, no matter what situation you might be facing in life.

Are you facing difficult times? Are you being accused of things you didn't do or being blamed for things of which you have no knowledge? Are you being mistreated or discriminated against? If you answered *yes* to any of these questions, this is the moment for you to turn your eyes to the blackboard — God's Word — and study each stroke of the Master. Once you see what He did and how He responded in situations similar to yours, it is then your task to copy Him. If you'll take this approach to the challenges you're facing right now that seem so distressing, you'll begin to see those situations as opportunities to become more like Jesus.

So make it your earnest goal to apply the principles of Jesus' life to your own life. Strive to pen the strokes of your moments on this earth to reflect each stroke of the Master. If you'll let the

Holy Spirit help you, it's possible for you to successfully walk through life as Jesus did. What a blessing that you don't have to figure it all out by yourself! Just study the strokes of the Master's pen, and press forward by faith to copy those strokes in the face of every challenge that arises.

By yourself, you cannot do it. But Jesus didn't leave you to face the challenges of life alone and without help. After purchasing the full price of your redemption, He ascended on High, where He now intercedes continually before the Father on your behalf (*see* Hebrews 7:25). And just as He promised, Jesus sent the Holy Spirit to dwell within you as your Teacher and Guide and to fill and empower you so you can walk as Jesus walked through every situation you could ever face.

Jesus did the hard part. All that He suffered, He suffered for you, leaving behind a perfect example for you to follow. As you respond with His wisdom and love in the face of every challenge, light *will* overcome darkness and God's purposes *will* be fulfilled. Victory will be the outcome *today* in every situation you face when, by God's grace and the help of His Spirit, you determine to copy the strokes of the Master!

MY PRAYER FOR TODAY

Father, I've been struggling with a difficult situation. I have prayed for wisdom; I sought the advice and counsel of others. But now I know that I need to seek the example of Jesus as it is revealed in the four gospels. Jesus is my Example and the One I am called to imitate. So, Holy Spirit, I am asking You to help me as I open my Bible to seek answers from the life of Jesus. Once I see what Jesus did and how He responded to situations that are similar to mine, I ask You to help me copy every stroke of His life. I know that if I will do what Jesus did, it will not only help me, but also it will positively affect those whom the devil has used to mistreat me.

I pray this in Jesus' name!

MY CONFESSION FOR TODAY

I confess that I am a serious disciple of the Lord Jesus. He is my Example, my Teacher, my Master, and my Lord. As a serious disciple, I study His life and endeavor to imitate His every response in my thinking, in my actions, and in my relationships. I regularly read my Bible to learn from the life of the Master. As I seek answers from God's Word, the Holy Spirit enlightens my eyes and gives me the answers I need to successfully navigate through the difficult situations and relationships I encounter in life. By myself I could never know how to effectively maneuver through all these minefields, but the Holy Spirit sees what I do not see, He knows what I do not know, and He is helping me walk unharmed through life with the actions and attitude of Jesus!

I declare this by faith in Jesus Christ!

QUESTIONS FOR YOU TO CONSIDER

1. How long has it been since you've read all four gospels? Can you remember the last time you did it? What impact did it have on your life?

2. What is the exact situation you are facing right now that personally challenges you? Is it a person or a group of people that seems to be the source of trouble for you? Do you *really* understand why they don't like you, why they don't enjoy your company, or why they disagree with you? Even if their point of view is wrong, have you tried to understand it?
3. How long has it been since you seriously prayed for the people who are troubling you? As you *pray* for them, rather than just *think* about them, the Holy Spirit may drop ideas into your heart that will help you break the barriers between yourself and them. Why don't you take a few minutes to pray for them right now?

APRIL 2

Following in the Footsteps of Jesus

For even hereunto were ye called:
because Christ also suffered for us,
leaving us an example, that we should follow his steps.
— 1 Peter 2:21

When Denise and I were first starting our traveling ministry many years ago, we would occasionally make time to stop at the Oregon coast to enjoy the sights with our young sons. We didn't have a lot of money back in those days, so we stayed at some relatively low-class hotels, but the good thing about those hotels was that they were located right on the edge of the beach. The rooms might not have been the nicest, but the locations were terrific!

Denise and I would take our young sons to walk, run, and play on the beach. It was such fun to stand in the water and watch the ripples of the sea come in and slowly wash the sand out from between our toes. We'd collect seashells, chase seagulls, climb the big rocks that jutted out into the ocean, and eat Dungeness crab for lunch every day. But the funniest thing about those trips was watching Denise and the boys as they tried to walk in my footprints!

I'd walk out front, and Denise would follow behind me, trying ever so carefully to step exactly in each of my footprints. It was hysterical watching her, because my stride was so much bigger than hers. She would nearly leap from one footprint to the next in order to exactly follow in my steps. But the most humorous moment was watching our small sons trying to step in the footprints I had left in the sand. The boys would stretch forward with all their might to reach the next footprint. They'd step short of my steps, jump to get to the next footprint, sometimes trip and fall, and so on. It is one of my favorite memories of their childhood.

The reason I'm telling you this story today is to illustrate the apostle Peter's words in First Peter 2:21. He wrote, "For even hereunto were ye called: because Christ also suffered for us, leaving us an example, that we should follow his steps." Peter told his readers and us that when we face hardships with people or circumstances that make us suffer, we must look to Jesus and "...follow his steps." In yesterday's *Sparkling Gem*, we studied the word "example" (*hupogrammos*) and learned that we must be committed to copying Jesus' every movement. But in First Peter 2:21, Peter took it one step further and told us that "...we should follow his steps." What does he mean by that phrase?

The word "follow" is the Greek word *epakoloutheo.* It is a compound of the words *epi* and *akoloutheo.* In this context, the word *epi* means *after*, and the word *akoloutheo* is the word that means *to follow.* When compounded into one word as they are in this verse, the new word means *to carefully follow after someone with the goal to replicate what he or she does.* It depicts a person so committed to imitating another person that he is willing to follow him exactly and to do whatever he does. This is a picture of true discipleship. The word *epakoloutheo* could only describe a person who is very serious about replicating someone else's life in his own. Although everyone will not heed it, this call to replicate the life of Jesus is a call that God has given to every child of God.

But as Peter continued, he used a word to explicitly show how closely we are to imitate the life of Jesus in our own lives. Peter went on to say that we should follow "in his steps." The word "steps" is the Greek word *ichnos*, a word that really means *footprints* — precisely like the footprints I left in the sand at the beach. It is the picture of us putting our feet exactly where Jesus first placed His feet, stepping in His very footprints and following His actions in every circumstance we face. The verse could therefore read, *"We must ardently follow Him with the goal of replicating His life in ours. Yes, we must be so committed to follow Him that we step in His very footprints."*

This means we must learn to walk in Jesus' steps, even if it seems His stride — *His standard, His example, His way of living and loving and forgiving* — seems much bigger than the level we're used to walking in right now. Like my small sons who tried so hard to walk in my footprints, we must be committed to leap from one footprint of the Master to the next until we have learned to easily match His stride and keep the pace He set while He walked the earth.

This must have been very encouraging for the early believers who were suffering so many injustices at the hands of the Roman government and pagan communities. By following the footprints of Jesus, it made it easier for them to know what to do, how to act, what to say, what they shouldn't say, and so on. Jesus' footprints were right there in the four gospels — all they had to do was read them and then do what Jesus had done when He was in a situation similar to theirs.

The truth is, no one was ever more mistreated than Jesus. When soldiers spat on Him, Pilate scourged Him, religious leaders laughed at Him, and He was even betrayed by His own disciples, He continued to walk in love and forgave them all. He set the chief example about how we should respond when we find ourselves in circumstances beyond our control. Therefore, in moments when we feel injustice is being carried out against us, it is imperative that we remember the example Jesus set for us and then "follow His steps."

So instead of giving in to frustration and letting your emotions get the best of you when you're having a hard time, look to Jesus' example and strive to walk exactly as He walked. Once you've found His footprints in the Word of God, pick up your feet and step forward by faith to follow His steps, which are clearly outlined. *With those footprints before you, you can do what He did, you can say what He said, and you can walk how He walked.*

If you will let the Holy Spirit help you, it is possible for you to successfully walk through this time in your life. *What a blessing that you don't have to figure it all out by yourself!* Just look at Jesus' steps in the sand, and stretch forward by faith to step in His footprints. By yourself, you can't do it. But if you will let the Holy Spirit help you, He will show you how to keep the Master's pace and match His stride through every challenge along the way to a victorious outcome!

MY PRAYER FOR TODAY

Lord, I thank You for setting the supreme example for me! Although You were abused, misused, and falsely accused, it never affected Your love or Your steadfast commitment to minister to the world. Today I make the choice to follow in Your steps as they are outlined in the Word of God. I refuse to allow my emotions to dominate me or to permit my feelings to be hurt. I make the decision to ardently follow the example that You left for me. With the help of the Holy Spirit, I will give my best efforts to walk in the footprints You left for me in the Word of God.

I pray this in Jesus' name!

MY CONFESSION FOR TODAY

I confess that I will move out of the place of hurt feelings and step forward to walk in the same steps that Jesus took. His steps are clearly outlined in the Word of God, so I will read the Word, study Jesus' life, and learn how Jesus responded to people and situations. With His example before me, I will do what He did, say what He said, and walk how He walked. Following in His footprints makes it much easier for me to deal with the circumstances at hand!

I declare this by faith in Jesus' name!

QUESTIONS FOR YOU TO CONSIDER

1. Has there been a time in your life when you didn't know how to respond to conflict or injustice that was being leveled against you?
2. When you look at the life of Jesus and see how He responded to people who treated Him unfairly, how do you fare in comparison to His example? By studying His example, what do you now see that you should do differently when you are confronted with a difficult situation?
3. Why don't you take some time to read through the gospels to see how Jesus responded to the criticism that was leveled against Him just before His crucifixion? Take notes of what you read, and see what you can learn about the godly way to respond to false accusations and undeserved blame.

APRIL 3

When You Don't Know What To Do, Entrust Yourself to God's Care

Looking unto Jesus the author and finisher of our faith;
who for the joy that was set before him endured
the cross, despising the shame, and is set down
at the right hand of the throne of God.
— Hebrews 12:2

When Jesus hung on the Cross, beaten almost beyond human recognition, He was subjected to intense, ugly verbal abuse. The soldiers at His feet scoffed, religious leaders laughed, and even a criminal being crucified nearby sneered at Him. In this eternally pivotal moment, all of creation should have rejoiced, for the Creator of the universe was paying the ultimate price for the redemption for mankind. It was the single greatest act of love the world had ever witnessed. But instead of comprehending the supreme price Jesus was paying that day, the crowd arrogantly jeered, mocked, and scorned.

Have you ever pondered how all of this ridicule affected Jesus' emotions when He was dying on the Cross? Let me ask you — what if *you* were hanging on the Cross and people laughed and mocked you as you died for them? How would *you* be tempted to feel at that moment?

Jesus' body had already been ripped to shreds by the vicious beating He received in the residence of Pontius Pilate. Roman soldiers in Pilate's court laughed at Him, mocked Him, and played humiliating games with Him. One by one, a whole cohort of soldiers took turns spitting on Him, slapping Him, and striking His face with a reed they took from a nearby fountain in Pilate's palace. It was extreme *verbal*, *mental*, and *physical abuse.*

Then the soldiers jammed a crown of thorns so firmly on Jesus' head that the long, sharp spikes perforated His skin and scraped across His skull, causing blood to stream down from His brow like a river until His entire face was covered with it. The thick, sticky blood matted His eyebrows and eyelashes, making it difficult for Him to see. Huge, nine-inch iron nails were driven through His hands and feet, which pierced His nerves and sent signals of pain throughout His entire body. The weight of Jesus' body hanging from those nails dislocated His shoulders, and His joints were pulled out of place. He struggled to breathe every breath as His lungs began to fill with fluids that would eventually suffocate Him.

Making this unimaginably horrific experience even worse was the fact that Jesus had been completely stripped naked and hung on that Cross humiliated before the hostile crowd. Putting one's naked body on public display was a great indignity in Jewish culture, thus making the ordeal especially shameful for Him.

Yet Jesus endured all of this agony, pain, and embarrassment willingly. Why? Because His death was the price demanded to purchase forgiveness and redemption for the very people who had done all of this to Him. He was dying for the very people who sneered at Him, for the criminals who laughed at Him, for the soldiers who mocked Him, for the religious leaders who demanded His crucifixion — *and for you and me.* (In *Sparkling Gems 1*, April 21-24, I wrote vivid descriptions of the scourging and crucifixion of Jesus. If you have not already read it, I encourage you to do so. It will give you a greater understanding of what Jesus endured to purchase your salvation.)

But how do you think Jesus felt about this experience at the time it was happening? Hebrews 12:2 gives us insight to this question. It says, "Jesus, the author and finisher of our faith, who for the joy that was set before him endured the cross, despising the shame, and is set down at the right hand of the throne of God."

First, I want you to notice that this verse says that Jesus "endured" the Cross. The word "endured" is from the well-known Greek word *hupomeno*. It is a compound of the words *hupo* and *meno*. The word *hupo* means *under*, and the word *meno* means *to abide* or *to stay*. When the two are compounded, the new word portrays *a person who is under some type of incredibly heavy load but who refuses to stray from his position because he is committed to his task.* Regardless of the load, opposition, stress, or weight that comes against him, he is *not* going to move. He is going to stay put in his spot and not surrender it to anyone for any reason!

This word depicts *one who refuses to bend, break, or surrender because he is convinced that the territory, promise, or principle under assault rightfully belongs to him.* It denotes *a refusal to give up*. One expositor has rightfully translated *hupomeno* as *staying power.* However, my favorite translation of the word *hupomeno* is *hang-in-there power*!

The fact that the Holy Spirit chose to use this word to describe Jesus' time on the Cross tells us emphatically this was not an enjoyable experience. Regardless of how difficult and humiliating the experience was, Jesus was committed to "endure" it because the shedding of His blood was the only way to purchase our freedom from Satan, sin, and the effects of the curse that Adam's disobedience brought upon the human race.

The Cross was so unpleasant that Hebrews 12:2 goes on to tell us that Jesus "despised" it. This is very important because it reveals exactly how Jesus felt emotionally about His time spent on the Cross. According to this verse, He "despised" the whole experience. The word "despise" is from the Greek word *kataphroneo*, a compound of *kata* and *phroneo.* The word *kata* means *down*, and the word *phroneo* means *to think*. When the two are compounded into one word, the new word means *to think down on something* or *to despise it*. It could be translated *to loathe*, *to spurn*, *to detest*, *to abhor*, *to have an aversion*, or *to find something revolting or repulsive*. The Cross was a degrading, crushing, and humiliating experience. In fact, crucifixion was the lowest, crudest, and most barbaric form of death in the Roman Empire.

Hebrews 12:2 goes on to tell us that Jesus despised the "shame" of this experience. The word "shame" is *aischune*, which depicted *disgrace*, *embarrassment*, or *humiliation*. In the New

Testament language, the word *aischune* carries mostly the idea of *shame*. By using this word, the author of Hebrews was telling us that the Cross was something that brought *shame* to Jesus. It was an act of *indignity* which *degraded*, *debased*, and *dishonored* Him.

Just before He died, Jesus cried out and said, "Father, forgive them; for they know not what they do" (Luke 23:34). In this amazing statement, I want you to take note of the word "forgive." It is from the word *aphiemi*, which means *to release*, as in *releasing a prisoner or setting someone free from an act they have carried out*. It is the decision *to not hold something against someone, but rather to liberate a person from the consequences of his actions*. When Jesus cried, "Father, forgive them," He was saying, "Father, *release* them..." or "Father, *do not hold this against* them...."

When you are facing unfair criticism or being blamed for something you didn't do, it is imperative that you keep your eyes fixed on Jesus and the example He set for you. He lived a perfect, sinless life and did not deserve the punishment that was laid upon Him. Yet He willfully carried *our* sicknesses and bore *our* diseases. And when that sin and sickness was laid upon him, He did not retaliate or strike back! The Bible tells us that "when he was reviled, he reviled not again; when he suffered, he threatened not; but committed himself to Him that judgeth righteously..." (1 Peter 2:23).

There are rare times when nothing can be done to change a situation, and we are required to be silent and trust God to take care of it. First Peter 2:23 says that when Jesus was reviled, He did not revile again, and when He suffered, He threatened not. The word "reviled" is the Greek word *loidoreo*, which means *to speak abusively*, *to insult someone*, or *to speak words that are crude and vile*. We would call this *verbal abuse*. However, when these kinds of words were hurled at Jesus, He didn't return them to his offenders. Instead, He remained silent and "threatened not" when He suffered — even though He could have called upon all of Heaven to deliver Him or to obliterate His enemies. The use of the word *loidoreo* in this verse emphatically means that Jesus didn't threaten his enemies when they began to threaten Him.

Instead, Jesus "committed himself to Him that judgeth righteously." The word "committed" in First Peter 2:23 is from the Greek word *paradidomi*, which means *to entrust*, *to hand over*, *to surrender*, or *to commit*. The fact is, there was no way for Jesus to escape the Cross without abandoning His divine mission on earth. Rather than fight it or becoming angry and vengeful toward His abusers, Jesus chose to turn His eyes to the Father and entrust Himself entirely into God's hands in that very difficult moment.

Likewise, if you are in a situation that you cannot change, you are called to follow Jesus' example and entrust yourself into the Father's care. Retaliating against your offenders or verbally returning words they have said to you will not help you or them. It will just make the situation worse. When you are in a situation that you have no power to change, you must pray for strength to endure the situation, and you must also entrust yourself to God who judges righteously. *You can be sure that God is watching, and He will not overlook your prayers of faith or the price you're paying for the love of Him.*

MY PRAYER FOR TODAY

Lord, I want to say thank You for sending Jesus to die for me on Calvary. What a terrible price He paid to purchase my freedom from sin. When He hung on that Tree, it was for me, and for this I want to say thank You from the depths of my heart. Today I ask You for grace to forgive those who have sinned against me, just as Jesus forgave those who sinned against Him. The devil has tried to make me bitter, but I know Your grace can make me better. Rather than focus on the injustice I have experienced, I am fixing my eyes on You and entrusting myself completely into Your loving care.

I pray this in Jesus' name!

MY CONFESSION FOR TODAY

I joyfully declare that God is my judge and He is watching everything that is taking place in my life right now. I do not have to worry or fret that God doesn't know what is happening, because I have entrusted myself into His care and He is lovingly watching over me. I will not fight those who have wronged me and I will not retaliate with ugly words. I have made the decision to follow the example of Jesus. So today, I confess that I am not abandoned, I am not alone, but I am resting safely in the arms of my Heavenly Father who deeply cares about me and all that I am going through in my life right now.

I declare this by faith in Jesus' name!

QUESTIONS FOR YOU TO CONSIDER

1. Has there ever been a time in your life when you knew that fighting back would accomplish nothing, and you knew that you needed to simply be silent and trust God to work on your behalf? When was that time in your life and what happened as a result of silently trusting God?
2. Can you think of someone who is going through a difficult season in life and needs to be reminded that God is watching and that He will take care of those who surrender themselves to Him? Do you need to pick up the phone and call that person today to encourage that person to keep surrendering his or her situation to the Lord?
3. What did you specifically learn from today's *Sparkling Gem* that was new for you?

God will not overlook
your prayers of faith or the price
you're paying for the love of Him.

APRIL 4

Jesus Endured the Cross

Looking unto Jesus the author and finisher of our faith;
who for the joy that was set before him endured the cross, despising the shame,
and is set down at the right hand of the throne of God.
— Hebrews 12:2

Right now believers on every continent of the world are preparing for the Easter season — one of the three biggest annual Christian holidays, with the other being Pentecost and Christmas. Regardless of where you live, Christians will be celebrating Easter and singing jubilant songs that commemorate the resurrection of Christ.

But before there was a resurrection, there was first the Cross. There could be no resurrection without the Cross that preceded it, and that Cross represents the most horrible event Jesus could have ever endured. Yet He endured it all without complaint — for you, for me, and for *all* who would later come to repentance.

Have you ever felt that you were thrust into a situation that you didn't ask for or didn't desire? Did you find that there was nothing you could do to escape it? How did you deal with the situation? How did you endure it? If that is a description of how you are feeling about life right now, then pay close attention to today's *Sparkling Gem*, because as you will see, this is precisely how Jesus felt when He hung on the Cross.

Jesus lived a pure, sinless life. If there was ever anyone born on this earth who didn't deserve the Cross, it was Jesus. However, it was part of God's plan for Him to procure the salvation that today we gloriously and freely possess!

Jesus accepted His assignment, but the Bible plainly tells us that He did not relish the experience. He had to *set* Himself to "endure" it as a part of the assignment the Father had entrusted to Him. Hebrews 12:2 says, "Looking unto Jesus the author and finisher of our faith; who for the joy that was set before him endured the cross, despising the shame, and is set down at the right hand of the throne of God."

This verse makes it abundantly clear that Jesus "endured" and "despised" the Cross. In yesterday's *Sparkling Gem*, we discussed what it meant for Jesus when the Bible says He "endured" the Cross. However, today I want to take that discussion further.

As we saw yesterday, the word "endured" is a translation of the Greek word *hupomeno*, which is a compound of the words *hupo* and *meno*. The word *hupo* means *under*, and the word *meno* means *to abide* or *to stay*. When the two are compounded, the new word portrays *a person who is under some type of incredibly heavy load but who refuses to stray from his position because he is committed to his task*. Regardless of the load, opposition, stress, or weight that comes against him, he is *not* going to move. He is going to stay put in his spot and not surrender it to anyone for any reason!

That word "endured" tells us emphatically that Jesus *refused to stray from His position.* If He had wished, He could have called upon 12 legions of angels to deliver Him and destroy His enemies (*see* Matthew 26:53), but He refrained because the Cross was the path of redemption that the Father had entrusted into His hands. His experience on the Cross was unimaginably horrific, yet it was the necessary price to be paid for the forgiveness of sin. If Jesus had shirked His responsibility and refused to accept the Cross as a part of His divine calling, then you and I would still be bound by our sin today.

I've never hung on a cross as Jesus did, and I can't even imagine the thought of it. However, there have been times when God has asked me to endure some very hard things that I could escape only by disobeying His instructions. Regardless of how difficult it was to be obedient, I had to keep my eyes fixed on the prize before me and endure the moment. And one thing I have found to be sure: On the path of obedience, difficult or painful moments eventually come to a conclusion — and when they do, resurrection and exaltation follow.

You may be enduring a difficult situation right now because God has called you to do a certain task. Or perhaps there is no other way out but to go *through* a situation rather than run the other way. Regardless, I encourage you to focus on the example of Jesus and learn from Him. He utterly despised the Cross; yet He endured it nevertheless as a necessary part of His assignment to procure our salvation. This may not sound like something that makes you want to shout. But when you endure to the end and accomplish your divine mission, I promise you'll be thankful that you did not throw in the towel earlier when you were tempted to give up.

I want to encourage you today to lift your eyes and *set* them on the goal before you. God's plan is not that you remain in this difficult place forever. His plan for you is a place of victory and resurrection! For a season — and only God knows how long that season is — you may be called to simply endure. But if you know you're where you're supposed to be, simply embrace the opportunity to trust God in the midst of it all and refuse to let any person or any devil from hell move you out of position! *With God's power, you can stay in the right place and get the job accomplished that Jesus has asked you to do!*

MY PRAYER FOR TODAY

Father, I look to Jesus in all things as my Example of how to live and to walk in a manner that is pleasing to You. Jesus endured the Cross for me and remained committed to His task without weakening beneath the weight of all that opposed Him. Because Jesus refused to abandon Your plan, even when it cost Him greatly, I will not run from my responsibility to obey Your plan for me, despite the difficulty of what I am facing. I draw upon the power of His might to declare that although I may feel weak, I am strong in Him. Just as Jesus endured His Cross, knowing that it was crucial to His obedience to and fulfillment of God's divine plan, I take up my cross and follow Him — knowing that as I endure to the end, I will see the salvation of the Lord on my behalf.

I pray this in Jesus' name!

MY CONFESSION FOR TODAY

I confess that no temptation is beyond my ability to resist it and no trial can come to me that is not common to man or beyond what I can endure. But God is faithful to His Word and to His own compassionate nature. He is at work in me, creating both the desire and the ability to do what pleases Him. I know and trust that He will not allow me to be pressed beyond the measure of my ability and my power to endure so that I can bear up under it patiently. I let patience have its perfect work in me so I can come out on the other side of this situation strong in character and in spirit, lacking nothing.

I declare this by faith in Jesus' name!

QUESTIONS FOR YOU TO CONSIDER

1. Can you recall a time when you were called upon to do something very difficult that your flesh didn't want to do, but you knew it was God's will for you to endure it and stay there regardless of how tough it felt at the time?
2. When you look back at that difficult moment, I am *sure* you had times when you didn't know if you could endure it. What do you think would have happened if you had quit and thrown in the towel? What would have been the result of caving in to that temptation?
3. Do you know individuals who are exactly where they are supposed to be and doing exactly what they are supposed to be doing, yet that place and time is accompanied with hardship? What can you say or do to encourage them to remain faithful in spite of the temporary hardness?

APRIL 5

Jesus Took Our Shame

Looking unto Jesus the author and finisher of our faith;
who for the joy that was set before him endured the cross,
despising the shame, and is set down at the right hand of the throne of God.
— Hebrews 12:2

We've looked at the word "endured" in Hebrews 12:2 and have seen what it meant for Jesus to endure the Cross for you and me. But Jesus didn't just *endure* it — *He actually despised the shame of it.* Today I want us to look at the words "despise" and "shame" in the original Greek language so that we can better understand exactly how Jesus felt when He was physically hanging on that Cross.

The word "despised" is a translation of the Greek word *kataphroneo*, which is a compound of the words *kata* and *phroneo*. On their own, the word *kata* means *down*, and the word *phroneo* means *to think*. However, when these two words are compounded, the new word means *to look down upon, think poorly of, despise, abhor, detest, disdain*, or *loathe*. This carries the ideas of *contempt, aversion*, or something so *repulsive* that one is almost unable to stomach the idea of it. It is something that is simply *repelling, revolting*, and *disgusting*. Thus, the Greek word *kataphroneo* used in Hebrews 12:2 emphatically lets us know that Jesus looked down upon the Cross with *repugnance*. He literally *"despised"* it.

The word "shame" is the Greek word *aischune*, which describes something that is *base, ugly, revolting*, and *grotesque*. By using this word, the writer of Hebrews was telling us that Jesus' experience on the Cross as He hung naked and broken in full view of the world was *disgraceful, deplorable, despicable, and reprehensible*. Paintings and sculptures of the Crucifixion always portray Jesus with a towel wrapped around His waist, but this was simply not the case. Romans were not so kind as to cover the male anatomy — Jesus was stripped of all clothing and hung naked before the jeering crowd. For a Jew who respected the human body as something made in the holy image of God and who abhorred the naked idols of paganism, this indignity was utterly *repugnant* and *embarrassing*.

Imagine if you were beaten to a pulp and then hung physically naked in front of your friends, family, coworkers, and acquaintances. How would you feel? According to the Greek word *aischune* used in Hebrews 12:2, the Lord Jesus felt a deep sense of "shame" and "embarrassment" in that horrific moment.

Jesus paid the price for sin, for sickness and disease, for mental suffering, and for shame. Just as Jesus endured the scourging to procure our physical healing (*see* Isaiah 53:5), He literally took our shame upon Himself to pay the price for any humiliation that would ever try to poison our lives. As my wife Denise writes in her book, *Redeemed From Shame*:

> Oh, how God wants us to experience His great love for us every moment of our lives! Because of His suffering on the Cross, He paid the ultimate price for us to experience His loving presence. This is possible not by any work of righteousness that *we* have done, but by trusting in what *He* has done.
>
> So don't listen to the lies of the devil about your past. Don't let him convince you to give up. Instead, seek God's face, and listen to the loving words of truth from God's Spirit that are there for you. Jesus' flesh was not ripped apart in vain. It was for your deliverance and freedom to become the person God planned for you to be!
>
> Jesus took all your shame and fear so you wouldn't have to be tormented by its wicked hold. In exchange, He freely offered you His glory and healing power. All you have to do is receive by faith what He has already given you. You are free from the bondage of shame in Him. Now it's time to *live free* in Jesus' Name![4]

---

[4] Denise Renner, *Redeemed From Shame* (Tulsa, OK: Harrison House, 2004), p. 61.

Have you ever felt publicly humiliated? Have you ever been ashamed because of something you've been through or because of something someone said? Have you felt the discomfort, pain, and even torture of embarrassment and humiliation?

If you've experienced these feelings, take comfort in the fact that Jesus felt them too. He took those emotions upon Himself as part of His sacrificial work on the Cross so that you and I could be set free. We don't have to be encumbered with feelings of shame for the rest of our lives. *He literally took our shame so we could be free from it!*

Regardless of what has happened in your past that might have made you feel embarrassed or ridiculed, know that Jesus took your shame upon Himself and set you free. Your freedom from shame and humiliation was included in His work on the Cross, and you *never* have to be tormented with those hellish thoughts again — because of Jesus!

MY PRAYER FOR TODAY

Heavenly Father, how can I ever begin to thank You for Your great plan of Redemption? Jesus not only became sin for me, He also bore for me the humiliation and pain of it in ways far deeper than anything I could ever imagine. I am overcome with gratitude to know that Jesus endured such unspeakable horror so I could know Your perfect love and be set free from the torment of fear and shame. Holy Spirit, teach me how to walk in the reality of this freedom and love so that I will cause others to know the power made available through Christ's sacrifice on the Cross.

I pray this in Jesus' name!

MY CONFESSION FOR TODAY

I confess that never again will I allow myself to wallow in self-pity because of the pain I feel, the loss I've endured, or the abuse I've experienced. Jesus knows exactly how it feels to be humiliated and shamefully treated in the most degrading ways. Because Jesus is personally acquainted with such pain and such mental and emotional anguish, He is able to fully sympathize with all my feelings. Therefore, with confidence I come boldly before His throne of grace to receive His help in just the way I need it most!

I declare this by faith in Jesus' name!

QUESTIONS FOR YOU TO CONSIDER

1. Shame is a horrible spiritual force that causes a person to be embarrassed of who they are. Have you ever felt this negative power? Did you know that Jesus paid for your shame as a part of His redemptive work on the Cross?
2. If you walked free of shame and embarrassment and never returned to it, how would that freedom affect your life? What would life be like if you never had to deal with those negative emotions?

3. Now that you know that Christ paid the price for your shame, can you think of anyone you need to share this message with so he or she, too, can be freed from the power of shame?

APRIL 6

The Joy Set Before Jesus!

Looking unto Jesus the author and finisher of our faith;
who for the joy that was set before him
endured the cross, despising the shame,
and is set down at the right hand of the throne of God.
— Hebrews 12:2

When a person initiates a new, huge endeavor, his passion to succeed in that endeavor strengthens him to keep his eye on the goal in front of him. For example, as an athlete starts a race, his desire to win that race helps him keep his eyes fixed on the finish line. While constructing a building, workers who keep their eyes on the architect's finalized rendering are encouraged to sustain the momentum of the building process. While writing this book you hold in your hands, I encouraged myself by keeping my sight fixed on December 31 — the *last Sparkling Gem* I knew I would write for this volume. With every new daily entry I completed, I moved closer to that goal, and it gave me courage to keep writing. As a result of my writing and staying on track, you are reading this devotional today.

But what do you think Jesus focused on when He was hanging on the Cross and enduring the agony and shame we discussed in the last three days of *Sparkling Gems*? You can imagine that He must have had moments when He thought, *I don't have to do this! I could call on legions of angels to deliver me! I could come down from this Cross!* What do you think motivated Him to remain there until the job was done?

Hebrews 12:2 tells us very clearly: "…who for the joy that was set before him endured the cross, despising the shame, and is set down at the right hand of the throne of God."

This verse says Jesus focused on "the joy" that was set before Him as He endured the Cross. Just like a runner focuses on the finish line, like a builder forges ahead to view the completed project, and an author anticipates the last written page of a book, Jesus was looking forward to "the joy" of finishing. I'm sure that as Jesus hung on the Cross, He looked out across eons of time and saw the faces of people who would be saved because of what He was doing. He saw you, He saw me — but what else did He see that motivated Him to stay faithful to the end?

The word "joy" in Greek has a definite article, which means this wasn't just joy in general, but it was *a specific joy*. What was it? The verse goes on to describe that joyous "finish line" that Jesus set His face like flint toward: "...who for the joy that was set before him endured the cross, despising the shame, and is set down at the right hand of the throne of God." Jesus had His eyes of faith *fixed* on the empty throne at the right hand of the Father that was reserved for Him once His victory was complete. Upon that throne, all enemies would be His footstool, and He would commence the next part of His high priestly ministry to intercede for everyone who would ever come to Him in time of need (*see* Hebrews 4:16).

Jesus had His eyes, His heart, His mind — His *whole being* — fixed on that highly exalted place. That was *the* joy set before Him. When sin and hell were defeated and Jesus was resurrected, *that* was the seat of authority He ascended into Heaven to occupy. And ever since that time, from that highly exalted position, Jesus has been serving as Lord of the Church and as the High Priest and Intercessor for every believer.

What is the goal in front of you that keeps you motivated to move ahead even when things are difficult? If you have no goal, it's likely you'll give up. That's why it is so important to know exactly where you are headed, what will happen when you get there, and what kind of victory you'll experience when you attain that long-awaited position. Just as Jesus needed a joyous outcome to be set before Him, I guarantee that you need one too.

- What are you building with your life?
- What keeps you motivated to stay on track?
- What will it look like when you finish it?
- What are you "writing" with your faith?
- What will the final chapter of your life look like because you've done what Jesus has asked you to do?
- What is the specific joy that is set before you?

Sometimes when you are working hard to do what God has asked you to do, it can seem overwhelming, but progress is gained one step at a time. The increments of forward movement might seem tiny, but no matter how big or small the steps, you can know that you are inevitably progressing toward the goal that God has set for your life.

When I was a young man, God showed me the purpose of my life, and that purpose has been in front of me ever since. In times of hardship, I've kept my eyes focused on that goal, because fulfilling that divine purpose is what my life is all about. Sometimes it seemed like all I could do was take baby steps — yet each step has been a step in the right direction. That's the way I've lived my entire life focused and moving in the direction of the purpose God has revealed to me.

If you get your eyes off the goal and start focusing on how small your steps are along the way, it is probable that you'll get discouraged and give up before you arrive. So today I want to encourage you to lift your eyes and look beyond to the joy, the victory, and the fulfillment of what God has planned for your life. Even Jesus needed a goal to help Him stay focused as He underwent intense suffering and hung on that Cross.

So today I exhort you to make a fresh consecration before the Lord to submit to His will for your life. Then exercise your authority in Jesus' name and *resist* the devil (*see* James 4:7)! And as you move forward in obedience to the Lord's voice, keep your eyes of faith *fixed* on the prize Jesus has set before you. That is what will sustain your determination to *stay in place* and *stay on track* until you can finally shout that you've reached your God-ordained goal!

MY PRAYER FOR TODAY

Father, I thank You for the example of faithful endurance Jesus displayed when He suffered the pain and the shame of the Cross for me. Jesus kept His eyes fixed on the joy set before Him, knowing He would occupy His seat at the right hand of the Father reserved for Him once His victory was complete. When You raised Jesus from the dead, Father, You raised me up also to be seated in Him. Lord Jesus, I worship You, and I fasten a steady gaze on You so that I will finish my course with joy to the glory of God!

I pray this in Jesus' name!

MY CONFESSION FOR TODAY

I confess that I am focused on the goal of completing God's plan for my life. I realize that I am not my own, but I belong to God. Therefore, I draw upon the mighty strength that is available to me in Christ — and by the help of His Spirit within me, I move daily with unwavering devotion in the direction toward the prize of fulfilling my divine purpose as God has revealed it to me.

I declare this by faith in Jesus' name!

QUESTIONS FOR YOU TO CONSIDER

1. What has God set before you as the main project or goal for your life?
2. If you don't know the purpose for your life, have you ever asked God to show it to you? According to James 1:5 (*see* February 17 and 18), God will answer this very important question for you *if* you've met His conditions.
3. Can you describe what a life with purpose would look like to you? How would it change the way you are living if you knew *exactly* what God's purpose is for your life?

What are you "writing" with your faith?
What will the final chapter of your life look like
because you've done what Jesus has asked you to do?

APRIL 7

The Exceeding Greatness of His Power to Us Who Believe!

And what is the exceeding greatness of his power
to us-ward who believe, according to the working
of his mighty power, which he wrought in Christ,
when he raised him from the dead....
— Ephesians 1:19,20

One day my wife Denise and I were talking to each other about the mighty power of God that works so profoundly in the lives of believers. As we talked back and forth, we were just in awe as we contemplated the power available to us as believers in Jesus Christ. We both looked at each other and quoted Ephesians 1:19,20 as the ultimate answer to what kind of power operates inside us. In that verse, the apostle Paul wrote, "And what is the exceeding greatness of his power to us-ward who believe, according to the working of his mighty power, which he wrought in Christ, when he raised him from the dead...."

Let's look at the phrase "exceeding greatness of his power," as these words were Paul's answer to describe how great is the power of God that works in us.

The word "exceeding" is the Greek word *huperballo*, a compound of the words *huper* and *ballo*. The word *huper* describes something that is *above* and *beyond* anything else. The word *ballo* means *to throw* or *to hurl*. However, when these words are used in conjunction with each other, together they depict an archer who *overshoots* his goal. He put so much energy into it that when he pulls back on his bow and releases his arrow, he *overshoots, overreaches, surpasses*, and *eclipses* his goal.

The word "greatness" is the Greek word *megethos*, a form of *mega*, meaning *great*. However, as *megethos*, this word would be better translated *vast*. This means that the power Paul is describing is *boundless, immense, limitless, measureless*, and *vast*. One could say that it is so mighty that it is simply beyond human ability to measure.

The word "power" is from the well-known Greek word *dunamis*, which describes *power* or *ability*. But very often in Classical Greek and in the Old Testament Septuagint, the word *dunamis* was also used to depict the assembled forces of an army whose combined strength *enabled* them to achieve *unrivaled* victories. These troops were so *strong* that they simply could not be resisted. But in addition, we find in Classical Greek and in the Septuagint that the word *dunamis* can also describe the *power* that is inherent in a certain aspect of nature. For example, the power in a hurricane would be described as *dunamis* power, because it is a *power* so *mighty* that *it is impossible to resist* or *impossible to defeat*.

So when Paul used these three words to describe the power of God that works in us — *huperballo, megethos, dunamis* — he was piling image on top of image to show how *overshooting* and *irresistible* is the *power* that works in us who believe. This power is so mighty it can neither be measured nor resisted. There is simply no human power in existence to compare to it!

The apostle Paul went on to say that it is the same "...mighty power, which he [God] wrought in Christ, when he raised him from the dead...." Paul was making it emphatically clear that no power has ever equaled or rivaled the power that was required for Christ's resurrection. It was the greatest manifestation of power that the universe has ever witnessed. It literally seized Jesus from death's grip, raised Him back into His body, and then continued to lift Him up through demonic principalities, powers, might, and dominion until He was seated at His throne at the right hand of the Father. No power in hell or on earth, and no principality or power in the heavens, was able to resist this demonstration of divine energy.

As Denise and I discussed this verse and all that it means, we felt an even greater sense of awe. What a thrill to realize that God doesn't just put a small dose of power inside us who believe. *He has placed the power of His Son's resurrection in us!* It is a power that utterly eclipses any other power. It is full, boundless, measureless energy — so mighty that no evil power can resist it. And to think God has made it available to those who believe! Now *that* is something for you to think about as you prepare for this Easter season!

MY PRAYER FOR TODAY

Heavenly Father, You held nothing back when You exercised Your mighty power in raising Christ from the dead. I am in awe that You not only raised me from death unto life by that same power, but You have also breathed that mighty power into me by the same Spirit who raised Christ. Holy Spirit, I acknowledge the presence of Your power within me. And I ask You to conform me more and more unto the image of Christ as I let that irresistible power of God work in me and through me according to the counsel of Your will!

I pray this in Jesus' name!

MY CONFESSION FOR TODAY

I confess that the mighty power of God that raised Christ from the dead dwells in me. That power, which is at work in me, is beyond measure. It is vast, boundless, immense, limitless, and measureless! The power that is in me now by the presence of the Holy Spirit eclipses all other power and cannot be resisted by any work of the enemy. Glory to God! Greater is He that is in me than he that is in the world!

I declare this by faith in Jesus' name!

QUESTIONS FOR YOU TO CONSIDER

1. Use your imagination to describe what it would have been like to experience the power at Christ's physical resurrection.

2. Have you ever considered that this same mighty power is resident inside you? If it's inside you, do you experience it in the situations you face every day? If not, what do you need to do to release God's resurrection power in your life?
3. How is the power of God manifested in the life of a believer? Take some time to think it over, and write your answers on a piece of paper so that you really ponder your answers.

APRIL 8

Financial Freedom!

But the fruit of the Spirit is love, joy,
peace, longsuffering, gentleness, goodness,
faith, meekness, *temperance*....
— Galatians 5:22,23

God has sown His Spirit and His Word into your heart, so you have every right to expect divine fruit to be produced inside you. The fruit that the Spirit produces is wonderful, godly fruit, overflowing with blessings and life. In Galatians 5:22 and 23, the apostle Paul listed the fruit of the Holy Spirit, writing, "But the fruit of the Spirit is love, joy, peace, longsuffering, gentleness, goodness, faith, meekness, *temperance*.... " Today I want to focus on the word "temperance" and see how we can cultivate this precious fruit in our lives.

In Greek, the word "temperance" is *egkrateia*, which is a compound of the words *en* and *kratos*. The word *en* simply means *in*, and *kratos* is the Greek word for *power*. When the two are compounded, the new word *egkrateia* means *in power*, *in control*, or *in balance* and pictures a person who is fully in command of his will, his urges, and his emotions. It is the idea of *self-control* and *discipline*.

The ability to exercise self-restraint (*enkrateia*) is absolutely crucial in all arenas of your life, including your personal finances, diet and physical exercise, productivity at work, or any other area where discipline is required in order to progress. However, because so many believers struggle with self-control in the realm of finances, I want to address this specific issue. If you will allow the Holy Spirit to work in this very important area of your life, I *know* He will help you become *financially temperate* and very prosperous as a result.

Managing your personal finances in a fiscally responsible manner is an essential part of being a person through whom God can work effectively. By doing so, you remain free from the bondage of unnecessary, frivolous debt and thus are able to pursue your calling without the hindrance and distraction of crushing financial obligations to creditors slowing you down. However, if you repeatedly succumb to your flesh and use your credit card to purchase items you don't need and can't afford, you will inevitably end up swamped in debt and financially ruined. The Holy Spirit wants to help you be temperate in the realm of your finances, as well as in every other realm. So once you've made a commitment to exercise self-control (*enkrateia*) and stay debt-free, know that with His help and by His grace, you can *stick* to your commitment!

If you feel that you're failing at exercising self-control with your finances — *or in any other area of your life* — simply ask for God's forgiveness, and you will be forgiven and cleansed (*see* 1 John 1:9). Then let the Holy Spirit help you develop a practical plan that will help you begin the journey toward becoming financially free and responsible by cultivating temperance (*enkrateia*) in your life.

One truth Denise and I have witnessed time and time again is that sowing seed into the Kingdom of God is one of the most important tools we have to get out of debt. Tithing opens the windows of Heaven. In Second Corinthians 9:6, Paul confirmed this principle, saying, "...He which soweth sparingly will reap sparingly; and he which soweth bountifully shall reap also bountifully."

As you ask the Holy Spirit for a plan for financial freedom, ask Him also to direct you in your giving to the work of God's Kingdom. In addition to taking natural, common-sense steps toward financial freedom, it's imperative that you honor God with your tithes and special offerings — for this is a vital key to obtaining freedom in the financial realm both now and in the future.

If you'll listen to the Holy Spirit, He'll help you put together a plan to exercise temperance in your life. If you'll stick with His plan, He will lead you to a place of glorious financial freedom and will help you bring discipline and self-control to every other area of your life. When you get to this place, you'll never want to go back! Denise and I have learned firsthand that the fruit of *temperance* not only provides freedom — it gives peace! I'm praying for you to make the decision to let the Holy Spirit develop this fruit in your life in a greater measure than ever before — *starting today*!

MY PRAYER FOR TODAY

Father, I recognize that fiscal responsibility and financial freedom are essential for me to be effective in my service to You. I repent of the poor choices I've made financially due to fear, negligence, lack of self-control, or ignorance. Holy Spirit, I ask You to show me Your plan and wisdom for my finances so I can be the blessing I desire to be for the Kingdom of God. Please bring to me the knowledge I need, and then grant me the understanding and self-discipline I need to gain a heart of wisdom. I make a decision now to do what You reveal to me. I am willing to sacrifice what I want now in order to obtain what I need to possess later. Father, it glorifies You for me to be fully supplied so I can do the work You have given me to do without hindrance or delay. I receive Your help, and I commit my way to You.

I pray this in Jesus' name!

MY CONFESSION FOR TODAY

I confess that I honor the Lord with my tithes and offerings, and I seek first His ways in everything — including my finances. I declare that I am not wasteful of my time or my money.

I acknowledge that wisdom is the principal thing in all the affairs of life. Therefore, I cultivate temperance by allowing this wisdom and patience to have its perfect work in me. I am diligent in business, obedient to the Word of God, and my finances steadily increase. I exercise wisdom in my sowing, saving, and spending. I am faithful in little, and God can trust me with much because I am proving that I am satisfied in Him and I no longer seek to gratify undisciplined impulses with my finances.

I declare this by faith in Jesus' name!

QUESTIONS FOR YOU TO CONSIDER

1. Do you know what it is like to be so bound by debt that you are barely able to get by on your salary? What were the circumstances that produced that situation? What are the steps that you know are needed to turn that situation around?
2. Have you ever asked the Holy Spirit to give you a financial temperance plan that will walk you out of any mess you might be in now into a life of freedom and liberty? If you don't know how to devise such a plan, why not ask someone you trust to help you develop one?
3. Are you so in debt that you can't regularly pay your tithe? Be honest! Doesn't it make you feel guilty before the Lord? When you're not tithing, you are living below God's plan for your life. Consider the joy you'll experience knowing that your financial temperance plan has brought you to a place where you can freely and regularly tithe!

APRIL 9

Similarities Between the Human Body and the Local Church

For as the body is one, and hath many members,
and all the members of that one body,
being many, are one body: so also is Christ....
— 1 Corinthians 12:12

I'm sure you realize that there is nothing accidental about God. He's very intentional and strategic in what He says to us and how He says it. Today I want to show you a specific example of this that I believe will help you. In First Corinthians 12:12-27, Paul likened the local church body to a physical body. It's one of those very intentional divine analogies that God uses to help enlighten us to how we are to operate according to His Kingdom, because there really are so many pertinent similarities between the physical human body and the spiritual entity called the Body of Christ.

In particular, I want to draw a comparison to how the human body and the spiritual church body respond to attacks. You see, the human body exhibits distinct symptoms when an infection begins to spread, and the same thing is true in a local church body. A local church will demonstrate many telling signs that a spiritual infection has begun to take root in its midst. It's so important to be aware of and sensitive to detect these signs so you can stay alert in prayer as a "watchman on the wall" to ward off the enemy's attacks — not only from your own life, but also from the lives of your pastors and your church family.

So let's take an in-depth look at the many parallels that exist between a physical infection that has invaded a human body and a spiritual infection that has invaded a local church body.

- Physical infection can be defined as the *injurious colonization of a human body by a foreign species that begins to utilize the host's resources to assist in its own infectious multiplication*. Once inside a human body, an infecting organism quickly begins to multiply inside its host. Normally, the human body has multiple systems of defense designed to protect the body from infection. But when the human body is physically weak, malnourished, or exposed to fatigue over a long period of time, the immune system is compromised, and the body becomes susceptible to infection. Ultimately, an infected person becomes *contagious* to others.
- Persistent infections occur when a body is unable to completely purge the harmful organisms after the initial infection. Such infections may appear to go into remission, but in actuality, the infectious organisms merely remain dormant in the body, fully capable of being reactivated if the immune system is weakened once again. For persistent infections to be eliminated from the body, serious, directed treatment is often required.
- Infection can be transmitted in a variety of ways, but the most common means is *horizontal transmission*, or *the direct or indirect transfer of an infectious organism from one person to another*. Transmission through *direct contact* may occur when a healthy individual comes into physical contact with an infected person's body or bodily fluids. This can occur in numerous ways, but two very common causes of direct transmission are unprotected sexual contact and breathing air that has been contaminated by an infected person's cough or sneeze.
- Infections can also be transmitted through *indirect contact*. This occurs when a person touches a physical object that an infected person has previously handled. Common examples would be actions as simple as touching the same furniture, doorknobs, or toys or sharing foods or liquids. Although a person may not directly contact an infected individual, environment alone can be sufficient to transmit infection in extremely contagious cases. In these instances, the germs can be so robust that they are able to survive outside the human body for long periods of time and still retain their infectious nature. This fact demonstrates the necessity to

thoroughly cleanse and *sanitize* any areas, items, or people that have been *exposed* to the environment of an infected person.

- The longevity of an infection is dependent on whether the infecting organism is transmitted from one person to the next. If this transmission is stopped, the infection is stopped. Therefore, it is essential to stop that transmission process.
- In order to stop an infection from being transmitted to others, an infected individual must be willing to undergo treatment. Even in the ancient world, medication was used to treat infected individuals. Although the medication may be distasteful and unwanted, it is absolutely necessary to annihilate the infecting organisms in order to stop the spread of disease to others.
- If an infection progresses to a point in a person's body that medicine alone is no longer sufficient to halt its advance, the infected person may need to submit to a surgical procedure. As unwanted and painful as this step is, it may be the only way to stop the spread of disease to the entire body. Removal or surgical correction is never easy to endure, but this procedure may save the life of a person in that dire condition.
- In most cases, it is relatively simple to avoid an outbreak of infection by making minor adjustments to one's lifestyle. For instance, germs thrive in unsanitary environments, so regularly cleansing one's hands and making an effort to live in a clean, sanitary environment are helpful in preventing infection. In addition, it is important to eat food that is well prepared, healthy, and clean since unhealthy, dirty food is often a major contributor to the transmission of infection.
- In the human body, some infections are easy to detect because they are accompanied by immediate symptoms, whereas others produce no symptoms until the infection has already spread inside its host. Bodily aches, tenderness to the touch, chills, fatigue, inflammation, fever, loss of appetite, nausea, pain, weight loss, and vomiting are all common, easily detectable signs of infection. These symptoms alert a person that a foreign entity has penetrated his body and is now multiplying inside.

So how does all this apply to a case of spiritual infection in a local church?

- When spiritual infection finds its way into a local church, it quickly begins to multiply inside that congregation unless it is quickly addressed and *stopped*. God has designed the Body of Christ to supernaturally withstand most attacks by the power of the indwelling Holy Spirit. However, if a particular congregation has undergone a difficult period and become fatigued, spiritually malnourished, and weak, that congregation's God-given "immune system" may become more susceptible to infection from deceptive doctrines. Ultimately, if these destructive forces are allowed to propagate within a church, they will gain strength and spread to the entire congregation, even though they may have initially been embraced by only a few.

- Persistent spiritual infections occur when a church is unable to clear itself of an initial outbreak. This chronic condition may seem to go into remission — but if true repentance hasn't occurred, it will only be a matter of time before difficult conditions cause that toxic poison to be reactivated in the congregation. If this situation isn't dealt with properly — if the infection isn't eliminated as soon as it *first* becomes evident within the congregation — the infection will simply go into "sleep mode" — and will be certain to reawaken at a later time. This is why it must be dealt with *immediately* and *directly* if it is to be permanently eliminated from the church body.
- In order to stop spiritual infection from metastasizing inside a congregation, the person spreading the disease must be willing to "undergo treatment" by submitting to authority and correction. If the church itself has become diseased due to a long-term toxic condition, the spiritually infected person may also be required to submit to a stricter discipline. In extreme cases, the only way to bring correction to a church may be to remove the person at the source of infection. Although unwanted and painful, this corrective action may prolong the life of the church.
- The prevention of spiritual infection is relatively simple in most cases. Making minor adjustments to one's lifestyle, avoiding temptations to compromise, refusing to bend on one's moral positions, spending time daily in prayer and the Word, and keeping one's heart right toward the local church are all critical elements in preventing outbreaks of spiritual infection. Furthermore, it is very important to be fed a balanced, well-prepared, untainted diet of God's Word.
- Churches experience distinct symptoms when they have been invaded by a spiritual infection. For instance, just as a physical body might experience a lack of energy or weight loss when it has an infection, a church body can experience a lack of power or a drop in attendance when a spiritual disease has infiltrated the congregation. Or in the same way that a person dealing with infection might experience a loss of appetite, a church usually experiences a diminishing of spiritual hunger when it is infected.
- There are other striking similarities between the symptoms of physical and spiritual infection. Inflamed, infected tissue often produces swelling and becomes hot and painful. The spiritual counterpart to this physical phenomenon would be the tendency for infected churches to experience swelling crowds of uncommitted believers with itching ears because a spiritually contaminated congregation often appeals to others with perhaps different but equally diseased "ideas." Church attendance may increase in size yet be completely devoid of healthy growth. But in an infected church, "quantity" fails to reflect "quality" as people flock only to what feeds their selfish interests. Eventually the blend of these inflamed, swelling ranks becomes a toxic soup that spills out to infect ever-increasing numbers of people.
- In addition, the tenderness or pain displayed in an infected physical body may manifest as a spiritual infection in a local body of believers as a combination of touchiness, agitation, and anger. This "soreness" is often reflected in the attitude

of spiritually infected individuals who become belligerent with anyone who questions their erroneous beliefs. Their touchiness is always on display because they view every conversation as a potential challenge to their perspective. They become insufferable and cantankerous, feeling the need to take on the world to prove their point and producing "dis-ease" and discomfort among all who even slightly bump into them. Their irrational words, attitudes, and actions resemble the disorientation of a fevered person who can make outlandish statements and reflect bizarre behavior because of the way the inflammation has affected his or her brain.

- A local church often views the symptoms described above as demonic attacks. Although this is definitely true in part, the church leadership must still determine how the devil found access into the congregation in the first place. Seeking God in earnest prayer is essential to obtaining an answer to this question. Once the answer is known, repentance is required to rid the local body of whatever is allowing the enemy to poison and destroy from within.
- The most difficult type of spiritual infection to detect and treat is when one or more church leaders within a congregation become infected. False doctrine that finds its way into the heart of one leader, if it is not corrected, will begin to pass to others, just as an infection is passed from one host to the next. If this transmission isn't stopped, it has the potential to eventually infect an entire congregation.
- A spiritual leader who is infected with false doctrine is only one person — but he is an influential person that touches many lives. If the infection in his soul isn't eliminated, it is likely that others will be contaminated through his touch. His diseased influence will spread like germs until it infects people who gather to worship. If correction doesn't come to his life, his words and teachings have the potential to become food that makes others sick. Because his influence is strong, it is likely that those who are close to him will pick up whatever has contaminated him and become infected with the same spiritual problems.

The point is that it doesn't take too many erring individuals to transmit sickness to a church body when they hold positions of influence.

In cases where spiritual infection is extremely contagious and dangerous, *quarantine* may even be required to prevent the infection from spreading throughout the rest of the congregation. The person who is the source of infection may not understand the severity of his condition, or he may refuse to put sufficient space between himself and others to prevent the spread of contagion. To avoid putting the entire congregation at risk, the infected individual may have to be removed from the midst of the congregation to stop the destructive poison from spreading further.

It might be difficult to imagine that a congregation with loyalty to Christ would simultaneously be infected with an internal spiritual disease. However, Satan has learned that if he can't destroy a church with external pressure, he has to attack it from within. Often believers have been so focused on combating the external opposition that they overlooked the greater enemy that had risen up in their midst.

We must be careful to guard against enemies not only from without, but also from infections that grow from within. Those internal infections are harder to deal with, because they come from people we love and who have been with us for a long time. So after we have made sure that *we're* not the source of spiritual infection through poisonous attitudes, offense, lack of self-restraint with our words, and so forth — we must stay alert to detect any sign of infection creeping into our midst. And as watchmen on the wall, it's our responsibility to pray that God's wisdom prevails in every situation — first, to stop the potential spread of infection within the local body, and, second, to do everything possible to restore those "infected" to wholeness once again.

MY PRAYER FOR TODAY

Father, I am amazed by the many similarities between the operation of the physical body and the local church body. I ask You to give my pastor and the spiritual leaders of my church the discernment to recognize when a spiritual infection has begun to fester inside the church, as well as the wisdom and insight to know how to deal with it before it becomes a bigger issue. Holy Spirit, You are the Spirit of wisdom, counsel, and might. Thank You for revealing not only to leadership but also to the local body how we are to deal with these issues so that we can walk in spiritual health and wholeness, free from spiritual contamination of any kind.

I pray this in Jesus' name!

MY CONFESSION FOR TODAY

I confess that I am a contributor to wholeness in the Christian community. The Body of Christ is healthier because I am in it. I think with a sound mind; I appreciate sound doctrine; I respect spiritual authority; and I am a contributor to the overall health of the Church. When I see that something is amiss, I bring it to the attention of spiritual leadership, and they have the God-given wisdom to know what to do in every situation. The Holy Spirit is our Leader. He is the great Restorer, and I declare that He brings order and restoration to every place where spiritual infection has tried to take root.

I declare this by faith in Jesus' name!

QUESTIONS FOR YOU TO CONSIDER

1. Have you ever seen a spiritual sickness try to spread throughout a local church?
2. When that occurred, what did spiritual leadership do to address the situation and to bring healing to the congregation? This is a very difficult question, I know, but what did you learn from the experience?
3. What did you learn from reading today's *Sparkling Gem*? Is there anything that is particularly relevant to what you are experiencing in your own local church?

APRIL 10

Making Time for Prayer

And straightway he [Jesus] constrained his disciples
to get into the ship, and to go to the other side
before unto Bethsaida, while he sent away the people.
And when he had sent them away, he departed
into a mountain to pray.
— Mark 6:45,46

When taking stock of the monumental issues facing the world today, many believers are tempted to succumb to worry, stress, and anxiety. However, living in a mental prison of fear and anxiety is not God's plan for your life. As a child of God, you can find peace, no matter what storm is raging all around you! Psalm 55:22 states, "Cast thy burden upon the Lord, and he shall sustain thee: he shall never suffer the righteous to be moved." *According to this verse, the way to remain in peace is to spend concentrated time in the presence of the Lord.*

Setting time aside to get quiet and seek God so you can hear His voice can be a challenge for busy people. Personally, I am the type of person who loves to be on the go all the time, and there have been times in my life when I neglected to take enough time to be quiet before the Lord. However, a few years ago, He spoke to my heart and called me aside for a special, intense time of prayer and seeking His face. I am so thankful that I heeded His call because that time with God opened my heart so He could show me the areas of my life that required change. During that special time of prayer, I pored over the Scriptures, and as I studied, I found there were many examples in the Bible of believers who sensed a "calling away." Moreover, I found that each person who obeyed this call to prayer and separated himself for a time of seeking the Lord received divine blessings as a result.

Even Jesus had times when He withdrew from the daily schedule of life to give Himself to consecrated times of prayer. An example can be found in Mark 6:45 and 46, which says, "And straightway he [Jesus] constrained his disciples to get into the ship, and to go to the other side before unto Bethsaida, while he sent away the people. And when he had sent them away, he departed into a mountain to pray."

Prior to the events described in this verse, Jesus had just miraculously fed 5,000 people, concluded one of the largest meetings of His ministry, and built momentum and excitement among His followers. In fact, the entire region was buzzing about the miracle of providing supernatural food for the entire multitude. *But how did Jesus respond to this astounding event?* He told the disciples to get on a ship and sail away; He sent away the crowds; and then He headed for the mountains to pray!

I want you to notice the word "straightway" in Mark 6:45. This word is a translation of the Greek word *eutheos*, which carries the idea of doing something *without any delays, intervening circumstances, or detours*. This word speaks both to the timing and the determination of Jesus. His response to a great victory was to withdraw without delay or interruption and get to a place where He could pray to the Father without interference. Jesus sent away the disciples and the multitude so that He might have time alone with God.

Next, notice the word "constrained" in the same verse. This is the Greek word *anagkazo*, which is a compound of the two words *ana* and *agkale*. *Ana* means *up*, and *agkale* means *arm*. When compounded, the new word paints the picture of a raised arm, which demonstrates force and authority. It literally means *to compel by force*. In light of the miracle that had just occurred in Jesus' ministry, I am amazed by the Gospel writer's choice of these two words "straightway" and "constrained" because it illustrates exactly how Jesus responded to that great meeting: He immediately — *with determined force* — caused everyone to leave Him alone so that He could pray!

With so much work to be done in our own ministry, I frequently feel compelled to just keep going strong without a break. But that is *not* what Jesus did. He recognized His need to stay in touch with the Father, even in the midst of successful events. And it's interesting to note that it was after His time with the Father that *Jesus walked on the water* and *commanded a storm to be still* (*see* Mark 6:47-51). I want to follow Jesus' example.

Anyone who knows Denise and me and is familiar with our ministry knows that we believe wholeheartedly in working very hard and giving 100 percent to the call of God. But there is a time when each of us must come aside to spend special time with the Lord and press into His presence so He can refresh us and renew us by His Spirit, just as Jesus did after He fed the multitude. So I have determined to carve out special time with the Father — to pray, to read His Word, and to fellowship with Him. I set aside time just for Him so He can search my heart and change me and so I can hear Him speak to me with no distractions and interruptions.

I know many people are facing struggles right now, and maybe this is a hard time for you as well. The only way you will get through this time victoriously is by spending time with the Lord and casting the weight of all your cares on Him (*see* Psalm 55:22). *Isn't it time for you to give God more time than you've been giving Him?*

If God is calling you to set aside some extra time for Him, you need to be prepared for your flesh to put up a fight! That's why it's going to take determination to do it. When other things try to scream for your attention and pull you out of that consecrated place, you have to be determined to stay there unmoved, because that is where your source of strength, your peace, and all your answers will come from.

So obey what the Holy Spirit tells you to do by going to *your* mountain to be with the Father — in other words, by coming aside every day to spend special time with Him. I guarantee you that your obedience will bring a great reward. As the author of Hebrews declares, "...He is a rewarder of them that diligently seek him" (Hebrews 11:6).

It is essential that you make a deliberate effort to regularly spend time in consecrated prayer. Start this week — start *today*. Start by giving Him at least a few more minutes each day. Then let your special time with the Lord grow and grow until you are finally experiencing quality time with God that surpasses anything you've ever known in your life. He will open your heart, remove the things that have troubled you and caused your defeat, refill you with the Holy Spirit, and give you *joy unspeakable and full of glory*!

MY PRAYER FOR TODAY

Father, with all that I have to do today, I cannot afford to miss spending time alone with You. I repent for the days I have sought to serve You in my own strength. I was busy, but not always fruitful because I failed to maintain my vital connection with You. Lord Jesus, I deliberately look to You, and I look away from all that would distract my attention from You. Father, I diligently seek You, and I thank You for rewarding me with a greater revelation of Your wisdom and Your ways. Holy Spirit, teach me to order my days with the Lord occupying first place. Please refill me today with Your power and Your joy, which is my impenetrable strength!

I pray this in Jesus' name!

MY CONFESSION FOR TODAY

I confess that I will daily spend time in the Father's presence. No matter how full my schedule may be, I will come to Him for direction and to be refreshed and renewed. I make God's Word my priority. I will not allow my flesh to lure me away from staying vitally united to the Vine because apart from Him, I know I can't do anything of eternal value. I set aside time to read the Word, pray, and fellowship with the Lord. I search my own heart on a regular basis and allow Him to change me so His anointing will flow pure and strong through my life.

I declare this by faith in Jesus' name!

QUESTIONS FOR YOU TO CONSIDER

1. Do you spend daily time with the Lord? How do you spend that time?
2. Do you have a daily Bible reading plan that helps you spend your time with the Lord? If not, a variety of reading plans are available online and are easy to find. Having a scheduled plan will help you feel like you are not having to figure it all out on your own.
3. I personally have a "place" where I go to read my Bible and to pray. It has become my "mountain" where I retreat from the busyness of life to be with Jesus. Do you have such a place? Where is it?

APRIL 11

Wherever Faith Is Present, the Impossible Is Doable!

...If thou canst believe,
all things are possible to him that believeth.
— Mark 9:23

Never underestimate the power of faith! What you believe determines what you receive, so make sure you are thinking and believing correctly.

Mark 9:14-29 tells the account of a deeply distressed father who learned the power of faith first-hand on the day he came to Jesus with his son, who was severely demon-possessed. This boy wasn't just demonically affected — he was being violently attacked by demon spirits that had repeatedly tried to kill him by throwing him into both fire and water. As far as the father was concerned, this situation was irreversible and impossible to cure. So in desperation, he brought his son to Jesus' disciples, but they were unable to help the man. After repeated, unsuccessful attempts to cast the demons out of this child, the disciples finally brought the boy to Jesus to see if He could cast them out.

In New Testament times, demon possession was considered to be the most impossible malady to cure. People, including religious leaders, were so powerless in the presence of demons that demon-possessed individuals were often chained up and left in remote conditions. A famous example of this in Scripture is the demoniac who was kept in the remote region of Gadara (*see* Mark 5:1-20). However, when this father in Mark 9:23 brought his severely tormented child to Jesus, he didn't see his son's condition as an impossible situation at all — because he believed Jesus had *power* over those demons. Jesus responded to this man's faith and said, "...If thou canst believe, all things are possible to him that believeth" (Mark 9:23). Because the father believed, Jesus cast the demons out of his son and returned the boy to his father as a normal child (*see* Mark 9:24-28).

That day Jesus taught this principle: If one can simply believe, anything is possible — even setting a possessed person free from demon spirits. *Wherever faith is present, the impossible is doable!*

This verse always makes me think of all the times people have presented me with seemingly impossible odds and said, "Rick, no one has ever been able to do what you're attempting to do. We know several who tried to do it in the past, but they failed and ended up in a mess. So be careful because it is unlikely that you'll be able to achieve such a huge undertaking!"

Over the years, that kind of gloomy, pessimistic prediction has been made to my wife Denise and me more times than we can count. With nearly everything that we've ever done, someone has tried to tell us the task was impossible. But in every case, they were wrong. I want to say it again — *wherever faith is present, the impossible is doable.*

When I hear someone say something is impossible, I inwardly laugh, because I *personally know* that we serve a God who does the impossible! Jesus said, "...If thou canst believe, all things are possible to him that believeth" (Mark 9:23). Jesus made it plain — if we will believe, all things will be possible to us!

The word "possible" is the Greek word *dunata*, and it expresses the idea of *ability, power, one who is able and capable*, or *one who is competent.* The word *dunata* shares the same root with the word *dunamis*, which is the Greek word for *power.* This emphatically tells us that there is a power that causes one to become able, capable, or competent for any task. When this explosive power comes on the scene and begins to operate in a person's life, it doesn't matter how unfit or unqualified he was before — this power supernaturally *energizes* him and makes him capable for the task set before him.

But who is the type of person who will accomplish impossible feats? Jesus clearly answered that question. He said, "...*All* things are possible to him *that believeth.*" The word "believeth" is the Greek word *pistis*, meaning *faith*. However, the tense used in this verse pictures a person who is *believing*. This is not someone who once had an experience of faith in the *past*; rather, it is *a person who is presently believing right now.* He didn't just believe in the past — he *is* a believer. His faith is *actively reaching forward right now* to grab hold of what God has promised. His faith is habitually, constantly, consistently, and unwaveringly straining forward to take hold of that desired goal he sees before him!

Faith is the spark that ignites the impossible and causes it to become possible. When a person's faith is activated, it sets supernatural power in motion that enables that person to do what he normally would never be able to do! This is why Jesus said, "...If thou canst believe, all things are possible to him that believeth." Once faith has been activated and remains activated, a person becomes enabled and empowered so that he is capable and competent to do whatever it is God has told him to do. That person can even do the impossible!

In my particular case, this means:

- When I receive a new mandate from God to push forward into new and uncharted territory, I look at the project from every angle, and then immediately begin renewing my mind to believe that I can do *anything* God has asked me to do. Even what seems to be impossible will be possible to me!
- If He has told me to do something — regardless of how big or how impossible it seems to the natural mind — I begin to tell myself that I can do it and that my eyes will see it come to pass.
- *After all, if it couldn't be done, why would Jesus ask me to do it?*

The fact is, in God *all* things are possible. Therefore, *it's up to you and me* to get our thinking in line with God's Word. And as we build up our faith to the level it needs to be for the new challenge, we experience an explosion of supernatural power in us that literally carries us over into the realm where impossible things becomes possible!

- Jesus made it very clear that we receive exactly what we believe.
- If I believe I can do the impossible, I will do it.
- But if I believe I *cannot* do the impossible, I will *not* do it.
- When I look at those who have warned me about all the things they thought couldn't be done, most of those people have done nothing.
- Because we dared to believe, today we are standing in the middle of many accomplished "impossible" assignments that others said could never happen.
- *Wherever faith is, the impossible is doable!*

Until that father in Mark 9 met Jesus, he had probably been surrounded with a group of people who gave him no hope and demonstrated no faith. Apparently even the disciples had a hard time believing that little boy could be set free. But as soon as that father got around Jesus and heard Jesus speaking words of faith, he believed — and as soon as the father believed, it was just a matter of minutes before that son was completely and totally set free. Once faith is activated, it often doesn't take long for the impossible to become possible!

So today I want to encourage you to believe that all things are possible. Push that doubt and unbelief out of the way — and if you must, find a new group of friends who will get into a position of faith with you. Then release your faith for the impossible to become possible!

MY PRAYER FOR TODAY

Father, I believe Your Word! I will not listen to the naysayers who haven't accomplished anything. They want to halt and entangle me with their fear and unbelief. It doesn't matter how unqualified I may have been, Your explosive, supernatural power will energize me and make me capable. Faith comes when I hear Your Word, and I am determined to release my faith through obedient action. Regardless of the difficulty or impossibility before me, I know that when faith is present, anything is doable. Holy Spirit, I ask You to help me instantly discern when someone is not in agreement with You so I won't allow their polluting doubt to sink down into my heart. I am determined to push doubt and unbelief out of the way. I believe God, and it will be exactly as He spoke it to me. I believe God, and all things are possible to me.

I pray this in Jesus' name!

MY CONFESSION FOR TODAY

I confess that my faith is not just past tense — I am a believer this very moment! My faith is actively reaching forward right now to grab hold of what God has promised. My faith is unwaveringly straining forward to take hold of that desired goal set before me! My faith ignites the impossible, causing it to become possible, and sets supernatural power in motion that enables me to do what others thought I would never be able to do. With confident expectation, I say it out loud repeatedly: I believe God, and all things are possible to me!

I declare this by faith in Jesus' name!

QUESTIONS FOR YOU TO CONSIDER

1. Have you ever attempted to do something that others said was impossible? How did their words affect you? Did they encourage you to believe or did they drag you down into unbelief and defeat?
2. Who is speaking into your life right now? When you look at the friends who speak into your life, are they people who have challenged the impossible and done it, or are they people who have done nothing and are telling you that you are going to do nothing too?
3. If the impossible happens where faith is activated, what is likely going to happen in your life if things continue the way they are going right now?

APRIL 12

Miracles Catch People's Attention!

And a great multitude followed him, because they
saw his miracles which he did on them that were diseased.
— John 6:2

Today I want to talk to you about miracles and the effect that God's power has on people's lives. Throughout our many years of ministry, Denise and I have seen countless miracles, and we learned long ago that miracles always have a *profound effect* on people! Let me relate to you an example that occurred in the early years of our ministry abroad just after the breakup of the Soviet Union in the year 1991.

During those tumultuous times, that entire region of the world was facing many serious economic struggles. Food supplies were rare; gasoline was almost nonexistent; and medicines and medical supplies were in short supply. Well-trained doctors could diagnose a patient's sickness, but people remained untreated because no medications were available. In fact, even basic medications such as aspirin were a treasure because they were so hard to obtain.

In the midst of this dismal state of affairs, Denise and I announced on television that we were going to hold a series of miracle services in Riga, Latvia. These would be our first meetings in Latvia, and we wanted to facilitate a powerful demonstration of God's power in this city. For two weeks prior to those big meetings, we broadcast advertisements for the miracle services many times a day on television. We had no idea what kind of effect the commercials would have, but we prayed that people would come to the meetings to hear the Gospel, receive a miraculous touch from God, and come to personally know Jesus Christ.

The long-anticipated day finally arrived, and we drove to the city to begin our series of meetings. When we arrived at the large rented auditorium, thousands of people were already in line, waiting to get into the building for the meeting. As Denise and I stood on the stage and looked out over the audience in that large hockey arena, we were stunned to see nearly 8,000 people! Many of these were sick people who had no means of obtaining desperately needed medicines and had therefore turned to the power of God as their only hope for physical healing.

Night after night, we saw mighty miracles occur before our eyes. Blind eyes were opened; epileptics were healed; and deaf ears were unstopped. And the greatest miracle of all was the hundreds of people who came forward to give their lives to Jesus at the conclusion of the meetings each night! By the end of that week, more than 7,000 people prayed to receive Jesus as their Lord. Then on the last night of those meetings, we witnessed one of the greatest miracles we have ever seen in our ministry.

Nineteen years earlier, a man in that crowd had become paralyzed from the waist down after falling from the roof of a house. On the first day of the meetings, we saw this man as he hobbled toward the stage on his crutches to give his life to Jesus. On the second day of the meetings, he came to receive the infilling of the Holy Spirit. On the fourth day, he showed up at the local swimming pool where we were baptizing people, and he was water-baptized. If nothing else happened, his life had already been completely transformed by the power of God.

But on the last night of the meetings, just as we closed the final service, I heard a noise to my left and turned to see what the commotion was all about. This paralyzed man had released his faith and thrown his arms into the air — and as his crutches hit the ground, the lower part of his body had come alive! *Now he was standing with no crutches to hold him up.*

Because of where the man was seated, the entire crowd turned to watch as he began to take his first steps in nineteen years. He took one step, then another, and then another — and with each step, he moved faster and faster. Soon he was running back and forth all across the front of the vast crowd that was gasping with shock at the miracle they were witnessing. *The entire crowd saw this miracle take place!*

After that remarkable event, I gave an invitation for the lost, and more people gave their lives to Jesus Christ that night than in any of the other services. Years later, people still recall that amazing miracle, and as a result of that miracle and the other miracles that took place during those meetings, multitudes believed in Jesus. Many of these people hadn't previously believed in the existence of God at all, but because of these miraculous demonstrations, they gave their lives to Jesus Christ!

God has always used miracles to attract people to Jesus Christ. Many such examples can be found in Scripture, but one of the greatest demonstrations of this truth is recorded in John 6:2, which says, "And a great multitude followed him, because they saw his miracles which he did on them that were diseased."

The word "great" in this verse is a translation of the Greek word *polus,* which refers to *a great numeric quantity.* This tells us that the crowd following Jesus was *really huge.* In addition, the Greek word for "multitude" is *ochlos,* which always describes *a massive crowd.* By using these two words back to back, John was emphasizing that the crowd following Jesus wasn't simply large — it was an *enormously massive group of people*!

This verse goes on to tell us that this group of people "followed" Jesus. The Greek word used here denotes *continuous, unbroken action.* Taking this into account, the first part of this verse could be translated, *"And a great multitude kept on following and following and following him...."* You see, there was something about Jesus' ministry that attracted these throngs of people. They didn't want to be away from Him, not even for a moment! They just kept on following and following and following Him everywhere He went!

Why was this massive multitude following Jesus? The verse tells us: "...because they saw his miracles which he did on them that were diseased." The word "because" is the word *hoti,* and it points to *the reason* the crowd was following Jesus. It says they were following Him "...because they saw his miracles...."

I want you to look at the word "saw" in this verse. This word means *to be a spectator, to notice,* or *to watch in full detail.* Just as one would sit and watch a play from a seat in the theater, this crowd watched intently to see every miracle Jesus was performing. Like spectators in a theater who are mesmerized by an amazing show, they didn't want to miss one act in this supernatural performance, so they followed Jesus to get a close-up look at the miracles that were constantly occurring in His ministry.

The verse goes on to say, "...They saw his *miracles* which he did on them that were diseased." The word "miracles" used here actually comes from the Greek word *semeion.* In the Greek world of the First Century AD, this word *semeion* signified *the official written notice that announced the final verdict of a court, the signature or seal applied to documents to guarantee their authenticity,* or *a sign that marked key locations in a city.*

Taking this into account, we find these miracles were *the final verdict* or *proof* that God was with Jesus. When that crowd saw the miracles, they knew those supernatural acts were *God's stamp of approval* on Jesus' ministry. These superhuman deeds were *the guarantee* that Jesus was anointed by God. The miracles He performed were like signs that declared, *"God is here! You are in the right place!"* They were comparable to *a signature* or *a seal* that *authenticated* and *guaranteed* that God was with Him. That's why these followers didn't want to be away from Jesus. *They knew Jesus had the stamp of God's approval!*

John 6:2 even gives us an idea of what kind of miracles primarily caught the attention of the crowd. It says, "And a great multitude followed him, because they saw his miracles *which he did on them that were diseased.*" The words "he did" come from the Greek word *poieo,* which often conveys the idea of *creativity.* This is important because in this context, *poieo* gives the suggestion of *creative miracles*. The use of this Greek word implies that extraordinary miracles of a creative nature were regularly occurring and that these miracles in particular were catching the attention of the crowd.

Furthermore, John recorded that Jesus was healing those who were "diseased." The word "diseased" comes from the Greek word *astheneo*. This word doesn't refer to people with minor ailments such as the common cold; rather, it depicts people who are physically *frail* or *feeble* due to some bodily condition. Their physical condition is so serious that it has rendered them unable to move about freely. *These were feeble, frail, broken people.*

However, when Jesus walked the earth, He carried the anointing to heal the sick — and He regularly healed people who were physically frail or feeble due to some bodily condition. The health of these people had deteriorated to the point that they had become weak and frail — but once Jesus touched them, they were restored to health!

Taking all these words into consideration,
an interpretative translation of John 6:2 could read:

"A massive multitude continually followed Jesus because they were constantly seeing the mighty signs He was performing on those who were sick. Those whose health was so deteriorated that they were physically frail were recipients of these mighty deeds that authenticated the fact that God was with Jesus!"

Those who followed Jesus during His ministry on this earth knew that something wonderful was always happening. People's lives were being changed; their health was being restored; and their purpose in life was being renewed. *Jesus was the best thing that had ever happened to every person who ever came in contact with Him!*

And Jesus is still the best thing that has ever happened to every person who comes in contact with Him *today*! He is the same yesterday, today, and forever (Hebrews 13:8), so why don't you go ahead and believe for miracles to start working in your life as they did in Jesus' life? When people see those miracles and experience the power of God, it will open their hearts to hear the Good News of Jesus Christ. *Miracles will get their attention, and then you can tell them about Jesus!*

Think of the profound effect that a single miracle would have on your circle of friends and the people you know. God wants to work through you! As a believer, you are anointed and commissioned to lay hands on the sick, and you have the right to expect to see those sick people get well. That's God's promise in Mark 16:18, so boldly claim it by faith and reach out to let His power operate through you to others!

Having witnessed so many miracles in our ministry, I want to encourage you to believe God for miracles in your own life and in the lives of those around you. When people see and experience the power of God, it makes them want to follow Jesus, just like the crowds who followed Him in John 6:2. Miracles are God's way of shouting, *"I am here and I love you!"*

It is sad that many people think Jesus' miracle-working power is only a thing of the past, because He is the same today as He was then. He is both able and willing now to do the same things He did when He walked the earth 2,000 years ago. Jesus hasn't changed. He wants to touch, heal, and restore people. That's why I want to encourage you to make room in your life for Jesus to perform His miracle-working, life-changing ministry through you!

MY PRAYER FOR TODAY

Heavenly Father, I am so thankful that Jesus came to earth to reveal Your will and to show us Your ways. Just as Jesus went about manifesting Your goodness by destroying the works of the devil, He is the same — yesterday, today, and forever. Father, it's Your goodness and loving-kindness that leads people to repentance. I make myself available to You as a vessel through whom Jesus can manifest Himself to others. Jesus was the best thing that ever happened to every person who ever came in contact with Him. Holy Spirit, bring people into contact with Jesus through me as You use my life. Demonstrate Your miracle power through my life to open hearts and change lives. Make me a vessel You can flow through to cause people's health to be restored and their hope to be renewed by a personal encounter with You.

I pray this in Jesus' name!

MY CONFESSION FOR TODAY

I confess that I give place for Jesus Christ to perform His miracle-working, life-changing ministry through me. When Jesus walked the earth, He went about doing good, healing all, and destroying the works of the devil. I am anointed and commissioned by Him to lay my hands on the sick in His name and to see them recover. That is God's promise in Mark 16:18, and I boldly claim it by faith as I yield to His compassion and reach out to others with confident expectation to see His miracle-working power released to others through my life.

I declare this by faith in Jesus' name!

QUESTIONS FOR YOU TO CONSIDER

1. What miracle do you need in your own life right now? What touch of God do you need in your family? What supernatural provision do you need in your job, your business, or your finances? If you will release your faith in Jesus, He will step in and work miracles in any situation you're facing!
2. Can you think of people in your life who are in desperate need of a miracle? Have you asked the Lord what part He may want you to take in releasing His miracle-working power through you into their lives or situations?
3. Have you prayed with those people about that need, expecting God to move on their behalf to see that miracle manifest? If you haven't, why not? Let the love and compassion of God flow through you as you pray for these individuals — always with faith believing you have received the answer!

APRIL 13

926 People Baptized in a Public Swimming Pool

Go ye therefore, and teach all nations,
baptizing them in the name of the Father,
and of the Son, and of the Holy Spirit....
— Matthew 28:19

In yesterday's *Sparkling Gem*, I related the story of the first large meetings that Denise and I conducted in the former Soviet Union. We held those meetings in Latvia's capital city of Riga. During that amazing week, approximately 8,000 people attended the meetings on all five nights — for a total attendance of 40,000 people. Just as people followed Jesus to witness the powerful, mind-blowing miracles He performed during His earthly ministry, we discovered that these precious people didn't want to go away once they had been touched by God's power. Miraculous power abounded all around us, and that week we witnessed several thousand people come to a saving faith in Jesus Christ!

However, during these meetings, I was deeply disturbed by one very important fact: These new believers needed to be water-baptized! In Matthew 28:19, Jesus proclaimed, "Go ye therefore, and teach all nations, *baptizing* them in the name of the Father, and of the Son, and of the Holy Spirit." Jesus didn't tell us to just preach to them; He commanded that we baptize them and get them moving on the road to discipleship! Jesus treated baptism like it was important, so I knew I needed to find a way to get these new believers into baptismal waters.

Before I continue with this story, let's look at the word "baptism" for a moment to see what it originally meant in the Greek. The word "baptize" is from the Greek word *baptidzo*, a word that originally meant *to dip and to dye*. For instance, in very early cases, the word *baptidzo* described the process of dipping a cloth or garment into a vat of color to dye it; leaving it there long enough for the material to soak up the new color; and then pulling that garment out of the dye with a permanently changed outward appearance. Likewise a person who comes to Jesus Christ can be likened to an old garment that needs to be dipped into a vat of dye so its color can be changed. However, the person isn't dipped into a vat of colored dye, but into the precious blood of the Lamb! This person is so totally transformed by Jesus' blood that he becomes a new creature. His countenance is so changed that he even looks different. You could say that this new believer has been supernaturally "dipped and dyed"!

What a new light this sheds on baptism! In Romans 6:4, the apostle Paul said, "Therefore, we are buried with him by baptism into death: that like as Christ was raised up from the dead by the glory of the Father, even so we also should walk in newness of life" (Romans 6:4). Water baptism is a symbolic proclamation of the fact that believers have been buried with Christ and raised with

Him. When a believer is placed in the baptismal waters, it symbolizes being immersed in one condition and coming out looking brand-new. In other words, it is a picture of what happened to that person when he got saved! This outward symbol represents the fact that he has been dipped in the blood of the Lamb, and now his entire life has been newly colored and transformed to be like Jesus!

According to Paul's instructions in Romans 6, this was the act of officially burying the past and starting a new life in Christ. At the time of those meetings, I fully understood that Christ commanded us to lead people into the waters of baptism as a public declaration of what God had done in their lives — in addition to preaching and leading people in a prayer of repentance. When we saw so many people get saved the first night, I knew we had to come up with a solution to baptize them.

To solve this problem, we rented a public swimming pool for three afternoons, and I announced that we would make water baptism available to each new believer and that we would instruct him or her about water baptism around the sides of the swimming pool before they entered it to be baptized.

We thought it would be extraordinary if 100 converts showed up to be baptized in a mid-afternoon service, but even at that, our team was ready to baptize 10 people at a time. We thought that with all the getting in and out of the pool, we could handle 100 people in one hour per afternoon if we were really careful with our time. We thought that if 300 of the new converts showed up over the course of all three afternoons, it would be a fabulous turnout — so you can imagine how stunned we were when more than 300 people showed up the *first* afternoon. There were so many people that we could not fit them around the edge of the pool in one teaching session, so we decided to divide the afternoon into three different baptismal sessions that each accommodated about 100 people. This meant we ended up baptizing a little more than 300 people in that *first* afternoon.

But on the *second* day, another 300-plus people came to the pool for water baptism — meaning the turnout had already exceeded 600 people! Then on the *third* day, we were stunned when an additional 300-plus people showed up to be baptized. By the end of those three afternoons, *we had water-baptized 926 people.* To be honest, we were both *spiritually elated* and *physically exhausted.* And we still had one more evening service to preach where more people would repent. That meant even more people would need to be water-baptized!

It was an amazing week in our lives. It was our first public event in the former USSR. Approximately 40,000 people attended, approximately 7,000 people repented and received Christ, countless notable miracles abounded, and we water-baptized 926 people in a public swimming pool! Little did we know that we were just getting started, but as you will see in tomorrow's *Sparkling Gem*, God had plans that we were unaware of when that week of meetings began!

So have YOU ever received water baptism?

I am amazed at how many believers think that water baptism is optional because Scripture never presents it as an option. Certainly it doesn't save us, but it is, in fact, the first step of obedience for a believer who wants to become a disciple. Jesus commanded that we receive water baptism in Matthew 28:19.

Since Jesus spoke of water baptism as the first serious step for a believer, it is essential that you not simply skip over this step, as so many people have done. I have seen over many years of ministry that people who neglect this divine command tend to let other vital requirements of their Christian walk slip through the cracks. *Don't let this describe you.* You've been washed in the blood of Jesus, and if you haven't already been water-baptized, it's time for you to go under the waters of baptism to declare publicly that the old man is gone and that you are now "dyed" in the blood of Jesus Christ! *Don't you want to do what Jesus has asked you to do?*

MY PRAYER FOR TODAY

Father, today I see more clearly than ever the significance of water baptism as a powerful demonstration of my spiritual transformation in Christ. Father, just as Jesus publicly obeyed You when He suffered and died to purchase my redemption, I obey the Lord's command to publicly proclaim through the waters of baptism that I have been washed in the soul-cleansing blood of the Lamb. I thank You that because Jesus died in my place and You raised Him to new life, I take every step to demonstrate that I am a disciple of the Lord Jesus Christ. Clothed in His righteousness alone, baptism symbolizes that I've been dipped and dyed in the crimson flood of Jesus' blood as I gratefully proclaim: I am a child of God!

I pray this in Jesus' name!

MY CONFESSION FOR TODAY

I confess that I am a new creation in Christ Jesus. Old things have passed away and through Him, all things have become new. Crucified with Christ, I follow the Lord into baptism to bury my old man in a watery grave. And when I rise up, it is as a demonstration of how Jesus saves.

I declare this by faith in Jesus' name!

QUESTIONS FOR YOU TO CONSIDER

1. At what age were you water baptized? What do you remember about that event? Were there changes you witnessed in your life as a result of publicly proclaiming your faith in Christ with the act of water baptism?
2. If you have never been water baptized, why not? What would prevent you from obeying the Lord in this very elementary first step of obedience? Did you inadvertently skip it because no one told you it was important?
3. Do you attend a church that regularly baptizes people? If not, why do you attend a church that doesn't obey a command of Jesus that is so clear and simple? If your church doesn't regularly baptize people, is it possible that you should ask your pastor for the church's position on water baptism?

APRIL 14

Starting a Church in a Former Communist Auditorium

But where sin abounded,
grace did much more abound.
— Romans 5:20

In yesterday's *Sparkling Gem*, I recounted the time we baptized 926 new believers in a public swimming pool during the first meetings we held in the former Soviet Union. But there is more to this amazing story! As I stood and looked at all the people being water-baptized that week, I heard the Holy Spirit say, *"What will you do with all these people now that they have been baptized?"* In that moment, it was like a streak of divine revelation pierced through my soul — and I knew that God was telling me to take responsibility for these new believers. Denise and I were being instructed by the Holy Spirit to start a church.

Soon afterward, we began searching for a location to start a new church. When Jesus started his ministry, He announced that He was anointed to preach the *good news* of the Gospel (*see* Luke 4:18), so we felt we should name the church the *Good News Church* because the Gospel was such good news! Especially in the wake of the collapse of USSR when there was so much bad news all around in this part of the world, we believed this name would signal the truth of what the Gospel is.

After being rejected by several locations that we had investigated as potential sites for our church, we learned that an old auditorium formerly used by the Communist Party was available if we wanted to rent it. Within hours of receiving that information, I went to that auditorium to see if it would work as our new church building. There I was — surrounded by 680 leather-padded, theater-style, Communist-red seats. An enormous chandelier hung from the ceiling with gigantic, matching light fixtures that surrounded the circular auditorium. The walls were adorned with emblems of the Soviet Union that included a huge cameo of Marx and Lenin adorning the top left and right of the stage. The back rooms of the stage were filled with Communist paraphernalia — including flags of every Republic of USSR, a gargantuan bust of Lenin, and a huge copper emblem that celebrated one of the anniversaries of the Communist party.

When I stood on that stage and looked out onto those empty seats, I understood that *this* was the location where Jesus wanted us to start the *Good News Church.* We contacted the new believers who had been water-baptized and invited them to a full week of meetings in the new location. From the onset of those meetings, the power of God literally burst into that place and established the Church of Jesus Christ in that part of the world!

During that first week, every chair was filled, and people crowded the steps and lined the auditorium each evening. The auditorium was packed to maximum capacity until the number of people attending overflowed beyond the limitations prescribed by the local fire department, and we had to begin holding multiple services each week to accommodate our burgeoning congregation. In the middle of that location — where Communist powers had once prevailed — the grace of God was being *poured out*!

That week I couldn't help but be reminded of the apostle Paul's words in Romans 5:20, where he wrote, "Where sin abounded, grace did much more abound." Paul said that sin "abounded" — from the Greek word *pleonadzo*, which describes something that exists in *abundance*. However, Paul went on to use comparative language to tell us that regardless of how immense sin and its dominion was in a person's life, it is *nothing* in comparison to the working of God's grace.

When I looked at that auditorium, I thought of how that building, like so many lives, was once dominated by a horrible working of sin. But regardless of what sinful decisions were made there, it is nothing compared to the grace now poured out upon us!

God's grace is being poured out in a measure that is way *above* and *beyond* anything that sin ever dreamed to accomplish. Paul said grace did "much more abound" — that was his inspired way of explaining the *profuse*, *lavish*, *bountiful*, and *overflowing nature* of God's grace!

The words "much more abound" are actually a translation of the Greek word *huperperisseo*, which is a compound of the words *huper* and *perisseo*. The first part of this compound is the word *huper*, which means *over, above, and beyond*. It depicts *something that is way beyond measure*. It carries the idea of *superiority — something that is utmost, paramount, foremost, first-rate, first-class, and top-notch; greater, higher, and better than; superior to; preeminent, dominant, and incomparable; more than a match for; unsurpassed, unequaled, and unrivaled by any person or thing*.

The second part of this compound is the word *perisseo*, which depicts something that *abounds* in an *extraordinary measure* or something so *profuse* that it can be likened to a river that is *overflowing* and *flooding* beyond its banks. It is so *full* that it simply *cannot be contained* in a single location. Thus, when these two words are compounded to form the word *huperperisseo*, it dramatically portrays grace as a force that is *measureless* and which can *never* be exhausted. So this verse could be understood to mean, *"Where sin existed in abundance, grace FAR exceeded it!"*

This is not only true of that location where our first church gathered in Riga, but it is also true of you. Sin may have once existed in abundance in your life, but the grace of God has far exceeded anything that the devil or any past sin ever attempted to fulfill in your life. The grace of God working *in you* is higher, preeminent, unsurpassed, and unrivaled by any past rule of sin in your life. God's grace *in you* is simply *measureless* and *inexhaustible!*

Just as the grace of God was poured out in that old Communist auditorium, it is now being poured out abundantly — *without measure* — in your life. This is your time to gloat over what God can do in a person's life. There you are, a former temple of sin, and now you have become a place where God with all His miracle-working power is at work. It leaves one *speechless* to consider what God has done and is doing in you!

MY PRAYER FOR TODAY

Father, although sin once dominated in my life, Your lavish, overflowing grace has abounded even more in me. Your grace far exceeds the work or influence of sin. Holy Spirit, I ask You to open the eyes of my understanding and help me begin to understand how to cooperate more fully with the grace of God that is at work in my life.

I pray this in Jesus' name!

MY CONFESSION FOR TODAY

I confess that the grace of God abounds in my life, teaching me to say no to ungodliness and yes to living a morally upright life in this present age. The grace of God working in me is unsurpassed and unrivaled by any past rule of sin in my life. In the areas of my life and thoughts where fear and other sins once held control, the grace of God released to me now holds the superior position, and I allow that grace to reign supreme.

I declare this by faith in Jesus' name!

QUESTIONS FOR YOU TO CONSIDER

1. When you survey your life and the areas where sin once operated in you without restraint, what differences do you see now because of the grace of God at work in your life?
2. How is grace abounding in your life? Describe the ways in which you are deliberately cooperating with the grace of God so its work can increase in your life.
3. What is the most notable change that you have observed in your thoughts and attitudes toward others due to the measureless grace of God overflowing the banks of your life?

APRIL 15

Machine-Gun Fire and a Cup of Tea!

But as many as are led by the Spirit of God,
they are the sons of God.
— Romans 8:14

It was the early 1990s — a time when supernatural doors were flying open for our TV ministry in nearly every corner of the Soviet Union. But one area that remained closed was Baku, Azerbaijan. Since this was a Muslim city, I had been strongly advised not to go there to negotiate for television time. Plus, the country of Azerbaijan was in a serious military conflict at the time. But despite what people were advising me to do, I sensed a strong leading of the Holy Spirit to go there. I simply *knew* that if I would put my feet on that land, God would open doors for us to broadcast the teaching of the Bible there.

We watched the news day by day to monitor what was happening with the military developments that were largely based around the capital city of Baku — where the largest TV tower in that part of the world was located. This tower was so huge, its signal covered not only Azerbaijan, but it reached all the way into the heart of Iran. For a door of this size to open would definitely require the supernatural grace of God — and it would also require divine courage to go there in the middle of an escalating military conflict!

A single day came when a temporary cease-fire had been declared, so we quickly purchased plane tickets for two team members and me. We called to set up an appointment with the director of the national TV station, and we raced to the airport so we could board our plane to Azerbaijan. Hours later, we landed in the capital city of Baku. After being vigorously searched at the airport, a private car picked us up and drove us directly to the broadcasting company of that nation.

When we entered the broadcasting building, we were escorted to a sitting area to wait for our meeting with the TV director. We were told that we would need to be patient because the cease-fire had been broken at almost that exact moment, and there was heavy machine-gun fighting all around the TV facility. A secretary asked us if we'd like a cup of tea, and we sat drinking our tea while we could hear gunfire at the other end of the hallway adjacent to the area where we were seated! At one point, a group of soldiers carrying machine guns ran hurriedly past us, disappearing through the door to an area outside where all the action was taking place!

Soon the door opened to the national TV director's office, and we were invited in for our scheduled appointment. To my surprise, the director was a woman. She held an unusual, very powerful position in a Muslim society. When I made my presentation about our TV programs, she responded, "Maybe you don't understand. We are a Muslim republic. Your programs can't be broadcast here. Plus, our signal reaches Tehran, and if we run your Bible teaching programs, it could offend our partners in Iran."

But this broadcasting endeavor had been on my heart a long time. So rather than take no for an answer, I insisted, "We've come a long way today. Will you please just look at one of our programs?"

The director kindly consented. It just so happened that the random program she chose to watch was part of a series on what the Bible teaches about how husbands should treat their wives. As we watched, I could see the Holy Spirit was touching her heart with answers she had been seeking for her own marriage.

When that program ended, she asked if we had Part Two of that series with us and could show it to her. By the end of the second program, the Holy Spirit had totally melted her heart.

She said, "How often would you like to broadcast these programs and what price would you like to pay?"

Right before our eyes — *with machine guns firing rapid-fire in the background* — God opened a door that would not have opened if we had not had the courage to go to Baku at that critical moment in history.

That day I learned once again that it takes courage and confidence if you want to walk through a door that has never opened for anyone else. *It also takes the leading of the Holy Spirit.* It was the Holy Spirit who led us there on that very day — the day a great door flew open for the proclamation of the Gospel of Jesus Christ!

In Romans 8:14, we are promised, "But as many as are led by the Spirit of God, they are the sons of God." I want to examine this verse in today's *Sparkling Gem*.

The Greek word for "led" is the word *ago*, which simply means *to lead*. But it must also be pointed out that this word forms the root for the Greek word *agon*, which describes *an intense conflict, such as a struggle in a wrestling match* or *a struggle of the human will*.

This illustrates the fact that although the Holy Spirit wants to lead us, our human will doesn't like the idea of being led. You see, it's the nature of the flesh to want to go its own way. Thus, when we choose to walk in the Spirit and let Him dictate our lives, His leadership over us creates a struggle of our will with our flesh.

An example of this kind of intense struggle is that dangerous trip to Baku. The Spirit of God inside me was telling me, "Go *now* — there is an open door for you *today*." But the flesh ranted and raved, "You're putting your life in danger! Don't do what the Holy Spirit is telling you to do."

Maybe that's how you've been feeling about your own life. You want to obey God and be led by His Spirit, but your flesh is interested only in self-preservation and going its own way. However, as a child of God, you must learn to walk with Him and stay in your place — *behind* the Holy Spirit, following His lead. You have to defeat every fight the flesh puts up to stop you from obtaining the supernatural results the Lord wants you to have.

If you really want to live a supernatural, Spirit-led life, there is no way around it. You have to deal with your flesh! The flesh wants to control you, so you must mortify, or defeat, the flesh and allow the Holy Spirit to have His way. The struggle may seem great, but it's the only way to live a fruitful Christian life.

I'm so thankful for that day many years ago when God empowered me by His Spirit and gave me the courage to get on a plane and fly to Baku. God knew what I didn't know — that a great open door was waiting for me. When we arrived and found the cease-fire had been broken, we could have turned around, gotten back on the plane, and headed home immediately. But we were *certain* the Holy Spirit was leading us. By God's grace, the fight with the flesh was won, and a great event occurred before our very eyes.

As we do the will of God in life, we must listen to natural advice, but we must never forget that the leading of the Spirit is the prime factor in yielding supernatural fruit and obtaining a Heavenly outcome.

MY PRAYER FOR TODAY

Father, I now recognize that every time I have ever struggled to do what You asked me to do, the reason behind the struggle was that I had allowed fear and carnal reasoning to hinder me. Father, I repent for yielding to the pull of my own flesh instead of to the direction of Your Spirit. I want to live a fruitful life. Holy Spirit, right now I yield to Your strength, and I receive the courage I need to step out by faith and follow Your leading so I can obtain a heavenly outcome to the glory of God!

I pray this in Jesus' Name!

MY CONFESSION FOR TODAY

I confess that I obey God and I am led by His Spirit. I put to death all self-interest and every fleshly thought to make decisions based on self-preservation. I belong to God! My life is His, and His strength is mine! I refuse to allow my flesh to stop me from obtaining the supernatural results the Lord wants me to have. I choose to do the will of God. I declare right now that in those moments when the struggle to stay on track with His plan seems great because I'm tempted to let natural reasoning pull me off course, I will not fall short but will fulfill all the will of God without wavering! Greater is the courage of God within me than any fear that rants against my mind or any opposition that rises against me in this world!

I declare this by faith in Jesus' name!

QUESTIONS FOR YOU TO CONSIDER

1. Have you ever been directed by the Holy Spirit to do something that made no sense to your natural mind? When was that? How did you respond? What was the result of your obeying what He instructed you to do?
2. Have you ever been in a place that seemed filled with danger, but God told you to be there, and it ended up bearing fruit for the Kingdom of God? When was that experience? What happened as a result of your obedience?
3. What is God asking you to do *right now* that is requiring a greater measure of spiritual fortitude for you to obey Him? Have you asked Him to give you the courage and inner strength to obey what He is asking you to do?

As a child of God, you must learn to walk with Him and stay in your place — behind the Holy Spirit, following His lead.

APRIL 16

Becoming a Living Sacrifice

I beseech you therefore, brethren,
by the mercies of God, that ye present
your bodies a living sacrifice, holy, acceptable
unto God, which is your reasonable service.
— Romans 12:1

It is no secret that the desires of your flesh are often in direct contradiction with God's plan for your life. When God calls for moderation, the flesh strongly cries out for excess, and it will fight tooth and nail to get its way. That is why the apostle Paul began Romans 12:1 by intensely *pleading* and *commanding* you to hear and follow through with obedience to his message. He wrote, "I beseech you therefore, brethren, by the mercies of God, that ye present your bodies a living sacrifice, holy, acceptable unto God, which is your reasonable service."

I especially want to draw your attention to the word "beseech" at the beginning of this verse. In Greek, it is the word *parakaleo*, which is a compound of the words *para* and *kaleo*. The word *para* means *alongside*, and the word *kaleo* means *to call* or *to beckon*. When these two words are compounded, the new word depicts *a person who comes alongside someone else, as close as he can get, and then begins to passionately call out, plead, beckon, or beg another person or group of people to do something*. In fact, the sense of pleading is so strong in the word *parakaleo*, one expositor has suggested that this verse figuratively shows the apostle Paul on his knees, pleading with his readers to hear what he is saying and to do what he is requesting. This is no mere asking; it is Paul *prayerfully pleading* for his readers to hear his petition and obey it.

However, it is important to note that the word *parakaleo* actually holds another layer of meaning. In New Testament times, this word was also used to describe military commanders who would passionately address their troops before sending them into battle. In this context, the word *parakaleo* means *to exhort*, and it depicts a leader urging his soldiers to take action, prepare themselves for a fight, and then brave the imminent battle with courage and a commitment to win, regardless of the difficulties that might lie ahead. This is no suggestion — *it is a command*! Thus, Paul's use of the word *parakaleo* in Romans 12:1 reveals that in addition to *earnestly pleading* with his readers, he was *commanding* them as a leader and exhorting them to obey his request. What Paul was about to convey to his audience would require great fortitude and commitment on their part, so it was vital that they entered this spiritual battle with great strength of courage.

What was this difficult and monumental task Paul was urging us to intentionally engage in to fully accomplish? It was to *present our bodies as a living sacrifice unto God.*

Paul continued, "I beseech you therefore, brethren, by the mercies of God, *that ye present* your bodies a living sacrifice...." The phrase "ye present" is a translation of the Greek word *paristemi*, and it means *to present a sacrifice* or *to dedicate something to the Lord*. In fact, it is the same word used in Luke 2:22 to describe the moment when Joseph and Mary *presented* Jesus to God and *dedicated* Him in the Temple. The verse states, "And when the days of her purification according to the law of Moses were accomplished, they brought him to Jerusalem, to *present* him to the Lord." The word "present" in this verse is *paristemi* — the same word used in Romans 12:1. Just as Joseph and Mary presented Jesus to God and *fully dedicated* him to His service, Paul was exhorting us to *present* and *dedicate* our human bodies to God.

Because of his choice of language, there is no doubt that Paul was referring to the human body when he urged his readers to "present your bodies a living sacrifice" in Romans 12:1. The word "bodies" is the Greek word *soma*, which specifically refers to the *physical body*. Paul was calling on believers everywhere to surrender their physical bodies to the service of God — to put their bodies on the altar and dedicate them to God as "a living sacrifice."

Paul knew this endeavor would be difficult because the human body by its very nature does not want to be laid on the altar. Flesh desperately desires to be in full control of itself and will actively resist God's cry for surrender. So like a military commander, Paul exhorted his audience to take charge of their physical bodies and to surrender them to God regardless of what their flesh was telling them to do.

Paul's language in this verse is peculiar, because in New Testament times, there was no such thing as a *living* sacrifice when it came to the sacrifice of animals. All sacrifices were *dead* and thus had no voice or ability to resist. When a sacrificial animal was killed on an altar, the act was final, and the animal couldn't protest or scream out after the fact that it didn't want to be sacrificed. Yet in Romans 12:1, God calls on us to present our bodies as *living* sacrifices. He seeks living human beings who belong wholly to Him and who choose to *stay* on the altar of their own free will. In other words, we are to be completely surrendered to Him, fully dedicated to His purpose, and living entirely *for* Him — *24 hours a day, 7 days a week.*

So take a moment to ask yourself the following questions:

- Do you struggle with surrendering your body to the Lord and remaining a "living sacrifice"?
- What do your physical habits reveal about the current state of your surrender to God?
- Does your body call the shots, or is Jesus the Lord of your body?

These questions may be difficult to acknowledge, but they are vitally important. If you find that it's difficult to keep your body dedicated to God, don't be too shocked or disappointed in yourself. Realize it's a challenge for everyone, but don't give yourself any slack! Make a quality decision today to continually recommit the ownership and lordship of your body to Jesus Christ as a living sacrifice.

As we've seen, it's what your Heavenly Father asks for — the total surrender of your body, its habits, and its actions. He wants you on the altar, *and He wants all of you.* He knows that it is as you willingly choose to adopt that position of utter surrender to Him that His Spirit will be able to work in you and through you to become everything He created you to be.

MY PRAYER FOR TODAY

Father, Jesus asked us why we call Him Lord, yet fail to do what He tells us to do. The one I obey is the one I truly serve. Today I see areas where I have allowed the voice of my flesh to call the shots. Instead of mastering and subduing my flesh into silence, I have silenced the voice of my spirit that calls for me to present my body as a living sacrifice in obedient surrender to You. Father, I humble myself beneath Your mighty hand, and I repent for the ways I have indulged the carnal mind, which is not subject to You. I judge that as rebellion and I refuse to give it place any longer. Father, I thank You for Your great mercy in opening the eyes of my understanding to see this as You see it. I choose to submit to You and to resist the devil's attempts to exploit my flesh to gain access to my life. You alone, Lord Jesus, have the right to lead me and conform my thoughts to Your will.

I pray this in Jesus' name!

MY CONFESSION FOR TODAY

I confess that I make a decisive dedication of my body and my faculties to the Lord. I choose to follow the example of my Lord Jesus, who learned obedience through the things He suffered by walking in continual obedience to the will of the Father. I choose to make a continual commitment to refuse to live life according to fleshly dictates. Although this may be the biggest fight of my life, I decide and decree that this is a fight that will be won as I yield to the power of the Greater One inside me!

I declare this by faith in Jesus' name!

QUESTIONS FOR YOU TO CONSIDER

1. Has there been a concrete moment you can recall when you presented your body to Jesus Christ as a living sacrifice? If yes, when was that moment? If no, why not do it today before you do anything else or go anywhere else? *It will change your life!*
2. In what areas of your life do you battle with surrendering your body to the Lordship of Jesus? What steps can you take to make this process of submission easier?
3. Why don't you make a list of the areas that you still need to surrender to the Lord? At least if you have a list, you'll be aware of what areas you need to present to the Lord and work on committing to Him.

APRIL 17

Making Wrongs Right

Therefore if thou bring thy gift to the altar,
and there rememberest thou that thy brother
hath ought against thee; leave there thy gift before the altar,
and go thy way; first be reconciled to thy brother,
and then come and offer thy gift.
— Matthew 5:23-24

Have you ever been hurt or offended, but tried to deal with the problem by pretending nothing was wrong? You made an effort to smile, regardless of whether you felt like it or not, and then forced yourself to put on a bright, shining, happy face as though nothing was bothering you. You smoothed the wrinkles out of your forehead, unfurrowed your eyebrows, and prayed that people didn't see reflected in your eyes the conflict that was raging in your heart.

You inwardly surmised, *If I can keep up this facade, no one will ever detect my disgust!* However, in spite of your efforts, the bottled-up hurt and offense inevitably surfaced. Perhaps you ran into the offender at church and said hello, but the other person didn't reply exactly as you thought he should. Maybe he simply didn't have time to talk because of a previously scheduled appointment, or maybe he was just being plain rude. In either case, your flesh slipped into a silent mode of self-justification, mud-slinging, and name-calling. Inwardly you may have thought poisonous thoughts like: *That's exactly what I expected from that person! I don't know why I even try! He'll never change!*

Suddenly you were consumed with negative feelings you couldn't control. You became a prisoner to your own emotions. Those negative thoughts kept rolling around in your heart and soul, tearing you up on the inside. By not bringing those wounded emotions into the light, you allowed them to fester in darkness and wreak destruction in your life. And to top it off, your inner ugliness revealed that you are just as "in the wrong" as the other person!

Learning how to deal with these conflicts, resolve them, and move in the love of God is key to achieving victory in our relationships and in our lives. We must deal with our hearts and then make sure our outward actions reflect a walk of love. Part of those outward steps may be going to your offender to confess your hurt — or acknowledge his or her hurt — and make your relationship right both with that person and with God. You might say, "But, oh, this is so hard and embarrassing to do." The truth is, doing the right thing is not always easy.

Our need to confess our hurt and make things right usually comes to our minds when we are in worship. In fact, that's the essence of what Jesus said in Matthew 5:23,24. In those verses, He told us, "Therefore if thou bring thy gift to the altar, and there rememberest thou that thy brother hath ought against thee; leave there thy gift before the altar, and go thy way; first be reconciled to thy brother, and then come and offer thy gift." Let's look at this verse and see what Jesus commanded us to do.

Jesus was saying that as you bring a gift to the altar — whether it's a financial gift, an act of worship, a prayer, or simply your decision to draw nearer to God — you may "remember" suddenly, in a flash of a moment, that there is an issue between you and another person. If an issue has suddenly been quickened to your mind when you come before God in prayer or worship, it is likely the Holy Spirit is speaking to your heart in order to bring an issue to your attention.

Maybe it is something you were not aware of, or maybe it is something that you've tried to ignore or just didn't want to face. But when the Holy Spirit quickens it to you, that is a game-changer. It makes you personally responsible for whatever He has revealed to you. And Jesus said that if you suddenly remember your brother has "ought against" you, it is your God-given responsibility to put forth the effort as quickly as possible to make it right.

In Greek, the word "ought" is the little word *ti*, which means *anything* at all. In other words, this doesn't have to be something that *you* would deem a major issue. If the Holy Spirit brings *anything* to your mind that wrongfully exists between you and a fellow believer — regardless of what it is, how big it is, or how small it is — Jesus commands you to leave your gift at the altar, go find that individual, and be "reconciled." It may seem like a minor issue. But if the Holy Spirit has quickened it to your mind, you need to treat the situation seriously and immediately get "reconciled" with that individual.

The word "reconciled" in Matthew 5:24 is the Greek word *diallassomai*, which refers to *mutual concession after mutual hostility*. The idea of *concession* is *giving up an argument, surrendering a point, conceding to someone else*, or *letting something go and refusing to let it be an issue*. In other words, even though the issue is not totally agreed upon, you have at least agreed to be "right" with each other.

The sad fact is that most of the problems that people hold on to and allow to wreak havoc in their lives are truly insignificant. Many people are sent reeling into a maze of emotions over meaningless issues, which they subsequently magnify and exaggerate in their minds to a point of absurdity — literally making mountains out of molehills. *We've all been guilty of this from time to time.*

If I were to ask everyone reading this to send me stories of silly conflicts they've experienced, I could fill pages and pages with their testimonies. We could sit and roar with laughter over the silly things that upset people and see just how foolish we all can be. If we then magnify our personal experiences by those of thousands of other people, we'll begin to catch a glimpse of how many hours of people's lives are dominated by senseless, meaningless, unimportant debate.

Most of life's conflicts fall into this category. They are small, temporary, ridiculous, emotional flare-ups that can later be seen in their true light — perhaps humorous or even stupid, but certainly not worthy of getting upset about.

However, these trivial conflicts can easily become serious when we refuse out of pride to admit our error, apologize, and let go of our offense. When pride comes into the picture and someone gets offended, a minor incident that should be laughed off will quickly become a wall that separates. Anytime something small becomes a major issue, we need to back up and reexamine what we are thinking and feeling. Therefore, look inward and ask yourself, *Is this problem really so serious, or are we letting this matter get way out of hand?*

Once you've done what the Holy Spirit has told you to do — and you've done all you know to do to clear the air and to make wrongs right — the last of verse 24 tells you what to do: "...Then come and offer thy gift." Hopefully, the other person has received you, but even if he or she doesn't, at least you can rest knowing you've done your best. You've done what is necessary to keep a clear conscience and a clean heart before God. Now it's time to enjoy sweet, unhindered fellowship in the presence of the Lord.

MY PRAYER FOR TODAY

Father, here in Your light, I see the light of Your truth shining on the reality of the nonsense I've allowed to become a dividing wall of offense. I acknowledge my part in this, and I repent of thinking and responding contrary to the love of God. I will not ignore the situation any longer or harden my heart in pride. In obedience to Your Word, I will humbly go to my brother with the sincere desire to make this right. This may be difficult and somewhat embarrassing, but a clear conscience and unhindered fellowship with You means more to me than anything. As I seek to make peace, I entrust the outcome to You, Lord.

I pray this in Jesus' name!

MY CONFESSION FOR TODAY

I confess that I keep a clear conscience toward God that is void of offense toward any man. I keep myself in the love of God as I continually seek peace and pursue it. I refuse to make mountains out of molehills and allow petty nonsense to escalate into an offense that will produce bitterness in me or in others. I am quick to repent and also quick to forgive. Holy Spirit, I ask You to quicken my heart any time I need to make things right with anyone for any reason. I commit to You that I will do what You tell me to do so I can live peaceably with everyone and enjoy unbroken fellowship with You at all times.

I declare this by faith in Jesus' name!

QUESTIONS FOR YOU TO CONSIDER

1. Have you ever been in a time of worship when suddenly your mind became aware of a relationship that needed to be made right — and that you needed to take care of it before you could proceed with anything else in your life?
2. Is there someone who has "ought against" you right now? Or who is that person whom *you* have "ought against"? Based on today's *Sparkling Gem*, what is Jesus asking you to do about it?

APRIL 18

Work While There Is Still Light To Work!

I must work the works
of him that sent me, while it is day:
the night cometh, when no man can work.
— John 9:4

Several years ago when I lived in downtown Moscow, I frequently used to walk to the local coffee shop in the morning to get a cup of coffee to start my day and to read the Russian newspaper. As I sat at a small table on the sidewalk just outside the coffee shop, I always watched the masses of people who walk by on this street. As they passed by, I couldn't help but ponder the fact that vast numbers of those precious people were going to hell, yet they were completely blind to their dire predicament.

Because of the former Communist government's long-term and violent suppression of the Christian faith, it's most likely that the majority of Moscow's huge population is uninformed about the very real hell that awaits them if they don't accept Jesus Christ as their Lord and Savior. For them, a storm is definitely coming with eternal ramifications, and it absolutely breaks my heart that so many don't even know it.

Think of it! Billions of unsaved people from every corner of the world don't realize that they are sitting directly on the brink of eternal judgment. Clueless to the consequences of sin, they blindly go about their lives as if nothing is amiss — eating, drinking, and taking care of their daily affairs while living a life separated from Jesus Christ. This is a very sad and sobering thought because the Bible plainly states in Romans 6:23 that "the wages of sin is death." And if nobody warns these people, eternal death assuredly awaits them in their future.

This is the primary reason Denise and I moved to the former Soviet Union with our family so many years ago. We were commissioned by God to proclaim the Gospel to this lost Russian generation — to warn them in advance that, if they receive the Lord, they can escape the judgment that ultimately awaits all unsaved humanity. We constantly proclaim this message on television, in books, in literature, in evangelistic meetings, and in church services. And we are so thankful that we have seen literally *millions* of people come to Christ through our ministry and thereby seal their eternal destiny with the Lord!

However, there are still *millions and millions* of lost people to reach who have never heard the good news that Jesus saves, and our job will never be complete until we have reached the largest number of souls possible with the Gospel of Jesus Christ. This problem is not specific to the former Soviet Union; the same is true in every nation of the world, *including the United*

States. Each and every unbeliever needs the saving message that saved and transformed your life and mine, and it is our job to warn them in advance so they can flee that judgment and find safe harbor in Jesus. It is imperative that we use the time given to us *now* to reach the lost and to work while there is still time to work!

In John 9:4, Jesus said, "I must work the works of him that sent me, while it is day: the night cometh, when no man can work." This verse is incredibly important because it contains a strong admonition for every serious Christian. *The attitude of Jesus expressed in this scripture must be our attitude as well.*

Notice first that Jesus said, "I *must* work...." The word "must" is the Greek word *dei*, which always carries the idea of *an obligation* or *a necessity*. This reveals that Jesus *urgently* and *strongly* felt that there was *no option* in the matter. It was *imperative, essential*, and *compulsory* that He properly use His time to reach souls. Thus, the first part of the verse could be translated: "*For Me, there is no option; what is before Me is certainly compulsory....* "

Then Jesus went on to say, "I must work the *works....*" The word "works" comes from the Greek word *ergadzomai*, which is a form of the word *ergos* that by itself simply means *works*. However, when the word *ergos* becomes the word *ergadzomai*, it depicts *intensified work* or *something that is completely energized*. This is not a light matter; it is something that *completely consumes* one's thoughts, attitude, and actions. Thus, when Jesus said, "I must work the works...," this phrase really carries this idea: *"I must give myself completely to the task before Me and do it enthusiastically and passionately....* "

But there is one more very important point. Jesus said, "I must work the works of him that *sent* me...." The word "sent" is from the word *pempo*, which means *to send as a messenger* or *to send on a specific mission*. This means that Jesus was no haphazard messenger. He was purposely sent by the Father for a specific reason, and He was accountable for how He performed His mission. This part of the verse, then, actually carries this idea: "*I was sent specifically for this mission, and I will answer to the One who sent Me for how I carry out this assignment.*"

Taken together, Jesus' statement could be paraphrased as follows:

> *"For Me, there is no option, for what is before Me is certainly compulsory. I was sent specifically for this mission and this moment, and I will answer to the One who sent Me regarding how I carry out this assignment. Therefore, I must give myself completely to the task before me and do it enthusiastically and passionately."*

Jesus was also very conscious of the fact that His time was short and that He had to give Himself wholeheartedly to the task assigned to Him while the opportunity was available. He said, "I must work...while it is *day*...." The word "day" is the Greek word *hemera*, and it describes the *daylight hours* when it is possible to see and to work without hindrance. Jesus went on to explain that "...night cometh when no man can work." The word "night" is the Greek word *nuktos*, and it describes the *darkness of night* when it is impossible to see clearly and therefore impossible to work.

Jesus knew that the opportunity before Him was limited. This is true of most opportunities God places before us. If we delay or hesitate too long, the opportunities God gives us will pass us by. It is urgent that we — *like Jesus* — make the decision to esteem every God-given opportunity as a special gift that *cannot* be wastefully squandered. Time is a precious gift, and opportunities for the Kingdom are open doors provided by God Himself. Therefore, if God has given you a space of time when you can freely work without hindrance, you need to embrace it as a God-given gift and fervently seek to fulfill what He has called you to do.

Think of how many people you know who were given a remarkable opportunity to do something tremendous, but failed to take advantage of the moment. Because of laziness, hesitation, fear, or a "take it easy" mentality, the opportunity given to those people slipped away and was lost. *Don't let this describe you!* If God has given you a moment when you can work to achieve something tremendous — or if an exceptional prospect stands before you that will enable you to make a difference in someone else's life — then like Jesus, you must give yourself *enthusiastically* and *passionately* to the task that lies before you. These kinds of opportunities are usually short-term, so you must seize the moment *now* while it is still day!

This is exactly how Denise and I feel about our work in the former Soviet Union. Right now the door is wide open for us to work without hindrance, and we fully comprehend that we must work passionately and enthusiastically during this time we've been given. Denise and I are not here on a vacation or a pleasure trip. We were purposely sent by the Father to win souls while it is still day, and we know that we will give account to Him for what we do with this precious opportunity He has given us.

Souls are *precious* to God — so precious, in fact, that He sent His only Son to the earth to redeem people with His blood. Since people are that precious to God, they must be precious to us as well. Therefore, let's use the God-given opportunities we have, regardless of where we live, to warn people that a life lived apart from Jesus will result in *serious* eternal consequences. Let's do all we can to bring them into the safe harbor we have all found in Jesus Christ!

MY PRAYER FOR TODAY

Father, wherever I may reside, I am on a mission field. I was sent when Jesus said: "Go into all the world and preach the Gospel." You have given me many opportunities to make Christ known through my words, the works of my hands, or the associations You have brought across my path. Each window of opportunity You opened before me was time-sensitive. Some I seized in swift obedience; others I let close through procrastination, laziness, or plain disobedience. Father, I repent for wasting time and opportunities because souls were affected or neglected by my choices. Holy Spirit, I ask You to help me be sensitive to the spiritual needs of others and to obey You quickly when You prompt me to release Your love and truth into people's lives. I make a fresh commitment to worship You by working to reach, warn, and rescue as many lives as possible so they can have eternal life in Jesus Christ!

I pray this in Jesus' name!

MY CONFESSION FOR TODAY

I confess that I will place first things first. I will reverence God and esteem what He values. People are precious to God; therefore, people are precious to me. Daily I will thank God for the gift of my salvation through Jesus Christ. I will also show Him my appreciation daily by doing all I can do to tell as many people as I can that there is a Heaven to gain and an eternal hell of never-ending torment to shun. I will not hesitate. I will not draw back. I am compelled to work while it is day, before the window of time closes and the hour comes when no man can work.

I declare this by faith in Jesus' name!

QUESTIONS FOR YOU TO CONSIDER

1. Do you ever think about the vast number of unsaved people you know? If you were one of them, wouldn't you want a good friend to tell you the truth about Jesus and thereby help you avoid eternal judgment?
2. Do you have a prayer list for people that are unsaved? Who is on that list? How often do you pray for them? If you were unsaved, wouldn't you want someone to be praying for you?
3. Are you sensitive to opportunities that the Holy Spirit gives you to share Christ with those who are unsaved? What is a recent opportunity that the Holy Spirit gave you to share Christ with someone?

APRIL 19

The Power of Money in the Realm of the Spirit

If therefore ye have not been faithful
in the unrighteous mammon,
who will commit to your trust the true riches?
— Luke 16:11

One of the biggest issues people face — and one that people pray to get victory over in their lives — is in the *financial realm*. If getting your finances into shape is one of *your* desires, I'm certain this *Sparkling Gem* will be very important for you.

As we first saw in the January 5 *Sparkling Gem*, how you handle your finances is a very spiritual issue. According to Luke 16:11, your finances — how you manage and respect them — is a test

God uses to assess whether you're ready for higher levels of blessing, prosperity, responsibility, and greater authority. In this verse, Jesus clearly taught that God watches how you manage your money, and that is what helps Him determine if you are ready for promotion. This is precisely what Jesus meant when He said, "If therefore ye have not been faithful in the unrighteous mammon, who will commit to your trust the true riches?"

It is very important for you to understand what Jesus is telling us in this verse. In the Greek, the word "faithful" is the word *pistoi*, which expresses the picture of a person who is known to be *faithful, responsible, conscientious*, and *trustworthy*. This is in comparison to a person who is *impetuous, thoughtless, rash, irresponsible*, and therefore *not trustworthy*. Therefore, this verse could be taken to mean: *"If you are impetuous, thoughtless, rash, irresponsible, and untrustworthy with unrighteous mammon, who will commit to your trust the true riches?"*

Whatever this "unrighteous mammon" is in this verse, it is so important that managing it *unwisely* has the power to disqualify us from receiving true riches from God. So it is very important that we understand what the "unrighteous mammon" is that Jesus is speaking about in this verse!

The word "unrighteous" comes from the Greek word *adikia*, which in this verse is used to convey the idea of something *unspiritual, common, worldly*, or *something that belongs to the realm of human beings*. The word "mammon" is the word *mamonas*, a very old Greek word that denotes *money* or *wealth*. When these words "unrighteous mammon" are used together as they are in this verse, it denotes *common, worldly money*, along with all of its buying power in this earthly sphere.

Furthermore, when Jesus referred to "true riches," the word "true" is the Greek word *alethinos*, which means *real, bona fide, genuine, indisputable*, or *authentic*. You see, money, which seems so powerful in this earthly realm with all of its buying power, is nothing compared to the power of God. Heavenly power and heavenly riches far surpass the power and authority of money. For those who have proven themselves faithful and reliable, God will upgrade the level of spiritual power and authority that operates through them. But according to Jesus' words in Luke 16:11, before God upgrades this level of spiritual power and authority in a person's life, first He watches to see how he or she manages money — that's the *big* test!

In other words, if you are not faithful, responsible, conscientious, and trustworthy with money — which is a lower form of power in this earthly realm — *why* would God promote you to greater levels of spiritual power, responsibility, and authority?

How you manage your money and what you do with it is far more important than you may have ever realized. It's good that you want to get your finances in shape and get out of debt, but you need to know that how you handle your money is a big test. If God finds you faithful with money, the lowest form of power in the world today, He will know you can be trusted with real spiritual riches that are unequaled in power.

Taken together, a correct interpretative translation of Jesus' words in Luke 16:11 could be rendered:

"If you are impetuous, thoughtless, rash, irresponsible, and untrustworthy with regular ol' money and all of its buying power in this earthly realm, who will commit to your trust the indisputable, true, bona fide riches?"

By listening to the Spirit of God, using common sense, exercising self-control, and planning your purchases in advance, you can live a life that is more debt-free than the way you're living right now. It will take determination to do it, but if you really want to become free of debt — and remain free forever — it is possible to achieve it.

But most importantly, you need to know this: If your spending habits are so out of control that you don't tithe and cannot give to other works that the Holy Spirit prompts you to support, you're failing the test God uses to determine whether you're ready to be promoted into higher realms of spiritual power, responsibility, and authority. *Your money is the big test that God uses to determine if you are ready for that next big promotion!* Since this is what Jesus meant in Luke 16:11, doesn't it make sense that you should take a fresh look at how you're using and managing your money?

So let me ask you this question: Since God *is* looking at how you manage your money, do you think He finds you faithful and therefore ready for a big promotion — or do you think God finds you lacking and therefore not ready for the next step up in His good plan for you?

Most of the world — *including the Christian community* — longs for more financial freedom and less debt. Especially at this time when so many people have been hit across the world with financial crisis, God's people are asking Him for wisdom and resolutions to very pressing financial challenges.

The fact is that most of the world is in some sort of financial debt. This means there are very few people who are financially free. Nations, families, and churches are all in debt. But just because the rest of the world has fallen into this trap, and lives like this doesn't mean *you* have to fall into this same pattern and become trapped by debt that dominates your life. You can make the decision once and for all to be financially freer than you've ever been before. If you will stick with your decision, God will help you reach your goals and make that freedom a reality in your life.

And by proving yourself faithful with "unrighteous mammon," God will know that you qualify for higher levels of spiritual power. It may seem to be a very simplistic view about money and divine power, but this is exactly what Jesus taught!

MY PRAYER FOR TODAY

Father, I take a fresh look at how I handle my finances. It is not Your will for me to be in bondage to anything — including and especially to debt. I make the decision once and for all to be financially freer than I've ever been. Holy Spirit, I ask You to reveal to me the ways I can exercise more wisdom and restraint in financial matters, so that you can count me trustworthy with the true riches of Your Kingdom.

I pray this in Jesus' name!

MY CONFESSION FOR TODAY

I declare that from this day forward, I will give more attention to listening to the Spirit of God, using common sense, exercising self-control, and planning my purchases in advance so I can live a life that is more debt-free than the way I'm living right now. I desire to be and to remain completely free from any financial hindrance so I can give and go without hindrance. In all my affairs, especially in the area of my finances, I commit to making choices that prove me to be a faithful steward of the natural power and influence God has entrusted to me so I can be trusted with true spiritual riches for the glory of God and the blessing of others!

I declare this by faith in Jesus' name!

QUESTIONS FOR YOU TO CONSIDER

1. If you were free of debt, what are the ways you would be able to allot more money to the Gospel and to meet the needs of others?
2. Do you struggle in obeying God with your tithe and offerings? Do bills and credit card interest payments affect whether or not you give your tithe and offerings to the Lord? If so, what specific changes do you need to make to assuage any guilt you might be carrying in your soul because you know you're robbing God (*see* Malachi 3:8)?
3. If you are handling your money wisely, can you see how it would show Jesus that you had reached a level of maturity that would mean you could be entrusted with true riches?

APRIL 20

Does God Ever Resist Anyone?

God resists the proud, but gives grace unto the humble.
— James 4:6

We live in a day and age when the discipline of the Lord is rarely addressed from the pulpit. However, His discipline is a clearly taught biblical principle, and if we don't respect it and willingly submit to it, we will assuredly discover its truth in a less pleasant manner. Pay careful attention to what you read today, because it can make a giant difference in what you experience in this life!

In James 4:6, James addressed believers who were not living according to God's plan. In some way, they were violating God's principles, and they were doing it blatantly. So James wrote to them and reminded them of the serious consequences of their behavior, saying, "God resists the proud, but gives grace unto the humble."

In this verse, we find that the word "resist" is the Greek word *antitasso*, a military term that depicts *the orderly arrangement of troops to successively wage combat against the non-compliant.* It is a deliberate, premeditated arrangement of military might to crush an enemy. The whole notion of the word *antitasso* in the context of James's message is that if the arrogant will not willfully bow, God will *arrange* events so that they will bow regardless of whether it is willful or forced. One way or another, the proud *will* bow. God, however, invites them to humble themselves willingly rather than be humiliated forcibly.

The word "humble" is *tapeinos* — a word, which in this case, describes *a person who was formerly arrogant but has become humble.* In other words, this individual previously succumbed to pride, but he came down from that haughty position to become *obedient* and *conform* his behavior to fulfill God's commands. Hence, *tapeinos* can accurately be translated *to make small, to reduce one's self-importance,* or *to humble oneself* from previous arrogance. According to James, those who do this on purpose — that is, believers who willfully submit to God's commandments and turn from their arrogant ways — will become recipients of "grace." In the context of James 4:6, it means that even though they had run afoul in their attitude toward His commandments in the past, they will receive "grace" to avoid the otherwise unavoidable discipline of the Lord *if* they willingly submit to God, come back under His authority, repent, and adopt an attitude of humility. That is why James exclaimed, "Submit yourselves therefore to God...."

The word "submit" is *hupotasso* — a compound of *hupo*, which means *to place one's self under another*, and *tasso*, which is the same word used above to describe *a deliberate arrangement of military forces.* Used together in one word, it becomes *hupotasso*, and it portrays an individual who willfully places himself under (*hupo*) authority. Rather than go his own way, he places himself back under command (*tasso*). There is nothing accidental or haphazard about it. He has chosen to come under authority and has willfully arranged himself under his commanding officer.

In these verses, James appeals to those who arrogantly disregard God's commands and urges them to realign themselves back under God's authority. James calls on them to fall in line, submit themselves again in obedience to God, and thus escape divine discipline. If erring individuals retain their current course of action, they will be met with divine discipline. But if they respond to Christ's plea and reposition themselves back under His authority and thus change their behavior, it is possible for them to avoid the divine discipline that Christ is preparing to lovingly carry out in their lives.

The discipline of the Lord is just as real today as ever before. If a child of God deliberately ignores God's Word and knowingly goes astray, God will graciously give him an opportunity (perhaps many opportunities) to come back home of his own free accord. But if that person is really a child of God and refuses to come into compliance with what He has set forth in His Word, then

God — out of great love for that person — will take other measures to bring him or her back home. It may not feel like it at the time, but this spiritual discipline is divine love in action!

MY PRAYER FOR TODAY

Father, I thank You for Your divine discipline. It is a safeguard to me and also proof of your great love. I ask You to help me see where my attitudes or actions are not in alignment with Your Word and Your ways. Father, I know that You resist the proud and I don't want to be resisted by You! I willingly choose to humble myself beneath Your mighty hand so that I won't be humiliated as a consequence of needing to change my ways.

I pray this in Jesus' name!

MY CONFESSION FOR TODAY

I confess that I am quick to hear and quick to obey. I walk humbly before God and His grace abounds in my life. I am not rebellious or stiff-necked, but I yield to the promptings of the Holy Spirit and I remain pliable in the Lord's hand, as I deliberately, day-by-day, keep His words before my eyes and I continually ponder them in my heart. I choose to cultivate a sensitive and obedient heart, and the Holy Spirit helps me to judge myself so I won't need to be judged.

I declare this by faith, in Jesus' name!

QUESTIONS FOR YOU TO CONSIDER

1. Have you ever experienced the discipline of the Lord? I'm talking about a moment when you refused to listen to what God was telling you, so God found another way to get your attention.
2. What is the primary way that God speaks to get your attention if you are willfully not listening? It's different for every person, so in what ways does God act that get *your* attention?
3. God's intention is love when He disciplines you or me. After you've received the discipline of the Lord, did you become aware of what the Lord's discipline had spared you from experiencing? How did it make you better understand that you are truly and deeply loved by God?

Even though believers ran afoul
in their attitude toward God's commandments
in the past, they will receive "grace" to avoid
the otherwise unavoidable discipline of the Lord
if they willingly submit to Him, come back under His authority,
repent, and adopt an attitude of humilty.

APRIL 21

Choose To Let It Go!

Forbearing one another, and forgiving one another,
if any man have a quarrel against any:
even as Christ forgave you, so also do ye.
— Colossians 3:13

Every day we encounter opportunities to get upset with people about something they did or said. If we let down our guard and indulge in these urges, we will live in a continual state of frustration and strife, and our spiritual lives will suffer dramatically. Sometimes it can be very difficult to convince our minds to overlook a perceived slight, forgive the offender, and move on with our lives. However, the Bible offers us a powerful strategy that can be used to cultivate peace in our relationships: We must learn to extend grace to others and to realize that *humans* act *human*.

In Colossians 3:13, the apostle Paul wrote, "Forbearing one another, and forgiving one another, if any man have a quarrel against any: even as Christ forgave you, so also do ye." This verse specifically outlines how we are to respond to people in our lives who disappoint or upset us. And since life is filled with disappointments, it's important for us to understand exactly what Paul meant when he wrote these words.

Paul began with the phrase, "Forbearing one another…." This word "forbearing" is from the Greek word *anechomai*, which means *to endure one another*, *to put up with one another*, or *to have tolerance of one another*. It is the opposite of acting intolerant or being short-tempered with other people. At some point along the way, we all become frustrated with our friends, family, coworkers, and acquaintances. In those moments, the most Christ-like attitude to demonstrate may be to simply *show forbearance* and *let it go*. That doesn't mean we have to compromise or ignore an obvious problem; however, it does mean that sometimes taking the higher road means *shutting our mouths* and *letting go* of the offense or disappointment.

That's why Paul said in this verse that sometimes *forbearing* or *putting up* with the people you interact with in life is the highest road you can take. So when your flesh gets offended or you find yourself wanting to nitpick someone about what you perceive to be his or her failures, take some time to get quiet before God and ask Him what to do. It may be that His highest will in that situation is for you to simply show forbearance and let go of the matter. Although loving confrontation is needed at times, it is not *always* the right course to take.

Paul went on to say, "Forbearing one another, *and forgiving one another*…." The word "forgiving" comes from the word *charis*, the Greek word for *grace*. It carries the idea of *wholeheartedly forgiving*, *freely forgiving*, or *readily forgiving*. This is a step beyond simply being forbearing; it requires our response to go to the next level as we choose to *freely and wholeheartedly forgive with no restraints and no strings attached.* Just as God has extended His grace to us so many times by freely forgiving us of our sins against Him, now the Holy Spirit instructs you and me to extend forgiveness to those who have wronged us or offended us.

In the latter part of this verse, Paul relayed the core of his message, saying, "…If any man have a quarrel against any, even as Christ forgave you, so also do ye." The word "quarrel" is a Greek word *mamphe*, which means *a complaint or grievance against someone* and usually depicts *a complaint that is backed with solid evidence.*

Perhaps someone failed to do what you expected him to do or acted in a manner that was below your expectations of him. Regardless of what you perceive that this person did wrong or what "quarrel" you have with him, the Bible commands you to forgive "even as Christ forgave you." *Isn't that what Christ did for you?*

It's difficult for me to imagine why any of us would refuse to forgive someone else for a perceived offense in light of how graciously God has forgiven *us*. Certainly we are *all* guilty or worthy of blame! *How could we ever forget that it was for our dreadful sin that Jesus died on the Cross?* Jesus bore unspeakable suffering by taking on punishment He didn't deserve — and He did it *freely* for us.

Now Paul urged us, "…As Christ forgave you, so also do ye." You and I didn't deserve the forgiveness we received, but God forgave us anyway. He forgave us for all we have done in the past, and His mercy is so boundless that He continues to forgive us in the present when we ask for forgiveness. *Now we who are forgiven have a responsibility to forgive.*

So if you're having a day filled with opportunities to get upset with people and you feel yourself sliding into a state of frustration and strife, take a moment to pause and meditate on the truths of Colossians 3:13. When you remember how much you've been forgiven by Christ — and by others whom you've deliberately or accidently wronged in the past — you'll realize you don't have a right to stay upset with *anyone*!

MY PRAYER FOR TODAY

Father, I repent for allowing myself to become angry, frustrated, and unforgiving. That is wrong and I refuse to yield to selfishness any longer. No matter what has been said or done, I have no right to harbor ill will — especially when You have commanded me to forgive others as You have forgiven me. Jesus, You paid a horrific price for my sins. Even as You hung dying on the Cross at Calvary, You prayed not only for me but also for the person I'm upset with now. Lord, I deeply apologize. If I had been focused on You instead of myself, I would not have become upset in the first place. Help me to see this person and this situation through Your eyes. I choose to get over this offense right now. I let this drop and I refuse to think on my feelings anymore. Instead, I will seek to honor You in this matter. Holy Spirit, teach me how to love as Jesus loved me.

I pray this in Jesus' name!

MY CONFESSION FOR TODAY

I confess that I take heed to myself and I refuse to walk in unforgiveness, bitterness, or strife. I cannot control what others may say or do, but I am responsible for the condition of my own heart. I do not give place to the devil by indulging selfish thoughts or emotions. Neither do I attempt to justify my own negative behavior in response to what upset me. Instead, I choose to give place to the love of God, which is shed abroad in my heart by the Holy Spirit who indwells me. And I make a daily decision to love and to forgive others as God through Christ has loved and forgiven me.

I declare this by faith, in Jesus' name!

QUESTIONS FOR YOU TO CONSIDER

1. Can you think of someone whom you wronged, intentionally or unintentionally, but regardless of your bad behavior, they took the high road and forgave you for it?
2. Maybe you have a personal quarrel with someone right now and can even claim to have evidence to back up your position. But is it really worth the lack of peace that it's creating in your life? Is this a fight you should be fighting, or would it be more productive to just let it go and forget about it?
3. Have you had other instances in your life when you got upset with someone and held on to it for a long time, but then you finally woke up and realized it wasn't worth the lack of peace, so you decided to forgive? How much precious time was wasted that could never be recaptured because you got upset? Have you considered that this may be something you're going through right now? Why don't you choose forgiveness, move on, and let the Lord deal with it in His own way?

APRIL 22

A Guaranteed Investment

But my God shall supply all your need
according to his riches in glory by Christ Jesus.
— Philippians 4:19

Over the course of the last few decades, it has become very apparent just how temporary and shaky the world economic system actually is. We have witnessed the stock market plummet multiple times in the United States and in many other major markets around the world as well. Global markets reeled in the wake of these dramatic events as established financial accounts were reduced or even obliterated in just a matter of hours.

These troubling economic events reveal the great importance of investing financially into the Kingdom of God. The truth is that investments made into God's Kingdom are the only ones that have an absolute guaranteed return. This truth is clearly outlined in Philippians 4:19, which contains one of the most important financial promises the Bible gives us as believers. It says, "But my God *shall* supply all your need according to his riches in glory by Christ Jesus."

Christians constantly claim this verse over their lives. But many do not understand the context in which Paul wrote this verse and exactly what it meant for both his Philippian audience and what it means for themselves. As you'll see in today's *Sparkling Gem*, this verse applies to *givers*. In fact, the historical context reveals that the promise contained in Philippians 4:19 can *only* be claimed by people who are givers. But for those who *are* givers, this is God's *absolute guarantee* of abundant financial blessing!

When Paul wrote his epistle to the Philippians, he was incarcerated in one of the worst prisons in the entire Roman Empire. However, because he was a Roman citizen, Paul had the right to receive and send mail. One day as he sat alone in that dark, dank prison, Paul received a letter from the church of Philippi. It had been hand-delivered by a Christian brother named Epaphroditus, and as Paul read the letter, he quickly read that Epaphroditus had also brought a *special offering* that the church of Philippi had sent to him.

In the Roman penal system, an imprisoned Roman citizen had the legal right for his friends or family to put money into a special "account" held in his name. He couldn't access the money while he remained in prison, but if he was finally released, those funds were given to him so he could have money to start his life over again. Therefore, it was common for family and friends to bring money to the prison and deposit it into the account of their loved one in case he was fortunate enough to be released at a later time.

When Epaphroditus came from the church of Philippi, he brought Paul a letter that let the elderly apostle know the saints were praying for him. In fact, Paul specifically mentioned their prayers of agreement in Philippians 1:19. And accompanying this letter was a special offering, which was placed into Paul's account at the prison so he would have money to start life over again when he was released back into society.

That financial gift meant a lot more than money to Paul. First, it meant his friends were so full of faith that he would be released that they were putting money into his account and *preparing* for his release. This was faith in action that brought encouragement to Paul. He called it "an odor of a sweet smell" (*see* Philippians 4:18), which simply meant their actions were like a breath of fresh air!

It was in response to the Philippian believers' offering and generosity that Paul wrote: "But my God shall supply all your need according to his riches in glory by Christ Jesus" (Philippians 4:19).

You have to remember that the Philippians had just given a sacrificial gift to Paul. In response to that gift, Paul said, in effect, "Because of what you have done, now look what God is going to do for you. He *is going to supply* all your needs according to His riches in glory by Christ Jesus!"

Paul wrote that God would "supply" all the Philippian believers' needs in light of their giving, just as He will do for us in light of *our* heartfelt giving. The word "supply" is the Greek word *pleroo*, which means *to fulfill* or *to make full.* In other words, if we have any kind of want or need in our lives, *God will take that want and fill it.* God doesn't have any kind of shortage in Heaven. According to Philippians 4:19, He fulfills our needs according to His "riches" in glory by Christ Jesus. The word "riches" is the Greek word *ploutos*, which describes *immense wealth* or *riches beyond imagination.* It is where we get the word for a *plutocrat*, which describes *a person who possesses riches so immense that they are seemingly immeasurable.* God is the original Plutocrat; He knows no lack and has no insufficiencies!

When you go out of your way to meet the needs of the Gospel, God will go out of His way to make sure *your* needs are met. It is the law of sowing and reaping restated in another way. In other words, when you meet the needs of God's Kingdom, He will see to it that your needs are met — *but* when God meets *your* needs, He will do it *lavishly, abundantly, excessively,* and *richly*!

I encourage you to quit thinking that God wants to give you just enough to help you scrape by. According to Paul's words in Philippians 4:19, God wants to bless givers beyond anything they could ask, dream, or imagine! He wants to completely *fulfill* all their needs! So if you're a giver, you truly have something to shout about, because Philippians 4:19 was written specifically for you. *It is yours to claim!*

In this time of uncertainty and instability in world financial markets, it's time for you to lay hold of this promise and believe God to release a divine supply of provision that is reserved especially for givers. This heavenly reserve has been set aside and kept for *you.* God is ready to open His heavenly account and lavishly demonstrate that He will be faithful to you, regardless of what is happening in the world markets. His goodness and His faithfulness are not affected by world economies — *and if you are a giver, you qualify for God to meet your needs right now*!

If you're not a giver, it's never too late to get started. Start today by sowing into the work of God at your church, in your neighborhood, or to a ministry like ours that is touching a part of the world with the Gospel. The moment you start sacrificially sowing is the moment you qualify for Heaven's resources! God is just waiting to see what you will do. And when He sees you move to action — *that* is the trigger that causes Him to swing into action and begin to pour out Heaven's resources to meet your own needs!

MY PRAYER FOR TODAY

Father, I believe it is Your will for my needs to be met, and, as a giver, I lay hold of Your promise to supply ALL my needs according to Your riches in glory by Christ Jesus. I admit that I have been anxious at times because I paid attention to financial markets as well as to my personal financial situation. But You, Lord, are my source. You are ready to demonstrate that Your goodness and Your faithfulness to me are not affected by world economies. I will continue to give sacrificially to the Kingdom of God, knowing that as I give, I activate the law of seedtime and harvest, and You will pour out Heaven's resources to meet my needs. I receive Your provision today because You are faithful.

I pray this in Jesus' name!

MY CONFESSION FOR TODAY

I confess that I am a sacrificial giver and I have something to shout about because Philippians 4:19 is mine to claim! I qualify for God's promise to supply all of my needs according to His riches in glory by Christ Jesus. I lay hold to God's promise, and He faithfully meets my needs lavishly, abundantly, excessively, and richly!

I declare this by faith in Jesus' name!

QUESTIONS FOR YOU TO CONSIDER

1. Did you know that Philippians 4:19 was written only for givers and that it is their special promise from God?
2. In what ways have you seen God fulfill the needs in your life? Why not take a few minutes to reflect and remember all the various ways God has supernaturally fulfilled your needs? Then you might make a list and put it in the back pages of your Bible as a permanent record of God's faithfulness to you as a giver!
3. What needs do you have right now? What would God have you do to trigger a release of divine answers into your life?

APRIL 23

Discerning God's Plan for Your Life

But as it is written, Eye hath not seen, nor ear heard,
neither have entered into the heart of man, the things which
God hath prepared for them that love him. But God
hath revealed them unto us by his Spirit....
— 1 Corinthians 2:9,10

From time to time, we all struggle to discern the best course of action for our lives. Which decision is right? Which is wrong? What job should we take? What university should we attend? Whom should we marry? Should we pursue a secular career or go into full-time ministry? These questions are common to us all and they go on and on and on.

In the Old Testament, knowing the will of God was truly difficult because the Holy Spirit didn't reside in people's hearts; therefore, they struggled tremendously to discover God's plan for their lives. In their efforts to uncover His will, people would seek special signs and divine signals. They'd even go visit prophets who lived in their region in an attempt to find answers and gain knowledge. God had prepared so many benefits for His people! But because the Holy Spirit didn't live in their hearts at that time, they struggled with knowing what He wanted them to do and were unable to see much of what He had provided for them or what His plan was for their lives.

However, the situation couldn't be more different today. As believers, we now have the Holy Spirit living inside our hearts — and He has come to reveal to us all the answers we need! Yet all too often, many Christians still live like people under the Old Covenant, depending on special signs, divine signals, or advice from others. Perhaps it is because they never developed their spiritual sensitivity or learned to recognize the voice of the Holy Spirit. Regardless, this should *not* be the case!

The Holy Spirit has come to dwell within us, and He wants to tell you and me everything we need to know!

In First Corinthians 2:9 and 10, the apostle Paul wrote to us about the Holy Spirit's ministry to reveal God's plan to us. He said, "But as it is written, Eye hath not seen, nor ear heard, neither have entered into the heart of man, the things which God hath prepared for them that love him. But God hath revealed them unto us by his Spirit...." Notice he declared that God has "revealed" His plan to us by His Spirit. The word "revealed" is a translation of the Greek word *apokalupsis*, which is a compound of the words *apo* and *kalupsis*. The word *apo* means *away*, and the word *kalupsis* is the Greek word for *a veil, a curtain*, or *some type of covering*. When compounded, they form the word *apokalupsis*, which is normally translated in Scripture as the word *revelation*. This new word literally means *to remove the veil* or *to remove the curtain* so you can see what is on the other side.

This word *apokalupsis* plainly refers to *something that has been veiled or hidden for a long time and has suddenly become clear and visible to the mind or eye*. It is the image of pulling the curtains out of the way so you can see what has always been just outside your window. The scene was always there for you to enjoy, but the curtains have blocked your ability to see the real picture. As soon as the curtains are drawn apart, you can suddenly see what has been hidden from your view. In that moment when you see beyond the curtain for the first time and observe what has been there all along but not evident to you — *that* is the picture of what the Bible calls a "revelation."

So Paul was proclaiming in this verse that when the Spirit of God came to dwell within us, one of His major missions was to remove the veil that once obstructed our view. The Holy Spirit is continually at work in us to help our eyes to see, our ears to hear, and our hearts to fully comprehend the specific, special plans that God has meticulously prepared for each one of us!

Keep this thought uppermost in your mind and heart in the days to come: The Holy Spirit — the Great Revealer — lives inside you, and He wants to reveal to you God's blessings, promises, provisions, and plans for your life! Thank God, you're not living like people did under the Old Testament. You don't have to look for special signs, divine signals, or a prophet to discern God's plan for your life.

Right inside your heart is the greatest Source of revelation on planet earth — the Holy Spirit! *If you will develop a spiritual sensitivity and learn to listen to His voice, He will reveal everything God has prepared for you so you can get on with your life and do exactly what He intricately planned for you to do!*

MY PRAYER FOR TODAY

Father, I thank You that the Holy Spirit is a Revealer of truth. He will lead and guide me into all truth and show me things to come. I thank You that I never need to worry or even wonder about what You want me to do in any area of my life. If I ask You for wisdom and open my heart to hear, the Holy Spirit will make Your will clear to me. I praise You for Your wonderful plan and for helping me fulfill my part in it for Your glory!

I pray this in Jesus' name!

MY CONFESSION FOR TODAY

I confess that the Lord guides me continually by His Spirit within me. I trust in the Lord with all my heart and don't lean to my own understanding. In all my ways I acknowledge His wisdom and His presence, and He meticulously directs my steps to follow the good path He has prepared for me!

I declare this by faith in Jesus' name!

QUESTIONS FOR YOU TO CONSIDER

1. Can you think of a specific moment when the Holy Spirit "revealed" an answer that you desperately needed to know? How did He reveal that answer to you?
2. Have you ever had a "revelation" — a moment when the Spirit of God supernaturally removed an invisible veil that obstructed your view of things — and when that view was removed, you could see everything you needed to see and know exactly what you needed to know?
3. What are you doing in your life right now that is a direct result of a special revelation from the Holy Spirit? Maybe it's more than one thing, so why not write down your thoughts and demonstrate to yourself just how much the Holy Spirit has revealed the will of God to you?

APRIL 24

Remembering Your First Love

Remember therefore from whence thou art fallen,
and repent, and do the first works; or else I will come
unto thee quickly, and will remove thy candlestick
out of his place, except thou repent.
— Revelation 2:5

As we walk with the Lord, there is always a danger that as each of us grows older in our spiritual walk and become more structured, polished, refined, and doctrinally developed, we will slowly start to forfeit the zeal and spiritual fire we once possessed. What we once held as precious has a tendency to seem routine over time, and as we become accustomed to God's precious Spirit in our lives, too often we unintentionally begin to simply "traffic" in the things of God.

I don't know a single mature Christian who hasn't had to fight this temptation, as the reality of the lost condition he or she was delivered from gradually becomes a distant memory. It's a subtle backsliding that occurs in the very act of serving God.

A good example of this is found in the story of the church of Ephesus, a renowned church in the Roman province of Asia (modern-day western Turkey) that was founded by Paul in the First Century AD. These early believers had come to Christ in a blaze of glory and, from the onset of their congregation, experienced profound demonstrations of God's power. They witnessed people delivered from idol worship, liberated from evil spirits, and many healed in a myriad of truly miraculous ways. Zealous for Christ, they had burned all their occult books and magical incantations — which were worth a small fortune — thus demonstrating a deep and sincere repentance in their willingness to completely sever their new lives from their pagan past.

In its early years, the church of Ephesus burned like a spiritual inferno. The Ephesian believers' vibrancy and excitement inspired the same passion in other churches and spiritual leaders throughout the Roman Empire. But as the years passed, the zeal the Ephesian church had once possessed for the things of God slowly ebbed away. Knowledge increased, but the believers' fiery passion for Jesus seemed to diminish. Undoubtedly, as the church grew, so did its members' schedules, routines, habits, customs, and traditions. The subtle backsliding that often occurs when Christians become involved in serving God seems to be precisely what happened to this great church. The Ephesian believers were so busy serving Jesus that they lost their intimacy with Him. It is also likely that they experienced a loss of joy in their service, since joy is impossible to maintain without a vital connection to the Savior.

Revelation 2:4 tells us that the Ephesian believers had lost their "first love." In other words, they had lost the simplicity and passion once associated with their early love for Jesus Christ. This tells us how far they had unintentionally drifted from the fire and zeal that once characterized them. For this reason, Jesus urges them to stop everything they are doing to "remember" the simple but precious relationship they had with Christ before they became so spiritually sophisticated. He says, "Remember therefore from whence thou art fallen, and repent, and do the first works; or else I will come unto thee quickly, and will remove thy candlestick out of his place, except thou repent" (Revelation 2:5).

The word "remember" comes from the Greek root *mneia.* In ancient literature, this word denoted *a written record used to memorialize a person's actions, a sepulcher, statue, monument, or tombstone.* It is very significant that the word *mneia* can be translated *a sepulcher.* This suggests that the Ephesian believers' early experiences with Christ had become *buried* by 30 years of activity. Jesus urged them to dig through all the clutter of their schedules, routines, and activities so they could "remember" their vibrant beginning. Like dirt on a grave, the busyness of ministry had buried what was once precious to them. By using the word "remember" — the Greek word *mneia* — Jesus implored them to unearth those early times when their faith was tender and new — to dig deep in order to recall and recover their powerful past. Once they remembered, they would be able to see how far they've drifted from the vibrancy that once marked their beginnings.

However, the word "remember" (*mneia*) also refers to *a statue* or *a monument.* This tells us that some memories should stand tall in our lives forever and never be forgotten. The purpose of a *statue* or *monument* is to put living people in remembrance of a significant historical event or person. That statue or monument is intended to *memorialize* a historical event or a deceased hero that future generations should never forget.

Statues, monuments, and tombstones are made of metal or stone; therefore, they endure many years without human effort. *But memories must be deliberately maintained and cultivated if they are to remain vital in our hearts and minds.* And if significant memories are not deliberately passed onto future generations, they become lost under the overgrowth of life, just like a neglected grave with no tombstone. It doesn't take too long before the location of such a grave to be completely lost. People will walk across it and not even know that the remains of a precious person lay buried beneath their feet.

In the same way, important memories are easily forgotten. Adults forget their childhood; nations forget their heritage; and Christians forget their early beginnings with Jesus. In Revelation 2:5, we discover that churches can forget their past. Years of activity and Christian service can so consume a congregation's energy and strength that they begin to forget the great work of grace God performed in their hearts. Weariness, busy schedules, and new programs to implement year after year all have the ability to wear down a body of believers — turning all their activity for God's Kingdom into spiritual drudgery, slowly reducing what was once fresh and exciting into a monotonous, religious routine. Soon the early memories of coming to Christ are buried under an overgrowth of activity and spiritual weeds. Once-thankful people begin to forget how wonderful God's grace was when it first touched their hearts.

The word translated "remember" is in the present active imperative, which means Jesus wanted the Ephesian believers *to be continually mindful* of their past. What God had done in their midst was a wonderful memory that needed to be memorialized among them for all generations. And if they took an honest look at themselves and compared their present to their past, they would see what Jesus knew about them — that they were *fallen* compared to the zeal and the spiritual passion that had once burned in their hearts.

The word "fallen" means *a downfall from a high and lofty position.* The Greek tense doesn't describe the process of falling, but rather one who has *already completely fallen* and who is now living in *an already completely fallen state.* For the past 30 years, the church at Ephesus had hosted the world's greatest Christian leaders, experienced the power of God, and become more advanced in spiritual knowledge than any other church of that time. The Christian world looked at this congregation as the ideal church. However, we must never forget that what can be carefully hidden from human eyes can never be concealed from Jesus' eyes. Hebrews 4:13 tells us that "...all things are naked and opened unto the eyes of him with whom we have to do." Christ is often not impressed with the things that impress us. He often sees a different picture than others see. Others may have been impressed with the heritage of the Ephesian church and its roster of famous personalities who passed through its doors — but in Jesus' eyes, it was "fallen."

If this illustrious church with its list of remarkable accomplishments could be called "fallen," it is clear that any church — regardless of its notable beginning or enduring fame — can also be "fallen." *This means one's past is not a guarantee for the future.* If an individual or a church is not completely devoted to doing whatever is necessary to retain spiritual passion, it is likely that over the course of the years, that passion will slowly dissipate, as was the case with the church in Ephesus.

Just as Christ spoke to the congregation at Ephesus, I believe He is compelling us to return to Him and rekindle the fire that once burned so brightly in our hearts. We need to unearth the precious memories of what our walk with Jesus was like at the beginning — and honestly see if we have retained that same passion, or if we've let it slip over the passing of time due to schedules, routines, or other reasons. *Jesus is calling us.* He cries out to everyone who has an ear to hear what He is saying.

Is it possible that Jesus is speaking to you today, asking you to reevaluate the condition of your own spiritual passion?

MY PRAYER FOR TODAY

Father, as I evaluate my own heart, I realize that I have allowed distractions and the cares of life to dull my passion for You. Somewhere along the way, I became more focused on working for You than walking with You. I repent and turn away from the prayerlessness and hardness of heart that led me to this state. Renew a steadfast spirit within me. Restore to me the joy of Your salvation; lift me up from the place where I've fallen; and uphold me by Your generous Spirit. Teach me afresh to reverence You and to truly love You by being a doer of Your Word and not merely a hearer only.

I pray this in Jesus' name!

MY CONFESSION FOR TODAY

I confess that I give to the Lord the glory due His name. I am His and my heart is wholly devoted and undivided in its affections. I choose the better part of being with Him above all else — that I may know Christ and become increasingly transformed into His likeness.

I declare this by faith in Jesus' name!

QUESTIONS FOR YOU TO CONSIDER

1. Can you think of a time when your spiritual passion burned more brightly than it is burning today? How were you different than you are today? Why not write two columns on a piece of paper, with the left column listing words and phrases that described what you were like earlier, and the right column to express words and phrases of what you are like in comparison today?
2. Do you recall a time when you were like a spiritual burning inferno? How would you describe your spiritual fire today? High, medium, low, gone, consistent?
3. Remembering the passion that once burned brightly inside you may take some time. Why don't you schedule a quiet time when you can let your mind drift back to those early days and let your heart relish those precious memories that first set your heart on fire?

APRIL 25

Preaching Is Not Always Easy!

Now while Paul waited for them at Athens,
his spirit was stirred in him, when he saw that city
wholly given to idolatry.
— Acts 17:16

I am honored to come from a family that has had multiple missionaries in our family tree and to be one of those whom the Lord has called in that capacity. Because I have observed various relatives make great sacrifices to fulfill their calling, I have gained great respect for people who leave their families and relocate to other parts of the world to preach the Gospel. Often they are required to live and minister in regions that are very dark spiritually. But as a result of their willingness to go where others don't want to go, the Church has been established and societies have been transformed. Thank God for such heroic men and women of faith! We must not forget to pray for those who are ministering on the front lines.

You may not live on the spiritual "front lines" as many missionaries have been required to do. But wherever you live, you have probably found that it is not always easy to preach the Gospel. The devil hates the Gospel, and he tries with all his might to extinguish its light. And because he can't put out the light itself, the enemy often attacks the *light-bearer* — the preacher. This is the reason we as ministers often find ourselves under attack. But regardless of the assaults that may be waged against us, we just need to stick to our mandate to preach and keep marching forward by faith. As we do, the forces of darkness that try to oppose us will eventually surrender to the shining light of truth!

One such occasion occurred when the apostle Paul entered the city of Athens. Athens was so spiritually dark that Paul's "...spirit was stirred in him, when he saw that city wholly given to idolatry" (Acts 17:16). I want to give you a brief glimpse into the environment Paul encountered the day he entered Athens nearly 2,000 years ago. I assure you that if Paul could preach in the midst of the wicked atmosphere of Athens, you can fulfill *your* ministry wherever God has called *you* to minister!

What Paul saw in the city of Athens was so appalling that the Bible says, "...His spirit was stirred in him...." In the Greek text, the word "stirred" is the Greek word *paroxuneto*, which is derived from the word *paraxusmos*, a compound of the words *para* and *xusmos*. The word *para* means *alongside* and carries the idea of *being close*. The second part of the word is the Greek word *xusmos*, which describes *something sharp*, such as a knife, and normally indicates *a very sharp situation*. When you put the two words together, the compound word describes *someone who has taken something so close to heart that it has become a sharply felt agitation to him*.

This word carries such a sense of agitation that the word *paraxusmos* has been translated *to call into combat*. I like this translation, because Paul didn't retreat when he saw the darkness of the city. Instead, he charged full-steam ahead to wage warfare against the evil forces of the city.

Preaching God's Word is the highest form of spiritual warfare, for the mighty two-edged sword called the Word of God has the greatest power available in this life to banish the forces of darkness from any environment! In the New Testament, the word *paraxusmos* usually means *to irritate*, *to incite*, *to anger*, *to inflame*, or *to enrage*. Based on multiple uses of this word in the New Testament (*see* Acts 15:39; Hebrews 10:24), we can easily ascertain that Paul was deeply troubled and ready to pull out his sword of the Spirit to fight because of the wickedness he saw all around him.

The verse goes on to tell us exactly what disturbed Paul so deeply: "...When he saw that city was wholly given to idolatry." The word "saw" is the Greek word *theoreo*, which means *to gaze at* or *to look upon*. From this same root, the word *theater* is derived. The usage of this word is important in this context. It tells us that idolatry was so visible that Paul perceived the whole city as a huge stage set for the practice of idolatry. When the verse says Paul "saw" the idolatry, the Greek uses a participle. This means it could be translated that Paul "...saw and continually kept on seeing...."

Yes, that's right! Everywhere Paul looked, he saw idols, statues, gods, and deities, for they could be found on every street and corner in the city of Athens. He found himself encircled with thousands of marble (but vividly painted flesh-colored), naked idols of Greek gods. As noted in the previous paragraphs, there were so many idols in Athens that the original Greek could literally be translated, "...he saw and continually kept on seeing..." that the city was "wholly given to idols."

That phrase "wholly given to idols" is from the word *kateidoolos*, a compound of the words *kata* and *doulos*. The word *kata* gives the idea of *domination* or *subjugation*. The word *doulos* is the word for *a slave* who is sold to his owner and has no say-so in his life whatsoever. This slave completely belongs to and lives to fulfill the wishes and desires of his master. When the words *kata* and *doulos* are compounded, the new word forms the word *kateidoolos* that is used in Acts 17:17. It means *to be completely dominated by, subject to, and sold out to the rule of idols*. In other words, the idols were the masters and the people of Athens were the slaves, living their lives under the dominion of idolatry. The worship of idols and multiple gods was so woven into the fabric of Athens that it literally dominated every part of the inhabitants' public and private lives.

One expositor says that the word *kateidoolos* can be translated *sunk in idolatry*, *rife with idolatry*, or *gross idolatry*. This makes sense, for it is a known fact from archeological findings and historical records that there were at least 30,000 idols on public display in Athens, not counting the thousands of miniature idols that were kept in people's private residences. There were so many "gods" in Athens that one First Century historian wrote that it was "easier to find a god than to find a man" in Athens!

It was into this environment that Paul entered in Acts 17. With the sword of the Spirit and the Word of God in hand, he began to preach and wage spiritual warfare!

I realize that extensive information about the ancient city of Athens has already been written. Nevertheless, I would like to elaborate just a little more to give you the backdrop against which Paul stood as he began his preaching ministry in this city that was rife with idols and sunk in depravity. I believe this is important for you to understand because you might be thinking that your city or territory is too dark and difficult to take for the Kingdom of God. But if you compare your environment to what Paul faced in Athens, you will realize something: If Paul could preach in that evil atmosphere, then you can also fulfill *your* ministry — no matter *where* God has called you.

Athens was an intellectual city. It had been home to many famous people over the centuries, including the dramatic writers *Sophocles*, *Euripides*, and *Aristophanes* and world-class historians such as *Herodotos* and *Thucydides*. In addition, seminal philosophers and orators such as *Socrates*, *Plato*, *Aristotle*, *Demosthenes*, and *Isocrates* had also called Athens home. As a city, it was celebrated for its literature, history, music, and philosophy, and it was here that the idea of *democracy* was first born. Yet it was also in this highly educated, sophisticated atmosphere that *homosexuality* abounded, especially among the upper class who considered it *fashionable* to practice homosexuality.

Even today Athenian homosexuality is visible in the vast quantities of ancient Athenian vases that have survived from that period. These vases are covered with renderings of warfare, sports, relationships, life in the sauna, etc. — and an enormous number of them graphically portray homosexual relationships in every sphere of life. The vast quantities of these depictions make it clear that *homosexuality* was considered "normal" in Athenian society.

The Acropolis, the central mountain around which Athens was built, was a vast religious complex covered with a multitude of temples dedicated to a multiplicity of gods, including *Apollo*, *Pan*, and *Asklepios* (the Greek god of healing). The great theater of *Dionysus* was also there — a theater so enormous that it could accommodate thousands of people per event.

The Acropolis temples and their sculptures were beautiful almost beyond belief. Every temple and statue was not simply the white marble facades that we see today in museums; rather, they were painted in brilliant colors. The columns and ceilings of the buildings were all painted blue, red, and green, and real gold was applied to all the building ornaments. The figures in friezes were painted to look real. For example, flesh-colored warriors fought on a bright red background, and the armor and horse trappings on the sculptures were actually made of bronze. Blues and reds predominated. The temples of the Acropolis buildings were *beautiful.*

But the most outstanding of all temples on the Acropolis was the *Parthenon* — a temple so breathtakingly magnificent that it was considered to be one of the Seven Wonders of the Ancient World. Deep inside this edifice was the monstrous statue of Athena. Forty feet in height, this massive statue was carved of wood and completely covered by ivory to represent flesh. She was also dressed in a huge garment that had substantial jewels and vast amounts of gold interwoven into its rich fabric. In her left hand rested an enormous shield made of bronze. In her right hand, she held a *Winged Victory* that was the actual size of a human being. Upon her chest was the breastplate of the gods, and around the base of her shield was a coiled serpent. On Athena's head was an immense helmet that gave the onlooker the impression that her power was unequaled, and all the gigantic weapons she wore were fashioned of the highest quality bronze.

A great altar was located at the front base of the statue. Upon this altar, nonstop sacrifices were made with as many as 100 or more oxen being offered at one time. Billowing swirls of smoke from all the sacrifices and incense used in worship filled the air, creating a mystical effect. Worshipers stood with mouths dropped open in awe as they looked up through the smoke at the majestic, gold-covered image and Athena's lifelike eyes peered down at them.

Athena was definitely the main focus; however, there were so many deities in this city that one ancient historian wrote, "A day in Athens without taking account of the gods and their temples would be a day spent with your eyes half-closed."[5]

Idols were on every street, at every street crossing, and at every prominent location in the city. The briefest stroll through the city would expose a visitor to countless gods. And none of this takes into account the diminutive temples built at the entrance of every house, where family members would place their own preferred idol and make sacrifices to it every day as a part of their daily routine.

All of this is just a brief taste of the wicked, dark, insidious idolatry that prevailed in ancient Athens. Now you can see why Acts 17:16 says, "Now while Paul waited for them at Athens, his spirit was stirred in him, when he saw that city wholly given to idolatry." As noted earlier, the word "stirred" tells us that Paul was *terribly troubled* by all that he saw around him in Athens. Making this even more offensive to him was the fact that he was a Jew and wasn't accustomed to idolatry at all. Idolatry was forbidden by God in the Ten Commandments. (Exodus 20:4 says, "Thou shalt not make unto thee any graven image....") Therefore, this abundant display of idolatry would have made Paul feel especially uncomfortable and troubled.

---

[5] William Stearns Davis, *A Day in Old Athens: A Picture of Athenian Life* (Needham Heights, MA: Allyn & Bacon, 1914), p. 204.

Nevertheless, Paul recognized that for that moment in time, he was in Athens for a reason. So rather than grumble that the city was too hard, too dark, or too spiritually challenging, Paul took advantage of the situation for the sake of the Gospel! Acts 17:17 tells us, "Therefore disputed he in the synagogues with the Jews, and with the devout persons, and in the market daily with them that met with him."

In other words, Paul found a place to preach and begin to declare the truth, thus combating the wickedness of the city! Acts 17:17 says he "disputed" in the synagogues and in the market daily. The word "dispute" comes from the Greek word *dielegeto*, which means *to dispute, to argue*, or *to contend.* The tense used means *to repeatedly dispute*. Because Paul did this repeatedly, we can assume that he probably ran into opposition. But he didn't tuck his tail and run! Instead, Paul kept pressing and pushing forward to reach into the hearts and minds of his listeners.

When God calls us to fulfill *our* assignment, we must be willing to do what He asks and to go where He sends us, even if it means we must work in places that are difficult or in cities and nations where it is spiritually hard. Yes, we may encounter challenging situations that make it difficult for us to do our job. But regardless, we must decide that, with God's help, we will push through each distraction or problematic situation and refuse to be affected by what we see, hear, or feel.

- What is the assignment God has given to you?
- Does it seem that you are in a hard and challenging environment?
- Are you tempted to give up because the opposition is great?
- Is your flesh recoiling from the place to which you know God has called you?

Don't give up and give in to your flesh! I guarantee you that if the apostle Paul could do what God asked him to do in a place as dark and difficult as Athens, then you can also do what God has asked *you* to do where you live! Your situation may be tough; nevertheless, you are probably *not* surrounded by 30,000 idols! So it's time to quit complaining about how difficult your situation is and make the rock-solid decision that you are going to conquer those evil forces and get the job done!

Never forget — you are not alone! You have the power of the Holy Spirit within and alongside you to help you fulfill your divine assignment!

MY PRAYER FOR TODAY

Father, I ask You to help me adjust my attitude about the difficult situation I am facing in life. I have been tempted to complain about how hard this assignment is. You have positioned me where I am for a reason. I repent for the times I have grumbled, complained, and entertained my feelings because I was relying upon my own strength instead of Your mighty power. Holy Spirit, You are my Helper and my Standby — I know that with Your power, I can do all things through Christ. From this moment onward, I ask You to help me focus my faith and confident expectation on You. Show me how to navigate my situation and my current station in life by the power of the Holy Spirit who will put me over the top every time!

I pray this in Jesus' name!

MY CONFESSION FOR TODAY

I confess that I am an overcomer and can do all things through Jesus Christ. I can do whatever He calls me to do; I can go wherever He calls me to go; and I can fulfill whatever assignment He gives me because His Spirit lives within me and is empowering me! I look away from all that would distract or discourage me as I look to Jesus, the Author and Finisher of my faith! What You have called me to do, You have equipped and enabled me to do! I will not complain about the difficulties of life. Instead, I choose to take advantage of every opportunity God has given me and to make the most of every situation I encounter in life. With God's help, I can turn any difficult situation into an opportunity for advancement and victory!

I declare this by faith in Jesus' name!

QUESTIONS FOR YOU TO CONSIDER

1. Can you think of a time when you were challenged by a problematic situation that seemed insurmountable, yet you were able to forge through the ordeal and turn it into a glorious victory?
2. What are you facing right now that tempts you to give up? After reading about what Paul encountered in Athens and how he refused to back down in the face of darkness, what changes are you going to make as you face your own situation?
3. Can you think of a time in your life when you almost gave up — but because you kept going, it resulted in a new opportunity opening up for you? What would have happened if you had given up rather than pressed forward?

APRIL 26

Never Insult Your Audience!

Then Paul stood in the midst
of Mars' hill, and said, Ye men of Athens,
I perceive that in all things ye are too superstitious.
— Acts 17:22

Once as I was listening to Christian television in the United States, I paused on one channel to hear what a particular minister was saying to his audience both at home and on air. As

I listened, I was amazed at the derogatory way in which he was speaking to people. He spoke to them as if they were idiots! This minister obviously thought the way he was preaching to people was funny or cute. But by "talking down" to his audience, he gave the impression that he was on a much higher level than they were and that they were honored to be able to sit under his magnificent and wise teaching.

I was totally turned off by the minister's preaching style and felt sorry for the people who had to listen to him each week! I thought, *I don't care if I ever hear this guy preach again!* The truth is, his message was *awesome*, but his delivery was *atrocious*! After all, who likes being spoken to in a condescending manner?

This is why it is so important for us to be careful in the way we reach out to people with the Gospel — *especially unbelievers*!

One of the best demonstrations of how to reach into the hearts of unbelievers is found in Acts 17:22, where Paul was addressing the high court of Athens on Mars Hill. Paul's preaching in that idolatrous court is a shining example to us all of how to cross cultural boundaries, how to appeal to unbelievers, and how to address people in a way that *opens* their hearts instead of closing them. This is Paul's clearest and most lengthy message directed toward a pagan audience recorded in the book of Acts. There is a wealth of lessons to be learned from his approach to these lost listeners that will help us cut across cultural barriers and direct our message into the hearts of the unbelievers God is calling us to reach.

The verse tells us, "Then Paul stood in the midst of Mars hill, and said, Ye men of Athens, I perceive that in all things ye are too superstitious."

First of all, Paul said, "Ye men of Athens...." The truth is, Paul was likely speaking to the most pagan crowd he had ever addressed in his entire life! These weren't just sinners; these were blatant sinners involved in the deepest, darkest secrets of the occult and, most likely, in depravity and perversion of the lowest nature. If he had taken the approach of some, he would have said, "You sinners and rebels!" However, had Paul taken this approach, he would have immediately closed the hearts of his listeners. He would have been viewed as an intellectual idiot, and the door to the Gospel in Athens would have been slammed shut!

What did it hurt for Paul to speak to these pagan leaders with dignity and respect? Whether or not he agreed with them, they were people made in the image of God Almighty, and they represented the highest court of the land. Therefore, although these Athenian men were sinners, Paul addressed them with respect and honor.

Second, Paul said, "Ye men of Athens, I perceive...." The word "perceive" is the Greek word *theoreo*, which means *to gaze at* or *to look upon*. This is the root from which we get the word *theater*. By using this word, Paul alerted the high court with the knowledge that he had been watching and studying them and their culture. This let them know that he had not shunned them or shut them out. As a guest in the city, Paul had watched them. As one might study a performance on stage, Paul had witnessed their city, their culture, and their religion.

Third, Paul said, "Ye men of Athens, I perceive in all things that ye are very superstitious...." I want to draw your attention to the word "superstitious," which comes from the Greek word *deisidaimonia*, a compound of the words *deilos* and *daimonia*. The word *deilos* means *fear* or *respect*, and the word *daimonia* is the word for *demons*, although in Classical Greek language, it could also be used to mean *gods*.

But Paul didn't say, "I perceive that in all things you are demonized and eaten up with black magic, witchcraft, Satanism, and demonic activity that will doom your souls to hell!" Instead, Paul appealed to the Athenian leaders on a much higher level. He said, "...I perceive in all things that ye are very superstitious...."

The Greek tense used for "superstitious" is comparative, which means Paul wasn't just calling them religious; he was actually telling them:

- "...You are *deeply* religious and devoted to your gods...."
- "...Compared to people I've met elsewhere, you are among *the most religious* I have ever encountered...."

Paul never said he agreed with them or their false doctrine. He just found something about which he could compliment them, thus building a bridge between them and himself. With this one statement, that bridge was built and Paul's audience received him with interest rather than as an enemy. This method kept the door open so he could deliver his entire message to the end, enabling him to shine the Gospel light into their world of darkness. All of Paul's listeners would not receive Christ that day. But because he took this approach rather than a negative, condemning, stone-throwing style of preaching, the Holy Spirit was able to reach into the hearts of some of those who heard Paul, and they gave their lives to Jesus Christ as a result.

The truth is, the people on that high court were not just idol worshipers. As long-term citizens of Athens, they were most likely *deeply religious* and *brazen* idol worshipers. Because the city was sunken into moral depravity, it is probable that these men on the high court also led morally depraved lives, as was characteristic of Athenians.

But attacking and insulting these men on the high court wouldn't have gotten Paul anywhere. So rather than insult them, he found common ground on which he could appeal to their souls and buy enough time to deliver the message of the Cross to them. As a result of his approach, there is no sense in this passage that the Athenian leaders felt attacked, talked down to, or insulted. Paul's approach in speaking to these lost men was so respectable that they permitted him time to explain the Gospel message in full. *Thus, this high counsel of men heard the Gospel of Jesus Christ clearly and intelligently in a respectable open forum.*

Paul didn't start his message with a confrontation of sin, but before he had finished speaking to that respectable crowd of judges, they had clearly heard the message and been confronted by God's requirement of repentance. Paul worked his way into God's demands as the message developed. If he had started there, it would have been like a slap in the face to his listeners, even though it was truth. That kind of direct approach would have been a sure-fire way to make certain that the crowd never heard another word he had to say!

When you treat people with heartfelt respect, it always keeps the door open, even when they don't agree with you. In fact, showing sincere respect is a door opener to *every* person's heart, regardless of culture, language, or skin color.

When we speak to people who are different than us or who lead a life far from the righteous standard God demands, we must remember that the way we approach them could determine whether or not they ever hear a full presentation of the Gospel. Even if they are sinners, they are made in the image of Almighty God and demand respect as human beings.

So rather than malign unbelievers with disrespectful or condemning words, ask the Holy Spirit to show you how to find common ground on which you can build a bridge into their hearts. *Building a bridge with the love of God is always going to be a much more effective way of reaching people for Him than slapping them in the face with ugly words that bring judgment!*

MY PRAYER FOR TODAY

Lord, I thank You for what I have just read. This has helped me rethink the way I am addressing people who are lost and living their lives without You. I ask You to forgive me for the times I have approached them in a condescending or a negative way, and I ask You to help me find a way to reach them that will build a permanent bridge between You and them. I pray for their hearts to be open as I share with them so I can shine the truth of Jesus into the dark recesses of their lives. You are the best at reaching all our hearts, Father, so I ask You to teach me to do this as You would do it.

I pray this in Jesus' name!

MY CONFESSION FOR TODAY

I confess that the Holy Spirit is teaching me how to reach people in a positive way with the message of Jesus Christ. I am kind, tender, sincere, and respectful in the way I speak to all people including people who are lost in sin. I declare that even though I walk by God's standards of what is right and wrong, I am not haughty or insulting to people who are different than I am. With God's help, I am learning how to reach out to those who are lost and without God and to those who are sinking lower and lower into a sinful lifestyle. Because of the respect and love I show to them as humans created in the image of Almighty God, their hearts are wide open to hear the truth that God is asking me to speak into their lives.

I declare this by faith in Jesus' name!

QUESTIONS FOR YOU TO CONSIDER

1. Can you think of a preacher or speaker who "talks down" to people when he or she preaches? Who is that person? Why do you think this person takes this approach when preaching to people who willingly came to his or her meetings?

2. As you read about Paul's approach to the judges on Mars Hill, what did you learn about your own approach to unbelievers? Based on what Paul did, what do you think you should do differently?
3. Can you think of some common ground you can use to build a bridge of mutual respect between you and the people you are trying to reach? Why don't you take a little time to pray and ask the Holy Spirit to show you that common ground so it can become the bridge you need to cross over into their hearts and share with them the life of Jesus?

APRIL 27

An Unlikely Sermon Illustration

For as I passed by, and beheld your devotions,
I found an altar with this inscription:
TO THE UNKNOWN GOD.
Whom therefore ye ignorantly worship,
him declare I unto you.
— Acts 17:23

In yesterday's *Sparkling Gem*, we examined Paul's tactful and effective ministry strategy as he sought to share the message of the Gospel with the highly educated pagan crowd on Mars Hill in the city of Athens. Today I want to focus on his *message*. As Paul stood in the amphitheater and looked into the faces of the Athenian judges who were listening intently to him, the Holy Spirit dropped a sermon illustration into his heart that was *pure genius*.

Paul began by saying, "For as I *passed by*…." The Greek word used here carries the idea of *a leisurely walk* or *a stroll*. This is a word that a tourist might use to describe *a peaceful, paced walk* on a sunny afternoon. The Greek tense used implies *multiple strolls* throughout the city, which means Paul has taken the time to observe Athens. As a visitor to this historical city, he hadn't closed his eyes to the city but had taken the time to experience its sights, its sounds, its smells — all the unique characteristics that made Athens what it was.

Paul went on to say, "…And beheld your devotions…." The word "beheld" is the Greek word *anatheoreo*, a compound of *ana* and *theoreo*. The word *theoreo* means *to look upon* or *to gaze at*, and it is where we get the word for *a theater*.

Like a huge theatrical stage, the entire city of Athens was staged for idolatry. Since idolatry was the biggest show in town, Paul had carefully observed it like a patron at the theater who watches every act of a play. He had studied the Athenians' devotion to idolatry and knew the level to which this city had sunk into this abominable practice. However, in Acts 17:3, this Greek word *theoreo* is compounded together with *ana*, a word that means *up*. Thus, the word *anatheoreo*, translated "beheld," actually means *to look upward*.

In addition to the thousands of small idols that people kept outside the front door of their private homes, Athens was filled with huge images that towered over the heads of those who passed through the city. These statues were so monstrous that as Paul strolled through the city, he had to *look upward* to see them! But instead of referring to these idols as the abominations they were, he calls them "devotions." The word "devotions" is derived from the word *sebo*, a Greek word that means *to stand in awe, to reverence, to worship*, or *to venerate*.

Calling those idols *abominations* would have gotten Paul nowhere. In fact, using that kind of terminology would have gotten him kicked out of court and evicted from the city! Rather than lose this God-given opportunity to speak to the brightest minds in Greece at that time and impact that city with the Gospel, Paul continued to build a bridge to his listeners. If he had said that the city's idols were abominations or cursed images, he would have been correct. But instead, he kindly called them "devotions," which means *objects of worship*.

As Paul took strolls through the city and observed city life, he could see that the people of Athens were genuinely in *awe* of their gods, as evil as these idols were. The Athenians truly *venerated* and *reverenced* the idols as *objects of worship*, even though they were nothing more than objects carved of wood and stone — a truth that Paul clearly stated later in his message. But at that point in his message, Paul chose to call them objects of worship, further widening the door of the listeners' hearts so they would receive the next vital point he wanted to make in his message.

Looking up at the listening judges, he went on to tell them that as he had passed through the city, he had "...found an altar with this inscription: TO THE UNKNOWN GOD." Then he continued, "Whom therefore ye ignorantly worship, him declare I unto you."

Knowing full well that idols were precious to the heart of every Athenian — especially to Athenians such as the judges who were seated before him — Paul reached deep into the world of Greek culture and borrowed *an idol* as the sermon illustration for the message he was about to preach. If Jewish leaders back home had known what he was doing, they might have fainted! Idols of *any* kind would have deeply offended the Jewish leaders in Jerusalem. But the Holy Spirit had shown Paul that the idol to the UNKNOWN GOD was a divine opportunity to declare to these Athenian leaders *the identity* of the UNKNOWN GOD! Paul then went on to brilliantly make use of this image made of stone to reveal the truth of Jesus Christ to his listening audience!

At this point, Paul had the judges transfixed by his message and shocked by his knowledge of vivid details about the city. Sensing Paul's sincere respect for them, the men gave him their undivided attention as he prepared to shoot the Gospel arrow deep into the darkness of their souls in such a way that it would penetrate their hearts.

Then suddenly — Paul did another astonishing thing! *Right in the middle of his message, he reached into classical Greek literature and quoted the Athenians' own poets and philosophers!* He said,

"For in him we live, and move, and have our being; as certain of your own poets have said, For we are also his offspring" (Acts 17:28).

Today we use this quote in the lyrics of certain Christian songs. But these words weren't written by Christians — they were written in a heathen context and then used by Paul to reach Greek hearts! The words were originally written by Aratus of Soli in Cilicia in 270 BC and by a Stoic philosopher who wrote a hymn to Zeus in approximately 300 BC. If Paul was trying to impress his intelligent audience, he had done it! They had just learned that this was a serious man — so educated that he could even quote by memory from Greek literature!

It was clear to Paul's audience that he had read other materials in addition to studying the Old Testament. Because Paul was not only highly educated, but also *well-rounded* in his education, he could therefore speak freely to this intellectual crowd.

When Paul was a young man studying at the University of Tarsus, he had no idea that he would one day stand before the highest court of Greece and use the information he was studying at that time. What a vivid example this is of our need to cherish what we are presently learning! It is very likely that God will call upon us to use what we have learned in times past to help fulfill our assignment now or in the future.

There are great lessons to learn from Paul's message on Mars Hill. What did he do right?

- Verse 22: *Paul addressed them respectfully*: "Ye men of Athens...." He could have called them wicked sinners, which would have been true — but he would have immediately lost his audience. Paul appealed to them on a higher level of respect and therefore got their attention.
- Verse 22: *He called them religious.* As we saw yesterday, this was a great compliment to them, which caused them to open their hearts to hear his message. Paul could have condemned them for being idol worshipers, but this would have shut their hearts and provoked them to evict him from the court and from the city.
- Verse 23: *He used an altar as the basis for his sermon.* This object that Paul borrowed from their own culture as his chief illustration surely caused these judges to draw nearer to hear what he had to say. He could have said that this altar was an offense to God, but instead Paul chose to use it as an illustration to lead his audience to the Gospel message.
- Verse 28: Paul *quoted the Athenians' own Greek poets and philosophers*, showing them that he was familiar with their culture, literature, and history. This surely impressed the Athenian judges and caused them to respect what Paul had to say. He could have decided to quote only from the Bible, but by choosing to quote from their own literature, Paul grabbed their hearts and provided a common ground that they could relate to.

Imagine how dumbfounded the judges must have been when they realized that the man before them was a man of *intelligence*, not just an ignorant preacher with weird ideas. By the time

Paul was finished, he had fully preached the Gospel from beginning to end. He had even given an invitation, calling on his listeners to repent!

As you reach the people to whom God has called you to minister, ask the Holy Spirit to help you find ways to connect with them so they will open their hearts to you and to the message you have to share with them. The Holy Spirit knows the key to every person's heart. He knows every culture and every nation, so *nothing* takes Him by surprise. If you are willing to listen to the Holy Spirit's direction and do what He tells you to do, He will show you how to build that bridge into people's hearts more quickly than you could have ever done on your own. *Just open your heart and receive what the Holy Spirit wants to show you!*

MY PRAYER FOR TODAY

Lord, I am so thankful that You teach me step by step how to be more effective in the way I witness and share Your love with people. You know the key to every person's heart, so I ask You to give me the key to reach into the hearts of those people You have laid on my heart. I know they are part of my assignment, and I will do whatever You ask me to do in order to reach them effectively. But I ask You to speak clearly to me. Help me understand the proper steps to take and the right things to do so their hearts will be open to receive the love You want to give them.

I ask this in Jesus' name!

MY CONFESSION FOR TODAY

I confess that I am growing wiser in the ways I share Christ with unbelievers. Because I pray and seek the assistance of the Holy Spirit, He is helping me, showing me how to touch people's lives in a way that opens their hearts both to me and to the love of God that I am commissioned to bring to them. I declare by faith that God's Spirit is guiding me and teaching me how to be more effective in my methods of reaching both the unsaved and those who are in deep spiritual need.

I declare this by faith in Jesus' name!

QUESTIONS FOR YOU TO CONSIDER

1. Can you think of effective methods the Holy Spirit has given you in the past that have been successful in opening the hearts of unbelievers so you could share the message of Christ with them? What were some of those successful methods?
2. As you think of the people God has placed on your heart right now, what can you do that will draw them closer to you and thus allow you to ultimately share the best news in the world with them? What acts of kindness can you show them that will make an impression on their hearts?
3. For whose salvation are you specifically praying at this time? If you haven't yet made a list of the unsaved people God has put on your heart, why don't you do it now to help you remember to pray for them every day?

APRIL 28

You Must Make the Most of Every Opportunity!

Therefore disputed he in the synagogues with the Jews,
and with the devout persons, and in the market daily
with them that met with him. And certain philosophers
of the Epicureans, and of the Stoics, encountered him.
And some said, What will this babbler say?
Others said, He seemeth to be a setter forth of strange gods:
because he preached unto them Jesus, and the resurrection.
And they took him and brought him to the Areopagus....
— Acts 17:17-19

Our son Philip is a very talented singer and songwriter, who loves to glorify the Lord with his music. Because of these God-given gifts, he was once invited to take part in one of Russia's most famous talent shows. As parents, Denise and I were thrilled that such an opportunity had been given to Philip, and we knew that this had to be a door opened to him by the Lord. What especially elated us was that he would be singing the song he had written entitled "Two Thousand Years Ago, There Was a Man From Galilee"! It is a powerful song that declares the life of Jesus Christ in a contemporary format.

On the night of the event, Denise and I arrived at the auditorium and walked into the building where the competition was to be held. We were immediately *shocked* at what we saw! The word "dark" doesn't even begin to describe what we saw and felt. It felt as if we had stepped into a cesspool of depravity! Through the years, we've been in a lot of difficult spiritual environments, but this one won the prize! We were literally taken back by the darkness that abounded all around us.

Walking up the stairs to the hallway that led to the auditorium, we could see dimly lit lights barely piercing through the cigarette smoke that filled the air. The smoke was so thick that we had to wave it out of our faces so we could see where we were going. Once we were seated, through the smoke, we could see prostitutes walking among the tables where the audience had been seated for the show. The prostitutes flaunted themselves to advertise their wares and to alert potential customers that they were available for business after the show. Then I looked over at the bar where drinks were being served. All the bartenders — young, handsome, muscular Russian men — had on *very* little clothing as they stood behind the bar so they could show off their toned bodies!

As I looked around the room that night, I told my wife, "This is a pretty grim place to be singing a song about the Gospel. I can't imagine the spiritual opposition our son must feel here. Do you think there is any chance he can win a competition in a place like *this*?"

Just before Philip went to the stage to perform, he came to our table and sat next to us. Denise and I encouraged our son to sing boldly and without compromise. Soon his name was announced, and we watched as he walked confidently onto that stage. In that very dark, wicked atmosphere, Philip picked up his trumpet and microphone, and with his band playing behind him, he belted out his song, "Two Thousand Years Ago, There Was a Man From Galilee"!

Denise and I were stunned by Philip's boldness — and astonished at the response of the crowd. The people applauded and applauded and *applauded.* In fact, Philip was given a longer ovation than anyone else who performed that night! Our son's boldness, courage, confidence, and refusal to be ashamed of what he believed literally knocked his listeners off their feet! To our surprise, Philip walked out of that building that night as the *WINNER* of that national event! And as a result of what happened in that very spiritually dark, sinister place, phenomenal doors of opportunity have opened up to him. The acclaim he obtained that night opened the door for him to preach and sing in places he would have never before dreamed possible!

This kind of response is exactly what the apostle Paul experienced when he was preaching in the market in the city of Athens. Acts 17:17 tell us, "Therefore disputed he in the synagogues with the Jews, and with the devout persons, and in the market daily with them that met with him."

This verse says that Paul disputed in the synagogue and in the "market" daily. We already know what a synagogue is, so I want to focus on that word "market." This word is a translation of the Greek word *agora*, which is the old Greek word describing *the place of commerce, trade, slave-trading, and debate.* The market was a place of commerce, but like all of Athens, it was also a spiritually dark, oppressive place. It was filled with and surrounded by:

- Explicit statues depicting the Greek gods.
- The constant, nonstop, mindless banging of drums coming from the temples of various gods that surrounded the market.
- People headed to the public baths for an afternoon of relaxation and accepted forms of sexual perversion.
- Prostitutes who gathered here to offer their services to the people coming to the public baths.
- Philosophers and debaters who gathered at one central location in the market to listen and argue about their beliefs and points of view.
- Slave traders selling and buying slaves right next to those who traded and sold livestock.
- People shopping for their food on their way to or coming back from one of the temples in the neighborhood.

This was the "market" where Paul preached in Athens! Certainly this wasn't the perfect atmosphere for preaching. But when a minister is pioneering a work or working in a territory where no one has gone before him, he sometimes has to take advantage of whatever opportunity is available to him. As Paul surveyed the city, it must have become apparent to him that the market was the best place for him to reach the people of the city — *so he made the most of the opportunity*!

As I travel the world, I often hear people speak about how "hard" their city is to reach with the Gospel. They tell me with great confidence that their city is among the most *un*churched, *un*religious, occultic cities in the world. But I can assure you with even greater confidence that very few ministers, if any, are preaching in cities "harder" than Athens! There was no church in Athens, so Paul took advantage of the only place available to preach — the Athenian "market." It was undoubtedly noisy and filled with a wide assortment of traffic and distractions. The market was a very difficult place for Paul to preach, yet he hung in there and preached "daily." Finally his message became so well known that he was eventually invited to address the most elite group of the city on Mars Hill.

One section of the Athenian market was reserved for philosophers and debaters, who came to draw a crowd and share their ideas. Because Athenians loved wisdom and the attainment of knowledge, people would always gather in this area to listen to the new ideas that were being publicly presented. Then one day when a crowd assembled together to listen as they always did, a newcomer — the apostle Paul — ascended the stone steps to the public podium so he could take his first turn at preaching to an Athenian audience. Thus began Paul's ministry in that city of "disputing daily" with those who gathered to listen in the debaters' section of Athens' market.

Acts 17:18 goes on to tell us, "And certain philosophers of the Epicureans, and of the Stoics, encountered him. And some said, What will this babbler say? Others said, He seemeth to be a setter forth of strange gods: because he preached unto them Jesus, and the resurrection."

According to this verse, three groups were listening to Paul that day:

- Epicureans
- Stoics
- Others

Let's find out more about these groups so we can better understand what kind of crowd Paul was preaching to in Athens.

First, there were the *Epicureans*. Epicureans were a group of people who didn't believe in an afterlife. Their philosophy declared that all there is to our existence is the earthly life we are living now. Therefore, we are free to do whatever fleshly thing we desire to do because there are no eternal ramifications for any earthly actions. The Epicureans are the ones who coined the famous phrase, "Eat, drink, and be merry, for tomorrow we may die." This was a popular philosophy in Athens because it permitted every form of variance, perversion, adultery, and lasciviousness.

The Epicureans were notorious for gross sensuality and depraved forms of behavior. Because they didn't believe in the afterlife or in any form of eternal judgment, they indulged in and encouraged fleshly excesses. Later as the influence of Christianity began to grow, they strongly resisted the Gospel message because of its demands for holy living and its declaration of a future judgment.

The second group in Acts 17:18 were the *Stoics*. Philosophically, the Stoics were diametrically opposed to the Epicureans. Whereas Epicureans encouraged fleshly indulgence and lack of restraint, Stoics taught extreme discipline, self-control, and self-denial. You could say that Stoics were the ultimate perfectionists, so consumed with self-perfectionism that they advocated suicide before failure. It was a completely self-consumed philosophy that focused on man's ability to attain perfection on his own. Later when the influence of Christianity began to grow, the Stoics resisted the Gospel message because it presented man as a sinner, unable to save or redeem himself, devoid of hope without God. Because of their prideful position that proclaimed their ability to attain perfection on their own merits, Stoics perceived the Gospel as an affront and an insult to their intelligence.

Both the Epicureans and Stoics called Paul a "babbler," which comes from the Greek word *spermologos*. This word is a compound of the words *sperm*, the Greek word for *seed*, and the word *logos*, the Greek word for *words*. But when they are compounded as in this text, the new word depicts *a person who seeds a crowd with words, thoughts, or ideas*. This means the Epicureans and Stoics were asking, "Who is this seed-sower who is seeding us with words, thoughts, and ideas that we've never heard before?"

These Greek philosophers didn't realize how right they were when they called Paul a "babbler"! Every day, he stood in the market preaching and thereby habitually seeding that crowd with the heart-piercing truth of God's Word. Paul stood at that public podium like a farmer, throwing his "seed-words" onto the ground of the people's hearts, believing that in some of the hearts of those hearers was good ground. Paul knew what Jesus taught during His earthly ministry — that some hearts are stony, some are shallow, and some are good ground that will produce a 30-, 60-, or 100-fold return. Paul was preaching with the hope that some of the Word he was preaching was falling on good ground that would eventually produce a harvest for the Kingdom of God.

The third group Paul preached to were called *others*. Whoever these people were, they were shaken by Paul's message and said, "…He seemeth to be a setter forth of strange gods…." Acts 17:18 reveals what upset this group: that Paul "…preached unto them Jesus, and the resurrection." These people had never even heard of Jesus!

This was the first time any Gospel preacher had ever been bold enough to venture into this environment to speak that name to these Athenians. So when these people heard about Jesus, Paul was telling them something they had never heard before. This was a very rare phenomenon, considering the fact that Athens was filled with man's wisdom, knowledge, and education. The crowd was hearing about a brand-new god, one they had never heard of before — in a city filled with deities, statues, and idols! This was almost *revolutionary*!

In that dark spiritual environment, the apostle Paul climbed up to the podium, opened his mouth, and began to preach, sowing the seed of God's Word into the hearts of that listening crowd. It wasn't the most convenient place to do it, but the market was the only pulpit he could find. So right there in the middle of the market — surrounded by idols, the swirling smoke of incense, the banging of pagan drums in the background, prostitutes trying to sell themselves, slave traders buying and selling slaves, and people purchasing various items in the market — Paul seized the moment and made the most of his opportunity to preach Christ to the people of Athens.

By his perpetual persistence, Paul eventually got the Athenians' attention! He seeded that crowd so regularly, so consistently, and with such great effect that Acts 17:19 says, "And they took him, and brought him unto *Areopagus*...." Just so you'll know — the Areopagus was the most prestigious place in the entire nation to share a new idea! Only the brightest and most astute, intelligent, and clever people were invited to speak in the Areopagus. When Paul started out in Athens, the Epicureans and Stoics found him intellectually offensive. But eventually, even the brightest minds of Athens wanted to hear what he had to say. *This was a big score for the Gospel!*

I want to encourage you today to make the most of every opportunity you have to preach the Gospel and fulfill your call. So what if you don't have an ideal place to do what God has called you to do? That doesn't mean you can't do it — it just means you have to get creative and find new ways to fulfill your assignment! If you are willing to open your mind and explore new methods and ways of reaching people, I assure you that the Holy Spirit is not short on ideas! He will show you *what* to do and *when* and *how* to do it so you can seed people's hearts and minds with the life-transforming power of the Word of God!

MY PRAYER FOR TODAY

Lord, I ask You to help me become more aware of special opportunities that arise for me to speak Your name and Your Word to people who have open hearts. Forgive me when I get so busy that I forget to tell others about Jesus. I realize that Jesus is the only real solution to life's problems and that I have a special responsibility to share Him with people who don't know Him yet. Holy Spirit, I can only do this if You empower me, so today I am asking You to strengthen me and grant me a new awareness when a door of opportunity stands before me. Give me the boldness to speak Jesus' name in a way that pierces the spiritual darkness and brings answers to those who are in need.

I pray this in Jesus' name!

MY CONFESSION FOR TODAY

I declare by faith that I am bold to sow seeds of truth and love everywhere I go. I am sensitive to God-given opportunities to share the name of Jesus and the Word of God with people who are in need. Because the fruit of the Spirit is produced in my life, I think of others; I see their needs; and I look for ways to help them find the answers they need. The Holy Spirit is my Helper who is always present to assist me as I listen to Him and follow His leading. I am making the decision today to open my heart wider than ever before so God can depend on me to see and help meet the needs of others. Starting today, I am persistent and bold to walk through every open door and proclaim the name of Jesus and the Word of God to those who need to hear God's truth, just as others once did for me!

I declare this by faith in Jesus' name!

QUESTIONS FOR YOU TO CONSIDER

1. Have you ever tried to reach someone with the Gospel who responded by looking down on you as if you were a "babbler"? When that person did this, did you retreat and stop speaking the truth, or did you press onward to sow the seed of God's Word into his or her heart?
2. If you don't have an ideal place to fulfill your ministry right now, is it possible that the Holy Spirit has another creative way for you to reach people that you haven't even thought of yet? Is it possible that you've been so locked into your "normal" mode of doing things that you haven't been able to receive the radical, revolutionary, successful plan that God wants to give you?
3. Why don't you take a few minutes today to quiet your spirit and allow the Spirit of God to speak to your heart and show you how to make the most of the opportunities that are available to you right now?

APRIL 29

Strange Gods and New Ideas

...And some said, What will this babbler say?
Others said, He seemeth to be a setter forth of strange gods:
because he preached unto them Jesus, and the resurrection.
And they took him and brought him to the Areopagus....
— Acts 17:18,19

When we bring new ideas to a foreign culture, it can create an unpleasant reaction among the local people. That's why we must be both careful and anointed as we take the Gospel into cultures that have never heard the Good News of Jesus Christ the way we are accustomed to preaching it.

This is the lesson I learned when I moved to a foreign land where words and actions are perceived differently than they are in the nation where I was born and raised. Words and phrases that had always been familiar to me were new and unknown to those I was trying to reach, and I had to be careful in my presentation, lest I turn people off instead of reaching their hearts with my message. For this reason, I had to learn to be very careful and aware of cultural perceptions, customs, and language as I ministered to the people to whom God has called me to give my life.

This principle doesn't just apply to missionaries living on foreign soil. There are many people in your own city who don't know God and who didn't grow up in church. You can't assume that they understand the words and phrases that are familiar to you as part of the Church world where you have lived much of your life. The Christian community uses wonderful, meaningful terminology that the world doesn't know or understand. For example, the words "amen" and "hallelujah" are dear and precious to us. But to a world that is lost in darkness, those words sound strange — and when you use them, it often makes people want to tuck their tails and run!

When unsaved people hear believers trying to reach them with "Christian-ese," it scares them! This is why we must be careful in the way we present ourselves when we are speaking the Word and representing the name of Jesus. There is no doubt that our message is true and unchangeable. But *we* are the "packages" who carry the message — and how lost people perceive *us* is often what determines whether or not the package is ever opened and the message is ever heard or received.

Certainly we are not to compromise the message or to apologize for who we are and what we believe. We should never back away from the gifts of the Spirit, from the supernatural, or from expressions of worship and praise *in church*. But when we are reaching out to people outside the faith, God expects us to use our heads in the way we approach them. To reach into a lost culture, we must remember that we are leaving the world of "church" and reaching into spiritual darkness to people who are part of a particular "lost" culture. That's why we must have the help and the wisdom of the Holy Spirit as we seek to reach those people with the message of Christ!

Paul's preaching in Athens clearly demonstrates the reaction that can take place when we cross cultures to bring the message of Jesus Christ. Considering the countless numbers of gods, idols, and various deities that were present in Athens, you might assume that Athenians possessed a high rate of tolerance for new gods that someone may have wanted to bring into the mix. But the fact is that Athenians were extremely dedicated to *their* Greek gods and had almost *no* tolerance for foreign gods. They were very committed to their culture and their way of thinking and easily took offense at outsiders who tried to come in and change them.

To get the full picture, you must understand the central role the Greek gods played in Greek life and society. One historian wrote that these gods were such an integral part of the lives of ancient Athenians that they were like members of the people's families!

When it came to foreign gods, the Athenians had an ambivalent attitude. On the one hand, there were many instances where they accepted foreign deities into their own pantheon. But at the same time, the Athenians had a fiercely protective side regarding their culture. This serious view about new gods and new ideas lets us know that the Athenians appreciated their culture. They didn't want an invasion of any foreign gods coming in that would mess up their history, ideas, and beliefs. So the Athenian mindset was to evaluate a new religion with great skepticism — and when Paul stood in the market and presented the message of Jesus, the Cross, and the resurrection, this message was *radical* to his skeptical Greek listeners!

It was completely unacceptable for an ancient Greek to venture out of mainstream idolatry and embrace a new god that, by His very nature as the Son of God, eradicated the validity of all their other deities. In fact, such an action was on the same level as a person who renounced

Greek citizenship to join an enemy force on its way to attack Athens! It has been written that if an Athenian rejected *their* gods in favor of a foreign god, it was the equivalent of *treason*.

From childhood, every Athenian was taught to obey the religion of Athena and to defend her, if needed, in battle. Athenians had worshiped the gods for generations and were very proud of them. They had been raised all their lives on the legends of their religion, and they fully believed that the gods were the reason for Athens' prosperity. The people were so devoted to their gods that even if someone privately didn't believe in them, he would still participate in worshiping them because it was a part of the city's culture.

Despite all this, the religion of Athens was quite elastic. Every man was free to develop his own creed for living and to fashion his beliefs to fit his own lifestyle, very much the way people are doing today. The Athenians were also very superstitious. They prayed to *Zeus* for rain, to *Hermes* for luck in their businesses, and to *Asklepios* for healing. They believed that if the gods were angry at a person, that person could not escape their wrath. On the other hand, if the gods looked favorably upon someone, they would give that person wealth, health, honor, long life, and prosperity for his children.

Even with all their elasticity in what they believed, Athenians were rock solid in their commitment to their religion. All public meetings, court sessions, and public events opened with a sacrifice to the gods. In fact, it was unimaginable that any important public or private act would be attempted without inviting the attention of the gods. For Athenians, it was second nature to talk to the gods and talk about them with others. It was a natural part of life to sacrifice to the gods and to invite them to participate in their daily affairs.

So when Paul stood in the market and preached "Jesus, and the resurrection" (Acts 17:19), he created an almost scandalous event! The listeners were so upset by what Paul was preaching that they exclaimed, "…He seemeth to be a setter forth of strange gods…" (Acts 17:19).

The words "setter forth" is from *katanggelos*, the Greek word for *a messenger*. This word *katanggelos* was frequently used to denote *a messenger sent from the gods or from God to bring a specific message to the people*. This was a correct perception of Paul, for he had indeed been sent by God to Athens to bring the life-saving message of Jesus Christ into the people's darkness and depravity! But when the Athenians in the market first heard the message, they were terrified by the name of Jesus and by the Gospel that Paul preached, accusing Paul of bringing them a message of "strange gods."

The words "strange gods" are translated incorrectly in the *King James Version*. The Greek words used here are *xenos* and *daimonian*. The word *xenos* is the Greek word for a *foreigner* or a *stranger*. Today it is where we get the word *xenophobia*, a term that describes *a fear of strangers*. But the word "gods" is from the Greek word *daimonian*, which literally means *demons*, even though in the Greek world it could also denote *gods*. I remember when I first studied this word *daimonian* many years ago and saw that it could be translated either *demons* or *gods*. I realized the Greeks had so many demons in operation that when demons spoke, the Greeks thought it was one of their many *gods* talking to them! Nevertheless, because this word *daimonian* literally means *demons*, this part of verse 19 could be translated, *"This messenger is introducing foreign demons into our midst!"*

Paul's never-give-up, never-back-up, never-retreat style of preaching created such an uproar in Athens that the day finally came when *"they took him and brought him to the Areopagus…"* (Acts 17:19). The Areopagus was a criminal court where people were often tried for murder or other serious crimes against society. However, it was also used, as in this verse, to determine whether or not new doctrines were considered legal. There was no higher court in Athens, and for Paul to be summoned to this court meant that he finally had gotten the attention of the city with his "daily" preaching in the market. The highest court in Athens, the most brilliant and respected minds in all of ancient Greece, wanted to hear Paul's Gospel message for themselves.

When Paul finally stood before this high court, Acts 17:20 tells us that those in attendance said, "And thou bringest us certain strange things to our ears: we would know therefore what these things mean."

Notice they said, "And thou bringest us certain *strange things*…." The words "strange things" is from the word *znidzo*, conveying the idea of *something that is startling, shocking, surprising, strange, or scandalous*. Paul's message of Jesus, the Cross, and the resurrection was so far out of the range of normality for them that they found it to be completely *scandalous*! To hear that God died on the Cross for mankind and shed His own blood for redemption — that was a *startling* message to their ears! They were *shocked* by Paul's words — but they were also so intrigued that they implored him, "…We would know therefore what these things mean." This sentence in the Greek conveys the listeners' deeply passionate longing to hear what Paul had to tell them! A paraphrased translation could be, "*Please, PLEASE, tell us!*" They didn't want Paul to hold back *anything*. Instead, they wanted him to make a full disclosure of the Gospel he had been preaching to the crowds in the market.

All around Paul were the brightest, most intellectual, and most sophisticated minds in Greece at that time. This was a huge open door for Paul. These judges of the land were pleading with him to fully explain his message. As the highest court of the land, these men were poised to listen. Then afterward they would be required to pass judgment on Paul's ideas that were so strange to their Greek way of thinking and to render a legal decision regarding him and his message.

How Paul performed on this judicial stage could determine the outcome of his life. This could be a great open door, or it could lead to a death sentence. It was in a similar court in this same city, at an earlier time in history, that Socrates was judged and condemned to death for indoctrinating young Greek students with new, non-Greek ideas. Certainly Paul, who was an extremely educated man, must have recalled Socrates' demise as he opened his mouth and began to expound to this high court about the redeeming and saving power of Jesus Christ. Yet Paul forged ahead boldly and preached one of the greatest and most anointed masterpieces that has *ever* been preached in the history of the Church (Acts 17:22-31)!

As Paul began to preach, every word had to be carefully chosen and spoken under the anointing of the Holy Spirit. There was no room for error in his words on that day.

The good news is that just as the Holy Spirit was with Paul, so will He be with *you* when you reach beyond your comfort zone to reach people who are different than you. Paul had no experience as a pagan. But because he depended on the Holy Spirit, he was able to effectively cross those cultural boundaries and reach into the Athenians' world with the saving message of Jesus Christ!

In the same way, God has anointed *you* to reach the people He has placed on your heart. They may be different than you; they may have a different skin color than yours; they may live in a different part of the world than where you were born; or perhaps they are live on a different side of town. But I promise you that the Holy Spirit holds the key to every person's heart. He knows how to reach people in every culture. And if you will lean on Him and carefully follow what He tells you to do, He will give you the method and the manner to reach a particular group of people, no matter how difficult it may seem to you. The Spirit of God knows the path to each person's heart, so learn to lean on Him as you go forth into new territory to speak His name!

Paul never backed down, never apologized, and never violated what he believed in order to preach to the Athenians. But he recognized that he was speaking to Greeks, so he ministered to them in words and phrases that they could understand. (In the next *Sparkling Gem*, we will cover Paul's message at the Areopagus in greater detail, and you will be greatly helped by seeing the smart, Spirit-inspired things Paul spoke of when he was beckoned to the highest court in Greece.) In the same way, you should never compromise what you believe when you are presenting the Gospel, but you must be smart in the way you package the message!

So pray diligently before you barge into new, unknown territory. Do your homework so you'll know the kind of culture God is calling you to reach. Then ask the Holy Spirit to give you His insights on how to reach the people in that culture. One thing you can know for sure: *If you follow the Holy Spirit's leading and do precisely what He puts in your heart to do, your rate of success will be infinitely higher than it would be if you tried to do it all alone!*

MY PRAYER FOR TODAY

Lord, I am so thankful that the Holy Spirit is my Guide and Teacher. Because the Spirit of God is in my life, I am not an orphan who has to figure out everything on my own. I am willing to follow You — to do whatever You tell me to do and to go wherever You tell me to go — but I am depending completely on You to lead me, anoint me, and empower me as I take the steps of faith that are directly before me. Lord, I am willing to take the message to the people You have called me to reach. But I am asking You to show me how to most effectively package my message so they will receive the life-changing truth of the Gospel!

I pray this in Jesus' name!

MY CONFESSION FOR TODAY

I confess that I am careful in what I do and what I say as I reach out to people who are lost. They don't know Jesus; therefore, I must learn to speak to them in a way that touches their hearts and souls. Holy Spirit, You are the One who knows every man's heart, so today I declare that You are giving me the keys, the words, the methods, and the ways to reach the audience that God has put on my heart. I have the message that saves lives, and the Holy Spirit is teaching me how to package the message so it will be received and people's lives will be redeemed.

I declare this by faith in Jesus' name!

QUESTIONS FOR YOU TO CONSIDER

1. Can you think of a time when you saw someone totally turn off an unbeliever because of the way he tried to reach that person? What did he do that was so ineffective? It would be good to write down your response so you can think about it and learn as much as possible from that experience.
2. Can you think of someone who effectively reaches unbelievers and has brought many people to a saving knowledge of Jesus Christ? What is this person doing that is so effective? I suggest that you take a few minutes to ponder this question; then write down the things this person does that causes people to be receptive to the Gospel so you can learn from his or her example.
3. What group of people is God calling *you* to reach? What do you know about these people? What do you know about their culture and their way of thinking? What are you doing to prepare yourself so you can be more effective in the way that you reach them?

APRIL 30

The Results of Paul's Preaching on Mars Hill

And when they heard of the resurrection of the dead, some mocked:
and others said, We will hear thee again of this matter.
So Paul departed from among them.
— Acts 17:32,33

There are a wide variety of reactions to the preaching of truth. I'll give you an example from my own life — a personal experience I will never forget when I received multiple mixed reactions to a message I preached. I remember how stunned I was at the different ways people responded to what I ministered. To me, the message was thrilling, life-changing, and powerful, and I was so excited about the prospect of preaching it. I could hardly wait for the day to come to deliver what God had put on my heart, since I anticipated that people would respond to it the same way it had affected me. However, when I preached the message, people's reaction was *not* exactly what I expected!

By the time I had finished preaching, it was obvious that some people were visibly blessed. However, others were upset and even furious with what I had said! Then there was a third group that wouldn't immediately respond one way or the other, saying that they wanted to put their opinion "on hold" and think about what I had taught for a while.

I was shocked. I wondered, *How in the world could this message produce such a mixed reaction, and how could it possibly anger people?* I assure you that my intention had *not* been to make anyone angry, but only to speak a word from God that would set people free.

I was so perplexed that I decided to make copies of the message and send it to several nationally known ministers I respected and ask them to listen to it and give me their reaction to the message. As I waited to hear from them, I wondered what kind of response they would give me to this message. As the written responses came back, one after another said, "Not only is this message needed, it is *very* needed — and I would like to schedule you to come preach it in my church!"

Anyone who has been in the ministry long can testify that there is often a mixed response to the teaching of truth. What thrills one person can be a source of irritation to another person. When I was a younger man in the ministry, this varied reaction was confusing to me. But through the years, I have learned to expect the preaching of God's Word to elicit different responses from different people.

Since you will one day stand before Jesus to give account for what you preach, it is crucial that you inwardly know you are saying exactly what He wants you to say; then you must trust the Lord with the results. As God's messenger, you are ultimately responsible to speak what He puts on your heart, regardless of the response from your listeners.

When Paul concluded his message in the Athenian court, he had a very mixed response to his sermon. Acts 17:32,33 tells us, "And when they heard of the resurrection of the dead, some mocked: and others said, We will hear thee again of this matter. So Paul departed from among them."

This verse tells us that "some mocked" when they heard Paul's message. The word "mocked" is derived from the Greek word *echidna*, which is the word for *a poisonous viper*. This word *echidna* is exactly the same word used in Matthew 3:7, Matthew 12:34, Matthew 23:33, and Luke 3:7, when Jesus referred to the religious leaders of his time as a generation of "vipers." By using this vivid word, the Holy Spirit lets us know that when Paul concluded his masterful message, one group was so furious that they wanted *to sink their fangs into him*! They were *livid* and *fuming* because of what Paul preached.

That was one reaction to Paul's message, but there were other reactions as well. Acts 17:32 goes on to tell us, "...Others said, We will hear thee again on this matter." This second group wasn't jumping and shouting, "Amen!" But the fact that they were open-minded and wanted to hear Paul again constituted a *significant* victory for the Kingdom of God. This means they were *interested* — and for judges in the highest court of this pagan land to be interested in the Gospel was a huge development!

This was a massive triumph for Paul's ministry. Sometimes when a door of opportunity remains open rather than slamming shut, that open door is in itself a great success. Sure, these Athenian judges didn't walk the aisle or pray the sinner's prayer. *But they wanted to hear more*, and that let Paul know that he still had an open door into their hearts.

Acts 17:33 says, "So Paul departed from among them." The Bible doesn't explicitly say how Paul felt when he walked out of the amphitheater. However, we do know that he had enraged one group, interested another group, and had no visible proof that anyone would be saved as a result of his preaching that day. It is likely that he felt like a failure or thought he hadn't performed as powerfully as he had hoped.

Although the response to his message was very mixed, there was a small group of notable people who not only heard it but were deeply touched by it. Acts 17:34 says, "Howbeit certain men clave unto him, and believed: among the which was Dionysius the Areopagite, and a woman named Damaris, and others with them." These people believed the truth they heard and desired to know more.

This verse tells us that "certain men clave unto him." I want you to especially notice the word "clave." This word is taken from the Greek word *kollaoo* — a word that means *to glue to, to cleave to, to adhere to, to attach one's self to*, or *to associate with*. There is no doubt that this word conveys the idea of *discipleship* and *faithfully following after someone else*. We know that these individuals were saved as a result of Paul's ministry that day, because this scripture tells us they "believed."

Among this group of new believers was "Dionysius the Areopagite." This man's name indicates that he was named in honor of the Greek god Dionysius, which tells us he had been reared in a *very* pagan home. The Bible also tells us that Dionysius was an *Areopagite*. This word is taken from the word *Areopagus*, which describes the highest court of the land. We therefore know that this newly saved Dionysius was one of the 12 judges who ruled in the highest court in the entire nation.

This man's conversion was no small victory! Because he was one of the 12 judges who ruled the land, he was well known in Athens and throughout all of Greece. The early Christian historian *Eusebius* later wrote that Dionysius became so rooted in the faith that he was eventually named the bishop of the church at Athens and died a martyr's death.

In addition to Dionysius' conversion, Acts 17:34 says that "a woman named Damaris" was also converted as a result of Paul's message in the high court. Although the Bible doesn't give us much insight into Damaris, we do know that, like Dionysius, she was a very wealthy aristocrat. The verse goes on to tell us, "and there were others with them." The original language implies that although this group was not huge, it was a notable group of people who were probably members of the upper class. The seed of God's Word became deeply rooted in their hearts, and they kept the fire burning in Athens long after Paul's departure.

I am sure that Paul must have been perplexed by the mixed reaction he received to his message that day. Just as was true in my case, some were blessed, others infuriated, and others held their reactions to themselves. If you were just counting numbers, it would appear that the message Paul delivered in the Areopagus was no great success. But although the number of people converted wasn't substantial, the *identity* of those converted was of great consequence.

By penetrating the upper class of Athens with the Gospel, Paul pierced the most difficult category of people to reach. These were people of *influence*, people of *power*, and people of *high regard*. Therefore, even though there were not vast numbers of new converts, the influential nature of those who *were* converted provided a significant advancement of the Gospel in Athens.

When you reach people with the message God puts on your heart, don't be misled by the various reactions people have to you and to your message. Know beforehand that some may be *glad* to receive what you say, and some may end up *mad* at you because of the message you have preached. What is most important is that you know *exactly* what God wants you to say or do and then faithfully stick with that message, regardless of the reactions you experience. You will ultimately answer to Jesus, so when you step out to obey what He has told you to do, do it to please *Him*!

Make the decision not to permit yourself to be disturbed or disappointed because the numerical response you anticipated is smaller than you hoped. Even if the numbers are small, it may be that you have reached the heart of someone who will one day have great influence and power. That would make your results very successful indeed!

You may not know for many years the full consequences of your obedience. So if you have done your best to say precisely what Jesus has asked you to say, know that you have nothing left to do but rest your case. Then you can leave the rest of the matter in *His* hands!

MY PRAYER FOR TODAY

Lord, I ask You to help me know exactly what I am to say, how I am to say it, and when I am to speak. Then once I have obeyed You, help me trust You with the results. I admit that I've been affected by people's reactions in the past and have allowed those reactions to influence my obedience in the present. Please forgive me for allowing the opinions of man to affect me, even when I know I've done exactly what You told me to do. Help me keep my eyes on You when I step out in faith to obey the prompting of Your Spirit in my heart.

I pray this in Jesus' name!

MY CONFESSION FOR TODAY

I confess that I am not negatively affected by people's mixed reactions when I speak the Word of God. People will always respond differently to truth; therefore, I put my trust in the Lord and keep my eyes on Him, not on the responses of people. I will do my best to speak His Word accurately, and I trust the Holy Spirit to assist me. He is my Helper, my Standby, my Assistant, and my Mentor, so I am depending on Him to teach me how to speak as I ought to speak. From this moment on, I will no longer worry or fret about the reactions of people when I do what I am instructed to do with a right heart. Instead, I will rest my case and then leave the results with the Lord.

I declare this by faith in Jesus' name!

QUESTIONS FOR YOU TO CONSIDER

1. Can you think of a time when you spoke exactly what God put on your heart, and it caused a wide variety of reactions that surprised you? Exactly when was that experience, and what was the message that seemed so controversial?
2. What did you learn from that experience when it was over? Did the Holy Spirit show you how you could have done better? What lessons did you appropriate from that experience?
3. Can you recall a time when you felt like you had failed in sharing the message God had given you? Did you later find out that God did remarkable things in people's lives as a result of the seeds you planted that day?
4. What conclusion can you draw when you see eternal fruit produced in people's lives from a time of sharing the truth that *you* thought was disastrous?

MAY 1

What God Thinks About You

Put on therefore, as the elect of God,
holy and beloved....
— Colossians 3:12

If you know Jesus Christ today, it is no accident. God personally *summoned you* to know Him. The fact is, God looked out into eternity and saw *you* — and He said, "I *want* you. I'm calling you *out* of this lost world to belong to Me!" God literally *chose* you for Himself, which ought to be one of the truths you speak to yourself every day!

How can we know that to be true? God gives us that assurance in Colossians 3:12, where it says, "Put on therefore, as the elect of God, holy and beloved...." This verse is very important for us to understand because it tells you and me *what God thinks of us*. This is vital for us to get into our hearts, because we need to know what God thinks of those whom He has redeemed.

Pay close attention as we dig into this verse. Let these truths sink deep into your heart — because they have the power to transform the way you think about yourself!

Colossians 3:12 begins by saying, "Put on therefore, as the *elect* of God...." This word "elect" is the first word that reveals what God thinks of us. It is the Greek word *eklektos*, which is a compound of the words *ek* and *lego*. The word *ek* means *out*, and *lego* means *I say*. When they are compounded, the new word literally means, *"Out, I say!"* In other words, God loved us so much that He *called us out* from a lost eternity and began the process of making sure we came to Christ. For that reason, the word *eklektos* can be translated *elected* or *selected*, carrying the idea that we are personally *chosen* by God.

The verse continues, "Put on therefore, as the elect of God, *holy*...." This word "holy" is the Greek word *hagios*, which in ancient times described *awe, respect*, and *reverence* for a holy place or a holy shrine — a place separated and set apart from other places. Consequently, the word eventually came to refer to something that was *separated from the rest of the world* and was thereby *sanctified, consecrated*, or *holy*. The use of this word in the New Testament tells us that once we came to Christ, the blood of Jesus *separated* us, *consecrated* us, and made us *holy*. He removed our past sins and threw them into the sea of forgetfulness, separating our sin from us as far as the east is from the west (*see* Psalm 103:12).

The word "holy" (*hagios*) means that God Himself *respects* you as a *holy dwelling place* for His Spirit. God sees you as *consecrated* and *sanctified, different* from others, so *special* that you are in a totally *separate* category from the rest of the world.

So the next time the devil tries to tell you that you're too fat, too skinny, too homely, not spiritual enough, undeserving, or inferior in any way, read the preceding paragraphs to him as a rebuke! Then the first thing every morning, look in the mirror and declare: *"I am holy! Jesus' blood separated me from my past! He wiped it out and cleared the slate! He threw my sin into the sea of forgetfulness and separated it from me forever. Now I am clean, set apart, and consecrated — and God Himself respects me as the temple of His Spirit!"*

All these things are absolutely true about you. That's why you must do your best to live in obedience to God's Word and to avoid grieving the Holy Spirit who resides within you (*see* Ephesians 4:30). Whenever you do anything out of order or anything that would bring grief to the Holy Spirit living within you, just confess your sin to the Father, and you will be immediately and completely cleansed by the blood of Jesus (*see* 1 John 1:9).

Next, Colossians 3:12 goes on to say, "Put on therefore, as the elect of God, holy and *beloved*...." This word "beloved" is the Greek word *agapao*, which comes from the word *agape*, the Greek word for *love*. The tense used in this verse is very significant, because it means God *has loved* us in the past; He *still loves* us in the present; and He *will continue to love* us in the future.

Do you remember moments in your past when you were so very aware that God loved you? Were there moments when you felt overwhelmed by God's forgiveness, acceptance, and tender care for you, even at times when you knew that you had done something wrong and didn't deserve His love? The psalmist David wrote that God's love is *unfailing*. In Psalm 36:7 (*NIV*), David said, "How priceless is your *unfailing love*...." In fact, David and the other psalmists were so aware of God's "unfailing love" to sustain them that they wrote about it *70 times* in the book of Psalms.

Are you still aware today that God loves you with an everlasting, unfailing love? God's love for you has never changed. He loves you *today* as intensely as He loved you yesterday! You may have done things that were not appropriate for a child of God to do. But nonetheless, you are His child, and He loves you with an everlasting love. Even if you've largely ignored God and you need to ask His forgiveness, He never forgets that the Holy Spirit lives in you, and He *respects* you as a dwelling place of His Spirit. And the *really* great news is this: God's love for you *tomorrow* will also be unfailing. It will never change. Even if *you* fail, God's love for you will *not* fail. His love is steadfast and unchanging toward His sons and daughters.

Before I finish this point about you being the "beloved" of God, I want to take some time to explain further what the word *agape* really means, since it is one of the Greek words Paul used in Colossian 3:12 to reveal what God thinks of you.

This word *agape* refers to what I call *high-level love*, for there is no higher, finer, or more excellent love than *agape* love. In fact, the word *agape* is filled with so much deep emotion and meaning that it is one of the most difficult words to translate in the New Testament. Trying to explain this word has baffled translators for centuries; nevertheless, I'm going to try to clarify the meaning of this powerful word.

Agape occurs when an individual sees, recognizes, understands, or appreciates the value of an object or a person, causing the viewer to behold this object or person in great esteem, awe, admiration, wonder, and sincere appreciation. Such great respect is awakened in the heart of the observer for the person or object he is beholding that he is compelled to love it. In fact, his love for that person or object is so strong that it is irresistible.

In the New Testament, perhaps the best example of *agape* is found in John 3:16: "For God so loved the world that he gave his only begotten Son, that whosoever believeth in him should not perish, but have everlasting life." In the phrase, "For God so loved the world," the word "love" is the word *agape*.

This means that when God looked upon the human race, He stood in awe of mankind, even though man was lost in sin. God admired man; He wondered at man; He held mankind in the highest appreciation. Even though Satan held mankind captive at that moment, God looked upon the world and saw His own image in man. The human race was so precious to God and He loved man so deeply that His heart was stirred to reach out and do something to save him. In other words, God's love drove Him to action.

You see, *agape* is a love that loves so profoundly that it knows no limits or boundaries in how far, wide, high, and deep it will go to show that love to its recipient. If necessary, *agape* love will even sacrifice itself for the sake of that object or person it so deeply cherishes. Thus, *agape* is the highest form of love — a self-sacrificial type of love that moves the lover to action for the sake of the beloved.

When you put together the meaning of these three words in Colossians 3:12, you gain a deeper revelation regarding what God actually thinks about you. He has personally chosen you; He has separated you from your sin; He respects you as the dwelling place of His Spirit; and He loves you so much that His thoughts are continually turned toward you, causing awe, admiration, and wonder to be drawn from His heart. *That is what God thinks about you!*

MY PRAYER FOR TODAY

Heavenly Father, I am in awe of Your great love toward me. Thank You that even before the foundations of the world, You looked into eternity and saw me personally. When You fastened Your gaze upon me, Your heart of love opened toward me and You deliberately chose me that I might know You. Holy Spirit, You are the treasure within my earthen vessel. Help me see myself as the Father sees me. Then empowered by the confidence of His love and favor, strengthen and guide me to walk as a continual demonstration of that love to others for the glory of Your name!

I pray this in Jesus' name!

MY CONFESSION FOR TODAY

I confess that I am personally summoned by God to know Him intimately. When God sees me, His great "agape love" for me compels Him to behold me with an admiring gaze as when one beholds a treasure with awe and wonder. I am the chosen dwelling place of God's own Spirit. Therefore, I am valued greatly and esteemed highly by Him. I believe and receive God's great love for me, and today I walk in the reality of its irresistible strength and power. I am continually aware of His love for me, and for that reason, I remain secure and my faith in Him never fails!

I declare this by faith in Jesus' name!

QUESTIONS FOR YOU TO CONSIDER

1. Describe a moment when God's unfailing love for you left you feeling overwhelmed and speechless. How did that moment and expression of God's love for you change your walk with God and your relationship with others?
2. As you meditate on how God thinks about you, how does that change the way you think about yourself?
3. Did you realize you were the special dwelling place of God and that God respects you as a consecrated dwelling place? If you really embrace that truth, how will that help to shape your self-image?

The human race was so precious to God
and He loved man so deeply
that His heart was stirred to reach out
and do something to save him.
In other words, God's love drove Him to action.

MAY 2

No One Is Higher!

Far above all principalities, and power, and might, and dominion,
and every name that is named, not only in this world,
but also in that which is to come.
— Ephesians 1:21

Once when I was browsing in an antique shop in Russia, I came across an old, folded document that was covered in elegant, elaborate Russian handwriting. I could see that it was authentic, so I asked the shop owner if I could hold it in order to take a closer look. As I carefully unfolded the paper, I saw much to my amazement that I was holding a personal letter written by a Tsar of Russia to announce the birth of his son! I was stunned to be holding such an important piece of Russian history in my hands.

The imperial insignia was still pressed into the broken wax seal, and on the back of the letter was an inscription with all the names and titles of this particular Russian Tsar. The beautiful handwriting described him as:

Emperor and Autocrat of all the Russias,
of Moscow, Kiev, Vladimir, Novgorod, Tsar of Kazan,
Tsar of Astrakhan, Tsar of Poland, Tsar of Siberia,
Tsar of Tauric Chersonesos, Tsar of Georgia, Lord of Pskov,
and Grand Duke of Smolensk, Lithuania, Volhynia, Podolia,
Finland, Jerusalem, [and so forth, and so forth, and so forth].

The point of these titles was clear: There was no higher name and no greater power than the Tsar of Russia in the realms of his rule. But when I saw this Tsar's amazing list of names, titles, and ranks, I immediately thought of how highly exalted Jesus is above all others — *including* kings and queens and nobility of every type. In fact, Ephesians 1:21 says that Christ's resurrection exalted Him to a position at the Father's right hand, "Far above all principalities, and power, and might, and dominion, and every name that is named, not only in the world, but also in that which is to come."

Let's take an in-depth look at this verse to learn exactly how exalted Jesus Christ is in this universe. First, we see that the apostle Paul declared that Jesus is exalted "above all...." In Greek, this word "above" is *huperano*, which means *high above* or *far above* and refers to both *rank* and *dignity*. In the context of this verse, it means quite simply that no one in the universe has a higher rank, name, or position than Jesus Christ! Furthermore, to affirm Jesus' highest position, Paul added the word "all," which is a translation of the Greek word *pas*, meaning *anything* and *everything*. By using these two words together, *huperano* and *pas*, he left no room for misunderstanding or doubt regarding his message — that Jesus Christ holds the highest and most exalted position in the entire universe. *He is literally "above all."*

Paul went on to describe the specific categories that Christ is above. First, he stated that Christ is "above all *principalities*...." The word "principalities" is from the Greek word *arche*, and it denotes *rulers of the highest level*. This encompassing term refers to *all* human rulers, including kings and politicians. However, it must be noted that the word *arche* is also used in Scripture to refer to *angelic beings*. This means Paul was declaring that Christ's exalted rank is far above all *human rulers* and *angelic beings*. The natural and the spiritual realms are both under the dominion of Jesus Christ, and there is absolutely no one in any realm more highly exalted than Him.

Paul then mentioned Christ's superiority over "powers." The word "powers" is the Greek word *exousias*. This word describes people who have received *delegated power*, and therefore is often translated *authorities*. In the context of Ephesians 1:21, this word *exousias* refers to people who hold public office and wield authority entrusted to them by their superiors or through an election. Paul was teaching that although these individuals yield substantial power and influence in the affairs of the world, their authority pales in comparison to that of Jesus Christ. At the time Paul penned these words in the First Century AD, this was a very dangerous and powerful statement to make, because Roman political powers were actively persecuting the Church and attempting to suppress the message of the Gospel. However, Paul wanted his readers to know that no matter what authority a politician might try to exert over the Church, Jesus had a rank that was even higher than the most powerful human authorities.

Next Paul wrote of "might," which comes from the Greek word *dunamis*. The word *dunamis* denotes *explosive power*, but it also was regularly used to describe the full strength of a military force. By using this word, Paul declared that Jesus is exalted in His authority and power even above all the military forces in the world today.

As if this list is not already complete enough, Paul added one more word. He stated that Christ is supreme above all "dominions." This is the Greek word *kuriotes*, which means *lordships*. It could refer to any world system, political, financial, or any system of any type. There simply is no system more high-ranking that the Lord Jesus Christ!

Finally, to make sure he has included everyone and everything on his list, Paul added "...and every name that is named, not only in this world, but also in that which is to come...." In one sweeping statement, Paul declared that Jesus is Lord over all. He is literally superior to rulers (*arche*), elected leaders (*exousias*), military powers (*dunamis*), and constitutional authorities (*kuriotes*). *He is literally Lord over all!*

Today that old Russian document I found in the antique shop is framed and belongs to a high-ranking politician in Moscow to whom I gifted it. It is a remarkable document about a dead Tsar who persists only in distant memory as a historical figure. In Russia's history, no one was more highly exalted than the Tsar; however, in all of human *history*, no one has ever been more highly exalted than Jesus Christ. He is alive today and sitting at the Father's right hand, where He reigns forever as:

King of kings, Lord of lords, The Blessed and Only Potentate,
The King Eternal, Immortal, Invisible, The Anointed One, The Christ,
The Messiah, The Chosen One, The Lamb of God, The Glory of God,
The Word of God, The Only Begotten of the Father, Emmanuel,
Son of Man, Son of God, Wonderful Counselor, Everlasting
Father, The Power of God, The Wisdom of God, The Only
Wise God, Prince of Peace, Redeemer, Chief Shepherd,
Great Shepherd of the Sheep, Great High Priest,
Universal and Supreme Head of the Church —
God in the Flesh!

MY PRAYER FOR TODAY

Lord, I acknowledge and declare that You are literally and utterly Lord over all! You reign supreme and powerful above everything and everyone that is or is to come. I worship and exalt You, Jesus. No one and nothing is equal to or greater than You! I reverence and submit to your Lordship, and I resist any work of the flesh or the devil that would defy Your Lordship in my life!

I pray this in Jesus' name!

MY CONFESSION FOR TODAY

I confess that Jesus is my Lord, and I exalt Him as Supreme Ruler over every area of my Life! Every title conferred upon Him establishes a specific victory in my life. Jesus rules as my Prince of Peace; therefore, anxiety, agitation, and fear may not dominate me. Jesus reigns as my Redeemer; therefore, sickness, poverty, oppression or any work of the enemy may not establish any control or influence over me. I walk in truth that Jesus alone is my Lord, and this truth makes me free indeed!

I declare this by faith in Jesus' name!

QUESTIONS FOR YOU TO CONSIDER

1. What does it mean to you personally when you say *"Jesus is Lord!"*?
2. What areas of your life do you need to surrender to Jesus' Lordship? Why not make a list so that you can pray over it and make it a matter of personal consecration?
3. The name of Jesus wields ultimate authority over all the works of the enemy. What situation in your life, family, or business needs to bow to the name of Jesus? How will you enforce the Lordship of Jesus in that situation?

MAY 3

Under His Feet!

And hath put all things under his feet,
and gave him to be the head over all things to the church.
— Ephesians 1:22

In the Egyptian Museum in Cairo, Egypt, there is an exquisite display of the treasures of King Tut (Tutankhamun) — the boy pharaoh who died at a very early age and whose tomb was discovered by Howard Carter in the year 1922. I've been to Tut's Tomb in the Valley of the Kings, and on multiple occasions I've seen the display of treasures found in his tomb that are on view in the Egyptian Museum. This museum is one of the world's greatest — filled with artifacts from the ancient world. However, of all the relics on display, there is something uniquely breathtaking about the treasures of King Tut. Each time I've been there, I've found myself especially fascinated by one group of items in the collection — the walking canes that were used by King Tut.

As one might expect, these canes are long and slender and are decorated with gold, silver, ivory, precious stones, and rare woods. They were not designed to fully carry the weight of an individual, but rather were intended to convey *symbolism* to anyone who saw Tut walking with these items in his hand. I first realized this fact when I took a closer look and saw the unique carvings on the bottoms of each of these canes.

These walking canes are each shaped like a shepherd's staff with a u-shaped hook on one end. However, instead of being placed at the top of the cane like a typical shepherd's staff, these hooks were formed at the base. Engraved along the length of each hook are images of conquered peoples from foreign lands lying prostrate on their stomachs with their arms reaching upward in adoration of the Pharaoh. Every time the pharaoh walked with his cane in hand, these figures literally rolled on the bottom of cane, symbolically bowing before him. This imagery conveyed a strong message — namely, that all of Egypt's enemies were defeated and directly *under the feet* of this mighty Pharaoh.

When I first recognized the meaning behind these carvings, I was reminded of the apostle Paul's words in Ephesians 1:22, where he wrote, "And hath put all things under his feet, and gave him to be the head over all things to the church." Paul's choice of words in this statement is very powerful, so let's take a moment to examine the original Greek language.

The word "under" in this verse is the Greek word *hupotasso*. This word was originally a military term meaning *to subjugate* or *to dominate*. It described forcibly subduing a conquered people and putting them in their place, and it is the exact idea that the images on King Tut's canes were designed to convey. However, Paul's use of this word in Ephesians 1:21 was not figurative or symbolic at all. Jesus Christ — through His death on the Cross, subsequent resurrection, and ultimate ascension on High — literally put every foe that ever existed *under His feet*.

Paul elaborated on this in Philippians 2:9, saying, "Wherefore God hath highly exalted him, and hath given him a name which is above every name; that at the name of Jesus, every knee should bow, of things in heaven, and things in earth, and things under the earth; And that every tongue should confess that Jesus Christ is Lord to the glory of God the Father (*see* Philippians 2:9-11). *Nothing* in the universe is more highly exalted than Jesus Christ. His throne rules above all — above all human authorities, military authorities, and spiritual authorities. There is simply no one who rules higher or more majestically than Jesus.

Today King Tutankhamun is wrapped in burial shrouds and encased in a coffin. He is dead, but Jesus sits exalted at the right hand of the Father, and all nations, principalities, and powers must forever bow before Him! That in itself is an awesome thought to consider.

But you also have this truth to digest and apply to your life today and every day as well: As you read on in Ephesians, you find out the Father raised *you* to sit with Jesus in the heavenlies, far above all principalities and powers (*see* Ephesians 2:6), and He gave *you* all the authority invested in His name! So *you* have something over King Tut as well, because the devil and all his demon forces are under *your* feet in Jesus' name! Let that truth sink in today — and determine to see and respond to every situation you face from that position of authority that Jesus gave you in Him when you received Him as Savior.

The devil's strategies are under your feet. As you respond more and more from that position of authority, you will see situations that looked messy or even impossible begin to turn around for the good of all involved — and all to God's glory!

MY PRAYER FOR TODAY

Father of glory, I thank You that when You raised Jesus from the dead, You raised me up and made me to sit down together with Him at Your own right hand. Father I honor You for the blood of Jesus Christ that purchased my salvation. Holy Spirit, teach me day by day to exalt the name of Jesus in every situation of my life, as I crush every strategy the enemy wages against me through the power of Christ's magnificent name!

I pray this in Jesus' name!

MY CONFESSION FOR TODAY

I am seated together in heavenly places with Christ Jesus, far above all rule and authority and power and dominion. My life is hidden with Christ in God. I am in Christ, and by His Spirit, Jesus Christ dwells in me. He is the Head of the Church, which is His Body on the earth. Since I am a member of His Body, as He is, so am I in this earth. In every situation, I honor the Head by exercising His authority to enforce His will upon the earth.

I declare this by faith in Jesus' name!

QUESTIONS FOR YOU TO CONSIDER

1. People often treat political leaders like their legacy will be remembered forever, but I challenge you to name the last ten presidents of the United States. Who among them held political office the longest?
2. Which king in the Old Testament was referred to as the king of kings? Nations literally bowed before him, and he changed the course of history. Can you name him?
3. Of all the kings who have ever ruled, Jesus is the longest ruling and most exalted. It is simply a fact that there will be no end to His Kingdom. What thoughts arise in your heart when you consider the power, glory, and stability that belong to our Lord Jesus Christ?

MAY 4

Where Does the Word 'Church' Come From?

But if I tarry long, that thou mayest know how
thou oughtest to behave thyself in the house of God,
which is the *church* of the living God, the pillar and ground of the truth.
— 1 Timothy 3:15

Today I want us to look at the meaning of the word "church" as it was understood in the First Century AD when the Church was first emerging. This teaching goes a little deeper than we usually go — but for lovers of the New Testament, it will be filled with insight and revelation.

The term that the Holy Spirit chose to describe the newly emerging Christian community was the Greek word *ekklesia.* This word is a compound of the Greek words *ek* and *kaleo*. The word *ek* conveys the idea of an *exit* or a *separation*, and the word *kaleo* means *to beckon, to call, to invite*, or *to summon.* When these two words are joined, they form the word *ekklesia,* which describes those *who are called and separated to a prestigious assembly*.

The earliest examples of the word *ekklesia* is found in writings about Athens, where it was used to denote a prestigious assembly of Athenian citizens who regularly met to discuss civil matters. At these meetings, the distinguished citizens determined laws, debated public policy, formulated new policies, argued and ruled in judicial matters, elected the chief magistrates of the land, decided who should be banished, and so on. To be *called out* from society and *invited* to be a *member* of this assembly was a great honor.

The reason the Holy Spirit chose the word *ekklesia* to describe God's people becomes more and more evident as one studies this subject. The New Testament meaning of *ekklesia* is clear: *The local church is a body of individuals who have been called out, called forth, and separated for the purposes of God.* The church is God's assembly in every town and city — composed of people who have been saved and called out to make eternal decisions that will affect the very atmosphere of their local region.

God never intended for the local church to be simply a quiet, hidden body of believers. Rather, He intended for a church to be His voice and ruling power in each community — a special assembly comprised of people who have been called out to make decisions that will impact the atmosphere of their local environment for God.

Therefore, when the New Testament used the word *ekklesia* to depict the local church, it is conveying an incredibly important message right from the start: God's plan for each congregation was not that they hide and cower in fear, but rather that they rise to a position of power and influence in the place where God had called them to fulfill their specific assignment for their region. The church was intended to be a brilliant beacon of light in the midst of dark and troubled towns, cities, and regions.

The believers in the early New Testament were suffering terribly as a direct consequence of persecution. Church meetings had to be conducted in secret because swift retribution would be brought upon them if their actions were ever made known. Yet despite the fact that these believers were suffering immensely and forced to meet in secret, Christ still acknowledged them for who they were — His *ekklesia*, called out from the world and separated to exercise spiritual power over the bleak and seemingly hopeless atmosphere that surrounded them.

Regardless of how dark and oppressive the situation seemed to be or how much these believers struggled, it didn't change Jesus' view of them. They were His precious, appointed *ekklesia* — His governing body in their respective towns, cities, and regions. *And that is still how Jesus views the local church!* Each body of believers has its own specific assignment, *and each believer is assigned to a specific ekklesia*! All local bodies fit within a larger common purpose: that of furthering the Kingdom of God on this earth by equipping the saints and being an influence of God's truth and righteousness to a lost world.

So I encourage you to ask yourself today: *Do I know in my heart that I am planted firmly in my God-ordained company of believers? Am I positioned in the ekklesia that holds His assignment for this season of my life?* Then renew your commitment to be all God has called you to be to help the *ekklesia* to which He has joined you extend its influence. As that local body extends His voice into the surrounding culture, the spiritual atmosphere of that region will be *changed* to the glory of His name!

MY PRAYER FOR TODAY

Father, I thank You for saving me and calling me to be a member of Your precious Church. Help me see Your Church the way You see it — anointed, precious, and powerful. I ask You to help me be faithful in the church where You have planted me so that I will flourish as I use my gifts and talents there and do all I can to be a positive contributing member. In conjunction with everyone else in our church, I ask You to help us be an expression of Your voice that affects the city where I live.

I pray this in Jesus' name!

MY CONFESSION FOR TODAY

I confess that I love the church where God has called me. I use my gifts and talents to help in the various ministries and departments of the church. I give my tithes and offerings there, as God commands me to do in His Word. I pray for my pastor and listen carefully as he preaches what he believes God has to say to us each week. When he looks for someone on whom he can depend, my pastor knows that I am one he can turn to rely upon. I declare that our church is growing, is getting stronger and stronger, and that we are becoming a greater light to our city.

I declare this by faith in Jesus' name!

QUESTIONS FOR YOU TO CONSIDER

1. So what did you learn *new* about the word "church" today? Was any of this new information and insight for you? What was the primary thing you gained from reading it?
2. How does what you read in today's *Sparkling Gem* affect your view of the local church and the role of your pastor?
3. After reading what a privilege it was to be a member of the early *ekklesia*, how does this affect your view of your membership in your local church?

MAY 5

The Ultimate Sign of Jesus' Return

For nation shall rise against nation,
and kingdom against kingdom:
and there shall be famines, and pestilences,
and earthquakes, in divers places.
All these are the beginning of sorrows.
— Matthew 24:7,8

For me, there is no doubt that we are living at the end of the Church Age. It is a fact that many world-shaking events will occur before the coming of the Lord, and we've already witnessed many of them. In recent years, the world has experienced many upheavals and disasters that have left many believers reeling and wondering if the coming of Christ is imminent. Fortunately, the Bible provides clear guidance on this topic in numerous passages throughout the Old and New Testament.

In fact, Jesus Himself prophesied about the state of the world in the last days. In Matthew 24:7 and 8, He said, "For nation shall rise against nation, and kingdom against kingdom: and there shall be famines, and pestilences, and earthquakes, in divers places. All these are the beginning of sorrows."

Notice the phrase "beginning of sorrows" in this verse. This word "sorrows" is the Greek word *oodin*, and it specifically describes *the labor pains a pregnant woman experiences before she gives birth*. However, Jesus called this period in time the "*beginning* of sorrows" — not the *end* of sorrows. The Greek word for "beginning" is *arche*, which in this particular case simply means a *starting point*. By using this word, Jesus was teaching that the events described in verse 7 would mark the beginning of an undefined period of time that would transpire before the coming of Christ. He does not give us a specific timeframe, but He does reveal signs and indicators that will let us know when we have entered into this turbulent period. It is important to understand that just because some of these events are occurring today, it doesn't mean we have reached the end — *it simply means the process has begun.*

As we approach the end of the Church Age, Jesus said the world will begin to feel stress and pressure like a woman preparing to give birth to a baby. Let's think for a moment about the process of giving birth. A woman's pains start slowly then gradually grow stronger and stronger. Finally, her whole body is pushing downward to deliver that child. At the last moment, the pains come quickly, and they are intense. This is the indicator that she is right at the moment of delivery.

Likewise, as the world comes closer and closer to the end of the age, the pains in the world will become greater. These pains will become more intense and more frequent. As these grow in intensity and frequency, they are a signal that we are approaching the time when Jesus will return for the Church.

The Bible outlines many events that will occur in the last days (*see* Matthew 24, Luke 21, and 2 Timothy 3), but does Scripture give us a primary sign that will mark the uttermost conclusion of the age and imminent return of Jesus? And if so, what is it?

The only sure sign of Jesus' imminent return is found in Matthew 24:14, where He proclaimed, "And this gospel of the kingdom shall be preached in all the world for a witness unto all nations; and then shall the end come."

The *very last sign* Jesus gave concerning *right before* His imminent return was the preaching of the Gospel all over the world. That's how we can get a good idea of how close we are to the return of Jesus: the extent to which the Gospel is being preached all over the world! Jesus clearly said that when the *Gospel* is preached unto all the nations, "*then shall the end come*." If we want to know how close we are to the coming of Jesus, we must *look to the nations*. How well we are penetrating and reaching them with the Gospel tells us how close we are to the end! When the whole world has had a witness of the Gospel, *then the end shall come* according to the Lord Jesus Christ.

We must be very careful as we approach the future. Jesus admonished us in Matthew 24:6, "See that ye are not troubled: for all these things must come to pass, but the end is not yet." We must not let the noises surrounding us throw us into a state of turmoil or panic. We are people of faith, and we know the end of the story before it even begins! We must keep our eyes on the Lord and our minds on the Word because we have a faith that overcomes the world (*see* 1 John 5:4)!

Jesus said the last, greatest sign of His return is when all the nations of the earth have had a witness of the Gospel. So don't let negative news reports make you think it's all over, because *it's not over until that last nation has had an opportunity to receive Jesus Christ as Lord and Savior*!

Since this is true, it makes sense, then, that the devil would be actively trying to make believers fearful about the future so they will stop sowing seed. It's to his advantage if he can get believers to succumb to a fear-riddled mindset of self-preservation and abort their harvests of financial well-being. Not only would that hinder the fulfilling of their own God-given callings and destinies, but it would also hinder the spread of the Gospel and thus delay the coming of Jesus.

Of course the devil doesn't want the nations to hear the Good News! *Do you realize how close we are to the whole world having heard the Gospel?* He wants to stop it and sidetrack us so we'll stop what we're doing!

By luring us to stop sowing seed, the devil also ensures that we jeopardize any future financial harvest in our own lives. Therefore, when times get hard and supernatural provision is needed, it won't be there because there is no seed in the ground to bless and multiply!

Don't let the devil do this to you!

Sowing seed will keep you financially blessed through any storm that lies ahead. If you allow fear to dictate your giving and forget the masses of desperate, unsaved people for whom Jesus died, you will only end up hurting yourself. *Your financial gifts have the power to save nations!*

Neither the wind nor the clouds of this dark spiritual climate are to determine our obedience to God! As Ecclesiastes 11:4 says, "He that observeth the wind shall not sow: and he that regardeth the clouds shall not reap."

We cannot let the political or financial climate of the world dictate whether or not we keep sowing seed to allow the Word of God to reach the lost nations of the world. There has never been a greater opportunity for spreading the Gospel across the world than right now. All over the planet, people are crying for someone to bring them the truth of Jesus Christ. The whole world knows something is happening; they just don't know what it is! They don't understand that the earth is crying out for Jesus to return. *So we must go tell them!*

The problems of the world are real, and we would be foolish not to prepare. But we are also foolish if we trust in riches and move into a self-protective mode. We must keep our hearts and priorities right, regardless of what we hear around us. We must not let the devil push us back into retreat. And we must keep pushing forward — aggressively reaching toward the goal of preaching the Gospel to the ends of the earth. When that goal is achieved, *Jesus will come*!

MY PRAYER FOR TODAY

Father, I thank You for the privilege of contributing toward the spread of the Gospel across the earth. I ask You to help me always put first things first. Help me focus on Heaven's priorities — souls — so that I will not become distracted by the cares of this life or the pressures and anxieties of this age. Teach me how to prepare for the difficult times to come without slipping into self-preservation. I submit myself to You, Father, and I resist the spirit of fear. As I receive Your wisdom and grace, I follow the Holy Spirit's guidance to do my part in building the Kingdom of God and hastening Christ's return.

I pray this in Jesus' Name!

MY CONFESSION FOR TODAY

I consistently sow financial seed into the work of preaching Jesus Christ among the nations. I strengthen the work of missionary outreaches throughout the earth through my participation in prayer and offerings. As I do my part to spread the Gospel, I am helping to hasten His return. I remain focused without distraction — and bold without fear — to occupy until He comes.

I declare this by faith in Jesus' name!

QUESTIONS FOR YOU TO CONSIDER

1. Do you believe the coming of Jesus for His Church is near? What makes you believe this? What are the signs that really speak to your heart, that make you believe Jesus is coming soon?
2. Do you regularly give to missions or to missionary organizations that are spreading the good news of the Gospel to the ends of the earth? Do you believe that you have a financial responsibility to give to missions?
3. How do you perceive that your giving affects people in other parts of the world?

MAY 6

Looks Can Be Deceiving!

Do ye look on things after the outward appearance?
— 2 Corinthians 10:7

Denise and I decided to attend an art auction in Moscow simply because we wanted to do something fun and different. We were not going to purchase art, but we thought it might be fun to observe how an event like an art auction would be conducted. We figured it would be a high-class event, so we dressed accordingly. We got into the car, headed across town, and arrived in the location where the auction was to be conducted. We arrived a little early, so we walked through the gallery — *flabbergasted* at the asking prices of the art that was to be auctioned that evening.

When it was time for the auction to begin, we made our way to our seats. Before everything started, I looked around to see what kind of people were there to participate that evening. By the way most people were dressed, I never would have imagined they had any money. Denise and I were the best-dressed people in the place, and we were there only as observers! From all outward appearances, we were the ones who looked affluent, and the people who had big money to spend looked like they had dropped by the auction on the way to a picnic!

When the auction started, it wasn't long until the auctioneer starting pounding the podium with his gavel. "SOLD!" he said, over and over again. The man sitting in front of me wore sneakers, jeans, and a wrinkled shirt, and he held in his hand a list of paintings he intended to "war" over and take home that night. I could hardly believe my eyes and ears as that young man lifted his auction card again and again to bid for pieces of art. Within moments, he had spent a fortune on paintings. But the final shock was when an unshaven and disheveled-looking man across the room from us paid nearly $1,000,000 for two abstract paintings that were so ugly, I wouldn't have hung them in our garage!

When the event was over, I meandered through the small crowd so I could get a closer look at the people who had paid these whopping prices for art that evening. None of them looked like he or she had any money. Most of them looked like they needed fashion assistance! From all outward appearances, I wouldn't have thought any of them had a dime to spare.

Denise and I went to the car to head home. When we got into the car and looked at each other, we were speechless at first. We just didn't know what to say about the enormous sums of money people spent more quickly than we could blink — or about the unimpressive way these enormously rich people were dressed that evening. One lesson we clearly learned that evening: *Looks can be deceiving!*

This experience made me ponder the number of people we encounter in life who are much more powerful *internally* than they look *outwardly*. Just consider the apostle Paul! We have no illustrations or photos of what Paul looked like, but from what he wrote about himself in Second Corinthians 10:10, we can surmise that he wasn't among the best-looking of his day. In fact, Paul actually quoted an opponent who laughed at his physical appearance and voice. Paul told them in essence, "I've heard what you've said about me. You say, '…His bodily presence is weak, and his speech contemptible.'"

The words "bodily presence" is a translation of the Greek words *parousia tou somatos*, which may be better translated, "the mere appearance of his body." Paul's opponents were not impressed with his physical body! They called it "weak." The word "weak" that Paul quotes here is the Greek word *astheneo*, which can mean *physically weak*, but it can also mean *dubious, defective, or questionable in appearance*. It could actually be rendered, *"the appearance of his body is a little puzzling."*

It appears that they were laughing at Paul's physical body; yet it was that same physical body that had carried the power of God wherever he went. The external "package" may not have been very impressive to the apostle's opponents, but it contained the dynamic power of God! So Paul warned them, "You better be careful about judging me by my exterior appearance, because when I come to you the next time, you will find out how much power is contained inside this body!" (to paraphrase Paul's words in Second Corinthians 10:2,11).

Apparently they were also laughing at Paul's voice or the way he spoke, because he said, "I hear you saying that my speech is contemptible." The word "speech" is the word *logos*, which means *words* but in this case most likely means his *voice* or possibly his manner of speech. The word "contemptible" is the Greek word *exoutheneo*, which means *awful, despicable, disgusting*, or *horrible*.

What was it about Paul's voice or his way of speaking that some people loathed so much? We don't know, but something in his manner of speech or what his voice sounded like made them say that listening to him was *disgusting*! Yet it was this voice that first preached the Gospel to them and brought them out of spiritual darkness into spiritual light! We don't know what Paul sounded like, but regardless of his voice's tenor, depth, or tone — and regardless of how Paul articulated his message — it had been the voice of this apostle that had been the vehicle to bring the knowledge of God's power and love to the Corinthians and to people all over the Roman Empire.

There may have been weaknesses in Paul's physical appearance and vocal abilities, but his interior was mighty and powerful. People could mock all they wanted, but his opponents were never able to match what he accomplished because he was so *inwardly* filled with divine power and revelation. His opponents may have been more physically attractive, but inwardly they simply couldn't measure up to what Paul carried within himself.

That night at the art auction, Denise and I outwardly looked like the ones who had money to spend, and the people who actually possessed the necessary resources to purchase that expensive art didn't look impressive at all. Judging by appearances, we would have missed it altogether. It was an amazing night of learning anew that a person's outward package may not always tell the truth about what he or she is carrying on the inside.

I want to encourage you not to judge yourself too harshly by your exterior appearance. Do all you can to make yourself look better. But when you're done with improvements and there's nothing else you can do, you must remember that your inward man is filled with the power of the Holy Spirit.

Remember this truth also when you meet others. It is simply a fact that you will meet some people who look very impressive but are inwardly empty. And you will meet others who look very unimpressive but are among those who will change the world! So determine today to judge first yourself and then everyone else you know in life not by external appearances, but by the heart, just as God does. That one decision alone will help you see more clearly in every situation and keep you from evaluating yourself and those around you according to low-level human standards!

MY PRAYER FOR TODAY

Lord, I admit that I've judged others by what they look like externally, and today I am asking You to forgive me. I'm sure that others have thought they could figure me out by what they see, yet have missed it many times. Please help me do all I can to improve my outward appearance, but help me remember that I carry Your power and the revelation of Your Word inside me and that there is more to me than meets the eye!

I pray this in Jesus' name!

MY CONFESSION FOR TODAY

I confess that I am the temple of the Holy Spirit and that the power and the life of God live inside me. I carry within me the authority of the name of Jesus; my voice is an instrument that speaks life; and I am filled with divine treasures. Just as I do not want others to judge me by my external appearance, I will no longer judge others only by what my eyes see. From this moment forward, I will remember and live by the truth that there is more than meets the eye in me and in those whom I meet.

I declare this by faith in Jesus' name!

QUESTIONS FOR YOU TO CONSIDER

1. Have you ever met individuals who totally disarmed you because from outward appearances, you didn't expect them to be as talented or gifted as you found out they were?
2. How does it make you feel if you think others are judging you entirely by outward appearances? Do you want to run and hide, do you feel embarrassed, or does it make you want to stand up on the inside and show them who you really are?
3. Make a list of Bible characters who seemed weak or whom people deemed insignificant yet God used them mightily as history-changers.

MAY 7

What Does Diligence Look Like?

...He is a rewarder of them that diligently seek him.
— Hebrews 11:6

Some people never see anything accomplished with their lives because they start and stop too many projects. But Hebrews 11:6 says that God "...is a rewarder of them that *diligently seek* him."

If you want to qualify for God's reward and you know He has called you to do something, you have to be completely committed to pressing forward all the way until you have fully accomplished the assignment. For this, you need *diligence* to stick with it.

In today's *Sparkling Gem*, I want us to take a look at this phrase "diligently seek" and see how diligence is absolutely necessary to see any dream, vision, or calling come to pass. According to this verse, those who diligently seek God and His will are eventually rewarded!

The phrase "diligently seek" is a translation of the Greek word *ekzeteo*, a compound of *ek* and *zeteo*. The first part is the Greek word *ek*, which means *out*, and the second word is *zeteo*, which means *to seek*. When these words are compounded, the new word means *to seek out*. As used in Hebrews 11:6, it means *to zealously seek for something with all of one's heart, strength, and might*. It conveys the idea of being *hard-working, attentive, busy, constant, and persistent in one's devotion to what he or she is doing*.

If you and I take our life assignment lightly — approaching it with a casual, easygoing, take-it-easy, relaxed attitude — we'll never go far in the fulfillment of our calling or dream. It takes hard work to achieve anything worthwhile, and complaining about how hard it is won't make the process any easier. I always say, "Live like a slug, and you'll eat dirt the rest of your life." So unless we want to "eat a lot of dirt," we have to make the decision to get up and put our hands to the plow! If you and I are serious about doing what God has told us to do, we must adjust our level of commitment and get to work. Being a hard worker is a part of being *diligent*.

If you and I want to see our dreams fulfilled, we must give our *full attention* to what God has called us to do. It must have our full consideration, our undivided attention, and our full mental and spiritual concentration. Ceaseless, around-the-clock, nonstop devotion is essential in order to be *diligent*.

When we are seriously pursuing what God has told us to do, we won't have time for wrong attitudes and wrong thinking. To remain diligent, we must be engrossed, totally absorbed, and fully engaged. We must immerse ourselves in faith, prayer, and meditation regarding God's call on our lives. All of this takes 100 percent of our focus and effort for us to accomplish what God has placed in our hearts. This is part of what it means to be *diligent.*

Being constant and consistent is also an essential quality needed to *diligently* pursue your God-given dream. Fickle, flighty, erratic behavior will never produce the fulfillment of God's will in your life. It takes consistency and determination to push aside the powers of hell and obtain the victory you desire. If you and I constantly fluctuate — wandering back and forth and in and out of faith — we will never reap anything enduring for the Kingdom of God. To produce powerful results, we must be *constant* in our commitments. We must be "steady-as-she-goes" — fixed, unchanging, and steadfast. It's all part of being *diligent.*

Persistence is also a key to remaining *diligent.* When a person is persistent, he refuses to relent. He is tenaciously immovable, even in the face of opposition, and unbending until his objective is achieved.

Withstanding opposition and braving adversity is just a part of the walk of faith. In order for us to resist attempts to abort our dreams, we must be *persistent.* This is the kind of commitment required to live and walk in faith.

With this in mind, Hebrews 11:6 could be read:

"God is a Rewarder of those who are hard-working, attentive, busy, constant, and persistent in their pursuit of seeking Him."

A casual approach will never get you to the triumphant end of the spiritual race God has placed before you. You have to give 100 percent of your focus and energy in order to press through the barriers that will stand against you to keep you from making it to the finish line.

Diligence and all that it entails is a requirement for you to get to a place of victory. So now that we've discussed what diligence looks like, it's essential that you make sure you're right on track in this area so you can fully accomplish what God has asked you to do. *Are you diligently seeking God and His will for your life?* This is the perfect day to make sure your answer is *yes*!

MY PRAYER FOR TODAY

Father, I realize that I can apply more concentrated effort in my pursuit of You and Your will for my life. Thank You, Lord, for revealing to me the areas where I need to make adjustments and how I need to make them. I ask You for clearer revelation of my life's assignment so I can walk with greater focus and commitment to fulfill that purpose — whatever may be required. Holy Spirit, I ask for and receive Your help to apply diligence and all that it entails. Strengthen me in my inner man to lay aside slothfulness in every area of my life so that I can experience the reward of those who devote themselves to seek Your will with all diligence. I receive fresh grace from you now, in Jesus' name!

I pray this in Jesus' name.

MY CONFESSION FOR TODAY

I choose to live diligently, and I refuse to live like a slug! I am zealous and persistent in my pursuit of God's plan for my life. Instead of being fickle, flighty or erratic, I am hardworking, attentive, busy, and constant! I give earnest attention to being a consistent doer of the Word of God. As a result, my mind is continually being renewed, and my thoughts are conformed to be in agreement with God's will. I inspect and evaluate my ways on a regular basis. As I do this, I am quick to make any adjustments necessary in order to persevere in the fulfillment of God's will for my life.

I declare this by faith in Jesus' name!

QUESTIONS FOR YOU TO CONSIDER

1. If you asked God whether or not He saw diligence working in your life, what would He say to you? Be honest with yourself, because God will be completely honest with you if you ask Him to help you answer this important question.
2. In what ways does your life demonstrate diligence? If you possess this quality, it should be recognizable in your daily life, so identify some ways you show diligence.
3. In what areas do you lack diligence, and what are you willing to do to bring diligence into those aspects of your life? It would be helpful for you to write your thoughts about this question on a piece of paper so your eyes can see them. That might be uncomfortable for you to do, but if you really want to grow in diligence, you must be willing to confront any area of your life where a lack of this quality still tries to define you.

MAY 8

Sin and Its Creeping Effect

Little children,
keep yourselves from idols.
— 1 John 5:21

When the apostle John was on the island of Patmos, he received seven messages to the seven churches in Asia. His spirit had been pierced by Jesus' words, and he vividly recalled the Lord's loving rebuke concerning the sin that was trying to *creep back* into some of those congregations. John knew from Christ's words that idolatry was trying to seep into the Church. The apostle understood that the willingness of believers to compromise jeopardized the Church's holiness, weakened the power of the Holy Spirit among them, and nullified their witness for Christ. Thus, the apostle solemnly admonished them, "Little children, *keep yourselves from idols*."

This was a strong admonition for believers to guard their lives against evil that was looking for a way to get back into the mainstream of their lives. John instructed his readers to "keep" themselves from idols and the disastrous implications of idolatrous worship — which was connected with all types of sinful, sexual, riotous behavior. Since First John 5:21 is the living Word of God, it also speaks to you and me: *We* are to "keep" ourselves from insidious evil and sin that would try to creep back into our own lives.

The word "keep" in this verse is the Greek word *phulasso*, a word that occurs at least 400 times in the Old Testament Septuagint and 31 times in the New Testament. In each instance, the usage of this word is indisputable. It describes the *guarding* and *protecting* of a thing, such as the guarding of a house, property, possessions, or even graves, and it denotes the *alertness* and *sleeplessness* of the person who is *on guard*. The word *phulasso* could also imply the *safekeeping* of something entrusted to someone, and it was often used in a military sense to describe a *garrison*, *a guard*, or a *sentinel*. To "keep" (*phulasso*) something demanded that a person be loyal to the task — never lethargic or lackadaisical. If that individual "fell asleep on the job," the consequences could be grave; therefore, he must be on *full alert* at all times.

The Greek word *phulasso* means we are to remain wide awake and stay on course to the very end. We are to defend ourselves against the evil just as a garrison defends a strategic position. We are to be the sentinels of our lives and of the Church.

When John commanded his readers to "...*keep* yourself from idols...," he was urging them *to stay on alert* regarding the danger of idolatry and sin. The tense used in First John 5:21 stresses *continuous responsibility*, which indicates this vigilance must be constantly maintained. Idolatry and other sin — and all their insidious effects — were so close that the believers needed *to continually stay alert* in order to remain free from their contaminating effects. It was absolutely essential that they stood firm, steadfastly refusing to compromise in the face of worldly pressures.

The believers in the First Century were *surrounded* with temptation. Pagan temples abounded with perverse sexual practices connected with idolatry. Those pagan temples were hotbeds of demonic activity and sinful actions. In order for Christians to stay free, they had to *decide* to stay free — that meant deliberately avoiding contact with these places. If they didn't maintain an alert attitude and stay continually alert, idolatry would creep back into their midst with devastating consequences. This is the reason why John called on believers to "keep" themselves from it — that is, to protect themselves from idols and to stay continuously alert about the need to be vigilant against idolatry's temptations.

Likewise, we must take John's words to *our* hearts and realize that it is our responsibility to protect ourselves from sin that would try to creep back into our lives. The world is full of sin — and as time progresses, the sin will get darker and more depraved. Society (without God) is gravitating toward normalizing even the most debased base instincts in order to make these things acceptable in society. Hence, it is essential that you and I stay fully alert to the creeping effects of sin.

We may not have actual idols to deal with in today's modern world, but sin is still a reality — and believers must avoid the pull to compromise with a world that is drifting further and further from the absolute truths of God's Word. Regardless of what the world says is acceptable, we still have an unchangeable compass — the *Bible* — which serves as our absolute and final authority in these last days until Jesus returns for His Church. Until then, we must hide the Word of God in our hearts so we do not sin against God (*see* Psalm 119:11).

You are the guardian and overseer over your heart, and it is up to you to make sure your heart stays sensitive to the Holy Spirit and to God's Word by setting aside time each day to spend with Him. It is up to you to do all you can to "keep" yourself from the creeping effects of sin in this crucial hour. And here's the good news: You are *well* able to remain steadfast and pure in every area of your life, because through Jesus, you have *everything* you need to hold on to that victorious testimony!

MY PRAYER FOR TODAY

Father, I hear what You are saying to me, and I take this responsibility deep into my heart. You have called me to be the guardian and sentinel of my life and to retain this vigilant position until the end of my spiritual journey. Forgive me for times when I have been spiritually slack. I pray for the Holy Spirit to empower me to remain alert and wide awake and to stay on track — completely unresponsive to and unaffected by sin and its creeping effects that are in the world. Regardless of what the world and society may say or do, I thank You for Your continual supply of supernatural strength to draw upon, Father, to keep myself from sin and to live my life according to Your Word.

I pray this in Jesus' name!

MY CONFESSION FOR TODAY

I confess that I am dedicated to obeying the Word of God and that I do not allow society or the world around me to dictate what is right or wrong. Sin is looking for a way to creep back into my life — and into the lives of all believers — but I have determined that I will remain on guard, as a sentinel of my life. God expects this of me and will hold me responsible for keeping my life free from the contaminant of sin and its creeping effects. With the help of the Holy Spirit, I will walk with God in a manner that is pleasing to Him and that is free of the sinful influence of the world.

I declare this by faith in Jesus' name!

QUESTIONS FOR YOU TO CONSIDER

1. Do you know any believers who have been morally compromised by the world and the thinking of society? As you consider their waywardness, what were the early signs that showed sin was creeping back into their minds and lives again?

2. What do *you* need to do to "keep" yourself from the moral and spiritual contamination that is in the world? What steps do you need to take to build a strong spiritual barrier between you and the creeping effects of sin?
3. Are there any areas where you've already been affected by the world? If so, what do you need to do to reverse this trend, to cleanse your life of it, and to get back on the straight and narrow path with the Lord?

MAY 9

Being in the Right Place at the Right Time

As many as are led by the Spirit of God,
they are the sons of God.
— Romans 8:14

When I was a young man growing up in the city of Tulsa, I always thought I would attend Oral Roberts University (ORU). ORU was and continues to be one of the premier Christian universities in the world, and it just happened to be located in my hometown. I was so fervent about attending ORU that I even began taking a class there while I was still in high school in order to try to get a jump-start on my education.

Finally the time came for me to graduate from high school, and I eagerly anticipated attending ORU full-time in the fall. However, one day as I was praying about my future, the Holy Spirit spoke to my heart and *forbade* me from attending. I was completely stunned!

"Why don't You want me to go to ORU, Lord?" I asked incredulously. "There's no better place for a young man like me than ORU."

The Holy Spirit answered, *"Because there are things I want to teach you that you can only learn somewhere else. You'll be in a good environment at ORU, but you'll miss the greater things that I want to impart to you that are important for your future.*

When I consider how the Holy Spirit worked with me as I faced the decision of what university to attend, I think of Romans 8:14. It says, "As many as are led by the Spirit of God, they are the sons of God."

The word "led" is the Greek word *ago*, a word that was used in the *agricultural* and *athletic* worlds. In agricultural terms, it described *a person who led an animal who was attached to the end of a rope*. Wherever the farmer led, the animal was *to follow*. But interestingly, it is also where we get the word *agonidzo*, which described the intense struggle of a wrestler as he fought an opponent. From this word, we derive the word *agony*. It depicts the struggle — or the wrestling — of two opponents, each who are fighting furiously to throw the other to the mat in defeat.

Romans 8:14 tells us that the Holy Spirit wants to *lead* us about, but often there is a *wrestling* between our flesh and our spirits. The Holy Spirit leads one direction, but because the flesh doesn't understand the leading of the Holy Spirit or doesn't want to obey, it throws us into a *struggle*. The Holy Spirit is willing to lead us — and He will make sure we are in the right place at the right time — but we may have to overcome the flesh in order to follow. To be honest, it was a very big struggle for my mind to yield to the leading of the Holy Spirit to forego ORU and to attend a secular university.

But as difficult as the decision was, I *knew* in my heart that I needed to follow the Holy Spirit's direction. So I made the choice to forego Oral Roberts University and enroll at a state university located a couple hours away from my hometown. As the school year progressed, it soon became apparent that by attending this secular institution, many new doors were being opened to me that might otherwise have been left shut if I had attended a Christian university. It was in this environment where I first began to get deeply involved in the ministry. My earliest experiences teaching the Bible publicly took place in the university church — and because I was constantly surrounded by unbelievers, I had opportunities to share Christ with people. These experiences emboldened me and familiarized me with the academic community's objections to the Gospel, which in turn sharpened my ability to be an effective witness for the Lord.

That university was also where I began to study Classical Greek in earnest. These studies allowed me to delve deeper into the Word of God by analyzing the New Testament in its original Greek form. Before long, believers at the university church I attended began to approach me if they had a question about the Greek New Testament. Through these interactions, I saw how I could fill a vital niche in the Body of Christ by using my understanding of New Testament Greek to open up Scripture in such a way that listeners could gain new insight about God's Word. The skills I gleaned from this discipline profoundly affected my entire life — reshaping my approach to studying the Bible and laying the foundations for my teaching ministry that would touch the lives of thousands of people across the world in the years to come.

When I look back on my years at that state university, I completely understand why it was God's will for me to attend a secular school. It was a necessary training ground that provided me with the foundational skills I needed to succeed in ministry, and I am very thankful for that experience. As wonderful as Oral Roberts University is, God wanted me at a secular university so He could impart certain truths that I personally could not have received in another environment. And to top it all off, I even met my wife Denise at the university church!

Your environment — *the surroundings and conditions in which you live and operate* — is so important! Being in the right place at the right time according to God's plan for your life is crucial as you seek to discover and fulfill His will for your life. God will use people, places, and the opportunities around you to shape you, sharpen your gifts, and prepare you to do His will.

As First Corinthians 12:18 (*NKJV*) teaches, "…God has set the members, each one of them, in the body just as He pleased."

Are you where God has directed you to be? It might be that the place to which you are called is outside of your comfort zone and you wish you could escape to somewhere else far away. However, if you know in your heart that God has spoken a word over your life, don't second-guess Him. Instead, trust that He is working to fully develop the gifts He has placed within you so you can fulfill your divine mandate. *God knows exactly what you need and where you need to be!*

MY PRAYER FOR TODAY

Lord, as I reflect on my life, I can see how You have led me at times when I didn't understand that I was even being led. You put me exactly where I needed to be. You surrounded me with the people who were essential for my training and preparation. I am so thankful that I allowed You to show me what to do and that You gave me the courage to obey. I ask that You reignite that willingness and courage in me right now as I follow Your leading again and again. I receive Your wisdom and strength to do Heaven's work upon the earth. I believe that You are doing everything to develop the gifts and callings in my life so that I can fulfill my divine mandate.

I pray this in Jesus' name!

MY CONFESSION FOR TODAY

I thankfully confess that God leads me even when I don't understand that I'm being led. He puts me exactly where I need to be and surrounds me with the people that are essential for my training and preparation. God's Spirit shows me what to do. He gives me courage to obey. And right now, He is reigniting that willingness and courage in me as I follow His leading again. He is doing everything to develop the gifts and callings in my life so I can fulfill my divine mandate!

I declare this by faith in Jesus' name!

QUESTIONS FOR YOU TO CONSIDER

1. Have you ever *thought* you knew where you were supposed to be, but God interrupted your plans and led you differently than you anticipated?
2. Although you may have been taken off-guard at how God led you, as you look back on that experience, can you see how important it was that God led you to where you were and to be with the people you were with? How did that place and those people help prepare you for the next season of your life?
3. Is God leading you differently *right now* than you had anticipated? Is it a place that is outside of your comfort zone?

MAY 10

Perilous Times Shall Come

This know also, that in the last days
perilous times shall come.
— 2 Timothy 3:1

Few people would question that we are living in dangerous and treacherous times. Especially for people without God, the last decades have brought fear and terror into the hearts of people around the world. Regardless of where you live — whether in the United States, Europe, Asia, or the former Soviet Union — people have been rudely awakened to the truth that the world is no longer the place it used to be.

This is definitely a different age, far removed from the world many of us remember as children. Even today it is difficult to imagine how things could have spiraled out of control so quickly; however, nearly 2,000 years ago when the apostle Paul wrote the book of Second Timothy, the Holy Spirit spoke through him to alert us that such a day would come. By the inspiration of the Spirit, Paul wrote, "This know also, that in the last days perilous times shall come" (2 Timothy 3:1).

The word "know" in this verse is a translation of the Greek word *ginosko*. The word *ginosko* is a common word that is normally translated *knowledge*. In this verse, Paul used *ginosko* in the present imperative tense, which means this message is something so critical that it must be known, must be recognized, and must be acknowledged. *Whatever the Holy Spirit is about to say, it is so important that hearing it is not optional — it MUST be known and understood.*

Paul then told us what we must know. He let us know that "perilous times shall come." The word "perilous" comes from the Greek word *chalepos*, a word that is used only two times in the 27 books of the New Testament. This word *chalepos* was used to denote spoken words that were *hurtful*, *harsh*, *cruel*, *ruthless*, *cutting*, *wounding*, and therefore *hard to bear*. But it was also used to describe animals that were *vicious*, *ferocious*, *fierce*, *unruly*, *uncontrollable*, *unpredictable*, and *dangerous*. In nearly every place where this word is used in secular literature of the ancient world, it depicts something said that is harmful or an environment besieged with high risk or danger.

The only other time the word *chalepos* is found in the New Testament is in Matthew 8:28, where Matthew used it to describe two demon-possessed men. Matthew 8:28 vividly tells us, "And when he was come to the other side into the country of the Gadarenes, there met him two possessed with devils, coming out of the tombs, exceeding fierce, so that no man might pass by that way."

This phrase "exceeding fierce" in Matthew 8:28 is actually a translation of this very same Greek word *chalepos*. Because the word *chalepos* is used to describe these two demon-possessed men, it categorically conveys that they were vicious, ferocious, fierce, unruly, uncontrollable, unpredictable, and dangerous. In fact, if you read the entire story in Matthew's gospel, it's clear that the people who lived in the region of the Gadarenes kept a safe distance between themselves and these two men because they knew that being in close proximity to them would put their lives in jeopardy. These two demon-possessed men were *chalepos — vicious, ferocious, fierce, unruly, uncontrollable, unpredictable,* and *dangerous.* But they represented no threat to Jesus because He knew that He had authority over them. Therefore, instead of running like everyone else, Jesus stood up against those dark forces and set those men free.

This brings us back to Second Timothy 3:1 where the Holy Spirit prophesies through Paul that "perilous times shall come." If you take all of the original Greek words into consideration, it delivers a potent message from the Spirit of God.

Taking the definitions of all these words into consideration,
Second Timothy 3:1 could be taken to mean:

> *"You emphatically must know what I am about to tell you! In the last days, periods of time will come that are hurtful, harmful, dangerous, unpredictable, uncontrollable, and high-risk...."*

The Holy Spirit warned us 2,000 years ago that the world would become a dangerous place at the end of the age. However, we had no idea how fast or how far it would spin out of control. But as we live in the world today, we are waking up to the harsh reality of a world that is exceedingly fierce.

Because the world "perilous," the Greek word *chalepos,* is used to describe the demon-possessed men in Matthew 8:28, I personally believe that the Holy Spirit was warning us that demonic activity will be released in the last days that will bring about hurtful, harsh, cruel, ruthless, cutting, wounding situations that will be emotionally hard to bear. As a result of demonic activity, the world will become a place that is vicious, ferocious, fierce, unruly, uncontrollable, unpredictable, and dangerous. We are living in a generation that faces threats that no other generation has ever known. *As always, the Holy Spirit was correct in what He was trying to tell us.*

- ➢ So how should we as believers respond to all of this?
- ➢ Should we stay in our houses, close the blinds, and hide from what's going on in the world?
- ➢ Should we never fly on a plane again or take public transportation?
- ➢ Should we stop sending our children to public schools?
- ➢ What should we do in response to these Spirit-predicted truths and the external reality that continually faces us in the world today?

Instead of retreating in fear, you and I must accept the challenge to step forward as Jesus did when He encountered the demon-possessed men of the Gadarenes. What terrified other people and made them retreat in fear is exactly what beckoned Jesus to action. In this hour, we must not retreat in fear!

The situation in today's world beckons you to action. This is the time for you to step forward and use the authority Jesus Christ gave you to bring deliverance, freedom, and peace to each place that the devil has tried to bring chaos, harm, hurt, hazard, and risk. The situation that exists in the world today is your opportunity to let the power and glory of God shine through you!

Read carefully the words of Isaiah 60:1,2. Accept the challenge of the Holy Spirit as He cries out to you and me: "Arise, shine, for thy light is come, and the glory of the Lord is risen upon thee. For, behold, the darkness shall cover the earth, and gross darkness the people: but the Lord shall arise upon thee, and his glory shall be seen upon thee"!

Although the world is sinking deeper into fear and darkness, this is our finest hour as children of God! So tell fear to leave you in Jesus' name, and embrace the opportunities you encounter along the way to bring deliverance and freedom to people gripped with fear by the news they hear each day. Think of it — God considers you well able to live for Him and to fulfill His purpose for your life, even in the midst of these perilous last days! Embrace the honor of that position in His plan, and determine to trust Him with your life and be who He needs you to be every moment of the day!

MY PRAYER FOR TODAY

Father, I thank You for choosing me to live in the last days when prophecies are being fulfilled before my very eyes. I ask You to help me keep a soft heart and not become hardened when others around me grow cold and hardened through the deceitfulness of this age. People everywhere need freedom, and deliverance from the torment of fear and pain. Instead of retreating into self-preservation mode, I will deliberately yield to Your heart for the hurting world that is all around me. Your love is shed abroad in my heart by the Holy Spirit who was given to me. Therefore, I give place to Your love within me to see them with Your eyes, to feel for them as You feel for them. I hear and respond to Your call that is beckoning me to step forward with the authority of Jesus to make a difference in the lives of everyone near to me.

I pray this in Jesus' name!

MY CONFESSION FOR TODAY

I declare by faith that I am anointed by God to live in this day and age! I am alive today for a purpose. God has chosen me to be a part of this special generation so that I can shine His glory and power into the darkness that exists in so many places and in so many people's lives. I will not allow fear to paralyze or intimidate me. Instead, I will allow God's goodness, power, and love to operate in me for the freedom, deliverance, safety, and preservation of those who are near me. I am fully equipped by the Holy Spirit to glorify God without compromise in these difficult times. God is depending on me to do my part to bring His authority, His peace, His rule, and His reign into every place where Satan wants to create hurt, harm, hazard, and fear. Jesus commanded me to occupy until He comes. Therefore, I choose to establish His Kingdom and to enforce His will on the earth as it is in Heaven!

I declare this by faith in Jesus' name!

QUESTIONS FOR YOU TO CONSIDER

1. Can you think of someone who is seized with fear because of the events happening in the world today? What effect has fear had on that person's life?
2. What does the Spirit of God want you to do to bring deliverance, freedom, and peace to people in your life who are tormented with fear? You have the answers they need — so what is He asking you to do to make a significant difference in their lives?
3. When you step into a situation where fear or panic exists, in what ways can you exercise the authority of Jesus Christ — publicly or privately — to bring peace and safety to that situation? Have you made a practice of doing this?

MAY 11

Living in the Last Days

This know also, that in the last days
perilous times shall come.
— 2 Timothy 3:1

It is simply a fact that we are living in the last days. All around us, the world is changing at a staggeringly rapid pace, and events long ago foretold in Scripture are unfolding before our very eyes. In light of the increasing turmoil in the world, it can be tempting for us to succumb to feelings of uncertainty or anxiety regarding the future.

But as we talked about in yesterday's *Sparkling Gem*, we as believers are to hold fast to God's higher perspective and take our place as victors in this hour — no matter *what* is going on around us! We don't have to wonder about what the future has in store. God's Word provides us with a clear picture of what we can expect in the coming years and gives us the spiritual tools we need to face these turbulent times and remain victorious. His Word also lays out our role in the midst of this gathering darkness: to live as children of light, reaching a lost generation with His love and His message of hope in Jesus Christ!

In Second Timothy 3:1, Paul wrote, "This know also, that in the last days perilous times shall come." Notice he said these events will occur in the "last days." The word "last" is from the Greek word *eschatos*. This word always points to the ultimate end of a thing — such as the last month of the year; the last week of the month; the last day of a week; *or the very extreme end of an age*. In other words, *eschatos* doesn't merely describe the last days in general; it depicts the *very last* of the last days. It was used in Classical Greek literature to depict *a place furthest away*, such as the very ends of the earth. It also signified something that is *final.* It is from this Greek word *eschatos* that we get the term *eschatology* — which is a theological term for *the study of last times.*

By using this word *eschatos* in this verse, the Holy Spirit is vividly declaring what characteristics will be indicative of society at the very last of the last days. Therefore, the depictions in the following verses of Second Timothy 3 are intended to be signposts that you have entered into the final stage of the last days. If you see these things occurring commonly or on a widespread basis, you are to take it as a signal that we have passed across the line and have entered into the final chapter of history as we have known it.

Thank God that by studying the Scriptures, we can identify where we are on God's timeline. Because God loves us, He spoke through the apostle Paul to enlighten our eyes and help us see what the world environment would be like in the concluding moments of the Church Age. Having this knowledge before us helps us live soberly with eternity in our view. Time is short, so we must use the time that remains wisely and shine the light of the Gospel into the lives of those whom Satan has blinded.

Because of the word *eschatos* in Second Timothy 3:1,
an interpretive translation of this verse could read:

"You emphatically must know what I am about to tell you. In the very last part of the last times — at the very end of the age and at the very last of the last days — hurtful, harmful, dangerous, unpredictable, uncontrollable, high-risk periods of time will come...."

As a committed Christian, you have a responsibility to live with your eyes wide open to the events that are occurring around you. And if you have friends or family who are unsaved and blind to the truth, it is time for you to fervently pray for God to open their eyes so they can see and know the truth! Because of the events described in Second Timothy 3, we know that we have already entered into the very last of the last days.

Soon Jesus will come, and everything will change forever. Until then, we have time to pray for those whom Satan has blinded. It's not that they are naïve — they are *blind.* Satan has blocked their view and affected their minds. They have no eyes to see. Eyes are created for them when the light of the Gospel, through the work of the Holy Spirit, touches their hearts and minds.

Are you the one God wants to use to share the Good News of Jesus with the people you encounter today so their eyes can be opened to the truth and find true hope in the midst of this turbulent time we live in? Maybe you should quit praying for someone else to do the job and accept the fact that God is asking *you* to share the Gospel with those who come across your path and need the saving power of Jesus Christ. And you don't have to do it on your own! He has thoroughly equipped and empowered you to be His witness to a lost world in these very last of the last days!

MY PRAYER FOR TODAY

Father, I recognize that I am living in the last of the last days. Your Word gives me a clear description of the end times and the characteristics that will be evident. Help me live more soberly than ever before with a constant awareness of eternity. Show me day by day how to fulfill my responsibility not only to pray for people to awaken to righteousness, but also to spread the Gospel to the uttermost parts of the earth, starting with those nearest to me now. I ask You, Father, to give me a spirit of boldness to speak and live without compromise. Jesus is coming, and soon everything will change forever. Help me to be prepared and to prepare others also.

I pray this in Jesus' name!

MY CONFESSION FOR TODAY

I confess that I live soberly in this hour. I set my affections on things that are eternal as I seek first the Kingdom of God and pursue His ways. I do not allow myself to become entangled in low-level living or distracted by the cares of this life. I give myself to prayer, to the study of God's Word, and to a lifestyle that honors God and blesses people. I keep myself in the love of God so that I remain strong in faith to please God in all things.

I declare this by faith in Jesus' name!

QUESTIONS FOR YOU TO CONSIDER

1. Do you know a person or a group of individuals who seem blinded to the fact that we are living in the last days? How does this spiritual blindness affect the way they are living their lives?
2. Do you pray for these people on a regular basis? If not, why don't you make a list of people you know who are lost and begin to pray for their salvation every day. Ask God to send someone to reach their hearts so they can know Jesus Christ as you know Him. *Aren't you glad someone prayed for you?*
3. Is it possible that *you* are the person God wants to send to them? Why wouldn't you want to tell them this good news so they can escape an eternity separated from God? What is holding you back from telling them the most important news they could ever hear?

Time is short, so we must use
the time that remains wisely
and shine the light of the Gospel
into the lives of those whom Satan has blinded.

MAY 12

Signs of the Last Days — A Self-Absorbed, Self-Consumed Society

For men shall be lovers
of their own selves, covetous….
— 2 Timothy 3:2

As you drive down the highway to a town or city, signs are regularly posted along the side of the road to keep you on track and help you monitor how far you are from your destination. Those signposts are guides, markers, and indicators, intended to point you in the right direction and keep you on track until you finally arrive at your destination. When you reach your journey's end, a prominent sign usually stands at the entrance of the town, which reads in large, bold letters "Welcome!" *When you see that welcome sign, it is the declaration that you have finally arrived!*

Similarly, in Second Timothy 3:2, Paul listed the events that will act as spiritual signposts, indicating that we are headed toward the very last of the last days. He wrote, "For men shall be lovers of their own selves, covetous…." If all of these events are occurring simultaneously, we need to take it as a big "welcome" sign that lets us know we are no longer journeying *toward* the last of the last days; we have finally *entered* them. If all of these things are in evidence in society around us, we are already there — *in the last of the last days.*

At the first of his list, Paul said, "For men *shall be lovers of their own selves….*" Speaking through the apostle, the Holy Spirit alerts us to the fact that one of the principal signs of the last days will be self-love, self-consumption, and selfishness. When Paul wrote, "...Men shall be lovers of their own selves...," he packed this announcement full of insight!

This verse presents the picture of people who are self-focused, self-centered, and self-consumed. These are self-absorbed people whose wants and needs are the very core and center of their world. Rather than live selfless lives in service to others, their first consideration is always their own self-interests and desires. Everything else takes a back seat to *their* needs being met.

Paul clarified this truth when he stated that they will be "lovers of their own selves." The phrase "lovers of their own selves" is very strange in the Greek language, because it is the Greek word *philautos* — a weird compound of two Greek words. The first of these Greek words is *philos*, a form of the Greek word *phileo*, which mean *to love* or *to be fond of someone else.* It denotes the *love, fondness, attraction*, or *romantic* feelings that people have toward one another. In fact, the Greek word for *kissing* also comes from this word *phileo.*

As you know, kissing is something you do with *someone else*; generally speaking, no one stands in front of the mirror and kisses himself. The word *philos* should *never* be used to describe oneself. However, in this verse, the word *philos* is used in conjunction with the Greek word *autos*, meaning *oneself.* Thus the compound word *philautos* does not describe the love, fondness, romance, or attraction for *someone else* — it refers to one's love and attraction for *oneself.*

This word *philautos* is the picture of complete self-absorption, self-focus, self-preoccupation, and self-love. When you pile all these words on top of each other — the words *eimi*, meaning *I am*, and the word *philautos*, depicting *inordinate self-consumption* and *self-love* — the message is plain: In the last days, society will be utterly consumed with itself.

With this in mind, I advise you to take a look at the world around you today. Do you see a high level of selfishness and self-centeredness permeating every sphere of society? If you do, you need to take heed! *This is a major sign that you have entered the last days.*

Next, Paul said that men will be "covetous" in the last days. This is a translation of the word *philarguros*, which is another strange adjective used to depict people in the last days. Similar to the word *philautos* described above, this word is a compound of the words *philos* and *arguros.* As we saw, the word *philos* refers to *love*, *fondness*, *romance*, or *attraction.* But the second part of the word is the word *arguros*, which is the old Greek word for *silver* or *money*. When these two terms are compounded as they are in this verse, the new word describes *a love of money.*

In ancient Greece, the word *philarguros* was often used to depict *covetousness*, *a love of money*, or someone who is *money hungry.* Even more specifically, it portrayed people who had funds available but were so self-absorbed that they refused to share their wealth with others. Thus, they were so involved in self-embellishment that they were miserly about using their money for others. By using this word, Paul let us know that at the end of the age, a lost society will be so self-centered, they will spend ridiculous sums of money on themselves. Being primarily preoccupied with themselves, they will spend, spend, and *spend* on themselves — constantly searching for ways to treat themselves to more and more while they give less and less for the sake of others.

A major sign that we have entered the last days will be an epidemic of this type of lavish self-spending by people who are self-consumed and self-absorbed. *When you look at the world around you, do you see society moving in this direction?*

This verse could be interpreted to mean:

"People will be self-consumed, self-absorbed, self-focused, and in love with themselves more than anyone else. As a result of this self-love, they will hoard money for themselves while spending very little to help others...."

Certainly God wants His people to be blessed and prosperous, but as riches increase, we must remember that the Bible warns us: "If riches increase, set not your heart upon them" (Psalm 62:10). Our goal is not self-consumption but to use the riches God gives us to fund the preaching of the Gospel around the world. Deuteronomy 8:18 says, "But thou shalt remember the Lord thy God: for it is he that giveth thee power to get wealth, that he may establish his covenant which he sware unto thy fathers, as it is this day." *Establishing His covenant on the earth is our greatest assignment!*

How do you know if you have fallen into the same trap of self-centeredness that is so prevalent in the world today? Let me ask you this question — if the Holy Spirit speaks to your heart and tells you to give, can you say no to the things you were planning to buy so that you can obey the Spirit's unction instead? Or do you find that you regularly hold yourself and your desires above the Lord's calling to help others?

If your first response is to obey the Holy Spirit, it is a sure sign that the self-consumed attitude of the world does not have a place in your heart. If, however, you find it hard to say no to your own creature comforts and regularly ignore the invitation of the Holy Spirit to help someone else, it is a sign that the attitude of the world is worming its way into your heart and soul.

We are in the world, but Jesus has called us to be different from the world. *Therefore, we must ask the Holy Spirit to help us guard our hearts lest we fall into the trap that the world has fallen into in these last days.*

MY PRAYER FOR TODAY

Father, I ask You to help me keep my heart free from materialism and to keep the Gospel as the greatest and highest priority in my life. I know that You want me to be blessed and to be financially and materially increased, but I don't want to set my heart on riches and fall into the trap of this lost world in these last days. Help me stay focused on souls — what You love most — and to do my part to help establish Your covenant in every part of the earth. With the help of the Holy Spirit, I know I can maintain the godly balance You desire for my life regarding possessions and finances.

I pray this in Jesus' name!

MY CONFESSION FOR TODAY

I am sensitive to the Spirit of God in regard to money, materialism, and riches. God wants to massively bless me, but He also wants me to make Him and the preaching of the Gospel worldwide the greatest priority in my life. Jesus gave His life for souls — and I must give my all to help see that those souls hear the Good News. Therefore, I will walk in balance in regard to money and possessions. I will pursue the things I know the Lord wants me to have, but I will not overstep and become so self-absorbed that I ignore the souls that need to know about the saving knowledge of Jesus. I refuse to be self-consumed, so I make the willful decision to let the Holy Spirit rule this area of my life.

I declare this by faith in Jesus' name!

QUESTIONS FOR YOU TO CONSIDER

1. When you read this *Sparkling Gem* today, did you think about the way the world lavishes upon itself with no restraint? Because of easy-to-get credit, people

spend money without even thinking of the ramifications of their expenditures. Do you think this signpost of the last days is evident in the world around you today?

2. What does your own spending reveal about you? Do you have a difficult time saying no to your flesh and practicing restraint and budgetary control? Have you fallen into the trap that the world is in by spending more and more all the time?
3. Have you ever sensed the Holy Spirit speaking to your heart that you have gone over the limit in spending on yourself and that you need to stop being so self-consumed? How did you respond? How will you respond in the future if He lets you know that you need to make an adjustment in this area?

MAY 13

Signs of the Last Days — The Rule of Situational Ethics and Disrespect for Parents

For men shall be...boasters,
proud, blasphemers, disobedient to parents....
— 2 Timothy 3:2

Today let's continue looking at the signposts the apostle Paul wrote about to let us know when we have entered the *very last* of the last days. If we see all of these signs simultaneously occurring in society on a widespread basis, the Holy Spirit wants us to know that we have crossed an invisible prophetic line and have now entered into *the very last of the last days.*

Under the guidance of the Holy Spirit, Paul next wrote that society at the end of the age will be filled with people who are "...boasters, proud, disobedient to parents..." (2 Timothy 3:2).

Let's begin today with the word "boasters." The Greek word used here is the *alazon* — a word that is only used in the New Testament twice: in this verse and in Romans 1:30. It expresses the idea of someone who is a *braggart* or *boaster.* However, this person is not just a braggart — he is *a liar*, for the Greek word *alazon* actually represents *a person so committed to his own self-promotion and agenda that he is willing to exaggerate, overstate the facts, stretch the truth, embellish a story, and even lie if it will get him a new position or goal that he desires.* Today we call this *situational ethics:* adjusting your morals, beliefs, and convictions to fit any situation. In essence, it is doing and saying whatever you must in order to further your agenda, even if it clashes with your conscience or convictions.

Unfortunately, this philosophy is precisely what is being taught in public schools across the world today. Moral absolutes have been replaced by floating ethics, and the rights and wrongs concretely stated by the Bible are now deemed obsolete. The truth of the Gospel is actively supplanted by the immoral minority, who want to remove the Bible from every courthouse and every place of government and to turn each nation into a secular society free from the rule of Scripture and the mention of God. Ask your own children or grandchildren about the situational ethics being promoted in school.

The only other place this word *alazon* is used in the New Testament is Romans 1:30, where Paul described a world that lives apart from God. According to Romans 1:29-31, a godless society is "filled with all unrighteousness, fornication, wickedness, covetousness, maliciousness; full of envy, murder, debate, deceit, malignity, whisperers, backbiters, haters of God, despiteful, proud, *boasters,* inventors of evil things, disobedient to parents, without understanding, covenant breakers, without natural affection, implacable, unmerciful...." Notice the italicized word "boasters" in the middle of this text. It is exactly the same word as in Second Timothy 3:2. But here we see this word "boasters" — the Greek word *alazon* — positioned in the middle of the godless deeds of a world that has thrown moral absolutes to the wind.

It is truly amazing that this anti-God culture will carry out all of these unrighteous deeds with a haughty, bold, proud, "we-know-better-than-you" attitude. That's why Paul next mentioned the word "proud." The word "proud" is the Greek word *huperephanos*, which is a compound of the words *huper* and *phanos.* The word *huper* means *above* or depicts something that is *superior.* The word *phanos* means *to be manifested.*

When the two words are compounded, the new word depicts a person who sees himself as *above* the rest of the crowd. This represents *an arrogant, haughty, impudent, snooty, high-and-mighty, insolent attitude* that thinks it is intellectually advantaged and therefore has the right to set the agenda for everyone else. *What an accurate description of those who would like to remove God from our lives and force their liberal agenda on the rest of us.* According to Paul's prophetic words in Second Timothy 3:2, this will be a mark of society at the end of the Church Age.

Paul elaborated by telling us that these high-minded, immoral agenda-setters will also be "blasphemers." The word "blasphemers" in Greek is the word *blasphemeo*, which can refer to blaspheming God, but most often means *to speak discourteously, slanderously, and reproachfully* or *to rail against by bringing abusive, debasing, degrading accusations against those with whom one does not agree.*

Peter used *blasphemo* in Second Peter 2:11 to describe people who are disrespectful of the things of God. People in this category see themselves as superior to those whom they deem to be resistant to change and stuck in a primitive mode of thinking — that is, moral absolutes that uphold righteous conduct. They disdain, mock, slander, and speak ill of them. That is precisely what the Spirit is forecasting about the end of the age as Paul laid out the telltale signposts that declare the last of the last days is upon us.

But wait — there's more! In the midst of this last-days society where situational ethics reigns and Bible absolutes are thrown to the wind, Paul prophesied it would produce an epidemic emergence of "disobedience to parents." The word "disobedient" in Greek is the word *aithpees.* The root of this word is *peitho*, which means *to persuade.* However, with the Greek prefix *a* attached to the front, this word *aithpees* takes on the opposite meaning. It carries the idea of being *unpersuadable* or *uncontrollable* and thereby *unleadable.* Thus, the phrase "disobedient to parents" in Second Timothy 3:2 actually carries the idea of *children that parents can no longer persuade, control, lead, or exercise authority over.* In other words, a day is coming when children will no longer be required to submit to or follow the orders and leadership of their dad and mom.

This problem is already widespread in the world today. Children speak disrespectfully to their parents; they don't want their rights violated by parents telling them what to do; and the court system has stood by the right of a child to sue his or her parents. Parents are so bound by the laws of the new moral agenda that they are fearful to discipline their own children, lest they be arrested for child abuse. Although some children have certainly been protected by such laws, the fact is that these laws have put the child in a superior position in the eyes of the legal system and weakened the leadership of the parents to teach, discipline, and lead their own kids. *Just as Paul prophesied, the day has come when parents are under pressure to surrender their parental authority to rule their own children.*

If you put all these words and phrases together, an interpretive translation of this verse could read:

> *"...These boasters are so committed to their own self-promotion and agenda that they are willing to exaggerate, overstate the facts, stretch the truth, embellish a story, and even lie if it will get them the position, advantage, or goal they desire. They are arrogant, haughty, impudent, snooty, and insolent. They disdain, mock, slander, and speak ill of anyone that stands in the way of their plans. And in this environment, parents will no longer be able to persuade, control, lead, or exercise authority over their children...."*

All of these are signposts that *the last* of the last days are upon us. Based on these scriptures and Greek word meanings, can you see the marks of the last days in the world today? *Does any of this sound familiar to you?*

Just because this is what will happen in the world in the last days doesn't mean it must happen to you. These are events that will occur in the lost world — *not* in the Church of the living God! We are in the world, but we are not *of* this lost world's system (*see* John 17:14-16). And since the Holy Spirit warned us of these things in advance, we must take heed to His prophetic word and take action to protect families and homes while we march forward with speed to preach the Gospel to people who are lost and without Christ.

This can be our greatest hour if we will keep ourselves pure in the love of God, live separate from the lost standards of the world, maintain the moral code of God in our hearts and homes, and shine the light of Jesus Christ into the darkness that has flooded into nearly every corner of society. People are looking for solutions to their deeply embedded moral dilemmas, and we have the answers they need — *so let's let our light shine brightly!*

MY PRAYER FOR TODAY

Lord, I am deeply moved by the accuracy of Your Word and Your long-planned desire to prepare us in advance for the developments that are happening in the world around us today. Thank You for loving us so much that You desired to tell us in advance what would happen in the last days. Because Your Word is so clear, I know exactly what I need to do to protect my heart, safeguard my home, and keep Your law alive and fresh in my mind. Holy Spirit, I ask You to help me stay free from the distorted reasoning of the world and to stay on fire with the love of God. And I sincerely ask You to help me reach out to others who have been affected by the lost and deceived thinking of the world and whose lives have been made shambles as a result of no moral law. They need Your Word and help — and I know that You are asking Me to be Your hand extended to them. So today I surrender my life to be Your helping hand to this hurting world around me.

I pray this in Jesus' name!

MY CONFESSION FOR TODAY

I boldly declare that regardless of what the world or society says, I will live my life according to the law of God. The world does not dictate my moral code or standard because I am a child of God. When the world around me mocks, laughs, or ridicules me for taking a stand that is contrary to theirs, I am empowered by the Spirit of God to stand strong and to remain true to my convictions. God's Word is unchanging — and just as the truth of His Word never changes, I will not change my behavior or my convictions to be like the world. Rather, I will live in a righteous manner to please God, and by so doing, my life will shine a great light to people who sit in darkness. Due to my conviction and godly life, I will be a beacon of hope and help to others who have been devastated by the lost immoral standards of the world.

I declare this by faith in Jesus' name!

QUESTIONS FOR YOU TO CONSIDER

1. As you read today's *Sparkling Gem*, did any of it sound like the society in which you live today? What part especially hit you as being relevant and pertinent to our modern-day world?
2. Can you think of any areas in your life or thinking where you have allowed the world to affect your view? Maybe you once held tightly to a strict moral code, but in recent years you have let some of your convictions slip to accommodate people who are different from you or people you like but who are living outside of God's will and His ways? What are those areas where you have compromised your convictions and beliefs?
3. In what way should you respond to what you have read today? Is the Holy Spirit tugging at your heart? If so, what is the Spirit of God asking you to do to get back in line with His Word and His unchanging truth?

MAY 14

Signs of the Last Days — Unthankful and Unholy

For men shall be… unthankful, unholy….
— 2 Timothy 3:2

In the 1970s, a book by a well-known Christian leader was published that shook the entire Christian community to its core. The reason it so deeply impacted so many people was the dreadful predictions it made about the future. Perhaps the most shocking prediction was that a day would come when sexual situations and homosexuality would be seen on television in people's homes. People were *aghast*!

The Christian community reacted sharply. Across the nation people resounded, "The man who wrote this book is obviously off in his predictions, because such things could never happen in America." But now years have passed, and what this man predicted is *exactly* what has come to pass. No one would have believed that the trash now seen and laughed at on television every night would become so commonplace that people wouldn't even be disturbed by it.

This downward spiral that has occurred in the moral code of Western society is hooked to another modern trend that we can trace through the years. Western nations — and especially America — are extremely blessed with financial prosperity and material possessions. So who could ever dream that people in such a blessed environment could be *ungrateful* for the blessings they possess? Yet instead of focusing on the blessings they have and thanking God for them, a lost and selfish world focuses on what they do not have — claiming they deserve more than they are getting.

As we continue looking at signposts of the last days outlined in Second Timothy 3, we see that an *unthankful attitude* is listed with *unholiness* as two major indicators that the final stages of the last days have begun. Paul told us that society at the end of the age will become "unthankful."

The word "unthankful" is a translation of the Greek word *acharistos.* The word *charistos* on its own simply means *thankful*, but when an *a* is attached to the front of it, it *reverses* the condition and turns it into an attitude that is *unthankful* and *ungrateful.* It is a picture of people who previously had a thankful heart but now are *unthankful* and *unappreciative.* They no longer focus on their blessings they have in their lives; instead, they fixate on what they *don't* have. These are people who have become *unappreciative* and *unthankful* and who live their lives *void of any sense of gratitude.*

The only other place where the word *acharistos* is found in the New Testament is Luke 6:35. There Jesus connects *unthankfulness* with *evil*, which lets us know that ingratitude is evil in God's sight. It is spiritually criminal to not be thankful for what we have.

The unsaved man is selfish because iniquity rules his heart. And a chief manifestation of iniquity is ingratitude, which is a symptom of selfishness. But Christians are not immune from a selfish, ungrateful attitude. Christians can also succumb to the sense of entitlement and selfishness that marks the spirit of this age.

You need to know that as long as an ungrateful attitude prevails in your life, you will never be happy. *Thankfulness is a prerequisite to happiness, because only a thankful heart can be a happy heart.*

Unfortunately, we live in a world today where people are so self-focused and self-consumed that they are rarely grateful for anything. In fact, people have been blessed with so much that they take their blessings for granted and don't even realize how fortunate they truly are. Rather than being *thankful* — the Greek word *charistos* — they are *unthankful* (*acharistos*), and Paul taught that this is a signpost of the last days.

Before we proceed to Paul's next point, I want to ask you:

- Are you grateful and thankful for what you have, or has unthankfulness begun to poison your spiritual life?
- How long has it been since you took time to thank God for what you *do* have?
- Taking your words and actions into account, would God count you to be among those who have thankful and grateful hearts, or would He count you to be among the ungrateful and unthankful?
- How long has it been since you considered your blessings and set aside time to specifically thank God for what He has provided in your life?
- When you are thankful, it not only changes your attitude, but it also transforms the environment around you. So isn't it time that you took time to thank God for His blessings in your life and thereby positively affect your attitude and environment?

One thing is clear: Unthankfulness and unholiness are connected. *One always leads to the other.* That is why Paul lists the word "unholy" immediately after the word "unthankful." When people stop expressing a heart of gratitude toward God, unholy attitudes inevitably begin to materialize, and these attitudes are soon followed by blatant unholy behavior.

Think of it — in our world today, nations that were established on godly principles have become infested with godlessness and wickedness. Things have changed radically even within the span of our lifetimes! In just a few short decades, society has devolved from sanctioning open prayer in public schools to outlawing God altogether in those places. Instead of acknowledging God as the Supreme Creator, society refuses to recognize Him at all. And when the recognition of God is removed, everything evil has room to take root and propagate. As long as a society recognizes God, it will live by a higher moral code — but when God is removed, man immediately begins to slide downward into sin and debauchery. *Unthankfulness always leads to unholiness.*

The word "unholy" that Paul used in this text is from the Greek word *anosios.* The Greek root, *nosios*, refers to that which is *holy, sacred, pure*, or *sanctioned by God.* However, when an *a* is attached to the front of the word, it *reverses* the condition. Just as an *a* attached to the front of the word *charistos* changes the meaning from *thankfulness* to *unthankfulness*, an *a* added to the front of the word *osios* changes its meaning to *unholy*, *unsacred*, *impure*, and *unsanctioned by God*. This word *anosios* describes a person who once was ruled by holiness, but who now has become dominated by the rule of unholiness. At one point, this individual revered that which was holy, sacred, pure, and sanctioned by God — but he became contaminated by the *unholy*, *unsacred*, and *impure*. He made the choice to embrace attitudes and actions that are *unsanctioned by God*.

In addition to describing that which is unsacred, the Greek word *anosios* ("unholy") can also be used to describe activities or actions that are *impure*, *ill-mannered*, *improper*, *unclean*, *indecent*, *coarse*, *vulgar*, *offensive*, *crude*, *lewd*, and *rude*. That book I mentioned earlier produced a sharp reaction from the wider Christian community when it was published in the 1970s because no one believed such things could happen in a God-fearing nation. Yet in the years since that time, that author's predictions have proven true, time and time again. God has been removed from classrooms and from public places — and the nation has slidden into a moral downward spiral. One visit to an evening of television will quickly show that which is *impure*, *ill-mannered*, *improper*, *unclean*, *indecent*, *coarse*, *vulgar*, *offensive*, *crude*, *lewd*, and *rude* is dominating the air waves and society. What was once considered vulgar is now widely considered appropriate subject matter for jokes and entertainment. What God calls unholy is what society thinks is funny. *What has happened to us?*

These are all signs of the last days.

However, just because you live in the last days does *not* mean that you should be affected by this moral downslide. By making God's Word your standard and upholding it in your life, you can stay free from the spiritual corrosion that is eating away at the world today. What is happening to a lost society does *not* have to happen to you or to your family.

To remain untouched by this moral degeneration, you must make the decision to keep your eyes on Jesus and live to please Him. Choose to make His Word the guide for your heart, and never permit yourself to entertain or find funny those things that God deems "unholy." This situation is not funny — *it is spiritually deadly and damning*. The world laughs while it goes to hell. Lost society is oblivious to the deception that is dragging it lower and lower into depravity and judgment. What is funny about this scenario? *Nothing!*

If society focused its gaze on God and kept Him in their minds, it would be more difficult for Satan's deception to work its plan in the world. But when man becomes unthankful — ceasing to acknowledge God and to be thankful for His abundant blessings — that is when he begins to sink into decadence.

**These words in Second Timothy 3:2
are so packed with meaning that this part of the verse
could be expanded and paraphrased to read:**

"...Although they were once thankful and appreciative, people will become void of gratitude and generally unappreciative of everything in the last times. As a result, impurity will

seep into society and cause it to become unholy — impure, ill-mannered, unclean, indecent, coarse, vulgar, offensive, crude, lewd, and rude, behaving and carrying on in a way that God would never sanction...."

The same effect can happen to you as a believer if you cease to recognize God and express thankfulness to Him. You see, a Christian may not slide into the same sins to which the world quickly succumbs, but ungratefulness, bitterness, and other heart-hardening attitudes will worm their way into your soul if you do not maintain an attitude of thankfulness and constantly recognize God's goodness in your life.

This is exactly why King David spoke to his own soul in Psalm 103:2, saying, "Bless the Lord, O my soul, and forget not all his benefits." In a moment of difficulty, David paused to remind himself that God had been good to him. By rehearsing in his mind all the good things that God had done in his life, it created in him a thankful and grateful heart.

So before you do anything else today, why don't you take a few minutes to be alone with the Lord and express your thankfulness to Him for the wonderful things He has done for you? If you are tempted to feel sorry for yourself or to think that others are more blessed than you, this is an indicator that you may have slipped into the sin of being more focused on what you *don't* have than you are on all the good things you *do* have — and on the wonderful things God has already *done* for you. The truth is, you have a lot to be thankful for if you'll just take time to think about it. *Regardless of what you are facing today — God has been good to you, and it's time to thank Him for His blessing in your life!*

MY PRAYER FOR TODAY

Father, I ask You to help me remember all the good things You have done for me! Forgive me for being so focused on what I don't have that I've overlooked what I do have. I refuse to be unthankful. Today I pause to rehearse all the good and wonderful things You have done in my life. I repent for allowing ingratitude and a lack of thankfulness to creep into my life when the list of things I have to be thankful for is so long that I don't know if I can even recall all of Your goodness. Thank You for being so good to me!

I pray this in Jesus' name!

MY CONFESSION FOR TODAY

I confess that I have a grateful and thankful heart! My soul blesses the Lord, and I forget not all His benefits toward me! The world around me may forget God's goodness, but I will not be guilty of this neglect. He saved me from sin; He rescued me from myself; He delivered me from harm and destruction; He has kept me safely through all kinds of situations in life; and He has given me His Word as His promise and His Spirit to empower my life and to help keep me free from sin. He has done so much for me! I make the decision right now that my mouth is going to be filled with His praises, and thankfulness will spring forth from my heart. By recognizing

Him and what He has done in my life, I will positively affect my attitude and super-charge my environment with the Spirit of God!

I declare this by faith in Jesus' name!

QUESTIONS FOR YOU TO CONSIDER

1. How long has it been since you made a list of the things you are thankful for that God has done for you? In order to keep your heart soft before the Lord, it is necessary for you to maintain a grateful attitude, so today I want to encourage you to take a little time to reflect on all God has done for you and to make a list of the things for which you are thankful.
2. As you've watched television, have you noticed how so much of what is broadcast into people's homes is impure, ill-mannered, improper, unclean, indecent, coarse, vulgar, offensive, crude, lewd, and rude? As you listen to unholy jokes or watch subject matter that is grievous to God, what effect does it have on you?
3. What changes do you need to make in your own life to be more pleasing to God in the way you live and think? What do you need to eliminate in order to keep your mind pure and your thoughts clean? Has the Holy Spirit been dealing with you about any areas you need to change — and if yes, what are those areas?

MAY 15

Signs of the Last Days — The Breakdown of Family Relationships

...without natural affection,
trucebreakers, false accusers...
— 2 Timothy 3:3

When I was a young boy, each night our family gathered around the table in the dining room for the evening meal. Mother cooked while my sisters and I set the plates and silverware on the table, and before we ate, Dad prayed a prayer of blessing over our meal. It was a wonderful family time that we looked forward to each evening. When we finished our meal, we washed, dried, and put away the dishes. Then we'd usually move to the living room to spend time together watching a couple of family-oriented TV programs.

We ate together, prayed together, spent our evenings and weekends together, went to church together, and even rode everywhere in the car together because we only had one car. If we spent time away from home, it was at the home of family friends or at a church function. So we were together most of the time, as were most families back in those days. But this is *not* the case for most families today.

Because most homes own multiple cars today, everyone often travels separately, following their various busy schedules. As a result, few families sit down to eat a meal together — and even if they do, it is rarely cooked at home but usually eaten at a restaurant. Families don't even watch television together anymore. Because they have so many televisions in their houses, they can all be home, yet not together, watching different programs in different parts of the house. Unfortunately, many families don't even attend the same church.

The truth is, if families are going to spend time together today, it won't usually happen unless they cancel something else and schedule time to make it happen. The day of families spending large amounts of time together has almost vanished in our modern-day world. But according to the signposts that Paul lists in Second Timothy 3, the deterioration of close families and marriages are developments that will occur in the last days.

Paul next told us that society will be "without natural affection...." The words "without natural affection" are a translation of the Greek word *astorgos* — from the word *storgos,* but with an *a* affixed to the front of it, which reverses the definition of *storgos.*

So what does *storgos* mean? It is the Greek word that describes *devotion to one's own family* or *an instinctive commitment to one's family.* But when an *a* is fixed to the front of this word, it describes *a lack of devotion or commitment to one's family.* In other words, it pictures a disjointed family that has lost the closeness it once possessed. The word *astorgos* that Paul used in this verse could be translated *unloving,* but with reference to an unloving, non-nurturing, uncaring family environment.

The traditional family relationships that once existed in abundance are threatened today by schedules, multiple jobs in one home, financial pressure, divorce, kids living with separate parents, multiple cars that help to create separate paths of each family member's life, multiple televisions per home, and so on. Parents go one direction, while children go another direction — and very often even Dad and Mom don't go the same direction. Thus, the family resides in one house together, but they don't share life together, and most often they don't even share a meal together unless they schedule it into their week.

Sociologists say this troubling trend has contributed to rebellion in children who feel neglected or unwanted; attention disorders in children who are rushed from one place to the next or who spend time watching television instead of enjoying time with their parents and siblings; and marital relationships deteriorating as a result of life moving so fast that husband and wife don't take time to connect and share their hearts and lives in a meaningful way. This problem today is epidemic. Just ask any schoolteacher about the state of children today — and teachers everywhere will verify that the family is in serious trouble.

This is one of the signposts that we have entered the last of the last days.

People who assert that the family situation today is no different than in previous times are either deliberately negligent or blind to the facts. We have only to read the statistics and reports of what is happening to the family to nearly be shaken to the core. *It is a sign of the times in which we are living.*

Thank God, those of us who love Him do not have to fall victim to this plight. By living according to God's Word and by making our families and participation in a local church a priority, we can build strong families even in these last days. If we *don't* take time to build our families right, we will unfortunately reap sad consequences. These are the last days; therefore, we are obligated to wisely build our families to resist the spiritual storms that are characteristic of this age.

Paul went on to tell us next that the deterioration of the family will be so rampant in the last days, families will be affected by "trucebreakers." The word "trucebreakers" is the Greek word *aspondos*, from the word *spondos*, meaning *a treaty* or *a covenant* but with an *a* attached to the front of it. This makes it the word *aspondos*, which is an unquestionable reference to *one who breaks a truce* or *one who breaks a covenant*. The word is difficult to translate from Greek, but almost all translators agree that this describes a covenant that is broken due to *irreconcilable differences*. In this verse, Paul had just been speaking about deteriorating family relationships. By using this word *aspondos* at this juncture, in all likelihood he was predicting a rampant outbreak of *divorce* in the very last of the last days.

Family relationships will decline to such a degree in the last days that it will give rise to a widespread epidemic of divorce. Lacking the commitment to work through problems, husbands and wives — who already are moving so fast that they are nearly living separate lives — will find it easier to just keep permanently moving in different directions rather than sticking it out and working through their problems. Paul even used the Greek word *aspondos* to let us know the claim of *irreconcilable differences* will be used as the main reason to divorce. The Holy Spirit prophesies through Paul that when divorce hits epidemic proportions, it is a signpost that the world has entered the final chapters of the last days.

Divorce is at an all-time high in world history. The introduction of *no-fault divorce* — otherwise referred to as *irreconcilable differences* — has been a huge contributor to the largest increase of divorce in history. Billions of dollars are spent annually on support payments, and tens of thousands of professional workers administer and enforce child-support arrangements. In short, divorce is sadly one of the biggest industries in the world today.

Knowing that we live in these last days, we who are married must stay before the Lord, keep a pure heart, and cleave to the spouse God gave us. If you struggle in your marital relationship, God's Word and the power of the Holy Spirit can mend it. Yes, it may take time and work. But in most cases, with God's help, you will find that you don't have to become another casualty of this trend toward divorce that is so rampant in the world today.

But if you have already fallen victim to this symptom of the last days, God's grace is present to fully restore. He loves you and cares deeply for the wounds this has inflicted on your soul and on the souls of your children. With the help of God and empowerment of the Holy Spirit, it is possible for you to fully recover from this trauma. *God is always present to help those who call on Him in time of need.*

Where divorce is rampant, the courts are overloaded with lawsuits — and this leads to the next point that Paul listed in his signposts of the last days. He wrote that society will experience a wave of "false accusers." Pay close attention to this point because I believe that you will find this *very interesting.*

The words "false accusers" in Greek is *diabolos,* which most often is translated as the word *devil.* In the context of these verses, however, it is used to picture people who *argue* and *debate* in a court of law in order to win material gain or to get legal advantage.

Just as the word "devil" means *accuser* or *slanderer*, Paul used this word to depict a time when people will excessively accuse, slander, and sue to gain material substance or to get legal advantage. Paul forecasted a time when, rather than sit down and work it out, people will overload the legal system with lawsuits because they find it easier and more convenient — or to their financial advantage — to accuse and sue rather than to settle their differences. In fact, it may seem as if the devil himself has taken over the legal system as more and more people join the frenzy and resort to suing each other.

Does this sound familiar to the world you live in today?

As I read Paul's list of signposts indicating that the last days have begun, I am simply *amazed* at the accuracy of the Bible. Paul told us that society would be "...without natural affection, trucebreakers, false accusers..." (2 Timothy 3:2). Two thousand years in advance, the Holy Spirit perfectly forecasted what would occur in society at the end of the ages.

All of these words and phrases in an interpretative translation could read:

> *"...Love and commitment for family will degenerate; divorce will become epidemic with irreconcilable differences being the major cause for separation; and the court system will be overwhelmed as people go overboard in their suing others and in being sued...."*

It's amazing to read, isn't it? Yet these are the days we live in. But God has not abandoned us to these turbulent times. We have the Word of God as our instruction manual; the Holy Spirit as our Teacher, Mentor, and Guide; and we have other brothers and sisters in the Christian community on whom we can lean for support and help when it is needed. With all that God has provided, we are well able to live victoriously for Him in these last times!

It's not time for you to throw in the towel in despair — it's time for you to throw up your hands with a shout of victory! You are truly a part of a chosen generation that is experiencing not only the end of the age, but also history's greatest opportunity to share the Good News of Jesus Christ and to help bring in a last harvest of souls before the age concludes. *What a privilege!*

So continually fortify yourself with God's Word; learn to let the Holy Spirit's power flow unhindered through you; and run your race with endurance all the way to the end. In the midst of all your other responsibilities before God, make a quality decision to set aside time to spend with family as a top priority so you can keep family relationships strong and healthy. And before you conclude your race one day, determine to do all you can to tell the Good News of Jesus to people so that when you make the big exit, you will take as many people with you as possible!

MY PRAYER FOR TODAY

Lord, I am so glad that You saved me and delivered me from the destruction that is at work in the lost world today. When I read your Word and watch what is happening in the world around me, I see how carefully You tried to warn us of these things and to prepare us to live victoriously in them. How can I ever thank You enough for so carefully revealing the future and the truth to those of us who love You and Your Word? Now that I really see what a pivotal time this is, I ask You to help me live each day wisely and not to waste a minute. And please teach me to take advantage of each opportunity when I can tell the Good News of Jesus' saving grace to people who are lost and in need of Him.

I pray this in Jesus' name!

MY CONFESSION FOR TODAY

I boldly confess that the Holy Spirit lives in me. Therefore, I am more than enough to face the challenges of living in these last days. It is no accident that I am alive right now. God chose me for this time; He needs me on the earth. I am anointed to break burdens, to destroy the yoke of bondage in people's lives, and to manifest the glory of God to all those who are around me. Thank You, Lord, for allowing me to see the end of the ages that the prophets saw by faith. I purpose to obey the Word of God, walk in obedience to the Holy Spirit, and see the glory of God manifested in my life.

I declare this by faith in Jesus' name!

QUESTIONS FOR YOU TO CONSIDER

1. In light of what you have read in today's *Sparkling Gem*, I want to ask, how is the condition of your family? Do you spend time together? Do you sit down and eat a meal together every day — or do you find your family all going in different directions and hardly ever spending quality time together?
2. What decisions and changes do you need to make to strengthen your family? What do you believe the Holy Spirit is asking you to do to undergird your home and to make it stronger?
3. Can you think of people who have been casualties of the trends you've read about today? Can you think of people who have suffered personal tragedy or loss that you can help, strengthen, or assist as they recover from the struggles they have gone through? Who are those people, and what should you do to show your love and concern to them?

MAY 16

Signs of the Last Days — Confusion Between What Is Right and Wrong

...fierce, despisers of those that are good....
— 2 Timothy 3:3

The material I am about to present concerns a subject that I normally wouldn't write about. However, it provides a powerful illustration of the depravity Paul prophesied would occur during the last days (*see* 2 Timothy 3:2,3), and I believe it serves as a wakeup call to the Church. Sometimes we need a stark reminder of the rapid degeneration of society's moral fabric that is occurring all around us at an ever-increasing rate so we don't grow complacent and just "go with the flow" of society's downward moral spiral. As the Church, we have a vital role to play in these perilous times as standard bearers of truth. So bear with me as I take on that role to share some disturbing but important information, and you will understand my point.

Several years ago, the Holy Spirit strongly impressed me to speak on the subject of abortion to my Moscow congregation. I had never once spoken on this subject in all my years as a minister, yet I knew the Holy Spirit was compelling me that this was a message my congregation needed to hear. I didn't know why the Spirit of God impressed this upon me so strongly until I began to do research about abortion in the former Soviet Union and the rest of the world. What I discovered simply *stunned* and *shocked* me.

I discovered that there have been nearly one billion abortions performed worldwide since the 1940s. At the time of this writing, it is more than the combined populations of the *United States*, *Central America*, *South America*, *Canada*, *Australia*, *England*, *France*, *Italy*, and *Greece*.

The greatest and most extensive killing in human history was not done by *Nero*, *Domitian*, *Hitler*, or *Stalin* — it was done by medical doctors who have murdered more than *one billion* babies through the act of abortion in the past 100 years. This is mass murder of the innocent, far worse than any holocaust or genocide. It is the annihilation of those who cannot scream to be heard, who cannot defend themselves, and who are thrown in the garbage can or whose body parts are "harvested" for material gain and other purposes.

When I first read these statistics, I shuddered to think of the defenseless lives that have been lost and the blood that has been spilled. But as I continued studying, I was truly amazed at the rationale of those who are pro-choice. Repeatedly they state that they want the rights of the mother to be protected — that if she doesn't want to have a baby, it should be her "right" to end the pregnancy. I kept wondering about the "rights" of the infant. *What about the infant's right to live?*

What is confusing about this logic is that in the same hospitals where abortions are performed at one end, surgeries are being performed at the other end on infants who are still in their mother's womb. On one end of the hospital they take a life; on the other end of the hospital they save a life — both in the womb of a mother. This is completely *illogical.* One hundred years ago when common sense still prevailed, no one would have thought this kind of reasoning to be normal. *This is a sign of the times in which we live.*

As I pondered on all of this, my mind went to Second Timothy 3:3 where Paul discussed the attitudes that will be prevalent in society at the end of the age. As I thought about the brutality of taking innocent lives — and doing it in such a sophisticated way in our nice, sterilized hospitals — I thought about the next point on Paul's list of signposts that we are in the very last of the last days. He goes on to inform us that society will be "fierce" in those days. *What does the word "fierce" mean?*

The word "fierce" is a strange word to describe today. This word would better be used to describe cannibals or barbarians. It is the word *anemeros*, derived from the word *nemeros*, which pictures something that is *gentle, kind*, or *mild*. But when an *a* is fixed to the front of the word — turning it into the word *anemeros* — this word changes dramatically. Rather than *gentle, kind*, or *mild*, it means *savage, vicious, uncivilized, violent, ferocious*, or *inhumane*.

When you think about the world today, much of it seems quite civilized and sophisticated *until* you remember the one billion babies who have been brutally ripped to pieces — savagely killed every minute of the day in beautiful, sterilized hospitals and clinics across the world. This is savagery of the worse kind; it is legalized murder on a scale so massive that no fiction writer of yesteryear could have imagined it. But this is not fiction; this is *reality*.

Today those who fight for the rights of unborn children are portrayed as primitive and unintelligent. This is the result of a massive public relations blitz to annihilate the opposition and reinforce the right to terminate the life of a child. Thus far, the courts have unfortunately ruled that a child's life can be terminated. The law has no defense for the child. I say all of this because of the next point Paul listed in Second Timothy 3. He went on to speak about "despisers of those that are good." *What does this phrase mean?*

The phrase in Greek is the word *aphiloagathos*, and it is a very strange Greek word. In its oldest and truest sense, it depicts *a society where law is not primarily intended to protect the rights of good people but rather is used instead to protect and defend the rights of offenders.* This word is so unusual, in fact, that it is never used anywhere else in the New Testament. Who could ever imagine a world where laws were used primarily to defend offenders and not to protect the rights of those who are good? Yet this is precisely what Paul prophesied in this verse.

This teaching doesn't apply only to abortion; it also could be applied to a wide range of situations where criminals are so aggressively protected that they go free while the innocent suffer. According to Second Timothy 3:3, the world in the last days will be *savage* and *inhumane*, and it will be *morally confused* as to what is right or wrong. *Can you think of ways that this has application to the world we live in today?*

If you have terminated the life of an unborn child — or if you know someone who has done this — there is forgiveness in Jesus Christ. The world today has drifted far from what is right on a wide range of issues, and I did not intend to highlight this one act in order to condemn anyone. Just as there is forgiveness for every grievance against God, there is forgiveness for you or for that person you know who made such a wrong decision. If you will ask Jesus to forgive you, First John 1:9 promises that He will forgive you and cleanse you from all unrighteousness.

When the world is morally confused about what is right and wrong, we cannot look to society to set our moral agenda. We must look to the Bible to be our guide and let it be the standard by which we live. I exhort you today to make a renewed commitment to live your life according to the truths set forth by the Bible and to reject any piece of society's errant moral code that is in conflict with the Word of God. *When this world system is over and gone, the Bible and its truths will remain — so align yourself with the eternal and unchanging standards and principles of God!*

MY PRAYER FOR TODAY

Father, I ask You to give me a heart for people who have been victimized by the floating moral standard that is trying to dictate what is right and wrong in the world today. Because they listened to the advice of the world, so many people have made decisions they later regretted — decisions that hurt their hearts and wounded their souls. Help me not to condemn them for past mistakes, but to assist them in receiving forgiveness, hope, and healing. I know that You stand with arms wide open to anyone who comes to You. I want to have the same heart and mind that You have, so help me be a beacon of help and hope to people who are looking for answers in these last days.

I pray this in Jesus' name!

MY CONFESSION FOR TODAY

I confess that I will base my life on the Word of God, and I refuse to be led by the loose ethical standards that are in the world today. As a child of God and a member of God's Kingdom, I live by a superior law and higher standard. I have made the choice that God's Word will be a lamp to my feet and a light to my path that I may not sin against God. Because the Holy Spirit lives within me, He will help me to walk in the paths of righteousness even in the midst of a world that is headed in a wrong direction. With His help and power, I can always do what is right and make correct choices for my life.

I declare this by faith in Jesus' name!

QUESTIONS FOR YOU TO CONSIDER

1. How would you help someone who carries guilt and condemnation for something he or she did wrong in the past? What would you say? How would you counsel that person? What scriptures would you use to help him or her release from the past, receive the forgiveness of God, and move forward in life?

2. Can you think of someone you know who has been deeply affected by something he or she did in the past? What have you done to help that person get over that hurdle so he or she can move forward?
3. As you read today's *Sparkling Gem,* what other areas did you think about where society is morally confused? I'm talking about areas that are wrong according to God's Word, but society tries to promote it as though it is acceptable.

MAY 17

Signs of the Last Days — Widespread Violence

This know also, that in the last days
perilous times shall come. For men shall be...
heady, high-minded....
— 2 Timothy 3:1,2,4

Many years ago, Denise and I took our sons to Rome for a study tour of the ancient world with a special emphasis on early Christian history. As we stood inside the great Roman Coliseum, we listened as our doctoral guide spoke to us at length about the barbarism and atrocities that were so loved and cheered by the Roman citizens who packed that great stadium nearly 2,000 years ago.

You're familiar with the scenes I'm referring to — gladiators fighting one another to the death and wild animals ripping people limb from limb, devouring them before the leering gaze of a bloodthirsty crowd. Most of us have seen such scenes in various movies at some point in our lives. Who could ever forget the movie *Spartacus* or *Gladiator* in which barbarians mercilessly killed each other as the Roman audience roared with delight!

But the fact is that these bloody events did not occur only in the city of Rome. Violent entertainment occurred in every place where the Roman Empire was established. From Rome to the northern shores of Africa, from Britain to the Middle East, scenes of violence were regularly performed and enjoyed as entertainment by adoring crowds who erupted with *thrilled delight* at the sight of human blood. The shedding of blood was the most popular form of amusement of that time! Although the Romans claimed to be the great educators and civilizers of the world, the truth is that in many ways, they were *barbaric.*

Today we look back at the Romans and wonder how they could have tolerated such barbarism. Their ancient ruins stand as memorials of a society that ran amuck with murder and brutality. It's amazing to realize that at the time when these enormous stadiums were packed with people cheering on such atrocities, the Holy Spirit foretold that a time at the end of the Church Age would come when violence would once again become a mainstream occurrence in society.

In Second Timothy 3:4, the Holy Spirit pointed His finger toward the future and prophesied that in the last days, violence would become more widespread and worse than it has ever been — *even more depraved than the events that occurred in the Roman Empire.* Paul wrote that society will become "heady" in the last days. The word "heady" is a poor translation of the Greek word *propetes*, a term used to depict *people so wholly given to violence that they become known for their violent, reckless behavior and hot-headed, emotional intemperance that exhibits a lack of self-control.* Based on this word, it is clear that the Holy Spirit was prophesying of a time when members of society in general would fully embrace violence and lose their ability to control their tempers.

Since the Holy Spirit chose the word *protetes* to describe a last-days generation, I want to ask you: *Is this current generation known for violence and intemperance?* When history looks back at our time, what will they write about us? We remember the Romans for the violence that filled their stadiums. But how will history remember *our* generation and our own forms of entertainment and what we tolerate as society in terms of violence against its weakest members?

Was the Holy Spirit correct to forecast that violence in the last days would be more widespread than at any other time in human history? Of course, we know that He is the Spirit of Truth, and He predicts the future with absolute precision and accuracy. So, of course, the answer to that question is *yes*!

Unfortunately, it is true that our present generation is the most violent generation in human history. It has far surpassed the Romans with its love of bloodshed that now dominates movies, television, music, video games, and the Internet. This is a generation that feeds on violence and is, not surprisingly, experiencing increasing levels of actual violence in every facet of society.

Because the Holy Spirit prophesied this trend toward increasing violence, He clearly felt it was important for us to be informed about these things before they happen. The Holy Spirit said that society in the last times would be "heady" — *protetes,* meaning *violent* or *known for violence.*

One need only look at the violence in the media today to see how accurate the Holy Spirit was in His predictions about the last days. The percentage of households containing multiple televisions and computers is at an all-time high. It is therefore not surprising that the potential for violent words and images coming into those homes from the outside is also exponentially rising along with an increasing thirst for violence in every form of media.

By age 18, the average young person will have seen hundreds of thousand acts of violence on television. This doesn't include the thousands of hours of secular music he or she will listen to. Since much of this music is violence-related, it means that words and ideas concerning acts of violence are being poured into the minds of teenagers. Studies have shown that such music may be a significant marker for substance abuse, psychiatric disorders, suicide risk, other tendencies to anger and violence, and alienation from healthy, formative relationships.

We know biblically that it's true: Whether positively or negatively, what a person continually sees and listens to will directly affect him in his soul, in his spiritual life, and in his walk with God. And the company a person keeps will affect him spiritually and influence the way he views God and others. Thus it stands to reason that while a person is isolating himself from good relationships that are formative in a beneficial way, he is connecting himself to wrong relationships that can cause him to be *mal*formed socially and emotionally.

Literally hundreds of studies on the effects of television and film violence have been done in recent decades — and the majority of these studies have reached the same conclusion: *Television and film violence leads to real-world violence.* One expert on child behavior concluded that to argue against this conclusion is like arguing against gravity. I agree with this.

Violent video games also have an effect on children and youth similar to that of violent television and film. Studies reveal that the more often children practice fantasy, *virtual* acts of violence on video games, the more likely it becomes that they will carry out *real-world* acts of violence. These violent games have been compared to simulators used in military training. Players — often very young children — are cast in the roles of shooters, earning points and commendations for each "kill." Consequently, children are being conditioned to expect violence to produce a corresponding reward.

Youth today are also exposed to violent words and actions online — in music and images on hundreds of websites that are created to foster bigotry and violence and to glamorize bloodshed. Music lyrics have become increasingly explicit concerning sex, drugs, murder, and violence against women. The accessibility to online sources of violence has become so vast, it is nearly impossible for parents to monitor what their children see and hear in this digitized age.

I've shared only some of the effects of violence in the media on our children and youth. I didn't even talk about these violent effects on the rest of society — the impact this exposure and influence is having on the increase in crime overall.

The fact is, this *is* the most violent generation that has ever lived. We may not fill a stadium to watch actual murders as the Romans did, but we are every bit as barbaric. In fact, this modern barbarism is even worse than the Romans. Think how desensitized the soul of society has become to think it normal to watch a movie filled with murder and bloodshed — or listen to music focused on violence — in the comfort of our own homes with our family and friends. Each one of us must ask ourselves, *Is this normal?*

Although the facts I've shared here are dismal, take courage and remember that as the world gets darker, Isaiah 60:1 prophesies that the glory of the Lord rises and shines on those who walk with Him. This is not the time to retreat and hide. It's the time to charge full-steam ahead to rescue the perishing and care for the dying! Those without Christ need to see His light shining through us!

If you are among those who find violence entertaining, I want to tell you that I am not writing this to condemn you, but rather to encourage you to take a good look at your soul and ask yourself: Have I become influenced and affected by the world in these last days?

What about your children? Do you allow them to watch acts of violence in the media, forgetting the effects it has on their souls in their minds and emotions? Do you really want your children to watch and listen to endless hours of bloodshed? If you will listen to the Holy Spirit, you will hear His voice pleading with you to turn off that violence so you and your children can maintain hearts free from the desensitizing decay of the world in these last days.

In connection with this, it must be pointed out that the apostle Paul next wrote that society will be "high-minded" — a word that is very important at this juncture. The word "high-minded" is a translation of the Greek word *typhoo,* which is where we get the word *typhoon.* When a typhoon comes, it covers the entire landscape and arrives with destructive winds. As it approaches, the sky looks ominous and foreboding, turning dark and turbulent. When the storm arrives on shore, everyone in close proximity is affected, except for those who fled from the storm or took adequate shelter.

As dangerous and destructive as typhoons are, the good news is, they never last long! They are short-lived and eventually pass! Likewise, the events that the Holy Spirit is describing may seem overwhelming as you read about them. But right in the middle of the text, He reminds us that none of this will last long. Just as a typhoon passes, these events will also pass. Those who have taken shelter in Jesus will be safe from the destruction that "lays waste" in the unbelieving world around us (*see* Psalm 91:6 *NKJV*)! *All of this will eventually pass away!*

An interpretive translation of these words in Second Timothy 3:4 could be taken to mean:

"People will be preoccupied with and known for their violence, but all of this will pass. Just as a storm appears on the horizon and brings destruction with it, these violent winds in society will not last long. As threatening as it may look, it will pass just as surely as storms always pass…."

In light of what the Holy Spirit has warned us about in this verse and our need to find shelter in Jesus and His Word, I want to remind you what the Bible tells us about Lot. Lot was a righteous man who was tortured in his soul because of his habitual seeing and hearing wrong things. Second Peter 2:8 says, "For that righteous man dwelling among them, in seeing and hearing, vexed his righteous soul from day to day with their unlawful deeds."

The word "vexed" in this verse is a translation of the Greek word *basinadzo,* which means *to torture.* You see, when Lot first moved to the cities of Sodom and Gomorrah, the evil sights he saw in those cities were a torture to his soul. But because he dwelt among them and saw their sinful deeds from day to day, after a period of time his soul was no longer tortured. In "seeing and hearing" their unlawful deeds "from day to day," his righteous soul became desensitized, and he acclimated to that evil environment. He completely lost his spiritual sensitivity because of the images that became so commonplace to him.

What a lesson the story of Lot teaches us! Especially in these last days when violence abounds, we must set a guard and stay vigilant regarding what we see and hear. The scenes and sounds we allow to enter our eyes and ears have the ability to either save us or desensitize our souls.

I encourage you to lovingly set down rules not only for your children, but also for yourself in order to guard your family's eyes and ears against messages of violence. If your hearts become hardened or desensitized by wrong images and messages, it will eventually have an impact on every part of your life. That's why Proverbs 4:23 says, "Keep thy heart with all diligence; for out of it are the issues of life." The *New Living Translation* says, "Guard your heart above all else, for it determines the course of your life."

There is nothing more important than the condition of your heart and soul — so take every measure you possibly can to avoid the spiritual desensitization moving across the globe like an epidemic in these last days. Above all, make sure that you fellowship with Jesus every day in the Word and in prayer. Nothing will help you more to stay sensitive and responsive to His heart in the midst of this violence-loving generation!

MY PRAYER FOR TODAY

Father, I am deeply convicted by what I have read today. I admit that I have allowed myself to watch movies and listen to messages that are detrimental to my relationship with You. I didn't mean to do wrong, but now I understand how damaging it is to permit wrong images to enter my soul. Holy Spirit, I am sure that I have grieved You by watching wrong images and listening to words and messages that You find foul, so today I repent. I ask You to please forgive me for grieving You, and I ask You to help restore my soul from any desensitizing effect that these things have had on me. I don't want to be like Lot who became desensitized by the things he saw and heard, so I am asking You to help me do what is right and to turn away from all contaminating influences that have the power to negatively affect my spirit and soul.

I pray this in Jesus' name!

MY CONFESSION FOR TODAY

I confess that I acknowledge my responsibility to watch over my own soul, and I will not permit the filth of this world or the violence so accepted in society today to tarnish God's work in my life. God wants my spirit to be sensitive, tender, and compassionate, but the constant images of violence dulls that sensitivity. Therefore I make the decision to turn off and walk away from any bombardment of images and sounds that will affect the spiritual sensitivity I need to be effective in this world for Jesus Christ. With the help of the Holy Spirit, I will do everything I can to make sure that no vile thing enters my eyes or my ears!

I declare this by faith in Jesus' name!

QUESTIONS FOR YOU TO CONSIDER

1. Have you noticed how scenes and stories of violence now fill television and movie screens? Does it grieve your spirit and hurt your soul to watch such things or have you, like Lot, become so acclimated to what you see and hear that it no longer affects you?

2. If the Holy Spirit has spoken to you today to stop tolerating such scenes and messages, what action are you going to take to obey Him? What steps is the Holy Spirit asking you to take to free yourself or your family from these soul-desensitizing images?
3. If you take an honest look at your movie cabinet in your home, how many of your films would Jesus be willing to watch with you? Since He lives in your heart by His Spirit, and you don't want to offend Him, would you be willing to "clean house" and remove those things that hurt Him and wound your own spirit?

MAY 18

Signs of the Last Days — Lovers of Pleasure More Than Lovers of God

...lovers of pleasure more than lovers of God....
— 2 Timothy 3:4

It can seem a little heavy when we're reading Paul's list of characteristics of society in the last days, especially when the Greek words he used in that text are expounded on and looked at more deeply, as we are doing in these series of *Sparkling Gems.* But one thing is sure: The Holy Spirit did *not* inform us of these details so we would be worried or afraid and hide from the world. *He forewarned us of these things in advance so we could spiritually reinforce ourselves to live victoriously and free until Jesus returns!*

The Holy Spirit considers it important for us to know these things in advance, or He wouldn't have dedicated so much time and space to this subject. That's why we must give heed to His words and study them out fully so we can grasp their meanings to the greatest extent possible.

As Paul continued to bring illumination regarding events that will occur in society in the last days, he next wrote that people will become "lovers of pleasure more than lovers of God." Let's delve deeply into these words and phrases today to see what gems of truth we can extract from the Greek that will broaden our understanding.

The words "lovers of pleasure" are a translation of the Greek word *philodonos,* which is a compound of two words, *phileo* and *hedonos.* The first word, *phileo,* is a well-known word that conveys the ideas of *affection* and *love.* It can denote an affection so deep that it even embraces the idea of *romance* and is from the same root word that means *to kiss.*

Frequently in the Greek language, the word *phileo* is compounded with other words to form new meanings, as it is with the word *philodonos.* The following are examples:

- *Philadelphos:* You may recognize this word because it is where we get the name of the great city of *Philadelphia* on the east coast of the United States. It is actually a New Testament word that is a compound of the words *phileo* and *adelphos.* The word *phileo* means *to deeply, profoundly, and affectionately love,* while the word *adelphos* is the Greek word for *a brother.* When compounded, they form the word *philadelphos*, which means *brotherly love.*
- *Philosophia:* The word *philosophia* is a compound of the word *phileo* and *sophos.* As noted, the word *phileo* means *to love* or to have *a deep, profound affection.* The word *sophos* is the word for *wisdom.* When these two words are compounded, they form the word *philosophia.* This is where we get the word *philosophy,* which describes *a deep and profound love of wisdom.*
- *Philoxenos:* The word *philoxenos* is a compound of the words *phileo* and *xenos.* The second part of this word is *xenos,* which is the ancient Greek word for a *stranger* or *foreigner.* When the words *phileo* and *xenos* are compounded, they form the word *philoxenia,* a word that expresses the idea of a person who has a special *love for strangers* or *love for foreigners.*
- *Philostorgos:* The second part of this word is *storgos* — the Greek word for *a commitment or devotion to one's family.* When the words *phileo* and *storgos* are compounded, the new word depicts *a person who has a deep affection and sense of commitment for his family.*
- *Philanthropia:* In this word, the word *phileo* is compounded with the word *anthropos,* the word for *mankind* or *humankind.* The word *anthropos* is where we get the word *anthropology* or an *anthropologist.* But when the Greek word *phileo* is compounded with the word *anthropos,* it depicts *a love for humanity.* From this, we get the word *philanthropist*, which describes *a wealthy person who generously gives his resources or money for the betterment of humanity.*
- *Philarguria:* Here we see the word *phileo* compounded with the word *arguria.* The word *arguria* is the old word for *silver* or *money.* When *arguria* is compounded with *phileo,* the new word *philarguria* depicts *a love of silver* or *an affection and love of money.*

In Second Timothy 3:4, Paul compounded the word *hedonos* with the word *phileo* to tell us people in the last days will become "lovers of pleasure." Because the word *phileo* means to have *a deep, profound love* and can convey the notion of *a romantic preoccupation*, this emphatically forecasts that people in the last days will be *preoccupied with and in love with the pleasure and the pursuit of happiness.* But let's look deeper at the word *hedonos* to get the full picture!

The word *hedonos* is only used five times in the New Testament, and each time, it conjures up the picture of people completely preoccupied with pleasure and who live for the gratification of their flesh and their own personal happiness. The English Dictionary says "hedonism" is *the doctrine that pleasure or happiness is the highest good; addiction to and obsession for pleasure as a way of life*. Paul used the Greek word *philodonos* to say that society in the last days will become "lovers of pleasure" or that they will become preoccupied and obsessed with the pursuit of their own comfort, pleasure, and happiness.

The truth is, there has never been a generation in history with more material goods or comfort than this present generation. Yet despite this glut of goods and pursuit of pleasure, the worldwide happiness index is the lowest on record, especially in the industrialized world where material goods abound.

It is very clear that self-centered living does not produce happiness. In fact, the highest rating on the happiness index is in developing Third World nations where goods are scarcer, but where commitment to "one's personal faith" is higher.

There is no doubt about it! Because Paul used the word *philodonos* — which means "lovers of pleasure" — he was emphatically declaring that people in the last days will be *obsessed* with pleasure.

It is unfortunate that even Christians are often obsessed with comfort and pleasure to such an extent that they don't want to be asked to do anything that would inconvenience them. But this should *not* be the case.

Here's the bottom line: God is more concerned about your obedience than He is about your happiness. Happiness is fleeting, but obedience to God and His Word produces a long-term joy that is unaffected and unwavering.

A doctrine has permeated the Church in recent years that says God wants them to be happy above all else. Such teaching ignores the fact that the Gospel frequently calls for us to die to ourselves, to deny ourselves, and to even pick up our cross and carry it (*see* Luke 9:23). Obeying this call of God to pick up our cross and carry it means that we will often be required to take the road of sacrifice — to humble ourselves and even lay down our "rights" for the sake of others.

This errant doctrine that we are entitled to be "happy" erroneously leads people to avoid any decision or take any action that inconveniences their schedule, plans, or comfort. This is ultimately a doctrine of selfishness that justifies self-focus and non-service. Yet if we obey the demands put forth by the Gospel, these demands will make our flesh suffer — for in order for us to walk in the Spirit and not fulfill the lusts of the flesh, it will necessitate that we mortify the deeds and demands of the flesh.

But according to Paul's words in Second Timothy 3:4, the pursuit of "happiness" will become the chief goal of people at the end of this age. Of course, God wants us to be satisfied in life, but that which Paul wrote about in this verse is far beyond that. It was a prophetic declaration that people in the last days will become completely consumed with themselves and that their own happiness will drive them to unequaled selfishness.

Second Timothy 3:4 says this love of pleasure will even supersede love for God. No one would ever claim to love pleasure more than God, but as my mother told me when I was growing up, *a person's actions speak louder than his words.* A person's actions always reveal the truth about what he or she loves most. This verse tells us that love of pleasure will become so widespread that people will be more devoted to their own pleasure and pursuit of happiness than they are in love with God.

Paul wrote that people will be lovers of pleasure "more than" lovers of God. The words "more than" are a translation of the Greek word *mallon*, which draws a drastic comparison between two points, denoting something that is *extremely different* in comparison to something else.

In context, this means people will be *excessive* lovers of pleasure — *much, much more* than they are lovers of God. In fact, their desire for their own pleasure will be so great that it will *far surpass* their devotion, respect, and service to God. In the last days, people's thinking will not be ruled by what is morally right or morally wrong or what is pleasing or displeasing to God, but by the question: *How will this decision or action affect my own personal comfort, pleasure, or happiness?*

God is not against our being blessed or enjoying nice possessions, as long as we hold them in our hands and don't allow them into our hearts. But when the acquisition of possessions becomes an obsession and takes first place in our lives, thereby affecting our obedience to God and His Word, it is wrong. In fact, it has become a form of idolatry. We have crossed a line that is a serious violation in the eyes of God.

The words "lovers of God" in Greek is the word *philotheoi.* The first part of this word is *phileo,* and as noted earlier, it means *to love* or *to be deeply affectionate.* The second part of the word is word *theos*, the Greek word for *God.* But when these two words are compounded, as Paul does in this verse, the new word pictures *people who are deeply and profoundly in love with God.*

Jesus said that at the end of the age, people would be preoccupied with buying, selling, etc. This will be the condition of the unbelievers in the last days, but it does not have to be *our* condition. Especially as we draw near to the coming of Jesus, we must do everything we can to guard our hearts and keep them free from selfishness and greed. We must focus on Jesus and keep our priorities aligned with His Word.

Soon everything in this world will pass away, and only those things that were done for Jesus will remain. In light of this awesome truth, it is imperative that we examine our hearts to determine our real spiritual condition. If we find areas that need improvement, the Holy Spirit will help us correct those areas that are out of sync with Him!

MY PRAYER FOR TODAY

Father, it is very clear that self-centered living does not produce happiness. As believers in Jesus Christ, we have been commanded to live according to the law of love — and love does not seek its own. Father, I repent right now for each time I have been more focused on doing what resulted in convenience for me rather than doing what produced obedience to You. Today I make a fresh commitment to deny myself, to pick up my cross, and to follow Jesus Christ as my Lord and example in all things. Holy Spirit, I ask You to open the eyes of my understanding and teach me to how to truly seek first Your Kingdom and not my comfort, to pursue Your holy ways instead of temporal pleasures.

I pray this in Jesus' Name!

MY CONFESSION FOR TODAY

I declare that nothing may surpass my devotion, respect, and service to God. I purpose in my heart that my thoughts and actions will reflect a sanctified heart that desires to please God rather than to gratify self-indulgent preferences for personal comfort or gain. I choose to be conformed to Jesus Christ and not to the culture of the world around me. I put first things first and establish my priorities based on what will honor God, build His Kingdom, strengthen His Church, and ransom lost souls for whom Christ died.

I declare this by faith in Jesus' name!

QUESTIONS FOR YOU TO CONSIDER

1. The Bible says people will become lovers of pleasure *more than* lovers of God. It is possible, then, that they love God, but they love pleasure and self-gratification more than they love Him. Have you considered what dominates your own thoughts, desires, and pursuits? In light of your answer to that question, which do you love more — God or pleasure?
2. Can you think of ways that entertainment has found its way into the local church so that people come to church more for entertainment than for God? What would happen if this entertainment factor was suddenly eliminated? What do you think would happen to church attendance?
3. It is easy to point a finger at others, but what is the Holy Spirit saying to *you* about this *Sparkling Gem* today?

A person's actions always reveal the truth about what he or she loves most.

MAY 19

Comfort and Edify One Another

Wherefore comfort yourselves together,
and edify one another....
— 1 Thessalonians 5:11

We all experience hardships from time to time. These hardships may be financial stress, strained relationships, poor health, a job that seems overwhelming, or another personal disappointment of some type. The list of things that cause difficult moments is endless. But at some point, everyone comes face to face with a moment when he or she wonders if they will "make it" through the event they are experiencing in life.

To be honest, I've felt those emotions many times. Over the course of our ministry, God has called my family to live in difficult environments and to do things that were far outside of our comfort zone. In fact, sometimes the task at hand was so difficult and challenging that it seemed utterly impossible in the natural realm. Although the Holy Spirit lives within me and I am very aware of this marvelous truth, the fact is that there were times when I needed a tender touch of encouragement to bolster my confidence and to reassure me that I was capable of fulfilling my divine assignment. Personally, no one in my life is more effective at this than my precious wife Denise.

Although others may not see it at the time, Denise knows when I am struggling inwardly to overcome a monumental task even as I keep doing all I can to press forward in faith. I couldn't begin to count the times Denise has tenderly placed her arm around me, touched my hand, or peered deep into my eyes and offered encouragement when I have felt challenged. Often the greatest comfort she gives is simply her silent, supportive presence. Words are wonderful, but words do not always bring comfort — especially *if* we already know all the answers but still feel frail and weak. How I thank God for Denise's love and accepting presence and the comfort she brings to my heart. In those moments when I have felt overwhelmed and so very alone, she was at my side, and simply knowing she was "there" brought strength to my soul.

All of this comes to my mind when I read Paul's first letter to the church in Thessalonica. Paul wrote them at a time when the congregation needed *comfort* in order to overcome the adversities that were buffeting them from every side. If anyone had ever faced trouble and trials, it was this church, and they really needed to be comforted and strengthened. Paul wasn't personally there to do it, so he urged them to do it for one another. He said, "Wherefore comfort yourselves together..." (1 Thessalonians 5:11).

Because of their newfound faith in Christ, they were going through many different types of hardships. Many were experiencing financial stress because they lost their jobs when they came to

Christ. Many others were being physically beaten or imprisoned and lived with the understanding that they might eventually lose their lives. Paul knew they were undergoing great hardship, so in this verse, he wrote and told them to "comfort" one another.

What does Paul mean when he says they were to "comfort" one another? The Greek word for "comfort" is *parakaleo.* Its primary meaning is *to comfort, to encourage,* or *to speak consoling words,* especially in times of difficulty or bereavement. It could also be used in militaristic sense to describe a commanding officer *exhorting* his troops before going into battle. Knowing that a serious conflict lies ahead of them, the commanding officer speaks words that stir and strengthen the troops before they march off into the fray. In the Old Testament Septuagint, the word *parakaleo* was used similarly to mean *to comfort, to show compassion, to encourage, to support,* or *to strengthen.* In total, this particular Greek word is used 109 times in the New Testament, mostly by Paul, and it encompasses all of the above meanings.

So when Paul told the Thessalonians to "comfort" one another — and thereby instructs us to do the same — he was telling them (and us) that we need to give encouragement to those around us who need it. Those who are in the middle of a battle especially need our strengthening words or supportive presence. Paul urges us *to hearten them, to cheer them up,* or *to give some kind of boost* that will help them make it further along the way. Sometimes that "comfort" may be speaking words that stir or impart strength, as a military officer does to strengthen the resolve of his troops. Or it could simply mean a silent, strengthening presence like my wife Denise gives me in my most difficult moments. We must never forget that often the mere presence of a friend or companion can bring great comfort to our hearts.

But that's not all that Paul told us to do. In First Thessalonians 5:11, he went on to say, "Wherefore comfort yourselves, and *edify* one another...." What does the word "edify" mean? This word is not common in today's vernacular, so what specifically was Paul telling us to do?

The word "edify" is a translation of the Greek word *oikodomeo* — which is a compound of *oikos* and *demoo.* The word *oikos* is the word for *a house,* and *demoo* is the word for *construction.* When they are compounded, the new word describes the *enlarging of a house,* as well as all that is entailed in the building process. To add to a house or building, one must plan ahead, implement ideas, use instruments, and make a sizable investment. Basically, this word describes a deliberate decision, as enlarging a house doesn't normally occur accidentally. Have you ever seen a house that was added to without a plan? It usually *looks* like a house that was built with no foresight!

Therefore, when Paul exhorted us to "edify one another in" First Thessalonians 5:1, he was telling us to be very deliberate about how we encourage others. Our actions and words should *encourage and build people up* — that is, *add to them, advance them, augment them, enhance them, or improve them* in some way. We should put great effort into making other people's lives richer, fuller, and better. Accidental edification is appreciated when it occurs. But Paul was not asking for occasional, accidental, haphazard edification; he was requesting a well thought-out plan that occurs with great deliberation.

You should view this task of edifying people who are feeling overwhelmed and challenged as a personal construction project. What plan do you have to personally help enhance the lives of those around you? Are you sticking with a plan that the Holy Spirit gave you, or are you just hoping for accidental encouragement and growth?

At the beginning of today's *Sparkling Gem*, I spoke of Denise's strengthening and encouraging presence in my life. I can testify that she has been very deliberate in her encouragement of me and very intentional in her efforts to be an instrument God can use to enhance my life. I have learned so much about this subject by watching Denise. Today I want to ask you:

- Has anyone ever comforted you during a difficult time?
- What was it like to experience that comfort? What did that comfort do for you personally?
- Can you describe a time when someone comforted you with spoken words or by putting an arm around your shoulder or by tenderly touching your hand?
- Can you recall when someone gave you strength to make it through another day simply being "there" for you?

The Thessalonians were facing great trials and tribulations, so Paul told them, "Wherefore comfort yourselves together, and edify one another...." He was asking them to be intentional in the way they helped each other.

So keep alert today, because the Lord may very well want to use you to bring your *intentional* encouragement and support to someone who needs it. It's a great day to bolster others' strength for the battle and make their lives richer, fuller, and eternally better through the strategic help of the Comforter Himself who lives within!

MY PRAYER FOR TODAY

Father, I thank You for the way You have often comforted me through encouragement from people you placed in my life at just the right time. Lord, You are the Father of mercies and the God of all comfort. I ask You to speak words of life and strength through me to the weary who come across my path. Holy Spirit, You are the Comforter. I yield to Your power and presence within me to bring deliberate and specific support to those who are in the middle of a battle or great trial. You know what they need — whether comforting words or silent support. I make myself available to You, Holy Spirit. Let my words be Your words — so full of wisdom and grace that they minister grace to people in their times of need. Make me an instrument of Your peace and comfort, that I may comfort others the way You faithfully comforted me when I needed it the most.

I pray this in Jesus' name!

MY CONFESSION FOR TODAY

I declare that my actions and words encourage and build people up. What I say and the way I live will advance, enhance, and improve the lives of others in some way. I put deliberate, well-thought-out effort into making other people's lives richer, fuller, and better. I look for ways to cheer them up or give them some kind of boost. I appreciate when I can accidentally be a blessing, but I purpose to deliberately and consistently be a blessing to every life I have the privilege to reach to the glory of God.

I declare this by faith in Jesus' name!

QUESTIONS FOR YOU TO CONSIDER

1. As you review your life, can you name a person who has been a special strength to you? If yes, have you ever taken time to express your gratitude to that person for the role he or she has played in your life?
2. Can you think of someone who needs your intentional help right now? What steps can you take to be encouraging to that person, perhaps even today? Ask the Holy Spirit to show you the steps you can take or the words you can speak that will enlarge that person's confidence and strengthen his or her hope.
3. If you are troubled by events happening in your life, have you asked anyone to pray with you or have you opened your heart so they will know that they need to be especially encouraging to you? To whom could you speak about the things you are facing right now?

MAY 20

Impartation!

For I long to see you, that I may impart
unto you some spiritual gift....
— Romans 1:11

Have you ever been with someone whose mere presence positively affected you, changed you, or took you to a higher level in the Lord? Do you know if your presence has ever affected anyone in that way?

When I think about this question, one particular minister immediately comes to mind. He is a precious and dear friend who has walked with God for decades, and I have known him closely for many years. When I am honored with the opportunity to spend time with him, I always walk away feeling spiritually richer and touched by Jesus. Being in his presence leaves me with the feeling that something spiritual has rubbed off on me and has been *imparted* to my life.

Similarly, Paul felt this way about the First Century believers in Rome. Even though he had never met the Roman congregation face to face, he was sure that if he could spend time with them, he would rub off on them too. In Romans 1:10, he wrote, "Making request, if by any means now at length, I might have a prosperous journey by the will of God to come unto you." Then in Romans 1:11, he told them, "For I long to see you, that I may impart unto some spiritual gift...."

Notice that Paul said, "For I *long* to see you...." This word "long" tells us how deeply Paul wanted to meet these believers. In Greek, it is the word *epipotheo*, which has the root *potheo*, meaning *desire*. However, it also has the prefix *epi* attached to it, which gives an *extra force* to the word, portraying a person who wanted something so much that he *intensely longed* for it. Very often this word depicts *an insatiable appetite* or *a craving* — and in the New Testament it is often translated as the word *lust*. The fact that Paul used this word to depict his longing to come see the believers in Rome tells us that he was *intensely yearning* to see them.

In verse 11, Paul provided at least one reason *why* he wanted to see them. He wrote, "For I long to see you, that I may *impart* to you...." Paul believed he had something spiritual to impart to his brothers and sisters in Rome. The word "impart" comes from the word *metadidomi,* which means *to impart* or *to transfer* something from one to another. Paul believed that if he could see the Romans, spend time with them, or perhaps lay hands on them, there would be an *impartation* of something spiritual to them. In the same way that I walk away spiritually richer after being in the presence of the man I told you about earlier, Paul was convinced that if he could spend time with the Roman believers, something powerful would be imparted to them. As a result, they would come away from that encounter feeling richer, fuller, and touched by Jesus.

These words of Paul in Romans 1:11 tell me that he was convinced God would use him as a channel to touch these believers in a way they had never been touched before. Paul was so confident about it, he actually wrote that he longed to see them, specifically stating that he wanted *to impart* something spiritual to them. What did he want to impart? That's a topic we will look at tomorrow.

But for today, I want to ask you: Who has had this kind of profound influence in your life? Has being in anyone's mere presence made you feel touched by Jesus? Who was that person? Perhaps the more important question is this: Have you ever made anyone else feel that way? How do you affect people when you are with them? In what condition do you leave them when it's time for you to say farewell?

There's no doubt that God wants to use us to positively impact people. Just as the apostle Paul was confident that God would use him to impart something rich and spiritual to the Romans, we need to spend time with the Father and allow Him to pour His presence into our personal lives so that when we are with others, there will be an overflow that rubs off on them and takes them to a higher place in the Lord!

MY PRAYER FOR TODAY

Father, I ask You to flood me to overflowing with Your Spirit. When people are in my presence, I pray that they will become more deeply aware of You and Your nearness. Let Your life and kindness be expressed through me in such a way that people receive a supernatural impartation and spiritual blessing that will cover and penetrate their hearts and lives with Your wisdom, goodness, and love.

I pray this in Jesus' name!

MY CONFESSION FOR TODAY

I confess that I walk in communion with the Holy Spirit daily. When people are in my presence, they are enveloped by the life of God that flows through me by His Spirit within me. The fragrance of Heaven overflows through my life so that when I am with others, the peace and love of God rests upon them and takes them to a higher place in Him.

I declare this by faith!

QUESTIONS FOR YOU TO CONSIDER

1. What plan do you have to personally enhance the lives of those around you?
2. Recall a time when you knew something was spiritually imparted to you by being with someone else. Was it a conversation that person had with you that deeply impacted you, or was it transferred by prayer and the laying on of hands?
3. Has anyone ever told you that you affected him or her that way? If so, when was it, and what was the event that caused that other person to feel so positively and spiritually impacted?

MAY 21

When God Calls You, He Also Equips You

Being confident of this very thing,
that he which hath begun a good work in you
will perform it until the day of Jesus Christ.
— Philippians 1:6

When God calls you, He will equip and prepare you to effectively complete your assignment on time. He will use every aspect of who you are and where you came from to bring about His will in your life. He factors in your background, your level of education, your past occupations, and everything else you've accumulated from your life experiences. Many times He will also lead you into new territory where you are surrounded by unfamiliar faces in order to teach you lessons that you couldn't learn any other way. *Perhaps no example of this is clearer than the life of the apostle Paul.*

Paul played a major role in the founding of the Early Church. God used him to write almost two-thirds of the New Testament, and his inspired epistles have guided the Body of Christ for nearly 2,000 years. However, when Paul first came to the Lord, he was very inexperienced in the arena of ministry. In order for him to accurately understand God's vision of the Church, he had to be adequately equipped and prepared. This period of training would not happen in the way Paul planned. He would have to go somewhere entirely unexpected.

Soon after his life-changing conversion on the road to Damascus, Paul traveled to Jerusalem, eager to connect with the disciples who resided there and begin his ministry. Given his background as a former rabbi who spoke fluent Hebrew, Jerusalem seemed to him like the natural choice to focus his efforts, since he was so intimately acquainted with the Jewish culture, tradition, and religious thought that permeated that city. However, God had called him to bring the Gospel to the *Gentile* world first and foremost, and Jerusalem's predominately Jewish environment could not adequately prepare him for this ministry.

Paul's stay in Jerusalem didn't last long. The Gospel message he had boldly proclaimed in the synagogues soon after his arrival enraged the local Jewish leadership, and they conspired to kill him. When the local believers learned of this plot against Paul's life, they helped him covertly leave the city and then sent him off to his hometown of Tarsus. There Paul remained until God was ready to usher him into the next phase of his calling, where the sure foundations of his ministry would be laid and his Christian walk would be strengthened by leaps and bounds.

The proving ground for Paul would be the city of Antioch, a major city located approximately 300 miles north of Jerusalem in modern-day Syria. Antioch was the third largest city in the Roman Empire during early New Testament times, with only Rome and Alexandria exceeding it in size. Situated on a crossroads between East and West, it was a thriving commercial center and a true melting pot of cultures and peoples. The city's population was also composed primarily of Gentiles — a very important factor for Paul, given the nature of his calling.

The multiplicity of cultures found within the thriving urban environment of Antioch naturally resulted in a colorful and diverse Christian community. When the Gospel was first brought to Antioch in the wake of Stephen's martyrdom, it was warmly received and the city experienced a revival as pagans and Jews alike left their old lives behind and accepted Jesus into their hearts. Before long, a thriving church was established as believers in Antioch began to actively evangelize their city and the surrounding region. During Paul's time with this congregation, he regularly ministered alongside Gentiles and learned to communicate effectively with them. These experiences would do much to equip him for the epic apostolic journeys that he would later embark upon across the Roman Empire.

From its onset, the church of Antioch had grown rapidly until it was second in size only to the church of Jerusalem. However, despite the distinction of these churches as having the two largest congregations in the mid-First Century, the two works were very different. Many of the believers in Antioch were Gentiles who came from pagan backgrounds, whereas the believers in Jerusalem were nearly all of Jewish ancestry.

Antioch's rich, diverse environment was the "right place" God chose to equip and prepare the apostle Paul for ministry. A brand-new move of the Spirit was taking place in that city, and by following God's calling to move there, Paul put himself in a position to receive an entirely fresh perspective of the Body of Christ. During his time in Antioch, he learned important lessons from what he saw and experienced that he could have never learned if he had stayed in Jerusalem. Following God's call led Paul to a place he would have never anticipated, but it was an essential step to equip him for the rest of his ministry.

Never forget the promise that Paul himself wrote to us in Philippians 1:6. It says, "Being confident of this very thing, that he which hath begun a good work in you will perform it until the day of Jesus Christ." Paul was certainly speaking from personal experience when he wrote this verse. According to Paul, God will begin a good work in us and will "perform" it until the day of Jesus' return for the Church. The word "perform" is the Greek word *epiteleo*, a compound of *epi* and *teleo*. The word *epi* adds *force* to the word. The word *teleo* means *to finish, complete,* or *conclude*. When the two words are compounded, the new word *epiteleo* shows that God is forcefully moving His plans for us in the right direction until we are finally complete! Paul started that verse with the word "confident" — the Greek word *peitho*. It means you can be *sure*, *convinced*, and *ever certain* of these things!

Likewise, God knows exactly where you need to be and who you need to be with in order to equip you for your life assignment — and He is working to get you exactly where you need to be! As He did in the life of Paul, God will use every aspect of who you are and where you came from to bring about His will in your life. He will use your background, your level of education, your past occupations, and everything else you've accumulated from your life experiences. And He may also lead you into places where you are surrounded by unfamiliar faces to teach you lessons that you couldn't learn any other way. One thing is certain: If God has called you, He will equip you for the task! *You can be sure of it!*

MY PRAYER FOR TODAY

Father, I am so thankful that since You have called me, You will also equip me for the task in front of me. You never call anyone that You do not also equip to do the job. Help me have an open heart so I'll know where and with whom I need to be in order to be in the environment that will prepare me for the next phase of my life. Help me see where I am right now with spiritual eyes and to hear with spiritual ears so I can receive the maximum preparation You want to provide for me. I know that Your hand is guiding me. And even if You lead me to places with unfamiliar faces, I know You are doing what is necessary to get me ready for the next God-ordained phase of my life.

I pray this in Jesus' name!

MY CONFESSION FOR TODAY

I confess that I respond to God's call on my life and I cooperate with how He is equipping me for the task ahead of me. I know that God never calls anyone whom He does not also equip to do the job. My heart is open to follow the leading of the Holy Spirit. God's hand is guiding me, and He is doing what is necessary to get me ready for the path that lies ahead! Therefore, I will be at the right place, at the right time, with the right people, in an environment that will prepare me for the next phase of my life. My spiritual eyes and spiritual ears are attuned to the Spirit so I can receive the maximum preparation that God wants to provide for me.

I declare this by faith in Jesus' name!

QUESTIONS FOR YOU TO CONSIDER

1. As you look at your life, can you see how God has used your life experiences to prepare you for what you are doing right now?
2. What has God used from your life experiences to prepare you for what you are doing? Consider your background, your education, and your past occupations. What else has He used to equip you for what He has called you to do in the future?
3. Has God led you to places where you were surrounded by unfamiliar faces to teach you lessons that you couldn't learn any other way? When was that experience and what did you gain from it?

MAY 22

Take Off Your Old Clothes!

That ye put off concerning
the former conversation the old man....
— Ephesians 4:22

From time to time, Denise will go through a "clean out the closet" phase — a very involved process in which she tries on everything she owns and then decides which articles of clothing she'll keep and which ones she'll give to someone else. It's a long process that finally ends with clothes stacked on our bed and all over our bedroom in piles, often with name tags of the women to whom she wishes to give each article of clothing. It is such a huge process that she usually invites a friend to help her do it, and it becomes a kind of "give away clothes" party.

I usually find out how deep the process is when it's time to go to bed and I can't get into bed because its covered with the clothes Denise is planning to give away — *or* I discover it when I get to church on Sunday and see a number of women in our church walking through our church auditorium wearing her clothes. I'm always so proud of Denise when she goes through such a phase, because her process is very involved, very deliberate, and very sacrificial.

Sometimes it makes me think about all the personal "stuff" people have in their hearts and attitudes that no longer fit who they are. Maybe these attitudes and mindsets fit who they were at one time, but now after the grace of God has done such a work in them, some of these don't fit who they are anymore. Some attitudes are simply out of date with what God is now doing in their lives. Some are just no longer desired. And to be truthful, some attitudes should have never been in their lives in the first place.

There are a multitude of sources from which attitudes end up in our personal lives as Christians. But eventually God calls on us to unload those old ways of thinking that are no longer fitting to who we are in Christ so that we can be fully free.

To be honest, many believers come right to the edge of real change, only to turn away at the last minute in defeat. They think they're ready to tackle their wrong thought patterns, wrong believing, and wrong attitudes. But just when they are on the verge of victory, they draw back in fear at the thought of what it will cost them to experience true transformation. The devil strikes them with an attack that sends them reeling emotionally and, as a result, they lose their grip on the Word and slip back into those old attitudes — putting them back into the closet to keep just a little longer. You see, these satanic attacks are purposefully designed to prevent believers from achieving victory in their lives. The devil wants to shake them up so badly that they'll never regain the momentum to start back on the path to permanent freedom.

The first step to instituting permanent change and getting free is by identifying what needs to go! I advise you to allow the Holy Spirit to bring conviction to your heart about the areas inside you that need to change. I'm talking about attitudes that are deadly to your victory, such as selfishness, bitterness, unforgiveness, anger, gossip, fear, insecurity, and remorse over the past. As you start this process of identification, it is also very important for you to make a faith declaration that you are going to walk free of these things and that you will not turn back!

Once you have identified the areas in your life that need to go and have declared by faith that you're going for total freedom, the next step is to make a decision to change regardless of the cost or pain involved. You must decide to lay aside your residual hang-ups, bad habits, and fleshly tendencies that block the true expression of your identity in Christ. In Paul's epistles, he admonished us, "But now put off *put off* all these…" (*see* Colossians 3:8).

This phrase "put off" is the Greek word *apotithemi*, a compound of the words *apo* and *tithemi*. The word *apo* means *away*, and the word *tithemi* means *to place or to lay something down.* When the two words are compounded, the new word gives the picture of someone who is *laying something down* while at the same time pushing it *far away* from himself. It means *to lay something down and to push it far away and beyond reach.* Thus, the word describes removal of something and putting so much distance between you and that old thing that you cannot easily reach out to pick it up again.

In Denise's case, that physical act of *apotithemi* entails putting those extra clothes she no longer needs into a suitcase, placing the suitcase in the car, and sending it to church to be given away to other women. Once those steps have been put into process, retrieval would be too painful so her process can't be undone. That's what we need to do with the old attitudes that are no longer fitting for the new creations we have become in Jesus Christ.

Paul specifically said, "But now put off all these; anger, wrath, malice, blasphemy, filthy communication out of your mouth, lie not one to another, see that ye have put off the old man with his deeds" (Colossians 3:8-10). These are things that are simply not compatible with the new creature you have become in Jesus Christ.

We must deliberately decide to change — *to remove*, *to lay aside*, and *to put away* attitudes and actions that don't please God and adversely affect our walk of faith or that have become out of line with what God is presently doing in our lives. We must choose to put so much space between us and those old things that retrieval is too painful — we'll never reach back to put them back into our "closet" or to wear them again.

I don't know about you, but this discussion makes me want to follow Denise's example regarding my spiritual closet!

Let's decide to do a serious inventory of what's going on in our spiritual lives to see what needs to stay and what needs to go. If there's anything in our lives that no longer fits who we've become in Jesus, it's time to determine whether it should be a part of our lives any longer.

It's the season to "declutter"! So why don't you start evaluating your life *today*, item by item if necessary, for the purpose of eliminating all those attitudes that are out of character with who you are in Jesus Christ? The Holy Spirit is speaking to your heart, and as you allow Him to work in you, He will help you get rid of residual hang-ups, bad habits, and fleshly tendencies that block the true expression of your identity in Christ!

MY PRAYER FOR TODAY

Father, as I conduct an inventory of my spiritual wardrobe, I realize that I've not always walked about clothed in Christ. I've worn mismatched attitudes that are too small because they have nothing to do with my identity in Christ and do not reflect Your greatness in any way. Lord, I repent for the times I've displayed myself haughtily in garments of self-righteousness, which are equal to filthy rags before You. Your work in my life has also exposed attitudes and beliefs that are out-of-date because You've opened my understanding. Reveal to me trait by trait what needs to stay and what needs to go. I open wide the door of my heart, and I ask You, Holy Spirit, to direct my attention to remove the attitudes or actions I've held on to that no longer fit who I have become in Jesus. I submit to Your work in my life, and I put on Christ so that every part of me is practically and effectively hidden in Christ in God.

I pray this in Jesus' Name!

MY CONFESSION FOR TODAY

I confess that I am a new creation in Christ Jesus. I have put off the old attributes of the flesh — anger, wrath, malice, blasphemy, filthy communication — and I put on the new attributes that are compatible with who I have become in Jesus Christ. Clothed in Christ, I wear peace, patience, kindness, faithfulness, and self-control as my garments. I regularly inspect my spiritual wardrobe to verify that I am no longer holding on to attitudes and actions that do not serve God's purposes in my life. I will not fall short of the grace of God by clinging to old patterns and mindsets that keep me dangling on the verge of victory but not moving into lasting change. I will strip off, lay aside, and discard anything that is a hindrance to my walking in all God has planned for me!

I declare this by faith in Jesus' name!

QUESTIONS FOR YOU TO CONSIDER

1. What is an area of your life that doesn't reflect who you have become in Jesus Christ? Maybe it's inappropriate language, a wrong attitude, or an area of unforgiveness. What are those areas that need to go? What are you going to do about it, starting today?
2. Do you have any old habits or attitudes that you walked away from in the past but didn't put enough distance between you and that old way of doing or thinking? Did you find yourself retrieving it and putting it back into your life again? What is that area of your life that needs to be dealt with all over again?
3. Do you have physical clothes in your closet that you never wear that would be a blessing to someone else. How long has it been since you've done a purge on your closet and ended up blessing others who have been praying for new clothes?

MAY 23

A New Set of Clothes!

...put on the new man....
— Ephesians 4:24

In yesterday's *Sparkling Gem*, I taught about "purging the closet" — essentially, ridding your life of anything that is incompatible with whom you have become in Christ Jesus. Today I want to switch gears and teach you how to put on new things that *are* compatible with living a holy, consecrated life! But before I delve into the Word, I want to relate an experience from my life that happened soon after I had finished writing yesterday's *Gem*.

After crafting the finishing lines of that *Gem*, my wife Denise and I embarked on a trip to Rome that we had been planning for quite some time. When we arrived, Denise asked if she could go shopping "just to look" and see what was in the clothing stores. Of course, I know that looking leads to buying, so I was mystified that she wanted to purchase more clothes since she had just purged her closet the prior week. In fact, when we left for Rome, a huge pile of her clothes was still stacked on top of our guestroom bed, waiting to be zipped up in suitcases and sent to our church where they would be donated for other women to enjoy.

But now Denise wanted to go window-shopping — which I knew would result in buying more clothes. *I just couldn't wrap my head around it.* After that multi-day closet purge, her closet was *finally* free of those old clothes, and now Denise was going to start filling it up again!

As Denise browsed through one particular shop for two hours, I sat at a coffee shop down the street and waited. The longer I sat there, the more frustrated I became. I wondered, *Why is she trying to find new clothes when she just got rid of so many clothes?* So finally I got up from my table and went to the store to confront her with my question. I asked, "Denise, you just spent days cleaning out the closet and getting rid of your old clothes. Can you explain to me why you are now trying to refill the closet with new clothes?"

She looked at me and responded, "It's about having clothes that fit who I am now. Those old clothes don't reflect who I am anymore. I need clothes that reflect what's going on inside my life right now!"

I walked out of the store, returned to the very same coffee shop, and continued waiting. As I sat there over a fresh cup of coffee, I really pondered what my wife had said. Finally, I called her on her mobile phone and asked, "Are we close to finishing at this shop?" She answered, "Please come here. I want to show you what I've found." Over the next 40 minutes, we had a fashion show as she tried on every piece of clothing for me that she had picked out — and I have to be honest, those clothes were *totally different* from anything she had in her "giveaway" pile at home. This deliberate stylistic shift attested to a deeper change in Denise. She is a unique, evolving individual, and the clothes she chose beautifully reflected the changes taking place in her. *I finally got it!*

This experience brought my mind right back to yesterday's *Sparkling Gem*, where we saw that the apostle Paul exhorted us to rid ourselves of attitudes that are incompatible with a godly lifestyle. However, this was not the totality of Paul's message. After he exhorted us to "put off the old man" in verse 22, Paul continued in Ephesians 4:24 by saying, "And that ye *put on the new man*, which after God is created in righteousness and true holiness." After telling us what to *take off*, Paul proceeded to tell us what to *put on* — that we need to acquire *new* spiritual clothes!

What exactly do these new spiritual clothes look like? Paul provided more detail in Colossians 3:12,13 when he said, "Put on therefore, as the elect of God, holy and beloved, bowels of mercies, kindness, humbleness of mind, meekness, longsuffering; forbearing one another, and forgiving one another…."

The phrase "put on" is a translation of the Greek word *enduo*, which was often used in ancient literature to denote a person *putting on a new set of clothes*. Thus, when it comes to spiritual matters, Paul was telling us it is not enough to simply remove residual hang-ups, bad habits, and fleshly tendencies that block the true expression of your identity in Christ. We must make a conscious effort to "put on" new attitudes and characteristics that are compatible with our new life in Jesus Christ.

And do you know what I've discovered from my own personal spiritual journey? The longer I walk with the Lord and the closer I become to Him, the higher He calls me and the more He encourages me to change my lifestyle in order to more closely reflect His character.

As I watched Denise try on all those new clothes in that shop in Rome, I thought of these verses. Inwardly I surmised, *Well, Denise "put off" a bunch of clothes that no longer matched her style, and now she is going to "put on" a whole new set of clothes that better fits her evolving style.* When I went to pay her bill, I looked at her and jokingly told her she was being scriptural. *She liked that response!*

Take a moment today to meditate on Ephesians 4:24 and Colossians 3:12,13 and see what God wants you personally to put on. The Holy Spirit wants to dress you in a new and better style, and He is the best Designer on planet Earth! He knows you; He knows Jesus; and He knows how to make you reflect the work Jesus has done inside your heart and life!

MY PRAYER FOR TODAY

Father, You are an amazing Designer! You have decorated and adorned all Your creation in stunning array! But nothing compares with the way You adorned Your children when You clothed us with Your own righteousness to showcase the beauty of Your holiness in a glorious display. I honor You, Father, by putting on the garments that Jesus died to provide for me. And I thank You that because of what Jesus has done, when I put on Christ, people will see and recognize Your goodness each time they look at me.

I pray this in Jesus' name!

MY CONFESSION FOR TODAY

I confess that I am a new creation in Christ Jesus. I have laid aside the old clothes of my former way of thinking and acting, and I have put on the new wardrobe prepared for me as a partaker of God's own nature. For my permanent new set of clothing, I put on mercy, kindness, humility of mind, gentleness, patience, and forgiveness. This new wardrobe will never wear out, and it will always be in style with God's best. Thank You, Lord, for clothing me with dignity and strength, and for making my way perfect as I put on your character like a garment of glory.

I declare this by faith in Jesus' name!

QUESTIONS FOR YOU TO CONSIDER

1. What kinds of changes do you sense the Holy Spirit is seeking to work outwardly in your life so that you become a greater reflection of His work inside your heart?
2. When you came to Jesus, He called you to repent and lay aside dead works, but He also called you to take on the character of Christ. Can you say that you demonstrate the character of Christ in your lifestyle? In what ways do you need to conform to Christ more?
3. When you look at the list of Christ-like garments that we are supposed to wear listed in Colossians 3:12 and 13, which ones do you think need the most attention in your life specifically?

MAY 24

Diversity in the Church

And the eye cannot say unto the hand,
I have no need of thee: nor again the head
to the feet, I have no need of you.
— 1 Corinthians 12:21

Have you ever wondered why people are the way they are?

We all come from different backgrounds, and to a certain degree, these backgrounds determine who we are, what we believe, how we think, and how we respond to any given situation. For example, a farmer from rural Arkansas will have a different outlook on life than a man who grew up in New York City. A boy who grew up on the inner-city streets of Baltimore is going to see life differently than a boy who grew up in Sand Springs, Oklahoma. Or a girl who grew up with her poor grandmother and whose mother had five husbands is going to view some things differently than a girl who grew up in a white-collar home and never knew anything but financial security and a solid home life.

Likewise, a believer's background in church will often have a strong influence on how he or she views different church issues, such as doctrinal debates, how worship should be conducted, or the proper roles of church government. For instance, if you grew up a Baptist like I did, you might see the Catholic Church as very formal. If you grew up as a Methodist, the Assemblies of God might seem radical to you. Or if you were raised in a Charismatic church, the Assemblies of

God may seem too "denominational" to you. *How we respond to these different spiritual environments largely depends on the spiritual environment we are most familiar with.*

A person's background is not an *excuse* for his or her behavior, but sometimes it is an *explanation.* Take your family background, for example. If you grew up in a home filled with love — where you were freely hugged, given kisses, and told, "I love you" — it undoubtedly affected the way you conduct your own household now that you're an adult with a family.

Personally, I was raised in such a home. My parents loved me, and I knew it. Even when they disciplined me, I was aware of their love. When I was in college and came home to see my parents on the weekends, I kissed my mom and dad when I arrived and before I returned to school. I even kissed them each night on the cheek before I went to bed. And today, decades later, I still kiss my mom before I leave her to return home. The way I was raised has impacted the way I raised my own children and the way I treat my wife. My family represents the most precious relationships I have in this world — and I believe they should be treated as such.

However, if a person grew up in a home where no one was touched, no one was kissed, and the words "*I love you*" were never heard, he may have a difficult time later on in life expressing affection toward his loved ones. Or if a person grew up with an abusive, alcoholic parent in a home riddled with strife and neglect, he might struggle with significant emotional obstacles, such as residual anger issues and a fear of rejection. Furthermore, a person's background colors his or her perception of the world. For example, a Christian who has been through divorce will have a different view of marital failure than a believer who is happily married, and a believer who was involved in drugs or crime before he or she received Christ might have a more tolerant view of people involved in those sins than a Christian who was raised in the Church and never dabbled in such destructive behaviors.

When we consider the fact that these factors are multiplied by millions of people and then mixed together in the Church, it is easy to see why conflict occurs. We get frustrated and lose our patience with others because we tend to think they should feel, see, and do things exactly like we do — but the truth is, they do not.

However, we must always remember that this diversity is not bad. *On the contrary, it adds variety and spice to the Church!* As members of the Body of Christ, we each have unique and important roles to play, and we must learn to appreciate and respect the views and opinions of others in the Church. Learning to deal successfully with other believers — to cope with their differences and learn to appreciate them — is one of the greatest achievements we can reach in life. We don't have to agree with every believer on every issue in order to be good Christians. A difference of opinion isn't always bad; in fact, sometimes it's healthy. A disagreement only becomes bad if we take it personally and become offended or hurt by it. Unity doesn't mean we blindly agree with each other like mindless robots, and silence and compliance don't necessarily spell unity.

In my own ministry, I sense great unity when our staff meets together to strongly discuss issues about which we all have different opinions. The energy and teamwork put forth as we each discuss a different point of view brings a tremendous sense of unity to our team. Even though we may not agree on every detail, we are unified in our attempts to find the right answer or solution.

As long as we live in imperfect human bodies, we can be sure that we will occasionally hit bumps in our relationships at home, at work, and at church. Those bumps are not disastrous unless we take them too close to our hearts and get hurt or bruised by them.

Many times relationships are difficult simply because of a difference in personality. Your personality is unique to you. Since there are so many different kinds of personalities, you will find that you may mix well with some but not as easily with others.

Until we learn to understand each other better, these differences become hindrances — *points of conflict*. What a pity to let our differences go on separating us when the things that distinguish us from each other could be helping us! The apostle Paul used the parts of a human body to demonstrate how each part is vital in order for a person to perform at his fullest potential. A body without all of its parts would be a deformity. Imagine a body without a nose or a body without feet.

Speaking to the church in Corinth, Paul wrote in First Corinthians 12:21, "And the eye cannot say unto the hand, I have no need of thee: nor again the head to the feet, I have no need of you." That phrase "no need of you" is the Greek phrase *chreian sou ouk*, which implies the thought, *I have no occasion to employ your services. You have nothing that is of any use to me.* Paul was stressing, "You cannot say you have no use for others in the Body of Christ. Paul's illustration is very plain to understand: *A body must have all of the parts in order to be complete.* A body without hands can think, but it can't touch. A body without eyes can smell, but it can't see where to walk. A body without feet may see where it needs to go, but it cannot walk because it has no feet to carry it. *Every part is necessary for the human body to function normally.*

It is the same concerning our relationships in the Church. We need a whole spectrum of personalities in order for us to be complete and to successfully perform in life.

What would life be like if everyone was exactly like you? There would be gaping holes and terrible deficiencies all around us. Rather than allow differences in personalities to rub us the wrong way, we need to let the Holy Spirit teach us to see the benefit that each person we meet has to offer!

MY PRAYER FOR TODAY

Dear Heavenly Father, You are so wise. You have placed every member in the body as it pleases You. According to Your divine plan, our differences are designed to complement and complete each other. Thank You for the relationships you have given me that are like iron sharpening iron. Holy Spirit, I receive Your wisdom and counsel on how to interact with others who are completely unlike me — and how not to allow differences in people to divide and separate me from them. Instead, I choose to yield to Your work by the Holy Spirit to allow our differences to produce a sanctifying experience in my life to conform me into the image of Christ for Your glory.

I ask this in Jesus' name!

MY CONFESSION FOR TODAY

I confess that I am positioned in the Body of Christ according to divine design. God is working through my unique gifts, talents, experiences, and personality to make me a blessing to people and to His Kingdom. I will not evaluate others for not thinking or acting in a way that I would prefer. The only standard of measure is the Word of God. Upon that common foundation, God Himself is building His Body with great diversity and distinction. Instead of comparing myself with others, which is not wise, I will develop the fruit of godly character and diligently apply my efforts to increasing in understanding and skillfulness in all I do so that I can be a valuable member in the Body of Christ.

I declare this by faith in Jesus' name!

QUESTIONS FOR YOU TO CONSIDER

1. Do you find that you are impatient with others who are different from you? Have you ever considered what life would be like if everyone was like you? Imagine how boring everything would be!
2. Is it possible that you need to loosen up a bit and quit being judgmental of others for doing things differently than you would do them? Is it possible that they have a piece of the puzzle that is different from yours and that without them, you would have a gaping hole in your life? Who is that person you're thinking about while you're reading this question?
3. What about your own background has made you see life a little differently than how others around you see it? Is it possible that some of your struggles originate because of how YOU view life differently than others?

MAY 25

Your Heart, Christ's Home

That Christ may *dwell* in your hearts by faith;
that ye, being rooted and grounded in love.
— Ephesians 3:17

From time to time, many of us get caught up in the challenges of life and sometimes fail to notice all that God is accomplishing in our midst. As we go through each day, we can become so fixated on our daily challenges and trials that we lose sight not only of what God *has done*, but also of what He *is doing* on our behalf.

Truly life can be overwhelming at times. But we need to remember that although we may experience momentary afflictions, our overwhelming victory in Christ is permanent and eternal. It's during those times when the shifting tides of life threaten to unnerve us or to displace our footing that we need to recognize the permanent stability of our True Foundation, Jesus Christ. He is our Strong Tower, our Shelter, and our Dwelling Place. We can count on that! But even more important is the fact that *He has chosen to make our hearts HIS permanent dwelling place.*

The apostle Paul emphatically declares this truth in Ephesians 3:17, saying, "That Christ may *dwell* in your hearts by faith; that ye, being rooted and grounded in love." That word "dwell" is the Greek word *katoikeo,* a compound of the words *kata* and *oikos.* The word *kata* means *down,* and the word *oikos* is the Greek word for *a house.* The word *oikos* could also be used in a larger sense to describe *a family clan* or *a larger social unit,* such as the *house* of David, or it could depict *a local community.* In the New Testament, the primary meaning of the word *oikos* is *a house or location where an individual, entity, family, or community permanently dwells.*

When *kata* and *oikos* are compounded, the new word *katoikeo* ("dwell") carries the idea of one who *permanently resides at a specific location.* Thus, Paul's use of this word implies not only that Christ establishes His physical residence in a faith-filled heart by the Holy Spirit, but also that He is *at home* and *permanently settled* there. That location has become *His dwelling place, His temple, His property, His place of permanent residence* — and He has become a perpetual, never-to-move-out Occupant!

Isn't that good to know? Christ's dwelling is *permanently fixed* within our hearts, and He has no intention of ever leaving us or abandoning us for another place of residence! That means He knows what we face every day, and He faces it with us. It is impossible for us to live without Jesus' attention to every detail in our lives, because He perpetually dwells inside us in the Person of the Holy Spirit. This also means there is no place to run or hide from Christ, because He literally goes where we go and is always present wherever we are. We are His *permanent earthly residence,* not merely a stop on His way to somewhere else!

Christ Himself is in every challenge we face, so we can rest assured that God is always with and in us. He is always present to sustain us, strengthen us, and guide us through this life. He never leaves or forsakes us. We are His permanent dwelling place.

It's no wonder that First John 4:4 declares, "Greater is He that is in you than he that is in the world!" Jesus Christ lives inside you! *Think of that as you get started today!*

MY PRAYER FOR TODAY

Heavenly Father, I am so grateful that by Your great love and kindness, in Christ I am Your temple, Your sanctuary. Your Spirit has His permanent dwelling in me individually and in Your Church collectively. From this day forward, I will make it a practice to remind myself that Christ in me is my Hope of Glory. As Your permanent dwelling place, I know I carry You into every situation I face, so I thank You that You empower me to walk honorably in all I do to the glory of Jesus Christ.

I pray this in Jesus' name!

MY CONFESSION FOR TODAY

I confess that when the shifting tides of life threaten to unnerve me, I remain stable and unmoved because I am anchored in the solid Rock, the Lord Jesus Christ. He is my permanent stability and my true foundation; therefore, my steps do not slide. The name of the Lord is my strong tower and my shelter. My life is hidden in Christ in God. And not only do I abide in Him, but He also dwells in me! I am the living temple of the Most High God. He has chosen to make my heart HIS permanent dwelling place. Knowing that He will never leave me or forsake me, I boldly proclaim: Victory is mine because greater is He that is in me than he that is in this world!

I declare this by faith in Jesus' name!

QUESTIONS FOR YOU TO CONSIDER

1. Have you ever thought about the fact that your heart is Christ's home in your life and that you are His permanent place of residency? Since that is the case, how should it affect the way you live?
2. Just think of the fact that you cannot run or hide from Christ, because everywhere you go, He goes with you. That means you never face anything alone or without Him facing it with you. Knowing that Christ is in you, what kind of affect does that have on you as you face different circumstances in life?
3. If you really believe that Jesus is greater in you than anything you'll ever face, then ponder what a victorious position this puts you in your life. Why don't you take a few minutes to meditate on Christ being in you and do it before you let any time lapse after reading this *Sparkling Gem* today.

MAY 26

Faith Stands Still!

But let him ask in faith, nothing wavering.
For he that wavereth is like a wave of the sea
driven with the wind and tossed.
— James 1:6

It is no secret that the devil will try to knock you back from your stance of faith when you are facing a difficult challenge. However, in this pivotal moment when he is pushing his hardest, you must be aware that you stand at a crossroads. You have a crucial choice to make: You can give up, *or* you can stand your ground and boldly declare, "I refuse to be moved off my position of faith! The Word of God is true, and I'm *not* going to back off!"

If you've had trouble standing firm in your faith against the pressure of the enemy in the past, don't feel condemned. Just receive this message as an encouragement from the Lord to get back on your feet and then go for it again! To experience a breakthrough regarding a difficult situation or a trap that you've struggled with for too long, you must take a bold stance of faith and then *stand still.*

Yes, it may take time for your answer to manifest. Just because your request is in accordance with God's will, the answer doesn't always come to pass quickly or without a hitch. There's a devil out there that doesn't want you to experience God's will for your life. You also have your own flesh to deal with, and flesh loves comfort — it does *not* like a challenge. Your faith may need to grow. God wants you to come to a higher level in the process of receiving the answer to your prayer.

Faith knows what it wants. It doesn't vacillate. It never moves. *Faith stands still in one spot.* So make your bold confession of faith: "God, this is what I want. This is Your will for my life, and I'm not moving until I receive the fulfillment of it!"

In James 1:6, James described the unwavering attitude a believer *must* have when he asks God for something in faith. It says, "But let him ask in faith, nothing wavering. For he that wavereth is like a wave of the sea driven with the wind and tossed."

First of all, James told us that we must "ask." The word "ask" is the Greek word *aiteo*, which means to be *firm* or *adamant* in *requesting* assistance to meet tangible needs, such as food, shelter, money, and so forth. The petitioner is so sure that his request is correct that he asks boldly and with an expectation to receive what he is firmly requesting. This depicts a person who speaks up, speaks out, and prays boldly and authoritatively.

Second, James said that we must ask "in faith." The Greek lays emphasis on the word "in" — as something that the person is locked into or as something that is immovable. In other words, this person is praying from a stable, immovable, decided position. He knows what he wants and isn't going to budge. Faith knows what it wants, and *faith stands still.* Faith doesn't waver.

Third, the verse says that we must ask in faith and not "doubt." The word "doubt" in Greek is *diakrinomai*, which means *to differ* or *to be at variance with one's self.* In other words, your mouth may be saying all the right words, but your heart is not really in agreement. It's just a mouthful of correct, empty words. Until your heart and mouth get into agreement, you are not really asking in faith, so James told us that we must ask with hearts that are in agreement with our mouths.

Fourth, James said that if we are not asking in faith — that is, if we are not standing firm in our position of faith — we are like unto a "wave" of the sea. The word "wave" is the Greek word *kludunai*, and it describes *the billowing sea*, or *one roll of waves after another*, or *the ever-changing sea.* Waves may look impressive, but they don't last long. And likewise, a person who doesn't stand firm in faith may temporarily look or sound impressive when he prays, but like a wave of the sea, his prayers and desires are ever-changing; and therefore he is not standing firm in a position where he can be blessed. *Faith stands still.*

In verse 7, James continued to say, "Let not that man think that he shall receive anything of the Lord." It's not that God doesn't want to bless this man; He *can't* bless this man, because the man doesn't stay in a position of faith long enough to receive an answer to his prayers. Like the waves of the sea, he is shifting all the time from one request to another about the same issue — and then when a little pressure is applied and he doubts, he shifts again.

Consider your own walk with God. Perhaps this is one reason a prayer request of yours hasn't been answered. Maybe you've never locked in with your faith on that particular need. Regarding what you've asked God for, do you change your mind or waver in doubt every few days — or even every year? Sometimes it does take years for certain answers for prayer to manifest. That's why it's so important to *focus* and *lock in* with your faith. You have to say, *"This is it!"* and stand still.

I suggest you say out loud: *"Faith stands still."* Say it again and again until that truth gets planted firmly in your heart. If you're moving around and wavering in your faith all the time, you make it difficult for God to bless you. But when you determine, "I'm believing God for this answer to come to pass, and I'm *not moving* in my stance of faith about it!" — then you position yourself as someone God can bless.

So decide today what you want and need based on what God promises in His Word. Then pray a prayer of faith, and determine that you're not going to move until you see that answer come into manifestation. Regardless of how long it takes or how difficult the process is, you are not moving again — because *faith stands still*!

MY PRAYER FOR TODAY

Father, I repent for the times I have made a declaration of sincere faith, but then allowed myself to waver because of something I saw or felt. I acknowledge that such vacillating is to be double-minded, and the double-minded person will not receive anything from the Lord. I acknowledge that without faith it is impossible to please You. And I choose to please You, Father! Therefore, because I believe that You reward those who diligently seek You, I purpose in my heart to remain fixed and stable in my position of faith until Your reward is fully manifested in my life.

I pray this in Jesus' name!

MY CONFESSION FOR TODAY

I confess that this is IT — today I focus, and I boldly REFUSE to move from my stance in faith! I let patience have its perfect work, and I do not vacillate! I am not tossed like a wave to and fro, but I stand firm in one spot — fixed, immovable, and determined. I am confident that I will see what I have believed because my faith is based upon God's Word, and His Word is His will. Therefore, this day I confess that the will of God shall be manifested in my life!

I declare this by faith in Jesus' name!

QUESTIONS FOR YOU TO CONSIDER

1. Is it possible that your prayers haven't been answered because you've changed your prayer request so many times? Be honest with yourself. If faith stands still until it receives what it has requested, has your behavior met the description of how faith behaves?
2. What scriptures are you standing on for the things you are requesting from God? I advise you to write down the scripture references that back up what you are requesting from God. When the devil tempts you to back off or to think that God won't answer, this will give you a foundation to stand on and repel his attacks.
3. Have you ever known anyone who habitually changes his or her prayer requests, as James says, like a wave of the sea, driven by the wind and tossed? What would you advise that person after reading today's *Sparkling Gem*?

MAY 27

The Importance of Honesty in Relationships

Wherefore putting away lying,
speak every man truth with his neighbor:
for we are members one of another.
— Ephesians 4:25

I want to talk about the importance of honesty in relationships and the need to deal with past offenses or hurt before they take root in your heart and breed bitterness. I'll warn you in advance that you will need to pray for wisdom after you read this.

Many times offense and hurt arise from moments when little problems get completely blown out of proportion. At the time, the issue seems so big and all-consuming, but deep down, you know in your heart that it's stupid and not worth that kind of attention. How often do these little, nitpicky hang-ups steal our time, rob us of our joy, and separate us from others — whether for a few moments, or several hours, or days at a time, or even longer? It is important that we learn to identify and address these minor problems before they escalate into something bigger that ultimately steals our time, robs us of our peace, and separates us from those we love.

Let's bring this a little closer to home. Is there anyone in your life right now with whom you're having a hard time getting along? Perhaps you have a close friend who has disappointed you.

Maybe a business acquaintance has rubbed you the wrong way. Or maybe there is someone at church you just can't stand. You don't know why you feel the way you do, but when you see them, you feel disgust and intolerance and want to turn the other direction. Perhaps someone has hurt you unintentionally by saying something that was thoughtless, or maybe their attack was entirely purposeful. Regardless of the motive, the person's words went into your heart like a dagger that you've never been able to completely pull out. You still feel the hurt, the wound, and the pain of his or her thoughtless words, actions, and deeds.

As a Christian, you already know what you *should* do in all of these cases: Ask the Lord to forgive you for your wrong attitude and help you change the way you see the people who have hurt or offended you. You should overlook their weaknesses, forgive them for their wrongs, forget about their characteristics or hang-ups that irk you so much, and then move on as though nothing ever happened to ruffle your feathers. It's also possible that you might need to prayerfully, honestly, and lovingly communicate with those people about what's bothering you.

That's what you should do. You know the Holy Spirit wants you to love them with the love of Jesus. However, the emotions you feel are so strong that you'd rather just look the other way and forget about those who have hurt you. Your flesh doesn't want to take the time and energy required to forgive them, show God's love to them, and do as much as you can to preserve or restore those relationships.

And have you noticed how your mind will constantly drift back to that moment when you were hurt, irked, or offended? Subconsciously, you keep rehearsing the whole event over and over again in your mind, examining every little point of what you said and what the other person said. It grates against you as if it just happened minutes ago, when in reality quite a space of time has elapsed and you should be well over it by now. But if the truth be told — you're not!

If this describes a true scenario in your life, it's time to let go of your hurt or offense and forgive the person who wronged you. Why is this so crucial? Because these attitudes left unchecked will form a root of bitterness that could eventually ruin your life (*see* Hebrews 12:15). But in order to free yourself from these destructive mindsets, you must first confront them head-on. You must be honest with yourself and with the person who wronged you.

Honesty is the name of the game when it comes to relationships. Learning to "speak every man truth with his neighbor" is a challenge for the most mature believer. Yet this is the mandate the apostle Paul gave us in Ephesians 4:25 when he said, "Wherefore putting away lying, speak every man truth with his neighbor: for we are members one of another."

Paul said that God requires believers to "put away" lying in their relationships. These were mature believers Paul was addressing, so it is unlikely they were lying outright. The Greek word for "lying" is *pseudos*, which really means *dishonesty*. Maybe they weren't outright lying. Maybe they just weren't being truthful or didn't know how to be truthful. Regardless of how the situation transpired, it had led to dishonesty. Paul called on them to learn how to speak the "truth" with one another. The word "truth" is *alethosi*. In this verse, it refers to *truthfulness* or *honesty* in relationships.

In spite of Paul's exhortation for honesty between the members of the Body of Christ, the Church is full of actors who pretend like everything is good when inwardly they are hurt or offended by the words or actions of another believer. They aren't trying to be dishonest; they're trying to be mature. They think that by not discussing the issues that bother them, they are being "spiritual." But this "silent spirituality" is *not* a sign of spiritual maturity. In fact, it often leads to the cultivation of hostile attitudes, resentment, and a hard heart toward the other party.

Most people choose to simply "grin and bear it" and think that by ignoring their hurt, it will somehow go away by itself. But it rarely happens this way. The hurt may hide itself deep inside the soul for a while, but the next time a similar situation happens with the same person, that old wound will start screaming again.

That's your signal that you have never really dealt with your heart toward that other person! You never really got over it; you just covered up the hurt.

Honesty might be difficult, but it's not more difficult than living with a bitter spirit and a bad attitude. Being honest with the one who hurt you may seem difficult at the moment, but when forgiveness clears the breach in the relationship, you are *free.* Holding on to silent resentment makes you a prisoner in your own mind and emotions.

Is the Holy Spirit speaking to you today about taking action to be honest with someone about a situation you've tried to ignore? Well, as I told you at the beginning of the *Sparkling Gem,* it may be time for you to pray for wisdom!

MY PRAYER FOR TODAY

Father, I thank You for the Holy Spirit whom Jesus sent to help me in this life. He is the Spirit of Truth who alone can lead and guide me into all truth. I receive His counsel and help to open the eyes of my understanding and grant me revelation knowledge as I search my own heart in the light of Your Word. Help me discern the areas where I have become dishonest in my relationships in an attempt to deal with hurts and disappointments. I believe that I receive Your help today as I purpose to change!

I pray this in Jesus' name!

MY CONFESSION FOR TODAY

Today I choose to yield to the love of God that is shed abroad in my heart so I can forgive and move forward with integrity and in truth. I recognize the importance of maintaining honesty in my relationships — and that it starts by first being honest with myself. I receive the help of the Holy Spirit, who teaches me how to speak the truth in love so that I may walk with integrity and that I may honor my Lord Jesus in all areas and relationships in my life.

I declare this by faith in Jesus' name!

QUESTIONS FOR YOU TO CONSIDER

1. Do you have a relationship that is dishonest because you do not know how to speak the truth to that other person? I'm sure you wouldn't want to lie, but has your ignoring of the truth really emerged into a dishonest relationship?
2. If you did what the Holy Spirit wanted you to do, what would it be? Do you think the Holy Spirit would tell you to ignore the situation or find a way to discuss it with that other person?
3. What actions will you take as a result of reading today's *Sparkling Gem*?

MAY 28

Don't Inflate the Truth About Yourself!

"If thou hast done foolishly in lifting up thyself…
lay thine hand upon thy mouth."
— Proverbs 30:32

Many years ago, Denise and I went on a cruise of the Caribbean Sea. We had never been on a cruise and didn't know what to expect. When we arrived for dinner the first evening, we assumed we'd be seated alone, but the maître d' seated us at a table with six young people in their early to mid-20s. Denise and I looked at each other and then at the six other people, and we realized we were the grandpa and grandma in the group. It wasn't exactly the *romantic* setting we had in mind, but it was the seating given to us for the evening so we decided to enjoy an experience with this young group of people.

These were university students who had decided to take a cruise together. So rather than talk about ourselves, we decided to listen and see what we could learn from this younger generation. The young female seated next to Denise glowed as she chattered away. She told Denise that she was studying Classical Greek and that her dream was to become an expert, having already attained a measure of that expert status compared to other students back home at the university. She went on and on about the marvelous characteristics of Classical Greek — obviously trying to impress us with how smart she was.

Then the young man seated to my right side decided it was his turn to chime in, and he began to quite literally rave about how brilliant he was with the Russian language. Believe me, *pride* was not hidden at that table! These young people — *according to themselves* — were absolutely amazing in their respective abilities! The man next to me went on and on about how he had studied Russian at the university for two years and that he spoke Russian so flawlessly that even native Russians couldn't even detect a foreign accent when he spoke! *Denise and I looked at each other in amazement, but never uttered a word in response or gave a hint that we are both Russian-speakers.*

Then a gorgeous young girl across the table spoke up: "Well, I guess it's my turn to tell who I am and what I plan to do. I am a soprano, and I plan to sing professionally at the Metropolitan Opera in New York City." *Oh my goodness, I thought I would fall off my chair any moment.* Even if she was a good singer, she was sitting at the same table as my wife, who really *had* the opportunity to sing at the Metropolitan Opera but had given up the opportunity for the ministry. This gorgeous young girl had no idea what kind of real opera singer was sitting right in front of her as she exclaimed how many awards she had won and how gifted she was at singing.

After the young people had gone around the table and they had all finished "sharing" their areas of brilliance and expertise, they looked at Denise and me — almost as if to say, *We know you are older and probably the least experienced, but...* And they kindly asked us, "Now tell us — what has been your past area of expertise?"

Denise spoke up first and said, "Well, my husband is a Classical Greek expert and has written best-selling books on the subject." The girl sitting next to Denise, who claimed such expertise at Classical Greek, nearly wilted. She said, "Well, I'm really not a real expert, like you are. Oh, how embarrassing."

Then I turned to the overly confident Russian-student to my right and said, "My wife and I have lived in Russia for many years, and we speak Russian fluently. How about if you and I speak a little Russian together?" He leaned back from the table and said, "Oh, I really don't speak that well. I feel a little put on the spot. I'd rather not speak in Russian right now."

Then the gorgeous blonde soprano looked at Denise and said, "And what about you?" I interrupted and said, "May I answer that question, because my wife may be a little timid right now to tell you. But she *is* an opera singer who holds concerts all over the former USSR and who personally gave up a career at the Metropolitan Opera when we decided to get married." The blonde's mouth literally fell open, gaping in shock.

I didn't want any of them to be embarrassed for grossly exaggerating the truth about themselves, but I felt a need to give a little advice about truthful presentations. Feeling they were all embarrassed, I said, "There's no need to be embarrassed in front of us, but you need to be careful how highly you lift yourself up in front of others, because it could put you in a *very* embarrassing situation. Speak well of yourself, but don't stretch the truth." Then I asked them to please pass the gravy, and we all moved on to other subjects. All in all, the evening turned out to be a wonderful time with a group of young, inexperienced university students.

When I read Proverbs 30:32, I remember that night. It says, "If thou hast done foolishly in lifting up thyself...lay thine hand upon thy mouth." God's solution in such a moment is simple: "...lay thine hand upon thy mouth" — or in other words, shut your mouth when you are tempted to gloat about yourself.

In the Septuagint, the Greek version of the Old Testament, the word "foolishly" is the word *euphrosune*, and it pictures *the abandonment of one to self-aggrandizing.* Thus, it is translated as someone who acts *foolishly*. It is the extreme picture of one who speaks too highly about himself, one who revels in his own accomplishments, or one who is ridiculously self-congratulatory, which is why sometimes it is translated as *mirth*. It is the most extreme version of *thinking too highly of oneself*. The word "hand" is *cheira*, the normal word for a *hand*, but here it pictures a person putting his "hand" on his mouth!

Especially when I was younger, I felt the need to impress others because I wanted people to think highly of me. I was probably guilty of the same thing that I saw these young people do who were seated at the table with us that night. However, as I've grown older and become more secure in the Lord and who I am in Christ, the need to impress others has become less important to me — and my relationship with Jesus and how He perceives me has taken the place of greatest importance in my life. As I become more sensitive to the Holy Spirit, I become increasingly aware of how grieved He is when we embellish the truth.

During a time of self-examination years ago when I took an extended time to look back on my life, there were many words I wished I could retract, but it was too late and too many years had passed. So I made the decision to be very careful from that point onward to say only those things that were true and honoring to Jesus. *Sometimes the best policy is to say nothing at all.*

So today I want to ask you — are you guilty of embellishing the facts? If you're still guilty of this sin of the mouth, Proverbs 30:32 may be the best advice for you: "If thou hast done foolishly in lifting up thyself…lay thine hand upon thy mouth." God's solution is very simple. Whenever you are tempted to exaggerate the truth — or to exaggerate your own importance — put your hand over your mouth until it becomes a settled practice in your life to rest in who you are in Jesus. In time you will ensure that in all things and in every situation, Jesus *alone* gets all the glory and honor for whatever you accomplish in this life!

MY PRAYER FOR TODAY

Heavenly Father, I repent for the times I have sought to impress people by inflating the facts rather than seeking to please You by simply telling the truth. To exaggerate my abilities or accomplishments is utterly foolish since people usually see right through it! I realize now that if I engage in self-aggrandizement, not only am I deceiving myself, but I am also attempting to manipulate others by controlling their perception of me through a lie. That is not the way I want to live! I now see that to blow things out of proportion in order to exalt myself before others is actually a symptom of fear, not confidence — and fear brings a snare. Holy Spirit, I ask You to forgive me for the times I've grieved You by exalting myself instead of exalting Jesus. I ask You to set a watch over my lips as I commit to place my hand on my mouth and to give all glory to the Lord Jesus Christ alone!

I pray this in Jesus' name!

MY CONFESSION FOR TODAY

I confess that I choose to resist the temptation to exaggerate the truth and embellish the facts in an attempt to make myself seem more important or accomplished than I am. To safeguard against foolish speaking, I will put my hand over my mouth. I am complete in Christ, and my sense of security in Him continually increases as my identity in Him becomes more and more established.

I declare this by faith in Jesus' name!

QUESTIONS FOR YOU TO CONSIDER

1. Can you remember a moment when you embellished the truth to make yourself look more important in the eyes of others? When was that, and did you ever repent for embellishing the truth?
2. What is most important in your life right now? Is it the opinions of what others or what Jesus thinks about you? Be honest, because Jesus already knows the truth anyway!
3. Have you ever been astonished at someone's willingness to exaggerate the truth in order to impress other people? If you hear someone embellishing the truth, what do you think is your responsibility? Should you simply be quiet and let it go or privately ask the person about it?

MAY 29

A Supernatural Answer to Prayer!

Again, I say unto you,
that if two of you shall agree on earth
as touching any thing that they shall ask,
it shall be done for them of my Father which is in heaven.
— Matthew 18:19

In the early 1990s, I was on a plane that was horribly overloaded with people, luggage, and boxes. So many air-safety rules were being violated on this particular flight! Pieces of luggage and boxes were strapped into the seats where people should have been sitting — and people were sitting on top of the boxes in the main aisle of the cabin. From my vantage point, I could see most of the plane's interior. As I watched the debacle, I saw people literally pushing luggage and garment bags away because they were hanging in their faces from the overhead compartments. Yet even with all the excess bags, boxes, and luggage already on the plane, the crew just kept loading more and more into the airplane bay. In fact, it came to the point where they were filling the bathrooms with luggage and boxes, and there were even suitcases stacked in the cockpit! *I had never seen anything like it.*

I happened to be seated toward the front of the plane near the flight attendants, and I actually heard one flight attendant tell her colleague, "This plane is dangerously overloaded. I'm afraid that we are going to fall from the sky." As I continued to listen, I heard one say that the pilot had taken a bribe from a company to transport a gigantic shipment of items to the destination city. He knew he was taking a risk, but he had already been paid and needed the money, so he chose to risk the lives of his passengers. It was all about a bribe to get as much freight on that plane as possible!

People on the plane reeked of fear because it was blatantly obvious that this plane was loaded beyond its weight limitations, and its maximum capacity was far exceeded. I could tell my traveling companion was also very uneasy about the situation. I turned to him and asked, "Do you think this plane is going to crash because it's overloaded?" He answered, "Yes, seems to me that we're headed for a crisis."

I quietly asked my traveling companion to join hands with me and pray. We acknowledged that wherever *two* or *three* were gathered in Jesus' name, He was there and that He would answer our prayers. So we prayed in the Spirit peacefully and confidently. We harmonized our hearts and spirits together — believing that if we were in any type of danger, God would do something to change the situation and protect us. We prayed according to Matthew 18:19, saying, "Lord, You said that if two or three of us would agree on earth as touching anything, you would hear us, and our Heavenly Father would do it. So Father, if this plane is in danger in any way, as I have heard this flight attendant say, then we ask You to please do something to change this situation and protect us from harm."

Within minutes after our prayer, a flight attendant abruptly came on the sound system and hysterically announced the plane would be evacuated due to a phone call that said there was a bomb on board. She said, "There has been a phone call indicating that there is a bomb on this plane. So please… *quietly, orderly…*begin disembarking this airplane as *quickly* as possible. *EVERYONE GET OFF THIS PLANE!"*

The panic in her voice caused panic to hit the whole plane. Suddenly everyone was standing up in front of their seats, fighting, screaming, and trying to force their way to the airplane's sole open exit. It was mass confusion! Because the plane was overloaded with luggage that was choking up the main aisle, people were jumping and leaping over boxes and bags as they fought each other to make their way toward the exit. Because of where I was seated, I couldn't move — there were too many boxes stacked around me — so I decided to just sit back and watch the people wage war with each other to try to get off the plane quicker than all the others. The sight was like none I had ever seen. *It was anything but quiet and orderly!* In fact, people were actually injured as they fought with each other to be the first off the plane!

When everyone was finally off the plane and transported inside the terminal, an airline official met us and said we were to wait for directions regarding what we should do next. Hours passed, and as I looked out the terminal windows toward our evacuated plane, I could see people completely emptying the plane of all boxes and luggage that had been recklessly packed into every available space. Finally, the plane was completely emptied, and officials and bomb-searching dogs thoroughly searched it from top to bottom. However, when they had finished, an announcement was made in the terminal that said, "No bomb has been found, so we are now reboarding the aircraft. But this time, we have decided that no excess luggage will be allowed. Please use your same ticket and take your same seat."

About an hour later, we were seated back in our same seats, and when the door closed for that flight to take off, it was a completely different scene. People were all seated in their ticketed seats; no luggage or boxes were in the aisles; and no excess bags or garments were dangling from the overhead compartments. It was like a totally different aircraft. The passengers on board were now quiet and peaceful because they, too, knew it was a safer situation than what had existed only a few hours prior to our reboarding. Decades have passed since this event occurred, but I still remember it as though it happened yesterday because events like that are not easily forgotten!

That day, my traveling companion and I prayed according to Matthew 18:19, which says, "Again, I say unto you, that if two of you shall agree on earth as touching any thing that they shall ask, it shall be done for them of my Father which is in heaven." According to this verse, all that is required is two or three people who "agree" as touching anything that they ask, and it shall be done for them of our Heavenly Father.

Let's take a closer look at this word "agree" to see exactly what Jesus meant when He made this declaration. The word "agree" is the Greek word *sumphoneo*, and it is a compound of *sum* and *phoneo*. The word *sum* means *with*, and the word *phoneo* means *to make a sound*. As you can imagine by simply looking at its two parts, this Greek word is where we get the word *symphony*. Thus, when we describe *agreement in prayer*, it is good to first think of a *symphony*, which is a musical piece made of different movements, instruments, and parts. The use of this word *sumphoneo* in the context of prayer is revealing, for it shows that when two or more believers get into agreement — each of them praying and adding their parts — it creates a supernatural movement that deeply touches the heart of the Father. This action is so powerful, in fact, that Jesus said it would result in the Father fulfilling any issue they addressed through prayer.

This is precisely what happened on the airplane that afternoon. In a moment of urgency, my traveling companion and I got into high-level spiritual agreement and prayed with such power and faith that *a movement of prayer* ascended from our seats to the Father's ears. When God heard our unified prayer, He was blessed by our faith and genuine agreement, and He literally swung into action to evacuate an entire airplane in response.

When you find yourself in a dilemma and need help from Heaven, find another believer who can get into agreement with you. Take turns praying, and pray together in the Spirit, letting your spirits mix and mingle and harmonize as they ascend to the throne of God to produce a symphony of prayer. When God hears this, it's only a matter of time until He begins to move Heaven and earth to answer your prayers!

MY PRAYER FOR TODAY

Heavenly Father, I thank You for the tremendous power You have enabled us to tap into through unified prayer. When we come together in agreement with faith in Your Word, I am grateful that You not only hear us when we pray in accordance with Your will, but You also answer to perform Your will and purposes in our lives. It pleases and honors You when Your people take advantage of this powerful type of prayer that enables our spirits to harmonize in faith as we come before Your throne of grace (Hebrews 11:6; Matthew 18:19) with each one of us adding our parts. Father, You have instructed us to pray with all manner of prayer (Ephesians 6:18). I will, therefore, pay attention to engage this type of prayer with another believer when dilemmas arise so that Your power can be released.

I pray this in Jesus' name!

MY CONFESSION FOR TODAY

I confess that I deeply touch the heart of my Heavenly Father when I create a harmonious sound of faith by entering into faith-filled agreement with another believer in prayer. I do not fear when difficulties suddenly appear. Instead, I tap the power of agreement in prayer! As each of us add our part in a harmonious symphony of unified prayer, our agreement with God's Word and with one another releases the supernatural power of God in our behalf.

I declare this by faith in Jesus' name!

QUESTIONS FOR YOU TO CONSIDER

1. Have you ever been in a desperate situation where you and a friend lifted your voices in powerful prayer and you saw almost immediate results? When was that experience? Is it something you could share with someone today to encourage someone else in his or her own experience with the Lord?
2. Can you think of an emergency situation from your past in which your life was in danger, but you cried out in faith and God heard your prayer and rescued you?
3. Have you ever experienced a moment of symphonized prayer — a supernatural moment when your voice was mixed and mingled together with another believer's voice, and it released currents of power from Heaven?

When two or more believers get into agreement,
it creates a supernatural movement
that deeply touches the heart of the Father
and is so powerful that it results
in the Father fulfilling any issue they address through prayer.

MAY 30

Use Every Possibility To Escape!

There hath no temptation taken you
but such as is common to man: but God is faithful,
who will not suffer you to be tempted above that ye are able;
but will with the temptation also make a way to escape,
that ye may be able to bear it.
— 1 Corinthians 10:13

People can be quite a mystery!

You finally think you have them all figured out, and then they do something that totally lets you down and blows your mind! You never would have dreamed in a million years that they'd do something so crazy or inconsistent. That's why you have to learn how to overcome the temptation to take offense or get upset every time someone disappoints or lets you down. You'll enjoy life much more if you learn to *forgive* and *overlook* people's inconsistencies, lack of commitment, unfaithfulness, temper tantrums, and mood swings — as well as all the other defects that are part of being human.

There are days when I don't even understand my own moods! Therefore, I know I have to show mercy when I see others act differently than I expected. When I'm tempted to get upset with Denise, my kids, or my associates in the ministry, I stop and remind myself that I'm not perfect either. I'm sure there are moments when these same people are just as bewildered by me as I am by them! I can't complain too much about others being a mystery because I'm such a mystery to myself sometimes. Oh, how I long for the day when I walk in the Spirit 100 percent of the time!

Even Christians who spend hours in prayer, read the Word, pray in the Spirit, and seek to live a holy life sometimes get in the flesh, doing and saying things they later regret. It's just part of being human. When we receive our glorified bodies and go to Heaven, all our inconsistencies, mood swings, and complex emotions will be gone. Until then, we have to stay in an attitude of forgiveness and extend the same mercy to others that we expect them to extend to us.

If you're going to get "bent out of shape" and lose your peace every time someone says or does something *below* what you expect of them, you will live your life constantly bothered, upset, and frustrated. Rather than focus on the inconsistencies and flaws of others, why not look in the mirror and let the Holy Spirit deal with you about the areas *you* need to change? It may be that God is using the people you think have done you wrong to expose a weakness in your own character that needs to change. Let God's Spirit teach you how to overcome those exposed faults.

Galatians 5:22 says, "But the fruit of the Spirit is love, joy, peace, longsuffering, gentleness, goodness, faith, meekness, temperance: against such there is no law."

As Christians, we must learn how to allow the fruit of the Spirit to operate in us regardless of the situation. When our relationships with others are going great — when we have no challenges, no problems, and no conflicts with anyone — it's not difficult to be kind, loving, longsuffering, and easy to get along with. The real proof of spiritual maturity isn't measured by the moments when our flesh is comfortable; *it is revealed when we run into a situation that rubs our flesh the wrong way*!

But what if you're dealing with serious offenses and hurts in your relationships? What if you've been abused, betrayed, or deserted by your spouse, stabbed in the back by fellow church members, or rejected by your parents, family, or friends? If you've experienced any of these hurtful situations, you know how the devil can try to use such an event to debilitate you. But it's time to move on and let the past be the past. If you carry wounds, bruises, and scars from previous hurts and offenses, you don't have to carry them anymore. *You don't have to live with the residual effect of what the devil did to you in the past.*

If you have harbored unhealthy attitudes, you must allow them to be recognized, uprooted, and removed by the Spirit of God. Otherwise, they will begin to produce vile fruit that has the power to socially isolate you and emotionally immobilize you. Bitterness, resentment, and unforgiveness become like a terminal disease when left untended, eventually eating away at your insides, turning you bitter, and destroying every relationship in your life.

In every one of these situations I've described, God will make a way for you to escape negative emotions and killer attitudes *if* you really want to escape them. First Corinthians 10:13 says, "There hath no temptation taken you but such as is common to man: but God is faithful, who will not suffer you to be tempted above that ye are able; but will with the temptation also make a way to escape, that ye may be able to bear it."

That word "escape" comes from the Greek word *ekbasis*, which is a compound word combining the word *ek*, meaning *out*, and *basis*, which means *to go* or *to walk*. When compounded, the new word carries the idea of *an exit* and literally means *to walk out*, as *to walk out of a difficult place*; *to walk out of a trap*; or *to walk out of a place that isn't good for you*.

So this is what you can know: In every situation where you face the temptation to take offense at someone's words or actions, you are the *only one* who can make the choice to jump through that escape hatch. The moment you make that decision, your journey to freedom has begun! If you'll say yes to the Lord, He will show you how to get out of your mess! You can *avoid*, *evade*, *dodge*, *elude*, *shake off*, *get out of*, and *break away from* every temptation to take offense. You *never* have to get dragged into destructive emotions, feelings, and attitudes.

So today the Lord is asking: *"Are you going to stay upset and offended, or are you willing to take the proper steps to escape from this emotional temptation and demonic trap? Are you ready to give up all unforgiveness and lay it at the foot of the Cross so you can walk free? Or do you want to continue clinging to resentment and turmoil, held hostage by spiritually, mentally, and physically crippling attitudes?"*

What is your answer? What are you going to do? God is waiting for you to decide, because you definitely have the option to receive the freedom He is offering you and to walk into a broad, new place of abundant living with the choice you make today!

MY PRAYER FOR TODAY

Dear Heavenly Father, I come before You right now and repent for having given place to the devil because of hurt and offense. I see now that the enemy set a trap for me to fall into temptation. I also ask You to forgive me for judging the faults and failings of others, when in fact my own impatience and carnality were on full display by the way I responded to their behavior. I ask You, Holy Spirit, to open the eyes of my understanding and reveal to me the ways I need to change so I am not susceptible to unhealthy attitudes that would keep me socially isolated or emotionally immobilized. I choose to walk away from the devil's traps, and I trust You to help me escape the net of temptation.

I pray this in Jesus' name!

MY CONFESSION FOR TODAY

I confess that I realize no one is perfect — and neither am I! I am not ignorant of the devil's devices to destroy my relationships. Therefore, I refuse to be held hostage by crippling attitudes of negativity and disappointment when others fall short of my expectations. When I am tempted to become offended by a deliberate act of betrayal, rejection, or wrongdoing, I will look to the Holy Spirit. He is my Helper, my Strengthener, my Comforter, my Counselor, my Teacher, and my Advocate! The Holy Spirit will show me how to escape this temptation and respond according to the wisdom and the will of God. He will help me keep myself in the love of God so my faith will not fail and the devil cannot overtake me through his wiles against both me and the person who sought to do me harm.

I declare this by faith in Jesus' name!

QUESTIONS FOR YOU TO CONSIDER

1. Can you think of a time when you were tempted to be dragged into a conflict for which there was no real solution, but the Holy Spirit told you to be quiet and let it pass?
2. If you are upset or offended, are you going to allow yourself to be dragged down by these negative mindsets, or are you willing to take the proper steps to escape from this emotional temptation and demonic trap?
3. Are you ready to give up all unforgiveness, laying it at the foot of the Cross, so you can walk free? Or do you want to continue clinging to resentment and turmoil, held hostage by spiritually, mentally, and physically crippling attitudes? Your answer is very strategic to the outcome of your life, so seriously consider this question!

MAY 31

Follow After Peace

Follow peace with all men, and holiness,
without which no man shall see the Lord....
— Hebrews 12:14

Do you have a difficult relationship in your life that has been poisoned by offense, bitterness, or misunderstanding? It doesn't matter who it is — your spouse, a sibling, a friend, an employee, or a member of your church — you will find vital keys to help you navigate the situation in Hebrews 12:14. The verse starts out by saying, "*Follow* peace with all men...."

That word "follow" is the Greek word *dioko*. This word was an old hunting term that meant *to follow the tracks of the animal* or *to follow the scent of the animal.* Just imagine a hunter decked out in all his hunting gear, and he's following the tracks of his prey. He's following the scent of the beast, and he's looking for every little branch that the animal may have broken. The hunter is *hunting, following,* and *searching for* that animal — and he is *not* going to stop until finally he gets his prey.

This word *dioko* is also translated as "persecute" in the New Testament. In other words, when someone was persecuted, it wasn't something done haphazardly or accidentally; persecution was very intentional and deliberate. The persecutor *followed* his intended victims. He *searched for* them. He *hunted* them. He *tracked* them *down. He was out to get them.*

Now the Holy Spirit uses this same word in Hebrews 12:14 and says, "*Follow* after peace with all men...." That means sometimes peace doesn't just come to us. In fact, *most* of the time, peace does *not* come to us. *We* have to do something to find peace with people. We have to *follow after* peace.

No matter how difficult a particular relationship in your life is, God is telling you in this verse what *your* responsibility is as a believer. You have to put on your hunting gear and make a firm decision to *do something* about that relationship according to His love that has been shed abroad in your heart (*see* Romans 5:5). Remind yourself: "I can't be responsible for what that person does, but I *am* responsible for what I do — and God has *required* me to do everything I can do to obtain peace in this relationship." Of course, sometimes when you do everything you can do, the other person doesn't respond. You can't answer for the other person, but you *are* going to answer for yourself.

So if you're struggling to have peace with someone in your life, take this verse to heart. It's time to put on your hunting gear and begin to look for anything you can do. Follow the tracks. Follow the scent. Look for every little broken branch. Look for anything you might possibly do that might lead to peace. *Follow the tracks of peace.*

Why is it so important that we follow after peace? The Bible goes on to tell us the reason in Hebrews 12:14: "Follow peace with all men and holiness *without which no man will see the Lord.*" That word "see" tells us that lack of peace serves as a blocker that stops us from being admitted into the immediate presence of God. Think how many times you've been in a service where God's anointing is present and people are being blessed, but you can't enter into it because you are so inwardly upset about someone or something. You see, these attitudes are blockers, and that is why the writer of Hebrews says without peace — or in the presence of strife — you will not be able to be admitted into the life-changing presence of God. Strife is a blocker. It will stop you from entering into the anointing. It will stop you from entering into blessing of any kind.

The Bible tells us to "follow after peace and *holiness.*" The word "holiness" is the word *hagias*. It means *to be separate* or *to be different*. In this particular case, the writer of Hebrews is telling us that we don't have the privilege of acting or thinking like the world. God calls us to a higher standard. The Holy Spirit lives in us, giving us the power we need to walk in forgiveness on a much higher level than the world. The Holy Spirit gives us the power to walk in freedom rather than the bondage the world walks in. We are called to follow after peace — to *hunt* it, *seek* it, *pursue* it — with *all* men. And we're called to walk *in holiness*, to behave differently than lost people behave and to walk in forgiveness, free from offense. If we fail to pursue that kind of spiritual walk and remain in strife and bitterness, we'll never really be able to experience the tangible presence of God.

Take a moment to look at your life. Think about those times when you've harbored bitterness and offense and allowed your heart to grow hard toward a person. It was very difficult for you to experience the sweet presence of the Lord during those times, wasn't it? That's what this verse is talking about.

God has called us to a higher level, and like it or not, this verse tells us what we have to do when we're dealing with difficult people in our lives who have hurt or offended us. If we're serious about being disciples of Jesus, we must determine to forgive every person and every offense. We have to respond differently than the world would respond. Then as much as is possible with us, we must actively *follow after* obtaining peace with every person.

And let me tell you, friend — the *only* way you're going to be able to do this is by spending time with Jesus. Ask *Him* what path you're to follow to obtain peace. No one understands this better than Jesus. He had enemies all around Him, yet He walked in peace with all men. Talk to Jesus, and He'll get you on the right track that leads to freedom from strife and offense and to an abiding sense of His presence every day of your life.

MY PRAYER FOR TODAY

Heavenly Father, Your Word is very clear on how I am to respond to people who have hurt or offended me. When I am dealing with difficulties in relationships, You expect me to take the responsibility of hunting down peace and pursuing it. I ask You to show me what path I am to take in this pursuit so that I can please You by walking in the high level of love You have already shed abroad in my heart by the Holy Spirit who was given to me. I will not allow hurt, bitterness, or resentment to separate me from Your immediate presence. I receive Your help, Holy Spirit, to maintain a pure heart so that not only can I see God, but also so that I can see others as He sees them.

I pray this in Jesus' name!

MY CONFESSION FOR TODAY

I confess that because the Holy Spirit lives in me, I have the power I need to walk in forgiveness on a much higher level than the world. The Holy Spirit gives me the power to walk in freedom from the bondage of bitterness and strife. God requires me to follow after peace — to hunt it, seek it, and pursue it — with all men. Therefore, because I am required to do it, I am equipped to do it. I yield to the Holy Spirit, and I walk in holiness and in consecration to God and His ways. I deliberately separate myself from ungodly attitudes and actions because I refuse to be separated from the presence of God.

I declare this by faith in Jesus' name!

QUESTIONS FOR YOU TO CONSIDER

1. Has there been a relationship in your life in which you have found it particularly difficult to maintain peace? Who is that other person? Do you know why it has been so difficult to keep that relationship peaceful? Do you remember how the whole mess began, and do you know what you would have done differently if you could start all over again?
2. Has the Holy Spirit told you to follow after peace with that person? Instead of waiting for him or her to come to you with an apology, why don't you put on your "hunting gear" and make the choice to start following after peace until you finally obtain it in that relationship? It may require some creative thinking and acting born of diligent prayer about the matter — but if the Holy Spirit tells you to do it, it means you can do it. *Go for it!*
3. Have you been getting signals from the Holy Spirit that you have unresolved issues of hurt or offense with another person? For instance, when you try to worship God, does a certain name keep coming up, causing unsettled thoughts that steal your joy and your ability to freely worship? Don't ignore those kinds of signs. That may be the Holy Spirit telling you that strife is at work in your life to keep you from enjoying the presence of the Lord. If it's always the same person over and over again, consider that a clear signal that there is some kind of issue between you and that person and that you should do everything you can to forgive that person and to seek his or her forgiveness and make that relationship right so you can freely enjoy the sweet presence of the Lord again!

The month of June is usually the month when the Church across the world commemorates Pentecost — the day that the Holy Spirit was poured out on the Early Church. So because this is a month when people normally celebrate Pentecost and the outpouring of the Holy Spirit, I decided to focus every *Sparkling Gem* in the month of June on various subjects related to the Holy Spirit.

These June *Gems* are not intended to make you into a theologian, but to lead you to a place where you can experience the Person, power, and work of the Holy Spirit in a new way. It covers teachings of Jesus about the Holy Spirit from John chapters 14, 15, and 16, as well as various other verses that give insight into the ministry of the Holy Spirit. The month concludes with a series of *Gems* that cover various topics related to the ministry of Holy Spirit in the New Testament.

Are you hungry for the things of the Spirit? I pray that the month of June becomes a "marker" in your own personal relationship with the Holy Spirit as He helps you unlock and experience new aspects of Himself — more than anything you have known of Him until this present moment. I encourage you to dedicate this month to getting much better acquainted with the precious Holy Spirit and much more sensitive to His voice as He guides you each step of the way into the Father's good plan for your life.

JUNE 1

Jesus and the Holy Spirit

He that believeth on me, as the scripture hath said,
out of his belly shall flow rivers of living water.
(But this spake he [Jesus] of the Spirit, which they that believe
on him should receive: for the Holy Ghost was not yet given;
because that Jesus was not yet glorified.)
— John 7:38,39

If anyone ever understood the ministry of the Holy Spirit, it was the Lord Jesus Christ. Jesus' earthly ministry was completely dependent upon the Holy Spirit. From His birth, nothing that happened to Him and nothing He did was apart from the power of the Holy Spirit. Moreover, when He sat down at the Father's right hand in Heaven, the first thing He did was send the Holy Spirit upon the Church on the day of Pentecost.

The ministry of Jesus and the ministry of the Holy Spirit are inseparable. In fact, when Jesus spoke of the Holy Spirit's future ministry to His Church in John 7:38 and 39, He was describing the Holy Spirit's present ministry through *Him* during His earthly ministry: "...Out of his belly shall flow rivers of living water. (But this spake he [Jesus] of the Spirit)...." The Greek word translated "flow" is a form of the word *rheo*, which pictures a rushing stream, so full that it actually overflows its banks.

This is how Jesus described His own relationship with the Holy Spirit as He walked this earth — and how He foretold the nature of the relationship that those who believed on Him would one day experience with the Holy Spirit after Jesus' death and resurrection. Jesus depended on the continual flow of the Holy Spirit's power, wisdom, counsel, and ability through Him and upon Him during His earthly ministry. And as He is, so are we to be in this world (1 John 4:17).

So let's take it further and consider these important facts about the workings of the Holy Spirit in the life and ministry of Jesus on this earth:

- Jesus was conceived by the Holy Spirit in the womb of the virgin Mary (*see* Matthew 1:18-20; Luke 1:35).
- Jesus' conception in Mary's womb was confirmed by Elizabeth, Mary's cousin, when she was filled with the Holy Spirit (*see* Luke 1:41-45).
- Jesus' dedication as a baby in the temple was accompanied by the supernatural manifestation of the Holy Spirit as Simeon, the priest, and Anna, the prophetess, prophesied over Him (*see* Luke 2:25-38).

- Jesus' public ministry was announced by John the Baptist, who, under the anointing of the Holy Spirit, declared that Jesus was the One who would baptize in the Holy Spirit and with fire (*see* Matthew 3:11; Luke 3:16; John 1:33; Acts 11:16).
- Jesus spoke of the baptism in the Holy Spirit and commanded the disciples to stay in Jerusalem until they had received this special endowment of power (*see* Luke 24:49; Acts 1:4,5).
- Jesus was empowered by the Holy Spirit at the Jordan River when He was baptized by John the Baptist (*see* Matthew 3:16; Mark 1:10; Luke 3:22; John 1:32).
- Jesus was given the fullness of the Spirit without measure (*see* John 3:34).
- Jesus was led by the Holy Spirit (*see* Matthew 4:1; Mark 1:12; Luke 4:1).
- Jesus returned from the wilderness in the power of the Holy Spirit (*see* Luke 4:14).
- Jesus stated publicly that His ministry was a result of the power of the Holy Spirit (*see* Luke 4:18).
- Jesus proclaimed that we must be born again by the Holy Spirit (*see* John 3:5-8).
- Jesus warned about the danger of blaspheming the Holy Spirit (*see* Matthew 12:31,32; Mark 3:28,29; Luke 12:10).
- Jesus taught about the work and ministry of the Holy Spirit (*see* Matthew 10:20; Mark 13:11; Luke 11:13; Luke 12:12; John 7:39; John 14:16,17; John 15:26; John 16:7-15).
- Jesus offered Himself upon the Cross, like a Lamb without spot or blemish, through the power of the Holy Spirit (*see* Hebrews 9:14).
- Jesus breathed the Holy Spirit into the disciples after His resurrection (*see* John 20:22).
- Jesus, once exalted to the right hand of the Father, poured out the Holy Spirit upon the Church on the day of Pentecost (*see* Acts 2:2-4, 2:33).
- Jesus instructed the disciples through the ministry of the Holy Spirit (*see* Acts 1:2).

Jesus and the Holy Spirit were always together when He was on the earth. If Jesus needed this kind of ongoing partnership with the Holy Spirit in order to accomplish His divine role in the earth, *you* must have that same partnership with the Spirit of God to fulfill what God has asked you to do. The Holy Spirit has been sent by Jesus to give you everything you need to be a victorious, successful, faith-filled, overcoming child of God in this world. With Him at your side, you are equipped for every situation you could ever face in life.

Because no one has ever known the Holy Spirit better than Jesus, we must look to see what Jesus had to say about His personality, His power, His gifts, and His character. In John 14, 15, and 16, the Lord Jesus Christ gives us important instruction about how to develop our own partnership with the Holy Spirit. If you are hungry for more of the Holy Spirit, carefully read every *Sparkling Gem* in this month of June, for it is totally dedicated to the ministry of the Holy Spirit!

MY PRAYER FOR TODAY

Father, my heart yearns to know the Person of the Holy Spirit more deeply and to experience His power personally. I ask You to reveal truths and grant me understanding so I can cooperate with and respond to the Holy Spirit's ministry in my life. Father, I desire to walk in the spiritual depth and fullness that Jesus made available to me when He prayed in John 14 that You would send the Helper, the Holy Spirit, to indwell me. I ask You to open the door for me to embark on a spiritual path that I've never been on before. I know that this is Your will for me, so today I come before Your throne boldly and confidently to receive this with gratitude and joy!

I pray this prayer in Jesus' name!

MY CONFESSION FOR TODAY

I confess that it is God's will for me to know the Person, power, and work of the Holy Spirit. In John 14, 15, and 16, Jesus taught explicitly about the Holy Spirit so that every believer could learn about the Spirit of God and knowledgeably respond to and experience His power. I recognize that this is why Jesus taught so much about the Holy Spirit's ministry in those three chapters. Therefore, I boldly declare that I will act on the truths I learn in the days to come about the Holy Spirit and His work in my life. I choose to cooperate with God as I embark on a new, deeper, and higher walk with God's Spirit than I've ever known before in my life.

I declare this by faith in Jesus' name!

QUESTIONS FOR YOU TO CONSIDER

1. Can you describe what you know about the Person, power, and work of the Holy Spirit? Honestly, how well do you understand the work of the Holy Spirit?
2. When you approach this subject, what feelings do you have? Excitement and anticipation — or bewilderment, intimidation, and fear?
3. Does your church allow the Holy Spirit to move in its church services? In what ways does the Holy Spirit operate there? Are gifts of the Holy Spirit in open manifestation in your church? What are these gifts?

Jesus depended on the continual flow of the Holy Spirit's power, wisdom, counsel, and ability through Him and upon Him during His earthly ministry. And as He is, so are we to be in this world.

JUNE 2

Jesus' Teaching in the Upper Room

I am not leaving you comfortless:
I will come to you.
— John 14:18

I was raised in a wonderful church where we were doctrinally taught very well. But as I grew older, I began to become more and more spiritually hungry. It seemed there was a gaping hole inside my heart, and I yearned for more than what I knew about the Lord. That is when I began to learn of teaching about the ministry of the Holy Spirit that was different from anything I had ever been exposed to previously. Hearing those fresh teachings changed my life because they introduced me to the supernatural ministry of the Holy Spirit in a way I had never before experienced.

Starting today, I want to begin talking to you about those teachings on the Holy Spirit that so dramatically changed my life. To begin, let's go to the Upper Room where Jesus gathered His disciples on the eve of His crucifixion; where He washed their feet; where He served them Communion; and where He took time to teach them about the ministry of the Holy Spirit. The teachings about the Holy Spirit that Jesus gave in the Upper Room will be the basis for what you are about to read in the first 20 *Gems* of June. Then the *Gems* from June 21 onward will be drawn from various other scriptures that I believe also teach us vital truths we must know about the Holy Spirit.

On that last night when Jesus was in the Upper Room with His disciples, He knew that He was leaving the world and that these moments were actually His *last* opportunity to teach them. There was a myriad of subjects Jesus could have taught His disciples that night, but He knew that in His absence, they would need a powerful, ongoing relationship with the Holy Spirit. Consequently, Jesus devoted His last opportunity to teach them about the ministry of the Holy Spirit. In John chapters 14, 15, and 16, we find teachings by Jesus that are devoted primarily to the Person, power, and work of the Holy Spirit. We don't know the amount of time it took for Jesus to teach His disciples about the Holy Spirit during His last night on earth with them, but it's clear from these three chapters that He dedicated a significant amount of time.

That evening Jesus told the disciples that He would soon be departing the world. By reading John 14, it is clear that the disciples were tempted to despair when they heard this heavy news. They were tempted to feel abandoned, so Jesus told them, "I am not leaving you comfortless: I will come to you" (John 14:18).

Let's begin by looking at the word "comfortless" used in this verse. The word "comfortless" is a translation of the Greek word *orphanos*, and it is where we get the word *orphan*. A literal translation would be, "I will not leave you as orphans...." But in the time of the New Testament, this word had a wider range of meaning, for it was also used to describe students who felt abandoned by their teacher. However, whether this Greek word was used to describe orphans who had lost their parents or students who felt abandoned by a teacher, it always conveyed the idea of a person who felt deserted by someone whom they trusted and to whom they looked for guidance.

Jesus promised that although He was leaving this earth, He was not abandoning His disciples. He would come to them through the ministry of the Holy Spirit, who would exactly represent Him to the disciples in every way. By sending the Holy Spirit, Jesus was sending a personal replacement to take His place among the disciples — One who would be with each of them all the time. This would be far better than when Jesus was on the earth and could only physically be in one place at a time. In fact, Jesus later said that the coming of the Holy Spirit would be far better for them (*see* John 16:7) because it would herald the unlimited presence of Christ in the earth. Through the work of the Holy Spirit, Christ could reside with every believer in every place on the earth simultaneously.

Once Jesus was exalted at the right hand of the Father, He took on the role of our Intercessor for all eternity (*see* Hebrews 7:25). Once seated, He poured out the gift of the Holy Spirit upon the Church (*see* Acts 2:33). Today the Holy Spirit is that Member of the Godhead who operates in the world. Christ is Lord *over* the Church, and the Holy Spirit carries out His Lordship *inside* the Church. We live in the age when the *Holy Spirit* operates in the world.

In Ephesians 1:13, the apostle Paul taught that the moment you receive your salvation, the Holy Spirit enters into you and serves as God's covenant seal on your life in Him. Therefore, if you have surrendered to the Lordship of Jesus Christ, the Holy Spirit has come to take up residency inside of you. Hear me clearly — the Holy Spirit *is* a Resident in the life of every person who has surrendered to the Lordship of Jesus Christ. In fact, Romans 8:9 says it is impossible to personally know God unless you have the Holy Spirit residing inside you. So rest assured, if you have come to that moment when you gave your life to Christ — that is, you surrendered to His Lordship — then the Holy Spirit has sealed you and has permanently moved into your heart. This means your heart is not just a hotel where He occasionally visits. *Your heart is His home.*

As glorious as it is that the Holy Spirit lives inside those who believe, this does not guarantee that they experience fellowship with Him. So today I'd like to ask you: What kind of *fellowship* do you have with the Holy Spirit? Is He a neglected Resident in your life, or do you actually experience regular, intimate fellowship with Him?

That night in the Upper Room, Jesus promised His disciples (and us) that when He ascended to Heaven, He would not abandon us like orphans or like students who had been deserted by their teacher. He promised that He would come to us through the ministry of the Holy Spirit, and Jesus kept His word! But just as any person must be recognized to be experienced, we must *on purpose* recognize the presence of the Holy Spirit if we are going to experience fellowship with Him in our lives.

If you have never stopped to recognize the Holy Spirit in your life or experienced what I call the fellowship of the Holy Spirit, today would be a wonderful time for you to begin! Just open your heart and say, "Holy Spirit, thank You for living inside me. Starting today I want to begin enjoying fellowship with You!"

MY PRAYER FOR TODAY

Holy Spirit, I want to begin enjoying fellowship with You. Since Jesus depended on You, I know that I need to depend on You too. So right now, more than ever before, I express my inner yearning to begin a new and deeper journey in learning how to have fellowship with You. I want to know You; I want to know Your power; and I ask You to come alongside and help me as Jesus said You would do!

I pray this in Jesus' name!

MY CONFESSION FOR TODAY

I acknowledge that because I am a child of God, the Holy Spirit lives inside me as a continual Resident. He longs to have fellowship with me and to reveal the depths of Jesus' love to my heart. I repent for the times that I have ignored Him and treated Him as an unrecognized Resident. From this moment onward, I confess that I will live with an awareness of His presence and that I will embrace the wonderful ministry that He has come to provide for my life.

I declare this by faith in Jesus' name!

QUESTIONS FOR YOU TO CONSIDER

1. Do you experience the fellowship of the Holy Spirit in your life? If yes, how would you describe the experience of fellowship with Him to someone else?
2. Can you recognize when the Holy Spirit is speaking to you? If yes, how would you describe the way you recognize His voice?
3. Have you had moments when the Holy Spirit led you in a supernatural way that dramatically affected your life? If yes, what were some of those moments, and what happened as a result?

JUNE 3

Jesus' Prayer

And I will pray the Father,
and he shall give you another Comforter,
that he may abide with you for ever.
— John 14:16

I can't begin to imagine how alarmed the disciples must have felt when Jesus told them that He would soon be leaving them. Jesus had often warned them that He would be leaving, but that evening in the Upper Room, as they spent their last hours together, the full weight of this reality began to dawn on the disciples — and it put them in a state of panic and dismay. John 14:2 tells us that Jesus was aware that their hearts were troubled.

It was natural for the disciples to feel sorrowful at the news of Jesus' imminent departure. Living and walking with Jesus was more than they had ever hoped for in this world. With Jesus at their side, their lives had been filled with adventure, excitement, joy, victory, power, healing, and miracles. What would life be like without Jesus? Would it ever be the same? Was this the end to their dreams?

Feelings of insecurity and uncertainty would have been normal for any human being in the disciples' position. They had grown dependent upon the physical, visible presence of Jesus — something we've never experienced and therefore cannot fully comprehend. But in the midst of the disciples' fears, Jesus promised them, "I will not leave you comfortless…" (John 14:18).

As we saw in yesterday's *Sparkling Gem*, the word "comfortless" is from the Greek word *orphanos*, which is where we get the word *orphan*. As noted before, the word *orphanos* could describe children who had lost their parents, or it could describe students who were abandoned by their teacher. In both cases, it is the picture of younger, less educated, less knowledgeable people feeling deserted by those they trusted and looked to for guidance.

Jesus had become a spiritual Mentor to the disciples. For more than three years, these men had walked with Jesus and depended entirely upon Him. During those three years, Jesus' voice had been the only voice they had followed. They walked in His footsteps, and they explicitly followed His directions. As a Mentor, Jesus had taught them everything — how to cast out demons, how to heal the sick, how to travel in ministry, and on and on. The full extent of the spiritual training Jesus imparted to His disciples includes far too many truths to list here. In fact, Jesus had taught them *everything* they knew regarding spiritual matters.

But in John 14, Jesus made it clear that He would be leaving His disciples. Later that night, He was to be arrested in the Garden of Gethsemane, judged before the religious leaders of the city, sent to be judged by Pilate, then by Herod, and then back to Pilate again. And following these harrowing experiences, He was to be scourged, crucified, and buried. All of these events would occur in a mere matter of hours from those moments when Jesus sat with them in the Upper Room and told them that He would be leaving. They simply had no idea how quickly He would be physically taken from them.

But Jesus knew. That is why it was so important for Him to take that last evening to teach the disciples about the ministry of the Holy Spirit. Jesus knew they would need to depend on the Holy Spirit as completely as *He* had depended on Him. So Jesus took His last hours to instruct them about the ministry of the Holy Spirit and introduce them to this spiritual Partner who would become their new Teacher and Guide in the world.

Jesus told the disciples in John 14:16, "I will *pray* the Father, and he shall give you another Comforter…." The word "pray" is the Greek word *eratao*, which was a legal word that described *a lawyer who would argue a case in a court of law*. It is interesting that this is the Greek word most generally used in the Gospels to describe Jesus' prayer life. This particular word indicates that it was so crucial for the survival of the disciples that the Comforter would be sent that Jesus was going to the Father to present His case in that matter. This case would be so concrete — *so clear and unmistakable* — that the Father would respond to Jesus' request by sending the Comforter, *the Holy Spirit*, as His replacement to the disciples.

Imagine how important the ministry of the Holy Spirit must be for Jesus! Jesus was making the case clear to the Father that He *must* send the Holy Spirit, for the disciples — and then later the Church — would not survive without the Holy Spirit's help and assistance. The very fact that the word *eratao* is used to describe Jesus' petition to the Father tells us that the coming of the Holy Spirit was imperative. Jesus treated this request as one of the utmost importance. And if Jesus treated this subject so importantly, then we must treat it with equal importance.

So I encourage you to seriously ask yourself this question today: *How importantly do I treat the subject of the Holy Spirit in my life?* And whatever your answer, make it your priority in the days ahead to learn how to cooperate with the Holy Spirit's work in your life on a deeper level than you ever have before!

MY PRAYER FOR TODAY

Holy Spirit, I admit that I have often neglected to acknowledge Your presence in my life. I repent, and I ask You to please forgive me. It's not that I've tried to ignore You; I have just been ignorant of Your role in my life and how deeply I have needed Your fellowship. I confess that I've even had fears about opening my heart more deeply to You because of things I've seen and heard others do that seemed a little strange. Forgive me for being closed to You when, in fact, I cannot live the Christian life without Your power and Your help. Right now I take the next step to invite You to move powerfully in my life. I take down all the guards, and I decide to trust You to bring Jesus closer to me.

I pray this in Jesus' name!

MY CONFESSION FOR TODAY

I declare that the Holy Spirit works mightily in my life. I am not afraid to surrender to the Holy Spirit's power. I acknowledge that I cannot successfully live the Christian life without His involvement, so I open every part of my life to Him and to His powerful workings. As a result, I am filled with spiritual power; I am supernaturally led by the Spirit of God because I am a child of God; and I am being transformed into the image of Jesus Christ. As a result of my fellowship and obedience to the Holy Spirit, my Christian life is filled with victory and adventure!

I declare this by faith in Jesus' name!

QUESTIONS FOR YOU TO CONSIDER

1. Have you treated your relationship with the Holy Spirit as seriously as Jesus treated it? If not, why not?

2. Do you attend a church where your fellowship with the Holy Spirit will be encouraged or discouraged? If your church does not encourage you to go deeper with the Spirit of God, why are you still attending that church?
3. What concrete steps can you take to start developing a deeper fellowship with the Holy Spirit? For example, you could read books on the Holy Spirit that will take you deeper in your spiritual walk, or you could listen to teachings on the subject of the Holy Spirit. What other things can you think of to do to enhance your fellowship with the Holy Spirit?

JUNE 4

Another Comforter!

And I will pray the Father,
and he shall give you another Comforter....
— John 14:16

As Jesus fellowshipped with His disciples that night in the Upper Room, He taught at length about the ministry of the Holy Spirit. In fact, He covered so much material that it took three chapters in the gospel of John to relate it! However, one of the most important points Jesus made is found near the beginning of all He shared with His disciples. He said, "I will pray the Father, and He shall give you another Comforter..." (John 14:16).

In today's *Sparkling Gem*, I want you to take note of the word "another." This is the Greek word *allos*, which means *another of the very same kind*. By using this word, Jesus was sending a clear message that when the Holy Spirit came, the Spirit would be just like Himself. The Holy Spirit would perfectly represent Jesus in every way and duplicate His life and ministry. He would mirror Jesus to such a degree, in fact, that whatever Jesus would say is *exactly* what He would say, and whatever Jesus would do is *exactly* what He would do. To the disciples, this statement must have been very encouraging because it let them know that the Holy Spirit's presence would make it seem as if Jesus was still there among them.

So when John 14:16 uses the Greek word *allos* to describe "another" Comforter, it tells you and me that Jesus was telling us, *"The Holy Spirit and I are identical in every way, so by having Him, it will be as if you still have Me!"*

Sometimes I hear people express how they wish they could have lived 2,000 years ago when Jesus walked the earth. But if we believe the words of Jesus in John 14:16 about the Holy Spirit and His likeness to Jesus, then we should not regret that we weren't there 2,000 years ago. Jesus taught that if the Holy Spirit resides within us, it is *identical* to having Jesus walk amongst us in the flesh.

So if you want to know what the Spirit of God is like, look to Jesus in the four gospels, for He taught that the Holy Spirit exactly mirrors His own character, power, and actions. This is another reason why it is so important for you to get the story of Jesus down deep into your heart. As you learn what the Master did, how He acted, and how He responded to different situations, it will help you to know the Holy Spirit better — for He and Jesus are identical in all of these ways. And whatever Jesus did is *exactly* what the Holy Spirit will lead *you* to do in every situation of life as you lean on His guidance and direction from within.

MY PRAYER FOR TODAY

Father, I thank You for speaking to me about how the Holy Spirit perfectly represents Jesus in my life. In light of this, I ask You to help me gain more understanding regarding the four gospels and their account of the life of Jesus. I understand that if I know Jesus better from the New Testament, it will help me become more familiar with the way the Holy Spirit thinks and acts. Now I understand that Jesus and the Holy Spirit are similar in every way, so I desire to open my heart to the Holy Spirit in the same way I open my heart to Jesus.

I pray this in Jesus' name!

MY CONFESSION FOR TODAY

I declare that reading the four gospels — and getting to know Jesus better through reading them — is a top priority in my life. According to what Jesus taught about the Holy Spirit, I now know that Jesus and the Holy Spirit are identical in how they think, act, and behave. Therefore, as I get to know Jesus better from the New Testament, it will prepare my heart and mind to better recognize and know the voice and promptings of the Holy Spirit in my life.

I declare this by faith in Jesus' name!

QUESTIONS FOR YOU TO CONSIDER

1. Since Jesus and the Holy Spirit exactly mirror each other in how they think, act, and behave, what are you doing to get to know Jesus better and prepare yourself to become more familiar with the Holy Spirit?
2. Do you have a Bible-reading plan to take you through the four gospels? Start searching for a plan to lead you through these four books of the Bible so you can become better acquainted with Jesus — His ways, His works, and His will.
3. Since Jesus and the Holy Spirit exactly mirror each other, how does this help you get to know the ways of the Holy Spirit better?

JUNE 5

The Comforter, Part 1

And I will pray the Father,
and he shall give you another Comforter....
— John 14:16

As Jesus taught His disciples about the Holy Spirit during their last night together in the Upper Room, He referred to the Holy Spirit as the "Comforter" on four separate occasions (*see* John 14:16, 14:26, 15:26, and John 16:7). For Jesus to repeat this title *four times* in the space of three chapters tells us that the point He is making must be very important. When a truth is repeated in quick succession in Scripture, it is always for the sake of emphasis. Here we find that Jesus was trying to penetrate His disciples' hearts — *as well as our own hearts* — with the truth of the Holy Spirit's role as a "Comforter" so they would fully understand this truth.

However, to fully comprehend the message Jesus was trying to convey, we must look to the original Greek language to understand exactly what the word "Comforter" means. This title is actually a translation of the Greek word *parakletos*, which is a compound of two Greek words, *para* and *kaleo*. Today I am going to focus on the first part of this compound word, the word *para*, and then tomorrow we'll discuss the second part of the word, *kaleo*.

Simply put, the word *para* means *alongside*, and it carries the idea of *near proximity* or *being very close to someone or something else*. However, this term is quite versatile and can thus be seen in a variety of contexts throughout Scripture. Let's look at several New Testament examples to glean a better sense of its meaning.

The Bible says in Luke 5:1, "And it came to pass, that, as the people pressed upon him to hear the word of God, he stood *by* the lake of Gennesaret." The word "by" in this verse is a translation of the Greek word *para*. Here it conveys Jesus' close proximity to the lake of Gennesaret. He literally stood *alongside* this lake as He preached to the multitudes. In Mark 5:21, which follows the account of Jesus casting out a legion of demons from the demoniac of the Gadarenes, this term is used in a similar way. Mark records, "And when Jesus was passed over again by ship unto the other side, much people gathered unto him: and he was *nigh unto* the sea." The phrase "nigh unto" is also a translation of the word *para*, and it tells us that so many people were pressing forward to touch Jesus that He couldn't even get away from the water's edge. He was forced to walk *alongside* the sea.

In Second Timothy 2:2, we see a different usage of the word *para*. Here Paul used it to describe his close relationship with Timothy, writing, "And the things that thou hast heard *of* me among many witnesses, the same commit thou to faithful men, who shall be able to teach others also." When Paul said, "...and the things thou has learned *of* me...," the word "of" is the Greek word *para*. This conveys powerful information regarding Paul and Timothy's relationship to one another. The elderly apostle was reminding Timothy, "You learned everything *para* me. I allowed you to get alongside of me."

As a current example from my own life, I could say that my wife is *para*, or *alongside*, me. She lives with me, talks with me, shops with me, travels with me, prays with me, pastors with me, and has reared our children with me. *She is always with me.* We are side by side, close at hand, and alongside each other all the time. When two people are close in this way, they profoundly affect each other — even to the point where they begin to share the same attitudes, feelings, personality traits, habits, and gestures. In fact, they eventually know each other so well that they don't even have to ask what the other person is thinking — *they already know.*

The spiritual mentor-disciple relationship Paul and Timothy shared was probably similar in certain ways to the kind of close relationship I just described. Paul and Timothy had walked together for many years, spreading the message of the Gospel throughout the Roman world. To some degree, Timothy no doubt had picked up some of Paul's gestures, mannerisms, and thoughts, and he probably even sounded a little like Paul when he preached. The close relationship they shared allowed the truths of Paul's life to be transferred into Timothy. That is a natural consequence of this kind of intimacy.

This level of closeness is exactly what the word *para* refers to where it is used to form the compound word *parakletos*, or "Comforter," in John 14:16 and the other three references listed above. Thus, we see that the Holy Spirit is *close by* and *alongside* each of us at all times. His relationship with us is not a distant one that requires us to beg and plead for Him to draw near. *He is always with us.*

As we saw in the June 1 *Gem*, the Holy Spirit comes to reside inside us at the very moment we receive our salvation. However, this is not the full story. The use of the word *para* in John 14:16 reveals that He also comes alongside us to assist us in our daily affairs and to bring the reality of Jesus Christ into our lives. From the moment the Holy Spirit takes up residence in our hearts, we can continuously rely on His partnership to help us overcome any obstacles we might face in life.

In other words, when you accept Jesus as your Lord and Savior, the Holy Spirit comes into your life to provide you with the assistance Jesus would offer if He was present in the flesh. Whatever Jesus would do to assist you, that is precisely what the Holy Spirit will do. He dwells in you as a permanent Resident *and* as the most reliable Partner you'll ever have in this life. That is why some newer versions of the New Testament translate the word "Comforter" as "Standby." The word "Standby" perfectly describes the Holy Spirit's close, side-by-side position in you from which He helps, empowers, leads, and guides you every step of the way.

There is no doubt that this word *para* describes *the alongside ministry* of the Holy Spirit. Perhaps you were raised in a wonderful Bible-teaching church just as I was, but you have never experienced this kind of intimate relationship with the Holy Spirit that I am describing to you. If not, today would be a great time to lift your hands and declare, "Holy Spirit, I receive You as my side-by-side Partner!" Then get ready for a divine adventure that never stops as He takes you to ever-higher levels in Him!

MY PRAYER FOR TODAY

Holy Spirit, I know You live inside me, but I never understood that You are also side by side with me as my Partner in life. I have treated you like an invisible Guest, when, in reality, You have been sent to me to be at my side as my Helper and Standby in times of need. Please forgive me for overlooking and ignoring You when You have been waiting so long to assist me in life. Today I throw open my arms and my heart, and I say 'Welcome, Holy Spirit" — I receive You as my side-by-side Partner who has been called alongside my life!

I pray this in Jesus' name!

MY CONFESSION FOR TODAY

I confess that from this moment onward, I am wide open to the ministry of the Holy Spirit. Jesus sent the Spirit to be my Helper, and I certainly need His help. I will no longer ignore Him or disregard His presence in my life. I open my heart, mind, and soul to His ministry, and I will endeavor to recognize His voice, His leading, and His guidance, and I will strive to receive His supernatural help.

I declare this by faith in Jesus' name!

QUESTIONS FOR YOU TO CONSIDER

1. Of course the Holy Spirit lives inside you! But have you experienced moments when it seemed like He was right alongside you — side by side — assisting you in decisions and actions that you needed to take? In what ways do you need to cooperate with Him more?
2. What were some of the times when you really experienced the "Standby" ministry of the Holy Spirit? Have you ever recalled those moments or shared them with someone else? Take a few minutes to tell a friend how you've experienced the ministry of the Spirit if your life.
3. After reading today's *Sparkling Gem*, what are you going to do differently to embrace the "alongside ministry" of the Holy Spirit in your life? In what area of your life do you most recognize the need for His help?

From the moment the Holy Spirit
takes up residence in our hearts,
we can continuously rely on His partnership
to help us overcome any obstacles we might face in life.

JUNE 6

The Comforter, Part 2

And I will pray the Father,
and he shall give you another Comforter....
— John 14:16

In yesterday's *Sparkling Gem*, we began our study of the word "Comforter," which Jesus uses *four* times in the space of three chapters (*see* John 14:16, John 14:26, John 15:26, and John 16:7) to describe the ministry of the Holy Spirit. We saw that the word "Comforter" is the Greek word *parakletos*, a compound of the Greek words *para* and *kaleo*, and by looking at the word *para*, we saw that the Holy Spirit is sent to come alongside us and help us navigate through our lives. Today we are going to look at the second half of *parakletos* — the Greek word *kaleo* — in order to discern how it fits with the word *para* and how we can glean an even deeper insight into the word "Comforter."

The word *kaleo* is a Greek term that means *to beckon* or *to call*. Paul used this word in Romans 1:1 when he said he was "*called to* be an apostle of Jesus Christ." This *kaleo* kind of calling carries a sense of *strategic purpose*, *specific intent*, and *concrete direction*. For example, God *calls* us *to* fellowship with Him, and He *calls* unbelievers *to* repentance and salvation (*see* Matthew 9:13). Likewise, both Paul and Peter used the word *kaleo* to describe God's *call to* salvation and ministry for themselves and others (*see* Romans 1:1; 8:30; 9:11,24; 1 Corinthians 1:9; 7:15; Ephesians 4:1,4; 1 Thessalonians 2:12; Hebrews 9:15; 1 Peter 1:15; 2:9).

The apostle Paul also used the word *kaleo* to describe his *call to* apostolic ministry (*see* 1 Corinthians 15:9; Galatians 1:15; 2 Timothy 1:9). When Paul heard this divine call on the road to Damascus, he was instantly imbued with a powerful sense of direction, purpose, and destiny and received a concrete direction for his life. Thus, we see that the word *kaleo* carries the idea of *summoning forth an individual to do something very specific*. We are called *to* salvation; we are called *to* the ministry; we are called *to* service in the local church, and so on. Simply put, the call is *to* something.

Returning to Jesus' message in John 14:16, we see that since *kaleo* forms the second part of the word *parakletos* ("Comforter"), God has called the Holy Spirit to do a specific work, and this calling has given the Holy Spirit purpose and direction. You might say it has given Him a job description.

What is the calling our Heavenly Father has given to the Holy Spirit? *He is called to be our Helper in this world*. This is His chief purpose and responsibility. This is His *calling*.

Now that we've seen this important aspect of the Holy Spirit's ministry, let's take a step back for a moment and review what we've learned about the Holy Spirit thus far:

1. *The Holy Spirit is close by us.*

We have seen that the Holy Spirit indwells and seals every believer at the moment of salvation (*see* Ephesians 1:13). But when Jesus referred to the Holy Spirit as the "Comforter" in John 14:16, He was specifically referring to a practical relationship with the Holy Spirit that we can experience on a daily basis. We do not need to plead or beg for the Holy Spirit to come near because He is always *alongside* us.

2. *The Holy Spirit has a calling.*

   Just as men and women are called *to* the ministry, the Holy Spirit received a specific calling from God the Father *to fulfill* a specific assignment in this world. Just as I, for example, am specifically called to write and to teach for the Christian community, the Holy Spirit is specifically "called" (*kaleo*) to come "alongside" (*para*) each believer *at all times.*

   This means the Holy Spirit is with you when you are in the lowest pits of despair, and He is with you when things are going well. He is with you when you to go bed at night, and He is with you when you get up in the morning. He is with you throughout your entire day. He is with you when you pray, and He is with you when you don't pray. He is with you when you behave maturely, and He is with you through your moments of immaturity. He is with you when you go to work, to the movies, or to church. *Everywhere you go, the Holy Spirit goes too.*

3. *The Holy Spirit has a job assignment.*

   The Holy Spirit's job is to help us! That may include convicting us of sin, empowering us for works of ministry, imparting spiritual gifts, healing other people through us, and so on. The Holy Spirit is responsible for carrying out this heavenly mission — not according to our own fleshly demands and desires, but according to the will of God, the One who called and sent Him to us. This means you and I can be assured that the Holy Spirit will never fail at His job of helping us because He knows that He will answer to the Father for the way He performs in His role of staying alongside to help us. We may fail to recognize Him, but He will not fail at the task the Father has given to Him.

You are probably very aware of your defects and all the areas where you need to grow. Can you imagine someone who is called specifically to be with you? That is the ministry of the Holy Spirit! His primary task is to be the *Parakletos* — *called* to be *alongside* you.

So today I ask you to receive the Holy Spirit as your Partner. Simply tell Him, "I am receiving you as my Partner. You were sent to be alongside me. You've been here all along, and I have not fully received You as I should. So today I open myself to You and embrace You, Holy Spirit. I thank You for coming alongside me and for accepting such an amazing call to be my Helper!"

MY PRAYER FOR TODAY

Father, my eyes are being opened to the wonderful ministry of the Holy Spirit. I am shocked that I never really understood what profound help You sent to me in the Person of the Holy

Spirit as my divine Partner. My heart is simply overflowing with thankfulness that You have sent the Holy Spirit into my life to assist me wherever I am and in whatever I am doing. Now I understand that He is called by YOU to be with me all the time. Please help me to be more cognizant of His presence and to honor His holiness as He comes to assist me in life!

I pray this in Jesus' name!

MY CONFESSION FOR TODAY

I declare that I receive the Holy Spirit as my Partner. I choose to acknowledge Him and to cooperate with His counsel and direction. I listen to Him; I pay attention to Him; and I obediently follow when He leads or prompts me to take action. For a long time, I didn't understand the power of this gift God gave me. But now I understand, and I will honor the Holy Spirit and His role as senior Partner in my life.

I declare this by faith in Jesus' name!

QUESTIONS FOR YOU TO CONSIDER

1. Of all that you read in today's *Sparkling Gem*, what truth stood out and meant the most to you? Why did it impact you more than anything else?
2. From what you read today, can you verbalize what is the primary "calling" of the Holy Spirit in this world? Try to put it into your own words to see if you really understood the teaching today — and if it blessed you, why not share it with someone else?
3. Can you think of moments when you were made especially aware of the Holy Spirit's presence at your side to help you? What was one of the most memorable of those experiences, and what was the outcome?

JUNE 7

The Heavenly Coach

And I will pray the Father,
and he shall give you another Comforter....
— John 14:16

Today as we discuss the ministry of the Holy Spirit, I'd like to give you my favorite translation of the word "Comforter" that encapsulates all the meaning we've learned thus far. There are many possible translations for the word "Comforter," but the one that seems to satisfy me the most is the word "coach," because it conveys the meaning of the Greek word *parakletos* so well. Jesus' words in John 14:16 could read: *"I will pray the Father, and He will give you another Coach...."*

The word "Coach" perfectly describes Jesus' role toward His disciples during the three years they had walked with Him. He had been their Leader, Teacher, Mentor, Revelator, Prophet, Miracle-Worker, Healer, Pastor, and Lord. They did nothing without Him, and *everything* they did, He had shown them how to do. He was the *center* of their lives, the *focal point* of their attention, and their Mentor in everything.

Jesus was the One who sent the disciples out to spread the message of the Gospel, and He imparted the message they preached. He gave them authority to cast out demons, and He taught them how and when to address demon spirits and lay hands on the sick. Jesus showed His disciples how to deal with religious leaders and how to conduct themselves as ministers of the Gospel. He taught them how to build a ministry and even how to handle money in the ministry (*see* Matthew 10:5-14). For three years, the disciples carefully followed the Master's orders and dared not take a step without consulting Him first. In the truest meaning of the word, Jesus had been their *Coach*.

But at that Passover Supper, Jesus was letting the disciples know it was time to leave them and fulfill His divine destiny on the Cross. So He told them, "I will pray the Father, and he will give you another Comforter...." Or as we've seen today, we can paraphrase it to say, *"I will pray the Father, and he will give you another Coach...."*

The good news is that the Holy Spirit has come to teach us everything we need to know — *if* we'll listen to Him as the disciples listened to Jesus. As we cooperate with the Holy Spirit and allow Him to do what He was sent to do in our lives, He will *coach* us as Jesus coached the disciples.

Just think! You have a Partner residing inside your heart who knows all the answers you need. He is ready to give you not only the winning game plan, but also the strength and courage you need to achieve victory!

So many people have known the Lord for years — which means the Holy Spirit has been living in their hearts all that time — yet they didn't know they were supposed to have this kind of dynamic partnership with the Holy Spirit I'm describing. But God *wants* us to know the Holy Spirit in a personal way. He wants us to begin relying on the Holy Spirit in the same way the disciples relied on Jesus. Just as Jesus was a Coach to His disciples during His time on this earth, we must think of the Holy Spirit as *our* Coach.

So what exactly does a coach do? Let's look at a few common examples:

- A baseball coach teaches you how to swing that bat and hit the ball. He shows you how to run from base to base and how to use your glove to catch the ball. He says, "Hold the bat at the base with your hands wrapped around it like this. Then when you see that ball coming, swing as hard as you can and hit that ball as far as you can!"

- An acting coach teaches you how to become an actor. He will coach you on how to become more convincing, more dramatic, or more comical, and he will even teach you how to cry when tears are necessary for a certain scene.
- A vocal coach will teach you how to sing, how to make your breath last longer, how to push air from your diaphragm, how to make a sound stronger, how to sing on key, and to how to sing in a way that truly represents the emotional content of the music. If you make a mistake while you are practicing, a vocal coach will stop you right in the middle of a song to correct you, instruct you, and then tell you to go for it again.

Fundamentally, a coach teaches, advises, corrects, instructs, trains, tutors, guides, directs, and prepares you for your upcoming assignment. If you are new at what you are doing, his *coaching* may include a little *coaxing* as you develop your confidence. A coach will encourage you as he shows you what you did wrong so you can do it right the next time.

Furthermore, a coach isn't there to hit the ball for you, sing the note for you, or play the scene for you. He's there to coach you so *you* can hit the ball, sing the note, and perform as you should. Like an apprentice learning a new job, if you will listen carefully, the Holy Spirit will direct and guide you. He'll show you what's needed. He'll open your eyes; impress your mind with supernatural direction; bring you up by the hand; and develop, foster, improve, and "break you in" on the things of God and the things of life.

As believers, we must learn to take the Holy Spirit's advice and follow Him implicitly, taking each one of our cues from Him. He must become our Heavenly Coach, and we must learn to accept His leadership and be willing to yield and concede to His divine guidance with no objections. If we will open our hearts to the ministry of the Holy Spirit, He will do everything that Jesus did. He will coach; He will teach; and He will be a Helper. He will be there to teach us how to pack our bags, how to travel, what to say, and how to pray for the sick. He will do everything that Jesus would do, because He is a *Coach* to us in the same way that Jesus was a Coach to the disciples.

Today I urge you to open your heart to the coaching ministry of the Holy Spirit. Simply say, "Holy Spirit, be my Coach." The truth is, He was sent to be your Coach whether you recognize it or not. But as you open your heart to the Holy Spirit — listening to Him and diligently following every aspect of His instruction in His role as your Coach in life — this I can promise you: It won't be long until you look back on who you were before you made the decision to allow the Holy Spirit to be your Coach, and you'll know beyond a shadow of a doubt that your decision started a process that has *completely* changed your life!

MY PRAYER FOR TODAY

Father, I thank You for sending the Holy Spirit to mentor, teach, advise, correct, instruct, train, tutor, guide, direct, and prepare me for my upcoming assignment. From this moment forward I am going to start thinking of the Holy Spirit as my personal Coach. I will open my spiritual ears to listen to His instruction, I will obey what He tells me to do, and I will carefully implement the instructions I hear Him speak to my heart and mind. You sent the Holy Spirit as a

Coach to teach me, so I don't have to figure everything out on my own. So from this moment onward, I position myself as a pupil to the Holy Spirit, who is my divine Coach.

I pray this in Jesus' name!

MY CONFESSION FOR TODAY

I declare by faith that I am a willing, obedient, and teachable apprentice of the Holy Spirit! He speaks to my heart, tells me what to do or what actions to take, and I do exactly what I am told to do. My courage to obey is getting stronger by the day. As a result of listening to the Holy Spirit and taking my cues from Him, I am growing in my walk with the Lord, developing more confidence and experiencing greater victories day by day!

I declare this by faith in Jesus' name!

QUESTIONS FOR YOU TO CONSIDER

1. Have you ever experienced a moment when the Holy Spirit coached you on what to say or how to act in a certain situation?
2. Here's an example: Has the Holy Spirit ever led you in the way you witnessed to an unbeliever? You naturally didn't know how to do it, but word-by-word and moment-by-moment, you felt led in what to say as you shared Christ with that person? Have you experienced such a moment in your life?
3. Can you think of an area where you need to stop trying to figure everything out by yourself and just allow the Holy Spirit to start coaching you on what to say and what actions to take?

JUNE 8

The Spirit of Truth

And I will pray the Father,
and he shall give you another Comforter;
that he may abide with you for ever; even the Spirit of truth....
—John 14:16,17

As you're learning more about the ministry of the Holy Spirit in these June *Sparkling Gems*, you may have thought at some point, *Following the direction of the Holy Spirit at this deeper level is a little unsettling for me. Honestly, it sounds a little scary to stop trying to manage the situations of life and entrust myself completely to His leadership. I can't even see Him! What is my guarantee that I can understand how to hear or to follow Him when the Holy Spirit attempts to lead me?*

These are reasonable questions to ask if you're not used to the idea of partnering with the Holy Spirit. In fact, when Jesus first told His disciples about the ministry of the Holy Spirit, similar doubts were probably swirling around in their minds. That's why Jesus made sure to take the time during His last night on earth to assuage their fears and give them a divine guarantee regarding the ministry of the Holy Spirit. In John 14:16 and 17, He said, "And I will pray the Father, and he shall give you another Comforter; that he may abide with you for ever; even the Spirit of Truth...."

Notice that Jesus called the Holy Spirit "the Spirit of Truth" in this verse. This is the first of *three instances* where Jesus refers to the Holy Spirit as "the Spirit of Truth" over the course of His teaching in John chapters 14-16 (*see* John 15:26 and John 16:13). *Three different times in three chapters!* By repeating this phrase over and over again, Jesus was driving a truth into His disciples' hearts — that the Holy Spirit is utterly trustworthy and would never mislead them or misguide them.

In each instance where Jesus referred to the Holy Spirit as "the Spirit of Truth," the word "truth" is a translation of the Greek word *alethes*, which describes *something that can be depended upon* or *something that is trustworthy, reliable, and true.* In the Old Testament Septuagint, this term often denotes something that is *faithful, sure, stable, and firm*, as opposed to something that is unreliable and uncertain. In addition, the word *alethes* is used in the gospels to depict *the uncovering of truth* as opposed to the deliberate hiding of truth. Taken together, these meanings emphatically show that Jesus promised the Holy Spirit would *always* be trustworthy, reliable, and true. The disciples could rest assured that the Holy Spirit would never deliberately conceal information from them that was vital for them to know.

When Jesus used the word *truth* to describe the Holy Spirit, it was the equivalent of saying, "You don't need to worry that He will lead you astray or that He will lead you wrongly. You can depend upon Him and you can trust Him." Jesus wanted the disciples to relax and understand that they could depend on the Holy Spirit to lead them correctly.

Many believers have a hard time following the leading of the Holy Spirit because they can't see Him or physically hear His voice. They say, "Oh, how I wish Jesus was here" or, "I wish Jesus would step through the door and tell me what to do in this situation."

But this way of thinking isn't in line with the Bible. It is time for you to rejoice that you have the Holy Spirit in your life because He will never mislead you! You may need to develop your ability to listen, but the Holy Spirit will always guide you to where you need to be. *He is the Spirit of Truth!*

This means you can be sure that when the Holy Spirit nudges your heart to do something, it is the right thing to do. When He puts a thought into your mind, it is a right idea. When He guides your spirit, He knows something you don't and is trying to lead you on the best possible path through the obstacles in your life. He is always the Spirit of Truth, and as the Spirit of Truth, you can rely on the fact He will never mislead you.

The bottom line is this: If we're going to experience real, supernatural Christian living, we must come to a place of surrender to the Holy Spirit. He is always trying to coach and direct us, even when we're not listening. He is always as close as our next breath, dwelling in our spirits — speaking, directing, encouraging, and trying to help us make the correct decisions in life. Whether or not we listen to Him, He is still there on the inside of us because that's the job assignment He received from the Father. So to the extent we decide to listen to our Heavenly Coach and follow His advice, that is the extent we benefit from the Holy Spirit's role in our lives.

We must learn to trust the Holy Spirit's leadership and do what He instructs us to do. He is a divine Coach sent by God to help us. For Him to help us, it requires our ears, our hearts, our trust, and our obedience. Anything short of this will produce inferior results, results far short of the supernatural life you really desire. Since He is the Spirit of truth, it means He is completely trustworthy — so put aside your fears and objections and begin to let Him do His job of coaching you. This is Jesus' guarantee!

MY PRAYER FOR TODAY

Father, I confess that I have been fearful about following the leadership of the Holy Spirit. Today I admit it; I confess it; and I turn from it. I want to experience the coaching ministry of the Holy Spirit in my life. The Holy Spirit is the Spirit of truth. Therefore, I know He will never mislead me. Starting today, I choose to put aside my apprehensions and surrender to the leadership of the Holy Spirit. With Him helping me, I will begin to follow His leading and let Him guide me through life.

I pray this in Jesus' name!

MY CONFESSION FOR TODAY

I confess that when the Holy Spirit inspires a thought in my mind to do something, it is right. When He nudges my spirit to do something, I can rest assured that He sees and knows something I don't know and is trying to guide and direct me according to truth. He is always the Spirit of truth and will never mislead me. I long for real, supernatural Christian living, so I confess by faith that I will surrender to the Holy Spirit. In this act of surrender, I give Him permission to be my Heavenly Coach and Counselor.

I declare this by faith in Jesus' name!

QUESTIONS FOR YOU TO CONSIDER

1. Have you ever really trusted the Holy Spirit's leadership in your life, or do you typically question whether or not you should do the things He has nudged you to do?
2. If you have been afraid to follow His leadership in the past, what belief about the Person of the Holy Spirit caused you to be fearful?
3. Can you think of a time when you ignored the Holy Spirit's nudge in your heart, only to discover later that it really was the leading of the Holy Spirit?
4. What was that experience, and what was the result of your not doing what He was prompting you to do?

JUNE 9

Learning To Follow the Leader

For as many as are led by the Spirit of God,
they are the sons of God.
— Romans 8:14

When I was a young boy, I used to play a game with my sister and childhood friends called "Follow the Leader." The rules of the game dictated that the leader had absolute authority to tell us what to do. I always wanted to be the leader, but my older sister would always end up in that coveted leadership role. The leader said what we could play, who would clean the house, and so on. We basically did *whatever* he or she told us to do. No wonder my older sister always wanted to be the leader!

When I think back on those playtime experiences as a boy, I am reminded of Romans 8:14, where the apostle Paul talks about following the leadership of the Holy Spirit. He wrote, "For as many as are led by the Spirit of God, they are the sons of God." In Greek, the sentence structure is actually reversed, so that it reads, "For as many as by the Spirit of God are being led, they are the sons of God." It puts the Holy Spirit at the first of the verse, and we are placed behind Him — a picture of our responsibility as children of God to "follow the Leader."

The Greek word for "led" is *ago*, which simply means *to lead*. However, I want to point out that this word is also the root for the Greek word *agon*, which describes *an intense conflict*, such as *a struggle in a wrestling match* or *a struggle of the human will*. Thus, we see that although the Holy Spirit wants to lead us, our human will doesn't like the idea of being led. The flesh always distrusts guidance or instruction given by a person in a position of authority, and it's human nature to want to call the shots and lead the way. Whether young or old, most people don't like the idea of being led. When I played "Follow the Leader" as a child, I didn't like being led by my sister and being told what to do. I'd rather have been in charge myself and called the shots as *I* saw them!

In the same way, when we make the decision to allow the Holy Spirit to dictate the course of our lives, it often produces a struggle between our will and our flesh. However, as children of God, we must learn to subdue the complaints of our flesh and stay in our place — behind the Holy Spirit as *followers*. We're not to be out front directing the Holy Spirit; we are to go *behind* Him, following His leading, direction, and guidance. The mark of a mature believer is his or her ability to sense where the Lord is leading and then to follow that leading.

The fact that the Greek word for "led" is also the root of the Greek word for *struggle* tells us that we will have to deal with our flesh as we begin to rely fully on the Holy Spirit as our Coach and Guide. Our flesh wants to control our lives, so we must say no to it and allow the Holy Spirit to have His way. Regardless of how great the struggle seems, this process of trusting the Holy Spirit's leadership is the only way to live a supernatural Christian life.

In a certain sense, we should make it our goal to be "tagalongs" to the Holy Spirit. We should continually follow along to see what He is doing, where He is going, and how He is leading — and then we should obey His leading implicitly. Just as Jesus emulated the Father's actions, we must be sensitive to the leading of the Holy Spirit and then follow His cues. In other words, we must "be led by the Spirit," which is both the responsibility and benefit of being a child of God. To become the mature Christians God wants us to be, we must have this practical relationship with the Holy Spirit.

The leading of the Holy Spirit is often subtle, taking the form of an impression or nudging in our hearts to do something. However, His leading can also be more dramatic, such as through a prophecy, dream, or vision, or simply through a voice speaking clearly to our spirits.

The truth is, learning to know the voice of the Holy Spirit and being led by Him should be one of your primary concerns as a growing, maturing child of God. It's all part of that lifelong pursuit to know Him and the power of His resurrection as you press toward the mark of the high calling in Christ Jesus!

MY PRAYER FOR TODAY

Heavenly Father, I want to learn how to become a "tagalong" behind the leadership of the Holy Spirit. I know You sent the Holy Spirit to be my supernatural Coach — but that His Help is only a reality to me if I choose to obey His leading. I admit that I have often struggled with obedience, and I ask You to forgive me. I really want to obey. Today I ask You to give me the strength of will and the inward surrender of heart to trust and obey the Holy Spirit and do exactly what He is trying to lead me to do.

I pray this in Jesus' name!

MY CONFESSION FOR TODAY

I declare that I am tuned in to the Spirit of God and that I boldly obey whatever He instructs me to do. Fear and lack of trust do not dictate my obedience to the Holy Spirit. He is the Spirit of truth. He will never mislead me or misguide me, and I am confident of His leadership over my life. Even when I do not understand the reasons why He is leading me in a certain way, I choose to obey Him. He is the Spirit of truth. Therefore, I am confident that He is directing me into the perfect will of God for every sphere of my life.

I declare this by faith in Jesus' name!

QUESTIONS FOR YOU TO CONSIDER

1. Can you truthfully say that that you are a consistent "tagalong" who follows behind the Holy Spirit? Or do you find that most of the time you are out front, trying to direct Him as to what should be happening in your life?

2. Have you ever experienced an inner struggle after making a decision to follow the leading of the Holy Spirit? Perhaps He nudged you to do something — or to refrain from doing something — and you found it very difficult to do so, even though you were certain it was His divine leading?
3. Have you ever experienced a struggle when the Holy Spirit instructed you to witness to someone, but you found it difficult to obey? Or perhaps you sensed the Holy Spirit's leading to give a sacrificial offering, and your flesh put up a fight against His instruction in your heart. Can you think of other instances where you had to mortify your flesh in order to obey what the Holy Spirit was directing you to do or not to do?

JUNE 10

A Different Kind of Leading

And when Jesus departed thence, two blind men followed
him, crying, and saying, Thou Son of David, have
mercy on us.... Then touched he their eyes, saying,
According to your faith be it unto you.
— Matthew 9:27,29

Today I want to further highlight Jesus' own supernatural partnership with the Holy Spirit. It's so important to grasp the fact that Jesus depended *entirely* on the Holy Spirit's guidance during His earthly ministry as He preached and performed miracles throughout the land. And with that in mind, let's focus in on this truth: *Everything* Jesus did in His earthly ministry worked! Every single sick person He laid hands on was healed. Every demon He cast out of a possessed person left for good. Even the dead rose to His command! *His rate of success was 100 percent.*

What was the key to Jesus' success? Just this: *He never took action unless He knew the Father through His Spirit was leading Him to do so.* Jesus never attempted to heal a sick person, cast out a demon, or raise the dead without first knowing that He was doing what He saw the Father do (*see* John 5:19).

An interesting example of Jesus' spiritual partnership with the Holy Spirit can be found in the account of the two blind beggars in Matthew 9:27-31. As it is related in this passage, two beggars heard Jesus walking by them and began to cry out to Him for healing. However, instead of stopping to heal them, Jesus continued on His way without even acknowledging their presence. As a result, verse 27 states they "...followed him, crying and saying, Thou Son of David, have mercy on us." Even though they were blind and couldn't see where they were going, these beggars were determined to follow Jesus until they got His attention, and the Bible says they were "crying." This word "crying" is the Greek word *kradzo*, which means *to scream, to yell, to exclaim*, or *to cry out*. In other words, the two blind beggars were exerting every ounce of their hearts and their efforts into using their mouths to make a *sound* that would cause Jesus to turn His attention on them so they could *get Jesus' attention*!

Think about this situation for a moment. It is a very unusual depiction of Jesus. There were two blind men who desperately wanted to be healed and were crying out to get Jesus' attention. Yet instead of stopping to help them, Jesus just continued on His way as though they weren't even there. Still they pursued Him relentlessly. Groping along in their darkness, the blind men screamed, yelled, and cried out at the top of their lungs: *"Have mercy on us! Have mercy on us! Have mercy on us!"* There was no way that Jesus didn't hear their cries, but He didn't stop to acknowledge their existence.

In Matthew 9:28, we see that these blind beggars followed Him all the way to the house where He was staying and continued to cry out, *"Son of David, have mercy on us!"* Finally, Jesus came outside and addressed them, "Do you believe that I can do this?" They answered, "Yea, Lord." Then Jesus touched their eyes and said, "According to your faith be it unto you," and their eyes were immediately opened (v. 30).

Although this passage of Scripture relates the story of a mighty healing miracle, it perplexed me for many years. Why didn't Jesus acknowledge them? Why didn't He immediately turn to heal them when He learned of their blind condition? What were the reasons behind His hesitation?

After meditating on this subject, I came to a realization. The only answer possible is that Jesus evidently did not sense the leading of the Holy Spirit in that moment to restore sight to those men. Otherwise, He would have stopped to do it, because as Jesus stated in John 5:19, He did only whatever He saw the Father do, regardless of His own inclinations. The good news is that those men were able to use their own faith to be healed, anyway, and their sight was miraculously restored. In fact, it is almost as if Jesus told them, "You are going to have to receive this on your own. Be it unto you according to your own faith."

Usually we think of the Holy Spirit leading us *to do* something; however, in the case of the two blind beggars, Jesus was led to do *nothing*. If He had been led to heal them, He would have healed them immediately, just as He had done on countless other instances.

So often we get caught up in following our own plans and miss out entirely on what the Holy Spirit is attempting to do and say through us. We get the ball rolling on a project, and then after our program is already well underway, we pray and ask God to bless what we have initiated — assuming it was His will in the first place. No wonder we often have such poor results! We must learn to let the Holy Spirit lead us just as He led Jesus.

If the Holy Spirit leads us to action, we should act — but if there is no leading, we should *do nothing*. Sometimes doing nothing is the right thing to do! I can think of many instances when I saw something that was a good idea — something I thought someone should do — but I felt no unction to do it, and knew I would be wrong if I did it. In those cases, someone else had to use his or her faith to get it done, and ultimately that task was completed — *but by someone else, not me.*

I'm sure that when Jesus first saw those two blind beggars, He felt tugged by compassion to immediately reach out and heal them. However, He did only what He saw the Father doing, and He initiated nothing without first being led by the Holy Spirit. *That is why His success rate was 100 percent!*

Instead of jumping into action every time you see a need, learn to put on the brakes, stop yourself for a moment, and wait until the Holy Spirit speaks clearly to your heart. It may seem as though this way of doing things takes longer, but the end results will be far more rewarding and long-lasting if you adopt Jesus' approach and rely on the guidance of the Holy Spirit rather than just going with your own preplanned program. *You'll find that your success rate will increase dramatically!*

MY PRAYER FOR TODAY

Father, I ask You to help me learn to be keenly sensitive to the leading of the Holy Spirit — paying attention not just to when I should take action, but also to when I should do nothing. I've never thought about the Holy Spirit leading me to do nothing, but I can see that sometimes it is not His will for me to take action because He wants to work in a different way, at a different time, or through someone else. I admit that I've often assumed I knew what the Holy Spirit wanted me to do and then acted presumptuously without even praying. Now I understand why my success rate has not been as high as I desire. Help me be like Jesus — taking action only when the Holy Spirit is leading.

I pray this in Jesus' name!

MY CONFESSION FOR TODAY

I confess that I am led by the Holy Spirit and that I refuse to jump into action simply because I see something that needs to be done or because I am aware of a need that should be met. I put on the brakes; I listen; and I wait for the Holy Spirit to speak to my heart. Because I take action when He speaks to me and I do exactly what He tells me to do, I experience His supernatural power and supernatural results in my life. I confess that I will endeavor to do things the way Jesus did — doing only what He knew was being initiated by the Father and the Holy Spirit!

I declare this by faith in Jesus' name!

QUESTIONS FOR YOU TO CONSIDER

1. Can you think of an instance when you assumed you were supposed to take action, but in actuality, the Holy Spirit had not led you to do anything at all?
2. Can you recall other times in the four gospels when Jesus didn't heal someone? What do you learn about being led by the Holy Spirit by studying those examples?
3. Have you ever done something out of compulsion? Perhaps you thought this task needed to be done and it cost you a lot, but ultimately it produced no results. As you look back on that experience, what did you learn from it?

JUNE 11

Your Heart Is Not a Hotel!

...For he dwelleth with you and shall be in you....
— John 14:17

Today I want to return to that night in the Upper Room when Jesus taught His disciples about the ministry of the Holy Spirit. As the disciples sat and listened attentively, Jesus explained that the Holy Spirit had been *with* them all along, but soon would be *in* them. As they had ministered at Jesus' side, the disciples had experienced an atmosphere of the anointing and had temporary moments when the Spirit of God would come upon them. However, they had never experienced the Holy Spirit living *inside* them.

Up to that moment in history, the Holy Spirit had only taken up permanent residence inside one Person — *Jesus*. Even the prophets, priests, and kings in the Old Testament never knew this glorious privilege. Under the Old Covenant, the Holy Spirit might temporarily come *upon* people to specially empower them for ministry and service, but this anointing was temporary.

So when Jesus told His disciples in John 14:17 that the Holy Spirit "shall be in you," it was a mighty statement! The phrase "shall be in you" is translated from the Greek words *en humin*, which can only be translated *in you*. At first glance, this may seem simple, but remember that the Holy Spirit had *never before* lived inside a human being. This was Jesus declaring that for the first time in human history, the Spirit of God was going to literally come inside believers and abide there! His presence would no longer be temporary or fleeting, as people in the Old Testament had experienced. The Holy Spirit was going to take up residency and dwell inside them *permanently* — to never move, never waver, and never pack His bags and leave for another location.

Prior to this statement in John 14:17, Jesus had described the Holy Spirit's role as a "Comforter" (v.16). As we saw in previous *Sparkling Gems* (June 2-6), this word is the Greek term *parakletos*, meaning *one called alongside* them. Now He takes it a step further and affirms that the Holy Spirit would actually live "in" them.

This is a central truth of the New Testament: If you have repented of sin and surrendered to the Lordship of Christ, then you have been born again and the Holy Spirit has come to live inside you. This is why the apostle Paul wrote, "What? Know ye not that your body is the temple of the Holy Spirit which is in you, which ye have of God, and ye are not your own?" (1 Corinthians 6:19).

I like to say it this way — *your heart was never meant to be a hotel.* God never intended for the Holy Spirit to be your *Guest.* The Holy Spirit has come to stay as a permanent *Resident* inside your heart, and He will be with you for the rest of your life. This is yet another reason why you should develop your partnership with Him. He has moved in, taken up residence, and is committed to staying with you until that glorious day when you are ultimately relocated to Heaven itself!

MY PRAYER FOR TODAY

Father, I thank You that the Holy Spirit is not a temporary Guest, but a permanent Resident inside my heart. Help me to remember this and to live my life in a way that honors His indwelling presence. Help me to live with the constant awareness that He is with me always. I am so thankful that He does not come and go and that He is not a fleeting relationship in my life. Help me to cultivate my fellowship with Him until I come to know Him deeply in my life on a practical level.

I pray this in Jesus' name!

MY CONFESSION FOR TODAY

I acknowledge and declare that God's Spirit dwells permanently inside my heart. He will never waver or pack His bags to move to another location. My heart is not meant to be a hotel, but rather a permanent residence for the Holy Spirit. The Holy Spirit is not a temporary Guest — He has come to indwell my heart for the rest of my life! He has moved in, taken up residence, and is committed to staying with me until I am ultimately relocated to Heaven itself!

I declare this by faith in Jesus' name!

QUESTIONS FOR YOU TO CONSIDER

1. Have you ever thought about how glorious it is that your heart is not a temporary location for the Holy Spirit, but rather His permanent dwelling place?
2. How should the awareness that your heart is the Holy Spirit's permanent dwelling place affect the way you live your life?
3. What kind of condition is your heart in for Him? What renovations do you need to make in your heart to make it more accommodating to Him, considering the Holy Spirit already lives inside you?

God never intended
for the Holy Spirit to be your Guest.
The Holy Spirit has come to stay
as a permanent Resident inside your heart,
and He will be with you for the rest of your life.

JUNE 12

The Teaching Ministry of the Holy Spirit

But the Comforter, which is the Holy Ghost,
whom the Father will send in my name,
he shall teach you all things....
— John 14:26

As Jesus continued teaching the disciples about the various roles the Holy Spirit would soon have in their lives, He told them that the Holy Spirit would also "teach" them. Let's look at that word "teach" in today's *Sparkling Gem* and see what Jesus meant when He chose this word.

This word "teach" is the Greek word *didasko* — a word that is used approximately 200 times in both the Old and New Testaments. It is used so often, in fact, that its meaning is *very* well established. But to make sure we hit the target correctly, we will take our meaning of *didasko* from *The NIV Theological Dictionary of New Testament Words*, which gives the primary meaning of this word as "*to teach, inform, instruct, demonstrate, and prescribe*." It continues, "The word is used typically for the relationship between teacher and pupil, instructor, and apprentice. What is taught may be not only knowledge, opinions, or facts but also artistic and technical skills, all of which are to be systematically and thoroughly acquired by the learner through the activity of a teacher."[6]

Thus, in the context of John 14:26, we see that the word *didasko* means the Holy Spirit has taken on the role of a Teacher, just as Jesus was a Teacher to the disciples. The Holy Spirit has become our Teacher, and we are His pupils. He is our Instructor, and we are the apprentices. Furthermore, the full extent of the Holy Spirit's teaching is deep and multifaceted. Not only was He sent to us to impart knowledge and facts, lessons from Scripture, and theological truths, but He also teaches us how to live our Christian lives with divinely artistic skill. Instructed by the Teacher who lives within each of us as believers, we receive lessons imparted as we spend time in the Word or prayer or through any aspect of our innumerable life experiences. If we are listening, the Holy Spirit is teaching us *constantly*. Our responsibility is to listen, to obey, and to internalize and put into practice the truths He is teaching us.

There are always people who claim that if you haven't been to Bible school, you are untaught and ignorant and therefore unable to be used significantly by God. However, this is simply not the case. It's true that Bible school can be an immensely beneficial experience, and it's good for you to read every book that you can read. But if you never go to a Bible school or read a teaching book, the Holy Spirit will still teach you, because He is ordained by the Father to do just that. *Teaching is a fundamental part of the ministry of the Holy Spirit.*

---

[6] Verlyn D. Verbrugge, *NIV Theological Dictionary of New Testament Words*: Abridged Edition, (Grand Rapids, MI: Zondervan Publishing House, 2000), p. 141.

Jesus told His disciples that when the Holy Spirit came, He would teach them, and today the Holy Spirit has been sent to teach *you*. If you're seeking the best Teacher in the world, look no further! If you are born again, you have the Holy Spirit — *the greatest Teacher in the history of the world* — living inside you. If you'll see yourself as His apprentice and cultivate your partnership together, He'll teach you everything you need to know to live successfully and victoriously for Christ!

MY PRAYER FOR TODAY

Lord Jesus, You said that when the Holy Spirit came, He would teach me all things I need to know. I am thankful for my pastor, my church, my books, and my various teaching materials — but there is nothing that could ever replace the teaching ministry of the Holy Spirit in my life. I admit that I've leaned on my own understanding on too many occasions, but starting today, I sincerely dedicate myself as a pupil and apprentice to the Spirit of God.

I pray this in Jesus' name!

MY CONFESSION FOR TODAY

I confess that I am in need of the Holy Spirit's teaching in my life. I am thankful that I don't need to beg for it or work to earn this work of the Holy Spirit. Jesus knew I needed divine instruction, and that is one reason why He prayed for the Father to send the Holy Spirit into the world. He is my Teacher, and I am His pupil. He is the Instructor, and I am the apprentice. I am serious about learning, and I take it as my responsibility to internalize and put into practice what He teaches me through diligent study and by application of His words in my life experience.

I declare this by faith in Jesus' name!

QUESTIONS FOR YOU TO CONSIDER

1. Have you ever experienced the teaching ministry of the Holy Spirit?
2. Can you clearly express the specific ways you've experienced the Holy Spirit's teaching ministry? Your ability to do that could help someone else who needs to learn how to benefit from this coaching and instructing role of the Holy Spirit in his or her life.
3. How do you internalize and put into practice the things that the Holy Spirit has taught you through personal study or life experience?

If we are listening,
the Holy Spirit is teaching us constantly.
Our responsibility is to listen, to obey, and to internalize
and put into practice the truths He is teaching us.

JUNE 13

The Reminding Ministry of the Holy Spirit

But the Comforter, which is the Holy Ghost,
whom the Father will send in my name, he shall teach
you all things, and bring all things to your remembrance,
whatsoever I have said unto you.
— John 14:26

Have you ever wondered how the four gospel writers separately recorded four gospels with no contradictions? With all the countless words the disciples heard Jesus speak, how did they ever remember them all accurately? It is absolutely remarkable to me when I think about each apostle's fantastic ability to remember what Jesus said and did. This leads us to the next responsibility God gave to the Holy Spirit — *to bring to our remembrance all the things Jesus said or taught.*

When Jesus taught about the ministry of the Holy Spirit, He said that *bringing what Jesus said to remembrance* would be a part of the Holy Spirit's ministry. In John 14:26, Jesus said, "But the Comforter, which is the Holy Spirit, whom the Father will send in my name, he shall teach you all things and will bring all things to your *remembrance*, whatsoever I have said unto you."

The word "remembrance" is a translation of the Greek word *hupomimnesko*, which is a compound of the words *hupo* and *mimnesko*. The word *hupo* in this particular case means *by* — as *to place something alongside* of something else. The word *mimnesko* means *to remember, to recollect, to remind, to regather*, or *to recall.* When these two words are compounded, the combined nuances depict *someone whose memory is awakened* or *one who is enabled to call something to mind.*

This is truly amazing to me. When I read the gospels and I see how the Holy Spirit brought explicit, vivid details to the remembrance of four gospel writers, I know that it would have been naturally impossible for all four of these men to so precisely recall everything they remembered on their own. However, the fact is that they were all listening to the same Holy Spirit who was bringing to their remembrance everything they had experienced with Jesus.

The Bible gives us a very clear example in John 12 of this "reminding work" of the Holy Spirit. In this account, Jesus was entering into Jerusalem triumphantly as people joyfully proclaimed, "Hosanna, Blessed is the King of Israel that cometh in the name of the Lord" (John 12:13). At the time this was happening, the disciples didn't realize Old Testament Scripture was being fulfilled before their eyes. But John 12:16 goes on to say, "These things understood not his disciples at the first: but when Jesus was glorified, then *remembered* they that these things were written of him, and that they had done these things unto him." This very clearly refers to the *reminding ministry* of the Holy Spirit.

After the Holy Spirit was poured out upon those who prayed in the Upper Room on the Day of Pentecost, one of the ways the Holy Spirit taught the apostles about Jesus was by tying Old Testament Scripture into events they had experienced with Him. Many things that hadn't been clear or hadn't made sense to them while Jesus was on earth were now being explained and defined as the Holy Spirit led them in Old Testament verses. As He inspired the apostles to write the New Testament, He clarified and revealed to them the significance of the Old Testament as it related to Jesus' ministry and calling, the newly emerging Church, and the future.

Furthermore, the gospels contain no errors. What we have in them is exactly what Jesus said and did. They were written as the Holy Spirit put Matthew, Mark, Luke, and John in remembrance of what Jesus said and did. How marvelous and fantastic it truly is to see how the Holy Spirit illuminated their minds to recall vivid details from Jesus' life and ministry. It is due to this wonderful *reminding work* of the Holy Spirit that we have the books of Matthew, Mark, Luke and John in our Bibles today.

This makes me know that we can never claim ignorance for not knowing Scripture. Part of the Holy Spirit's ministry is to bring to our memory exactly what verses we need — *when* we need them. If our partnership with the Holy Spirit is strong, we can lean upon Him the moment our memory fails us, because it is His responsibility to remind us of the Word of God. When we are in the midst of a difficult situation and don't know what to do, the Holy Spirit will reach into the Word of God that is stored in our hearts and minds, and He will withdraw the exact verse or truth we need and put us in remembrance of it at just the right moment.

Perhaps this particular reminding work of the Holy Spirit is best illustrated in parts of the world where the Bible is illegal. My family lives in the former Soviet Union, where the Bible was forbidden for more than 70 years. I am constantly in awe as I meet leaders and entire churches that had only one Bible over a span of many years. Sometimes it was a hand-copied version with torn and tattered pages from decades of use. Those yellow, tattered pages of the Word of God meant everything to them.

It is the most amazing thing to see people who have had limited access to the Bible and yet know it so well. They can quote it and remember it better than people in free countries who have several Bibles in their homes and the opportunity to read them every morning and every night. There is only one explanation: *the Holy Spirit.* He is doing exactly what Jesus said He would do — putting them in remembrance of the Word of God. This is especially true where the Word of God, although it may be scarce, is embraced and esteemed. When a person has given precious care to reading and meditating on the Word day and night, the Holy Spirit has the wherewithal to call to remembrance what that person has read and assimilated in the deepest parts of his being. That is one of the Holy Spirit's responsibilities as our Partner in this world.

Today I want to encourage you to open your heart to this reminding ministry of the Holy Spirit. If you say you have a difficult time memorizing Scripture, open your heart to the ministry of the Holy Spirit because He wants to put you in remembrance of everything that Jesus said.

And He will help you recall everything you need to remember that Jesus said to you — exactly on time and exactly at the right place. That's part of His *reminding ministry* to you and to me.

MY PRAYER FOR TODAY

Father, I am so thankful for the wonderful work of the Holy Spirit to put me in remembrance of the words and acts of Jesus Christ. I confess that there have been times when I found it difficult to remember scripture verses, but now I understand that in times when my memory fails me, the Holy Spirit will step forward to help me remember exactly what needs to be brought to my attention. I will no longer claim a poor memory but will now embrace this special reminding ministry of the Holy Spirit!

I pray this in Jesus' name!

MY CONFESSION FOR TODAY

I confess that the Holy Spirit brings to my memory everything I need to recall about the life, words, and acts of Jesus Christ. I have the mind of Christ working in me because the Holy Spirit lives in me and is helping me. Part of His ministry is to remind me of everything that Jesus said or did, and I declare that because of the Holy Spirit's faithfulness to remind me, I recall everything I need to — on time and in every situation where it is needed.

I declare this by faith in Jesus' name!

QUESTIONS FOR YOU TO CONSIDER

1. Can you think of a time when you couldn't recall a verse or a passage of Scripture, and then it suddenly came to your mind at exactly the right moment? When was that? How did it affect you when you remembered it so correctly?
2. Is this reminding ministry of the Holy Spirit a brand-new concept to you, or have you already been aware of His function to remind you of things Jesus said or did?
3. Everyone has a responsibility to memorize Scripture. If this is difficult for you, do you see more clearly after reading this *Sparkling Gem* how the Holy Spirit is ready to help you with this? As you plant the Word in your heart and determine to set certain scriptures to memory, He will be faithful to bring those words to your remembrance!

The Holy Spirit will help you recall everything you need to remember that Jesus said to you — exactly on time and exactly at the right place.

JUNE 14

The Testifying Ministry of the Holy Spirit

But when the Comforter is come,
whom I will send unto you from the Father,
even the Spirit of truth, which proceedeth
from the Father, he shall testify of me.
— John 15:26

When I was growing up, our church had regular visitation nights when we paid a visit to people who had recently attended our church or we visited the homes of unsaved people so we could present Christ to them. I literally hated those evenings of visitation and witnessing. The word "hate" is not too strong of a word, because this is precisely what I felt at the time. I *hated* it.

I loved Jesus with all of my heart, but getting into the car to go knock on doors to talk to people I'd never met in my life and read them a tract that they weren't interested in hearing wasn't my idea of having a good time. Other Christians had the same problem too. I know, because our pastor constantly had to coax our congregation to come to Sunday school visitation and nights of witnessing.

Nevertheless, I knew I was supposed to be a witness for Jesus. I can remember piling into my Sunday school teacher's car, looking at the list of names we were to visit, and then going to knock on all those doors. I felt powerless, defeated, and joyless as we went, and although many believers would never want to admit it, they feel the same way about witnessing that I did.

The truth is, there is no true witnessing without the work of the Holy Spirit. We must have the Holy Spirit's help as we testify. However, the good news is that Jesus said, "He [the Holy Spirit] *shall* testify of me."

You see, the Holy Spirit loves to testify of Jesus. As a result of His deep love, adoration, and affection for Jesus, He loves to talk on and on about Him. So when you partner with the Holy Spirit and allow Him to work through you, testifying becomes natural and simple instead of forced and difficult. It becomes an *overflow* of your relationship with the Holy Spirit.

In Acts 1:8, Jesus told the disciples to stay in Jerusalem to wait for the power of the Holy Spirit, He said, "But ye shall receive power, after that the Holy Spirit is come upon you: and ye shall be witnesses unto me both in Jerusalem, and in all Judea, and in Samaria, and unto the uttermost part of the earth." Notice He said that the disciples would be witnesses "after" the Holy Spirit came upon them. To witness and testify powerfully about the resurrected Christ, supernatural power is required. Hence, without the Holy Spirit's assistance, it is almost impossible to testify with confidence about Jesus Christ.

Before the Day of Pentecost, the disciples were similar to many Christians today. Rather than advancing upon the lost world with the message of Christ, they were hiding behind closed doors (*see* John 20:19). Unlike the great spiritual army they were supposed to be, they were simply "holding out" in a room, hiding for fear of the Jews.

Yet Jesus said the Holy Spirit would "testify" of Him, not make us fear-filled cowards! That word translated "testify" comes from the Greek word *martureo*, which means *to witness* or *to give a good report*. It's where we get the word *martyr*, referring to someone who obtains a righteous testimony as a result of his willingness to accept suffering or death rather than renounce his faith in Jesus. That kind of courage comes only from the supernatural ability of the Holy Spirit, empowering the believer to testify of Jesus, regardless of any pressure or opposition, no matter how severe.

It was not until Acts 2 that the disciples comprehended the greatness of the Holy Spirit's ability to empower believers to testify. The witness of Jesus Christ literally *blasted* out of their mouths as they hit the streets of Jerusalem, fully yielded to the Holy Spirit. In addition to supernaturally declaring "the wonderful works of God" in other languages (*see* Acts 2:11), they proclaimed the Word of God intelligently in their own language to a people they had been afraid of the day before!

A good example is seen in the story of the apostle Peter. After he received the infilling of the Holy Spirit on the Day of Pentecost, he was transformed! Standing before an enraptured crowd, Peter boldly proclaimed, "Ye men of Israel, hear these words; Jesus of Nazareth, a man approved of God among you by miracles and wonders and signs, which God did by him in the midst of you…ye have taken, and by wicked hands have crucified…whom God hath raised up, having loosed the pains of death…therefore being by the right hand of God exalted" (Acts 2:22,23,33). *This was supernatural witnessing! This was supernatural proclamation!*

Certainly there is nothing wrong with preplanned evangelism, door-to-door visitation, or evangelism programs that teach you the basics of witnessing. But when those programs are carried out without the power of the Holy Spirit, they are often dry, dead, and unsatisfying. Real witnessing or testifying of Jesus Christ can only be done by the power of the Holy Spirit!

Why lean on your own understanding when it comes to witnessing? Why reduce this powerful moment to a mere program? The Holy Spirit was sent to testify of Jesus! No one knows how to testify better than He does.

If you are afraid to witness, as I was when I was younger, I urge you to open your heart to the Holy Spirit and let Him release His power through you to become a witness for Christ. As you surrender your heart and mind to the Holy Spirit's control, witnessing will turn from stressful drudgery into a joyful, rewarding, and exciting adventure!

MY PRAYER FOR TODAY

Lord, I admit that I am one of those who has been uneasy and fearful about witnessing in the past. I've felt so uncomfortable — afraid that I'll say the wrong thing or that someone will ask a question I can't answer. I've been controlled by fear and dread when it comes to sharing my faith with others. In fact, I've even tried to avoid it, even though I know that I am commanded to be a witness for Jesus. I realize now that all that fear, frustration, and anxiety was the result of my attempt to do Your will in my own strength without the enabling power of the Holy Spirit. Starting right now, I want to do my best to surrender to the Holy Spirit — and let Him release His testifying ability through me. Holy Spirit, You love to talk about Jesus, and You know precisely the words to speak because You hold the key to every person's heart, so speak through me to others and touch the part of their hearts that is ready to hear and receive the truth of the Gospel. I thank You, Holy Spirit, for making me an effective fisher of men!

I pray this in Jesus' name!

MY CONFESSION FOR TODAY

I confess that I am NOT afraid to witness for Jesus Christ. My testimony is powerful. People want to hear it. Because the Holy Spirit is my Partner, He knows exactly how to start every conversation, how to touch each heart, and how to win each person to Jesus Christ. I do not do this on my own, but I do it in partnership with the Holy Spirit. The Holy Spirit is jubilant when it comes to the subject of Jesus, and He releases that joy-filled attitude victoriously through me as I open up and testify of Jesus to others! I receive the power of God that makes me an effective witness for Him!

I declare this by faith in Jesus' name!

QUESTIONS FOR YOU TO CONSIDER

1. Have you been afraid to witness? Have you ever thought about why this is such a fearful thing for you to do? Maybe it would be good for you to think through this question and come up with a conclusion you can pray about.
2. There is special supernatural power available to help you share Christ with others. Have you ever experienced that supernatural power in a specific situation? What was that situation?
3. Who do you know that is unsaved and needs to hear the message of Jesus right now? Is it a friend, relative, coworker, or an acquaintance? Don't you want that person to know Christ as you know Him? Why not yield to the Holy Spirit and let Him testify through you to that person? He'll show you when and how to do it!

JUNE 15

The Convicting Ministry of the Holy Spirit

And when he is come, he will reprove the world of sin,
and of righteousness, and of judgment.
— John 16:8

In the Upper Room, as Jesus continued teaching about the ministry of the Holy Spirit, He said, "And when he is come, he will reprove the world of sin, and of righteousness, and of judgment" (John 16:8). Let's talk about what Jesus meant when He said the Holy Spirit would "reprove" the world of sin.

The word "reprove" is the Greek word *elegcho*. It means *to expose, to convict, or to cross-examine for the purpose of conviction* — as in convicting a lawbreaker in a court of law. The Holy Spirit will begin to deal with the heart of an unbeliever, and by the time He is finished, that lost, sinful soul will feel exposed and convicted. As the Holy Spirit enables that person to hear the Word of God for the first time, the razor-sharp sword of the Word will penetrate his soul until he feels as if he has been cross-examined on a witness stand. Finally, the court will be adjourned, the verdict announced, and he will *know* on the inside that he is guilty of sin.

This is *precisely* what a sinner feels when the Holy Spirit convicts him of sin. It is amazing how long a sinner can live without conviction or godly sorrow for his behavior — how long he can be nearly numb to any sense of wrongness regarding his sinful actions. The Bible says that sin has made unbelievers to be hardhearted, spiritually blind, and past feeling (*see* Ephesians 4:18,19). But those factors change instantly when the Holy Spirit touches the human soul and exposes its sinful condition. Exposed, naked, confronted — that is exactly what a sinner feels when the Holy Spirit wakes him up to his true spiritual condition.

It is the work of the Holy Spirit to convict sinners of their lost condition. The whole world stands guilty before God (*see* Romans 3:19), but the lost don't realize they are guilty until that moment when the Holy Spirit reveals it to them.

Jesus stated, "No man can come unto me, except the Father...draw him" (John 6:44). This drawing of a person's heart to Jesus is done through the work of the Holy Spirit. Jesus reminded us of this when He said, "And when he is come, he will reprove the world of sin" (John 16:8). Without the work of the Holy Spirit to expose our sinful condition, we would still remain in darkness today, eternally lost and without God.

It is amazing to me that a person can be in sin, and even understand that he is in sin, yet nonetheless fail to grasp the real eternal consequences of what that means. He can even be in a church service where he hears about sin and acknowledges that the sermon is true and that he's a sinner — yet leave that service and continue living the same lifestyle he did before he got there.

But something happens when the Holy Spirit begins to work in that person's soul. He lovingly cross-examines that person, until finally He brings him to a place of confrontation. It is at this point that invisible scales fall from the person's eyes, and he truly sees for the first time that he is in sin. This is something that can only be revealed by the Holy Spirit. When *He* convicts of sin, the sinner *absolutely* knows that he is a sinner.

Once the Holy Spirit has lovingly brought that person to the place where he finally sees it for himself, the person has a choice: Will he stay in sin, or will he repent and turn toward God? Helping that person reach this point of decision that has such eternal consequences is the purpose of the Holy Spirit's convicting ministry in his life.

It is frustrating to share Christ with family and friends and to feel as if you are "hitting a brick wall." You share, talk, and plead with them to receive Christ, yet it seems they just can't hear what you are saying. Even though they may acknowledge they are sinners, they may not seem to be too deeply disturbed by the implications of this fact. They just press on as though they were numb to or ignorant of the spiritual deadness in their lives.

But the Bible clearly teaches that a lost person is "dead in trespasses and sins" (Ephesians 2:1). Don't forget that dead people don't feel anything. Spiritually dead people especially don't feel the conviction of sin. It requires a special, supernatural work of the Holy Spirit to rouse the human consciousness to realize its sinful condition.

How can you make a dead man see? How can you cause a dead man to feel? How can you convince a dead man that he needs to change? Thank God for the convicting work of the Holy Spirit! Only through the convicting power of God's Spirit can a spiritually dead man be awakened and beckoned to Christ.

Friend, it was the Holy Spirit's call that touched your soul, awakened you to your sinfulness, and beckoned you to Christ. Once you were brought to this place of undeniable conviction and you recognized that you were a sinner, the Spirit invited you to receive Jesus as your Savior and Lord. At that divine moment, your soul heard the Holy Spirit say, "Awake thou that sleepest, and arise from the dead, and Christ shall give thee light" (Ephesians 5:14). And in that next moment, you were born again!

What a miracle it was when God raised our spirits from spiritual death to spiritual life. In fact, there is no greater miracle! The convicting work of the Holy Spirit is part of the foundational work that He does in our lives, but it's certainly not the last! Tomorrow we'll look at His work to "convince" us of our God-given righteousness. Don't miss it!

MY PRAYER FOR TODAY

Heavenly Father, I know Jesus Christ today because of the convicting work of the Holy Spirit. I remember when You first awakened me to my sin — a realization that had never gripped me before. But when I saw my spiritual condition, I really understood that I was lost and needed to be saved. Thank You for the convicting work of the Holy Spirit and for bringing me to a place where I could be saved. I could have never arrived there on my own, so today I want to say thank You! And I trust You to complete that work in the lives of those for whom I pray to come to a saving knowledge of You.

I pray this in Jesus' name!

MY CONFESSION FOR TODAY

I confess that the Holy Spirit is working in the lives of my family, friends, coworkers, and acquaintances to bring them to a place where they really see and understand their lost condition and need for salvation. Jesus Christ died for them, and He sent the Holy Spirit to draw them to Jesus. If the Holy Spirit prompts me to testify to them, I will do so, for the Holy Spirit knows how to touch each and every heart. I declare that they will finally hear, understand, and come to a saving knowledge of Jesus Christ because of the convicting and converting power of the Holy Spirit at work in their lives.

I declare this by faith in Jesus' name!

QUESTIONS FOR YOU TO CONSIDER

1. Can you remember when you were first struck by the reality of personal sin and separation from God? Where were you, and what situation produced that awareness?
2. When you awakened to your need to turn from darkness to the light, how long did it take before you turned to Jesus in repentance to receive Him as your Savior and Lord?
3. What unsaved individuals are on your prayer list right now? Can you think of someone who was praying for you before you came to Christ?

How can you make a dead man see?
Thank God for the convicting work of the Holy Spirit!
Only through the convicting power of God's Spirit
can a spiritually dead man be awakened
and beckoned to Christ.

JUNE 16

The Convincing Ministry of the Holy Spirit, Part 1

And when he [the Holy Spirit] is come, he will reprove…
of righteousness…because I go to my Father,
and ye see me no more.
— John 16:8,10

When I was a young man, I struggled with condemnation, constantly fearing that I wasn't really saved. I didn't grasp the idea of a God-given righteousness. I felt that I had to prove my worth to be acceptable to God. But one day the Holy Spirit began dealing with me, supernaturally *convincing* me of my Christ-imparted righteousness. And, friend, I want to tell you from the Word *and* from personal experience that being convinced of righteousness is just as supernatural as being convicted of sin.

The word "reprove" in John 16:8 is the Greek word *elegcho*. As we saw in yesterday's *Sparkling Gem*, it means to cross-examine a person on a witness stand until he is brought to a place of utter confrontation where he cannot deny the facts. We saw yesterday how the Holy Spirit has an *elegcho* ministry with sinners, bringing them revelation of their spiritual condition to the point where they cannot deny the fact that they are lost, without God, and in sin. At that point, they then have the opportunity to repent and to receive Christ.

But in the very same way, the Holy Spirit cross-examines us as believers and convinces us of our righteousness! The Bible says that we are the righteousness of God in Christ Jesus (2 Corinthians 5:21). It is very difficult for the human mind to comprehend and accept, because our natural thinking says we're not righteous. And it's true — on our own, we are *not* righteous, but we have been declared righteous because of the blood of Jesus.

Rather than struggle in an effort to become righteous — a state you will never be able to attain on your own — the Holy Spirit wants to open your eyes. He wants to bring you to a point where you see and understand, beyond a shadow of a doubt, that you are not trying to *become* righteous; rather, you have been *declared* the righteousness of God in Christ Jesus. The day you understand that and are utterly convinced that this is an actual fact, it will begin to radically change how you pray, how you feel about yourself, and how you carry yourself. Why? Because you will see and act like one who has become the righteousness of God!

What a wonderful work God did for us! He sent Jesus to die in our place and to take our sin upon Himself. Then God exerted all of His mighty power to raise Jesus from the dead, seat Him at His own right hand, and send the Holy Spirit to live in us so we could actually *become* the righteousness of God in Christ. Yet if there is any subject in Scripture about which

Christians will often argue, it is this issue of righteousness. Most Christians are so conscious of their own sinful nature that they have great difficulty embracing the truth that they have been declared righteous. If you were to tell them they are righteous, they'll likely respond by telling you how bad they are.

Sinful nature always clings to what is worst and most negative. It will always gravitate downward, never upward. That is the nature of the mind that isn't under the control of the Holy Spirit. The sinful flesh, if not mortified by the sanctifying power of God's Spirit, will follow its negative leanings all the way to the grave. If abandoned to your flesh, you'll never believe a good report; you'll never believe God is doing a good work in you; and you'll certainly never believe you have been made the righteousness of God in Christ.

Negative, base, sinful thinking has been a part of our humanity for so long that it requires a special convincing work of the Holy Spirit to make us realize the supernatural work that God has done inside us. When the Father says, "You're My child, and I've made you righteous," we must receive the Holy Spirit's special work of convincing us of our rightstanding with God. If we don't, our negatively charged mind and emotions will retort, *It's not so! I'm unworthy. I'm unholy. I'm so pitiful!*

Too many Christians fall into this trap. But that is like throwing the compliment back in God's face! These people love the Lord, but they fail to understand and esteem the work He has done for them — a work that cost Him greatly! He put forth His best work to redeem them and make them "new creations in Christ Jesus" (*see* 2 Corinthians 5:17) — and yet they have nothing good to say about themselves!

The Bible tells us explicitly that we are "...his workmanship, created in Christ Jesus..." (Ephesians 2:10). Another version of that verse could read, *"We are a product of His very own, marvelously created in Christ Jesus — created under the influence and control of His divine power."* This is a powerful, life-changing truth, but it requires the Holy Spirit to move this truth from our *heads* to our *hearts*. Just as the Holy Spirit must *convict* the sinner of his lost condition, He also must *convince* us of our position of rightstanding with God!

We are so negative in our old, fleshly nature that it really does take a supernatural work of the Spirit to cause us to comprehend our new condition in Jesus Christ. This realization that we have been made righteous is just as supernatural as the lost man recognizing that he is lost.

I can remember when the Holy Spirit woke me up to this truth many years ago. Driving down the street, feeling totally unrighteous, I was listening to a teaching on righteousness — when *suddenly* my mind began to grasp what I was hearing. It was as if someone took blinders off my eyes and earplugs out of my ears. For the first time in my life, I was seeing and hearing — *really* seeing and *really* hearing — that God had declared me righteous in Jesus Christ. The truth was going straight to my heart by the power of the Holy Spirit! I heard it! I understood it! My inward man was leaping for joy as the Spirit of God illuminated my understanding about righteousness. Right then He *convinced* me of the truth, and I was set free!

If you struggle with your self-image and feelings of condemnation, you need the Holy Spirit to do His convincing work in your life. Only He can open your eyes to *really* see and your ears to *really* hear who you have become in Christ Jesus. Once your eyes and ears have been opened and you understand you have been made righteous, you will never throw the truth back in God's face and argue with Him again. Now when the Holy Spirit reminds you that you've been made righteous, you will cry out with joy, "Thank You! That's exactly what I am!"

You don't have to keep being negative about yourself all the time. You don't have to beat yourself over the head, constantly reminding yourself of how unworthy you are. Jesus Christ made you worthy! He made you righteous! He made you a new creation! *Let the Holy Spirit do His work to convince you of these glorious realities!*

MY PRAYER FOR TODAY

Father, I ask You to bring me to that place of realization where I really understand the righteousness that has been imparted to me through Jesus Christ. I don't want to struggle with guilt and condemnation anymore. Since Jesus was made sin for me that I could be made the righteousness of God in Him, help me to step into that place of awareness and remain there, forever free!

I pray this in Jesus' name!

MY CONFESSION FOR TODAY

I declare by faith that I am the righteousness of God in Christ Jesus. I didn't earn it or deserve it, but by faith I repented, and I received righteousness as the gracious, free gift of God. I do not struggle with my past. It has no hold on me. I am, in fact, a new creature, totally new in Christ Jesus. The Holy Spirit has done His work to convince me of my rightstanding with God, and I am free from the past forever!

I declare this by faith in Jesus' name!

QUESTIONS FOR YOU TO CONSIDER

1. Have you struggled with self-condemnation and self-judgment? If yes, what benefit has it produced in your life?
2. Has there ever been a moment when the Spirit opened your eyes and "convinced" you that Christ had made you righteous? If yes, what was the immediate result of that revelation?
3. If you were to describe people who are sin-conscious or righteousness-conscious, how would you describe these two groups of people?

JUNE 17

The Convincing Ministry of the Holy Spirit, Part 2

And when he [the Holy Spirit] is come,
he will reprove the world of sin,
and of righteousness, and of judgment....
Of judgment, because the prince of this world is judged.
— John 16:8,11

Today I want to continue talking about the supernatural convincing work of the Holy Spirit. In the previous two days, we've seen how the Holy Spirit convicts the sinner of his sin — a supernatural work that cannot happen apart from the work of the Holy Spirit. We've also seen how the Holy Spirit convinces a Christian of his God-given righteousness — something that a believer will not completely comprehend until the Holy Spirit reveals it and brings that person to the undeniable fact that he has been *made* the righteousness of God in Christ Jesus.

But there is one more convincing work of the Holy Spirit mentioned in John 16:8,11. It says, "And when he [the Holy Spirit] is come, he will reprove the world of sin, and of righteousness, and of judgment.... Of judgment, because the prince of this world is judged." This describes the Holy Spirit's work to convince and remind us that although Satan may seem to have free rein at the moment, his ultimate fate is settled and his doom is sealed. He is the *loser* at the end of the day.

If all we do is sit and listen to the news, it's likely that it will leave us in a despondent state as we wonder what in the world is going to happen. Moral codes are changing; laws are changing; politics are changing — and it seems much of the Church itself is negatively changing. If we dwell on all these negative changes, we will soon become despondent with despair. But a glorious part of the ministry of the Holy Spirit is to convince us that the "prince of this world is judged" (*see* John 16:11). That means the devil isn't going to win! His judgment has already been pronounced, and part of the Holy Spirit's ministry is to remind us and convince us of this fact.

Let's look at the terminology Jesus used when he called Satan "the prince of this world." The word "prince" is the Greek word *ho archon*, a title used to describe *a ruler* in a particular realm that can be translated as the word "prince." The word "world" is the Greek word *kosmos*, which emphatically does *not* describe the earth, universe, or planetary systems. Instead, it denotes *culture*, *society*, and the *systems* in which mankind lives and functions. It denotes systems, such as education, entertainment, government, and every human sphere, as the places — the *kosmos* — where Satan operates. The word *kosmos* is the identical word that the apostle Paul used in Second Corinthians 4:4 when he referred to Satan as the "god of this world." It pictures Satan as being the ruler of the *lost culture* and *lost systems* that dominates every sphere of mankind. Those systems are where Satan temporarily operates and exercises his power. I say that he operates there *temporarily* because Jesus said his rule has been "judged."

The word "judged" is the Greek word *krino*. The word *krino* was used in a judicial sense, even in a court of law, to mean the decision has already been weighed and decided. There is no more debating of this issue. The decision is made, and the case is closed. All that remains is pronouncement of the verdict, which is *judgment*. And Jesus said that part of the Holy Spirit's ministry would be to convince you and me that Satan is condemned without the possibility of escape.

This means, my friend, that the bad news we see in the world today is temporary. Jesus is Lord, and everything we see around us won't last very long. Christ completely and utterly defeated Satan through His death on the Cross and His resurrection. Now it's only a matter of time until the clouds break and Jesus comes through the eastern sky — *and everything changes*!

When you're tempted to despair because of what you hear and see, that is the moment you need to say, "Holy Spirit, please — remind me that the prince of this world is judged." He will bring you to an absolute place of conviction that will put your feet on solid ground and cause you to *know* beyond any shadow of a doubt that the prince of this world is judged and that you really are on the winning side!

MY PRAYER FOR TODAY

Father, I thank You that Jesus conquered Satan through His death on the Cross and His resurrection and that Jesus is truly Lord over all! The ministry of the Holy Spirit in my life is a daily reminder to me of this glorious fact. Especially today, when it seems so many things are changing and it looks like evil is winning so many battles, I rely upon this special convincing ministry of the Holy Spirit that the prince of this world is judged — and from this condemnation he has no possibility of escape. Thank You, Holy Spirit, for keeping me in remembrance of the truth that Jesus is Lord now, that He is Lord tomorrow, and that He will always be Lord of all!

I pray this in Jesus' name!

MY CONFESSION FOR TODAY

I confess that Jesus is Lord over everything in this world. When I am tempted to fear or to give sway to the bad news that is going out over the airwaves all the time, I will stand tall, throw my shoulders back, hold my head high, and boldly declare that Jesus is Lord and Satan is the loser! I declare that the decision has already been made, the court is closed, and Satan's doom is sealed. Jesus is coming back soon, and everything will change!

I declare this by faith in Jesus' name!

QUESTIONS FOR YOU TO CONSIDER

1. Have you ever had moments when it felt like the world was morally crumbling all around you and it made you feel hopeless? What do you say or think on to counteract the temptation to go down that dark road in your emotions?

2. What do you do when you hear other believers speak almost endlessly about how bad things are getting? Do you remind them that Satan's doom is sealed and that things we see are only temporary? Or do you join in and begin complaining with them? What *should* you do in that case?
3. Have you ever heard the Holy Spirit speaking to you to take heart because the real truth is that Jesus is Lord and everything else is temporary? Is the Holy Spirit trying to assure you of this, but you keep getting caught up in the bad news you hear? What should you do differently to keep your focus on the winning side?

JUNE 18

The Guiding Ministry of the Holy Spirit

Howbeit, when he, the Spirit of truth is come,
he will guide you into all truth....
— John 16:13

In most Middle Eastern countries, ancient ruins are scattered throughout the land, dating from biblical times. To visit these sites, it is required that a person be accompanied by an "official guide." These guides are certified by the government and undergo a rigorous certification, which must be renewed annually. The process requires guides to receive ongoing education and training in a variety of subjects, such as history, art, and archeology, in addition to earning their initial degrees. Official guides are not simply individuals who snapped a "tour guide" badge on their shirt or jacket; they are highly trained specialists who invested years of study in order to obtain and maintain that hard-earned status.

To make a tour interesting for a group, a guide must know how to communicate effectively and give clear instructions concerning where to go, what to stay away from, and so on. Hiring good guides can be expensive because they have spent so many years studying and training. However, their expertise is invaluable. As they lead people through a site, tour guides impart information that can be obtained only through many years of studying — a commitment that most people obviously cannot make.

In many large, complex sites, such as the ancient ruins of Ephesus and Pergamum in modern-day Turkey, it would almost be foolish to try to see these sites without a certified guide. These sites are huge, and parts of the ancient roads are deteriorated, twisted, rocky, and potentially dangerous. In fact, there are so many paths to take that an uninformed person could easily get confused and lost along the way. However, with a good guide at your side, you can rest assured that you will not get hurt or lost as you explore, and you'll conclude your experience with a wonderful memory of a trip well executed.

With this example in mind, let's look at John 16:13, where Jesus told His disciples, "Howbeit, when he, the Spirit of truth is come, he will guide you into all truth...." In this verse, Jesus used the example of a tour guide to describe the guiding ministry of the Holy Spirit in our lives. Just as a guide leads a group through a historical site, the Holy Spirit wants to guide us through life.

The word "guide" in John 16:13 is the Greek word *odega* — a word that describes *a tour guide* or *one who would lead you on an excursion*. As we have seen, a tour guide is a professional who has gained an intimate knowledge of a site you want to see through years of dedication and experience. He knows all the shortcuts and all the points of interest, and he can relate its history in depth. Your willingness to allow the guide to lead and your willingness to follow his directions will save you from making mistakes and drawing incorrect conclusions about where you are, where you are headed, and what are you are seeing.

This Greek word *odega* describes the guiding ministry of the Holy Spirit in our lives. Jesus was informing us that if we are willing to listen to the Holy Spirit and to follow His instructions, He will act as a Guide for our lives. Like the tour guides discussed in the example above, the Holy Spirit knows what lies ahead of us. He knows the obstacles we should avoid; He sees our ultimate destination; and He knows God's plan for our lives down to the smallest detail. The Holy Spirit knows every route God desires for us to take — and if we are willing to follow the Spirit's leading, He will give us a wonderful and memorable experience along the path of life.

My friend, I want to tell you that the Holy Spirit deeply desires to guide you in life. If you'll let Him lead you, He will offer you sound guidance in every sphere of your life. If you listen to His voice, He will tell you the career you should choose, the person you should marry, and the place you should live. He is the only One who knows the future; therefore, He is the only One who is truly qualified to lead and guide you.

Divine guidance is one of the biggest challenges we face in the Christian life. However, Jesus explicitly said that the Holy Spirit is here to lead and guide us every step along the way. What a relief and security it affords us to know that God the Father has charged the Holy Spirit with the responsibility of leading and guiding us to the right place at the right time — every single time. And He also warns us *away from* certain people, places, and situations. This is His job! Without His direction, we are incapable of discerning where we should go in life, the people with whom we should surround ourselves, and the best timing for our endeavors.

However, in order for this to happen, we have to make an effort to listen to the Holy Spirit's voice and be willing to follow His instruction. If we will do that, we'll find that the Spirit of God is leading us, just as He did the apostles in the book of Acts!

Today I urge you to open your heart to the guiding ministry of the Holy Spirit. Trust that He is the Spirit of Truth who will not mislead you. "Take the hand" of the Holy Spirit and tell

Him from your heart: "Holy Spirit, I trust You from this moment forward to be my Guide every step of the way!"

MY PRAYER FOR TODAY

Holy Spirit, I open my heart to Your leading and guiding in life. I repent for foolishly having tried to lead myself through difficult decisions and questions, when you were always right there, wanting to lead me along the way. You know the plan of God for me down to the smallest detail, and from this time forward, I will do my best to consult You and to yield to Your guidance for my life. You know everything about me, my future, and which steps I need to take next. Rather than try to figure it all out on my own, I entrust myself to you as my official Guide to lead me each step of the way!

I pray this in Jesus' name!

MY CONFESSION FOR TODAY

I declare by faith that I am led by the Holy Spirit. He was sent to lead and direct me, and I am learning to hear His voice, to recognize His leading, and to allow Him to be the Senior Guide in my life. I know that as a result of being guided by the Spirit, my life is going to be more adventuresome and filled with less mistakes, for the Holy Spirit is the Spirit of Truth, and He will never lead me down a wrong path. Holy Spirit, I'm ready — let's get started today!

I declare this by faith in Jesus' name!

QUESTIONS FOR YOU TO CONSIDER

1. Can you think of a moment in your life when the Holy Spirit supernaturally led you through difficult decisions and questions? When was that experience, and have you ever shared it with anyone else?
2. How do you recognize the guidance of the Holy Spirit? If someone asked you to describe what it is like to be led by the Holy Spirit, how would you put it into words? Why don't you practice describing it so you'll be ready to help someone else understand what it is like to receive guidance from the Holy Spirit?
3. What situation are you facing right now that requires supernatural direction? How will you let the Holy Spirit guide you down the path that lies before you?

The Holy Spirit is the only One who knows the future;
therefore, He is the only One
who is truly qualified to lead and guide you.

JUNE 19

The Prophetic Ministry of the Holy Spirit

Howbeit, when he, the Spirit of truth is come,
he will guide you into all truth: for he shall not speak
of himself; but whatsoever he shall hear, that shall he speak:
and he will shew you things to come.
— John 16:13

There is no second-guessing when it comes to the leadership of the Holy Spirit. That's what Jesus stressed as He continued teaching His disciples about the ministry of the Holy Spirit. In John 16:13, Jesus said, "Howbeit, when he, the Spirit of Truth is come, he will guide you into all truth: for He shall not speak of Himself; but whatsoever He shall hear, that shall He speak: and He will *shew* you things to come."

The word "shew" in this verse is the Greek word *anagello*, which means *to announce* and describes *a vivid showing* or *a pronouncing of events.* So we see that part of the ministry of the Holy Spirit is *to announce* future events to us — and to show them to us with great clarity. The Holy Spirit does *not* portray a blurry picture of the future. If we listen to Him, He will vividly show us things to come so we can plan our lives according to His will.

This aspect of the Holy Spirit's ministry is evident in nearly every book of the Bible. For example, when the apostle Paul described the events that will occur in society at the end of the age (*see* 2 Timothy 3), he was writing under the prophetic ministry of the Holy Spirit. Likewise, the Holy Spirit is the One who imparted the vivid details to the apostle John concerning end-time events recorded in the book of Revelation.

However, this "revealing" ministry of the Holy Spirit is not relegated to Scripture. Jesus was speaking to *every* believer when He spoke of the Holy Spirit showing us things to come. If what Jesus taught is true — *and it is* — a significant part of the Holy Spirit's ministry is to reveal details about future events. He wants to prophetically speak to you and prepare you for your future. He wants to show you details about your future and the future of your family that He believes you need to know.

Open your heart today to the revealing work of the Holy Spirit. If anyone wants you to be prepared, it is the Holy Spirit, your Helper and Coach. He does not want you to be taken off guard by *any* situation you might encounter in life.

Simply avail yourself to Him by spending time in prayer every day without distraction. Linger in God's presence long enough to get your mind quiet and your heart open to hear. Then ask Him, "Holy Spirit, show me things to come in my life, in my business, and in my family. Reveal to me what I need to know to navigate every future situation that I will face with Your wisdom. I purpose to follow Your leading every step of the way."

MY PRAYER FOR TODAY

Holy Spirit, today I receive You as One who speaks into my life to show me things to come that I really need to know. I've tried hard to figure out things on my own. Forgive me for not developing my trust in You the way I should have in this area of my life. Starting right now, I ask You to fulfill the prophetic role of Your ministry in my life and to show me things to come. I know You want me to know how to plan my life, how to circumvent demonic attacks, and how to be prepared for every phase of my journey in You. Your Word promises that as I keep my spiritual ear tuned to You, You will show me exactly what I need to know about every step in front of me. I believe You and I gratefully receive Your ministry in my life day by day.

I pray this in Jesus' name!

MY CONFESSION FOR TODAY

I confess that my ears are open and that my spirit is attuned to the voice of the Holy Spirit. Jesus said that He would show me things to come, and by faith, I embrace the prophetic ministry of the Holy Spirit in my life to show me everything I need to know about my future. I am not left to figure anything out on my own. The Holy Spirit speaks to my heart about things to come. I listen to His directions, and I make plans to do what He shows me. This spares me wasted time, helps me avoid mistakes, and puts me on a solid path that leads to His highest will for my life.

I declare this by faith in Jesus' name!

QUESTIONS FOR YOU TO CONSIDER

1. One of the Holy Spirit's roles is to show you things to come. Have you learned to let the Holy Spirit speak prophetically to you about your future, or have you just tried to figure it all out on your own?
2. Can you think of a time when the Holy Spirit *did* tell you something about your future and you believed Him — and as a result, it gave you direction and saved you lots of valuable time and effort?
3. Can you think of a time when the Holy Spirit clearly spoke to you, impressing your spirit with vital information, and you discounted and ignored it — only to understand later that it really was the Holy Spirit trying to show you something about your future that you really needed to know?

If anyone wants you to be prepared,
it is the Holy Spirit, your Helper and Coach.

JUNE 20

The Glorifying Ministry of the Holy Spirit

He shall glorify me: for he shall receive
of mine, and shall shew it unto you.
— John 16:14

Do you find the ability to express yourself in worship to God *easy* or *difficult*? Is it easy for you to lift your arms and audibly worship the Lord, or do you feel self-conscious and think about the possibility that people might be watching you? Do you hesitate to worship in the presence of others but find it easy to worship at home when no one is watching?

As Jesus prepared to depart from this world and sat in that upper room teaching His disciples about the Holy Spirit and His various roles, one of these roles He stressed that the Holy Spirit would carry out is *the ministry of glorifying Jesus*. Jesus said in John 16:14: "He shall glorify me: for he shall receive of mine, and shall shew it unto you."

The word "glorify" is the Greek word *doxadzo*, which can be translated in a variety of ways depending on its context. It can be rendered *to extol, to praise, to magnify, to worship, to give honor, to give adulation*, or *to express one's fame or repute*, and in John 16:14, it actually encompasses the full range of these meanings.

Thus, when Jesus said, "He [the Holy Spirit] shall glorify me…," He expressly meant that the Holy Spirit's role is to *extol, magnify, glorify*, and *worship* Him. In fact, one of the Holy Spirit's chief roles is to give *adulation* and *fame* to Jesus — to *glorify* that name that is exalted above every other name (*see* Philippians 2:9). The Spirit of God doesn't seek to draw attention to Himself in any way. Rather, He points everyone toward Jesus and leads us in rapturous worship of our exalted Savior.

Because the Holy Spirit is an invisible, non-material Spirit Being, He cannot glorify Jesus in the way the Lord desires without using someone as a vessel through which to work. By now, I'm sure you can guess that the vessel He chooses is the one in which He lives — *you*! How does the Holy Spirit fulfill His responsibility to glorify Jesus through you? He heals the sick, casts out demons, leads lost people to a saving knowledge of Jesus, and so on. However, one of the most effective, magnificent avenues through which He glorifies Jesus is in those moments when your heart is full, your hands are raised, and your whole being is caught up in worshiping Jesus the Lord.

By His very nature, the Holy Spirit is a *Glorifier* and a *Worshiper*, and when He is free to work in your life as a believer, it's very obvious because you *will* glorify Jesus. If you will allow the Holy

Spirit to be loosed inside your life, you will find yourself wanting to throw your hands in the air, move your feet, and lift your voice to Heaven with praise and worship — completely oblivious to who might be watching or judging you. The Holy Spirit seeks to glorify Jesus in every aspect of your life, including your conversations, your behavior, and your relationships. He wants your lips to be filled with *Jesus, Jesus, Jesus.*

The Holy Spirit's primary task is to reveal Jesus to you — and He'll take you to Jesus on a level that you've never known before. He's just waiting for you to surrender and to take the plunge into this spiritual experience. Believe me when I tell you that you'll never be the same.

If you've had a hard time abandoning yourself in worship in the past, today is the day for you to begin. I urge you to take a moment right now and pray, "Holy Spirit, You are a Worshiper, so I yield to You. I ask You to help me remove all my inhibition as I do. I ask You not only to glorify Jesus in my behavior, my conversations, and my life, but right now in a time of worship, I ask You to glorify Jesus through me."

If you prayed this prayer, just yield to the Holy Spirit and watch what He will do in you. Right now while no one is watching, lift your arms to Heaven and begin to express your thanksgiving to Jesus. Allow the Holy Spirit to fill you and take you into a realm of worship that you've never known before.

The Holy Spirit's primary task is to reveal Jesus to you — and if you let Him, He'll take you to Jesus on a level that you've never known before. He is there with you in this moment, and He's just waiting for you to surrender and to take the plunge into this spiritual experience. *The time and place for you to start is right now in the privacy of your own home.* He's waiting for you — *so why not start today?*

MY PRAYER FOR TODAY

Father, I thank You that the Holy Spirit reveals Jesus — and I ask You to help me abandon my inhibitions and enter into the freedom of worship. I know that there are realms of worship that I have never experienced, but today I am opening myself to those realms and asking that the Holy Spirit unleash worship in me as never before. I surrender myself to be an instrument of worship and, Holy Spirit, I ask You to take me on an adventure as I learn to worship Jesus as You reveal Him to me on a level I've never experienced before.

I pray this in Jesus' name!

MY CONFESSION FOR TODAY

I declare that my entire body — all that I am — is an instrument that the Holy Spirit uses to magnify and to exalt the name and Person of Jesus Christ. Inhibitions have no part in my worship. I am free to express my adoration and love for Jesus — the One who is higher than all others and whose name is more highly exalted than any other name. Inhibitions must go from me in Jesus' name, for I am liberated to worship Jesus in the power of the Holy Spirit!

I declare this by faith in Jesus' name!

QUESTIONS FOR YOU TO CONSIDER

1. Has been there a moment when you threw off all restraint and worshiped Jesus in the power of the Holy Spirit? When did that experience occur, and has anything stopped you from entering into that type of worship again?
2. What happened inside you when you threw off those restraints and fully entered into the worship of Jesus? What did the Holy Spirit do inside you that changed you forever?
3. What would you say to someone who has never experienced freedom in worship? What has it done for you, and what will it do for them?

JUNE 21

Spiritual Adultery!

Ye adulterers and adulteresses,
know ye not that the friendship of the world
is enmity with God?
Whosoever therefore will be a friend
of the world is the enemy of God.
— James 4:4

Up to this point, we have covered Jesus' teaching on the ministry of the Holy Spirit in John 14, 15, and 16, and we've learned how to develop a more intimate and personal relationship with the Holy Spirit. Now we're going to shift our focus to another vital aspect of the Holy Spirit's ministry found in the New Testament.

As you will see in the days to come, the Holy Spirit lives within us like a Divine Lover. When believers allow the things of the world to usurp the place that should belong only to Him, the Holy Spirit — like a violated spouse — feels hurt and grief. It's therefore vital that we gain a deeper understanding of how sin affects the indwelling Holy Spirit so we can purpose to change any permissive attitude toward sin that may linger in our lives and to live holier and more consecrated before Him in love.

In James 4:4 and 5, James referred to the nature of the believer's relationship with Christ and the indwelling presence of the Holy Spirit in the believer's heart. He wrote, "Ye adulterers and adulteresses, know ye not that the friendship of the world is enmity with God? Whosoever therefore will be a friend of the world is the enemy of God."

Throughout the New Testament, believers are most often referred to as "brothers and sisters." Yet here James referred to his readers as "adulterers" and "adulteresses." Imagine if a great spiritual leader wrote to you and called you an adulterer or adulteress! This is especially strong language when you consider that James was writing to Jewish believers, who could have been stoned for committing adultery. In fact, James couldn't have said anything more shocking or outrageous to his audience! However, this adultery he was referring to was not a physical act, but rather a *spiritual adultery* that they had committed by giving their hearts to things other than Jesus Christ.

The Greek word for "adultery" is *moichalis*, and it carries all kind of connotations. *Unfaithfulness*, *impurity*, and *violating a commitment to marriage* are just a few. This word paints the picture of a wounded spouse who feels rejected, betrayed, misled, and deceived because the sanctity of his or her marriage relationship was recklessly thrown away by the act of adultery. All of these ideas are embedded in the Greek word *moichalis*.

So what had these believers done to be addressed in such a way? James explained, "Ye adulterers and adulteresses, know ye know not that *friendship with the world is enmity with God...*?"

To illustrate James' point, let me share an example from my own life. In the early years of our marriage, Denise and I led a single-adult ministry in a large denominational church. During this time, we developed a program to help single adults who had recently gone through a divorce. As we listened to the concerns of these precious believers, we discovered that most of these people felt like they were outcasts from the Church. So we made it a point to open our hearts and emphasize "life after divorce" as a primary message of our ministry. Soon newly divorced people came to us from all over to receive ministry, love, acceptance, and healing. It was one of the most gratifying, yet troublesome, periods of ministry we had ever experienced.

It was gratifying to see people who had been so rejected and wounded being healed by the love of Jesus Christ. However, it was very troublesome to hear the pain many of these believers felt as a result of being betrayed by someone they loved and trusted. Day after day, we would sit and listen as each one shared his or her story. Out of approximately 100 cases, nearly all sounded similar — so similar, in fact, that eventually I could almost finish most of their stories for them.

Again and again, these emotionally bruised people lamented, "I just don't understand how he could do that to me. After all these years of being faithful to him, raising our children together, and working to help him through school, I don't understand how he could hurt me like this." Or, "How could she do this to me after I've given her so much? I gave her my love, my attention, all that I knew to do. How could she do this to me?"

These intense, painful emotions are exactly what Jesus felt toward the believers James addressed in James 4:4. After all that He had done for them, they had been unfaithful to their sacred relationship with Him as the Bride of Christ by embracing a sinful relationship with the world.

In tomorrow's *Sparkling Gem*, I will explain in depth what the believers did to prompt James to refer to them as "adulteresses" so that you never have to cross that line yourself. But today, why don't you take a moment to look inwardly and carefully examine your life. Do you see anything that would cause the Holy Spirit to feel violated by your actions? After all He has done for you — regenerating you, filling you, and sanctifying you — I *know* that you would never want to intentionally cause the Spirit of God pain and sorrow. So make sure that you are living in such a way that will always give Him pleasure, not grief!

MY PRAYER FOR TODAY

Holy Spirit, I repent and ask You to forgive me for all the times I've walked too close to the world and violated Your holy indwelling presence by allowing sinful actions and attitudes to persist in my life. I am truly sorry, and today I repent before You. I ask You to strengthen me with Your mighty power to walk with a higher discernment and with the spiritual awareness to know when I am doing something that is grievous to You. I want to honor Your presence and honor You by the way I treat You with my life.

I pray this in Jesus' name!

MY CONFESSION FOR TODAY

I confess that I live a life that is pleasing to the Holy Spirit. When I do something that hints of displeasure to Him, I quickly recognize it and repent of it. I do not permit wrong attitudes and actions to rule me. Instead, I surrender to the fruit of the Holy Spirit, and it produces the life and character of Christ in my own life. Day by day, I am becoming more sensitive and spiritually aware of the things that displease the Lord, and I am learning to walk a higher walk in Him.

I declare this by faith in Jesus' name!

QUESTIONS FOR YOU TO CONSIDER

1. Are there any areas of your life that are out of sync with the Holy Spirit's indwelling presence? What are those areas? If you are aware of them, is there a reason you have tolerated them instead of repenting and getting your heart right with the Holy Spirit?
2. When the Holy Spirit is grieved because of our attitudes and actions, our own spirits are grieved as well. Have you felt grief and sorrow in your own heart when you did things that were displeasing to the Lord?
3. What are some of the areas in which you've made progress and no longer habitually repeat sins as you once did? If you've had victories, you need to remember them and thank God for them!

JUNE 22

Friendship With the World

Ye adulterers and adulteresses,
know ye not that friendship with the world
is enmity with God...?
— James 4:4

As we saw yesterday, James began James 4:4 by calling his readers "adulterers" and "adulteresses" — which is strong language to use when addressing believers! James obviously wanted to get their attention. In some way, they had violated their relationship with Christ. They had been unfaithful; they had crossed the line and given a part of their hearts and souls to the world around them. By calling them "adulterers" and "adulteresses," James was saying that whatever they were doing was the equivalent of *spiritual adultery.*

James probingly asked his readers, "...Know ye not that the friendship of the world is enmity with God...?" The word "know" is *oida.* It refers to firsthand knowledge that these believers should have already possessed. In this case, it means, "Don't you know?" "Don't you understand?" "Haven't you grasped by now?" Then he continued, "...Know ye not that friendship with the world is enmity with God...?"

The word "friendship" is the word *philia*, a noun taken from the word *phileo*. The word *phileo* describes *affection*, *attachment*, *devotion*, *endearment*, or *familiarity*. It can be used to portray the *intense sentiment* between two or more people. It was most often used to denote a relationship that was *dear*, *precious*, and *valuable*. In fact, it carried such a feeling of *endearing affection* that the word *philema* comes from it, which is the Greek word meaning *to kiss*. There is no doubt James meant that these believers' tie to the world had never been fully severed. In some manner they were still being attracted to the world — to such an extent that its influence was encroaching on their relationship with the Lord.

Worldliness is a serious thing with the Lord, and it tries to wrap its arms around all of us. If we begin edging in on worldliness with the way we live our lives, the Holy Spirit will warn us to break that wrong relationship with the world and return to Him.

If you want to have a quick wakeup call, just take a little time to think of the things you tolerate in your life today that you would never have tolerated ten years ago. For example, do you watch movies today that you would have considered a sin ten years ago? Are you more permissive in your thinking about sin now than you used to be? Are there any areas of your life where you used to be more on fire and less compromising than you are right now? Do you pray and witness as you much as you once did? You may as well be honest with God because He knows your real spiritual condition anyway.

You can't bluff God by making up excuses. At least when you're honest with God, you put yourself in a position where He can deal with your heart. Once you're being truthful with yourself and with Him, you can begin to repent and return to being on fire for Him the way He desires you to be.

We could all admit worldliness in some area of our lives, but if we don't deal with the areas as the Holy Spirit leads us, over time we will become more conformed to the world than to Jesus Christ. Being a friend of the world doesn't happen overnight. It takes time. It's a very slow, seductive, and methodical process as our thinking, behavior, and outlook on life grows to look more and more similar to the world than to that of Jesus.

The Bible says that a Christian who is entangled with the world is at "enmity" with God. The word translated "enmity" is the Greek word *echthra*, meaning *hostility* or *enmity*. Allowing the world to encroach on your relationship with God is a very serious thing in His view. The word "enmity" tells us that this is very serious!

Today I want to ask you: *Are you on fire for Jesus as you once were?* Or have the things of the world slowly begun to douse the flames that once burned so brightly for the Lord? Are you free of the world, or has its attraction lured and seduced you from Christ? Would Jesus say that you are completely committed to Him, or would He say you are sharing His rightful place with other things? *Who or what is the central focus of your life?* If you consider yourself to be a serious Christian, these are very important questions for you to answer today!

MY PRAYER FOR TODAY

Father, I want to burn brightly and live on fire for You. I ask You to search my heart. If worldliness has found a place in my heart and soul, today I repent of it. I turn toward You to walk in holiness and sanctification unto You. I can see how worldliness can slowly creep up on me, and I ask You to forgive me for allowing the lure of the world to affect me. It wasn't intentional. I repent for allowing myself to become distracted and for not keeping first things first. I got busy and involved, and before I knew it, I had sunk to a spiritual low that I detest. I ask You to refire me and help me return to my first love and to keep You in that position for the rest of my life.

I pray this in Jesus' name!

MY CONFESSION FOR TODAY

I declare by faith that I am on fire and burning brightly for the Lord. I live in the world, but I am not a part of it. It has no lure on my heart and soul. Every day I am growing more passionate to know Christ practically, through experience for myself, and to become more fully committed to Him. Jesus Christ is the Object of my heart's desire — and I refuse to ever live the kind of life that would make Him want to say I am guilty of spiritual adultery.

I declare this by faith, in Jesus' name!

QUESTIONS FOR YOU TO CONSIDER

1. Are you burning as brightly as you once burned for the Lord? If not, what happened to cause you to lose the fire that once burned so brilliantly in your heart?
2. In order for you to return to that place of spiritual fire and passion for Christ, what do you need to change or sever from your life? The Holy Spirit has already been speaking to you about it, so it shouldn't be hard for you to answer this question. So what do you need to change?
3. If you were asked to describe a worldly Christian, how would you do it?

JUNE 23

Grieve Not the Holy Spirit

And grieve not the holy Spirit of God, whereby ye
are sealed unto the day of redemption.
— Ephesians 4:30

Today I want to talk about grieving the Holy Spirit, which I am certain none of us wants to do. That's why it's so important for us to know what the Bible says about grieving the Holy Spirit — so we know how to avoid that pitfall! So let's look at Ephesians 4:30, which says, "And grieve not the holy Spirit of God, whereby ye are sealed unto the day of redemption."

I want to especially draw your attention to the word "grieve" in this verse, which is the Greek word *lupete*. This was a word that described *pain* or someone that was *wounded* by someone else. It could be used to depict the emotions of a betrayed spouse — feeling deceived, lied to, misled, hurt, wounded, and abused. All of these portray the emotions of a spouse who has discovered that her or her mate has been unfaithful and feels very *hurt, grieved,* and *wounded.* The word *lupete* would describe all of those painful emotions.

We find the word *lupete* was used by Paul to describe how we affect the indwelling Holy Spirit when we embrace worldliness. There is no doubt as to what Paul was telling us. When we cease to make our relationship with the Holy Spirit the number-one priority in our lives and let other things take His rightful place, it hurts and deeply grieves Him. After all He has done for us, it is simply grievous to the One who dwells within us whenever we do anything to yield our hearts and souls to worldliness.

The Holy Spirit is the One who lives in us, leads us, guides us, teaches us, reminds us, comforts us, seals us, sanctifies us, empowers us, and works to produce the character of Christ in us.

He has been sent to reveal the will of God, which is the mind of Christ and to give us the victory Christ won through the Cross and His resurrection. The Holy Spirit is here for us. *That is why He was sent.* Therefore, when we ignore Him, turn a deaf ear to Him, or consistently disobey what He nudges us to do, it grieves Him. It would grieve you, too, if *you* were the Holy Spirit.

But let's be even more *specific* about what grieves the Holy Spirit. The verses preceding and following this one about grieving Him say to put away "lying" (v. 25), "let not the sun go down upon your wrath (v. 26), "neither give place to the devil" (v. 27), "steal no more" (v. 28), "let no corrupt communication proceed out of your mouth" (v. 29), and, finally, "let all bitterness, and wrath, and anger, and clamour, and evil speaking, be put away from you, with all malice (v. 31). *All* these things "grieve" the Holy Spirit.

Unfortunately, Paul was speaking to Christians when he wrote these verses. That means *Christians* were doing these things! They were lying, holding on to grudges, giving place to the devil, stealing, talking evil about one another, giving bitterness a place in their hearts, being angry, and having malice toward each other. No wonder the Holy Spirit was grieved!

The fact that Paul used the word "grieve" — the Greek word *lupete* — tells us that the Holy Spirit felt wounded by these believers. He felt like a spouse who was being dragged through the mud by an unfaithful mate. After doing all that He had done within them, how could they now give in to their flesh in such an ungodly manner?

We need to remember that Someone lives inside us whose name is the Holy Spirit. The reason He is called the Holy Spirit is that He is holy. Romans 1:4 actually calls Him "the spirit of holiness." That is who He is, and that is what He has come to produce in our lives.

You would never think of throwing mud and garbage all over a beautiful cathedral. Your conscience wouldn't bear the guilt of knowing that you had personally desecrated a finely decorated church building! Yet the temple of the Holy Spirit called *you* is much more valuable to God than a fine church building!

The Holy Spirit doesn't live in buildings. He lives in each of *us* as believers. Yet in spite of this, we throw garbage into our lives and drag Him through the mud, never thinking of how it must grieve the Spirit of Holiness who lives inside us.

According to Ephesians 4, the sins that we find most difficult to resist are usually inward attitudes such as grudges, bitterness, anger, or malice. But we shouldn't harbor these attitudes in our lives for even a minute, if for no other reason than because we know they grieve the Holy Spirit.

The next time you want to hold resentment in your heart toward someone, ask yourself the question, *Is this attitude going to grieve the Holy Spirit in my life?* If you simply make yourself more aware of the Spirit's indwelling presence, it will help you change the way you think and live. It will most definitely help you think before you talk and act!

Remember that the Holy Spirit lives inside you. What you do in your life today, you do to Him as well. Where you go today, you take Him with you. When you go to the movies, He goes with you. What you look at on the Internet, He watches with you. When you choose to sin, you are dragging Him with you through that filth. Do you really want to grieve Him? Of course not! So make a decision today to never forget — the Holy Spirit lives inside you, and He deserves your utmost respect and honor in all you say and do!

MY PRAYER FOR TODAY

Holy Spirit, I repent for the times that I have subjected You to ugliness and ungodliness that I have tolerated in my life. I am truly sorry. It is my heart's desire to honor You and Your holy presence in all I do and say. After all the wonderful things You have done in me to change me, to restore me, and to make my life better, I am so sorry that I have ever done anything that would bring pain or sorrow to You. I repent — and that means I am changing my behavior, and I am going to start right now.

I pray this in Jesus' name!

MY CONFESSION FOR TODAY

I confess that I live continually aware of the Holy Spirit's indwelling presence in my life. I am very aware that He lives inside me — so much so that this realization impacts how I live each day. Choosing to deliberately give Him my attention helps me live in such a way that my life brings honor to Him. I am so thankful for my salvation and the infilling of the Holy Spirit and for the daily power He provides to me. The last thing I'd ever want to do is to bring pain and sorrow to the Holy Spirit because I tolerated ungodly attitudes or behaviors in my life. I declare that from this moment onward, I am going to live with the consciousness that the spirit of holiness lives in me!

I declare this by faith, in Jesus' name!

QUESTIONS FOR YOU TO CONSIDER

1. Have you ever been aware of a moment when you brought pain to the Holy Spirit by your attitudes or actions? Have you knowingly done something you knew was wrong — and you knew it caused the Holy Spirit to be grieved?
2. What actions do you need to take in order to stop whatever you've been doing that brings Him pain?
3. If you were advising another believer about what to do in these cases, what advice would you give him or her? In what ways can you apply the same advice to yourself?

Remember that the Holy Spirit lives inside you.
What you do in your life today,
you do to Him as well.

JUNE 24

The Permanent Indweller of Your Heart

Do ye think that the scripture saith in vain,
The spirit that dwelleth in us lusteth to envy?
— James 4:5

According to James 4:5, the Holy Spirit came into our hearts as a Permanent Indweller. It says, "Do ye think that the scripture saith in vain, The spirit that *dwelleth* in us lusteth to envy?"

The Greek word for "dwelleth" is *katoikidzo*, a compound of the words *kata* and *oikos*. The word *kata* carries the idea of *settling down*, and the word *oikos* is the word for a *house*. Taken together, the new word means *to take up residency* or *to dwell in a house*. This word carries the idea of *residing permanently*. In other words, this word would never describe a transient or one who came to live in a place only temporarily. This is the picture of a person who has settled into a home with no intention of *ever* leaving.

In other words, when the Holy Spirit came to live in you, it wasn't for a short period of time. When He came, He came to *stay*. From the moment you made Jesus your Savior and Lord, the Holy Spirit made your heart His permanent home. He has, so to speak, hung His own pictures on the walls, moved His furniture in, and settled down into a nice, big comfortable chair. He has no intention of ever moving out to leave your heart vacant while He finds somewhere else to live.

Think of that! The Holy Spirit doesn't come only to visit occasionally. Your heart is His *home*. Meditate on this truth, and determine to live each moment of the day with a deep sense of awareness of the Holy Spirit's indwelling presence. Welcome His fellowship; talk to Him; and yield to Him as He prays through you and gives you guidance and direction. A deeper realization of the Permanent Indweller who lives on the inside of you will help you stay on track and continually move forward in your walk in Christ!

MY PRAYER FOR TODAY

Holy Spirit, I am so thankful that my heart is Your home! I worship You for taking up residency inside of me! The thought is almost too glorious for my mind to comprehend! I welcome Your fellowship. Teach me how to talk with You, yield to You, and cooperate with You as You pray through me, giving me guidance and direction every day. I ask You to please open my understanding to a deeper realization of Your permanent indwelling so I stay on track spiritually and continually move forward in my walk in Christ!

I pray this in Jesus' name!

MY CONFESSION FOR TODAY

I am thankful to declare that the Holy Spirit is not a guest who occasionally comes to visit me. He moved into my recreated spirit to permanently abide with me. He regenerated and renovated me, and He brought His power and glory along with Him when He moved inside me. I am the permanent home for the Spirit of God.

I declare this by faith in Jesus' name!

QUESTIONS FOR YOU TO CONSIDER

1. Since your heart is the home of the Holy Spirit, what do you need to do to make Him feel more comfortable there? What changes do you need to make to accommodate His holy presence?
2. So many times I've heard songs that invite the Holy Spirit to come and visit us, but that isn't even scriptural! He lives *inside* us. We are not a temporary place He comes to visit. Can you think of songs that might be unscriptural along these lines that we sang with all of our hearts in the past, not realizing we were singing unscriptural songs?
3. A guest in a hotel doesn't have many rights, but when you *live* in a house permanently, it becomes *your home* and you have rights there. What kind of rights does the Holy Spirit have as a Permanent Indweller in your heart?

JUNE 25

A Divine Lover

Do you think that the scripture saith in vain,
The spirit that dwelleth in us lusteth to envy?
— James 4:5

In yesterday's *Sparkling Gem*, we looked at the word "dwelleth" in James 4:5. It says, "Do you think that the scripture saith in vain, the spirit that dwelleth in us lusteth to envy?" The next word in this verse that we must consider is the word "lusteth."

For the most part, the word *lust* has a very bad connotation in our minds. We think of sexual lust, for example, as something that must be eradicated from our lives. We think of a greedy kind of lust as an excessive desire for material possessions. Lust is something we don't want to admit exists in our lives. On the contrary, we think of lust as something we want to get rid of.

But James tells us that the Holy Spirit has *lust* — and because He is the Spirit of holiness (*see* Romans 1:4), we know that the lust of the Holy Spirit must be a healthy, godly kind. Understanding this point is so important that we must stop and see exactly what James is trying to say to us here.

The word "lusteth" is taken from the Greek word *epipothei*, which is a compound of two Greek words — *epi* and *pothei*. The word *epi* adds *force* to the word, and the word *pothei* means *an intense desire* or *yearning*. When compounded, the new word describes *an intense, excessive yearning for something*. Usually this word is used to indicate something that is morally wrong or sinful.

For example, this word could be used to picture a drug addict who daily requires a new "fix"— enough drugs to carry him into the next day. When the last fix wears off and his body is desperately crying out for a new infusion of chemicals, the drug addict nearly doubles over in pain, yearning for the next injection. Everything in him is focused on getting those chemicals. He is *consumed* with his need for more. The word *epipothei* could describe that kind of desperate yearning.

The word *epipothei* could also be used to describe the behavior of a sexual addict. Going from one sexual experience to the next, he is driven to keep going and going. In this case, the desire is so abnormal that enough is never enough. The desire can never be satisfied. People with such an addiction are raging with lust to have more and more sexual encounters of some type.

It is interesting that James would use the word *epipothei* — translated "lusteth" — to describe the Holy Spirit in this verse. Why would James do this? Does the Holy Spirit truly lust? Why would James use such a word?

It's important to understand that this word "lust" doesn't refer to something bad unless it is used in a bad connotation. It can be used in a good way. James 4:5 demonstrates this truth by telling us that the Holy Spirit Himself "lusteth." In other words, there is something that the Holy Spirit is *yearning after* — something He *passionately longs to possess*. One expositor has translated this verse to read, *"The Spirit that dwelleth in us has an intense yearning…."* But what does the Holy Spirit yearn for so strongly?

After all the Holy Spirit has done in us, it should be no great shock to discover that He is in love with each believer He indwells. The fact that the Spirit of God views our mixing and mingling with the world as adultery should alert us to the intense love and affection He has for us.

The Holy Spirit was sent to be our Helper and Comforter. Although He does many other things, His primary job is to help us find Jesus Christ, help us grow as Christians, help us witness, help us worship, help us understand God's Word, and so on.

Everything the Holy Spirit is to us — our Indweller, our Sealer, our Sanctifier, and the Power of our new life in Christ — is encompassed in His deep love for us. His work, His attention, His gifts, His power, and His Word are all directed toward us. We are the objects of His love and affection. As a Divine Lover who lives on the inside of us, His love and affection are single-heartedly focused on us. He passionately yearns to fulfill His responsibility to the Father to help, to teach, to guide, and to empower us.

James used the word *epipothei* to describe the Holy Spirit's intense desire to possess us and fill us. This word emphatically means the Holy Spirit wants more and more of us. When it comes to you and me, He can never get enough!

I have walked with God for many decades. Over the years, I have learned one important thing about my relationship with God: It doesn't matter how much I surrender to His sanctifying power today, by tomorrow He will be asking me to surrender more. Every second, every minute, every day, every week, and every year that passes by, my eyes are illuminated to new areas of my life that have never been surrendered, and each time the Holy Spirit asks me to yield those areas to His control.

During the altar call when I was saved, the congregation was singing the famous song "I Surrender All." Ever since that time, I've been surrendering all as the Holy Spirit convicts me and shows me areas where I've never fully surrendered. I first called Jesus "Lord" decades ago, but I'm still learning to accept His Lordship in various areas of my life. It doesn't matter how much I think I've surrendered or how yielded I think I've become, there is always more to surrender and more He desires to possess of my life.

Likewise, the Holy Spirit desires to possess you — *all of you*. This desire is so intense that it almost appears excessive compared to natural, human lust. He is absolutely focused on changing you, empowering you, conforming you to the image of Jesus Christ, and helping you fulfill God's plan for your life.

The amazing thing is that the Holy Spirit dwells within each of us as believers, thinking of and concentrating on each of us all at the same time! He is always looking for ways to help us in our walk with God. The Holy Spirit is consumed with a flaming, passionate desire to fill us up with His love and affection and to possess ever more of us.

Let the Holy Spirit love you! Let Him control you! Let Him exercise His authority in your life! Let Him flood you with His divine desire! Every intention He has for you is good, holy, and pure. How can you go wrong by surrendering your life, your mind, your family, your spouse, your children, your business, your ministry, your actions, and your behavior — everything that you are and everything you have — to the Holy Spirit?

The Holy Spirit "dwelleth" in us, and He "lusteth" for us. Meditate deeply on these two truths, and you will come to understand in a more profound way than you ever have before what it means to have the Spirit of Almighty God Himself permanently abiding within you and passionately yearning for you.

The Holy Spirit will *never* be satisfied with a shallow fellowship; He is in constant pursuit of true communion with you. So make a decision today that from this day forward, you will start satisfying the Holy Spirit's passionate yearning for you to know Him intimately on a deeper, more sustained level than you ever have before!

MY PRAYER FOR TODAY

Father, I thank You that the Holy Spirit is absolutely focused on changing me, empowering me, and conforming me to the image of Jesus Christ as He helps me fulfill God's plan for my life. I am amazed by the Holy Spirit's ability to think of and concentrate on each of us all the time as He continually looks for ways to help each of us in our walk with God. I surrender every area of my life to You today, even areas I've never surrendered before. And tomorrow when You reveal other areas I need to surrender, I'll surrender those areas as well. I know the Holy Spirit wants to fully occupy my heart and my life — and I am ready to yield!

I pray this in Jesus' name!

MY CONFESSION FOR TODAY

I confess that I am surrendering more and more of my life to the Holy Spirit every day I live. Every day I am seeing new areas that need to be surrendered, and with the help of the Holy Spirit and the grace of God, I am surrendering those areas. I will not stop surrendering as long as I live on this earth, because I know that every day, the Holy Spirit will show me another area I need to yield to Him. With His help, I will give Him greater access to every part of my life and being so He can have full, unhindered expression through my life to the glory of God the Father!

I declare this by faith, in Jesus' name!

QUESTIONS FOR YOU TO CONSIDER

1. Can you think of areas you've never surrendered to the Holy Spirit's sanctifying power? What are those areas? Wouldn't it be wise for you to make a list so you could begin to pray over those areas of your life in which you know the Holy Spirit is asking you to more fully surrender to the Lordship of Jesus Christ?
2. What did you learn about the "lust" of the Holy Spirit by reading this *Sparkling Gem*? Please take a few minutes to think through this question. It's important, because it will help you identify what the Holy Spirit really wants.
3. I don't know about you, but every day I am becoming more aware of areas I've never surrendered. I thought I had surrendered all to Jesus when I got saved. But the older I get and the more mature I become, I realize there is so much more to surrender. What about you? What areas has the Holy Spirit pinpointed in your life over the past months that He has asked you to more fully surrender to God?

JUNE 26

The Desire of the Holy Spirit

Do ye think that the scripture saith in vain,
The spirit that dwelleth in us lusteth to envy?
— James 4:5

Imagine the emotions of a young man who discovers someone else has captured the heart of his sweetheart. That's the same feeling James was describing when he wrote, "The spirit that dwelleth in us lusteth to envy." In the last two *Sparkling Gems*, we've seen how the Holy Spirit dwells in us and passionately yearns for us. But today, let's look further at the word "envy" to see what it means in this particular verse.

This word "envy" comes from the Greek word *phthonos*, which was frequently used in literature from the New Testament period, thus enabling us to know precisely what it means. The word *phthonos* means *jealousy* — an emotion so strong that it tends toward taking vengeance upon someone. The young man who lost his lover feels jealous and has a deep desire for his former relationship to be restored. He also most likely bears some malice toward the romantic thief. He is envious of the relationship that has replaced the one he used to have with the one whom he loves and desires to have again.

This should make James 4:5 clear to us. The Holy Spirit is a Lover. He is preoccupied with us. He wants to possess us totally, and He passionately desires our affection to also be set on Him. When we walk and talk like unbelievers and give our lives to natural pursuits, the Holy Spirit feels like a lover who has been robbed. He feels jealous for His relationship with us to be restored. He has divine malice for the worldliness that has usurped His role in our lives. And He is filled with a godly envy to see things put back the way they should be.

When you put all three words together — *dwelleth*, *lusteth*, and *envy* — this paints quite a picture. The Holy Spirit is not a passive partner. He *aggressively* and *actively* pursues us. When we give a piece of ourselves to something or someone else's control, He wants to seize it and bring it back under His divine control. He even has godly malice toward our preoccupation with other things.

**With all of this in mind,
James 4:5 could be read this way:**

"The Spirit who has come to settle down, make His home, and permanently dwell in us is moved by an all-consuming, ever-growing, passionate desire to possess us — and He is envious and filled with malice toward anything or anyone who tries to take His place in our lives."

We live in the world, work in the world, and function as human beings in the world. There is no way to get around that. Jesus didn't pray that we would be *removed from* the world, but that we would be *kept from* the world (*see* John 17:15). There is nothing wrong with going to work, buying a house, purchasing a new car, or enjoying beautiful clothes. Those things are part of living an abundant life on this earth. They are not wrong unless they consume and preoccupy our thoughts.

Let's not forget that all kinds of things can preoccupy our thinking. If we're called to the ministry, even our ministerial responsibilities can so occupy our thoughts that we seldom think of the Holy Spirit or focus on cultivating our relationship with Him. Yes, that seems like a contradiction. However, it's very possible to be so involved in good works that we hardly ever slow down long enough to spend time with the Lord, read His Word, and listen to what His Spirit wants to say to our hearts. Sometimes it's just the cares of this life that pull us away from the Holy Spirit. We can get so busy and so committed to doing so many things, even *good* things, that our continual busyness deteriorates our spiritual life.

Amazing as it is, even good things, if taken to an extreme, become adulterous in the eyes of the Lord. Only He knows how to balance us, but we have to open our hearts and our spiritual ears to listen to His counsel. That's why it's so crucial to set aside time to spend with Him every day.

So don't tell yourself that you have too much to do to spend time with the Lord each day. When it comes right down to it, you basically do what you want to do. If having communion with the Holy Spirit is a priority, you'll make time for Him. If it's not a priority, you won't make that time. It's that simple.

Perhaps you're reading this today and thinking, *I have so much to learn about the Holy Spirit. I didn't know I was supposed to intentionally have communion with Him. I didn't know I could depend on Him as my Comforter. I didn't know I could grieve Him with my attitudes. I didn't realize how important it is for me to develop a closer fellowship with the Holy Spirit!*

If that is you, you're in a great position today — standing at the threshold of a whole new realm of God in your life! His Word promises that if you draw closer to Him, He will draw closer to you (*see* James 4:8). I can't help but wonder how many Christians die and go to Heaven — and then find out how much they missed because they never experienced a real partnership with the Holy Spirit. *Don't let that be your story!*

MY PRAYER FOR TODAY

Holy Spirit, there is so much for me to learn about You I never knew before. Today I open my heart — as wide as I know how — and I ask You to teach me about You and Your ministry to my life. I want to be a vessel You work through, so please help me become that vessel. Jesus sent You to be with me and to indwell me. You are preoccupied with me, and You passionately and rightfully desire my affection to also be set on You. I repent for the times I allowed the cares of life or desire for other things to steal my attention and affection away from You. For each and every time I've violated my relationship with You in any way, please forgive me and know that from this day forward, I am turning toward You with my whole heart and soul.

I pray this in Jesus' name!

MY CONFESSION FOR TODAY

I boldly confess that I am going to pursue a deep, intimate relationship with the Holy Spirit, and I will not stop until I've attained it. He already lives inside me, but I want to know Him and the power He continually makes available to me. I've lived my Christian life largely in my own power, but from this point forward, I want to live it fully in the power of the Holy Spirit.

I declare this by faith, in Jesus' name!

QUESTIONS FOR YOU TO CONSIDER

1. Before you read today's *Sparkling Gem*, did you know the Holy Spirit is envious and jealous over His relationship with you? How does that realization affect your understanding of His ministry to your life? In what ways will it change how You respond to the Holy Spirit in the future?
2. Is there an area of your life to which you're more committed than to your relationship with the Holy Spirit? If so, just know He is going to go after that area and bring it back into balance. So why don't you get started by making a list of those areas that fit in that category, and then invite the Holy Spirit to help you get those areas realigned according to *His* priorities?
3. Godly jealousy is a good thing — but have you ever considered that there is such a thing as godly malice that the Holy Spirit feels? What "reasons" have you used to justify giving more of your attention to those other things at the expense of your communion with Him? How will you begin to eliminate those excuses, starting today?

JUNE 27

Your Spiritual Interior Is Magnificent!

What? Know ye not that your body is the temple of the Holy Spirit
which is in you, which ye have of God, and ye are not your own?
For ye are bought with a price: therefore glorify God in your body,
and in your spirit, which are God's.
— 1 Corinthians 6:19,20

When teaching on the indwelling presence of the Holy Spirit, I sometimes say that when the Holy Spirit moved into our hearts, He hung pictures on the wall; He put rugs on the floor; and He settled into a comfortable chair inside our hearts. But He has done much more than that! He has taken our spirits, once dead in trespasses and sin, and raised them to new life, recreating them into a marvelous temple of God.

Obviously, what the Holy Spirit accomplished in our salvation was not just a decorating job. He created a dwelling place on the inside of us that is so wonderful, so marvelous, so fantastic, and so outstanding that the Holy Spirit — the Third Person of the Godhead — was willing to make it His home! Paul referred to this miraculous work in First Corinthians 6:19 and 20, when he wrote, "What? Know ye not that your body is the temple of the Holy Spirit which is in you, which ye have of God, and ye are not your own? For ye are bought with a price: therefore glorify God in your body, and in your spirit, which are God's."

The word "temple" is taken from the Greek word *naos*, which always describes *a highly decorated shrine*. It paints the picture of a beautiful cathedral with tall, vaulted ceilings, marble columns, granite floors, hand-carved woodwork overlaid with gold and silver, crystal chandeliers, silver candelabras, and burning incense around the front of the altar.

Being raised in a Protestant denomination, I was accustomed to the interior of a simple Protestant church. We had pews, a baptistry, an attractive carpet, and heavy oak pulpit furniture. That was our style of church decoration. It was nice, but moderate and simple.

The first time I ever entered a cathedral, I nearly fell over! I was just a small boy when I participated in my uncle's wedding at a large Catholic church in our city. I remember walking down the aisle of that church building, awestruck by the high ceilings and the beauty of the statues and paintings.

In my journeys from one end of the former Soviet Union to the other, I often stop to see large Russian Orthodox church buildings. The architecture; the craftsmanship; the gold, the silver, and precious stones; the inlaid marbles; the painting and icons — the talent and gifting required to create all that beauty is so much more than I could ever imagine! Some of these buildings are nearly unbelievable in terms of size and visual grandeur. To say they are spectacular is a great understatement.

This is precisely what Paul meant when he wrote that we were "temples" of the Holy Spirit. It is warm and cozy to think of the Holy Spirit making Himself at home in our hearts, but because Paul used the word *naos* ("temple") in First Corinthians 6:19 to describe us, he was painting a very different and much more magnificent picture of our spiritual interiors.

The Holy Spirit performed the ultimate miracle when He came to dwell in our hearts. He came to occupy our spirits, which were dead in trespasses and sins (*see* Ephesians 2:1) and then He quickened us together with Christ (Ephesians 2:5). In that miraculous moment, He created us to be like God in righteousness and true holiness (Ephesians 4:24). The work inside us was so glorious and perfect that when it was all finished, He declared we were His workmanship created in Christ Jesus (Ephesians 2:10). From start to finish, we were apprehended by Him, regenerated by Him, and molded and fashioned to be a magnificent temple, fit for the Spirit of God Himself to make His permanent habitation.

The change in our previously dead spiritual nature is truly miraculous. He resurrected it with glory and power and recreated us to contain the revelation, holiness, splendor, righteousness, the fruit of the Spirit, the gifts of the Spirit, and the life and character of Christ. He adorned our inner man until, spiritually speaking, we became a shrine unto God!

Inwardly we are so beautiful and magnificently created that Almighty God, through His Spirit, is willing to take up permanent residency within us. What kind of home do you think God would require? Would He desire a shabby shack of dirt and sticks? No! He has built for Himself an unspeakably beautiful temple, fit for His glory, within our hearts!

MY PRAYER FOR TODAY

Father, I thank You for the amazing work You have done inside my heart. By Your Spirit, You took my spiritually dead condition, raised me to life, and moved into my heart. My spiritual interior has been recreated and embellished so richly that You were even willing to take up residence within me. I am not a shabby shack made of dirt and sticks, but a magnificent temple that You have built for Yourself. You recreated my spirit, and then You adorned my inner man with Your revelation, holiness, splendor, righteousness, the fruit of the Spirit, the gifts of the Spirit, and the life and character of Christ Himself! Holy Spirit, help me gain a deeper revelation of what You have done inside me than I've ever had before.

I pray this in Jesus' name!

MY CONFESSION FOR TODAY

I confess that because of the new birth, my spiritual interior has been miraculously and marvelously recreated to be a suitable residence for the indwelling presence of the Holy Spirit. I am a magnificent temple where the Holy Spirit dwells. Inside me are the power, glory, and splendor of the Holy Spirit. God's meticulous attention to detail within my inner man was so glorious and perfect that when it was all finished, He declared me to be His workmanship created in Christ Jesus. I may not see this manifested yet in my outward appearance, but inwardly this is exactly who I am. I will therefore stop speaking poorly of myself. Instead, I will honor the Lord by speaking words in agreement with the mighty work He performed in my inner man, and I will begin to speak words that honor my body as the temple of the Holy Spirit!

I declare this by faith in Jesus' name!

QUESTIONS FOR YOU TO CONSIDER

1. Have you ever pondered what your spiritual interior must look like in order for the Holy Spirit to be pleased to dwell there? Why don't you stop and reflect on this question? It could revolutionize the way you see yourself!

2. Are you guilty of judging yourself by your exterior appearance instead of by your interior reality? Is it possible that you've been putting your focus on the wrong part of you? *Think about that!*
3. Why don't you take time to think of the supernatural work the Holy Spirit has done within you, such as regenerating your spirit, filling you with His power, and so on. How would it affect your confidence and boldness to walk through the situations of life if you continually meditated on what the Holy Spirit has done *in* you rather than what you'd like to change about your exterior appearance and characteristics?

JUNE 28

God Made an Investment in You!

But we have this treasure in earthen vessels,
that the excellency of the power
may be of God, and not of us.
— 2 Corinthians 4:7

Most people struggle with poor self-images. We see ourselves as unworthy shacks built of mud and sticks. We certainly do not see ourselves as the highly decorated shrines of the Holy Spirit that we talked about in yesterday's *Sparkling Gem*!

Paul was aware of this, too, and that is why he commented, "But we have this treasure in earthen vessels, that the excellency of the power may be of God, and not of us" (2 Corinthians 4:7).

Paul used several key words in this text. First, he said, "But we have…." The Greek word used here is *echomen*, and it can be translated *we hold* or *we possess*. It is in agreement with the phrase "earthen vessels," which is the Greek word *ostrakinos*, describing *small, cheap, easily broken pottery*. This particular kind of pottery was considered to be weak, fragile, and easily replaceable.

By using the word *echomen* in connection with *ostrakinos,* Paul is making a strong statement regarding our real spiritual condition. He says that we hold or possess some kind of treasure in vessels that are small, cheap, easily broken, and replaceable. This is how he described our physical bodies. And — he was right! The human body is fragile. A wrong diet can kill it; working too hard can break it; too much pressure can damage it; and even after caring for it your whole lifetime, it still dies.

The greatest minds, the most creative inventors, the highest intellects, the most colorful writers, and the most dynamic politicians are all subject to physical death. Eventually the human body breaks under the stress of age, and the vessel that carried such incredible talent and potential is reduced to unrecognizable dust, totally valueless. Some human vessels break earlier, and some last longer — but eventually they all break; they all collapse; and they all return to dust.

Here is the amazing part: We "earthen vessels" contain something Paul called a "treasure." The word "treasure" is the Greek word *thesauros*. It describes a treasure so rich and immense that it could never be expended. This would be the treasure hunter's greatest dream. This, my friend, refers to the precious Holy Spirit, which God has deposited inside us!

From natural appearances, we may look weak, fragile, and valueless. Certainly we don't look like a place where God would hide His greatest treasure. Paul wrote this verse with a sense of amazement: *"We hold this immense, incredibly rich, inexhaustible treasure in these human bodies of ours that are so easily broken and expended!"*

If you were God and possessed a treasure that was infinitely grand, would you place it in something as unreliable as you are? But that is precisely what He did. This is part of the miracle of our salvation. What we see with our eyes is the outer casing of weak humanity. *But contained in that fleshly, carnal, short-lived body is the very power that created the universe and raised Jesus from the dead!*

The point is this: After recreating us in Christ Jesus; after turning our previously dead spirits into temples so marvelous that God Himself is willing to live in them; and after placing His greatest treasure in our hearts, do you think the Holy Spirit is going to walk off and leave His investment for the enemy to plunder? The emphatic answer to that question should be obvious to you by now! *Never!*

MY PRAYER FOR TODAY

Father, thank You for putting Your Spirit inside me. Yes, it's true that my body is weak, fragile, and temporary. Yet You have chosen to place Your immense, incredibly rich, inexhaustible treasure in this fragile human body of mine that is so easily broken! Help me, Holy Spirit, to understand this wonderful truth so I can more effectively yield to and cooperate with You. Open my spiritual eyes so I can truly see the wealth You have deposited inside me!

I pray this in Jesus' name!

MY CONFESSION FOR TODAY

I confess that I am the repository of the Holy Spirit! When God was choosing a place for His Spirit to take up residence, He chose me! Although my physical body may be a clay earthen vessel of human frailty, He has chosen to reside deep within me so the grandeur and surpassing greatness of Christ in me, the Hope of Glory, will be shown to be arising from Your sufficiency and not from me. My spiritual eyes are being opened, and I am realizing more and more every day that God has put His greatest gift in me!

I declare this by faith in Jesus' name!

QUESTIONS FOR YOU TO CONSIDER

1. When did the Holy Spirit first come into your life? This is a very doctrinal question — one that you need to get right because it establishes your foundation for belief.
2. When the Holy Spirit moved into you, what qualities and characteristics did His divine life impart to you? In what ways are you tapping into them and applying them in the various areas of your life?
3. Is there any other place the Holy Spirit lives outside the human spirit? Why has the Holy Spirit chosen to indwell you?

JUNE 29

The Holy Spirit Is Our Seal and Guarantee

In whom ye also trusted,
after that ye heard the word of truth,
the gospel of your salvation:
in whom also after that ye believed,
ye were sealed with that holy Spirit of promise.
— Ephesians 1:13

In Greek and Roman times — and in certain places still today — if a package was to be dispatched to another location, it *first* went through a series of investigations to make sure the contents were not flawed, broken, or shattered. The sender would examine every single piece of the contents to make sure each one was whole and intact. This means the process of examining every little fragment of the contents was extraordinarily important for the one charged with *sealing* the shipment. If everything was whole and intact, the sender would pour hot wax on the crease of the package and then carefully push the insignia of the owner into the wax, signifying that all the contents were in perfect order. That "seal" was called a *sphragidzo* — the exact same word used in Ephesians 1:13, where the Bible says we were "sealed" with the Holy Spirit on the day we believed in the Lord Jesus Christ.

This insignia on the package was important for several reasons. It was the *insignia of the owner* of the package. No one would dare break into the sealed package to disturb the contents, especially if this owner was a high-ranking person, for the consequences of such an action would be severe.

Furthermore, that insignia, or "seal," was *the guarantee that the package would be delivered to its final destination*. It was like the highest postage stamp one could put on a package. The seal guaranteed that it would arrive at its ultimate destination unharmed.

Last but not least, that insignia *guaranteed that everything in the package was in order* — nothing was missing, broken, inferior, or shattered. Everything was whole and complete.

As I've noted, this Greek word *sphragidzo* ("seal") is precisely the word used in Ephesians 1:13, where Paul wrote, "…In whom also after that ye believed, ye were *sealed* with that holy Spirit of promise."

This tells us that when we believed and were born again, God examined us to make sure we were made completely new and whole, and He found no flaws, no defects, and no shattered places. God saw that we were truly a product of Christ's own making and were complete in Him. In fact, we were *so* complete that, figuratively speaking, Christ poured His "wax" onto our hearts and spirits and then pressed the insignia of the Holy Spirit into us, giving guaranteed proof through the Spirit's indwelling presence that we belong to God and will make it to our ultimate destination — *Heaven*.

You and I may feel that we've had a few bumps along the way, but the Holy Spirit is the *guaranteed proof* that we will eventually make it to our heavenly home! Regardless of how the devil or life may try to assail against us, the Holy Spirit is "postage-paid sufficient" to get us all the way to our Lord Jesus one of these glorious days!

MY PRAYER FOR TODAY

Father, I thank You for sending someone to preach the Gospel to me — and for giving me the faith to believe it. I am in wonder and amazement that as soon as I believed, You gave me the Holy Spirit. The Spirit's presence in me is absolute, guaranteed proof that I belong to You — and I am so thankful that You pressed the insignia of the Holy Spirit into my heart and spirit, which means "postage-paid." Because of this precious work You've done in my life, I rejoice that one day I will reach my destination to be with You in my heavenly home!

I pray this in Jesus' name!

MY CONFESSION FOR TODAY

I confess that I am complete and whole in Jesus Christ. After I believed, God saw that I was truly a product of Christ's own making. God made a full examination of me to make sure all parts were complete and that I was whole in Jesus Christ. Then He gave me the gift of the Holy Spirit, who will be with me all my life as a guarantee. He is the proof that I am a child of God. He is the evidence that I am born again. And His presence in my life is the guarantee that I will make it one day to my heavenly home!

I declare this by faith in Jesus' name!

QUESTIONS FOR YOU TO CONSIDER

1. According to the Bible, you received the Holy Spirit the day you surrendered your life to Jesus Christ. Can you recall the change that occurred inside you when God made you His temple and sent His Spirit to dwell within you? What were some of the immediate changes you experienced?
2. When you read that God checked you out — that He investigated you to make sure you were really born again and whole — and found that you *were*, what does that mean to you? Think of it: *God found no defects!*
3. If you've ever wondered if you will actually make it to Heaven, you can put that thought away forever *if* you have the Holy Spirit living inside you. He is the "postage-paid," absolute guarantee that you will make it to your heavenly home. When you think about that, how does it make you feel?

JUNE 30

The Holy Spirit Is Like Wind

And suddenly there came a sound from heaven
as of *a rushing mighty wind*,
and it filled all the house where they were sitting.
— Acts 2:2

Having grown up in Oklahoma, my family members were all well aware of the power of the wind. If atmospheric conditions were right, we'd hear the city sirens begin to blare — warning everyone to run for cover because severe winds or a tornado was imminent. At the sound of those sirens, I remember my mother commanding me to get off the porch and into the house to seek shelter. Running for cover was the last thing I wanted to do, because I loved watching how the low-level clouds would suddenly turn eerily dark. The latent power of wind simply mesmerized me. The fact that the wind could not be seen but could be felt — and the added fact that it was so unpredictable — made me want to stay on the porch so I could feel the wind in action.

But at my mother's urging, I would eventually head for cover with the rest of the family, usually in a small, enclosed area of the house that could potentially withstand a hit, like a bathroom or closet. We'd shut the door and wait. When the sirens stopped blaring, that's when we knew the storm had passed. Many times we emerged from our hiding place to find large tree limbs strewn across our yard that had been carried there from blocks away. Sometimes we would see huge trees that the wind had ripped up from their roots. Very often after these storms, we'd venture out to discover that roads were impassable because of debris — trees, limbs, and power lines that had been knocked down by the wind and scattered across the roads. Electrical sparks would spit fiercely into the air from where electrical lines had been severed, so we would drive around them or look for alternative routes until electric crews arrived to repair the fallen lines.

We're all aware of the potentially destructive power of wind. But if properly harnessed, wind can also bring tremendous benefits. Think how much it would impact the world if there were no wind. The earth would be stagnant, stinking from pollution and from the normal decaying process that is occurring on the planet.

Just think how essential wind has been to the very development of civilization. For example, if there were no winds, exploration never would have occurred. Consider the great ships of the past that had no mechanical or nuclear energy to drive them, yet they glided across oceans with ease as their great sails caught the winds. The world was explored and conquered by men who "set sail" and traveled the globe, fueled by the force of the wind.

In fact, if no wind were blowing, there would be no movement. Windmill blades would never turn — and the production of materials would be slowed and diminished. Wind is essential for progress to be made. Without wind, we would be hundreds of years behind where we presently are in history.

Wind cannot be seen, but its effects can be felt and heard — *just like the Holy Spirit.* We cannot see Him, but we can feel the effects of His presence and His power. On the Day of Pentecost, Acts 2:2 says, "And suddenly there came a sound from heaven as of a rushing mighty wind, and it filled all the house where they were sitting." Today I want us to look at the comparison of wind to the Holy Spirit in this verse to see what we can learn about why the Spirit came in this manner on the Day of Pentecost and what this means to you and me.

In Acts 2:2, 120 disciples were gathered in the Upper Room, waiting for the promise of the Father as Jesus had commanded them (*see* Acts 1:4). The Bible says that as they were waiting, "suddenly" there came from Heaven a certain sound. The word "suddenly" was translated from the Greek word *aphno*, which carries with it the idea that something took them *off-guard* and *by surprise*.

Acts 2:2 goes on to say, "...Suddenly *there came* a *sound*...." This phrase "there came" is a translation of the word *ginomai*, which in this case describes something very similar to the Greek word *aphno* — *something that happens unexpectedly or that catches one off-guard.*

The word "sound" in this verse is the Greek word *echos*. This is the very word that is used in Luke 21:5 to describe *the deafening roar* of the sea.

Verse 2 continues, "...A sound *from heaven*...." The phrase "from heaven" is from the Greek words *ek tou ourano*. The word *ek* means *out*, and *tou ourano* means *of Heaven*. This leaves no doubt that this sound had originated and emanated from Heaven itself.

Then Luke compared this sound from Heaven to a "rushing, mighty wind." The word "rushing" was translated from the Greek word *pheromones*, the present-passive participle of *phero*, which means to be *carried, borne*, or *driven* and agrees with the idea of *something borne or driven downward very loudly*. When this sound from Heaven came, it was *loud* — so loud that the writer used the word "rushing" to describe what Jesus' disciples heard that day in the room where they gathered.

Furthermore, the Greek text also uses the word *biaias* for "mighty," a word that could be better translated as *violent*. Hence, this "sound" thundered like the roaring of a sea or a mighty wind that swept downward very loudly and violently.

The word "wind" itself comes from *pnoe*, which describes wind so loud that one may be tempted to cover his ears from the overpowering noise of it. This means when the Spirit was poured out, it was no quiet affair. It was loud, noisy, and violent — not violent in terms of *destructive*, but rather it was *strongly felt*.

Just as wind moves ships, empowers engines, drives windmills, and disperses pollution from the earth — when the Holy Spirit moved on the Day of Pentecost, He released *power* strong enough to transform 120 disciples into a mighty force for God!

When the wind of the Spirit blows upon a near-dead church, it can blow life back into that congregation again. When all of our organizing is done and is nearly perfect, yet we still lack power, it is the wind of the Holy Spirit that can blow strongly upon us and cause a vision or organization to come alive with the life of God.

If you are someone who desires a "quiet" relationship with God, I must warn you that when the Holy Spirit's wind blows, it is rarely a quiet affair. It is usually noisy and attention-attracting — or as we've seen, it's a powerful force that sweeps downward from Heaven like the roaring of the sea.

When God formed man, He formed him perfectly. But man had no breath in his lungs until God breathed the breath of life into him (*see* Genesis 2:7). Likewise, when the Church was assembled on the Day of Pentecost, it had no power until the Holy Spirit breathed into that assembly. When that loud *"boom"* exploded overhead in the room where they were gathered, the power of God came upon 120 disciples, and they became an *empowered, mighty force* in the earth as a result.

Wind is a good word to describe the power of the Holy Spirit. Change happens when winds blow — and when the Holy Spirit moves, He brings change like wind. Energy is produced by wind — and when the Holy Spirit moves in this manner, He supplies supernatural energy. He empowers us to do what we could not naturally do on our own. *Oh, how we need the supernatural wind of the Holy Spirit!*

MY PRAYER FOR TODAY

Father, I thank You for the movement of the Holy Spirit that comes to empower me and to make me alive to minister and represent You on the earth! So many times I do everything that needs to be done organizationally, but life and power remain missing. Today I personally ask You to blow Your wind upon me, upon my church, and upon the mission organizations I support so they will all be "moved" by the Spirit and supernaturally empowered to do the work of the ministry!

I pray this in Jesus' name!

MY CONFESSION FOR TODAY

I boldly declare that I will not be satisfied until a fresh wind of the Holy Spirit has blown upon me to give me divine life and divine energy. Without this life, I can only do what human power can do, but when the Spirit blows His divine wind upon me, suddenly I am empowered to do what I could have never done before. Today — right now — I am opening myself to the rushing mighty wind of the Holy Spirit. I confess that I am a ready recipient, and I am receiving a fresh infilling of this divine wind to empower me for God's service.

I declare this by faith in Jesus' name!

QUESTIONS FOR YOU TO CONSIDER

1. Can you think of a time when you did everything naturally that could be done, but you still lacked the power to do the work of the ministry? Do you feel that way right now? If yes, what are you going to do about it after reading today's *Sparkling Gem*?
2. Have you ever had a moment when the Spirit's wind moved upon you — and suddenly you were supernaturally empowered like never before in your life?
3. If you know someone who feels spiritually stagnant, how would you encourage him or her after what you have read in today's *Sparkling Gem*?

Change happens when winds blow —
and when the Holy Spirit moves,
He brings change like wind.
Energy is produced by wind —
and when the Holy Spirit moves in this manner,
He supplies supernatural energy.
He empowers us to do
what we could not naturally do on our own.

JULY 1

Study To Be Quiet

And that ye study to be quiet,
and to do your own business….
— 1 Thessalonians 4:11

When I was a young boy, Grandpa and Grandma Renner lived two blocks from our house. Almost every day, I'd go visit them. When I'd arrive at the back gate, I'd yell out, "Grandpa!" — knowing that he was probably somewhere in the backyard or doing something interesting in his garage. When he heard my voice, Grandpa would quickly appear from seemingly nowhere and cheerfully open the back gate so I could follow him to see what he was doing in the yard or garage.

I also always knew, without even asking, where I would most likely find Grandma Renner. I could almost be sure to find her talking on the telephone — a beige rotary telephone that sat right next to a notebook filled with the names and phone numbers of her dearest friends. I can vividly remember hearing her say, *"Hello…this is Ethel…."* Within minutes, the gossip would begin — something she was committed to as seriously as Grandpa was to his yard and garage! Then as soon as that conversation ended, she'd pick up her pencil, put the eraser end into the circles on the rotary dial, and begin dialing the next girlfriend on her list to start the whole gossipy conversation all over again.

There was Grandpa — working contentedly in the garage and minding his own business, fully satisfied. Meanwhile, Grandma was in hot pursuit of knowing everyone else's business! As much as I loved Grandma, it was just a fact that she was continually repeating what she had just heard from someone else and expressing her opinions about people's personal issues that were none of her business.

Unfortunately, talking about other people's private affairs is a characteristic of the fallen human nature. I shudder to think how many people's reputations have been scarred or stained because of false information spread from person to person by those who didn't know what they were talking about or who really had nothing to do with the matter. Even if they had "inside information," it still wasn't their business.

This inclination of human nature to stick its nose where it doesn't belong is not new. Two thousand years ago, the apostle Paul told the Thessalonians, "And that ye study to be quiet, and to do your own business…" (1 Thessalonians 4:11). What does it mean to *study* to be *quiet*?

The Greek word for "study" is *philotimeomai*, a word that means *ambition*. This means Paul was actually telling readers to be *ambitious* about being quiet. Before we proceed further, let's look deeper at this Greek word and learn more about what it means to you and me when used in conjunction with the idea of being quiet.

This word *philotimeomai* pictures an individual who is *totally committed to obtaining or achieving a specific goal.* He is determined to reach it, and he is enthusiastic about his pursuit of it. He has a strong, inward yearning to attain it that drives and motivates him — *propelling* him toward his goal. He is absolutely fixated on obtaining the object of his desire and *will not stop* until he gets it. He simply *won't* let go of his commitment to attain it.

Although we usually think of ambition of this sort in a negative sense, Paul used it here in a positive context to describe a person who is totally committed to do whatever it takes to be "quiet." The word "quiet" is the Greek word *isuchadzo*, which refers to *keeping to your own business instead of prying into other people's affairs.* By using this word in this verse, Paul was calling on his readers to refuse to be *busybodies.* Someone whose behavior fits that description might be known for eavesdropping, snooping into other people's business, intruding into others' personal matters, prying into the affairs of others, and gossiping about other people. In other words, someone who behaved himself in this manner would definitely fall into the category of a *busybody*!

We are to follow Paul's admonition: *"Make it your ambition — that is, give it your fullest and most enthusiastic effort — to stay out of other people's business...."* Then he continued, "...And to do your own business...." In other words, instead of poking around in matters that have nothing to do with us, we are to keep our mouths shut, keep our eyes from wandering, and focus on our own personal affairs. We don't have a right to delve into the private matters of other people for whom we have no responsibility. In such cases, we need to take a firm stand and refuse to allow gossip or hurtful information to enter our ears. *Period.*

This must have been a problem for a few believers in the church of Thessalonica, because Paul addressed busybodies several times in his first letter to them. In each case, he reprimanded them, even telling others to disassociate with those who acted in such a manner.

Today I ask you to look at your own life and see if you need to make an adjustment in this area. If people were talking about and delving into *your* private affairs, wouldn't you appreciate it if they stopped it — completely refrained from doing it? *Of course you would!* So I encourage you to decide today to obey these scriptures and give the same courtesy to others that you would want them to give to you.

And if there are people in your life who do this — those who try to use your ears as garbage receptacles to receive trashy information — politely tell them that you're not going to listen any longer. This may offend them at first, but it will also make them think twice before they open their mouths. And remember, if people gossip about others to you, they won't think twice about gossiping about *you* to others. It's just so much better to obey God and determine to never let yourself get into that kind of conversational trap!

MY PRAYER FOR TODAY

Lord, I repent for the times I've allowed my tongue to communicate words ignited by the flesh and for giving place to devilish discussions that were not inspired by the Holy Spirit who indwells me. Words of gossip and slander proceed from a polluted heart. To speak such words destroys reputations and relationships — and taints the hearts of those who hear them. Holy Spirit, I ask You to cleanse me from all defilement and from twisted speech and inappropriate communication. Please set a watch over my lips and create in me a clean and quiet heart.

I pray this in Jesus' name!

MY CONFESSION FOR TODAY

I declare that life and death are in the power of the tongue. Therefore, I will not use my tongue to insert hell's suggestions into people's ears, but rather speak God's will and promote God's perspective. Because out of the abundance of the heart the mouth speaks, I choose to fill my heart with God's words, and I cultivate a quiet spirit that is trained to wait upon God. I will heed His direction concerning when to speak, what to say, and when to remain silent. In that blessed quietness, confidence and discernment shall be my strength. I do not speak about or involve my opinion in matters that are none of my business. And I do not allow others to bring gossip to me wrapped in the guise of a prayer request. Like Jesus, I speak only the words I hear my Heavenly Father speak. His words are love-filled and life-producing, releasing health and strength in me and in the hearts of those who hear them.

I declare this by faith in Jesus' Name!

QUESTIONS FOR YOU TO CONSIDER

1. Have you been guilty of talking about other people for whom you have no responsibility and therefore no reason to discuss their personal lives? If your answer is *yes*, what actions are you going to change as a result of reading today's *Sparkling Gem*?
2. Often when people talk about others, they dress up their negative words in the guise of a prayer request. Isn't it possible to address a prayer need without talking about another's private affairs? How can you request prayer without divulging private information or delving into other people's personal matters that don't concern you?
3. What would happen if you told those people who gossip that you aren't going to participate in that kind of conversation any longer? After all, it's almost certain that they are also talking about you.

JULY 2

Caring for the Fatherless

Pure religion and undefiled before God and the Father is this,
to visit the fatherless and widows in their affliction,
and to keep himself unspotted from the world.
— James 1:27

In Russia, we have a significant outreach to people who are poor, needy, and forgotten. This includes outreaches to orphans, to the developmentally disabled, to the blind, and to large numbers of people who are addicted to drugs or alcohol. Regardless of *why* people are in this condition, we have a God-given responsibility to do whatever we can to help them spiritually, materially, and socially — and to show them the love of Christ.

I could tell many stories of those we have helped, but one remarkable story comes to mind — a small boy whom we'll call Sasha for the sake of confidentiality.

Sasha was deserted as a small boy and raised by dogs. Although it seems almost too bizarre to believe, those dogs accepted that small child and raised him as a member of their pack. He lived with them and was fed and cared for by them for years before he was discovered by social workers, who placed him into the care of an outreach based out of our Moscow church.

In Russia, when a child is discovered who was raised by animals, social workers say that such a child has a "Mowgli" syndrome. It's a term taken from "The Jungle Book" regarding the small boy who, as the story goes, was lost in the jungle as a baby and raised by animals. So when little Sasha came into the care of our outreach, he came with that "Mowgli syndrome" designation because he had been raised by dogs and had no memory of ever living with a human being.

When the outreach based in our church decided to take him, it was a huge commitment of time, attention, and love to help him transition from a world of dogs into a human environment. But they accepted the challenge. Today that little Sasha is a young man with a fabulous future. Because someone loved him enough to receive him, he is a shining example of God's restorative powers!

In James 1:27, we are told, "Pure religion and undefiled before God and the Father is this, to visit the fatherless and widows in their affliction, and to keep himself unspotted from the world." Denise and I have seen so many lives like little Sasha's transformed because we have always taken seriously the Lord's command to live according to God's definition of "pure religion." Today I want to talk about a certain aspect of that definition: our responsibility to show God's kindness to the fatherless.

But let's begin by looking at that phrase "pure religion." It is a translation of the Greek words *threskeia kathara*. The word *threskeia* depicts *religious service* and includes *religious acts*. The second word in this phrase is *kathara*, which in this case simply means *clean*. Taken as one phrase, the new word literally means *clean religion*. By using these Greek words, James was describing religious actions that are "undefiled" before God.

The word "undefiled" is the Greek word *amiantos*, which refers to actions that are *free of contamination* and therefore *acceptable* with God. But what was James about to describe that *is* approved and accepted by God? *What are these acceptable actions?*

James continued, "Pure religion and undefiled before God and the Father is this, to visit the fatherless and widows in their affliction…." The word "visit" doesn't mean just to wave hello to them in passing. It is the Greek word *episkeptomai*, and it means *to look upon, to physically visit*, or *to provide help for those in need*, and it was even used to denote *the provision of medical care*. James then specified the target that we are to care for: "…the fatherless and the widows in their affliction…."

The word "fatherless" is the Greek word *orphanos*, and it is from this term that we derive the word *orphan*. However, the English usage of the word "orphan" is more limited today than it was during the First Century AD when James wrote this verse. In New Testament times, the word *orphanos* described not only children left without a parent, but it also included the idea of *abandonment*. Perhaps the parents are still living, but the children are abandoned and left to themselves with no parental care or guidance. In Russia, this category is often called *social orphans* and refers to children with living parents who have abandoned them. For all intents and purposes, they are fatherless and motherless. In fact, this Greek word *orphanos* could even be used to describe adults who have suffered abandonment.

James used the word "affliction" to describe the living situation of this category of people. This is the Greek word *thlipsis*, which depicts *pressures* that make it difficult to cope with life. This hardship may include housing, food, medical needs, or other physical needs that leave a person suffering in life. As you will see in tomorrow's *Sparkling Gem*, James included physically needy widows in this category of people.

Of course, every situation isn't as desperate as little Sasha's. Yet every need that fits this category is acute, and James wrote that if we are interested in living out a religion that is clean and acceptable before God, we must turn our attention to the fatherless and motherless and to those who have been abandoned in life. God's commandment to us is not just to wave hello to them and wish them better luck. He actually wants us to focus our attention on them, physically visit them, help them, and provide them with the medical care they need.

If you don't know how to personally get involved in helping those who have been abandoned, ask your church for advice or look for a ministry that specializes in helping the poor and needy. People often talk about how bad religion is. But according to James, there is a clean, uncontaminated form of religion — and the Lord commands us to do whatever we can to get involved in it!

MY PRAYER FOR TODAY

Father, I want to demonstrate my faith in You with actions that reflect Your character. You are a Father to the fatherless and the Source of hope to the hopeless. You said that those who give to the poor are lending to You. You are watchful over the defenseless, and You take note how they are treated. I thank You for reminding me today that pure, undefiled religion is lived out by loving those who are in need. Through the demonstration of my love, I am directly participating in the expression of Your own heart toward them. And by loving them, I am offering genuine worship to You. Thank You, Father, for allowing me the privilege to be an extension of Your hands so others may know Your goodness practically through experience for themselves.

I pray this in Jesus' name!

MY CONFESSION FOR TODAY

I confess that I live out a religion that is clean and acceptable before God. I give attention to the fatherless and motherless and to those people who have been abandoned in life. When I encounter the fatherless who have been abandoned, neglected, and left bereft of any support, I do not simply wish them well. I inquire of the Lord how I can personally give aid and provide help for them.

I declare this by faith in Jesus' name!

QUESTIONS FOR YOU TO CONSIDER

1. What do you do to help the poor and needy? Have you ever visited people in need?
2. Do you regularly give offerings to help support ministries that reach those who are in dire circumstances? Whom are they helping? What are they doing with the offerings you send to them? Do you know?
3. Whom do you know who has been abandoned in life? How could you reach out to these individuals with an expression of friendship? Maybe you don't have finances to give, but you could call them, check on them, visit them, and show genuine compassion to them. Who is that person or group of people?

If we are interested in living out a religion
that is clean and acceptable before God,
we must turn our attention
to the fatherless and motherless
and to those who have been abandoned in life.

JULY 3

A Man Who Remembered

Pure religion and undefiled before God and the Father is this,
to visit the fatherless and widows in their affliction,
and to keep himself unspotted from the world.
— James 1:27

Just to the west of Tulsa, Oklahoma, is a city called Sand Springs — a small town that was constructed with the single wealth of a man named Charles Page. Page's father died when he was young, and he saw the struggle that his widowed mother experienced as she cared for him and his siblings. As a young man, Page got a job working in the oil industry, but soon he went into the drilling business for himself. Page hit his first oil gusher in 1905 when he was 45 years old — one that began to quickly produce up to 2,000 barrels of oil per day. Soon he hit another gusher and then another — and it wasn't long before he became immensely wealthy at a relatively young age.

Page remembered his mother's financial struggles after his father died, so he chose to devote the bulk of his wealth to help *orphans* and *widows*. In 1908, he purchased land west of Tulsa and in the middle of that enormous territory, he began the construction of Sand Springs, Oklahoma — the town where I grew up. But Page's purpose was *not* to build a city just for the sake of building a city. He dreamed that this city would become a hub for his real dream, which was *Sand Springs Home* — a well-financed orphanage that would care for orphans until adulthood. To assure that the orphans raised at *Sand Springs Home* would have jobs after they set off on their own, Page constructed the city of Sand Springs. He began to negotiate with steel, glass, and porcelain industries to move to his new city so that kids from his orphanage would have good employment opportunities when they became adults.

In addition to *Sand Springs Home*, Page also dreamed of constructing a widow's colony to care for widowed women. So in 1912, Page began construction of *Sand Springs Widows' Colony*, a large area that had 40 houses for widowed women with children who could live there freely at his expense. All of this was provided as benevolence because Charles Page remembered the burden of poverty that his own family experienced when his father died unexpectedly.

I am familiar with this story because I grew up in Sand Springs and also because my Grandfather Miller was personally hired by Charles Page to lead the orchestra and band for *Sand Springs Home*. Through my grandfather's connection to Page, my mother as a small girl spent many days and weekends at *Sand Springs Home*, where she personally witnessed how generously this man treated these orphans and widows.

When I entered high school myself, I became keenly aware of how well the children from *Sand Springs Home* were treated. They were well-dressed and well-groomed, and at Christmas time they received what seemed like mountains of gifts that were provided by funds left after the death of Charles Page. If they did well in school, there were funds available to help them go to college or university. What Page did for these orphans and widows — the long-term planning that he prepared for them — was simply remarkable and has impacted thousands of people's lives for the better since he first began to put his dream into action in 1908.

Today I want to talk to *you* about assisting needy widows. But first, let's talk about what the Bible means when it refers to widows. The word "widows," which James used in James 1:27, is *chera*, a word that uniquely describes *widows* in the traditional sense of the word. It is the same word used by Jesus in Matthew 23:14 and Luke 4:26, which both clearly describe women who were bereft of their spouses due to death. James used the word "affliction" to describe the condition of this category of widows.

As we saw yesterday, the word "affliction" is a translation of the Greek word *thlipsis*, which depicts *pressures* that make it difficult to cope with life. This hardship may include housing, food, medical needs, or other physical needs that leave a person struggling to get up and face each day. According to James 1:27, we as believers have a God-given responsibility to reach out and help widowed women who are struggling due to the loss of a spouse. It is good, clean, and acceptable before God for us to visit and assist widows in these circumstances.

I realize we live in a day and age when insurance pays death benefits, the government often assists women who have lost their spouses, and many widows today are not suffering financially. However, there are still many widowed women who suffer great financial and social need when their spouses die, and God commands us to do whatever we can to be a blessing to them in their times of suffering. Since this is the command of God, I want to ask you: What are you doing to help widows in need?

You don't have to be rich and wealthy like Charles Page was in 1908. The truth is, there are many wealthy people who never help anyone. Page helped because he remembered his mother's own difficulty and chose to make a difference with his resources. What he did took great passion and long-term planning — which tells us that his giving was not based on emotion or just a "fancy of the moment." It was deeply felt compassion that was expressed in action that has continued to impact people's lives ever since his charitable work first started. I don't know the spiritual status of Charles Page's soul, but I know that his works continue to speak long after his death. What Page did was "clean religion" — something that God both encourages and endorses!

MY PRAYER FOR TODAY

Father, I am deeply stirred to begin formulating my long-term plan to bring real, measurable help to people in need through sincere acts of charity. You specified needy widows and orphans as people for whom I should take compassionate responsibility when their needs are brought to my attention. I ask You, Lord, to show me who and how to help. I commit to prove my faith by my works, as I live out the "clean religion" that honors You the most.

I pray this in Jesus' name!

MY CONFESSION FOR TODAY

I confess that I actively pursue a life marked by the "clean religion" that God both encourages and endorses. I do not ignore the plight of orphans and widows in need. I deliberately take action in well-planned ways to provide help and to produce change that will make a positive difference in their lives for the glory of God!

I declare this in Jesus' name!

QUESTIONS FOR YOU TO CONSIDER

1. After reading today's *Sparkling Gem*, what actions are you going to take to reach out to widows who are in need? Have you ever done anything special to help a woman who has lost her spouse?
2. Do you personally know a woman who has suffered financial and material loss as the result of her husband's death? Who is that woman? Do you even know if she has financial need?
3. What would Jesus do if He knew of a widow in dire financial straits? Would He simply wave at her and wish her well, or would He do something to assist her?

JULY 4

Praying for Those in Authority

I exhort therefore, that, first of all, supplications,
prayers, intercessions, and giving of thanks,
be made for all men; for kings,
and for all that are in authority;
that we may lead a quiet and peaceable life
in all godliness and honesty.
For this is good and acceptable
in the sight of God our Saviour....
— 1 Timothy 2:1-3

Even if we don't like the way things are going in our government, we *must* obey the apostle Paul's exhortation in First Timothy 2:1-3 to pray for our governmental leaders. Before you dismiss Paul's instructions to pray for those in authority as too simplistic, remember that he lived at a time of grossly immoral governmental leadership and that he ultimately was martyred by Nero — the very "king" he asked people to pray for! In First Timothy 2:1-3, Paul declared, "I exhort therefore, that, first of all, supplications, prayers, intercessions, and giving of thanks be made for all men; for kings, and for all that are in authority; that we may lead a quiet and peaceable life in all godliness and honesty. For this is good and acceptable in the sight of God our Saviour...."

Paul gave us *six prayer commands* in these verses that God expects us to obey — regardless of who is calling the shots politically. In this passage of Scripture, he clearly defined guidelines for us to follow when we pray. Rather than rush to God with accusations, complaints, grumbling, protestations, and whining, we are to follow the positive approach in prayer Paul provided. He began by saying, "I exhort therefore, that, first of all, *supplications*...."

1. A Right Attitude

The word "supplications" is a translation of the Greek word *deisis*, which describes the *attitude of one who beseeched a king*. Access to a throne was a great privilege in the ancient world, so when an individual approached a king, he showed *respect* and *gratitude* for the privilege.

As Paul began to outline his instructions regarding how we should pray, he reminded us of the kind of attitude we ought to have when we draw near to God. Before we utter a single word in prayer, we must clearly understand in our hearts that we have been afforded a *great privilege* to access the throne room of God. Regardless of the thoughts swirling around in our minds or the complaints we may be harboring in our souls, we need to come into God's presence with hearts of *respect* and *gratitude*. We certainly are not to enter His presence ready to unabashedly spew ugly, disrespectful, or slanderous words at Him as though it's *His* fault that things aren't going the way we wished they were going!

Therefore, the first thing we need to do when we prepare to pray for our government is *get our attitudes right*.

2. A Prayer of Personal Consecration

As Paul continued, he wrote, "I exhort therefore, that, first of all, supplications, *prayers*...." The word "prayers" — the Greek word *proseuche* — literally means *an exchange or a surrender* and pictures a person who comes into the intimate presence of God to consecrate himself as *a first matter of priority*.

So Paul affirmed that our first responsibility as believers before we ever utter a request or a complaint regarding others — *before we utter anything else at all* — is to enter the presence of God and get our own attitudes and thoughts right before Him. Then with clear hearts we can receive *His thoughts* and know *His ways* in the place of prayer. When our own attitudes are corrected and realigned, it usually changes the way we pray concerning others, because our words reflect the Father's heart instead of our own personal preference or opinions.

Everything must be surrendered to God and the power of His Spirit before anything else is spoken to Him in prayer.

3. A Prayer of Intercession for Others

Once a believer has dealt with his own wrong attitudes and his need of consecration, Paul wrote what to do next. He said, "I exhort therefore, that, first of all, supplications, prayers, *intercessions....*"

The word "intercessions" is the Greek word *huperentugchano*, which means *to appeal to God on behalf of someone else.* Once you have dealt with your own attitude and consecrated yourself to the will of God, you are in a position to appeal to God about someone else.

Perhaps you sense the Holy Spirit's leading to pray for someone who is unable to pray for himself, such as a novice believer who simply doesn't know how to pray effectively, or for a government leader whose spiritual condition and unwise decisions are negatively affecting masses of people. In other words, you sense the Holy Spirit's leading to assume an *intercessory position* and to focus your prayers toward a specific individual or situation. And if you have made sure your own heart is clear of clutter, you can pray for others in this way while remaining free from any selfish agenda or wrong attitude.

4. A Prayer of Thankfulness

Paul continued in his list of prayer guidelines by saying, "I exhort therefore, that, first of all, supplications, prayers, intercessions, *and giving of thanks....*" According to this verse, you are also to give "thanks" while you are in God's presence. This phrase "giving of thanks," which is a form of the Greek word *eucharistos,* depicts *an overflowing, grateful heart.*

Let's be honest — it's difficult to be grateful and thankful when you are harboring a complaining attitude at the same time! God knows this. So He instructs you to allow thankfulness to flow from your heart, which will literally shift your "inner atmosphere" during your time of prayer.

So before you start griping about a political leader — or anyone else for that matter! — first take time to think of reasons you can be thankful regarding that person. This will change your tone and make you more effective in prayer. And rest assured — *God will appreciate your change of attitude!*

5. A Prayer for Everyone

Paul continued, "I exhort therefore, that, first of all, supplications, prayers, intercessions, and giving of thanks, *be made for all men....*" The word "all" means we are not to show favoritism or to be picky about the people we pray for. Regardless of their spiritual status or political affiliation, we are to pray for "*all* men." This is a good test, because if there is someone you think you can't pray for, it probably indicates a problematic attitude inside you that needs to be consecrated to God. This is very important to understand, because your inability to pray for someone actually reveals a deep need for change in *you.*

6. A Prayer for Governmental Officials

Next, Paul said that we must pray for "*for kings.*" If anyone needed prayer, it was the unsaved kings who possessed lofty positions of power and authority in the First Century AD! But Paul broadened the scope of this divine command by saying that we are to pray for *all* who are "in authority." The word "authority" used here is *huperarche* and depicts *prominent governmental officials*. Ponder that for a moment. That means we are to pray for *all* prominent governmental officials — *even* those whom we don't care for at all! Paul told us the reason for all this praying is "...that we may lead a quiet and peaceable life in all godliness and honesty. For this is good and acceptable in the sight of God our Savior...."

Most believers in New Testament times had no option to vote, so they did what they *could* do and followed Paul's six prayer commands. I'm sure if they had been given the right to vote, they would have rushed to the polling booths to cast their votes. But the only vote they could cast was in prayer — so they prayed! Since their governmental leaders were entrenched in power and there was nothing they could do to change it, these early believers took their role in prayer very seriously. And ultimately the power of those prayers brought about change far greater than any election day could ever produce!

Remember — our democratic system allows us to vote, and we must exercise this cherished right. But once the election is over, we have to face the fact that the men and women who have been placed in positions of power are there because of the democratic system that elected them. They represent the choice of the people who put them there. If we are unsatisfied with the outcome, our opportunity is coming again a few years down the road to change the situation. Yet even so, our greatest effectiveness will be found as we enter God's presence in the authority of Jesus' name and fulfill these *six prayer commands* given by the Holy Spirit to the Church through the apostle Paul!

MY PRAYER FOR TODAY

Father, I cherish the right to vote. It is a freedom that cost the lives of many. At the appointed time, I will exercise that privilege to make my voice heard via my voting ballot. However, I realize that I don't have to wait for an upcoming election to cast my vote for righteousness. I take my place in prayer, in obedience to Your Word, and with the help of the Holy Spirit, and I pray with all manner of prayer and supplications. Seated together with Christ Jesus and by the authority of His name, I pray with confidence according to Your will, knowing that You hear me.

I pray this in Jesus' name!

MY CONFESSION FOR TODAY

I confess that I exercise my rights on earth and in Heaven. I pray for those in offices of governmental authority as I exercise my authority in Christ through prayer. I operate according to the divine law of love, and I refrain from criticism and negative speech. Instead, I speak words in agreement with the will of God and the establishment of righteousness in my land.

I declare this in Jesus' name!

QUESTIONS FOR YOU TO CONSIDER

1. Do you have the right to vote? If so, do you appreciate it? Do you actually vote, or are you among the millions of people who no longer go to the polls and just trust that everyone else will do the voting?
2. How often do you pray for those who are in authority? Often people feel free to criticize leaders, but they fail to pray for them. Which category do you fit into? If you are one who criticizes only, how will you change after reading today's *Sparkling Gem*? Will you begin to pray for those who are in authority?
3. Without looking back at what you read today, can you recall the six prayer commands that Paul gave to us? Since these are commands, it would be good for you to memorize them so you can make them a regular part of your prayer life.

JULY 5

I Signed a Contract, a Widow Heard From God, and the Lord Gave the Increase!

I have planted, Apollos watered;
but God gave the increase.
— 1 Corinthians 3:6

I had worked laboriously for an "open door" to Channel One in the nation of Ukraine — the premier TV channel that broadcast into every home in the country. However, regardless of how hard I tried, it seemed that access to this massive station eluded me. But one day, I received a phone call from a man who said he had an "inside" contact at Channel One and that if I would meet him at a certain location in Kiev, he would accompany me to the station and introduce me to the top leadership of that channel. So at the appointed time, I met him — it was almost like a clandestine operation — and he did exactly as he promised. He walked me through the open door that I had been seeking for years.

I found myself standing in an executive TV office with the two men who had the final say-so about which programs would or would not be broadcast on Channel One. After a few minutes of talking, they said, "We've reviewed your programs, and we're ready to accept them as part of our daily broadcast schedule."

I almost lost my breath. Did they *really* say what I just heard? Were these men actually offering me the possibility of broadcasting our programs to the *entire* nation *every* day of the week? As far as I knew, this opportunity had never been given to anyone else. But now the door had flung wide open and was standing *right in front of me* as open and passable as it could be! *This was a God-ordained moment.* I knew that God was beckoning me to trust Him and to walk through this door.

When they told me the cost per broadcast, I didn't have that kind of money or anything even close to it. But the door was open, and God was urging me to put my name on the "dotted line" of the contract. So I asked for a few minutes to be alone with my associate who was with me. Once we were alone, we bowed our heads, clasped hands, and prayed for the courage to accept this step of faith. I told my associate, "I don't have the money to pay for this, but I know God has opened this door, and I am supposed to sign this contract. I don't know where the money will come from, but I *must* sign this contract and trust that God will speak to someone *somewhere* to help pay for this huge opportunity."

When we finished praying, I had deep peace that despite the fact that I didn't have the money to take this step, God wanted me to sign the contract. So when the men reentered the room and asked what we had decided, I boldly told them, "Of course, we are going to broadcast! So give me that contract, and I'll sign it."

After reviewing the contract, I took a pen in hand, gulped a deep breath, and signed that piece of paper. It was a huge leap of faith for me, but I had the awesome inward witness that we were about to experience the supernatural provision of God in a measure we had never seen before. God was going to show Himself strong to us and provide every cent that was needed to broadcast on this massive TV channel. As a result, *every* person in *every* home in that nation where there was a television would be able to hear rock-solid Bible teaching *every day of the week*!

But that's just half the story. At the exact time I was signing that contract, a ministry partner — a widow who had faithfully given smaller offerings for many years — received surprise information that she had received a large inheritance. She had always told the Lord, "If You'll trust me with money, I'll use it to finance the preaching of the Gospel." God heard her, knew she was serious, and did exactly what she prayed. He supernaturally put a large sum of money into her hands. When she received that inheritance, she said, "Lord, I'm going to help Rick Renner preach the Gospel to the former Soviet Union!"

When we later looked at the calendar and compared the times on both sides of the world — we discovered that at the exact moment I was signing that contract, this woman was receiving the news about her inheritance! I signed the contract, and literally *simultaneously*, God put the money into the hands of a widow who had made Him a promise.

Before the first payment was due for that massive TV outreach, we had all the finances we needed to pay the bill. God had entrusted that widow with the money necessary to cover the cost of those first broadcasts — and she kept her promise to steward her finances for the preaching of the Gospel.

Actually, this woman supported our TV outreach for many years. As a result, our Bible teaching programs went into *every* home in that nation *every* day. Over time, we received millions of letters from people who watched the programs, who gave their lives to Christ, and who began to regularly correspond with our ministry for help to further develop their lives in Christ.

As I think back on this experience, I see how every person played such a vital role for this miracle to be brought to pass. I signed the contract — but I didn't have the money to pay for it. God gave finances to a faithful widow — and she supplied the money to pay. Each time I ponder this experience, I'm always reminded of what the apostle Paul wrote in First Corinthians 3:6: "I have planted, Apollos watered; but God gave the increase."

Paul knew his role was that of a "planter," which is the Greek word *phuteuo* and means *to plant*. Paul's statement was a clear reference to his founding of the Corinthian church. He was anointed to forge into new territory and challenge the powers of darkness in order to *plant*. Paul was endowed with the anointing to push open doors and find opportunities — and to plant seeds for the Gospel that would grow into churches.

Apollos, on the other hand, was anointed differently for ministry. He was specially called *to come behind* Paul and to "water" and "nourish" what Paul had planted. The word "watered" is the Greek word *potidzo*, which means *to give drink, to water*, or even *to imbibe*. It portrays one who nourishes what has been planted, thus providing the sustenance it needs to grow.

Of course, we know that God ultimately gave the increase, bringing forth what Paul planted and Apollos watered — and causing growth to come in the Corinthian church.

As I look at First Corinthians 3:6, I see these three elements in the Channel One miracle: *First*, I was the planter who was anointed by God to sign the contract. That was an essential first step. *Second*, our blessed partner, a widow, was called and anointed to "water" the seed I'd planted (the signing of the contract) with her finances. She was assigned a very important portion of the process, and she willingly did her part.

Third — and most important — was God, the Partner who was ultimately responsible for all of it. Paul said, "...But *God* gave the *increase*."

The word "increase" in First Corinthians 3:6 is a form of the Greek word *auxano*, which simply means *to increase* or *to grow*. The form of this word used in this instance indicates the *continuous blessing* of God upon the work of Paul and Apollos, with God as their chief Partner in the process.

One theologian has said, in effect, "We can till the ground, plant the seeds, pull the weeds, and lavishly water what has been planted, but *only* God can provide the blessing, sunshine, and environment to make it all grow."

It simply takes every one of us doing his or her different job — with God's blessing on it — for doors to open and harvests to be reaped. Divine connections are essential for completing a divine assignment. And respect for every person for the role he or she plays — including God and His role — is so important. Most of us realize that even if we all did our respective parts to make supernatural things come to pass, nothing of value would ever grow without God providing His continuous blessing. So *all* the glory goes to God for what is produced in our lives.

In the case of the contract with Channel One, after that man helped me make contact with the leaders of that TV station, God used my associate and me to negotiate the deal, my hands to sign the contract, and a widow to sow finances into the project. And, most importantly, God's hand of blessing was on it throughout the entire journey. Those elements all working together produced a harvest of salvations from our TV programming that will last for all of eternity.

If you're trying to complete a God-given project alone, I pray that today's *Sparkling Gem* has spoken to your heart about the need for divine connections with other people — and the absolutely essential need for God to be your chief Partner in making everything you do grow and become prosperous. If you do not have those connections right now, I pray that God will divinely connect you to others who will come alongside to help you complete the assignment He has called you to fulfill — *in Jesus' name*!

MY PRAYER FOR TODAY

Father, I see that it takes divine connections to make a project of faith come to pass and bear fruit. Many times I have felt discouraged because it seemed I had to complete a God-project alone. Father, I ask You to connect me with others who will respond to Your voice and help cause Your supernatural plan to come to pass. I receive God-ordained help to complete the assignment You have given me. I ask You to strengthen me and those with whom You will connect me so that together we can do our respective parts under Your direction to fulfill what You want each one of us to do!

I pray this in Jesus' name!

MY CONFESSION FOR TODAY

I confess that I am obedient and faithful to the direction of the Lord when He gives me an assignment. And I declare that with each divine assignment He gives me, God also ordains obedient and faithful people who are positioned with me to see that assignment through to completion. Just as Paul planted, Apollos watered, but God gave the increase, we each do our part by the direction of God as we give all glory to His name!

I declare this by faith in Jesus' name!

QUESTIONS FOR YOU TO CONSIDER

1. Can you think of a moment when you obeyed the Lord, but you didn't know how God was going to do what He was instructing you to do? When was that and what happened?
2. Have you ever had an experience when *you* took a step of faith, and God used an unexpected person to supply the provision you needed to make your step of faith come to pass?

3. Were you filled with enthusiastic excitement at the moment you committed yourself to a huge project in faith — or did you feel a sense of hesitancy? What did you experience as you "signed your name on the dotted line" and made a commitment that would require *the supernatural provision of God*?

JULY 6

Living on Borrowed Time!

But let patience have her perfect work....
— James 1:4

In the early days just after the collapse of the Soviet Union, our family settled in the nation of Latvia, where we first started our ministry in the former Soviet Union. At the time, the government of Latvia was especially fearful of spies and therefore paranoid about foreigners, so they did not like our being there. Because we had so much TV equipment, it was rumored that we were a CIA group sent to spy on the activities of the nation. Thus, we were very unwelcome by many influential people who occupied high positions of authority within the Latvian government. But we *knew* that this was the place where God had called us to start our work in the former USSR, and we were determined not to be moved by fear or to be bullied out of that nation.

As is often the case in a foreign country, living in Latvia required a visa. The man in charge of immigration at the time did not like us — so he would only issue us a visa that lasted one day, three days, five days, or *maybe a week* at a time! Then at the end of that very brief period, we had to start the entire visa process all over! It was like the devil was trying to wear us down and run us out of town. But we knew that we had been called to be there, and we would not give up.

Actually, there were *several times* when our visas expired, and we had to plead with officials to issue us another one. When they'd finally grant our request, the new visas would often be valid for a mere 24 hours! That meant we had only one legal day to "rest" and breathe a sigh of relief before we had to initiate the process all over again.

Denise and I still have our old passports from back in those days, and they are *filled* with pages and pages of Latvian visas. We had so many visas that we ran out of space in our passports several times, and the U.S. Embassy would sew in extra pages to make room for *more visas*!

It was just like we were living on borrowed time. Every night when we went to bed, and every morning when we woke up, we were talking and praying about visas so we could stay where we knew God had called us. It was undoubtedly one of the biggest fights we had ever faced — and this fight continued unabated for several years! Space prevents me from articulating how much pressure it put on us. While we were producing TV programs, starting a new church in Riga, and answering mountains of pieces of mail from TV viewers, this visa problem was constantly in the background hassling us. It literally affected every area of our lives.

But after years of being hassled, vexed, and beleaguered, an abrupt change *suddenly* came! For some reason, which we never discovered, someone in the very top echelon of the government said, "*Enough is enough* that we have done to this family." To our surprise, we were granted a *three-month* visa; then a *six-month* visa; then a *one-year* visa; and, finally, our entire family was granted *permanent residency*! The battle was over — and that meant we could fully focus on the task of taking trusted Bible teaching across the entire former USSR. By God's grace and the virtue of patience, we had endured and outlasted the enemy's onslaught.

Many believers in the early centuries had a favorite character trait, which they called the "queen of all virtues." It was the Greek word *hupomeno*, and it appears throughout the New Testament. One example is in James 1:4, which says, "But let *patience* have her perfect work...." The word "patience" in Greek is *hupomeno*.

The word *hupomeno* is a compound of two words, *hupo* and *meno*. The word *hupo* means *under* or *by*, and the word *meno* means *to stay* or *to abide*. When compounded, they form the word *hupomeno*, one of the strongest words in the New Testament. It depicts a person who knows he is in the right place — hence, regardless of the pressure, assaults, or restraints that are forced upon him, he has decided that he will not *bend*, *bow*, or *break* under that pressure. He has simply decided that this is his spot, and nothing is going to move him from it. *It is an unrelenting decision to hold fast to that spot and not be moved for any reason.*

Whether we're talking about me and my family and the situation we faced in Latvia or something you may be facing in your ministry, business, or education right now — it is a fact that there are forces at work to try to move us out of our places. The devil does not want us to realize our long-sought victories. That is why we must have *hupomeno* — *staying power* — that comes with a firm decision that we will *hang in there* and never *surrender*, *succumb*, or *quit*.

This word is such a vital part of my life and my thinking that I actually wear a baseball cap with the word *hupomeno* monogrammed across the front panel. It is found throughout the New Testament, and as we have seen, the early saints esteemed it as the queen of all virtues. This tells me that we still need to possess this *lasting power* today! That's why I focus on it so much in my own life.

You see, when *hupomeno* is working in your life, it's not a question of *if* you will win; it's just a matter of time *until* you win! Eventually, the enemy himself gets tired and surrenders. And when he flees, everything you've believed to see will begin to come together. So I encourage you to hang in there and refuse to give up! Let *hupomeno* be a central feature of your life. Eventually the pressures will let up and subside — and when they do, your answer will come. In that day and hour, you'll be so glad you stood your ground and didn't surrender to the pressures that were trying to wear you down and push you out of position in your pursuit of God's plan for your life!

MY PRAYER FOR TODAY

Father, when You gave me the assignment I'm working on, You supplied everything that I would ever need to fulfill it! I thank You for sufficient grace, wisdom, ability, provision, help from others, and Your very own stick-to-it power! Father, I come before You now and ask You to fill me full and afresh with Your Holy Spirit. I ask You to anoint me with fresh oil and to strengthen me with a fresh touch of Your power so I can allow patience to have its perfect work in me. I am not willing to let go, loosen my grip, or grow slack. I know that I am in the right place at the right time, and I refuse to budge for any reason! Holy Spirit, I receive Your help. And by the power of God's grace undergirding me, I will hold fast and see this assignment through to the end.

I pray this in Jesus' name!

MY CONFESSION FOR TODAY

I boldly confess that staying power is at work in my life! It's not a question of if I will win — it's just a matter of time until I win! No matter how long I have to stand my ground, I will not give up and quit. I will not cringe in fear or bow out because of attempted bullying, intimidation, or harassment. The enemy is the one who will have to surrender in exhaustion. And when he flees, everything I have believed to see will come together before my eyes as everything that opposed and tried to withstand my efforts falls away before the invincible greatness of my God!

I declare this by faith in Jesus' name!

QUESTIONS FOR YOU TO CONSIDER

1. Have you ever felt as though pressures were trying to bully you into giving up on your dream or whatever God has told you to do? How did it affect you, and how did you respond?
2. Have you ever been put in a position where you were hassled as you tried to do the will of God? Have the opposing opinions of family and friends ever threatened to pull you off course as you pressed forward to do what God called you to do? How did you handle it?
3. Did a breakthrough eventually come for you? What caused the breakthrough, and how were things different on the other side?

When HUPOMENO is working in your life,
it's not a question of IF you will win;
it's just a matter of time UNTIL you win!
Eventually, the enemy himself gets tired and surrenders.

JULY 7

A Revelation!

But God hath revealed them unto us by his Spirit:
for the Spirit searcheth all things,
yea, the deep things of God.
— 1 Corinthians 2:10

For years I searched for a way to reach the very large elderly population in Moscow, Russia, where we live. They are a very specific generation, and I had never understood the key to touching them in large numbers. I knew there was a way to do it, but I didn't know that way. To be honest, I had nearly bent my brain trying to think of how "I" could reach them! I didn't realize it at that time, but I had worked so hard thinking on my own that I hadn't involved the Holy Spirit very much in obtaining the answer!

I'll never forget the day I looked out the living room window of our apartment in downtown Moscow — and there on the street that ran parallel to the Kremlin was a massive demonstration of pensioners, widows, and elderly, looking like they were having the greatest party of their lives! Some of them were carrying signs with Communist slogans like they did in the old Soviet Union. Some even carried huge photos of Lenin and Stalin, waving them over the heads of the crowd.

As I leaned out our window to get a better glimpse, I heard music from the Soviet era being played, and I saw that many of these pensioners were actually dancing in the streets to the music. Although most people in the West remember Communism as an evil entity, these elderly people grew up in the USSR and remembered it as the time of their youth. They were reveling in the memories of earlier times when they were younger and life seemed easier than it had become in their old age.

I told Denise, "I want to go downstairs, get out on the street, and experience those elderly people!" Within minutes, I had my winter coat on; I pressed the button on our elevator to take me down to the street; and I nearly flew out of the door of our building to quickly join that big demonstration. My eagerness to join the pensioners on the streets wasn't because I agreed with Communist dogma; I just wanted to share the experience with these thousands of lively elderly people!

When I stepped into the huge throng of senior citizens, I suddenly found myself engulfed by elderly people who were behaving like teenagers. All around me was a mass of white-haired senior citizens who had seized the moment to step into earlier memories of life in the USSR. For several hours, they really "whooped it up" on the central street of downtown Moscow! It was so invigorating to see them enraptured in their memories that I lingered among them until several hours had passed and the crowd finally began to dwindle down. As I walked home toward our apartment, the streets were covered with confetti and large banners with Soviet slogans that lay scattered on the ground.

As I stood there pondering the whole experience, I cried out, "Holy Spirit, please show me how to reach this generation!" Before I got back to our apartment, God had marvelously opened my heart and mind to a new idea of how to reach this older generation, and before I stepped back into our elevator, God had given me a plan to reach them. He imparted to me a revelation that when later acted on, enabled us to build what is now one of the largest senior adult ministries in the world.

It all began with an idea from the Holy Spirit that was birthed in my heart when I was not expecting it. It had started out as just an ordinary day that then developed into an unusual set of circumstances that I shared with thousands of elderly people. And in the midst of that unexpected situation, suddenly the Spirit of God showed me something to do that I had never thought of before. It was like a supernatural beam penetrated my mind, and I could see what to do. Since that moment, years of fruit born from the implementation of that idea have proven that it truly was a revelation from the Lord.

I had always prayed for a way to reach the senior population in Moscow because they represented such a large part of the city. But I would have never been smart enough to dream up the idea that the Holy Spirit dropped into my heart that afternoon on the streets of Moscow. And not only did the Holy Spirit give me an inspired idea, but He also injected me with the courage I needed to obey it. In one split second, I had both the idea and the courage to do what the Holy Spirit had shown me. Insight for the plan and the faith to move forward on it came simultaneously, and the outcome in the years since that moment has been truly profound. Through this outreach that was birthed in my heart in that moment years ago, many thousands of senior citizens have gotten saved and experienced the love of God. The path to reaching them was so simple and so powerful, yet I had never seen it before that moment.

Very often we think so long and hard about how to do certain things that need to be done — when all along, the Holy Spirit knows exactly how to do it. The Holy Spirit sees and knows everything. He knows the key to every heart. He knows the secret to every success, whether in ministry, education, family, or anything else. If we will listen to Him, the Holy Spirit will reveal exactly what we need to know for every situation we face in life. The question is — *are we listening?*

In First Corinthians 2:9, Paul wrote of the restrictions normally placed on our minds, but in First Corinthians 2:10, He told us that part of the Holy Spirit's ministry is to remove those restrictions so we can see what we normally could not see on our own. He says, "But God hath revealed them [hidden things] unto us by His Spirit...."

The word "revealed" is the Greek word *apokalupsis*. The root word is *kalupsis*, which describes something that is *veiled* or *hidden* to the human eye and mind. It is there, but it isn't seeable or knowable. It's like an entire lawn that is beautiful, green, and landscaped, but because the curtains inside the house are closed, you are unaware of the beauty that is right outside for you to see.

But in First Corinthians 2:10, the word *apo* is added to the front of the word *kalupsis*, and that little addition of *apo* means the curtain that once hid our view has been *removed*. Suddenly what was *unseen* becomes *visible*, and what was *hidden* becomes *revealed*. This is the reason *apokalupsis* is translated as something *revealed* or as a *revelation*. And Paul stated that this was a strategic part of the Holy Spirit's ministry — to take hidden things that we cannot know on our own and reveal them to us.

On that day when the Holy Spirit spoke to me on the streets of Moscow, it was as if He held the strings on an invisible curtain that had blocked my ability to see how to reach that older population. When I cried out to Him for answers, He lifted that curtain, and I *instantly* saw what I had never seen. In a split second, I had an answer to a question I had been asking for years. It wasn't something I sat around and concocted on my own; it was something *revealed* to me as the Spirit removed the invisible veil that had separated me from the answer I had been seeking.

God has blessed our ministry enormously over the years, and I am the first to tell you it isn't because we are so smart. If Denise and I have done anything right, we have *listened*. We discovered that if we'll remember to ask the Holy Spirit for help, He will always be there to show us that which we're not smart enough to figure out on our own.

I don't know what answer you've been seeking, but I know *who* has the answer! The Holy Spirit sees everything and knows everything — including those things that your mind would never see or know on its own. Perhaps you've been seeking answers about your marriage, your business, your children, an important relationship — the list could go on and on. You may have been seeking answers for years, but you just couldn't see what to do.

In my own case, all those years the Holy Spirit had the answer I had been seeking, but I was so busy trying to brainstorm ideas by myself that I hadn't allowed the Holy Spirit to operate in His revealing ministry on my behalf.

Today I want to encourage you to open your heart to the Holy Spirit in a new way. He is present with you right now, holding the strings to the curtain that has blocked your view. This may be the very moment that He pulls those strings and you see what you've been searching for so long. Instead of brainstorming and trying to think it through on your own, look to Him — and get a revelation of what the Holy Spirit wants to happen next!

MY PRAYER FOR TODAY

Father, I thank You for revealing the hidden things to me by Your Spirit. I repent because I recognize that too many times, I have tried to think through what to do instead of relying on You for wisdom and divine insight. Holy Spirit, You see and know everything, and You know the key to every heart. You know the secret to every success, whether in ministry, education, family, or anything else. From this day forward, I make a decision to listen to You. I know You will reveal exactly what I need to know for every situation I face in life. And now, as never before, I am listening!

I pray this in Jesus' name!

MY CONFESSION FOR TODAY

I confess that the Holy Spirit not only gives me inspired ideas, but He also injects me with the courage I need to obey Him and to act on those ideas. I receive insight for the plan of God for my life, and I release my faith to move forward on that plan by the strength of the Holy Spirit within me.

I declare this by faith in Jesus' name!

QUESTIONS FOR YOU TO CONSIDER

1. What answer are you desperately seeking that you've never been able to discover on your own?
2. Have you been brainstorming so hard that you've forgotten to involve the Holy Spirit in your pursuit? Is it possible that He's been speaking to you, but you haven't been listening? Do you realize that today the Holy Spirit has the strings to that invisible curtain in His hands, and He's just waiting for the opportunity to show you what you've been seeking?
3. Can you think of a moment when an idea supernaturally dropped into your mind — something you could have never thought of by yourself, but it was exactly the answer you were seeking?

JULY 8

A Broken Wrist on the Road to the Temple of Aphrodite

And be ye kind one to another,
tenderhearted, forgiving one another, even as God
for Christ's sake hath forgiven you.
— Ephesians 4:32

Today I'd like to begin by telling you about an amazing event that occurred when Denise and I were in Greece some years ago — an experience that taught me a lot about the impact kindness has on others.

While visiting the ancient city of Corinth, Denise and I decided to take the long walk up the rocky road that led to the acropolis where the Temple of Aphrodite once stood. Having taught on the book of Corinthians for many years and knowing the historical influence that this location once had on the people of Corinth, I wanted to ascend that arduous peak to see that ancient site with my own eyes. But as we walked higher and higher, we understood that this would take far more time than we had planned, so we turned around and headed back down the mountain, descending the same slippery slope we had climbed.

As we descended, I suddenly felt my foot slip out from under me. With lightning speed, I slammed onto the rocky surface of that ancient road. And the instant I hit the ground, I *knew* I had broken something in my left hand and wrist. In a matter of seconds, my left wrist had swollen to twice its normal size — and because I am left-handed and a writer, I understood that the consequences of this could be serious. Denise took me by the arm and slowly we descended that road until we arrived at the car. I could see the look of shock on the driver's face, as he very carefully helped me into the car and then drove like a madman to get me to a hospital in Athens.

As the car sped down the highway toward the hospital, my hand and wrist continued to swell larger. Denise and I knew that I was in a serious condition in a foreign country. About an hour later, the driver pulled up to the emergency entrance of a hospital and ran inside to get help. He soon reemerged with an English-speaking group of medical attendants, who took us into an emergency room filled with people who were also waiting for emergency care. When I saw the large number of people who were in line before us, I nearly despaired. As a writer, I didn't want my ability to type to be affected by this incident, and I knew this could become a really serious injury if I didn't get help fast.

Denise and I were instructed to "take a seat" in the long, noisy hallway, filled with other people also waiting to see a doctor. Then suddenly a nurse waved for us to quickly follow her, and she escorted us right past the registration desk, past scores of people, and into a small room, where she told us to sit and wait. In just a few minutes, a doctor appeared who spoke a little English. He summoned a team together, and they began to examine my hand and wrist so they could determine what to do with me. Although I was on foreign soil in a very crowded, noisy hospital, the kindness and care the medical staff showed me was amazing. They literally escorted us from the car, into the building, past long lines of people who were waiting, and into a private room, where doctors urgently treated me with compassionate care.

After X-rays, it was determined that I needed emergency surgery, so we made plans to fly to Tulsa, where our U.S. office is located and our extended family resides. There I could recuperate for several weeks. So with the Greek doctors' permission and a lot of very serious instructions (they explicitly told me how to carry my hand in order to travel), the following day Denise and I boarded an airplane that took us to America, where the required surgery was performed. A medical team inserted a metal plate with seven screws into my wrist to put me back together again!

Although it has been years since that accident happened, every time I look at my hand and wrist, I see the large scar from the surgery that is still visible, and it causes me to remember the great *kindness* that was shown to me in that experience. If people had been unkind or uncaring, it would have made the situation much more difficult. But their kindness changed the atmosphere and the outcome of the entire predicament for me.

When I look at that scar on my left hand, I am reminded of that moment when tender care was provided to me, and I am thankful for it. But I am also convicted by it, for we as Christians should be known for this type of kindness. The apostle Paul commanded us to demonstrate kindness to one another. In Ephesians 4:32, Paul said, "And be ye kind one to another…."

When Paul said, "Be ye…," the Greek describes an ongoing process. The idea is to *"start where you are and continuously work at it; be constantly becoming kind…."* This tells us that this trait can be cultivated. If you're not a naturally kind person, this doesn't mean you can't develop this trait. Kindness (gentleness) is a fruit of the Holy Spirit listed in Galatians 5:22. If you will yield to the Holy Spirit and let Him do His work inside you, He will produce this valuable fruit through your life.

Oh, let us surrender to the indwelling Holy Spirit! As we yield to the Spirit of God's work in our lives, He makes it easier for us to demonstrate the kindness of Jesus Christ toward others. It may take time, but if we start where we are and continuously work at it, we can begin to produce a great harvest of kindness in our lives!

But what do I mean by kindness?

In Ephesians 4:32, the Greek word for "kindness" is *chrestos*. This well-known word portrayed *helpfulness*, *warm-heartedness*, and *a willingness to show goodness from the heart* to others — a trait so admirable in the ancient world that it was viewed as a characteristic that everyone should seek to possess. You could say that *chrestos* pictures a person *who is attentive to the needs of others*, *who is beneficial and helpful to others*, or even who is *considerate of other people and their needs and demonstrates this kindness in some way*.

This word acutely describes the attitude Jesus wants to produce in us by the power of the Holy Spirit. Christ wants us to be so conformed to His image that we will be moved with compassion when we see someone who is in need. We will no longer be able to stand idly by and watch a need go unmet but will treat it with the most urgent and loving care.

That is what I experienced the day I slipped on the acropolis above Corinth and broke my wrist — a great demonstration of *compassionate kindness*. I don't know the spiritual status of those who helped me, but I know the attributes they demonstrated to me that day match the descriptions of what Paul commands us to cultivate in our lives.

As noted before, if you don't think these qualities naturally flow from your life, that's all right, because the Holy Spirit lives inside you! And if you will yield to Him, He will cause kindness to flow out of you in an ever-increasing demonstration of His unconditional, compassionate love!

MY PRAYER FOR TODAY

Father, I earnestly desire for the character of Christ to be fully formed in me. I ask that You help me cultivate the fruit of kindness Jesus displayed as He was moved by divine compassion as He went about doing good. Holy Spirit, teach me how to display the Father's heart and character to those in need of Your kindness the most. Lord, it is Your lovingkindness that leads men to repentance and draws them to You. Today I commit to love others as You have loved me by the power of Your Holy Spirit within me.

I pray this in Jesus' name!

MY CONFESSION FOR TODAY

I confess that I let my roots grow down deep into Christ and that His life in me enables me to produce the fruits of righteousness that glorify His name. I choose to yield to the Holy Spirit and to let Him do His work inside me. As I surrender to the Holy Spirit's work in my life, He helps me demonstrate kindness. I allow God to do His sanctifying and transforming work throughout all my personality. Day by day, I yield to the Holy Spirit's presence to help me demonstrate the kindness of Jesus Christ in my life for the glory of God the Father!

I declare this by faith in Jesus' name!

QUESTIONS FOR YOU TO CONSIDER

1. Can you recall a moment when someone showed you special kindness at a difficult time? When was that moment? What kind of impression did that act of kindness make on your life? Have you ever thanked that person for the kindness he or she showed to you at that moment?
2. Are you known by others as a kind and compassionate person? Are these traits lacking in your life? Are these areas that the Holy Spirit wants to develop and cultivate inside you?
3. Has there ever been a moment when you were so inwardly moved by a person or need that you had to get up and do something about it? That is the movement of *compassion*. What were the circumstances leading up to that moment, and what was the harvest?

JULY 9

Jesus Christ — the Same Past, Present, and Future!

Jesus Christ the same yesterday, and to day, and for ever.
— Hebrews 13:8

Do you ever feel like the world is shifting and swirling so fast that it is different from one day to the next? It is simply a fact that we live in an age when everything seems to be changing before our eyes. In fact, technology develops so quickly that if I listed devices that represent the "new" technology of today, whatever I wrote down would be outdated before this book is printed!

Not only have we seen technologies change quickly, but we have also seen politics and political parties, national and international boundaries, and currencies change — and the list goes on and on. And in the midst of this climate of sweeping changes that the world is caught up in, scores of people have been swept into a seismic shift in core biblical values and morals, even concerning the most basic tenets of faith. These changes are occurring at an alarming rate, but we should not be surprised by it, because the Holy Spirit warned us 2,000 years in advance that this would occur in the very last part of the last days. Perhaps the shock we feel is that so many are abandoning former positions of faith to embrace new ones at what seems to be such lightning speed.

In the midst of this ever-changing environment, it is good to remember that there is one thing that never changes — and that is *Jesus Christ*! He was in the past *exactly* who He is in the present and *precisely* who He will be forever! That's why Hebrews 13:8 says, "Jesus Christ is the same yesterday, and to day, and for ever." Today I want us to focus on this verse, because it shows the *immutability* of Jesus Christ!

The Greek word for the "same" emphatically states that Jesus Christ is *unchangeable*! What good news this is in a world where things are changing at lightning speed! Jesus Christ is the one Person we can depend on to be the same, regardless of the time or the spirit of the age. We don't need to refigure who Jesus is, what He thinks, or what His message is, because He is the *same* — and everything He represents is the *same* — yesterday, today, and forever!

The word "yesterday" is the Greek word *exthes*, and it depicts *all time that ever was up until this present moment*. It describes *the past*. The word "today" is the Greek word *semeron*, and it means *today* or *at this very moment* or *this current age*. It depicts *the present*. But in the Bible when the words "yesterday and today" are used in one phrase, as they are used here, it also portrays *continuity*.

The words "yesterday and today" are an Old Testament expression to denote *continuity* (*see* Exodus 5:14; 2 Samuel 15:20). So here we find that Jesus isn't one way in the past and another way in the present. Whoever He was in the *past* is exactly who He is in the *present*. There is *continuity* in Jesus Christ! Therefore, if you discover Jesus of the *past*, you have also discovered Jesus of the *present*, and you have discovered Jesus of the *future*, because *He is continuously the same*. The word "forever" in Greek means *into all the ages of the future*. This phrase depicts *all future time to come*, including all ages that will ever be known. Hence, it describes the *future*.

Hebrews 13:8 carries this idea:

"Jesus Christ is exactly the same in the past, in the present, and in the future."

I don't know about you, but I am so thankful that Jesus Christ is the same yesterday and today and for all future ages! With all the sweeping changes happening in the world right now, I thank God that Jesus isn't one of them! Whoever He was in the past is who He is in the present and who He will be forever!

So in light of this wonderful truth, I want to advise you to dig deep into your Bible — particularly into the four gospels where Jesus is so vividly portrayed. The Jesus you find in the four gospels will be the same forever. What Jesus said and did in those four gospels is exactly what He is saying and doing now. So if you come to know the Jesus of the gospels, you will come to know the Jesus of today, because He is exactly, identically, and precisely the same!

MY PRAYER FOR TODAY

Father, in the midst of this ever-changing world environment, I am so thankful that Jesus Christ never changes! He was in the past exactly who He is in the present and precisely who He will be forever! Lord, I am in awe of Your unchanging love and Your unending mercy. In a society that is morally, politically, and economically shifting, I boldly proclaim: On Christ the solid Rock I take my firm stand! Truly all other ground is sinking sand. Help me, Holy Spirit, to stand strong for You, no matter who around me may abandon their position of faith.

I pray this in Jesus' name!

MY CONFESSION FOR TODAY

I confess my agreement with what the Bible declares in Hebrews 13:8: Past, present, and future — Jesus is exactly the same! Today I receive the stabilizing victory and strength that His unchanging faithfulness brings to my life in every area. No matter who or what may change, my hope is built on nothing less than Jesus' blood and righteousness!

I declare this by faith in Jesus' name!

QUESTIONS FOR YOU TO CONSIDER

1. Since Jesus is *exactly* the same today as He was in the four gospels, what does that tell you about His will concerning healing the sick?
2. Since Jesus is *exactly* the same today as He was in the Old Testament, what does that mean about where He stands on issues of morality?
3. Since Jesus is *exactly* the same today as He will always be, how can you better predict His future actions, responses, and behavior?

We don't need to refigure who Jesus is, what He thinks, or what His message is, because He is the same — yesterday, today, and forever!

JULY 10

Tons of Mail!

From whom the whole body fitly joined together
and compacted by that which every joint supplieth,
according to the effectual working in the measure
of every part, maketh increase of the body
unto the edifying of itself in love.
— Ephesians 4:16

When our television ministry first began in the former Soviet Union, Denise and I thought it was appropriate to encourage people who watched our TV programs to write to us and tell us about their prayer needs. And we promised that our team would *personally* read each letter and that we would *personally* write them back.

But we simply had no idea of the mountains of mail that would come so quickly into our office from every far-flung corner of the USSR. Before we could hardly catch our breath, we had 800,000 unread letters packed in boxes stacked on top of more boxes. An entire large room in our office was filled from floor to ceiling with boxes and boxes of unread mail that desperately needed to be read and answered, *as promised.* The fact is, we were overwhelmed by the response. Worse yet, our staff was so small that as hard as they worked to get through this mail, we simply had neither staff nor equipment to answer such huge numbers of letters in an expeditious manner. We only had a handful of computers for data entry, so these 800,000 letters would have to be answered by hand!

As noted above, I had made a promise on TV that if people wrote, we would read each letter and answer them. But *how* were we going to keep that promise with the mail growing by boxes each day? Then someone on staff suggested that we schedule a number of all-night weekend "mail parties" — working all night long and simultaneously celebrating this great breakthrough of reaching so many thousands of TV viewers.

It really was worth throwing a party because we *were* seeing a miracle before our eyes with each new huge box of mail that was carried into the office. People from all over that part of the world were responding to my invitation to write. So having a "party" to celebrate this miracle — and combining it with a team effort to catch up — seemed like a fun and great idea. We reasoned that if we put our whole effort into it, perhaps we could catch up on the mail!

A series of weekends were chosen, and *everyone* who served in any capacity on the team — workers in the mail department, TV producers, secretaries, guards, drivers — participated in multiple all-night mail-party events. One group of people would open the letters, put data into the computers, and pass the letters on to readers, who read and answered each letter by hand. Once the letters were answered, they were passed on to a group who stuffed envelopes, licked stamps, and sealed the letter. Finally, the last group organized the thousands of letters into batches addressed to each country of destination in order to fulfill the obligations of our local Soviet-style post office.

It took nearly one month to do it, but by being committed — and by every person doing his part joyfully — we were able to supernaturally answer all that mail and catch up with the new incoming mail. Not only that, but afterward God enabled us to purchase additional computers so we would never have to answer mail by hand again.

This series of mail parties was one of the biggest catch-up operations I've ever witnessed! And throughout each overnight marathon, I encouraged the team from Ephesians 4:16 — a very powerful verse about team participation and supernatural energy to get a job done. It says that "...the whole body fitly joined together and compacted by that which every joint supplieth, according to the effectual working in the measure of every part, maketh increase of the body unto the edifying of itself in love."

We can't examine every part of this verse today, but I want you to especially notice the central section of this verse, where it talks about the whole body being "...fitly joined together and compacted by that which every joint supplieth, according to the effectual working in the measure of every part...."

What a picture of teamwork! That's why I chose to use it to encourage our team as we dove into that mountain of mail back in those early days.

The phrase "being fitly joined together" is a translation of the Greek word *sunarmologeo*, a word with three parts. The first part of the word is *sun*, which denotes *cooperation* and *partnership*. It pictures *something that is done in conjunction with someone else*.

The second part of the word, *armos*, is a medical term for a *physical joint* in the human body. The last part of the word is *logos*, which in this case means *to frame* or *to specify*. When compounded, the new word depicts *a joint that works in conjunction with another specified joint*. In other words, these two joints are made to function with each other — and when they do so correctly, the results are extraordinary.

The word "compacted" is *sumbibadzo*, a word that describes the *sinews* and *ligaments* that hold all the joints together and cause them to function as a *single unit*. These sinews and ligaments are essential to keep all the joints held securely in their places to do their proper job of providing *motion* and *mobility*.

The words "every joint" are a poor translation from the Greek word *aphe*. It should be translated "every part." It describes *every individual part* of the body. This tells us that *every part* — that is, *every member* of the Body of Christ — has a specific place where he or she is to be joined and to work in cooperation with other parts of the Body. Every single member, *every part*, of the Body of Christ is to work in cooperation with its other parts. *This describes a team experience.*

Furthermore, when each part is in its proper place, functioning with the other parts it is called to work with, it begins to "supply." The word "supply" is *epichoregeo*, a word that describes *a lavish provision of what is needed.* (For more on the origins of the word *epichoregeo, see* the January 2 *Gem* in *Sparkling Gems 1.*) The use of the word *epichoregeo* in this context tells us that when every member of the Body of Christ is properly connected to other members and working correctly, *a supernatural, lavish supply of divine energy is activated to fully accomplish the purposes of God.* That is why Paul went on to say, "according to the effectual working of every part…."

The words "effectual working" of "every part" underscores everything we've already seen above. The words "effectual working" are a translation of the word *energeia,* where we get the word *energy,* and in this context, it refers to *divine energy.* It is *the supernatural ability to get something done.* The phrase "every part" is *en metro,* meaning *in measure.* This means that every person has his part, his measure, or his contribution. And when every part or every member is in his place, a release of divine energy takes place that results in a supernatural ability to get a job done!

It also tells us that no single member can do everything on his own. He can only do his part *in measure* alongside the other members to whom he is joined. But when every person is joined and doing the full measure of what he can do, it results in divine ability being released in the Body of Christ.

I used this verse to encourage our team because we all needed to get in our places, connected by sinews and ligaments — by *commitment* — and do the part that was assigned to us. If we would do this, I knew that it would cause a release of supernatural energy that would enable us to quickly do what normally would have taken many months to do. Because my team operated in full cooperation, we looked at those boxes and boxes and piles and piles of mail with joy. Team members got into their respective places and stayed there to do what they were assigned to do. As a result, the task was accomplished in minimal time, and we kept our promise to personally answer each letter!

Those letters from Soviet TV viewers were so precious to me that I never allowed them to be disposed of until recently — when I realized that we had a whole warehouse that was filled with tons of old mail from those earlier days. Each letter represented a precious soul, and it was so hard for me to let them go. When we finally did decide to dispose of them, after many years, it was all together more than 100 tons of mail that we shredded and burned. And to be honest, I kept several boxes as precious memories of a notable moment in the history of our ministry.

What type of task do you have in front of you today that can *only* be accomplished if a team comes together to make it happen? Do you find yourself, as I did, with something that grew more quickly than you anticipated and has nearly overwhelmed you? Whom has God called to join with you through deep commitment? I assure you that if you find a team who will accept the challenge and who will cooperate together, it will release the divine energy of the Holy Spirit — and He will supernaturally supply whatever you need to get the job done!

MY PRAYER FOR TODAY

Father, I thank You that You have placed me in my right place in the Body of Christ so every part can work effectually. I thank You, Father, that I am not alone to do the things You've asked me to do and that You have set each one of us in the Body as it pleases You for the fulfillment of

Your plan and Your purposes. Although I may see certain projects that You have assigned me to fulfill, my primary function may be to join myself to another person's assignment in order to see it achieved victoriously. Regardless of whether it is my assignment or a project someone else is called to lead by Your direction, I yield myself to You and ask You to reveal to me my function according to Your design and where I fit for the purpose of Your plan. I ask You to equip me by Your grace to maintain the commitment to stay there, to provide all the mobility and support I can to make the project move forward, and to see a supernatural release of the Holy Spirit's energy to accomplish what I could never do on my own!

I pray this in Jesus' name!

MY CONFESSION FOR TODAY

I declare that the Holy Spirit is clearly and regularly speaking to my heart, showing me where I am to fit and how I am to function in the Body of Christ. Regardless of how much I may want to function on my own, I realize that God has not asked me to do it all by myself. I am equipped according to the measure that has been assigned to me. I declare that I know where I fit, that I know how to function there, that I am committed to the task, and that the Spirit of God supernaturally and lavishly releases His divine power to enable all involved with the assignment to each do their part in moving forward to accomplish His will together for His glory!

I declare this by faith, in Jesus' name!

QUESTIONS FOR YOU TO CONSIDER

1. Do you know where you are supposed to be connected in the Body of Christ and how you are to function in that place?
2. Have you ever experienced genuine, Spirit-led teamwork that draws its strength from the Holy Spirit and releases His divine energy to get things done in a supernatural manner?
3. When did you experience that? Are you working as part of such a team right now? Describe the qualities of the team you have worked with or are working with now that helped produce supernatural results.

When every member of the Body of Christ
is properly connected to other members
and working correctly,
a supernatural, lavish supply of divine energy
is activated to fully accomplish
the purposes of God.

JULY 11

It's Time To Shake It Off and Get Back on the Playing Field!

Take heed to yourselves:
If thy brother trespass against thee, rebuke him;
and if he repent, forgive him.
— Luke 17:3

When I was a young boy, I had a baseball coach who really disliked me. No matter how hard I tried to please him, he poked fun at me and tried to embarrass me in front of my teammates. His words and behavior would hurt me deeply, but I can remember my father telling me to forgive him. My dad would gently urge me to "grin and bear it" because these things happen in life. So when my coach insulted me, I'd do my best to forgive him and then muster the strength to wipe away my tears and walk back onto the ball field. It was wrong of that baseball coach to treat me in that way, but his negativity provided a good learning experience to help prepare me for life. I'm so thankful my father taught me to forgive, get back on the field, and not let the words of others affect me too much.

In life, we will experience many moments when we are tempted to leave the playing field because of the way others have treated us. But just like my father taught me, we have to forgive those who wrong us instead of letting a root of bitterness take root in our hearts. Sometimes the only course of action available to us is to "grin and bear it" and resolve not to throw in the towel on account of someone's hurtful words or actions. Life is beckoning us to do great and adventurous things, and we can't let the actions or words of a few people sidetrack us from what God has planned for our lives!

In Luke 17:3, Jesus gave instruction for how we are to respond when we *perceive* that someone has done something wrong to us. I emphasize the word *perceive* because our *perception* may be incorrect — but whether it is right or wrong, it is still our perception. So what are we to do in such moments? Should we ignore it? Should we let it continue to eat away at us? Or should we take some other route altogether?

Jesus began His instruction by saying, "Take heed to yourselves...." Jesus commanded us to deal with ourselves before we respond to anyone about a perceived wrong. Jesus then continued by telling us how to proceed once we have gotten a grip on our own emotions, saying, "...If thy brother trespass against thee, rebuke him; and if he repent, forgive him."

The word "trespass" means *to violate* or *to cross a line*. In the context of this verse, it refers to *crossing a line with one's words or actions in a way that leaves the other person feeling hurt and violated.* When we perceive that someone has "trespassed" against us, we are to first take a moment and get a grip on our own emotions. However, if you still feel that someone has crossed a line with his words or behavior after you've taken the time to think over the situation and pray about it, the next course of action is to lovingly confront the behavior that you've found inappropriate.

Specifically, Jesus said we are to "rebuke" such a person. In English, this word sounds very strong and harsh; however, in the original Greek, the tone is much softer. The word "rebuke" is a translation of the Greek word *epitimao*, which describes *a frank but gentle way of politely telling a person that he has done something that you perceive to be wrong.*

You see, confrontation doesn't have to be ugly. If you address your offender from a place of love, the conversation can actually be a healing experience. Simply say, "My feelings are hurt, but I recognize that I might have misconstrued your intentions. I need to tell you about it and ask you if this is really how you meant to make me feel." When you go to someone in this way, the person will often express regret for his actions and ask for forgiveness.

Now, let me mention here that in Mark 11:25, Jesus came at the subject of forgiveness from a different angle and made it clear that God expects us to forgive others, no matter what, if we want our prayers to be answered. But today let's focus on what He said in Luke 17:3 about how we should respond to our offender if he repents. Jesus continued, "...If he repent, forgive him." This word "repent" is the Greek word *metanoeo*, a compound of the word *meta*, which denotes a *change*, and the word *nous*, meaning *mind*. When the two words are compounded, the new word depicts *a person who changes his mind and, ultimately, his behavior.*

Jesus was saying that if your offender apologizes for his actions and promises to try not to do it again, you are to "forgive" him. Jesus never said that the offender had to meet *your* requirement for repentance, so don't require what Jesus didn't require. If your offender expresses true sorrow for his words or actions and asks for forgiveness — if he exhibits a change of mind and heart about his actions — you are to forgive him and to let it go.

The truth is, God has already given you all the faith you need to forgive others when they offend or hurt you, whether or not they ever apologize or seek reconciliation themselves. But you still have to make the decision to *use* that faith to pull out every root of bitterness while it's still a little seedling. Don't wait to "lay the axe to the root" until you have a huge tree of anger and bitterness defiling your life!

That brings us to the word "forgive." What does it really mean to forgive? The word "forgive" is the Greek word *aphiemi* — a simple, yet powerful word that means *to dismiss*, *to release*, or *to let it go*. In other words, if your offender offers you a sincere apology and asks for forgiveness, Jesus says you need *to let it go*! Rehashing the issue is not an option. Don't waste your time and energy on something that has been dealt with according to the Word. Rather, put a smile back on your face, and get back on the playing field of life.

But what should you do if the same person offends you again in the same way? Jesus said, "And if he trespass against thee seven times in a day, and seven times in a day turn again to thee, saying, I repent; thou shalt forgive him." Or to paraphrase this statement in modern English: *"And if he violates and crosses a legitimate boundary seven times in a day, and seven times a day repents for his behavior, you are to let it go."*

If a person repeatedly hurts you after apologizing and asking for forgiveness, you might be tempted to judge his repentance as insincere. However, you must be careful not to put yourself in a position where you are judging the character of a person's heart. That is only for God to decide. Perhaps God is dealing with a difficult aspect of his character or with his dealings with other people. Or maybe the person was truly sorry, but he just keeps stumbling again and again.

If the person is willing to acknowledge his error and ask for forgiveness, Jesus said we are obligated *to forgive* them every single time. We must *dismiss it, release it*, and *let it go*.

Jesus' message may be a difficult pill to swallow in the heat of a conflict, but when you consider your options, it is the only path that makes sense and brings peace into your life. Would you rather be in strife constantly with a person who upsets you? Would you prefer to harbor unforgiveness and develop a hard heart? Of course not. Hardening your own heart will never change the heart of your offender; it will just produce problems in two people's lives instead of one. It's far better to let the offense go as many times as necessary and keep your own heart pure and free.

The devil wants to sidetrack you with little problems that will knock you out of the game of life, but you don't have to let him do it. Follow Jesus' instructions, and you will achieve victory in your relationships. If you perceive that someone has wronged you, pray about it, frankly and politely confront the situation, and then give that person the opportunity to repent and ask for forgiveness. Your job is to let the offense go and be free of it. And no matter how many times that person offends you, Jesus requires you to forgive him each and every time.

It's time for you to shake it off and get back on the playing field of life!

MY PRAYER FOR TODAY

Father, I am not willing to be sidetracked by little problems that the devil has orchestrated to knock me out of the game of life. He has no new strategy. I recognize that his repeated ploy has been to insult, bully, and offend me in such a way to trigger and provoke my emotions to take over my thoughts about myself or others. The devil's goal was for me to ensnare myself in the trap of bitterness, unforgiveness, and fear so I'd remove myself from the plan or assignment that You set before me. Father, I repent for the times I have let that happen. I was so focused on the hurt I felt from a perceived wrong, I forgot that the bigger picture was Your plan and my position in it. Holy Spirit, I receive Your help to follow Jesus' instructions to forgive even when it seems to be for the same thing over and over again. When I'm confronted with a perceived wrong, help me do more than merely "grin and bear it." I ask You to strengthen me to focus on the joy of victory as I refuse to cling to offenses!

I pray this in Jesus' name!

MY CONFESSION FOR TODAY

I confess that I guard my heart. I do not allow it to become hardened through bitterness because of offenses. But I keep myself in the love of God so my faith will not fail. In that position, the enemy cannot provoke me to stumble or remove myself from the game of life by choosing to walk in the flesh rather than stay in the Spirit. I follow the example of my Lord Jesus who, when He was ridiculed, chose to forgive. I follow His example and obey His command to forgive so I can live in victory above all the schemes of the enemy.

I declare this by faith, in Jesus' name!

QUESTIONS FOR YOU TO CONSIDER

1. Is there a specific person who continually hurts your feelings? How do you deal with it when that person has done something that has hurt you? Do you harbor bad feelings against him, or have you learned how to politely talk to him about his behavior?
2. If that person expresses regret and sorrow for hurting you, are you able to let it go and walk away from it? Does it upset you if he doesn't meet your expectations according to what you believe repentance should look like? Are you able to accept the simplest apology and let it go?
3. Have you ever hurt someone and later found out about it, only to feel stunned to hear how that person *perceived* that you treated him? When you found out what this person felt, were you thankful he was honest with you so you could make the relationship right? When was that experience and what can you learn from it as you lovingly confront those you think have wronged you?

JULY 12

An Overcoming Attitude!

I can do all things through Christ
which strengtheneth me.
— Philippians 4:13

It seems we live in a world where negativism is the rule of society. Many people think the worst, believe the worst, and constantly talk about worst-case scenarios. But that shouldn't be the case for believers. Those who bear the name of Christ should walk as He walked — full of faith and confidence in the Father.

The best example of this kind of overcoming attitude is found in Philippians 4:13, where the apostle Paul wrote, "I can do all things through Christ which strengtheneth me."

If anyone had a reason to be dominated by the flesh at that moment, it was Paul. Think of it — he was in a *horrible* prison and facing *terrible* circumstances. But rather than let his flesh dominate him with negativism, Paul used a number of powerful Greek words to declare that he had the upper hand over all the natural challenges that were around him — and that he could do anything through Christ who strengthened him.

Although Paul was in a horrible predicament at the time he wrote the book of Philippians, he declared, "I can do all things through Christ which strengtheneth me!" I want us to look at this verse today, because it is loaded with insights about having an overcoming attitude.

When Paul said, "I can do," the phrase is a translation of the Greek word *ischuos*. In Classical Greek, Old Testament Greek, and New Testament Greek, that word denotes the strength and power of gods. But when *ischuos* was noted to operate in individuals, it caused them to be superior to others, to be champions and victors. It gave the upper hand in every situation so that individuals operating in *ischuos* prevailed in every circumstance.

Furthermore, Paul adds, "I can do all things...." The phrase "all things" is from the Greek word *panta*, the word *pan* with *ta* attached. The word *pan* is an *all-encompassing word* that includes *everything* and *excludes nothing*. The little word *ta* denotes even the *smallest* of things. So when Paul uses the word *panta*, he is proclaiming that through Christ, he has the upper hand over everything with nothing excluded, including even the most minute details.

An interpretive translation would read:

> *"I have the ischuos power operating in me, and it causes me to be superior — a champion, a victor! This ischuos gives me the upper hand in every situation I face and causes me to prevail in every circumstance...."*

But Paul went on to say, "I can do all things through Christ which strengtheneth me." The word "strengtheneth" in Greek is a translation of the word *endunamounti*, a present active participle of *endunamoo*. The word *endunamoo* is a compound of *en* and *dunamis*. The word *en* means *into*, such as in placing water *into* a vessel, and *dunamis* means *power*. But more importantly is to note that *dunamis* depicted *the forces of an entire army*. In fact, the Old Testament Septuagint, the word *dunamis* was primarily used to picture *the combined forces of a complete military*.

So when these words *en* and *dunamis* are compounded, the new word *endunamoo* pictures *the power of a whole army being deposited into a person*. Making this even more significant is the fact that Paul used it in the present active participle, which means he was declaring this type of power was presently acting in him and would continue to express itself through him. He was telling us that deposited into his spirit, and at his disposal, was the equivalent of *an entire fighting army*.

So the full verse could be interpreted as follows:

"I have the ischuos power operating in me, and it causes me to be superior — a champion, a victor! This ischuos gives me the upper hand in every situation I face and causes me to prevail in every circumstance, And it is all through Christ, who has filled me and continuously infuses me with the strength of a whole army!"

If Paul could write this in the horrific situation he was in at that time and really mean it, there is absolutely nothing you face that you can't overcome too. God's *ischuos* power is available to you as well, to cause you to be superior, to be a champion — a victor — and to have the upper hand in every circumstance you face. When He filled you with the Holy Spirit, He infused you with the ability of a whole army (*endunamoo)* — and He continues to infuse you with that strength at this very moment.

Your flesh may try to tell you that there's no chance you'll make it through what you're facing. That flesh will try to tell you that you might as well give up and throw in the towel, because there's no hope for you. But that's *your* moment to take charge over your flesh, command it to get into subjection, and release the power of God that's been mightily deposited inside you! Soon you'll find a supernatural flow of divine power coming forth from your inner man that will give you the upper hand in whatever situation you find yourself.

Rather than being dominated by your mind, body, and negative emotions, you'll find that you have become a mighty instrument in God's hand through whom His power can and will operate! *Regardless of what you face, you'll have an overcoming attitude that prevails in every situation!*

MY PRAYER FOR TODAY

Father, I submit my body, mind, and emotions to You as Your exclusive instruments to be filled with Your Word, Your Spirit, and Your mighty power for Your holy purposes. I yield to You, Holy Spirit, and I cease to be a slave to my body and emotions. I ask You to make me a mighty instrument in Your hand to achieve the divine destiny You have placed in my heart to be fulfilled for Your glory!

I pray this in Jesus' name!

MY CONFESSION FOR TODAY

I confess that I have God's mighty power operating in me, which makes me a superior victor and champion over every trick and attack of the enemy. I let the Word of Christ dwell in me richly, and I walk in submission to the leadership of the Holy Spirit. The power of God at work within me gives me the upper hand in every situation I face and causes me to prevail in every circumstance through Christ, who fills and continuously infuses me with the strength of a whole army!

I declare this by faith in Jesus' name!

QUESTIONS FOR YOU TO CONSIDER

1. Can you think of a time when the power of God rose up inside you and pushed all your negative thinking out of the way to give you the upper hand in your situation? When was that time in your life?
2. Did you realize that when you received the infilling of the Holy Spirit, the strength of an entire army came into you? Have you ever felt that strength before? When was that, and what did it feel like to you?
3. What do you need to do to take charge of your body, mind, and emotions so they stop taking charge over you?

JULY 13

No Open Doors!

Neither give place to the devil.
— Ephesians 4:27

Have you ever felt like you were under spiritual attack or that the devil was trying to wage a vicious warfare against your very existence? Today I want to talk to you about doing all you can to keep every door shut to the enemy so he is unable to find easy access into your life.

I can personally testify to many attacks that have come against our ministry and family as we have pressed forward to take new territory for the Kingdom of God over the years. I have learned that the enemy is always looking for ways to sabotage anything that is of significance to the overall plan of God. Therefore, we have had to stand our ground and fight many times. Part of a long-term protection plan against the enemy's attacks has been making sure that we left no open doors for the enemy to find easy access to us or our ministry. Believe me when I tell you that the devil is trying to find a way to sabotage everything good — so we don't need to help him by leaving a door open for him!

Even as I write this, I am thinking of Denise and her habit of locking the doors every night before we go to bed. Even when she is home during the day, she keeps the doors locked. No one enters our home who isn't invited. When someone arrives, they must ring the doorbell to announce his or her arrival. After we invite the visitor in, the door is locked again. Denise's safeguarding of our home once seemed over-protective to me, but then came the time when a stranger tried to enter our home, which made me very thankful that my wife was so careful about keeping the doors locked. I can assure you that it would be *very difficult* for someone to enter our house without permission.

The one time a stranger tried to find entry into our home, an employee escorted him off the property. Even so, the intruder lingered a long time behind our home, waiting for our attention to drop so he could try once again to get back onto the property. But we stayed alert and didn't relax our guard until that intruder was long gone. Had we not been diligent to stay alert on that occasion, I'm sure it would have been only a short time before the person started trying to find entrance to our home again. But a locked door and an alert attitude kept our home from being penetrated by an unwanted guest.

It may seem like a simplistic example, but an "open door" is exactly what the devil is looking for in each of our lives. If we are diligent to keep the doors to our lives locked, it makes it much more difficult for the devil to find access to us. This is one reason the apostle Paul wrote, "Neither give place to the devil" (Ephesians 4:27). This verse is full of insight about how the devil operates, and it explicitly tells us what our part is in keeping the devil from finding a way into our lives. Let's look at this verse and see what it tells us.

First, when Paul wrote, "Neither give place to the devil," it was *not* a suggestion; it was a *command.* If you've ever come under spiritual assault and found the devil in the middle of your affairs, you know that it's much easier to stop the enemy at the doorway than to try to find a way to extract him once he has found an access point to worm his way into an area of your life.

That's why Paul so urgently warned you to give the devil no "place." In other words, keep on alert so the enemy can't freely access your life. Believe me, just like the stranger who lingered in the back of our property, waiting for us to drop our guard and relax our level of alertness, the devil will linger a long time to see if you are truly serious about keeping him out of your life.

When Paul told us to give the devil no *place,* that word "place" is the Greek word *topos.* It describes *a specific, marked-off location.* But rather than a physical location that we use a map to identify, this "place" may refer to a rough spot in our relationships, our finances, our thoughts, or our personal habits or to lingering areas of disobedience. Whatever it is, *it's an identifiable location that the devil seeks to find and use as an open door into our lives.*

If the door is closed, you're already in good condition. If it's locked because you are living a life of holiness and obedience, you are even in better condition. But if you are living loosely, you need to know that the door is not only unlocked — it is likely standing wide open, literally inviting the enemy to come in and wreak havoc in your life! This is why you must be so circumspect in answering the question: *Are there any open doors I need to close that allow the enemy access to my life?*

We need to be serious about our lives because the devil is always looking for a door, a window, or a crack — *an entry point* — through which he can access us. We must circumspectly look at our lives to see if there is any area we have left open or unguarded that has allowed the devil to find a way to attack us. These types of "places" are the open doors he seeks in our lives.

The word "devil" in Ephesians 4:27 leaves no question about the devil's intention to attack us as believers. It is the Greek word *diabolos,* which is a compound of *dia* and *ballo.* The word *dia* means *through,* as in *all the way through an object.* This second part of the word "devil" is from the word *ballo,* which means *to throw, to hurl, to inject,* or even *to beat.* When these two words are compounded to form the word *diabolos*, the new word categorically means that the devil is one who *strikes repetitiously* — trying to find a way to break through into our worlds and mess up our lives.

This word *diabolos* vividly reveals the devil's tenacity. He is so committed to our destruction that if he doesn't easily find his way into our lives, he will linger and wait for us to drop our guard so he can try again, perhaps from another vantage point. The Greek emphatically means he'll even try to *beat* his way inside if that is what is required of him.

The devil is more committed to attack than most of us are to withstand him. That's why he is often so successful in the warfare he wages against us. And that is why the apostle Paul commands us to give him no "place."

Since we know the devil is going to try to find a way to gain entry into our lives, we must use the weapons of warfare God has given us to resist him (*see* Ephesians 6:10-18). But it is likewise essential that we diligently and continually *keep* watch over our lives on a sustained and continual basis, looking for any open doors we may have left open that would make it easier for the enemy to find entrance.

One thing is certain: Living a life of obedience shuts every door and makes it very difficult for the devil to find entry into our lives. On the other hand, we must also acknowledge that if we are living in disobedience in any area of our lives, those areas may become the very entry points by which the devil gains access to try to disturb our peace and stop our forward momentum.

I realize that many attacks we experience can be attributed to the devil acting in accordance with his own evil nature. But the truth is, many times *we* have left a door open that allows the enemy to find his way into our lives and launch his fiery darts from an inside position. It's up to us to do all we can to shut every door and to make sure they *stay* shut. And during those times we are under attack, it would behoove us to ask: "Holy Spirit, is there any area in my life where I've left a door open and allowed this intruder to find his way in?" Before we take authority over the devil in the name of Jesus, let's do all we can to *find the access point and STOP him at the door*!

If you are under attack, you can stand strong in the Lord, confident that the weapons of warfare given to you will enable you to successfully repel the enemy in the name of Jesus Christ. But if you have knowingly, negligently, or ignorantly left a door open that allows the enemy access, there is always the possibility of a successful attack against your life. So I urge you to follow Denise's example. Spiritually *close the door* — and then *keep it locked* so no demonic attack will find its way into your affairs!

MY PRAYER FOR TODAY

Father, I thank You for the spiritual weapons of warfare that You have given me to resist my enemy, the devil. I see that it is essential to diligently survey my life to see if I have left any open doors that would make it easier for him to find entrance into my life and circumstances. Holy Spirit, I ask You to help me live a life of obedience so I can shut every door to deny him access. I ask You to open up my understanding as You shine the light of Your Word into my life. Help me identify and deal with areas of disobedience that may become the very entry points the devil seeks to penetrate to rob me in some way of the goodness of God manifested in my life.

I pray this in Jesus' name!

MY CONFESSION FOR TODAY

I confess that the weapons of my warfare are mighty to keep my mind protected and my life secure against the onslaughts of the wicked one. I am alert, and I keep a watchful eye on myself to guard my heart and the borders of my own life with the protective barrier of obedience to the Word and to the Spirit of God. I am not negligent but diligent to keep the doors to my life open only to God and completely closed to the devil.

I declare this by faith in Jesus' name!

QUESTIONS FOR YOU TO CONSIDER

1. Can you think of an area of your life that is currently under attack because you have left a door open? Is it possible that there is an area of disobedience the devil has been able to use to find easy entrance into your life?
2. If you can identify such an area, what will you do to close that door? What concrete steps will you take to safeguard yourself against future successful assaults?
3. Have you studied the weapons of God in Ephesians 6:10-18? Do you know what weapons God has given you to stand up and fight against the attacks of the devil? If not, I highly advise you to take time to study my book *Dressed to Kill*, as it explicitly describes how the devil attacks, what these spiritual weapons are, and how to use them!

JULY 14

An Unforgettable Funeral!

Likewise reckon ye also yourselves
to be dead indeed unto sin,
but alive unto God
through Jesus Christ our Lord.
— Romans 6:11

When I was first starting in the ministry, I served as an assistant pastor in a denominational church. Because I was in training for ministry, the senior pastor wanted to teach me how to conduct funerals. To instruct me, he took me to funeral after funeral so that I'd learn how to handle myself in delicate and difficult situations.

One funeral in particular was an experience I shall never forget. In fact, even today I can still vividly picture it in my mind's eye. It was a funeral conducted for an unsaved family whose son had tragically died in an accident. The sorrow and remorse in that room was so thick that it could nearly be cut with a knife. Perhaps there is nothing sadder than a funeral with a room full of unbelievers. They have no hope, and when they lose a loved one, it is truly a catastrophe because their lack of hope overwhelms them. But even worse than attending such a funeral is being called upon *to conduct it*!

As the mother approached the casket to tell her son goodbye one last time, I watched as she crawled *into* the casket with that dead body. She was so overwhelmed with grief that she clutched that dead body tightly, pleading, *"Talk to me! Talk to me! Don't leave me like this!"* Funeral workers had to pull her out of the coffin and escort her to the limousine that waited to take her and the rest of the family to the cemetery for the burial.

That early experience is forever etched in my memory. I've never forgotten that pitiful sight when this mother gripped her son's dead body in her arms and begged it to speak to her one last time. But that body was not going to talk to her. It was *dead.* The empty shell that lay in that casket was the deceased, expired, finished shadow of a man who had once lived but now was gone. There was no heartbeat, no breath in his lungs, and no pulse in his wrists to detect. The clock had quit running for that man's life, and there was no turning the clock back to make it start ticking again. It was a "done deal." This man's life had *expired.* All the mother's pounding on her son's lifeless chest wasn't going to wake him up!

As I drove off to the cemetery that day to conduct the gravesite rites, everything I had seen in the funeral home that morning rolled over and over in my mind. The permanence of death and the inability to produce a response from a dead body particularly stayed in my mind. I thought of how that sorrowing mother tried so hard to get that dead body to respond to her, but it simply could not respond because it was dead. As I meditated on this whole scenario, the Holy Spirit began to speak to my heart from Romans 6:11. It says, "Likewise reckon ye also yourselves to be dead indeed unto sin, but alive unto God through Jesus Christ our Lord."

What a glorious thought that is! Our old man is "dead" to sin because of the work of Christ on the Cross!

As soon as I got home from the gravesite service, I reached for my Greek lexicon and looked up the word "dead." As I expected, it was the Greek word *nekros,* which is the Greek word for a *corpse* — in other words, a dead body with no heartbeat, no breath in its lungs, and no pulse to feel in its wrists. It doesn't matter how loud you scream at it, pull at it, or pound on its chest, it's impossible to get a response or reaction because its life is expired. Its life has ceased. In God's mind, *that* is how dead we are to our past and to the sinful impulses that once ruled our lives. In God's mind, who we used to be is *never* to be revived.

According to the Greek text, that part of Romans 6:11 could be translated, *"Continually consider yourselves to be dead to sin."* In other words, if sin tries to act up, we are to keep reminding sin that it is has *no* power over us. The word "reckon" that is used in the *King James Version* is the Greek word *logidzomai*, which means *to count*, *to deem*, or *to consider*. Paul used it in the present imperative case. This means it is a *command* that must be acted upon *continually*. Putting all of this together means that we are *commanded* to *continually* deem our old selves — that is, the personality that existed before Christ — to be as lifeless as a corpse with no life left in it. It is as dead as dead can possibly be, which means you are *not* who you used to be. That person who once lived is dead, lifeless, gone, and buried forever in the mind of God. *This means you are free of your former identity.*

So if your old identity is dead, *who are you now*? Romans 6:11 says that you are "...alive unto God through Jesus Christ our Lord." The word "alive" is the Greek word *zoontas*, a present active participle of *zao*. When *zao* becomes *zoontas*, it doesn't just refer to life, but to *overflowing life*, *profuse life*, *life abundant*! It is truly the picture of one who is living to the fullest. And because it is a participle, it means this is *forever* who you are in Christ!

This overflowing life is a permanent condition in Him! There's no reversal to our old identity. When we died to sin, God quickened us alive with Christ for all of eternity. Therefore, we are forever alive unto God *because* of what Christ Jesus has done for us! We are new individuals with completely new identities. *We are in Christ Jesus!*

When I closed my Greek lexicon and paused from my studying, I thought, *Wow — that was a lot to get out of an experience at a funeral!* And to be honest, I've been getting something out of it all these decades since that funeral occurred! It is impossible to exhaust the revelation in Romans 6:11, which declares the old man is dead and an entirely newly created man has arrived in Christ. But that, my friend, is the case!

Who you once were is not who you are now. Today you are a new creature in Christ Jesus, and the person Jesus has made you has become your forever-new identity! It's a good time to shout, *"Amen!"*

MY PRAYER FOR TODAY

Father, I thank You for the fresh breath of Your Spirit that has swept across my heart. I praise You for giving me new understanding of my identity in Christ. I am overflowing with gratitude to You as I realize that Your great plan of redemption truly caused old things to pass away and all things to become new for me in Him. Through Your great mercy, I was crucified with Christ. When I accepted that exchange, my spirit was recreated by the life of Christ that filled me and made me an entirely new creation in Him. Now with my life hidden in Christ, the old me no longer exists, and this body, once devoted to sin, is now the dwelling place of Your Spirit. My body has no right to dictate my attitudes, actions, or appetites because I am free to reckon it dead. I am forever new because of You. Holy Spirit, I ask You to help me walk in the newness of this life so that I will be an instrument You can use to demonstrate the reality of Christ's life in me, the Hope of Glory on the earth!

I pray this in Jesus' name!

MY CONFESSION FOR TODAY

I joyfully confess that I am not who I once was. Today I am a new creature in Christ Jesus, and the person Christ has made me to be now is my new identity! I am forever alive unto God because of what Christ Jesus has done for me! I continually deem my old personality that existed before I was born into Christ to be as dead as a corpse with no life left in it. I am not the person I used to be. That person who once lived is dead, lifeless, gone, and buried away forever in the mind of God. I am free of my former identity forever!

I declare this by faith in Jesus' name!

QUESTIONS FOR YOU TO CONSIDER

1. Do you believe you've ever *really* had a revelation that your old man is dead and that you are a totally new individual because of what Christ has done for you?
2. Just think of it — nothing about who you were before your conversion really applies to you now. Do you see more clearly how radical salvation actually is after reading this *Sparkling Gem*?
3. How does it affect you to think that before God, you are a completely brand-new person and that you will never revert to the personality of your old nature again? How will this affect the way you choose to think and act from this day forward?

JULY 15

God Rewards Your Sacrifices

Therefore, my beloved brethren,
be ye steadfast, unmoveable,
always abounding in the work of the Lord,
forasmuch as ye know
that your labour is not in vain in the Lord.
— 1 Corinthians 15:58

I know that you face many demands, but today I want to remind you that God has watched what you have done for His work, and He will reward you. All the time, effort, and finances you have sown into the advancement of the Gospel are before His face — and He is faithful to remember and to reward you for what you have done. In First Corinthians 15:58, Paul wrote, "Therefore, my beloved brethren, be ye steadfast, unmovable, always abounding in the work of the Lord, *forasmuch as ye know that your labor is not in vain in the Lord.*"

Notice especially the last part of the verse that declares your labor is not in vain in the Lord. The word "labor" is the Greek word *kopos*, which can refer to *the most exhausting kind of work or effort.* Because this word is used in this context, it tells us that sometimes it is not easy to obey what the Lord tells us to do; sometimes it is very difficult to obey Him. In fact, there are times when it requires great effort to walk in obedience. But this verse promises that our labor has not been in vain!

I think of all the times the Lord has asked me to do something that was very difficult. Yet because I have always wanted to obey the Lord, I have done my best to follow His instructions, regardless of how hard it was or how much it required of me or of my family. Building our work in Russia has not been an easy task. But God called us to do it, so Denise and I and our sons have given 100 percent of our lives to this divine mandate. Since that is what God has asked of us, that is what we decided we were going to do.

Regardless of where you live or what you believe God has asked you to do, it is important that you give your whole heart and soul to your divine assignment. Even if it is difficult sometimes, you must keep pressing forward toward your God-given goal in obedience to the Lord. And whenever the way of obedience seems difficult, you need to remind yourself once again of His promise that "your labor is not in vain in the Lord."

The word "vain" is the Greek word *kenos*, and it depicts *something that is empty, void, or wasted.* This is God's promise that anything you do for Him is never a waste! When the devil tempts you to think that no one is noticing what you are doing or that no one appreciates what you do — that is the moment for *you* to remember that nothing done for the Lord is ever a waste! Every effort, every deed, *everything* you have ever done in obedience to Him will be credited to your heavenly record!

Don't let the devil discourage you. Dig in your heels and remind him that you are standing in faith on God's promises! Declare with confidence that God is going to be faithful to meet every need in your life because you have faithfully sown your time, effort, and finances. And never forget: *Nothing you ever do for the Lord is a waste!*

MY PRAYER FOR TODAY

Father, I am grateful for this reminder that You pay attention to my response to Your assignment for my life. You are very aware of where I am in life, and You see what I do to express faithfulness to You. Thank You for strengthening me with Your might in those times when I felt discouraged and wondered if my labor was in vain. I rejoice in Your all-sufficient grace that never fails to cover me in the midst of the difficulties and hardships I may encounter while obeying You. Lord, I ask You to help me be conformed more fully to Your faithful ways, so when my heavenly record is read before You, I will receive a crown to place at Your feet on that day.

I pray this in Jesus' name!

MY CONFESSION FOR TODAY

I declare that I am steadfast, immovable, always abounding in the work of the Lord, because I know that my labor in the Lord is not wasted. God is aware of all that I say and do for His glory. He openly sees my heart's motivation for what I have said and done, and He will reward me accordingly. I do not live my life for the praises of man. The prize I seek is God's approval. Therefore, I set my focus daily to live a life that will matter for eternity as I labor to see the will of God done on earth as it is in heaven.

I declare this by faith in Jesus' name!

QUESTIONS FOR YOU TO CONSIDER

1. Can you think of an area where you have labored especially hard for the Lord, and you've been tempted to think that it is all in vain? How did today's *Sparkling Gem* encourage you to keep going?
2. Would you describe your position of faith as being immovable, or have you been up and down in your walk of faith? What changes do you think you need to implement in your spiritual life to become more stable and enduring?
3. Do you have anyone who can stand in faith with you and encourage you as you wait for God's plan to come to pass in your life? Are they people who can pray with you and encourage you to dig your heels in deep until you see God's reward?

JULY 16

Don't Play Around the Edge of a Dangerous Cliff!

What say I then? That the idol is any thing, or that which
is offered in sacrifice to idols is any thing? But I say
that the things which the Gentiles sacrifice, they sacrifice
to devils, and not to God: and I would not that ye
should have fellowship with devils.
— 1 Corinthians 10:19,20

It cannot be overstated just how important idol worship was to the pagans of the ancient world. People were intoxicated with the worship of their gods and goddesses. Pagan temples were built in vast numbers in cities everywhere, and idol worship permeated every facet of life.

For believers at the time, it was unavoidable to live in that world and not occasionally walk by an idol, since they were positioned in homes, on streets, and in key locations throughout every city. These environments were spiritually dangerous, and Paul strictly forbade any believer from setting foot on their premises.

However, shunning temples posed a challenge for certain believers in New Testament times because the best meat in town was sold on temple grounds. After meat had been offered as a burnt sacrifice to an idol, temple workers removed it from the altar and placed in the temple meat market, where it was sold for public consumption. So to purchase the best meat in town, one had to physically go inside a pagan temple and look over the meat selection. As a result of this exposure, some began to fall back under the old influences from which they had been delivered.

Paul knew that being so physically close to those spiritually dark environments was too great a risk for these believers. So he urged them to stay away from those sites, lest they fall back under the influence of the demonic powers from which Christ had delivered them. He wrote, "Wherefore, my dearly beloved, *flee* from idolatry..." (1 Corinthians 10:14).

The word "flee" in this verse is the Greek word *pheugete*, which means *to run as fast as possible* or *to take flight.* Furthermore, the tense Paul used for this word conveys that his readers were *to constantly flee* from idolatry with no exception. He was emphatically stating that idolatry should never be tolerated under any circumstances — *not then, not now, not ever.* These environments were simply too detrimental for believers who had already been delivered from a life of idolatrous practices.

As an analogy, consider a person who has been delivered from alcohol. Once Christ set him free, it would be foolish for him to meet people in a bar because that environment might *lure* him back into the habit of drinking again. A bar is simply a dangerous environment for an individual who has been set free from an alcoholic addiction. Common sense says he shouldn't go there.

Another example would be someone who has recently quit smoking. Hanging out with smokers would create a temptation to light up a cigarette and start smoking again; therefore, common sense dictates that it is better for someone who formerly smoked cigarettes to stay away from those who still smoke so he or she can remain free. That may mean choosing a new set of friends, but severing these ties from the past is a far better option than slipping back into bondage with cigarettes.

When Paul addressed the subject of idolatry in First Corinthians, he made it clear that an idol in and of itself is nothing. Rather, it was the *environment* in which idolatry was practiced that was so dangerous because demonic activity permeated it. In the dark, spiritually charged environment of these pagan temples, the spirit realm was stirred up under the guidance of the priests and priestesses, and demon spirits were drawn to these grounds like moths to a flame.

It is a biblical command to flee from the presence of evil because it is foolish to blatantly put ourselves at risk in a detrimental environment. We may not fall off the edge of a cliff simply by standing near it, but playing around the cliff's edge greatly increases the danger of slipping. Keeping a safe distance from the edge assures us that we will *not* slip and fall. Therefore, although we rejoice in the truth that declares, "Greater is he that is in you than he that is in the world" (1 John 4:4), we must also remember the same epistle likewise commands us, "Little children, keep yourselves from idols" (1 John 5:21).

There is great potential spiritual damage and harm that you can subject yourself to by simply being in a wrong spiritual environment where there is an evil influence.

Christ required that believers live a life of holiness and use spiritual common sense to stay away from the crumbling edge of a spiritually dangerous cliff. He had called them *out of* darkness *into* His marvelous light (*see* 1 Peter 2:9), and He knew that skirting around the edges of darkness was *not* the way for His children to flourish. Thus, the Holy Spirit pleaded with New Testament readers through the apostle Peter: "As obedient children, not fashioning yourselves according to the former lusts in your ignorance: but as he which hath called you is holy, so be ye holy in all manner of conversation; because it is written, Be ye holy; for I am holy" (1 Peter 1:14-16).

Living far from the edge of darkness, evil, and worldliness is what Christ demands. By adhering to this command, those early believers who were once bound by a lifestyle of darkness and sin could continue enjoying the freedom that Christ had purchased for them on the Cross with His own blood.

The same is true for us today. We need to use common sense about where we go and with whom we choose to spend our time. Christ has set us free, but just because we're free doesn't mean we can play around the edge of the cliff!

MY PRAYER FOR TODAY

Father, I ask You to help me use common sense to know the places that I need to avoid to maintain my spiritual freedom. I know that I am free. I know that Christ's power in me is greater than any force around me. But Your Word clearly teaches me to avoid those detrimental environments that once held sway in my life. So in obedience to Your Word, I deliberately choose to change my way of doing things, lest I place myself in spiritual jeopardy. Holy Spirit, I ask You to help me be sensitive to discern when I am in a wrong place or with a wrong group — and to show me how to graciously leave when I know it's time for me to be going!

I pray this prayer in Jesus' name!

MY CONFESSION FOR TODAY

I confess that I will no longer intentionally place myself in positions that are too close to the edge of the cliff. Christ has set me free, but I don't need to play around or fellowship in the sinful places from which Jesus liberated me. I admit that I've made this mistake in the past, but I will not make it any longer. The Holy Spirit within gives me wisdom and common sense to recognize when I'm in a detrimental environment, and He gives me the courage to exit these situations so I can keep moving forward.

I declare this by faith in Jesus' name!

QUESTIONS FOR YOU TO CONSIDER

1. Since most of us do not live in places where actual idolatry is practiced today, what is the application of these truths for you and me?
2. Can you name environments or places that you need to avoid because they would tempt you to fall back into old patterns or habits from which Christ has already delivered you?
3. Do you know anyone who was freed from sin, but fell back into it as a result of hanging out at the wrong places with the wrong people?

JULY 17

Your Problem Is Nothing Special

There hath no temptation taken you
but such as is common to man:
but God is faithful,
who will not suffer you to be tempted
above that ye are able;
but will with the temptation also make a way to escape,
that ye may be able to bear it.
— 1 Corinthians 10:13

In these uncertain times, many people are facing huge challenges that have left them feeling like they're stuck in a trap with no way out. Maybe you're feeling this way too. However, I have good news for you! There's a means of escape from *every* trap, whether it was laid by the devil, by external circumstances beyond your control, or even by your own mistakes.

There are many different kinds of traps people struggle with that span all walks of life. For example, any type of addiction can be a serious trap, such as overeating, substance abuse, illicit sex, or some other destructive behavior. Left unchecked, turmoil in your relationships, whether past or present, can also cause mental anguish and make your mind feel trapped in an emotional prison. Or it could be a discouraging prognosis from your doctor regarding an illness you've been battling that overwhelms you with feelings of hopelessness and negativity.

A financial trap can feel particularly crushing. In fact, it can seem like the deepest ditch of all because it affects your emotions, your mind, and your relationships. When you don't have enough money to cover your mortgage, car payments, credit card payments, or utility bills month after month, it's easy to let worries about money consume your thoughts. Let me tell you — that is *not*

God's will for your life. He wants to deliver you out of that financial trap and bring you into abundant provision and blessing. And He knows just how to do it!

First Corinthians 10:13 gives *God's* perspective on all the problems you are facing right now. The apostle Paul wrote, "There hath no temptation taken you but such as is common to man: but God is faithful, who will not suffer you to be tempted above that ye are able; but will with the temptation also make a way to escape, that ye may be able to bear it." The phrase "such as is common to man" is a translation of the Greek word *anthropinos*, which literally means *commonplace to humans*. So Paul was telling us that no matter how overwhelming, suffocating, and insurmountable your trap might seem, it is merely a common human problem that has already been faced *and overcome* by countless people and believers in the past.

Every human being has the same basic needs and faces the same type of problems and temptations in life. However, it is an insidious trick of the devil to plant the false assumption in your mind that *your* need is a special case. If he succeeds in doing this, it will be vastly more difficult for you to overcome your obstacle, since you'll view it as a one-of-a-kind problem that you alone have to face. You'll assume that none of God's principles apply to your situation because it is so *huge*, *unique*, and *special*. And when someone gives you an answer for your situation from God's Word, you'll just nod and say, "Yes, I know that's what the Bible says, but my case is an exception. It has all kinds of unique complications that make it especially hard to deal with."

This is wrong thinking! It is imperative that you stop looking at the trap you're in as something that no one else has ever experienced. During my years as a minister, people have often come to me for counsel and said, "My situation is very unique, an especially difficult case. It isn't like other problems." However, as they begin to share their situation with me, I quickly find that it's the same problem countless others have faced in the past and are facing today.

How you look at the problem will determine how quickly you get out of it! If you look at it like it's huge, unique, and special, you'll have a very hard time getting over it.

So how *should* you look at your problem? Simply address the trap that is holding you hostage and declare, "This is *not* a special problem. In the history of mankind, I'm not the first person to face this type of challenge, and I won't be the last. There are countless other people facing problems far more difficult than mine, yet they smile and maintain their joy in the midst of the challenge and end up victorious on the other side! This is just a common problem that many people have conquered before me — and I'm going to be the next to do it!" When you adopt this attitude, you position yourself to quickly escape the trap you're in by reducing the size of your problem in your mind into something manageable and conquerable.

Paul concluded First Corinthians 10:13 by saying, "...But God is faithful, who will not suffer you to be tempted above that ye are able; but will with the temptation also make a way to escape, that ye may be able to bear it." *God is faithful to make a way of escape for you.* He will show you how to get out of any trap you might find yourself in right now. There *is* a way out, and God has given you His Word and His Spirit to guide you every step of the way.

Make the decision today to align your thoughts, words, and attitudes with God's Word about any problem you are currently facing. Then, step by step, begin walking out of that trap — until that glorious moment when you arrive on the other side, free and victorious!

MY PRAYER FOR TODAY

Father, as Your child, I am special and unique — but my problems are not. There is nothing new under the sun. Every temptation I have faced or ever will face has already been experienced by others. But more importantly, it has already been faced and overcome by the Lord Jesus Christ. Father, I rejoice that You are faithful to Your promise not to allow me to be tempted beyond what I may be able to bear, but with each temptation, You will also make a way of escape for me. Thank You for showing me the path prepared to get me out of traps that try to drain my hope and cause me to doubt and fear that I may never be free of it. I set myself in agreement with Your Word and Your Spirit to guide me out of my problems and into Your plan for me.

I pray this in Jesus' name!

MY CONFESSION FOR TODAY

I declare that there is no temptation that may try to overtake me that isn't already common to mankind. I refuse to see any problem as too big to solve. I confess that every situation has a solution and it can be conquered by the wisdom of God. Today I make the decision to align my thoughts, words, and attitudes with God's Word about any problem I may face. I know my Father God will always provide a way of escape for me from every temptation. Therefore, I listen to His voice and expect His Word and His Spirit to illuminate and direct my steps as I begin walking out of every trap until I arrive on the other side, free and victorious!

I declare this by faith in Jesus' name!

QUESTIONS FOR YOU TO CONSIDER

1. Are you facing a problem right now that you have been tempted to "glorify"? Instead of blowing it out of proportion in your mind and your emotions, how are you going to shift the way you think about it?
2. Have you been guilty of saying your problem is special and therefore unsolvable, even by operating the principles outlined in God's Word? After reading today's *Sparkling Gem*, do you see how important it is to downsize your problem in your thinking?
3. When your flesh tries to convince your mind that your problems are insurmountable and enormous, how are you going to respond?

JULY 18

Uncomfortable Questions That Are Healthy To Ask Yourself

Examine yourselves, whether ye be in the faith;
prove your own selves....
— 2 Corinthians 13:5

Second Corinthians 13:5 tells us to "examine ourselves" from time to time to see if we are in the faith. This is especially true as we witness the direction society is going in these last of the last days.

That word "examine" is the Greek word *peiradzo*, which actually refers to an *intense examination.* This could include a test by fire, a test based on questions, or a test that includes some type of *self-examination.* A test of self-examination is the most pain-free option, even if you must ask yourself questions that require answers that are uncomfortable to confront.

So today why don't you do a little self-examining and see how well you fare? Open your heart, be honest, and talk to yourself and to God about these questions. They are designed only to help you consider possible areas where you may need to change.

➤ **What do you give to God financially?**

Since actions speak louder than words, take a look at your financial giving and see what it reveals about whom you love most. Do you give the tithe, as commanded by Scripture, or do you regularly make excuses for not giving and use the money elsewhere for personal pleasures or other things?

If you are honest today, what would you say that your giving reveals about your love for God?

➤ **What do you do with your time?**

Do you make spending time with God a top priority in your life? Or do you complain that you do not have time to pray or read the Bible, yet you somehow make lots of time to visit with friends, watch television, go to the movies, and do other things that you want to do?

If God Himself looked at your life and measured what you love most by the things you dedicate your time to, what would He say?

- **What do you do to serve others?**

  It's amazing how many people claim to love God, but never have time to serve Him in a practical way in a local church. Words are easily spoken, but actions prove a person's sincerity.

  By looking at your life, would God say that your actions prove you are more devoted to your own needs and interests, or that your life demonstrates you are in love with God's Church?

- **When you pray, what do you pray about? Do you pray about yourself only, or do you pray for the needs and dreams of others?**

  It is easy to think of your own needs and desires, but how often do you focus your prayers on the concerns of others? When you pray, does God hear you primarily praying for yourself, or does God hear you praying for other people too?

  If God were to give a report about the things He hears you pray about, would He report that you are an unselfish person who is concerned about the needs and dreams of others, or would He report that you are concerned only about yourself and your own needs?

- **What personal sacrifices do you make to serve the Lord?**

  How long has it been since you gave something up or changed your schedule to help someone else or to walk in obedience to God's plan? Can you honestly say that you are picking up your cross and dying to your own interests in order to serve others and to make a difference in someone else's life?

  If God opened the books to reveal the sacrifices you have made for Him or others, would the record reveal that you care deeply for God and live in obedience to His commands, or would it show that you are unwilling to inconvenience your life in any way or sacrifice any of your private plans?

- **What do your spending habits reveal about you?**

  When you look at the money you spend on your hobbies, personal possessions, and other non-essentials, and then compare it to the amount of money you invest in the Gospel, what does it reveal about your love for God and concern for others who need to hear the saving message of Jesus Christ? We can all mislead ourselves to think we are generous, but if God Himself gave His view of what your spending habits reveal about your priorities, what would He say about you?

  Would God say the Gospel is most important to you, or would He say that your spending habits reveal that your driving motivation in life is simply pursuing comfort and pleasure?

- **What are you sacrificing to be obedient to God?**

  Is there anything you are laying down in order to walk in obedience to God and His Word, or would you have to honestly say that you don't sacrifice much for God or others? Are you willing to be inconvenienced to help someone else or to serve in the church, or are you unwilling to jeopardize your own comforts and pleasures?

Would God say your life reveals that you are willing to pick up your cross to do what God asks of you, or that you do everything you can to avoid letting anyone or anything inconvenience you?

➢ **What does your lifestyle reveal about your priorities?**

Does your daily lifestyle reveal that you love entertainment, pleasure, comfort, and happiness the most? Are you consumed with yourself and your own needs and offer no service to anyone else if it requires you to sacrifice your time, energy, or comfort? Or can you honestly say that you are living your life primarily for Jesus, fulfilling His plan for you in these last days?

If God were to comment on your lifestyle, would He say that it is dedicated to Him and to fulfilling His plan? Would your priorities match those of a selfish or unselfish lifestyle?

A day is coming when the truth about you will be known! The secrets of the heart will be made manifest, and the truth will be laid bare before God. So wouldn't it be much wiser for you to let God deal with your heart now — to expose those areas of your life and thinking that need to be changed so you can be more conformed to the mind of Christ?

If you let the Holy Spirit deal with you now and bring about the necessary changes in your life, you will be able to confidently and joyfully look into the eyes of Jesus on that day you stand before Him. And you will be known as one who loved Him most of all in these last days when so many were caught up with being "lovers of pleasure more than lovers of God" (2 Timothy 3:4)!

MY PRAYER FOR TODAY

Father, I come before You now as humbly as I know how, and I ask You to shine the light of Your Word into every hidden place of my heart to reveal my true motives to me. Disobedience produces self-deception, and, Father, I realize that actions speak far louder than words. I have often praised You with my lips, yet my heart was far from You as I rationalized and justified my self-seeking priorities with self-deluded excuses for being a lover of self more than a lover of God. Holy Spirit, I ask You to help me judge myself and lay aside every weight and sin that can so easily trip me up. More than anything, I desire to please You, Father, and to honor the Lord Jesus who gave His life for me. Today, like Jesus, I choose Your will above my own. I yield all I am and all I possess to You for Your exclusive use. I am not my own. I belong to You. I have been bought with a price, the precious blood of Jesus Christ. Therefore, I yield to Your transforming power more than ever before. On the day I stand before You and the books of my life are opened and read, I will receive a crown to set at Your feet, just as I lay my life before You now.

I pray this in Jesus' name!

MY CONFESSION FOR TODAY

I declare that I examine myself in the light of God's Word and I apply what the Holy Spirit reveals. I refuse to delude myself with reasoning that is contrary to truth. I choose to be a doer and not merely a hearer who listens to the Word but refuses to internalize its meaning or to act on the truth. I respond to wisdom's voice, and I bring my life into alignment with God's purposes and plan. I choose to agree with God; therefore, I walk in harmony with His will and His ways. I don't waste my life. I keep my focus on Jesus and on eternity. On that great day when I stand before Him, my reward will be that in this life, I was fruitful for His glory because I obeyed.

I declare this by faith in Jesus' name!

QUESTIONS FOR YOU TO CONSIDER

1. Did the questions in this *Sparkling Gem* stir you to self-examination and repentance, or did they provoke anger? If anger, why did they make you angry?
2. Did the Holy Spirit actually cause you to pause on one or more of these questions to reflect more deeply on what it was asking? If so, which question in this self-examination really stood out to you?
3. What area(s) do you feel the Holy Spirit is speaking to you about that you need to address and change? We each have areas that we need to work on, but just between you and God, which areas are you convicted about?

JULY 19

'No Bible — No Food!'

...Man shall not live by bread alone,
but by every word that proceedeth
out of the mouth of God.
— Matthew 4:4

Many years ago, I was living at such a furious pace that the only time I really opened my Bible was to prepare something to preach. The inspired Word of God was only passing through my brain in much the same way textbook material would go in when I used to cram for a test in school. In other words, I wasn't studying to learn; I was studying to "pass." The Word wasn't really going *into* my heart.

It's a very difficult thing to admit that this had become the way I was dealing with the Word of God — reading it and preparing my heart at the last minute. But the Holy Spirit spoke to me and convicted me that this was wrong. As God spoke to me, I made a fresh commitment that there would be no higher priority in my life than His Word. And from that time until the present, I have lived with a self-imposed rule: *"No Bible — no food."* In other words, I made a personal commitment that if the Word of God did not go into my heart first thing every morning, then no food at all would go into my body. I simply made a decision to put the Word of God first and make it my highest priority, even "*more than my necessary food*" (*see* Job 23:12). This is not a biblical rule. It's my own made-up rule that I needed to establish discipline in my own life.

Matthew 4:4 says, "…Man shall not live by bread alone, but by every word that proceedeth out of the mouth of God." Why do we eat "bread" or natural food? We eat food because that's what our body needs to maintain strength and health. And just as our body needs food every day, our spirit needs the Word of God every day for our *spiritual* health and vitality.

I want us to pause for a moment to look deeply at Matthew 4:4. Notice that this verse says we live "by every word" that comes out of the mouth of God, which is the Greek phrase *epi panti rhemati.* I want to take this phrase apart piece by piece so that you'll get the full impact of what Jesus was teaching us.

The word "by" is the Greek word *epi*, which means *on*. The word "every" is the Greek word *panti*, and it means *every*. It is a compound of two words: *pan*, which means *all*, and the word *ti*, which denotes *the smallest, most miniscule detail.* Hence, it is *every little piece*. The word "word" is the Greek word *rhemati* and it is *plural* for the word *rhema*. It depicts *living words.*

When all these words are used as in Matthew 4:4, perhaps a better rendering might be that man lives by *"feeding on the constant stream of* rhema — *living words — coming toward him from the mouth of God and by consuming all of it, every little piece down to the smallest detail…."*

This verse clearly teaches that we are to take every word of Scripture into our hearts and souls and feed on it. Every little nuance of the Word of God has power in it and brings nourishment to our lives. Just as we *must* have physical food to survive and thrive, so our spiritual nature *must* have God's living Word as our daily sustenance if we are to live in His abundance and thrive. It is essential that we live "on" the Word of God if we want to spiritually flourish. To ignore or neglect our spiritual need for the Word is the equivalent of denying our bodies the food that they need to grow, develop, and prosper in health.

David said, "Thy word have I hid in mine heart, that I might not sin against thee" (Psalm 119:11). Whether we're talking about a Christian who lived in the First Century or one who lives in the last days of the ages, the answer for living in a sin-darkened society is the same. We must become "people of the Book," continually receiving God's *rhema — living words* — words that He is speaking to us through His Word and His Spirit into our hearts and minds so the very substance of God can be released into our lives. We have to open up God's Word like we would open a treasure and allow *who* is inside the written Word to flow within us. This Word is the only thing that will heal us and make us whole, protect our families, and help set our children and our marriages on a blessed, right course.

I encourage you today to renew your commitment to the Word of God like never before. Commit to Him that in these last days, you'll fill your mind with His creative, restorative substance — His very Person and nature — which will provide you with healing, wholeness, deliverance, protection, and all the answers you need for life. Then the life that resides in you will flow out to others and create a river of blessing for them to participate in and enjoy!

MY PRAYER FOR TODAY

Father, I receive what I read today as a personal exhortation TO ME to renew my commitment to consuming the Word of God on a daily basis. I need "every word that proceeds from the mouth of God," for it brings healing, wholeness, deliverance, protection, and it provides all the direction I need for my life. I ask You to forgive me for letting my commitment lapse, but today I make a new commitment that the Word of God will be the highest priority in my life, more than my daily necessary food.

I pray this in Jesus' name!

MY CONFESSION FOR TODAY

I make a new commitment today that the Word of God will be the highest priority in my life and that I will consume it on a daily basis. I will fill my mind with His creative, restorative substance — His very Person and nature — which will produce healing, wholeness, deliverance, protection, and all the answers I need for my life. I will put first things first and open up God's Word like a treasure to allow the Living Word who indwells the written Word to flow within me. God's Word is the light and life that will make me whole, protect my family, and help set my relationships on a blessed, right course. I confess that I will allow the life of God's Word in me to flow out to others and create a river of blessing for them to participate in and enjoy!

I declare this by faith in Jesus' name!

QUESTIONS FOR YOU TO CONSIDER

1. Be honest — how often do you read your Bible? God already knows the truth, so it's good for you to level with yourself about this question. Is it enough to keep you spiritually strong? If you ate natural food the way you consume the spiritual food of God's Word, what would your physical state be like?
2. Do you have a daily Bible reading program to help guide you as you read through the Old and New Testament? If not, why not find one online, or ask your pastor what daily Bible reading plan he would recommend for you?
3. What do you experience when you read the Bible? Do you sense that God is speaking to you?

Our spiritual nature must have God's living Word as our daily sustenance if we are to live in His abundance and thrive.

JULY 20

Why Spiritual Gifts?

For I long to see you, that I may impart
unto you some spiritual gift, to the end
ye may be established.
— Romans 1:11

We saw earlier (*see* the May 20 *Gem*) that the apostle Paul deeply yearned to meet the believers in Rome because he believed that if he could spend time with them or perhaps if he could lay hands on them, there would be a spiritual *impartation* to them. As we discussed then, the word "impart" in Romans 1:11 is the Greek word *metadidomi,* which means *to transfer something from one to another*. The only reason Paul would use this word was if he believed he had something inside him that could be transferred to the Romans. Paul believed in what he had in himself, and he was sure that if he could get to them in person, that spiritual substance he carried would rub off on them!

As Paul continued in Romans 1:11, he made it very clear regarding *what* he wanted to impart. He specifically stated that he believed if he could spend time with them, it would result in the impartation of a "spiritual gift" to them. The word "gift" in this verse is the word *charisma* — and it is derived from *charis*, which is the Greek word for *grace*. When *charis* becomes *charisma*, it depicts something that is *given* or *imparted* by *grace.* This is why certain people call themselves *Charismatics* — indicating that they claim to be *gifted* with the gifts of the Holy Spirit, or at least that they place a significant emphasis on the gifts of the Spirit in their expression of worship.

Historically, the word *charisma* was used to describe that moment when the gods *graced* or *donated* supernatural *ability, favor,* or *power* to an individual. Thus, this word *charisma* meant a *gracious gift* — and that is exactly how it should be interpreted in the New Testament. A person who has received a *charisma* has received a *donation* or an *enablement* from God that equips him in some supernatural manner.

Thus, when Paul wrote that he wanted to impart a spiritual gift to the Romans, he was saying that if he could see them in person, God would impart a *charisma* — a divine gifting — to them.

Paul continued to say, "For I long to see you, that I may impart unto you some spiritual gift, to the end ye may be established" (Romans 1:11). The word "established" comes from the Greek word *steridzo.* It describes something *fixed* and *solid*, like a column that holds up the roof of a house. It could also be rendered *to brace*, *to shore up*, *to bolster*, *to support*, or to *uphold*, and it fundamentally describes the act of adding *strength* and *support* to something that already exists.

In ancient times, the word *steridzo* was also used to describe a rod that was driven into the ground next to a grapevine to support the grapevine as it grew upward and flourished. That stake gave upward direction to the vine and supported the clusters of rich grapes that hung from the vine. The vines were *reinforced* and *supported* by the rod that the vine grew and twined around.

This illustration perfectly encapsulates how I feel when I am around seasoned men or women of God. After being in their presence, I spiritually feel like an iron rod has been hammered into the soil of my heart that helps me keep growing upward in the right direction. I feel *reinforced* and *stronger* as a result of being with them. They help me keep my focus where it ought to be, and this all contributes to fruitfulness in my life.

In our backyard in Moscow, Denise and I have grapevines that grow along the fence. As usual, they started out as little twigs that looked very unattractive. But our gardener was certain of their growth, so he acted in faith and firmly hammered tall metal rods next to each little twig. When I asked what those rods were for, he informed me that each rod would provide direction for the vine to grow upward. It was hard to imagine that those tiny little sticks poking out of the ground would one day need such a tall rod to grow on, but he was right! Eventually the vines twined around the rods, growing upward toward the light. Those rods *reinforced* the growth process — and it wasn't too long before the vines were producing healthy clusters of grapes.

That's what the gifts of the Holy Spirit are intended to do for us — to *establish* us, to *reinforce* us, to make us *stronger*, and to help us *grow* so we can then *bear much fruit* for the glory of Jesus and for the furtherance of His Kingdom!

MY PRAYER FOR TODAY

Father, I am so grateful for the privilege of being around seasoned men or women of God. After being in their presence, I spiritually feel like an iron rod has been hammered into the soil of my heart that helps me keep growing upward in the right direction. I thank You for the blessing of being reinforced and stronger as a result of their influence. Holy Spirit, help me follow their example in Christ so I can keep my focus where it ought to be, and produce greater fruitfulness in my life.

I pray this in Jesus' name!

MY CONFESSION FOR TODAY

I confess that the gifts of the Holy Spirit are at work on my behalf to establish me, to reinforce me, to make me stronger, and to help me grow. I walk with the wise, and wisdom surrounds and saturates me so that I can bear much fruit for the glory of Jesus and the furtherance of His Kingdom!

I declare this by faith in Jesus' name!

QUESTIONS FOR YOU TO CONSIDER

1. Can you recall a moment when you felt spiritually reinforced simply by being in the presence of someone who was older and more seasoned in the Lord?
2. What fruit was produced in you as a result of that righteous influence?
3. Are the gifts of the Holy Spirit in manifestation in your congregation? If not, is there a reason why they are not manifesting in the church? Is the manifestation of these gifts permitted? Do you know what your church believes about the gifts of the Holy Spirit?

JULY 21

Three Types of Churches Will Appear in the Last Days

Repent; or else I will come unto thee quickly,
and will fight against them with the sword of my mouth.
— Revelation 2:16

Today the Church is facing a crisis of morals. More and more, society has no stomach for spiritual or moral absolutes. Pastors and spiritual leaders who decide to "take a stand" and preach the Gospel in its pure, unadulterated form are derided as irrelevant and intolerant hate-mongers.

The public reaction to biblical truth is often so adverse that many pastors are hesitant to take strong positions on issues of morality, even though these truths are clearly stated in the Word of God. Rather than answer difficult moral questions, they are tempted to dodge the questions and skirt around the issues in an attempt to avoid conflict.

This same issue plagued the Early Church nearly 2,000 years ago. Toward the close of the First Century AD, there was a group of spiritual leaders who intentionally "watered down" the message of the Gospel to make it less demanding and more accommodating to other points of view. Because the culture couldn't stomach the idea of a strict exclusionary faith that claimed to be above all others, this group of spiritual leaders attempted to entice Christians to make their faith more inclusive of everyone else's beliefs.

The problem grew so rampant at the close of the First Century AD that Christ issued a strong rebuke to the people who were spreading this toxic doctrine when He supernaturally appeared to the apostle John. Addressing these erring spiritual leaders, Jesus sternly warned, "Repent, or else I will come unto thee quickly, and will fight against them with the sword of my mouth" (Revelation 2:16).

The word "fight" in this verse is the Greek word *polemos*, a well-known Greek word that describes *a full-scale battle that is fought until victory is achieved.* This emphatically means that Christ is not willing to surrender His Church to *anyone*, and He will fight for His Church until it is solidly back in His hands. He *refused* to stand idly by and let these individuals corrupt His Church. If errant spiritual leaders did not repent of their *active* or *passive* tolerance of this false teaching, Christ would rise up against them with His mighty sword.

Christ's warning to the Early Church applies to the Church in all ages, and it is clear to see why His words are especially relevant to believers today. Although there are many God-fearing pastors, preachers, and spiritual leaders in the modern Christian community, a host of spiritual leaders are replicating the grave errors made by errant leaders in the First Century. In pulpits and congregations around the world, truth is being watered down and altered to reflect the inclusive values of a changing culture. In many congregations, pure, sound doctrine has been completely replaced by soft, "feel-good" messages, and the majority of people in the pews are ignorant of even the most elementary tenets of the faith.

Despite their ability to communicate masterfully, many modern-day ministers lack a basic education in fundamental Bible principles or have simply chosen to avoid teaching sound doctrine in favor of more popular motivational messages. To be direct, it appears that some have been duped into taking a politically correct position on many biblical truths instead of declaring truth — because the truth would put them on a collision course with the society that surrounds them.

This drift away from the Bible has created a doctrinal vacuum in the Church — a void currently being filled with dynamic business ideas, financial advice, and motivational messages instead of the Word of God that the Holy Spirit is bound to honor with signs and wonders. It is certainly true that some of the motivational messages delivered from the pulpit are beneficial in people's lives, but this help is temporary and can often be found in a book by some psychological guru. When everything is said and done, only the Bible has the power to permanently transform.

Unfortunately, what we currently see and feel is only the beginning of the rift that is developing within the Church world. Unless a major revival occurs, this rift will only grow deeper and wider. If repentance doesn't melt the hearts of people throughout the Church world, it will eventually seem like there are three churches:

- A Church that holds fast to the truth and faces the brunt of opposition because it refuses to bend.
- A Church in the middle trying to "ride the fence" through accommodation in order to avoid persecution and societal rejection (*see* Revelation 2:12-17).
- A lukewarm, "Laodicean-like" Church (*see* Revelation 3:14-22) that has allowed compromise to run its full course, stripping it completely of the power of God and leaving Jesus standing on the outside.

It is not too late for the Body of Christ to make a recovery. In fact, it is never too late as long as there are believers who are willing to hear and hearken to what the Holy Spirit is saying to the Church. However, in order for the Church to receive the divine power it needs for correction, change, and restoration, it must undergo a transformation from the highest to its lowest levels.

The Bible makes it clear that if spiritual leaders refuse to take a stand for truth in these turbulent times, Christ will fight against them with His mighty sword. This is a battle that they cannot win. Absolutely no one may mitigate the truth of the Gospel — even for the purpose of purchasing peace with the world around them. The only true recourse is to surrender to the Holy Spirit and do what is right, even if it is wrong in the eyes of the world.

Early believers endured bullying, ridicule, imprisonment, and were even put to death because they refused to conform to the world that surrounded them on all sides. Although some believers collapsed under this pressure, many steadfastly resisted this coercion to conform and held fast to their faith. God has always had His remnant — those who will not bow to external pressures. In these last times God will have that remnant once again, and those who refuse to fear or to compromise their faith in Jesus Christ will experience previously unknown levels of the power of God as a result of their commitment to stand by truth.

I realize this is a very different type of *Sparkling Gem*, but I felt it necessary to write and memorialize what I believe are the greatest struggles facing the modern Church. I encourage you to stay faithful in praying for those believers and spiritual leaders who refuse to succumb to the pressures of the age and stand by absolute, biblical truth, regardless of what the world around them dictates. Why not make a fresh consecration to the Lord today that *you* will always be counted among that faithful number? Make a quality, immutable decision for your own walk with God: *"From this moment forward, there's no fence left to ride! Compromise in my commitment to Jesus is NOT an option!"*

MY PRAYER FOR TODAY

Dear Father, I ask You to help me understand the relevance of this word I've read today. I pray that You will strengthen the present leadership of the Body of Christ to stand for the absolute truths of God's Word even if that stance places them in direct opposition to the world. I ask You to raise up strong leaders in the Christian community who will lead the way and courageously stand for truth, regardless of the price that must be paid. I pray for my pastor and for other spiritual leaders. Father, I ask You to help them hear what the Spirit is saying and grant them boldness to call the Church to a time of holiness and separation, even if it is opposed to the voice of the world around them.

I pray this in Jesus' name!

MY CONFESSION FOR TODAY

I boldly confess that I will stand by the truth of God's Word, regardless of what the world around me tries to dictate as morally right or wrong. A day will soon come when we will all stand before Christ's high court of reckoning and give account for how we upheld truth or how we forfeited it to accommodate the world around us. I have made my decision! Regardless of what the world says or what names it calls me, I am going to stand by the Christian values that have guided the Church for 2,000 years. Truth has not suddenly changed — it is society that has changed. I am determined to stand by biblical truth regardless of the price I must pay.

I declare this by faith in Jesus' name!

QUESTIONS FOR YOU TO CONSIDER

1. Today's television programs often depict homosexuality as the norm. Can you think of other examples in modern society where biblical truths are undermined and exchanged with a new code of ethics?
2. As a Christian do you believe you should merely go with the flow of what's happening, or is it your responsibility to uphold the absolute truth of the Gospel?
3. If it personally costs you to take a strong moral stance that is in line with God's Word, are you willing to pay that price? How far are you willing to go in your commitment to biblical truth?

JULY 22

Prove All Things

Prove all things....
— 1 Thessalonians 5:21

I once bought a violin that I was sure was an authentic Stradivarius violin. Of course, if it was real, it was worth several million dollars. Before I purchased it, I studied documents about how to recognize a real Stradivarius compared to a well-made copy. After convincing myself that I had found a real Stradivarius in a remote antique shop in Russia, I purchased it. But after an examination by a violin expert, it proved to be nothing more than a very old, fabulous fake. Only an experienced eye would have been able to discern that it wasn't authentic. Today that fake Stradivarius hangs on the wall in one of my offices as a reminder that everything that looks real *isn't* real and that it's important not to eagerly believe everything we see and hear.

I share this example because someone in the church at Thessalonica claimed to possess the gift of prophecy, but it wasn't the authentic gift of the Spirit. It was an imitation, but it so closely resembled the real gift of prophecy that people in the church had been affected by it. When Paul wrote First and Second Thessalonians, he addressed this issue. Someone was claiming to speak by the gift of prophecy — and whoever this person or this group of people were, they had apparently prophesied that Jesus had already secretly returned and that the Thessalonian believers had missed His return. Because of this error that Paul sought to correct, we now have the apostle's teaching on the return of Jesus Christ, as recorded in First Thessalonians 4:15-18 and Second Thessalonians 2:1-17.

The church in Thessalonica had already suffered terribly due to persecution, so the hope of Jesus' return was very precious to them. We are not sure who was upsetting them, but whoever the person or persons were, they must have been influential, because it seems many believers took their prophecies seriously that Jesus had already come and they had missed His return. The Thessalonian believers panicked, thinking they had missed Jesus' return. The prophetic utterances must have closely resembled what a real prophetic message sounds like, because it seems the congregation as a whole took it very seriously.

This deeply upset the Thessalonian believers, as it would upset you if someone you respected convinced you that Jesus had secretly come and that you had missed it. When these believers finally figured out that Jesus hadn't come yet, they were so distressed by these *inaccurate prophecies* that they were tempted to turn a deaf ear to *all* prophetic utterances. But closing their hearts to prophetic utterances would have been a wrong response. Even though they had been exploited by bogus prophecy, the value of genuine prophecy hadn't changed. It was still a real gift from God that they needed. If they shut their hearts to it, it would have robbed them of fresh words from the Holy Spirit that were a part of their necessary supply from Heaven.

Many of us have been negatively affected by inaccurate prophecy at one time or another. But that doesn't mean all prophecy is wrong or untrustworthy. Lots of things are used inaccurately in life. For example, a car can be driven in such a reckless manner that it results in a collision — but that doesn't stop us from getting in our cars. It simply makes us more aware of our need to drive more carefully and responsibly. If we decided to never drive a car again because someone was once fatally wounded in a car accident, that would be an irrational response.

When Paul wrote to the Thessalonians, he didn't put a "ban" on all prophecies because of this negative prophetic experience; he simply told them to check their hearts regarding what they heard and to test prophetic utterances *before* they embraced them. He told them, "Prove all things…" (1 Thessalonians 5:21).

The word "prove" is the Greek word *dokimadzo*, which means *to approve after testing.* In other words, don't simply believe everything you hear. Test it *before* you accept it.

The word *dokimadzo* was used in various ways, but one significant way was to describe the process of testing coins to see if they were *real* or *counterfeit.* The counterfeit coins look very authentic — and there was such an abundance of counterfeit coins in circulation in ancient times that it became an accepted practice to test coins to determine if they were real or counterfeit. If tested and proven phony, they were rejected. Only if the coins were tested and proven authentic were they approved, pronounced good, recognized for use, and put into public circulation to be accepted for payment. *That* is where the word "prove" comes from that Paul used in First Thessalonians 5:21.

By using this word *dokimadzo* in the context of false prophecies that were being circulated among believers in the city of Thessalonica, Paul was urging these believers to treat every prophetic utterance with caution. He didn't tell them to *reject* these utterances, but to *test* them.

As noted above, we need prophetic ministry, but we have a responsibility to test the content of the utterances spoken to us to ensure they originate from the heart of God. Just because someone says, "Thus saith the Lord," does not mean it is a genuine prophetic utterance. It could just be the product of a person's mind, given out of spiritual immaturity. Or in some cases, it could represent a conscious attempt to deceive, just as that fake Stradivarius I purchased was a deliberate attempt to copy something that was real. In both the natural and spiritual realms, the process of testing is crucial to ensure that only the authentic is received.

So if you have been the recipient of fraudulent prophetic utterances in the past, let that experience be a lesson to you and then move forward! Add it to your list of experiences that provided a spiritual education! But don't let it cause you to back off from legitimate and biblically sound prophetic ministry, which is vital and needed both by you as an individual and by the Church at large. Learn from it and move on. Draw on the wisdom and discernment of those who are older and seasoned in the Lord to teach you how to recognize the difference between the real and the counterfeit. That is what Paul was trying to teach the Thessalonians when he told them to "Prove all things…."

The gift of prophecy is real — described as a gift of the Spirit in First Corinthians 12:10. We *need* this manifestation of the Holy Spirit to be active among us; in fact, Paul exhorted us in First Corinthians 14:1 to actively desire that the Holy Spirit use us in the manifestation of that specific gift.

So cultivate a sensitive heart so you can test every utterance that claims to be inspired by Heaven, just as Paul encouraged us to do in First Thessalonians 5:21. And once you've proven a word to be authentic, do your best to *embrace* it, meditate on it, and wage a good warfare with it in the name of Jesus!

MY PRAYER FOR TODAY

Heavenly Father, I thank You for teaching me common sense regarding the gift of prophecy. The apostle Paul clearly told us to test all things, and I confess that I have received "words" without testing them in the past. But rather than reject all prophetic utterances because some have turned out to be false, today I assume responsibility to test and to prove what is spoken over me. I don't want to miss anything that the Holy Spirit has to say specifically to me, so I refuse to reject the gift of prophecy. But I thank You for helping me as I follow a commonsense approach to the manifestation of this gift from this moment forward. Please help me learn how to recognize what is real and what is counterfeit.

I pray this in Jesus' name!

MY CONFESSION FOR TODAY

I declare by faith that I am growing in my personal discernment of spiritual things. I am not as naïve as I once was. I am learning to recognize what is real and what is counterfeit. I release every bad experience I've ever had with so-called prophetic manifestations, and I open my heart and my mind to the true gift of prophecy that comes from the Holy Spirit. God gave this gift for my edification and for the building up of the Church, and I refuse to reject it because of past bad experiences. With the help of the Holy Spirit, I am becoming wiser and more discerning in my ability to separate the false from the true.

I declare this by faith in Jesus' name!

QUESTIONS FOR YOU TO CONSIDER

1. Have you ever heard a so-called prophetic word that sounded authentic, but in the end, you realized it was erroneous? When did you have that experience, and what effect did it have on you?
2. Has the gift of prophecy been an avenue of God's blessing in your life in times past? Have you learned to test words given to you before you receive them as inspired by the Lord? What is your method of knowing whether or not you have heard a bona fide word from the Spirit of God?
3. If you have felt abused by the gift of prophecy, are you ready to release that bad experience to the Lord and start over again in the way you determine the validity of prophetic words that are spoken? Do you see that God wants this gift to operate within the Body of Christ, but He wants you to use your head when it is in operation?

JULY 23

Hold Fast to That Which Is Good

Prove all things; hold fast to that which is good.
— 1 Thessalonians 5:21

Years ago I was invited to have lunch with a man who said he wanted to talk. As I sat with him, he began to tell me the many reasons why he had abandoned believing in the gifts of the Holy Spirit. At first, I thought maybe he just needed someone to talk to about his doubts, but soon I realized this man was deeply bitter. I finally understood he had asked me to lunch in an attempt to dissuade me, and whoever else would listen, from believing in the gifts of the Holy Spirit.

As I listened to this man, I silently asked the Lord for wisdom to help him. I could tell from the man's words that he had been disappointed in the past by leaders. Out of hurt, he dismissed them all as a bunch of Charismatic misfits. Like many have done in times of disappointment, rather than separate disappointing behavior from truth, he mixed the leaders and their poor behavior all into one big bag and then rejected the whole lot of them.

But taking this approach is illogical. It's like someone saying, "You know, I ate food once and got food poisoning, so I've made the decision that food is bad and I'll never eat food again."

If you go without food, eventually you'll die, so choosing to reject all food because of one bad experience would be a fatal decision. Maybe you need to be a little more selective in where you eat or what you eat, or perhaps you need to learn a little more about how to correctly prepare your food — but you cannot avoid food if you wish to keep on living.

Bad experiences surrounding false prophecies often have negative consequences, and regretfully do occur in the Christian community. But instead of throwing out our legitimate beliefs, as this man had done, we must obey the words of the apostle Paul in First Thessalonians 5:21. When he wrote to the believers in Thessalonica, Paul was speaking to Christians who felt very disappointed and confused as a result of individuals who had misused the gift of prophecy. Because the Thessalonian congregation was tired of this abuse, they were tempted to throw out the spiritual gift of prophecy altogether — no longer allowing it to operate in their church. So Paul wrote and told them, "Prove all things; *hold fast* to that which is good."

As we saw in yesterday's *Sparkling Gem*, Paul taught that we have a God-given responsibility to "prove" the prophetic words that are spoken over our lives. God doesn't expect us to blindly accept every prophecy as from the Lord. But once we have determined that a word we received is legitimate and sound, we must "hold fast" to it because there is something we are to do with that word from the Lord. Paul was so convinced of the importance of authentic prophetic utterances that he urged Timothy to "war a good warfare" with the prophecies that had been spoken over his life (*see* 1 Timothy 1:18).

I think of words from the Lord that He has spoken to me over the years concerning our ministry. These words have been tested, proven, and shown to be legitimate. Denise and I have walked this walk long enough to be able to discern in our spirits the difference between a real prophetic utterance and a bogus prophetic utterance. And like Timothy, Denise and I have waged warfare with some of the prophetic words that have been spoken over our lives. Certainly prophetic utterances are *not* equal to the Bible, but they have been guideposts that have helped navigate our journey through good times and bad.

Yes, misguided words are given from time to time. But when prophetic words are spoken over our lives that are proven to be legitimate, we need to *"hold fast"* to them!

The words "hold fast" in First Thessalonians 5:21 are a translation of the Greek word *katecho*, which is a compound of the words *kata* and *echo*. The word *kata* means *down*, and the word *echo* means *to hold* or *to embrace*. When compounded, the new word means *to hold firmly* or *to hold down* lest the desired object slip away from you, or *to take possession* of a thing. It is the picture of figuratively wrapping one's arms around an object and refusing to let it go. It clearly means if we don't deliberately embrace these prophetic words and make them our own, they can slip away from us. Therefore, Paul urged us to hold sound prophetic words very tightly and to refuse to let them go.

Paul also specifically told us that we are to hold fast to that which is "good." The word "good" is from the word *kalos*, which in this case, denotes something that is *sound* and in *order*. It's been *tested*, *proven*, and shown to be *authentic*. It is therefore to be accepted, like a coin that has been tested and proven and therefore worthy to be put into public circulation. It is *attested*, *dependable*, *genuine*, *reliable*, and *true*. This is the nature of a prophetic word to which God charges us to "hold fast."

What words have been spoken over you that you know are legitimate words from the Lord? Has life tried to seize them away from you? In order for those words to come to fulfillment, it will require you to *hold fast* to them — because the devil and the cares of this life have a way of trying to steal the words God has spoken over your life. Just think of the Old Testament characters who received prophetic words, such as Abraham or Joseph. Imagine how determined they had to be to *"hold fast"* to the words they had received from the Lord in order to see their fulfillment!

Likewise, you must *wrap your arms around* those prophetic utterances spoken over your life that you know in your heart are legitimate. Just because a word birthed in Heaven is faithfully delivered to you does *not* mean it will automatically come to pass in your life. That word God has given you will more than likely *test* you — just as the word of the Lord tried Joseph until the time of its fulfillment (*see* Psalm 105:19). But that doesn't matter when you've already decided you're going to stay in faith until you see the manifestation of what the Lord has spoken to you. You just dig your heels in the ground, *hold fast* to that which is good, and refuse to ever let *anything* take it away from you!

MY PRAYER FOR TODAY

Heavenly Father, I thank You for speaking clearly to me about my life. I confess that there have been times when I've been tempted, out of weakness and weariness, to let go of Your prophetic utterances over my life. Today I am encouraged to wrap my arms around those promises You made to me and to not let them go until I see their fulfillment. With the help of Your Spirit, I will prove all things and hold fast to that which is good!

I pray this in Jesus' name!

MY CONFESSION FOR TODAY

I declare that I will do what God has told me to do. Many forces have tried to stop me, but the Word of God is working mightily in me and it will accomplish God's will in my life. I wrap my arms around those prophetic words that I have proven to be true, and I refuse to surrender to the negative forces that try to take them away from me. I will remain steady and on course until I see the manifestation of what God has spoken to me.

I declare this by faith in Jesus' name!

QUESTIONS FOR YOU TO CONSIDER

1. Can you think of an authentic prophetic word that has been spoken over your life? When was it spoken over you? By whom? Where were you? What was your immediate response to it? How do you know that it was authentic?
2. Did you find that you have had to hold tightly to keep hold of that word from the Lord for your life lest it slip away from you?
3. What method did you use to test that word to ensure that it was worthy of acceptance and action in your life?

JULY 24

A New Name — A New Beginning

...To him that overcometh
will I give...a new name....
— Revelation 2:17

Very often in ancient society, a person received a "new name" when he achieved a new status or advanced to a higher level of society. The bestowal of a new name normally accompanied a person's elevation, ennoblement, or social promotion, and with it came rank, privilege, and, frequently, the right of inheritance. That new name marked a distinct change in an individual's status, which could potentially impact his lineage for generations to come.

We see this many times in Scripture. The Bible records many accounts of God conferring new names upon believers when they underwent life-changing spiritual transformations. Take, for instance, the Old Testament examples of *Abraham* and *Sarah*. When God changed Abram's name to Abraham, it marked a new beginning in his life — a spiritual *advancement* or *elevation.*

The name *Abram* means *father*, which reflected his status as the head of his household. However, when Abram entered into a covenant with God, God changed his name to *Abraham,* meaning *a father of many nations.* This new name memorialized their covenant together and reflected Abraham's new, God-ordained status in life (*see* Genesis 17:4).

As further affirmation of His promise to Abraham, God also changed the name of Abraham's wife from *Sarai*, which means *quarrelsome*, to *Sarah*, meaning *princess*. Genesis 17:15,16 records this event: "And God said unto Abraham, As for Sarai, thy wife, thou shalt not call her name Sarai, but Sarah shall her name be. And I will bless her, and give thee a son also of her: yes, I will bless her, and she shall be a mother of nations; kings of people shall be of her." The new names that God gave to Abraham and Sarah did not in itself change them. Rather, it reflected the change God was performing *in* them. It marked the *end* of one chapter and the *beginning* of a new life. Consider that Abraham was 99 years old when God gave him a new name, and Sarah was 90. *If anyone's life demonstrates that it's never too late to change, it is the life of Abraham or Sarah.*

We find another powerful example of God bestowing a new name in the story of Jacob. The name *Jacob* means *supplanter*, and it denoted the mischievousness of this man's original character. In fact, when Jacob and his twin brother Esau were born, Jacob came out of the womb gripping Esau's heel in his hand — demonstrating the intense competition that existed between the two brothers even while they were still in the womb. However, after Jacob's encounter with the angel at Peniel, God changed Jacob's name to *Israel*.

Genesis 32:27 and 28 records: "And he [the angel] said unto him, What is thy name? And he said, Jacob. And he said, Thy name shall be called no more Jacob, but Israel: for as a prince hast thou power with God and with men, and hast prevailed." The name Israel means *one who is triumphant with God* or *one who prevails with God*. Some scholars even translate it as *God rules, God judges*, or *prince of God*. Thus, it is clear that the new name Israel signified a moment of surrender in this man's life and his character. Like Abraham and Sarah, the "new name" in itself didn't change Jacob, but it marked the moment when one chapter permanently *closed* and a new chapter *opened* that would affect the entire history of mankind.

We can even see instances of new names that were bestowed upon individuals in the New Testament. First, there was *Simon*, whose name was changed to *Peter* after he had a revelation of Jesus Christ (*see* Matthew 16:18). The day Simon was given the new name Peter, which comes from the Greek word *petra*, for *rock*, marked a transformational moment in this disciple's life. He is not remembered as *Simon*, but by his newly given name *Peter*.

We find a New Testament example in the story *Saul of Tarsus*. Prior to his conversion, Saul was an extremely arrogant man. To get a sense of how prideful he was before he came to Christ, we can look to his own words in Philippians 3:4, where he essentially stated that no one had more reason to boast in the natural than himself. However, at some point after his life-transforming experience with Jesus Christ, God changed his name from *Saul* to *Paul*, meaning *small* or *humble*. On the other side of his divine encounter on the road to Damascus, Saul was clothed with a new identity — and today we remember this apostle not as Saul of Tarsus, but by his new name *Paul*.

Then there is *Joses* — a Levite from Cyprus — who was an unknown believer until he gave a large financial contribution to the church in Jerusalem, which brought him to the attention of the apostles. They changed his name to *Barnabas* to reflect what he had become to them (*see* Acts 4:36,37). The name Barnabas meant *encourager*. The changing of Joses' name didn't change him, but it reflected a *new* status he had obtained as an "encouragement" to the apostles. Today he is not remembered as Joses of Cyprus, a name no one even recognizes, but by the new name bestowed upon him — *Barnabas* — a name that defined the gifts and calling God had placed on his life.

Each of the new names from these Old and New Testaments examples marked new beginnings and profound changes of character in the lives of the individuals who received them. Likewise, we experienced a *transformational shift* in our lives when we surrendered to the Lordship of Jesus. Although our names might not have been legally changed, Jesus dramatically redefined our lives when we chose to follow Him — and we are not the same people we used to be!

Today as I wrote this *Sparkling Gem*, I asked my wife Denise, "If God gave you a new name to reflect who you are, what do you think your new name would be?" She reflected for a few moments and then answered, "If God gave me a new name, I think my name would be Redeemed!" *What name do you think God would give you to describe who you are today in His eyes?*

MY PRAYER FOR TODAY

Father, I thank You for the transformational change You have worked in my life since I committed my life to Jesus. You have worked so many miracles in my life and changed me so much. I give you all the honor and glory for what you have done. When I think about how my life used to be and compare it to how my life is today, I cannot imagine living without You. Thank You for redeeming me, saving me from destruction, and giving me a new spiritual status in Your family!

I pray this in Jesus' name!

MY CONFESSION FOR TODAY

I declare that I am totally different from how I used to be. Since I've committed myself wholly to Christ, He has worked miracles in my life and character. I thankfully confess that since I've belonged to Jesus, I've had multiple transformational moments in my life. The Holy Spirit is working inside me continuously — to change me and to take me to a higher dimension in every aspect of my life. If anyone needs to thank God for working miracles in his or her life, it's certainly me! I thank You, Heavenly Father, for the dramatic changes that You have worked in me!

I declare this by faith in Jesus' name!

QUESTIONS FOR YOU TO CONSIDER

1. Can you think of anyone else in the Old or New Testament who had a name change that reflected a transformational moment in their lives?
2. If you were to receive a new name to describe who you are now, what do you think that name would be? What name do you think would describe you, your gifts, and your calling? What would you *want* that new name to reflect about you?

3. Can you think of five names that God calls us in the Bible? For example, the Bible calls you *Beloved* (*see* Philippians 2:12) and *Called* (*see* Romans 1:6). What other words does God use in the Bible to denote who you are since that transformational moment when you surrendered your life to Christ?

JULY 25

Always On Guard!

… Abstain from pollutions of idols,
and from fornication….
— Acts 15:20

We must never forget that the devil is always on the prowl, waiting for us to drop our guard and fall asleep on the job so he can stealthily find an entrance into our lives. In our moments of lethargy and complacency, we are especially vulnerable. The enemy is constantly poised to exploit any perceivable weakness, and when he makes his move, it is often with devastating consequences. Therefore, we must perpetually remain on guard — diligent, wide-awake, and doing our part to protect ourselves from the evil lurking in the shadows.

Specifically, this means we must be *vigilant* about not exposing ourselves to environments that have spiritually negative consequences. An integral part of being vigilant is to stay away from *places*, *events*, and *people* that are detrimental to our spiritual lives.

For instance, this means:

- Staying away from immoral films that stir carnal passions and arouse temptation.
- Avoiding people who freely drink alcohol, since the situation could open a door for the enemy to lure you into a new bondage or one from which you've already been delivered.
- Separating from "loose" Christians who have a lower standard of holiness and lack passion for God and the things of God.

The Bible makes it clear that it is our duty to avoid anything that is opposed to a life of holiness. By doing so, we fulfill our part in protecting ourselves from the evil in the world. *This is our responsibility, and God expects us to fulfill it seriously.*

Much like today, the Early Church was literally surrounded on all sides by things that could easily lure new believers back into a life of sin. Pagan temples were one of the most prominent temptations in New Testament times, since these cult sanctuaries were central to life in the

Roman Empire. Essentially functioning as "cultural centers," temple grounds hosted numerous community events, including festivals, ceremonies, and even open marketplaces. However, these temples were also dark cesspools of *demonic activity*, *idolatry*, and *fornication*, which made it imperative for early believers to stay as far away from them as possible.

In Acts 15, we read that the Early Church leadership convened in Jerusalem to discuss what to expect of new converts who abandoned paganism and came to Christ. After much deliberation, the council arrived at a decision, which Peter summarized in Acts 15:19,20: "Wherefore my sentence is, that we trouble not them, which from among the Gentiles are turned to God: but that we write unto them, that they abstain from pollutions of idols, and from fornication, and from things strangled, and from blood."

Peter announced new converts should "...abstain from pollutions of idols, and from fornication...." The word "abstain" in this verse is the Greek word *apecho*, which means *to deliberately withdraw from*; *to stay away from*; *to put distance between oneself and something else*; or *to intentionally refrain*. The word "pollutions" is a translation of the Greek word *alisgema*, which depicts something that is *defiled*. Part of the activities of idolatry included "fornication." This is from the Greek word *porneia*, the Greek word that was used to describe *any sexual activity outside the context of God-ordained marriage*.

The rites of idolatry were often connected to immoral sexual acts, which God condemned. These rituals were *lewd*, *indecent*, *obscene*, *vulgar*, *degenerate*, and *profane*. Therefore, it was essential for new believers to *distance* themselves from the environments where these things occurred because it had the power to infect, sicken, and nullify them spiritually. This is exactly where the devil wanted them to be, knowing that if he could get believers into that old environment again, he could possibly drag them back into bondage, dilute their spiritual power, and negatively affect their witness.

You see, most believers had been saved *out of* that immoral pagan lifestyle, and to return to a blatantly pagan environment for a social event was flirting with temptation. Roaming about a pagan temple with all its spiritually poisonous activities could ultimately bring ruin into their lives. To be in that environment certainly was *not* being diligent to protect themselves against the evil that is in the world. Early believers needed to stay away from these dark environments at all costs — *even* if all their friends and neighbors went there. It just wasn't the place for Christians to be *if* they intended to remain spiritually free.

The spiritual leadership in Jerusalem made the decision under the inspiration of the Holy Spirit that we *all* need to be careful about the *places*, *events*, and *people* we allow in our lives. Those who belong to Christ do not need to deliberately expose themselves to films that cause temptation, hang out in bars where there is a strong temptation to drink, or spend time with "loose" friends who have adopted a worldly view that Christ opposes.

Is today's *Sparkling Gem* a wake-up call for you to be more vigilant about where you go, what you do, and whom you spend time with? If nothing else, let the Holy Spirit speak to you about walking in greater spiritual freedom and holiness.

My friend, there are places, events, and people that are spiritually detrimental to your future. Rather than put yourself in jeopardy by allowing these things in your life, it is safer to *put distance* between them and yourself.

Since the devil is on the prowl, it is *essential* always to remain on guard — diligent, wide-awake, and doing our part to protect ourselves from the evil that is in the world. This means putting distance between ourselves and *any* individual, activity, or atmosphere that could contribute to our spiritual demise.

So I ask you today — are you sensibly putting space between yourself and detrimental *places, events*, and *people* that aren't healthy for you? That was God's requirement 2,000 years ago — *and it is still what the Holy Spirit requires of you today!*

MY PRAYER FOR TODAY

Father, I ask You to reveal to me the places, events, or people I specifically need to avoid in order to stay spiritually strong. I want to be a witness to the freedom You have brought into my life. But if I am not strong enough to be around the former places and people and not be affected by them, I need the courage to say no to the invitations that would negatively affect me. Give me the wisdom to know those whom I can help influence and those whom I deliberately need to avoid. I know that the Holy Spirit has the answer, and He wants to help me make the right decisions. So Holy Spirit, teach me how to be vigilant and sensible about my spiritual life, as this will affect everything about my future.

I pray this in Jesus' name!

MY CONFESSION FOR TODAY

I confess that I am vigilant and fully aware when it comes to my spiritual life. I know that the devil is on the prowl, looking for an entrance into my life. Therefore, I am very sensible about where I go, what I do, and whom I see. I guard my heart carefully because nothing is more important than my spiritual life. God expects me to put distance between myself and anything that will potentially cause negative spiritual ramifications in my life. I love Jesus more than I love anything else. Therefore, I have chosen to walk the straight and narrow path, surrounding myself only with people and activities that edify my spirit. I will build close fellowship only with those who are like-minded about following Jesus Christ in a spirit of holiness!

I declare this by faith in Jesus' name!

QUESTIONS FOR YOU TO CONSIDER

1. Do you know any believers who started out strong in their new walk with Jesus, but became sidetracked by being in the wrong places or surrounding themselves with people who had compromised themselves with the world?
2. Are there any places, events, or people you need to rethink your relationship with after reading today's *Sparkling Gem*? Are you influencing them to come

closer to Jesus, or are they dragging you back into sin and defeat? If you are being negatively affected by those places, events, or people, is it possible that you need to put distance between yourself and those things?

3. What steps do you need to take to make a break with those places, events, or people? Have you asked the Holy Spirit to give you a plan to start restructuring your time, such as where you go and with whom you spend your life? If you haven't already begun asking for help in this area, why not ask today?

JULY 26

The Responsibility of Speaking for God

And I was with you in weakness,
and in fear, and in much trembling.
— 1 Corinthians 2:3

Our Moscow church waited many years to have its own building, and when that moment finally came and we moved in, it was a time of great rejoicing. The building had been constructed debt-free, and it was one of the few church buildings of its type in Russia. I was so awestruck by what God had done that when I first approached the pulpit to preach, I found myself *trembling*.

I have always felt comfortable speaking to people from the pulpit. However, when our congregation moved into the new facility, I understood that the transition held more significance than a simple change of venue. The whole scope of our ministry had been elevated, and I had a palpable awareness that I was being held to a higher level of accountability. Every word I spoke from that pulpit had to be accurate, at least to the best of my ability, because it would be carried far and wide on television and the Internet, and the impact would be great.

In the week prior to the official move, I was gripped by a sense of electric anticipation. I pored over my notes again and again, trying to discern if there was one last truth that I needed to share from the pulpit. When Sunday finally arrived, I rose up early that morning, reviewed all of my notes again, drove to the church building, and entered the main auditorium with the full knowledge of what God was expecting in my delivery. Stepping up to the platform, I could literally feel myself *tremble* as I approached the moment when I was to speak behind that pulpit as the oracle of God to our church congregation.

Speaking for God is a great responsibility for any preacher of the Gospel, and the older I get, the more aware I am of the magnitude of this responsibility. I do not always tremble when

I speak, but there are certainly moments when I do. The apostle Paul must have felt similarly at times, because he referred to a "great trembling" that he experienced as he prepared to preach to the pagan audience in the city of Corinth. In his first epistle to these Corinthian believers, Paul reflected, "And I was with you in weakness, and in fear, and in much trembling" (1 Corinthians 2:3).

When Paul first stood up to preach before that crowd of pagans, he was about to begin his public ministry in Corinth — a city rife with paganism, immorality, and demon spirits. Paul knew that he was totally dependent on the power of God and would have no success in Corinth without it. Therefore, he was overwhelmed with a sense of *utter dependence upon God.*

Paul actually says that in that moment, he experienced "much trembling." This is a translation of the Greek phrase *en tromos polloo.* The word *en* means "in" and describes the state of being that he was "in" when he began his ministry to the Corinthians. What was that state of being? Paul told us with the preceding Greek word, *tromos*, which means *to shake*, *to quake*, or *to tremble.* He even told us the extent to which he was trembling by adding the word *polloo*, which describes *a large magnitude* or *a great quantity.* Together these words emphatically tell us that Paul literally "shook" as he stood up to preach to the Corinthians.

But what would make Paul feel such a great trembling? He had stood in front of large audiences and preached the Gospel on numerous occasions throughout the Roman Empire. So why did he feel such a strong inner shaking then?

Paul had just come from Athens, where his success as a preacher of the Gospel had been limited (*see* Acts 17:32-34), and it is likely that he felt that he had failed there. He was also very aware of his own shortcomings as an eloquent public speaker (*see* 2 Corinthians 10:10). Knowing that refined oratory skills were important to a Greek audience, Paul may have felt overwhelmed by his inadequacy of speech as he remembered his experience in Athens and prepared to publicly declare the Gospel to the Corinthians. And as if these feelings were not enough, Paul was very aware that enemies were present in the crowd, lying in wait to attack him over the slightest verbal misstep. Any of these factors may have contributed to the "great trembling" he felt that day.

However, in spite of the emotions that tried to engulf Paul at that pivotal moment, he made a decision that proved to be key to the outcome of his entire ministry from that moment onward. He determined he would know nothing among the people except the simple message of Jesus Christ crucified for them (*see* 1 Corinthians 2:2) — and then he went on to preach in the power and demonstration of the Spirit (v. 4). In the end, the apostle's ministry in Corinth was an amazing success that led to the establishment of one of the most important congregations in the Early Church. His feelings of inadequacy produced an utter dependence upon the power of God that resulted in a message that was accompanied by supernatural manifestations — which proved far more successful than any elegant oratory skills.

Over the years I have come to realize that if such a powerful apostle like Paul felt weakness and trembling from time to time, others who are called to do something significant for God may also feel such emotions when it is *their* moment to stand up and be counted. That was precisely what I felt when I stood in the pulpit of our new Moscow church during those first weeks — totally insufficient without the power of God assisting me. But in spite of that tangible sense of my own natural deficiencies, I have also sensed an increased level of God's power manifested every time the Gospel is proclaimed from the platform of our new church building. *To God be the glory! It is all for Him and His purposes!*

So how does this apply to you?

When you are called upon to do something new — something that seems bigger than you or outside of your capabilities, yet you *know* it is *your* assignment — that is the moment for you to push aside those feelings of deficiency and turn to the sufficiency of the Holy Spirit. Prepare as well as you can, but when the time comes for you to stand, to speak, to sing, to witness, or to testify, lean upon the Holy Spirit and His power.

Train and prepare as much as you can, but make room for the Holy Spirit to do *His* part that only He can do. You may feel "great trembling" at that moment, but if you'll make room for the power of God to operate, you'll see Him work with convincing proof that is far more effective than anything you could do on your own. In fact, you'll be utterly amazed at the things God works through you!

MY PRAYER FOR TODAY

Father, I admit that I've had moments when I shook to the core when it was time for me to stand up and publicly speak, sing, testify, or to take a public position on an issue. Today I surrender to the power of the Holy Spirit. Holy Spirit, I ask You to do the supernatural part that I cannot do. I'll train, prepare, and present my body to You as a living sacrifice. As I do my part, I ask for and yield to Your help as You step forward to do the part that only You can do. I am completely and utterly dependent on You.

I pray this in Jesus' name!

MY CONFESSION FOR TODAY

I confess that I have felt weakness, fear, and great trembling at times when I've been called to stand up and be counted in a significant way. But from this point onward, I will do my best to train, study, and prepare so that when my moment comes to step forward, I will lean upon the Holy Spirit and not on my preparation alone. I will make room for the Holy Spirit to work, and I declare that He will work through me with supernatural, convincing powers that are far more effective than anything I could have ever done in my own strength!

I declare this by faith in Jesus' name!

QUESTIONS FOR YOU TO CONSIDER

1. Have you ever had a "great trembling" moment in your life? When was that moment, and what about that event caused you to feel such trembling? Did you experience the power of God in that experience? What did you learn from that experience?

2. The next time you are called to stand up and do something that will be viewed publicly or significantly, what will you do differently than the last time? What did you learn from your last experience that will make you act differently the next time an opportunity arises?
3. Can you think of other Bible personalities who had "trembling" moments in their lives, but who experienced the power of God? Who were they? Can you make a list of them by name?

JULY 27

What Is a Plague?

And straightway the fountain of her blood
was dried up; and she felt in her body
that she was healed of that plague.
— Mark 5:29

Do you know anyone that has ever been subjected to a plague? Have you ever had a plague afflict you? Technically, *what is a plague*?

We tend to use this word "plague" to describe worldwide pandemic outbreaks, but that is not the way it is used in Mark 5:29, which tells of a woman who had an issue of blood for 12 years. Specifically, Mark 5:29 says that when this woman touched Jesus, she was healed of her "plague." Yet this woman's sickness was not contagious, nor was it imminently life-threatening, since she had been sick with it for 12 years. So today I want to tell you about how I discovered the meaning of the word "plague" in the New Testament and why this was such an important discovery to me.

As a university student, I suffered tremendously from allergic reactions. In fact, a simple change in the weather could affect my whole body. To combat the pollens in the air and my body's reaction to them, I went to the university infirmary twice a week to receive allergy injections in both arms. As I had grown older, my allergies had progressively gotten worse and worse until they nearly controlled my life. One day when I was praying for an answer to these debilitating allergies, I began to delve into the story of the woman with an issue of blood in Mark 5, whom the Bible says had a "plague."

When I picked up my Greek New Testament to study this story in depth, I was quite struck to see the Greek meaning of the word "plague" used in Mark 5:29. It really gave me insight that helped me know how to pray more effectively for myself — and through this insight, I ultimately received healing and have never had an allergic reaction since! I believe this Greek word study will help you, as it helped me, to be more effective when you are praying about ailments that afflict you or others whom you know and love. At the very least, it will give you something to think about!

Before we delve into Mark 5:29 and the meaning of this word "plague," let's first briefly review the story of this woman with the issue of blood.

According to Mark 5, this woman was sick for 12 years, and she had spent all her money on physicians. However, instead of getting better, she only grew worse (*see* Mark 5:25,26). Then one day she heard of Jesus and set out to find Him. She came up from behind him in the crowd and reached out and touched the hem of His garment. Immediately, power flowed out of Jesus into her — "and straightway [immediately] the fountain of her blood was dried up; and she felt in her body that she was healed of that *plague*." According to these verses, this was a 12-year affliction that simply wouldn't go away or permanently respond to any type of medical treatment. Perhaps this woman would get better temporarily, but then it would recur again — much like the allergies that afflicted me for many years earlier in my life.

When I looked up the word "plague" in my Greek New Testament, I was shocked. I ran every reference to make sure I was understanding it correctly. I studied the historical usage of the Greek word for "plague" to be certain I was seeing this accurately. And I found that this word did not describe a pandemic disease at all. It was the Greek word *mastigos* — a very unusual word to be translated "plague." But once I studied it out and carefully thought through its usage, it made perfect sense, as I believe it will to you too. The word *mastigos* — translated "plague" — is a word that is borrowed from the world of *torture*.

Specifically, the word *mastigos* denoted the act of recurrently beating a prisoner or victim. Once the person's wounds had mended, the torturers would bring them back to the whipping post, where they were struck again and again and again. These beatings were sporadic but constant, and although they were not serious enough to kill the victim, it kept them in constant pain and misery. It was torment and abuse — a scourge that caused great suffering and prolonged anguish.

I'm sure you can see why this word was used to describe the condition of the woman with the issue of blood, for her ailment struck her again and again for 12 long years. She experienced a sporadic, regular attack of this condition all those years. It was a physical torment that would not go away but just kept coming back again and again and again.

I found it extremely interesting that *this* was the original meaning of the word *mastigos* — the word "plague" — that was used to describe this woman's long, protracted ailment. Let's think about this scenario for a moment. This woman didn't die from her affliction; it simply kept her life torn up for years. This was a "plague" that struck this woman over and over and over again. She'd feel better — and then suddenly that affliction would reappear to strike her again.

By the time we read of this poor woman in Mark's gospel, she had been afflicted with this recurring ailment for 12 long years. Physicians tried to help, but there was simply nothing they could do to permanently relieve the misery that this woman had lived with for more than a decade of her life. It wasn't serious enough to kill her, but it made her life continually miserable.

But when she touched Jesus with her faith, she was instantly made well of that torturous, recurring affliction!

So what is a "plague" as it is referred to in Mark 5:29? It is an ailment, sickness, or affliction that regularly strikes an individual again and again. It is a recurring condition that is not serious enough to kill but that continually keeps the individual sick and miserable. It is a sick, demented, elongated devilish attack upon an individual's physical body that causes discomfort and pain. Thus, this word *mastigos*, translated "plague," would describe chronic conditions such as *migraine headaches, rashes, allergic reactions, high blood pressure, foot fungus*, and so on. These are conditions that come and go, can last for years, and rarely permanently respond to medication or the treatment of physicians.

When I saw how the word *mastigos* was used to describe the woman with the issue of blood and then compared it to my own allergic condition, which had gone on for years with no relief, I understood that I was being victimized by the devil's multiple, recurring attacks against my body. When I understood that this was more than a medical condition — *it was a premeditated spiritual attack* — I took authority over it in Jesus' name and broke its power over my life. And I have *never* had another allergic episode since that moment!

Medicine is an important tool in administering aid to physical suffering. However, throwing medicine at a spiritual attack can at best bring only temporary relief; the symptoms will inevitably come back again because you are dealing with an attack and not an entirely physical problem. This was a great revelation for me, and it resulted in my physical healing. I stood up to each attack and resisted it in Jesus' name until those recurring allergic reactions stopped. The power of Satan that was attacking me was literally broken, and I've been free ever since.

Today you can take that same revelation to stand against the enemy's recurring attacks against *your* body. It's time to live *free*! *No* weapon formed against you shall prosper in Jesus' name — including every recurring physical condition that falls into this tormenting category called "plague"!

MY PRAYER FOR TODAY

Father, I thank You for the power in the name of Jesus. Today I use the name of Jesus to break every demonic attack against my body. I have suffered long enough with the afflictions that have assailed me. Starting today, I stand up against them with the name and the blood of Jesus Christ, and I command the devil to take his hands off my body!

I pray this in Jesus' name!

MY CONFESSION FOR TODAY

I confess that healing belongs to me because Jesus purchased it in my redemption! Greater is He that is in me than he that is in the world, and I authoritatively command the enemy to remove that whip that He has used to strike me and to keep me continually sick. I break the burden of its binding yoke by the power of the anointing of Jesus Christ in His mighty name!

I declare this by faith in Jesus' name!

QUESTIONS FOR YOU TO CONSIDER

1. Do you have any sporadic yet regular sicknesses that afflict you? Have you ever considered that these may be the result of devilish attacks against your body?
2. If you've used medicine with no results, like the woman with the issue of blood, have you ever considered that a spiritual answer may be what you need for your physical ailment?
3. What is your response to this *Sparkling Gem*? Has it given you illumination to a situation in your own life and body? How does it affect your view of the recurring sicknesses that have afflicted you for a long period of time?

JULY 28

'Do Not Deny My Faith!'

I know thy works, and where thou dwellest,
even where Satan's seat is:
and how thou holdest fast my name,
and hast not denied my faith....
— Revelation 2:13

Today I want to encourage you from the words Jesus used to address the believers in the First Century who were also experiencing pressure to bow to society and its demands. Christ commanded the early believers to remain faithful in the face of opposition. It is the same message that He is speaking to Christians today!

Early believers were bombarded daily with opportunities to deny their faith. Yet even in the face of these immense external pressures, there was always a *core group* of steadfast individuals who refused to waver in their commitment to Christ — and the same is true today. This company of believers simply would not cave in to the unrelenting intimidation brought against them. It was for this reason that Jesus declared, "...and thou holdest fast my name, *and hast not denied my faith....*"

The words "hast not" in this verse are a translation of the Greek word *ouk*, which essentially means *no*. However, the form of the word used in this verse is an exclamatory word expressing *a strong, emphatic no.* Thus, we see that the *King James Version* does not carry the full weight of the message conveyed in the Greek text, which actually reads as if Christ raised the volume and tone of His voice in order to make a resounding proclamation of these early believers' commitment.

Christ continued by saying, "…Thou…hast not *denied* my faith…." The word "denied" is the Greek word *arneo*, which is usually translated *to deny, to disown, to reject, to refuse*, or *to renounce.* This word *arneo* commonly referred to a person who had become unfaithful in a relationship and subsequently *disavowed, forsook, walked away from*, and *washed one's hands of* that other person. *The New International Dictionary of New Testament Theology* offers insight into the reasons behind such a total rejection: "The motive for denial is usually fear of others, fear of suffering ridicule or persecution, or anxiety about what others will think."

As persecution intensified during the latter years of the First Century, some believers chose to deny Jesus and abandon their faith in order to escape tribulation. Fear of other people's opinions and ridicule, fear of persecution, and even fear of death were all factors that contributed to this decision. Jesus, however, chose not to address these defectors in Revelation 2:13. Instead, He raised His voice to affirm the faithful core who did *not* disavow Him in their time of struggle. When Jesus said, "…thou…hast not denied…," He was essentially saying, "*When you had the opportunity to break your vow and walk away, you did not do it.*"

Notice that Christ specifically said, "…Thou...hast not denied *my faith*…." In the Greek text, there is an emphasis on this phrase "my faith" that reveals how Jesus truly feels about the message of the Gospel. These words are the Greek phrase *ten pisten mou*, which could literally be translated *the faith of me.* Of course, in English, the order of these words doesn't make much sense, but in the Greek, this phrasing is deliberate and logical.

The first word in the phrase *ten pisten mou* is the word *ten*, which simply means *the.* This word is a definite article, which always points to something very specific. In this instance, it appears directly in front of the word *pisten*, which is the Greek word for *faith.* Therefore, when these two words are used in conjunction with one another, they denote *a specific set of beliefs, a specific doctrine, a specific creed*, or *a specific faith.* It clearly refers to *the* faith, or the body of truth comprising the New Testament. It was this truth that Satan hated and wanted to destroy, and it was this truth that these dedicated believers refused to deny.

In order to convey how personally He feels about *the faith*, Jesus followed the word *pisten* ("faith") with the word *mou*, which is the Greek word for "my." Like its English counterpart, *mou* always denotes *ownership* and *possession.* When *mou* is used in conjunction with the phrase *ten pisten*, an accurate translation could read *my faith, the faith that belongs to me*, or *the faith that I hold closely.*

The Gospel not only comes *from* Christ, but it is also *firmly in His possession.* Jesus is the *Originator*, the *Giver*, and the ultimate *Supervisor* of the faith; therefore, it is incredibly precious to Him.

We are the recipients of the truth of the Gospel and its amazing benefits, but Christ is the One who paid for it with His blood to make it available. *What One bleeds for, another lives for* — and Christ shed His own blood for the truth of which we freely partake.

Even if the spirit of our age tries to lure us into modifying the message of the Gospel to pacify the shifting whims of our society, we must firmly proclaim the faith in its purest form. The faith didn't originate with us, and we don't have the right to modify it in any way.

You are destined to live as a shining light in the midst of a lost generation. But that destiny can only be fulfilled as you hold fast to the truth of Jesus Christ and *refuse* to compromise your stance or conform to the world, regardless of any pressure you face to do otherwise. *THAT* is something for you to think about — and to make a rock-solid decision about *TODAY*!

MY PRAYER FOR TODAY

Father, I want to be a part of the remnant that refuses to bend to the pressures of society in these last days. Although there is pressure to modify what we believe and to be less committed, Your Word has never changed; therefore, I know that You have not asked me to change my position or what I believe. Please help me to be strong in these times and to impart strength to others who are feeling the same pressure to conform to the dictates of society in these last days.

I pray this in Jesus' name!

MY CONFESSION FOR TODAY

I declare that neither society nor the courts will determine the standard by which I live and that I will live according to the teaching and dictates of the Bible. There is no doubt that society is trying to force me to change the way I think and believe, but I hold fast to the name of Jesus and to the teaching of the Word of God. It has been correct for thousands of years, and it remains the unerring guide for my life. I recommit myself to living according to the teaching and the standards of God's Word, even if it puts me at odds with what society is trying to tell me to do.

I declare this by faith in Jesus' name!

QUESTIONS FOR YOU TO CONSIDER

1. Describe some opportunities that you see presented for believers to deny their faith in society today.
2. The Gospel is Christ's message and no one has the right to change it. In what ways are society and even the courts attempting to change and twist the Gospel of Jesus Christ?
3. Give some examples in which your life is in direct contrast to the way the world encourages people to live and to believe.

JULY 29

Come Boldly to the Throne of Grace!

Let us therefore come boldly unto the throne of grace,
that we may obtain mercy, and find grace to help
in time of need.
— Hebrews 4:16

I can't begin to count the times that I've felt pressed into a hard place and didn't know what to do. But in those moments, I've learned to lean upon the promises made to us in Hebrews 4:16. It says, "Let us therefore come boldly unto the throne of grace, that we may obtain mercy, and find grace to help in time of need."

Today I want us to look at the words "boldly," "obtain," "find," and the phrase "help in time of need." I am sure that these words are packed with awesome insights that will absolutely thrill your heart and will give you such peace!

The verse begins by saying, "Let us therefore come *boldly*...." The word "boldly" comes from the word *parresia,* an often-used Greek word that was used in ancient times to refer to *freedom of speech.* It normally depicts a person who *speaks his mind* and who does it *straightforwardly* and with *great confidence.* In New Testament times, freedom of speech was restricted, and people who violated the rules were punished. The word *parresia* that is used in this verse depicts a *frankness* that was so *bold,* it was often met with resistance, hostility, and opposition. It just wasn't acceptable to speak so candidly. Therefore, when someone freely spoke his mind and thoughts, such outspokenness was met time and again with scorn or rebuke.

Because the Holy Spirit uses the word *parresia* in Hebrews 4:16, it tells us several important things. First, we know that whenever we approach the Lord in prayer, we need never fear that we are *too frank, too bold, too forthright, too honest, too outspoken,* or even *too blunt* when we bare our hearts to Him or request His help. We should never be irreverent, but neither do we need to be ashamed to speak exactly what is on our hearts. When you go to the Lord, He *wants* to hear exactly what you have to say!

Second, the use of the word *parresia* — which was used to give us the encouragement to speak boldly to God in prayer — tells us that God will not rebuke us for telling Him exactly what we think. Even if we are wrong, it will not bother God when we're honest with Him. He may correct us or take us to the Word to help fix our wrong thinking and believing, but He is always glad when we come to Him and speak freely from our hearts.

As the verse continues, it exhorts us to "…come boldly unto the throne of grace, that we may *obtain* mercy, and find grace to help in time of need." We all need mercy, so now let's look at the word "obtain" to see how we can obtain it!

The word "obtain" comes from the Greek word *lambano*. It can be translated a couple of ways, depending on how it is used in the text. For example, it can mean *to seize or to lay hold of something in order to make it your very own,* almost like a person who reaches out *to grab, to capture,* or *to take possession* of something. In some cases, it means *to violently lay hold of something in order to seize and take it as one's very own.* At other times, it depicts a person who gently and graciously *receives* something that is freely and easily given.

How easily you receive from God may be determined by your own personal circumstances or inward struggles that affect the ease with which you receive God's help. If your mind is tormented or you feel the world is pressing hard against you, it may be more difficult for you to receive — not because it's difficult for Jesus to give, but because it's difficult for you to focus on what He wants to give you. In that case, it may mean you have to reach out and *forcibly lay hold of* the help God offers.

The truth is, Jesus is willing to simply give you what you need, and all you have to do is open your heart and by faith *receive* it. But if exterior forces seem to be pulling you in countless different directions, it may take a deliberate act on your part to shove those external pulls out of the way and reach out by faith *to lay hold of* the mercy that Jesus offers you. *Lay hold of it, take it,* and *make it your own* so you can *receive* the mercy Jesus wants to give to help you in your situation.

But don't stop with obtaining mercy, because the verse continues to say that you can also "*find* grace to help in time of need."

The word "find" is a translation of the often-used Greek word *eurisko.* The word *eurisko* simply means *to find.* It expresses the idea of a discovery that is made by *searching.*

Usually the word *eurisko* points to a discovery made *due to an intense investigation, scientific study, or scholarly research.* There's nothing of *chance* left to this kind of investigation. After working long hours and searching for a long time, the time and effort finally pay off as the researcher finds what he has been seeking! In that ecstatic moment of euphoria, he shrieks, *"Eureka!"* — which means, *"I found it!"* In fact, the word "eureka" is derived from the word *eurisko* that is translated "find" in Hebrews 4:16, informing us of the joy experienced when a seeker finds what he has sought for so long.

Maybe you've sought God's help for a long time. Perhaps you've prayed for it and searched for it. You've heeded Jesus' word to ask, seek, and knock (*see* Matthew 7:8; Luke 11:10). And you've been persistent like the woman who knocked on the judge's door and never gave up (*see* Luke 18:1-8). You have knocked and knocked and knocked — and you have sought and sought and sought. Finally, the door opens and you receive the help you needed. You have every right to shout, "*Eureka!* I've found it! I've received it! I have it!"

After you seek, God promises that you will capture exactly what you need from Him, so don't stop seeking it until you have finally laid hold of it and have made it your very own!

But there is something else very important about the word *eurisko* that I must point out. This word doesn't just describe a discovery made for yourself; it can also mean *to acquire something for someone else.* For example, do you know someone in need of some kind of help?

- Do you know someone who needs physical healing?
- Do you know someone who needs deliverance?
- Do you know someone who needs peace of mind?
- Do you know someone who needs a healing in his or her marriage or family?
- Do you know someone who needs a financial breakthrough?

Because the word *eurisko* also means *to acquire something for someone else*, it means you can go to Jesus, the Great High Priest, and seek Him for help on behalf of others. You can obtain help for those who are in need — those who need healing, those who need deliverance, those who need relief from mental torment, those who need wholeness in their marriages and families, and those who need a financial breakthrough. Not only can you take your own needs to the Lord, but you can also take *their* needs to Him to obtain the help *they* so desperately need. This means the Lord wants to hear about your needs *and* the needs of those you love and hold dear to your heart.

But now let's look at the phrase "help in time of need." The phrase is a translation of the Greek word *boetheia,* a word with a military connotation. The word *boetheia* can be translated *to help*, as *to help a person with his or her needs*, but the military connotation of this word adds much more meaning and makes it really powerful.

In the world of the early New Testament, it was a military word that beckoned soldiers to battle. That word was *boetheia*, which was first and foremost a military word that depicted the exact moment when a soldier heard that his fellow fighter was entrenched in battle, captured, or struggling. Once alerted to this situation, the soldier quickly went into battle to fight for the safety and well-being of his fellow fighter. For that soldier, just hearing of a fellow fighter in need was all that was necessary to beckon him into battle. He spared no effort to deliver his brother as he went into action to rescue him and bring him back into a place of safety, security, and protection.

The Holy Spirit uses this same word to tell us that when we get into trouble and we tell Jesus about it, He goes into battle like a Mighty Warrior to be our defense and to secure our deliverance!

When Jesus fights, He is always on the winning side. So the next time you're struggling, don't try to slug it out all by yourself. Instead, go to Jesus and tell Him your situation. He will go to battle for you and fight until you are delivered and free! This is the kind of "help" Jesus wants to provide if you will present your needs to Him in faith. *Why fight alone when the greatest Warrior in the universe is willing to fight for you?*

For the last 2,000-plus years, Jesus has been seated at the Father's right hand, where He ever lives to make intercession for anyone who comes to Him by faith (*see* Hebrews 7:25). The Lord has been fighting for every believer who has come boldly and honestly to Him in prayer. If you are willing to seek His assistance and not stop until you get it, Jesus will step up to the plate and fight for you. More than 2,000 years ago, Jesus died for you, but today — and right at this very moment — He is living to fight for your every need!

Isn't that some of the best news you've ever heard in your whole life? Jesus is just waiting for you to present your needs to Him and to ask for His help. So why don't you take a few minutes right now to present your needs to Him? Don't worry that He will rebuke you for being too honest. He is beckoning you to come boldly to His throne to obtain mercy and to find grace to help in your time of need!

MY PRAYER FOR TODAY

Lord Jesus, I come to You boldly with the needs I am facing in my life. I have wrongly lacked confidence and failed to be straightforward about them with You, but now I understand that You want me to be frank, forthright, and direct with You about these challenges I am facing. Thank You that You don't rebuke or scorn me for being bold — and thank You for stepping forward as a mighty Warrior to help fight my challenge with me. Today I am coming to You boldly, and I am expecting You to step forward to fight in my defense!

I pray this in Jesus' name!

MY CONFESSION FOR TODAY

I declare that I obey the Lord's charge to pray boldly and forthrightly when I come to the throne of God's grace. He bids me to come, and today I accept His invitation to come boldly and to declare my each and every need. With the help of the Holy Spirit, I will lay hold of the answers that I need and my exterior circumstances must change as a result of this time at the throne of God's grace. Jesus will step forward as my Mighty Warrior to fight for me. He is just waiting for me to issue Him the invitation to step into the fray with me and to manifest His victory in this battle!

I declare this by faith in Jesus' name!

QUESTIONS FOR YOU TO CONSIDER

1. Can you think of a time when you boldly approached the throne of God and received help in your time of need? When was that experience? What happened as a result of boldly asking for help?
2. Are there others you know who need you to do some asking for them today? Who are those individuals who really need you to bring their names before the throne of grace?
3. Is there a moment you recall when Jesus stepped forward like a Mighty Warrior and fought for you when you were in need? When was that moment? Wouldn't it be good for you to meditate on His faithfulness to you today? It will help stir you up for the victory that you need right now.

JULY 30

Christ-Like Attitudes We Must 'Put On'

Put on therefore, as the elect of God, holy and beloved,
bowels of mercies, kindness, humbleness
of mind, meekness, longsuffering....
— Colossians 3:12

Let me challenge you today: Set aside some quality time to be alone with God and make this specific request of Him: "Father, I ask You to show me what areas of my life need to be adjusted so they more accurately represent the attitude of Jesus Christ." And as you begin a search with that question in your heart, I suggest that you begin with Colossians 3:12, where Paul described the Christ-like attitudes we need to implement in our lives.

Paul wrote, "Put on therefore, as the elect of God, holy and beloved, *bowels of mercies, kindness, humbleness of mind, meekness, longsuffering*." Paul's choice of wording for each character trait is very specific, so let's take time today to deconstruct them to better discern his exact meaning of each one.

To begin, I want to focus on the phrase "bowels of mercies," which sounds very strange in today's vernacular but conveys a powerful message. It is a translation of two Greek words, *splagnon* and *oiktirmos*. The word *splagnon* refers to *the inner organs of a human body*, or more specifically, *the bowels*, and the word *oiktirmos* denotes *compassion* or *a deeply felt urge to help relieve some kind of pain or sorrow*.

Before I elaborate further on the Greek word *splagnon* ("bowels"), I must ask you to pardon me in advance for being so blunt with my explanation. However, it is important to consider the function of bowels in order to understand the reason why that word is used in connection with "mercy" and "compassion" in the New Testament.

Physically, when your bowels move, you feel it *deeply*. When the process is done, the bowels have made *a physical deposit* and rid the body of human waste. The purpose of these feelings, however, is not superficial — they are a sign that the intestines are working to push waste through the system and out of the body.

Thus, by using the word *splagnon*, Paul was saying that *deep feelings of compassion* should do more than merely provoke pity for a person's situation; they should spur you to action. When these feelings begin to well up deep within your spirit, you must surrender to them and let them work through your inner man until they manifest through your words and actions. As you do this, God's Spirit simultaneously works through you to reach out and make a spiritual deposit into those who are suffering, sorrowful, or going through a difficult time in their lives. To feel that inner pain without taking any action simply produces no benefit.

It's interesting to note that "bowels of mercies" is the very first Christ-like attitude that Paul listed in Colossians 3:12. Throughout the four gospels, the Greek words *splagnon* and *oiktirmos* are frequently used together to describe moments when Jesus was "moved with compassion." The Bible tells us that when Jesus experienced this feeling, compassion flowed from deep inside Him to help multitudes, heal the sick, or otherwise demonstrate God's kindness to people who were in need (*see* Matthew 14:14-21; 15:32-38; 20:34; Mark 1:41,42; 6:34-44; 8:2-9; Luke 7:13-15). By listing this quality first, Paul was urging us not to focus on our own needs but rather to turn our attention outward to others who are in trouble and allow our hearts to feel their pain until we are *inwardly touched*!

Is there someone you know who needs a touch of God's compassion? That divine compassion is deposited deep inside *your* spirit, and if you will yield to it, it will flow from the deepest part of your being to heal, change, deliver, and bring relief to that person in need. So I exhort you: *Please don't shut off your bowels of compassion!* If you sense the urge growing and building inside your spirit to alleviate another person's pain, *let that compassion flow* and bring him or her the delivering power of God.

The next attitude Paul told us to put on in Colossians 3:12 is "kindness." This is a translation of the Greek word *chrestotes*, which means *to show kindness* or *to be friendly to others*. In Greek history, it often depicted rulers, governors, or others in positions of leadership and authority who were *kind*, *mild*, and *benevolent* to their subjects. Anyone who demonstrated this quality of *chrestotes* was considered to be *compassionate*, *considerate*, *sympathetic*, *humane*, *kind*, and *gentle*. Elsewhere in Scripture, the apostle Paul used this word *chrestotes* to depict *God's incomprehensible kindness* for people who are unsaved (*see* Romans 11:22; Ephesians 2:7; Titus 3:4). One scholar has noted that when the word *chrestotes* is applied to interhuman relationships, it conveys the idea of being *adaptable* to others.

When *chrestotes* is working in a believer, that believer strives to become *adaptable* to the needs of those around him rather than harshly requiring everyone else to adapt to his own needs and desires. This is so contrary to the flesh, which says, "Excuse me, but if you don't like me the way I am, that's tough! This is the way I am, and if you don't like it, you can just get out of here. I'm not changing for anyone!"

When the Holy Spirit produces "kindness" in you, your entire mode of thinking will change. You'll begin to ask people, "How can I be different for you? Is there any way I can change that will help you? Is there anything I can do better for you? How can I serve you to meet your needs more effectively?"

When you become *adaptable* to meet the needs of other people, a supernatural work of God takes place in your heart, and you grow substantially in your spiritual walk as a result. If this kindness *hasn't* started to work in you yet, today would be a great day for you to ask the Holy Spirit to start producing this Christ-like attitude in your life!

Paul continued in Colossians 3:12 by urging us to allow "humbleness of mind" to develop in our lives. The Greek word used here is *tapeinophrosune*, a compound of the words *tapeinos* and *phronos*. The word *tapeinos* is translated *humility*, and it depicts the attitude of *one who is humble, lowly, and willing to stoop to any level that is needed*. The word *phronos* simply means *to think*. When these two words are compounded, as in this verse, the new word portrays the attitude of someone who is unassuming and not self-promoting. It suggests a person who is *modest* and *unpretentious*.

Does "humbleness of mind" operate in your life? Jesus was known for stooping to the level of everyone around Him in order to minister life to them. Had He seen Himself as "better" or "more deserving" than others, He never would have died on the Cross for you and me. *Kindness* is also a Christ-like attitude that the Holy Spirit strongly desires to produce in all of our lives. Is it working in you right now, or is this an area in which you need to allow the Holy Spirit to work more deeply in your character?

In this remarkable list of Christ-like attitudes found in Colossians 3:12, Paul next mentioned "meekness." Most people assume that if a person is *meek*, he must be *weak*. However, this is a grossly incorrect view of the word "meekness." In reality, "meekness" is one of the strongest attributes a person can possess, because it refers to a unique strength that dramatically impacts everyone it touches. In fact, in the ancient world, meekness was considered to be a high and noble ideal that people aspired to attain in life!

The word "meekness" is the Greek word *prautes*, which describes *a person who is forbearing, patient, and slow to respond in anger* or *a strong-willed person who has learned to submit his will to a higher authority*. This isn't a *weak* person; it's a *controlled* person. A meek individual may possess a firm will and a powerful character, and he may have his own strong opinions. However, he has fundamentally learned how to bring his will under control. When confronted by an injurious situation, a meek person doesn't react with a rash or angry outburst, flying into a rage and throwing a temper tantrum. Instead he responds with kindness, gentleness, mildness, or even friendliness.

In rare instances, the word *prautes* ("meekness") was used in Classical Greek literature to describe wild animals that had become tame because the word correctly conveys the idea of a wild, fierce will being brought under control. Thus, the meaning of this word extends to the idea of *an individual who remains in control of himself in the face of insults or injuries*. In the Greek language, the word *prautes* also conveys the idea of a high and noble ideal to be aspired to in one's life.

In addition, the word *prautes* was used in a medical sense to denote *soothing medication to calm the angry mind*. Thus, we see that a meek person doesn't project the countenance of one who is offended, upset, angry, or reactive to insults or injuries. Instead, his response is so gentle and mild that it acts as a soothing medicine for an angry or upset soul in an unsettling situation.

The flesh loves to rage out of control, but "meekness" makes you *careful* and *controlled* even in difficult circumstances. Instead of flying into a rage and throwing a temper tantrum at every perceived slight, you're able to remain silent and keep your emotions and temper in check. Your very presence will become *God's soothing medication* for angry, upset people, and you will impart peace to situations that previously were unsettling and unstable. And if you find yourself in a situation that you fiercely believe is wrong, you're still able to remain silent until the appropriate moment to speak or until you've been asked for your opinion. You know how to control yourself and your emotions.

Last in Paul's list of Christ-like attitudes is the word "longsuffering." This is a translation of the Greek word *makrothumia*, which is a compound of the words *makros* and *thumos*. The word *makros* indicates something that is *long*, *distant*, *far*, or *remote*. The word *thumos* is often translated *anger*, but it also embodies the idea of *a strong and growing passion* about something. When the two words are compounded, they form the word *makrothumia*, which refers to *the patient restraint of anger*, *longsuffering*, *forbearance*, or *patience*.

The idea of *makrothumia*, or "longsuffering," can be compared to a candle with a very long wick that allows it to burn for a long time. In a similar way, a person who is *longsuffering* is ready to forbear and patiently wait for people to "come around," listen to counsel, make progress, and ultimately implement change in their lives. Walking in *makrothumia* is a part of our Christian responsibility. We have an obligation before God not to be short-tempered with people who struggle or fail. Instead, we are to forbear with them and help them succeed!

Longsuffering is so different from the way the flesh wants to react. Flesh gets easily angered, blows up, loses its temper, says things it later regrets, and doesn't want to give the same mercy it demands from others. That is the exact opposite of the response God wants us to have when facing difficult situations. In fact, He commands us to make longsuffering a key characteristic in our lives!

This one verse holds so much insight into the question that we need to answer before God: *What areas of my life need to be adjusted so they more accurately represent the attitude of Jesus Christ?* Any or all of these qualities we discussed above may represent some of those areas that need to be adjusted in our lives. The good news is that the Holy Spirit lives in us, and each character trait discussed today is a fruit He wants to produce in our lives. All He needs is our cooperation.

So I encourage you: Make the decision today to yield to the Holy Spirit on a continual basis, and allow Him to produce these Christ-like attitudes inside you!

MY PRAYER FOR TODAY

Holy Spirit, I am so thankful that You live inside of me to produce the attitudes of Jesus Christ in my life. Today I have been convicted regarding areas in my life where I need to grow and change. I ask You to release Your divine power inside me to produce the attitudes and the attributes of Jesus' character in my life. Let Colossians 3:12 become a reality inside me as the very nature and life of Jesus becomes replicated in me!

I pray this in Jesus' name!

MY CONFESSION FOR TODAY

I boldly confess that I am changing every day as I surrender to the indwelling power of the Holy Spirit. He is convicting me of areas where I need to be more Christ-like, and I am responding to what He reveals to me about the areas I need to change so I can become more conformed to the image of Jesus Christ. I am not powerless. I am not a victim to my ugly old nature. The

Spirit of God indwells me, and He gives me the power to change in these areas where He is speaking to my heart!

I declare this by faith in Jesus' name!

QUESTIONS FOR YOU TO CONSIDER

1. Can you think of a time when God's compassion tried to flow through you, but you reasoned yourself out of yielding to that inner urge? Were you later sorry that you denied the love of God to be expressed through your life?
2. Take a moment to examine the way you respond to insults, injuries, or volatile situations. Do you find that you are often a contributor to a heated and potentially explosive atmosphere? Or does your presence bring peace into the midst of the conflict? When others say or do something that could offend you, do you quickly retort with a harsh answer, or are you able to control your emotions and temper, remaining silent until a more appropriate time to speak?
3. Do you "suffer long" with others who struggle in some area, or are you easily angered and irritated when people don't "get it right the first time"? Have you ever said something rude to someone else who was genuinely trying his best to succeed at something yet had failed? Were you later convicted of your own failures and shortcomings? Do you remember others who practiced longsuffering toward you when you needed it? What about those who *didn't* demonstrate longsuffering? How did their attitudes or behaviors help or hinder you?

JULY 31

Five Things To Do Every Day To Keep Yourself Strong

Be careful for nothing; but in *every thing*
by prayer and supplication with thanksgiving
let your requests be made known unto God.
— Philippians 4:6

Over many years and through many experiences, I have learned that I have to be *proactive* to keep my spiritual life strong and healthy. We can't ignore our spiritual life and expect it to remain strong. Just as our bodies need regular care and attention, our spiritual lives need a maintenance schedule in order to remain healthy.

I want to give you five principles that Denise and I have learned over the years to keep us strong and vibrant. These five principles have become essential elements in our daily lives — and they have resulted in our being continually strengthened to accomplish the tasks the Holy Spirit has entrusted to us. These five elements are very simple, but if you will do them faithfully, I am fully convinced that your life will be strengthened in every way.

1) Every day spend time with God in the morning.

In Psalm 5:3, David wrote of his commitment to spend time with God every morning. He said, "My voice shalt thou hear in the morning, O Lord; in the morning will I direct my prayer unto thee, *and will look up*."

I want you to particularly notice the italicized portion of this verse: "...and will look up." I have learned that if we don't begin our day by "looking up," our natural tendency is to start by looking *down*. By the time we read our text messages on our mobile devices each morning, read our emails, answer a few phone calls, listen to the morning news, or simply contemplate everything that is on our "to do" list for that day — our emotions can pull us into a downward spiral before we ever even leave home!

David understood this. He was surrounded with enemies outside his home and even among his own family members. David knew that he needed to start each morning "looking up" before his flesh had an opportunity to take him down.

Similarly, *you* need to start every day with the Lord "looking up." You accomplish this by focusing your attention on the Word each morning and by spending some concentrated time in prayer.

Making the Lord and His Word your first focus each day will be a lifeline for your spiritual strength. Ignore this element of your spiritual walk, and you'll end up troubled, nervous, worried, and lacking spiritual power in your life. Make this a daily habit, and you'll be at peace. You'll be infused with confidence, and you'll experience power to overcome the daily problems you face in life. Making a commitment to do this may require that you get up earlier or that you to go to bed earlier. But making the Lord your first focus every day will absolutely change your life.

I start every day of my life exactly as I am suggesting to you. When I wake up, I grab my cup of coffee, head to my chair in our TV room, sit down with my Bible, and immediately begin to put God's Word into my heart and soul. It feeds me, keeps me on track, and helps my heart stay tender before the Lord.

One day without God's Word is all it takes for the hardening process to begin in your heart. That's why it's so crucial that you hold yourself as an alert watchman on the walls of your heart, carefully guarding what comes in its "gates," as well as your level of intake of the Word versus the level of outflow. Proverbs 4:20-23 states the divine warning concerning this: "My son, attend to my words; incline thine ear unto my sayings. Let them not depart from thine eyes; keep them in the midst of thine heart. For they are life unto them that find them, and health to all their flesh. Keep thy heart with all diligence; for out of it are the issues of life."

And while you're already sitting there with your Bible, you should take time to pray! That's a crucial part of "looking up" to get your heart set on the Lord at the beginning of the day. Philippians 4:6 says, "Be careful for nothing; but in *every thing* by prayer and supplication with thanksgiving let your requests be made known unto God." The word "everything" is from the Greek *panti*, and it embraces *everything*. It is an *all-inclusive word* — including the finest, most minute details.

My advice is that you:

- Pray before you read your Bible, and ask the Holy Spirit to speak to you.
- Pray as you read your Bible, and ask the Holy Spirit to plant what you are reading deep into your heart and soul.
- Pray every day for a few minutes with your spouse.
- Pray with your children before they leave the house.
- Pray before you drive your car or travel on any other means of transportation.

I have implemented these simple guidelines in my own prayer life, and they have added great strength to my walk with God.

In First Thessalonians 5:17, Paul tells us to "pray without ceasing." The words "without ceasing" come from the Greek word *adialeiptos*, which means *without interruption, without taking a break*, or *continuously*. The only way you can do this is to develop a lifestyle of prayer. Starting early in the morning is the best way to get started — and then you can keep it up throughout the rest of the day.

2) Every day spend time feeding your spirit on other godly sources.

When Paul was in prison writing the last letter he would write, he told Timothy, "When you come…bring my books…" (2 Timothy 4:13 *NLT*).

Paul asked for books — books he could read to strengthen his own spirit as he waited in prison for his execution. Paul was filled with revelation and knew the Lord better than any of us, yet he still longed to read and to grow as he waited to depart to be with the Lord. He could have said, "Forget it — I'll be in Heaven soon anyway!" But Paul understood that as long as he was alive, he needed to feed his spirit.

Never forget that *growing people are reading people*. It's usually true that people who are stagnant in life don't spend much time reading what others have written.

It is simply a fact that reading is like fertilizer to a garden. The more you read good books, the more your mind and spirit expand and your inward capacity grows. And it doesn't have to be hours upon hours of reading. It can be a chapter a day from a book that causes you to dig deeper or that challenges your mind and spirit to grow. The point is to make a deliberate effort to read on a regular basis in order to bring growth to your spirit and mind.

If you are an auditory learner more than a reader, you can do the same thing by taking a few minutes each day to listen to an audio series or audio books as you drive your car or work around your house. One of our sons showed me a group of teaching CDs he had been listening to as he drives his car all over Moscow. It impressed me. Why not use the valuable time you spend in your car to feed your spirit and produce strength in your life?

What you put into your mind will determine what you think, what you believe, and, ultimately, what will happen in your life. That principle can work both negatively or positively, so apply it to your advantage by regularly reading or listening to words that will lift your spirit and help change your circumstances to conform to God's will. If you say you don't have time to do that, I suggest that you log the time you spend watching television programs in a given week — programs that do nothing to nurture and grow your life spiritually. You'll see that you really do have time to invest in your own spirit by feeding on other godly sources.

3) Every day spend some time in quietness.

Proverbs 27:19 says, "As in water face answereth to face, so the heart of man to man." Just as you see your reflection when you look into a pool of water, you can see and hear your own heart when you get quiet enough to listen.

I am convinced that the failure to do this is one reason people get confused in life. They get so busy that they no longer are in touch with themselves — what they believe, what they need, and what they feel. Instead, they just keep moving through life like robots.

But you need times of deep contemplation in order to stay in touch with your own heart. Perhaps journaling will help you process your thoughts, as it does for some people, and articulate your ongoing conversations with God.

In Psalm 37:4, David wrote, "Delight thyself also in the Lord; and he shall give thee the desires of thine heart." We all want the desires of our hearts — but if we are not in touch with our hearts, how can we even know what those desires are? The fact is that *much activity with no pause leads to spiritual dullness and confusion.* You need a few minutes of "quiet" every day.

Where can you find a time and place for quiet contemplation? If you don't have a place to be quiet, consider these possibilities:

- Take a walk to let the quietness of the outdoors become a sanctuary for your spirit.
- Get up before other people in your house are awake and let that time of quietness fill your soul with peace.
- Go into the bathroom, if necessary, and shut the door!

Finding a few minutes of quietness has become a very integral part of my life. It is essential for me to stay in touch with my own heart and the deeply imbedded God-given desires in my spirit. It helps to chase away inner turbulence and to bring the peace of God to the forefront of my mind.

Psalm 46:10 says, "Be still, and know that I am God." God commands us to be still because He knows how much we need this for the health of our spirits and souls.

To get started spending time in quietness each day as a habit, consider setting aside even as little as five minutes every day to be alone and allow God to minister strength to you through a concentrated time of quietness.

4) Every day spend some time with those who strengthen you.

Hebrews 10:25 says, "Not forsaking the assembling of ourselves together, as the manner of some is, but exhorting one another...." People tend to think this verse refers to attending church, and that's true. You need to be faithful to attend church; after all, you are a part of the Body! Your church family needs you, and you need what others have to give you. In the Body of Christ, there is a mutual exchange of strength that occurs in fellowshipping with other believers that you absolutely need.

However, for me personally, I need more than a weekly meeting with an auditorium full of people. That corporate worship time is essential, but I also need people who speak into my life — to encourage me, to check on me, and to hold me accountable in various areas of my life. These times of fellowship can be done by telephone, by email, by Skype, or by a number of means that are available today — *or* by the old-fashioned way of personally meeting together!

There are six people who speak deeply into my life — and I speak with at least one of them every day and nearly all of them at least once a week. With all that I am required to give of myself to others, I have found a great need to have people who impart spiritual wisdom and insight into my life. It helps keep me strong and healthy. The primary one who does this is Denise — but in addition to my precious wife, I have come to treasure five men who fill this vital role in my life.

These five men remind me of God's faithfulness. They remind me to keep my eyes on Jesus, and they encourage me to keep marching forward in obedience to Jesus' call on my life. Yes, I could probably do it without them, but I'm so thankful I don't have to! I deliberately and purposefully stay in touch with these precious men. I don't wait for them to call me. I actively pursue these relationships, because I know I need them and that God wants to strengthen me through them.

Who speaks into your life with this kind of authority? These types of relationships need to be identified, pursued, developed, and maintained, for they will serve to make you stronger in your walk with God.

5) Every day take time to stop throughout the day to acknowledge God.

Psalm 119:164 says, "Seven times a day do I praise thee because of thy righteous judgments." This is something you can stop and do several times a day that requires almost no effort. But I promise — doing so will radically change your life.

I personally take pauses throughout each day to recognize God's presence in my life. I have a program on my mobile device that "chimes" like a church bell intermittently throughout the day — and regardless of where I am or what I am doing, when I hear that "chime," I pause to recognize God's presence in my life and to thank Him for being in control.

When so much seems to be going on beyond your control, it's good to pause and acknowledge that God is on the throne and is righteous in all His judgments — regardless of what you see, what you feel, or what others are doing or are failing to do. Pausing to recognize this at various points throughout your day will energize your atmosphere and keep you "connected" in your soul to the Living One!

There is nothing more important than your relationship with God. Please prayerfully consider how you can implement these five life-changing elements in your life every day. Making these five principles a part of our daily lives has truly changed Denise and me — and we know they will add so much strength to your life as well.

MY PRAYER FOR TODAY

Father, I thank You for speaking to me today about areas where I need to be more proactive in guarding my spiritual life to make sure that I stay spiritually strong, healthy, and vibrant. I understand that to keep my spirit in strong condition will require time and energy and perhaps the sacrifice of other good pastimes. There is nothing more important than my relationship with You. How I walk with You affects every other area of my life. Help me take this seriously and apply these principles to my life. Show me how to get started, because I know that my spiritual condition is vital to the rest of my life and to the lives of those You have positioned me to influence for Your glory.

I pray this in Jesus' name!

MY CONFESSION FOR TODAY

I confess that I am proactive in keeping my spiritual condition strong, healthy, and vibrant. I do not ignore my spiritual life. Just as I feed my body every day and have certain regimens in place to care for my physical condition, I am careful to attend to the needs of my spirit and soul. As a result, I am spiritually strong; I am spiritually healthy; and my heart is vibrant. I am disciplined, committed, and careful to keep my spiritual condition in top-notch shape!

I declare this by faith in Jesus' name!

QUESTIONS FOR YOU TO CONSIDER

1. What did you honestly think when you read this *Sparkling Gem* today? Did you feel overwhelmed by the list of five things to do, or do you believe that these are elements you can apply to your life?
2. Perhaps you already do some of these things in your daily life. Which ones are already essential elements in your life? Which one do you need to implement immediately?
3. To implement these suggestions, or even a partial list of them, what changes will you have to make in your daily schedule? I suggest that you look at the main points of this *Sparkling Gem* once again, and choose which elements you can most easily adapt to your life. The point is to get started.

AUGUST 1

Do You Feel Like You've Hit a Brick Wall?

...We were pressed out of measure, above strength,
insomuch that we despaired even of life:
But we had the sentence of death in ourselves,
that we should not trust in ourselves,
but in God, which raiseth the dead.
— 2 Corinthians 1:8,9

Are you currently facing hard times in your life? Today I want to encourage you from the Word of God and show you how to tackle these difficult circumstances and emerge victorious. The devil will try to convince you that you're a failure, that your life is over, and that nothing good lies ahead for you; however, *this simply isn't true.* These emotions are temporary and fleeting, and the enemy is trying to use them to hold you back and keep you from experiencing the fulfilled life that God wants you to enjoy.

Although we don't like to admit it, we all occasionally have times in our lives when we hit a brick wall, so to speak. We don't know what to say, what to do, where to turn, or even how to pray. Sometimes it seems as if we've hit a dead end and everything is *finished, over,* and *done with.* If you've ever been in a place like that, you know what a hard place this can be! These feelings usually arise when we think that we've failed, that people have misunderstood us, or that we've been unfairly judged. However, even when we've made serious mistakes, these setbacks are rarely as irreparable as they seem.

I understand that these emotions feel very real in the moment. When others tell you that your situation is not as bad as you think or that you need to remember to be grateful for all the good in your life, it may even make you angry. Their comments may be right, but because you're the one in the midst of the trial, you still feel hopeless. Somehow you've found yourself caught in a storm and you don't know how to put one foot in front of the other to make your way out of it. You may feel like nothing you do pleases anyone, so you question why you should even try.

In truth, it doesn't matter if the emotions you are experiencing stem from real personal failure or from circumstances outside of your control. It's still your responsibility to get up, brush yourself off, and start moving forward again in your walk with God! Think about it — your entire faith is based on *resurrection.* The resurrection power of God is inside you, and it can lift you up above all the jumbled emotions and turmoil — into a better place than you've ever known in your life!

There have been many moments in my own life when I felt overwhelmed by circumstances and challenges. Usually those are the times when the devil seized the opportunity to whisper, *There is no way out. You have no way to crawl out from where you are. You're trapped with no escape.* However, his words of discouragement and despair have *never* proven to be true! Although it may have taken longer than I anticipated to reach my goal and required me to grow to new levels of faith, there was always a way to do whatever Jesus had asked me to do, and I ultimately found victory in every challenge.

If we stick with our assigned tasks and keep moving forward — even if it's one step at a time — we will always win! And after we've pressed beyond our struggles into victory, we'll always be thankful we didn't give up!

When I am facing challenges in my life, I always derive immense strength from Paul's words in Second Corinthians 1:8 and 9, where he wrote, "...We were pressed out of measure, above strength, insomuch that we despaired even of life: But we had the sentence of death in ourselves, that we should not trust in ourselves, but in God, which raiseth the dead." Paul wrote these verses when he felt trapped by crushing ordeals in his ministry, and his words tell me that he didn't know if he would survive. How thankful I am that God didn't hide the apostle's difficult moments from us!

Paul's words in Second Corinthians 1:8 and 9 teach us what to do when we feel like we simply cannot make it any further in our own strength or that we're no match for the challenges we're facing. We simply *must* surrender to the resurrection power of God! That's what the apostle Paul did when he found himself face to face with life-threatening situations. When Paul wrote, "...We had the sentence of death in ourselves...," he was at one of those dead-end places that I'm talking about today. In fact, the situation he faced was so acute that he compared it to a sentence of death. That's dramatic language!

The word "sentence" is the Greek word *krino* — a word that usually referred to a jury who had just handed down their *final sentence* in a court of law. You could say that it denoted *a verdict* or *a final sentence* pronounced as the result of a court trial. After all the evidence had been presented and the judge had examined all the facts, a *final verdict* was issued by the court.

By using this word "sentence" or *krino*, Paul told us that so many problems were stacked against him and his companions that, by all appearances, it seemed like there was no way for them to escape or even to survive. It looked as if they'd hit a dead-end, as if everything was *finished*, *over*, and *done with*! Paul went on to say that it looked so insurmountable that, as far as he was concerned, it seemed there was only one possible outcome — *death*!

But in spite of how bad things appeared, Paul didn't die, nor did he fail at fulfilling the job God had given him to do. It may have looked like it was the end of the road for Paul, but it was really the beginning of a new supernatural flow of divine power into his life. That's why he went on to say that through it all, he learned not to trust in himself, but in God who raises the dead.

Paul had been under intense pressure, but right in the midst of this horrible situation, God's resurrection power was released inside Paul and he was rescued! Paul said it was so dramatic that it was almost as if he and his companions had been *raised from the dead*.

When you don't know what else to do but turn to God, that's usually when His resurrection power can begin to operate in you in the greatest way. You see, in God there's no such thing as *a hopeless situation*. That dead-end place you may be facing right now can become a place of new beginnings!

Let me tell you, people all around you are struggling right now. The devil is telling them that they won't make it. But they *will* make it if they choose to turn their focused gaze to Jesus, and you will too! Your victory may not come as you thought, but God is with you, and He will get you through whatever it is you're facing if you'll surrender to the Holy Spirit's resurrection power inside you.

This is *not* the end for you! God has a marvelous plan for your life, and the devil simply doesn't have the power to hijack what He has planned. Remember — if the devil has tried to tell you that you're a failure, that life is over, and that nothing good lies ahead of you in the future, it's not true! What you're feeling will pass, and better days are ahead. *Just determine to lay hold of the resurrection power of Christ in you, and let it lift you up above the storm into a brighter and better place!*

MY PRAYER FOR TODAY

Father, I thank You for Your marvelous plan for my life. I praise You because the devil is powerless to hijack it. I turn my attention from my failures and fix my gaze upon Jesus, who is the Author and Finisher of my faith! My victory might not be coming to me exactly as I expected — nonetheless, my victory is on the way. I surrender to the power of the Holy Spirit and allow Him to flow through me to bring me to a place of victory!

I pray this in Jesus' name!

MY CONFESSION FOR TODAY

I confess that when I don't know what to do, I turn to God for direction and help, and He releases His wisdom in me. There is no such thing as a hopeless situation. When I feel that I am facing a dead end, God's power turns it into a place of a new beginning. What I am facing is not the end for me — it is, in fact, the starting point for a glorious new beginning. When the devil tries to tell me that nothing good lies ahead for me, I remind him of the future that is awaiting HIM! I confess that the resurrection power of Jesus Christ has already lifted me far above his attacks and that a brighter and better future awaits me!

I declare this by faith in Jesus' name!

QUESTIONS FOR YOU TO CONSIDER

1. Have you ever felt that you came to a dead-end place in your life, only to find it was the beginning of an entirely new chapter, which turned out better than anything you had ever previously known?
2. How do you respond when the devil tries to attack your mind with thoughts of failure and defeat? Do you submit to his insinuations and fall into despair, or do you rise up in the power of the Spirit to take those thoughts captive?
3. How would you advise someone whose mind was under assault with thoughts of failure and defeat? How would you instruct them to take authority over those thoughts?

AUGUST 2

Grace-Given Gifts

As every man hath received the gift,
even so minister the same one to another,
as good stewards of the manifold grace of God.
— 1 Peter 4:10

Every person has been bestowed with *grace-given gifts* that were not earned, but rather divinely imparted by God's grace. This is a biblical truth, whether or not we realize it or even want to agree with it. These are not gifts bestowed for the purpose of boasting — they are given and released and activated *to reveal God to man*. And *you* have these powerful gifts inside you, just waiting for you to take ownership of them and *use* them!

In First Peter 4:10, Peter wrote, "As every man hath received the gift, even so minister the same one to another, as good stewards of the manifold grace of God." Today I want to look at that word "stewards" as it pertains to the grace of God and these "grace gifts" that we have received from Him.

The word "stewards" in First Peter 4:10 is from the Greek word *oikonomos*, which is a compound of the words *oikos* and *nomos*. The word *oikos* is the Greek word for *a house*, and *nomos* refers to *the rule of law*. These two words used together literally mean *the rule of the house*. But in Greek culture, the word *oikonomos* was specifically used to describe the *household manager* of a wealthy, upper-class home. This *oikonomos*, or *household manager*, was responsible for keeping law and order in the house. The owners of the house had found this person faithful and therefore elevated him to the powerful ruling position of chief manager over their personal property and private affairs.

In Greek culture, this chief manager was accountable for overseeing the house itself, the gardens surrounding the house, the contents inside the home, and the assets and treasures of the family. He was also in charge of distributing wages faithfully and on time to the other servants and employees who worked in the house. For the master of the house to give this much responsibility to one person was a great trust, and the master demanded that his household manager faithfully perform according to his expectations.

By using the word *oikonomos* in this verse, Peter profoundly declared that when God placed His grace-given gifts inside each of us, He was making us the stewards of His own personal treasures. Because of this, He expects us to be faithful managers of the gifts He has entrusted to our care. We are to use our gifts as God intended when He bequeathed them to us. In other words, He expects us to use our gifts faithfully and on time to meet the needs of those around us and to do it in such a way that He receives all the glory.

Taking all the Greek words into consideration that are contained in this verse, First Peter 4:10 carries the idea that every single one of us, *without exception*, has received grace-given gifts from God. We must embrace what God has placed inside us, taking ownership of it and doing our best to use our gifts to meet the needs of others. God has entrusted us with great spiritual treasure by placing these special gifts in our lives, and He is depending on us to be faithful with this weighty responsibility.

If you've believed and acted like so many others, just sitting around waiting for the perfect moment when you could begin using your God-given talents — *now you know that you've been using the wrong approach*! It's time for you to recognize what God has placed inside you and to begin using those gifts as God expects you to do. You've been waiting on God to do something special, but He already did it when He placed those gifts in your life. It's up to you to start releasing them now for the benefit of those around you!

I can tell you this from my own personal experience and from my experience with others over the course of my ministry: Those who wait for some fantasy-like moment to occur so they can step out and use their gifts usually end up very frustrated. They wait and wait — seemingly endlessly — when God, who gave the gifts, has already given them permission to use those talents for Him. In fact, He has *commanded* them as stewards of His grace to get about the task of managing those grace-gifts and using them to meet the needs of others.

So I encourage you, if you've been waiting on a special moment to step out and use your grace-gifts for God — don't waste any more time! *The Holy Spirit within you has already enabled and empowered you, so start making the most of your divine equipment that's just waiting to be released!*

MY PRAYER FOR TODAY

Heavenly Father, I am so thankful that You have placed grace-given gifts inside of me. I understand that You have made me the steward of these divine treasures. You expect me to faithfully manage these gifts that You have entrusted to my care. Father, I ask You to teach me how to use these gifts as You intended so I can meet the needs of those around me and do it in a way that gives all the glory to Jesus. Give me a pure and understanding heart so I can exercise these gifts wisely and with great responsibility!

I pray this in Jesus' name!

MY CONFESSION FOR TODAY

I confess that God has given me gifts of His grace that are powerful and have the ability to make a difference in the lives of other people. God expects me to do something with these gifts, for He gave them to me for the purpose of building His Kingdom. I refuse to let another day pass without allowing these grace-given gifts to be expressed through me. This divine equipment has been given to me in order to help others, so I will not sit by idly while others are in need! God will move through me and use this supernatural equipment, not only to meet people's needs, but also to help them come through their situations with victory.

I declare this by faith in Jesus' name!

QUESTIONS FOR YOU TO CONSIDER

1. Are you aware of the grace-given gifts God has placed in your life? If so, what are those gifts? Can you identify them? What are you doing to cultivate them?
2. How do you allow those gifts to operate? Can you give a personal testimony of what happens when this divine equipment operates in you and how it affects other people? How has God used these in your life to make a difference in someone else's life?
3. Is it possible that there are grace gifts in you that you have never allowed to manifest because you've been afraid to step out in faith? What is stopping you from letting these marvelous treasures do what God intended for them to do?

AUGUST 3

A Lesson From Snakes!

...Be ye therefore wise as serpents....
— Matthew 10:16

Over the years in our ministry, I have discovered *timing* to be extremely important. I have certainly found it to be true that we need to act when favor is obviously on our side. But let me also say that wonderful opportunities can also come packaged with difficult challenges.

Knowing exactly which opportunities to take — and which ones to let pass us by — has been one of my personal challenges in the former Soviet Union. One day I was seeking the Lord about several opportunities that were presenting themselves. The Lord said to me, *"If you're going to survive and do what I've called you to do in this part of the world, you have to learn to think like a snake."*

At first, these words caught me off guard. But immediately Matthew 10:16 came to my mind: "Behold, I send you forth as sheep in the midst of wolves: be ye therefore wise as serpents, and harmless as doves." In this verse, Jesus commanded His disciples — as He is commanding us today: *"Be as wise as serpents."*

The word "serpent" is the Greek word *ophis* and it simply describes *a snake of any type*, but it is used here as a sign of *cunningness* or *cleverness.* Matthew 10:16 had always perplexed me because I had previously thought of a serpent as being only evil. But as I meditated on this verse more deeply, I began to gain new insight about what Jesus was saying. He was saying serpents are "wise," and we need to take a lesson from them!

If you're a little squeamish about the subject of serpents or snakes, just stay with me for the next few moments so you don't miss the full impact of what Jesus was telling us. He is the One who chose to use a serpent to make His point!

Let's consider the behavior of serpents to see how Jesus' statement about these creatures in Matthew 10:16 relates to *timing.* First, serpents blend into the environment when they move into a new territory. Rather than announce their presence, they lay low, stay quiet, and blend into their surroundings. In fact, you could walk right past a snake and not know you're close to it!

Most snakes have the ability to be nearly invisible because they were designed to be *camouflaged.* This camouflage serves as a protective "covering." Even the fiercest aggressor could pass by, but the serpent would not likely be noticed because it blends so well into the landscape.

The camouflage gives the serpent latitude to find its way around new territory — to move about freely while "evaluating" a new situation. Serpents will assess a situation to identify places of shelter so they can settle into a new environment. They find hiding places to protect themselves from attack. They also observe where to find the easiest prey. When all of these assessments are made and the facts are assimilated, the serpent is ready to act. But this "settling in" is a key time for a serpent.

Can you see the parallel between the behavior of a serpent and Jesus' strategic plan for us when we are entering new territory for Him? *Jesus said there's wisdom to glean from such a study!*

As I carefully pondered the behavior of serpents, I understood exactly why Jesus used this example. This analogy applies to all of us in regard to our families, businesses, ministries, or any other opportunity God places before us in which we must implement His strategies in order to establish His victory on the earth.

When God calls us to do something new — to move into a new territory or seize a new opportunity — it is wise for us to move slowly and carefully into that new phase of our lives. A common mistake is to act too fast. Acting hastily, before all the facts are gathered and assimilated, often leads to erroneous decision-making. In fact, one serious mistake can cause us to lose out on an opportunity altogether. Better to *lay low*, *stay quiet*, *blend into the environment for a while*, and *learn from the facts we observe.*

Let me give you a perfect personal example of how the "wisdom of a serpent" served Denise and me so well when we launched out to begin our ministry in the former USSR.

When Denise and I and our family moved halfway around the world, we took time to learn the customs and the culture of that new territory. We knew it would take time to understand everything we would see and experience, so we moved slowly and very carefully. Although we immediately saw opportunities for ministry, we decided to first watch and gain as much knowledge as possible of the new environment and the circumstances we found ourselves in at that moment. In retrospect, I can assure you that for us, acting too fast would have certainly meant making some poor decisions that we would have greatly regretted down the road.

In the first few months we lived in the USSR, we made little noise and were hardly noticed. This allowed us the ability to move about freely and without disruption. We visited churches unannounced. We wandered in and out of different parts of the city, where we began to observe and ascertain the spiritual condition of this new territory. Before I made any grand announcement that we were going on television, I first wanted to know something about television in that part of the world. The best way to learn — especially at that volatile time in those nations — was to do it covertly.

During this time of acclimating ourselves to our new home, we also observed that many American missionaries were announcing great plans that never developed or got off the ground. Many of those ideas were wonderful — and perhaps they were even from God. But because these missionaries acted before they understood the full picture, they ruined their testimony and lost glorious opportunities to bring the Gospel to places where it was needed so badly. These sincere men and women were trying to take ground for the Kingdom of God that they really knew nothing about. They hadn't taken the time to learn.

It is very unwise and a waste of Kingdom resources of money and time to start fantastic projects without first understanding the challenges, risks, and dangers. Many people have been hurt because of someone getting in a hurry and acting too quickly.

Denise and I knew that moving slower may take more time initially — but in the end, it would produce more stable, serious, and lasting results. We made the choice to move "slow and steady": to gather all the facts we could, analyze the accumulated information, and then seek the Lord in prayer, listening for what He might have to say to us through those facts. Only then would we make announcements concerning our plans. I can't emphasize it enough: To move ahead more quickly than we did in those early days would have proven a harmful mistake!

Most mistakes in forging new territory for the Gospel are avoidable. God is a strategic Planner who delights in giving you the wisdom you need in *whatever* venture you're undertaking for Him.

Your part is to move forward by His grace and according to His guidance. As you do, you will be well able to secure the victory He has planned for you in that new territory and season.

So I strongly advise you to take your time in any new venture for Jesus — and be sure of the actions you take. Before you act on that opportunity publicly, I suggest that you first do the following:

- Learn the "landscape" of your new environment.
- Determine what kind of attacks could potentially come against you.
- Take time to really understand the opportunities around you.
- Make sure you are completely informed of all the pertinent facts about your new environment — facts that will help you adjust smoothly and move forward in fulfilling your new assignment without unnecessary delays or detours.
- Pray diligently about the information you gather, and seek the Lord's wisdom on how that information applies to your assignment.

That is how you emulate the strategy of the serpent, taking advantage of your "settling in" time. Then when the right moment comes and opportunity strikes, you can seize your divine moment with the grace and favor of God!

But how can you be sure you'll recognize the right moment to strike? That's what I want to talk to you about in tomorrow's *Sparkling Gem*. Jesus was being very deliberate and strategic when He instructed us to act as "wise" as a serpent, and there's still more to learn from this example. *So don't miss tomorrow — it could be a game-changer for your life!*

MY PRAYER FOR TODAY

Heavenly Father, I take heed to Jesus' instructions to be as wise as a serpent when surveying new territory for the Kingdom of God. Father, You are the ultimate Strategist, and You leave no detail unattended in Your great plan! As I follow your specific instructions, I will be able to avoid unnecessary difficulties or destruction. Lord, I ask You to show me Your ways and grant me a wise and understanding heart. Teach me how to walk in great discretion with accurate discernment. I want to finish the assignment You've given me, so I am willing to move slow and steady to avoid harmful mistakes. Thank You for giving me the wisdom I need for each venture You have set before me. Then when the time is right, I will seize the moment by Your grace to fulfill the outcome You desire.

I pray this in Jesus' name!

MY CONFESSION FOR TODAY

I confess that I am as wise as a serpent yet harmless as a dove. Your gentleness, oh, Lord, has made me great! You give me wisdom and sound counsel before I publicly act on my God-given opportunities. I pay close attention to the strategies of the Lord, and I learn the "landscape" of the environment where He wants me to establish His Kingdom. I follow the strategies of God while remaining discerning of and alert to the tactics of the enemy. I am diligent to pray out the plan of God so He can alert me to the enemy's potential attacks against me. I take time to understand my God-given opportunity, and I make sure that I am completely informed of all the facts I need to help me adjust smoothly and move forward in fulfilling my assignment without unnecessary delays or detours.

I declare this by faith in Jesus' name!

QUESTIONS FOR YOU TO CONSIDER

1. Have you ever had a golden opportunity placed before you, but you acted too quickly and lost that opportunity because you were not well informed enough to seize it yet?
2. There is wisdom in becoming acclimated to new surroundings without making too much fanfare. The results could be disastrous if you parade about and make your presence and intent known in a new environment too soon before you become familiar with your surroundings or your purpose in it. Have you ever had the experience of becoming hasty in a new situation that ultimately sabotaged the reason you were sent there in the first place? How did you recover your ability to function, or did you?
3. What Bible examples can you think of that demonstrates taking time to acclimate to a new environment before launching out to do something new?

AUGUST 4

The Importance of Timing

...Be ye therefore wise as serpents....
— Matthew 10:16

Yesterday we began looking at what Jesus had to say about being "wise as serpents." Today I want to continue because there is more truth to glean from this verse. The word "wise" in Matthew 10:16 is the Greek word *sophos*, and it depicts *special insight* and *a wise approach* to a matter. According to Jesus, serpents are "wise" in the way they do things, and there is something we can learn from their actions.

One particular aspect we can learn from the serpent's behavior is *the importance of timing*. This is so key to fulfilling any assignment that God may give us, because *knowing when to act* is as important as *knowing when to lay low*.

For a serpent, this knowledge is key to its very survival. When prey passes before the serpent, it instinctively knows when its time to strike. If it waits too long, the opportunity will pass irretrievably, and the serpent will go hungry.

So what can you learn from the serpent in this arena? When it's time for *you* to act, you must put aside all fears, emotions, and second-guessing — and *seize the moment*!

I have seen so many young ministers fast, pray, and wait for that golden moment of divine opportunity to come to them. Then at last, that time arrives! A great door of opportunity stands directly in front of them. It's time to act. But rather than seize the moment and walk through that door, they pause to pray just a little bit more. God brought them *exactly* what they'd been praying for so long, but because they hesitated, they lost the opportunity. When they finally got around to saying yes, it was too late.

Let me give you another personal example.

Back in 1993, I earnestly prayed and sought God to open television ministry wider to us. One day I received a phone call from the top directors of a national television station in the former Soviet Union. They asked me to meet them and talk about putting my program on national television. My associate and I booked the next available flight and flew to meet those two powerful men in their offices.

My heart was filled with anticipation as the plane carried us to that meeting. *Was this the opportunity I'd prayed for? Was it actually happening? Was God really answering my prayer?*

I had a sense that something great and awesome was about to transpire, and I could hardly wait to arrive at the meeting to hear their proposal.

I had already done my homework. I had studied the statistics about the full reach of the TV channel on which they were about to offer me time. I spoke with pastors and churches throughout my region to find out what they thought of that channel. My time of "lying low and blending into the environment" had given me the "wisdom" I needed when I stepped into that meeting with those directors. I was equipped for this long-awaited conversation.

Armed with information and supported by the prayers of our partners, the meeting began. Those directors asked me, "Would you like to broadcast on our national channel and penetrate every single home in the nation with your program?"

This is exactly what I had been praying and waiting for — *for such a long time*! The opportunity of a lifetime was sitting on the table in front of me in the form of a TV contract. I held my composure, not wanting them to know how excited I was at this chance to reach every home with the Gospel. I waited to hear how much this divine door of opportunity was going to cost our ministry each month.

When I heard the price of the time slot they were offering me on that channel, at first I felt some hesitation. Fear tried to form in my mind that we wouldn't be able to come up with the cash each month. Yet I knew a door had opened before me *that had never been offered to anyone else before*! Only God could open such an incredible door for the Gospel. There was no doubt that He was orchestrating the entire event.

My head and logic said, *"Don't do it,"* while my spirit said, *"DO IT NOW!"* In my heart, I knew it was the moment to strike and seize this opportunity. Within a few minutes, I picked up an ink pen and signed my name on the dotted line. National television had fallen into my hands!

Within days of signing that contract, politics radically changed, and if I had not seized this divine opportunity at that exact moment, I would have lost it. Just one week later, that same wide-open door would have been tightly closed. Because we seized the moment at *just the right time*, our television program was locked into a contract that this new government had to honor! As a result of acting at the right time, our television program and our ministry became one of the most powerful spiritual forces in that part of the world. Since 1993, when we walked through that door, we have made a strong impact to affect that nation with the teaching ministry God has given us!

I thank God that I had the spiritual guts to act at the right moment. I had already prayed and prayed. Then there came a time to seize the moment and *strike*!

The Lord has taught me over the years that there are moments to "lay low" — and there are other moments to "strike fast." Surely, this is a key part of what Jesus meant when He told us to *"be wise as serpents"* (Matthew 10:16).

You may be asking, "But how do I know when it's a time to lay low or to take action and seize the moment?" The Holy Spirit will lead you and cause you to know — if you will be sensitive to follow His leading. And believe me, if you will listen to and follow Him, He will *guide you past every obstacle*, *camouflage you from every attack*, and *show you exactly when to take action* in your family, your business, your church, or the assignment God has given you.

Romans 8:14 says, "For as many as are led by the Spirit of God, they are the sons of God." The word "led" is the Greek word *ago*. It means *to be gently led about* and was the same word used to describe a man leading his cow about on a rope. The farmer is the leader, and the cow is merely the follower. The cow doesn't argue with the farmer; the animal simply trusts and follows.

This is how we are to follow the leading of the Holy Spirit. He is the Leader!

Many people are afraid to obey what the Holy Spirit puts in their hearts to do. Fearful that they will be led astray or that they will make a mistake, they sit on the sidelines and watch other people achieve success, while they remain right where they've always been.

But let me assure you from very personal experience: *You can trust the leading of the Holy Spirit!*

In John chapters 14-16, Jesus called the Holy Spirit "the Spirit of Truth" four separate times! It seems that Jesus thought this was a truth worth repeating! Jesus was emphatically assuring us that the Holy Spirit *will not* lead us in a wrong direction. He is "the Spirit of Truth" on whom we can rely.

If the Holy Spirit is prompting you to take action *now*, it's because He sees and knows something you may not see. Let the Holy Spirit become your eyes and ears to key moments and divine opportunities for your life, family, business, or ministry.

Timing has been a major key to the success of our ministry, and it is the key to your success as well. Denise and I are not brilliant enough in ourselves or by our own reasoning to figure out the right timing for everything we've been able to do in the former USSR. We give God all the glory, because we know our timing has been directed by the Holy Spirit, not by us. Denise and I have depended on the Holy Spirit's leading through the years, and as a result, we have walked through many strategic doors at key moments. We've learned that when He says, *"NOW!"*— He really means exactly that!

So don't move too fast, and don't hesitate when the time is right to act. And now you know what Jesus meant when He commanded us to *"be wise as serpents"*!

MY PRAYER FOR TODAY

Heavenly Father, I thank You that You are faithful to lead me in the direction I should go and in the decisions I must make. Help me recognize when it's time to lay low and blend into the landscape and when it is time to strike! I have prayed for divine opportunities, so when they present themselves to me, help me to recognize them and to have the courage to step out by faith to accept the assignment. Holy Spirit, I know that You are a faithful Leader, so today I put my trust in You to lead me in each and every step that I take!

I pray this in Jesus' name!

MY CONFESSION FOR TODAY

I confess that I am wise as a serpent! I know when to lay low, how to blend into the landscape, how to learn my new territory, and how to discern and recognize when a God-given opportunity passes my way. Fear does not hold me back. Hesitation does not stop me. Because I have prayed and done my homework in advance, I am well prepared for that golden moment when God gives me the opportunity for which I've waited for so long. The Holy Spirit is my Leader, and He is leading and guiding me every step of the way.

I declare this by faith in Jesus' name!

QUESTIONS FOR YOU TO CONSIDER

1. Have you had a moment in your life when the Holy Spirit instructed you simply to lay low and blend into the environment, so that you could learn more about your new territory? When was that, and what was the result of that course of action?
2. What spiritual disciplines and practices have you built into your daily life to develop your discernment and sensitivity to the leading of the Holy Spirit? Do you read your Bible, meditate in the Word, and pray daily? If not, what steps

can you take to make your personal time with the Lord a non-negotiable necessity in your daily schedule?

3. Can you identify your own patterns and tendencies for taking action on something God has put in your heart to do? Do you move quickly, or do you procrastinate after you know what to do? What steps do you plan to take to ensure you are moving in sync with the Holy Spirit's leading to avoid a misstep or mistake?

AUGUST 5

Self-Discovery: Why God Tests You

By faith Abraham, when he was tried, offered up Isaac:
and he that had received the promises offered up
his own begotten son, of whom it was said, That in
Issac shall thy seed be called: Accounting that God
was able to raise him up from the dead....
— Hebrews 11:17-19

I know from firsthand experience that when God asks you to sacrifice something precious, it can be very difficult to come into compliance with what He is asking you to do. The flesh rebels every step of the way, and the mind tries to argue, as if it knows better than the Lord. Therefore, when your will collides with God's divine plan for your life, you must make a conscious decision to exercise *obedience* and follow His leading, no matter what.

There are critical moments when you must make the choice to do what God asks, whether or not you understand it. When you fully *abandon* your natural inclinations and *defer* to God's will, you will be elevated to brand-new levels of success and victory that you have never before attained.

Let me share an example of this kind of deference and obedience from my own life. When God first asked my family to move to the USSR, I knew He had something truly wonderful in store for us. However, my flesh didn't relish the idea one bit. Night after night, I lay in my bed and listened as my mind told me that this move was the stupidest notion I'd ever considered in my life and that if I really carried through with this absurd idea, I would lose everything. I was having an ongoing inner dialogue with God about the matter. I remember asking Him, *Are You REALLY asking me to sacrifice everything that we've worked so hard to achieve?*

At the time God called us to move overseas, our ministry in the United States was finally taking off after years of struggle and hard work. However, just as we were experiencing the first trappings of success, God asked us to lay aside our dream because He wanted to do something new through us. This was a pivotal moment in our lives! We didn't understand the full scope of His divine plan, so we had to choose to defer to His voice and trust that He was leading us on the right path.

Have you experienced a similar moment in your own life? If not, I guarantee you that a time will come when you will be called on to step out and follow God's leading, even though you don't fully understand His design. However, it is important to remember that when God asks you to sacrifice something precious in your life, He always has your best interest at heart, and He is trying to use that experience to reveal something to you about your life so that you can go forth and do the will of God with confidence.

A clear example of this biblical truth is clearly seen in the Old Testament story of Abraham. After waiting approximately 25 years for God's promise of a covenant child to come true, Abraham and Sarah finally became the proud parents of their son *Isaac.* When Isaac was born, Abraham was 100 years old, and Sarah was 90 years old.

Everyone knew this baby was a *miracle*! How many 90-year-old women do you know that have given birth to a baby? It was so fantastic that even Sarah said, "God hath made me to laugh, so that all that hear will laugh with me. And she said, "Who would have said unto Abraham, that Sarah should have given children suck? For I have born him a son in his old age" (Genesis 21:7).

Try to imagine for a moment the sight of a 90-year-old woman breastfeeding a baby. You can understand why Sarah said everyone who saw it would laugh — *it was absurd* to the natural mind! Yet everyone who saw this mother and child together was filled with joy because it was such a demonstration of God's faithfulness to keep His Word. In fact, this blessing brought so many people joy that Abraham and Sarah named the baby *Isaac*, meaning *laughter.*

Abraham had personally given up a lot to accommodate the promise of God in his life. He knew that Isaac was the seed through whom God was going to bless the nations of the earth, as God had promised in Genesis 12:2,3 and Genesis 15:4,5. All of Abraham's hopes and dreams rested in *Isaac.*

However, after Abraham had spent years watching his son grow into a God-fearing young man, the Bible says that God came to him and commanded him to offer up Isaac as a burnt sacrifice! Genesis 22:1 and 2 records: "And it came to pass after these things, that God did tempt Abraham, and said unto him, Abraham: and he said, Behold, here I am. And he said, Take now thy son, thine only son Isaac, whom thou lovest, and get thee into the land of Moriah; and offer him there for a burnt offering upon one of the mountains which I will tell thee of."

In Hebrews 11:17, the writer of Hebrews offers another account of these events, saying, "By faith Abraham, when he was *tried*, offered up Isaac...." This verse tells us that God "tried" Abraham that day on Mount Moriah when He commanded him to sacrifice Isaac as a burnt offering on the altar.

This word "tried" is from the Greek word *peiradzo*, which describes *an intense examination that is done to prove the fitness of an object.* For example, *peiradzo* was used to describe the fiery process of testing and removing impurities from metal in the ancient world. These tests ensured that the metal would be strong and durable, and that any object crafted from metal would hold up under pressure. In addition, *peiradzo* also described the process of testing coins to determine if they were authentic or counterfeit. In early New Testament times, counterfeits often looked so similar to the genuine article that only a test would reveal whether a coin was real or fake. Therefore, people regularly tested their money to see if it had worth.

The word *peiradzo* most often described the process of testing an object to reveal its true quality, and this is precisely how the word is used in Hebrews 11:17, where the verse says Abraham was "tried" by the Lord. The fact is, the Lord already knew that Abraham's faith was sound and real. But when Abraham drew his knife to slay his son, Abraham himself learned something important about his own faith and level of consecration. He discovered that he was willing to do whatever the Lord asked him to do. There was nothing counterfeit or lacking about Abraham's obedience to God; his commitment was real and authentic.

You see, God never tests you to learn new information about you. He doesn't need to "test" to find out something new because He already knows it all. Rather, He is trying to show you something about *you* — to make you more self-assured and confident as you go forward to do His will. Every test you are going through is being done for your own self-discovery — lessons learned *if you go through those tests correctly* to give you confidence as you proceed to do the will of God for your life.

When God called my family to relocate to the former USSR back in 1991, my willingness to say yes to God revealed something to me about myself that I needed to see and know. *It showed me that my commitment to God was real.* This experience was a *peiradzo* — a test designed to reveal the imperfect areas of my life that required attention and to prove to me that I was the type of person God could depend on. He already knew this about me, but I personally needed to know it deep down in my spirit.

I am so glad my family said, "Yes!" when God beckoned us to leave the United States and move to the former Soviet Union. Even though it initially felt like we were sacrificing everything to do it, the truth is, we didn't lose *anything*. What God has given us in our new home overseas is far greater than any home, possession, or dream that we *thought* we were relinquishing. From the very outset, God had a wonderful plan for the Renner family.

When God asks us to lay something on the altar of sacrifice, we can know there is something bigger and better He wants to put into our hands. But as long as we're clutching what we have right now, we're not free to receive the great things He wants to give us next.

Realize that whatever you're doing today may simply be the training ground for your future. Don't allow yourself to get so cemented in what you're doing that you can't move forward to the next step God has in store for you. And if it ever seems like God is asking you to make a huge sacrifice, just remember: This is just His way of freeing you so He can give you something better and greater and make you more productive for the Kingdom of God. *You can trust Him!* And as you keep your heart free and your emotions untangled, you'll be able to move forward whenever His Spirit beckons you to take the next step in His good plan for your life!

MY PRAYER FOR TODAY

Father, I am thankful to know that You already know everything about me and that You don't need to put me through a test to find out whether or not I'm genuine. Now I understand that You are trying to show me something about myself. Help me to embrace the tests that help me to learn what kind of person I am. Holy Spirit, I ask You to help me cooperate with Your working in my life so that I will become the type of person You can use to expand and build Your Kingdom. That is my heartfelt prayer.

I pray this in Jesus' name!

MY CONFESSION FOR TODAY

I confess that I am alert to recognize when God is testing me to show me something I need to know about myself. He already knows all the answers about me and nothing takes Him by surprise. But I need to know about me. I need to know that I am willing to obey and do whatever He asks me to do. I need to know that I am authentic and genuine in my faith. What He is asking me to do is for me to gain revelation about myself. It is information I need to know so that I can proceed with confidence and boldness as I push forward toward God's plan for my life.

I declare this by faith in Jesus' name!

QUESTIONS FOR YOU TO CONSIDER

1. After reading today's *Sparkling Gem*, do you see that God tests you to reveal something to you about yourself? God already knows all the answers and doesn't need a test to find out something about you. So what do the tests you've undergone reveal about you that you need to know?
2. How do you think Abraham felt after he passed his test on Mount Moriah? What did he discover about himself and his own willingness to obey God?
3. What test are you going through right now? Do you now understand that God already knows the answers, and He's trying to show something to you about you? What is He trying to show you?

When God asks us to lay something
on the altar of sacrifice,
we can know there is something bigger and better
He wants to put into our hands.

AUGUST 6

Jesus the Great Philanthropist

How God anointed Jesus of Nazareth
with the Holy Ghost and with power:
who went about doing good, and healing
all that were oppressed of the devil;
for God was with him.
— Acts 10:38

In today's *Sparkling Gem*, I feel especially led to highlight a truth from Acts 10:38 that has deeply impacted my life. Although I had read this verse hundreds of times, I was amazed when I saw this truth because I'd never realized before what I'm about to tell you, nor had I ever heard anyone teach about it. Since then, this one revelation has had a huge effect on Denise and me and the way we conduct our ministry.

Acts 10:38 says, "How God anointed Jesus of Nazareth with the Holy Ghost and with power: who went about doing good, and healing all that were oppressed of the devil; for God was with him." What I want to share with you today concerns a very real aspect of Jesus' ministry you may have never thought about before.

Most people focus on the part of this verse that describes the healing and deliverance ministry of Jesus — both of which are, of course, so very important. But there's something else in this verse that's also very significant, and I overlooked it for many years. Then one day as I was studying my Greek New Testament, my eyes fell on a particular Greek word in this verse and I began to study it. What I learned completely opened up a part of Jesus' ministry I had never considered. I'm talking about the phrase that says Jesus "went about *doing good*."

I was truly taken aback when I saw the words "doing good" in the Greek language because I'd always thought the phrase in this context was just a descriptive summary of healing the sick and delivering those who were oppressed by the devil. But those words actually refer to a *completely different* aspect of Jesus' ministry — and one of the largest and most profound parts of His ministry on the earth. I wondered how it was possible that I'd never heard anyone teach about something that provided such an eye-opening view right into the heart of Jesus!

The words "doing good" in Acts 10:38 are a translation of the Greek word *euergeteo*, an old word that denotes a *benefactor*; a *philanthropist*; *one who financially supports charitable works*; or a *person who uses his financial resources to meet the needs of disadvantaged people*. This word was used only to portray the provision of food, clothes, or some other commodity to meet a physical or material need. Thus, the use of this word in Acts 10:38 emphatically means that a part of Jesus' ministry was comprised of meeting the physical and tangible needs of people who were disadvantaged in some way.

Of course, we know that Jesus performed *supernatural miracles* of provision — such as the time He multiplied five barley loaves and two fish to feed a large crowd of thousands of people (*see* John 6:1-13). However, the word *euergeteo* in Acts 10:38 tells us that His ministry also provided *natural, material* help to people who were in need.

By reading the four gospels, it becomes evident that Jesus' ministry possessed enormous financial resources that came from various places. Besides offerings that were received, Luke 8:2 and 3 says there was a group of very wealthy women who supported Jesus' work (*see Sparkling Gems 1,* November 18). Another indication of Jesus' significant resources is the fact that He had a treasurer — His disciple, Judas Iscariot — who was responsible for handling the ministry finances.

In John 12:3, it is recorded that Mary used a pound of expensive spikenard — a rare scented oil — to anoint Jesus' feet. Judas asked Jesus, "Why was not this ointment sold for three hundred pence, and given to the poor?" (v. 5). We can infer from Judas' words that Jesus' ministry had a philanthropic outreach to the poor, over which Judas had been placed in charge as treasurer.

Acts 10:38 makes it even more clear that a significant outreach of Jesus' ministry was to provide physical and material assistance to people in need. The use of the word *euergeteo* explicitly tells us that Jesus used His resources to do *good works,* such as caring for the poor and helping feed the needy. Thus, He set an example for us today to be involved in meeting people's basic human needs as He enables us to do so.

Acting in "goodness" is a characteristic of God's nature. In Acts 10:38, Luke mentioned this philanthropic aspect of Jesus' ministry in connection with His healing ministry — in the very same sentence. The Holy Spirit was conveying the message that God is just as interested in helping the poor and needy with physical and material assistance as He is in supernaturally healing their bodies. Thus, we can know that helping meet the physical needs of others — performing similar acts of goodness — is just as much a part of Jesus ministry today as it was when He "went about doing good" in His earthly ministry almost 2,000 years ago.

Jesus longs to do it all — to physically heal sick bodies, to deliver those who are spiritually oppressed, and to help meet the meets of the poor. *Jesus is still a Philanthropist!*

I don't know why this would ever be a surprise to us. Whether we fully realize it or not, we've all experienced God's tender care in our lives. From the beginning of the Old Testament to this moment, He has cared for the needs of His people and has made provision for those who come to Him in faith — including you and me. Jesus is the same yesterday, today, and forever (Hebrews 13:8). So it makes perfect sense that He would demonstrate this same caring nature both through His earthly ministry then and through His Body, *the Church*, today.

Furthermore, Galatians 5:22 tells us that one of the fruits of the Spirit is "goodness." This word is translated from the Greek word *agathusune*, which comes from the word *agathos*, meaning *good.* But when *agathos* becomes the word *agathusune*, it means *goodness in the sense of being good to someone.* This word portrays a person who is *generous, big-hearted, liberal,* and *charitable.* We would call this person *a giver.*

This means one of the characteristics of the Holy Spirit — and one of the fruits He longs to produce in our lives — is the demonstration of care for others in physical and tangible ways. When we exhibit this characteristic by demonstrating care to others, we are acting like God Himself!

By listing this word "goodness" as one of the fruits of the Spirit in Galatians 5:22 and 23, God lets us know that He wants us to be selfless and use our resources to help change people's lives. This is absolutely contrary to the flesh, which would consume every spare dollar on itself. But when the Holy Spirit is working mightily in us, He shifts our focus from ourselves to the needs of those around us. The fruit of the Spirit called "goodness" creates in us a supernatural urge to reach beyond ourselves to meet the natural needs of others.

The truth is, when a believer is walking in the Spirit, the Holy Spirit opens his eyes to see the needs of humanity, and that person's heart is moved to meet those needs. *This is why there's no greater benefactors or philanthropists in the world than those who are filled with the Spirit of God.*

There are so many human needs in this world, and no one person, ministry, or organization can meet them all. But we are each responsible to respond to the nudge of the Holy Spirit to help those He brings across our path. If we'll each respond to the distinct nudges we feel from Him — one by one, many needs will be met. And through those acts of goodness, Jesus will touch hearts in a very tangible way.

Throughout the Scriptures, you can find that helping those in need is deeply significant in God's eyes. My own heart has been gripped by the number of passages that promise His supernatural help and blessing to those who demonstrate care for the disadvantaged and the poor. For example, Psalm 41:1 and 2 says, "Blessed is he that considereth the poor: the Lord will deliver him in time of trouble. The Lord will preserve him, and keep him alive; and he shall be blessed upon the earth: and thou wilt not deliver him unto the will of his enemies."

Since Acts 10:38 became such a revelation to me, Denise and I have been obeying the promptings of the Holy Spirit when He quickens us to meet the needs of those in trouble. We call this aspect of our ministry our *rescuing* outreaches. Through this part of our work, we are reaching out to literally rescue the hurting and perishing with both the physical and spiritual help they need. As I already said, we know we can't physically help everyone. But when it's apparent that God has brought certain people across the path of our ministry for us to help them, we do our best to obey His Spirit's promptings.

Since the time we first saw this profound truth in Acts 10:38 about ministering to the needs of others, Denise and I have accepted our responsibility to preach, teach, lay hands on the sick, and pray for *spiritual* needs to be met. But we have also embraced our role to help meet the *physical* needs of humanity and to be like Jesus, who was and still is *the world's greatest*

Philanthropist. We are so thankful for every opportunity to share God's Word, but we also count it an honor that He would use us to extend a hand of mercy to people who are in need.

I encourage you to make the commitment today to be a prompt doer of the Word when the Holy Spirit nudges your heart to do something extra in this area of meeting the material needs of those less blessed than you. It's another way you can be as Jesus is in this world — as you go about doing good, led each step of the way by the Spirit of God!

MY PRAYER FOR TODAY

Father, I ask You to help me become more like Jesus, who was the world's greatest Philanthropist! Help me not just to say I love people, but rather to show them love by my actions and deeds. Open my eyes to see the needs of those around me — and even to see how I can give of my finances to help people in other parts of the world. Since this was the heart of Jesus, it should be my heart too. Holy Spirit, I ask You to help me become like Jesus and do all that I can both spiritually and physically to meet the needs of those You bring across my path.

I pray this in Jesus' name!

MY CONFESSION FOR TODAY

I confess that God is using me to meet the physical and material needs of others. When God brings someone across my path who is hurting, I willingly respond to the Lord's direction concerning how He wants to use me to help meet his or her need. I can't help everyone, but I can and will help those He leads me to help. I obey the Holy Spirit's promptings and do what He instructs me to do. I am an extended hand of mercy to people who are hurting and disadvantaged. When the Holy Spirit needs someone to make a difference in another person's life, He knows He can count on me to be available!

I declare this by faith in Jesus' name!

QUESTIONS FOR YOU TO CONSIDER

1. What are you doing to help meet the physical and material needs of others? Does your church have an outreach to help the poor and needy? If not, could you respectfully ask your pastor why there is no philanthropic ministry to help the less fortunate? Jesus helped those in need, so shouldn't we be doing it too?
2. What are some ways you can begin to practically give help to those who are hurting and in need? Do you have any clothes you could give to someone else? Could you prepare a meal for a family that might be struggling or disadvantaged?
3. Can you think of a time when someone helped you through a rough financial time? What kind of impact did it make on you? Have you considered that maybe it's time for you to do the same thing for someone else?

AUGUST 7

Embrace Your Grace!

According to the grace of God
which is given unto me, as a wise masterbuilder,
I have laid the foundation, and another buildeth thereon.
But let every man take heed how he buildeth thereupon.
— 1 Corinthians 3:10

Have you ever struggled with the grace that God placed on your life? Have you ever wished you could be like someone else instead of the person God made you to be?

Many believers struggle with this issue. They aren't satisfied with the grace on their own lives, and they wish they could have the grace of another person.

For example, a pastor may grow tired of preaching to the same faces week after week as he leads his local congregation. Soon he begins to dream of being a traveling teacher or an evangelist who journeys across the world to proclaim the Gospel in new places. Or on the flip side, a traveling evangelist or teacher may grow tired of constantly moving around and wish that he could be given the pastoral grace that would allow him to settle down in one spot. However, as long as a person yearns to be someone other than who God made him to be, he will never feel satisfied or fulfilled in life.

Romans 12:6 tells us that we all have "...gifts differing according to the grace that is given to us...." Therefore, it's vital that we as believers endeavor to discover our own particular grace and then, once we have found it, to embrace it and pursue it with fervor!

In First Corinthians 3:10, Paul described the grace that was placed on his own life. He said, "According to the grace of God which is given unto me...." I want to draw your attention to the word "according" in this verse, which in Greek is the word *kata*. This Greek word always describes *a downward force* or *something that is subjugating, dominating, or conquering*. By using this word *kata*, Paul was literally saying, *"I have been conquered by this particular grace that is on my life."*

Think of how difficult it must have been for Paul to accept his grace as an apostle to the heathen cities of the Roman Empire. Many of the cities to which he traveled were rife with immorality and demonic activity. The city of Corinth, for example, was one of the most wicked cities of that time, yet Paul still boldly entered that city to proclaim the light of truth in the face of unspeakable darkness. When he first traversed the long road that led into Corinth, he walked past intricately carved idols that lined the road on each side. These statues — most of which were naked — had been vividly painted, with great attention paid to even the smallest details, to make them appear as vibrant and lifelike as possible. Thus, when Paul walked down on that street into the city of Corinth for the first time, flanked by brightly colored idols on all sides, it was as if he was walking through a corridor of living pornography.

However, despite the monumental challenges that lay ahead of him in Corinth, Paul didn't back away from his divine calling or waste his time wishing he could borrow the grace of another man. Instead, he boldly marched into this wicked city, and with the grace that was on his life, Paul literally pushed the powers of hell out of the way. And as a result of his perseverance and determination, the apostle gave birth to the church of Corinth, which would grow to become one of the greatest churches of the First Century. It was in this city that he would also meet Aquila and Priscilla, who became the greatest partners in ministry he would ever have.

In city after city, the apostle Paul pushed the powers of hell out of the way — confronting principalities and powers, demonic manifestations, and pagan temples — in order to lay the foundations for new churches. He did this in Corinth, in Ephesus, in Thessalonica, and many other cities. This was his grace. And just as each church became established, the Holy Spirit would direct him to turn over the congregation to someone else and then move on to do it again.

The very fact that Paul used the word *kata* in First Corinthians 3:10 implies that he struggled with his grace — just as many of us have struggled with ours. However, he finally came to a place where he quit struggling with the anointing God had placed on his life; in fact, he opened his heart and *embraced* it. Paul testified in his epistle to the Corinthians that this grace dominated his life.

In my own life, I have an anointing to minister to the people in the former Soviet Union. Time and time again, this grace on my life has enabled me to accomplish what other people could not, and since Denise and I first moved to the former USSR in 1991, we have repeatedly overcome obstacles that others have described as insurmountable. For instance, when Denise and I moved to Moscow to establish a church in that city, countless people warned us that we would fail. They'd exclaim, "Moscow was the center of world Communism. Demonic powers and principalities loom in that city! It is the graveyard of preachers!"

Everywhere we turned, we heard these kinds of reports, but I knew I had the grace to accomplish this work for the Lord. And because I embraced my grace and pursued the calling of God on my life, I have since reaped the abundant rewards of obedience. In fact, ministering in Moscow has been one of the most enjoyable endeavors I have ever undertaken in my life, and the church we started continues to grow by leaps and bounds.

It is such a joy when you finally know and accept your grace. When you reach this point, you no longer feel threatened by or envious of the grace of anyone else. You are able to confidently say, "This is my grace! Other people can't do what I do, and I don't have to do what they do because that is their grace."

Thank God, we're not all the same! Each one of us has been given equally unique and important gifts. Whether you are a pastor or an usher, a businessman or an artist, you are an essential member of the Body of Christ. Your grace defines your place. So discover your grace, embrace it, and then allow it to dominate your life!

MY PRAYER FOR TODAY

Father, I thank You for the unique grace You have placed upon my life. I am gifted differently than others, and You have called me to do what You have not called others to do. To do this job effectively, you have anointed me and equipped me in a distinctive way for the job. Today I ask You to help me surrender to the grace that you've placed on my life and to quit struggling with who You have called me to be!

I pray this in Jesus' name!

MY CONFESSION FOR TODAY

I declare that I am content in the grace of God that is on my life. God has called me, anointed me, and graced me exactly for what I am doing. Who I am and what I am doing is no mistake. I have stepped into God's glorious plan for my life, and His grace has equipped me uniquely and effectively for what I am doing. Day by day, I become more comfortable with the grace of God that dominates my life!

I declare this by faith in Jesus' name!

QUESTIONS FOR YOU TO CONSIDER

1. Do you know what is the specific grace that God has placed upon your life? If yes, what is that grace? How would you describe it?
2. How is your grace different from the grace that is on other people's lives?
3. Has it ever been a struggle to accept the place that God's grace has defined for your life? If yes, why has it been a struggle?

AUGUST 8

Is It Time To Recommit To Your Promises?

Redeeming the time....
— Ephesians 5:16

It has been eight months since families and friends around the world gathered to celebrate the New Year. Millions of people at that time were thinking about changes they needed to make in their lives as they began a brand-new calendar year. I think we all know that although this was a time when many people made commitments or *resolutions* to change, many of those commitments haven't yet been acted on, even eight months later.

Maybe you've done better than others at keeping the commitments you made at the beginning of the year. But I'm sure you'd agree that you still have progress to make in order to fully walk out those commitments you made to move forward in various areas of your life.

Instead of living in regret about those commitments that remain completely or partially neglected, this is a good time to follow through on what you uttered before the Lord at the beginning of the year. Making excuses or throwing a pity party won't help you. In fact, it will make things even worse, pulling you into a state of discouragement and self-condemnation. It's so much better to just lift your hands and rejoice that you still have *four more months* in this year to keep your commitments with the strength and grace that God provides!

But to effectively make those changes, you're going to have to get serious about doing what you said you'd do before the Lord. Four months is a significant amount of time, but it's not a vast amount of time for you to make forward progress in those areas. Don't let the devil lie to you and tell you that it's too late. It's *not* too late. *You can do it!*

To be forthright, I've got my own list of commitments I made to the Lord at the beginning of this year that I have yet to fulfill. I've made progress on some, and no progress on others. But I've determined that I'm going to follow my own good counsel! I have my eyes fixed on these four remaining months, and I intend to step up my focus on fulfilling the things I committed to do. It's a good time to reset my commitment and get serious about doing what God has put on my heart to do!

The next four months represent time for a brand-new start — a new opportunity to attain new victories. This is a golden moment for you to begin reaching forth to the wonderful possibilities before you!

Let me encourage you with one of my favorite verses of Scripture. Ephesians 5:16 commands us to get in the habit of "redeeming the time" Time can be lost or wasted, depending on what we did with it. But if we have wasted or lost time along the way, the end is not over! Ephesians 5:16 clearly says we can "redeem" time.

The word "redeeming" in this verse is the Greek word *exagoridzo*. The word *agoridzo* is the Greek word for *a marketplace* that's cluttered with products and vast opportunities to spend more time and money shopping there than one ought to use. It was the same then as it is today. If a person isn't careful, he can become lost roaming through the shops of the market, wasting precious time. But that word *ex* means "out" and is where we get the word *exit*. When *ex* is added to the word *agoridzo* to form *exagoridzo*, it paints the picture of finding what you need, purchasing it, and getting out of the marketplace quickly. In other words, do what you need to do, and then make an *exit*!

In this phrase "redeeming the time," the word "time" is *kairos*. In this context, it refers to the brevity of time that we have available and our need to be time-conscious in the way we conduct our lives. It depicts someone who is learning to make full use of time because he is conscious that time is limited and he must use it wisely. Paul was saying that by implementing diligence and commitment, we can buy back time that we have frivolously lost along the way.

The good news is this: If we've became sidetracked in the fulfillment of promises that we made to ourselves or to the Lord — if our lives have become so cluttered that we have become lost in the maze of our objectives — we can still *reverse* this condition. Through our recommitment to ourselves and to the Lord, we can buy back time that has been lost, wasted, or forfeited this year thus far. And with the Holy Spirit's supernatural help, we can accomplish in *a short time* what we did not accomplish in the first eight months of the year. We can *redeem that time* and get back on course!

Ask the Holy Spirit to help you win new victories in the remaining four months of this year! Reach forward to achieve those dreams and longings you've put off again and again. Throw open your arms and your heart, and welcome the wonderful future Jesus has waiting for you! Through the power of the Holy Spirit, He will help you shrug off wasted or lost time, redeem it — buy it back — and fulfill the commitments you made eight months ago. With God, all things are possible, so release your faith in the wonderworking power of God. *Press forward* toward the victories that are awaiting you!

MY PRAYER FOR TODAY

Heavenly Father, I thank You for this needed encouragement in my life today. I was nearly discouraged because I hadn't accomplished the things I promised myself at the first of the year that I would do. But I still have four months of this year left to attain some significant progress in various areas of my life. So I'm going to shake off all regret, yield to the workings of the Holy Spirit in my life, and go forward in Jesus' name. With His help, I am determined to make progress in those areas in which I know the Lord wants me to experience growth and change!

I pray this in Jesus' name!

MY CONFESSION FOR TODAY

I confess that I make a fresh commitment again to advance and make progress in my life and to achieve significant victories before the calendar hits December 31. The victories I long for are victories that the Lord desires for my life. He is with me. He is for me. He gives me overcoming power to accomplish these goals and dreams. I embrace His grace, and I repent for not making progress as I should have made. Today I turn my energies and my attention to the future. I plan to end this year with achievement and success!

I declare this by faith in Jesus' name!

QUESTIONS FOR YOU TO CONSIDER

1. Have you taken the time to make a list of the things you'd like to accomplish in the next four months? If not, I encourage you to set aside some time to pray and

seek the Lord regarding what He wants you to achieve before the end of the year.

2. If you failed to accomplish important tasks or goals due to a lack of commitment so far this year, have you taken time to repent before the Lord? It's important to do this so you can "clear the slate" and start the rest of the year with a right heart before God. Not only will He forgive you, but He will also give you the grace and strength to move forward and attain in Him what you never thought you could achieve on your own.
3. Are there any changes you need to make (e.g., in your environment or in your relationships) so you can start implementing these resolutions to finish this year right? Perhaps you need to clear an area of your home just for praying and studying God's Word. Or maybe you need to gently withdraw yourself from friendships that are toxic and emotionally and spiritually unhealthy. Ask God, and the Holy Spirit will guide you and show you what to do.

AUGUST 9

Christ's Warning to Erring Leaders

Repent; or else I will come unto thee quickly,
and will fight against them
with the sword of my mouth.
— Revelation 2:16

I have such a heart for spiritual leaders in the Body of Christ. As one who is called to stand in a leadership position myself, I have a burning desire to see men and women raised up who are leaders of integrity and who are taking a steadfast stance of faith on God's Word. These are qualities that God requires in His leaders, and the world desperately needs leaders of a pure heart and strong faith. That's why Jesus takes it *very* seriously when a spiritual leader falls into error and leads others into that same error.

In Revelation 2:16, Christ was speaking to erring leaders in the Early Church about the toxic influence they were having on those under their spiritual care. A group of spiritual leaders in a local body were leading others astray, teaching them that a little compromise with the world — *worldliness* — would not be detrimental to the spiritual life of the congregation. These leaders propagated among the people a belief that a lifestyle that could "bend" with the times might help them obtain a measure of peace with their pagan neighbors. In essence, this false teaching advocated that separation from the world was not required for the Christian community.

Jesus was firmly against what these errant leaders were teaching; His warning to them is clearly recorded in Revelation 2:16. And for nearly 2,000 years, Christ's words have sounded a clear alarm for *all* spiritual leaders who, whether intentionally or unintentionally, lead the flock of God into a position of accommodating the world.

In today's *Sparkling Gem*, we'll look at the warning that Christ spoke to erring leaders nearly 2,000 years ago. And we'll see that He is *still* issuing this same alarm to spiritual leaders who deviate from sound doctrine today.

In Revelation 2:16, Christ told these erring leaders, "Repent; or else I will come unto thee quickly, and will fight against them with the sword of my mouth."

Knowing the tender graciousness of Jesus, I'm confident that before issuing such a stern admonition, He had spoken to these leaders previously about their wrong behavior. Surely He had warned them of the grave error of their ways and had given them many opportunities to change. But after they had ignored the pleadings of the Holy Spirit, Christ's words became very serious as time began running out for these leaders to respond appropriately and repent.

As we see in Revelation 2:16, a time eventually came when Jesus' tone of voice changed, and He called on that group of leaders to repent "or *else.*"

The word "repent" is the Greek word *metanoeo*, which is a compound of the words *meta* and *nous*. The word *meta* means *to turn*, and the word *nous* is the word for *mind, intellect, will, frame of thinking, opinion*, or *one's general view of life*. When *meta* and *nous* are compounded, the new word depicts *a decision to completely change the way one thinks, lives, or behaves*. Thus, when Jesus used this word in Revelation 2:16, He was adamantly and forthrightly calling on those who were in error to *change*. He was commanding them to stop accommodating the unbelieving world and assimilating that mindset into their midst.

Today the voice of Jesus is still crying out for the Church to repent of worldliness and carnality. As is true in each generation, we have a choice today to harden our hearts and turn a deaf ear to the Holy Spirit — or to allow Him to deal deeply with us and produce true repentance in our hearts and souls. Although Christ is always ready to transform His Church, no true transformation can occur unless we are willing to hear what His Spirit is saying to us. And once we do hear that divine message, we must be willing to respond with humble obedience.

The vast majority of the early believers had repeatedly proven themselves faithful to Christ, even when faced with intense opposition from the pagan government and the unbelieving local community. Yet in their midst were errant spiritual leaders who had become a polluting and adulterating influence on the entire congregation. In Revelation 2:16, Christ issued a stern warning to this latter group, declaring, "Repent; or else *I will come unto thee quickly....*"

The phrase "I will come" in verse 16 signaled that Christ's patience with those in error was rapidly reaching an end. This was His final warning — *a final opportunity to repent* — before He would begin moving in their direction, wielding "the sword of His mouth" — His sharp sword with two edges (*see* Revelation 1:16; 2:12,16). If those church leaders accepted Jesus' call to repent and turn from their erroneous position, they would be spared. But if they refused to heed His call to repent, Jesus emphatically warned them: "I will come to you."

The words "to you" come from the Greek word *soi*, which conveys a sense of strong exclamation. That phrase literally means, *"I will come to YOU!"*

There was no misunderstanding Christ's warning to those erring leaders: If they refused to heed His words and abandon their doctrine of compromise, He would make a direct path to them and personally deal with their sin. The time for repeated warnings was coming to an end.

Jesus' words were a solemn proclamation to those leaders that they should not misinterpret His past delays in judgment as His tolerance of their sin. For Christ to speak in such strong words reveals that He had already warned them and given them opportunities to respond. But because they had repeatedly ignored His pleas, the opportunity to avoid judgment was swiftly coming to a close. By lifting His voice loud and clear, Christ was providing one last chance to repent and thus avoid the repercussions of His discipline. This was an act of love — a merciful plea to those who were leading others astray to *repent* and *change* — before He would take a more severe course of action.

The word "quickly" in the phrase "I will come unto thee quickly" is from the Greek word *tachus*, which describes *a swift, high-speed movement*. This word emphatically denotes that the clock was ticking and time was running out. When the sword of justice would finally fall, Christ would not leisurely enact judgment; rather, Christ would come to them with sudden, unhesitating swiftness.

Christ continued his warning by saying, "Repent; or else I will come unto thee quickly, *and will fight against them....*"

The word "fight" comes from the Greek word *polemos*, which was a well-known word used throughout Greek literature to describe *an organized and often prolonged military conflict designed to defeat an opponent*. In other words, *polemos* was no mere skirmish — it was *an all-out war*! By using this word, Jesus let these believers know that the situation in their church had grown so grievous that He was armed and ready to engage those individuals in battle.

The time for negotiating had come and gone. Just as a powerful nation sends a pre-war declaration to its weaker enemies, calling for their surrender before they are crushed in battle, Christ was calling for the unconditional surrender of those errant leaders. If they chose to defy Him, they would suffer the consequences of a divine assault and experience the sword of His mouth. If these erring leaders finally refused to hear what the Holy Spirit was saying and repent, Jesus declared He would "fight *against* them."

The word "against" is the Greek word *kata*, which describes something that is *dominating* or *subjugating*. In this instance, it depicts a *full force* that comes to completely *subdue* and *conquer*. Based on Jesus' prior experience with these leaders — and the fact that they had not yet repented — we can conclude that Christ didn't expect them to respond in obedience to His command. Thus, He warned them that He was going to exert His authority and retake the church for Himself, one way or another. They could repent and surrender, or they could be crushed. Either way, Christ was going to have His way in His Church.

Revelation 1:16 and 2:12 both portray Christ as having a sharp sword with two edges. However, in Revelation 2:16, Jesus says, "Repent; or else I will come unto thee quickly, and will fight against them *with the sword of my mouth*."

The word "sword" in all three of these verses is the Greek word *rhomphaia*, which is a very unusual word to be used in the context of the Roman world since the *rhomphaia* was not a Roman weapon. Rather, this sword originated in Thrace, a region near Asia Minor, and it was so horrible that it was feared above all others, even by Roman soldiers. This weapon was essentially a very sharp, often double-edged, sickle-shaped blade affixed to a long pole. The ruthless effectiveness of the *rhomphaia* against Roman armies was the result of the sword's capability to cut through thick armor and its long reach. This allowed the soldier who wielded it — often in a back-and-forth, hacking motion similar to a farmer using a sickle — to penetrate even the tightly compacted formation of the Roman infantry.

Therefore, when Jesus used the word *rhomphaia* to describe His spiritual weaponry against those erring leaders, He was referring to one of the most feared weapons of the ancient world. This was no accident; rather, it was a clear declaration — and a serious warning — that if those in error chose *not* to repent, Christ would extend His mighty sword into their midst and *remove* them.

In light of the truths found in these verses, my thoughts go directly to Eli, Israel's high priest, and the fact that God removed him and his two sons from the ministry *in a single day* because they wouldn't repent of their evil ways (*see* 1 Samuel 2:12-4:18). They had been given ample opportunity to repent — but, ultimately, a time came when toleration was no longer acceptable. Although God's mercy gave them a great amount of time to repent and change, they rejected each offer afforded them. Then time ran out. As a result, God's sword of judgment swung into action, and they were each removed from their positions of spiritual authority.

This is a sobering account from Scripture with a very serious message. We *must* pray for our spiritual leaders — that they will hear the voice of the Holy Spirit and respond to His leading and correction when it is needed. We are living in a day and hour when the Church is sadly compromising on many levels. This is a time — perhaps above all other times — when God's spiritual leadership needs to stand up on the side of His unchanging truths. If there are spiritual leaders who will not respond to the repeated call and correction of God, Christ Himself will deal with them with the sword of His mouth to bring whatever level of correction is necessary.

So let's commit to praying diligently for those who are in authority within the Church. Never has it been so crucial that our leaders hear clearly and heed the Holy Spirit as they lead God's flock in the way that Jesus would have them lead.

MY PRAYER FOR TODAY

Heavenly Father, I pray for the spiritual leaders over my life. I pray that they will be quick to hear and prompt to obey Your Voice. I ask You to strengthen them with might in their inner man, that they will remain unbending in their commitment to the unchanging truths of Your Word, even if it means they must take a stand that is different from the spirit of the age around us. In this day when morals and beliefs seem to be changing on every side, give my pastor and spiritual leaders the fortitude and courage to stand firm in their commitment to the unchangeable truths of Your Word.

I pray this in Jesus' name!

MY CONFESSION FOR TODAY

I confess that those who are spiritual leaders over my life walk in divine wisdom, counsel, and might. They are marked by integrity and free from compromise, standing with unwavering commitment to God's unchanging truths as revealed in the teaching of the Bible. Regardless of what society says, what the courts declare, or what the spirit of the age dictates, my leaders are led by the truth of the Bible and the Spirit of the Living God. I declare that they are sensitive to God's voice; they are quick to be corrected when it is required; and they will stand the test of time. They are anointed to minister in these last, very critical days of this age!

I declare this by faith in Jesus' name!

QUESTIONS FOR YOU TO CONSIDER

1. Can you think of other examples from the Bible when God took action against erring spiritual leaders? Who are those examples?
2. In your life, have you seen a spiritual leader whom the Lord disciplined or removed because he was leading the flock into spiritual error and refused to repent?
3. If you see someone in leadership who is leading others in error, how do you think you should pray for him or her? How would you want someone to pray for you if you were in his or her place?

Never has it been so crucial that our leaders hear clearly and heed the Holy Spirit as they lead God's flock in the way that Jesus would have them lead.

AUGUST 10

Coming to the Lord One Step at a Time

...He fell down at Jesus' knees, saying, Depart
from me; for I am a sinful man, O Lord.
— Luke 5:8

As you live your life, it's likely that you will come face to face with people at all kinds of different spiritual levels. You may find that you end up spending time with:

- People who are actively pursuing a closer relationship with Jesus.
- People who have recently recommitted their lives to Christ and are excited about living for Jesus.
- People who are nonchalant or noncommittal about their relationship with God.
- People who have gone astray from the walk they once had with Jesus.
- People who are religious or churchgoers but are still unsaved.
- People who are lost and don't know the message of Christ.

I was really surprised by the number of times Simon Peter had to encounter Jesus *before* his life was changed. And if we include his encounter with Christ when he fell to his knees and recognized Jesus' lordship, that means he had *four different encounters* with Christ *before* he was changed. I had never chronologically put it together until recently, so it struck me when I realized how many encounters it took to bring Simon Peter to a place of conversion, where he turned from his own ways and completely submitted his life to the Lord. We will look at each of those four encounters in this *Sparkling Gem*.

This tells me that sometimes people come to know the Lord one step at a time. Of course, we know that the act of receiving eternal salvation is a one-time event. When I talk about steps and stages, I'm referring to the various encounters people might have with God *before* they finally surrender their lives to the lordship of Jesus Christ.

Let me show you that progression in Simon Peter's life — how he moved from the moment he first heard about Jesus to an eventual encounter that totally changed his life. As you read this *Sparkling Gem*, think of people you know — especially those who may be in one of these various stages in their own encounter with Jesus Christ.

1. Simon Peter's *first encounter* with Jesus.

The day after Jesus was baptized by John the Baptist, Jesus was walking nearby and John exclaimed, "Behold the Lamb of God!" (*see* John 1:36). Verses 37-40 relate that two men heard John and that one of them was *Andrew*, whose brother was *Simon* (later referred to as *Simon Peter* or *Peter*).

This passage goes on to say that Andrew and the other unnamed man followed Jesus to see where He was staying. Jesus could see them following, so He told them, "Come and see." Verse 39 goes on to tell us that the two men spent the entire day with Jesus. Afterward, Andrew went to fetch his brother Simon in order to bring him to Jesus (v. 41).

Thus, Simon's *first encounter* with Christ was this secondhand information that he heard from his brother Andrew. At this point, Simon had never personally met Jesus. All he knew of Him was what his brother had told him: "We have found the Messiah!" At long last the Savior had come, but Simon had only secondhand knowledge about Him.

This describes the spiritual state of many people in the world. These individuals may have heard about Christ from family and friends. They know *of* Jesus, and they know *about* Him; however, they've never personally *met Him*. That kind of secondhand knowledge is *not* enough to bring a person into the Kingdom of God.

That's where *our* responsibility begins. Just like Andrew, you and I must take the initiative to make sure our friends and family members have more than secondhand knowledge about Jesus. A person must have a personal encounter with Jesus Christ in order to go to Heaven — not just "head knowledge" about Him or the ability to say, "I know who Jesus was historically."

As Andrew did for Simon, so must we do everything we can to bring our friends and family to Jesus — which leads us to the next point.

2. Simon Peter's *second encounter* with Christ.

In John 1:42, we read about Simon Peter's *second encounter* with Christ. Simon came to the place where Jesus could be found, and it seems that he lingered and listened to Him. We know that Jesus and Simon had a conversation; however, there is no record that a life-transforming conversion occurred in Simon's life at that time.

Although Simon's heartfelt conversion occurred some days later, as is recorded in Luke 5 (which we'll discuss later), this second encounter was his *first personal introduction* to Jesus. During this encounter, Jesus even told Simon that his name would be changed to Peter, indicating that soon he would have a change of character. However, this change didn't occur at that moment. This second encounter was merely Simon's introduction to the Savior and His message. Again, we see that Simon was *close* to the Kingdom of God but not yet actually *inside* the Kingdom of God.

I urge you to do for your family and friends what Andrew did for his brother. Invite them to a place where they can hear the message and learn more about the Savior. They may have already heard the message from you, but now is the time to take them to church or to a smaller gathering where Christians celebrate Jesus. Taking someone to a place where the Gospel message is presented may seem like only a small step, but this step may be needed to bring about the change of heart that will make a difference for eternity.

Just as Jesus introduced the idea of a *character change* to Simon Peter in that first personal encounter, this may be a way to introduce your lost friends to the truth that Jesus can totally change their lives. Even if they don't get saved during this first introduction to Jesus, remember, Simon's real inward change also didn't happen the first time he personally met Jesus.

I feel impressed by the Holy Spirit to say that there are many who take this particular step and get stuck there. In other words, they go to church or to a meeting searching for truth — and they come very close to the truth. In fact, they are in the very vicinity where a life change can occur. But because no one ever tells them about the need to repent of their sins and surrender their lives to Jesus Christ, they end up *religious* but *unsaved*. Unfortunately, churches are filled with people who have come close to the Kingdom of God but have never entered it.

These people go to church, know the words to the hymns and songs, and often even pay their tithes. But because they've never recognized their sinful state and repented of their sins, they live on the edge of God's Kingdom without ever entering it. As a result, their character has never changed. They are simply religious, unsaved people.

You may discover people in your circle of family and friends who fit in this category. Ask God to give you an opportunity to bring them all the way to repentance and to a true saving knowledge of Jesus Christ.

3. Simon Peter's *third encounter* with Jesus Christ.

Luke 4:38 tells us that after several days, Jesus went to Simon Peter's house. This was a *third step* for Simon as he drew closer and closer to truly knowing Jesus Christ.

Simon Peter's mother-in-law was sick with a fever. But when Jesus arrived, verse 39 says that He "...stood over her, and rebuked the fever; and it left her...." Instantly, this woman was healed. In fact, the verse goes on to say that "...immediately she arose and ministered unto them." The phrase "ministered unto them" most likely means that after Jesus healed Simon's mother-in-law, she felt so well, she immediately got up and cooked dinner for them!

That same night, word spread through the city that Jesus was spending the night at Simon Peter's house, and people got excited. Luke 4:40 tells us what happened next: "Now when the sun was setting, all they that had any sick with divers diseases brought them unto him; and he laid his hands on every one of them, and healed them."

Right in Simon Peter's own home, he experienced God's power. This was no longer secondhand information. Simon had not only witnessed the miraculous healing of his mother-in-law, but he'd also seen multitudes of sick people healed by Jesus' touch that same night. This was the *next step* leading toward the transformation that would occur soon afterward in Simon's life. God's power was all *around* Simon, but the change he needed at his core had not yet occurred *in* him.

This makes me think of people I've seen through the years who have attended meetings where God has demonstrated His power right in front of them. These people have experienced answers to prayer and have tasted of God's power — *but they've never been changed at their core.* I wonder how many people have grown up in church, where they saw and heard so much about God's love and power, yet never allowed the truth they heard to sink into their hearts and bring them to a saving knowledge of Jesus that changed their nature. People who fit that description are thus *unsaved.* In life, it's reasonable to assume that you'll come into contact with many people who are in this category of "*churched* but not really saved."

Keep your heart sensitive to the Holy Spirit about this issue. He may use you to lead someone who fits this description into a saving knowledge of Christ. One thing is for sure: A change at *the core* is essential to enter the Kingdom of God. If no real change of character has occurred at a person's core, it's likely he or she has never been born again.

Luke 4:44 tells us that after this evening of miracles, Jesus left Simon Peter's house and began to travel and preach in the synagogues of Galilee. It isn't known how much time elapsed between the miracles that occurred at Simon's house and his next experience with Jesus. However, Luke 5:1 tells us that some days later, Simon encountered Christ *a fourth time.*

4. Simon Peter's *fourth life-transforming encounter* with Christ.

First, Simon Peter obtained "secondhand" knowledge of Jesus. Second, he went to a specific place where he was introduced to Jesus. Third, he personally experienced the power of God. Then in Luke 5:1-11, we read the story of Simon's *fourth encounter* with Christ — the encounter that reached so deep into his core that it transformed his life. *The result of this fourth encounter was that Simon Peter totally committed his life to the cause of Christ.*

The moment came when Jesus stepped into Simon Peter's boat and used it as a pulpit to preach to a large crowd. Simon's *surrendering* of his boat to Jesus was the first time he had ever given something to Jesus — and that's when Jesus stepped deeper than ever into his life. When Simon surrendered the use of his boat to Jesus, he had *no idea* where that would take him. But after preaching to the multitude from Simon's boat, Jesus told him: "...Launch out into the deep, and let down your nets for a draught" (Luke 5:4).

Simon Peter was a professional fisherman and had just fished all night with no results. But he chose to obey Jesus, saying, "...At thy word I will let down the net" (v. 5). Verse 6 relates, "And when they had this done, they inclosed a great multitude of fishes: and their net brake." In fact, the catch was so enormous that it "...filled both the ships, so that they began to sink" (v. 7).

Such an enormous catch couldn't be attributed to coincidence or a freak accident. Simon Peter had been fishing all his life, but he had never seen anything like this — and neither had anyone else. This encounter with Christ pushed Simon into a rock-solid faith as "...he fell down at Jesus' knees, saying, Depart from me; for I am a sinful man, O Lord" (Luke 5:8). Peter recognized his sinfulness and called Jesus "Lord." This is the Greek word *kurios.* Peter's use of this word lets us know that at this moment, he finally recognized Jesus as having supreme spiritual authority and surrendered his life to Christ.

It was this final experience that caused Simon Peter to see Christ's holiness and his own sinfulness. When Peter saw this miraculous catch of fish, he *really knew* that *God Himself* was in the boat with him. In that moment of revelation, he called Jesus "Lord." This fourth encounter totally *changed* Peter and *reset* his goals for life. However, this life-transforming experience happened:

- *After* Simon Peter had learned that Jesus was the Messiah.
- *After* Jesus had spent time in Peter's home.
- *After* Peter had seen Jesus miraculously heal his mother-in-law.
- And *after* he had witnessed Jesus healing multitudes outside his own home.

One might think that these previous encounters would have been sufficient to bring Peter to the point of conversion. However, it took this final experience to cause him to drop to his knees and *fully acknowledge* the Lordship of Jesus Christ. As a fisherman, Peter knew that the amazing size of this catch of fish was an *unquestionable* miracle. Consequently, this fourth encounter was so life-altering that he never returned to a life of fishing again. From that moment on, Peter followed Jesus.

As you come in contact with so many different people, it is likely that you will spend time with people who are like Simon Peter before that fourth encounter: They just need *one final touch* to bring them to a rock-solid faith in Christ.

Like Peter, these people may mentally know who Jesus is and may have seen demonstrations of His power; however, they have never actually recognized their need to repent of their sins and submit to the Lordship of Christ. *Are you the person the Holy Spirit wants to use to reach out to the people in your life who need this encounter so you can bring them into the family of God?*

MY PRAYER FOR TODAY

Father, I see now that some people — including notable people like Simon Peter — come to know You one step at a time. Help me to recognize how I can be used to bring people closer to You. Show me what to do, what to say, and what steps to take to introduce people to a knowledge of Jesus Christ that will change them at their core. Give me wisdom to lead my friends and acquaintances to a knowledge of Jesus that will transform them from the inside out.

I pray this in Jesus' name!

MY CONFESSION FOR TODAY

I acknowledge that many people come to the Lord one step at a time. While only one experience is needed to bring a person to true conversion, it often takes many experiences to bring a person to that one experience that changes them forever. I confess that I am an instrument that God uses to share Christ, to bring people to a knowledge of sin, and to bring them to a place of repentance that changes them at the very core of their being.

I declare this by faith in Jesus' name!

QUESTIONS FOR YOU TO CONSIDER

1. As you read about Simon Peter and how he came to the Lord one step at a time, did you think about anyone you know who is coming closer and closer to the Lord, but still lacks that final experience of repentance that changes him at his core? Who is that person? What can you do to help bring that individual to that final place of genuine conversion?
2. What was your own experience of coming to the Lord? Did you instantly come the first time you heard about the need to repent, or did it take time and multiple experiences for you to come to a place of repentance and faith in Christ?
3. Is there any person whom you are actively introducing to the Lordship of Jesus Christ? Who is that person? How close is he or she to making that final commitment to the Lordship of Jesus Christ?

AUGUST 11

The Importance of Truthfulness

...Speaking the truth in love....
— Ephesians 4:15

Being truthful with others is one of the most important qualities the Lord has taught me over the years. Ephesians 4:15 tells us we are to "speak the truth in love."

As the leader of our ministry, I *expect* my team to be honest with me and to speak truthfully. Even if I don't always like what they say, their honesty guarantees a clear and truthful relationship between us.

However, if someone on my staff were to tell me one thing and then tell a fellow employee something entirely different, it would create distrust between that staff member and me. If that happened, I wouldn't know whether I could really count on that team member to be honest with me.

This is precisely what the Bible is talking about when it says that those chosen to be deacons cannot be "double-tongued" (*see* 1 Timothy 3:8). The Greek word for "double-tongued" is *dilogos*, and it means, *two-worded.* It presents the picture of someone who says one thing to one person about a situation, but then says something altogether different about it to someone else. This "double-tongued" individual is either *inconsistent* in what he tells people, or he is just simply *dishonest.*

Sometimes this characteristic of being "double-tongued," or *two-worded*, indicates that a person is a people-pleaser. He wants everyone to like him, so he agrees with whomever he is with at the moment. This person may be concerned that if he takes an opinion contrary to his immediate audience, he will lose favor or influence with them. So instead of speaking his true convictions in an attitude of love, he finds himself violating his conscience. Beyond just remaining silent if he doesn't agree with something that others say, he actually verbalizes *agreement* with those in his presence, knowing that what he says is not really what he believes.

This trait of being double-tongued is a serious character flaw. And the Bible is very strong in telling us that a person who possesses this trait should not be used in leadership. A leader who tells the pastor, "I believe you're right" and then tells the church members, "I believe the pastor is missing it this time" is not being a blessing to the pastor. In the end, he creates *confusion* and *suspicion*.

It's a blessing to always know where I stand with a person and to never wonder if that individual really means what he or she says. When I can always count on a person to tell me exactly what he or she thinks, a foundation of trust can be established that is very important if we're going to build a long-term relationship in the ministry.

My team is *very* honest with me. Because they are honest with me, I trust them *incredibly*. I know I can depend on their straightforward, truthful responses. Denise and I are visionaries — we are "idea people"! But we need the perspective of others to help us see all the details that must accompany a vision in order to bring it to pass. We need their honest input in our lives. That's why God sent us our team.

Please remember on this subject of truthfulness that we are called to speak the truth *in love* — *not* to "bludgeon" each other in the way we communicate what's on our minds! We must ask God to teach us how to present the truth in a manner that makes it easier to receive.

One reason that truth is rejected is the inappropriate way it is sometimes packaged. When truth comes bundled with harsh tones of judgment, criticism, and condemnation, it can cause the recipient to put up a wall of defense as a safeguard against the attack. But when truth comes wrapped in patience, tenderness, and love, it is much easier to receive.

This does *not* mean honesty is always easy. Taking the path of truthfulness can be very difficult. However, it is always the clearest and most noble path to take.

Sometimes the biggest challenge we face in this area isn't speaking the *truth*; it is speaking the truth *in love*, as Ephesians 4:15 commands. So let's look in greater detail at the *manner* in which we are to speak truthfully with each other.

In my own experience, I've learned that the truth in itself isn't as hard to hear as the *wrong way* in which it is sometimes spoken. I think you know that cold water thrown in your face would not be a very enjoyable experience. In fact, it may be such a chilling encounter that you become tempted to respond in kind and throw water right back!

When you are required to confront someone and speak the truth, remember the principle of doing unto others as you would have them do unto you (*see* Matthew 7:12). In other words, be mindful to speak the truth in love to that other person as you would want to have truth spoken in love to *you*. Ask yourself this question: *How would I want the truth spoken to me?*

- Brutally?
- Harshly?
- Impatiently?
- Kindly?
- Gently?
- Humbly?

If you're in a situation in which you must confront someone with the truth, imagine how you would respond to that same truth if it were being presented to *you*. Then try to picture what would help you receive it in the easiest way that would bring growth to your life and be a blessing. As you ponder these ideas, what you discover will create a path for you to follow to speak the truth in love into someone else's life. As you follow that path, you will most likely end up treating that other person correctly — with dignity and respect — as you tell him or her what you perceive to be the truth.

If you are the one in charge in your family, ministry, or organization, you must set the example by being truthful with the people who live, serve, and work under you. When you are truthful, people will know you are being straight with them. Even if they don't like everything you say, they will know they can always depend on you to tell the truth when they need to hear it and not "fudge" about it. If you are truthful, you will set the standard for integrity, truthfulness, and *trust* among all the members of your team.

Certainly, my own teams in Russia and the United States have many areas in which we can grow more. I'm not claiming that we carry out *speaking the truth in love* perfectly! But we sincerely attempt to walk honestly and openly with one another. I need what my team members have to impart to me — and they need what I have to impart to them! I personally count these people very valuable in my life and ministry. I want to do everything I can do to obey God in my attitude and conduct toward them — and that includes speaking the truth in love.

MY PRAYER FOR TODAY

Heavenly Father, I find speaking the truth in love to be difficult. I don't always know how to do that effectively, and at times I'm concerned that I might hurt someone's feelings or that I may be rejected. To do what I've read today will require a higher level of spiritual maturity in my life. Holy Spirit, I am asking You to help me know when to speak, when to be silent, and how to speak the truth in a way that is truthful, loving, and a blessing to those who listen to me. And help me to be open and receptive when people express the truth in love to me too!

I pray this in Jesus' name!

MY CONFESSION FOR TODAY

I confess that I am honest with people about the things I express to them. I do not lie. I do not shade the truth, but I kindly and lovingly answer them in truth. Because they know I am truthful, they trust me and know that they can always depend on me to be truthful with them. Likewise, I confess that I am grateful when people speak the truth to me. God gives me the grace to listen, and He gives me the wisdom to discern what is true and what is just their opinion. I need truthfulness and honesty. Therefore, I choose to accept other people's candid relationship with me as a blessing to my life!

I declare this by faith in Jesus' name!

QUESTIONS FOR YOU TO CONSIDER

1. Are you honest in your relationships, or do you conceal what you really feel about things? Maybe you're afraid to be honest. What is the root of that fear?
2. How do you feel when someone lovingly tells you the truth about something? Do you appreciate it, or do you resent it?
3. When was the last time you really expressed truthfully what you felt about something, and what was the response to your truthfulness? Did you tell it in love, or did you bludgeon the listener(s) with your words?

AUGUST 12

Pleasing the Lord Above All Else

For the appeal we make does not spring from error
or impure motives, nor are we trying to trick you.
On the contrary, we speak as those
approved by God to be entrusted with the gospel.
We are not trying to please people but God,
who tests our hearts.
— 1 Thessalonians 2:3,4 *NIV*

In First Thessalonians 2, Paul gives a detailed account of his personal motives in ministry. Although he wrote from the perspective of an apostle, his message pertains to all believers regardless of the specific calling on their lives. I believe that it would be good for every one of us if we stopped from time to time to take account of our own motives for *why* we do what we do in fulfilling the call of God on our lives. Filled with wonderful nuggets of truth, First Thessalonians 2 is a vast *treasury of wisdom* because it not only reflects on what Paul's motives were, but also on what they were *not*. So for the next few days, I want us to examine what Paul wrote about right and wrong motives for being in the ministry.

Although Paul and his ministry team remained in Thessalonica for only a short time, Paul's ministry greatly impacted the Thessalonian church. During this short, intense visit, a deep bond was forged between Paul and the church members in that city. In First Thessalonians 1:5 and 6, Paul wrote about that time with the Thessalonian believers: "For our gospel came not unto you in word only, but also in power, and in the Holy Ghost, and in much assurance; as ye know what manner of men we were among you for your sake. And ye became followers of us, and of the Lord, having received the word in much affliction, with joy of the Holy Ghost."

Notice in the above passage, Paul ministered the Word of God in the power of the Holy Spirit and with much boldness. His ministry had such an impact on these people that they literally became "followers" of Paul and his ministry team. In the Greek, the word for "followers" is *mimetes*, which means *imitators*. Because Paul had made such a strong impact upon this church with both his message and personal life, the Thessalonians began to *imitate* Paul and became examples of his ministry to the believers in the surrounding areas.

But it was more than just words that Paul imparted — he imparted his very life to these people by building a relationship with them. Paul's ministry to the Thessalonian church was powerful because of the relationship he had developed with them during the short time he was with this body of believers.

We see this truth illustrated in First Thessalonians 2:1, where Paul wrote, "For yourselves, brethren, know our entrance in unto you, that it was not in vain." The word "entrance" in this verse is from the Greek work *eisodon*, which is a compound of two words, *eis*, which means *into*, and *odon*, from the word *odos*, which refers to *a road*. When Paul put these two words together, he was describing his entrance into the Thessalonian church in terms of *relationship*. In essence, he was saying that he had journeyed on a road that took him straight into their hearts.

By using this particular word "entrance," Paul was describing the happy and successful ministry he enjoyed there in the church. In turn, the people in that church opened their hearts to Paul, and Paul experienced powerful ministry in that city.

After describing his "entrance" into the Thessalonian church, Paul goes on to define his personal motives for ministry. The first motive he mentioned was his desire first and foremost to please God. Paul's first responsibility as a believer and as a minister was to live a life pleasing to the Lord. And this is no less true for us as believers and ministers today.

In First Thessalonians 2:4, Paul wrote, "But as we were allowed of God to be put in trust with the gospel, even so we speak; not as pleasing men, but God, which trieth our hearts." Notice the word "pleasing" in this verse. It's the Greek word *aresko*. In early Greek history, this word was found very frequently on grave markers of civil servants. In his career, a civil servant's mind was on serving others. When the word *aresko* was used on the grave marker of one of these servants, it meant the deceased person was a wonderful, pleasing civil servant.

This word *aresko* carries the connotation of *virtue*, *joy*, and *delight*. Basically, it portrays the idea of being a virtuous person who is exceedingly pleasing. Again, it was originally used to describe civil servants or individuals who loved serving people and who gave their entire lives to the service of others.

Paul used this word *aresko* to describe himself. In essence, he was saying, "I'm called to *serve* people. Although Paul had a desire to be pleasing to those he served and ministered to, his *first* and *chiefest* priority was to please God.

There's a great lesson in that for us as ministers and as believers today. We're called to *serve* people, but not necessarily to *please* them.

There can be a very thin line between pleasing man and pleasing God. As servants of the church, we naturally want to be pleasing to the church. We want to serve the church, and we want to make the Gospel palatable so people can receive it. Yet on the other hand, we can't water down the Gospel to please some people — because, first and foremost, we're to please God.

By using the word *aresko*, Paul was defining his primary motive in ministry. Although he was called to be a servant of the Church and to be pleasing to the Body of Christ, his chief responsibility was and always would be to be pleasing to God *first*. Paul had to be virtuous and delightful to *Him* before he could be truly pleasing to anyone else. So while Paul was called to serve the church, his eyes continually remained on the Lord.

This principle not only applies to anyone in the ministry, but also to every one of us as believers in every walk of life. We must make sure our first goal is to please God, even when it means that what we're doing with our lives might not please everyone around us. Our highest aim should be to fulfill His purposes for our lives and to make as many inroads as possible into people's hearts with the truth of the Gospel and the love of God as we go through each day. We are to give them not only the Word of God but also our own personal example of abundant life in Jesus, lived before them in a way that would make them want to imitate us. Oh, how I pray that God uses you and me in such a powerful way, each and every day!

As we continue this study over the next few days, take a little time to look at your own heart and examine the motives of why you do what you do. Although you want to be satisfactory to everyone you serve, your highest ambition should be to please the Lord.

Love the people and please the Lord — that has to be our goal!

MY PRAYER FOR TODAY

Father, as I serve You and Your Church, help me to always keep the balanced perspective that I am to love the people — but I am to please the Lord! As a servant of the Church, I always want to serve in a high-level, satisfactory manner, but my highest aim must be to please You above all else. Help me to find inroads into people's hearts, to give them Your Word, and to be a personal example that's so godly that they would want to imitate it.

I pray this in Jesus' name!

MY CONFESSION FOR TODAY

I confess by faith that I deeply love people, but I live to please the Lord. Satisfying Jesus with my love for His people and my service to others is my highest aim. I want to be a vessel that God works through to touch others and take them higher. As a result, God gives me inroads to people's hearts and minds to pour the Word of God into them and live a godly example before them that they will want to imitate!

I declare this by faith in Jesus' name!

QUESTIONS FOR YOU TO CONSIDER

1. Who was the person who affected you immensely when you first came to Christ? What qualities in that person found an "inroad" to your heart and mind?
2. Who are you influencing right now? Have you been too busy to be involved in the development of another Christian? If so, what do you think the Holy Spirit would have you do about that?
3. Are you living the kind of Christian life that someone else would want to imitate?

AUGUST 13

A Cloak of Covetousness

For neither at any time used
we flattering words, as ye know,
nor a cloak of covetousness; God is witness.
— 1 Thessalonians 2:5

As Paul shared his priorities and motives in ministry, he also talked about what *didn't* motivate him in ministry — namely *financial gain*. In First Thessalonians 2:5, he wrote, "For neither at any time used we flattering words, as ye know, nor a cloak of covetousness; God is witness." In this verse, Paul specifically dealt with the issue of money in ministry, and he emphatically conveyed that his motives for ministry were not financial gain from those who followed his ministry. Instead, the apostle strove to keep his motives for ministry pure.

If Paul hadn't made this his first motive — to please God and not man — he would have been vulnerable to becoming a man-pleaser and using "flattering words" to exact some kind of selfish gain from the people he ministered to. But Paul's primary focus was on pleasing the One who called him and who sent him to the precious people in Thessalonica.

The same quality should be true of us. Our motives for serving God should be pure and unadulterated, rooted solely in a heart desire to please Him through the fruits of our labor as we do what He asks us to do.

Let's study verse 5 more closely. What exactly does it mean for someone to use "flattering words"? This phrase comes from the Greek word *kolakeia*, which means *to "butter up" someone by saying things he or she wants to hear.* Usually, when someone "butters up" another person, he is putting himself in a position to take advantage of that individual. The word *kolakeia* — "flattering words" — also means *to say things with an insincere motive.*

In other words, when you're using *kolakeia*, your words are just a vehicle to get you what you want. They hold no genuine meaning and are spoken for no other reason than that.

But in these two verses in First Thessalonians 2, Paul was saying he didn't do that to the congregation in Thessalonica. He didn't butter them up so he could get something out of them. He didn't just say good things about them or tell them how wonderful they were to receive some kind of selfish gain. Paul wasn't insincere in his dealings with the believers in the Thessalonian church; instead, he spoke truthfully to them as he interacted with them and ministered to them.

Now let's look at the next phrase Paul used in this passage: "cloak of covetousness." The word "cloak" is the Greek word *prophasis*, which can be translated as *a pretense* or *something that is phony or not real.* The whole idea behind this word *prophasis* is that a person will be whatever he needs to be to receive some kind of gain from others.

Prophasis describes a person who is constantly changing, not according to his conviction, but according to how he can gain something from someone else. This is why the Bible calls it a "cloak." It is a *covering* or a *pretense* — something that isn't real.

The Bible calls this cloak a "cloak of covetousness." I believe that a better translation would be *"a cloak for the sake of covetousness."* In this verse where Paul wrote, "For neither at any time used we flattering words...nor a cloak of covetousness...," he was actually referring to *the exploitation of people for gain.*

The word "covetousness" in First Thessalonians 2:5 is translated from the Greek word *pleonexia*, which is used in this scripture to describe *monetary greed.* The word *pleonexia* carries a few ideas that tend to build upon each other, as in a progression.

- *First*, it simply means *to have more.*
- *Second*, it portrays the concept of *expanding* — to have more and more and more.

- *Third*, it carries the idea of *overreaching for more than you need.*
- *Fourth*, it depicts *control*. In other words, at some point, you aren't reaching out for the thing you want more of anymore — now that thing has reached out and grabbed you. Now it has gained control of *you*.

This word covetousness describes a man who has money in the heart. He "thinks" money. In fact, he thinks about money almost all the time. He *eats, drinks, and sleeps* money! Money becomes just about all he wants to talk about. When he goes to bed at night, he's thinking about money — and when he gets out of bed in the morning, his first thoughts turn to money. When he talks to people, he sees currency on their foreheads! He's constantly looking for more money, and he sees everything — every encounter, every relationship, and everything he does — as an opportunity to turn a buck.

It is this attitude of covetousness that Paul emphatically rejected. His motive for preaching was not to pretend to be something he wasn't in order to make financial gain from the people God had given him to care for and minister to. *And neither can it be our motivation for serving others!* Furthermore, people are smart — and if they sense that you are after their money and not their hearts, it won't be long until they will send you on your way!

So make the decision today that you will always be someone who speaks from an authentic, pure heart and seeks only to edify the listener and glorify God, never to receive monetary gain or advantage for yourself. As you make that your constant practice, people will come to know that they can trust the source! They'll receive your words as genuine, and the power of love behind your words will minister to people's hearts as God intends!

MY PRAYER FOR TODAY

Father God, everyone needs money, including me — but I ask You to keep my motivation for serving others free from the contamination of greed for money. Scripture is full of examples of people who were spoiled and suffered ruin because they let money become a motivator for ministry. I thank You for meeting my needs according to Your riches in glory by Christ Jesus. Keep my heart free from ever serving people with money as a motivator. For my own needs, I look to You, and I trust You to provide for me every step along the way!

I pray this in Jesus' name!

MY CONFESSION FOR TODAY

I boldly confess that money is not and will never be my motivation for ministry. If making money is what it's all about, I need to go elsewhere and do something else. God has called me to serve people purely and to trust Him to meet my financial needs and obligations. I look to God, not people, as my Source to meet my needs!

I declare this by faith in Jesus' name!

QUESTIONS FOR YOU TO CONSIDER

1. Have you ever known someone whose motive for ministry was financial gain? What happened to that person in the end?
2. When you look at people whom God has brought across your path, do you see them as a financial opportunity or as a ministry opportunity? *Your answer to this question is very important!*
3. Have you been hurt by someone whose driving motivation was money? Have you forgiven them? If not, you need to forgive them and release that experience so you can move forward in your walk of faith!

AUGUST 14

Living in the Limelight

Nor of men sought we glory,
neither of you, nor yet of others,
when we might have been burdensome,
as the apostles of Christ.
— 1 Thessalonians 2:6

Another pitfall that has short-circuited the call of God in lives of others is a desire for glory or fame. But neither money nor fame was Paul's motive for pursuing ministry. Paul's primary pursuit was to please God. He genuinely loved God and the people God had called him to reach.

In First Thessalonians 2:6, Paul said, "Nor of men sought we glory, neither of you, nor yet of others, when we might have been burdensome, as the apostles of Christ." The Greek tense makes it clear that Paul was saying he didn't habitually seek glory from men; it wasn't his pattern of operation. Then Paul got more specific by using the phrase "neither of you, nor yet of others." In a general sense, Paul wasn't seeking glory from people. And in a specific sense, he wasn't seeking glory from those he knew personally, including the church members in Thessalonica.

Paul's statement in verse 6 was what I call a futuristic statement. Paul was saying, "I haven't sought glory in the past; I'm not seeking glory from you now; and I'm not going to seek glory from anyone else in the future." Paul simply wasn't interested in the limelight — in receiving the glory of men.

This is a great test and temptation for anyone who becomes well known. *It is a test that must be passed.* If having the adulation of men is important to you, it will eventually become a noose that hangs you — as you'll end up doing or saying anything to get attention and adulation.

Proverbs 29:25 (*NKJV*) holds a powerful warning to us along this line. It tells us that "the fear of man brings a snare...." Being overly concerned about what people think of us and fearing their possible rejection of us is actually a dangerous trap of the enemy that he uses to try to control us. It will either muzzle and silence us from speaking the truth when necessary, or provoke us to say what people want to hear — instead of the word of the Lord they *need* to hear.

Either way, seeking adulation and praise from man is a deceptive trap, and the source is fear. And fear always works to nullify faith, which is essential for you to please God! So make sure your goal is always to stay pleasing to the Lord above all else and all others. It's that pure desire of your heart to please Jesus that will keep you free every day from the trap of seeking praise from men!

MY PRAYER FOR TODAY

Father, I know what it's like to live for the honor and adulation of men, and I do not want to live in that kind of slavery ever again. It's a trap to fear man, to live constantly to please man, and to live for the praises of people. My utmost goal is to live to serve and please You. If I can live in the light of Your glory, I'll be so thankful — and that will be a glory that never passes with time. That is the true limelight my heart cries out for!

I pray this in Jesus' name!

MY CONFESSION FOR TODAY

I confess that I do NOT live for the glory and adulation of men. I appreciate being appreciated, and I am glad when people are thankful for what I do — but I live to please God. Daily I present myself before God as a living sacrifice to be acceptable unto Him, while I rely upon His grace to help me maintain a balance in my life of appreciating what others say and do while living exclusively for God and for His approval!

I declare this by faith in Jesus' name!

QUESTIONS FOR YOU TO CONSIDER

1. Have you ever lived with the adulation of men as a goal for your life? Do you know what it's like to live in their pleasure or displeasure? I assure you, it is easier to live a life pleasing to God than to try to be pleasing to all the different kinds of people who are in your life!
2. The Bible says that the fear of man is a trap. Have you ever experienced that trap? Do you know what it's like to live in the fear of man? Have you been delivered from it? If yes, how were you delivered?

3. If you've lived for the limelight of man and then experienced what it's like to "fall out of the limelight," how did it affect you? Did that experience give you a new perspective of what is and isn't important?

AUGUST 15

The Heart Motive of Love

So being affectionately desirous of you,
we were willing to have imparted unto you,
not the gospel of God only, but also our own souls,
because ye were dear unto us.
— 1 Thessalonians 2:8

In the past few *Sparkling Gems*, we've seen how Paul was not motivated by money or glory in his efforts to serve God and spread the Gospel throughout the Roman Empire. However, since he wasn't interested in fame or fortune, what exactly *was* his motive for ministry? What was the driving force behind the sacrifices Paul made and the time and energy he spent to preach the Gospel and disciple believers? Today we will conclude our study of First Thessalonians 2 by examining the answer to these important questions.

To be pleasing to the Lord was Paul's highest aim, and the primary focus of his ministry was *relationship*. He genuinely cared about the people he was ministering to, and in verse 7, he described his feelings for them. The last thing he wanted to do was abuse them; rather, he wanted to see them grow. He said, "Nor of men sought we glory, neither of you, nor yet of others, when we might have been burdensome, as the apostles of Christ. But we were gentle among you, even as a nurse cherisheth her children" (1 Thessalonians 2:6,7).

In verses 6 and 7, Paul drew a comparison between what he *wasn't* and what he *was* in terms of his attitude and conduct toward the people in the Thessalonian church. Instead of being "burdensome," he was "gentle." Like a mother feeding her children, Paul drew them close to his heart to feed them the Word of God and nurture them. All he wanted to do was love the Church. This passage of Scripture paints a very beautiful bond of love and trust — one that should exist between every minister and those whom God has placed under his charge.

In First Thessalonians 2:8, Paul continued, "So being affectionately desirous of you, we were willing to have imparted unto you, not the gospel of God only, but also our own souls, because ye were dear unto us."

What did Paul mean when he said he was "affectionately desirous" of the believers in Thessalonica? This phrase is taken from the Greek word *homeiromai*, and this word is extremely important because it tells us a lot about the heart of the apostle Paul. The word *homeiromai* was primarily found on the grave markers of children that had died, and it describes what the parents felt for their child. It indicates *a deep longing* or *an affectionate, fervent desire* to see the child one more time.

By using this word, Paul was conveying his deep desire to see these Thessalonian believers just one more time. He loved them very much, and like a parent who longs to see again a child who has died, everything within the apostle Paul longed to be able to visit the church of Thessalonica and minister again face to face to these believers whom he held so close to his heart.

Because Paul was so affectionate in his attitude toward the people in Thessalonica, he further expressed, "...We were willing to have imparted unto you, not the gospel of God only, but also our own souls, because ye were dear unto us" (1 Thessalonians 2:8).

When someone is dear to a person, that person is willing to go to great lengths to bring benefit to that loved one. Here Paul was saying that his desire for the Thessalonian believers' spiritual welfare was so great that he had a "willingness" in his heart to impart to them as much of himself as he could. The word "willing" in this verse is from the Greek word *eudokeo*, which means *to seek something that is pleasurable.* This word carries the idea of something that is *delightful and wonderful.*

Because Paul loved this church so much, he was pleased to do anything and everything he could for them to help them grow and develop as believers in Christ. This was not something he was being forced to do; it was something that flowed from his heart and brought him a great sense of joy.

What did Paul want to impart to this church? Verse 8 says, "...to have imparted unto you, not the gospel of God only, but also our own souls...." The word "imparted" is the Greek word *metadidomi*, which carries the idea of *exchange.* By using this word, Paul was saying he was willing to give a part of himself to them, but he wanted something in exchange: He wanted the church in Thessalonica to give a part of themselves to *him.* In other words, Paul wanted to have a *relationship* with the believers to whom God called him to minister.

This is such a crucial lesson for us to learn from Paul's ministry to the Thessalonians — one that will help us remain focused and effective in our own priorities and motives as we fulfill our divine callings. Paul wasn't in the ministry to get rich or to become famous. Rather, he sincerely wanted to please the Lord with his whole heart. And as a result, he was focused on the needs of the people to whom he ministered. The one thing he sought was an authentic relationship with people so he could minister to them more effectively. Not moved by greed or glory, Paul gave his whole heart to God and to the church.

Every one of us must reflect from time to time on our motives and priorities in serving others. Using First Thessalonians 2 as a guide in examining ourselves will help us maintain steadfastness of character and a deep devotion to God and His people that we need to carry on effectively and with power.

So here's a parting thought to ponder as you interact with the people in your life each day: When God's love for others is a burning compassion in your heart — and not merely a concept understood and accepted in your mind — you will look for ways to bless and help others grow and develop into all they can be in Christ *because of your love for Him*! You won't feel forced or compelled to do it as a requirement or for the sake of appearances or what others may think of you. Your desire to please the Lord by walking in His ways will help you see people as He sees them. And it's your ability to see through Jesus' eyes that will help you treat each person as *He* would treat them. That's the key to living life from a heart motive of unconditional love — and that's the key to pleasing Him!

MY PRAYER FOR TODAY

Father, I want my priorities to be correct about ministering to people. You deeply care for Your people, and I want that same love and compassion to be exactly what motivates me. Help me search my heart and put aside any other ulterior motive so that the care of Your people is the number-one priority on my heart. I am so thankful for the people who have genuinely cared for me and who continue to care for me. I consider it an honor to show genuine love, concern, care, and compassion for my brothers and sisters in the Christian community.

I pray this in Jesus' name!

MY CONFESSION FOR TODAY

I confess that I love God's people and that I am doing all I can to help them grow in their knowledge of Jesus Christ. There are many things that vie for my attention, but I have decided that none is as important as ministering to the Lord and to His saints. Because the Holy Spirit has shed the love of God into my heart, I have a deep-seated, genuine love, concern, care, and compassion for the saints in the Christian community. I love God's people and my love for them is growing greater all the time!

I declare this by faith in Jesus' name!

QUESTIONS FOR YOU TO CONSIDER

1. Do you really care for people? Even more important, what would God say about the way you demonstrate care for people?
2. The Holy Spirit has shed the love of God abroad in your heart, but it has to be released to effectively minister to other people. Are you allowing that God-deposited love to function and flow through you to others?
3. What are you doing to help others grow in their relationship with Christ? What would *God* say you are doing to help others grow in their relationship with Christ?

AUGUST 16

God's Testimony of Your Heart

For ye remember, brethren, our labour and travail:
for labouring night and day, because we would not be chargeable
unto any of you, we preached unto you the gospel of God.
Ye are witnesses, and God also, how holily and justly and
unblameably we behaved ourselves among you that believe:
As ye know how we exhorted and comforted and charged
every one of you, as a father doth his children,
That ye would walk worthy of God, who hath called
you unto his kingdom and glory.
— 1 Thessalonians 2:9-12

What was the apostle Paul's top priority in life and in ministry? It was to love God and to please Him *first*. Paul loved people, but his first responsibility was toward the Lord — to love, to obey, and to do that which was pleasing to *Him*.

We've looked at the importance of having the right motives in ministry, and I discussed at length what Paul's motives for ministry were *not*. Paul wasn't motivated by an insatiable desire to get richer and richer and richer. Neither was he motivated by a desire to be popular with people and to receive the accolades of men. The desire for riches and the praise and adulation of others didn't move Paul or influence his behavior and actions. The apostle Paul simply wasn't interested in fame or glory.

So what *did* Paul want? *He wanted to please God.*

An inordinate desire for money and fame is a snare that has enslaved many God-called ministers of the Gospel who allowed themselves to be sidetracked and their faith shipwrecked because they became errant in their hearts concerning their motives for ministry. But Paul labored to keep his heart's motives pure and his relationship with God as his highest priority.

It's very important that we establish our priorities as believers — and especially as ministers of the Gospel — because anyone can *say* he's putting God first and claim to have the right motives in ministry. But not everyone can actually make this claim before God, as Paul did, with God as his witness.

In First Thessalonians 2:4,5,10, Paul wrote, "But as we were allowed of God to be put in trust with the gospel, even so we speak; not as pleasing men, but God, which trieth our hearts. For neither at any time used we flattering words, as ye know, nor a cloak of covetousness; God is witness.... Ye are witnesses, and God also, how holily and justly and unblameably we behaved ourselves among you that believe."

Notice in these verses that Paul makes the following statements:

- "Not as pleasing men, but rather God, *who tries our hearts*" (v. 4).
- "At no time did we use flattery, *as you know*" (v. 5).
- *"God is a witness"* (v. 5).
- "*You are witnesses, and so is God* of how we behaved ourselves with you" (v. 10).

What was Paul saying? He was saying, "*You* know it — and *God* knows it. You are all our witnesses that we behaved ourselves as holy, just, and blameless among you."

Let's look again at the phrase "...God is witness" in verse 5. That word "witness" is translated from the Greek word *martus*, which was the very word you would use to describe *a witness on the witness stand in a court of law.*

What do we know about a witness who is sworn in by an officer of the court to "tell the truth, the whole truth, and nothing but the truth"? By an oath the witness makes before God, that person must tell the truth! So Paul was saying, in effect, "You know that this is true. If you could put even God on a witness stand and 'swear Him in,' He would say the exact same thing about my motives in ministry."

That's what Paul said in verse 5. Then in verse 6, he also made it clear that he wasn't in the ministry for fame or glory — *or* for the praise and adulation of men.

Paul was no doubt answering allegations against him as a minister of the Gospel. You need to know that there will be times when your own motives will be questioned as well.

Each one of us must examine our hearts so thoroughly that we can answer boldly and confidently, as Paul did, and lay every allegation to rest with the truth. Paul didn't defend his ministry with words that he only *wished* were true. Instead, he defended his life and ministry before God and man — *as if both were witnesses on a witness stand,* sworn in to tell the full, complete truth about Paul's motives and desires concerning ministry and those he ministered to.

If God were to take the witness stand to testify about *you,* what would He say? What would be the witness of God about you? It's a sobering thought, isn't it? But you can determine today that you are going to do all you possibly can each day of your life to keep your heart pure.

As I reach the end of this *Sparkling Gem* today, I feel compelled to examine my own heart to make sure my motivations are God-pleasing and that I am truly people-loving. *Why don't you join me in making a self-evaluation of these crucial issues of the heart?*

MY PRAYER FOR TODAY

Father, I want my heart to be aligned with Your heart so I can confidently lay to rest any allegation against the truth. Holy Spirit, I ask You to help me evaluate myself to see where I stand on these issues of motivations and priorities that are so vitally important to You and to Your Church. I want my heart to be clear and clean about how I see and treat people. If there are areas where I need to change, I ask You to reveal them to me. Help me as I step forward to make things the way they ought to be.

I pray this in Jesus' name!

MY CONFESSION FOR TODAY

I confess and acknowledge that God not only observes what I say and do, but also He takes note of the intent and motivations of my heart. I am open to correction, therefore, I hear and obey the Holy Spirit when He speaks to me about changes I need to make in my life. And when the Holy Spirit speaks to me, He gives me the will and the power to make the changes He requires of me. My goal is to love God, to please Him first, and to keep my heart pure so that if God took the witness stand to testify about me, He would be able to say that I am walking worthily of His call upon me and that I am doing it by the power of His Spirit instead of the vain energy of my flesh. I establish my priorities as a believer in such a way that God Himself can testify that I pursue Him and His will for my life with all my heart, soul, and strength.

I declare this by faith in Jesus' name!

QUESTIONS FOR YOU TO CONSIDER

1. Can you say your chief goal in life is to please the Lord, or are you motivated to please people to influence what they think about you?
2. If God took the witness stand to truthfully witness about you, what would He testify about you, your character, and your desire to please Him above all others?
3. Is there any area of your life that is out of sync with your desire to please God above all else? Is there some other person or goal that means more to you than pleasing the Lord? If something comes to mind, recognize that today the Holy Spirit is calling you to lay that area of your life on the altar and fully surrender it to God.

The desire for riches and the praise and adulation of others didn't move Paul or influence his behavior and actions. The apostle Paul simply wasn't interested in fame or glory. So what DID *Paul want? He wanted to please God.*

AUGUST 17

The Privilege and the Responsibility of Ministry

But we were gentle among you,
even as a nurse cherisheth her children.
— 1 Thessalonians 2:7

Today we are going to continue looking at what Paul wrote about his ministry to the church in Thessalonica. Paul was greatly moved by his love for this particular church. He was highly motivated to give of himself and to do whatever was necessary to impart to them the truths they needed to put down their spiritual roots and to grow and develop in Christ.

To do all that, Paul had to very quickly develop a genuine relationship with those church members. Paul actively sought out a relationship with these believers in the short time that he was with them — and that relationship was marked by certain characteristics, which we will look at in depth today.

Paul felt privileged to be called into the ministry and to reach the Gentiles for Christ (*see* 1 Timothy 1:12), but he also felt a great *responsibility* toward his calling and toward those to whom God had called him to disciple and minister. Paul's role was one of a spiritual father, and he took that role and responsibility very seriously.

In regard to this role, he wrote, "But we were gentle among you, even as a nurse cherisheth her children" (*see* 1 Thessalonians 2:7). Notice Paul's *gentle* approach with these people. He wasn't harsh or demanding — rather, he *nurtured* these church members as a mother would nurse her child.

The word "nurse" is from the Greek word *trophos*, which literally means *a wet nurse*. In ancient Greece and in other cultures around the world, a wet nurse was not the mother of a child — rather, she was a woman called in to nurse a baby for its mother. By using this term "wet nurse," Paul was defining his relationship with the believers at Thessalonica.

In essence, Paul was saying, "Some of you came to know the Lord through my ministry, and I have nursed you as my own children. Some of you were won to the Lord by others, — they have entrusted you into my care, and I've nursed you as though you were my own. Regardless of whether you came to the Lord through my ministry or someone else's, you were all young in the Lord, and I treated you as though you were my children."

As a mother cherishes her children, Paul cherished the believers in Thessalonica. The word "cherisheth" is from the Greek word *thalpo*, which means to *warm*, *hold*, *cuddle*, *be tender toward*, and *nourish*. It carries the idea of holding an infant in one's arms and taking care of it — rocking it, helping it fall asleep, feeding it, and teaching it how to eat.

When a mother "cherishes" her child, she cradles that small child in her arms, feeds him, and makes him feel safe. By using this natural comparison, Paul was describing his attitude toward the church. He cared for them like spiritual infants that God had placed in his arms.

What tenderness we see here in the apostle Paul's attitude toward these young believers! Paul didn't see this church as just another new thing he was doing. Instead, he saw it as a new "baby" God had dropped into his life. Because Paul loved the Thessalonian church with his whole heart, he treated it tenderly, just as a mother would treat a brand-new baby. His responsibility was to nurse it, or feed it, and treat it with tremendous care.

We need to ask ourselves: How do we care for the new believers that God has brought across our path? Do we treat them with tenderness, as Paul treated the Thessalonians? I believe that today the Holy Spirit is imploring us to think carefully about this question. and to do all we can to help them get established firmly in the faith until they become strong. That's the heart of the Father, and we are called to demonstrate His heart through our lives. *What an honor!*

MY PRAYER FOR TODAY

Father, I want to be sensitive to the needs of new and younger believers. Help me to pay special attention to those who are new. Even if I didn't personally win them to Christ, help me to do whatever I can do to help them get on a strong path toward maturity if I see they are young, tender, and needy. Help me not to be self-absorbed with my personal interests but to put aside my own desires and respond to the needs of younger believers as a priority. Oh, Holy Spirit, help me to understand the great honor and privilege it is to minister to anyone, and especially to those who are young and new.

I pray this in Jesus' name!

MY CONFESSION FOR TODAY

I confess by faith that I am sensitive to the needs of new and young believers. I do not see it as a burden to minister to them. I am thankful for those who ministered to me, and I count it a great privilege and responsibility to return this blessing by ministering to others who are young and new in the faith. I declare that the love of God in my heart is growing and multiplying and my concern for others is increasing. None of this is possible without the work of the Holy Spirit. So, Holy Spirit, I thank You for helping me grow in this area of my life.

I declare this by faith in Jesus' name!

QUESTIONS FOR YOU TO CONSIDER

1. Is there a new or young believer whom God has recently brought across your path? What are you doing to help him or her get established in the faith?

2. When you were young in the Lord, who was the person who really paid attention to helping you get established in your faith? Have you ever taken time to personally thank that person for what they did for you?
3. Can you think of a Bible character who helped someone else get established in the faith? Who is that person?

AUGUST 18

Love the Church as Christ Loves the Church

So being affectionately desirous of you,
we were willing to have imparted unto you,
not the gospel of God only, but also our own souls,
because ye were dear unto us.
— 1 Thessalonians 2:8

In First Thessalonians 2:7, Paul wrote about the need for believers to tenderly care for each other, saying, "But we were gentle among you, even as a nurse cherisheth her children." Notice he chose the word "cherisheth" — the Greek word *thalpo* — to describe his feeling toward the believers in Thessalonica. He used this same word in Ephesians 5:25-29, so let's look at those verses to see further how the word *thalpo* carries the idea of *tender care* and *nourishment.*

In Ephesians 5:25-29, Paul wrote, "...Even as Christ also loved the church, and gave himself for it; that he might sanctify and cleanse it with the washing of water by the word, That he might present it to himself a glorious church, not having spot, or wrinkle, or any such thing; but that it should be holy and without blemish. So ought men to love their wives as their own bodies. He that loveth his wife loveth himself. For no man ever yet hated his own flesh; but *nourisheth* and *cherisheth* it, even as the Lord the church."

The word for "cherisheth" in this text is also *thalpo*, the same Greek word Paul used in First Thessalonians 2:7 to describe his ministry to the Thessalonian church. With this one little word *thalpo* ("cherisheth"), Paul shared with us the secret behind his success in ministry: *The way Jesus Christ treats the Church is the way we should treat it!*

Clearly, Jesus loves the Church. He pulls it close to His side and feeds it. He protects it. He nourishes and cuddles it like a tiny infant in His arms. The Church is the most priceless thing in the whole world to Jesus. He shed His blood to bring it forth. He sanctified it with His blood, and He's coming back for it one day.

As a result of His tender love for the Church, Jesus gave the Holy Spirit and the fivefold ministry gifts to minister to the Church. Jesus' heart is full of grace and mercy for His Church, and there are even times when He has pity on it. Jesus is patient with the Church when it makes mistakes, and He nourishes it so that it will grow.

Just as Jesus is full of tenderness for the Church, so the apostle Paul was tender and gentle toward the churches he was charged with ministering to. And we are to be tender and gentle toward those under our care too. That's why Paul said, "So being affectionately desirous of you, we were willing to have imparted unto you, not the gospel of God only, but also our own souls, because ye were dear unto us" (1 Thessalonians 2:8).

When Paul used the phrase "ye were dear unto us," he was conveying how important these church members were to him. In fact, the Greek word for "dear" is *agapetos*, which actually means *beloved*.

Very early in Greek history, this word was used to describe *the admiration that a man had for an object of beauty*. But it wasn't just any old art object. In fact, the idea behind this word was that the object was so intensely beautiful that it drew affection out of the man's heart. The onlooker or observer of this beautiful work of art was so taken by the object that he couldn't simply look at it — he *gazed* upon it and became affected by it. Deep admiration and appreciation came out of his heart because he was so moved by what his eyes beheld. He didn't have the words to adequately express all that he felt because of the beauty of this object.

Then in verse 9, Paul described what his love for this church looked like as he expressed it in his words and actions. He said, "For ye remember, brethren, our labour and travail: for labouring night and day, because we would not be chargeable unto any of you, we preached unto you the gospel of God" (1 Thessalonians 2:9).

As Paul wrote about his labors, travail, and the many sacrifices he had made to minister the Gospel to the Thessalonian believers, he was not doing it to make them feel badly or even to make himself look good. Paul was still baring his soul. He was showing them the "why" behind all his laboring and sacrificial giving. He was still revealing his motivation for ministry.

Apparently, no one else had ever made the kinds of phenomenal sacrifices for the Thessalonian saints Paul had made. That church had never before seen such an operation of God's love. This is why Paul's ministry there would stand out in their minds as such a great memory. Paul wrote, "...Remember, brethren, our labour and travail: for labouring night and day."

Let's look at the phrase *"our labour and travail."* The word "labor" is from the Greek word *kopos*, which refers to *intense physical labor* or *wearisome toil*. And the word "travail" is from the Greek word *mocthos*, which refers to *trouble*, *pain*, or *struggle to overcome difficulties*.

What was it that caused Paul to go through such labor and travail?" The answer is *love*. It was for *love* that Paul and his ministry team suffered these things and didn't quit or give up despite the *trouble*, *pain*, and *struggle to overcome difficulties* they experienced.

Do we love other believers the way Paul and his team loved them? Are we willing to undergo whatever is necessary to complete their faith and bring them to a higher relationship with Jesus? The truth is, one of our very highest priorities in life should be the building up of other brothers and sisters in the Lord. And if that isn't one of our greatest priorities today, let's ask the Lord to develop that desire in our hearts!

MY PRAYER FOR TODAY

Father God, I thank You for Your love which is already shed abroad in my heart by the Holy Spirit. I desire to deliberately give expression to that love more than ever before. I ask You to expand my own capacity to be filled with Your own undying love and passion for the Christian community that surrounds me. I pray that You would open the eyes of my understanding so I can comprehend how precious they are to You, and as a result, they would become so precious to me. Thank You for the example of Jesus, the apostle Paul, and others, who have gone before me and demonstrated how to love and sacrifice for others. I ask You to forgive me for the times I've been selfish and have held back on giving my time and effort to help others. Help me to grow in my personal understanding and acquaintance with Your great love for me, so that I can love others as You have loved me.

I pray this in Jesus' name!

MY CONFESSION FOR TODAY

I confess that God fills me with an undying love and passion for the Christian community. I comprehend how precious they are to God; therefore, they are precious to me. I devote myself to walk in love toward others and to willingly sacrifice for them. I repent for the times I've been selfish and have held back from giving my time and effort to help others. I commit from this moment forward to be less selfish and to be more giving, just as God gives Himself to us in the ways we need Him the most.

I declare this by faith in Jesus' name!

QUESTIONS FOR YOU TO CONSIDER

1. Can you think of anyone who made serious sacrifices for you to be able to advance as you were growing in your Christian faith? Were they extremely patient with you in your younger years? *Now isn't it time for you to do this for someone else?*
2. To whom much is given, much is required. In what way have you sought to honor that person's investment into your life and spiritual development?
3. What is the greatest sacrifice you've ever made for another believer? Who was that believer? What was the result of the sacrifice you made for him or her? How did your sacrifice change him or her? How did your sacrifice change you?

AUGUST 19

Nurturer and Mentor

As ye know how we exhorted and comforted
and charged every one of you,
as a father doth his children....
— 1 Thessalonians 2:11

In First Thessalonians 2:7, Paul described his relationship to the Church in terms of the relationship that exists between a mother and a child. But in verse 11, he paints a different side to his ministry toward the Church. Here, Paul is taking on the role of a *father* in their lives.

He wrote, "As ye know how we exhorted and comforted and charged every one of you, as a father doth his children..." (1 Thessalonians 2:11).

Paul was saying that you can't be a mother all the time in ministry. Sometimes you have to fill a *fatherly* role. He was implying that there is a time to *cuddle* and a time to *spank* — a time to *caress* and a time to *correct*. In a spiritual sense, Paul had taken on the roles of both mother *and* father in the lives of the Thessalonian believers.

In verse 11, we see how this fatherly ministry of Paul functioned. First, Paul "exhorted" the people. This is the Greek word *parakaleo*. Next, he "comforted" them, which is the Greek word *paramutheomai*. Finally, he "charged" them. The word "charged" is the Greek word *marturomai*. These three words mean three very different things, and they are all very important.

First, I want you to notice that the Greek words translated as "exhorted" and "comforted" both begin with the word *para*, which again indicates *relationship*. Although Paul was speaking here to an older group in the church, he was still by their side, continually exhorting them, walking with them, teaching them, and speaking to them. That was a part of Paul's ministry even for those who were more spiritually mature.

When Paul performed his fatherly ministry, he *exhorted*, and he *comforted*. The Greek word for "comfort" carries the idea that even if your father can't physically be at your side, you should still live in the godly manner he taught you.

Here, Paul was calling the believers to a lifestyle of responsibility. Now that some of them were grown, they were responsible to live the Christian life, or a life that was honoring and pleasing to God.

Finally, Paul "charged" them in verse 12: "That ye would walk worthy of God...." That is ultimately where Paul was taking the Thessalonian Christians. His deepest desire was to see them walk steadfastly with God. The word "walk" in Scripture always refers to *stability* or to *an ongoing relationship*. So Paul's primary purpose was to see these believers grow up in the things of God and to maintain their spiritual walk.

In verses 19 and 20, Paul summed up this great textbook chapter on ministry by concluding, "For what is our hope, or joy, or crown of rejoicing? Are not even ye in the presence of our Lord Jesus Christ at his coming? For ye are our glory and joy."

What can we conclude from Paul's writings in First Thessalonians 2? More than anything else, Paul desired a relationship with the Thessalonian church so that he could minister to them effectively. And the same will be true for us today: As we give our hearts completely to God, He will enable us to give our hearts to the people in our lives, and we'll experience powerful ministry among those to whom we are called (*see* 1 Thessalonians 1:5).

Nothing gave Paul more pleasure and delight than to see these young Christians in Thessalonica maturing in their relationship with the Lord. Paul's greatest glory and joy was the calling that God had placed on his life and the people God had placed in his care. That's a priority and motive we can emulate with confidence, and God will reward our own labors and bring rich increase both to us and to those under our spiritual care.

Are you ready to get started? If yes, ask the Holy Spirit to help open your eyes to those He is calling you to help strengthen and encourage in the faith. The Lord will give you wisdom and will empower you to extend His hand of love as you comfort, encourage, and strengthen them in their faith. *It will be one of the greatest joys of your life!*

MY PRAYER FOR TODAY

Father, my heart is stirred as I ponder the need for and importance of nurturing and mentoring young believers as they are growing up in the Lord. How thankful I am for the Christian leaders who mentored me and who helped me mature in the Lord Jesus Christ. I think of my pastor, who led me and corrected me at the right times in order to help me grow up. Holy Spirit, I ask You to help me and other Christians to take our place and strengthen and encourage young believers who need spiritual fathers and mothers in their lives.

I pray this in Jesus' name!

MY CONFESSION FOR TODAY

I confess I have wisdom from the Lord, and the Holy Spirit gives me the counsel I need to help young Christians mature in their relationship with the Lord. I find great joy in praying, teaching, serving, and helping others mature in the Lord. To see Christ formed in young believers is a priority. Therefore, I yield to the ministry of the Holy Spirit so that I can be a vessel for Him to fill and flow through in order to bless and strengthen those under my spiritual care.

I declare this by faith in Jesus' name!

QUESTIONS FOR YOU TO CONSIDER

1. How did you meet the person who became your spiritual mother or father? In what ways did that person influence you the most?
2. In whose life are you serving such a role right now? What individuals are you helping to grow — loving them, correcting them, and helping them to develop in their faith?
3. Can you think of a few specific ways you can comfort, exhort, or strengthen the faith of the people in your life? What steps can you take today to start implementing these ideas in your relationships?

AUGUST 20

Deflation and Inflation

Therefore take no thought, saying,
What shall we eat? or, What shall we drink?
or, Wherewithal shall we be clothed?
...For your heavenly Father knoweth
that ye have need of all these things.
But seek ye first the kingdom of God,
and his righteousness; and all these things
shall be added unto you.
— Matthew 6:31-33

On the day our family moved to the Soviet Union, we settled into our rented house and went to bed for some much-needed rest. When we awoke the next morning, we heard a news report that prices on all basic food commodities had soared *500 percent* during the night-time — the *very day* after we arrived! Not only that, but all the 50-ruble notes had been declared void, so if you had 50-ruble notes, you simply possessed pieces of paper that held no value whatsoever.

Unfortunately, on the day our family arrived, we also exchanged 1,000 U.S. dollars for rubles so we would have the currency of the land to get us started living in that part of the world. And the person who performed that transaction had exchanged our $1,000 *exclusively into stacks of 50-ruble notes — which were now worthless*!

In addition, stores were depleted of the most basic items, and pharmacies were completely empty. I mean, there was *nothing* at all on those shelves. It was also rare to find a gas station that had any gasoline to purchase. The entire infrastructure of the Soviet Union had fallen apart.

People were fearful that they would not be able to find bread. Therefore, when bread was finally shipped to our town, lines quickly formed all the way around the block. Basic products, such as flour, sugar, milk, and eggs, could only be purchased in small, limited quantities — and *only* if people had ration coupons that were allotted to them by the government. But ration coupons were given to citizens only, so our family wasn't able to obtain them.

Yet through all this initial hardship and shock, God made a way for us to have everything we needed.

Admittedly, some of those earliest days were spent like scavenger hunts — looking for a gas station that actually had gasoline, searching for basic food items, and hunting down necessary paper products such as toilet paper. We faced *many days* when currency shops had no rubles to exchange. And if we had no rubles, we couldn't buy products even if we *could* find them. Then once we'd find rubles, after losing $1,000 in the exchange market, we would only exchange small amounts of dollars to avoid another hardship like that first one. It was a precarious time that required an increased sensitivity to the Spirit of God to know when and how to act just to carry out basic business from day to day.

Today you may not be living in the dire circumstances we endured when we first moved to the USSR. But it's a fact that people are facing difficult financial times all over the world. Products are more expensive than they used to be, and it isn't certain which way the economy is headed. Perhaps you are also feeling the brunt of this financial volatility. But rather than let a spirit of fear control you, this is the time for you to stand strong on Jesus' teaching in Matthew 6:31-33.

Throughout the years of our own lives and ministry, there have been many times when Denise and I have not known how we were going to pay for what God was asking us to do. Yet we have learned that if we will seek the Kingdom of God first, as Jesus taught us, everything else will come into place as needed.

During those early days of our life in the former USSR — and every time God has asked us to do something bigger than our bank account could pay for — we learned to reflect on Jesus' teaching in Matthew 6 where He taught us about trusting God in times of need. Jesus said, "Therefore take no thought, saying, What shall we eat? or, What shall we drink? or, Wherewithal shall we be clothed.... For your heavenly Father knoweth that ye have need of all these things. But seek ye first the kingdom of God and his righteousness; and all these things shall be added unto you" (Matthew 6:31-33).

Notice Jesus said, "Therefore take *no thought....*" Pay close attention, for these words "no thought" are very important for you and me. The word "thought" is preceded by a *negative imperative*, which means this is a *command* of Jesus *not* to do something. The word "thought" is the Greek word *merimnao*. It denotes *anxiety, care, concern*, or *worry* — or it depicts a person who is *deeply troubled*. This person is *worrying* about how his basic needs will be met.

By using a *negative imperative* with the word *merimnao*, Jesus was literally saying, "*Don't worry*, for your Heavenly Father knows that you have need of these things."

I can personally testify that God has been faithful in our lives and ministry from the very beginning to this present moment. Even when Denise and I didn't know how our most basic needs would be met when we first moved to the USSR, God was faithful and on time to meet every one of those needs. And through times when God has required us to take monumental steps of faith that were beyond our financial capabilities, He has caused the necessary finances to come in, doing for us by His Spirit what we could not do for ourselves.

And let me also tell you that fretting, worrying, and being troubled never added one cent toward meeting our need or helped take us further toward our goals. That doesn't mean I wasn't *tempted* at times to fret or feel worried. But I have learned over the years that God is well aware of every need we face and of every cent that is required. And He is *far* ahead of us — working in ways we can't even imagine — to make sure everything we need comes to us on time.

In Matthew 6:33, Jesus said, "Seek ye first the kingdom of God and his righteousness; and all these things shall be added unto you." My son Philip Renner paraphrases it this way: *"Put God first, and everything else will come your way!"* All I can say to that is *amen*, as that is *exactly* the teaching Jesus was trying to drive into our hearts and minds when He spoke those words!

What about you today? Are you straining and worrying over things you can't change or do anything about? Are you aware that God is knowledgeable of your situation? How is worrying going to help you change one thing for the better? It won't! That's why Jesus commanded you, "*Don't worry*, for your heavenly Father knows you have need of these things."

Today I encourage you to cast your burdens, troubles, worries, and cares on the Lord — and to seek Him and His Kingdom first, above all else. Then watch as He provides everything that you've been tempted to worry and fret about obtaining. God is faithful to provide for His own. He will be faithful to provide everything you need as you trust wholly in Him!

MY PRAYER FOR TODAY

Father, as I reflect on my life, the truth is that You have been faithful to me from the very beginning. I repent for every time I yielded to the temptation to worry and fret instead of trusting You. Father, I ask You to please help me grow up and mature in this area of my life. I have no reason to ever doubt You, for You have always been faithful to me. Help me remember Your faithfulness rather than focus on the needs that seem so large and insurmountable. Your name is Faithful — and You will be faithful to me now and always!

I pray this in Jesus' name!

MY CONFESSION FOR TODAY

I confess that I do not worry about God's provision for my life. God has always been faithful to me, and He always will be faithful. Faithful is one of His names. He will always sustain all those who trust in Him and cast their burden on Him. Likewise, God will sustain me and help me. Even if my eyes cannot see the way, I know He is going to do it. Everything that I see is subject to change. Therefore, I focus my attention on the unchanging Word and the faithful character of God. I cast my burden on Him, and I trust Him to meet the needs of my life and to help me do the large tasks He has commissioned me to do!

I declare this by faith in Jesus' name!

QUESTIONS FOR YOU TO CONSIDER

1. Can you think of a time when you didn't know how your needs were going to be met? Were you tempted to worry and fret? Did the worrying and fretting help you — or just send you into a tailspin of more worrying and fretting? In the end, what happened? Was God faithful to meet your needs?
2. Name one specific time when you thought you wouldn't make it, but then God miraculously provided what you needed. Did you stop to thank Him for His provision? Have you ever shared it with anyone else in order to encourage that person in the situation he or she is facing?
3. I encourage you to read Psalm 103. Then ask yourself, What are the many ways these verses have been manifested in my life as the Lord has shown His goodness and faithfulness to me?

AUGUST 21

The Experience of a Lifetime!

He that findeth his life shall lose it:
and he that loseth his life
for my sake shall find it.
— Matthew 10:39

When our family first arrived in the former USSR, we disembarked the airplane to find Soviet soldiers standing all around the landing strip with machine guns in arm — *a brand-new sight for our family*! Those soldiers tried to rush us along to leave the runway area and get inside the terminal. But I had predetermined that when we landed, the first thing we were going to do was drop to our knees, kiss the ground, and ask God to put a love in our hearts for this new homeland where He had called us.

With soldiers watching very cautiously, I led my family in dropping to our knees. We joined hands and leaned down together to literally kiss the ground! Then I led us in a prayer of committal for protection and provision. And I earnestly asked God to put a love in our hearts for this new part of the world and the people who lived here.

At that time, Denise and I thought we would be living here for a one-year period. Nevertheless, we intended to pour ourselves into the work for that span of time, and we desired to be filled by God in our hearts for these precious souls. So we kissed the ground and prayed.

When we finally stood to our feet, those soldiers with machine guns had nearly encircled us. I'm sure they had never seen anything like that before. Using their guns to point the way, they directed us toward the terminal, and we understood that it was time for us to get moving. But that moment of bowing to the ground on our knees in prayer was such a divine moment for our family. We were accepting God's call and asking for His favor to do what He had commissioned us to do with power and grace.

Inside the airport, the luggage belts were broken, so suitcases and boxes were being thrown upward through a hole in the floor into the luggage area. We had brought suitcases plus 32 boxes, many of which were filled with breakable items. So I was running around as quickly as I could to try to catch our items as they were being tossed into the air.

When we were finally allowed to leave the airport, we were escorted to a decrepit van, and a driver drove us over bumpy, broken roads to a grey-looking, neglected little town that would be our first home in the USSR. As we unloaded our luggage and the boxes from the vehicle and carried everything into the house, we discovered the house that had been provided for us had no heat — and this was during a *very* cold Russian winter. We were freezing in that ice-cold house! We were so cold during those first nights, until the heat finally came on, that all five of us crammed into one tiny bed to try to stay warm.

As I look back on it, I realize that if we had not dropped to our knees immediately and surrendered our lives to this new place, we could have become quickly discouraged. But instead, we found each challenge invigorating and fun. When we discovered the grocery stores were void of food and that finding basic necessities would be a serious challenge, we didn't let it discourage us. Instead, every day turned into an adventurous scavenger hunt! God amazingly filled our hearts with rejoicing, and every difficulty became an opportunity for another joy-filled experience.

Our sons didn't groan or complain that life was difficult, and Denise and I were not sorry that we had led our family to this part of the world. Although we faced serious challenges, we decided to make each one a fun learning experience. As a result, we fell in love with all of it — with the people, the land, and even the problems and the challenges. That moment of kissing the ground and consecrating this new season of our lives to the Father on the runway had really done something in our hearts. Regardless of how broken and neglected everything around us seemed to be, we fell in love with that country and the people who lived there.

Within two months, we realized that God had given us a *life commitment* to this part of the world, not a simple one-year engagement. At the time of this writing, we have lived in the former Soviet Union multiple decades and have seen the Holy Spirit's supernatural fruit as thousands have received Christ, grown in the Spirit, and found their places in local churches — many of which we helped start. *It has been the experience of a lifetime*! And our sons — now full-grown men with families of their own — grew up experiencing a book of Acts kind of childhood by living in this spiritual environment.

Especially at the beginning, we could have tucked our tails and run back home to the United States because even just basic living in the former USSR was extremely challenging. But because we had surrendered to God — and had given Him our all to do what He wanted with our lives in that part of the world — what would have been hard and burdensome became a daily adventure that continues to enrich our lives today.

I want to ask you today: Have you surrendered to what God has called *you* to do?

Let me remind you of the words of Jesus in the second half of Matthew 10:39: "...He that loseth his life for my sake shall find it." Pay close attention to these words, for they are so very important if you really want to experience God's fullness during your life journey.

The word "loseth" was translated from the Greek word *apollumi*, which literally means *to release* — as to release one's rights to something. It is the picture of the *full surrender* of one's life. But the key is not just forfeiting your own dreams and desires, but rather doing it "for Jesus' sake."

At the time God called my family to the Soviet Union, I had personal dreams of what I wanted to accomplish through our ministry in the United States. But God called me to lay that down — that is, to *release* it. He beckoned me to surrender my dream for His *greater* dream for my life — and to do it for His sake.

To be honest, I couldn't begin to imagine how great a dream and life God had planned for me. I didn't understand it. All I knew was that the Spirit of God was asking me *to release* my own preconceived dream and to follow Him into the unknown plan He had for my life.

Now I understand that if I had refused to release my own dream and had rejected God's call to fulfill *His* dream, I would have missed the amazing adventure He had not only for me, but also for our whole family and the millions of lives He has touched as a result of our obedience. But because I released my plans for Jesus' sake and for *His* purposes, we found something far greater than anything we had ever dreamed or imagined.

Jesus promised, "...He that loseth his life for my sake shall *find* it." The word "find" is the Greek word *eurisko*, which means *to find* or *to discover*, and it is where we get the word *eureka!* This word pictures the euphoric feeling a person experiences when he discovers something magnificent. His heart and soul, and perhaps even his mouth, exclaim, *"Eureka!"* It is the jubilant expression of one who shouts out, *"I found it!"*

For multiple decades, my heart has been exclaiming, *"Eureka!"* regarding this treasured call God has placed on our lives to reach the Russian-speaking peoples of this part of the world. When I think of what life would be like if we had rejected the Lord's call and simply stayed with our ministry in the U.S., it nearly breaks my heart. We would have missed the amazing adventure that God had planned for our lives.

By asking us to release or surrender — *apollumi* — our dreams to Him, He was never trying to take something from us; He wanted to give us something wonderful. But to receive what He desired to give, we first had to *release* what we were holding on to and *surrender* to what He wanted to do in and through us. As a result of trusting Him and doing what He asked — instead of stubbornly holding on to what *we* wanted to do — God has gloriously allowed us to be part of one of the greatest missions epochs in the history of the Church.

When this all started, I didn't understand what exactly Jesus had in mind for us. All I knew was that He wanted me to release my own plans and surrender to *His* plan for our lives. Ever since we yielded and obeyed, we've been rejoicing, even in hard times! What a grand and glorious adventure God had in store for us, and I'm so thankful we didn't miss it!

What about you? What is God asking you to release so He can give you something far greater? I assure you that God is not trying to deprive you of anything. He wants to give you something bigger and better than your imagination could ever conceive. He simply needs your agreement to release your own ideas and to surrender to what He has waiting for you. Jesus Himself said, "… He that loseth his life for my sake, shall *find* it." When you step out of your own realm into Jesus' realm of possibilities, you'll find yourself forever grateful that He gave you the courage to say yes when His call to "lose," or surrender, your life came to you!

MY PRAYER FOR TODAY

Father, I don't want to hold on to my life and, as a result, miss the great adventure You have planned for me and my family. Forgive me for not trusting You — and help me put all fear and doubt aside as I "kiss the ground" of my calling. Help me allow Your power and love to sink deep into my heart for what You are asking me to do. I repent for hesitating and holding back out of a sense of self-preservation and a fear of the unknown. Today I fully surrender my life and my future to You.

I pray this in Jesus' name!

MY CONFESSION FOR TODAY

I confess that I will not hold back on the Lord any longer. Whatever He wants me to do, that is what I will do. In the past, fear of an uncertain future has hindered me, but now I know that God has only a wonderful adventure in store for me and my family. I rebuke the spirit of fear that has restrained me, and I put my trust fully in the Lord as I step forward by faith to kiss the ground of God's calling on my life. I declare that God will put a deep-seated love in my heart for what He has called me to do. I'll never look back in regret but will only rejoice that I finally and fully surrendered to the call with which He has entrusted to me.

I declare this by faith in Jesus' name!

QUESTIONS FOR YOU TO CONSIDER

1. Denise and I made a deliberate choice to fully surrender to the call of God on our lives in the former USSR. It was a big decision and a huge step of surrender,

but it was *essential* in order for us to begin the exciting journey God had planned for us and our family. Have you fully yielded to the call of God on *your* life, or is there something holding you back? If there is something hindering your full surrender, what are you going to do about it?

2. Have you been honest with God about your feelings — your fears, your concerns, and your questions — regarding this step of faith He is asking you to take? If you'll open your heart and cast your cares on Him, the Father promises to lift that burden and give you peace. Why don't you stop right now, and for the next few minutes, cast all of your cares and concerns onto Jesus? Let Him give you His peace that surpasses all natural understanding (*see* Philippians 4:7)!
3. Do you actually think Jesus would lead you where He wouldn't provide for you? If you're worried about provision, put that worry away once and for all — for where God calls, He also provides!

AUGUST 22

Why Do People Sometimes Collapse in the Presence of God?

And when I [John] saw him [Christ],
I fell at his feet as dead....
— Revelation 1:17

Over my years of serving God, I have noticed that often when people have encounters with God, they physically fall. Sometimes they fall forward, and at other times they fall backward. Still at other times, they simply collapse onto the ground. I have seen this in many meetings — and I experienced it as a young man. I can tell you, the experience was *real.*

My experience occurred the first time I ventured out from my Baptist church and attended a Pentecostal type of service. Just prior to that, I had been released from the hospital, where I had been diagnosed with a kidney condition — one that I was born with — that was very serious. It was so serious that to try to correct it required surgery that was considered life-threatening. When the man praying for the sick in this Pentecostal meeting invited the sick to come forward, I went to the front to be prayed for, not having any idea what would happen.

When the minister laid his finger on my forehead, I felt the power of God come on me. My legs collapsed out from under me, and I crumpled to the floor. I could feel the power of God radiating from one end of my body to the other end.

When I finally stood to my feet, I had been completely healed of the condition. That healing was later verified by my physician — and in the decades since that event occurred, I have *never* had a reoccurrence of that medical condition. I was *supernaturally* and *permanently* healed by the power of the Holy Spirit when I fell to the floor.

The Old and New Testaments tell of those who fell to the ground when they encountered the strong presence of God.

- Genesis 17:3 records that Abram *collapsed* when God spoke to him.
- Joshua 5:14,15 tells us that Joshua *collapsed* when he experienced the presence of the Lord.
- Ezekiel 1:28 and 3:23 say that Ezekiel *collapsed* when the glory of the Lord appeared to him.
- Daniel 8:17 and 10:15 state that Daniel *collapsed* on the ground when he encountered the glory of God.
- Matthew 17:6 records that when God's glory was manifested to *Peter, James, and John*, all three of these men *collapsed* to the ground.
- Acts 9:4 and 26:14 reveal that Paul *collapsed* to the earth when he saw Christ on the road to Damascus.
- Revelation 1:17 tells that the apostle John *collapsed* at the feet of Jesus at the beginning of his vision on the island of Patmos.

Let's look at John's experience on the island of Patmos. Revelation 1:17 says, "And when I [John] saw him [Christ], I fell at his feet as dead...." The word "fell" is from the Greek word *pipto*, which means *to fall from an upright position*. It is used occasionally to describe those who fall in battle — which, of course, could mean a falling forward or backward or a crumpling to the ground. In John's case, he fell at Jesus' feet.

Revelation 1:17 says that John fell as one "dead." The word "dead" is the Greek word *nekros*, which is the word for a *corpse*. In other words, in one split second, it seemed that all the life had gone out of him, and he *crumpled forward* (*pipto*) at the feet of Jesus. As it is with many cases in which people experience God's glory, John's legs buckled under him and the strength was drained from his body as he fell in the presence of God.

So if you hear of someone crumpling to the floor in the presence of God, don't be too surprised. There are a lot of scriptural examples for people falling or collapsing when they come into contact with God's supernatural power. I advise you to look at each of the scriptural examples I just shared and search this out for yourself. This "falling" may not be a common event in your church, but it has scriptural precedence, and it still happens. As I noted, it has undeniably happened to me.

If you're standing in a prayer line to receive prayer, and you feel the strength go from you — surrender to it and let the Holy Spirit perform a divine operation. This may even happen in the privacy of your own home.

For me, the experience of collapsing in God's presence was *real*, and it resulted in a permanent healing in my body. God has used such moments in other people's lives to remove bitterness, hardness of heart, and to perform all kinds of "spiritual surgeries."

Who can guess what is happening in the heart, soul, or body of a person when he or she experiences this tangible touch of the Holy Spirit? Perhaps it is an operation of God's power to do something in the person that couldn't be dealt with any other way.

If this experience has never happened to you, just tell God today that you are willing for Him to work in your life any way He sees fit. And if that means you will one day have a supernatural encounter with His power that is too strong for you to remain upright, just say, "Amen, Lord! I'm hungry to receive more of You — whatever that means and whatever that looks like in every situation!"

MY PRAYER FOR TODAY

Father, I know that You love me deeply and that Your love for me is not proven by physical manifestations such as falling down under the power of the Holy Spirit. But I want to thank You for the times I have come into contact with Your strong presence to such an extent that I could physically feel the result of it. I open my heart for You to move in my life in any way that You wish — and I ask You to forgive me for being skeptical in the past when I've heard of such experiences in others and have doubted it. From this moment onward, I am open for You to make Yourself known to me in any way You desire.

I pray this in Jesus' name!

MY CONFESSION FOR TODAY

I confess that I experience the power of God in my life and that my heart and my mind are open to experiencing His presence in whatever way He wishes to manifest Himself to me. I am willing to be changed by the power of God, regardless of whether I remain on my feet or lie on the floor. I am open to the Holy Spirit, and I desire to yield fully to His divine operation inside me. I long for it; I pray for it; and I claim it!

I declare this by faith in Jesus' name!

QUESTIONS FOR YOU TO CONSIDER

1. Have you ever known a person who came into such strong contact with the power of God that he or she crumbled to the floor as a result? Who was that person? Why don't you ask that individual to tell you about the spiritual significance of his or her experience?

2. Can you think of any other examples from the Old or New Testament in which individuals fell when they came into the strong presence of God?
3. Has this experience of falling under the power of God ever happened to you? If yes, how did it affect you? Do you know what God imparted to you or said during that encounter with Him?

AUGUST 23

A Promise to Those Who Are Overcoming

...To him that overcometh will I
give to eat of the hidden manna....
— Revelation 2:17

Right now you may feel that insurmountable odds are arrayed against you. However, let me assure you that you are not the first person to feel this way. If you stay in faith and refuse to budge, it's only a matter of time until you will outlast the attacks of your enemy the devil. This is God's promise to you as a believer! Furthermore, if you are steadfastly committed to overcome, Christ promises special supernatural nourishment for the battle. That's what I want to talk to you about today — *supernatural nourishment for those who are overcomers*!

This subject is so rich that it will take two *Sparkling Gems* for me to cover it fully, so stay with me today and tomorrow on this subject. Believe me, if you need strength in the midst of the fight of faith — whether it is *spiritual, physical, mental*, or *emotional* — God has supernatural nourishment that He will provide you. All He requires is that you draw near to His table to feed on the supernatural sustenance He longs to give you.

There is no better way for me to begin this subject than to go right to the words of Christ in Revelation 2:17. In that verse, Jesus addressed believers who were facing many obstacles that they needed to overcome — including unsaved relatives, friends, associates, and coworkers who didn't understand their new faith and who antagonized them for being different. He was *very* aware of the extreme difficulties they were facing — just as He is aware of the challenges faced by every believer in every age, including your own. To each believer who stands fast in the faith and refuses to give up, Jesus promises, "To him that overcometh will I give to eat of the hidden manna...."

Today I want us to look at what it means to "overcome." The word "overcometh" comes from the Greek word *nikao*. It refers to *a victor*, *a champion*, or *one who possesses some type of superiority*, and it can be translated *to conquer*, *to defeat*, *to master*, *to overcome*, *to overwhelm*, *to surpass*, or *to be victorious.* This word was often used in Greek literature to portray athletes who had mastered their sport and ultimately reigned supreme as champions in the games. It could also describe a military victory of one foe against the other.

The word *nikao* denotes a complete victory over the opposition that Christians were facing on all fronts. By using this word, Jesus was calling upon those early believers to rise up like a mighty spiritual army to defeat the enemies that threatened them on every side.

Today Jesus is calling *you* to rise up like a mighty warrior as well! And He isn't just calling you to do it — He provides the strength you need to do it phenomenally.

Winning the victory in a battle requires the greatest level of commitment and determination. This is true in natural war, and it is true in the spiritual realm. In order to receive an overcomer's reward, the early believers whom Jesus addressed in Revelation 2:17 had to pay the price to overcome.

It is also important to note that the tense of the Greek word translated "overcometh" in this verse speaks of *a continuous action.* It isn't acceptable to win a single battle but then lose the war because of a slack, unguarded attitude. Christ was calling on believers to continuously *remain* victorious. He was admonishing them, as He does each of His children up to the present day, *to be permanently and consistently undeterred in their efforts to overcome and to obtain a lasting victory over sin in their lives.*

Jesus still calls on us all to be *overcomers.* This is imperative for us to understand. It is to be our continual and unrelenting goal to maintain our victorious stance in every possible sphere of life as long as we are on this earth. And for us who are in the process of overcoming — when it seems that we've given all we have and that no more strength remains — Christ promises to nourish us with "manna."

To understand the special significance of this imagery, it is necessary to recall what is known about manna from the Old Testament. That is what we will look at in tomorrow's *Sparkling Gem.* Today I want to ask you: *What obstacles are you facing right now that Christ is urging you to overcome?* Is it a personal challenge that no one knows about but the Lord? Is it a family matter, job problem, financial difficulty, health issue, or relational issue? Is it something you are fighting in your mind? Or are you in the process of overcoming a sin or habit that has encumbered your life for a long time?

Regardless of the obstacle that challenges you, turn to Jesus Christ! He overcame everything in life, and He understands every fight and foe you face. By His Spirit, He will empower you to stand strong until the fight is won. Not only that, but He will give you the fortitude to maintain the victory once it has been achieved. He's not interested in you merely winning a skirmish; He wants you to win the final victory and *maintain* that victory once it is achieved. And as you will see in tomorrow's *Sparkling Gem,* if you'll make the decision to overcome, He'll provide supernatural nourishment to keep you strong all along the way!

MY PRAYER FOR TODAY

Father, You are calling me to live in overwhelming victory. Through You, I can be a conqueror who gains the mastery over all opposition. Forgive me for the times I focused more on the struggle opposing me than on the victory You have already won for me. I am a victor, not a victim. I realize that You want me to see myself as a victor, a champion, one who has completely defeated my enemies. You have made provision for me to continuously maintain that victory in my life through the Holy Spirit. I make an intentional decision to draw upon Your power in me. I'm willing and ready to jump in the fight and finish it to the end in the strength of Your might!

I prayer this in Jesus' name!

MY CONFESSION FOR TODAY

I confess that Christ calls me to overcome, and He gives me the power to do it. He would not ask me to do something I cannot do. But I can overcome only through the mighty power of the Holy Spirit, so I declare that I yield to the Person of the Holy Spirit who indwells me. I am a willing vessel for the Holy Spirit to release His supernatural power through me. He causes me to rise above my difficulties. His power enables me to put my foot on the enemy's neck and command him to back down. The enemies I face hear my voice of authority and see my commitment — and as a result, they back off from their attack, because greater is He that is in me than he that is in the world!

I declare this by faith in Jesus' name!

QUESTIONS FOR YOU TO CONSIDER

1. What immediately comes to mind as the big issue you are trying to overcome in your life right now? Is there an area in your life you've identified as an issue you need to focus on? Now that you've identified that issue, what specifically are you going to do about it?
2. What issues that used to hamper your life have you already overcome? I'm talking serious issues from the past that are no longer a concern to you today. Don't forget those victories! They will encourage you as you focus your faith on overcoming the current obstacles you're facing.
3. Is there any area of your life in which you gained victory but let it slip away from you over a period of time? What are you going to do to retake that area of your life and then sustain that victory from this time forward?

Regardless of the obstacle that challenges you,
turn to Jesus Christ! By His Spirit, He will empower you
to stand strong until the fight is won.

AUGUST 24

A Superabundant Supply of Heavenly Angels' Food

To him that overcometh will I
give to eat of the hidden manna....
— Revelation 2:17

In yesterday's *Sparkling Gem*, we saw that Jesus expects us to *overcome*. And this "overcoming" is not just a one-time event. He has given us the power and the authority to *consistently maintain* victory in the areas where we have experienced victory through His grace.

To those of us who are currently in the process of overcoming and who need sustenance to keep us strong in battle, Christ promised "manna" as nourishment to continually strengthen us. In Revelation 2:17, He said, "To him that overcometh will I give to eat of the hidden manna...." Let's look at this "manna" to understand exactly what Christ promised us and *how much* of that divine supply He is willing to provide to keep us strong along the way as a reward for our obedience.

To understand manna, we must return to the Old Testament book of Exodus, where it is recorded that manna first appeared. Approximately two months after the Israelites left Egypt, their food stores began to run low and supplies were rationed. God told Moses, "Behold, I will rain bread from heaven for you..." (Exodus 16:4). The word "bread" in the Old Testament Greek *Septuagint* is the word *man hu*, or *manna*, an unusual word that had never been used before. It is a Greek word that describes a heavenly provision of supernatural sustenance *like bread*.

When that "manna" first appeared on the ground, no one knew what it was, how it originated, or how God provided it. Every time the Israelites took it in their hands and lifted it to their mouths, they were partaking of a divine phenomenon with no natural explanation. God graciously provided supernatural sustenance to sustain them in their time of need. Certainly they had other forms of food, but there was something so supernatural in this manna that it supplied what no natural food could provide. *It was a supernatural substance that had the ability to meet whatever need was present.*

These qualities also describe the supernatural sustenance God provides for us today. We don't always know how He imparts His divine supply to us, but we are thankful when He does. With each touch of His hand on our spirits, bodies, and minds, we are strengthened, refilled, and replenished. It is supernatural provision! And God superabundantly supplies whatever we need. Our part is to draw near to His table, pull up a chair, and open our hearts to Him. As we do, God serves us a veritable *feast* of His power!

Let's look again at the manna God so amply supplied to His people under the Old Covenant. Psalm 78:23-25 records that God "...opened the doors of heaven, and had rained down manna upon them to eat and...man did eat angels' food...." The psalmist told us several important truths about this supernatural provision:

- The doors of Heaven were opened (v. 23).
- When the doors were opened, manna rained upon them (v. 24).
- Manna was the food of angels (v. 25).

First, the psalmist wrote that when the manna fell, the "doors of heaven" were opened. This phrase "doors of heaven" refers to a heavenly portal that opens at God's command. The first mention of it in Scripture is in Genesis 7:11, where the Bible says that "...the *windows* of heaven were opened..." and rain started *falling*. That phrase "windows of heaven" is a reference to the same portal referred to as the "*doors* of heaven" in Psalm 78:23. In fact, so much rain fell through this portal over the course of 40 days and nights that Genesis 7:19 records, "And the waters prevailed exceedingly upon the earth; and all the high hills, that were under the whole heaven, were covered."

Second, the psalmist recorded in Psalm 78:24 that when this manna began falling, it "rained down." This shows that when Heaven's portal opens, whatever comes through does so in *super-abundant* measures.

Let me refer to rabbinical literature for a moment. That literature asserts that manna fell in the wilderness each day in such abundance that one day's supply of manna would have been enough to feed the children of Israel for 2,000 years!

However, despite this overabundance, God forbade the Israelites to take more than one day's supply per person except in the case of the Sabbath, in which case they were allowed to collect two days at once in order to avoid breaking the Sabbath laws. Each person was limited to an *omer*, or approximately six to seven pints, which was gathered each morning. If anyone gathered more than what God prescribed, the extra became filled with maggots.

This was doubtlessly a great test of obedience for many people, since the human tendency would have been to hoard manna just in case it didn't fall again. However, hoarding manna would have caused the Israelites to trust in their *supply* rather than trust in *the God who supplies.* By gathering only a single day's ration, it meant that they had to trust God anew for His faithful provision each day.

It is impossible to know exactly how much manna came pouring through that portal during those 40 years, but one can make a rough estimate. If the Israelites numbered approximately 3,000,000 people, as many Bible scholars believe, it is estimated that they needed *4,500 tons* of manna every day. If they gathered 4,500 tons a day every day for 40 years, that means an estimated *65,700,000 tons* of manna supernaturally appeared on the ground over that period of time.

However, for the children of Israel, this miracle was an everyday event that occurred for 40 years. In fact, an entire generation of young children was born during that time period who grew up thinking it was *normal* for 4,500 tons of manna to appear each morning out of thin air (*see* Exodus 16:35)!

God instructed the children of Israel not to hoard manna, but rather to trust Him to provide them with the sustenance they needed each day. The manna that rained daily in the desert was an ever-present reminder that God was faithful and would not lead them on a path that lacked His provision.

Likewise, we need to trust that God will touch us *every day* with the power and substance we need to be strong overcomers! He simply needs our availability. He is willing to give, but He needs hungry *takers*!

We read from Psalm 78 that, first, the "doors of heaven" were opened when all that manna fell. Then, second, the psalmist says the manna "rained down." When Heaven's portal opens, whatever falls through it does so *superabundantly*.

Third, the psalmist recorded that manna was "angels' food" (*see* v. 25), which explains the extraordinary effect it had upon those who ate it. Theologian Albert Barnes noted that manna was "...food so directly and manifestly from heaven that it might be supposed to be the same kind that was eaten there, and that had now been sent down by a special miracle for man; food so delicate and so free from the ordinary coarse properties of food, that it might be supposed to be such as angels feed on."[7]

In order for us to do what God asks us to do, we must regularly eat of His table and receive of His grace. He provided manna to sustain His people in the wilderness. In the same way, Jesus promises divine sustenance to believers who overcome. Jesus' offer of "manna" in Revelation 2:17 to those who overcome was a declaration to believers throughout the ages that He provides nourishment in times of need and that at His table, the food never runs out.

There is a divine supply of provision for us — a supernatural, heavenly touch — that will replenish and strengthen us, enabling us to overcome the most difficult circumstances. But we must continually draw near to His table and eat the heavenly "bread" He has set before us.

Jesus promises to provide *spiritual provision* and *replenishment* to every one of us who will come to His table with faith to receive. He is sufficient to provide the spiritual refreshment and nutrients needed to strengthen us through tough times to accomplish our assignment. God's grace is available to us, just as daily manna had been available to the children of Israel during their trek across the desert. If they will but come to His table, Christ will provide everything they need.

When Christ offered "manna" to these believers, He was not referring to a mere one-time taste of heavenly power. Rather, He was offering them a consistent supply of spiritual nourishment that would enable them to forge ahead, regardless of the opposition. And no matter what they faced, that supernatural sustenance would empower them to outlast the challenges that surrounded them.

---

[7] Albert Barnes, *Notes on the Bible* (Blackie & Son, London, 1884-85; Reprinted by Baker Books, 1996), Psalm 78:25.

Just as manna was provided to sustain God's people in the wilderness, He has divine provision for you today and every day! If you will draw near to His table and eat the heavenly bread He has set before you, Christ will personally provide the manna you need — *a divine touch* — to strengthen and replenish your spirit so you can finish your race and complete your divine assignment. *He will provide the manna you need to stay strong for the journey!*

Are you ready to pull up your chair to God's table and let Him set a feast of heavenly bread before you that will fill you with a fresh supply of His awesome power? God is willing to give you this divine sustenance every single day, but you must be willing to proactively *come* to His table to take in this strengthening supply!

MY PRAYER FOR TODAY

Heavenly Father, I am thrilled to know that You are so concerned about my well-being. How can I do anything but praise and thank You? You have demonstrated that You care so much for me that You would provide me with the daily bread I need to keep my life strong. Today I make the decision to draw near to Your table and to eat of the heavenly bread that You have set before me — bread that never runs out! Your supernatural strength is my sustenance. I partake of Your presence as my necessary food. You have called me to overcome, and Your sustaining touch keeps me strong in the battle. I know that as You strengthen me with Your might, I will be continually replenished, sustained in times of difficulty, and enabled to move obstacles out of my way.

I pray this in Jesus' name!

MY CONFESSION FOR TODAY

I confess that God provides the spiritual nourishment that I need to overcome the obstacles and difficulties that try to hinder me in life. Each day as I consciously walk with an awareness of God's presence within me, I am replenished, strengthened, and enabled to conquer any foe that shows up along the way. God's power touches me physically, spiritually, and emotionally and fills up those areas that have been depleted due to a long struggle. God's grace is available to me every day just as daily manna was available to the children of Israel during their trek across the desert. The Lord spreads a table before me even in the presence of my enemies. When I come to His table, Christ provides everything I need. With God's daily touch on my life, I am revived, refreshed, and ready to continue the fight until I can shout, "Amen! The victory has manifested because the battle was already won!"

I declare this by faith in Jesus' name!

QUESTIONS FOR YOU TO CONSIDER

1. How does God regularly refill and replenish you to keep you strong for whatever fight you are engaging? Can you explain that replenishing process?
2. How often do you come to God's table? Are you taking in this *Bread of Heaven* every day? How often do you read your Bible? If you ate natural food in the same quantities that you are eating spiritual food, what kind of physical condition

would you be in? Would you be spiritually fit or malnourished? If you're going to eat, you need to pull up a chair and get in a position to receive that heavenly food. The Word of God will give you the strength you need.

3. Do you have a daily Bible-reading plan to help you stay on track in your reading of God's Word? If not, plans are widely available on the Internet, free of charge, or perhaps at your church bookstore. I encourage you to find a daily Bible-reading plan and let it help guide you in your consumption of God's Word on a daily basis.

AUGUST 25

Refuse To Give Up and Quit!

And let us not be weary in well doing:
for in due season we shall reap, if we faint not.
— Galatians 6:9

I've told you before, but today I sense a leading to tell you again — you *must* stay steady and on track with the assignment the Lord has given to you! Believe me, I know what it's like to get tired of staying steady and holding the course. But those moments when you're tired and tempted to quit are the exact times when you need to grab hold of the power of God and determine that you are not going to stray from your course until you've finished what God asked you to do!

In moments when weariness tries to get the best of me, I meditate on Galatians 6:9, which says, "And let us not be weary in well doing: for in due season we shall reap, if we faint not." The word "weary" in Galatians 6:9 is the Greek word *egkakos* — a compound of *en*, which means *in*, and *kakos*, which describes something *evil*. Here it actually depicts *a person who is tempted to throw in the towel and quit, thus surrendering to evil*. In this verse, God commands you and me *not* to surrender to any temptation to give up. He promises that in "due season," a harvest will be reaped if we won't quit — the manifestation of what each of us is believing for *will* come if we will not cave in and give up.

Notice that God says the manifestation comes in "due season." This tells us that each seed has *its own set season* — a specific, individual time when the seed will produce its harvest. Even if multiple seeds of various kinds are planted at one time, each has *its own season* to be reaped, depending on the seed. One seed produces in one set season, and another seed is reaped in a different set season. But no matter what season our seed is to be reaped in, God promises that if we are consistent — if we steadfastly keep sowing our seed into the ground and refuse to let weariness take us down — a time will come when "we shall reap."

The words "we shall reap" describe *a future, fixed event.* So if a seed has been sown, a harvest is guaranteed to happen — *if* we stay on course. This is why Paul continued, saying, "...if we *faint not.*" The word "faint" is a Greek word that pictures *a person who has become so weary that he gives up and forfeits what he'd been waiting so long for and what he was so close to reaping.* Pressures applied against such a person caused him to become tired and weary. As a result, his grip slackened, and the thing he'd held on to and hoped for slipped from his hands. The result was *loss.* In the case of Galatians 6:9, he lost *a harvest.*

The most common thing that causes one to loosen his grip is *weariness.* That's why Paul urges you not to throw in the towel in times of spiritual, physical, or mental exhaustion. It's exciting to plant seeds of faith, and it's *really* exciting when harvest comes. But in order to reach that point of reaping, you must hold on tight to what God has told you and remember that your seed has a set season when it *will* produce if you don't disrupt the process.

Often people are tempted to quit believing because they get *tired.* Maybe you have felt this very same temptation. But God promises you in Galatians 6:9 that if you will remain steadfast, your time of waiting will eventually produce a harvest — the manifestation of what you've been waiting for and believing to see.

We're all believing for something and sowing seeds toward it. I don't know what you're trusting God for in this season of your life. Perhaps no one knows but you because you've kept it between you and the Lord. Maybe it's a financial harvest, a breakthrough in a relationship, or a healing or restoration in some area. Maybe this harvest is taking longer than you'd anticipated or expected. But I want to reassure you that God's Word and His promises are absolutely true — and if you will just *refuse to give up and quit,* it's only a matter of time until your long-awaited blessing arrives!

MY PRAYER FOR TODAY

Father, I have been sowing seeds and waiting for my harvest for quite some time. It is true that I have been tempted to become tired and weary of waiting. So today I thank You because You said those who wait upon You shall renew their strength! I thank You for renewing and replenishing me as I patiently wait for my harvest. Your Word promises that it will come in due season. Holy Spirit, strengthen me with Your mighty power to stay the course until my due season arrives. I receive fresh grace to remain steady and on track with the project that You have assigned to me to complete! In those moments when I'm tempted to be tired and quit, help me remember that I can grab hold of Your power and not stray from my God-assigned purpose!

I pray this in Jesus' name!

MY CONFESSION FOR TODAY

I confess that I refuse to give up in times of spiritual, physical, or mental exhaustion. I will reach that point of fulfillment when I reap because I will hold tightly to what God has told me. God promised me in Galatians 6:9 that if I will remain steadfast, the manifestation of what I've been waiting for and believing to happen will come. On the basis of this promise, I

REFUSE TO GIVE UP AND QUIT. I declare by faith that it's only a matter of time until my long-awaited blessing arrives. Instead of caving in to weariness and the temptation to quit, I will lift up my hands in thanksgiving. I make the choice to praise God with a grateful heart as I keep thanking God for the harvest He has in store for me!

I declare this by faith in Jesus' name!

QUESTIONS FOR YOU TO CONSIDER

1. What harvest have you been sowing seeds toward? What exactly is the harvest that you are waiting for right now? How long have you been waiting?
2. Have you ever considered that you could be right on the edge of receiving what God has prepared for you, and that is why the devil has geared up his attack against you? Could it be that the devil is trying to push you to the edge of quitting because he knows you're about to receive that long-awaited blessing?
3. Do you know anyone who waited a long time for their "due season" before it finally came? Can you think of a Bible character who waited a long time for his or her dream to come to pass, but it eventually happened, even against all odds?

AUGUST 26

The Day We Traveled With 85 Trained Killers!

Are they not all ministering spirits, sent forth to minister
for them who shall be heirs of salvation?
— Hebrews 1:14

October 3, 1993. It was our wedding anniversary, and Denise and I were in Murmansk, Russia, located just north of the Arctic Circle. We had been ministering there in one of the largest churches in Russia at the time. After several days of wonderful meetings, we concluded the last evening service and returned to the apartment where we were staying. Our plan was to begin preparing for our trip home early the next morning. As we packed, we decided to turn on the television to see the late-night news.

We sat nearly frozen in disbelief as we learned that there had been a major coup in the city of Moscow! The image of the Russian Vice President appeared on the TV screen before us. Looking disheveled, this man morbidly glared into the TV camera and stated that a coup had begun in Moscow and that Russia's newly gained democracy was about to be lost. We were stunned when we heard him "beckon" people to go into the streets to fight using whatever they could find from their homes as weapons to oppose the pro-Communist faction — especially in the area near Red Square — that was trying to seize control.

While we had been busy ministering in Murmansk, a major conflict had erupted in Moscow. There was a clash between then President Boris Yeltsin and a pro-Communist political faction that had violently seized control of the Russian White House and had barricaded themselves inside it, refusing to come out.

The Russian White House is situated in front of the massive Novoarbatsky Bridge along the banks of the Moscow River. I found it so interesting that the entire day while we had been busy with church activities in another city, Boris Yeltsin had been busy ordering army tanks to line up on that bridge, point their cannons directly at the Russian White House, and shoot to drive those occupants out of the building! By the end of the day, those tanks had blown the top half of the structure nearly completely off. But although democratic forces shelled the White House with one bomb after another, the rebels refused to surrender their position.

It was late at night, and Denise and I sat in front of the TV dumbfounded and perplexed about what we should do. The mayhem in Moscow was spreading to other locations, and we didn't know what Moscow airports would be like the following morning. Moscow was our only connection to Riga, Latvia, where we lived at the time. We didn't know if flights would be canceled — or even if there would be potential attacks at the airport. And God only knew what might develop in the nighttime as we slept!

We arose early the following morning, took a car to the airport, and went inside to see if we could make our flight to Moscow en route to Riga. When the time came for passengers to board the plane, Denise and I were the *only two* passengers they allowed to embark. Everyone else with tickets for that flight was denied access to the plane!

The airline attendants seated us in First Class on the very front row of the plane. Denise and I were somewhat amused and discussed quietly that it looked like we had the whole plane to ourselves. That's exactly what we thought as that large Russian aircraft took off from that runway and began to ascend — that we were the only two passengers aboard the flight.

To this day, we still don't know why we were the only two passengers allowed to board that flight, *but that is exactly what happened.* We speculated that perhaps the person in charge knew us from our nationwide television program — or that we had received special treatment because of our American passports. All we could do was guess. But for the duration of that flight from Murmansk to Moscow, Denise and I sat alone on what looked to be an empty aircraft, musing over our strange situation.

That entire, very large commercial airliner was completely empty — except for us and the flight crew! At least that's what we thought *until* it was time to disembark. When we arose from our seats to leave, the flight attendant abruptly pulled back the curtain that concealed the whole back half of the airplane. To our utter amazement and shock, there stood in front of us 85 Black Berets, Russia's highest-trained land-combat soldiers!

What a scene that was! It looked like 85 "Rambos" standing there, with machine guns hanging off their shoulders, handguns strapped to their waists, strips of hundreds of rounds of ammo draped around their necks, giant knives fastened to their boots — and their faces completely smeared with greasy black "war paint"!

Denise and I stood there, nearly paralyzed, for what seemed like minutes. As much speculating as we had entertained about why we were alone on that flight, the thought never crossed our minds that we were *not* alone — and that we had flown all that distance to Moscow with 85 trained killers!

Sitting in the car that transported us from the plane to our terminal, we watched spellbound as those soldiers quickly disembarked that plane in unison and boarded jumbo helicopters that we later learned were assigned to fly them to the Russian White House. By the time we entered the terminal and made our way through passport control, we saw on TV monitors those same 85 soldiers being lowered by ropes onto what was left of the roof of the White House!

We later discovered that those killer troops were ordered to retake the Russian White House, arresting rebels who surrendered and shooting those who didn't. By the end of that standoff, 124 rebel soldiers had been killed and 348 had been wounded by those Black Beret soldiers — soldiers with whom Denise and I had unknowingly flown on a plane!

At times in life, we've likely all been oblivious to what's happening around us. Had Denise and I known we were flying with 85 trained killers that day, we would have experienced some apprehension about getting on that flight. But we *thought* we were the only two people on board. We actually enjoyed the experience, laughing and talking during the entire flight to Moscow. We only realized 85 "Rambos" were riding with us when it was time to disembark. By that time, it was too late to worry because we had already arrived safely at the airport in Moscow!

As Denise and I watched the monitors from inside the airport terminal and saw those soldiers being lowered into the remains of the White House, we hardly spoke a word. We were stunned that we had been that close to those armed and trained killers and yet completely unaware of it. As we awaited our next flight, we each sat quietly, pondering the events that had just taken place. It wasn't until we were securely on board our flight to Riga that we finally began to talk again. Excitedly, we began talking about the situations we all find ourselves in at times that we don't fully comprehend until later. And we particularly talked about the ministry of *angels* — that just as those Russian killer soldiers had been dispatched to restore order and peace, God sends His angels on "covert missions" to oversee and protect us in times of danger and uncertainty.

Hebrews 1:14 says, "Are they not all [angels] ministering spirits, sent forth to minister for them who shall be heirs of salvation?" You and I are the heirs of salvation, so this means that angels are sent forth to minister to *you* and *me*. But what exactly does the phrase *"sent forth to minister for them"* mean?

Notice the verse includes the word "minister" in some form twice. It says, "Are they not all *ministering* spirits, sent forth to *minister* for them who shall be heirs of salvation?" In both cases, the words "ministering" and "minister" are a translation of the Greek word *diakonos*, which depicts *high-level, top-notch service* of various kinds. As we look at the ministry of angels in the New Testament, we find that angels provided especially high-level, top-notch service to the saints when they experienced various types of need.

The following is a condensed list of activities that angels perform. Please keep in mind that this *Sparkling Gem* is about God's care over us when we are oblivious to things that are happening around us. In such moments, angels step in to provide certain kinds of high-level, top-notch service for us — including the list of angelic assignments that follow in this teaching. Of course, angels also have other roles, but for the purposes of this discussion, we will focus on the role of angels to minister to believers — heirs of salvation.

Angels Meet Physical Needs

Matthew 4:11 and Mark 1:13 tell us that when Jesus concluded His 40-day fast in the wilderness, angels appeared to Him and ministered to Him, thereby *meeting Jesus' physical needs* after that 40 days of fasting and being tempted by the devil. In both of these verses, the word "ministered" is a translation of the Greek word *diakonos*. Wherever this word is used in the New Testament, it pictures *a servant whose chief occupation is to meet some kind of physical or tangible need.*

Angels Give Strength

The Bible provides many examples of angels strengthening the weary, but the best New Testament example is found in Luke 22:43, where an angel strengthened Jesus in the Garden of Gethsemane during the most difficult time of His earthly life. It says, "And there appeared an angel unto him from heaven, *strengthening* him." This word comes from the Greek word *enischuo*, a compound of the words *en* and *ischuos*. The word *en* means *in*, and the word *ischuos* is the Greek word for *might* or *strength*. When these two words are compounded, the new word means *to impart strength*; *to empower someone*; *to fill a person with physical vigor*; or *to give someone renewed vitality*. In other words, a person may have been feeling exhausted and depleted, but suddenly he receives a robust blast of energy that instantly *recharges* him.

This means that when Jesus' disciples and friends couldn't be depended on in His hour of need, God provided an angel who *empowered*, *recharged*, and *imparted strength to* Jesus, thus renewing His vitality so He could victoriously face the most difficult hour of His life. Thus, Luke 22:43 provides a vivid New Testament example of how angels strengthen the weary.

Angels Can Give Supernatural Guidance

Examples of how angels provide supernatural guidance are abundant in the New Testament. Matthew 2:13 says an angel appeared to Joseph in a dream and told him to quickly take Mary and the young Christ Child into Egypt because Herod would seek to kill Jesus. Later when Herod died, an angel appeared in a dream to Joseph in Egypt, informing him that Herod was dead and that he and his family could return to Israel (Matthew 2:19-23). In both of those instances, the supernatural angelic guidance occurred in dreams.

In Act 10:3, we find an example of angelic guidance that also changed the course of history. An angel appeared in a vision to an Italian centurion named Cornelius who lived in Caesarea.

Although Cornelius was unsaved at that moment, God heard this man's prayers and intervened on his behalf by providing angelic guidance. The angel who appeared to Cornelius instructed him to send his servants to Joppa to summon Peter and his companions to come to him. When Peter arrived at Cornelius' residence, the apostle preached the Gospel to those who were present. All who heard Peter repented and were filled with the Holy Spirit. At that historic moment, the door to salvation was opened to the Gentiles, and the Gospel message began to go forth into the Gentile world.

Angels Provide Protection and Deliverance

The Old and New Testaments are filled with evidence that God assigns angels to guard and protect His people. For instance, Psalm 34:7 says that angels encamp around those who fear the Lord to deliver them. Psalm 91:11 promises that God will give His angels charge over His people to keep them in all their ways. We see a New Testament example of how angels guard and protect God's people in Acts 5:17-20. In this account, the high priest rose up against the apostles and had them arrested and thrown into prison. Verses 19 and 20 say, "But the angel of the Lord by night opened the prison doors, and brought them forth, and said, Go, stand and speak in the temple to the people all the words of this life."

A few chapters later in Acts 12, we find the story of Peter being arrested and thrown into prison. After Herod ordered the beheading of James (*see* Acts 12:1,2), he saw that many Jews approved of his action. Therefore, in order to garner more support and popularity with the angry mob of Christian-haters, Herod gave the order for the apostle Peter to be arrested next. The authorities may have recalled the previous time when a group of apostles miraculously escaped from prison because this time Peter was delivered to "four quaternions of soldiers" (Acts 12:4).

A "quaternion" refers to a group of *four* Roman soldiers. So four quaternions — or four different groups containing four soldiers each — successively took turns guarding Peter throughout the night. Verse 6 tells us that Peter was sleeping between two guards in that prison while two other guards stood watch at the prison door. Suddenly the angel of the Lord came into the prison cell and awoke Peter from his sleep, telling him to rise up quickly and leave the prison. Instantly, the chains that held Peter were loosened and fell to the ground.

Not only did the angel of the Lord set Peter free from the chains that held him, but it seems the angel also temporarily blinded the guards so they were unaware of what was happening. Peter followed the angel through the first and second ward until he came to an iron gate, which supernaturally opened in front of him without anyone touching it. An angel delivered the apostle from the horrible destiny that had awaited him at the hands of Herod.

Angels Perform Superhuman Feats

Perhaps the best New Testament example of angels performing superhuman feats is when the angels rolled away the massive stone that lay before Jesus' garden tomb. Matthew 28:2 says, "...The angel of the Lord descended from heaven, and came and rolled back the stone from the door, and sat upon it." The word "stone" is the Greek word *lithos,* which simply means *a stone.* It is known, however, that the stones placed in front of such tombs were immense in their dimensions — impossible for a human being to move without the assistance of several people.

Another remarkable example of an angel's superhuman strength is recorded in Revelation 20:1-3, where John writes: "And I saw an angel come down from heaven, having the key of the bottomless pit and a great chain in his hand. And he laid hold on the dragon, that old serpent, which is the Devil, and Satan, and bound him a thousand years, and cast him into the bottomless pit, and shut him up, and set a seal upon him, that he should deceive the nations no more, till the thousand years should be fulfilled: and after that he must be loosed a little season."

At the appointed time, an unnamed angel will seize Satan, bind him with a great chain, shut him in the bottomless pit, and seal it so he can't escape. No natural human being would ever be able to perform such a feat, but this passage of Scripture clearly states that a day is coming when an angel will singlehandedly accomplish this task — scriptural proof of the great power heavenly angels possess.

And to think — such "ministering spirits" are dispatched to "minister" to those who will inherit salvation. *That's you and me!* God has specifically sent angels forth to meet our physical needs, to give us strength, to supernaturally guide us at times, to provide us with protection and deliverance, and to perform superhuman feats on our behalf.

Flying from Murmansk to Moscow with 85 hidden trained killers — while Denise and I were completely oblivious to that fact — reminds me that wherever we are and whatever we're doing, we have a group of "ministering spirits" that are assigned to watch over us and care for us. In fact, looking back on that incident, I realize that a "special-forces unit" of angels is always assigned to Denise and me! And these trained spiritual combatants pose *a far more formidable threat* to unseen devilish forces than the threat those 85 trained soldiers posed to rebels occupying the Russian White House that day!

If you look back over your own life, I'm sure it won't be difficult to recall moments when you experienced angelic assistance to help you overcome in the midst of what you were enduring. You may not have seen those ministering spirits with your physical eyes or even felt their presence, but it is certain they were there, for that is God's promise to you and to me in Hebrews 1:14!

MY PRAYER FOR TODAY

Father, I want to thank You for the many times You have given Your angels charge of me to protect, provide for, and guide me when I was confronted with difficulties or was completely unaware of the situations I had unknowingly wandered into or of the danger that surrounded me. I am reminded of how Your ministering spirits have met my needs; brought me help; strengthened me when I was exhausted both physically and emotionally; and kept me safe in the midst of circumstances that could have produced certain harm or even taken my life. Time after time, You've held me safe through the watchful care of Your ministering angels. Lord, I love You. You have shown me great mercy, and each day I find new reasons to praise and glorify You as a faithful Keeper of covenant in my life.

I pray this in Jesus' name!

MY CONFESSION FOR TODAY

I confess that time after time, in ways I seldom realize, God dispatches angels to assist me. These ministering spirits surround me and keep me safe, and they never fail to step in to deliver me even when I don't know that I am in harm's way. Whatever my situation, and regardless of the need, angels are assigned to protect, provide, strengthen, and guide me in all my ways of obedience to the Lord.

I declare this by faith in Jesus' name!

QUESTIONS FOR YOU TO CONSIDER

1. Have you ever been in a situation in which you were oblivious to what was happening around you, but you later discovered that God had dispatched an angel or angels to protect you in some way?
2. Can you recall a specific experience of God's miraculous, delivering power in your life? When was it, and what happened? How did you respond?
3. When you consider that experience, what does it reveal to you about the tenderness of God to watch over you and protect you? Have you ever told anyone about that moment of divine protection?

AUGUST 27

Thou Hast Left Thy First Love

Nevertheless I have somewhat against thee,
because thou hast left thy first love.
— Revelation 2:4

On April 24, I wrote a *Sparkling Gem* called "Remembering Your First Love." Today I'd like to take that *Gem* a step further — to really develop what Jesus had to say in Revelation 2:4 when He spoke to His precious church in the city of Ephesus.

In Revelation 2:4, Jesus told the church of Ephesus, "*Nevertheless* I have somewhat against thee, because thou hast left thy first love." The word "nevertheless" is a translation of the Greek word *alla*, which essentially means "*BUT*...."

Despite all the outstanding commendations Christ had just given to this church, there was one point that was *not* commendable. Jesus was so dismayed and disconcerted by this one serious defect that He told the Ephesian believers, "...*I have* somewhat against thee...."

The words "I have" are a translation of the Greek word *echo*, which means *I have* or *I hold*. In spite of all the remarkable features that made the Ephesian church so outstanding, there was one area where these believers had failed, and it was so bothersome to Christ that He *personally held it against them*. The phrase "against thee" is very personal, informing us that Christ was *deeply disturbed* by something He knew about this church.

Jesus then declared to the Ephesian believers, "Nevertheless I have somewhat against thee, *because thou hast left thy first love*" (Revelation 2:4).

The word "love" in this verse is the Greek word *agape*, which we have studied before. This word *agape* is so filled with deep emotion and meaning that it is one of the most difficult words to translate in the New Testament. The task of adequately explaining this word has baffled translators for centuries; nevertheless, an attempt will be made here to clarify the meaning of *agape* and then to apply it to the context of Revelation 2:4.

As I have stated before in previous *Gems*, *agape* occurs when an individual *sees, recognizes, understands, and appreciates the value of an object or a person*, causing him to behold this object or person in great esteem, awe, admiration, wonder, and sincere appreciation. Such great respect is awakened in the heart of the observer for the object or person he is beholding that he is *compelled* to love. In fact, his love for that person or object is so strong that it is *irresistible*. This kind of love knows no limits or boundaries in how far, wide, high, and deep it will go to show love to its recipient. If necessary, *agape* love will even sacrifice itself for the sake of that object or person it so deeply cherishes. *Agape* is therefore the *highest, finest, most noble*, and *most fervent* form of love.

In addition, the Greek sentence structure of this verse is very different from the *King James Version* previously quoted. The original Greek literally states, "...*because your love, the first one, you have left.*" The phrase "the first one" is a clarification of what type of love Jesus was describing. This phrase comes from the Greek words *ten proten*, which modifies *agape* to mean *first love* or *early love*. Jesus used this phrase here to remind the church in Ephesus of the esteem, awe, admiration, wonder, and appreciation that was first awakened in their hearts for Him when they received Him as their Savior many years earlier.

Like young people who fall in love, the Ephesians *fell hard* when they first came to Christ. Their hearts were captivated with their love for Jesus. There were no limits to what they would surrender to Him, no boundaries to their obedience. They were willing to sacrifice and leave behind anything to follow Him.

Acts 19:18,19 described the Ephesian believers' early act of public repentance, when they burned their occult fetishes and attempted to amputate every connection to the past that would hinder their new lives in Christ. The repentance of these new believers was so deeply rooted in their hearts that it produced a radical, far-reaching, profound transformation that completely altered their way of living. They were *fervently* in love with Jesus and completely sold out to Him — with no sorrows, regrets, or reservations.

But by the time the apostle John saw the exalted Christ on the island of Patmos, decades had passed since the Ephesian believers first repented — and in the vision, Christ issued them this stern warning: "Your love, the first one, *you have left*." The phrase "you have left" is from the Greek word *aphiemi*, which denotes *the voluntary release of something once held dear* or *to neglect, to ignore*, or *to leave something or someone behind*. Although the Ephesian believers were still committed to Christ, doing everything "for his name's sake," they no longer had the deep passion and fervency for Him that had once consumed their hearts. Over the years, as they became more doctrinally sophisticated and astute, their simple but profound *first love* for Jesus had somehow dissipated and slipped away from them, even though they never stopped faithfully serving Him.

It seems that after fighting spiritual battles year after year — testing false apostles, training leaders, starting new churches, overseeing entire groups of churches, and dealing with spiritual wolves who were constantly trying to ravage their ministry base — the Ephesian congregation became so focused on protecting their church that they were no longer able to enjoy their relationship with Jesus as they had many years earlier. This was still a remarkable church, but the spiritual fervency that had characterized this body of believers in the past was now missing. It was for this reason that Jesus was so deeply disturbed. The blazing fire that once characterized the Ephesian believers had gradually waned until it became little more than a smoldering flame.

It often happens that the first generation of Christians during a move of God experiences dramatic salvations as that segment of the Church is born in the power of the Spirit. However, the second generation, raised in a Christian environment, often doesn't experience the same radical deliverance their parents did. Of course, it should be the goal of all believing parents to raise their children in a godly environment; however, they can never stop working diligently to keep the fires of spiritual passion burning.

As each successive generation becomes more accustomed to a Christian environment — learning to speak the language of the church, sing the songs of the church, and act the way "church" people should act — it becomes easy for the younger generations to slip into a mindset of familiarity. Too often this can produce apathy in people's hearts, ultimately leading them to take the redemptive work of Christ for granted. Therefore, the potential for spiritual fires to die down and become a pile of smoldering embers increases dangerously with each new generation. The only way for each local body and its members to avoid that process is to become unrelenting in their commitment to retain their spiritual passion for Christ.

There is no clearer example of this vital principle than the illustrious church of Ephesus, which was perhaps the finest congregation that existed in the First Century. Although only a few decades had passed since the birth of this church, the fervency that once gripped these believers' hearts had waned. The spiritual fire that once blazed in their midst was gradually diminishing into a flickering flame, replaced instead by orthodoxy, creeds, and dogmas — a form of religion that lacked the power known by the earlier generation (*see* 2 Timothy 3:5).

If this could happen to the church of Ephesus, it must be taken as a warning for the Church in every generation. We must regularly allow the Holy Spirit to search our hearts and reveal whether or not we are still on fire for the Lord as we once were. It may be a painful revelation to realize that we have become doctrinally sophisticated yet powerless. However, if we are willing to remember from whence we have fallen and then to repent, we can be spared the tragedy of becoming irrelevant to our generation.

As I conclude today, my own heart is stirred. Oh, let each of us examine our own heart to see if we have let anything slip in our fervent pursuit of Jesus. And if we discover that we have left our first love in any way, let's take every step necessary to fan the fire within until it blazes hot and high for Him the way it did when we first came to know Jesus Christ!

MY PRAYER FOR TODAY

Father, as I read how the church at Ephesus subtly shifted its focus from walking with You to working for You, I'm struck by the realization of how easily our attention can fasten on what we do for You instead of on You for who You are. Lord, I repent for how I've allowed the cares of life and my concern for other things to harden my heart and dull the fervency of my passion for You. When I compare how I am today to how I was when I first came to Jesus, I must admit that I've become doctrinally sophisticated yet spiritually powerless. I confess my sin of idolatry because I've allowed other things to become enthroned in my heart. Holy Spirit, I humbly ask You to work in me, to ignite within me a white-hot fervor for Jesus like I've never known. Bring me to a place where my chief desire is to know Him, to love Him, to walk with Him, to serve Him, and to please Him in the pure power of holiness.

I pray this in Jesus' name!

MY CONFESSION FOR TODAY

I declare that I am in love with Jesus Christ. He is the center of my life. My love for Him consumes me and motivates every part of my life. I started out in the fire of God, and I will end in the fire of God. I allow the Holy Spirit to search my heart regularly to reveal my true spiritual state. I refuse to become doctrinally sophisticated yet powerless and irrelevant. I confess that I am overwhelmed with the love of Jesus. My heart is increasingly captivated by Him. Every day, every week, and every year that passes, I grow more deeply in love with Him. Soon I'll meet Him face to face. Each morning I awaken with greater determination to live my life for that moment when I look into His loving eyes. Oh, what a day that will be — but until then, I want to be consumed with His fire!

I declare this by faith in Jesus' name!

QUESTIONS FOR YOU TO CONSIDER

1. If the church of Ephesus could lose its first love, then Jesus' message to them in Revelation 2:4 must be taken as a warning for the Church in every generation. Allow the Holy Spirit to search your heart and reveal whether or not you are still on fire for the Lord as you once were.
2. Have you ever had the painful realization that you had become doctrinally sophisticated yet spiritually powerless? If you are willing to remember your first love and repent, you can be spared the tragedy of becoming irrelevant to your generation.
3. Why don't you take a moment to examine your heart and see if you have let anything slip? If you discover that you have left your first love in any way, take every step necessary to return to the flaming fire of passion you had in your heart when you first came to know Jesus Christ!

AUGUST 28

Remember!

Remember therefore from whence thou art fallen,
and repent, and do the first works....
— Revelation 2:5

Have you ever sensed the Holy Spirit pleading with you to return to the on-fire love you had for Him when you first received your salvation? As we saw in yesterday's *Sparkling Gem*, that is precisely what Jesus did with the church of Ephesus when He diagnosed their spiritual condition and told them that they had left their first love (*see* Revelation 2:4). However, Jesus didn't just diagnose their spiritual condition — He also showed them the steps they needed to take in order to reverse their course and rectify the situation. This is seen in Revelation 2:5, where Jesus told the Ephesian believers how to return to the white-hot passion they'd possessed in the early years of their salvation. He said, "Remember therefore from whence thou art fallen, and repent, and do the first works...."

Notice that Jesus urged the congregation in Ephesus to do three things to correct their deteriorated spiritual condition: 1) *remember*, 2) *repent*, and 3) *do the first works*. These three key points are packed with meaning, so I will take my time to properly explain each one. In the next few *Gems*, we will study what Jesus meant when He told the Ephesians to *repent* and *do the first works*, but today I want to focus on the word *remember*.

The Ephesian believers had lost their "first love" — the simplicity and passion that marked their early love for Jesus Christ. This tells us how far they had unintentionally drifted from the spiritual zeal that once characterized them. For this reason, Jesus urged them to stop everything they were doing in order to "remember" the precious fellowship they used to enjoy with Him before they became so spiritually sophisticated.

The word "remember" is a translation of the Greek word *mneia*, which in ancient literature denoted *a written record used to memorialize a person's actions, a sepulcher, a statue, a monument*, or *a tombstone*. The fact that the word *mneia* can denote a *sepulcher* is very significant in the context of Revelation 2:5, because it suggests the Ephesian believers' early experiences with Christ had become *buried* by years of activity.

Like dirt on a grave, the busyness of ministry had buried what was once precious to them. So by using this word *mneia*, Jesus implored them to dig through the clutter of their schedules, routines, and activities and unearth the early memories of their faith when it was tender and new. Once they recalled their powerful past, they would see how far they had drifted from the spiritual fervency that had marked their beginnings. Only then would they be in a position to make the necessary adjustments in their lives to recover their excitement and passion for the things of God.

Furthermore, because *mneia* ("remember") also refers to *a statue* or *a monument*, we see that certain memories should forever stand tall in our lives and never be forgotten. The purpose of a *statue* or *monument* is to *memorialize* a historical event or a deceased hero so that future generations will never forget. Most statues, monuments, and tombstones are made from durable materials like metal or stone, and they endure for many years without effort or upkeep. Generations can come and go, but statues and monuments persist, allowing people to gaze upon the faces of deceased heroes and read the inscriptions that describe their past actions and contributions. As long as a statue or monument remains in its place, it will stand as a reminder to future generations.

Memories, however, must be deliberately maintained and cultivated if they are to remain vital in our hearts and minds. If significant memories are not deliberately passed on to future generations, they become lost under the overgrowth of life, just like a neglected grave with no tombstone. It doesn't take long before the location of such a grave is completely lost. People will walk across it without even knowing that the remains of a precious person lie buried beneath their feet.

Like an unmarked grave, important memories can be easily forgotten. Adults forget their childhood; nations forget their heritage; and Christians forget their early beginnings with Jesus. In Revelation 2:5, we discover that churches can forget their past. Years of activity and Christian service can so consume a congregation's energy and strength that they begin to forget the great work of grace God performed in their hearts. Weariness, busy schedules, and a constant stream of new programs to implement all have the ability to wear down a body of believers — turning their activity for God's Kingdom into spiritual drudgery and reducing what was once fresh and exciting into a monotonous, religious routine. If they are not careful, they risk forfeiting their zeal and spiritual fire and allowing what was once precious to become routine. Their early memories of coming to Christ can become buried under an overgrowth of activity and spiritual weeds, making them forget how wonderful God's grace was when it first touched their hearts.

This is actually a common struggle among spiritually mature believers. In fact, it is difficult to find a single mature Christian who hasn't had to fight this temptation as his or her sinful past gradually fades into a distant memory. They become accustomed to the precious Holy Spirit in their lives, and too often they unintentionally begin to simply "traffic" in the things of God. It's a subtle backsliding that occurs in the very act of serving God.

In the early years of the Ephesian church, the vibrancy and excitement of the Ephesian believers inspired the passion in congregations and spiritual leaders throughout the years. But as the years passed, this zeal for the things of God slowly ebbed away. Knowledge increased, but the believers' fiery passion for Jesus diminished.

Undoubtedly, as the Ephesian church grew, so did its members' schedules, routines, habits, customs, and traditions. They were so busy serving Jesus that they lost their intimacy with Him, and it is likely that they experienced a loss of joy in their service, since joy is impossible to maintain without a vital connection to the Savior. Therefore, it was essential for the Ephesian believers to recall their point of departure from their first love if they were to return to the vibrant relationship they once experienced with Christ. They needed to pause everything they were doing and gratefully remember:

- Their deliverance from idol worship.
- Their liberation from evil spirits.
- The many miraculous healings that occurred in their city.
- The great bonfire where they burned all of their occult books and magical incantations.
- Their public act of repentance before a pagan crowd.

Having put themselves in remembrance of their glorious history, the Ephesian believers would be able to move forward in their relationship with Jesus and "repent." We'll look more at what that word means in tomorrow's *Gem*.

So have you allowed the busyness of *serving* God to bury the excitement you felt for Jesus when you were first saved? If so, take Jesus' words to heart and *remember* your first love. Clear away the weeds and clutter of life from those memories, and let them stand tall like a monument in your mind!

MY PRAYER FOR TODAY

Father, I never want to forget the amazing things You did in my life when I first came to know You many years ago. Forgive me for allowing the clutter of my life to bury precious memories that I should never forget. From the start of our relationship, You have proven Yourself faithful to me. I need not ever bury that or forget it when I get busy. Holy Spirit, today I ask You to help me "declutter" the memories of my past and revive those precious memories that I need to hold clear and dear.

I pray this in Jesus' name!

MY CONFESSION FOR TODAY

I declare that I do not easily forget the things that God has done for me. I have personally experienced the faithfulness of God, and I remain thankful for all that He has done for me. Weariness, busy schedules, and a constant stream of new responsibilities do not blur God's faithfulness to me. My spiritual life is not full of drudgery, nor is it reduced into a monotonous, religious routine. I am spiritually alive, vital, and eager for God to move in my life!

I declare this by faith in Jesus' name!

QUESTIONS FOR YOU TO CONSIDER

1. Do you ever take time to "remember" the things that the Lord did for you in the early years when you first came to know Him? What does it do for you when you recall those precious moments?
2. What has the Lord recently done for you? How has He delivered you, rescued you, or saved you? Have you taken time to thank Him for all that He's done for you?
3. Memories must be cultivated and maintained. What are you doing to cultivate and maintain your sweet memories of your past times with Jesus? How do you plan to share those experiences with your friends and loved ones?

AUGUST 29

'From Whence Thou Art Fallen'

Remember therefore *from whence thou art fallen….*
— Revelation 2:5

In yesterday's *Sparkling Gem*, we saw that Christ confronted the illustrious church of Ephesus about the fact that they had left their first love. He urged them to put everything on pause and to *remember* the fiery love they'd had for Jesus when they first repented several decades earlier. Although they were perhaps the largest and most sophisticated church in the world at that time, they had lost the wonder of it all as they became consumed in the busyness of ministry. That's why Jesus told them that they needed to "Remember therefore *from whence thou art fallen…*" (Revelation 2:5).

It is important to note that Greek word translated as "remember" is in the present active imperative, which means Jesus wanted the Ephesian believers *to remain continually mindful* of their past. What God had done in their midst was a wonderful memory that needed to be memorialized in their congregation for all generations. But if they took an honest look at their hearts and compared their present to their past, they would see what Jesus knew about them — that they had *fallen* from the zeal and spiritual passion that had once burned in their hearts. Regardless of the adulation the Ephesian church received from other churches and spiritual leaders throughout the Roman Empire, Jesus could see the true state of this body of believers. Therefore, He admonished them, "Remember from *whence* thou art fallen…."

The word "whence" is the Greek word *pothen*, which *points back in time to a different place or a different time*. It is intended to draw one's attention to a specific moment or experience in the past to see what life was once like. In addition, the word "fallen" means *a downfall from a high and lofty position*. The Greek tense doesn't describe the act of falling; rather, it refers to one who has *already completely fallen* and who is now living in *a completely fallen state*.

For the past multiple decades, the church at Ephesus had hosted the world's greatest Christian leaders, experienced the power of God, and become more advanced in spiritual knowledge than any other church of that time. In fact, the Christian community at the time viewed this congregation as the ideal church. However, we must never forget that what can be carefully hidden from human eyes can never be concealed from Jesus. Hebrews 4:13 tells us that "…all things are naked and opened unto the eyes of him with whom we have to do." Jesus is often unimpressed with the things that impress us because He sees a different picture than we do. Others may have been impressed with the heritage of the Ephesian church and its roster of famous personalities — but in Jesus' eyes, the church was "fallen."

This is reminiscent of the apostle Paul's words in First Corinthians 10:12, where he said, "Wherefore let him that thinketh he standeth take heed lest he fall." The word "thinketh" comes from the Greek word *dokeo*, which in this context means *to be of the opinion*, *to reckon*, *to suppose*, or *to think*. In this verse, the word *dokeo* expresses the idea of what a person *thinks* or *supposes* about himself. There is nothing to verify if that individual's opinion is correct — only that it is the prevailing opinion he has regarding himself.

The word "standeth" comes from the word *istemi*, which simply means *to stand*, *to stand fast*, *to stand firm*, or *to stand upright*. But when the words *dokeo* and *istemi* are combined in the same thought as Paul used them in this verse, the phrase could be read: *"Wherefore let anyone who has the self-imposed opinion of himself that he is standing strong and firm…."* Then Paul added the next critically important words: "…Take heed lest he fall."

The words "take heed" are from the Greek word *blepo*, which means *to watch*, *to see*, *to behold*, or *to be aware*. The Greek tense indicates the need not only *to watch*, but also *to be continually watchful*.

The word "fall" in First Corinthians 10:12 is a form of the same word Jesus used in Revelation 2:5 when He told the believers in Ephesus that they were already fallen. This word depicts one who *falls into sin*, *falls into ruin*, or *falls into some type of failure*. In other words, this isn't merely the picture of someone who stumbles a little; it depicts *a downward plummet that causes one to tragically crash.* This verse could therefore be interpreted, *"If anyone has the opinion of himself that he is standing strong and firm, he needs to be continually watchful and always on his guard lest he trip, stumble, and fall from his overly confident position — taking a downward nosedive that leads to a serious crash."*

Spiritual smugness is an attitude that deceives a person into thinking more highly of himself than he ought to think (*see* Romans 12:3). Often this self-congratulatory attitude emerges among those who "think" they are more advanced, educated, or spiritually sophisticated than others. It is a spiritual pride that blinds one from clearly seeing his own areas of shortcoming and need the way he once did and causes him to be overly impressed with himself.

It is vital that we take this as a divine warning that directly pertains to our own walk with God. We must understand that our own opinion of ourselves or the high opinion of others concerning us is not a trustworthy measure. Proverbs 16:2 says, "All the ways of a man are clean in his own eyes; but the Lord weigheth the spirits." According to this verse, flesh is always prone to be self-congratulatory and to excuse its own failures and weaknesses. But there is nothing hidden from Jesus' sight; He sees it all from the beginning to the end. All the public relations in the world will not change what Jesus sees in a person's heart. Therefore, it is what Jesus Christ knows about us that is most important — *not* what we think about ourselves or what others think or say about us.

The church of Ephesus had a glorious past and a famous name. It was large, well-known, and recognized by others as a spiritual center and a model church. Nevertheless, Jesus saw the situation very differently from what human eyes could see. If Jesus could call this illustrious church with its list of remarkable accomplishments "fallen," it is clear that any church, regardless of its notable beginning or enduring fame, can also be "fallen." *This means one's past is not a guarantee of one's future.* If an individual or a church is not completely devoted to doing whatever is necessary to retain spiritual passion, it is likely that over time, the initial passion will slowly dissipate, as was the case with the church of Ephesus.

That is why Jesus lovingly pointed the Ephesian believers backward in time, reminding them of the spiritual vibrancy they once possessed but had lost. Then He enjoined them to take action to rekindle their fire. If they would recognize the religious routine into which they had fallen — and allow this knowledge to produce conviction of sin about their backslidden condition — they could repent and turn the situation around.

I covered the subject of repentance in the March 17-21 *Gems.* However, this subject is so vital in the Church world in this present hour that I am going to cover it again in the following *Sparkling Gem.* If there was ever an hour to issue a clear teaching on the need for repentance — what it is, how it is done, and what the effects of true repentance are — it is in the hour in which we live.

Oh, how far the Church has drifted from the simple, powerful, fiery beginnings of revival that once burned in the hearts of early believers! Today Christ is speaking from the Scriptures and calling His people to repent, just as He called on the church of Ephesus to repent nearly 2,000 years ago. Let's hear what the Spirit is still speaking to His Church!

MY PRAYER FOR TODAY

Dear Father, I confess that the Church — with all of its sophistication and technology — seems to be lacking in great demonstrations of the power of God. But rather than take a critical role, I admit that I am a part of this great Body of believers, and that, I, too, need to remember from whence I have fallen. Help us to remember the early days, the early passion, the early fire that burned in our hearts. Help us to do a corrective self-analysis of where we are compared to where we were. There have been so many wonderful advances, and I recognize that, but there is a simplicity and fire that is missing. Lord, restore it to us and help us burn brightly and simply as we once did.

I pray this in Jesus' name!

MY CONFESSION FOR TODAY

I confess that admitting what is wrong is the first step in repentance. Therefore, I repent for allowing the busyness of life and worldliness to usurp the place in my heart that belongs only to the Lord. I press in to receive a fresh visitation of the Holy Spirit's power and the heartfelt willingness to receive it with open arms. I confess that I am open-hearted, willing, and ready for the Lord to restore His Church to the power that He destined for it to possess!

I declare this by faith in Jesus' name!

QUESTIONS FOR YOU TO CONSIDER

1. Can you recall an earlier time in your Christian life — a simpler time — when you relished and cherished the gifts of the Holy Spirit and could hardly wait for a move of the Spirit? What changed?
2. Do you attend a church where the moving of the Holy Spirit is appreciated? If God wanted to mightily move on your congregation, would it be welcomed or rejected? Does that response reflect your personal belief and desire?
3. How would you honestly gauge your own spiritual life? Are you more advanced than you once were, or are you "fallen" compared to the fiery passion you once had in your earlier life with Jesus?

There is nothing hidden from Jesus' sight;
He sees it all from the beginning to the end.
Therefore, it is what He knows about us
that is most important —
NOT what we think about ourselves
or what others think or say about us.

AUGUST 30

Repent!

Remember therefore from whence
thou art fallen, *and repent....*
— Revelation 2:5

In this modern age, people want to be comforted and told that everything is going to be all right. But the truth is, some things are *not* going to be all right in people's lives unless they make a decision to *repent* and change. In those cases, it is sometimes up to us to love people enough to be honest with them, no matter how painful it is for them to hear the truth. This type of spiritual pain is good for people to experience because it makes them aware that things are not right between them and God.

You may remember from the March 18 *Sparkling Gem* that the word "repent" is the Greek word *metanoeo* and means *a change of mind, repentance*, or *conversion.* The Septuagint used this word in the Old Testament to depict the prophet's call to the people *to turn* or *to change their attitudes and ways.*

In the New Testament, *metanoeo*, or "repent," has the same meaning, but the force is much stronger. It demands a decision *to completely change* or *to entirely turn around in the way one is thinking, believing, or living.* This word "repent" gives the image of a person changing from top to bottom — a total transformation wholly affecting every part of a person's life.

Because Christ loves us, He often confronts us with painful truths about ourselves and then calls on us to repent. At that point, we must make the decision to turn from the sin in our lives and remove every action, attitude, or relationship from our lives that grieves Him and hurts us.

In Revelation 2:5, Jesus didn't mitigate the truth; rather, He had a straightforward confrontation with the Ephesians as He told them that they had allowed their relationship with Him to slip. This congregation was viewed as the model church — an example for churches throughout other parts of the Roman Empire. Nevertheless, Jesus said its members and leadership were "fallen" compared to what they had experienced earlier with Him. The passionate, on-fire relationship they had once enjoyed with Jesus had slipped away as they became lost in the sophistication of ministry.

When the pastor of the Ephesian church heard this message from Christ, it must have pained his heart; yet it was his responsibility as the *messenger* of the church to pass this message on to the entire congregation. One can only imagine the pain these early believers felt when they heard Jesus' words to them, urging them to put everything on pause and to take the time to remember the intimate relationship they had enjoyed with Him in the past. It must have profoundly affected the Ephesian congregation when they compared their passionate love for Christ in those earlier days to the body of believers they had become — spiritually sophisticated but distant from the Lord in their hearts.

Psalm 51 provides a vivid example of genuine repentance and is, in fact, called David's psalm of repentance. In this psalm, one can sense not only David's *sorrow* but also his *decision to change*. In verse 17, he wrote about a heart that is broken over sin: "The sacrifices of God are a broken spirit: a broken and a contrite heart, O God, thou wilt not despise." The word "contrite" is the Old Testament expression for someone who is genuinely repentant for what he has done. This is a person who has recognized his wrong, decided to change, and now desires to live uprightly.

This was the spiritual condition to which Christ was calling the congregation of Ephesus. He confronted them with the truth: that although they had continued to serve Jesus and to faithfully go through the motions, little by little their spiritual zeal had begun to wane. Then He compelled them to acknowledge — just as He compels us today — that they needed to *repent* and return to Him, thereby rekindling the fire that once burned so brightly in their hearts.

When necessary, Christ calls entire churches to repent. Besides the churches in the book of Revelation, another scriptural example is the Corinthian congregation, to whom Paul brought correction for their many acts of carnality. When the Corinthian believers received Paul's first letter and recognized that God was speaking to them through the apostle, they were moved with fear to purge themselves of the sin in their midst that had grieved the Holy Spirit. This willingness to change was the *proof* that true repentance had occurred. The indisputable transformation that occurred in the Corinthian church was sufficient evidence for Paul to declare in his second letter that they had cleared themselves in the matters where they had previously been wrong (*see* 2 Corinthians 7:9-11). God's goal in confronting His Church is always to produce cleansing, transformation, and restoration.

Today Jesus is still crying out for the Church to repent of worldliness and carnality. As is true in each generation, today we have a choice: to harden our hearts and turn a deaf ear to the Holy Spirit, or to allow Him to deal deeply with us and produce genuine repentance in our hearts and souls. Although Christ is always ready to transform His Church, no transformation can occur unless we are willing to hear what His Spirit is saying to us. And once we do hear that divine message, we must be willing to respond with humble obedience, just as the Corinthian church did.

This was the case for the church at Ephesus. Jesus was calling this congregation to recognize their fallen state and to take visible steps to demonstrate that they were sincere about restoring their passion for Him. But how does a fallen church, or a wayward believer, restore that fire that once burned so brightly? That is exactly what we will discuss in tomorrow's *Sparkling Gem*!

MY PRAYER FOR TODAY

Father, I thank You for speaking to me about my need to repent — that is, to change the way I've been thinking and living. Truthfully, I've been consumed with serving You more than I have been consumed with just loving You, as I once did in the past. I've become so busy that I don't read my Bible as I once did; I don't pray as I once did; and I've drifted from the passionate fire that once burned in my heart. I am busy and involved, but my relationship with You is distant compared to the intimate communion we once shared years ago. For all this I repent. Today I hear Your voice calling me back into meaningful fellowship. Forgive me for my spiritual lethargy, and set me ablaze with the Spirit of God!

I pray this in Jesus' name!

MY CONFESSION FOR TODAY

I declare that I am on-fire for Jesus Christ. I have repented for allowing a lukewarm attitude to work inside me, and I ask God to make me a bonfire for the Kingdom of God! I confess that I burn with passion and with the power of God. I am consumed with a desire to see lost souls come to Christ. I long to see the power of God even more than I once did. I humble myself before the Lord. I hear His voice, and I submit myself to God and to His service in a fresh, new way.

I declare this by faith in Jesus' name!

QUESTIONS FOR YOU TO CONSIDER

1. What were you like when you *first* repented and came to Christ? What were you like when you were *first* filled with the Holy Spirit? If you compare who you are today, compared to who you were back then, what would be the big difference?
2. First John 1:9 guarantees cleansing for believers who confess sin and repent. *It literally guarantees cleansing!* What does that verse mean to you? I'll tell you up front that it means a lot to me!
3. What are the fruits of repentance? In other words, what are the outward signs that a person has genuinely repented? Can you make a list of all the things that accompany real repentance?

AUGUST 31

Do the First Works!

Remember therefore from whence thou art fallen,
and repent, and *do* the first works....
— Revelation 2:5

It's not enough just to say "you're sorry." That is not genuine repentance. Real repentance, as described on March 18 and 19, describes an *inward* change that results in an *outward* change. Real, inward repentance shows forth evidence that repentance has occurred. Jesus told the church at Ephesus that they needed to repent and "do the first works." That word "do" refers to the outward actions I am describing — *the outward proof of repentance.*

The word "do" is the Greek word *poieo*, a word that is used 568 times in the New Testament; thus, its meaning is well established in New Testament writings. It literally means *to do*, but it actually conveys much more. This word *poieo* describes all types of *activity*, particularly the idea of *creativity*. For example, the Greek word *poietes* — a form of the word *poieo* — is the source of the word *poet*, which denotes one who has the extraordinary ability to write or create a certain literary form. Thus, this word describes *doing* that produces *results*.

Because the word *poieo* is connected to the creative activity of an author, poet, or painter, let's pause to consider what is required for this type of creative person to produce excellent work. It takes concentration and commitment for a poet to write a poem or for an artist to paint a masterpiece. The person must free himself from all distractions so his mind, emotions, and talent can focus on the specific project before him. When an author or artist can concentrate exclusively on a creative assignment, he is able to put forth an all-out effort and release his full potential to produce a masterful work. Although it may be true that a great work can be produced with intermittent interruptions, the removal of distractions for the purpose of a more concentrated focus enables one to achieve the best results with greater speed.

This is significant in light of Revelation 2:5, where the tense of the word *poieo* calls for *urgent* and *quick* action. Anything less than a serious response would be found insufficient. Therefore, great effort, prayer, and concentration would be required if the Ephesian believers were to return to their first love and replicate the works that accompanied their early faith.

It is obvious that Christ expected the best from these believers — which would only be achieved if they responded to Him with their best effort. And because the Greek tense demands urgent and quick action, it is certain that Jesus wasn't willing to wait endlessly for them to respond. If they didn't heed His words, they would lose their position of spiritual leadership in Asia (*see* Revelation 2:5).

But what specifically was Jesus commanding this church to do? He told them in verse 5: "Remember therefore from whence thou art fallen, and repent, and do *the first works*...."

The phrase "first works" comes from the Greek words *prota erga*. The word *prota* means *first* or *early*, and the word *erga* means *works*, *deeds*, or *activity*, conveying the idea of *work that is produced by consistent and tireless effort*. Although the *King James Version* translates this Greek phrase as "first works," it could actually be interpreted, *"the actions that were indicative of you at the first"* or *"the things you did in the very beginning."*

Jesus commanded them to return to their "first works." He was referring to the words, deeds, and activities that characterized the Ephesian congregation at the beginning of their spiritual journey when they first fell in love with Jesus Christ.

What were these "first works" that once distinguished the church of Ephesus? Scripture reveals several characteristics of this prominent church in its early beginnings:

- They possessed a great spiritual hunger (*see* Acts 18:20).
- They enjoyed rich fellowship among the brethren (*see* Acts 18:27).
- They had an eagerness to repent and to receive what God had for them (*see* Acts 19:1-6).
- They cherished the Word of God (*see* Acts 19:8).
- They sacrificed their religious reputation for Jesus (*see* Acts 19:9).
- They were committed to applying God's Word to their lives (*see* Acts 19:10).
- They were receptive to the power of God and to the gifts of the Spirit (*see* Acts 19:11,12).
- They loved Jesus and the wonder-working power associated with His name (*see* Acts 19:17).
- They were quick to confess their sin and turn from their evil works (*see* Acts 19:18).
- They severed all connections with a pagan past at great personal cost (*see* Acts 19:19).
- They were publicly persecuted for the sake of Christ (*see* 1 Corinthians 15:32).
- They were faith-filled (*see* Ephesians 1:15).
- They were known for their love of the brethren (*see* Ephesians 1:15).

All of the qualities listed above characterized this passionate, vibrant congregation in its early years. The fact that Christ called for them to return to doing these "first works" doesn't necessarily mean they had become completely void of these attributes. However, it is evident that the intensity of their zeal had radically diminished. Thus, Christ urged them *to remember*, *to repent*, and *to do the first works* for these reasons:

- *Remembering how the fire of God once burned in their hearts was essential.* Only by remembering what they used to be could the Ephesian believers realize how far they had drifted.
- *Repentance was God's requirement.* An acknowledgment and confession of sin was the place to begin. If they were willing to humble themselves and repent, it would lead to their restoration and spare them from impending judgment.
- *Repentance demands proof.* A person who confesses his sin with no intention of changing is doing nothing more than admitting his guilt. He is *not* exhibiting genuine repentance. True repentance is always accompanied by corresponding actions. Regarding the Ephesian believers, Jesus made it clear that the proof of *their* repentance would be a return to a passionate pursuit of intimately knowing Him.

In Revelation 2:5, Jesus continued with His message to the Ephesian believers: "Remember therefore from whence thou art fallen, and repent, and do the first works; *or else I will come unto thee quickly…*"

The words "or else" would be better translated, *"and if not."* The Ephesian church had a decision to make, and Christ anticipated that they would do what He asked of them. But *if* they did not, He warned them, "...I will come unto thee quickly...."

The phrase "I will come" is a translation of the Greek word *erchomai,* which describes an event that would indeed take place *if* the Ephesian believers didn't meet Jesus' requirements. If they failed to do what He asked of them, they could expect Him to come to them with judgment, for the issues at hand were far too serious to ignore. The choice had been set before the congregation at Ephesus: They must repent, or Christ would remove them from their place of prominence among the other churches.

There is no Greek word in the original text for this word "quickly"; rather, it was added by the translators to help convey the urgency of the situation. Yet even as Jesus gave the Ephesian church this urgent warning, He also gave them the time frame they needed to respond to His request.

In the apostle John's vision of the exalted Christ, he saw that Jesus' feet were "like unto fine brass" (Revelation 1:15). Brass in Scripture represents judgment, which tells us that Christ was prepared to bring judgment if necessary. But brass or bronze is heavy; therefore, it is difficult to quickly move an object made of these metals. The fact that Jesus' feet appeared as made of bronze clearly sent the message that when Christ moves to bring judgment, He does *not* rush. Rather, He moves slowly in that direction, providing ample time for the repentance that will prevent the impending judgment.

Nevertheless, Jesus made it clear to the Ephesian congregation that if they resisted His pleadings, He would have to come to them in judgment. Thus, He warned them, "I will come unto thee quickly." The phrase "unto thee" (or "to you") is the Greek word *soi,* which means *directly to you.* The use of this word *soi* made Christ's warning to the Ephesians extremely *direct* and *personal.* The time allowed for repentance had already been set, and Jesus was walking toward them with His feet of bronze. If His voice was ignored, the outcome would be inevitable: *Judgment would surely follow.*

At the conclusion of Revelation 2:5, Jesus said, "Remember therefore from whence thou art fallen, and repent, and do the first works; or else I will come unto thee quickly, and will remove thy candlestick out of his place, *except thou repent.*"

The grammar used here implies again that Christ rebuked the Ephesian congregation with an expectation that they would repent; however, this outcome wasn't certain. This tells us how far the church of Ephesus had regressed in its spiritual passion. Jesus' warning to these believers was very direct, personal, and clear. Yet they had drifted so far from the fiery love for Him they had once known. The seeds of institutionalized religion seemed to have already begun to control them so much that Christ didn't say with absolute certainty that they would pass this test.

What about you? Is Jesus speaking to you today, calling you to return to a simple, passionate love for Him? Will you respond and pass the test? These questions that I've asked you in the past few days of *Sparkling Gems* are very important. Christ is watching, and He is waiting to see how you will respond to the dealings of His Spirit. If you've become stagnant and cold, are you going to respond by returning to the fires of His Spirit that once burned brightly within your heart — or are you going to remain as you are? Only you can answer this question — but be assured, *Jesus is awaiting your response today!*

MY PRAYER FOR TODAY

Father, I am deeply convicted by what I have read today. I recognize that You are calling me deeper and higher, and it is my responsibility to follow the leading of the Holy Spirit and to respond to what I have read. I repent for backsliding — for letting my once passionately intimate relationship with you slip and be replaced by other worldly concerns. I admit that I've done this, and I confess my sins and repent according to I John 1:9 and I receive full forgiveness. Now that I am free, I reclaim what I have lost, and I move forward to obtain what You have for me in the future.

I pray this in Jesus' name!

MY CONFESSION FOR TODAY

I confess that I repent for allowing worldliness and other things to take the place that belongs only to You. I lay hold of a new level of commitment that results in renewed love for You. You are watching and waiting to see how I will respond to the dealings of Your Spirit. I profess that I return to my first love.

I declare this by faith in Jesus' name!

QUESTIONS FOR YOU TO CONSIDER

1. Take an honest examination of your spiritual state: Do you possess a great hunger for the things of God? Do you cherish and prize God's Word above all else? Are you eager to repent or turn away from wrongdoing so you can stay in proper alignment with God?
2. Has the intensity of your spiritual zeal radically diminished? Are you in passionate pursuit of knowing the Lord intimately? If your fervor for the Lord has diminished, what caused that change? What must you do to return to your first love?
3. A person who confesses his sin with no intention of changing is doing nothing more than admitting his guilt instead of exhibiting genuine repentance. What do you need to repent of? What corresponding actions must follow your decision?

What about you?
Is Jesus speaking to you today, calling you to return to a simple, passionate love for Him?
Will you respond and pass the test?

SEPTEMBER 1

The Solution to Offense: FORGIVENESS!

...If thy brother trespass against thee,
rebuke him; and if he repent, forgive him.
— Luke 17:3

I was once offended by a missionary who lied to me and led me into a web of deceit that hurt me deeply. What really hurt was that I had trusted this man and had such a high regard for him. But when I discovered what he had done — and that he had done it deliberately — it was like a knife had been plunged into the depth of my soul. Every time I saw that brother and how casually and unrepentant he behaved about what he had done, the devil twisted that knife in my back another turn and caused that deeply intense pain to be inflicted all over again.

I really didn't know what to do to resolve the situation. I felt the missionary should be held accountable for what he had done to Denise and me and to our ministry — but there was no way to hold him accountable that we could find. So he just drifted away freely, facing no consequences for the deep wound he had caused in my heart.

One day as I lay in my bed, pondering this situation, the Holy Spirit spoke to my heart and said, "Rick, your only option is to let it go. If you hold on to this pain and hurt, it will imprison you to your emotions and hinder you from making the forward progress I want you to make in life."

Was the Holy Spirit really telling me to just let it go and act like what this minister had done never happened — while I continued to rub shoulders with him from time to time at meetings that we were both required to attend? This seemed like a most difficult thing that the Lord was asking me to do!

Meanwhile, the offender felt no guilt for what he'd done. He suffered no pain for the suffering he had inflicted on us. He was free in his mind from the entire matter! He didn't wrestle with a single thought about his betrayal of a fellow minister and brother in the Lord. Instead, *I* was the one who was bound, consumed with negative thoughts and feelings of hurt, pain, and offense. It was like this man had no conscience — and that ate away at me too.

Have you ever held on to an inward offense instead of dealing with it quickly? If so, you know that it has a way of eating away at your soul — spoiling your outlook on life, adversely affecting your view of others, and, of course, negatively impacting your spiritual life. Furthermore, when you allow offense to fester in your soul, you become less and less guarded with your own words about your offender. It's not long until you start *talking* about the other person who offended you rather than *praying* for him or her, because as the Bible teaches, out of the abundance of the heart, the mouth speaks.

Have you ever been guilty of telling others about a negative thing that another person said or did to you? If you did, were you aware that you were defiling your listeners? You were staining their thoughts with a negative opinion that could change how they see and respond to the person who offended you. Every time those who heard your words encounter your offender in the future, they will likely remember that report you gave them.

This is precisely how gossip-fueled scandals are created, many of which cause irrevocable damage. No one wins when bitterness is allowed to take root and then spring up to defile many.

Instead of being free in my own situation, I found that my mouth had become a vehicle to say ugly things about this man every chance I got. Maybe my words were not so direct and caustic, but they left an impression for any listener to understand that I had serious doubts about the integrity of this leader. Without directly accusing him, I was purposefully casting a shadow on his integrity.

Finally, a day came when I sat down with this man — one of the most difficult things I had ever done — and expressed my feelings to him. To make sure there was a witness, I brought along another ministry leader to listen to both of us and judge the situation. After hours of conversation, rehashing the story over and over again, it was obvious that my offender was not repentant or even slightly sorry for what he had done. This led me to a choice: I could stay hurt and in bondage to my pain forever, or I could choose to let it go and walk away free. "Letting it go" is exactly what the Holy Spirit had already told me to do!

That night, I was reminded of Jesus' words in both Luke 17:3 and in Mark 11:25. In Luke 17:3, He provided a solution: "…If thy brother trespass against thee, rebuke him, and if he repent, *forgive* him." Then in Mark 11:25, Jesus gave the full solution: "And when ye stand praying, *forgive*, if ye have ought against any…."

I had rebuked this missionary in the presence of another leader, yet it made no difference. But even though he had not repented, my options were *still the same*! I could remain in emotional bondage to the pain he had inflicted — or I could forgive him and walk away from that table free, even if he *never, ever* recognized the extent of the damage he had done to us.

Jesus expects us to take the mature role and to forgive others, regardless of how they behave. The word "forgive" is the Greek word *aphiemi*, which means in modern terms *to let it go*. Rather than be held hostage by what someone has done to you, or by what you may *think* that person has done to you, Jesus says, "*Aphiemi* — let it go."

But often the only way you can truly *dismiss, release*, and *let go o*f an offense is to get into the presence of the Lord and let Him help you. Just go to Him and say, "Father, I'm not willing to be bound by this offense. I refuse to be imprisoned by these feelings of hurt, rejection, or humiliation. Right now before You, I choose to let it go in the name of Jesus."

You are the only one who has the authority to rip the root of bitterness and offense out of your own heart. If you're ever going to be free, move forward, and live fully in the power of God, you're going to have to release the offenses that you've allowed to build a stronghold in your heart.

Also, please be aware that bitterness doesn't just hinder your walk with God. It will also impede your fellowship with others. The fact is, if you're bound by offense against one person, that bondage will affect your other relationships as well, because the poisonous attitudes you carry in your heart against one person will affect how you respond to everyone else.

You may have suffered a hurt or offense in the past that harmed you terribly. In fact, it may have robbed you of something that can never be returned or restored. But if you refuse to forgive — to let go of anger, animosity, and bitterness — that offense will continue to work its destruction in your life. A past-tense problem will become a present-tense issue when you refuse to let go of your bitterness. If you don't get over that past offense, you will give it the power to damage and even destroy your future as you drag it along like a bag of garbage or toxic waste. At some point, you have to just let it go and get over it for your own benefit and for the benefit of those around you.

I don't know what may have happened to you in the past or what offense you may be holding against someone else right now. But I want you to know that you can walk free of those negative, unhealthy attitudes and emotions *if* you'll make the decision to exercise your authority over your own heart and mind. Someone may commit an offense against you by speaking or acting inappropriately toward you without your provocation. But you cannot be offended unless you *take* the offense to yourself. You *always* have a choice.

It is a difficult lesson to learn, but learn it you must. There is no other way to move forward in God. When an offense is hurled at you, you are to deal with it scripturally the best way you can. But if you cannot bring it to a peaceful resolution, you are called to *let it go*. As you do, you will walk away *free* — free to be all God intended for you to be as you pursue the destiny He ordained for you.

So make the choice today regarding every past offense, hurt, or disappointment: "This day I *let it go*, and I walk away *free*!"

MY PRAYER FOR TODAY

Father God, I repent for the offense I have harbored in my heart toward people. I see now that offense has held me in a prison of my own making. I have been tormented by it, and it has kept me from making spiritual progress as I should. Rather than allow offense room to continue festering in my heart and soul, today I make the choice to let it go. I forgive my offenders, and I extend the same grace to them that I want others to give me. Right now I receive freedom as I choose to walk away from the offenses that have held me in bondage for so long!

I pray this in Jesus' name!

MY CONFESSION FOR TODAY

I declare by faith that I am an offense-free person! Others' actions, or lack of actions, do not have the power to put me into a state of bitterness and offense. To be offended requires my agreement, and I will no longer agree to stay in a state of unforgiveness and offense. I release those who have violated me in the past, and I will never bring it up again to them, to others, or to myself. I completely and freely forgive them. As a result, I am a free person with no oppressive, parasitic appendages hanging on me any longer!

I declare this by faith in Jesus' name!

QUESTIONS FOR YOU TO CONSIDER

1. Have you ever held on to an offense that sabotaged your present or future? How long did you allow that offense to adversely affect you before you finally decided to let it go and be free of it?
2. Do you know any individuals right now who are held in a spiritual prison because they won't forgive people that they perceive have done something wrong to them? After reading today's *Sparkling Gem*, how should you minister to them to help set them on a path of freedom?
3. Is it possible that those who have offended you didn't even know they offended you? Has the devil perhaps conjured up a bogus issue in your mind to steal your peace and rob your joy? And even if the offense is real, don't you think it's time to obey Jesus and *let it go*?

SEPTEMBER 2

My Hallowed Place

And in the morning, rising up a great while
before day, he [Jesus] went out, and departed
into a solitary place, and there he prayed.
— Mark 1:35

Every day when I rise in the morning, I go to the kitchen to get a cup of coffee, I grab my Bible, and I head to a hallowed place of prayer in our home. I shut the door to that room, which happens to be the TV room. There I have a leather chair that has become my daily meeting place with God each morning. Recently I looked at that chair, and it is practically ruined with "scratches" — crease marks — from the thousands of hours I have sat upon it as I've prayed. But those marks are precious to me because they represent countless hours I've spent sitting there, seeking the face of God and letting Him saturate my heart. Those scratches memorialize the place where I meet with God every morning unless I'm traveling abroad. (When Denise and I are traveling, we both rise early and seek out separate places where we each can pray privately just as we do when we are home.)

Denise kindly understands that as long as the door to our TV room is shut in the mornings, I am in fellowship with the Holy Spirit, reading my Bible, and allowing the Word of God to search my heart and soul to bring me into closer alignment with Jesus. Denise graciously never interrupts — unless it's for some urgent reason — for she knows that this time alone with God will make me a better Christian, a better husband, and a more devoted follower of Jesus Christ.

On days when I must be at morning meetings at our Moscow Good News Church — or on days when we are filming TV programs — I arise even earlier, because I simply cannot forgo this time with the Lord. So even on those days, I can be found there in the TV room — the door closed — seeking God and studying His Word before any of these other events take place.

I have learned that I cannot have productive days without this time with the Lord. During those early morning times, I pray and I pour out my heart to God with thanksgiving for all He has done in my life. I pray fervently for partners and for others who are on my prayer list. I virtually never start a day at home without sitting in that beloved chair to seek the face of God and to allow God's Spirit to search my heart and bring me to a more intimate experience with Jesus.

When I think of this "hallowed" place that I have set apart for seeking God, my mind always goes to Jesus and to the fact that He would rise early in the mornings to seek a solitary place where He could be alone with the Father and the Holy Spirit. We read of this in Mark 1:35, where the Bible tells us, "And in the morning, rising up a great while before day, He went out, and departed into a solitary place, and there he prayed."

When the verse says that Jesus rose up "a great while before day," the Greek actually says He arose while it was still dark. His disciples may have still been sleeping — but Jesus sought a secluded place where He could enter into fellowship with the Holy Spirit. He understood that the strength and anointing He needed depended on His fellowship with the Father and the Holy Spirit. So Jesus made it His highest priority to withdraw from the disciples and from the multitudes *very early in the morning* to spend time fellowshipping with the Father and the Holy Spirit without interruption. When everyone else was finally rising, He had already been touched and strengthened by God and was ready to emerge with a fresh touch of the Holy Spirit's power on His life.

Because Jesus and the disciples were constantly on the move from one location to another location, He did not have the luxury of having the same leather chair to retreat to each day as I do. The place where He spent time in prayer was frequently different. But one thing that was true of each location is found in Mark 1:35, where it says that Jesus always sought a "solitary" place where He would not be disturbed.

Actually, Mark 1:35 says he "departed into a solitary place." The word "departed" is a form of the Greek word *aperchomai*, which, in this case, means *to seek distance away* from other things.

Jesus may have walked to the top of a mountain, or into a ravine, but it was some place that was distant from His disciples and the multitudes. He deliberately sought "space" between Himself and others for this private time of prayer.

Mark went on to say that when Jesus arose, He went to a "solitary" place. The word "solitary" is the Greek word *ermos*, which describes a *deserted* place. To put it into today's vernacular, we could say it was *a remote spot*, *a place that was out of the way*, *somewhere off the beaten track*, *an obscure site*, or *an unfrequented location*.

In other words, Jesus sought for a place where no one would accidentally find Him and disturb this solitary time in prayer. This demonstrates just how vitally important it was to Jesus to find time alone where the Father could speak to His heart and He could pour His heart out to the Father and fellowship with the Holy Spirit.

I don't have a mountain to climb to find a remote location, and there are no ravines near my house. So I use what is next best — a room in my home that I have designated as "off-limits" during the time that door is closed. And during those "off-limit" times, I have deep and meaningful fellowship with the Father and the Son and the Holy Spirit. And just as Jesus emerged from His solitary times renewed in power, I come forth from my daily times refreshed, reinvigorated, filled with new ideas, and empowered for my day.

Such moments of solitude with God are critical to the daily victory of every believer!

I want to ask if you have a "solitary place" where you "depart" — that is, where you put distance between yourself and others so you can have isolated time with the Lord? He longs to have this time with you — and you *must* have it if you are to live as an overcoming, victorious, empowered child of God.

If you answered yes, where is your solitary place where you meet with God? If your answer is no, I urge you today to begin seeking a place where you can develop this meaningful time with God in prayer!

For me, it all happens in a scratched-up leather chair in my TV room — a chair that bears all the marks of the time I've spent alone with God. And I can tell you for sure that if *you* really want to have this type of solitary time with the Lord, He will show you where, when, and how to do it!

MY PRAYER FOR TODAY

Heavenly Father, I make a fresh commitment to start each day by lifting my voice to You. Each morning, Lord, I will rise and present my life to You, waiting expectantly for what You will speak to my heart. I ask Your forgiveness for all the times I foolishly launched into my day without having read your Word, sought Your face, or consulted the Holy Spirit whom You sent to be my Counselor, Helper, and Guide. Father, how arrogant and misguided of me to believe I could walk effectively in wisdom and truth without having submitted myself to You first. Only through rich fellowship with You can I produce fruit that remains. Forgive me for mistaking busyness for fruitfulness. I abide in You and let Your words abide in me. I treasure the words of Your mouth more than my necessary food. Holy Spirit, I ask You to help me order my day and to keep it set around giving my time with the Father first place from this day forward.

I pray this in Jesus' name!

MY CONFESSION FOR TODAY

I confess that I do not neglect my time in a "solitary place" with God. I deliberately designate an off-limits time and place where I can have deep, meaningful, and uninterrupted fellowship with the Father, the Son, and the Holy Spirit. Just as Jesus arose a great while before day to meet with the Father and then emerged from His solitary times renewed in power, I come forth from my daily times refreshed, reinvigorated, filled with new ideas, and empowered for my day. These moments of solitude with the Father keep my heart sensitive and yielded to Him while equipping me to possess my daily victory in the power of His might!

I declare this by faith in Jesus' name!

QUESTIONS FOR YOU TO CONSIDER

1. Do you have a "solitary place" where you meet with God every day? What time of the day do you set aside for this special moment? Is it in the morning, at lunch, or in the evenings before you go to bed?
2. It may be hard for you to rise early, but I strongly suggest that you develop a discipline of rising early before your day gets started so that you can be touched, refreshed, and empowered for whatever you will face each day. What earlier time could you start getting up to spend this time in prayer?
3. Do you feel that you actually know how to fellowship with the Lord in prayer? If not, don't be embarrassed. Get an online Bible-reading plan and start there, fellowshipping with the Lord as you read His Word. As the Holy Spirit speaks to your heart about certain verses, stop and reflect on them. Let His words sink deep into your heart. That is an excellent starting point!

Jesus sought for a place
where no one would accidentally find Him
and disturb His solitary time in prayer.
This demonstrates just how vitally important
it was to Jesus to find time alone
where the Father could speak to His heart
and He could pour His heart out to the Father
and fellowship with the Holy Spirit.

SEPTEMBER 3

Jesus in Our Very Midst — Even When We're Separated by Miles

For where two or three
are gathered together in my name,
there am I in the midst of them.
— Matthew 18:20

Denise and I fully believe in the promise of Jesus in Matthew 18:20. It says, "For where two or three of you are gathered together in my name, there am I in the midst of them." We have experienced the presence of Jesus for years as we and other believers have gathered in His name. What a sweet presence fills our hearts as we come together in His name and seek His face.

We've experienced the presence of Jesus at church, at conferences, in prayer meetings, even at work with other believers — and now we're experiencing Him in a new fashion every Monday night as Denise and I, along with one or more of our sons, welcome people to our online "Home Group" that is broadcast by Internet across the face of the earth. We "gather together in Jesus' name" — and Jesus is there in the midst of us all over the world.

Some years ago, the Holy Spirit dropped an idea into my heart to start an online Home Group every Monday night and to invite people from around the world to join us. In the years we have done this, we have seen God touch so many people's lives. The Word has been taught; miracles have occurred; and God has supernaturally linked people together online from all over the earth. And Jesus has been in the midst of us even as we all tune in from our various locations across the globe.

We actually webcast our online Home Group twice every Monday — once in English for the English-speaking world and once in Russian for the Russian-speaking world. People join us from all over the planet for this time when we teach the Word of God and share our life experiences from our hearts. This Home Group has truly become an online family and a time that our family and our Home Group members have come to cherish each week. In fact, one of our greatest personal joys is to have people come up to us when we are traveling and speaking in churches and conferences across the world and identify themselves as Home Group members. It's like we have a brief, fabulous family reunion "on the spot" as we finally meet face to face!

On this very night as I write this *Gem*, we broadcasted one of our Home Group meetings. As soon as it was over, I immediately left the TV studio to put my thoughts on paper. The very air in our TV studio was electrified by the presence of Jesus as people tuned in from all over the earth to participate in an international online time together in Jesus' name. I always begin by introducing ourselves, and then I remind our Internet family of the promise of Jesus in Matthew 18:20. Jesus said, "For where two or three are gathered together in my name, there am I in the midst of them." Jesus said nothing about being in the same room in order to experience His presence. *He simply said we had to be gathered together in His name!*

There are a handful of us who actually gather in the TV studio and produce the Internet broadcast for the Home Group. But in addition, there are *very large numbers* of faithful Home Group members who sit in front of their computers all over the world, joining with us as we all seek the truths of God's Word together. Some view the webcast alone, and others watch with their spouses and families. There are even entire prayer groups who come together around a computer to join in!

Again, Jesus never said we all had to be gathered in one room. He simply promised that if we were "gathered together in His name," He would be in the "midst" of us. Through the amazing development of the Internet, scores of us gather in Jesus' name — and Jesus honors His Word by manifesting His sweet presence in the TV studio and in every home across the world where people are gathered online with us. *It is a truly amazing experience!*

Notice that Jesus said His presence would be in our "midst" anytime two or more are gathered together in His name. That means if you're in the car with a Christian friend, Jesus is *there* with you. If you are at restaurant with several Christian brothers and sisters, Jesus is *there* with *you*. If you are at church, assembled with the entire congregation, Jesus is *there* with you. If you are on the telephone talking to a Christian friend and calling on Jesus to be the center of the conversation, Jesus is *there* with you!

The Greek word for "midst" is *meso*, which means *right in the very center* or *right in the very midst.* It is Jesus' guarantee that we if are gathered together in His name, for His purposes — regardless of *how* we are gathered — He will be right there with us in the power of His mighty name!

Before the development of Internet, I had always limited this verse to church services, conferences, seminars, or prayer meetings, etc. But now the limit has been removed entirely. Anyone who deliberately gathers — in any shape or fashion — in the name of Jesus will experience the *presence* of Jesus in their midst. Believers on every continent of the world can gather simultaneously through the Internet in His wonderful name. And even though thousands of miles separate them, Jesus will manifest His presence in the heart of each person at the same time! *What a miracle!*

Today I want to encourage you to seek out fellowship with other believers through whatever means you can — over the phone, by Internet, by text or chat, at church, etc. — and ask Jesus to be there at the *very center* of your fellowship. Even if it's only two or three of you, He will always be faithful to show up and manifest His goodness in your midst by His Spirit. It's His promise to you and me, and there is nothing to be compared to the sweet presence of Jesus among believers who are gathered in His name. *Do it today!*

MY PRAYER FOR TODAY

Father, I thank You for the promise Jesus made in Matthew 18:20 — that if two or three gather together in His name, there He would be in the midst of them. There is nothing even remotely comparable to the sweet presence of Jesus in the midst of Christian fellowship. It makes me want to ask You to forgive me for the times that I haven't made a better effort to gather with other believers. I really need that sweet presence of Jesus that is experienced in Christian fellowship — and I'm so thankful that Jesus manifests Himself to those who gather in His name. Help me to be more consistent about my commitment to gathering in Jesus' name with other brothers and sisters. And thank You for revealing and manifesting Yourself to us in such a precious way!

I pray this in Jesus' name!

MY CONFESSION FOR TODAY

I confess that I need the sweet presence of Jesus that is manifested specially as brothers and sisters gather together in the name of Jesus. The Lord Jesus promised that He would be there among us as we gather in His name — and I commit to gathering regularly with others who are also seeking His face. Thank You, Lord, that You did not say we had to all be in the same room at the same time. You said simply that we had to gather at the same time in Your name, and Your precious presence would be there with us. I declare that I need that "corporate" presence of Jesus and that I will therefore take advantage of every opportunity to gather with other believers in Jesus' name!

I declare this by faith in Jesus' name!

QUESTIONS FOR YOU TO CONSIDER

1. What did you learn from today's *Sparkling Gem*? Had you ever considered the wide ramifications this promise from Matthew 18:20 held for you and me?
2. In what ways do you sense the sweet presence of Jesus when you are gathered with other believers in His name?
3. Have you ever experienced Jesus' manifested presence in a setting other than a typical prayer meeting or church gathering? Where did that occur? How did that experience minister to you?

Anyone who deliberately gathers —
in any shape or fashion —
in the name of Jesus will experience
the presence of Jesus in their midst.

SEPTEMBER 4

Six Suggestions To Help You Get Into a Place of Faith

But without faith it is impossible to please him....
— Hebrews 11:6

I am so glad Denise and I chose to obey God when He called our family to move from a comfortable life in the United States into the unknown challenges of ministering in the former Soviet Union. I vividly remember that difficult time when I struggled with the growing awareness of that divine call. However, I ultimately came to the place where I knew there was no way around it. If we were going to obey God and walk in divine alignment with His plan and purpose for our lives, we'd have to obey His leading and move halfway around the world to the former USSR.

A verse that really helped me back in those days — and that still helps me today — is Hebrews 11:6. It says, "But without faith, it is impossible to please Him [God]...." The word "without" is the Greek word *choris*, a word that means to be *outside* of something — like *outside* the city limits or *outside* the house, as opposed to inside the city or inside the house. It should actually be translated, "But *outside* of faith...."

This word describes faith as a location — a place where you can live "in" or live "out" of. The Greek literally means, "But *outside* of the place of faith, it is impossible to *please* Him...."

Furthermore, the word "please" is the Greek word *euarestesai*, a compound of the words *eu* and *arestos*. The word *eu* means well, as in something that is *well* — and the word *arestos* means *enjoyable* or *pleasing*. Together they describe *the pleasure one feels from seeing something that is especially excellent or delightful.*

So when you take all these different meanings into account, Hebrews 11:6 can be translated: *"Outside of the realm of faith, it is impossible to bring delight and pleasure to God...."* The flip side to this statement is that when you are living "in" a place of faith — that is, if you are where God has called you and doing what God has asked you to do — you bring pleasure to the Lord.

For Denise and I to live in a place of faith, it required us to be where God was calling us — and that was the former USSR. In the years that we have lived in this part of the world, God has asked us to do many things that required us to have "faith." Each time, we had to decide to stay "in" the place of faith until the assignment was accomplished. Regardless of how difficult the task was or how long it took us to do it, we knew we had to be committed to stay "in" the place of faith until the job was done. According to Hebrews 11:6, God has been observing us — and as long as we've stayed "in faith," it has brought delight and pleasure to His heart. *That has been our great motivation to stay "in" faith!*

If you want to fully follow God's plan for your life, you must find out where God wants you to be. Then you must get in alignment with God's call and stay there until the task is fulfilled. It is only from this position of solid, unequivocal alignment with God's will that you can know you are pleasing God!

But you have to get started! So in today's *Sparkling Gem*, I want to help you know how to start moving toward that all-important goal of being "in" faith with the tasks and assignments God gives to you. It may be that you don't know where to begin your tasks of faith, so I want to help you learn how to get started and to discover where you'll find God's will for your life.

I want to offer six suggestions that can help you get moving in the right direction. If you don't already have concrete direction, I've discovered that it's best for you to first find a place to serve; then as you serve, God will start giving you a vision for your own life. So here are my simple six suggestions:

1. **Decide to *start.***

   Look around you and assess the various needs you see. Decide which needs you may be able to help meet. Prayerfully determine how your talents, gifts, and money can best reach souls and bring them into God's Kingdom.

   Then go for it "full throttle"! Actively set your faith on fulfilling the task. Believe for blessing to come upon it. Make it a priority in your prayer life, praying and serving as if the entire project depended on you.

2. **Decide *how* you are going to start serving.**

   Seek guidance from the Lord regarding *how* you're supposed to move forward. What is God specifically telling you to do? Is it something at church, with a ministry, or on your own? Are you supposed to start by giving *financially* to the work of the Lord? It takes fuel to run any ship, so your finances provide a powerful means of serving. Giving is one of the most effective ways to help promote and advance the cause of the Gospel.

3. **Decide *where* you are going to serve.**

   Don't take just any opportunity that comes along. Instead, ask the Holy Spirit to show you *where* you are supposed to serve. Once the Lord shows you, go for it with all your heart. Don't be a low-level performer at anything God calls you to do. Give your best to the assigned task and remember that there's a reward awaiting you in the future.

4. **Decide what *level of commitment* you are willing to make.**

   Don't *overcommit* yourself by promising to do something that isn't possible for you to do. Even if your heart wants to say, "Yes, yes, I'll do that," step back and ask, "Is this realistic? Will I be able to do what I'm committing to?"

Evaluate how this level of commitment fits in with all the other commitments you've already made. When you commit to do something, people think they can depend on you. So if you back out of your commitment later because it's too much for you to handle, you mess up the plan for everyone else involved. It's better to move slower in the beginning so you can make sure you're making the right decision.

Before you make a financial commitment to a church or ministry, make sure it's a commitment you can really keep. If your heart is crying out to give financially, act on that desire.

However, first analyze what amount you can actually give. If you have the ability to give large amounts, go for it! But if you need to start by giving smaller amounts because your financial resources are limited, that's all right too. It's better to commit to an amount that is actually achievable than to make a financial commitment that is larger than your current ability to fulfill.

5. Decide to make a habit of *sowing seed* — and start immediately.

Galatians 6:7 says, "...Whatsoever a man soweth, that shall he also reap." This law of sowing and reaping works for everyone in the world. *What you sow is exactly what you are going to reap.* It may take awhile, but harvest day is coming if you've been planting seeds along the way. So decide to become a sower immediately — *and start sowing those seeds today!*

You also need to decide *what* you are going to sow. Since Galatians 6:7 says, "...Whatsoever a man soweth, *that* shall he also reap," it's very important to know what you want to reap. Determining what you want your harvest to be is the best way to determine what you should sow.

For instance, if you need time, you should sow time. If you need love, you should sow love. If you need friendship, you should sow friendship. If you need money, you should sow money. This is a law of God that always works. So look at what you need to reap, and then start sowing your seed accordingly.

You need to decide *where* you're going to start sowing seed. As you make that decision, I urge you to make sure that you sow your seed into *good* ground. By that I mean you should sow seed into a church, ministry, or Christian organization that is truly accomplishing something profitable and good. Don't throw your seed into ground that doesn't produce excellent fruit. Look for fruit-producers. Once you find them, you'll know where you should plant your seed.

I also strongly recommend that you sow your seed into what you want to become. I plant my seeds into ministries I believe in and into ministries from which I want a particular harvest. The Bible promises that we become "partakers of the grace" that rests on any ministry we sow into (*see* Philippians 1:7). Therefore, I carefully choose where I sow my seed. I sow into ministries that have something I desire for myself. In other words, the grace that is on that ministry is the grace that will flow back into my life.

6. Decide that you will not *stop* for any reason.

Galatians 6:9 continues, "And let us not be weary in well doing: for in due season we shall reap, if we faint not." Keep your eyes on the prize, and don't allow weariness to knock you out of the game! The Bible promises that your due season is coming. Even if it looks like it's taking too long for your harvest to come back to you, hang on tight and keep doing what you know God wants you to do. Your "due season" is on its way.

In the process of receiving that expected end, keep your level of expectancy *high*. God promises that your "due season" *will* come if you don't faint and give up. So don't let the devil or discouraging circumstances maneuver you out of the manifestation you've been waiting for. The moment you're on the brink of your "due season" of God's plan for your life, that's usually the time the devil tries the hardest to get you to quit!

These six principles of God's Word always work — *in every country, in every culture, and for every person.* If you will follow these principles, they will work for you to get you on the path that leads to your divine destination.

I urge you not to waste any time just sitting around and waiting for something to happen. It's time for you to jump into action and expend whatever level of energy is necessary to move forward in fulfilling what God has put in your heart to do. And if you don't know how to get your own dream moving yet, take this time to sow your time, talent, and money into someone else's God-given dream. Remember, the law of sowing and reaping is always in operation. *What you do for someone else is exactly what will come back to you!*

So if you don't know where to start in your own journey of faith, I pray that these six suggestions are helpful to you. Once you start moving, serving, and giving, I am sure that the Holy Spirit will begin talking to you about your own faith assignment — which may be entirely to help someone else. Whatever your divine assignment entails, God will make it very clear to you as He observes you staying faithful. These six suggestions are very simple, but if you put them into practice, it won't be long until you begin to hear God speak some concrete direction to you. Then you'll begin to understand where you need to be and what you should be doing to stay "in" the place of God that makes Him smile when He looks at you!

MY PRAYER FOR TODAY

Father, I thank You for this practical help on knowing how to get started on finding my place of faith. I want to know Your will; I want to follow it; and I want to stay "in" that place of faith until I hear You tell me that I've faithfully finished the task You've assigned to me. Help me know where to start, where to serve, what to sow, and where to sow my seed. I know that the six suggestions outlined in today's Sparkling Gem will help me get started, so Holy Spirit, let's do it — I am ready to get started today!

I pray this in Jesus' name!

MY CONFESSION FOR TODAY

I confess that I am not a person who just sits around, wondering about God's will for my life. Until He speaks to me, I will implement these six suggestions in my life. I will start; I will know how and where to serve; I will determine the level of commitment I can make right now; I will sow my seed; and I will not stop. I fully expect to see harvests coming back to me from every direction. I refuse to sit idly and wonder what I should do. I will find a place to serve and sow, and I will get started. As I take these steps of faith, I'll begin to hear God's voice speak to me specifically about my own place of faith — and when I hear it, I'll obey and stick with it until I hear the Lord say the job is done.

I declare this by faith in Jesus' name!

QUESTIONS FOR YOU TO CONSIDER

1. Do you *know* what God has told you to do with your life? If not, have you considered serving someone else or somewhere else until your vision becomes clear to you? Are you serving somewhere now? Where are you serving?
2. Have you ever been "in" faith, and then slowly moved "out" of faith to the degree that you had to repent and get back in faith again? When was that experience? Is it something you are going through right now? How do you plan to get back "in" faith again?
3. Of the six suggestions you read about today, which of them are you already doing? Which ones do you need to implement?

SEPTEMBER 5

'Spiritual Curb Appeal'

Moreover he must have a good report
of them which are without....
— 1 Timothy 3:7

Sometimes I hear people remark, "What people think of me is not important. It's only important what God thinks of me, and that's all that I should be concerned about."

Today I want to explore this statement, especially for those who hunger to be used by God in a greater way. As you will see, what others think of you is very important if you want to be effective in reaching and helping other people. Your "spiritual curb appeal" determines whether or not people will listen to you or let you lead them, or if they will walk away in disgust. Let me give you an example from my own life.

Years ago I was prepared to invest a large sum of money on a particular project, so I spent weeks researching to understand the best place to make this investment of my time and money. I read advertisements and browsed the Internet to see what I could learn about different places where I could do this business. Finally I found what sounded like the ideal place to take our business. However, this was such a serious investment that I sensed the need to first go there to personally check it out before I made such a large transaction. I told my wife, "From everything I've read, it seems to me that this is a top-notch professional place to do business."

But when I actually came to the place to see if this local business met my expectations, I was *shocked*. There I was, ready to make a large transaction that was very serious to me. But when I saw how the employees were dressed, I wasn't so sure I *wanted* to do business there. Their clothes were sloppy; their hair was disheveled; the shoelaces on their tennis shoes were untied, and it looked to me like the official company uniform included shoddy-looking, baggy sweaters. I was dressed far more nicely than any of them!

I sat down to speak to a representative, and it was evident that he really knew what he was talking about. But to be truthful, the entire time the man was talking to me, I kept thinking, *Why am I talking to a man who didn't comb his hair before he came to work and whose shoes are filthy? I don't feel good about trusting a man who doesn't even care what he looks like to his clients!* As smart as he sounded and as great as that group claimed to be, they lost my business because I just couldn't bear the idea of investing my money with a group of people who looked so unprofessional. Even if they were geniuses, their "curb appeal" was so unprofessional that I decided *not* to do business with them.

Whether we like it or not, most people make their choices based on information received by their five senses. What people *see*, *hear*, *smell*, *taste*, or *feel* affects *everything*. What they perceive with their senses determines what they receive or reject; what they eat or refuse to eat; what they listen to or shut their ears to; what they watch or what they turn off; what they buy or what they walk away from; what they enjoy or what they loathe. People are affected by what they *see*, *hear*, *smell*, *taste*, and *feel*. If it doesn't look good, sound good, smell good, taste good, or feel good, it isn't going to sell very well. This is usually true regardless of how good a product is. It isn't going to sell very well if it doesn't appeal to the senses because people are affected by these things.

This is why it is so imperative that you understand what people perceive about you *is* very important. If you do not have the right "curb appeal," people will not listen to you or follow you. If they are turned off by you, your behavior, or your personal presentation, they will be less inclined to let you be their leader. It is just a fact that people *are* affected by how you dress, how you talk, how you treat others, how you work at the job, and yes, even by your personal appearance. *Think of what an impact a first impression has on you when you meet a person!*

This issue of what people think is so important that when the apostle Paul told Timothy how to choose leaders, he told the younger minister that it was imperative to choose leaders who "...have a good report of them that are without..." (1 Timothy 3:7).

The words "good report" is derived from two Greek words, *kalos* and *marturia.* The word *kalos* means *good, beautiful, noble, enjoyable,* or *pleasing.* The word "report" in Greek is derived from the Greek word *marturia.* This word has an array of meanings, depending on how it is used, but in this verse, it means *a testimony* or *a witness.* When used with the word *kalos,* the entire phrase means *a good witness* or *a good testimony.*

However, because the word *kalos* means *good, beautiful, noble, enjoyable,* or *pleasing,* it conveys the idea of a person whom others *enjoy* and who has a testimony of being *pleasant* or *pleasing.* In other words, this person has *a good reputation* in the sight of others. There is nothing offensive or displeasing in his behavior, temperament, or presentation that would discredit him in other people's sight. According to Paul, it is mandatory that potential leaders have this kind of testimony. *What others think about them is very important!*

But look what Paul said next. He wrote that if a person desires to be a leader, it is especially required that he or she has a good reputation with "them that are without."

The word "without" is the Greek word *exouthen,* and it refers to people who are *outside,* such as those who are *outside of Christ.* It refers to people who are *non-Christian.* Paul says a man or woman shouldn't even be permitted to be a leader unless non-Christians think highly of them.

It doesn't matter how much Gospel you preach to non-Christians, how many tracts and books you leave on their desks, or how much literature you send them in the mail — unbelievers are affected by what they *see, hear, smell, taste,* and *touch.* This means *your life is your primary pulpit.* If you are a leader or aspire to a leadership position, you must understand this and recognize that people are actively observing the message you present with your life. That is why it's so important that your "curb appeal" be Christ-honoring and spiritually appealing to people who are watching you.

Think for a moment about leaders of influence who have many people following them. People generally don't follow those of whom they have a low opinion; rather, they follow people whom they respect and of whom they hold a high opinion. This shows the power of influence and the importance of people's perceptions. A person's reputation and his personal behavior are so powerful that these factors determine whether or not a crowd will follow him. In fact, if a person's "curb appeal" isn't right, people will seldom listen to or follow him or her, regardless of how gifted that person might be.

Sometimes I hear people remark, "What people think of me is not important. It's only important what *God* thinks of me. That's all I should be concerned about." When I hear that, I know these are the remarks of individuals who have had no experience in leading people. If anyone intends to help people and affect masses in a positive way for the Kingdom of God, that person will have to learn this principle called *curb appeal.*

The fact is, what people perceive about us *is* very important, for it determines whether or not they will ever listen to us!

So let me ask you:

- Do you have a testimony that you are a positive, optimistic, cheerful, faith-filled, hardworking, dependable team player who is enjoyed by others?
- Do non-Christians prefer not to work with you because you frequently display a negative attitude and often give a lazy performance on the job?
- What is your "curb appeal" with unsaved people who see you every day?
- Do people in the church see you as a person they can depend on, or do they view you as undependable and not serious about your commitment?
- How is your "curb appeal" to people in your Christian community?
- Do your fellow believers look to you for help when it's needed, or do they bypass you because their opinion of you is so low that they have discounted you altogether?

I encourage you to think a little deeper about this subject, especially if you want to be used by God to touch other people in this life. And if your present circle of friends doesn't understand this vital principle, you may need to develop a *new* circle of friends who do understand it! It's too important to just ignore the implications, because *you can influence people for God only to the extent that people have a high opinion of you.*

So I encourage you today: Ask the Lord what specific steps you could begin to take to spruce up your "spiritual curb appeal"!

MY PRAYER FOR TODAY

Father, I repent for thinking that other people's opinion of me is unimportant. Help me live such a powerful, balanced, godly, dependable life that others will look to me as a tower of strength they can rely on. My life is my pulpit, and how I live before others will determine whether or not they respect me. If they do hold me in respect, the door will stay open for me to lead them and to influence them with the Gospel of Jesus Christ. So starting today, I am changing the way I think and embracing the truth that other people's opinions about me are very important!

I pray this in Jesus' name!

MY CONFESSION FOR TODAY

I confess that I have a positive influence on the people around me. I have a testimony that I am a cheerful, optimistic, faith-filled, dependable, and hard-working team player who is enjoyed by others. Because I do my best to live according to the Word of God, I have a good reputation with others in both the non-Christian world and in the Christian community. People respect me, honor me, believe me, trust me, and want to follow me because they have witnessed that I am solid, dependable, and reliable. Because the Holy Spirit is working in my character to transform my mind and conform me to the image of Jesus Christ, I have a good testimony with everyone I know and meet.

I declare this by faith in Jesus' name!

QUESTIONS FOR YOU TO CONSIDER

1. Have you ever known a Christian who said all the right words, but whose life didn't match the things he said or preached? How did that person's hypocrisy affect you and others who were watching?
2. Would you want to follow obediently someone you don't respect? Why not?
3. What do people think of you? Do they have a high opinion of you and therefore want to know more about your faith, or do they quietly disrespect you? If you are bold enough to do it, why don't you dare to ask a few people for honest answers to this question!

SEPTEMBER 6

Jesus Christ, Prince of the Kings of the Earth!

...the prince of the kings of the earth....
— Revelation 1:5

We live in an age when darkness is increasing all over the face of the earth. But as we face this looming threat, we need to remember that Jesus Christ is Lord over all. Nothing takes Him by surprise because He has known everything that has and will ever occur before He even created earth. The rulers of the darkness of this world may think they are in charge, but Revelation 1:5 declares that Jesus Christ is "the prince of the kings of the earth." Therefore, He rules over all the affairs of mankind. We may not always see His hand or understand His movements, but Christ is in charge nonetheless.

This means that no matter what political party, president, or ruler holds power or what verdicts the courts mete out, Jesus Christ's ultimate authority over the kings of the earth remains *uncontested.* Others may command an earthly sphere of influence for a limited time, but Christ's rule supersedes and outlasts them all.

Today I'd like for us to look at the apostle John's description of Jesus as "the prince of the kings of the earth" and see exactly what it tells us about our Lord and Savior as He rules today! The word "prince" is the word *archon*, a Greek word that denotes *one who holds the highest and most exalted position.* That emphatically means Jesus is truly Lord over *all.*

Furthermore, the word "kings" is a form of the Greek word *basileuo,* which means *to rule* or *to reign.* However, the form of the word used in Revelation 1:5 not only refers to human *kings* or *rulers*, but also to *governments*, which tells us Jesus' power is greater than any human government. Human governments may think they are in control, but Jesus is exalted far above them, and He calls the shots. In time, every opposing force will be eliminated, and Jesus will remain high and lifted up!

It is significant that John used this terminology to depict Jesus in the beginning of the book of Revelation. As he wrote these words in the latter years of the First Century AD, early believers were suffering greatly at the hands of evil rulers. So John reminded them — *and us* — from the onset of his message that Jesus holds the ultimate authority and commands the final say in all matters. John boldly proclaimed that Jesus is *the most highly exalted King* and that *He possesses supreme power and authority* — more than any *ruler* or *government* that will ever exist in the earthly sphere.

Even in the darkest hours or the bleakest situations, the efforts of evil will always be thwarted by the prevailing power of Jesus Christ. Nearly 2,000 years of Church history have proven beyond a shadow of a doubt that darkness doesn't have the power or authority to silence the voice of Jesus Christ and His Church.

When Jesus appeared to John as the risen and exalted Christ, He imparted a powerful message to believers in all ages — He is *the* King of kings! He holds the highest seat of power; He possesses dominion over all; and His Kingdom will never cease. Other kings and governments will come and go, but Jesus' Kingdom is everlasting and supersedes all others. *There is no better reason to proclaim "AMEN!"*

MY PRAYER FOR TODAY

Father, I am so thankful that Jesus is Lord over all, and that includes my life! Your Word is coming to pass at a rapid pace in these end times: Darkness is increasing; morals are sliding; laws are changing for the worse; and society is rapidly degenerating. But seated above them all is Jesus — the King of the kings of the earth. When all is said and done, rulers may have a temporary say-so in the affairs of man, but Jesus ultimately rules over all. Help me not to despair when I see evil prosper and to remember that Jesus has not lost His grip on the situation. He really IS Lord over all!

I pray this in Jesus' name!

MY CONFESSION FOR TODAY

I boldly confess that Jesus Christ is not only the King of kings, but the Prince of all the kings of the earth (see Revelation 19:16;1:5). There is no higher power or authority than Jesus Christ. His throne is exalted above all others. Human powers come and go, but the Kingdom of Jesus Christ endures forever. I declare that 2,000 years of Church history have proven that Jesus is highly and forever exalted, and that He will have the ultimate say-so in the affairs of mankind. I may not see how His hand is moving, but none is greater than or equal to Him. Jesus Christ rules over all, and He is directing the affairs of mankind to fulfill His divine purpose!

I declare this by faith in Jesus' name!

QUESTIONS FOR YOU TO CONSIDER

1. Have you despaired over the darkness that permeates society and the governments of the world? Are you ever tempted to think that darkness is in control? How can you best resist that temptation?
2. What did you learn from today's *Sparkling Gem*? If you were to tell others about what you learned today, what truths would you share with them?
3. Why don't you shut your eyes and let your imagination take you to the highest Heaven for a moment? Picture Jesus Christ above all the kings of the earth, seated there on His highly exalted throne!

SEPTEMBER 7

Faithfully Doing the Small Things

For by the grace (unmerited favor of God) given to me
I warn everyone among you not to estimate and think
of himself more highly than he ought
[not to have an exaggerated opinion of his own importance],
but to rate his ability with sober judgment,
each according to the degree of faith
apportioned by God to him.
— Romans 12:3 *AMPC*

When I was first getting started in the ministry, I was so excited and filled with confidence. In fact, I thought I could accomplish anything — and I naively thought I could do it all by myself without help from anyone else. I'll never forget the time I tried very hard to impress an older gentleman who had been in the ministry for more than 50 years. I confidently told him about all the areas in which I excelled and all the things I was capable of doing. The older and much wiser leader listened attentively and then responded, "Son, I believe you can do great things. I'm just not convinced you can do *small* things, or that you'd be able to work with anyone else."

Being young and inexperienced, I was initially shocked at this older minister's answer. But decades later, I now savor the wisdom he spoke to me that day. Time and experience have taught me that God watches to see how we serve in the small things and how we work with others. The way we manage the small things in our lives proves whether or not we are worthy of being entrusted with greater responsibility. That means "small things" really aren't so small at all! My experience has also shown me that nothing great is accomplished by a single person; it takes many hands to do a great job. Those who work alone *rarely* accomplish anything significant.

In Romans 12:3 (*AMPC*), Paul says, "For by the grace (unmerited favor of God) given to me I warn everyone among you not to estimate and think of himself more highly than he ought [not to have an exaggerated opinion of his own importance], but to rate his ability with sober judgment, each according to the degree of faith apportioned by God to him." I really like the *Amplified* translation of this verse. Paul used the Greek word *huperphroneo*, a compound of *huper* and *phroneo*. The word *huper* means *over*, *above*, or *beyond*, and the word *phroneo* means *to think*. Compounded, the new word carries the meaning as translated in the *Amplified* — *to think of oneself more highly than he ought to think* or *to have an exaggerated opinion of one's own importance*.

In verses 4 and 5 (*AMPC*), Paul provided us with a balanced view of our different roles and showed us that we are each a vital part of a much greater whole. He wrote, "For as in one physical body we have many parts (organs, members) and all of these parts do not have the same function or use, so we, numerous as we are, are one body in Christ (the Messiah) and individually we are parts one of another [mutually dependent on one another]."

We see from Romans 12:4 that Paul likened the Church to the human body. This analogy sounds simple, yet it is so profound! Hands are different than ears; a mouth is different than a nose; and so on. The different parts of the body are all unique, yet they're all equally important and interdependent. The same is true for the Body of Christ. Even Christ — the Head of the Church — is dependent on His Body. We as believers worship and take directions from the Head, but ultimately the Head needs the Body to do what the Head tells it to do.

Let me give you an example from my own life. I'm a writer, and the gift in my life that will have the longest-lasting impact is *teaching* through *writing*. I believe that the words I write will long outlast me. An example is the book you hold in your hands. This book and the many other books I have authored will continue to minister to people long after I am in Heaven. However, these books don't just supernaturally show up on the shelves of a bookstore one day. The book you are reading came to pass because I sat down at my computer one day and started typing. When it was time for me to write, the information came from my brain through billions of nerve cells in my spinal cord, activating the muscles in my arms and every bone in my hand. My fingers began to move on the computer keys, transferring thoughts to words in print as information flowed through my body at lightning speed.

This process happens so fast that we can't conceive or comprehend it. You can't see a single one of those nerves because they're invisible to the eye. But if you ripped those nerves out of your body, *nothing* could be produced.

In addition to my work as the author, there are editors, researchers, and other talented people who help craft these books. Each book goes through multiple levels of editing, typesetting, proofreading, and design. Someone must send the manuscript to the printer and ensure that the printed books are delivered on time. Contacts are made with distributors, and then *finally* the books are delivered to bookstores, where someone unpacks them and displays them on bookshelves. Eventually they are sold by someone who works at a sales desk. My name appears on the cover because I undertook the monumental job of writing the book, but if I were the only one involved in the process, those words would be nothing more than a file on my computer. *Yes, there are many necessary parts to the successful publishing of a book, and every part is important.*

The same is true with our TV ministry. Denise and I are the faces seen on our television program and on the Internet all over the former USSR. However, there are also cameramen who stand behind cameras, editors who edit programs, and individuals who contact the TV stations and ensure the programs are delivered on time. It takes a dedicated team of people working interdependently toward a common goal to produce this TV program and see that it reaches the masses with the teaching of God's Word.

My own part in writing books and recording TV programs is crucial, but it's only a "part" of the total process. Nothing would happen if I didn't do my part, but my part would be fruitless without the help of others fulfilling their own vital roles. Keeping this in mind helps me appreciate everyone else's role as much as I value my own in an assignment. It also helps me remember that we are interdependent upon each other in the Body of Christ.

Consider all the "invisible" members in the Body of Christ who work for the Lord behind the scenes. I'm talking about those you never see on a platform, behind a pulpit, or over the airwaves on a television broadcast. *Every* part of the Body of Christ is vital and necessary. Oh, how we need to be thankful for the invisible people who play critical roles in the functioning of the Body of Christ! They are just as important as the more visible roles people play, and often, they are even more important!

Paul makes this truth abundantly clear in Romans 12:6 (*AMPC*), where he wrote, "Having gifts (faculties, talents, qualities) that differ according to the grace given us...." *Every person has been given a grace to employ in service to God and the Body of Christ.* You may feel drawn to practical areas of service. Perhaps you're called to teach others, or maybe you're particularly gifted at encouraging people. Or maybe you're especially motivated by compassion to rescue the lost and hurting.

Whatever gifts and graces God has given you, I highly encourage you to find your place in His house and serve. Don't despise the "lowly" acts of service you may be called upon to fulfill along the way — they will qualify you for greater places of responsibility.

MY PRAYER FOR TODAY

Father, I am amazed by Your design for the Body of Christ, with each of us interdependent upon the other. Alone we can do our small parts, but together we can accomplish a greater goal. I ask You to help me really see and understand this truth. I repent of the pride that has tried to creep in to make me despise small things or to hinder me from cooperating with others to fulfill my part in Your plan. I confess that these are areas where I need to grow. Father, You resist the proud, but You give grace to the humble. I ask You for Your grace to help me reach new levels in these areas so I can glorify You and be a true blessing to others.

I pray this in Jesus' name!

MY CONFESSION FOR TODAY

I confess that I am well aware of my interdependence with others in the Body of Christ. You called us as a whole Body so that we may work properly and accomplish greater goals. I am not willing to be independent in the way I operate. By the grace of God working in me, I submit myself to God and resist the temptation to overestimate myself. I will appreciate those who are called alongside me to work, and I will humbly esteem their great value to God and also to me. The visible and less visible members are equally important, and as I walk with God, I am becoming ever more aware of my need to do my part, along with those who are called by God to do their own part.

I declare this by faith in Jesus' name!

QUESTIONS FOR YOU TO CONSIDER

1. What do you do independently that requires no one else's participation but has a great impact on many people?
2. What do you do that requires the cooperation of others in order to reach masses or even to be effective at reaching small groups of people?
3. What gifts do you have that are effective and far-reaching all by yourself?
4. The "small things" are qualifiers for larger assignments in the eyes of God. Have you learned to be faithful at doing small, almost unnoticeable assignments?

SEPTEMBER 8

Are We So Busy Serving That We've Missed What Really Matters?

I know thy works, and thy labour, and thy patience,
and how thou canst not bear them which are evil:
and thou hast tried them which say they are apostles,
and are not, and hast found them liars:
And hast borne, and hast patience,
and for my name's sake hast laboured, and hast not fainted.
— Revelation 2:2,3

Whether we want to admit it or not, it is simply the truth that every one of us as believers must make a *firm* commitment to retain our fire and passion for the Lord. Busy schedules, work, problems, and challenges in life have a way of wearing us down and dimming the flame that burns in our hearts for Jesus. There's only one way we can make sure this doesn't happen in our own lives: We must stay firmly committed to do whatever it takes to retain our fire, no matter the cost.

This was the core of Jesus' message to the church of Ephesus when He appeared in a vision to the apostle John (*see* Revelation 2:2-7). The Ephesian believers were full of good works and were widely respected for their soundness in doctrine — and Jesus commended them for it.

In Revelation 2:2 and 3, Jesus said, "I know thy works, and thy labour, and thy patience, and how thou canst not bear them which are evil: and thou hast tried them which say they are apostles, and are not, and hast found them liars: And hast borne, and hast patience, and for my name's sake hast laboured, and hast not fainted."

But after praising the church of Ephesus for its stellar performance, its faithful adherence to truth, and its excellence in doctrine, Christ went on to say in verse 4, "*Nevertheless....*" The word "nevertheless" served as a warning signal to the Ephesian congregation, letting them know that something else mattered to Jesus even more than all their good works. Then He continued, "Nevertheless I have somewhat against thee...." The word "against" is the word *kata*, which in this case means, "I have one thing *against* you — *a downward strike, a negative point, or a mark against you.*" Essentially, it describes something that was obviously not in the Ephesian believers' favor.

The believers of the Ephesian church had fallen into the trap of busyness in ministry at the expense of fervency in fellowship with the Lord, and Jesus rebuked them for it. And His message is no less relevant and urgent for us today than it was when He first delivered those words to the apostle John for the church at Ephesus on the island of Patmos almost 2,000 years ago.

Productivity for God must never take the place of passionate love for Him. Christ requires us to be both productive for Him *and* passionate about Him. Yet it is easy to become so consumed with the busyness of the ministry that we fail to stay focused on our passionate love for Christ.

I learned this during a period of several years that Denise and I maintained an extremely busy schedule, which eventually escalated to an unsustainable pace. There were times I could only vaguely recall what country I was in when I'd awaken during the night. I was trying to accomplish as much as I could for the Lord, but I was moving at a pace He never intended.

For so long, Denise and I had stayed continually busy doing good things with excellent results. Lives were changed, and the Kingdom of God was furthered. But my spiritual fervor had dimmed, and it became clear to me that God was calling me to come aside and get still before Him. So I recommitted myself to reviving the fire of God in my own heart.

Speaking from my own experience, I urge you to take a moment to evaluate yourself and ask yourself the following questions:

- Are you just going through the motions in your ministry?
- Have you come to a place where you substitute more activity for times of stillness in the presence of the Lord?

- When you do attempt to get quiet before God, is your body still while your mind continues to race with thoughts of all you want to do or need to accomplish?
- Do you remember with longing what it was like when you first fell in love with Jesus and were so thankful for your salvation?
- What were your habits and devotional life like when the flame of your passion for Jesus burned with the highest intensity?

These are the kinds of questions every one of us should ponder, allowing them to sift through the embers in our souls and stir us to rekindle the flame of our first love for Jesus. When we take the time to do whatever is necessary to revive and retain spiritual fervor and freshness in our relationship with the Lord, our hearts will find renewed satisfaction in our walk with Him and in the ministry He has called us to fulfill. But more importantly, the Lord will be satisfied with *us*, because He will find us to be men and women after His own heart. And when all is said and done, nothing else could please Him more.

MY PRAYER FOR TODAY

Father, I desire to retain the fire in my heart that I had when I first came to know You. Life has become busy, and I confess that somewhere along the way I allowed the busyness of it all to dim the fire in my heart. Although I've become more experienced and professional, I am less passionate than I used to be. I repent for this, and I confess that it is wrong. Holy Spirit, I ask You to help me return to the place of my first love. I have lost sight of loving You more than anything else. For this I repent, and I ask You to forgive me. Purify my heart so that Your presence will ignite a flame in me until You are the highest priority and goal in my life.

I pray this in Jesus' name!

MY CONFESSION FOR TODAY

I confess that I refuse to allow my productivity for God to take precedence over my passionate love for Him. I will not offer diligence toward duty as a substitute for devotion toward Him as I approach my God-given assignment. I return to the place of my first love. I commit to pull away often from the busyness of life and ministry so I can be still in the presence of the Lord in order to maintain a vital connection with Him. I will not attempt to serve God without a fresh touch of His Spirit upon me. In the morning I will lift up my eyes, my heart, and my voice unto the Lord while I wait until His Word speaks to my heart in a fresh way for each new day. From that place of union with Him, I will stay focused on what really matters.

I declare this by faith in Jesus' name!

QUESTIONS FOR YOU TO CONSIDER

1. Do you spend time with the Lord as you once did, or do you find that setting aside time to be with Him is getting more and more difficult for you to do? What does this tell you about the temperature of your spiritual life?

2. If Christ evaluated you by the questions asked in today's *Sparkling Gem*, how do you think He would answer the questions?
3. What changes do you need to make in your life to return to Christ as your first, passionate love?

SEPTEMBER 9

Standing Together To Overcome the Darkness

This know also, that in the last days
perilous times will come.
— 2 Timothy 3:1

I've dedicated numerous *Sparkling Gems* to Second Timothy 3 in this second volume (*see* May 10-18). The reason for this is that I am *convinced* we are entering the *last* of the last days and that the days ahead will be the most challenging period the Church has ever faced. In this verse, Paul prophesied, "This know also, that in the last days perilous times will come." This word "perilous" is the Greek word *chalepos*, which means *dangerous* or *difficult*. It is translated in Matthew 8:28 as "exceedingly fierce." So when Paul prophesied by the Spirit that the last days would be "perilous," he was saying that the end times would be *dangerous*, *difficult*, and *exceedingly fierce*.

This truth was reinforced in me several years ago as I traveled by airplane across the Atlantic Ocean. As I looked out the window of the plane, I saw a vision unfold before me. It was as if someone suddenly pulled a cord to draw back a curtain separating the natural realm from the spiritual realm, and an entirely different picture came into clear view. Before me, I saw what appeared to be ominous, swirling black clouds spreading rapidly across the landscape of the world. I understood that I was seeing demonic forces that are currently attempting to spread and exert their influence.

I immediately turned to Denise and said, "The spirit realm just opened up before me, and I witnessed a vast buildup of demonic activity occurring over the nations of the world. It is an attempt to wage war for the control of the nations just before the Second Coming of Jesus."

This supernatural vision made a great impression on me as I considered the seriousness of this hour, and it alerted me to step it up in my God-given role as a leader in His Church and *call the Body of Christ to action*. This is a time when we in the Christian community should not only pray more — we should also work together closely to see God's purposes brought forth on the earth.

In these last days, everything that can be shaken *will* be shaken. Since judgment begins at the house of God, we must first be certain our own lives are lived worthily so that, having preached to others, we ourselves don't become castaways. We then have the divine duty to lead others in taking a righteous stand, actively engaging the forces of darkness, and claiming the nations in Jesus' name.

If you are in a leadership role in your church, I encourage you to work on implementing the following steps both in your personal life and in your church to a greater degree than ever before. These steps will strengthen your spirit and prepare others to stand firm against the enemy's strategies in the days ahead.

1. Increase your prayer in your church, ministry, and personal life. If you're too busy to pray, you are too busy.
2. Be open to establishing increased order and accountability in your church or ministry. Christians are usually in one ditch or the other, creating either a dogmatic order that steals their liberty in Christ or an overly relaxed tolerance that unleashes lawlessness and chaos.
3. Besides encouraging fellowship with believers from other parts of the Body, find new avenues to work together with other Christians to accomplish the business of God's Kingdom.
4. Walk in faith, regardless of the circumstances!

As for the clouds I saw in the spirit, they were very dark and perilous. But I want to exhort you not to allow fear to grip your heart as you witness what is happening in the world around you. We have been called by a mighty and all-powerful God, and together we are exceedingly able to meet every challenge!

Long ago the prophet Isaiah declared what the role of God's people would be when darkness blanketed this world system in the last days: "Arise, shine, for your light has come, and the glory of the Lord rises upon you. See, darkness covers the earth and thick darkness is over the peoples, but the Lord rises upon you and his glory appears over you. Nations will come to your light, and kings to the brightness of your dawn" (Isaiah 60:1-3 *NIV*).

Our role is clear: We must stand together to drive back the darkness with the light of the Gospel so Jesus can be exalted and the transforming power of God can be displayed to this generation as never before. It's our honor to have a part in bringing in this end-time harvest of souls. But to fulfill our respective roles in this divine plan, we must refuse to slow down or weaken our stance of faith *until the whole earth is filled with the knowledge of God's glory* (*see* Habakkuk 2:14)!

MY PRAYER FOR TODAY

Heavenly Father, I ask You to help me assume my role in prayer as we charge forward into the last of the last days. In these last days, everything that can be shaken will be shaken. Holy Spirit, since judgment begins at the house of God, I ask You to help me as I examine myself. I want to be certain that I live my own life worthily as I ought so that after having preached to others, I myself won't become a castaway. Lord Jesus, I embrace my divine duty to build the Kingdom of God until You return and to lead others in taking a righteous stand to actively withstand the forces of darkness by the power of Your mighty name! Strengthen me with Your wisdom, counsel, and might to accept my responsibility to pray and to live with unflinching conviction. Father, although spiritual darkness seems to blanket the nations, You promised that the knowledge of the glory of the Lord would cover the earth as the waters cover the sea. So I refuse to allow fear to grip my heart. By the power of Your might, I know that I am exceedingly able to meet every challenge, no matter what is happening in the world around me! The darker the hour, the greater the opportunity for Christ in me — the Hope of glory — to shine brightly and be revealed to a dying world that needs His life!

I pray this in Jesus' name!

MY CONFESSION FOR TODAY

I confess that I live a life of increased prayer and consecration to God. In those moments when I may be tempted to think I'm too busy to pray, I will recognize that I'm just too busy and that something has to go — but it won't be my time in the Bible or in prayer! As the days grow darker spiritually, I will become even more accountable to my church and to fellow believers because we are stronger together. I receive the wisdom of God that protects me from falling into either a ditch of legalism or of lawlessness. I keep myself in the love of God and find new avenues to work with other Christians to build God's Kingdom. Because I increase my time spent in the Word of God, my faith increases regardless of circumstances, and I continue to pray for those in authority. It is an honor to help gather in this end-time harvest of souls. Therefore, I confess that I take my place to drive back spiritual darkness with the light of the Gospel so Jesus can be exalted and the transforming power of God can be displayed to this generation as never before. I refuse to slow down or weaken my stance of faith until the nations come to His great light and kings to the brightness of His dawn!

I declare this by faith in Jesus' name!

QUESTIONS FOR YOU TO CONSIDER

1. Have you sensed that we are entering the darkest time in the history of mankind? What is your Christian responsibility in regard to shining the light of the Gospel during this time?
2. How do you shine the light of the Gospel in a society that is deteriorating? Can you state specific ways that you can effectively shine your light in the darkness?
3. In what ways do you know that God is stirring your heart to shine His light to your family, friends, and associates?

SEPTEMBER 10

The Power of Agreement

…If two of you shall agree on earth
as touching any thing that they shall ask,
it shall be done for them of my Father
which is in heaven.
— Matthew 18:19

When our family moved to Moscow in September 2000, we were new to the city and didn't have close friendships with other local pastors simply because we didn't know them yet. As often happens when a new church starts, some people from other churches began to visit our church, and the other pastors didn't appreciate that fact. They were concerned that their people would relocate to our church. This didn't actually happen as much as the pastors predicted, but I fully understood their concern. On one hand, they were glad we moved to Moscow. But on the other hand, they weren't too happy about the concerns it raised for them.

Yet as time passed, it became necessary for those of us who pastor in Moscow to work together on various issues that concerned us all. As we got to know each other better, fears and suspicions melted away, and an amazing thing occurred — we started to value each other's gifts and strengths and genuinely care for one another as friends! Soon key church leaders in the city began to reach out to Denise and me and warmly receive us.

When our ministry decided to purchase and renovate a new church facility in Moscow, these local ministers encouraged us with one accord to take that huge step of faith, which has since proven to be a successful venture in God's plan for our ministry. Years before when we first arrived in Moscow, some of these very ministers had opposed our coming to start a new church. Today we're all linked together in a vital way that has benefited everyone involved. We're not just "brothers and sisters in the Lord" — *we are friends.*

In Matthew 18:19, Jesus taught about the enormous power that exists when believers get in agreement with each other. He said, "…If two of you shall agree on earth as touching any thing that they shall ask, it shall be done for them of my Father which is in heaven."

The Greek word for "agree" in this verse is *sumphoneo*. It means *to agree together, to make a bargain,* or *to come to an agreement.* It is the Greek word from which the word "symphony" is derived. A symphony orchestra combines many diverse instruments under the direction of a skilled conductor to produce a beautiful, musical masterpiece, and its impact extends far beyond what any one instrument could achieve on its own. This imagery paints a perfect analogy for the Christian community as God intended it to be.

My own ministry has been powerfully enriched because I am a part of a "symphony orchestra" of ministers in the city of Moscow. The unified front of this group has made an impact that could never have been as great if each of us had tried to accomplish the same goals individually. Over the years, we have spoken to each other in ways that have positively changed our attitudes, doctrines, and practices. Do we always agree on finer points of doctrine? No! But we're the family of God, and we act like it. After all, we don't always agree with our natural family members either — but we're all still family, tied together by blood and birth. The same thing is true in the family of God. We were all purchased by the blood of Jesus and born of God's Spirit. As Paul said: "There is one body, and one Spirit...one God and Father of all.... But unto every one of us is given grace according to the measure of the gift of Christ" (Ephesians 4:4-7).

I feel privileged to have experienced the power of agreement when church leaders reach out to each other in esteem and respect for each other's gifts and callings. And I can tell you this — I wouldn't want to work in God's Kingdom any other way. Unity among the brethren reflects the heart of the Father, and *He* says that where unity prevails, the anointing of His presence saturates and commands His blessing to manifest in their midst (*see* Psalm 133)!

MY PRAYER FOR TODAY

Father, I am so grateful that unity reflects Your heart and causes the anointing of Your presence to saturate us and manifest Your blessing in our midst. Enormous power exists when believers get in agreement with You and with each other. Holy Spirit, I ask You to teach me and the body of believers You have planted me in how to operate just like a symphony orchestra. I ask this also for the Body of Christ at large. As many instruments combined with a wide array of sounds, help us yield to Your direction as a skilled Conductor so that all those sounds blend together into a beautiful musical masterpiece. Help us symphonize in faith and unity more and more so we may have greater power in prayer and action and make a phenomenal impact on the listeners that extends far beyond what any one instrument could achieve on its own.

I pray this in Jesus' name!

MY CONFESSION FOR TODAY

I confess that I contribute to the unity the Father desires the Body of Christ to operate in. I refuse to adopt an adversarial role when He has called me to do everything I can to achieve unity. We have more that unites us than divides us, so I choose to focus on the things that bring us together instead of the things that drive us apart. I thank You for the support I've found from other believers and ministers, and I ask You to help me be a support to others who are stepping out in faith to do what You have asked them to do.

I declare this by faith in Jesus' name!

QUESTIONS FOR YOU TO CONSIDER

1. Can you think of a time when the Body of Christ really got behind you and supported an idea that God birthed in your heart? What did their support mean to you?
2. On the other hand, can you think of a time when it seemed no one would get in agreement with what God had revealed to you? Did that make it difficult to forge ahead?
3. Were there also times when you could have been more supportive of others than you were? What do you think of that now? Have you repented for being unsupportive when your encouragement could have made all the difference in the world for those who were stepping forward in faith?

SEPTEMBER 11

Five Different Crowns of Reward

Henceforth there is laid up for me
a crown of righteousness,
which the Lord, the righteous judge,
shall give me at that day: and not to me only,
but unto all them also that love his appearing.
— 2 Timothy 4:8

At the time that the apostle Paul wrote Second Timothy, he was imprisoned in Rome, awaiting the moment of his own execution, which would be death by decapitation. However, when we read his final words in Second Timothy 4:8, we discover that Paul wasn't focused on his own death, which would indeed be gruesome. He looked beyond that event to that glorious moment when Jesus would personally step forward to give him a "crown of righteousness" as a reward for his faithful service.

Today I want us to look at this word "crown." The New Testament mentions *five* different types of crowns that will be given to Christians as rewards for the various ways they ran their race of faith. But before we look at all five different types of crowns, first let's look at the word "crown" to see exactly what kind of crown the New Testament is talking about. In each instance where it is mentioned, it is the same Greek word. The Greek word for a "crown" in these verses is not the word for a royal diadem, as a king would wear. Rather, it is the Greek word *stephanos*, which describes *the crown given to athletes — most notably, runners — after they had run their race or finished their contest victoriously.* It was generally referred to as *a victor's crown.*

At the conclusion of a contest or race, a winner was declared, and a "crown" was placed on the champion's brow that was made of pine or olive branches and leaves. Although the crown wasn't made of expensive material, it was highly valued as a public recognition of the skill, commitment, discipline, endurance, self-control, self-mastery, and training that had enabled the athlete to win the competition. Being awarded the *victor's crown* brought a person great acclaim, honor, and respect in the eyes of an adoring public. Therefore, it was every athlete's chief aim to obtain this crown.

For Christians who ran their race of faith, wholly giving themselves to pursuing God's plan for their lives, there could be no greater reward than Jesus Christ Himself personally placing this *victor's crown* on their brow. This is in fact the promise that Christ makes to Christians who have endured to the end and victoriously finished their race of faith. A day is coming when Jesus will step forward, dressed in the regal splendor of the exalted King of kings, and He will place a *victor's crown* upon the heads of those who had steadfastly run their race to the very end. The Savior Himself will personally place this priceless reward upon the brows of the faithful.

As noted previously, there are *five* different types of crowns mentioned in the New Testament. Each of these crowns is a specific and distinct reward for Christians who have faithfully fulfilled God's call on their lives.

1. First Corinthians 9:25 refers to a *crown of incorruption.* Paul described this as a special crown given to believers who practiced *physical self-governance* and therefore ran a successful race in life. Those who practiced self-discipline and refused to let the flesh hinder their race of faith can look forward to receiving this precious reward.
2. First Thessalonians 2:19 refers to the *crown of rejoicing.* Theologians often refer to this as the *soul-winner's crown,* as it is a crown given to those who brought others to Jesus Christ. Oh, think of the joy those who have brought others to Christ will experience when they receive a *crown of rejoicing* or *a soul-winner's crown.*
3. Second Timothy 4:8 refers to the *crown of righteousness.* This crown is specially designated for those who longed for Jesus' appearing and lived holy lives in anticipation of His return. This is the crown that Paul referred to when he wrote about his own death and the crown that Jesus would give to him.
4. First Peter 5:4 refers to the *crown of glory.* This is often called the *pastor's crown* because it is a special reward that will be given to shepherds who faithfully pastored and taught God's people. You would do well to read First Peter 5:4 and to personally see this special crown that will be given to faithful pastors.
5. James 1:12 and Revelation 2:10 refer to the *crown of life.* This crown is often referred to as the *martyr's crown* because it is given to those who suffered for

their faith, those who died for Christ, or those who were committed to finishing their race of faith regardless of the difficulties they encountered in this life.

Athletes who prepared, trained, and won their competitions were highly regarded. Likewise, Christ will give *special honor* to those who victoriously ran their race of faith to its conclusion. On that day in our future, Jesus Christ will stand, step forward to us as we bow before Him, and place one of these respective crowns on our brows if He has found us faithful to the task that was assigned to us.

There are believers who are still in that fight right now, and their struggle has been great. Paul was still in his race when he wrote Second Timothy 4:8. But rather than focus on his imminent execution by decapitation, Paul chose instead to focus on the crown of righteousness that the Lord would soon be placing upon his brow.

Similarly, if you are running in a fierce race of faith that is requiring every ounce of your spiritual, mental, and physical strength, I encourage you to lift your eyes to Heaven and see Jesus with your crown in His hands. One day your race will be finished, and if you made it all the way to the end, He'll place that crown on your head — a *victor's crown* for one who finished his race of faith!

To be honest, sometimes I am tempted to yield to weariness or to wonder if the fight has been worth it. Other times I know I'm looking at difficult times on the road directly before me. In these vulnerable moments, I often lift the eyes of my faith and focus on the moment when the King of kings will place a victor's crown on my own head because He found me faithful. Thinking of that makes me want to stay in the race and finish it all the way to the end! *How about you?*

MY PRAYER FOR TODAY

Father, Your Word clearly teaches that when we see Jesus in Heaven, He will have a special "reward" in His hand — a victor's crown — to place upon our heads. But more important to me than receiving a crown is that I please You. To receive a crown from You will be a blessing, as it is Your recognition of what I have done, and it will be a treasure that I can lay at Jesus' feet on that day. But the greatest reward for me will be knowing I have run a race that brought You pleasure!

I pray this in Jesus' name!

MY CONFESSION FOR TODAY

I declare that I will run my race of faith all the way to its final conclusion. There will be no dropping out of the race halfway along the God-ordained course of my life. I'm in this to finish it and to bring glory to the name of the Lord Jesus Christ. I am thankful that because I will be faithful to the end, on the day I see Jesus, He will give me a victor's crown. But most of all, I want to see the satisfaction in His eyes that I've run a race of faith that has brought glory to His name. His glory is my highest goal and the reason I am running in this race of faith!

I declare this by faith in Jesus' name!

QUESTIONS FOR YOU TO CONSIDER

1. Do you envision running your race of faith in a way that will take you all the way to the finish line? Are you giving it all the spiritual, physical, and mental strength you can muster to run that race like a champion?
2. By looking at the five different types of crowns that Christ will give to faithful champions, which crown do you think you will receive when you see Jesus face to face? *Which crown would you like to receive? What decisions are you making to ensure that you do receive it?*
3. When you think of seeing Jesus face to face, what thoughts immediately come to your mind? Is this an event that brings joy to your heart and mind, or does it cause you to be fearful? What reasons are behind your reaction to this very important question?

SEPTEMBER 12

Do Things Right the First Time!

For which of you, intending to build a tower,
sitteth not down first, and counteth the cost,
whether he have sufficient to finish it?
Lest haply, after he hath laid the foundation,
and is not able to finish it,
all that behold it begin to mock him.
— Luke 14:28,29

I have it on my heart today to share a vital principle from the Word of God that will help ensure your next endeavor in God has a successful outcome. Over the years, I've seen how so many believers like to blame the devil for just about everything that goes wrong in their lives. But although the devil certainly does try to wreak his share of havoc and destruction in Christians' lives, everything bad that happens cannot be blamed on demonic attacks. I have discovered that a believer's defeat can often be attributed to a lack of planning and preparation.

Jesus spoke of this crucial principle in Luke 14:28,29, saying, "For which of you, intending to build a tower, sitteth not down first, and counteth the cost, whether he have sufficient to finish it? Lest haply, after he hath laid the foundation, and is not able to finish it, all that behold it begin to mock him."

Jesus began this verse by underscoring the importance of *sitting down* and *counting the cost* before beginning a project. The phrase "sitteth down" comes from the Greek word *kathidzo*, which depicts *someone who sits down and takes a long time to seriously contemplate the project he is about to initiate*. Part of that contemplation process is counting the cost of the endeavor. The phrase "counteth the cost" is the Greek word *psiphidzo*, which means *to count* or *to calculate* the *real cost* of the project *before* it is commenced. This process includes the careful consideration of not only the monetary cost involved in fully accomplishing the assigned task, but also of *all* that will be necessary in order to complete the task — time spent, physical effort expended, relationships impacted, etc.

Furthermore, the word "finish" is *apartismos*, which means *to bring a project to completion*. According to Jesus, it is very important to have the foresight *before* you get started on a project to ensure that you *have the wherewithal to finish it*. Getting started on a task is easy, but if you don't have a solid financial and logistical plan in place, you will see very little progress.

Jesus continued in Luke 14:29 by saying, "...Lest haply, after he hath laid the foundation, and is not able to finish it, all that behold it begin to *mock* him." This word "mock" is the Greek word *empaidzo*, which means *to ridicule*, *to mock*, or *to taunt someone*. According to Jesus, if you give up on your project before it is complete, bystanders will *ridicule* and *taunt* you. And even if bystanders don't mock you, the devil will most certainly accuse you of being a stupid failure who can't finish what you start. Therefore, the wise course of action is to avoid this cast of accusing voices altogether by developing a meticulous plan well in advance. By sitting down and seriously contemplating the logistics of your project — what it will cost, where the money will come from, how much help you'll need, and so on — you will know exactly what you need to see your endeavor through to completion.

Allow me to share an example from my own life. My wife Denise and I have lived in the former Soviet Union since the early 1990s. During this time abroad on the mission field, we've seen *many* missionary families come and go. In fact, of all the families who moved to the former USSR in the early 1990s to share the Gospel, we are the only family that remains as far as we can tell.

Certainly it's true that some missionaries left because God called them to take the next step in their ministries and move to a new location. However, time and time again, Denise and I watched people leave prematurely because of unresolved personal issues that they didn't take care of before they moved their families across the world. They would quit their jobs and move their entire families to Russia *without counting the cost*. And as a result, they would become so distracted by unresolved problems back home that they couldn't focus on their work on the mission field. There is no doubt that these people were called to the mission field. But because they didn't take care of their personal responsibilities, they couldn't complete what God had called them to do.

There are a multitude of reasons why these well-meaning people were forced to leave the mission field early. Each reason is an example of failure to count the cost and to do things right from the start. The following list represents a few of the issues we've seen derail the ministries of missionaries overseas:

- They left before their house was sold or rented, leaving a huge financial responsibility weighing on their shoulders.
- They left before appointing someone to pay their bills, creating a financial mess that ultimately required them to return home.
- They left before raising any financial support. A missionary must have strong faith for sustained financial provision, but common sense in this arena is also very important.
- They left before working out problems with relatives, such as who would care for their elderly parents in their absence. Having this as an unresolved issue forced them to abandon the mission field and move back home as soon as their elderly parents needed care.
- They left before resolving serious issues in their family relationships. I can assure you of this: If a missionary family launches out with unresolved issues in their marriage and relationships, the mission field will expose those problems. The pressures of personal issues can create so much stress on a family that it disrupts their ability to minister effectively and can even lead to the dissolution of the family.

For those who did things wrong and failed to count the cost before leaving on their faith journey, these people lost a lot of time and money and suffered a great deal of unnecessary emotional wear and tear. Only a few times have we seen any of these missionary families return. Most became so sidetracked that they never made it back to the mission field where God called them.

Through observation and personal experience, Denise and I have learned that it may take a little longer to do things right the first time around, but nothing is as difficult as abandoning your divine call because you didn't count the cost and do what you should have done in the beginning. *Doing things right the first time is the smartest, cheapest, and best way to live!*

I am so thankful that we have been able to continue our ministry in the former Soviet Union because we took the time to sit down and count the cost. We know that if we do things wrong, we'll only have to backtrack and fix the problem, so we do our best to get it right from the very start of every assignment. We haven't been successful 100 percent of the time, but with the help of God's Spirit and sound counsel, we've been successful most of the time. For this, we give glory to God! We have peace in our hearts that our family members are secure, and we strive to keep our relationships with our partners alive so they feel connected to our ministry.

As a result, Denise and I have been free to focus on the task before us without unnecessary distractions that might pull us away from the call God has placed on our lives. Remaining in this place of freedom requires a great deal of effort. Often it has meant spending less money or moving slower than planned with certain projects. But in the long term, our efforts have empowered us to keep pressing forward into new and uncharted territory.

So today I strongly encourage you to do what Jesus said: Sit down and contemplate the total cost of the task or assignment that lies ahead of you *before* you begin. Count the cost from every angle to make sure you will truly be able to finish with excellence what you started out of obedience. You can do whatever God has called you to do — as long as you take heed to His words and do it *His* way!

MY PRAYER FOR TODAY

Father, I thank You for the common-sense approach that I've read today. I know that You have called me to do significant things with my life, so I accept the challenge to sit down and calculate the costs before I get started. The last thing I want is to start something I can't finish and give others a reason to mock me or to deride Your holy assignment. I do not want to create an opportunity to hear the accusing voice of the devil or the mocking voices of doubters or non-believers. So help me use my mind, seek wise counsel, and take each step of faith carefully and methodically. I receive Your supernatural assistance to do every natural thing You've called me to do.

I pray this in Jesus' name!

MY CONFESSION FOR TODAY

I declare that I start every project by first sitting down to seriously contemplate the cost and the effort it will take to complete it. I ask You to help me think through every step that is required to finish this project. I will start this assignment with the full assurance that this is correct. I am confident and persuaded that I will finish what I have started because I fasten my attention and take my direction from Jesus, who is both the Author and the Finisher of my faith!

I declare this by faith in Jesus' name!

QUESTIONS FOR YOU TO CONSIDER

1. Do you personally know anyone who started a project that he was unable to complete? How did people respond to that event? When that person announced his next project, did people believe or doubt him?
2. When you hear the phrase "count the cost," what does that mean to you personally for the future plans you are currently praying about? It would be good for you to count the *total* cost — financial, physical, emotional — needed to complete the project you are planning to start.
3. It is the strong spirit of a man that sustains him and enables him to endure. What steps have you taken to build new habits into your walk with God that will increase your spiritual stamina and consistency and ensure that you will be able to finish with even greater strength than when you began your assignment?

SEPTEMBER 13

In Days of Difficulty, We Have the Answer!

Then the disciples, every man according to his ability,
determined to send relief unto the brethren
which dwelt in Judaea.
— Acts 11:29

I have no doubt in my mind that we are facing the most serious time in the history of mankind. Jesus warned of impending floods, earthquakes, and wars as we approach the end of the age. These calamities will become more and more frequent in the days ahead — but how we deal with them is up to us. We can respond in fear, or we can be prepared and rise up in faith to seize the hour for the spreading of the eternal Gospel.

There are numerous instances in Scripture where believers prepared themselves for difficult times after being forewarned. In Matthew 24:1-8, Jesus Himself warned the Early Church that trying circumstances lay ahead in their future, and instead of succumbing to worry and panic, these believers continued to believe and work and prosper. Another example is found in Acts 11:27-30, which tells of believers in Antioch who were warned by the Spirit of an impending famine and then began to set aside food and prepare for the coming crisis.

Notice that when these believers heard this warning from the Spirit, they were "determined" to take action. The Greek word for "determined" is *horidzo*, which means *to be bound* or *to be obligated.* In other words, these believers didn't hoard their prosperity in times of need. Bound by a sense of covenant obligation as fellow believers, they *determined to act.* Working together in unity, the believers in Antioch prepared a relief offering to send to the church in Jerusalem so the money could be distributed to believers in need. The action of the Antioch congregation before a time of crisis made them God's agents of provision and deliverance for others when the crisis actually occurred.

Today the Church's response to crises is often fractured, disorganized, and negatively influenced by poor doctrine. In the face of an impending catastrophe, one camp's strategy is to run and hide, whereas another will deny that the crisis even exists at all. Both of these strategies ultimately produce the same result: They prevent the Church from demonstrating God's manifold wisdom to the world.

There's no way to avoid the end-time prophecies outlined in the Bible — troubles *will* increase on the earth in the days ahead. However, these troubles are prime opportunities for those of us who know God and are called according to His purposes. By God's power, we can walk in faith through every fiery trial and become sources of supernatural provision to meet the needs of those who are suffering, demonstrating His love, grace, and wisdom to those who don't yet know His saving power in their lives.

Even if days of darkness lie in the future, these are not days to fear. Rather, they are opportunities for you rise up as a man or woman of faith and do great things for the Kingdom of God. These are days for you to demonstrate that you are a member of the Church of Almighty God and that you will meet the needs of the lost and hurting. Just as God used the church of Antioch to meet the severe needs of believers in Jerusalem — this is *your* moment to shine! But in order to be God's hand of deliverance and provision, you must plan and prepare. *Are you praying about how to prepare so God can use you mightily in these last times?*

MY PRAYER FOR TODAY

Father, there is no doubt in my mind that we are living in the last of the last days. The challenges in our future are unlike any faced by the previous generations. Jesus warned of impending calamities as we approach the end of the age. He did not warn us of these difficulties to scare us but to prepare us. Holy Spirit, I trust You for the wisdom I need in order to plan and be prepared in every area of my life for what lies ahead. I ask You to make me Your hand of deliverance and provision for others as You equip and enable me to meet the severe needs of those who are suffering in these difficult times.

I pray this in Jesus' name!

MY CONFESSION FOR TODAY

I confess that God has not given me a spirit of fear, but of power, love, and a sound mind. Therefore, I am well organized and prepared for any dark days that lie ahead. I rise up in faith and boldly seize the hour for the spreading of the eternal Gospel. I remain sensitive to and in touch with the Spirit of God, and He teaches me how to prepare as He leads me according to truth and shows me things to come. God has blessed me so I can be a blessing to others. I have resolved to be an expression of God's hope and blessing; therefore, He will bless me with resources and provisions that I can share with those who are in need.

I declare this by faith in Jesus' name!

QUESTIONS FOR YOU TO CONSIDER

1. Have you ever considered how God wants to use you to help people in times of distress? In what ways are you prepared to help people in times of distress? What steps could you take to get better prepared?
2. Think of how God used the church at Antioch to help suffering believers in Jerusalem. Because God spoke to them — *and they listened* — they were prepared to help those who were in need. Are you listening to what the Holy Spirit is telling *you* about the days to come?
3. Joseph is a great example of a believer who prepared for difficult times. Because He listened to God's voice and prepared, Joseph was a blessing in hard times. In fact, God used him to provide for an entire nation! Can you think of ways to emulate Joseph and prepare to help the people God has placed in your life?

SEPTEMBER 14

God's Law of Giving and Receiving

But this I say, He which soweth sparingly
shall reap also sparingly; and he which soweth bountifully
shall reap also bountifully.
— 2 Corinthians 9:6

In recent years, many people have been forced into positions of financial hardship as they struggle to keep up with an unpredictable, ever-changing global economy. People from almost every walk of life have been affected by the rising cost of living. Families scramble to keep up with house payments, car payments, insurance costs, school costs for the kids, credit-card payments, and a myriad of other monthly expenses.

This economic instability has also adversely affected churches, ministries, and mission organizations. When things get tough in the economy, many believers simply cut back on their giving to God, choosing not to set aside their tithes or give special offerings to ministries or charitable organizations. This decline in giving has had catastrophic consequences in the Kingdom of God because preaching the Gospel and establishing churches require money. Regardless of what is happening in the economy, there is a lost world that desperately needs to hear the message of Jesus Christ — and when people cease to give to the work of God, it hinders the outreach to lost souls.

The Bible makes it clear that tithes and offerings are not optional for us as believers. In fact, we have an even greater responsibility to be consistent and faithful in difficult times. God is watching — *and His law of giving and receiving always works*!

Right now believers all over the world are faced with these questions:

- In light of current financial challenges, will I remain faithful and unmoving in my financial commitment to the work of the ministry?
- What does this time of financial hardship reveal about me and my commitment to steadfastly sow into the work of the ministry?
- Will the giants move my faith, or will my faith move the giants?

Allow me to share an example from my own life. My parents' response to these challenging economic times stands out to me as a wonderful example of being consistent regardless of what is happening in the economy. Perhaps no one understands the challenge of making ends meet on a limited budget more than retirees. My father is now in Heaven, so today I will give you the vibrant example of my mother. Although she lives on a fixed income and makes many difficult financial decisions, she has never stopped giving to the work of the Lord.

My mother has always been careful with money, but now that she lives on a fixed retiree's income, she thinks twice before she gets in the car to drive to the grocery store or pharmacy. Instead of casually driving down the street to run a single errand, she combines errands to avoid driving when it isn't absolutely necessary in order to save on gasoline expenses. She is extremely careful with her expenditures.

Nevertheless, she has always resolved that regardless of what happens in the economy, she will not cut back in her giving to the ministry. She knows that if she and others don't stay on track with their giving, it ultimately affects souls that need to hear the Gospel and be saved. My mother has never considered her giving into the work of the ministry as something that could be "opted out of" in order to cut expenses.

I want to encourage you to take the same stance of faith as my mother. Be unmoved in your commitment to support the work of God, regardless of what is happening in the economy. Every time you write a check for the furtherance of God's Kingdom, *He is watching.* He sees each time you cut back on something else but refuse to skimp on your tithes and offerings. *God sees it all, and He takes note of your love, devotion, and unwavering commitment to support His work.* As a result, God will provide for you in ways that your natural resources could never provide. *God will multiply your seed back to you in ways you could never expect or anticipate.*

In Second Corinthians 9:6, the Holy Spirit said through Paul, "But this I say, He which soweth sparingly shall reap also sparingly; and he which soweth bountifully shall reap also bountifully." Paul wrote in terms of *seed* when he spoke about giving to the work of God. Since this is the metaphor the Holy Spirit gives us, we need to consider what it means. What does a farmer — a sower of seed — do to guarantee that he will have a harvest in the fall of the year?

If a farmer puts seed into the ground, he is guaranteed to have a harvest. But what if he says, "It's too hard to plant right now, so I'm going to hold on to my seed and not plant it this year"? Or what if he decides, "I'm going to eat my seed because I have so little of it"? These faulty decisions will guarantee that the farmer is going to experience a crisis at harvest time — because if no seed is planted in the ground, there simply will be no harvest.

The future of a farmer is completely dependent on getting his seed into the ground, and any farmer who fails to do this is guaranteeing his own crop failure. Therefore, regardless of how hot the weather or how difficult the task, a farmer must plant seed if he wants to reap a harvest. This is God's law of sowing and reaping.

The law of sowing and reaping applies to every sphere of life, including finances. It supersedes natural laws and natural economic crises. Even if the world around you suffers financially, sowing seed into the Kingdom of God will bring you protection and blessing. *This is God's promise to you.*

One of the best examples of God's people being blessed in times of crisis is the account of the children of Israel when God delivered them out of Egypt. God's people were *blessed* and *protected* while the world around them suffered. Although plagues ravaged the Egyptians, those plagues never touched the children of Israel because they hearkened to the voice of the Lord and did exactly what He instructed them to do.

The world around the Israelites was falling apart, but *their obedience to God's Word created an invisible wall that protected them from the destruction* that crippled and laid waste to Egypt. If Israel had not obeyed God's commands, that invisible wall would never have been erected and they would have experienced the same plagues the people of Egypt did. It was their obedience that *set them apart* and *saved them* while the godless world around them suffered terribly.

If you and I stay on track financially and give to God's work, regardless of how difficult it seems to be to do so, we will be divinely protected, supernaturally provided for, and guaranteed a blessing multiplied back to us. Like natural seed, it may take awhile for the crop to grow, but God promises in Second Corinthians 9:6 that if we put seed into the ground, we *will* reap. If we sow sparingly, that is how we will reap. But if we sow bountifully, God promises that we will reap bountifully. The level we reap will be completely determined by the level we sow.

If you and I are sure of where God wants us to sow and how much we're supposed to sow, we must stay steadfast in our obedience to give! We must first make sure we're putting our seed in ground that will produce good fruit. Then we are to determine *not* to refrain from giving, regardless of the current economic climate or forecast.

Just keep your eyes faithfully fixed on Jesus in this matter of giving. Carefully obey His command to tithe, to give offerings, and to sow seed. As you do, He will cause harvests of blessing to come to you, despite anything that is happening in the world around you. *This is God's promise to you!*

I'm very aware that many are worrying about the economy and wondering what's going to happen in the future. But don't let that happen to you! A spirit of fear will cause you to back off and retreat from doing what God commands — and that will put you in a negative cycle that brings a curse instead of a blessing. If you want to stay in a cycle of blessing, you must take authority over fear in the name of Jesus and then trust God as you obey His command to give, for that is His method of bringing you a harvest. Don't shrink back; keep pressing forward; keep your eyes on Jesus; and believe for a good harvest to come from the seed you have sown into good soil.

If you do what is right and obey God's command to give, you needn't worry about the future because the law of sowing and reaping *works*. This universal law assures a harvest of provision for you, for your family, and for your business, regardless of what happens in the world around you. *And that, my friend, is good news!*

MY PRAYER FOR TODAY

Heavenly Father, I thank You that the law of sowing and reaping works regardless of what is happening in the current world economy. Your Word commands me to give tithes and offerings, and I obey what Your Word tells me to do. You said that if I love You, I will keep Your commands. By giving, I am demonstrating my love to You. It is a part of my worship. I thank You for keeping Your promise that if I give, it will be given to me again. It is part of Your personal promise to me, and I thank You for being faithful to perform Your promise in my life.

I pray this in Jesus' name!

MY CONFESSION FOR TODAY

I confess that I am consistent and faithful when it comes to giving tithes and offerings to the work of the ministry. People need to hear the Good News of Jesus Christ — and I commit to using my money to preach the Gospel and to mature new believers in their faith. When it comes to my contributions, I declare that God can count on me. If there is any area that needs to be cut back in my expenses, it will not be in the area of my tithes and offerings. I will be faithful, and God will multiply my seed back to me. My time of harvest will come, and it will never be late. God is well aware of my situation, and He will keep His promise of sowing and reaping to me!

I declare this by faith in Jesus' name!

QUESTIONS FOR YOU TO CONSIDER

1. During times when the world economic situation is challenging to you, do you remain faithful to give your tithes and offerings, or do you see this as an optional choice to stop or to reduce your giving? Do you see yourself giving to God for *His* purposes or merely to men?
2. Have you considered what happens to churches and ministries — the work of the Kingdom — when people stop giving? The needs of the ministry continue regardless of what is happening in the economy. So if everyone cut back, how would it affect the ability of the ministry to carry out the work of Jesus in these times?
3. Can you think of a time when you were tempted to cut back on your giving, but you decided to remain steadfast, and in the end, you saw God multiply your seed back to you in some way that you could have never anticipated?

Don't shrink back; keep pressing forward;
keep your eyes on Jesus; and believe for a good harvest
to come from the seed you have sown into good soil.

SEPTEMBER 15

Planes, Trains, and Automobiles

In journeyings often, in perils of waters,
in perils of robbers, in perils by mine own countrymen,
in perils by the heathen, in perils in the city,
in perils in the wilderness, in perils in the sea,
in perils among false brethren....
— 2 Corinthians 11:26

The difficulty of travel when we first moved to the Soviet Union cannot be exaggerated. For example, because the whole USSR was gripped with deficits multiple decades ago, people never knew if they'd be able to find gasoline for their car. In the town where Denise and I lived, there was rarely gasoline at the gas station. The only reason we could drive our car was that we found a man who filled the Russian Army tanks with fuel. He siphoned gas on the side and sold it to drivers for $20 for five gallons.

But starting out with a tank of gas was no guarantee that you'd make it to your destination. You could be en route to some destination with a full tank of gas at the onset. But along the way when you needed to refill, you would drive into gas station after gas station that had big signs on the pumps that read, "CLOSED: NO FUEL!" It was a definite challenge to travel by car!

Then there were the trains! Russian trains today are beautiful and a delightful experience, but back in those early days after the fall of the Soviet Union, passenger trains were *filthy*. A person nearly needed waders to go into the restroom because the urine was so deep on the floor of the toilet stalls. Drunks drank vodka like water; drunken people physically fought each other; gypsies roamed the train cars and robbed travelers; and cockroaches scrambled across the floors.

In addition, the trains rarely ran on schedule, which meant there was a strong chance you would show up late for whatever kind of meeting you were trying to get to. It only cost about 25 cents to take a train back in those early days, but you more than paid for the inexpensive ride by having to put up with the inconveniences — the filth, the thieves, and the drunken fights. Add to that the frequent delays, and it took hours upon hours in the most unpleasant conditions to reach your destination by this mode of travel.

Finally, there was traveling by airplane. Today Russia has some fine, world-class airlines, but in the early '90s, getting on a Russian airplane was a *real adventure*! I actually experienced times when I was seated next to someone who had a dog or goat on the plane with him! And the food — if you could call it food — was nearly thrown at you by flight attendants, who didn't know *anything* about serving customers. I was once on a plane when the engines caught on fire. And on another flight, the flight attendants actually warned us that there would likely be a drop in cabin pressure because one of the doors had a broken seal!

Furthermore, ticket agents took bribes in those days and oversold seats on planes. One time I was on a plane that was so overloaded, a nursing mother was seated in the cockpit and the kitchens had people seated on the cabinet countertops and on the kitchen floors! My seat — which had been reserved and purchased in advance — was occupied by someone else when I arrived on board. So the flight attendant seated me in the coat closet on top of a crate of Pepsi bottles, which was crammed next to a rose bush that someone was taking to his home in the next city. And try to imagine it — before the flight took off, the flight attendant shut the curtain to the coat closet, *so I sat in darkness the whole flight!* By the end of that flight, my bottom felt sore from being poked by pop bottles, and my arms were scratched all over by the thorns on that rose bush.

As I remember those experiences that happened so many years ago, they remind me of what the apostle Paul wrote of his own travels in Second Corinthians 11:26, where he stated that he had been "…in *perils* of waters, in *perils* of robbers, in *perils* by mine own countrymen, in *perils* by the heathen, in *perils* in the city, in *perils* in the wilderness, in *perils* in the sea, in *perils* among false brethren…."

In this verse, Paul repeats the word "perils" *seven times* as he tells about what he faced as he traveled in his apostolic ministry. The word "perils" is from the Greek word *kindunos,* which simply means *danger* — telling us that traveling to preach the Gospel in the First Century AD was often a dangerous affair.

First, Paul says that he faced "perils of waters." The word "waters is *potamos,* which is the Greek word for *rivers.* Hence, we know that there were moments in his travels when Paul and his team had to cross dangerous rivers that could have jeopardized their lives. Dry riverbeds in that region of the world quickly swell to overflowing during flash floods — a constant danger to those who were traveling by foot.

Second, Paul says that he faced "perils of robbers." The word for "robbers" is *listes,* and it depicted *bandits* that lay alongside the roads and robbed those who were traveling alone or in small groups. According to Paul's testimony in this verse, he faced bandits at some point during his apostolic journeys.

Third, Paul says that he faced "perils of my own countrymen." The word "countrymen" is the Greek word *genos,* which is where we get the word *genes.* Paul was saying that he had been in danger at the hands of people who were from his own ancestry. We know by reading the book of Acts that the Jewish community continually assaulted Paul and his team and put them in great danger.

Fourth, Paul says that he faced "perils by the heathen." The word "heathen" is *ethnos,* and it referred to *pagans.* The pagan world was fiercely opposed to the message Paul and his companions preached, and as we read in the book of Acts, they were often confronted with dangerous situations at the hands of pagans.

Fifth, he says "perils in the wilderness." The word "wilderness" in Greek is *heremia,* and it denotes *an isolated, desert place.* Such places were often confronted when one traveled by foot, and they could often prove to be dangerous because there was little water and no sustenance.

Sixth, Paul says that he faced "perils in the sea." Acts 27 records one concrete dangerous event that Paul faced while he was at sea. However, Second Corinthians 11:25 says that he suffered shipwreck *three* times. That means there are two shipwreck events that are not even recorded in the Book of Acts!

Seventh, Paul says that he faced "perils among false brethren." The key to this phrase is the word "false" — the word *pseudos*, which implies the idea of *pretend* brothers. They feigned to be in Christ, but in fact they were not. Perhaps they were spies or other enemies sent into the Church to try to obtain information about Paul and his team. The text does not make it clear who these particular false brothers were, but it makes it clear that they were a "peril" to Paul's ministry.

In all seven instances we've seen, the word "peril" is the word *kindunos*, the Greek word for *danger*. This tells us that traveling as a Gospel preacher in Paul's time was not always grand and glorious. There were constant threats, which had to be held off with faith and a determination to proceed regardless of the risks involved. Much of what Paul faced in his travels is not even recorded in the Book of Acts!

As I faced my own struggles in the earlier years of ministering in the former USSR, I took courage from Paul's testimony in Second Corinthians 11:25. I am certain that ministers of the Gospel over the past 2,000 years have read these words and have similarly taken heart that their own particular struggles were not unique — and that if Paul could face such threats and go on to minister in God's power and anointing, they could do it too.

Today I want to assure you — you can do *whatever* God has told you to do. The devil may try to thwart God's plan for your life or hinder you along the way, but if you'll stay in faith and keep pressing forward, these obstacles will move aside, and you will do exactly what God has told you to do!

I would encourage you to read the rest of Second Corinthians 11 to see what else the apostle Paul encountered as he traveled to do the work of apostolic ministry. The devil tried to oppose him, hinder him, and thwart him from making progress in every way possible. But Paul pushed through each attack and every moment of opposition, and he did precisely what God called him to do. *Let that be your testimony too!*

MY PRAYER FOR TODAY

Father, I thank You for the power of God that sustains me when I am in rough places. The devil has tried to hinder me, oppose me, and thwart Your plan for my life. But I've kept my eyes focused on the goal that You have given me — and as a result, You have empowered me to keep going forward regardless of the opposition that I have encountered. Today I ask You to empower me by the Holy Spirit to tackle and overcome every hindrance that I am facing. I thank you for this divine power that always helps to make a way!

I pray this in Jesus' name!

MY CONFESSION FOR TODAY

I confess that greater is He that is in me than He that is in the world! The devil and the world itself may try to limit and hinder me from fulfilling God's plan for my life, but I declare that I will not be defeated, nor will I allow the devil to have delight in mastering my life. With the name of Jesus, the power of God, and the endurance of the Holy Spirit, I will press forward by faith until I have gone where I am supposed to go and have done what I am supposed to do!

I declare this by faith in Jesus' name!

QUESTIONS FOR YOU TO CONSIDER

1. What have you faced as you stepped forward to follow Jesus Christ and accomplish what He has called you to do? If Paul faced dangers, it shouldn't surprise us if we face them too!
2. How have you experienced the delivering and saving power of God as you've stepped out to obey God with your life? Can you think of times when you shouldn't have made it, but His quickening power reached out and rescued you, empowering you to keep forging ahead?
3. Have you read the rest of Second Corinthians, in which Paul relates the whole account of what he endured as he traveled in his apostolic journeys? As you do, realize that if Paul could overcome these things, you can overcome what you are facing too!

SEPTEMBER 16

By Invitation Only!

To all that be in Rome, beloved of God,
called to be saints....
— Romans 1:7

Growing up in our church, it was our custom after the sermon concluded to give a public invitation for people who felt some kind of "call" from God. As the piano played and an atmosphere was created for people to respond to the dealings of the Holy Spirit, the pastor often asked, "Is God *calling* you today?" People would come to the front of the sanctuary, meet the pastor, kneel at the altar, and receive prayer for the various invitations that were made. Whether it was a call to salvation, a call to rededication, a call to join the church, or a call to the ministry — people sensed the Holy Spirit drawing them to respond to Him in those services.

If we know Jesus Christ, God has called each of us — and that call is very special. But what does it actually mean to be *called*? This is what I want to talk to you about today. I want us to begin by looking at an example of the word "called" in Romans 1:7, where Paul wrote, "To all that be in Rome, beloved of God, *called* to be saints...."

The word "called" is the Greek word *kaleo*, which means *to beckon, to call, to invite*, or *to summon*. Although the word *kaleo* can simply mean *to call*, it is often used to convey the idea of an *invitation*. Those who are *called* or *invited* should view the invitation as a privilege and a prestigious honor to be treasured, prized, and revered.

The New Testament abounds with 148 examples of this word *kaleo*. Two notable examples are found in Matthew 22:2-10 and Luke 14:7-24. In Matthew 22, the word *kaleo* is used in Jesus' parable to describe a special invitation extended by a king who was asking people to attend a great marriage feast. Such royal events were closed to the public; a person couldn't attend without being *invited*. Receiving an invitation to attend this type of special occasion was therefore considered an honor.

In Luke 14:7-24, Jesus taught two parables in which various forms of the word *kaleo* are used 12 times to denote invitations given to people to attend a wedding and a great feast. Both parables in this passage of Scripture emphatically convey the idea of the great *honor* and *privilege* bestowed on a person who was *called* or *invited* to such an event.

The apostle Paul used the Greek word *kaleo* and its various forms 49 times in his epistles. For instance, he used this word *kaleo* to describe God's *call* to repent — to be set free from spiritual darkness and the world of sin and to become a part of His family. This divine *call* comes to each person when God opens his or her spiritual ears to hear the Gospel's invitation to salvation. When the Holy Spirit opens a person's spiritual ears to truly hear the Gospel message, that is precisely when God's invitation is extended to him or her.

As believers, we must *never* forget that we couldn't have come to the Lord if He hadn't opened our spiritual ears and invited us to become a part of His family. Yes, Jesus died for all, but only the Holy Spirit opens spiritual ears to hear the invitation to become a part of God's family. Our being called into the family of God was at *His* initiative. Our part was simply to respond to the invitation He was offering us.

As a mature believer, I now understand what was happening at the altar of our church when I was a young man. God's Spirit was touching hearts, calling and inviting them to make various changes or commitments. Then people, by His grace, were responding to the invitation that the Holy Spirit was extending to them.

So why don't you take the time to ask yourself, *What is it God is calling me to do for Him?* Whatever invitation you have received from Heaven — whether it is the call to salvation, to the ministry, or to any other assignment for the furtherance of God's Kingdom — it is your responsibility to recognize the honor of the invitation and to answer His call with a willing and obedient heart. Whatever the Holy Spirit is saying to you, you can know this for sure: *It's a good day to say YES to the Lord!*

MY PRAYER FOR TODAY

Father, I thank You for opening my spiritual ears to hear the call You first issued to me when You called me to repentance and salvation. I understand that I "heard" that call only because You opened my spiritual ears to hear. How I thank You for that divine act of grace in my life! And now, Father, I ask that my spiritual ears remain open so that I can continue to hear the invitations You extend to me when You call upon me to do new tasks and assignments. Help me not to be so busy that I don't hear You. It is my sincere prayer that my spiritual ears remain open to hear You, and that when You speak, I am quick to obey what You have called and invited me to do!

I pray this in Jesus' name!

MY CONFESSION FOR TODAY

I joyfully confess that God speaks to me and that I hear Him when He speaks. He has opened my spiritual ears, and I have the ability to hear when He calls and invites me to do something new and special. When God asks me to do something or beckons me to a new task, I do not argue. I choose to quickly agree with God so that I can walk continually with Him. I consider it an honor and a privilege whenever God allows me the opportunity to do something in His service.

I declare this by faith in Jesus' name!

QUESTIONS FOR YOU TO CONSIDER

1. Do you remember the first time God opened your spiritual ears, and you heard Him call you to repentance and salvation? When was that time? Do you remember the specific place and date?
2. Are your spiritual ears open? Are you cultivating a sensitive, listening heart that stays tuned in to the Holy Spirit's leadings in your spirit? You may be sensing a new calling that He is extending to you in this season of your life. Is there a new invitation to take on a new task or assignment?
3. To be honest — and we must be honest if we're going to grow in the Lord — is there any call that He has extended to you that you have not obeyed? It's never too late to repent for that, and to immediately begin to follow the instructions that the Holy Spirit has extended to you. What is that call that you are supposed to be fulfilling?

Take the time to ask yourself,
"What is it God is calling me to do for Him?"
And whatever the Holy Spirit is saying to you,
it's a good day to say YES to the Lord!

SEPTEMBER 17

The Lifting of Holy Hands

I will therefore that men pray every where,
lifting up holy hands....
— 1 Timothy 2:8

I can remember as a young boy when I would sit next to my Grandmother Bagley in church. I would take her hands in mine, and I'd run the tip of my index finger along the bulging blood vessels in her elderly hands. I was amazed at how I could push the vessels one way or the other, and how easily her wrinkly skin moved when I pressed against it. I was particularly fascinated by the liver spots that covered ever-increasing sections of the skin on her upper hand. As I looked at her hands, they told me that her life had not been an easy one.

I've always enjoyed looking at hands because the condition of people's hands tells so many stories about their lives. If people have worked hard, manual-labor jobs over the course of their lives, it can be seen in their hands. If people have served in a top-level professional job, it can usually be detected in the softness they have been able to retain in their hands. Hands tell stories. They are indicative of one's life.

Think of it! With our hands, we embrace loved ones; we work in our employment; we handle property; we make money; and we touch every sphere of our lives. There is nothing pertaining to our daily lives that we don't put our hands to in some way.

With people's hands, both good and evil is done. With hands, others are helped, sin is committed, and communication is carried out. Hands are required in every area of our lives, and they represent us in every way. Thus, our hands become *symbolic* of our lives.

The apostle Paul stated, "I will therefore that men pray every where, lifting up holy hands..." (1 Timothy 2:8). When we lift our hands to Heaven, we therefore present *everything we are*, *everything we have done*, and *everything we have* to God. When you or I lift our hands in worship, we are lifting up our families, our loved ones, our relationships, our work, our money, and *everything else* to God.

But Paul specifically said that he wished all men everywhere would lift up "holy" hands. The word "holy" is the Greek word *hosios*, which describes something that is *consecrated* or *dedicated* to God. Thus, when Paul wrote of lifting up "holy" hands, he was expressing his deeply felt longing that men everywhere would present themselves as *dedicated* and *consecrated* to God.

When you lift your hands to Heaven, *what does God see*?

- Does He see a life that is consecrated and dedicated?
- Does He see sin or compromise?

- ➢ Does He see sacrifice?
- ➢ Does He see commitment?

Paul's prayer was that men everywhere would do whatever is necessary to present *dedicated, consecrated, holy hands* to the Lord — which means to present their *dedicated, consecrated, holy lives* to Him.

So pause for a moment today and look at your hands. What do you see when you look at them? An even bigger question is this: What does *God* see when He looks at your hands? One thing is for sure: Your hands are not just skin and bones — they are *symbols* of your life. So each day make sure that you lift up holy hands and give glory to your faithful God. Then offer your hands as holy instruments unto Him, to do His will and to reach out to others with His unconditional, unchanging love!

MY PRAYER FOR TODAY

Father, You are stirring my heart today to offer myself to You as a holy instrument to do Your will. I realize now that the lifting of my hands to You represents bringing my life to You in yielded surrender. You are calling me to a higher level of dedication, and when I lift my hands to You, that action represents a life lifted in consecration to Your glory. When I look at my hands, help me think seriously about the adjustments I may need to make so I can lift up my life to You in worship with confidence and without compromise.

I pray this in Jesus' name!

MY CONFESSION FOR TODAY

I proclaim that every day I dedicate myself more and more to Jesus. Today I make a fresh decision to live a life that is consecrated to the purposes of God. Every day I choose to set my attention and affection on Jesus and to allow the Holy Spirit to reveal to me areas of my life that Jesus longs for me to surrender. I release those areas to His control and submit them to the Lordship of Christ. When I raise my hands in worship, I raise hands that represent purity, dedication, consecration, and total surrender to the will of God!

I declare this by faith in Jesus' name!

QUESTIONS FOR YOU TO CONSIDER

1. The apostle Paul prayed for men to present themselves as living sacrifices, consecrated to God. Can you confidently say that your life is a consecrated life?
2. What do you need to do differently and specifically to live a life of consecration? Take a moment to examine your heart and to determine those areas where you know that your ways do not line up with God's ways. First John 1:9 tells you how to experience a deep cleansing by the blood of Jesus so you can dedicate your life to the Lord in a fuller way.

3. What specifically did the Holy Spirit speak to you about today as you read this Sparkling Gem? What action is He leading you to take as a result?

SEPTEMBER 18

What Are You Doing With Your Time?

Redeeming the time,
because the days are evil.
— Ephesians 5:16

It's interesting to me that the most successful of wealthy investors and a homeless, penniless man on the street have one thing in common: Each has only 24 hours in a day.

In this natural world, *time* is the very essence of our lives. To a large degree, the way we use time defines who we are. Because that is true, the issue of how we utilize our time becomes supremely important.

It's true that the way we utilize our money is a measuring rod of what we value most in life. But although financial stewardship is important, the way we spend our *time* is even more important. For example, many wealthy moguls will ignore their families for weeks, months, and even years, and then try to "buy" the affections of their loved ones with money and material wealth. This is rarely, if ever, a successful undertaking. It seems that no amount of money they spend can compete with spending their most precious commodity — *time* — on the ones they love.

Time is one of our most valuable resources. Money can be replaced. Financial shortfalls can be made up in the following quarter or fiscal year. But nothing can replace time. *Once it is gone, it is gone forever.*

The good news is that the apostle Paul said we can "redeem the time" (*see* Ephesians 5:16). The word "redeem" is the Greek word *exagoridzo*, which in this context means *to buy back* time. You may have lost time by merely wasting it or by using it on things that weren't important. But the great story of redemption is that *your story isn't over*. With God's help, time can be *redeemed* — that is, bought back by personal carefulness and by stewarding what time remains.

Today we live in age of distractions. It's not that we're necessarily idle or lazy. But so many things vie for our time and attention that we can become distracted from important and essential things. For example, nonstop media entertainment and electronic gadgets fill our modern lives, constantly luring us away from the truly important things of life. Part of the act of prioritizing is identifying these types of time-wasters and eliminating them from our routines — or at least reducing the amount of time we spend focusing on those activities.

Media and gadgets are not bad or wrong in themselves, but often they take far too much of our time from matters that should be our *real* priorities, such as time with the Lord, family, work, and friends. The key is balancing all our priorities, and that means knowing what needs to be done at what time and being able to put other things on hold that are nonessential or less important at the moment.

The ability to properly manage your time and to establish sound, balanced priorities is one of the most critical keys to experiencing a stable, fruitful life as a believer and a leader. So I encourage you today to prioritize your time by carefully identifying the things that are most essential to your life. Once you've determined your top priorities, focus on those areas and let other, less important pursuits fall into place beneath what you truly value most. As you learn to use your time wisely, not squandering it but making the most of the life God has given you, you will surely find the fulfillment He desires you to experience in every area of your life.

MY PRAYER FOR TODAY

Father, I ask You to help me understand what my top priorities should be and then give me the discipline to live according to those guidelines. Help me discern when something is actually a distraction that will pull me off task so I don't become entangled in activities that are either unnecessary or possibly even a hindrance to the main thing You want me to accomplish. I repent for the times I have allowed procrastination and laziness to waste valuable time. Those are not habits that I want to continue in my life. Teach me to focus and prioritize as You help me cultivate new habits and patterns that produce Your desired results in my life. Today I make a fresh commitment to steward my time with diligence and to trust You to guide my choices so I can make the most of every moment.

I pray this in Jesus' name!

MY CONFESSION FOR TODAY

I confess that I am diligent, productive, and undistracted as I give my time and attention to the most important priorities in my life. I maintain keen focus on the assignment before me. I keep my ears open to the Holy Spirit's guidance to follow His wisdom in all I set out to do. Therefore, I am productive and organized. I believe that I receive lasting fruitfulness as the reward of how I invest my time.

I declare this by faith!

QUESTIONS FOR YOU TO CONSIDER

1. Can you think of time-wasters in your life? Is it too much time on the Internet, texting people, or watching television? What is there in your life that is taking too much of your precious time and thereby robbing you of the ability to be more productive in the areas that matter most?

2. Have you ever asked the Lord to help you form a set of priorities for your life? If yes, do you live by that list of priorities? If not, why not?
3. How many hours a day do you spend on less important pursuits that should be used more productively?

SEPTEMBER 19

Your Most Valuable Partner

So then neither is he that planteth any thing,
neither he that watereth; *but God that giveth the increase.*
— 1 Corinthians 3:7

What has God called you to do that you never dreamed you would be doing? I've learned that as we walk with God as our most important Partner in life, we often find ourselves doing what we would have never thought possible.

In 1992 — just after relocating my family to live and minister in the former USSR in the fall of 1991 — God miraculously opened a door for Denise and me to begin a television broadcast that would transcend the 11 times zones of the former USSR. (This was launched with the signing of a supernatural contract, as I related in the July 5 *Gem.*) We didn't realize at the time that our step of faith to start that one program was actually the inception of what would become the first Christian TV network in the territory of the former USSR.

Decades later, we are still broadcasting our own TV programs in addition to other programs that we broadcast for other ministries. Seven days a week, 24 hours a day, we broadcast to a viewing audience of millions of people! Over all these years, we have literally broadcasted hundreds of thousands of hours of Bible-teaching TV programs all across this vast land. By the grace of God, I am thoroughly convinced that it has made a permanent impact on the spiritual environment of the former USSR. So much teaching of the Bible has gone into homes that the Church in this part of the world will *never* be the same.

Since we started broadcasting in 1992, we have received millions of letters and correspondence from people whose lives have been changed by the powerful teaching of God's Word via the airwaves. It is no exaggeration to state that several million people have come to Christ as a result of our television network. Books have been distributed free of charge by the millions. We give all the glory to God for what has happened and for what will ensue, and we are thankful for the gifts of our partners who have worked hand in hand with us so we could establish and continue to fulfill this mighty work.

To do all of this has taken faith, courage, finances, equipment, a skilled technical team, and a group of giving partners who have stood by us through the years so we could consistently and professionally reach the multitudes who live in spiritual darkness. In addition to the technical expertise needed, this assignment has also required a large team of dedicated employees who read and answer every single letter that is received from those who correspond in response to the programs.

This is no small undertaking and requires a *"1,000-percent"* commitment from everyone involved, despite the obstacles and setbacks that invariably occur with such a monumental task. Hell does not sit silent as you take the life-saving message to those in darkness, so you must also stand ready to combat spiritual enemies that come to oppose you. And I'd be remiss if I didn't say that God's mercy and grace remain the most important factor in this mix!

We can buy the finest equipment, produce the highest quality programs, and purchase the best time slots available on television — but if God doesn't supply *His* part, it will all be to no avail. I am reminded of Psalm 127:1, which states: "Except the Lord build the house, they labour in vain that build it: except the Lord keep the city, the watchman waketh but in vain."

In First Corinthians 3:7, Paul also stated this truth: "So then neither is he that planteth any thing, neither he that watereth; *but God that giveth the increase*." As we saw in the July 5 *Sparkling Gem*, the word "increase" is from the Greek word *auxano*, which simply means to *increase* or *grow* — and in this context indicates *the continual blessing of God*.

But let me go into greater detail today concerning this word "increase." The form of the Greek word *auxano* that Paul used to write this passage denotes something that is *amplified*, *augmented*, *enlarged*, or *enhanced*. It carries the idea of something that *escalates* and *multiplies*. It clearly means that even though one plants and another waters, it is God who causes the vision to blossom, to become larger, and to grow strong and healthy.

Another way to say it is that we can nurture the soil, plant the seeds, and water what has been planted, but only *God* can produce the sunshine and weather conditions to cause growth. Therefore, even with all the faithful people who do their essential parts, *God* is still the most important Partner in whatever it is we are called to do!

So whatever God has called *you* to do, give it your very best, but never forget the crucial role of prayer and the reality of your utter dependence on God as your number-one Partner in life. Just like a farmer, you can prepare the ground and plant the seed of God's Word; then you can water and nurture the seed that was sown. But *only God* can produce the sunshine and weather conditions necessary to bring the growth that is needed. Therefore, in the end, He gets the glory for all increase!

Today I urge you to make sure you have these two essential ingredients — prayer and complete trust in God — thoroughly integrated into the mix of what you are doing. Remember that you have no Partner comparable to the One who called you, for He is the ultimate Source of all true increase!

MY PRAYER FOR TODAY

Dear Father, I thank You for reminding me again today that even as I do my part, I have to always remember that I must trust You to do Your part or no increase will come to what You have called me to do. I promise to nurture the soil, plant the seed, pull the weeds, and water what is planted — but I look to You to provide the sunshine and proper weather conditions to produce the increase I need. I understand that one plants, another waters — but only You give the increase. Thank You for bringing this back to the forefront of my mind today and for encouraging me to remember that You are the crucial ingredient in all that I do! In the end, we can do all our parts, but the increase is totally dependent on You!

I pray this in Jesus' name!

MY CONFESSION FOR TODAY

I boldly confess that I will do what God has asked me to do. I will nurture the soil, plant the seeds, pull the weeds, and water what has been planted — and I will do it faithfully with others who work alongside with me. But no results will be gained if God does not join Himself to what we are doing. So today I look to God as the great Provider of increase. He will provide the sunshine and weather necessary to make these seeds and acts of faith grow. Without Him, I can do nothing, but with God as my primary Partner, it is guaranteed that I will see and experience increase!

I declare this by faith in Jesus' name!

QUESTIONS FOR YOU TO CONSIDER

1. Have you ever attempted something without God's involvement and experienced poor results? Perhaps you put time, energy, and attention into the project but forgot to bring God into the mix. What did you learn from that experience? What will you do to prevent that from happening again?
2. On the other hand, can you name a time when you *remembered* that God is your primary Partner? As you did your part while leaning upon God as your Partner, how did you experience supernatural increase?
3. From what you have read today, what changes are you going to make in the tasks and projects that are in front of you? What difference will this *Sparkling Gem* make in the way you do things?

You have no Partner comparable
to the One who called you,
for He is the ultimate Source of all true increase!

SEPTEMBER 20

Special Mercy for the Overwhelmed

To Timothy, my dearly beloved son:
Grace, *mercy*, and peace, from God the Father
and Christ Jesus our Lord.
— 2 Timothy 1:2

Have you ever felt overwhelmed by what you were facing in life? I'm sure the answer to that question is yes. And certainly you know that you are not the only person who has faced what felt like insurmountable odds. There have been millions before you who felt the same, but with God's help, they survived, tackled the odds, and even came out on top.

Tough times come to everyone at some point, but the storm eventually passes for those who are determined to navigate it *God's* way. And to help His people "get to the other side" safely, God provides *special mercy* for the overwhelmed. That's what I want to show you in Scripture today.

The apostle Paul wrote the epistle we call Second Timothy at a time when his young son in the faith was facing insurmountable odds. Nero was ruling as emperor; believers were being persecuted for their faith; many people were deserting the Lord; and others were defecting from the Church. At the moment that Paul wrote this letter to Timothy, Timothy was serving as pastor in Ephesus — a major city in Asia where persecution was raging. Surviving every day was a challenge for believers in that region, and Christian leaders, of course, especially felt the brunt of it. By reading the words of Second Timothy, it is clear that Paul was trying to comfort the overwhelmed heart of this young Christian leader and provide him with some spiritual help and strength.

In the opening lines of that letter, Paul wrote, "Paul, an apostle of Jesus Christ by the will of God, according to the promise of life which is in Christ Jesus, to Timothy, my dearly beloved son: Grace, *mercy*, and peace, from God the Father and Christ Jesus our Lord" (2 Timothy 1:1,2).

When Paul wrote a letter, he normally used a greeting that included the words *grace* and *peace*. Paul deviated from that greeting only *three times* out of all his 13 New Testament letters. The first instance was in First Timothy; the second was in his epistle to Titus; and the third was here in Second Timothy 1:2. In all three of these instances, Paul was writing to someone who felt overwhelmed by their situation. In each of those instances, Paul added the word *mercy* to his greetings. He told them, "Grace *and mercy* and peace be unto you."

When Paul penned his first epistle to Timothy, the younger minister had just assumed the leading role in the rapidly growing church of Ephesus, and he felt *overwhelmed* by his new responsibilities. Because of the awesome task at hand, Timothy needed to be reminded that God's *mercy* was available to help him in his situation. So when Paul wrote to Timothy the first time, he added the word "mercy" to his salutation.

When Paul wrote to Titus, he had just left Titus on the island of Crete to establish a church among the island's unruly inhabitants. The people of Crete had such bad reputations that Paul even quoted one of their prophets as saying, "...The Cretians are always liars, evil beasts, slow bellies." Amazingly, Paul agreed with this assessment, asserting, "This witness is true..." (Titus 1:12,13). It would have been very difficult for Titus to lead a congregation among people like that! Titus surely felt *overwhelmed* by his assignment. He needed to know that a special measure of *mercy* was available to him for his difficult task. So when Paul wrote to him, he added the word "mercy" to his salutation.

When Paul wrote Second Timothy, Timothy was once again feeling *overwhelmed* — not because of a large, growing church, as had been in the case in Paul's first letter to him, but because his congregation was in decline, people were suffering persecution, and a spirit of fear was trying to attach itself to him (*see* 2 Timothy 1:7). So when Paul wrote to him, he again altered his salutation to include the word *mercy*. Right from the start of his letter, he wanted to remind Timothy that God's mercy was available to the overwhelmed, so Paul wrote, "...Grace, *mercy*, and peace...."

Isn't it good to know that when God calls you to do something difficult — something that threatens to overwhelm you or make you feel inadequate — He inserts extra *mercy* between the grace and the peace? *There is a special measure of mercy to those who feel overwhelmed by their trials in life.* This was especially good news for young Timothy, and it's good news for you too!

When God's mercy works in your life, it may manifest as a renewed sense of courage and inner toughness to make it to the next day. That may not seem very spectacular — but think how much more difficult it would be if you didn't have that special touch of mercy!

It would be good for you to reflect on the ways you've already experienced God's special mercy during difficult times in your life or in the lives of others. When you bring to your remembrance those times His mercy was demonstrated in your life right at the moment it was needed, it fortifies your expectation to receive a manifestation of God's mercy in the midst of your present challenge as well.

If you feel overwhelmed by what you are facing in life, I want to assure you that God is well aware of it and He has not abandoned you. Whether the issue is financial, relational, work-related, health-related — *whatever* may be the root cause of what you are facing, you can be assured of this: God has special mercy that He is ready to make available to help you through this difficult time. Thank God for His *grace* and *peace* — but if you are feeling overwhelmed, receive by faith His special *mercy* to help you make it through victoriously to the other side!

MY PRAYER FOR TODAY

Father, I am so grateful that when You call me to do something difficult and it tempts me to feel inadequate, You insert extra mercy between the grace and the peace in my life. Holy Spirit, I receive a special measure of mercy to undergird me in the times when I feel overwhelmed by the trials of life.

I pray this in Jesus' name!

MY CONFESSION FOR TODAY

I confess that when my heart is overwhelmed, I go to the Rock of my salvation to partake of His mercies that are new for me every morning. I confess that His mercy is at work in my life right now. Today I walk with a renewed sense of courage, persistence, and inner toughness because God's all-sufficient grace, mercy, and peace are being multiplied to me.

I declare this by faith in Jesus' name!

QUESTIONS FOR YOU TO CONSIDER

1. Do you recall a time when you were especially overwhelmed by events in life and you experienced God's mercy in a special way that helped you make it through that difficult season? How did God demonstrate His goodness to you in that time?
2. Have you ever observed someone who received a special touch of God's mercy? What was the manifestation of that mercy? What was its effect on that person's life?
3. What are you facing right now that makes you a candidate for another dose of God's special mercy? Since God is always willing to give you a special touch of His mercy, why don't you open your heart and allow the Holy Spirit to minister that to your heart and soul today?

SEPTEMBER 21

Riches Are Not Always Measured in Dollars and Cents

I know thy works, and tribulation, and poverty,
(but thou art *rich*)....
— Revelation 2:9

When the renowned theologian St. Thomas Aquinas visited the Vatican in the Thirteenth Century AD, Pope Innocent IV invited him to view the breathtaking treasures that had been amassed by the Church. With great pride, the pope told him, "No longer can the Church say, 'Silver and gold have we none'!" To this, St. Thomas Aquinas answered, "Holy Father, that is very true indeed. But neither can we say to the poor and afflicted, 'Rise, take up your bed and walk!'"

It is good for us to remember that some of the poorest churches in history have been spiritually *rich* and some of the wealthiest churches in history have been spiritually *poor*. Church buildings may be adorned with gold, silver, and treasures, but they are often vacant of the true riches of the Holy Spirit. A church's coffers may be filled and its congregation may include many wealthy people, but that is no guarantee that the church is truly rich. In God's eyes, many financially prosperous churches are actually *spiritually famished*, while some financially poorer churches are *spiritually rich*.

It is simply a fact that riches are not always measured in finances or precious treasures. An example is in the First Century church of Smyrna. The church of Smyrna was experiencing severe persecution. Members of their congregation had been tortured, imprisoned, and even killed for their faith in Jesus. In addition, many believers had been robbed or had their livelihood destroyed as they were ostracized from the community. The combination of these trials had left them financially broke. Yet Jesus told them, "I know thy works, and tribulation, and poverty, (but thou art *rich*)...."

The word "rich" is the Greek word *plousios*. It depicts one who is *extremely wealthy*. A person who is *plousios* isn't merely rich — he is *very* rich. This was the word Jesus used when He told the church of Smyrna, "...But thou art *rich*...." There are many less tangible yet infinitely more valuable forms of riches that cannot be purchased with money — and in regard to those riches, the church of Smyrna was extremely wealthy.

A study of the word *plousios* in the New Testament shows that it can also refer to *spiritual riches*. Jesus had already made it clear in Revelation 2:9 that the church of Smyrna was impoverished materially and financially. Although the Smyrnean believers were materially poor, Jesus clearly stated that they were spiritually *very* rich.

These believers may have been deprived in terms of worldly goods, but they were *rich* in many other ways. They had forfeited their creature comforts, and all legal protection had been removed from them, causing them to lean on their fellow believers for support. This brought about a rich, meaningful level of fellowship that is less prevalent in countries where believers' rights are protected and the need for close-knit relationships isn't felt as intensely. The love of Christ permeated the church as its members spiritually and emotionally lent encouragement and help to each other during their time of great need.

Words can't describe the tenderness of the Holy Spirit that was present when these early believers gathered in illegal underground meetings to worship Jesus. It is no wonder they greeted each other with a holy kiss every time they met together (*see* Romans 16:16), for whenever they departed from a meeting, they were never certain they would see each other again. The entire congregation lived in a hostile environment where the threat of arrest, seizure, or death was constantly imminent. As they held hands to pray or lifted their hands to worship quietly so they wouldn't be heard and caught, these believers shared a depth of spiritual commitment and covenant relationship rarely experienced in today's world where such concepts are often viewed as radical and strange.

For the Smyrnean church, tribulation had come in many forms. Jobs were lost; property was seized; and slander destroyed their reputations. They were made outcasts by both Jews and pagans. But in the midst of it all, these believers experienced a different kind of richness — one that can't be measured in worldly wealth. It was a richness of the Holy Spirit's presence, a richness of patience, a richness of strength to endure, a richness of faith, a richness of love among the saints, and a richness in spiritual rewards for their steadfastness in the face of adversity. And in experiencing a death to self, the church of Smyrna had come to know the mighty power of the resurrected Christ. Although these believers had suffered great tribulation and had been reduced to abject material poverty, they were *plousios* — magnificently rich — in all of these other, less tangible ways.

Sometimes believers' obedience to God places them "outside" the world's favor. In those cases — especially when Christians suffer the loss of revenue or material possessions — God compensates His people with other types of riches that are infinitely more precious.

So don't make the mistake of thinking riches can always be measured in financial terms. There are elements of your faith that make you wealthy in ways beyond your natural comprehension — in ways that cannot be measured in money.

MY PRAYER FOR TODAY

Heavenly Father, I thank You that spiritual riches go beyond dollars and cents. Financial wealth can be obtained and lost, but spiritual riches are enduring. Although I am thankful for the ways You have blessed me financially, I know the riches of this life are fleeting. Therefore, I ask You to help me walk worthily of my rich spiritual inheritance that possesses a value exceeding anything this world can offer. I rejoice in knowing that spiritual riches outlast this life and that this is the wealth I can take with me to Heaven.

I pray this in Jesus' name!

MY CONFESSION FOR TODAY

I confess that God meets my financial needs according to His riches in glory by Christ Jesus. But in addition to having my financial needs met, I am also spiritually enriched by the gifts of the Holy Spirit and by the love of God within me that makes me more than a conqueror — no matter what I may face. I have rightstanding with God Himself by the blood of Jesus; an abiding peace that surpasses natural understanding; and a wellspring of joy that provides me with an endless source of strength. I boldly confess that I am spiritually rich and superabundantly blessed by the riches of God in my life.

I declare this by faith in Jesus' name!

QUESTIONS FOR YOU TO CONSIDER

1. Can you recall a time in your life when you had less financially, but because of your relationships and the presence of the Lord in your life, you felt spiritually rich? When was that time?
2. If you are more financially blessed and more independent now, do you miss some of the closeness you experienced when you were less financially blessed? Or can you say you are as spiritually rich today as you were back in those days?
3. How would you express spiritual riches? What does that term mean to you?

SEPTEMBER 22

All Scripture Is Given by Inspiration of God

All scripture is given by inspiration of God….
— 2 Timothy 3:16

In Second Timothy 3:16, Paul wrote these precious words about the Bible: "All scripture is given by inspiration of God…." Today I want us to look at the word "inspiration" to see exactly what the original language conveys to you and me.

The word "inspiration" comes from the Greek word *theopneustos*, a compound of two Greek words, *theos* and *pneuma*. The first word, *theos,* is the word for *God*; the second half of the word is *pneuma*, which comes from the Greek root *pneu*.

The root *pneu* communicates *a dynamic movement of air.* For example, it can mean *to blow*, as *to blow air.* It was actually used to portray a musician who *blew air through an instrument to produce a musical sound.* There are also places where it is used to picture the *emitting of a fragrance*. Furthermore, this root word could be used to depict *the projection of emotions.*

But when the root *pneu* becomes *pneuma*, it carries an additional range of meanings — including *life*, *force*, *energy*, *dynamism*, and *power.* The Jews considered *pneuma* to be the *powerful force* put forth by God to create the universe and all living things and also the *force that continues to sustain creation*. In the Old Testament Septuagint, *pneuma* demonstrates moments when God would *move mightily upon a person, enabling him to do supernatural feats.*

When this word *pneuma* is compounded with *theos*, the new word is *theopneustos*, which literally means *God-breathed* and is where we get the word "inspiration." The word *theopneustos* is the picture of *God breathing His own substance into something*. Just as a musician would blow on an instrument to produce a distinct sound, God mightily moved on those who wrote the Scriptures, causing them to temporarily become instruments through whom He expressed His heart and will. They were the writers, but God was the Great Musician who breathed upon them, His instruments. Thus, the Bible is God's message delivered through human writers to us.

And just as the word *pneuma* can carry the idea of *a fragrance*, the Word was breathed from God and thus carries *His very essence and fragrance* within it. Since the word *pneuma* can also portray *the projection of emotions*, we know that God projected the totality of His emotions into the Word when He inspired its writing. Therefore, the Word not only conveys an intellectual message, but it has *God's heart* in it as well. And the *pneuma* of God didn't create the Scripture and then depart from it. This power — the same *pneuma* power that originally created and continues to sustain the universe — is still inside God's Word, upholding and empowering it to be just as strong as the day it was given.

What does all this mean to you personally? You can know that as you give the Word of God a prominent role in your life, that anointed Word, infused with the heart of Almighty God Himself, will bring the music and the fragrance of Heaven into your life and home and literally change the atmosphere.

Think about it — the Bible you own contains the very *life*, *essence*, *energy*, and *dynamic force* of God Himself! If you'll get hungry for more of Him and determine to meditate on this truth long enough to tap into it, God Himself will come pouring out of the Bible into your life and situation. The *power* held inside the Word will blow mightily upon you and upon the situations that surround you — and when that happens, *everything* will change!

MY PRAYER FOR TODAY

Dear Lord, I am so thankful that the Bible is filled with your power and life. When I pick it up and read it, I am receiving the very life of God into my being. Father, help me to become more disciplined when it comes to reading Your Word. Each word contains Your very life, essence, energy, and dynamism in it. It contains the power and answers that I need for every situation that I am facing in my life. Please forgive me for not reading it as often or as much I should. Holy Spirit, I receive Your strength today to make and to stay faithful to a new commitment to take the Word of God into my heart EVERY DAY so that it can nourish and sustain my heart and my soul.

I pray this in Jesus' name!

MY CONFESSION FOR TODAY

I confess that I value the Word of God as the most important priority in my life. I keep it before my eyes, I put it in my ears, and I speak it out of my mouth. The Word of God dominates my life decisions and guides my path. I hide it in my heart so that I do not sin against God. As I read the Bible, it releases the essence, energy and dynamism of God Himself into my spirit, soul, and body. God's Word revives me, rejuvenates me, and replenishes me. The very force of heaven invades my life as I take the Word of God into me!

I declare this by faith in Jesus' name!

QUESTIONS FOR YOU TO CONSIDER

1. If the Bible is so important to you, when and how often do you read it? Do you treat it like it is important, or is reading it something you do *if* you have extra time to do it?
2. What happens inside you as you read the Word of God?
3. What time of the day do you personally find is the best time for you to set aside time to read your Bible? Different people have different Bible-reading habits. What are yours?

SEPTEMBER 23

Equipped To Navigate Stormy Last-Days Seas

All scripture is given by inspiration of God,
and is profitable for doctrine, for reproof, for correction,
for instruction in righteousness: That the man of God
may be perfect, throughly furnished unto all good works.
— 2 Timothy 3:16,17

In yesterday's *Sparkling Gem*, we looked at the power that is resident in the Word of God, by studying the phrase, "For all scripture is given by inspiration of God..." (2 Timothy 3:16). Today let's go further to see what else Paul had to say about the power of God's Word.

When Paul wrote to his second letter to Timothy, he gave Timothy the *ultimate remedy* for the problems that were assailing his congregation in Ephesus. In Second Timothy 3:16 and 17, he wrote, "For all scripture is given by inspiration of God, and is profitable for doctrine, for reproof, for correction, for instruction in righteousness: That the man of God may be perfect, throughly furnished unto all good works."

In verse 17, Paul told Timothy — and every believer — that when someone seriously applies the truths of the Bible to his life, those truths will "thoroughly furnish" him unto all good works. The words "thoroughly furnished" come from the Greek word *exartidzo*, which means *to completely outfit* or *to fully equip*.

At the time this verse was written — just as is true today — there were simple boats that weren't designed to go very far and that certainly wouldn't survive a storm at sea. On the other hand, there were other boats that were fully equipped with sails, rudders, and other types of equipment — ships designed for long-distance sailing and for making it through the worst storms. With this in mind, the Greek word *exartidzo* pictures a simple boat whose owner chooses to *outfit and equip that ship with gear.* As a result, a once-simple boat becomes *completely equipped* and *fully supplied,* giving it the ability to sail through rough waters, travel long distances, and survive even the worst of storms.

We are living in a season of storms in these last days. Like it or not, times have become turbulent; the waves are getting higher; and it is essential that we be adequately equipped for these times. Those who are "thoroughly furnished" are the only ones who will successfully make it through the storms of life. If this exhortation was needed in the early days of the Church, imagine how much more needed it is in these latter times!

God places a crucial choice before you: Ignore what He says in His Word, and remain unequipped for this hour we live in — *or* make God's Word the sole authority in your life, and steadfastly obey its commands. If you will choose the latter route, you will become *thoroughly furnished* to go the whole distance and to make it through any storm that comes your way. You'll be *well-equipped and outfitted* to stand your ground, maintain your position, complete your journey with joy, and experience victory with the assignment God has given you to fulfill.

It's up to us to make the Bible our absolute authority and allow it to thoroughly equip us. As we do, we will safely sail through these times and rise above the waters of destruction to take our God-ordained position in His plans and purposes. God's Word will cause us to be buoyed above the perils of this hour, sustaining us in victory when everything around us seems to be sinking!

MY PRAYER FOR TODAY

Father, I thank You that the Word of God thoroughly furnishes me to rise above the perils of this hour. There is no doubt that turbulent waters are in front of us, but the Word of God makes me well-equipped and outfitted to sail through the densest darkness and to sail across the greatest storms. Without Your Word, I am ill-equipped to travel long distances or to survive strong storms, but with Your Word working in my life, I have all the spiritual gear I need to make it all the way to my ultimate destination. Thank You for giving me Your Word — for equipping me with everything I need to sail through rough waters and to survive even the worst of storms!

I pray this in Jesus' name!

MY CONFESSION FOR TODAY

I acknowledge that we are living in a season of storms in these last days. Like it or not, times have become turbulent, the waves are getting higher, and only those who are adequately equipped will make it to the other side. I boldly confess that I will not only begin the journey, but in Christ I am "thoroughly furnished" and will complete it. Because the Word of God is hidden in my heart and is a light unto my path, I will not fall, I will not stumble, and I will not sink. The Word of God enables me to ride high above the waves, and it will take me all the way to the other side to God's ultimate destination for my life.

I declare this by faith in Jesus' name!

QUESTIONS FOR YOU TO CONSIDER

1. From your own observation and experience, how would you describe the difference in the life of a believer who rarely reads his Bible and that of a believer who regularly reads his Bible and takes it deep into his heart?
2. Think of a time in your own life when your intake of the Word was less than it should have been. How did your failure to regularly feed on the Word affect you during that time in the different areas of your life, such as your intimacy with the Lord, mental and emotional well-being, physical health, finances, relationships, etc.?
3. From your own personal experience, how would you describe the effect that a regular, rich diet of God's Word has had on your life during those times when you have been faithful to spend daily time fellowshipping with Jesus in prayer and in His Word?

SEPTEMBER 24

A Boy With a Battered Brain

How God anointed Jesus of Nazareth with
the Holy Ghost and with power: who went about doing good,
and healing all that were oppressed of the devil....
— Acts 10:38

During our early years in the former USSR, I preached a series of meetings in Riga, Latvia. Several thousand people showed up for these special services — many of whom were first exposed to our ministry through our TV program — and our team witnessed thousands of people come forward to surrender their lives to the Lordship of Jesus Christ. It was absolutely *thrilling* to see people's response to the Gospel message.

After all the meetings were concluded, the local church leader who organized the event came to me and asked me to pray for his disabled teenage son. His boy had suffered severe, permanent injuries after being physically beaten by a gang of hoodlums. In fact, they smashed his head into the concrete street so many times with such force that his brain had become dislodged from his skull. He was literally a boy with a battered brain. The father asked me if I would pay a visit to their home to pray for their son's miraculous healing, so we went to their home to meet the young man.

When my eyes first fell upon that poor boy, I was utterly shocked to see what that gang of hoodlums had done to him. Severe tremors shook his entire body, and he seemed unaware of anything going on around him. He didn't even know we were there. His battered brain caused him to exist in a coma-like state. He just lay in a chair in the corner of the house, where he quivered and shook uncontrollably. The doctors had already pronounced that there was no hope and that he would be a vegetable for the rest of his life. According to medical science, this condition was irreversible.

However, during the previous week of meetings, we had experienced many miraculous healings and witnessed mighty, life-changing demonstrations of God's power. So with a whole week of miraculous events behind me, I looked at this young man with eyes full of faith. And his parents, who had witnessed the same miraculous events, were also full of expectation for God to do the impossible for their son.

I moved forward, laid my hands on the young man, and commanded him to be healed in the name of Jesus. I ordered his brain to correctly reattach to his skull and commanded the horrific trembling to stop. Yet regardless of how confidently or loudly I prayed or how much authority I felt I was exercising in Jesus' name, absolutely nothing happened when we were done praying. The young man was still a sorry-looking heap of trembling, quivering flesh — shaking uncontrollably and still unaware that we were even there to pray for him.

As I told the father and mother farewell, I felt their great disappointment that nothing instantaneous had happened — and I was deeply dismayed as well. I was so full of expectation for God's healing power to be imparted, but from what I saw with my eyes, nothing happened except that we had raised our voices in prayer and laid hands on him with no results. The events of that day disappointed me deeply and threw me into a state of bewilderment, because I fully expected the young man to be healed and fully restored as a result of our visit. To be honest, I couldn't shake the image of that young man shaking so uncontrollably and our seeming powerlessness to do anything about it — and that disappointment stayed with me in the months and years that followed.

Three years later, I returned to the same city to preach again, and the father who had organized our earlier meeting came to see me. I asked about his son's condition, and he said, "Oh, we never told you, but the day you laid hands on him, his condition slowly began to change. It started the day you prayed over him — little by little, his violent shaking and uncontrollable quivering stopped. Today he is totally whole and back to living a normal life!"

The man continued: "Our son's recovery started immediately after you left. It took a few months for it to be complete, but over that brief period of time, God completely restored him!"

I was *stunned.* For three years I carried sorrow in my heart about that young man, not realizing that when I prayed three years earlier, healing power went into him, and slowly — little by little, step by step — it began to completely restore his broken body and battered brain. I asked the Lord for insight into how this happened, and I was led to Acts 10:38, where the Bible says, "How God anointed Jesus of Nazareth with the Holy Spirit and power, who went about doing good and healing all who were oppressed of the devil."

I had read this verse and quoted it on many occasions. But this time, my eyes were especially focused on the word "healing," and I understood that the Holy Spirit wanted to show me something important that I needed to understand about the healing ministry. So I opened my Greek New Testament to Acts 10:38 to see what this word "healing" meant in the Greek. And to my surprise, it was the Greek word *iaomai*.

This word *iaomai* is a very ancient word for "healing" — so ancient that it was even used in Homer's time. It mostly denoted *healing that came to pass over a period of time*. It is for this reason that the word *iaomai* is often translated throughout Greek history as a *treatment* or *cure* or *remedy*. Thus, it depicts a sickness that has been *progressively healed* rather than instantaneously healed.

When I saw this, I began to look for other examples of *iaomai* in the New Testament, and I discovered that this word is used 23 times in the Gospels and the book of Acts to denote miraculous acts of power that were *progressive*, rather than instantaneous. It unmistakably tells us that there are many people who, from the moment they are touched by God's power, begin to *amend* or be *cured*. In other words, this means that all healings are *not* instantaneous; certain people are *progressively restored* to health over a period of time. They become *better* and *better* until ultimately they are completely *cured*. Although this type of healing is not instantaneous, it is nonetheless miraculous.

The picture of *iaomai* is similar to a physician who gives medicine to a sick patient and expects the medication to do its invisible, internal work to produce a remedy for a physical problem — but with supernatural results. When this type of healing power is at work, the person praying for the sick may not see immediate results. But that person can be confident that because he has prayed in faith, healing power has been imparted. The complete manifestation of healing may take time. But if God's power has been imparted and received by the person's faith, that healing power has started its invisible, internal work to reverse the sick person's condition and bring him or her back to a healthy state of being.

When the Holy Spirit quickened this truth to my heart, I understood that this is precisely what happened to the boy with a battered brain! When I prayed for him, I did it in faith and sensed an impartation of the Spirit. However, I saw no immediate change — and therefore, I became discouraged. But as we have seen already, that boy progressively began to get better day by day after I prayed for him, until finally his brain returned to normalcy and he was completely *cured*.

Perhaps you've prayed for someone, fully expecting to see an immediate change, but like me, you walked away disappointed because you didn't see immediate, miraculous results. Now you have new insight from the Word to help you hold fast to your faith! Based on the usage of this Greek word *iaomai* in Scripture, you can know for certain that when you pray for a person in faith, a supernatural impartation of healing power does take place! Whether or not you see an immediate change, the divine "medicine" has been administered in faith, and that healing power will progressively work in that sick person to eventually reverse the individual's condition and restore him or her to wholeness again.

So today I want to encourage you to lay your hands on the sick and release your faith that they will be healed. Don't allow what your eyes see in the present moment to affect your faith. If you don't see instant results, bolster the faith of those whom you've laid hands on. Let them know that they received a dose of healing power that works like divine medication! And if they will continue to stand strong in faith for the full manifestation of their healing, they will progressively see that healing manifested until they are fully well!

Praise God for those moments when we see instantaneous results! But let's not forget that sometimes the Lord works through *iaomai* power. In those moments, the results may be delayed, but they will come nonetheless — and that manifestation of God's healing power is just as miraculous as any other!

MY PRAYER FOR TODAY

Father, I thank You for the healing power of Jesus Christ. Whether it works instantaneously or progressively, healing is miraculous, and I am so thankful that You heal those who believe. Help me embrace the fact that although many are healed instantaneously, many are also healed progressively. Rather than be moved by what I see in front of me, help me to believe that when I pray in Jesus' name and release my faith for a person's healing, divine power is released into that person, and day by day they will progressively be restored to health.

I pray this in Jesus' name!

MY CONFESSION FOR TODAY

I confess that God uses me in the healing ministry. Some people are healed instantly when I pray, while others are healed progressively over a period of time. Regardless of whether the healing is instantaneous or progressive, it is miraculous, and I am thankful for God's healing touch. I will lay my hands on the sick, fully expecting divine power, like divine medication, to enter their bodies and work inside them until their condition is reversed and they are restored to health again.

I declare this by faith in Jesus' name!

QUESTIONS FOR YOU TO CONSIDER

1. Can you think of examples from the Bible where people were healed over a period of time? Who are some of those examples?
2. Have there been instances when you prayed for individuals to be healed, and their condition started to improve after you prayed for them — but because it wasn't instant, you didn't recognize it as a result of the divine healing power imparted when you prayed?

3. Do you know individuals who need healing right now? Did today's *Sparkling Gem* strengthen your confidence to know that when you lay hands on them, healing power will be imparted to work in their bodies until their health is restored, regardless of what you see?

SEPTEMBER 25

Do Not Budge From Your Post!

Preach the word;
be instant in season, out of season....
— 2 Timothy 4:2

In the book of Second Timothy, the apostle Paul gave a long, detailed description of the things that would become more and more prevalent in the last of the last days (*see* May 10-18 *Gems*). Later in that same letter, Paul gave this charge to the younger minister: "Preach the word; *be instant in season, out of season*..." (2 Timothy 4:2).

The word "instant" is from the Greek word *ephistemi*, and it means *to stand at your post.* The word *ephistemi* is a *military* term. That's important because standing at your post entails *engaging in spiritual warfare.* I won't delve into a deep study of the subject of spiritual warfare here, but I will say that declaring the Word of God in faith is the highest level of spiritual warfare there is. That's why it's especially important for a preacher, or *any* believer who has God's Word planted deeply in his heart, to stand *and to keep on standing* at his post without moving an inch!

The declaration of God's Word from the pulpit is another form of spiritual warfare. The preaching and teaching of the Word can have a life-changing, yoke-destroying effect on people's lives. When the Gospel is proclaimed, the power in those words of truth penetrate the hearts of people who are in sin. The Word of God breaks down strongholds, releases the supernatural power of God, and transforms minds and lives as it changes eternal destinies.

That's why Satan is always after the pulpit! He attacks it not so much because of the individuals who stand in the pulpit, but rather because of what they declare from their position in Christ and the authority Jesus has delegated to them as ministers of the Gospel. The enemy wants to stop the light from going forth because of the high level of warfare that's effectively demonstrated when truth penetrates the human spirit and enlightens a person's mind.

There's power in the proclamation of the Gospel to snatch a person right out of a lifetime of bondage and plant his feet firmly on the right path. On that path is everything that person could ever need: light for his feet, freedom for his mind, strength and resolve for his will, and vision for a bright future. *That's* what God's Word can do! It is therefore no wonder that Satan tries to stop the preaching, teaching, and ministry of the Word! Mental, emotional, and spiritual strongholds are *demolished* when the Word of God is proclaimed!

Now you can better see why Paul would go to such great lengths to urge and admonish Timothy to "stay put" — to remain in his place of ministry, or *to stay at his post.* It's obvious that he wouldn't exhort Timothy to stay put somewhere unless the younger minister was being tempted *not* to stay put. Believers in the church of Ephesus were suffering intense persecution for their faith in Christ. But Paul said to Timothy, "*You* be instant!" In other words, Paul was exhorting him, *"Stay at your post! Don't leave the position where God placed you!"*

Paul's next words — "in season, out of season" — give us further clues to help us understand why remaining continually stationed where God has placed us is so important. The phrase "in season" was translated from the Greek word *kairos,* which basically means *in good times.*

For those of us in the ministry, it's so much nicer to preach when everyone in the congregation is on our side and thinks we're great. We love it when everything in the church or ministry is running smoothly with no challenges to distract us. Those are good times! But when people in the church start gossiping about us and about each other, when newspapers are writing stories about us or a family member that are untrue, or when our well-being — or the well-being of our families — is threatened either financially or physically, those are not very good times.

That's why Paul said that we need to stay at our posts *even* when things seem to be "out of season." That phrase was translated from the word *akairos*, and the prefix *a* puts a negative spin on *kairos*. It means *when things have changed and they are NOT so wonderful.* The whole phrase could be translated: *"in good times and bad times!"*

What are you supposed to do when pleasant times begin to shift? What do you do when dark storm clouds begin to form in skies that just moments before were clear and blue? *You do the same thing you were doing before when times were good!* You remain at your post, refusing to budge!

In fact, Paul wrote previously in Second Timothy 3:14, "But *continue* thou in the things which thou hast learned and hast been assured of, knowing of whom thou hast learned them." In other words, Paul was telling Timothy, "Don't you budge! Don't move from the place where God has called you. *Stay put!*"

Paul wrote these words to Timothy, but through these Spirit-inspired writings, He is also saying to us: "Stay at your post and don't budge an inch! Stay there and do what God has told you to do when times are good — and if times turn bad, remain steady and unflinching!"

One thing is sure: As you determine to remain faithful to your divine call and to the place where God has assigned you — *as you decide to stay put and refuse to budge an inch* — He will empower you with inner strength that enables you to see it through to a glorious conclusion!

MY PRAYER FOR TODAY

Father, I hear You saying, "Stay at your post, and don't budge an inch! Stay there, and do what I have told you to do. Be faithful when times are good — and if times turn bad, remain steady and unflinching." I know that if I'll remain faithful to the call and to the place where You have called me, You will empower me with inner strength and sufficient grace that will enable me to see my calling through to a glorious conclusion! So, Holy Spirit, I receive Your fortitude to withstand the pressure to give up, give in, and throw in the towel. Strengthen me with the might I inwardly need to stay put and see my assignment through to completion!

I pray this in Jesus' name!

MY CONFESSION FOR TODAY

I confess that God strengthens me with His might to be faithful, steadfast, and persevering. When times are good or when times are tough, I am consistently constant. I stay put, no matter what. I will not be moved in my committed stance. The grace of God is teaching me how not to be provoked or lured to move away from my post. I keep my focus fastened on Jesus, and my roots grow down deep into Him. His stability keeps me grounded and enables me to be faithful to the call and to the place where God has planted me.

I declare this by faith in Jesus' name!

QUESTIONS FOR YOU TO CONSIDER

1. Where has God called you that requires you to have inner fortitude to "stay put"? Are you remaining faithful to stay in that place, regardless of whether the times are good or bad?
2. Can you think of a time when the conditions for what you were doing were nearly perfect, but then suddenly or slowly the atmosphere changed and it became more difficult? What did you do when things turned more difficult? Did you stay put, or did you relinquish your God-given place to someone else?
3. What about right now? Are you in a good season or a difficult season? Are you allowing yourself to be filled and refilled with the Holy Spirit so that you have the inner strength you need to finish to a grand and glorious conclusion, *regardless* of what things feels like right now?

As you determine to remain faithful to the place where God has assigned you, He will empower you with inner strength that enables you to see it through to a glorious conclusion!

SEPTEMBER 26

Last-Days Deception

For the time will come
when they will not endure sound doctrine;
but after their own lusts
shall they heap to themselves teachers,
having itching ears;
and they shall turn away their ears from the truth,
and shall be turned unto fables.
— 2 Timothy 4:3,4

Today I'd like to talk to you about what the apostle Paul wrote to Timothy right after exhorting him to stay by his post, regardless of the external pressures that would try to bump him off course. There is a strategic sequence to Paul's words that apply specifically to the believers of this generation.

Paul went on to describe the unique challenge that believers would face as a last-days deception occurs inside the Church. He wrote that at the end of the age — in the period just before Jesus returns — large numbers of people in the Body of Christ would be led astray.

Remember — the Holy Spirit didn't tell us this to scare us, but rather to prepare us so we would not succumb to these devil-inspired tactics to affect the Church in the very last of the last days. That makes the message of these verses particularly significant for those of us born into this present-day generation of the Church.

Paul wrote, "For the time will come when they will not endure sound doctrine; but after their own lusts shall they heap to themselves teachers, having itching ears; and they shall turn away from the truth, and shall be turned unto fables" (2 Timothy 4:3,4). The word "time" in verse 3 was translated from the Greek word *kairos*, which depicts *a specific season*. Paul said, "This specific season shall come." The tense is futuristic, pointing to *a season in the future*, or to events that will occur in the very last part of the last days.

In this end-times season, the Holy Spirit said increasing numbers of people in the Christian community "...will not endure sound doctrine..." (v. 3). Even now, this is taking place as many are gravitating toward teaching and preaching that is more motivational and psychological than Bible-based.

The Holy Spirit doesn't indicate how many will be pulled in this wrong direction, but the word "they" in the Greek language implies *large numbers* of people. According to Paul's prophetic utterance, a portion of the last-days Christian community will simply no longer endure the sound teaching of Scripture. In fact, the word "endure" is the Greek word *anecho*, which denotes *no ability to put up with or to have no tolerance for.*

The words "sound doctrine" in Second Timothy 4:3 are very telling. The Greek word for "sound" is *hugiaino*, and it indicates something that is *wholesome and healthy* and that produces *a healthy state of being.* The word "doctrine" refers to the *long-held teachings and tenets* of the Christian faith.

Thus, the Holy Spirit foretold of a specific end-time season when a segment of the Christian community would not only lose their appetite for sound doctrine, but they would also actually develop a *distaste* for it. Instead, they would acquire a distinct taste for doctrine that is unwholesome, preferring a self-help style of teaching over the teaching of sound doctrine.

In Second Timothy 4:3, Paul forecasted a moment when large numbers of people will no longer have a stomach for sound doctrine. Instead, "...after their own lusts shall they heap to themselves teachers, having itching ears…." The word "lusts" describes *desires* or *whims.* In other words, this part of the verse could be translated, *"But after their own desires shall they heap to themselves teachers, having itching ears."*

Paul unequivocally stated that a generation will arise in the very last days that will reject age-tested truth in favor of teaching that is more in step with the times. According to the Holy Spirit, teachers will appear on the scene in a specific *kairos* season to satisfy the hankerings of a generation that adheres to the world's progressive approach. What these spiritual leaders teach will appeal to people's emotions and intellect instead of to the deepest part of their being where actual transformation takes place. Because these teachers will speak what the crowds want to hear, they will enjoy great popularity among this audience of listeners.

In Second Timothy 4:3, Paul went on to say that this last-days generation will "heap" to themselves such teachers. The word "heap" is the future active indicative tense of the Greek word *episoreuo*, which points to *piles* of "teachers" who will appease an end-time audience with messages to suit them and the whims of the times.

Paul said that these teachers will satisfy the "itching ears" of the people. The words "itching ears" is used figuratively to depict a person (or a crowd of people) who wants to hear something *new* as compared to what he has already heard and known. Having his "ears" filled with something he wants to be told is the only thing that relieves this "itching-ear" syndrome.

As a result of this strange period that will develop in the last part of the last days, Paul said many "…shall turn their ears away from the truth, and shall be turned unto fables" (2 Timothy 4:4). This "turning away from the truth" is the rejecting of absolute biblical truth — the time-tested interpretation of the Word of God.

Is it possible we are currently witnessing this turning away from truth that the Holy Spirit predicted nearly 2,000 years ago? Are we seeing in our own day an accommodating attitude toward the world that produces a brand of Christianity that melds into the environment around it?

Paul wrote that an erring end-time group would discard fixed truth and replace it with "fables" — the Greek word for *fantasies*. By using the word "fables," Paul inferred that what this group of last-days orators taught would resemble fantasy. These teachers would substitute *"fables"* for the authentic teaching of the Bible that calls for repentance from sin and a change of behavior that is befitting God's Word.

The craving and demand for these fanciful messages by those with "itching ears" will produce large numbers of newly fashioned teachers with *restyled* messages. The mixture of truth and falsehood these teachers deliver will eventually lead a large segment of people into a distorted perception of who the Christ of Christianity really is.

You might say, "Brother Rick, that sounds like a lot of really *bad news*." But I need to tell you that in the haze of this deception that Paul prophesied about, another group of spiritual leaders will arise. Paul wrote about these leaders, calling them "...blameless and harmless, the sons of God, without rebuke, in the midst of a crooked and perverse nation, among whom ye shine as lights in the world" (Philippians 2:15).

Since there also will be a group of believers emerging who will hold to the ageless Word of Truth and proclaim its timeless teaching, let's make sure *that* is the group to which we belong! In spite of the difficulties these men and women may endure for proclaiming the Bible as utter truth, they will nevertheless stand firm, their feet solidly planted on the integrity of God's Word.

That, my friend, is the group you want to be a part of in these end times!

As I said at the beginning of today's *Sparkling Gem*, Paul forecasted that a time would come when a deception would occur inside the Church — in the period just before Jesus comes. Again, the Holy Spirit did not tell us this to scare us — but to prepare us, lest we fall into this trap ourselves. It is time for us to dig our heels deep into the truth of God's Word, refuse to budge from its life-transforming truths, and do all we can to teach and proclaim it to those around us!

MY PRAYER FOR TODAY

Father, I thank You that the Holy Spirit warned the Christian community about error seeking to secure a foothold inside the Church in the last of the last days. This motivates me to become even more committed to the solid teaching of the Word of God than ever before in my life. I ask You, Holy Spirit, to help me listen with a discerning ear to what I hear and take into my spiritual ears. What I spiritually digest determines my spiritual health, so please help me consume spiritual teachings that are wholesome and profitable to my spiritual life.

I pray this in Jesus' name!

MY CONFESSION FOR TODAY

I confess that I am excited God has chosen me to be a part of this last-days' generation! The Holy Spirit inside awakens me to what teaching is right and what teaching is wrong — and I have a spiritually discerning ear to know what I should accept and what I should reject. I further declare that I will NOT be a part of the "itching-ear" generation. Instead, I have a heart for the solid, time-tested teaching of the Word of God. On this Word of Truth I stand, and I will not move or even budge. Where God's eternal Word is concerned, I will allow no room for negotiation!

I declare this by faith in Jesus' name!

QUESTIONS FOR YOU TO CONSIDER

1. How would you personally determine whether a teaching you hear is wholesome and healthy for your spiritual life? What is the measuring stick you use to determine if what you hear will produce lasting, godly results in you?
2. Have you heard teaching produced by restyled teachers, who appease the multitudes with teaching that is more psychological than it is Word-based?
3. After reading today's *Sparkling Gem*, what do you sense that God expects you to do? Can you make a list of ways you should be more discerning about whom you listen to in the last days in which we live?

SEPTEMBER 27

Be an Immovable 'Pillar' in the Work of the Lord

Therefore, my beloved brethren, be ye stedfast,
unmoveable, always abounding in the work of the Lord,
forasmuch as ye know that your labour is not in vain in the Lord."
— 1 Corinthians 15:58

Often when I read the above verse, I think of a precious lady named Nina Reeves, who is now in Heaven along with the multitudes of other faithful saints. Let me tell you a little about Nina and how she impacted my life and the lives of many other people.

Nina served in the nursery at our church when I was growing up. She served in that capacity for more than 60 years and held hundreds of babies, including my sisters and me and all my friends. Finally, Nina went to Heaven at the age of 92. When she passed away, she was in good health and was still serving *every week* in the exact same church nursery room where she had held me as an infant.

When I think of Nina, the word *pillar* comes to my mind. To think that she forfeited her right to sit in church services for 60-plus years so parents could sit in the main church services to receive the teaching of the Word — that is *amazing* to me. I'm sure there must have been times when Nina must have felt that her ministry was unimportant — just caring for babies in the most isolated room of the nursery. Surely there must have been moments when the devil or even her own mind would tell her, "*You're just a nursery worker.*" But the fact is, her service ultimately impacted the lives of countless people for eternity. Part of the fruit of my own ministry, I'm sure, will be accredited to Nina Reeves.

In First Corinthians 15:58, the apostle Paul wrote, "Therefore, my beloved brethren, be ye stedfast, unmoveable, always abounding in the work of the Lord, forasmuch as ye know that your labour is not in vain in the Lord." Today I want to look at Paul's message in this verse and encourage you in the heroic work you are called to do as one of God's "pillars." You may be tempted to think your role is not very important, but there will come a day in Heaven when God will display your part in His plan through the ages on Heaven's "movie screen," and you will see the great effect you had on others because you were "steadfast" and "unmovable."

The word "steadfast" is the Greek word *hedrios*, and it conveys several meanings. First, it means *to be stationary*, such as something that sits in one place for a long, long time. It also describes something that is *firm* and *steady*; thus, this word was frequently used in connection with *foundations* in buildings. Furthermore, it describes something that is *strong*, *unbendable*, *unbreakable*, and *permanent*, such as a *strong column* that holds up a roof.

Therefore, when the Holy Spirit through Paul urges us to be "steadfast," He is calling on you and me to be totally *reliable* — not shaky or undependable. We should be *stationary* in the roles where God has called us to serve. We shouldn't be quickly shaken or easily lured to some other place or task. We must be like *pillars* in the place where we've been called to serve in the house of God.

See yourself as a pillar that others can depend on to be totally reliable. *You are called to be a pillar!*

Notice First Corinthians 15:58 also exhorts us to be "unmoveable." This word is a translation of the Greek word *ametakinetos*, which refers to *something that is not capable of being moved from one place to another place*. In other words, once you've said yes to the call of God on your life, you should be a *permanent fixture* in that place where God has called you to serve.

Satan will always attempt to sidetrack you and me and anyone else whom God calls to do a job. The enemy will try to use discouragement and a host of other tactics to move us off course from our God-assigned place of service. That's why it's imperative that we make up our minds to be a *permanent fixture* in that place where God has called us to serve. You and I must be thoroughly dedicated to fulfill our assignment and carry on and follow through until the task is done the way the Lord expects it to be done.

The apostle Paul went on to say, "Therefore, my beloved brethren, be ye stedfast, unmoveable, always abounding in the work of the Lord, *forasmuch as ye know that your labour is not in vain in the Lord.*" The word "labor" in this verse is the Greek word *kopos*, which describes *the most exhausting kind of work or effort*. By using this word, Paul was stating that sometimes it isn't easy to do what the Lord asks us to do. In fact, there are times when it requires great effort to walk in obedience. I can personally testify that it's taken great commitment and fortitude to do what God has asked me to do — *and to stick with it to the end.*

Before Paul concluded First Corinthians 15:58, he reminded us of a vital principle we must never forget! He said, "...Forasmuch as ye know that your labor is not in *vain* in the Lord."

Please pay special attention to that word "vain." It is the Greek word *kenos*, and it depicts something that is *wasted.* This is God's promise to you that *anything* you do for Him is *never* a waste! So when your flesh or the devil whispers to you and tempts you to think that no one notices or appreciates your efforts, that your job is insignificant, or that you are wasting your time — *that* is the moment for *you* to remind yourself and the devil that nothing done for the Lord is ever a waste. Every effort, every deed — *everything* you have ever done in obedience to His instructions — will be accredited to your heavenly record!

I began today by telling you about a precious lady named Nina, who served 60-plus years in the church nursery. Once she knew where God called her to serve, Nina never moved from that place. She was *steadfast* and *immovable.* And even though she may have been tempted to think of herself as insignificant or to listen to what the devil may have told her, she stuck by her commitment and became a pillar in that church and a personal hero to me. Today in Heaven, I guarantee you that Nina doesn't regret those 60-plus years of serving in the nursery. She now sees with her own eyes the tremendous fruit that was reaped because *she found her place and stayed in it.*

That is the legacy of Nina Reeves — and that should be our legacy as well. We must always remember that nothing we ever do for the Lord is a waste. And as we remain steadfast as immovable pillars in the place where God has called us to serve, we can trust Him to remain faithful to *us* to repay — in His time and in His perfect way!

MY PRAYER FOR TODAY

Lord, I ask You to help me know the place where I am supposed to serve and to use my gifts and talents. Help me accept Your assignment with joy, regardless of what it is or where it is, and to keep my eyes fixed on my heavenly reward. In times when it gets tough and my flesh screams to be released from my assignment — or in those moments when the devil tries to tell me that my part is insignificant — please help me dig in my heels and refuse to move from that place where You have called me.

I pray this in Jesus' name!

MY CONFESSION FOR TODAY

I declare that I am of value to God and to His plan to touch people. I am reliable, steadfast, and immovable in what God has asked me to do. Even if the devil tries to tell me that I'm not making a difference, I declare that I am making a difference in the lives of others. My time, talents, and gifts are a blessing to others. And I boldly confess that nothing I ever do for Him is wasted!

I declare this by faith in Jesus' name!

QUESTIONS FOR YOU TO CONSIDER

1. Can you think of faithful people who have served year after year in the same place? Who comes to your mind? Have you ever taken time to go out of your way to express your gratitude to these faithful servants of the Lord for the way they have served?
2. Would anyone think of you when creating a mental list of faithful people? What have you done consistently over years that has eternally impacted other people's lives?
3. If you haven't served consistently in any position in your church or in some ministry organization, why not? Why don't you make a list of ways you can serve? It may take some creative thinking to do it, but take time to ponder how you use your time, talents, and energies to make a difference in the lives of other people.

SEPTEMBER 28

There's a Bomb on the Plane!

Are they [angels] not all ministering spirits,
sent forth to minister for them
who shall be heirs of salvation?
— Hebrews 1:14

Today I want to talk to you about the ministry of angels, and how they work to protect and deliver us in times of trouble. Let me begin by retelling a part of a story that I related to you in the May 29 *Gem*, and I want to add a story at the end to demonstrate the point even stronger.

I had long wanted to visit the city of Vorkuta, located above the Arctic Circle in Russia. It was one of the major cities where Joseph Stalin deported believers during a raging period of persecution. There Christians were incarcerated in huge prison camps and forced to work deep under the earth in dangerous coal mines, where they dug the coal that fired the massive coal-burning factories and trains of the Soviet Union.

I sensed that it was a divine assignment to visit Vorkuta at that time. Because of its notorious place in history for Christian believers, I wanted to talk to the TV director that covered that large area in order to obtain a contract for broadcasting our TV program. I also intended to find out how many believers still lived there and what we could do to be of assistance to them.

As I related in the earlier *Gem*, my seat on the airplane was at the front of the plane near the flight attendant station, and I was seated next to a window, which made it possible for me to see everything happening outside of the airplane. My particular seat faced the tail of the plane, so I could also see everything that was happening inside the aircraft.

First, all the passengers boarded. Then I watched out my window as cargo handlers began to load cargo into the underside of the plane. I was shocked at the amount of boxes, suitcases, and cargo they were putting into the cargo hold. In fact, it was so overfilled that when it came time to shut the doors to the cargo hold, it took several men to shut it, because the overflowing cargo was pressing against the door.

Meanwhile, inside the plane from where I was seated, I watched as airport workers piled boxes, boxes, and *more* boxes in the tail of the plane, until the rear end of the plane — that is, the kitchen and the toilets — were no longer visible or accessible. After that, they began piling luggage and boxes into empty seats, and then they started stacking them from the back to the front of the center aisle of the plane. The extra cargo filled the cabin all the way from the very back to where I sat in the front of the plane!

Because I was seated close to the flight attendants, I could hear their conversations. I overheard one flight attendant say to another, "I'm getting off this plane, because it's so severely overloaded that I'm afraid this plane is not going to make it."

Yet I *knew* I was supposed to go to Vorkuta. *So what should I do?* I thought. I bowed my head with those who were traveling with me, and we prayed, "Lord, if this plane is going to crash, please do anything needed to get us off this plane!"

Just as we finished praying, a flight attendant frantically yelled, "Everyone — as quickly as possible — get off this plane! We just received a phone call that there's a bomb on this plane!"

People started fighting with each other and shoving their way to the airplane door. At last when everyone was off the plane, and we were inside the terminal, a public announcement was made, which declared that the entire plane was being unloaded so the authorities could search for a bomb. After hours of our waiting and wondering what to do next, another public announcement was made over the intercom, saying, "After searching the aircraft, we found no bomb on the plane. It was a false threat. However, we have decided that when we all reboard the aircraft, *no extra luggage or boxes* will be permitted. Only the suitcases of passengers will be permitted on this airplane."

My companions and I stepped into the plane and reseated ourselves in the same seats that had been assigned to us. People looked relieved, peaceful, and thankful that the plane was no longer overloaded. I heard the same flight attendant who had earlier threatened to get off the plane tell his colleague, "Now we'll have a safe flight."

This brings me to what I want to share today about the delivering and protective ministry of angels — because I asked myself that day, *Who was that mysterious phone caller who said there was a bomb on the airplane?* Who caused the airplane to be so quickly emptied, leading to the fortuitous decision to remove all that dangerous extra cargo? I wondered, *Is it possible that an angel was the unidentified mystery caller?*

Hebrews 1:14 declares, "Are they [angels] not all ministering spirits, sent forth to minister for them who shall be heirs of salvation?" According to this verse, angels are "sent forth to minister" on behalf of those who belong to the family of God.

The word "minister" is the Greek word *diakonia*, a word that depicts *high-level service.* It is important to note that rabbis in New Testament times used a very similar phrase to describe what they called "angels of service or ministry" — angels whom they believed were assigned to protect individuals and deliver them from harm.

Let us be confident that part of the angelic ministry is to ensure a believer's safety from dangerous and harmful things. Certainly that day at the airport, something inexplicable happened that saved the lives of my team and everyone else who was on that airplane. There were five believers on my team. I would not be surprised if that event was some type of angelic intervention to spare our lives from tragedy. *In fact, I truly believe this is what happened.*

Especially during the time period when Hebrews 1:14 was written, believers were often forced to physically move from one place to another and were regularly caught in difficult circumstances. But "ministering spirits" — that is, angels — were sent forth to "minister" to them. These angels provided the highest level of service available to help these believers and protect them from harm as they were en route from one place to another.

The phrase "sent forth" in Hebrews 1:14 is a translation of the Greek word *apostello*, which describes *one who is dispatched on a mission.* Therefore, these angels spoken of in this verse are purposefully dispatched on a mission to serve and protect the heirs of salvation. It was, and it remains, the mission of angels to serve the needs of the saints and to provide them protection.

Even as you read this, perhaps you can think of people who were in the direct path of harm until something happened to divert their course, and it was that change of direction that spared them from a catastrophic event. I am reminded of a time when our eldest son Paul had a car accident in Moscow. He hit a pole, and it turned the car over multiple times, totally crushing the vehicle. Yet all three people in that car walked away unharmed! The street-side pole was destroyed; the car was completely crushed. But the three people traveling in the car were unscathed. It was truly *miraculous.*

When Denise and I saw the car, we cried, because we realized there was no human way that death could have been avoided. It was clear to us that our son and his companions had been protected by angels who were assigned to protect them and save them from harm.

So today I want to encourage you to know that there are angels on assignment, sent to minister to you and to protect you in times of danger. To qualify for this angelic protection,

Hebrews 1:14 states that one must be an "heir of salvation" — or one must be a child of God. So if you have made Jesus the Lord of your life, you qualify — and it's time for you to recognize that angels have been assigned to you and to call upon them as you travel and traverse the twists and turns of your life.

Now every time I enter a plane, I lay my hands on its exterior and thank God for the angels who are traveling with me and who are assigned to keep me and all those traveling with me from harm. Knowing that God has provided such protection has kept me in peace on many occasions when I could have been inwardly disturbed in difficult situations. I keep in mind that Psalm 34:7 declares, "The angel of the Lord encampeth round about them that fear him, and delivereth them."

This is a good day to take a few minutes to reflect on the times when your life has been spared by the divine intervention of God and His angelic hosts. Or perhaps you can think back to times when the lives of people near and dear to you were divinely protected. If they are heirs of salvation and the way they were spared was absolutely miraculous, you can know that they lived to tell the story because of angelic intervention. Angels were sent on assignment to travel with them and to protect them.

Although we certainly don't worship angels, I think it's right for us to thank God for providing this *high-level service* to keep us and protect us from harm!

MY PRAYER FOR TODAY

Father, I thank You for assigning angels to protect me from harm. I am grateful for Your promise to send angels on a special mission to protect, minister to, and help the heirs of salvation. Since I'm an heir of salvation, I qualify! I am so thankful to know that I have angels assigned to keep watch over me and that they will serve me with the highest-level service possible. So rather than let fear try to grab hold of me in times of hardship or potential danger, I will give thanks to You for the angels who are present and on active duty — sent on a mission to protect and minister strength and help to me when I need it most!

I pray this in Jesus' name!

MY CONFESSION FOR TODAY

I confess that God sends His angels to guard me. These ministering spirits are as flames of fire and they are on a specific mission to protect the children of God. Wherever I go, angels are on assignment to go with me and to surround me and keep me safe. Because these angels hearken to the voice of God's Word, I speak the Word and believe in its power — knowing that angels watch over those words to perform them. Although I cannot visibly see them, I have angelic traveling companions who are with me all the time in every situation I face. According to Psalm 34:7, I am surrounded by the angels of the Lord, and He delivers me from harm!

I declare this by faith in Jesus' name!

QUESTIONS FOR YOU TO CONSIDER

1. Can you think of moments in your own life when you were miraculously, inexplicably spared from tragedy? Do you see now that angels are assigned to protect you?
2. Do you know others whose lives were protected unexplainably? Were the situations they found themselves in potentially catastrophic — yet instead of suffering tragedy, were they protected from harm?
3. Can you think of situations in the Bible where angels provided safety, protection, or deliverance from danger?

SEPTEMBER 29

Have You Ever Felt Like a 'Scapegoat'?

...We are made as the filth of the world,
and are the offscouring of all things unto this day.
— 1 Corinthians 4:13

Has anyone ever tried to blame you for problems that had nothing to do with you? Maybe it was a fellow employee who blamed you for something *he* failed to do. Maybe it was a fellow church member who failed at *his* responsibility, but didn't want to look unfaithful, so he shifted the blame on you for something you didn't do. Or maybe you can remember a time when your siblings pointed their finger at you for something *they* did, and as a result *you* were punished instead of them!

If you've ever been accused or blamed for something you didn't do, you know what a miserable experience it is. There is nothing worse than to be made a scapegoat for someone else's misdeeds. If this has ever happened to you, you know how victimized you can feel when you are accused of something you didn't do!

Shifting blame to someone else started all the way back in the Garden of Eden when Adam pointed his finger at Eve and blamed her for his failure to obey God. When sin entered the human race, one of the first manifestations of sinful nature was Adam's refusal to accept responsibility for his choices and for his attempt to blame his wife for his failure.

When people don't want to face the consequences of their own failure, they often look for someone else to blame. They point the finger at others and say, *"They are the reason we are in this mess!"* By pointing their fingers away from themselves and shifting the blame to someone else, they attempt to deflect the punishment they deserve themselves.

Of course, such blame-shifting is unjust. Yet as long as we live in this fallen world that has the devil and the influence of ungodly men, such acts of injustice will continue. When Jesus comes and sets up His Kingdom on the earth, all injustice will come to an end. But until that time, injustice *will* occur in many forms. And if you or I are ever treated unjustly — for instance, if we're ever blamed for something we didn't do — we must know how God expects us to respond to the situation.

Think of the believers who lived in the pagan Roman Empire and who faced injustice on a daily basis. They were constantly blamed for things they didn't do. If the weather was bad, the pagans often blamed the Christians for the bad weather. If the empire was grappling with financial troubles, the Christians were typically the ones blamed for the financial woes. When the city of Rome burned to the ground — an event most likely instigated by Nero himself — Nero pointed his finger at Christians and blamed them for starting the fire rather than face the consequences of what he had done. (*See* Volumes One and Two of my *Light in Darkness* series for an in-depth look into the challenges early believers faced as they lived for Jesus.)

Early Christians were a threat to the devil and to the domain of darkness. So from the beginning, Satan inspired people to hate believers and to blame them for all types of heinous deeds that had *nothing* to do with them. They became "scapegoats" that society used to blame for all their ills and problems.

As happened to many believers during the time when the New Testament was being written, the apostle Paul and his traveling companions were often charged falsely with deeds they didn't commit. Paul told us about this in First Corinthians 4:13 when he wrote, "...We are made as the filth of the world, and are the offscouring of all things unto this day." This verse is very insightful, but it requires a study of the original Greek words to fully understand the message contained in it.

This verse is very powerful. Not only does it give us a glimpse into the challenges Paul and his associates physically faced, but it lets us know how they emotionally felt when these things happened to them. No one likes being called the "scum of the world," but that's in essence what Paul and his team members were called. The apostle Paul wrote on behalf of his team to explain how the world had treated them with utter contempt. When he wrote, "...We are made as the filth of the world," he was painting a *very* strong picture!

The phrase "the filth of the world" is taken from the Greek word *perikatharma*, a compound of the words *peri* and *kathairo*. The word *peri* means *around*, and the word *kathairo* means *to cleanse* or *to purify*. The latter word depicts the removal of disgusting grime, like the dirty ring left on the sides of a bathtub when dirty water is drained. If that filth is allowed to remain on the bathtub very long, it becomes hard, crusty, and difficult to remove. At that point, getting rid of that hardened "ring around the tub" requires determination and a lot of hard work. It means someone has to get on his hands and knees and *scrub*! Only after a lot of persistent, nonstop scouring can that hardened, grimy ring around the tub be eliminated.

This is the idea Paul conveyed when he said that he and his traveling companions had been treated like "the filth of the world." Instead of appreciating these Gospel preachers for all they had done to bring light into darkness, the unbelieving world has repeatedly tried to wipe them out! In the world's view, these ministers of the Gospel were *the scum of the earth*.

In addition to conveying the idea of actual grime, the words "the filth of the world" was also one of the lowest, crudest derogatory statements that could be made about someone. To call someone "the filth of the world" was a *terrible* insult!

Furthermore, the "filth of the world" was a phrase used to describe low-level people in society, such as criminals deemed unworthy to live. If a city had a chain of bad fortune, public officials would give the order for the "filth of the world" — low-level criminals — to be rounded up and publicly sacrificed. They believed that if this societal *scum* could be exterminated, it could reverse a city's bad fortune.

When Paul said that he and his team were treated like "the filth of the world," he let us know that they had been blamed for many things that had nothing to do with them. Over and over again when something wrong happened, someone would likely cry out, *"It's the preacher's fault!"* Rather than thank Paul and his team for the many sacrifices they had made, the world treated these believers with the same disdain they would a dirty ring around a tub that needed to be wiped out. In addition to leveling terrible insults at them, large segments of the pagan population believed if they could just get rid of Christians, it would somehow bring good luck back to them again.

But Paul went on to say that they were treated like the "offscouring of all things." The word "offscouring" is a translation of the Greek word *peripsema*, which depicts *the ardent and ferocious process required to remove filth and grime*. No one wants to live in the middle of filth, and no one wants to take a bath in a tub covered with grime! When the situation gets sufficiently distasteful, someone will eventually step forward to say, *"Let's do something about this sickening dirt! Let's get rid of it!"* The word "off-scouring" depicted that moment when the world cried out, *"Enough of these Gospel preachers! They've brought too much bad luck on our lives! Let's get rid of this filth!"*

The Romans and Greeks frequently looked for someone they could blame for society's problems and ills. They regularly pointed their fingers at low-level criminals — the so-called "scum of the earth" — and as noted above, they accused them of bringing bad luck on the citizenry. These people were viewed as bad omens that needed to be stamped out and eliminated. So from time to time, publicly elected officials gave the order for low-level people, criminals, and societal "scum" to be rounded up and executed, especially in times of plague, war, famine, or other catastrophes. They falsely believed that *scrubbing out this scum* from society would put an end to their bad luck.

Paul used these same vivid phrases to tell us what the world was saying about him and his associates. Although he was preaching and doing the good works of Jesus, he wrote that the world viewed them as scum that needed to be removed. They and other believers were blamed for all kinds of problems and calamities. The unsaved world actually believed they would be far better off if these light-bearers were exterminated.

When Paul wrote that believers are the "filth of the world"
and the "offscouring of all things,"
this verse could be interpreted:

> *"The world views us like dirt that needs to be wiped off, and they are doing everything they can to scrub us out of society. We have become the scapegoats for everyone's problems. They point their fingers at us and blame us for everything wrong in the world. What they would really like to do is permanently get rid of us!"*

Has anyone ever tried to blame you for problems that had nothing to do with you? Have you ever been accused or blamed for something you didn't do? Have you ever had your good name smeared by people who talked badly about you? Have you ever felt "victimized" by others? *Remember that you are not alone!*

There are others who have faced more difficult times than you are facing right now, but they didn't stop serving or stop loving, nor did they abandon what God had told them to do. They kept their eyes focused on "...Jesus the author and finisher of our faith; who for the joy that was set before him endured the cross, despising the shame, and is set down at the right hand of the throne of God" (Hebrews 12:2).

During times like these, you *must* keep your eyes fixed on Jesus and remember that He also endured the assaults of men. He completely understands any emotion you feel about the situation you're facing. If you will go to Him and talk to Him about what you are experiencing and feeling right now, His Spirit will comfort your heart and give you wisdom about how to respond — *if* you should respond at all.

Today — in fact, *right now* — I encourage you to take a few minutes to talk to Jesus about any false accusations or unjust treatment you're receiving. I guarantee you that no one can understand your situation, provide wisdom and instruction, or comfort your heart better than Jesus can!

MY PRAYER FOR TODAY

Father, I am so glad that Jesus understands what I am going through when I suffer verbal abuse or ridicule or when I experience unjust discrimination. It is so emotionally difficult to be blamed for things that have nothing to do with me, yet I face this from time to time. Instead of becoming bitter and hardhearted toward those who wrong me in this way, I ask You to give me a heart full of love for them. In my own flesh, I am unable to forgive and love them as I must, but with Your Spirit's help, I can love even the most unlovely person. So today I'm asking You to fill my heart with forgiveness, love, and compassion for those who have dealt unfairly with me.

I pray this in Jesus' name!

MY CONFESSION FOR TODAY

In Jesus' name I confess that I forgive the people who have deliberately misused me, abused me, and falsely accused me. If they really understood what they were doing, I believe they would never have done such a terrible thing. Instead of letting my heart get hard and bitter, I am turning to the Holy Spirit for help. He will soften my heart; He will help me forgive; and He will fill me with love and compassion for those who have tried to victimize me. Just as Jesus forgave those who crucified Him, today I am choosing to forgive those who have done wrong to me. With the help of the Holy Spirit, I can do this and I WILL do it.

I declare this by faith in Jesus' name!

QUESTIONS FOR YOU TO CONSIDER

1. Has there been a time in your life when were made a scapegoat for someone else? If not you, have you ever seen someone else made to be a scapegoat and blamed for things for which he or she was not responsible?
2. Have you ever had someone speak derogatory words to you or behind your back? When you heard it or learned about it later, how did it affect you? Were you able to forgive and go on, or did it wound you?
3. As a Christian, how do you think Jesus would have you respond to such occurrences? Forget about the advice of the world around you, and think about how Jesus would respond to such an attack. What do you think *He* would do?

SEPTEMBER 30

It's Time for You To Start Using the Gifts and Talents God Has Given You!

As every man hath received the gift,
even so minister the same one to another,
as good stewards of the manifold grace of God.
— 1 Peter 4:10

On August 2, we talked about the "grace-given gifts" that have been divinely imparted to each one of us by God Himself. Today I'd like to take that discussion a step further to help you get started *today* in activating the giftings on the inside of you on a daily basis so you can fulfill your part in God's great plan of revealing His love to man.

Here is a key to releasing your God-given grace gifts: It is something you can do on purpose. You don't have to wait around for the elusive "perfect moment."

Often people wait and wait for the "perfect time" to launch their business, their ministry, or their big dream in life. But the truth is, very few successful people began the pursuit of their call with that kind of an ideal moment. In fact, what most people would refer to as spectacular success stories actually began very "unspectacularly." If you study the lives of individuals who have made a significant contribution to this world, you'll find that often their journey began with just a simple decision to *get started*.

Certainly you can choose to wait around and wish for a "perfect moment" to come when the skies part, lightning bolts strike, and beams of glory land all around your feet to signal that your moment has arrived. But if this is what you're waiting for, I want to tell you that you will probably be waiting a very long time! That just isn't the way God does things in the vast majority of cases.

When I was a young man, I daydreamed of the time when my ministry would begin and I could start using the gifts and talents I had received from the Lord. I would lie in bed at night and envision the day when I would finally step up to the plate and begin my ministry. Then one day as I was praying, the Holy Spirit spoke to my heart. He told me that it was time to quit fantasizing and *get started*! I had always thought I was waiting for that perfect moment to take the first step. But all the while, God was waiting for *me* to get up and start doing something with the gifts He had placed in my life!

I knew I had a gift to teach the Bible — and since that was what God had equipped me to do, I decided to use my gift! I invited my friends to a Bible study that I would lead on the university campus where I was studying. I knocked on doors, handed out leaflets, and started to intensely prepare to teach my very first public, verse-by-verse study in the New Testament. Today I still have the notes I prepared for the first series I ever taught, and I treasure those notes. They are memories from those early days when I was just getting started in the ministry. My beginning was small, so small it was almost *unnoticeable*, but it was *a beginning*.

Everyone has to have a beginning — including you! If you know what God has gifted you to do, don't wait around and lose precious time as you wait for a hypothetical, fantasy-like "perfect moment" to get started. Instead, why not put your hand to the plow and begin to use your gifts right now? Once you take that step of faith, God will have something to bless. But as long as you do nothing, you're not giving Him anything to prosper!

This is precisely why Peter wrote, "As every man hath received the gift, even so minister the same one to another, as good stewards of the manifold grace of God" (1 Peter 4:10). Today I want us to look deeply into this powerful verse.

First, I want you to notice that Peter said, "As *every man* hath received the gift…." The words "every man" are translated from the Greek word *hekastos*, which is an all-inclusive word that literally means *every single person, no one excluded*. This undeniably means that every person who has been born of the Spirit and who declares that Jesus is Lord has been supernaturally endowed with gifts from God. Because the word *hekastos* is used, it emphatically means that *no one is excluded* from these God-given gifts. Even the person with the lowest self-esteem is mightily gifted by the Spirit of God but simply unaware of the powerful gifts that reside inside him.

If you think that *you* are not gifted, you are wrong! The usage of the word *hekastos* in First Peter 4:10 clearly means that you, too, are endowed with magnificent, God-given gifts.

Peter went on to say, "As every man hath *received* the gift...." Pay careful attention to the word "received" in this verse. It comes from the Greek word *lambano*, which is used 258 times in the New Testament. It means *to receive into one's possession* or *to take into one's own control and ownership*. It carries the idea of *taking hold of something; grasping onto something;* or *embracing something so tightly that it becomes your very own*. When used in connection with God-given gifts, as Peter uses it in this verse, it portrays God as the Giver of gifts and us as the receivers. Then once we receive the gift of God, He sees it as our responsibility *to accept and take ownership of that gift as our own*.

Then Peter wrote, "As every man hath received *the gift*...." The word "gift" in this verse is the word *charisma*, derived from the word *charis*, the Greek word for *grace*. But when the word *charis* becomes *charisma*, it speaks of *grace-given gifts*. In other words, these are not gifts earned or deserved; rather, these are gifts imparted supernaturally and divinely by God's grace.

Thus, there is no room for boasting or self-glory in the possession of these magnificent gifts, for these are not natural talents developed by one's own ability. These are supernatural graces that are divinely imparted by the Spirit of God. According to this verse, God has graced every child of God with miraculous gifts that are beyond his or her own natural ability. Once released and activated, these gifts bring the life-changing power of God into manifestation to meet and answer human need.

Yes, even *you* have these powerful gifts inside — just waiting for you to take ownership of them and *use* them!

Peter continued, "As every man hath received the gift, even so minister the same one to another...." This word "minister" comes from the Greek word *diakoneo*.

This Greek word portrays *a servant whose primary responsibility is to serve food and wait on tables*. It presents a picture of a waiter or waitress who painstakingly attends to the needs, wishes, and desires of his client. It is this servant's supreme task to please clients; therefore, he serves honorably, pleasurably, and in a fashion that makes the people he waits on feel as if they are nobility. *This is a committed, professional server who is fanatically dedicated to doing his job on the highest level possible.*

By choosing this Greek word *diakoneo*, Peter alerted us to the fact that God expects us to be radically, passionately committed to using the gifts He has given us in such a way that pleases Him and meets the needs of others. That is why Peter continued by saying, "As every man hath received the gift, so let him minister the same *one to another*...." God intends for us to use our gifts to minister to one another. These gifts are not given for self-glory or self-promotion, but for the benefit of the larger Christian community and the world around us.

What about you? Are you using your grace-given gifts to minister to the needs of those around you?

Peter concluded this verse by saying, "As every man hath received the gift, so let him minister the same one to another, as good *stewards* of the manifold grace of God." The word "steward" is from the Greek word *oikonomos* and was specifically used to describe the *household manager* for an upper-class, wealthy home (*see* August 2).

By using the word *oikonomos* in this verse, Peter shows us that God has indeed made us the stewards of His own personal treasures and He expects us to give Him glory by using our gifts *wisely* and *on time* to meet the needs of those around us.

Taking all these Greek words into consideration, we could paraphrase this verse to read:

"Every single one of you without exception has received a grace-given gift from God. Embrace what God has placed inside you. Take ownership of it, and do your best to use that special gift to meet the needs of one another. God has entrusted a lot to you by placing those special gifts in your life, and He is depending on you to be faithful with this great responsibility."

God gives you gifts and talents, and then He expects you to use them, regardless of their size. As you do, He will begin to bless the work of your hands. However, if you choose to wait for the "perfect moment" to develop before you ever do anything with your gifts, you'll probably *never* get started! Don't waste any more time — *it's time for you to start making the most of divine equipment inside you that's just waiting to be released!*

MY PRAYER FOR TODAY

Lord, I want to thank You for placing spiritual gifts in my life. These gifts were given by You, and my heart's desire is to use them as You intend for them to be used. Forgive me for the time I've wasted waiting for the perfect moment before I got started. Help me now as I step out in faith to start using these gifts in ways that will benefit those around me. I know that Your gifts have power, so as I release these precious treasures, I ask that Your power will also be released to meet the needs of the people whose lives I touch. Today I willfully recognize the gifts You have placed inside me, and I make the choice to let these gifts begin to operate through me!

I pray this in Jesus' name!

MY CONFESSION FOR TODAY

I confess that God's grace works mightily in my life and those mighty gifts have been placed in my life through this divine grace. Although in the past I have put myself down and lightly esteemed my value in the Body of Christ, I have made the decision to recognize, embrace, and take ownership of the marvelous gifts inside me! God expects me to be responsible in my stewardship of these gifts, so I will be meticulous and faithful in the way I allow these gifts to operate through me!

I declare this in Jesus' name!

QUESTIONS FOR YOU TO CONSIDER

1. Do you know which gifts God has graced you with? What are those gifts that He wants to operate in your life? Have you ever made a list of the ways you believe God wants His grace to flow through your life to others? If not, it would be a good idea for you to do this so you can affirm the gifts, imparted by the grace of God, that reside in you!
2. What results have you observed from the times you allowed your God-given gifts to operate in your life? How have these gifts benefited and helped others? What impact did those gifts have on others when you allowed them to freely operate through you?
3. Can you think of people who have been waiting a *long* time for the "perfect moment" to come so they can get started in life? Are they still waiting?

OCTOBER 1

God Makes the Impossible Possible!

(As it is written, I have made thee
a father of many nations,) before him whom
he believed, even God, who quickeneth the dead,
and calleth those things which be not
as though they were.
— Romans 4:17

Right now autumn is settling in where I live in Russia. The air is cool and crisp, and the leaves are beginning to change colors and fall to the ground. It is absolutely beautiful! During the fall season, I am often reminded about an experience that happened many years ago when I was out in the backyard raking leaves with my two older boys. Paul, our oldest son, was busy helping me dig piles of dead leaves out from under an overgrown bush when Philip, my second son, called out to me, "Daddy, please come here!"

As I turned and looked over at Philip, I watched as he took a small, withered branch that had fallen off a tree and began to poke it down deep into the soil. As I walked over, he began to gather dirt around the base of the broken branch and then proceeded to pat the dirt as hard as he could to make sure the dead limb would not fall over. Then he reached over to pick up large, dead leaves out of the pile we had raked and started trying to reattach the dead leaves to the dead branch. Amused by what I had seen, I asked, "Philip, what are you doing?"

He answered, "Daddy, God's beautiful little tree broke and died. Will you please ask God to make this dead branch come alive again?"

Of course that branch was dead and gone, but the Holy Spirit used this moment to speak to my heart about Romans 4:17, which tells of God's marvelous ability to "quicken the dead" and to "call those things that are not as though they are." It reads: "(As it is written, I have made thee a father of many nations,) before him whom he believed, even God, who quickeneth the dead, and calleth those things which be not as though they were." God may not be in the business of making dead branches come to life again, but He certainly *does* reverse impossible situations in the lives of His people.

The word "quicken" in Romans 4:17 is the Greek word *zoopoieo*, which is a compound of the words *zoon* and *poieo*. The word *zoon* denotes *a living creature*, and the word *poieo* means *to do* or *to make* and most often conveys *creativity*. When those two Greek words are combined, the result is *zoopoieo*, an incredibly powerful word that literally means *to make alive*, *to infuse life in*, *to resurrect*, or *to empower with divine life*.

What an amazing message! God has the ability to inject resurrection power into any failing circumstance in your life, and most importantly, He absolutely *wants* to do it!

Next, I want to draw your attention to the word "dead" in this verse. It is the Greek word *nekros*, which literally refers to *a lifeless corpse*. This is vital to understand because it emphatically shows that no matter how *cold*, *dead*, and *lifeless* your situation might seem, God can and will empower you with divine life if you will stand firm in your faith and seek His face.

Consider the Old Testament example of Abraham and Sarah. They were physically "dead" as far as their ability to bear children was concerned. Yet when God's Word came to them, faith was imparted and their aged bodies were supernaturally empowered to bear children. Or think back to Joseph who, through dreams and visions, received a great vision for his own personal life. For all practical purposes, it probably seemed as though his dream had died on the day his brothers sold him into slavery. But God took that shattered dream and supernaturally made it come to life years later. Once again, God proved that He is the God who quickens the dead and calls those things that are not as though they are!

When my son asked me to pray for that little branch to come to life again, I immediately thought of all the humanly impossible situations people face in their personal lives. To them, their problem is just as irreversible as that dried, broken, and withered branch. Without a miracle, their situations are hopeless, and for all practical purposes, their hopes, dreams, and aspirations are "dead."

Naturally speaking, these people have problems that seem impossible and beyond repair — but with God, *all things are possible*! He knows how to take broken dreams and resurrect them! He knows how to take dashed hopes, withered vision, and dried-up callings and restore them to life again.

We serve an awesome God who specializes in taking humanly impossible situations and turning them around for His glory. As James 1:17 (*AMPC*) so aptly states: "Every good gift and every perfect (free, large, full) gift is from above; it comes down from the Father of all [that gives] light, in [the shining of] Whom there can be no variation [rising or setting] or shadow cast by His turning [as in an eclipse.]" God's perfect will is to shower you abundantly with "good and perfect gifts." *That is His will for your life!*

So don't despair just because your situation looks impossible. These matters are not beyond the reach of God, and all He asks is for you to have faith. Hebrews 11:6 tells us, "But without faith it is impossible to please him: for he that cometh to God must believe that he is, and that he is a rewarder of them that diligently seek him." God wants to bring new life to those areas that you thought were beyond repair. He desires to "quicken" your dreams, hopes, and aspirations and restore you to wholeness in every area — your mind, your body, your finances, your marriage, your relationships, etc.

Jeremiah 33:3 says, "Call unto me, and I will answer thee, and shew thee great and mighty things, which thou knowest not." We have a miracle-working God who is available *right now at this very moment* to start a supernatural work of resurrection in your life. With man, this may be impossible — but with God, *all things are possible*!

I think of the people who thought our ministry in the former Soviet Union would never be possible. But God was just waiting for someone to believe Him and act on His Word. The powers that once controlled this part of the world are gone, and now the Gospel light is starting to shine where darkness once reigned. When I think of the attacks the devil has tried to throw against us and the finances we've needed to fulfill this assignment, it makes me stop and thank God for His supernatural ability to move above the natural realm and do what others said could not be done!

God is our Great Provider. He is the Great Quickener of dead dreams. He is our Great Physician, our Great Redeemer, and our Great Restorer. He is more than enough to meet every need, and He can turn any dead situation around!

Do you need a miracle in your life today? Do you need a dying situation to be empowered and resurrected with divine life? Let today be the day that you believe God to quicken your dream *back to life* again!

MY PRAYER FOR TODAY

Father, I am so thankful that You are our Great Provider, Great Quickener, Great Physician, Great Redeemer, and Great Restorer. There is absolutely nothing that You cannot do. I ask You to breathe new life into my visions and dreams that have been on the verge of death. You are the great power of the Resurrection, and I ask You to release Your resurrection power into my situation and turn it around. I know this is impossible in the natural — but with You, I know that all things are absolutely possible!

I pray this in Jesus' name!

MY CONFESSION FOR TODAY

I confess that the resurrection power of Almighty God is working in me to reinvigorate my visions and my dreams and to bring them back to life again. Despite what seemed to be against me and against the fulfillment of what God promised He would do with my life, God will show me His greatness and His glory. I will see the miracle come to pass. I boldly declare it will come to pass. God's quickening power is at work on my behalf, and it's at work inside me right now!

I declare this by faith in Jesus' name!

QUESTIONS FOR YOU TO CONSIDER

1. Can you think of a person in the Bible who thought his dream was over, but in fact, God resurrected it and made it come to pass? Who was that person?
2. Can you think of someone you personally know who fought and fought, and it seemed the fight was lost — but then the power of God resuscitated the life back into that dream again and it came to pass?
3. What vision or dream are you waiting to see come to pass? Has the devil tempted you to think you're done and it's over — that your vision or dream will never come to pass? Why don't you make a list of all the Bible characters you can think of who came to the end of their dream, only to see it come alive again? I think this little exercise will surprise and encourage you!

OCTOBER 2

The Humility of Christ

Who [Jesus], being in the form of God,
thought it not robbery to be equal with God:
but made himself of no reputation,
and took upon him the form of a servant,
and was made in the likeness of men:
and being found in fashion as a man,
he humbled himself,
and became obedient unto death,
even the death of the cross.
— Philippians 2:6-8

One of the most amazing passages in the Bible to me is Philippians 2:6-8, in which Paul demonstrates the humility of Christ. The apostle Paul described it this way: "Who [Jesus], being in the form of God, thought it not robbery to be equal with God: but made himself of no reputation, and took upon him the form of a servant, and was made in the likeness of men: and being found in fashion as a man, he humbled himself, and became obedient unto death, even the death of the cross."

Consider Paul's words in Philippians 2:6-8. These are probably the strongest verses about *humility* in the New Testament, and they demonstrate that Jesus' behavior has always been marked by humility.

When Paul wrote that Jesus existed in the "form" of God, he used the Greek word *morphe*. This word *morphe* describes *an outward form* — meaning that in Jesus' preexistence, He looked just like God. Jesus wasn't just a component of God, nor was He a symbol of God. In reality, He *was* God. As the eternal God Himself, Jesus possessed the very shape and outward appearance of God — a form that included great splendor, glory, power, and a divine presence so strong that no flesh could endure it.

But Paul said that Jesus "...made himself of no reputation..." (Philippians 2:7). This phrase comes from the Greek word *kenos*, which means *to make empty, to evacuate, to vacate, to deprive, to divest*, or *to relinquish*. The only way Jesus could make this limited appearance on earth as a man was to willfully, deliberately, and temporarily let go of all the outward attributes of His deity. For 33 years on this earth, God divested Himself of all His heavenly glory and "took upon him the form of a servant."

The phrase "took upon him" perfectly describes that marvelous moment when God laid hold of human flesh and took that form upon Himself so He might appear as a man on the earth. The words "took upon him" are from the Greek word *lambano*, which means *to take, to seize, to catch, to latch on to, to clutch*, or *to grasp*. This word reveals that God literally reached out from His eternal existence into the material world He had created and took human flesh upon Himself in "the form of a servant."

The word "form" in this phrase is exactly the same word that describes Jesus being in the form of God. It is the Greek word *morphe*. This means that just as Jesus in His preexistent *form* had all the outward appearance of God, He also existed in the exact *form* of a man — appearing and living on this earth in the same way as any other man. For a brief time in His eternal existence, Jesus emptied Himself of outward divine attributes and literally became like a man in every way.

Paul then said that Jesus took upon Himself the form of a "servant." This is the Greek word *doulos*, which refers to *a slave*. Paul used this word to picture the *vast difference* between Jesus' preexistent state and His earthly life.

Out of His deep love for you and me — His profound yearning to see us redeemed from spiritual death and its eternal consequences and to reconcile us to Himself — Jesus was willing to leave His majestic realm of glory to enter the world of humanity. He came down to our level so He could become an effective High Priest on our behalf. Shedding all His visible attributes of deity that were too much for man's flesh to endure, Jesus clothed Himself in human flesh and was manifested as a man on the earth.

All of this required the greatest *humility* ever witnessed since the creation of the world. But Philippians 2:8 reveals that even more humility was required of our Lord to fulfill the plan of God for the redemption of man: "And being found in fashion as a man, he humbled himself, and became obedient unto death, even the death of the cross." That word "fashion" is the Greek word *schema*. This is very important, for this word was used in ancient times to depict *a king who exchanged his royal garments for the clothing of a beggar for a brief period of time*.

This is precisely what occurred when Jesus left the majestic realms of Heaven. It is the true story of a King who traded His royal garments and took upon Himself the clothing of a servant. But the story doesn't stop there. Jesus loved us so much that He "...humbled himself, and became obedient unto death, even the death of the cross" (v. 8).

The word "humbled" is the Greek word *tapeinao*, and it means *to be humble, to be lowly*, and *to be willing to stoop to any measure that is needed*. Think of the humility that would be required for God to shed His magnificent glory and lower Himself to become like a member of His own creation! Consider the greatness of God's love that drove Him to divest Himself of all His splendor and become like a man.

When this verse says that Jesus humbled Himself "...unto death, even the death of the cross," the word "unto" is from the Greek word *mechri*, which means *to such an extent*. The word *mechri* is sufficient in itself to dramatize the point that this level of humility was shocking. However, the verse goes on to say that Jesus so humbled Himself that He was willing to suffer "...even the death of the cross." The word "even" is the Greek word *de*, which *emphatically* means *even*. The Greek carries this idea: *"Can you imagine it! Jesus humbled Himself to such a lowly position and became so obedient that He even stooped low enough to die the miserable death of the Cross!"*

It is truly an awesome concept for our human minds to grasp. The Almighty God, clothed in radiant glory from eternities past, came to this earth for one purpose: so He could one day humble Himself to the point of dying a horrible death on the Cross, thereby purchasing our eternal salvation. All of this required *humility* on a level far beyond anything we could ever comprehend or that has ever been requested of any of us. Yet this was the reason Jesus came.

Jesus is now sitting at the Father's right hand and arrayed in splendor beyond human imagination — but His humility still remains intact, consistent, and unchanged. It is one of the chief characteristics of His nature. He *was* humble; He *is* humble; and He *will always be* humble, just as Hebrews 13:8 says, "Jesus Christ the same yesterday, and to day, and for ever."

As I write this *Sparkling Gem* today, it makes me want to take a good look at my own life to see if I demonstrate the characteristic of *humility* that is so evident in the Person of Jesus Christ. Does it affect you the same way to read of Jesus' willingness to stoop to any measure required to purchase our redemption? That, my friend, is love and humility beyond comprehension.

May the humility of Christ also be produced in our lives!

MY PRAYER FOR TODAY

Dear Heavenly Father, I am left speechless when I consider the humility that Christ demonstrated when He left the realm of eternal glory. To know that He was made in the likeness of a man, and then died the death of a Cross — and that He did it all for me — leaves me in awe of Your goodness and love. If Christ had not been willing to lay aside His glory and to come to earth as a man, I would have remained lost and unsaved. Father, how I thank You for sending Jesus – and for the example that Christ has set for me and for all believers to cultivate the characteristic of humility as evidence of Your love in our lives.

I pray this in Jesus' name!

MY CONFESSION FOR TODAY

I confess that Almighty God, clothed in radiant glory from eternities past, came to this earth to die a horrible death on the Cross to purchase my eternal salvation. This required humility beyond anything I could ever comprehend, yet this was the reason Jesus came. Jesus now sits at the Father's right hand, arrayed in splendor beyond human imagination — but His humility remains intact, consistent, and unchanged. He was, He is, and He will always be humble, just as Hebrews 13:8 says, "Jesus Christ the same yesterday, and today, and for ever." I confess that I am yielding to the Holy Spirit's work to produce this same Christ-like humility in my life as well.

I declare this by faith in Jesus' name!

QUESTIONS FOR YOU TO CONSIDER

1. What was the primary thing you learned by reading today's *Sparkling Gem*?
2. Had you ever considered the great humility it required for God to become a Man and to die the death of a Cross? What does this mean to you now that you've pondered it?
3. In what area of your life do you lack humility? In what ways can you cooperate with the Holy Spirit to help you develop this Christ-like characteristic in your life? Invite the Holy Spirit to bring His transforming power to reveal and remove any attitude in your heart that grieves Him because pride is at the root of it.

Consider the greatness of God's love that drove Him to divest Himself of all His splendor and become like a man.

OCTOBER 3

A Promise to Overcomers

...To him that *overcometh*....
— Revelation 2:7; 2:11; 2:17; 2:26; 3:5; 3:12; 3:21

We all have things that we need to overcome in life — whether it's trouble in relationships, weight gain, health issues, financial difficulties, problems at work, or mental attacks in the mind. But regardless of what obstacles oppose us, Jesus called us to be committed to becoming an *overcomer*!

When He spoke to the Church in Ephesus in Revelation 2:7, Jesus cried out, "He that hath an ear, let him hear what the Spirit saith unto the churches; To him that *overcometh* will I give to eat of the tree of life...."

The subject of this *Sparkling Gem* is not the tree of life, as that would require an entire *Sparkling Gem* all by itself. But today we are looking at the word "overcometh" — a word that Christ used when He spoke to all seven churches in the book of Revelation. They were *all* called to be overcomers (*see* Revelation 2:7; 2:11; 2:17; 2:26; 3:5; 3:12; 3:21).

The word "overcometh" is the Greek word *nikao*, which denotes *a victor*, *a champion*, or *one who possesses some type of superiority*. Often this word was used to portray athletes who had gained the mastery of their sport and ultimately reigned supreme as champions in the competition. It might also refer to a military victory of one foe over the other. The word *nikao* can be translated *to control, to conquer, to defeat, to master, to overcome, to overwhelm, to surpass*, or *to be victorious*.

It is important to understand that the word *nikao* can describe either *an athletic victory* or *a military victory*. This means Jesus was conveying two messages. First, He told these early believers that the only way to defeat the foes they faced was for them to maintain the attitude of an athlete. To win the contest before them, they had to eliminate all spiritual apathy and prepare for the toughest competition they had ever engaged in. Nothing less than a full commitment would be sufficient to master the exterior adversaries and interior struggles they were facing. Whether Jesus' imagery referred to a runner, wrestler, discus thrower, or any other type of First Century athlete, His message was clear: Only a thoroughly committed believer will win *a victor's crown.*

Because the word *nikao* was also used militarily to depict the absolute crushing of an enemy, Jesus' words held a second meaning: He was calling believers to rise up like an army to attack and defeat the external and internal enemies that threatened them. Spiritual complacency and the lack of passion were intolerable enemies of their faith that had to be conquered. They were to *wage war* against the weaknesses Christ had brought to their attention. Winning this victory would require the highest level of determination they had ever known, for apathy and complacency are always the most difficult enemies for a person or a church to conquer.

It must also be noted that the tense for "overcometh" speaks of *a continuous and ongoing victory.* This means Christ wasn't urging these believers to run a temporary race or to fight a short-term battle. He was demanding a commitment to start and to *remain* in the race until the finish line was reached — to attack and defeat their foes and then to *remain* victorious over their enemies. Thus, Jesus was actually asking them, as He asks each of us, *to be permanently and consistently undeterred in overcoming and obtaining victory in every area of their lives.*

Christ commands believers throughout all generations to be overcomers. Christians are to make it their continual and unrelenting goal to maintain victory in every possible sphere of life as long as they live on this earth.

Have you made the commitment to be permanently and consistently undeterred in obtaining every victory in your life? *Why not start by making that commitment right now?*

MY PRAYER FOR TODAY

Father, I hear what Your Spirit is speaking to me today. You are calling me to jump into the race and stay in the race until I reach the finish line. You are calling me to fight the good fight of faith — and to maintain the victory once it has been won. I recognize that for me to do this, I will need to be permanently and consistently undeterred to overcome and obtain victory in every sphere of my life. Father, this is a level of commitment far greater than I've ever demonstrated in my life. Holy Spirit, I ask You to help me forge ahead. By Your strength, I know I can and will do it.

I pray this in Jesus' name!

MY CONFESSION FOR TODAY

I declare by faith that I am an overcomer in Jesus Christ. He has given me His Spirit. I have His Word. And He overcame the devil at the Cross and the resurrection — then He gave me His name to use. There is no reason I can't overcome the troubles I've had in my relationships, my weight, my health, my finances, or any other struggle that I've had. With the Spirit's help, I am strong; I am stable; I am undeterred. In Him I win and maintain the victory!

I declare this by faith in Jesus' name!

QUESTIONS FOR YOU TO CONSIDER

1. What ongoing battle is in your life that you *know* it's time for you to overcome?
2. What are you going to have to do differently than you've done in the past in order to achieve this victory and then maintain it in this area of your life? This is a serious question, so give serious thought and prayer to your answer.
3. To win the contest before you, have you committed to eliminating all spiritual apathy from your life and to preparing for the toughest competition you've ever engaged in? Nothing less than a full commitment will be sufficient to win this victory.

OCTOBER 4

The Devil Can't Curse What God Has Blessed!

How shall I curse, whom God hath not cursed?
or how shall I defy, whom the Lord hath not defied?
— Numbers 23:8

I want to share with you about an interesting character in the Bible who actually tried to curse God's people. He attempted unsuccessfully to do it multiple times — which proves that *the devil cannot curse what God has blessed*! The example of Balaam shows that witchcraft, divination, and curses simply have *no impact* on people who are walking with the Lord.

Let's learn more about this man named Balaam. There are numerous sources that describe his origin, but the Bible is our most solid source, and it identifies Balaam in Numbers 22. Balak, king of the Moabites, heard that Israel was approaching his territory. Balak feared that his kingdom would be defeated by Israel's army. Verse 5 states that Balak "...sent messengers therefore unto *Balaam*...."

Balaam's lineage is difficult to determine because the Bible doesn't tell us where his family came from. The greatest bulk of what is known about Balaam comes from ancient Jewish commentaries. These ancient sources affirm that he was well known in his time and that he played an influential role as a diviner and soothsayer. One Alexandrian commentator described Balaam as a "master" diviner and foreteller of great renown.[8]

The city of Alexandria was a long-time center of Egyptian witchcraft, sorcery, wizardry, enchantments, incantations, magic, and spells — and the educated Jewish scholars from this city were very familiar with these practices. They had seen occult practices during their sojourning in Egypt, and they knew the difference between a *mere apprentice* and a *master* of sorcery. Thus, for an Alexandrian Jew to write that Balaam was renowned for his dark skills indicates Balaam possessed a profound level of expertise as a master sorcerer.

The most famous Jewish scholar was Josephus, whose writings are still considered the most accurate extra-biblical historical account of Jewish history ever written. He wrote, in effect, that Balaam was among the greatest of the prophets at that time.[9] That is a remarkable statement, since Balaam lived during the same time as the prophet Moses. But whereas Moses was an instrument for the *power of God* in the earth, Balaam was an instrument through which the *kingdom of darkness* found access in the earthly realm.

The use of the word "prophet" in the writings of Josephus should not be misunderstood. In this context, "prophet" does not refer to a spokesman of God, such as Moses or Elijah, for

---

[8]Philo, *De Vita Moysis*, I.48.
[9]Josephus, Flavius. *Antiquities of the Jews*, IV.VI.2.

Balaam's practices were diametrically opposed to the way God manifested Himself through His prophets. In fact, Deuteronomy 18:10-12 and Leviticus 19:26 enumerates God's prohibitions regarding occult practices, such as those practiced by Balaam. Josephus simply used the word "prophet" in a general sense to denote *one who was able to foresee the future*. Pagans often used this word "prophet" to denote anyone who was a vocal instrument of the spirit realm. In this sense of the word, Josephus' description of Balaam was very much in line with what the Bible tells us about this controversial "prophet."

According to Scripture, Balaam was a diviner who operated with powers of divination (*see* Numbers 22:7; 23:23). Other common names for "diviners" include *foretellers, seers, soothsayers, consulters of familiar spirits, enchanters, necromancers, wizards, witches, voices through which the spirit realm speaks, mediums,* and *clairvoyants*.

The ancient world was full of diviners, but it seems none was more notable than Balaam during his time. Balak's own kingdom of Moab almost certainly had a plethora of diviners. But because none was capable of cursing Israel, he sent emissaries nearly 400 miles to plead with Balaam to come and curse the people of Israel on his behalf.

If diviners enjoyed a past record of success, they could demand high prices for their divination, and Balak knew that hiring a sorcerer as notable as Balaam would be very expensive. However, the Moabite king was prepared to pay whatever sum was required to coax Balaam to come and curse Israel. Therefore, he sent his emissaries to Balaam, offering to "promote" him with "great honor" (*see* Numbers 22:17). Verse 18 implies that Balak was willing to pay Balaam a great fortune — perhaps even "a house full of silver and gold" — to perform this service of cursing a nation of people.

We know Balaam was revered as a great diviner and soothsayer, known far and wide for his abilities to bless or curse, because in Numbers 22:6 (*NKJV*), Balak told Balaam, "...For I know that he whom you bless is blessed, and he whom you curse is cursed." Balak was *certain* that Balaam would be able to curse Israel — *but Balaam could not do it.*

Balaam tried three times to speak a curse upon Israel, yet he did not have the power to do it. Balaam finally was forced to tell Balak, "How shall I curse, whom God hath not cursed? Or how shall I defy, whom the Lord hath not defied?" (Numbers 23:8). Scripture tells us that every time Balaam opened his mouth to speak a curse, a blessing came out instead (*see* Numbers 23:10-12). Finally, after failing repeatedly to place a curse on Israel, Balaam conceded that divination was no match for the power of God. It was at this point that he told Balak, "For there is no sorcery against Jacob, neither is there any divination against Israel..." (Numbers 23:23).

It was simply impossible for a curse to be pronounced where God had pronounced a blessing! It was true then, and the same is true today.

Balaam serves as a reminder of God's divine protection. Balaam — one of history's most famous sorcerers — was unable to penetrate God's protective shield that held fast and secure around His people. Even today, there are some who allege that people involved in the occult have the power to curse believers. However, Scripture clearly teaches that *no one* has the power to curse what God has blessed. The story of Balaam serves as a perpetual reminder that what God has blessed is *blessed*, and that fact cannot be reversed.

If you are in Christ and walking in obedience to God's Word, you are safe, secure, and sealed in the protective blood of Jesus — and the power of that divine protection can never be breached by someone operating under, or in cooperation with, the powers of Satan. You need never be fearful of any curse assailed against you or your loved one, no matter how dark or "powerful" the vessel through which the curse tries to come. The occult has never been, *and will never be*, a match for the power of God that is inside a believer. This is precisely why the apostle John wrote, "...*Greater* is he that is in you, than he that is in the world" (1 John 4:4)!

I encourage you today to cast off fear of the devil or fear of *anything* that anyone has told you about the possibility of being cursed. If you are in Christ, you are *the blessed of the Lord* — and what God has blessed, no one can curse!

MY PRAYER FOR TODAY

Father, I rejoice that because I am in Christ, I am the blessed of the Lord and protected by the blood of Jesus Christ. The devil does not have the power to curse what God has blessed. Holy Spirit, I receive Your help to walk in obedience to the Word of God and to shun anything that would violate the supernatural shield of protection that surrounds my life.

I pray this in Jesus' name!

MY CONFESSION FOR TODAY

I confess that I am safe and shielded by the blood of Jesus Christ. When God placed me in Christ, He surrounded me with divine protection that cannot be breached. No demon, no devil, no evil worker has the power to speak any kind of curse on my life. I am curse-free because Jesus Christ bore the curse for me in every form, that I might become the blessed of God forevermore. I do not live in fear of the devil, and I rejoice that greater is He who is in me than he that is in the world!

I declare this by faith in Jesus' name!

QUESTIONS FOR YOU TO CONSIDER

1. Had you ever considered the impossibility of Balaam's attempt to curse God's people? How does it affect you to know that there is no divination strong enough to work against the people of God?
2. What did you learn about Balaam that you never knew before?
3. Before today, did you think that Balaam was just a backslidden prophet of God or did you understand that he was a sorcerer? How does the truth of his identity affect your understanding of what took place?

OCTOBER 5

Waiting for That Last Person To Repent

The Lord is not slack concerning his promise,
as some men count slackness; but is longsuffering to us-ward,
not willing that any should perish, but that all
should come to repentance.
— 2 Peter 3:9

Today I want to encourage you to remember something about the patience and longsuffering of our Lord. Jesus Christ is still on the throne as King of kings and Lord of lords, regardless of the events that are occurring around the world. We may not see exactly how He is moving — or know everything that He is doing — but Christ is fully in charge and is moving by His Spirit around the planet to take us toward final prophetic fulfillments. As we will see in Second Peter 3:9, God is presently holding back His judgment *until one last person* repents. Just think of it. One last person will repent before that moment on God's prophetic timeline begins, and then judgment will fall on this planet and God will deal with a world gone astray.

To our natural eyes, it seems like society is degenerating at an ever-increasing rate. Laws are being implemented that are antagonistic toward people of faith, and Christians are increasingly labeled as *intolerant* because they refuse to endorse the activities of a morally bankrupt world. Therefore, it is important for us to remain aware that Christ is still seated on His throne in Heaven, ruling over the affairs of mankind. No matter how turbulent the waters around us may seem, Christ has never moved from His highly exalted seat of authority. The Day of Judgment is near, but Christ waits lovingly and patiently for one more soul to repent before that prophetic moment occurs and judgment falls.

While we wait for that final moment of God's reckoning with the affairs of men, it can be discouraging to see ungodly men run the transactions of government. So we must remember the fact that God's Word promises a day will come when *every man* will stand before the throne of judgment. We must pray for ungodly men to come to the knowledge of the truth, but we must also never forget that those who resist and oppose the truth will not escape the consequences of their actions. *A time will inevitably come when every man will be called into Christ's high court of reckoning.*

Only mercy restrains Christ from taking immediate action against evildoers. He is well-equipped to eliminate those who oppose the truth, but His mercy endures forever. This truth is very clear in Second Peter 3:9, where Peter wrote, "The Lord is not slack concerning his promise, as some men count slackness; but is *longsuffering* to us-ward, not willing that any should perish, but that all should come to repentance."

I want to look at that word "longsuffering" with you. It is the Greek word *makrothumeo*, which is a compound of the words *makros* and *thumeo*. The word *makros* depicts something that is *long*, and *thumeo* is the word for *anger*. When compounded, the new word *makrothumeo* is the picture of *the long restraint of anger* — thus the reason it is often translated as *patience* or *longsuffering*. But it is actually the picture of *God holding back His anger*.

Why does God hold back so long when it seems that judgment should come more quickly? Peter wrote the reason: God is "...not willing that any should perish, but that all should come to repentance." He is holding out for *one last person* who will repent before the clock stops ticking and time runs out.

From the signs around us, it would seem that this event will happen during our lifetime. I personally expect to see the Rapture — the "catching away" (*see* 1 Thessalonians 4:17) — of the Church during our lifetime. Afterward, great bowls of God's judgment will be poured out upon the earth. But God is loving, patient, and kind. He longs for one more person to repent before that prophetic moment in history begins, so He restrains His anger toward the godlessness in the world as He patiently waits.

Wouldn't it be wonderful if *you* were the one who led that last person to the Lord before the judgment cycle begins on the earth? Consider the joy of knowing that God used *you* for such a historic moment. Don't say it couldn't be you, because it's going to be *someone* who brings that last soul into the family of God! And when this grand moment occurs and the very last person repents in this current age, the long-awaited judgment will begin. To be honest, it could happen anytime.

MY PRAYER FOR TODAY

Heavenly Father, my heart is stirred today to pray for my unsaved friends, family, and acquaintances. The Bible has long foretold that a day of judgment is coming, but I've never thought about it so deeply as I've thought about it today. Thank You for being patient with the world — and for being so merciful that You are waiting for more people to repent before the clock stops ticking and time runs out. Father, I want to be open and available for You to use me to share the witness of Jesus with those who are unsaved. And if I was the one You used to bring the last person to Christ, I would be overwhelmed by the privilege of doing so!

I pray this in Jesus' name!

MY CONFESSION FOR TODAY

I confess that we are living in the last days. The time is soon coming when the prophetic clock will stop for this age. When it does, the Church will be caught away, and the judgment cycle will begin on the earth. I declare that from now until then, I will do all that I can to share Jesus with my unsaved friends, family, and acquaintances. God's longsuffering causes Him to wait for one last person to repent, and I will do all I can to bring as many souls as I can to the Lord before this age ends and the next age begins.

I declare this by faith in Jesus' name!

QUESTIONS FOR YOU TO CONSIDER

1. Have you ever wondered why the judgment of God is often delayed for so long? After reading this today, how would you now answer that question?
2. Have you ever thought about the fact that every man will be called into Christ's high court of reckoning one day? How does that realization affect the way you conduct your own life?
3. What friends, family, and acquaintances are you concerned about because they are unsaved? Have you ever tried to share Christ with them? Why don't you ask the Holy Spirit to open a door so you or someone else can share Jesus with them?

OCTOBER 6

The Holy Spirit's Role in Removing Obstacles From Our Lives

Likewise the Spirit also helpeth our infirmities:
for we know not what we should pray for as we ought;
but the Spirit itself maketh intercession
for us with groanings which cannot be uttered.
— Romans 8:26

Has there ever been a time when you just didn't know how to pray about some kind of challenge, or when you were in a predicament and you didn't know how to get out of it? Maybe you've come before the Lord and prayed, "Father, I'm not even sure if I know what the desires of my heart are. Please help me pray."

We all experience moments like these at one time or another. That's why I want to share with you about the Holy Spirit's responsibility toward us regarding prayer. We find a wealth of information about this in Romans 8:26. Right now I want to point out a few important truths in verse 26, and I'll continue the discussion about these verses in tomorrow's *Sparkling Gem* as we continue to look at Romans 8:27.

Romans 8:26 begins, "Likewise the Spirit also helpeth our infirmities: for we know not what we should pray for as we ought...." That word "helpeth" is extremely important because it conveys the idea of real partnership and cooperation and paints the picture of two individuals working together to get the job done. The Greek word translated "helpeth" is actually a compound of three Greek words. The first word is *sun*, meaning *to do something in conjunction with someone else*. The second word is *anti*, which means *against*. The third word is *lambano*, which means *to take* or *to receive*. When these three words are joined, the new word, *sunantilambano*, means *to take hold of something with someone else, gripping it together as tightly as possible, and throwing your combined weight against it to move it out of the way*.

For instance, suppose you walk out of your front door one morning and discover that someone has placed a huge boulder in the middle of your driveway during the night. You walk over and push on that boulder to move it out of your way, but it's too heavy and you can't budge it. Then you try to move it from the other direction, but no matter how much you tug and pull, you can't get the job done by yourself. So what do you do? You call a friend and ask him for help. He comes over, grabs hold of that boulder with you, and together the two of you press against it with all your strength until you have moved the boulder out of the way.

This Greek word *sunantilambano*, translated "helpeth," powerfully conveys this same idea of partnership and cooperation to remove an obstacle. It tells us that the Holy Spirit literally becomes one with us in the task of removing every obstacle. In the midst of our weaknesses when we are inadequate to get the job done, the Holy Spirit says, "Let me grab hold of that hindrance with you, and you and I will push against it together until it is moved completely out of your way."

In this way, prayer becomes a twofold partnership between you and the Holy Spirit. When that really becomes a revelation to your heart — when you realize that your prayers are not something you're responsible for alone — it will forever change your prayer life.

Verse 26 goes on to say, "Likewise the Spirit also helpeth our *infirmities*...." It is the Greek word *asthenia*, which would better be translated "weaknesses." It is used to describe people who are *sickly or ailing in their bodies, minds, or emotions*. Frequently it is also used to describe people who are *spiritually weak*.

Thus, we see that the Holy Spirit comes to help us because we are *asthenia*. We are simply too weak — physically, mentally, spiritually — and by ourselves we don't have what it takes to get the job done. This is why we need our Partner to help us. We simply cannot pray like we need to by ourselves. So the Holy Spirit comes to assist us in prayer, throwing His weight against our weaknesses to remove them from our lives. The truth is, according to this verse, we cannot remove anything from our lives without the Holy Spirit's assistance. And that is why He comes to bear this responsibility for us, assisting us in removing anything in our lives that is ailing — whether it is frailty in the body, a sickly mental state, or a weakness in our spiritual walk.

I don't know about you, but I'm thankful that the Holy Spirit is willing to become a Partner with me to remove those weaknesses when I'm not able to remove them by myself!

Romans 8:26 continues, "Likewise the Spirit also helpeth our infirmities: for we *know not* what we should pray for as we ought...." In other words, we just don't have the "know-how" when it comes to prayer. We confront situations in which we simply don't know how to accurately view or pray about a difficult situation or decision we're facing.

This verse says we know not "what" we should pray. That word "what" is a Greek word *ti*, which depicts *a very little thing*. This tells us that we don't know the fine points, the hidden problems, the intricate details of what is involved in the matter we're praying about. Left to ourselves, we simply don't have the ability to see the whole picture in a comprehensive view. We don't have the know-how to deal with the smallest details and the entirety of possible challenges and problems that might arise regarding the situation.

Is there a specific way to pray about each instance that comes into your life that will remove every obstacle and foil the enemy's strategies against you in that situation? The next phrase in verse 26 sheds some light on that question: "…For we know not what we should pray for *as we ought*…." That word "ought" comes from the Greek word *dei*, which means *necessary*. Thus, this phrase refers to something that *must* be a certain way. So this part of verse 26 could be translated, "…We do not know how to pray *according to the need, as is necessary to pray*, or *as that need exactly demands*."

Some needs demand a different kind of prayer. And this verse here says that without the Holy Spirit's cooperation in prayer, we don't know how to pray as each need demands. But thank God, His Spirit comes to remove our weaknesses and to *help* us in our inadequacy to know what to pray!

How does the Holy Spirit actually help us? We know from the word "helpeth" that He partners with us in prayer, grabbing hold of the obstacle and pushing against it in conjunction with us to remove that satanic blockade. Now let's look at the very end of verse 26 to learn more about how He helps bear the responsibility in prayer for us: "…But the Spirit itself [Himself] maketh *intercession* for us with groanings which cannot be uttered."

The word "intercession" is an interesting word. It's the Greek word *huperentugchano*, which means *to fall into with*. It is the picture of a person who comes upon someone who has fallen into some kind of quandary. Upon discovering the trapped person's dilemma, he swiftly swings into action to rescue and deliver the one who is in trouble. This word *huperentugchano* also carries the idea of *coming together in experience* or *meeting with*. Finally, it can mean *to supplicate*, which denotes *a rescue operation in which one snatches and pulls a person out of imminent danger*. So we could translate the phrase, "the Spirit itself maketh intercession for us" this way: *"The Spirit Himself falls into our situation with us"*; *"the Spirit Himself meets us in a common experience"*; or *"the Spirit Himself supplicates for us, rescuing us from our weaknesses."*

Here we gain more insight into the way the Holy Spirit comes to your aid. As you're walking through life, things may seem to be going fine. But then the devil digs one of his holes in the path ahead of you that you don't even know is there. You take a step, and before you know it, you fall headlong into the hole. Now you're all scuffed up, covered with dirt and bruises, trapped at the bottom of a pit.

You can do one of two things at this point. You can feel sorry for yourself and stay at the bottom of that pit — or you can say, "Holy Spirit, this is where You come in. I don't know how I got here, and I don't know how to get out of here. I need Your help!"

So let's say you choose the second option. What does the Holy Spirit do after He meets you in your common experience at the bottom of the hole? He begins to supplicate for you — to move on your behalf to rescue you. When you say, "Holy Spirit, I need You to help me," He answers, "That's what I'm here for. I am here to bear the responsibility of helping you in prayer." And there at the bottom of that pit, the Holy Spirit takes hold together with you in prayer against the hindrances that are preventing your deliverance.

Have you ever prayed when you're in the pits? Your zeal is not exactly at a high level at that point. You might feel discouraged and confused about why you fell into that hole in the first place. You're bruised and dirty, and you may have spent most of your prayer time voicing your negative emotions about the whole situation to the Lord. But then the Holy Spirit meets you right where you are in the midst of your trouble and begins to help you in your weakness. He says, "I'm here with you. I'm going to grab hold of this problem together with you, and we're going to press against it until it moves out of your life."

All of a sudden, something rises up on the inside of you, and you sense a renewed strength to go after that problem in prayer. You throw back your shoulders, lift up your head, and pick up the spiritual weapons God has given you to win this battle and overcome the enemy's strategies in your life!

What just happened to you? The Holy Spirit grabbed hold of your weaknesses and helped you push them out of the way! This is His responsibility. And He'll keep pressing with you against that problem you're facing until it is moved out of your life and you're out of that pit for good!

Aren't you thankful for this wonderful work of the Holy Spirit in your life? Whatever challenges you're facing in these uncertain times, of this you *can* be certain: Right now He is making intercession on your behalf, and He's not going to stop until every obstacle to your victory has been moved out of the way!

If you've been feeling like you've fallen into a pit and you don't know how to climb out, just remember who's down there with you, ready to help. Then begin to pray, knowing that the Spirit of God will make you strong where you are weak and help remove every obstacle that hinders your forward progress in Him.

MY PRAYER FOR TODAY

Father, I thank You for the insight I've gained into how the Holy Spirit comes to my aid. When it seems that I have fallen headlong into a hole, I can call out to the Holy Spirit for help and He will meet me in my experience. Thank You, Holy Spirit, for moving on my behalf to rescue me. At the bottom of every pit, You take hold together with me in prayer against the hindrances that attempt to prevent my deliverance until they move out of my life. Father God, I thank You for assuring my victory through the power of Your Spirit at work in me.

I pray this in Jesus' name!

MY CONFESSION FOR TODAY

I confess that each time I say, "Holy Spirit, I need You to help me," He answers, "That's what I'm here for. I am here to bear the responsibility of helping you in prayer." If ever I happen to fall into a hole, or if I feel discouraged and confused about why I fell into that trap in the first place, the Holy Spirit meets me right where I am in the midst of my trouble and begins to help me in my weakness. The Holy Spirit is always here with me, and He grabs hold of my problem together with me. We press against it together until it moves out of my life completely!

I declare this by faith in Jesus' name!

QUESTIONS FOR YOU TO CONSIDER

1. Have you ever experienced a moment when the Holy Spirit fell into a situation with you and interceded for you — rescuing you from an obstacle when you could not rescue yourself?
2. How would you describe it when the Holy Spirit has joined you as a Partner to bring forth your deliverance from an all-encompassing problem?
3. Do you know the delivering, empowering partnership of the Holy Spirit? If you've never experienced it yet but simply tried to get out of problems by yourself, why not start today to let the Holy Spirit step in as your delivering Friend?

OCTOBER 7

Our Partner in Prayer

Likewise the Spirit also helpeth our infirmities:
for we know not what we should pray for as we ought;
but the Spirit itself maketh intercession for us
with groanings which cannot be uttered.
And he that searcheth the hearts knoweth
what is the mind of the Spirit,
because he maketh intercession
for the saints according to the will of God.
— Romans 8:26,27

Today I want to continue talking to you about the Holy Spirit's role and responsibility in your life in the area of prayer. Yesterday we looked at several truths about this subject contained in Romans 8:26. Now I want to address how the Holy Spirit can intercede for and through you when you're grappling with your inadequacies in prayer.

I shared that the word "intercession" is the Greek word *huperentugchano*, which means *to fall into with*. This word "intercession" in the Greek conveys the idea of *a rescue operation* and paints the picture of a person who comes upon someone who has fallen into some kind of quandary. Upon discovering the trapped person's dilemma, he swiftly swings into action to rescue and deliver the one who's in trouble.

This word *huperentugchano* carries the idea of *coming together in experience* or *meeting with*. It can also mean *to supplicate*, which denotes *a rescue operation in which one snatches and pulls a person out of imminent danger*. So we could translate the phrase, "...the Spirit itself [Himself] maketh intercession for us..." like this: *"The Spirit Himself falls into our situation with us, meeting us in a common experience and rescuing us from our weakness."*

Now let's look at the word "groanings" in this verse. It is the Greek word *stenagmos*, which means *deep inward sighs* and could be translated *to vent*. The picture this word paints is similar to a teapot of water placed on a stove. As you turn up the flame and the water begins to boil, the teapot lets out some steam and that little pot begins to whistle.

This Greek word *stenagmos* gives us insight into how this *"intercession for us with groanings"* takes place in us. We think our world is falling apart — that our fiery trial is so unbearable that we're going to be consumed by the heat of that test. Of course, the devil stokes the fire in an attempt to convince us that we're never going to walk free from that place of testing. And, indeed, we can begin to think it's all over for us. But little do we know that as those flames are heating up, the Holy Spirit on the inside of us is getting angrier and angrier about the looming obstacle the enemy has placed before us. Then — *suddenly* — the Holy Spirit *vents*! The Holy Spirit *sighs*, and incredible prayers come rising up out of us. The Bible describes them as *"groanings which cannot be uttered."*

Now what does this mean, "which cannot be uttered"?

First, I want to ask you — if someone stood before you and began groaning in agony, would you be able to hear him or her? All things being equal, yes, you would hear that person groaning.

There have been times in my life when I've gone before the Lord with a problem, and I've groaned so hard in prayer that although my prayer was uttered with my mouth, it was expressed without, or apart from, natural language or speech. In other words, I prayed with "groanings which cannot be uttered."

We see an example of this in Jesus' prayer life (*see* March 14), when He stood before Lazarus' tomb and "groaned in the spirit, and was troubled" (John 11:33). What Jesus was experiencing wasn't just a matter of human emotions, but a deep, inward form of prayer when Jesus' spirit hooked up with the Holy Spirit in a powerful, supernatural expression of the Father's will.

These "groanings which cannot be uttered" can also refer to speaking, or praying, in other tongues. This phrase in the Greek simply indicates that what is uttered doesn't make sense to the human mind. So, you see, this has nothing to do with silent thoughts or with silent groanings and sighings. Rather, the groanings in Romans 8:26 are supernatural utterances that proceed from your spirit and come forth from your mouth as the Holy Spirit rises up within you to lift you up and rescue you from your plight. *This is the responsibility of the Holy Spirit as your Partner in prayer!*

Second, the first part of this verse says, "Likewise the Spirit also *helpeth* our infirmities…." As we saw yesterday, the Greek word for "helpeth" — *sunantilambano* — conveys this same idea of partnership and cooperation. In the midst of our weaknesses when we are inadequate to get the job done, the Holy Spirit comes and says, "Let Me grab hold of that hindrance with you, and you and I will push against it together until it is moved completely out of your way." This is how prayer becomes *a twofold partnership between you and the Holy Spirit.* He does this thing *with* you — in fact, He can't do it *without* you!

In the trials of life and the situations you find yourself in that seem impossible and overwhelming, you must participate with the Holy Spirit as He intercedes on your behalf. The Holy Spirit is in you — in your spirit — grabbing those problems along with you. The devil may turn up the heat, but, all of a sudden, the Holy Spirit begins to shove back and *vent*! And like that teapot on a hot stove, as you're praying, you might make some noise!

Romans 8:27 tells us how the Holy Spirit knows just what to pray to get the job done: "And he that searcheth the hearts knoweth what is the mind of the Spirit, because he maketh intercession for the saints according to the will of God." The word "searcheth" here is similar to the Old Testament word "looketh" used in reference to God as He instructed the prophet Samuel to anoint a king from the household of Jesse (*see* 1 Samuel 16:1-10). After Jesse had called in his sons, Samuel looked at Jesse's firstborn, Eliab, and said, "…Surely the Lord's anointed is before him" (v. 6). However, God saw things differently: "But the Lord said unto Samuel, Look not on his countenance, or on the height of his stature; because I have refused him: for the Lord seeth not as man seeth; for man looketh on the outward appearance, but the Lord *looketh* on the heart" (v. 7).

As Samuel looked at each one of Jesse's sons who had gathered before the prophet that day, the Lord said to Samuel, "No, it's not him. He's the wrong man for the job. You're looking at outward characteristics, and you think you know what you want. But I look inwardly, at the *heart.*"

Both of these words "looketh" in First Samuel 16:7 and "searcheth" in Romans 8:27 indicate that God is looking for something that we wouldn't think to look for. He looks beyond the surface — beyond what is shallow — right down to the need at the very deepest point.

The word "searcheth" in Romans 8:27 is translated from the Greek word *ereunao*, and it literally means *to investigate, to examine*, or *to sift*. It paints a picture of someone who's going through stacks of material looking for something, so he carefully *investigates, examines*, and *sifts through* the materials as he searches for what he needs.

Verse 27 continues, "…He that searcheth the hearts *knoweth what is the mind of the Spirit….*" The word "spirit" in verse 27 is capitalized in the *King James Version*, but this word is not a proper noun in the Greek. You'd have to translate this Greek word in the context of the setting — and in this particular setting, the word "spirit" refers to the human spirit, not the Holy Spirit. In other words, the Holy Spirit who searches a person's heart knows the "mind" of that person's spirit.

Before we look at what the Holy Spirit knows about the mind of a person's spirit, let's look more closely at what it is He's looking for as He "searcheth the hearts." First, we know that He's looking inward — within the heart — not outward, or just at the appearance of things. Second, we know He's *investigating* and *examining* as He looks upon the heart. That's how He knows the "mind" and the deepest, truest desires of a person's human spirit.

Why do we need Someone to help us pray? Because we simply don't know how to pray "as we ought" (v. 26)! For example, do you really know what the deepest desire of your heart is? Even if you think you know, could you agree that there's probably a deeper desire of your heart than you're even aware of right now? Well, the Spirit of God searches — *investigates, examines, and sifts* — through your heart for what He needs in order to pray for you. He looks for things you don't even know to look for — things that, naturally speaking, you don't have the ability to search out on your own. And He who searches the heart "...knoweth what is the mind of the Spirit..." (v. 27).

The word "mind" in this verse is translated from the Greek word that means *frame of thinking*. The Holy Spirit knows the mind of your spirit because He's *examining and sifting —investigating* your heart to discover the will of God embedded deep within your innermost frame of thinking. The Holy Spirit is searching to see what your spirit desires or what dreams God has planted in your heart. And when He finds the deeply laid plans of God on the inside of you, He begins to pray about them according to God's will.

Of course, you may already have a measure of understanding concerning some of those plans, but there's no way you can instantly, automatically understand everything there is to know about them. But the Holy Spirit *examines* and *investigat*es your heart and knows how to intercede effectually on your behalf regarding all that He finds there. Now you can see how valuable the Holy Spirit's role is in your prayer life. This intercessory work *has* to be His responsibility because He's the only One capable of accomplishing it!

Now let me ask you — have you ever been so perplexed by some challenge or dilemma that you said, "Lord, I don't even know how to pray about this situation"? Are you facing difficulties right now at your workplace, in your business, in your family, or in your finances? Whatever situation you find yourself in, the Holy Spirit's job is to *fall into that situation with you* and *launch a rescue operation* to deliver you out of confusion or danger and into the perfect will of God.

You may not know how to pray "as you ought," but the Holy Spirit knows how to make intercession for you! He knows how to *examine* and *investigate* your heart until He takes hold of the frame of thinking of your spirit. You may be wondering, *What am I going to do about this situation in my family?* But the Holy Spirit knows just what the Lord wants to do. You may be concerned about a situation at work, and you're asking, *What about my job?* Well, the Holy Spirit knows. Maybe you're staring at a crossroads in your life, wondering which way to turn. The Holy Spirit knows!

I'm so thankful for the beautiful intercessory work of the Holy Spirit in my life. I can't even recall all the times He has made intercession on my behalf to strengthen me in my weakness when

I faced my own quandaries and crossroad moments and didn't know what to do. And He wants to do the same for each one of us.

The Holy Spirit wants to help you pray about the deep, God-given desires of your heart. He knows better than you do what the plan of God is for your family, your job or business — and *all* the dreams He has placed in your heart. That means He knows about plans you may not yet be aware of. But the Holy Spirit hovers over those dreams and plans, and He knows the *frame of thinking* of all the secret places of your heart. Just ask, and the Holy Spirit will help you make the discoveries you need to know about your life and your future!

MY PRAYER FOR TODAY

Heavenly Father, I simply don't know how to pray as I ought! I have to acknowledge that I don't even know what the deepest desire of my heart is. Thank You for the Spirit of God who searches, investigates, examines, and sifts through my heart to discover the will of God that is embedded deep within my innermost being. Holy Spirit, it is my will to cooperate with You as You search to find the deeply laid plans of God inside me and to pray about them according to God's will. Thank You, Holy Spirit, for interceding effectually on my behalf. I cannot even begin to calculate the value of Your great intercessory work in my prayer life.

I pray this in Jesus' name!

MY CONFESSION FOR TODAY

I confess that I am grateful for the work of the Holy Spirit in my life. He makes intercession on my behalf to strengthen me in my weakness when I face crossroad moments and don't know what to do. Just as the Holy Spirit hovered over the waters when God created the earth, He hovers over my life to help me pray about the deep, God-given desires of my heart. The Holy Spirit knows better than I do what the plan of God is for my family, for my job or business — and for all the dreams He has placed inside me. He knows all the secret places of my heart. I simply ask Him, and the Holy Spirit helps me discover the precise wisdom I need to know in prayer about my life and my future!

I declare this by faith in Jesus' name!

QUESTIONS FOR YOU TO CONSIDER

1. The Holy Spirit knows how to search for the exact will of God for your life. Have you ever allowed Him to do His investigative work in your heart to reveal the Father's plan for you?
2. There are so many desires buried deep in your heart, but the Holy Spirit knows how to locate them, unearth them, and reveal them to your mind. Have you experienced this revealing work of the Holy Spirit in your walk with God?
3. We are helpless without the assistance of the Holy Spirit. Have you opened your heart to yield to the Holy Spirit so that He can be the Helper He was sent to be in your life?

OCTOBER 8

A Father's Bad Influence

Then certain of the vagabond Jews, exorcists,
took upon them to call over them which had evil spirits
the name of the Lord Jesus, saying, We adjure thee by Jesus
whom Paul preacheth. And there were seven sons of one Sceva,
a Jew, and chief of the priests, which did so.
— Acts 19:13,14

Today I want to talk to you about the spiritual role of fathers — and the immense impact they have upon the lives of their children. I want to use an example from Acts 19 to make the point, and I ask you to seriously consider the ramifications of what you are about to read. This is not a passage that is normally used to teach about the influential role of fathers, but it tells of a father who started out right but who went astray and, in doing so, led his seven sons astray with him.

Acts 19:13-17 relates this account:

Then certain of the vagabond Jews, exorcists, took upon them to call over them which had evil spirits the name of the Lord Jesus, saying, We adjure thee by Jesus whom Paul preacheth. And there were seven sons of one Sceva, a Jew, and chief of the priests, which did so. And the evil spirit answered and said, Jesus I know, and Paul I know; but who are ye? And the man in whom the evil spirit was leaped on them, and overcame them, and prevailed against them, so that they fled out of that house naked and wounded. And this was known to all the Jews and Greeks also dwelling at Ephesus; and fear fell on them all, and the name of the Lord Jesus was magnified.

Acts 19:13 specifically uses the word "exorcists" to describe the activity of Sceva and his seven sons. The word "exorcists" is derived from the Greek word *exorkidzo*, which depicts those who *adjured*, *implored*, and *begged* demon spirits to obey. With no real authority over the spirits, these exorcists resorted to their spells, charms, incantations, and magical names to try to coax evil spirits to cooperate with them.

Acts 19:14 goes on to tell us that the father of these seven sons was a man named Sceva. It says, "And there were seven sons of one Sceva, a Jew, and chief of the priests, which did so."

"Who was Sceva?" This man's identity has been a subject of great debate among biblical scholars over the years. There is *no record* that a "chief of the priests" of the Jews ever lived in Ephesus. Hence, there are scholars who believe the Greek word used for "chief priest" indicates that Sceva was a renegade Jew who had backslidden from his Jewish roots and had become involved in the worship of Artemis at Ephesus. Therefore he was, or had been at some time, a chief priest *in the worship of Artemis.*

Making all of this even more interesting is the fact that the name "Sceva" isn't a Jewish name. It is a Hellenized version of a Latin word that means *left-handed* — which in the vernacular of the First Century was slang that referred to someone who was *untrustworthy*, *perverse*, *reprobate*, *a wretch*, or *a scoundrel*. It is entirely possible that the name "Sceva" wasn't even this man's real name. It may have been a fictitious name inserted by Luke, the writer of the book of Acts, to express his opinion of this *apostate Jew* who converted to paganism and practiced it with his seven sons.

If these suggestions are true, the text would then convey the following idea: *"And there were seven sons of one Sceva, a Jew — a wretched, reprobate scoundrel who advertised himself as being great and who served as one of the high-ranking priests in the worship of Artemis — a man known for practicing pagan exorcism with his seven sons."*

With all this in mind, it seems likely that this Jewish man named Sceva converted to paganism and practiced occult rituals forbidden by the Old Testament — and then led his seven sons into the same practice. It is the perfect example of a man who has wandered away from the truth — and certainly a poor spiritual example of a father. Because of his own abandonment of the Word of God, this man led his sons right along with him into a backslidden spiritual condition — to the point that they even became involved in the activities of the occult.

When I meditate on this passage of Scripture, it always makes me want to pray for fathers in this critical hour. I pray that fathers will be spiritual leaders in their homes and will lead this next generation in the direction of a deep commitment to Christ and an authentic, intimate relationship with the Person and power of the Holy Spirit.

If you know a father who is leading his children astray by a wrong example, pray for him to change. God can change even the hardest heart. And if you are a father or mother of this next generation, make it a matter of serious prayer and determine to wake up to the awesome responsibility God has charged you with to lead and provide a godly influence for your children and the younger generations in your life. You have the potential of changing young lives as you lead others through your authentic and godly example.

If you are a father or mother, you are able to help teach your children to walk in obedience to Jesus and the Word of God. Let the example of Sceva stress again to you the incredible influence you have on your children. Then make a fresh commitment today to be a *godly* influence that leads your children in one direction only — on God's good path that leads to *life*!

MY PRAYER FOR TODAY

Father, in this critical hour, it is so important for parents to adhere closely to the Word of God in order to guide this young generation along the path that fulfills Your plan for their lives. I pray for myself and for other fathers and mothers who represent Your Kingdom — that our hearts will remain steadfast and strong in the truth of Your Word. We will not be like Sceva, who led his sons astray because of his own wayward and hardened heart. Instead, we will be true spiritual leaders in our homes so that we can not only teach our children with right words, but also train and lead them by the example of our lives in the direction of a deep commitment to Christ and an authentic, intimate relationship with the Person and power of the Holy Spirit. I make a fresh commitment today to be a godly influence in my children's lives, always pointing them to the path that leads to life!

I pray this in Jesus name!

MY CONFESSION FOR TODAY

I confess that I accept my divinely ordained responsibility as a parent to lead as a godly influence for my children and the younger generation in my life. I have the potential of changing young lives as I live an authentic example of the character and the ways of God the Father before them. I continually rely upon Heaven's wisdom to help me teach my children to walk in obedience to Jesus and the Word of God. I make a fresh commitment today to be a consistent example of obedience and love who leads my children in one direction only: God's good path!

I declare this by faith in Jesus' name!

QUESTIONS FOR YOU TO CONSIDER

1. Can you think of parents who wandered from the Lord and thereby affected the spiritual direction that their children took in life? What commitments have you made to the Lord to make sure you never wrongly influence those who look to you as an example or a guide?
2. Can you think of specific ways you can strengthen the godly example you are called to live before your children and the young generations?
3. What did you learn new from today's *Sparkling Gem* that has never been explained to you before? How will that truth affect your life from this day forward?

OCTOBER 9

Demonic Intelligence — No Match for the Power of Jesus!

And the evil spirit answered....
— Acts 19:15

Yesterday we saw how seven exorcists attempted to add the name of Jesus to their repertoire of magical incantations. As the story unfolds in Acts 19, we find that the seven sons of Sceva had a major confrontation — *an unsuccessful one* — with a demon-possessed man in Ephesus. As noted earlier, these exorcists saw Paul successfully using the name of Jesus to exercise authority over demons. Hoping to expel demons from a man in Ephesus, they added the name of Jesus to their list of magical names, even though they had no personal relationship with Jesus.

According to Acts 19:15, their attempt was futile. In fact, the verse says that the demon indwelling the man challenged them: "And the evil spirit *answered* and *said*, Jesus I know, and Paul I know; but who are ye?"

The actual structure of the Greek text says, "And *answering*, the evil spirit *said*...." The Greek tense tells us this was *not a single answer*; rather, the demon spirit that possessed the man verbally responded to each attempt the seven exorcists made to drive it out. Thus, the spirit was *answering* each time they tried to use a new magical name, spell, or incantation to drive it out. This, of course, tells us that evil spirits have *intelligence* and the ability *to speak* and even *to converse.*

This ability of evil spirits to speak is evident in the four gospels and in the book of Acts. A study of the Scriptures makes it clear that demon spirits are intelligent:

- They can possess specific information about things, places, or people.
- They can know the names of people.
- They have the ability to indwell a human being and engage that person's vocal apparatus to terrorize others, to blaspheme, to challenge, to make requests, and to scream, shriek, and cry out.

Vivid examples of evil spirits possessing intelligence and having the ability to speak can be found in Matthew 8:29 and Mark 5:7-12, where we read about the demoniac of Gadara. This tortured man was indwelt by a legion of demons that demonstrated both *intelligence* and the *ability to speak.* Mark 1:23-25 relates another example of this phenomenon. In this instance, evil spirits in a man spoke so *freely* that Jesus had to command them to stop talking and be silent.

Then in Mark 1:34, we are told that many sick people and those possessed with demons gathered to be healed and delivered by Jesus. The evil spirits referred to in this verse were so *fluid in speech* that Jesus actually had to forbid them to speak so they wouldn't reveal who He was before the time. These are just a few New Testament examples demonstrating that demons have both intelligence and the ability to use the vocal organs of the person in whom they dwell.

Going back to Acts 19:15, we read that this man had an "evil spirit." All demons are evil, but the word "evil" in this verse is the word *poneros.* If used in connection with animals, the word *poneros* depicts *ferocious, savage,* and *dangerous beasts.* Likewise, when this Greek word is used to describe *spirits* that indwell people, these spirits are *ferocious, savage, dangerous,* and *malicious* to those in whom they dwell and bring *harm* and *danger* to those who are in close proximity to them.

First, the evil spirits often create harmful and self-injuring behavior. The New Testament has many examples of such savageness. One example is found in Luke 9:37-39, where Luke tells us of a boy who periodically experienced demonic attacks that were injurious. Luke described it like this: "And, lo, a spirit taketh him, and he suddenly crieth out; and it teareth him that he foameth again, and bruising him hardly departeth from him" (v. 39). Matthew related the same account in Matthew 17:14 and 15, adding that the evil spirit would hurl the boy into fire and water. This was *ferocious, savage, dangerous,* and *malicious* treatment by the demon spirit against the one it possessed.

Another example is found in Mark 5:5, where we find the demoniac of Gadara, who was continually wandering in the mountains and among the tombs, crying out and "cutting himself with stones." He continually wandered around that isolated region, crying out in pain and agony while slicing his body with sharp stones — and it was all the result of the "evil spirits" that indwelt him. It is no wonder that these spirits are called *poneros* in the Greek, for they truly are *evil.*

But this description of the destructive impact of demonic control in a person's life should not cause us any fear. In my years of ministry, I have occasionally found myself in a confrontation with a demonized person. Just like the stories referred to in the Bible, I have heard demons speak, and I have seen them exercise physical power beyond human ability. But in each case, I have also seen them *wilt* and *shrink* when the name of Jesus is employed against them. We must remember that Jesus taught, "And these signs shall follow them that believe; *In my name shall they cast out devils...*" (Mark 16:17).

If you really know Jesus as your Lord and Savior — if you are in Christ — you can be sure that you have authority over demonic powers in the power of His name. Unlike the exorcists who used magic and incantations to manipulate the spirit realm and failed, you are empowered by the Holy Spirit, and you are given the name of Jesus to take authority over and to cast out demons. You are empowered by the Spirit of God and have real God-given authority in the spirit realm!

I am so thankful that the Bible clearly shows us that demonic powers shrink back at the name of Jesus. In fact, spirits are so fearful of that name that James 2:19 says demons "tremble" in the presence of faith and the name of Jesus. The word "tremble" is the Greek word *phrisso,* which means to *bristle,* as when the hairs stand up on a person's neck when he is suddenly "spooked" or startled by an unexpected noise, etc.

This means that even though demons may have intelligence to speak and power to be able to put forth superhuman strength, none of that helps them when they find themselves in the presence of a believer exercising his authority by faith in the name of Jesus. That prospect sends them into shock, panic, and dismay. Figuratively, it causes the hair to stand up on their necks. It *terrifies* them!

As a believer, you have the Holy Spirit living in you and you have the name of Jesus Christ to use at your disposal. That means you are in a position to make demons tremble! And it doesn't stop there. You also have the power to cast them out in Jesus' name, just as promised by Christ in Mark 16:17.

So the next time you find yourself in the presence of evil, don't *you* shrink back in fear. Release your faith and lift your voice to take authority over the devil's strategies in the name of Jesus — and as you do, you'll send those evil, malevolent powers scurrying away in terror! Then as you release the peace and the love of God in Jesus' name, His power will go into operation to calm those who had been adversely affected by that demonic oppression and turn that situation completely around according to God's purposes and to His glory!

MY PRAYER FOR TODAY

Father, I am inspired and thankful to learn I have authority that is given to me because of my relationship with Jesus Christ and His matchless name that He has entrusted to me. When I encounter situations where demonic power is present, I thank You for giving me the boldness to take authority and to expel those powers in Jesus' name!

I pray this in Jesus' name!

MY CONFESSION FOR TODAY

I confess that greater is He that is in me than he that is in the world. The devil is minor compared to the awesome power of Christ that indwells me. When I speak the name of Jesus, empowered by the Holy Spirit, the spirit-realm listens and obeys. I am in Christ, and Christ is in me. When I speak in Jesus' name against demon powers, it is like Christ is speaking through me!

I declare this by faith in Jesus' name!

QUESTIONS FOR YOU TO CONSIDER

1. Have you ever had an experience with demonic intelligence like Acts 19:15 depicts? When was that experience, and what happened?
2. What did you learn from today's *Sparkling Gem* that you never knew about demons and our authority over them? This is a very important subject for Christians, so we need to know what the Bible teaches (*see* Ephesians 6:10-18)!
3. Have you ever had an experience binding or casting out a demon spirit? When did that happen? What was the result?

OCTOBER 10

A Demonic Recognition

And the evil spirit answered and said, Jesus I know,
and Paul I know; but who are ye?
— Acts 19:15

The evil spirits in the demon-possessed man in Acts 19 were very familiar with both Jesus and the apostle Paul. However, the demons did *not* recognize the seven sons of Sceva who were trying to exercise authority over them. We can know this from the original Greek in Acts 19:15, where the evil spirit responded to the seven exorcists: "…Jesus I know, and Paul I know; but who are ye?"

The words translated "know" in those two phrases — "Jesus *I know*" and "Paul *I know*" — are two distinctly different words in the Greek text. In the phrase, "Jesus *I know*," the word "know" is the Greek word *ginosko*. The word *ginosko* has a wide range of meanings, depending on the context in which it is used. The foremost meaning of *ginosko* was *to recognize a person or a thing, to acknowledge*, or *to have a full comprehension about the person or thing being acknowledged*. There is no question that the use of the word *ginosko* here means the wicked spirit that inhabited this man *admitted, conceded*, and *affirmed* that the name "Jesus" was *well known* to it. Like all evil spirits, this demon *was familiar* with Jesus — it *fully comprehended* and *acknowledged* who Jesus was — and had possessed this knowledge for a long time. So when the evil spirit said, "Jesus I know," it was saying, in effect, "*...Jesus I know and fully comprehend with absolute certainty....*"

On the other hand, in the phrase, "and Paul *I know*," the word "know" is translated from a completely different Greek word. It is the word *epistamai*, which describes *a knowledge obtained by outward observation*. In other words, Paul's reputation was growing as one who had authority over demons, and it had captured the attention of the spirit world in Ephesus. Local demons were "tuning in" to observe Paul's activities.

The word *epistamai* implicitly reveals that the dark spirit world in Ephesus had recently become familiar with Paul's ministry. The apostle's activities were a great threat to the demonic forces over that city, and they were taken aback by his spiritual power. Therefore, the evil spirits of the territory were *scrutinizing* this newcomer and *carefully watching* him move through each situation as one who possessed great authority. This word *epistamai* also implies that these demonic spirits were *spying* and *conducting surveillance* on this newcomer who had invaded their dark stronghold — so they could stay aware of what Paul was doing and look for ways to oppose him. The word *epistamai* therefore carries the idea: "*...and Paul I know because I have recently become familiar with him by carefully following and observing his activities....*"

But then the evil spirit asked the seven sons of Sceva an interesting question: "But who are ye?" This question should be understood in the context of the entire verse. The reader should understand the text to mean: "*Jesus I know and fully comprehend with absolute certainty, and Paul I know because I have recently become familiar with him by carefully following and observing his activities. But I have no idea who you are! In fact, we know nothing about you! We don't recognize you or your authority at all!*"

One would think that demonic forces would recognize exorcists who regularly delved into occult practices; however, the evil spirit in the man didn't recognize these exorcists at all. But oh, what a glorious thought that this spirit knew the name of *Jesus* and knew *Paul* because Paul was in Christ and was an authorized user of Jesus' name!

You fit that description too! If you are *in Christ*, you are an authorized user of the name of *Jesus* and the power of the Holy Spirit! James 2:19 says that demons "tremble" when they hear that name. As we saw yesterday, the word "tremble" would be better translated that they are "spooked" or "terrified" when they hear the name of Jesus spoken with bold faith by an authorized user!

If you are a Christian indwelt by the power of the Holy Spirit, you have all power in Heaven and earth given unto you (*see* Matthew 28:18). You are authorized to speak on behalf of Jesus and to take authority over any evil presence that comes your way. And it *must* obey!

MY PRAYER FOR TODAY

Father, I am thrilled and grateful to learn of the authority that I have in the name of Jesus Christ. I am so thankful that I am a real, born-again child of God — and that You have authorized me to use Your power and Your name at any moment that it is required. I need never be afraid of the devil because demons recognize that the power of God inside me is greater than all of them put together. Thank You for encouraging me to be bold when I sense the devil is trying to manifest his presence or wage an attack!

I pray this in Jesus' name!

MY CONFESSION FOR TODAY

I declare that the Son of God lives inside me — and I am in Him — and when I am required to speak to an evil presence and command it to go, that evil spirit recognizes Jesus' voice speaking through me. I am not afraid. I do not give way to fear. I do not listen to communication that would incite anxiety or fear. I receive from strong, Word-based teaching resources, like this one today, in order to build my faith and prepare me to take action when it is needed!

I declare this by faith in Jesus' name!

QUESTIONS FOR YOU TO CONSIDER

1. Have you ever thought about how sad it is that people involved in the occult are playing with powers that will ultimately work against them? Do you know someone personally who is operating under this kind of self-deceived influence?
2. Demons know the name of *Jesus* — and if you are *in* Jesus, they know your name too. So let me ask you — have you ever had an experience where a demon spirit recognized you and obeyed your authority? Or have you heard of someone else who had that type of experience? Where was it, and what happened?
3. How would you recognize a demonic presence in your immediate surroundings?

Demons tremble when they hear the name of Jesus spoken with bold faith by an authorized user!

OCTOBER 11

Illegitimate Authority and a Demonic Attack

And the man in whom the evil spirit was *leaped* on them,
and *overcame* them, and *prevailed* against them,
so that they fled out of that house
naked and wounded.
— Acts 19:16

As we continue looking at Acts 19, we find the evil spirit in this man was inflamed by the seven exorcists' feeble and ineffective attempts to cast it out. The evil spirit unexpectedly seized the full use of the possessed man's body to physically attack and injure them. Acts 19:16 tells us, "And the man in whom the evil spirit was *leaped* on them, and *overcame* them, and *prevailed* against them...." Those exorcists had encroached on demonic territory that they didn't know how to handle! Let's look at those words *leaped, overcame,* and *prevailed*, because they tell a huge part of this story.

When the text says the man "leaped" on them, it is the Greek word *ephallomai*, which means *to leap upon*, *to jump upon*, or *to pounce upon*, as a panther leaps on a weak and defenseless animal. This word carries the idea of abruptly taking a victim by surprise, which means these exorcists were completely taken off guard by this attack. Not only did the demon-possessed man leap on them, but the verse also says that he "...overcame them, and prevailed against them...."

The word "overcame" is a translation of the word *katakurieuo*, a compound of the words *kata* and *kurios.* The word *kata* carries the idea of a force that is *dominating* or *subjugating*, and the word *kurios* is the Greek word for a *lord* or *master.* When compounded into one word, the new word means *to completely conquer*, *to master*, *to quash*, *to crush*, *to subdue*, *to defeat*, *to force into a humiliating submission*, or *to bring one to his knees in surrender.*

The word *katakurieuo* leaves no room for misunderstanding — this was a *humiliating defeat* for these seven exorcists. Their defeat was so complete that the verse goes on to say that the evil spirit "*prevailed* against them." The word "prevail" is a translation of the Greek word *ischuos*, which describes a *mighty* individual, such as a man with such muscular strength or physical power that he could defeat any opponent.

It is indisputably clear that evil spirits have the ability to supernaturally energize those in whom they dwell. When they do, the demonized individuals may exhibit inexplicable physical strength. One of the best examples of this is found in Mark 5:3,4. Here we read again about the demoniac of Gadara, who was so supernaturally energized that no one could bind him, not even with fetters and chains. If people were successful enough to attach the fetters and chains around this man, he was so empowered by demons that he could tear those heavy iron chains to pieces and get free almost without effort. Absolutely no one could tame him or bring him under control — *except* Jesus.

The demons that inhabited this man who lived among the tombs in the Gadarenes were violent beyond any human's ability to control. It must be noted that ancient Greek literature used the word *daimonian* — the word "demon" — to portray a person who is *mad* or *insane*. But this is not only the classical Greek view. The New Testament also shows that those who were possessed with evil spirits were *mad* and often afflicted with *physical illnesses*. This is why Matthew 4:24 says, "...They brought unto him [Jesus] all sick people that were taken with divers diseases and torments, and those which were possessed with devils, and those which were lunatick, and those that had the palsy; and he healed them."

Please get the revelation of this, because it is crucial. Jesus had *absolute* authority over evil spirits when He walked this earth. Then He gave the authority to cast out demons in His name to all those who trust in Him (*see* Mark 16:17). *This was the secret of Paul's success.* But these seven sons of Sceva were *not* believers; they were simply exorcists trying a new formula. And they soon discovered what happens to those who try to wield spiritual authority they don't possess. Those men were *no* match for the demons that indwelt the demoniac at Ephesus!

As the seven exorcists commanded the evil spirit to leave the man, suddenly the evil spirit seized the man's body and demonically energized it, and the man surged forward like a fierce wild animal and pounced upon them. After being severely beaten and battered, all seven of those men fled the scene in fear. Verse 16 says, "...They fled out of that house naked and wounded."

The word "fled" in Greek is *ekpheugo*. This word is a compound of the word *ek* — meaning *out*, as to *exit* or *leave* a place — and the word *pheugo*, which means *to flee* or *to run swiftly*. When these two words are compounded, the new word conveys the idea that those seven sons of Sceva *got out* of the house *as quickly as they possibly could*, making a mad dash or *a fast exit*. And no wonder they wanted to get out so quickly — they had been injured and had even lost their clothes in the attack!

The verse says the seven men fled out of "that house," referring to the house where the demoniac was kept. The wording of this phrase implies that this was a well-known house. It wasn't just *a* house; it was *the* house where this savage man lived. It was the place everyone avoided and stayed far from, for too much fear was associated with it and with the violent activities that took place there. And at that moment, it was the exorcists themselves who were escaping from "that house" in great haste!

When the men ran out of the house, Acts 19:16 says they were "naked and wounded." The word "naked" is *gumnos*, an often-used Greek word that simply means *physically naked*. The word "wounded" is *traumatidzo*, which means *to cause injury or harm* and is where we get the words *trauma* and *traumatized*.

We don't know the exact details of this demonic attack, how long it lasted, or how badly these seven sons of Sceva suffered. We do know, however, that by the time they exited the house, they were *naked, physically wounded*, and *traumatized*.

When people heard that these particular exorcists had miserably failed to exorcise the demon, it was big news in Ephesus. Everyone heard how the evil spirit acknowledged the name and authority of Jesus and even knew the name of Paul, Christ's servant — yet did *not* recognize these famous professional exorcists. So even in this worst-case demonic scenario, God's purposes prevailed as it was noised abroad that only the name of Jesus had been recognized and respected by the demon world, bringing attention to that name all over the city of Ephesus and throughout the surrounding region (*see* Acts 19:17).

I assure you that the kingdom of darkness knows *your* name as well. As a child of God, you have the legitimate authority to wield the name of Jesus like a weapon in your hand against everything the enemy might try to throw at you. And when you exercise that authority in faith, every demon that has been sent to harass you will flee in terror! *Hell knows you and trembles when you stand in the power of the name of Jesus!*

MY PRAYER FOR TODAY

Father, what an awesome thing to realize that the demons not only recognize Jesus' authority — they also recognize the authority of those who know Jesus. Of course, Jesus stripped Satan of all his powers (Colossians 2:15) and it should be no surprise to me that he is terrified of Jesus' name and those who had been authorized to use it. But I am especially thankful to You for bringing me out of the bondage of darkness, for translating me into the kingdom of Your dear Son, and for giving me authority in the name of Jesus Christ!

I pray this in Jesus' name!

MY CONFESSION FOR TODAY

Demons may have authority over unsaved people, but I boldly confess they do not have authority over me and others who are in Christ Jesus. I never have to fear a demonic attack like the seven sons of Sceva experienced because the devil is the one who is running from me when I use the Spirit-empowered name of Jesus! I refuse to shrink in fear, and I refuse to let the devil intimidate me, because I have the presence of the Greater One living inside me!

I declare this by faith in Jesus' name!

QUESTIONS FOR YOU TO CONSIDER

1. In your lifetime, have you ever heard of anyone who came under a demonic attack similar to the one we read about in Acts 19:16 today?
2. I once had a demon-inflicted man pick up a table and try to throw it at me, but he strictly obeyed me and put it down when I authoritatively spoke to him in the name of Jesus. Have you had any experiences where demons have quickly obeyed when you used Jesus' name?
3. What faith-building stories can you recall of believers exercising authority over demon spirits?

OCTOBER 12

Jesus Is Glorified!

And this was known to all the Jews and Greeks
also dwelling at Ephesus; and fear fell on them all,
and the name of the Lord Jesus was magnified.
— Acts 19:17

In the past few *Sparkling Gems*, we've seen how the pagan population of the city of Ephesus was *very* preoccupied with the magical power of secret names, spells, and incantations. It was very significant to the citizens of the city that the demon possessing the demoniac, who was apparently well known in Ephesus, *knew* the name of Jesus. No one else had ever been able to help this demon-possessed man. But the evil spirit that had taken control of this tormented individual actually *spoke* and *admitted* to knowing the name of Jesus. This would have signaled to the pagan population that the name of Jesus contained great power. And the fact that the demon even acknowledged Paul would have also given the apostle a higher level of authority in the eyes of the people.

As a result of this event, a new preeminence was immediately given to the name of Jesus in Ephesus, and Paul's influence increased. Acts 19:17 describes the impact this incident had on those who heard about it: "And this was known to all the Jews and Greeks also dwelling at Ephesus; and fear fell on them all, and the name of the Lord Jesus was magnified."

The Bible doesn't specify how the news of this event quickly reached both the Jewish and Greek communities in Ephesus, but we know that it did. Perhaps there were eyewitnesses of the event who told others about it. Or perhaps those who had hired the seven sons of Sceva reported this event to friends, who then spread the news to others. Maybe there were firsthand witnesses of the incident who heard the screams of the exorcists and saw them running naked from the house.

Regardless of how the news was spread, it made a significant impression on both Jews and Greeks. Both groups were impressed that the name of Jesus was known by the evil spirit that inhabited this man. As a result, this verse states that "…*fear* fell on them all…."

The Greek word for "fear" is *phobos*, which in this case describes a *reverential fear, hush*, or *amazement* that literally *fell* on the residents of the city. It brought a speechless sense of awe to the entire community — and a heightened awareness of the name of Jesus. This is why the verse goes on to say, "…And the name of the Lord Jesus was magnified" (v. 17).

It must be noted that Luke referred here to the "*Lord* Jesus," not just to "Jesus." The word "Lord" is the Greek word *kurios*, meaning *lord* or *supreme master*. This violent episode between the demon and the seven sons of Sceva had demonstrated that Jesus alone has the power and might to demand respect of evil spiritual forces. By calling him "Lord Jesus" in this context,

Luke revealed to us that Jesus came out of the ordeal as the Champion. As a result, His name was "magnified" — *enlarged*, *expanded*, and *maximized* — throughout the city.

Thus, the failed attempt of the seven exorcists was an event used by God to bring attention to the name of Jesus and to escalate the pace of the work for His Kingdom in Ephesus. Large numbers of conversions took place as people turned from their occult deeds with genuine acts of repentance.

There is no question that the power of God was being unleashed in the heart of this dark pagan city and that its foundation, which had been established on the bedrock of idolatry, was being shaken to its very core. Life in Ephesus was being eternally impacted by the power of the Gospel, and many who lived in the region would never be the same again.

This is what happens when the power of God is in manifestation! It shakes people to their core and they know without any doubt that they have come into contact with the highest level of supernatural power.

Doesn't this make you want to see the power of God manifest in your city, in your church, or in your ministry? *Nothing brings glory to the name of the Lord Jesus Christ more than His divine power being unleashed through faith in full operation!*

MY PRAYER FOR TODAY

Father, I want to see Your divine power unleashed in my city, in my church, and in our ministry. Nothing brings glory to the name of the Lord Jesus like a miracle or a supernaturally heaven-sent manifestation of divine power. Forgive me for restraining the manifestations of the Holy Spirit when He has longed to demonstrate the power of God. I am sorry and so wrong for fearing what people will think — when in fact, this is the very thing that will make the greatest impression on people. I ask You to help me from this moment forward to surrender to the great working of Your power and that this type of manifestation will cause the name of the Lord Jesus to be magnified!

I pray this in Jesus' name!

MY CONFESSION FOR TODAY

I admit that the fear of man — and what other people think — has caused me to hinder the power of God from operating as God wants it to operate in our city, in our church, and in our ministry. However, from this moment forward, I confess that I am throwing open my arms to receive the supernatural assistance that heaven wants to give in terms of signs and wonders. Such signs and wonders were sent to draw people to Jesus, not deter people from Jesus — so I am going to stop wondering what people think and I'm going to become an instrument for the power of God to bring signs and wonders into manifestation!

I declare this by faith in Jesus' name!

QUESTIONS FOR YOU TO CONSIDER

1. Have there been times when God wanted to move supernaturally, and you hindered it or stopped it because you were afraid of what people would think?
2. From what we've studied in today's *Sparkling Gem,* do you see that such power magnifies the name of Jesus and brings people closer to the Kingdom of God? Do you understand that your fear of people's reactions has been altogether inaccurate?
3. The next time you sense the leading of the Holy Spirit to operate in the gifts of the Spirit or to unleash the power of God, what are you going to do? It's going to take a firm decision, one that you'll stand by, so what is your truthful answer?

OCTOBER 13

When It Comes Right Down to It, Whose Law Will You Obey?

Not forsaking the assembling of ourselves together….
— Hebrews 10:25

In today's *Sparkling Gem,* I want to share some history with you about where believers met to worship when the law forbade them to do so. *I think you will find this little history lesson to be very interesting!*

Hebrews 10:25 commands believers to meet together regularly. However, during New Testament times, Roman law expressly forbade believers from congregating. Although there were periods of reprieve in different regions of the empire in the early centuries of the Church, it was generally illegal for Christians to come together anywhere in the Roman Empire — including the privacy of their own homes. Those who were caught doing so often faced severe reprisal.

These restrictions put believers in a difficult position. Although Scripture instructed them to obey, honor, and pray for the authorities of the land (*see* Romans 13:1,2), their government wouldn't permit them to obey God's commands. As the new laws took effect, *Christians found themselves being forced to choose between obeying the law of God or following the law of man* — just as Peter and John had to decide whom they would obey when the Sanhedrin commanded them to stop preaching in the name of Jesus (*see* Acts 4:19). When Roman or local laws were in line with God's law, early Christians diligently obeyed them. *But if a law conflicted with the principles clearly outlined in God's Word, most believers chose to obey God over the government's mandates.* This choice was not without consequence, however, because it gave rise to accusations that Christians were insubordinate lawbreakers.

As a result of Roman authorities passing laws that forbade gatherings that were not sanctioned by the government, it quickly became difficult for believers to find safe locations where they could worship together in peace. Early Christians had to be creative in the ways they met and in the way they communicated where their meetings would be held. One method they used to communicate with each other was secret imagery that pagans didn't understand.

An example of this secret communication was a special symbol that believers would often scratch into the marble pavements of public places. This symbol was essentially a circle with a series of intersecting lines at its center, somewhat resembling an eight-spoked wheel. To the eyes of the public, these drawings looked like mere children's games that had been scratched into the pavement — but to believers, this symbol was actually a secret code. If one separates the lines from the circle, one finds that this symbol is actually composed of five Greek letters — **ΙΧΘΥΣ** — that overlap one another. In Greek, this sequence of letters is *icythus*, the Greek word for *a fish*, but to Christians, these letters hidden within the circular *icythus* symbol conveyed so much more.

The word **ΙΧΘΥΣ** is an acronym for Ἰησοῦς Χριστός, Θεος Υἱός, Σωτήρ, which means: **Jesus, Christ, God, Son, Savior.**

- **"Ι"** is the first letter (*Iota*) of the word **Ἰησοῦς** — which is the Greek name **Jesus**.
- **"Χ"** is the first letter (*Chi*) of the word **Χριστός** — which is the Greek word for **Christ**.
- **"Θ"** is the first letter (*Theta*) of the word **Θεός** — which is the Greek word for **God**.
- **"Υ"** is the first letter (*Upsilon*) of the word **Υἱός** — which is the Greek word for **Son**.
- **"Σ"** is the first letter (*Sigma*) of the word **Σωτήρ** — which the Greek word for **Savior**.

Soldiers and political officials might have thought this symbol was a mere street game, but in reality, it was a secret code designed to help believers connect with each other and coordinate meetings. For instance, if it was scribbled next to a shop, it might have conveyed that the shop owner was a Christian. If it was drawn next to a home, it might have indicated that a Christian gathering was secretly being held there. Wherever this symbol was inscribed, it sent the message that believers were nearby.

Because of the law forbidding unauthorized gatherings — which included members of this upstart Christian sect — Hebrews 10:25 put believers in direct opposition to the law. Consequently, they were often driven to assemble in secret meetings, which they frequently disguised to look like something else. Using emblems like the circular *icythus* symbol, believers were able to covertly communicate where they lived or worked with each other. And by regularly changing the place and time of their meetings, they made it difficult for authorities to catch them.

Congregations rarely met at the same place for long, choosing instead to constantly move to new secret locations in order to avoid detection. Church meetings in the First Century were mostly conducted in private residences, and just like today, the homes of believers could come in all sizes. Some places were quite modest, whereas others were large enough to accommodate a small congregation. In Acts 20:7-12, we read of a boy who fell from a window of a third-floor apartment where Paul was preaching to a local congregation. This reveals that even apartment buildings could be used for church use if the circumstances were right.

As the years passed and forces continued to mount against Christians, they were often forced to become even *more* covert about the locations of their meetings. For example, in the mid-Second Century at the trial of Christian leader Justin Martyr, he admitted to the Roman magistrate that he had been conducting meetings in a room located above a bathhouse in Rome.

Since Roman bathhouses were notorious cesspools of sinful activities, it might seem highly unusual that a respected church leader like Justin Martyr would choose to meet with other Christians there for purposes of teaching or corporate worship. However, the strategic potential of such a meeting place should be considered. This may have been an ideal covert location for Christian gatherings simply because it *was* such an unlikely possibility.

Another place where believers met in secret was in suburban cemeteries on the outskirts of the cities. These were considered ideal meeting places because they were largely hidden from the eyes of hostile governmental authorities.

By the Second Century — and some scholars believe there is evidence for as early as the late First Century — believers began to use underground catacombs for the burial of their dead. Although there were few rich Christians in the earliest years of the Church, later some wealthy Christian landowners granted permission for underground tombs to be built on their land. Some of the larger rooms in these underground chambers became another means used by early believers to assemble together in secret.

Especially during periods of fierce persecution in the Second and Third Centuries, these underground catacombs sometimes provided an effective "cover" for Christian meetings because they gave the impression that these believers were merely a group of people gathered for a funeral ceremony. In fact, at times actual funerals became legal opportunities for Christians to gather.

Roman soldiers were superstitious about the dead and were afraid to enter the catacombs, so some of the larger chambers in these underground systems became ideal locations for believers to meet on occasion without fear of authorities watching what they were doing. Deep beneath the earth, those burial quarters would be transformed into places for worship, testimony, and the teaching of God's Word — a place where believers could strengthen each other's faith before reemerging into the sunlight. But even these Christian burial grounds came to be officially forbidden to believers.

So we see that because of the hostile forces arrayed against the Church during the first three centuries of its existence, it was a matter of survival for early believers to find concealed places where they could meet to worship, hear God's Word, and fellowship with one another. It's not so different than the way the Church operates today in countries where governments are hostile to the Gospel.

We should never take for granted how fortunate we are to be able to attend church without the threat of death or imprisonment. This privilege has cost and continues to cost others highly. *Let's pray for God to give us a renewed love for the local church — and a firm decision that if we have to choose between obeying man's laws or God's laws, we will always choose to obey God rather than man!*

MY PRAYER FOR TODAY

Father God, I realize that it is better to obey You than man. I didn't realize the pressure that early Christians faced just to meet together. Because we have so much freedom, I often forget that there are Christians around the world today who are persecuted simply for attending church. As we face the days ahead of us — when laws passed by high courts may conflict with the law of God — give us the courage to stick by Your law and do what You say. This will take great strength of will, so I ask You, Holy Spirit, to give me the inward fortitude to do what is right, regardless of what the world around me says.

I pray this in Jesus' name!

MY CONFESSION FOR TODAY

I confess that I am committed to carrying out the instructions outlined in the Word of God. The thinking of the world and society may change, but God's Word is unchanging — and I will stick by the Word of God, regardless of the way the world around me tries to dictate my actions or influence my beliefs. I am filled with courage; I am overflowing with confidence; and I have the power of the Holy Spirit. The Lord is my strength and my personal bravery. The Word of God is a high tower of strength to me. Regardless of what man says or the price it will cost to obey, I will do what God's Word commands.

I declare this by faith in Jesus' name!

QUESTIONS FOR YOU TO CONSIDER

1. Do you think of or pray for Christians in other parts of the world who are presently suffering for their faith? Have you ever thought about what it costs them simply to attend a church service?
2. Our freedom is so abundant, and we have lived in freedom for so long that it's hard for us to imagine losing it. But if the government suddenly put restrictions on your practice of faith, how would you respond? Would you obey the courts, or would you obey the Word of God?
3. I live in Russia where there was a time when believers had to meet covertly. If you had to meet covertly to worship with other Christians, would you do it, or would you fall out of fellowship to avoid persecution?

OCTOBER 14

Put On Love

"And above all these things put on charity,
which is the bond of perfectness."
— Colossians 3:14

Can you imagine loving with such a pure love that you expect nothing back in return and it's *impossible* for you to feel hurt or let down by the response of the recipients of your love? You don't love them for the purpose of getting something in return; you shower them with love simply because you love them. That love is entirely possible, because it's God's *agape* love, and He has shed His love abroad in your heart by the Holy Spirit (Romans 5:5). This is why I call *agape* a *high-level love*. It is a love that has no strings attached, a love that loves simply and purely — *the God-kind of love.*

In today's *Sparkling Gem*, we are going to look at this God-kind of love through Paul's words in Colossians 3:14, where he commanded us, "And above all these things put on charity, which is the bond of perfectness."

The phrase "put on" is a translation of the Greek word *enduo*, a common term that was used in New Testament times to denote *the act of putting on a garment or a piece of clothing*. Although clothing styles have changed innumerable times over the millennia, the process of putting on your garments has always been the same. If you're going to dress properly for the day, you have to make the choice to look into the closet and select the clothes you wish to wear. Then you have to deliberately take that outfit off the hanger and slip it onto your body. Your clothes won't jump out of the closet and onto your body without your help. If you are going to wear them, you have *to put them on*!

In the same way, Paul says we are to "put on love." This word for "love" is the Greek word *agape* — a complex term that I call *high-level love* because there is no higher, finer, or more excellent love than *agape* love. As we have studied before, this kind of love occurs when an individual *sees, recognizes, understands, and appreciates the value of an object or a person,* causing the viewer to *behold this object or person in great esteem, awe, admiration, wonder, and sincere appreciation*. Such great respect is awakened in the heart of the observer for the object or person he is beholding that he is *compelled* to love. In fact, his love for that person or object is so strong that it is *irresistible*. If necessary, *agape* love will even sacrifice itself for the sake of that object or person it so deeply cherishes. Thus, *agape* is the highest form of love — a self-sacrificial type of love that moves one to action.

In First John 3:16, we are urged to possess *agape* for each other. It says, "Hereby perceive we the love of God, because he laid down his life for us: and we ought to lay down our lives for the brethren." This plainly means that we are to love and appreciate each other just as fully and freely as God loves us.

The Father loved us to the point of *self-sacrifice*. In the same way, we are to *agape* our brothers and sisters to such a great extent that we would be willing to lay down our lives for them or forgive them for wrongs we perceive they have committed against us. *We are to love others with no strings attached.*

You may ask, "But how can I possess such love? Is it really possible for me to exhibit that kind of love for other people, including those who have offended or hurt me?"

Because the seed of God's Word has been sown into your own human spirit, this divine love is within you all the time. If you will let the Spirit of God release it from your heart, you will begin to experience this fruit of the Spirit called *agape* as it swells up from deep within. And as you allow God's love to flow out of your life to others, it will transform your character to become more like Jesus Christ.

But this kind of love is something you have to "put on" if you're going to experience it. This love is always inside you — but it's like clothing hanging in the closet. The clothes are yours, but you've got to walk to the closet, open the door, take the clothes off the hanger, slip your arms through the sleeves, and then begin to push the buttons through the buttonholes. You never get dressed by accident. It's always a result of your decision and action.

Likewise, God has placed this amazing love deep inside you — in your "heart-closet," so to speak. But you are the only one with the power to open the doors to that place where it is kept, take it off the hanger, and start putting it on. Furthermore, when you are tempted to take that love off and put it back in the closet out of anger or disappointment, remember that you alone can decide to adorn yourself in this *agape* love of God. So open your heart, reach inside, pull it out, and be determined to get dressed in the *agape* love of God. In fact, God commands it!

So refuse to let anger, frustration, and intolerance rule you — and take this command of God very seriously. Slip on the garment of *agape* love, and *keep* it on! God *is* love; in fact, it's the very essence of who He is. And just as Jesus is the perfect reflection of the Father's love (*see* John 15:9), so are you called to be a reflection of Jesus' love. First John 4:17 declares, "...As he is, so are we in this world"!

Now that you know this type of divine love is inside you, you can deliberately and *on purpose* open the doors to your "heart-closet" to take it out and put it on! This will enable you to walk in love, regardless of the situation you find yourself in. Don't you agree that it's time for you to get dressed in the love of God today?

MY PRAYER FOR TODAY

Lord, I thank You for the love of God that has been shed abroad in my heart by the Holy Spirit who was given to me. Releasing this love is a choice, and I repent for the times I've chosen to walk in anger, frustration, or intolerance instead of choosing to put on love as You've instructed me to do. I thank You for Your great love for me. Jesus said I will prove to be His disciple when I release His love toward others. Thank You, Lord, for the gift of a free will. I honor You with it by choosing to put on agape love. I will give no place to the devil by keeping myself clothed in the love of God.

I pray this in Jesus' name!

MY CONFESSION FOR TODAY

I confess that the incorruptible seed of God's Word is sown into my spirit. Therefore, God's agape love is planted within me. I deliberately choose to put on that love as a garment. Clothed in the love of God, I walk into each situation covered with the God-kind of love that never fails, fades out, or comes to an end. In every situation I face, I am equipped to love others as God has loved me – purely from the heart, with no strings attached!

I declare this by faith in Jesus' name!

QUESTIONS FOR YOU TO CONSIDER

1. Have you had moments when you *decided* that you were going to walk in love instead of offense or anger? Isn't it a victorious moment when you make the right choice? What is stopping you from making that choice today?
2. Have you ever "half-walked" in love — as if you got your arm into one of your shirtsleeves, but then something happened that caused you to jerk your arm out of it and say something disparaging to someone else? What did you do to recover from that and to repair the hurt you may have caused?
3. Are there individuals with whom you need to be careful that you don't get out of love? Who are they? Have you put them on a prayer list and determined to make praying for these people a part of your daily prayer time?

OCTOBER 15

An Example of Turning One's Ears From the Truth to Fables

And they shall turn away their ears from the truth,
and shall be turned unto fables.
— 2 Timothy 4:4

In our home in Russia, Denise and I have several black, lacquered boxes that are precious Russian works of art. They were painted using a centuries-old technique, and each box contains up to 16 layers of papier-mâché. The work is so intricate, in fact, the scenes on these boxes were painstakingly painted with a brush containing only one hair! Then when the painting was finished on one of these boxes, the artist would burnish it with the tooth of a wolf.

Four main schools taught and performed this method, and when the art form first began in Russia, the intricate scenery on these boxes primarily consisted of religious icons and scenery depicting religious events and nobility. But the art changed after the 1917 Bolshevik Revolution. Under Communism, the artists who masterfully created these works of art were no longer allowed to paint religious themes because atheism had become the "religion" of the State.

Because these artists still possessed their amazing talent and desired to continue creating these magnificent boxes, they stopped painting religious iconography and began painting fairytales instead. They continued to work in the same artistic style, but new subjects began to appear on the boxes. In addition to painting scenes from popular fables or painting depictions of mythical characters, these artists were commissioned to paint pictorials of the revolution, Soviet labor, industrial giants, and Communist party leaders. So these gifted artists didn't stop *painting*; they simply stopped painting the truth!

Every time I look at one of these boxes in our home, I think of a generation of artists that changed — and I also think of a generation of God-called ministers, many of whom the Bible says *will* change. Having once preached the truth, they will begin preaching something other than the pure truth they once ministered.

The creators of those old lacquer boxes kept practicing their art, but they changed and began to do it differently. Similarly, the Bible prophesies that some ministers in the last days will keep practicing their vocation, but they'll begin to do it differently. They'll possess the same God-given gifts, talents, anointing, and calling they always had — but because of people's "itching ears" (*see* 2 Timothy 4:3), these men and women of God will turn away their ears from the truth and will turn instead to fables, or *myths*.

Let's look first at First Timothy 1:3 — Paul's earlier warning to Timothy, his son in the faith: "As I besought thee to abide still at Ephesus, when I went into Macedonia, that thou mightest charge some that they teach no other doctrine."

The words "other doctrine" are especially significant. The word "doctrine" is the Greek word *heterodidaskalos*, which is a compound of the words *heteros* and *didaskalos*. The word *heteros* means *of a different kind*. The word *didaskalos* means *teaching*. So when these two words are compounded, it means *teachings of a different kind* — indicating *incorrect teaching*. When Paul made this charge to Timothy, he was in essence saying, "...That you might charge some that they not engage or participate in *teaching of a different kind*."

Well, what about this "teaching of a different kind"? It was teaching, all right. In fact, it sounded so much on the surface like real Bible teaching that Paul used the word from the Greek *didaskalos* — the Greek word for "doctrine" — to describe it. So it sounded like doctrine, but Paul was warning Timothy to *listen carefully* — because this teaching had a different ring to it. It was doctrine *of a different kind*. It had been twisted and altered from its original state.

In First Timothy 1:4-6, Paul continued, "Neither give heed to *fables* and endless genealogies, which minister questions, rather than godly edifying which is in faith: so do. Now the end of the commandment is charity out of a pure heart, and of a good conscience, and of faith unfeigned." Then in verse 6, he said, "From which some having swerved have turned aside unto vain jangling."

The word "swerved" in this verse comes from the Greek word *astocheo*, which means *to miss the mark* or *to deviate from truth*. So if a minister has swerved from preaching correct doctrine, it means he or she is not hitting the target any longer. The words "turned aside" are translated from the Greek word *ektrepo*, a medical term that describes *a bone out of joint*. If you've ever had a bone out of joint, you know firsthand that the experience is a very *painful* one!

Similarly, Paul was telling us that when a minister swerves and turns aside from truth — teaching something other than the truth he previously taught — it's like a bone that's out of joint. And just as a bone that's out of joint affects the whole body, naturally speaking, when a minister gets out of joint with his doctrine, it affects the entire local body that he is a part of.

So many are hungry for the pure teaching of God's Word but they're not receiving it because much of the solid teaching that was taught to earlier generations has been replaced by motivational sermons — or *teaching of a different kind*. But when the Bible is taught correctly, it has a sobering effect on people. It helps them keep their own heads on straight. It helps them win in the circumstances of life and to bear fruit to the glory of God. And it stabilizes them in times of great instability and uncertainty.

Especially because we live in the last days when the Holy Spirit prophesied that some leaders would go astray in their doctrine, we must pray for God to raise up skilled, solid Bible teachers who will feed the pure Word of God to people whose hearts are crying out for it. God's people need good teaching, so let's be united in prayer for God-sent leaders who will not twist or alter what the Bible says in order to appease a crowd with "itching ears." Let's pray for bold preachers who will refuse to revert to motivational messages instead of preaching the Word of truth. Nothing is more powerful than truth, mixed with the anointing of the Holy Spirit.

That's what I think of when I look at the black lacquered boxes that we have on display in our home in Moscow. I keep them in view as a beautiful reminder that I am never to deviate from the original call of God on my life or from putting out a sound message that has the power to transform people's lives!

MY PRAYER FOR TODAY

Heavenly Father, I know that we are living in the last days. I ask You to help me keep my head on straight when it comes to the preaching and teaching of the Bible. This is a day when truth is being traded for motivational messages, and many in the Church don't even know the basic tenets of the faith anymore. I ask You to help me stay on track with solid Bible teaching. Keep me rooted and grounded in the Word of God, I present myself to You to use as a source of strong teaching for people who are new in the Lord or who are simply hungry for deeper and balanced teaching!

I pray this in Jesus' name!

MY CONFESSION FOR TODAY

I confess that I have been taught the Word of God and that I stand on a strong, stable doctrinal foundation. My spiritual senses are so exercised that I am able to discern true teaching from myth-like teaching. My heart goes out to those who are not able to discern the difference, and I will do everything in my ability to help put people on a strong doctrinal foundation that will hold them up in the times ahead. I am thankful for the Word of God that has been placed in my life. I honor it. I cherish it. And I accept the responsibility to help share it with others.

I declare this by faith in Jesus' name!

QUESTIONS FOR YOU TO CONSIDER

1. Where did you receive your doctrinal foundation? Who taught you the basic doctrines and tenets of the Christian faith? Do you value what they taught you — and have you ever taken the time to personally thank those people for placing you on such a rock-solid foundation?
2. Can you think of an example of a teaching that has heresy in it, but people at large have accepted it, because they don't have enough Bible teaching in their own lives to be able to discern the difference between good and bad spiritual food? What is an example that quickly comes to your mind?
3. Have you been accused of being spiritually "stuck" because you don't go with every wind of doctrine that blows through the Church? When Paul talks about enduring afflictions from other believers (*see* 2 Corinthians 11:26), do you understand what he is talking about? Have you ever experienced that from other Christians?

OCTOBER 16

Do What Is Honorable to the Name of Jesus Christ

Now I pray to God that you do no evil,
not that we should appear approved, but that you
should do what is honorable....
— 2 Corinthians 13:7 *NKJV*

It is a sad reality that some Christians have earned bad reputations for being dishonest. As a result of their dishonest, dishonorable words and actions, others were negatively affected.

The truth is, we have a God-given responsibility to hold up the name of Jesus in all our words and our deeds. Our lives should demonstrate that we are honest and that we do those things that are honorable to Jesus' name. This is why Paul wrote to the Corinthians, "...I pray to God that you do no evil, not that we should appear approved, but that you should do what is honorable..." (2 Corinthians 13:7 *NKJV*).

Over the years in our ministry, Denise and I have had our "fair share" of dealing with dishonest Christians as we've pressed forward to take new territory for the Kingdom of God. It is amazing how such individuals can smile with so much enthusiasm and glee while knowing in their hearts that they're scheming to do something dishonest. Thankfully, this group of people constitutes a *minority* of believers — yet this small minority can leave a bad taste in one's mouth and have a widespread negative effect, especially if the person they've wounded tells others about the ordeal.

In moments when we experience the unpleasantness of someone's dishonorable behavior, it would be wise for us to remember that even Jesus had an insincere person — Judas Iscariot — on His team. So it should not surprise us if we occasionally experience a disappointing personal encounter with a fellow Christian. From time to time, it simply happens — and when it does, we must forgive and move on without spreading the bad news to others whom it will disappoint and hurt. Only those who are in authority need to be informed when such an event occurs.

If this happens to you, I advise you not to slip into a mode of judging those who let you down. They may simply be believers whose minds are not yet renewed to truth and right behavior. Down the road in their Christian walk, after God works in their hearts and minds, they may repent and come back to ask your forgiveness. So when you have a disappointing experience with a fellow Christian, it's vital that you keep your own heart free of judgment and bitterness. Instead of letting that bad experience get the best of you, focus on your own actions and make sure that *you* are not among those who portray a bad image of believers in Jesus Christ!

As Paul closed his second letter to the Corinthians, he told them, "Now I pray to God that you do no evil...but that you should do that which is honorable..." (2 Corinthians 13:7 *NKJV*). In light of today's conversation so far, let's look a little deeper at this verse.

The words "now I" are a translation of the Greek word *echometha*, which would be better translated, "Now we...." It tells us that this was not the prayer request of Paul singularly — rather, his entire apostolic team was praying for honorable behavior among the readers of the apostle's letter. As a city, Corinth had a bad reputation for being swindlers and cheaters. Paul's entire company was concerned about the behavior of the Corinthian believers. And they prayed against it, believing that the Christians in Corinth would conduct their lives in a way that reflected integrity, honesty, and honor.

Paul wrote specifically that they prayed the Corinthians would "do no evil." The word "evil" is from the word *kakos* — a word that describes something that brings harm and thus produces bitterness in the recipient or recipients of the evil actions or conduct. *Kakos* denotes something that is unfair, unjust, or destructive — thus, as noted, the result of this kind of behavior leaves a bitter taste in the mouth of the one to whom the "evil" was done.

In Greek, when Paul wrote the words "do no evil," he used a strong form of the word "no"— meaning he was giving a very *strong prohibition* against those "evil" kinds of actions and activities. This tells us that Paul was not making a mere suggestion; he was giving a command to his readers to come up higher in their motives and actions.

For the believer, Paul simply left no room and no excuse for a lack of integrity. Likewise, the Holy Spirit is speaking to us today through this verse, telling us that we must also do nothing that is deliberately or knowingly wrong — or that would cause embitterment in another person. Instead, Paul commanded us, "...That you should do what is honorable..." (2 Corinthians 13:7 *NKJV*).

The word "do" is a form of the Greek word *poieo*, which carries the idea of *creativity*. In other words, if finding a way to do something right, good, fair, and honorable doesn't come to you easily, ask the Holy Spirit to help you get creative about ways to do what is helpful and beneficial to others.

The *King James Version* translates the word "honorable" as "honest." The word "honest" is from the Greek word *kalos*, and it describes something that is done *with good in mind* or *in a noble or honorable way*. It denotes something that is *unblemished* and *pure*. We might say that *kalos* carries the idea of actions that are *ethical*, *principled*, *morally correct*, *upright*, or *full of integrity. Kalos* denotes *the highest and finest kind of aspiration* — the desire to do something in the *most correct* and *honest* manner.

In summation, the Holy Spirit — speaking through the apostle Paul — pleads with us to do that which is honest, honorable, and good. He strongly urges us never to deliberately do anything that would cause hurt to others. In fact, He warns us that there is no place for this type of behavior in the life of a committed Christian. We must constantly remember that what we do reflects on the good name of Jesus. If we're tempted to do something that lacks integrity, we need to pull back, repent, and ask the Holy Spirit to help us speak the truth and to do what is just, fair, helpful, and beneficial to those who could be affected by our actions.

I urge you to read the questions that follow and sincerely ask if there is any area of your life that needs to be changed concerning showing honor to Jesus' name. The Holy Spirit is right there inside you to open your eyes to anything that needs to be corrected. He simply needs a heart that is willing to see the truth and to respond to what He shows you and tells you to do. Open your heart and let the Holy Spirit help you. Refuse to do *anything* that is morally or ethically questionable. Allow Him to help you set your heart on behaving uprightly in your words and deeds.

MY PRAYER FOR TODAY

Holy Spirit, after reading today's Sparkling Gem, I am more determined than ever before to yield to You — the Spirit of Truth — in every area of my life. I commit to be honest and forthcoming in all my dealings with people in my life. If I've ever caused harm to a fellow Christian or hurt the reputation of Jesus' name, I ask You for forgiveness. As I look back on my life, I can't think of a time when I've done this intentionally. But perhaps I have a poor memory. So just in case I've been guilty in some way of dishonoring the name of Jesus or grieving the Person of the Holy Spirit by my poor actions and behavior, I repent and ask You to forgive me so the slate will be clear in my life!

I pray this in Jesus' name!

MY CONFESSION FOR TODAY

I declare that I will not be involved in any type of sinful shenanigans that would hurt the testimony of Jesus' name or that would cause people to retreat from fellowshipping with His Church. I will walk worthily of the calling that has been given to me. I will walk in integrity and be forthright, even if it costs me personally to be honest and truthful. I declare that I will not deliberately do evil to anyone, but I make it my aim to represent the Lord Jesus Christ in a noble and honorable manner in all things!

I declare this by faith in Jesus' name!

QUESTIONS FOR YOU TO CONSIDER

1. Can you think of a time when some fellow believer did some questionable things that hurt his or her Christian testimony? When was that? In the end, what happened? Were people hurt by this person's lack of Christian integrity?
2. Has there been a time in your own life when you acted manipulatively to get what you wanted? Were you truthful, or did you twist the facts and the story, in order to gain some kind of advantage? Did the Holy Spirit convict you that this was wrong? Did you ever go back to those individuals with whom you were dishonest and ask them for forgiveness?
3. Can you recall someone who was spiritually damaged because of something a Christian did that was full of dishonesty and ulterior motives? Did that person who was hurt write everyone else off because of that one experience? Have you ever done anything to attempt to restore that believer back into fellowship with a church?

The Holy Spirit is right there inside you to open your eyes to anything that needs to be corrected. He simply needs a heart that is willing to see the truth and to respond to what He shows you and tells you to do.

OCTOBER 17

THE CROSS! Foolishness or the Power of God?

"For the preaching of the cross is to them that perish foolishness;
but unto we which are saved it is the power of God."
— 1 Corinthians 1:18

Since Jesus rose from the dead, different people have responded differently to the preaching of the Cross. Some reject it, while others receive the message by faith and thus experience the power of God. Paul referred to this dichotomy of response when he wrote, "For the preaching of the cross is to them that perish foolishness; but unto we which are saved it is the power of God" (1 Corinthians 1:18).

The word "foolishness" in this verse is from the word *moria*, which means *foolish*, *stupid*, or *unintelligent* and describes *unacceptable behavior, thought, or speech*. From this word *moria*, we derive the word *moron*. To the Greek and Roman mind, to believe in Christ and in His Cross *alone* as the way to salvation was the belief of a *moron*. This kind of exclusive and "narrow" behavior, thought, or speech was simply unacceptable. When confronted with the message of the Gospel, a pagan of that time would have forthrightly exclaimed, "It is *stupid, unintelligent,* and *unacceptable* to believe that Jesus is the *only* way to God."

Paul continued in First Corinthians 1:18, saying, "...Unto we which are saved *it is the power of God*." The word "power" is the Greek word *dunamis*, which is most often used in ancient literature to depict *military might* or *the ability to conquer*. In fact, it is used 210 times in the New Testament to denote *strength* and *conquering ability*. For those who don't believe in Jesus and have never experienced the delivering and conquering power of the Gospel, this message may seem to be foolishness. But those who have repented and have entered into covenant with Jesus Christ know the delivering, conquering power of these mighty words. It is no foolishness to the redeemed — *it is the lifesaving power of God*!

In the early days of the Church, the message of the Cross — backed with the power of the Spirit — produced life wherever it found open hearts to receive its eternal truth. It ignited new birth in the hearts of men, broke the yoke of spiritual bondage off of people's lives, brought healing to bodies and minds ravaged by sickness and disease, and delivered people of defiling demonic influences from their previous pagan environment.

There was, there is, and there always will be wonder-working power in the message of the Cross. It may seem primitive or foolish to those who do not believe — but to those of us who are saved, this is the power of God unto salvation. For us, it is clear: There is salvation in no other.

Jesus is the *only* name given to man by which we can be saved (*see* Acts 4:12). The Cross is still the power of salvation to those who believe!

MY PRAYER FOR TODAY

Heavenly Father, I am thankful for the life-saving, transforming power of the Cross of Christ. Thank You for sending Jesus to die on that Cross to pay the price for my freedom. Thank You that the Holy Spirit opened my spiritual ears to hear and that my heart believed the message. I gratefully rejoice that the Cross is still the power of God to us who believe.

I pray this in Jesus' name!

MY CONFESSION FOR TODAY

I confess that my life has been changed by the power of Jesus Christ and His death on the Cross. That Cross has become the wisdom and power of God to me. Because of the Cross, I am freed from sin, bondage, sickness, and disease. It has been, is now, and will always be the power of God to me and to all those who believe. I am not ashamed of the Gospel of Jesus Christ that proclaims the power of the Cross. I am attentive and available to the Spirit of God so He can use me as He desires — both to proclaim and to demonstrate the power of the Cross so that men may receive the saving knowledge of its truth!

I declare this by faith in Jesus' name!

QUESTIONS FOR YOU TO CONSIDER

1. Do you remember the first time you heard the message of the Cross preached? Where were you, who preached it, and what effect did it have upon you?
2. In what ways has your life been changed since you first heard the message of the Cross, and the power of Christ was released in you? Do you continue to meditate upon what Christ accomplished for you through His death, burial, and resurrection?
3. Do you know anyone who thinks the message of the Cross is foolishness? Do you pray for that person's eyes to be opened to the truth?

In the early days of the Church,
the message of the Cross —
backed with the power of the Spirit —
produced life wherever it found open hearts
to receive its eternal truth.

OCTOBER 18

What Impression Do You Leave With Others?

Look not every man on his own things,
but every man also on the things of others.
— Philippians 2:4

As a pastor, one of the saddest realizations I've had to face over the years is that many people think of themselves disproportionately more than they think of anyone else. They are often self-consumed, but they don't even realize it. They think of themselves, talk about themselves, worry about themselves, spend money on themselves, think and talk about their needs, and so on. They don't *deliberately* act this way; they are simply *self-absorbed.* In fact, I can't imagine anyone acting like that on purpose! To be perfectly honest, this kind of attitude and behavior is so repulsive that I find myself trying to run from such individuals because I just don't want to get caught up in a conversation with them.

I'm not talking only about church members; some of the most self-consumed people I've ever met have been in the ministry. It shouldn't be that way — but often it is the case. They want to tell you all about their ministry, their outreaches, and everything else great that they are doing. What's so sad is that these same people often never ask a single question of the person they're talking to in order to know more about him or her. It's usually a one-sided conversation about what matters to *them* — because that is who is uppermost on their hearts and minds: *themselves.*

It doesn't take too long to figure out when you're with that kind of person, because the person's mouth quickly reveals the truth about what is in "the abundance of their hearts" (*see* Matthew 12:34). Even as I write this, specific individuals come to mind. When I see them, I immediately begin to look for an exit or a way to avoid them — because I know that once they "capture" me, I'm going to be a prisoner to their conversation. They are so self-consumed that I can't even break into the conversation to say I need to be going for an appointment or previous engagement.

Often the conversation ends and these individuals have never asked a single question about what the Lord is doing in our lives or ministry — *except* to say, "Oh, I've talked the whole time and never let you tell me anything about what *you're* doing." And that's all right with me because I don't think they really cared, or they would have made room for it in the conversation.

Over the years, I've had to come face to face with the fact that there are just some people who are that way, and they seem to be *stuck* in that rut of self-absorption. I'm not being critical or judgmental; I'm simply making a sad observation that's forthright and honest. Some people are simply all about themselves with seemingly no capacity or ability to leave room in their lives for others. Even if the other party *tried* to interject something about himself in the conversation with people who fit this description, they wouldn't listen very deeply because their thoughts are too involved with themselves.

It is unfortunate that this kind of behavior should exist in the Christian community, because we, more than any other group of people on earth, should *live* to know more about others and how to serve others. If we are totally consumed with ourselves, we are missing the point of the Christian life in a very big way.

The apostle Paul must have faced this same disappointing experience with people, because when he wrote Philippians 2:4, he referred to this type of behavior among believers and urged them to put a stop to it. He said, "Look not every man on his own things, but every man also on the things of others." The original Greek is very strong and should be taken as a prohibition!

The word "look" is the present active participle of the word *skopeo*. The word *skopeo* means to *intensely focus* on something. In this case, Paul was talking about people who were completely fixated on themselves. But he forbade them to act like this, and that's why he used a negative prohibition in conjunction with it. It's just not right for Christians to be so self-absorbed that they focus only on themselves and never ask a thing or pose a care about anyone else. And I'll tell you the truth — people will generally try to avoid dealing with this particular character defect. They'll try to run from it!

That's why Paul continued to say, "Look not every man on his own things...." The words "every man" is the Greek word *hekastos*, which literally means *every man* — no one excluded. In other words, regardless of who you are or how much you've done with your life, it's wrong to be so completely self-absorbed that all you can see is yourself and your own deeds and needs.

This applies to *everyone*! Thus, this verse should be taken as a *rebuke* to those who constantly focus on and talk only about themselves. And it serves as an *encouragement* to get our eyes off ourselves and to remember to think of others and to show concern about them too.

Paul continued, "...But every man also on the things of others." Notice Paul began with "but every man *also*." This is a transition that emphatically tells the reader that it is right to also focus on others — on things besides himself and his own interests.

The words "every man" is the same word *hekastos*, meaning *every man with no one excluded.* A more literal translation would read, "*But let every single one of you....*" Then Paul added to his inspired instruction, saying that we should focus "...also on the things of others." Rather than focus on ourselves, *every single one of us* should be focused intensely on the things of others!

The words "the things" in this verse is the Greek word *ta*, which means the *things* of others — and that would include *anything* that the other person involved in a social setting wanted to share. However, the problem often is that the other person never gets an opportunity to talk because the one who is so self-focused absorbs all the time there is to talk and to share. Then when it's time to part, there is no mutual caring or sharing because one person dominated the whole conversation.

This is extremely selfish and often hurtful to the "captive" member who was overlooked in the conversation.

Paul was grateful for his relationships with Timothy, Luke, Epaphroditus, and other members of his team who genuinely cared for him. He listened to them, and they likewise listened to *him*. There was a mutual sharing and caring between them. I, too, am thankful for the people in my life who want to hear what I think and feel — and they know I genuinely want to hear what they think and feel as well.

Self-centeredness is easily detectable, because such people usually don't maintain long-term friendships. The truth is, others can smell the odor of self-consumed focus in their every word, and it's an invisible stench that repels.

If you've ever been trapped in a conversation with a person like this, you know exactly what it's like to wish you could somehow escape! But rather than focus on the misdeeds of others, let's all look in the mirror and make sure that *we* do not fall into this self-absorbed category of people that we're talking about today.

When we leave a person and a conversation, let's endeavor to leave the fragrance of Christ's love in our wake. Let's make it a goal to leave that conversation knowing that we did our best to get better acquainted with that person's heart and to discover more of the Father's heart for his or her life. Let's deliberately show those we speak with the attention they deserve and leave them wondering why we never have much to say about ourselves! *I think that is what Jesus would do!*

MY PRAYER FOR TODAY

Heavenly Father, how many times have my thoughts, words, and actions been focused on me, my problems, or my preferences? Whether I did this privately or even more regrettably with others, I repent for such selfishness. Father, my utmost desire is to reflect You to others, just as Jesus did when He walked on the earth. You are Love, my Father. Therefore, I ask You to help me leave the undeniable fragrance of Your goodness and love upon every life that I touch.

I pray this in Jesus' name!

MY CONFESSION FOR TODAY

I confess that the love of God is shed abroad in my heart by the Spirit of God who dwells within me. Therefore, I am not haughty, arrogant, conceited, or inflated with pride because I walk in humility, patience, and kindness that God's own loving nature reproduces in me. I choose to walk in God's love, and that sets me free from fear, which includes carnal craving for self-exaltation, self-protection, self-promotion, and any attitude that exalts fleshly preference above godly character and priorities. When others leave my presence, they sense that God's love has encouraged and lifted them higher than they were before. And when I encounter people who are so self-absorbed that they cannot see beyond themselves, God's love shines so brightly through me that their hearts are touched and stirred to seek Jesus more deeply and to be like Him.

I declare this by faith in Jesus' name!

QUESTIONS FOR YOU TO CONSIDER

1. Have you ever been trapped in a conversation you couldn't seem to get out of — being dominated by a person who talked incessantly about himself or herself?
2. When you leave a person, do you know more about that individual, or did he or she only hear about you and what you were doing in life?
3. How do you think Jesus behaved when He was with people? Did He show interest in them or talk only about Himself?

OCTOBER 19

The Queen of All Virtues

But let *patience* have her perfect work....
— James 1:4

Today I want to talk to you again about *patience*. Early Church leaders called this remarkable godly trait the "queen of all virtues." They understood that if you had patience, it was never a question of whether or not you would win a battle — it was only a matter of *when* you would win it.

That is a true statement that is borne out in Scripture, and Denise and I have certainly proven the spiritual effectiveness of patience in our own lives and ministry. I've said so many times that the Greek word for "patience" is one of my favorite words in the New Testament! How we all need this extraordinary quality working in our lives today.

Let's look at this word "patience" to see why Early Church leaders valued this characteristic so highly.

As we have seen, the word "patience" comes from the Greek word *hupomeno*, a compound of the words *hupo* and *meno*. The word *hupo* means *under*, as to be *underneath* something that is very heavy. The word *meno* means *to stay* or *to abide*. It describes *a resolute decision to remain in one's spot*; *to keep a position*; or *to maintain territory that has been gained*. But when the words *hupo* and *meno* are compounded to form the word *hupomeno*, the new word portrays *a person who is under some type of heavy load, but who refuses to stray from his position because he is committed to his task*. Regardless of how heavy the load, how fierce the opposition, how intense the stress, or how much weight is thrown against him, this person is inwardly resolved that he is *not* going to move. He is committed to stay put, and he will never surrender for any reason.

In the earliest years of the Church, believers faced long periods of unremitting persecution. They were confronted by a host of hostile powers that were arrayed against them. The pervading immoral culture, pagan religions, secular government, unsaved family and friends — all of these external forces put constant pressure on the early believers to forfeit their faith and return to their old ways.

But the early believers firmly believed that if they had *hupomeno*, they would survive and outlast all the opposition. This is why they referred to this spiritual characteristic as the "queen of all virtues." It was believed that if Christians possessed this one virtue, they could survive anything that came against them. Believers understood that if *hupomeno* was operational in their lives, the question was no longer *if* they would overcome their battles, but rather *when* that victory would come.

The sense of determination inherent in the word *hupomeno* is clearly seen when it is used in a military sense to portray soldiers who were ordered to maintain their positions, even in the face of fierce combat. Their order was *to stand their ground and defend every inch of territory that had been gained.* To do that, the soldiers resolved to courageously do whatever was required to fulfill the assignment — *no matter how difficult the challenge.* Their goal was to see that they survived every attack and held their position until they had outlasted the resistance. These soldiers had to indefinitely and defiantly stick it out until the enemy, realizing the soldiers couldn't be beaten, therefore decided to give up and retreat. Thus, the word *hupomeno* conveys the idea of being *steadfast, consistent, unwavering,* and *unflinching.*

The *King James Version* translates the Greek word *hupomeno* as "patience," but a more accurate rendering of this word would be *endurance.* A good way to translate this word *hupomeno* in modern terms is *staying power* or *hang-in-there power.* Both of these interpretations correctly express the concept behind *hupomeno,* because it is the attitude that *hangs in there, never gives up, refuses to surrender to obstacles, and turns down every opportunity to quit.*

If a person has *hupomeno* working in his life, it means he is committed to standing by his faith, his task, or a principle of truth, regardless of the price to be paid. This person possesses a steadfast, tenacious attitude that refuses to crumble or concede to defeat. Nothing can change his mind or sway his determination to maintain his position — not external circumstances, other people's words, or any other attempt to manipulate or change his stance.

Likewise, for you to survive the seemingly unremitting pressure and opposition that Satan or life itself wages against *you,* it is essential for you to have *hupomeno* — that persistent, steadfast, tenacious spirit that refuses to crumble or concede to defeat. If you possess this quality, you will not surrender in the face of pressure or capitulate to the forces that attempt to stamp you out. It may seem like you are facing the impossible, but if you refuse to budge or give an inch, the opposition will eventually move off — and you will score a major victory in your fight of faith!

MY PRAYER FOR TODAY

Father, I draw upon the might of Your invincible life within me, and I ask You to help me cultivate Your character trait of this never-give-up kind patient endurance in my life. Help me rely upon and release the power of the Holy Spirit so that I do not bend or surrender in the face of pressure — or capitulate to the forces that have tried to conquer me. I ask You, Holy Spirit, to infuse me with Your mighty power in my inner man so that I will be strong and enduring. Fill me with Your staying power — Your divine hang-in-there power — to outlast the odds and to eventually win the battle that has been arrayed against me. It's just a matter of time until the opposition folds and goes away, but I need patience to stay in the fight until that glorious moment of victory occurs. I receive Your help today!

I pray this in Jesus' name!

MY CONFESSION FOR TODAY

By faith, I declare that I have the inner fortitude to outlast every skirmish that the enemy has tried to array against my life. Because the Holy Spirit is inside me, I am tougher than any circumstances I face. I do not bend. I do not break. The Lord is my Strength and my impenetrable Shield; therefore, I do not yield to the pressures that try to move me from His promises for my life. Patience works in me — and that means I have been fortified with God's very own hang-in-there power that never surrenders an inch of what He has promised to me.

I declare this by faith in Jesus' name!

QUESTIONS FOR YOU TO CONSIDER

1. Can you recall a time in your life when you won a battle simply because you were patient and lasted longer than the attack?
2. When the pressure let up and you finally won that particular fight, were you glad that you hadn't thrown in the towel and quit?
3. What battles are you facing right now that will require you to exercise patience until you win?

To survive the seemingly unremitting pressure
and opposition that Satan or life itself
wages against you, it is essential
for you to have HUPOMENO *—*
that persistent, steadfast, tenacious spirit
that refuses to crumble
or concede to defeat.

OCTOBER 20

Is It Time for a Personal Evaluation?

For unto every one that hath shall be given,
and he shall have abundance:
but from him that hath not shall be taken away
even that which he hath.
— Matthew 25:29

A business consultant who gave high-dollar lectures to large companies once asked me, "Rick, how are you able to accomplish all that you do in your ministry? It seems like God keeps handing new assignments to you."

I was blessed by this man's view of our ministry, as he was a very serious businessman who had seen a lot over the course of his career. As I pondered his compliment, I was reminded of Jesus' teaching in Matthew 25:29, which says, "For unto every one that hath shall be given, and he shall have abundance: but from him that hath not shall be taken away even that which he hath." The word "abundance" in this verse is the Greek word *perisseuo*, which means *to abound* or *to have something in excess*. In some places in the Greek New Testament, it carries the ideas of *something that is given generously* or *something that is overflowing, plentiful, or even superabundant.*

As I look back on all our years of ministry, I believe the word "abundance" perfectly describes the many assignments that God has given me. When it seems there is no more in us to take on new assignments, that is often when God opens a marvelous new door and beckons us to walk through it. These past adventures of faith and obedience have built a strong foundation for our ministry, which enables us to do more and more with the help of our well-trained team. Although there is still much room for growth, the strides we've made over the years in our personal lives, in our spiritual walks, and in the structure of our organization have put us on solid ground and demonstrated to the Lord that we are capable of doing more. So "more" is exactly what the Lord continues to give us!

In Matthew 25:29, Jesus teaches that how you perform in your current endeavor determines whether or not God gives you greater, more significant responsibilities in the future. God is watching you right now to see if you will prove yourself faithful in your present task because it shows Him whether or not you can be trusted with a big promotion. *Your future is contingent on your attitude and job performance in the present!*

Therefore, it's important that you take a thorough look at yourself and honestly evaluate your condition. Ask yourself the following questions:

- *Am I giving my present job 100 percent of my effort?*
- *If I was looking for someone to fill a position of great responsibility, would I want to hire someone who has my attitude and work ethic?*
- *Do I finish projects, or do I drop the ball along the way?*
- *Can I be trusted with money?*
- *Do I handle my money in a way that shows I appreciate its value and power?*
- *Does my life and attitude reflect the qualities that would make God want to choose me?*

Your honest answers to these questions should help you determine whether or not you are the kind of person to whom God wants to give additional responsibilities in the future. Don't despair if your answers are less than satisfactory. Simply determine to make necessary adjustments in your life and become the kind of person God looks for when He needs someone to fulfill an assignment from Heaven!

One thing is certain: God does not choose lazy people who sit around doing nothing. Think about it. Why would He call someone to do *His* work when that person hasn't successfully done his or her own work?

There is not a single example in Scripture of God *significantly* using a person who was idly sitting around and wasting time when He called them. All the men and women of God in the Bible were already busy doing something when God spoke to them.

Consider Jesus' parable in Matthew 25:14-30, which tells of the master who gave talents to three of his servants. Jesus says that when the master returned from his long trip, he expected to see *increase* and *productivity* as a result of his gifts. The two servants who were faithful and worked hard were richly rewarded. However, Jesus describes the servant who brought no increase or productivity as "unprofitable." The Greek word for "unprofitable" is *achreios*, which means *useless.* It is the picture of a person who contributes so little that he is essentially *worthless*, and it reveals a lot about how Jesus views lazy people.

Through this parable, Jesus teaches that faithfulness and hard work is commendable in the Kingdom of God. When God needs someone to do something for Him, He looks for hard-working, faithful, "use-what-they-have" individuals who have already demonstrated worth. These people already know how to handle money; they know how to work; and they know how to stick with the job until it's done. Maybe they are still growing in these areas, but they have done enough to demonstrate to God that they can be trusted with more.

The Bible is loaded with examples of men and women of God who exude these qualities. The following list provides a few examples of strategic, well-known, key Bible personalities who were *already* successful *before* God called them, and there are many, many more found in Scripture.

- *Noah* was successful and righteous *before* he was called to build the ark.
- *Abraham* was successful and rich *before* God called him to become the father of faith.

- *Joshua* was successful as Moses' associate *before* God called him to be the leader of Israel.
- *Gideon* was successful as a leader *before* God called him to lead the Israelite armies.
- *David* was successful as a shepherd *before* God called him to be the king of Israel.
- *Daniel* was successful in Nebuchadnezzar's court and walked in integrity *before* God called him to be a prophet.
- *Matthew* was successful as a tax collector *before* Jesus called him to be His disciple.
- *Peter* was a successful fisherman and businessman *before* Jesus called him to be His disciple.
- *Luke* was a successful doctor *before* he was called into the ministry.
- *Paul* was a successful politician and religious leader *before* God called him into the apostolic ministry.
- *Timothy* was successful as Paul's associate and disciple *before* he became the pastor of the church of Ephesus.

This is just a small, representative list of the many similar cases I could show you from both the Old and New Testaments. God called these individuals because they had already proved their work ethic through their previous endeavors. By observation, He knew each of them could be trusted with a greater assignment.

You might try to put together a list of people who were doing *nothing* when God chose them for a big assignment. If you do, I believe you'll have a very difficult time assimilating such a list. I actually tried once to compile one, and I couldn't think of anyone who was used significantly by God but was doing nothing when He called him.

Maybe you think you have enough on your plate already, and that may be a fair point. But know that when God finds someone faithful, He likes to give that person more responsibility because He knows He's finally found someone He can trust. Therefore, don't be too surprised if more is given to you in "abundance." Just consider it the harvest of faithfulness and a demonstration of God's trust in you!

I encourage you today to conduct a deliberate self-evaluation to see how you're doing in your walk with God and where you need to grow and change. As God observes your willingness to yield to the necessary process of preparation, He will know when you are ready for more.

MY PRAYER FOR TODAY

Father, I pray that You will help me honestly evaluate myself and my performance. Even more, I ask for Your grace to help me see where I need to change. I receive Your empowerment to make the necessary adjustments so You can trust me with more responsibility. In those areas where I have not done well, I ask You to forgive me, and I receive Your forgiveness. With the power of the Holy Spirit and my decision to change, I believe that I'll make forward progress in my life and that You will put more on my plate because You've seen that I am faithful with what I'm doing right now.

I pray this in Jesus' name!

MY CONFESSION FOR TODAY

I confess that I am faithful with what God assigned me to do right now. God is watching me; He is evaluating my performance; and He sees that I am doing the best I can with the knowledge and experience that I possess. I confess that I am willing to grow and change in the areas where I have not done well. I refuse to shut my eyes to the truth, and I will be honest with myself about the areas I need to change. God's Spirit is helping me — and with His help, I will become a vessel that God knows He can depend on and use.

I declare this by faith in Jesus' name!

QUESTIONS FOR YOU TO CONSIDER

1. Take a moment to think about people whom God called upon to do great things. Can you think of any who were doing nothing at the time that God called them?
2. Based on the conclusion that God gives more to people who are doing well with what he has already given them to do, how do you evaluate yourself? Are you a candidate to whom God would consider giving more responsibility?
3. As you evaluate yourself honestly, what are the areas that you know need to change?

OCTOBER 21

Stop Murmuring and Disputing With God When He's Trying To Change You!

For it is God which worketh in you both
to will and to do of his good pleasure. Do all things
without murmurings and disputings.
— Philippians 2:13,14

Would you like to see some real, deep changes occur in your character and behavior? Maybe you've tried to do it on your own, but feel you have failed time after time. Well, today we will look at Philippians 2:13, which emphatically tells us that God is not only interested in helping us change, but it is His express will to take what we are and make us better!

Philippians 2:13 says, "For it is God which worketh in you both to will and to do of his good pleasure." Let's begin by looking at that word "worketh" before we go any further, for it is a Greek word that will make you want to shout with a voice of victory if you really understand and embrace it!

The word "worketh" is the Greek word *energeo* — the word from which we get our word *energy*. In Greek, however, it describes much more than that. It means *the divine energy put forth to effectually bring forth a tangible, noticeable change*. Plus, Paul writes it as a present active participle, which means this word describes the unequivocal will of God to put forth power *constantly, in every moment, active at every second* that will change our character and behavior *permanently*.

Of course, God is thrilled when we come to Christ just as we are, but He is not satisfied that we *stay* the way we are when we first come to Him! Furthermore, God knows that we cannot change ourselves. So the moment we surrender to the Lordship of Christ, it triggers a release of power — a supernatural flow of divine energy to bring forth changes that make us more like Him!

In fact, the verse continues to say that it is His "good pleasure" to do this in us. The words "good pleasure" are translated from the word *eudokia*, which is a compound of the words *eu* and *dokia*. The word *eu* means depicts *a feeling of deep satisfaction* — and the word *dokia* is the word for God's *pleasure*.

Compounded into one word, the new word means it gives God the *deepest gratification* to take us with all our quirks, blemishes, and inconsistencies — the mess we were when we came to Christ — and unleash His divine *energeo* in order *to effectually and productively bring forth a tangible, noticeable change* in our lives that is *permanent*. And as I noted before, Paul writes this as a present active participle, which means God *in every moment* is releasing this divine power to change us. There's never a second that God isn't working deep in our hearts, souls, and character to bring us forth as more mature sons and daughters of God — to be more like Him.

We all have areas in which we need a character adjustment, and about which we often cry out in prayer for God to change us. To this prayer, God gladly complies and expends a flow of supernatural power to change us. But when He begins to work deeply in our character to bring about those much-needed changes, that is often when our flesh begins to murmur and dispute with God. While we cry out for permanent change, our flesh doesn't enjoy what God has to do to change us!

I could give many examples of how the flesh starts to grumble when God goes to work to change it, but for the sake of space and time, let me give you just three examples that you'll clearly understand.

Consider the process that people have to go through when they have been a gossip who run their mouths about other people all the time and God's power inside goes to work to teach and train them to keep their mouths shut. They have been in the habit of gossiping and being busybodies for a long time. Now suddenly God is telling them, "Keep your mouth shut and stay out of other people's business"!

Obeying that command can be a difficult thing for people like that to do. In fact, it can be so difficult that the flesh may rebel at first — and perhaps even for a long time. The power that is trying to effect a deep and permanent character change is working — but rather than be compliant, those individuals may be tempted to murmur and even dispute with God about how hard it is to keep their mouths shut!

Or how about people who have been in the habit of overeating all their lives? Now God speaks to their hearts and says, *"Enough is enough. I am going to effect a change in this area of your life."*

At first, people may be thrilled that God is going to help them. But when the help begins and God says, "Shut the refrigerator, walk away, and don't take another bite," their flesh may recoil at what God is asking them to do. Their flesh screams for more and can even be manipulating in its attempts to get and have more — but they can sense that the Holy Spirit is firmly telling them, *"NO!"*

The fact is, God is releasing the power to effect the change that these individual have long desired. Compliance and obedience would actually make the process of change flow much smoother and be much easier. But the flesh puts up a fight and often even murmurs and disputes with God, making the change take longer and become more difficult.

Let's also use the example of people who don't know how to put away the credit cards but continue to *spend, spend, spend* even when their behavior places their financial life in jeopardy. Then they ask God to help them. Now "help" is there in the form of God's *divine energy* working inside them.

But the next time these individuals go shopping and the Spirit of God rises up like a standard against that bad habit, the flesh also tries to rise up. Flesh recoils at any form of newly imposed discipline!

The Holy Spirit gently but firmly tells these believers, *"You don't need this, and you don't need that — you don't need any of this. Put your credit cards away and go home."* But they resist what they know the Lord is speaking to their hearts. They may even begin to argue with Him. Once again, compliance and obedience would bring forth a quick transformation, but the flesh doesn't like to be told what to do.

It's interesting that the word "murmur" is the Greek word *goggusmos*, which is the expression of dissatisfaction, grumbling, or muttering negatively in a low tone of voice. In other words, your murmuring may not be an out-loud arguing with God. Rather, you may just harbor a silent resentment and resistance to what He is trying to do inside you.

The word "disputings" is the Greek word *dialogismos*, and it depicts an inward skepticism or inward criticism — a questioning of what is being demanded. It also depicts rebellion against God's work inside us. It is the very word that is used in the Old Testament Greek Septuagint to depict the rebellion of God's people against His commands.

- The fact is, the gossiper can stop gossiping.
- The overeater can stop overeating.
- The person who spends money irresponsibly can change his spending habits.
- WHATEVER the problem is, *it is subject to change.*

Why am I so confident that all of these issues you might have in your life — and other issues besides — are subject to change? Because it is God who "...worketh in you both to will and to do of his good pleasure" (Philippians 2:13). The power you need to change is already inside you, just waiting for your compliance and obedience. When you stop moaning and groaning and disputing with God — and you stop muttering in a low-toned voice against what He is asking you to do — you will be on your way to experiencing the *energeo* of God to assist you in whatever change you need to make. If you will surrender to the power that is at work in you at this very second, instead of putting up a fight, you can conquer any character flaw, and God's mighty power will *change* you to become more like Him!

So what are you going to do? If you have been muttering and rebelling at what God's power is resident in you to do, today is a fine day to surrender to that ever-present power and let the Holy Spirit transform you, set you free, and make you the person you always wanted to be!

MY PRAYER FOR TODAY

Father, as I surrender to the Lordship of Christ, my act of obedience triggers a release of power and a supernatural flow of divine energy to produce change and transformation until I am shaped into the image of Christ. Lord, I ask You to make my thoughts agreeable to Your will while Your mighty power is trying to effect a deep and permanent character change within me. I make a decision right now to be compliant and to obey You as You work in me by Your Spirit to make me be the person You created me to be!

I pray this in Jesus' name!

MY CONFESSION FOR TODAY

I confess that God is working in me to will and to do according to His good pleasure. The power I need to change is already inside me, just waiting for my compliance and obedience. When I stop moaning and muttering and disputing with God about what He is asking me to do, I see His hand at work in my life. When I stop putting up a fight and surrender to the power that is at work in me at this very second, I can conquer any character flaw as God's mighty power changes me to become more like Him.

I declare this by faith in Jesus' name!

QUESTIONS FOR YOU TO CONSIDER

1. Can you think of areas in your life where the Holy Spirit has been working in you to make some changes, but your flesh has been putting up a fight to resist His work?

2. Do you see more clearly that even though God has released His divine *energeo* — divine energy — to effectively and permanently change you, it still requires your compliance and obedience for His power to effectively operate in your life?
3. Can you name specific areas in your life where you have been murmuring and complaining about the changes God is requiring of you? If the answer is yes, are you able to explain to yourself why have you been making it more difficult for those needed changes to take place in your life?

OCTOBER 22

What Race Is God Asking You To Run?

"Being confident of this very thing,
that he which hath begun a good work in you
will perform it until the day of Jesus Christ."
— Philippians 1:6

After years of searching for a permanent location for the *Moscow Good News Church*, our ministry finally found a facility that would suit our needs — that is, it would meet our needs *after* total reconstruction. I put the vision before our church to purchase it, and we started to believe for the funds needed to acquire it and then totally renovate it.

I likened our situation to the Israelites' divine assignment to possess the Promised Land. Just as Joshua's spies outlined the obstacles they encountered when they came back from scouting out the land, I didn't hesitate to outline the challenges that lay before our congregation. I related the facts with clarity, but like Joshua and Caleb, I made it clear that God would give us victory over every obstacle or giant along the way. The issue was not how big the giants were; the matter revolved around God's faithfulness to perform His promises and our obedience to enter into and receive the promise He had given us.

The fact is, what we were stepping out by faith to do required God's supernatural blessing because completing this mammoth vision far surpassed our natural abilities. Yet we were certain this was God's plan. Therefore, we fixed our eyes on Jesus, and we were fully convinced that He would supernaturally enable us to accomplish this mighty deed. Then we jumped in to run that race of faith. With our eyes fixed solely on the prize, we committed to do what God had asked us to do and to not stop until we had reached the finish line.

This grand undertaking required every ounce of our *faith*, *strength*, and *might*. It demanded the highest level of faith for finances that Denise and I had ever released in our lives. It required our concentration and our intercession. However, we knew that God had watched us for years, and that He knew He could count on us or He wouldn't have entrusted us with such a magnificent assignment.

I also knew that just as God entrusted Denise and me with the task of heading up this project, He had entrusted many faithful partners to contribute financially. God explicitly told me that people would generously help us — and that He would abundantly bless those who participated in the project. We knew the same grace that was on us would also be on our partners, and God would *supernaturally* grace them to *supernaturally* give.

The Lord assured me that unusually large gifts would be given to help Denise and me so that this huge assignment was not a burden. Gifts and offerings would be given to help us establish this Gospel center in the heart of Russia, and Heaven would keep records of every gift given. Those gifts would be credited to people's heavenly accounts that await them there!

I have often reflected on God's faithfulness to our ministry as we ran that race of faith. He perfectly and completely fulfilled every single one of His promises to us. Although the challenges were terrific, we accomplished the vision! When we are all in Heaven one day, the fabulous building that we now occupy in Moscow will still be filled with people worshiping Jesus. From the grandstands of Heaven, Denise and I — along with all those who financially gave — will rejoice that we didn't shrink back from His command. With God's grace, we ran the race and finished it!

What race is God asking you to run in your own life? Does it seem *huge, gigantic, massive,* and *colossal* to you? When you ponder what He is asking you to do and the ramifications of your obedience, does it *rattle* you, *shake* you, or make you *shudder*? Does it *excite* you, *stir* you up, *stimulate* you, and *thrill* you to know that God trusts you to believe Him for the impossible?

Each one of us has come too far to shrink back from God's command now. It's too late to turn around and run the other direction. As we near the last of the last days, there's no place for fear or timidity. The time is short, and God is looking to each of us to fulfill His plan for these last generations. God is depending on you and me, and we must give our lives to do exactly what He is asking. There is nothing more important in life than heeding His voice and doing what He is requiring.

God could choose anyone, but He is choosing you. So whatever your task or assignment is, think about what an honor it is that God would use you to accomplish such a feat! You must push aside fear, reach deep inside to the anointing and power of God that resides within you, stand on His promises of provision and strength, and step forward by faith to see it done. *You will never know what God can do unless you do something that gives Him the opportunity to show you!*

As the children of Israel prepared to cross the Jordan River into their Promised Land, the river was at flood stage — its highest stage of the year. Yet God commanded Joshua to instruct the priests to step right into the river! God assured him that if he did, the water would supernaturally part so that he and the priests and the rest of the Israelites could pass through on dry ground.

Imagine what Joshua must have felt. People were watching him and the priests, looking to see if the water would part as their leader had promised. Every eye in Israel was peering at Joshua in speculation. But this wasn't Joshua's moment to shrink back in fear — it was his moment to obey!

Standing on the brink of the Jordan River with its dangerous waters rising higher and higher, Joshua obeyed God's command, and the priests lifted their feet to make that first brave step into the raging, overflowing waters. As they obeyed, the waters parted just as God had promised. The Bible tells us, "And the priests that bare the ark of the covenant of the Lord stood firm on dry ground in the midst of Jordan, and all the Israelites passed over on dry ground, until all the people were passed clean over Jordan." (Joshua 3:17)

It took one man's courage and obedience for those waters to part — and because of Joshua's willingness to obey, all the Israelites passed into their land of promise. *That, my friend, shows the power of one person's obedience.* Your own obedience affects many lives! When you obey, it impacts *many* people and paves the way for others to inherit God's promises as well.

This is not to say that obedience to God is always easy or without challenges. I'm sure Joshua had to *fight* his thoughts, *battle* his emotions, and *constantly refuse* to give in to the trepidation that tried to flood his mind as he followed those priests into the raging river. Had Joshua listened to those thoughts and emotions that certainly assaulted his mind, he never would have obeyed. Just as you and I must do, he pushed all of it out of the way and boldly stepped out. And in the moment Joshua committed to obey, he experienced the intervening, supernatural, history-making power of God!

Those who stand on the banks and simply watch will never experience the power of God as Joshua did that day. If they want to see and experience God's power, they must be willing to get up, get out, and do exactly what God is asking them to do.

Certainly, there will be a season for you to develop a dream or vision so it can take root in your heart. However, eventually a time will come when you must stop thinking about it and start taking action. If you don't, your dream will remain in the realm of fantasy and imagination. But when you finally act on that dream and step forward to do what God has asked of you, *that* is the moment you will see God move into action and part the waters before you!

I'm so thankful that Denise and I — along with our staff, our church, and our partners — put our feet into the waters in front of us. We thought, prayed, planned, and talked about it for years. Then God asked us to take action and obey. He had given us assignments in the past that we obeyed, and we had experienced His power as a result. Because of our past obedience, we were equipped and prepared by Him for the greatest step we had ever taken to that point. *How could we do anything else but obey Him this time?* With man it is impossible, but with God, *all* things are possible (*see* Mark 10:27)!

Today this is true for you too!

- ➤ Has God given you an assignment?
- ➤ Is God asking you to start a new business?

- ➢ Has He assigned you the task of reaching your unsaved family and friends?
- ➢ Do you think God is calling you to pursue higher education?
- ➢ Is His Spirit calling you into the ministry?
- ➢ Do you feel the tug of God in your heart to become a bigger financial giver?

Accomplishing what God is asking of you may seem impossible to your natural mind, but it's not impossible with Him! Whatever God is telling you to do, think it over and pray about it *a lot*! Then there will come a moment — maybe that moment is *now* — when the time of thinking and preparing must stop and action must commence. God will one day speak to your heart and say, *It's time to get off the banks of the river and lift your feet to step into the waters. If you'll do what I say, I assure you that you will see My power as never before!*

If you know it's time to step out in faith, you must take your eyes off the raging, turbulent waters before you and fix your eyes on Jesus Himself. He is the Author and Finisher of your faith (*see* Hebrews 12:2). You can be sure that what He starts, He will always finish. That's why Paul said, "Being confident of this very thing, that he which hath begun a good work in you will perform it until the day of Jesus Christ" (Philippians 1:6).

The word "confident" is from the Greek word *peitho*, which means to be *fully persuaded* or *fully convinced.* Paul is literally saying, "I am *fully* and *completely persuaded* and *convinced*...that he which began a good work in you will perform it until the day of Jesus Christ." The word "perform" is the Greek word *epiteleoo*, which is a compound of the words *epi* and *telos*. The word *epi* gives *force* to the word. The word *telos* describes something that is *accomplished*, *culminated*, or *fulfilled.* However, the way it is used in Greek, it emphatically means that God Himself will move you toward the goal, and He will not stop until you have reached the end.

That means God is with you at the beginning of your journey, in the middle of your adventure, and He will empower you to make it all the way to the finish line. You may not always feel like you're an overcomer, but God's grace is moving you — one step at a time — toward your land of promise!

Joshua's obedience resulted in all of Israel passing over into their land of promise. And think how *your* willingness to obey will make the way clear for others to follow and to see, touch, and taste the power of God in their lives! When you obey God, it brings His power into play on a scale far greater than you could have ever dreamed or imagined. However, such power belongs only to those who obey.

- ➢ What is your life assignment?
- ➢ What is the step of faith you need to take to fulfill your own destiny?
- ➢ What promise awaits you on the other side of the river?
- ➢ What is stopping you from taking the next steps to get there?
- ➢ Is it time for you to stop just thinking and start acting on what God has given you to do?

Denise and I know what it means to accept a faith assignment; therefore, we understand what you may be feeling as you step out in faith to obey what God has told you to do. We assure you that God will protect you and supernaturally provide everything you need to accomplish the job He is asking you to do.

As Denise and I lifted our feet and stepped forward by faith to do this seemingly impossible task, we understood that it was our assignment and that God had long been preparing us for this moment. He was depending on us to obey. He is likewise depending on *you* to hear His voice and to do what He is telling you to do right now.

What race is God calling you to run? What river is He calling you to pass over? I deeply believe that God will empower you to do the most radical, supernatural thing you have ever done in your life. It may seem as impossible as crossing the Jordan at flood stage, but His grace and power will pick you up and carry you toward the goal, and He'll bring you all the way to completion!

If that describes you, and if you do exactly as God instructs you to do, your obedience will "split open" the Spirit realm and bring the supernatural power of God into your life on many levels. I'm convinced that your obedience will trigger *miracles* in your own life and in your family, relationships, health, finances, and business — including the fulfillment of things you've sought, prayed for, and desired to come to pass for many years.

So I must ask you — *what do you hear the Spirit of God asking you to do*? Whatever it is, your obedience will result in a manifold blessing of His power to increase you in every area of your life and to make you a blessing to many others for generations to come!

MY PRAYER FOR TODAY

Father, I hear You beckoning me to step forward by faith, and I am inspired to do what You are telling me to do. I've been in a preparation season for a long time. I thank You that you are finally telling me its time to step forward, to put my feet into the river's waters and to see Your supernatural power make a way for me to enter into the land You promised to me and that You've been speaking to me about. Thank You for having confidence in me. With the Holy Spirit living inside of me, the two of us together can challenge the impossible and do the unthinkable! By faith, I am stepping forward — and I thank You for carrying me toward the finish line and helping me complete what You have put into my heart!

I pray this in Jesus' name!

MY CONFESSION FOR TODAY

I declare that the impossible is moving out the way for me. God has been preparing me a long time to do more than I've been doing. He has tested me, watched me, prepared me, and now it's time for me to take the big leap of faith and move forward toward the goal He's put in my heart. It's a miracle, but He is carrying me toward the finish line and He will make sure I get all the way to the conclusion. I give God all the praise and glory, for He prepares me, empowers me, and carries me toward that place He has ordained for me to be!

I declare this by faith in Jesus' name!

QUESTIONS FOR YOU TO CONSIDER

1. What impossible goals have you accomplished by the grace of God? As you look back over your life and think of the things you've done, what are those things that you never could have done on your own? Why don't you take time to make a list and then thank God for His fulfilling power working in your life?
2. What are the goals that are still directly ahead of you? Have you jumped in the race and decided that you're going to pass over the raging waters that stand before you? Or are you struggling with the desire to shrink back in fear and timidity?
3. Can you think of a single instance when God has not been faithful to you? Why don't you take a few minutes to meditate on all the times God has taken you from where you were to where you needed to be?

OCTOBER 23

The Applause of God

Therefore judge nothing before the time,
until the Lord come, who both will bring to light
the hidden things of darkness, and will make
manifest the counsels of the hearts: and then
shall every man have praise of God.
— 1 Corinthians 4:5

Located in the very heart of Moscow, Russia, just minutes away from the Kremlin, is the world-famous Bolshoi Theater. It hosts some of the finest opera and ballet productions in the entire world, and world-class singers and dancers regularly grace its stage. My wife loves opera, and I occasionally take her to the opera as a gift.

I am always in awe of the wonderful, God-given talents of these performers. However, one aspect about these operas that has always impressed to me is the response of the audience when they hear a singer who gives an outstanding performance. When the performance concludes, the enthusiastic crowd rises to their feet and boisterously thunders, *"Bravo! Bravo! Bravo!"*

As they shout their approval, they also clap their hands together in unison to give a mighty applause that seems to go on forever!

When the evening's performance finally draws to a close, the singers return to the stage for one last bow to the audience. As they walk past the curtain, the crowd rises to its feet and begins to riotously cheer and applaud once again, and from all over the front of the auditorium, patrons vigorously fling huge bouquets of flowers at the feet of the artists. Within a few moments, piles of flowers are scattered across the front of the huge stage. As the applause and adulation begin to wind down, beautifully dressed ushers walk onstage to personally deliver magnificent bouquets that were bought for the singers by devoted fans who wanted to show their appreciation through an extravagant gift.

At the end of the night when the curtain falls for the last time, the singers return to their dressing rooms to change out of their costumes and have their cosmetics removed, and the audience files out of the theater to go home.

Ultimately, this experience persists only as a memory in the minds of those in attendance. The rounds of applause, praise, approval, and adulation were wonderful while they lasted, but they never last long and are soon forgotten. However, there is an applause that will last for all of eternity — *and that is the applause that comes from God Himself.*

A day is coming in your future when you will be called on stage before God to give account for your life. Sitting in the audience, He will watch as the activities of your life are reviewed. In First Corinthians 4:5, the apostle Paul wrote about that moment, saying, "Therefore judge nothing before the time, until the Lord come, who both will bring to light the hidden things of darkness, and will make manifest the counsels of the hearts: and then shall every man have praise of God." This verse clearly reveals that the secrets and motivations of your heart will be made known as you stand before God on that day.

Notice the last phrase of First Corinthians 4:5, which says, "...And then shall every man have *praise* of God." This word "praise" is translated from the Greek word *epainos,* which actually means *applause*. However, it isn't singers, ballet dancers, or entertainers who are being applauded in this verse — it is believers who have lived holy, consecrated, dedicated, obedient lives.

Paul used the word *epainos* to evoke a very strong image. By using this word, he let us know that a day is coming when we will give account for our lives. On that day, if we have lived right before God and the motives behind our service were pure, we will receive praise from the Lord Himself. It will be as if He rises to His feet to give *a round of applause* and *a standing ovation*! In fact, Paul's imagery is so strong that the verse could be loosely interpreted, *"...And at that time every man will have the applause of God."*

Think of God rising to His feet to give a standing ovation! Can you imagine the thunderous sound of His hands clapping as it reverberates and echoes throughout all of Heaven! That is precisely the picture the apostle Paul paints for that day when faithful believers stand before

Him! The magnitude and nature of that divine applause will far surpass anything given by a human audience!

The truth is that much of your hard work and preparation unto the Lord is done in secret behind closed doors. When you accomplish something for Him, people are often unaware of your actions or perhaps simply forget to show their appreciation. However, according to Paul's teaching in First Corinthian 4:5, a day will come when God Himself will personally rise and thank you for everything you have done in the name of Jesus for the advancement of the Gospel.

There is a massive, silent army of believers today whose work for the Gospel goes unrecognized in the public eye. Yet they are the engines that drive the Church and empower the advancement of the Gospel. Although they remain unseen, unrecognized, and often neglected, the fruit of their work is eternal, and Jesus sees it all. And a day will come when they receive the great applause from the King of kings Himself as He personally thanks them for their service.

The applause of men is a reward that is very short-lived and soon forgotten, but the applause of God lasts for all eternity. If you do what Jesus has called you to do and you do it with a right heart, you, too, will receive His eternal reward. As you stand before Him on that glorious day, any hardships you may have endured will dissipate before your eyes, and you will have the eternal gratification of knowing that you pleased the Lord. And as Jesus gives you *His* version of a standing ovation, I guarantee you that it will be the *ultimate* reward!

MY PRAYER FOR TODAY

Father, You see everything. You are not unjust. You know how I have worked for You and how I have shown my love for You by caring for other believers. When I am tempted to be discouraged and to think that no one appreciates me, remind me that You know exactly what I am doing and why I am doing it. I know that You take note of what I do for Your Kingdom, and Your approval is what I desire. Holy Spirit, You are my Helper. I receive Your wisdom, counsel, and might to do my work for Jesus in the most excellent, professional manner possible. Thank You for Your power that enables me to serve the Lord in such a manner that one day He'll rise to give a round of applause for what I've done and how I've done it.

I pray this in Jesus' name!

MY CONFESSION FOR TODAY

I confess that I work as unto the Lord, whether or not men see my labor. Although it is nice to be thanked, I don't work for the applause of men. Rather, I am laboring to please the Lord, and my priority in life is to serve Him in a manner that is honoring of Him. I devote 100 percent of my energy and efforts to glorify Jesus in all I do. With the help of the Holy Spirit, I purpose to satisfy His heart with my service and my heart motives behind my service. On that day when I am called to give an account for my works, I will stand boldly and unashamedly before Jesus because I will know I've given my best here in this life.

I declare this by faith in Jesus' name!

QUESTIONS FOR YOU TO CONSIDER

1. Do you have times when you feel that no one acknowledges the hard work you are doing for the Lord? In moments like these, are you tempted to feel unappreciated?
2. Can you think of other believers who are giving every ounce of their energies to serve the Lord but are rarely thanked for their service? Have you ever gone out of your way to express your gratitude to them for what they do?
3. Wouldn't it be a good idea to take a few minutes today to list the people you should thank for their service to the Lord? It would take you only a few minutes to make this list, but if you thank these people, it will mean so much to them. *Wouldn't it mean a lot to you if someone went out of his or her way to say thank you to you today?*

OCTOBER 24

What Is an Apostle?

And He Himself gave some to be *apostles*....
— Ephesians 4:11 *NKJV*

When I was growing up, I was told there was no such thing as a *living apostle.* Our denomination taught that all the apostles died at the end of the "Apostolic Age" — along with *miracles, signs and wonders,* and *gifts of the Holy Spirit*! To my young mind, the term "apostle" belonged to a group of 12 legendary men who walked with Jesus 2,000 years ago. Once they died, that was the end of that!

But over the past decades, we have learned that much denominational teaching was wrong. Miracles, signs, wonders, and gifts of the Holy Spirit are still "alive and well." Prophets, also previously considered relics of the past, are recognized and honored. No one would argue that the Church is also blessed with fiery evangelists, powerful pastors, and profoundly God-gifted teachers. But now — at the end of the age — it is finally being recognized that *the apostolic gift* still exists.

The apostolic gift has always been around, but the theology I grew up hearing wouldn't sanction someone being called an apostle. To call someone an apostle seemed ludicrous and arrogant. Everyone "just *knew*" there was no such thing as an apostle — and to call a person by this name was almost considered a blasphemous insult to the first 12 apostles.

So thanks to our scholarly ancestors who read and spoke Latin, we reverted to calling apostles by the Latin name *missionaries.* But "missionary" is not a correct term in this context. The only reason we called apostles *missionaries* was the fear of retribution for calling them *apostles,* as they often should have been called.

I am *not* implying that everyone who is a missionary is an apostle. Some people are called to be missionaries — people who sense a need to go on a mission to help the work of God. This work is very beneficial and needful, but it does not in itself constitute an apostolic call. Often these are truly missionaries and not apostles — people sent by the local church or their denomination to help in some way on the mission field.

An apostolic call originates in *a divine revelation and encounter with Jesus Christ.* As Paul said, his calling was "...not of men, neither by man, but by Jesus Christ...." (Galatians 1:1). These precious apostolic gifts may not have always been recognized as *apostles,* but they have always been present in the Church throughout history, and they are present and active in the Church in this hour. Ephesians 4:11-13 says that all the fivefold ministry gifts — *including the apostle* — will be present and active "till we all come in the unity of the faith...."

The Church of Jesus Christ *cannot* reach full maturity unless *all* of these Christ-given gifts are imparting their unique portions to the Church. Like the other fivefold ministry gifts, the gift of apostleship is an *essential element* to carry the Church upward to her destiny as a "...glorious church, not having spot, or wrinkle, or any such thing..." (Ephesians 5:27).

But before we go any further into this teaching about the role of *apostles* in today's world, let's back up and study where this word *apostle* comes from. Today we'll look at the Greek meaning of the word, and tomorrow we'll look at the various historical usages of this word "apostle" in New Testament times. You may be very surprised to see the various ways this word was used and how they all had application to a New Testament apostle.

The Greek word for "apostle" is *apostolos,* which is a compound of the words *apo* and *stello.* The preposition *apo* means *away,* and the word *stello* means *to send.* When the two words are combined, they form the word *apostolos,* meaning *one who is sent away.* This Greek word appears 79 times in the New Testament. The root of *apostolos* is the word *apostello,* a word that appears no less than 131 times in the New Testament and more than 700 times in the Old Testament Greek Septuagint.

At first, it may seem that the definition of this word *apostolos — one who is sent away* — denoted one who had been dismissed, set aside, or rejected. However, this word didn't refer to a person sent away in dishonor or disgrace. Rather, the word *apostolos* was a term of great honor that referred to *a person who was personally selected, commissioned, and sent on an assignment on behalf of a very powerful government or individual.* This person wasn't merely sent off; he was *empowered, invested with authority,* and then *dispatched to accomplish a special task.*

So when we talk about apostles, we are discussing individuals who are *appointed, empowered, invested with authority by the Lord,* and *then dispatched to do a special task.* And their task is *the establishing of the Christian community in places where it had not existed heretofore.*

There is a lot for us to see on this subject, so tomorrow we'll look more deeply at the historical meaning of the word "apostle." I pray these *Sparkling Gems* will open your eyes to a greater understanding of this gift and how desperately we need this gift to be active in the Body of Christ today!

MY PRAYER FOR TODAY

Father, I ask You to help me recognize those who are apostolic gifts — those who have apostolic callings — in the Body of Christ. We need all fivefold ministries — apostles, prophets, evangelists, pastors, and teachers — for the building up of the Church. If one of these is missing, there will be a certain portion of Christ's impartation missing from the Church. I ask You to help me be open-minded to the reality of the apostolic ministry gifts and to honor them in our midst.

I pray this in Jesus' name!

MY CONFESSION FOR TODAY

I confess that apostles, prophets, evangelists, pastors, and teachers are all present and active in the Body of Christ. I am open to each of these impartations of Christ. Because I am open to them, I will be a recipient of the grace of God that is delivered through each of these. I will receive ministry from apostles, prophets, evangelists, pastors, and teachers — and it will contribute to my edification, growth, and to the building up of the Body of Christ!

I declare this by faith in Jesus' name!

QUESTIONS FOR YOU TO CONSIDER

1. Do you personally know anyone who stands in an apostolic anointing? Who is that person? Why would you say he is apostolic? What is the evidence that makes you believe this person carries an apostolic calling?
2. How will what you've learned in today's *Sparkling Gem* influence the way you respond to and receive from the apostle's ministry in the future?
3. Are you clear about the distinction between missionary and an apostle or "sent one"? How would you describe that distinction?

The word APOSTOLOS *was a term of great honor that referred to an individual personally selected, empowered, and invested with authority and then dispatched to accomplish a special task.*

OCTOBER 25

The Historical Meaning of the Word 'Apostle'

And He Himself gave some to be *apostles*....
— Ephesians 4:11 *NKJV*

Today I want to cover some of the historical usages of the word "apostle." You will see that it had many uses in the Greek language of early New Testament times, and you'll also see how all these uses have application to a New Testament apostle. I believe this discussion will not only enrich your understanding of this ministry gift, but it will also help you more fully receive from this gift that, among other purposes, is given to help establish and strengthen you in the faith. And if you've ever sat under a true apostolic ministry, you will probably recognize the operation of that gift by many of the distinct characteristics that are found within the meaning of the word *apostolos*.

The Admiral of a Fleet of Ships

During the time of the ancient Greek orator Demosthenes (384-322 BC), the word *apostolos* was a naval term that described *an admiral, the fleet of ships that traveled with him, and the specialized crew who accompanied and assisted the admiral.*[10]

The fleet would be sent out to sea on a mission to locate territories where civilization was nonexistent. Once an uncivilized region was identified, the admiral (called the *apostolos*) — along with his specialized crew and all their cargo and belongings — would disembark, settle down, and work as a team to establish a new community. Then they would begin the process of transforming a strange land into a replica of life as they believed it should be. Their purpose was total *colonization* of the uncivilized territory.

Within this special fleet of ships were both the personnel and the cargo required to establish a new culture, a new life, and a new community. When that fleet pulled up to shore, it contained workers trained to build roads, construct buildings, and teach uncivilized natives how to read, write, and function in a new kind of social order. Thus, the admiral became the team leader for the construction of a new society.

Once the job was completed, a majority of the team members got back on the ships and launched out to sea again to find another uncivilized area and repeat the entire colonization process all over again. Thus, we find that the word *apostolos* described an admiral or team leader who led a team to establish new communities in uncivilized territories.

---

[10]David Francis Bacon, *Lives of the Apostles of Jesus Christ* (New Haven: L. H. Young, 1836), p. 8.

You can easily see how this definition had application to a New Testament apostle, whose primary task was to travel with an apostolic team to establish the Church in places where the Church was non-existent. This is one historical usage of the word *apostolos* that has bearing on its meaning in the New Testament.

A Passport or Travel Document

The word *apostolos* was so closely associated with the idea of traveling that it also eventually became synonymous with *a passport* or *a travel document.*

If a person wanted to exit a country, he had to possess a travel document that was essentially *an exit visa* or *a passport.* This legal document was called an *apostolos* — the same word translated "apostle." The document guaranteed *the right of passage and the ability to move freely from one place to another*.

When the word *apostolos* was applied to early New Testament apostles, it implied that an apostle was a *spiritual passport* that gave believers *right of passage* into heavenly realms and into deeper spiritual truths. One can certainly see that those who were under the apostleship of Paul were taken into realms of revelation that they could have never attained on their own. His ministry was a *spiritual passport* that gave them *right of passage* into spiritual revelation.

It should be noted that any person who operates in a genuine apostolic calling will lead people into new spiritual realities.

An Ambassador or Envoy

The word "apostle" also described a person who had the authority to act much the same way an *ambassador* represents his government to another government. This classical and secular meaning of the word *apostolos* meant *an envoy sent to do business on behalf of the one who sent him*. Thus, a governmental apostle served as a *personal representative*, *emissary*, *messenger*, *agent*, *diplomat*, *ambassador*, or *charge d'affaires*.

This person officially possessed the clout and influence to *speak* and *act* in the place of the one who sent him on his assignment. So when the ambassador — *apostolos* — spoke, his words were counted as the words of his sender. When the *apostolos* acted, his actions were interpreted as those of his sender. The connection between the sender and the person who was sent was almost inseparable.

This reveals the New Testament apostle's position to *speak* and *act* on behalf of the Lord. This is a governmental position within the Body of Christ, and as such, an apostolic ministry gift should be received as one with great spiritual clout and the backing of Heaven.

It is very important for you to understand this truth and its powerful implications. You see, when a genuine apostle ministers, he is authorized by Heaven not only to lead you into new spiritual realities, but also to help mobilize you into position to fulfill your unique function in the Body of Christ!

But we are only getting started, as there is so much more to learn about the word "apostle" and how it is applied in the New Testament. In tomorrow's *Sparkling Gem*, you're going to discover a surprising new answer to the question "How many people in the New Testament were called apostles?"

The answer to this question may shock you and open you to the reality that there are still apostles functioning in the Body of Christ today. They may not be called or recognized as apostles; nonetheless, they carry an apostolic calling and anointing. *Don't miss tomorrow — it will be a real eye-opener!*

MY PRAYER FOR TODAY

Father, what I've read today describes a whole world of information about the function of the apostolic ministry both in the New Testament and today. I thank You for accurate knowledge that reveals the enormity of Your great plan and the significance of every distinctive part of the Body of Christ. Lord, I ask You to open the eyes of my heart to see and understand more about the role and value of this fivefold ministry gift overall and to me personally, because I want everything You have to offer me and Your Church!

I pray this in Jesus' name!

MY CONFESSION FOR TODAY

I confess that I believe in and honor the ministries of prophets, apostles, evangelists, pastors, and teachers according to Ephesians 4:11, which says that each ministry gift, including the apostolic ministry, is essential for the growth and the building up of the Church. So I will embrace in my life this aspect of Christ's character and function that He expresses in His Body through each ministry gift to the Body of Christ! As a result, I grow strong in my own identity in the part I am ordained to fill as a member of the Body.

I declare this by faith in Jesus' name!

QUESTIONS FOR YOU TO CONSIDER

1. Historical definitions of the word *apostolos* shed light on the function of the apostle's ministry. What is the modern application of the three definitions shared in today's *Sparkling Gem*?
2. Have you ever observed the work of an apostolic team that traveled extensively to establish churches in new places? Have you ever been a part of such a team either directly or by supporting it in prayer or with your finances?
3. As you've read these descriptions of how apostles work, do you recognize that certain individuals or ministries whom you've known were actually doing an apostolic work that you did not realize at the time?

OCTOBER 26

How Many Apostles Are Named in the New Testament?

And He Himself gave some to be *apostles*....
— Ephesians 4:11 *NKJV*

Today we continue our study of the word "apostle." By the time of the New Testament, the word *apostolos* was already an old word with quite a lengthy history. It carried many shades of meaning — all of which overlapped each other and were interrelated, as we have seen. So when people in the Early Church heard or read the word "apostle," it is likely that they understood an apostle to be a person who was specially selected, commissioned, and sent by the Lord to represent Him for the purposes of the Kingdom: to build up, draw forth, speak out, align, govern, strengthen, and establish His Church as His unique agent on the earth.

Early believers were also probably aware that the apostle was a pioneer and a chief overseer, responsible for opening up new territory, both physically and spiritually, for Kingdom purposes. They would have known him as one who provided passage from one spiritual dimension to another as he took a church to new levels in its spiritual growth that it could never reach apart from the apostolic anointing.

Believers recognized the apostle as one who had the anointing, authority, and spiritual backing to *get things accomplished* for the furtherance of God's purposes. He wasn't just the implementer of pragmatic ideas and strategies. Rather, a true apostle carried within him *supernatural insight and revelation* that was vital for the growth and the building up of the Church.

Over the centuries, the question "Who is a true apostle?" has been something of a theological conundrum for many scholars. Some insist that only the original 12 were true apostles, whereas others argue that the apostolic ministry has continued since the death of Jesus' original 12 apostles. But let me give you a concise way of looking at this subject.

In Luke 6:13, Jesus called together His disciples and from among them, He chose 12 men whom He called apostles. They are listed by name in Matthew 10:2-4. In Luke 9:1-6, Jesus sent forth these 12 apostles to preach the Gospel, heal the sick, and cast out demons. But in the next chapter, Jesus appointed 70 more people and "...sent them (*apostolos*) two by two..." (Luke 10:1).

When Judas died, Acts 1:25,26 tells us that Matthias was chosen to take his place among the original apostles. Paul was also an apostle, as he testifies of in multiple places throughout the New Testament.

So the Greek word *apostle* is used to describe the original 12, another group of 70, plus Matthias and Paul — and then 11 others:

1. Apollos (*see* 1 Corinthians 4:6-13)
2. Epaphroditus (*see* Philippians 2:25; "messenger" is *apostolos* in the Greek)
3. James, the Lord's brother (*see* Galatians 1:19)
4. Barnabas (*see* Acts 14:4,14; 1 Corinthians 9:5,6)
5. Andronicus (*see* Romans 16:7)
6. Junia (*see* Romans 16:7)
7. Titus (*see* 2 Corinthians 8:23; "messenger" is *apostolos* in the Greek)
8. An unnamed brother with Titus (*see* 2 Corinthians 8:18,23)
9. Another unnamed brother with Titus (*see* 2 Corinthians 8:22,23)
10. Timothy (*see* 1 Thessalonians 1:1; 2:6)
11. Silas (*see* 1 Thessalonians 1:1; 2:6)

If you were to take the entire list of those who were sent forth apostolically in the New Testament, there are at least 83 people in the New Testament who are called "apostles." All of this makes it very clear that apostolic ministry has continued beyond the original 12 apostles. Just as prophets, evangelists, pastors, and teachers have continued for 2,000 years, the apostolic gift has also continued; it has simply been more or less unrecognized.

You may wonder why this information is relevant to you personally and to the Church at large today. But consider it this way: If the Scriptures reveal that there was a multiplied increase in the apostolic ministry in the Early Church — from 12 to 83 — who were called apostles, *how much more* will Jesus Christ continue to give this gift to men for the purpose of building His Church?

And this would be especially true in these last days before Jesus returns! Great preparation and equipping is taking place in the Church to prepare all of us as end-time believers to be His bold, sold-out, Holy Spirit-empowered witnesses on this earth before He comes. We as a Body *need* to receive the powerful benefits given to us by God through the operation of the apostolic anointing!

MY PRAYER FOR TODAY

Lord, I am amazed at this list of people who were sent forth as apostles in the New Testament. I now wonder about and have a new desire to better understand the gifts You have set in Your Body as it pleases You. Help me, Holy Spirit, to understand not only my own spiritual gift but also the authentic gifts in those around me — including the apostolic gift whom You've sent to build up, draw forth, speak out, align, govern, strengthen, and establish Your Church as Your unique agent on the earth. I want to humbly and completely cooperate with and draw from the apostolic anointing that rests on those You have genuinely called to this ministry so that I can experience the fullness of Your intent when You gave gifts unto men.

I pray this in Jesus' name!

MY CONFESSION FOR TODAY

I confess that my appreciation for and knowledge about the valuable apostolic ministry is expanding. My perspective is adjusting concerning the supernatural function of authentic ministry gifts — and of the apostle in particular. I see that it is worthy of my study and consideration. I want everything that God has for me, and if this is part of God's plan for the Church, my heart is longing for it too.

I declare this by faith in Jesus' name!

QUESTIONS FOR YOU TO CONSIDER

1. Were you surprised by the lengthy list of people in the New Testament who were sent out as apostles? What is your initial reaction to this information?
2. How many people over the centuries who were called missionaries do you think were actually God-called apostles? Have you ever thought about it? Why do you think many apostles were never recognized for being apostolic?
3. Why do you think it is important to recognize and acknowledge the true ministry gift upon a person's life? Whom do you know *right now* to be true apostles? Is their apostolic gift acknowledged, or are they referred to as something else?

OCTOBER 27

Supernatural Patience and Endurance

Truly the signs of an apostle were wrought
among you in all patience....
— 2 Corinthians 12:12

Here is an important fact to know about the apostolic ministry: God didn't leave it to us to *guess* who is a true apostle and who is not! I'm thankful for that! In Second Corinthians 12:12 the apostle Paul wrote by the Holy Spirit about the signs that will help us discern correctly whether an apostle is in our midst. He said, "Truly the signs of an apostle were wrought among you in all patience, in signs, and wonders, and mighty deeds."

The word "signs" is the Greek word *semeion*. It was used in the vernacular of secular business to describe *the official written notice that announced a court's final verdict*. This word also described *the signature or seal applied to a document to guarantee its authenticity* and *a sign that marked key locations in a city*. This secular word was carried over into New Testament language — as Paul used it, for instance, in Second Corinthians 12:12.

By using the word *semeion*, Paul declared that certain signs exist as the *final verdict* to prove a person's apostleship. These accompanying proofs are like a *signature* or *seal authenticating* and *guaranteeing* that a person is an apostle. They provide authentication — verifiable proof — and should accompany every person claiming to carry the apostolic mantle.

Thus, Paul was telling us that if the "signs" he listed are evident in a person's ministry, those signs may be the *announcement*, *guarantee*, or *proof* that this particular person is an apostle.

The marks of an apostle that Paul listed in this verse are not all-inclusive. However, they serve as a good starting place in describing the signs that point to an apostolic call. Just as a highway sign lets you know you are coming closer to a particular city or destination, these particular signs in a person's ministry may be evidence that you're looking at a person who has a genuine apostolic call on his or her life.

In Second Corinthians 12:12, Paul wrote, "Truly the signs of an apostle were wrought among you in all patience, in signs, and wonders, and mighty deeds." The word "truly" comes from the Greek phrase *ta men*, a phrase that means *emphatically* or *indeed* and could be translated, *Of a certainty*! By using this phrase, Paul's message was loud and clear: If a person is apostolic, it is certain that he will have these particular signs in his ministry.

Let's focus today on the first sign Paul listed as a sign of true apostleship, "patience," and tomorrow we'll look at the rest of the signs listed. Patience is an attribute that most people overlook, yet it is just as supernatural as healings and miracles. It comes from the Greek word *hupomeno*, which we've seen depicts *a person's supernatural ability to hang in there and to stay put no matter what forces try to stop him*.

People with an apostolic call on their lives must often do frontline work in environments that are difficult and even hostile to the Gospel. An example would be the city of Corinth — one of the world's most wicked cities in the First Century — where God called Paul to establish a church. In order to fulfill this divine call, Paul had to resist the demonic powers of that city and all the other forces arrayed against him. This assignment therefore required a special God-given endowment of *patience* — the supernatural ability to *stay put* regardless of the pressure or opposition one encounters.

Paul knew that God had given him the supernatural ability to remain steadfast in the midst of the intense resistance that came against him in Corinth. In fact, Paul was so impacted by the divine grace that enabled him to *stay put* in such a hostile environment that he was inspired to include it as one of the marks, or signs, of an apostolic ministry.

Such patience is also evidenced in the fact that an apostle is uniquely graced to encompass all five ministerial offices, as needed, in order to establish a church and develop the ministry gifts within believers. Therefore, for a time, the apostle will operate prophetically, as an evangelist, in a pastoral capacity, and as a teacher. He may minister consistently as a pastor or teacher, but it will be with a higher level of authority than the pastoral or teaching ministries.

Only a divine endowment of patience and endurance can give a person a sufficient measure of strength and courage to keep him pressing forward when it seems as if all of hell is raging against him. Paul testified that the *hupomeno* ability to *stay put* while laying a foundation and then building upon it — which includes establishing divine order and strengthening the saints, often in the face of potential discouragement or intense opposition — is both remarkable and supernatural. Thus, he listed this attribute as the first sign that always accompanies true apostolic ministry.

In the July 6 *Gem,* I related our own experience with "staying put" despite all odds in an account of our earliest days in the former Soviet Union in Latvia. We were some of God's "sent ones," commissioned to help reestablish the Church in that part of the world.

From the outset, we faced stubborn opposition from the government in that nation. While we were busy producing Christian TV programs, starting a new church, building leaders in the ministry, and answering mountains of mail from TV viewers and those we were ministering to, we found ourselves having to renew our visas multiple times in a week — *and sometimes every day of the week*!

Because the person in charge of visas didn't like us and refused to renew our visas for longer periods time, life became very difficult for Denise and me and our ministry. At times, our new visas would be valid for *only 24 hours*! That meant we had only one legal day to "rest" and breathe a sigh of relief before we had to initiate the process all over again. It was undoubtedly one of the biggest fights we have ever faced — and this fight continued *unabated* for *years*! The pressure this ordeal put on us was enormous. It was constantly in the background hassling us and affecting every area of our lives while we worked diligently to fulfill our assignment.

The enemy was using that man in the government to try to weary us and run us out of that nation. But we knew that we had been "sent" there by God. And by the grace of God, we remained among those precious Latvian people "in all patience" (*hupomeno*). We were determined not to be moved out of that nation. And as I wrote in the July 6 *Gem*, after years of being hassled, vexed, and beleaguered by that man in the visa department, an abrupt change finally came! By God's grace, we had endured with patience and outlasted the attack of the enemy. I can therefore say emphatically both from the Word and from personal experience: *Patience and endurance are supernatural signs that accompany the apostolic office.*

Paul said, "*Truly* the signs of an apostle were wrought among you in all patience...." In Greek, this word "truly" is *ta men*, meaning *emphatically*, *indeed*, or *of a certainty*. It is as if Paul was putting an exclamation mark on the indicators that immediately followed. In other words, a person's supernatural ability to stand strong and steadfast as he fulfills his divine call to establish the Church, regardless of the opposition that comes against him, is truly — *emphatically* — one of the evident, undeniable signs in the life of someone with an apostolic call.

Although you may not have an apostolic calling, this same divine impartation of *hupomeno* is a part of your inheritance as a child of God! You have on the inside of you the ability to endure through difficulties while holding fast to your faith, no matter what obstacles you encounter along the way! *Hupomeno* is yours to lay hold of because you belong to the Kingdom of God. So why not make the decision to become an expert at *hanging in there* by faith to do God's will, *no matter what* from this day forward!

MY PRAYER FOR TODAY

Lord Jesus, thank You for giving the gift of the apostle to Your Church to establish and strengthen us in doctrine and in the personal and practical knowledge of Your wisdom and ways. I thank You, Lord, for the divine endowment of patient endurance that You impart to the apostle to be able to build and advance the Kingdom of God. Holy Spirit, since this supernatural quality of endurance and staying power is mine also as a child of God, I place my trust in You and fully expect You to lead me in triumph through every obstacle and challenge. By the power of Your anointing within and upon me, I ask You to spread the fragrance of the knowledge of God through my life everywhere I go, to the praise and honor of my Lord Jesus Christ.

I pray this in Jesus' name!

MY CONFESSION FOR TODAY

I confess that I have staying power! This divine impartation is part of my inheritance as a child of God! I have within me the supernatural ability to endure difficulties and to persevere through challenges while holding fast to my faith. When I encounter hostility or obstacles, the Lord Himself is my strength and personal bravery. The Lord steadies and directs my steps, enabling me to make progress in times of trouble, testing, suffering, or great responsibility. Amid all these things, no matter what I may face, I am more than a conqueror through Jesus Christ, and I always triumph in surpassing victory through Him!

I declare this by faith in Jesus' name!

QUESTIONS FOR YOU TO CONSIDER

1. Did you ever think of patience and endurance as supernatural abilities? How do you view these qualities now?
2. Can you think of a time in your life when you sensed a supernatural impartation of *hupomeno* strength that enabled you to endure a difficult situation until you could come out on the other side victoriously? What was that experience, and what spiritual lesson did you learn from it?
3. What situation are you facing now that requires supernatural staying power? You can do all things through Christ who strengthens you! Read and think on what Philippians 4:13 means for you personally.

OCTOBER 28

The Signs of a True Apostle

Truly the signs of an apostle
were wrought among you....
— 2 Corinthians 12:12

Today we'll look further at the indicators the apostle Paul listed that point to a true apostolic call on a person's life. The Holy Spirit inspired Paul to inform the Church of these clues to a true apostolic ministry so that we as believers would know how to discern and receive from this crucial ministry gift. Paul wrote, "Truly the signs of an apostle were wrought among you in all patience, in *signs*, and wonders, and mighty deeds" (2 Corinthians 12:12).

The next criterion after "patience" that Paul mentioned is "signs." He wrote this verse to the Corinthians, yet there is no clear record in the book of Acts of his working signs and wonders in Corinth (*see* Acts 18). However, because of this statement, we may assume that miraculous signs *were* wrought through Paul in Corinth similar to the signs God performed through him in other cities — such as:

- Restoring strength to the limbs of the lame (*see* Acts 14:8-10).
- Casting out demons (*see* Acts 16:16-18).
- Transferring God's healing power through aprons or napkins taken from Paul's body to the bedridden who couldn't attend his meetings because of their physical conditions (*see* Acts 19:11,12).
- Raising the dead (*see* Acts 20:9-12).
- Healing the sick (*see* Acts 28:8,9).

People mistakenly get the impression that Paul's ministry was continually visited with miracles of this nature. But if one carefully and honestly examines the book of Acts to determine the regularity in which these types of supernatural signs occurred, you will find that these events did not occur nonstop in Paul's ministry, but rather at pivotal and crucial moments when miracles were needed to open the door for the Gospel even wider. These were supernatural signs intended to grab the attention of listeners and to serve as proof that the Gospel message they were hearing was true.

In addition to these miraculous signs, Paul also listed "wonders" and "mighty deeds" as indicators that a person has an apostolic call on his or her life. The word "wonders" is the Greek word *teras*. The word *teras* was used in classical Greek times to depict the *fright*, *terror*, *shock*, *surprise*, or *astonishment* felt by bystanders who observed events that were contrary to the normal course of nature. Such occurrences were viewed as miracles, and people believed they could only take place through the intervention of divine power. These miraculous events were so shocking that they left people *speechless, shocked, astonished, bewildered, baffled, taken aback, stunned,* and *awestruck* — and therefore in a state of *wonder.*

This is the reason the word *teras* is most often translated as the word "wonders" in the New Testament. It describes occurrences so out of the ordinary that people are left in a state of *perplexity, amazement,* and *wonder* as a result.

But Paul didn't stop with the word "wonders." He went on to say, "And mighty deeds." The word "and" is the Greek word *kai,* which could — and probably should — be translated *even,* causing the phrase "mighty deeds" to actually *amplify* the word "wonders." Thus, the phrase could be translated "wonders, *even mighty deeds.*" In other words, Paul was saying that these "wonders" were so amazing, they were truly "mighty deeds."

The phrase "mighty deeds" is a translation of the word *dunamis,* the Greek word for *power.* It is from this word that we derive the English word "dynamite," which is a very appropriate usage of this Greek word. Indeed, *dunamis* power carries the idea of *explosive, superhuman power that comes with enormous energy and produces phenomenal, extraordinary, and unparalleled results.* The word *dunamis* depicts "mighty deeds" that are impressive, incomparable, and beyond human ability to perform. In fact, this very word is used in First Corinthians 12:10 when the apostle Paul lists "the working of miracles" as one of the gifts of the Spirit. Thus, the word *dunamis,* as Paul now uses it in Second Corinthians 12:12, denotes *miraculous power* or *miraculous manifestations.*

Keep in mind that the word "wonders" refers to people being shocked or stunned by events that don't occur in nature or by experiences that are out of the flow of normal life. Because Paul connected it to the phrase "mighty deeds" — the Greek word *dunamis,* referring to *superhuman or miraculous powers* — we know that he was referring to instances when the laws of nature are overruled or suspended by the supernatural power of God. In some way, God Himself intervenes in the laws of nature and does something that could never occur in the natural realm.

There were many instances of "mighty deeds" in Paul's ministry pertaining to miraculous healings that could never have occurred naturally or with the assistance of medicine. Whenever God's power intervenes to reverse a physical condition that medical science defines as incurable, this can technically be defined as *a miracle.*

But in addition to the supernatural power that flowed from Paul to others to work healing miracles, there were also some truly amazing instances when God's power intervened on *Paul's* behalf. We find an example of this in Acts 16, when Paul was miraculously released from his jail cell in Philippi after a remarkable earthquake shook the prison and set him free.

Acts 16:24 tells us of a time when Paul and Silas were in an "inner prison" and their feet were "fast in stocks." As the two apostles began to pray and sing songs of praise to God in the middle of the night, "...suddenly there was a great earthquake, so that the foundations of the prison were shaken: and immediately all the doors were opened, and every one's bands were loosed" (v. 26).

Consider how strange this occurrence was that night. This earthquake shook the prison, opened all the doors, and caused the chains to fall off the prisoners. Yet it seems that not one brick fell, for there is no record of any damage to the actual building. In fact, this appears to have been such a regional earthquake that it affected only one building in the entire city. Only the prison where Paul and Silas were confined apparently felt the impact of this particular earthquake!

When people heard about this landmark event, the news left them in a state of *wonder*. In other words, they were left *speechless, shocked, astonished, bewildered, baffled, taken aback, stunned,* and *awestruck*. Certainly this earthquake would qualify as a "mighty deed" — a miraculous event — that occurred in the life of the apostle Paul.

Another example of a mighty deed occurring in Paul's life can be found in Acts 28:3, when Paul was shipwrecked and marooned on the island of Melita. On that rainy day as Paul was gathering sticks to build a fire, "…there came a viper out of the heat, and fastened on his hand." When the barbarians saw the deadly, venomous viper hanging from the apostle's hand, they expected Paul to swell up and suddenly fall down dead (*see* v. 6). But instead, verse 5 tells us that Paul "…shook off the beast into the fire, and felt no harm."

The deadly poison of that snake should have killed Paul. But as the powerful venom surged through the apostle's circulatory system, God's power intervened, overruling and nullifying the venom so that it had no adverse effect on Paul whatsoever! On the other hand, this "wonder" had a *huge* impact on those who were standing nearby, watching in amazement. Instead of seeing Paul fall dead, these people saw "…no harm come to him..." (v. 6). They were so shocked by this miraculous event that a major revival erupted, through which many people from every quarter of the island came to Christ. This would therefore definitely qualify as a "mighty deed" occurring in the life of the apostle Paul.

Writing about his many experiences in ministry in Second Corinthians 11, Paul tells of being shipwrecked three times, severely beaten on five different occasions, traveling on dangerous roads and across treacherous rivers, and so forth. If it hadn't been for God's power sustaining Paul and intervening on his behalf, many of these experiences would have ended in the apostle's death.

We must note the time Paul was stoned in Lystra and left for dead. Religious Jews were professionals at stoning people to death. Therefore, it's very significant that Acts 14:19 tells us that certain Jews, "…having stoned Paul, drew him out of the city, supposing he had been dead."

After pummeling Paul's body with stones, these Jews dragged him out of the city and left him to be eaten by animals. But Acts 14:20 goes on to tell us, "…As the disciples stood round about him, he rose up…." This was a *mighty deed* — a special working of God's miraculous power that seems to have actually raised Paul from death itself.

Those who have an apostolic call on their lives serve God on the front lines of His Kingdom, facing challenges and difficulties beyond what others might encounter. These individuals must forge their way and make significant inroads into the enemy's territory. Therefore, miracles — *those undeniable moments when God's power intervenes in the natural course of events* — are required and will always be evident in the lives of those whom God has called to be apostles.

God imparts supernatural strength for the apostolic pioneer to endure the fight of faith required to fulfill his assignment. And throughout the assignment, whenever needed, God shows up to perform signs, wonders, and mighty deeds — not only following the anointed preaching of His Word, but also on behalf of His obedient "sent one" in order to ensure that the divine assignment is completed. As a result, people's lives are transformed to the glory of Jesus Christ and the building of His Church!

MY PRAYER FOR TODAY

Father God, I praise and magnify You, for You alone are the God of miracles. Your mighty wonders cannot be contained or explained by any natural power or force of nature. Lord Jesus, You said supernatural signs would follow the preaching of Your Word. I pray that ministers and believers everywhere who proclaim Your Word will also walk in mighty demonstrations of Your awesome power to authorize them as they enforce Your will. Lord Jesus, as we approach the day of Your returning, I expect an increase in signs, wonders, and miracles — not only through Your people, but also on behalf of Your people to protect them and to prevent their assignments from being cut short as they live in consecrated service to Your divine will.

I pray this in Jesus' name!

MY CONFESSION FOR TODAY

I confess that Jesus Christ is the same yesterday, today, and forever; therefore, I know that He continues to confirm His Word with signs following just as He said He would. The supernatural power of my Almighty God is still on display today through miracles, signs and wonders that manifest outside the realm of ordinary events — and they do so both through me and on my behalf to the glory of God the Father!

I declare this by faith in Jesus' name!

QUESTIONS FOR YOU TO CONSIDER

1. What other signs and mighty deeds can you think of that marked the apostle Paul's life and apostolic ministry? Why not take a few minutes and make a list of what comes to your mind?
2. We find examples of God protecting and delivering His people through miracles, signs, and wonders in both the Old and New Testament. Can you recall a time when God intervened in your own life through a demonstration of His power and love that could not be explained as merely a natural event?
3. You may not be an apostle, pioneering for the sake of the Gospel. But in Mark 16:17 and 18, Jesus described specific signs that would follow those who believe. Take a moment to read these words of Jesus and then ask yourself if these signs have ever followed *you*.

OCTOBER 29

Why Would Anyone Claim To Be an Apostle if He Wasn't?

And He Himself gave some to be *apostles*....
— Ephesians 4:11 *NKJV*

Why would anyone claim to be an apostle who was not? In the Early Church, it seems there were many individuals who deliberately claimed to be apostles because they understood the *weight* and *influence* that accompanied this title. If a person was an apostle — the Greek word *apostolos* — they knew that this position held enormous authority and that those who carried this title could obtain leverage in the Church. Therefore, they coveted this title and intentionally claimed it as a way to gain control and exert power over God's people.

What an apostle said carried great weight within a church or even within an entire group of churches. Whoever could lay claim to the apostolic title would be able to influence what happened in the lives of many people. For a genuine apostle, this was a serious responsibility that he exercised with holiness, fear, and prudence. But for a person with impure motives, this position of authority represented an opportunity to obtain power for the sake of selfish gain.

Many imposters therefore moved in on the scene like predators in Paul's day — waiting for the opportunity to seize a fledgling church through deception and then claim it for themselves.

In fact, false apostles frequently followed Paul from city to city, lying in wait until he left town. Then they would begin implementing their heinous plan of ruining Paul's reputation and claiming the territory for themselves. This is what Paul referred to when he wrote that there was assigned to him "...a thorn in the flesh, the messenger of Satan to buffet me..." (2 Corinthians 12:7).

The word "thorn" is the Greek word *skolops*. It could refer to either a *thorn* or a *splinter* that gets under the skin and causes a constant irritant. Paul specifically identified these "thorns" or "splinters" as "the messenger of Satan." These were individuals who were such a constant hassle to Paul that he called them Satan's messengers.

Paul endured many afflictions during his ministry, and many of them were a result of these false ministers who fiercely opposed him and constantly tried to displace his position of authority over the flock of God in the local churches. They wanted Paul out of the picture so they could usurp his place of prominence. Therefore, they attempted to discredit the apostle, hoping to shift the spotlight to themselves by boasting that their revelations were superior. Paul alluded to these sheep-stealers in Second Corinthians 11:5 (*NIV*) when he sarcastically referred to them as "super-apostles" and scoffed at their claims of hyper-spirituality.

This is precisely the same reason people with false motives claim apostleship today. It is all about control. These self-inspired claims are evil and are usually monetarily motivated. The apostle Paul had no tolerance for those who claimed to be apostles but were not. They were constantly battling Paul for his relationship with a church or group of churches.

Pretentious self-promotion is a key disqualifier for the kind of leadership God blesses. In fact, the Lord Himself will resist the proud and self-seeking while giving grace, favor, and peace to those who humble themselves beneath His hand. Let's do all we can to make sure our motives are in line with the characteristics that qualify the authentic and not disqualify the counterfeit ministers who never passed their tests in God's classroom of integrity.

MY PRAYER FOR TODAY

Father, I thank You for the common sense shared in these Sparkling Gems to keep me safe from influence of imposters and spiritual predators. Thank You for helping me to be wise and to keep my eyes wide open about who I receive as a spiritual authority in my life. I realize that I must be accountable to someone in my life, but I ask You to give me discernment about who that person should be!

I pray this in Jesus' name!

MY CONFESSION FOR TODAY

I confess that my natural and spiritual eyes are wide open, along with my natural and spiritual ears. I am sensitive to the voice and leading of the Holy Spirit and I do not fall victim to unscrupulous people who flatter others for personal gain. I pay close attention to what I hear and see. If anyone has ulterior motives for wanting spiritual authority in my life, the Spirit of Truth illuminates my understanding so I can see and recognize it. The Spirit of God within my spirit will bear witness to alert me so I will know when I have come across the real deal!

I declare this by faith in Jesus' name!

QUESTIONS FOR YOU TO CONSIDER

1. Have you ever seen a so-called spiritual leader take advantage of others? Were you hurt by that leader's actions? Have you forgiven him or her? Have you truly moved on and let it go?
2. I want to tell you that there are more real ministers of the Gospel than counterfeits. It would be a good exercise for you to name all the real ministers of the Gospel that have been a blessing to you over the course of your life. You'll discover that they far outweigh those who have a negative influence.
3. If someone in the ministry financially took advantage of you, did your spirit alert you to it in advance, but you ignored it? In most cases, our inner man knows when something is amiss, but we have to listen in order to be protected. If you consider your own situation, did you feel an inner alert telling you to be careful?

OCTOBER 30

Apostolic Authority Is Relational, Geographical, and Territorial

And He Himself gave some to be *apostles*....
— Ephesians 4:11 *NKJV*

The very nature of apostolic ministry lends itself to being relational, geographical, and territorial. Let me tell you what I mean — *and then you can think about it*!

The apostolic call is based on *relationships*. For instance, although Paul was universally respected in the Early Church as an apostle, he was *not* an apostle to every First Century church. He was an apostle only to those with whom he had an *apostolic relationship*.

Churches in other cities and regions acknowledged Paul's apostleship, but he was not *their* apostle. Other believers respected Paul as an excellent minister, a beloved brother in the Lord, and an able leader. But he only had apostolic responsibility for the churches he had helped start and those for whom he served as mentor, teacher, and father in the faith.

Thus, Paul's apostleship was limited to those for whom he bore direct spiritual responsibility and with whom he had a unique relationship. This would have included the churches of *Ephesus, Colossae, Corinth, Galatia, Hierapolis, Laodicea, Pergamum, Philadelphia, Philippi, Sardis, Smyrna, Thyatira,* and others. Paul's relationship with these churches is the reason we have the books of First and Second Corinthians, Galatians, Ephesians, Philippians, and Colossians. Paul wrote these letters because he was directly responsible for the spiritual well-being of these believers and because he had a unique apostolic relationship either with them or with their local leadership.

One example of Paul's apostolic relationship with local leadership was the church in Colossae. Although there is no evidence that Paul personally founded the Colossian church, we know that he sent Epaphras as his *personal emissary* to fulfill that assignment. Under Paul's orders and spiritual covering, Epaphras traveled to Colossae and started the church. Once the Colossian church was established, the congregation received Paul as the apostle to that church *based on his relationship to Epaphras.*

Paul was very aware that he wasn't an apostle to everyone. That's why he wrote, "Not boasting of things without our measure [or out of our territory]...not to boast in another man's line of things made ready to our hand [for example, not to take credit for another person's apostolic work]" (2 Corinthians 10:15,16). Paul was careful not to cross over into another man's territory if it might produce confusion about who was supposed to give direction to certain churches or to whom those churches were accountable (*see* 2 Corinthians 10:13,14). This tells us that Paul not only *possessed* authority, but he also *respected* the authority and territory of others.

This also explains why Paul told the Corinthians, "If I be not an apostle unto others, yet doubtless I am to you..." (1 Corinthians 9:2). The word "doubtless" is actually the Greek word *gar,* and it means *indeed.* It is an affirmation of his apostolic relationship to them. A better translation would be "indeed I am to you!" Paul knew that his apostleship was *limited, geographical,* and *relational,* so he concentrated on those with whom he knew he had this special, "indeed" God-given relationship.

Paul frequently had to defend his apostleship because of these deceitful workers who swarmed in, trying to exert authority over entire regions of churches that he and other apostles had established and to which they had imparted their lives. Apostleship was power, so those with impure motives sought to invade Paul's territory and claim his fruit, seeing it as an effective way to exploit someone else's work for themselves.

Those who coveted the apostolic position used every imaginable method to attract, tempt, lure, entice, and seduce the churches under the realm of authority of genuine apostles. In Paul's case, the imposters couldn't find a legitimate reason to accuse the apostle, so they used slanderous and even stupid accusations as they tried to persuade the churches to reject Paul and submit to *their* authority instead. For example, these false apostles:

- Accused Paul of being unimpressive in appearance and a poor public speaker (*see* 2 Corinthians 10:10; 11:6).
- Accused him of financially taking advantage of the churches (*see* 1 Corinthians 9:14,15).
- Endeavored to lure the churches back into the noose of legalism by accusing Paul of being loose in his doctrine of grace (*see* Galatians 1:6,7).
- Asserted that Paul's revelations weren't as deep as theirs, prompting Paul to remind his readers that he was the one who actually had a direct revelation of Jesus Himself (*see* 1 Corinthians 9:1).

These usurpers of apostolic authority were after Paul's territory — and in order to get what they were after, they set out to *discredit* Paul. This is why Paul frequently started his letters by saying, "Paul, an *apostle* of Jesus Christ" (*see* 1 Corinthians 1:1; 2 Corinthians 1:1; Galatians 1:1; Ephesians 1:1; Colossians 1:1).

Wherever Paul's apostleship was being threatened by false apostles, he rose up like a spiritual father to defend his position. His children in the Lord were in jeopardy, and his relationship with them was at stake. Paul's deep sense of responsibility and his love for the flock wouldn't allow him to remain silent. Rather, it drove him to speak up and wage war if needed against the imposters who were trying to invade his geographic realm of influence. Paul was determined not to allow those deceivers to destroy his credibility so they could steal and ravage the sheep under his care.

It is sad to say, but there are people who misuse the ministry for their own personal gain of some type. Whether it's for prestige or monetary reasons, it is innately wrong. When this kind of deceit occurred in Paul's day, this Early Church apostle rose up to defend the churches, as well as his apostleship. Paul's one desire was to protect the flock that God had placed under his charge against wolves that only sought to devour the sheep to gratify their self-absorbed lust for control.

In this, Paul revealed the power of the apostolic relationship that provides the foundational mortar for the "house" God has called an apostle to build. Whatever the assignment that particular apostle has been sent to fulfill, it will be defined by some form of divine boundaries, whether they are regional, geographical, or spiritual in nature. And within that marked-out territory assigned by the Lord, the true apostle will stand guard over the relationships he is called to steward within those boundaries. His heart's fervent desire will be to protect, teach, and strengthen the people — ensuring that they become firmly established in God's Word, not swayed by external forces or opposition — so they in turn can take *their* place and do their part in fulfilling the apostolic assignment.

Perhaps now you can see more clearly what was in God's heart in giving the apostolic ministry gift to the Body of Christ. Certainly it is not more important than the other four ministry gifts, but it *is* crucial in its unique purpose and function. As we recognize and esteem this gift operating throughout the earth in this hour, we actually help the Body of Christ — and ourselves personally — receive the full benefits of the apostolic ministry, thus becoming more and more equipped to do all the Church is called to do before the return of our soon-coming King!

MY PRAYER FOR TODAY

Father, I ask You to help me use my head and not just react according to my emotions, when it comes to who is leading me spiritually. You have given me a mind that You expect me to use, and I pray for the wisdom to think carefully and clearly about those to whom I give the right to lead me spiritually. I thank You for my pastor and for my church. Nonetheless, I know that I must keep my eyes open and my heart in tune with Your Spirit about anyone to whom I yield oversight in my life.

I pray this prayer in Jesus' name!

MY CONFESSION FOR TODAY

I confess that I have a good head on my shoulders! My heart is open to the Spirit of God, and my mind thinks soundly and clearly. I rely on God's wisdom and counsel, and He causes my thoughts to be in agreement with His will. I have a strong foundation of God's Word in my heart and mind; therefore, I am not easily misled because that Word illuminates my understanding. When something is wrong, an alert goes off inside me that warns me to be careful. I am not suspicious or quick to accuse, but I am sensitive to what is happening spiritually. I thank God that the Holy Spirit produces in me the mind of Christ, and the mind of Christ helps me to think soundly and accurately.

I declare this by faith in Jesus' name!

QUESTIONS FOR YOU TO CONSIDER

1. I have been misled before because I was innocent and naïve, but those experiences have made me wiser and smarter. I am thankful for every experience I've had in my spiritual journey. What are some of the experiences you've had that have made you a little wiser?
2. What advice would you give someone who was just starting his walk with the Lord and is very pure in his thinking about everything and everyone? Without poisoning him with bad stories, what helpful advice would you give him about whom to follow as a spiritual leader and how to guard himself against deception?
3. As you've recalled the difficult experiences that became your occasion to gain wisdom, sift through your heart to determine if you detect a root of bitterness toward anyone who was a part of that experience. Release all who hurt you and let them go from the offense you've attached to them. You will be amazed by the way that act of obedience and love will propel you forward in the plan of God for your life.

OCTOBER 31

False Apostles and Deceitful Workers

For such are false apostles, deceitful workers….
— 2 Corinthians 11:13

Today is the last *Sparkling Gem* on the subject of apostleship. I have sensed the need to cover this material because this topic is so rarely addressed. I pray that it has been a blessing to you and that it has caused you to deeply think about spiritual leadership — the need for it and the need to be careful about whom you choose to follow spiritually.

In Second Corinthians 11:13 and 14, Paul described the growing problem of false apostles. He said, "For such are false apostles, deceitful workers, transforming themselves into the apostles of Christ. And no marvel; for Satan himself is transformed into an angel of light."

The phrase "false apostles" comes from the Greek word *pseudapostolos*, a compound of *pseudes* and *apostolos*. The word *pseudes* carries the idea of *any type of falsehood*. It can picture *a person who projects a false image of himself, someone who deliberately walks in a pretense that is untrue*, or *someone who intentionally misrepresents facts or truths*. In every instance where this word is used in the New Testament, it portrays *someone who misrepresents who he is by what he does, by what he says, or by the lie or misrepresentation that he purports to be true.* The second part of the word is *apostolos* — which, of course, is the word for an *apostle.* Therefore, the word *pseudapostolos* actually describes *a pretend apostle* or *someone who intentionally represents himself to be an apostle even though he knows he is not.*

Paul called these false apostles "deceitful workers." The word "deceitful" comes from the Greek word *dolios*, which is derived from a root word used to describe *bait that is put on a hook to catch fish.* It conveys the idea of *craftiness, cheating, cunning, dishonesty, fraud, guile,* and *trickery intended to entrap someone in an act of deception.* Like a fisherman who carefully camouflages a hook with bait, these counterfeit apostles lured sincere believers closer and closer until those believers finally "took the bait." And once the hook was in their victims' mouths, the false apostles "pulled the hook" and took congregations, even entire groups of churches, captive.

Paul said these individuals were deceitful "workers." This word "workers" is taken from the Greek word *ergates*, a word that denotes *someone who actively works at what he is doing.* This indicates that nothing was accidental about this act of deception and that these false apostles put forth great effort to impersonate real apostolic ministry.

Paul said these deceitful workers were so skilled at the art of deception that they were able to "transform" themselves into the apostles of Christ. The word translated "transform" in this verse is the Greek word *metaschimatidzo*, which means *to disguise oneself, to deliberately change one's outward appearance,* or *to masquerade in clothing that depicts a person as different than he really is.* Paul was referring to individuals who intentionally attempted to pass themselves off as apostles, knowing full well that they were not. He was describing a blatant act of deception.

At that time, such a large number of people were professing to be apostles that the Ephesian church developed certain criteria — *a paradigm* or *model* — to determine who *was* and who *was not* an authentic New Testament apostle. The problem was serious in the Ephesian church, and that church was serious about correcting it. This prompted Jesus to tell the Ephesian believers, "...Thou hast tried them which say they are apostles, and are not, and hast found them liars" (Revelation 2:2).

The word "tried" points to *a thorough and serious investigation.* It means *to try, to examine, to inspect, to investigate, to scrutinize,* or *to put to the test.* The leadership of the church wanted to guard the reputation of the true apostolic gift and protect the members of their congregation from pretenders who sought to lead them astray. This leadership was so serious about it that they developed a "test" to prove whether or not a person really had an apostolic calling. This should show how powerful the apostolic call is — for if the church at Ephesus was testing people to see if their call was real, it meant they felt a need to protect those who had a *bona fide* apostolic calling.

This last *Sparkling Gem* in this series is *not* intended to promote suspicion of leadership in the Church, but rather to encourage discernment. The apostolic call is so important to building up the local church that those who imitate this call for the sake of personal gain should not be tolerated in a congregation. And if a person has an authentic call, a test or a little scrutiny won't hurt or diminish it. In fact, it will only *prove* that the call is genuine and authentic, which will then open the way for you to open your heart and receive the rich benefits of the apostolic anointing whenever it is present in your midst!

MY PRAYER FOR TODAY

Father, help me trust those who are over me in the Lord to know how to test and try those who come to minister to our congregation. I trust my pastor and the leadership of our church. Nevertheless, I pray for You to guide them and to give them wisdom as they open the doors of our church to ministers who are new to us. I ask You, Lord, to heighten their spiritual discernment so that they can clearly distinguish when everything that glitters is not gold, and everything that looks spiritual is not necessarily of God. Help our overseers to have the wisdom of God in whom they invite to minister to our congregation.

I pray this in Jesus' name!

MY CONFESSION FOR TODAY

I confess that my pastor and the leadership team of our church are spiritually sensitive about those whom they invite to minister to our congregation. They are diligent to pray and seek the Lord; therefore, I can rest at peace that whomever may be invited to stand in our pulpit is anointed to impart something from Heaven that will strengthen and establish us to do the will of God from the heart. I am so thankful that this responsibility is not mine, but I pray for them. I declare that those who are called and equipped to exercise stewardship and give an account for my soul in the Lord walk in the wisdom and spiritual fortitude they need to make right choices for our congregation, so when they stand before You they can hear You say, "Well done!"

I declare this by faith in Jesus' name!

QUESTIONS FOR YOU TO CONSIDER

1. Do you trust your pastor and spiritual leaders to make right choices concerning those whom they invite to minister in the pulpit of your church? If not, why don't you trust them, and why are you attending that church if you don't trust their spiritual oversight?
2. Do you take responsibility for what you spiritually receive into your own heart, or do you just naïvely receive whatever is dished out for you to consume spiritually?
3. Pastors do have a great responsibility to make sure a special speaker is spiritually right with God. Are your pastors careful about those whom they invite to minister in your church? If you are a pastor, are you doing what is necessary to be watchful over your flock in this way?

NOVEMBER 1

More End-Time Ministry Advice

But watch thou in all things, endure afflictions,
do the work of an evangelist,
make full proof of thy ministry.
— 2 Timothy 4:5

Today I want to give you some *end-time ministry advice* — advice that is very pertinent for the present times. You might want to go back and review what we discussed in the September 26 *Sparkling Gem*, because it is foundational to what I will share with you today. As we saw, the Holy Spirit prophesied in Second Timothy 4:3,4 that doctrine would change in the last days.

The Holy Spirit inspired these writings in Second Timothy 4 to *prepare* us for what lies ahead, much of which is already happening right now. He told us that when it comes to our stance on the infallible, incorruptible Word of God, we should be dedicated to correct interpretation and to teaching and preaching that is done with the power of the Holy Spirit.

This is very important instruction for us in a day when people are abandoning the sound teaching of doctrine. Regardless of what others do, we must decide that we will remain *clear channels* for the truth, even if it means we must put up with accusations that we are too traditional and stuck in the past. *This is God's command to us.*

Then Paul wrote in verse 5, "...Make full proof of thy ministry." The Greek word for "full proof" is *plerophoreo*, which simply means *fulfill*. Paul was urging Timothy to complete his ministry and bring it to its fullness. Although Paul was addressing Timothy directly, he was also talking very specifically to *us* — to those who would be alive at the end of the age. I believe this refers to our generation, and it certainly explains why we see so much nonsense going on in the world around us concerning the way people think and believe. This kind of deluded thinking and believing has even crept into the Church.

The pure preaching of doctrine is often replaced today with motivational speaking — nice, uplifting messages. In fact, the majority of people in modern congregations are ignorant of the most elementary aspects of New Testament doctrine. And *very often*, those who occupy the pulpits — although they may be masterful communicators and rate highly among motivational speakers — are equally uneducated in basic Bible principles. Many of those who do know the Bible don't preach it as strongly as they once did because it's not as popular as other types of messages. The result of this compromise is a drift from the Holy Scriptures. And this drift *continues*, seemingly unabated, while the doctrinal vacuum in the Church is being filled with motivational messages and "new-and-improved" church-growth programs. *Yet when everything is said and done, only the Bible has the power to permanently transform a life.*

Friend, the Bible has not changed. It's still sharper than any two-edged sword (*see* Hebrews 4:12), and it's still the answer for everyone, whether it's in written form or on your computer or smart phone! The Bible is still the Word of God that has His very breath infused within it. And if you'll take it into your heart and release it, it will put you on your feet again. It will heal your body, deliver your mind, and bring peace and order to your children and your household!

So much of what "creeps" into your home today is just a treadmill of information designed to keep you in a continual state of learning, never able to come to the knowledge of the truth (*see* 2 Timothy 3:6,7). So if I could leave you with some valuable end-time advice today, it would be to *continue in the truth you know — found in God's holy, infallible, incorruptible Word.*

You can rest assured that the Word of God *is*, *has been*, and *always will be* unchanging, and it will produce fruit in you if you will abide in it. God's Word will perfectly equip you to stand strong, unfaltering, and unwavering in the days that lie ahead. Your part is simply to abide in His truth and *continue* in that which you have learned from Him.

MY PRAYER FOR TODAY

Father, I thank You for this reminder of the dire need to guard my heart and spirit against the whims of the times that have adversely affected the Church. I don't feel fear because of this teaching; I feel prepared by it. I am thankful to You for loving me so much that You put such clear, sound warnings in Scripture to protect us in these last days. Help me be open to what You are doing and closed to what leads away from the pure teaching of doctrinal truth.

I pray this in Jesus' name!

MY CONFESSION FOR TODAY

I confess that I exercise discernment when it comes to my consumption of spiritual teaching. I know that what I put into my eyes and ears affects what I believe and what I receive — so I put a filter upon my eyes and ears to make sure only truth finds access to my mind and heart. Lord, I am thankful that You have chosen me to live in these last days, and I count it an honor that You trusted me with this privilege. While so many people struggle to know what is right or wrong — doctrinally or morally — I declare that Your Word is burning and alive in my heart and will keep me walking in the light, enabling me to bring answers to people in a way that will offer them spiritual help and relief.

I declare this by faith in Jesus' name!

QUESTIONS FOR YOU TO CONSIDER

1. Have you ever expressed your thankfulness to your pastor for providing solid Bible teaching in your church every week? He works very hard to provide a full spiritual meal, and it would be such a blessing for you to personally thank him. He would appreciate it.

2. If you attend a church where the Bible is not taught much anymore, why are you attending that church? Don't you agree that you need to be where you can hear the clear, sound teaching of the Word of God?
3. Can you explain the basic tenets of the Christian faith? Could you pass a doctrine test? If yes, amen. If no, what should you do to change that?

NOVEMBER 2

Can You Do What You're Doing in the Name of Jesus?

And whatsoever ye do in word or deed,
do all in the name of the Lord Jesus....
— Colossians 3:17

As you know, the Holy Spirit lives inside you if you have been born again, and your body individually is His temple here on the earth (*see* 1 Corinthians 6:19,20). After Jesus died for you, washed you with His blood, and placed His Holy Spirit inside you, don't you think you should think once, twice, or *more* about everything you do?

The Holy Spirit — your internal Resident — is right there with you all the time. And whatever you say, do, watch, or participate in, you involve Him because He lives inside you. So if you can say and do things, knowing those words and deeds will bless the Holy Spirit and honor the name of Jesus, then go right ahead and say and do them. But if you are even a bit concerned that what you say or do will grieve the Spirit or bring dishonor to the name of Jesus, you should refrain from it.

In Colossians 3:17, the apostle Paul said, "And whatsoever ye do in word or deed, do all in the name of the Lord Jesus...." Let's look at this verse a little deeper today.

The word "whatsoever" is translated from the Greek phrase *ti ean*. The word *ti* describes *the most minute, miniscule detail*. This is important, because it tells us God is concerned about every action in our lives — not only the large ones, but even the smallest. The word *ean* generalizes the subject to mean *whatever*. But when *ti ean* are used together, it can be translated *whatsoever*, as the *King James Version* records it. But it is important for you to know that included in this word "whatsoever" is the picture of *every little detail*, even the smallest, *most minute, miniscule detail.*

This verse continues, "And whatever you do...." The word you "do" is a form of the Greek word *poieo*, which has a wide range of meanings in the New Testament. Here, however, it infers *any action* that one does. It is another word with wide-range meaning, which tells us that we must be careful about *whatever* we say and do, for every little action has an impact on our internal Resident, the Holy Spirit, and on the honor we should bring to the name of Jesus with our lives.

Colossians 3:17 continues, "And whatever you do in word...." The word "word" comes from the Greek word *logos*, and it depicts *spoken words*. This means that our words have an impact on the indwelling Holy Spirit and the manner in which we honor the Lord Jesus.

In other words, there are some types of verbal communication that should *never* come out of the mouth of a committed Christian. We read about this in Ephesians 4:29,30, where we are commanded, "Let no corrupt communication proceed out of your mouth, but that which is good to the use of edifying, that it may minister grace unto the hearers. And grieve not the holy Spirit of God...."

I want you to especially notice it says that we must not allow "corrupt" communication to proceed out of our mouths, for it "grieves" the Holy Spirit. The word "corrupt" is the Greek word *sapros*, which describes anything that is *rank, foul, putrid, rotten, corrupt,* or *worthless*. This could include gossipy language or simply putrid talk. Ephesians 4:30 says that it "grieves" the Spirit when a believer talks like this. The word "grieve" is *lupete*, and it means it *deeply pains* the Spirit when a believer talks in this fashion.

This tells us that when a Christian uses corrupt language — which could include anything that doesn't minister life to someone else — or any language that is rotten and worthless, it grieves the Holy Spirit and brings dishonor to the name of Jesus. Thus we must avoid being gossipy or using language that is not worthy of Jesus' name or the Holy Spirit's indwelling presence.

But the verse goes on to say, "And whatever you do in word or deed...." The word "deed" is a form of the Greek word *ergos*, which refers to our *actions* or *deeds*. This would include our treatment of others, how we handle our money, what we do with our time, what we look at on TV or on the Internet, etc.

"Deed" — *ergos* — is all-inclusive of *everything*, making it impossible to give a full list of "deeds" here. But if you will listen to the indwelling Holy Spirit, you will know when your actions or deeds grieve Him. When that occurs, simply back off, immediately repent, and resolve not to do it again.

Paul continues in Colossians 3:17, "And whatever you do in word or deed, do all in the name of the Lord Jesus...." The word "all" in Greek is the compound word *panta* — which is the word *pan*, meaning *all*, with the affixed *ta*, referring to *everything*. Thus the word *panta* means *all things* — nothing excluded. We are to do everything we do — nothing excluded — in the name, or to the honor, of our Lord Jesus.

- ➢ If the movies or TV programs you want to watch don't give honor to the name of Jesus...
- ➢ If what you're watching on the Internet doesn't give honor to the name of Jesus...
- ➢ If the words you are speaking don't give honor to the name of Jesus...

- If *anything* you want to do doesn't give honor to the name of Jesus…
- *THEN DON'T DO IT!* It's just that simple.

We need to examine our lives and see if we are living in a way that honors the indwelling Spirit and the name of Jesus.

The truth is, you probably already know what you do that doesn't honor the Holy Spirit and the name of Jesus. You may have hardened your heart so you don't feel conviction about it anymore — but if you are serious about your walk with God, you must turn from these things that grieve Him and renew your tenderness to the Holy Spirit and your honor for the name of the Lord Jesus Christ.

If your heart has already been hardened in an area that causes you to do and say things that are displeasing to the Holy Spirit and dishonoring to the name of Jesus, it will require your solid commitment — not based on feelings or emotions — for you to return to your first love (*see* Revelation 2:4). You must decide with steadfast determination that you are returning to a life *and a lifestyle* that pleases the Holy Spirit and brings honor and glory to Jesus' name.

It's difficult to soften a hardened heart, but if you make the decision to do it, you can do it — and the flames that once burned in your heart will begin to blaze for Jesus again. When those fires are blazing, you'll never want to do anything to offend the abiding Holy Spirit or to bring dishonor to the precious name of Jesus.

Today I urge you to take a good look at your words and actions and see if they bring honor or dishonor to the Holy Spirit and to the name of Jesus. If you have fallen in an area, ask the Holy Spirit to help renew you and bring you back to a place of tenderness, where you would never want to do anything to offend His presence or Jesus' precious name. If you are willing, He is willing to start the process of renewing and refreshing you today. *Why not get started now?*

MY PRAYER FOR TODAY

Father, I examine my life to see if I am living in a way that honors the indwelling Spirit and the name of Jesus. Help me recognize the attitudes and actions that don't honor the Holy Spirit or exalt the name of Jesus in my life. I ask You to forgive me and to help me to become sensitive in spirit if I have hardened my heart through unbelief and disobedience. Lord, as honestly as I know how, I am serious about my walk with You, so I ask You to please help me to turn away from anything that grieves You.

I pray this in Jesus' name!

MY CONFESSION FOR TODAY

I confess that I make it my aim that whatever I do in word or deed, I do all in the name of the Lord Jesus. I take every thought captive to do His will, and I endeavor to think, speak, and act in a way that only gives honor to my Lord Jesus Christ.

I declare this by faith in Jesus' name!

QUESTIONS FOR YOU TO CONSIDER

1. Can you honestly say that you are living a life that causes the Holy Spirit to dwell comfortably inside you and that gives honor to the name of Jesus?
2. If the Holy Spirit brings an area of your life to your attention in which you've been grieving Him with your words or deeds, what will you do as a consequence? How will you respond?
3. Is the Holy Spirit comfortable with every place you go and everything you watch?

NOVEMBER 3

When Five Psychiatrists Were Assigned To Study Me!

Then went the Pharisees, and took counsel how
they might entangle him in his talk.
— Matthew 22:15

In the early years of our ministry in the former Soviet Union, a group of local psychiatrists determined among themselves that I was using a high level of hypnosis to control the people who attended our church. They stated that my level of hypnosis was so developed that I could even manipulate and control people who read my monthly teaching letters that we sent to television viewers. They suggested that as people read my letters, an amazing hypnotic power dramatically affected the readers, causing the readers to *want* to do what I had encouraged them to do in my letters. Of course, we know it was the power of the Holy Spirit at work, but this was their secular interpretation of what they were observing in our church members and TV viewers.

These psychiatrists were so convinced of these hypnotic powers that they paid a visit to the Department of Religion to express how gravely concerned they were about the level of hypnosis I was using to control people. I was unaware that I was "the talk" of this group until we received a call from the Department of Religion to inform us that five unidentified psychiatrists would be covertly attending all of our church meetings for three months to study the method of hypnosis I was using to control my entire congregation. Of course, since I know nothing of hypnosis, I was amazed! All I had done was teach the Word of God verbally and in written form — under the anointing of the Holy Spirit — and it was producing results in people's lives!

I must tell you — when you know that five psychiatrists are somewhere out in the crowd, listening carefully and trying to find something against you so they can accuse you before the government, it can try to play with your mind. It tends to make you very self-conscious about what you do or say lest it be misinterpreted.

At first, I found myself very guarded in nearly every statement I made, very aware of the psychiatrists who were somewhere in the crowd, listening to "catch" me in something that I did or said publicly. But then I remembered Jesus and the time when the Pharisees listened carefully to Him in order to try to "catch" Him in His words so they could bring an accusation against Him. Knowing that Jesus had experienced the same thing, I turned to the Master to learn how to deal with the situation.

Matthew 22:15 says, "Then went the Pharisees, and took counsel how they might entangle him [Jesus] in his talk." The word "council" is the Greek word *sumboulion*, which describes *a mutual agreement to devise a course of action with harmful or evil purposes.* This tells us plainly that the Pharisees were very deliberate in their actions. They met together, agreed on a mutual course of action, and then proceeded to try to catch Jesus off-guard and "entangle" Him in His talk so they could find a reason to charge Him.

Reading this story personally helped me because it sounded so much like the five psychiatrists who were scattered throughout our congregation. I knew that if Jesus could stand successfully against the Pharisees, then the Holy Spirit could empower me likewise to stand strong and stable in the face of these psychiatrists whose sole purpose was to *prove* that I was controlling and damaging people with hypnotism.

Matthew 22:15 plainly states that this group of Pharisees wanted to "entangle" Jesus in his talk. The word "entangle" is a form of the Greek word *pagideuo*, which can be translated *to ensnare*, *to catch in a trap*, or *to acquire information about an error or fault with the purpose of causing harm*. It carries the idea *to catch off-guard* or *to catch in a mistake*.

Other translations of the New Testament put it like this:

- "Then went the Pharisees, and took counsel how they might *ensnare* him in his talk" (*American Standard Version*).
- "Then the Pharisees went and conspired together plotting how to *trap Him* by [distorting] what He said" (*Amplified Bible*).
- "Then went the Pharisees and held a counsel how they might *ensnare* him in speaking" (*The Darby Bible*).

The Greek wording in this verse emphatically means they purposefully tried to catch Jesus with tricky questions. But Matthew 22:18 says Jesus "perceived" what they were doing. The word "perceived" is *ginosko*, and it means that *He knew*, *He surmised*, and *He perceived* their wicked intent. Rather than be threatened by them and their presence in the crowd, Jesus boldly addressed them — so boldly that "when they had heard these words, they marveled, and left him, and went their way" (Matthew 22:22).

The word "heard" is a participle, which denotes *continuous action*. This means the Pharisees stayed for a considerable period of time and listened to what Jesus had to say as He poured forth the truth in utter boldness. Yet when all was said and done, they had caught Him in no trick, so in the end, they just "marveled" and went their way. The word "marveled" is the Greek word *thaumadzo*, which means Jesus' detractors were *so shocked* at what they heard and how He delivered His message that they were rendered *speechless* and *struck with awe*. Jesus *completely disarmed* them.

This also revealed to me that Jesus didn't change His behavior or His message to fit the doubters in the crowd. In fact, knowing that they were present, Jesus poured it on even more strongly — and as a result, they eventually left Him and, for that time at least, bothered Him no more.

Once I had a deeper understanding of the way Jesus handled this situation, I knew that I was expected to respond like He did. Rather than cower in fear because these five psychiatrists were there, I was to preach more boldly and more fearlessly than ever before. This wasn't a time for me to be self-conscious.

So I decided if those doctors wanted to know what kind of power was operating through me, it was time to give them a very vivid demonstration! For three months, I poured out the Word of God in power and with the conviction and anointing of the Holy Spirit. When the three months were complete, the psychiatrists left, went their way — and filed their reports of what they had observed.

I personally saw those reports. In them, they indicated that they could not explain either the boldness or the effect of the message — and they suggested that it was something that superseded the powers of hypnotism. A few of them had been so helped during those three months that they continued to attend our church for a period of time to receive more help! Oh, what I learned from that experience!

Just like Jesus, we are not to change the way we present ourselves or our message simply because of who is in the audience or because of whom we're talking to at the moment. We have no need to apologize for what we believe or for the power of God that works through us. If we shrink in fear, they will perceive it as weakness, but if we stand forth boldly and pour out what we really believe with the convicting power of the Holy Spirit, it will silence our critics.

Once I was seated on an airplane next to a fabulously well-known, foul-mouthed actress. I thought, "Oh, great, what will I tell her if she asks what I do?" But I decided not to retreat. I was going to be direct and honest and then leave the results with the Lord.

The woman responded to my frankness when she heard that I was a Gospel preacher — and when she heard me describe my family and how we all serve together, she began to weep over the condition of her delinquent daughter and son. For three hours I counseled her from the Word of God about steps she could take to redirect the detrimental path they were currently taking. She was not offended; she was helped. If I had squirmed and sheepishly told her what I did, I am certain she would have shunned me. But my frank, bold response threw open the door for a conversation, which I pray helped her with her children and her personal spiritual life.

Never forget that when you are true to the Word of God and your Spirit-inspired convictions of who you are, the Holy Spirit will be right there to empower you through every situation! The Spirit — working through you — will protect you and render your accusers silent and leave them better off for having been with you!

MY PRAYER FOR TODAY

Father, I ask You to forgive me for the times I've allowed myself to be affected by people I knew were in the crowd or by whom I was talking to in a moment. Help me stand fearless and true to You, to Your Word, and to who I am. I have no reason to be embarrassed or ashamed or to squirm from fear of what man thinks of me. Just as Jesus boldly spoke to the Pharisees who tried to catch Him, help me be bold in moments when I am tempted to be weak or to draw back. Your soul takes no pleasure in those who draw back, so I refuse to be intimidated! Your righteousness makes me as bold as a lion. Therefore, since God is for me, I will not fear any mere man who may come against me!

I pray this in Jesus' name!

MY CONFESSION FOR TODAY

I confess that just like Jesus, I will not change how I present myself or what I believe when I know opponents are listening to me, looking for something negative to say about my faith. I have no need to shrink down or apologize for what I believe or for the power of God that works through me. I will stand forth boldly and pour out what I really believe with the anointing of the Holy Spirit empowering me. I will be true to the Word of God, steadfast in my convictions, and unashamed as I present the Gospel by the power of Christ in me!

I declare this by faith in Jesus' name!

QUESTIONS FOR YOU TO CONSIDER

1. Can you think of a time when you really felt put on the "spot" because of your faith? Did you stand firm in what you believe, or did you cower in fear and retreat?
2. Have you ever had someone intensely question you about what you believe? How did you respond? How would you respond if it happened today?
3. Has there been a moment when you were afraid to stick with who you really are, but you did it anyway and found the other person was receptive to you and to what you had to say?

We have no need to apologize for what we believe or for the power of God that works through us.

NOVEMBER 4

Saul of Tarsus — Proof That God Can Reach Anyone!

Who was before a blasphemer,
and a persecutor, and injurious....
— 1 Timothy 1:13

Sometimes I hear people say, "I just don't know if So-and-so can come to Christ. They are so hardhearted and far from God!" If you've ever said this about a person in your life, today I want to give you hope. We're going to look at what kind of person Paul was before he came to Christ — and I believe you'll see and understand that if God could save Saul of Tarsus (who became known as the apostle Paul), then He can save *anyone!*

In First Timothy 1:13, Paul described himself *before* his conversion to Christ: "Who was before a *blasphemer*, and a persecutor, and injurious...." Although Paul was a strictly religious Jew before he surrendered his life to Jesus, he admitted that he had been guilty of blasphemous behavior. The word "blasphemy" is the Greek word *blasphemia* — and it does *not* primarily refer to speaking irreverently about divine matters. It has a broader meaning that refers to *any type of debasing, derogatory, nasty, shameful, ugly speech or behavior that is intended to humiliate someone else*. Paul used the word "blasphemer" to describe his own past words and actions when he purposefully *mistreated* and *humiliated* believers for whom he had no tolerance.

Before Paul's conversion to Christ, he persecuted believers in Jesus Christ with a vengeance. To make sure readers understood how atrocious his treatment of Christians was before his conversion, Paul then clarified what he meant, stating that he also used to be a "persecutor" and "injurious."

The word "persecutor" comes from the Greek word *dioko*, which means *to pursue* or *to ardently follow after something until the object of pursuit is apprehended*. It was the very word used to depict a hunter. By using this word *dioko*, Paul revealed that he aggressively pursued Christians to capture or kill them like a relentless hunter tracking the scent of an animal.

Proof of this is found in the book of Acts. For instance, Acts 7:57,58 states that Paul (then called Saul of Tarsus) was present at the stoning of Stephen: "Then they cried out with a loud voice, and stopped their ears, and ran upon him with one accord, and cast him out of the city, and stoned him: and the witnesses laid down their clothes at a young man's feet, whose name was Saul." Also, from Paul's testimony before King Agrippa, we know that he cast his vote for the death of many believers. The apostle told Agrippa, "...Many of the saints did I shut up in prison, having received authority from the chief priests; and when they were put to death, I gave my voice against them" (Acts 26:10).

There is no doubt that before Paul came to Christ and was still known as Saul, he was such a *scourge* to the Church that believers everywhere had heard of his vengeance (*see* Acts 9:21). Saul was obsessed with a sense of duty to eradicate Christians and to cleanse this "filth" from the Jewish community. In fact, when Paul later described his behavior before his conversion in First Timothy 1:13, he used the word "injurious" to explain the maliciousness of his past behavior.

The word "injurious" is the word *hubristes. The New Linguistic and Exegetical Key to the Greek New Testament* states: "The word [*hubristes*] indicates one who in pride and insolence deliberately and contemptuously mistreats, wrongs, and hurts another person just to…humiliate the person. It speaks of treatment which is calculated to publicly insult and openly humiliate the person who suffers it."[11]

Although Paul laid claim to being among the most religious Jews (*see* Philippians 3:5,6), his use of the word *hubristes* in First Timothy 1:13 reveals that hatred raged in his heart. Paul acknowledged that his loathing of Christians was once so intense that he derived personal pleasure when *humiliation* and *pain* were inflicted on them. Whereas the word "blasphemer" reveals that he once *verbally humiliated* believers, the word "injurious" indicates that his *physical behavior* toward Christians was *shameful* — and that he enjoyed doing it. Both his words and actions were intended to *debase, defame, dehumanize, depreciate, drag down, malign, mock, revile, ridicule, scorn, slander, slur, smear*, and *vilify* believers.

When Paul was still Saul of Tarsus, he discriminated against believers, treated them with hostility, dehumanized them, and even contributed to their deaths (*see* Acts 8:3; 9:1; 26:11). He was moved with rage to extinguish the spreading flame of Christianity. However, one encounter with Jesus on the road to Damascus was all it took for Saul's heart to be emptied of rage and hatred and filled instead with a deep love for the Church he had so horribly persecuted and humiliated in the past.

In a split second of time, this man who had been such an enemy of God and the Church was converted to Christ and totally transformed. When people heard that he had come to Christ, it was hard for them to believe at first, because he had been such an ardent persecutor of the Church (*see* Acts 9:21). But his conversion was *real* — and it *proved* that *if* God could save Paul, then God could save and change absolutely anyone! If there was ever a situation where it seemed impossible for someone to be saved, it would have been Saul of Tarsus — but one encounter with Christ changed everything in a split second.

So what about your friend, acquaintance, relative, coworker, and so forth, who seem so distant from God? Are they so far that they cannot be reached and changed? No, Paul's testimony affirms that God can reach any heart, regardless of how hard it is or how far that person has wandered from God. *So don't give up hope!* Keep praying and believing for your lost loved ones to come to a saving experience with Jesus Christ. *If it can happen to Paul, it can happen to anyone!*

---

[11] Cleon L. Rogers, Jr. and Cleon L. Rogers III, *The New Linguistic and Exegetical Key to the Greek New Testament* (Grand Rapids, MI: Zondervan Publishing House, 1998), p. 488.

MY PRAYER FOR TODAY

Heavenly Father, I thank You that Your saving power can reach any person, regardless of how deep they are in sin, how hardhearted they are, or how far from You they may have wandered. Your mercy extends to every person, and Your salvation was meant to save every person! I thank You for giving me hope for my friends and loved ones through the testimony of the apostle Paul. Today I pray for my friends, acquaintances, and relatives who are far from God. I pray that the Holy Spirit will direct their paths into an encounter with the living Christ that will suddenly transform their lives for eternity!

I pray this in Jesus' name!

MY CONFESSION FOR TODAY

I boldly confess that my friends, acquaintances, and relatives are on a collision course with Jesus Christ — and that they are going to be saved and changed in a split-second experience with Him. Although they are not walking with God and seem hardhearted right now, God is working mightily to invade their lives and to bring His saving power into their spirits. They may not know it, but they are on the verge of salvation! By faith I call them out of darkness and into the light of God's Kingdom, where His righteousness, peace, and joy will cause them to increasingly yield to the Lordship of Jesus Christ until their lives fully manifest His glory on the earth.

I declare this by faith in Jesus' name!

QUESTIONS FOR YOU TO CONSIDER

1. Whom are you praying for to receive salvation? Do you have a prayer list of people that you believe will come to faith in Christ? How often do you pray for these people?
2. When you read of the salvation of the apostle Paul, do you think of others who are now in Christ, who had once been far from God? Who are those people? Is one of them you? Can you say that if *you* could be saved, anyone can be saved?
3. How long has it been since you've shared your testimony with someone who does not know the Lord? Can you think of people who would be open to hear your story? Is there a reason you haven't shared your testimony with them? Do you realize that your story could be the final stroke that brings them into the kingdom of God?

If there was ever a situation
where it seemed impossible for someone to be saved,
it would have been Saul of Tarsus —
but one encounter with Christ
changed everything in a split second.

NOVEMBER 5

The Night I Broke a Pew During Church!

These things write I unto thee, hoping to come unto thee shortly:
But if I tarry long, that thou mayest know how thou oughtest to behave
thyself in the house of God, which is the church of the living God,
the pillar and ground of the truth.
— 1 Timothy 3:14,15

Growing up in church, there were many opportunities for my parents to teach me how I ought to behave in the house of God. Today I see that many parents are *not* teaching their children about these things, and it's a shame. Children must learn to respect the house of God and the atmosphere where God works among people corporately.

But children must be *taught* this kind of appropriate behavior in order to learn it; it doesn't come to them naturally. When I was a boy, my church friends and I didn't always do so well at behaving correctly in church. But each time I erred, I paid for it handsomely when the service was over and my father and mother disciplined me at home!

For example, there was the notorious Sunday night service when we kids were seated on a cracked pew in church. Every time we bounced up and down on that pew, it squeaked. I was a young boy at the time, and the thought of making our seat squeak every time I bounced on it just elated me! So I started vigorously bouncing — *up and down, up and down, up and down*. My friends sitting with me joined in the fun, and we all bounced *until* I (and everyone else in the auditorium) heard a huge, cracking noise like the splitting of timber. It was our pew cracking *all the way through*, from one end to the other!

As that pew split and cracked, it sloped down to the ground — and everyone sitting on it slid onto the floor and under the pew in front of us! It was quite a sight and sound, interrupting the whole service as men, women, and children came crawling out from under the pew in front of us to find another seat in the auditorium.

I knew that I was going to be in serious trouble after church that night — and I was right! My father gave me a *strong lesson*, never to be forgotten, about how I was to behave in the house of God!

Then there was another time when, during a Wednesday night service, a group of us boys skipped the service and — for some unknown, unexplainable reason — decided to climb onto the roof of the church auditorium just for fun. We each scaled the wall of one side of the building and scrambled all the way to the peak of the main auditorium — while the service was simultaneously being held!

We boys all noticed what a cool, "hollow" sound we could produce if we stomped on the roof, so we started entertaining ourselves by stomping and stomping — *until* the side door of the auditorium was flung open, and *the pastor himself* emerged! He called out to us to get off the roof and find our seats in the service!

That was another night I'll never forget! I paid a dear price not only for skipping the service, but also for interrupting the preaching of the Word and the work of the Holy Spirit taking place inside the auditorium beneath our stomping feet!

Another memory of my behavior in church as a young boy is from a time when my parents sang in the church choir. Choir rehearsal was always after the Wednesday night service. While my parents practiced with all the other adults, the Renner kids and some other kids of parents in the choir had nothing to do. So we would run around the church, scamper around the auditorium, and often prove to be a distraction to the choir rehearsal, which was led by our pastor.

One Wednesday night, we kids were especially disruptive, so our pastor yelled, "Renner kids and all you other kids, get up here!" We shook at his tone of voice because we knew that we had crossed a line that night and were about to get in trouble. We all stood before him on the church platform waiting to be rebuked. But instead of scolding us, he said, "I'll give you a dime to leave the church building and go across the street to the gas station to buy a soda. But you have to promise to stay out of the auditorium until rehearsal is over."

A soda! That was a big deal when I was a youngster, so we excitedly extended our palms toward him as he placed a dime into the hands of all us Renner kids and the other kids who were with us. We then ran down the aisle of the church, burst through the auditorium doors, and headed across the street to the gas station, where we each inserted our dime into the pop machine and bought ourselves a soda as the pastor suggested.

But when we returned home that night my father had a serious talk with me about my behavior in church. And *every time* I misbehaved in the house of God, he used the opportunity to teach me about right and wrong behavior in church. Because of my parents' instruction as I was growing up, I learned how to behave appropriately in church — and that helped me know how to teach my own sons when Denise and I became parents.

This reminds me of First Timothy 3:14 and 15, where Paul wrote, "These things write I unto thee, hoping to come unto thee shortly: But if I tarry long, that thou mayest know how thou oughtest to behave thyself in the house of God, which is the church of the living God, the pillar and ground of the truth." In verse 15, Paul was addressing wider issues that affected the whole house of God. But there is a principle in this verse I wish to discuss: We "ought" to know how to behave in the house of God!

The word "ought" in verse 15 is the Greek word *dei*, which describes *a necessity* or *something that isn't optional*. In other words, this is *mandatory behavior*. The word for "behaveth" is from the

Greek word *anastrepho*, which means *to conduct oneself appropriately*. It is simply inappropriate to be disrespectful in the house of God or to act unbecomingly in the presence of other believers who are trying to seek God or to prepare for His work.

Paul said it is *obligatory* that we behave appropriately when we are in the house of God. This is something that must be taught and imparted, and it is why I am so dismayed at parents who do not teach their children how to behave properly when they are in church. Frequently children talk loudly, sit lackadaisically, or even move about the auditorium with no restrictions from their dad or mom.

We once had parents in our Moscow church who refused to discipline their son and teach him to sit quietly and listen during the service. They actually allowed him to run all over the auditorium, which disturbed everyone who was trying to hear the Word of God. These parents had been counseled multiple times about this problem, but to no avail. The disruptive behavior of their children continued without parental correction.

One Sunday, I'd finally had enough of the outrageous behavior of this child — although I realized the problem was not really with the child; it was with *the parents* who refused to discipline him. So I called the parents aside and told them that if they would not enforce a measure of order with their son when they came to church, they would no longer be welcome because they were so disruptive to others. That was the last time they ever came to our church.

This unchecked behavior in the house of God isn't true only of children. We live in a society that has increasingly drifted so far from God that when people finally do come to church, they often talk out loud during the service, loudly chew gum, write notes back and forth to one another, send text messages on their phones, and do other things that are disruptive and disrespectful. As more mature believers, it is our God-given responsibility to gently teach them to respect the house of God and how to behave while they're in church.

In early New Testament times, people were attending church for the very first time since they were newly converted. Neither men nor women knew how to behave in church and had to be taught. But they *were* taught, as we can see in First Timothy 3:15. Paul knew that people had to learn how to behave in the house of God; thus, he addressed the issue in this verse.

I ask you today to look at your own children or grandchildren and determine if they behave respectfully when the Word of God is being preached or taught. Do they move freely about during the service, write notes, chew gum, or do other things that are distracting or disruptive to the preaching of the Word and moving of the Spirit?

The house of God is a cherished place where we assemble corporately to worship Him, grow in Him, and serve Him together to further His purposes. That's why it's so important to allow Him to teach us — so we can then teach others that it is a place where respect and honor are *mandatory*. I encourage you to make a decision today that you and *your* house will always fit that description when in church, behaving in a way that helps others hear the Word of God and that does not disrupt the moving of His precious Holy Spirit!

MY PRAYER FOR TODAY

Father, I ask You to help me behave appropriately when I am in the house of God — not only when I am in a service, but also to behave appropriately as a Christian. May my lifestyle and behavior bring glory to the Lord Jesus Christ. Forgive me for the times I have acted out of order or done things that were inappropriate or disruptive. Help me develop a personal discipline in the way I conduct myself not only when I am in the house of God but also in every area of my life because I am, in fact, Your temple, and Your Spirit resides within me. Therefore, I desire to conduct myself worthily as I ought at all times in a dignified manner that reflects You, giving both You and the sanctuary where Your people gather the full respect that is due according to Your will.

I pray this in Jesus' name!

MY CONFESSION FOR TODAY

I confess that I am mannerly, honoring, and respectful when I am in the house of God. I listen attentively, and I do not disturb others who are trying to hear the Word. I honor God in my behavior. When I see others, either young people or adults, who are disruptive and dishonoring, God shows me how to respectfully teach them how to behave and to conduct themselves in church. Because I am serious about my life with Christ, I behave seriously when I am in the house of God!

I declare this by faith in Jesus' name!

QUESTIONS FOR YOU TO CONSIDER

1. If you grew up in church, can you recall times when you had to be corrected and taught how to behave in the house of God?
2. When you see how others behave inappropriately in the house of God — sending text messages to other people, talking out loud, and so forth — do you ignore it, or have you found a polite way to teach them that their behavior is incorrect?
3. Nothing is more serious than the proclamation of God's Word and the moving of the Holy Spirit. What things have you witnessed that can disturb these holy moments?

The house of God is a cherished place where we assemble corporately to worship Him, grow in Him, and serve Him together to further His purposes.

NOVEMBER 6

I Witnessed an Astounding Miracle!

Then Philip went down to the city of Samaria, and preached
Christ unto them. And the people with one accord gave heed
unto those things which Philip spake, hearing and seeing the miracles
which he did. For unclean spirits, crying with loud voice, came out of many
that were possessed with them: and many taken with palsies, and that
were lame, were healed. And there was great joy in that city.
— Acts 8:5-8

On April 12, I told a bit of this story, but it so impacted my life that I want to share it in greater detail today and give you the reason why miracles often occur on a massive scale, or among large crowds of people.

It was the conclusion of five amazing days of meetings — the first large public meeting that Denise and I had ever conducted in the former USSR. Of the 32,000 people who attended the event, 7,000 people came forward to receive Christ and 926 people received water baptism — and we witnessed *scores* of healings, miracles, and deliverances. The meeting reminded me of Acts 8:5-8, which says:

> **Then Philip went down to the city of Samaria, and preached Christ unto them. And the people with one accord gave heed unto those things which Philip spake, hearing and seeing the miracles which he did. For unclean spirits, crying with loud voice, came out of many that were possessed with them: and many taken with palsies, and that were lame, were healed. And there was great joy in that city.**

In those five days of meetings, we preached Christ to 32,000 people, and the people literally "gave heed unto" the things that we preached. As a result, we saw *miracles* that week — including the expulsion of many unclean spirits that cried out as they were expelled from people by the delivering power of Christ. Many who had various types of sickness were healed, including the lame. And just as Acts 8:8 says, there was great joy as a result of all these happenings.

Yet there was one man who was obviously in need of a miracle, but had not received a healing touch in the meetings. He came into the meetings each night after the meeting had started so he could get to his reserved seat without fighting the crowds that swarmed into the big auditorium. Because he came in late each night, I saw him each evening. I couldn't help but notice his desperate and sad physical condition and the distorted look of pain in his face.

I later learned that this man had been paralyzed from his waist down as a result of falling off his house 19 years earlier. For 19 years, he had used crutches like legs. He would swing his body on his crutches as he slowly moved forward one "crutch step" at a time. Once he would finally reach his seat each evening, he would collapse into his chair, exhausted from his "crutch walk." Because he had come in *after* the rest of the crowd was seated, many people had watched him come into the auditorium each evening and — they were aware of his extremely disabled condition.

That week we had witnessed many instantaneous miracles. Ears of the deaf were opened. And as Christ came into people's hearts, we literally heard demons scream as the power of Christ drove them out. It was everything I had read about in the book of Acts, but it was happening *here and now* — in our meeting! Denise and I were speechless at the wonder-working power of God we saw in those services.

Now it was the last night. Oh, how I longed for that paralyzed man to receive a miraculous touch. As that last meeting concluded, I stood to dismiss the crowd and bid them farewell. Suddenly I heard a lot of commotion to my left, and I turned to see what the disturbance was all about. I turned at the exact moment the man on the crutches suddenly shot straight up from his chair and threw his crutches into the air!

Before I could even catch my breath, the man jumped and began walking — *free of crutches*! The bottom half of his paralyzed body had suddenly come alive. This was the first time this man had walked in 19 years without the assistance of his crutches. He literally went walking and leaping and praising God all the way to the front of the auditorium, where he threw his crutches on the stage and then stood there *jumping* for joy!

There was a crowd that night of approximately 8,000 people. When they saw this miracle happen right before their eyes, hundreds *rushed* the stage for more prayer. Only God knows how many more people received miracles that night.

When the auditorium authority said it was time to shut down the meeting, people didn't want to leave and had to be forcibly directed out of the arena and onto the street. People clung to us, asking for more prayer, but it was time to leave, so we quickly left the stage through a private back hallway and a door that opened right to our transportation. However, when we exited that exterior door, several hundred people had already surrounded our vehicle, wanting one more opportunity to receive prayer.

Later as I meditated on the miracles we saw that week, I kept going back to Philip's experience in Samaria in Acts 8. It specifically says, "...The people with one accord gave heed unto those things which Philip spake..." (v. 6). This is precisely what had occurred with us, so I opened my Greek New Testament to study what these words meant in the Greek.

The words "one accord" is *homothumadon*, a compound of *homou* and *thumos*. The word *homou* usually points to *a moment* when something happens at *one time* or *simultaneously*. The word *thumos* here carries the picture of *passion*. The people were *excited* about what Philip was preaching. The Greek word tells us they were completely *stirred up* and *excited* about what they were hearing. And it wasn't just *a few* of them, but all of them *at once* were caught in the moment — *in an eruption of thrill*.

The crowds were so enraptured by what Philip was preaching that Acts 8:6 says they "gave heed" to the things he was speaking to them. The words "gave heed" are from the word *prosecho*, a compound of the words *pros* and *echo*. The word *pros* means *near*, and the word *echo* means *to hold* or *to embrace*. When the two words are compounded, the new word *prosecho* means *to hold near* or *to draw near*. It is the idea of *giving one's full attention* to what is being spoken and heard — and *drawing as near to it as possible*. In other words, all those people under the sound of Philip's preaching were *fixated* on and *undistracted* from his message.

Prosecho can also be translated *to give one's full attention* to a matter, *to apply the mind* to a thing, or *to give serious consideration and contemplation* to what is being heard. This was not a light-listening moment in Philip's ministry in Samaria — *those people were listening with 100 percent of their hearts and souls!*

No wonder Philip's crowd experienced so many miracles! Romans 10:17 says, "So then faith cometh by hearing, and hearing by the word of God." As they listened so intensely to the message of Christ, faith came *exploding* into their hearts — and where faith explodes, the supernatural takes place.

This truth, by the way, provided my answer for why we saw so many supernatural signs and wonders in that big meeting in the USSR. The crowd was *fixated* on every word we preached from that stage. And where the message of Christ is *really* heard, faith comes. That explains why miracles started occurring all over that vast auditorium. The people heard, believed, and received.

This shows how important it is that you *really listen* when the Word of God is being preached. If you're talking to your neighbor, writing notes, sending text messages, thinking of something else, or merely not listening, the Word can have *great* effect on the people all around you, yet have *no* effect on you. If you want to see the supernatural, you *must* be totally focused on the message that's being preached, for faith comes by hearing — *really hearing* — the Word of God. And when the message has been heard and embraced by 100 percent of a hearing heart, the environment becomes right for the supernatural to start taking place!

MY PRAYER FOR TODAY

Father, first of all, I repent for each and every time I've been where the Word is preached, yet I disrespectfully allowed myself to be distracted by other things in my mind by writing notes, by sending text messages, or by visiting with my neighbor. Father, Your words are life. Each one contains the power to save, to heal, to deliver, to transform, and to make all things new. Forgive me for not giving Your Word the full esteem and utmost regard. I've been wrong for not totally focusing on the message being preached. For this, I truly ask You for forgiveness. I ask You to help me discipline my mind to focus as I respond with ears to hear and a heart to receive what is being preached so that the message will impart faith to my heart!

I pray this in Jesus' name!

MY CONFESSION FOR TODAY

I boldly confess that each time the Word of God is preached, I give it my full concentration. I refuse to be dull in my hearing or to negatively influence the atmosphere of a meeting with hardness of heart and unbelief. Instead, I shove all other thoughts aside, and I fixate on the Word being declared to me. As a result, faith is ignited in my heart, for faith comes by hearing — really hearing — the Word of God. As I mix my faith with what I hear, I not only see and experience supernatural results in my life, I also affect the atmosphere and help create an environment for the supernatural power of God to explode around me so others can hear and be healed, saved, or transformed by the Word of God. Such supernatural occurrences were not meant just for Bible times. They are for anyone in any generation who will draw near to the Word, focus on it, and receive an influx of faith. And I confess that this is a description of me!

I declare this by faith in Jesus' name!

QUESTIONS FOR YOU TO CONSIDER

1. Have you ever been in an atmosphere where miracles were taking place? How did it affect you? What kind of miracle did you personally observe?
2. From what you've read today, can you describe how vitally important it is for you to allow no distractions when you're hearing the Word of God preached?
3. What can you do personally to help create an atmosphere for the Word to have a great effect both on you and those around you? What do you need to stop doing while the Word is being preached so that you can be more attentive and get more out of the message?

NOVEMBER 7

Forewarned and Prepared by the Spirit of God

Fear none of those things
which thou shalt suffer:
behold, the devil shall cast
some of you into prison....
— Revelation 2:10

God loves you so much that *if* you will listen to His Spirit, He will *forewarn* and *prepare* you for things to come — whatever it is that you are to face. A perfect example of this *forewarning* and *preparing* is found in Revelation 2:10, where Jesus said, "Fear none of those things which thou shalt suffer: behold, the devil shall cast some of you into prison, that ye may be tried…."

At the time that Jesus spoke these words, He was speaking to the church at Smyrna, who was suffering great persecution. He was *forewarning* them so they would be *prepared* by knowing that some of them are going to be put into prison and tried. Rather than let this event take them by surprise, Christ wanted them to know in advance, so He lovingly informed them of what the future held.

Being put in prison is a harrowing ordeal under any circumstance. But to be thrown into a Roman prison was a horrid prospect to contemplate. Thus, with great love, Christ forewarned the church of Smyrna that the devil was going to use this experience to test the commitment and steadfastness of their faith.

The word "tried" is the Greek word *peiradzo*, which describes *a calculated test deliberately designed to expose any deficiency*. By using this word, Jesus made it clear that the hardships these Christians would endure were intended to test them to see if their faith was genuine. They had confessed Jesus as Lord, and soon Satan would "try" them to discover if their commitment to Christ's Lordship was truly sincere. Just as the devil tempted Jesus in the wilderness (*see* Matthew 4:1-11; Luke 4:1-13), the enemy was now preparing to tempt these believers with persecutions beyond anything they had ever endured or imagined.

Believers throughout the Roman Empire were undergoing persecution as well. When the apostle Peter wrote to the believers in Pontus, Galatia, Cappadocia, Asia, and Bithynia, he referred to the fiery trials that were testing *their* faith: "That the trial of your faith, being much more precious than of gold that perisheth, though it be tried with fire, might be found unto praise and honor and glory at the appearing of Jesus Christ" (1 Peter 1:7).

Both Scripture and experience confirm that a faith declaration often triggers a devilish attack. Satan's purpose was to test the sincerity of these believers' faith to see if they would break under pressure. Therefore, Christ warned the church that these present and imminent attacks would verify whether or not they were really committed to the faith they had publicly declared. If there was any deficiency in their faith, those fiery trials would expose it, for the devil would design this calculated test to break them. Some would succumb to his attacks and recant their faith — but the majority of those who were to be "tried" would endure and prove themselves faithful, even unto death.

Jesus had more to say about what was to come: "Fear none of those things which thou shalt suffer: behold, the devil shall cast some of you into prison, that ye may be tried; *and ye shall have tribulation…*" (Revelation 2:10).

The word "tribulation" reveals how intense these fires of testing would be. It is the Greek word *thlipsis*. The word *thlipsis* conveys the idea of *a burden that is crushing, debilitating, or overpowering*. Most often, the word *thlipsis* was used in connection with *displays of extreme hostility* or *torture*. Christ used the word to forecast *a time of distress, oppression, pressure, and stress*. This word "tribulation" may be understood as a clarification of the word "tried." The tests the church of Smyrna was about to endure would be *crushing*, *debilitating*, and *overpowering*, resulting in *great distress*, *oppression*, *pressure*, and *stress*.

It is interesting that although Christ told these believers, "Fear none of those things which thou shalt suffer...," He didn't hesitate to tell them that very difficult times awaited them. Jesus knew that Satan was about to unleash a horrendous onslaught against these believers to attack their faith — but He also knew they could endure this test because their faith was indeed *genuine*.

Jesus then went on to promise that this time of tribulation would last only for a limited period of time. He said, "Fear none of those things which thou shalt suffer: behold, the devil shall cast some of you into prison, that ye may be tried; and ye shall have tribulation *ten days*..." (Revelation 2:10).

Jesus knew that the intense, impending bombardment would seem unending to the congregation. So when He asserted, "...Ye shall have tribulation *ten days*...." The phrase "ten days" was meant to give encouragement and hope to the suffering church — letting these believers know that their hardships wouldn't endure forever. Theologian Albert Barnes noted that the reference to "ten days" refers to "a short time; a brief period; a few days."[12] Bible scholar Henry Alford suggested, "The expression is probably used to signify a short and limited time."[13] Christ is so kind and merciful that He forewarned the believers in Smyrna of this time of persecution so they wouldn't be taken by surprise. And as He promised, that time of tribulation *did* come to an end!

Hard times are inescapable in this life, but God's power *always has* and *always will continue* to sustain those who are determined to be faithful to Him. Even if the fires of adversity rage and it seems as if they will never cease, those trials are temporary and will eventually come to an end. Almost 2,000 years of Church history have proven that the persecuted Church always comes forth purer than gold and mightier in the Spirit. The spiritual darkness may seem overpowering at times as Satan fiercely attempts to blot out the light of truth. But as John 1:5 promises, the light cannot be held perpetually under the domain of darkness. Victory belongs to those who endure to the end (*see* Matthew 10:22).

History bears witness that the Spirit of God always warns His people in advance when difficult times are coming. There are abundant historical records spanning the centuries that relate accounts of believers and missionaries in hostile nations throughout the world who were forewarned by the Holy Spirit of future hardships. Such divine warnings are intended to prepare believers to face the impending challenges, *if* they will hear and heed the voice of the Spirit.

Jesus lovingly prepared His people for the turbulent times that awaited them. It is imperative that in *your* time, you keep your heart open so that you can hear what the Spirit of God is saying to you about *your* future. There is one thing for sure: His goal is *always* to cause you to triumph (*see* 2 Corinthians 2:14). If you'll keep your ear tuned to Him, He will be faithful by His Spirit to *forewarn* you and *prepare* you for the times to come — and then He will empower you to walk through every single situation as *more* than a conqueror in Him (*see* Romans 8:37)!

---

[12] Albert Barnes, *Notes on the Bible* (Blackie & Son, London, 1884-85; Reprinted by Baker Books, 1996), Revelation 2:10.

[13] Henry Alford, *Greek Testament Critical Exegetical Commentary* (Boston: Lee & Shepard, 1878), Volume IV.

MY PRAYER FOR TODAY

Father, I thank You that Your love for the Church is so strong that You forewarn and prepare us for the days ahead. Please forgive me for the times when You tried to warn me but I didn't listen — and help me open my heart to hear what You are saying to me now about the times to come. Regardless of what the future holds, I know that You are Lord of all and that You made me to be an overcomer. I pray for a flood of the Holy Spirit's power to be unleashed in my life in these last days so that I will have everything I need to brave any storm and emerge victorious on the other side!

I pray this in Jesus' name!

MY CONFESSION FOR TODAY

I confess that my spiritual ears are open and I am attuned to what the Holy Spirit is telling me about the present and the days ahead. The future will not take me by surprise, because I am listening to the Holy Spirit, and He reveals to me what I need to know. Jesus promised that the Holy Spirit would show us things to come, and I declare that my spirit is wide-awake and alert to hear the Spirit's forecast about the future. I am filled with the Holy Spirit; therefore, He gives me all the strength and energy I need to outlast any storm the devil ever tries to send my way. With the help of the Holy Spirit, I will come out on the other side of any difficulty as an overcomer!

I declare this by faith, in Jesus' name!

QUESTIONS FOR YOU TO CONSIDER

1. Are you aware of any times in history when the Holy Spirit warned people in advance that difficult times were coming? Can you think of other examples in the Old or New Testament when the Spirit of God forewarned and prepared people for coming difficult times?
2. What is the Holy Spirit saying to you about your future? What does the Bible prophesy about believers living in the last days?
3. If the Holy Spirit and the Word of God speak directly about the life before you, what steps should you take to prepare for those times? What steps can be taken right now to be sure you ride through any storm victoriously?

*As John 1:5 promises,
the light cannot be held perpetually
under the domain of darkness. Victory belongs
to those who endure to the end.*

NOVEMBER 8

Jesus Has Overcome the World!

...In the world ye shall have tribulation:
but be of good cheer;
I have overcome the world.
— John 16:33

What *good news* that is to know — Jesus has *overcome* the world! John 16:33 has been a source of strength and encouragement to Christians for nearly 2,000 years — and it still speaks to us today as we face difficult periods in our lives. Jesus assures us, "In the world ye shall have tribulation: but be of good cheer; I have overcome the world."

Think about that! Regardless of what challenge or trial you or I face in the days to come, Christ declared that our correct position of faith is to "be of good cheer" because He has overcome it already!

You may say, "But you don't understand the difficult time I'm facing right now. Has Christ really overcome *everything* that I will face in life?" Yes, everything — including the most difficult moments of your life!

To make the point, John 16:33 uses the word "tribulation." Let's look at this word "tribulation" to see exactly what Jesus was saying to us. In Greek, it is the word *thlipsis*, a word that describes *distress*, *affliction*, or *trouble* that is very intense. Jesus declared that He had overcome all of these. However, by using this word, Jesus recognized that times would not always be easy for those who choose to follow Him. Yet regardless of what the world or the devil tries to throw at us, Christ soundly declared — and still declares *today*, "...But be of good cheer; I have overcome the world!"

The words "good cheer" come from the Greek word *tharseo*. A more accurate rendering would be *"take heart!"* — and it also conveys the idea of *"be courageous!"* It is a word spoken to strengthen someone who was facing a hardship or trial. If you translate the verse more literally, Jesus said, *"In this world you will go through some distressing times, but take heart and be courageous...."*

Then Jesus went on to assure His disciples, "...I have overcome the world." The word "overcome" comes from the Greek word *nikos*, which can be translated *to overcome* but is also the word for *victory*. However, the grammar used in this verse doesn't imply a single victory; rather, it denotes *a continuous, abiding victory* both now and in the future. Therefore, the idea presented in Jesus' statement could be interpreted, *"I have overcome the world; I am overcoming the world; and I will always be overcoming the world."*

Let the memory of these words provide great encouragement and strength to you whenever you face difficult times. Even if it seems like the entire world is trying to wipe you out, you can hold on to the promise that Jesus *has overcome* the world; He *is overcoming* the world; and He *will always overcome* the world. So regardless of what you are facing today, you can hold fast to that knowledge by faith: Jesus has already overcome the world — and He is with you to help you enforce the victory you possess in Him in the midst of *whatever* you are facing.

So instead of letting the devil discourage you with thoughts that there is no hope or that you cannot overcome the struggles that seem to be attacking you from every side, grab hold of the truth and declare that Jesus is with you and that you *will* — with Jesus' help — overcome the world too!

MY PRAYER FOR TODAY

Father, I thank You that You sent Jesus — and that Jesus has overcome the world in every respect. Regardless of what the devil tries to do, Jesus has already overcome it. I do not have to lose heart or be discouraged. I can lift my head, throw my shoulders back, and rejoice, because Jesus has overcome the world and deprived it of its power to harm me. I am more than a conqueror through Jesus Christ, who has given me His overcoming power to make me triumphant in this life!

I pray this in Jesus' name!

MY CONFESSION FOR TODAY

I boldly confess that Jesus Christ is Lord over all! Jesus is Lord over every foe and every enemy I face in my life. Jesus didn't partially overcome the world; He completely overcame it. And because I am in Christ, I share in this glorious victory! Jesus said to take heart and to be courageous, so today I take heart and face the future with courage. I am not a victim to my circumstances because Jesus died on the Cross, defeated the enemy, and rose from the dead victorious over all. He has literally overcome everything that needs to be overcome, and now He shares that glorious victory with me!

I declare this by faith, in Jesus' name!

QUESTIONS FOR YOU TO CONSIDER

1. In what areas of your life are you overcoming right now?
2. Have you ever pondered the truth that Jesus already overcame everything you will ever face and that He will give you His overcoming power? Do you know how to receive that overcoming power? If so, how?
3. In what ways did the Holy Spirit speak to you as you read this *Sparkling Gem*?

NOVEMBER 9

When Paul's Friends Saved His Life

And when Paul would have entered in
unto the people, the disciples suffered him not.
And certain of the chief of Asia,
which were his friends, sent unto him,
desiring him that he would
not adventure himself into the theatre.
— Acts 19:30,31

The book of Acts relates an interesting story about the apostle Paul in which he was about to endanger his life until his friends stepped in, took control of the situation, and saved him from danger. Today I want to tell you about that event — and as you read, I want you to think about the times God has used family, friends, or acquaintances to save you from mistakes you were about to make!

We find the account in Acts 19. A huge demonstration against Christians took place in the Great Theater of Ephesus. Concerned about the negative impact that the Gospel was having on their businesses, angry rioters took to the streets and dragged several of Paul's companions into the theater (*see* v. 29).

When Paul heard what was happening, he wanted to rush into the demonstration and join his detained friends. The Bible doesn't tell us *why* he wanted to do this. Maybe he thought he could save them from being hurt, or perhaps he wanted to be alongside them because they were his traveling companions.

However, regardless of Paul's motivation, the Bible tells us that his friends immediately stepped in to convince him otherwise. Acts 19:30,31 records: "And when Paul would have entered in unto the people, the disciples suffered him not. And certain of the chief of Asia, which were his friends, sent unto him, desiring him that he would not adventure himself into the theatre."

Notice verse 30 states that Paul "...*would* have entered in unto the people...." The word "would" here is a translation of the Greek word *boulemai*, meaning *to counsel, to advise,* or *to exercise one's will* about something. In this context, it means that after thinking through all the consequences of his decision, Paul *counseled* himself and *made up his mind* to enter the theater. Fully realizing that doing so could place his life in jeopardy, Paul still concluded that he should join his friends in their plight.

Verse 30 goes on to say that Paul "…would have entered in unto the *people*…." The word "people" is the Greek word *demos*. In this context, the word *demos* refers to *a large mass of people*. The Great Theater of Ephesus seated approximately 24,000 people — and the use of the word *demos* in verse 30 indicates that the seats were nearly packed by the time Paul decided to join the fray. As the screams and shouts of the rioters reverberated throughout the city, people came from every quarter of Ephesus to investigate the source of the disturbance.

As Paul began to make his way toward the Great Theater, Acts 19:30 says, "…The disciples suffered him not." When this verse states that the *disciples* prohibited Paul from entering the Great Theater of Ephesus, it refers to *ardent* followers — serious students who believed in Paul and felt a strong allegiance to him and to his ministry. Therefore, when they saw that the apostle had determined to enter the theater, they took action to *stop* him.

It is natural that Paul wanted to join his ministry associates when they potentially faced trouble in the theater. However, although this act of courage may at first appear heroic, it *could* have resulted in Paul's premature death and the end of his ministry. If he had done as he planned and suffered death as a result, the loss of his ministry at that time would have been a devastating blow to the work of God's Kingdom.

These verses provide a vivid example of how God often uses friends and disciples to stop us from making mistakes that may have devastating consequences. Paul's desire to enter the theater may have seemed like the right thing to do at that moment. But the apostle had much more work to do, and those who were committed to him and his ministry stepped forward — possibly against his will — to stop him from making a mistake that could have had life-threatening ramifications.

And it wasn't only Paul's disciples who tried to stop him from entering the theater. Even pagan unbelievers who respected the apostle knew that this wasn't the right thing for him to do. Acts 19:31 says, "And certain of the chief of Asia, which were his *friends*, sent unto him, desiring him that he would not adventure himself into the theatre."

The "certain of the chief of Asia" is a translation of the word *Asiarch*, which is a title derived from the word *Asia* and *archos*. The word *Asia*, of course, referred to that region of the world. The word *archos* is the Greek word that describes *someone of a high rank or position*. When the two words were compounded, the new word became a particular title given to ten high-ranking men throughout Asia Minor as representatives of the Roman emperor.

This is a very important point because it reveals that Paul's ministry had permeated the lofty classes of society. Just as Jesus had been a friend to sinners and tax collectors, Paul was a friend to the local *Asiarch* — a prestigious unbeliever who served the emperor. This man had been sufficiently exposed to Paul to develop a strong respect for him. So when the Asiarch suddenly became aware of Paul's intention to enter the theater, he and his high-ranking associates took action to prevent him from being personally injured as a result of such a rash action.

Paul was a spiritual man, but God used others to redirect Paul's steps and prohibit him from taking a detrimental course of action — as the Lord often does with His people. In this case, He came from every direction, using both believing disciples and high-ranking pagans to stop Paul from taking a step that could have resulted in tragedy.

Acts 19 doesn't tell us whether or not Paul agreed with those who protested his intention to enter the theater. Regardless of how the apostle felt about the situation, however, it remains a fact that their actions stopped the apostle from acting on a potentially tragic decision. I'm sure when the event was finished, Paul was thankful for the actions of his friends that intervened on his behalf that day.

Can you think of a time when God used family, friends, or associates to help navigate you through a difficult time or to redirect you when you were about to make a fateful decision? Or maybe there was a moment when God used *you* to do this for someone else.

We may *not* always appreciate it when our friends act on our behalf, but when the situation calms down and we see things from a different perspective, we often realize that God was using our friends to spare us. Later we are *thankful* that God used them to help us when we didn't see things so correctly.

Why don't you stop and thank God today for the family, friends, and acquaintances that God has used in your life in a similar way?

MY PRAYER FOR TODAY

Heavenly Father, I acknowledge and repent for being stubborn. I admit that my decisions have not always been right, and there have been moments when You have used friends and associates to stop me from acting in a way that might harm me. At the time, I didn't like their advice and their actions, but after I calmed down I came to realize that You had intervened in my life by using them to help redirect my steps. Thank You for loving me so much that You would use others to help navigate me through difficult moments. I am so grateful for the friends and influences You've positioned along my path in life who have helped me when I didn't even know I was going the wrong way. My heart is filled with thanksgiving for this today!

I pray this in Jesus' name!

MY CONFESSION FOR TODAY

I confess that I walk among the wise, and I give attention to the voice of wisdom. God loves me so much that He will place people around me who speak truth to me and help me when I don't even know that I need help. When I am about to make a wrong decision or take an action that could be detrimental to me, they speak up and I listen to what they have to say. I declare that I will be open-hearted to them and will hear the voice of God speaking to me through friends when I need His voice to come to me in that way!

I declare this by faith, in Jesus' name!

QUESTIONS FOR YOU TO CONSIDER

1. Can you think of a time when God used certain people in your life to spare you from a wrong decision that you were about to make? When was that experience, and how did God use them to stop you from going in a wrong direction?
2. Have you ever taken time to thank that person(s) for loving you enough to step forward and to act on your behalf — even if they risked your friendship to do so? What if they had said nothing? What would have happened? Don't you think it's right for you to take the time to call them, write them a note, or find some way to express your thankfulness to them for what they did?
3. Has God ever used *you* to spare other individuals from making a bad decision? When was that event? What would have happened if you had just let them do what they had planned to do? Were you later thankful that you had the courage to speak up and act on their behalf?

NOVEMBER 10

Jesus Is Not Ashamed of His Church!

...And being turned,
I saw seven golden candlesticks;
and in the *midst* of the seven candlesticks
one like unto the Son of man....
— Revelation 1:12,13

We live in a day and hour when some people act as if they are *embarrassed* to be affiliated with the Church. Perhaps something happened at their church that disappointed them with that local body and its leadership. But regardless of the reason, they have distanced themselves from the Church.

But I want to tell you that even though the Church as a whole has many imperfections, Jesus is *not* ashamed of His Church!

We may be tempted to feel dismayed about the carnality that sometimes seem so pervasive in the contemporary Church, but it's important for us to remember that Jesus paid the highest price of all for the Church, He loves His people, and He still remains in the *midst* of them. In fact, when the apostle John recorded the vision He had in the book of Revelation, he wrote that He saw Jesus standing right in the *midst* of the seven candlesticks, which were symbolic of the Church. This means Christ was standing right in the *midst* of the Church when John saw Him in this vision.

Revelation 1:12,13 says, "…And being turned, I saw seven golden candlesticks; and in the *midst* of the seven candlesticks one like unto the Son of man…."

The word "midst" is the Greek word *mesos*, which can be translated as *in the midst*, *in the middle*, or *in the center*. Thus, this word portrays Jesus standing right in the *very center* of the Church. The seven churches in the book of Revelation were most likely the leading congregations of Asia. Yet despite their prominent status, these local churches had problems — some of which were of a *very* serious nature. Nevertheless, Jesus didn't distance Himself from these churches. Regardless of their imperfections and problems, He stood *right in the very midst* of them.

This close proximity infers that Jesus is not ashamed of His Church, even though it is comprised of flawed human beings. In fact, having purchased their redemption through His death and resurrection, Jesus is delighted to abide in the midst of His blood-bought people!

In the vision, John saw Jesus standing like a Great Overseer in the *midst* of the seven golden candlesticks, His eyes focused on them. This explains Jesus' intimate knowledge about each of these seven congregations and the reason He would later say to each of them, "I *know* thy works" (*see* Revelation 2:2; 2:9; 2:13; 2:19; 3:1; 3:8; 3:15).

This word "know" that appears in all these verses is the Greek word *oida*. It comes from a Greek root that means *to see*. Thus, the word *oida* in these scriptures describes what Jesus had *seen personally*, not what He had obtained from an outside source. This was knowledge based on *personal observation*. By standing in the midst of the seven golden candlesticks — or in the midst of those seven churches — Jesus was in a position *to see* everything that happened in those churches, both good and bad.

This should be taken as both an encouragement and a warning to the Church of every age. As the Head of the Church, Jesus stands in the midst of His people, lovingly overseeing everything that transpires, both positive and negative. He knows from *personal observation* every victory won, every misstep taken, every challenge faced, and every demonic attack withstood.

- Regarding the congregation in Ephesus, Jesus could *see* their labor, patience, and intolerance for false doctrine — but He could also see that they had lost their first love.
- Regarding the congregation in Smyrna, Jesus could *see* their tribulation and poverty — but He could also see that they were struggling with a fear of future calamity.
- Regarding the congregation in Pergamum, Jesus could *see* the demonic activity that confronted believers on a daily basis, as well as the price many of them were paying to remain firm in the face of opposition. But He could also see that the

damnable doctrine of the Nicolaitans was trying to influence the church and lead its people astray.

- Regarding the congregation in Thyatira, Jesus could *see* that they were hard-working; that they were dedicated to works of charity and to serving people in need; and that they demonstrated patience and excellence in whatever they undertook to do for the Lord. But He could also see that a woman named Jezebel was seducing God's people with damnable doctrines that endorsed loose living and ungodly morals.
- Regarding the congregation in Sardis, Jesus could *see* that they had enjoyed a strong beginning in their faith. But He could also see that their steadfastness was slipping and that they were in danger of drying up spiritually and becoming completely ineffectual.
- Regarding the congregation in Philadelphia, Jesus could *see* that they had rare opportunities and open doors to declare the Gospel. But He could also see that they needed to hold fast during challenging times.
- Regarding the congregation in Laodicea, Jesus could *see* nothing positive. He saw that they were neither hot nor cold, rebuked them for their self-sufficiency, and pleaded with them to open the door and allow Him back inside their church once more.

In every case I just noted, the word "see" in the corresponding verses is the Greek word *oida* — which is used *seven times* to affirm that Christ knew all of this by His *personal observation* of these local churches. Christ was so close — so centered on these congregations — that all of these conditions were visible to His eyes. But notice this: The blemishes did not turn Jesus away. He still stood in the midst of the Church, for He loved it enough to pay for it with His own blood.

Likewise, Jesus stands in the midst of His people *today*, overseeing all the activities that transpire among them. He sees both the *good* and the *bad*. He sees their love, faith, patience, and commitment. He also sees the actions that are out of line with His character and His plan for the Church. And as has been true throughout the centuries, if His people will listen, they will still hear the voice of Jesus, urging them to hear what He is saying to His Church and to repent wherever repentance is needed.

But Christ is *not* ashamed of His Church — He is standing right in the *very middle* of it! In spite of its imperfections, *Christ loves His Church*!

If you know those who are embarrassed of the Church (and maybe that describes *you*), help them remember — or remind yourself — that Christ in all His holiness and perfection is *not* ashamed. Rather, He draws near to oversee the Church, to pray for it, and to bring the correction that it needs. Jesus has not abandoned His Church, and He *never will*!

MY PRAYER FOR TODAY

Father, I thank You for reminding me of Your great love for the Church in spite of all of its present blemishes, flaws, and imperfections. Forgive me — and forgive others — when we have been judgmental of Your precious Church and have been ashamed or embarrassed of it. We have actually been judgmental of ourselves because we are Your Body, the Church, members one of another. You are right in the midst of the Church; therefore, I refuse to criticize what You have given Your life for and invested Yourself in so completely. I thank You for bringing correction and encouragement to my heart today. I repent for any judgmental attitude about your Church or its leadership, and I receive Your forgiveness. Help me keep a right heart attitude.

I pray this in Jesus' name!

MY CONFESSION FOR TODAY

I boldly confess that I love the Church of Jesus Christ, and I am thankful to be a member of it. I regret holding a critical attitude, and I repent of it right now. I make the decision to change the way I see the Church and how I speak about the Church. Most of all, I make the decision to pray for the Church. Christ loves the Church as His own Body, therefore, I refuse to despise Christ Himself by ill-esteeming His own Body — of which I, too, am a part! Since Christ is in the midst of the Church, I set my affection and devotion in the midst of the Church. I acknowledge this, I accept it, and I conform my beliefs and my actions to this declaration of faith. With the help of God's Spirit working in my heart and mind, I will maintain a good, positive, faith-filled attitude toward the Church and its leadership, especially when I see imperfections that seem glaringly obvious to me. Who am I to judge another man's servant? Before his own master he rises or falls, but God is able to make him stand. My responsibility is to pray so that I am not judged in the same critical way.

I declare this by faith in Jesus' name!

QUESTIONS FOR YOU TO CONSIDER

1. Do you know anyone who got "turned off" by the Church, became critical of it, and, as a result, stopped going to church altogether? Who is that person? What can you do to woo that individual into fellowship with the saints again?
2. Have you ever realized that as long as human beings are members of the Church — including *you* and *me* — it will be flawed? If you think about it, it's a great work of grace that Jesus' blood washed us and cleansed us and that He placed us inside His Church. He accepted us in the *Beloved* and made us a part of His Body. Isn't that a miracle for us to ponder?
3. If you've been negative about the Church and have spoken about it negatively to others, did you ever think about the ramifications that your negative words could have on others — how your remarks could also make *them* negative about the Church? If you've participated in such negative conversations, what should you do *now* to make it right?

NOVEMBER 11

The High Priestly Ministry of Jesus

And in the midst of the seven candlesticks
one like unto the Son of man,
clothed with a garment down to the foot,
and girt about the paps with a golden girdle.
— Revelation 1:13

When John received his vision of the exalted Christ while imprisoned on the island of Patmos, the elderly apostle took note of several prominent features of Jesus' appearance. One such feature was His garment. In Revelation 1:13, he wrote that Christ was "…*clothed with a garment down to the foot*…." Today we will take a careful look at this phrase and see what it tells us about the Person of Jesus and why it matters to *you* as a child of God.

The word "clothed" is derived from the Greek word *enduo*, a term that referred to *one who is dressed in a garment.* But it must be noted that the Greek tense used in Revelation 1:13 implies that this particular garment was conferred upon Christ *once and for all.* He was given this garment by the Father and will be thus clothed forevermore. The Greek tense literally means Jesus *was* clothed; He *is* clothed; and He *will always be* clothed with this particular garment that reaches "down to the foot."

The phrase "down to the foot" is a translation of *poderes*, a Greek word used only this one time in the entire New Testament. It describes a robe that *flows all the way down to the ankles but leaves the feet exposed.* The word *poderes* is also used seven times in the Old Testament Greek Septuagint to describe *the attire of the high priest.*

Perhaps the best example of this word *poderes* is found in Exodus 28, where God told Moses how to make "holy garments" for Aaron and his sons, who would serve as priests. The priestly garment was to be made of gold, blue, purple, and scarlet thread and fine woven linen. It was to reach down to the ankles, exactly like the robe Christ was wearing in John's vision. For this reason, one symbolic meaning of the garment Jesus wore in John's vision was to portray Him in His role as our Great High Priest!

- Hebrews 3:1 (*NKJV*) declares that Jesus is the "High Priest of our confession."
- Hebrews 4:15,16 describes Jesus Christ as the High Priest who can be touched with the feelings of our infirmities, a truth that has been a comfort to believers throughout the centuries. In these verses, God calls each of us to come boldly before the throne of grace to obtain mercy and to find help in our time of need from Jesus, our High Priest.

- ➢ Hebrews 5:5,6 reveals that the office of High Priest was conferred upon Jesus and that His priesthood will remain "forever" after the order of Melchisedec.
- ➢ Hebrews 7:24 states that Jesus' role as our Great High Priest is "unchangeable."

The ministry of Jesus Christ as our High Priest is one of the most important themes of the New Testament. Jesus *was* clothed with priestly garments; He *is* clothed with priestly garments; and He *will always be* clothed with priestly garments — because He is *forever* the High Priest of our confession.

The way Jesus was clothed when He appeared to John sent an extremely important message to the apostle and to the Church at large. John was about to receive Jesus' messages for the seven churches in the Roman province of Asia, some of which would contain correction and stern yet loving rebukes from Christ in response to wrong beliefs and behaviors that were emerging in these congregations. However, by appearing to John as High Priest, Jesus' intercessory ministry was the prominent feature the apostle noticed before anything else. It proclaimed that Jesus was the Great High Priest who was praying for the churches.

We saw in the September 6 *Sparkling Gem* that Jesus revealed Himself in Revelation 1:5 *first* and *foremost* as the Prince and Supreme Sovereign of the kings of the earth. But in Revelation 1:13, He appeared as High Priest, thus affirming that He was standing in His priestly role, interceding for the churches He was about to discipline and correct. Before He appeared with feet of bronze, representing judgment, He appeared as the Great High Priest who was praying for them — that they might repent *before* He needed to apply His feet of judgment.

But John's description of Jesus' "garment down to the foot" also portrayed the intercessory ministry of Jesus, which will never change. This is an office that was once and for all conferred upon Christ and is *unchangeable.* Jesus *was, is,* and *will always be* interceding on behalf of the Church that He purchased with His own blood.

Hebrews 7:25 declares that Jesus lives to make intercession for us. Dressed in His high priestly garments, He sits in the holy presence of the Father and intercedes on our behalf.

That means Jesus is praying and interceding for you *right now.* So what is stopping you from coming to Him today with the needs and desires that are on your heart? Jesus *was, is,* and *forever* will be your Great High Priest. *He is waiting for you to come boldly into His presence to present your needs and desires!*

MY PRAYER FOR TODAY

Father, I thank You that Jesus is in Your Presence as my Great High Priest, where He ever lives to make intercession for me and for those who belong to Him. I thank You that I have no need to be ashamed or embarrassed when I come to You through Him, because He has thrown open the door and invited me to come boldly to the throne of grace to receive help and assistance in my time of need. I am so thankful for this high priestly ministry of Jesus — that He was, is, and forever will be my Great High Priest!

I pray this in Jesus' name!

MY CONFESSION FOR TODAY

I declare that Jesus is my Great High Priest. Seated at the right hand of the Father, He lives to make intercession for me. Jesus, my High Priest, is touched with the feeling of my infirmity. I have no need to be ashamed or embarrassed when I come before the Father through Him, because He has given me unrestricted access and invited me to come boldly to the throne of grace to obtain help in my time of need.

I pray this in Jesus' name!

QUESTIONS FOR YOU TO CONSIDER

1. What needs and desires should you boldly present to Jesus at the throne of grace? He is waiting for you — so what is stopping you from coming to Him with those needs and desires?
2. Can you imagine Jesus dressed in high priestly garments in the presence of the Father, where He ever lives to make intercession for those who come to Him by faith? Why don't you put everything on pause for a moment and try to mentally picture the image of Jesus in this capacity, waiting for you to come to Him?
3. What does it mean to you when the Bible says we can "come boldly" to the throne of grace? What does the word "boldly" communicate to you?

NOVEMBER 12

Eyes as a Flame of Fire

...His eyes were *as a flame of fire*.
— Revelation 1:14

In several previous *Sparkling Gems*, we studied the revelation of Jesus that John wrote while imprisoned on the island of Patmos (*see* January 27,28; March 15; August 22,31; September 6,8,21; November 10,11). Today I want us to focus on another important part of this supernatural vision. As John tried to focus his eyes on the brilliant image before him, one can only imagine how he might have strained to see through the bright light to the Person behind it. In Revelation 1:14, the apostle described the powerful moment when he finally gazed into the eyes of the risen Lord, declaring, "...His eyes were *as a flame of fire*."

The words "his eyes" are a translation of the Greek phrase *ophthalmoi autou*. The word *ophthalmoi* is the plural Greek word for *eyes*, and it is where we get the word *ophthalmology*. The word *autou* simply means *of him*. When the two words are used together as one phrase, they carry a sense of wonder, as if to mean there was something about *Jesus'* eyes that was *unique* and *different* from the eyes of all others. The Greek structure should literally be translated "the eyes *of* him" — emphasizing the fact that Jesus' eyes were unequaled, unsurpassed, unmatched, and unlike anyone else's eyes.

John says that when he looked into *those* eyes, they were "as a flame of fire." The Greek word for "flame" is *phloz*, which describes *swirling, whirling, flickering flames that bend, twist, turn, and arch upward*. The word translated "fire" is *puros*, the Greek word for *a burning fire*. Thus, the phrase "flame of fire" depicts *a brightly burning fire with flames swirling, whirling, flickering, twisting, turning, and arching upward toward the sky*. This, then, is not a depiction of *heat* but of the *character* of fire.

Many readers misread this phrase and conclude that Jesus had real fire *in* His eyes. But John didn't say that. He said that Jesus' eyes were "as" a flame of fire. That word "as" means *like, similar to*, or *with the same effect as* fire. To understand what John was trying to communicate here, it is necessary to stop and think about the effect that a campfire or a fire in a fireplace has upon a person who stares at it for any length of time. The longer a person looks into a fire, the more the flickering flames have a *magnetic, mesmerizing* effect on his eyes, mind, and senses. Soon the person gazing into the fire gets lost in the swirling, turning, twisting flames that flicker back and forth as the wood crackles and pops and the flames reach upward and disappear out of sight. The fire has its own character, both captivating and sedating, drawing people near to watch the dance of its flames as it gives out its warmth.

These seem to be the qualities of fire that John thought of when he peered into Jesus' eyes and became *transfixed* by what he saw. Although he had looked into those eyes thousands of times nearly 60 years earlier, something was different about *these* eyes. In the vision, Jesus' eyes were *compelling, irresistible, riveting*, and *gripping*. They exuded *intelligence* and *magnetism*.

Like the flickering flames of a fire, those eyes drew John closer and *captivated* him completely. John must have been drawn by the warmth and love pouring forth from Jesus' eyes. Yet that wasn't all John saw, for Jesus' eyes also burned with a searching gaze, looking intently into the seven churches in the book of Revelation to see and address their specific needs and problems.

"Fire" is an important symbol in Scripture and frequently represents *purification* and *judgment*. Which effect of divine fire we experience depends wholly on our response to God. If we as individuals, or as the Church at large, submit to the pleadings of the Holy Spirit and "hear what the Spirit saith unto the churches," we will experience the *first* type of fire — a holy fire intended to purify and to make us more like Christ. The first fire is unavoidable for a Church that is submitted to the Lordship of Christ and to the dealings of the Holy Spirit; however, cooperating with this fire does *not* result in severe discipline.

On the other hand, if we resist the pleadings of the Holy Spirit and stubbornly continue to act in ways that are contrary to Christ's character, there is a *second* type of fire that burns up chaff and consumes everything that stands opposed to God. Of course, God is merciful, and even this kind of fire is an act of His love and mercy. Consuming everything that is wrong and displeasing to Christ, this fire clears the way for genuine repentance so individuals or churches can rebuild with proper methods and behaviors that are compatible with Jesus' nature.

Jesus' intense, searching eyes, which seemed "as" a flame of fire, captivated John's attention and signaled to the apostle that the Head of the Church had examined the seven churches in Asia and was preparing to deliver a potent message. Some of these churches were about to be encouraged by the words of Christ — such as the churches of Smyrna and Philadelphia, which received *no* correction at all. The other five churches — Ephesus, Pergamum, Thyatira, Sardis, and Laodicea — were about to be warned of impending judgment if they didn't repent. As King and Head of the Church, Christ had every right to search the churches and require them to change.

This may explain why Jesus appeared to the apostle John first as King (*see* Revelation 1:5) and second as the Great High Priest (*see* Revelation 1:13). Five of the seven churches were on the verge of judgment, and Jesus, their Great High Priest, was interceding for them. The very fact that He came to warn them meant He did not want to judge them. If they were willing to hear the Holy Spirit's voice and repent, they could avoid the fires that bring judgment. What happened next would depend on whether or not the churches chose to hear the Savior's pleading and submit to His commands. The type of fire these churches experienced would depend on their response — but the fire of God *was* coming.

How we respond to the dealings of God determines which kind of fire we will experience. Will it be a fire that purifies and takes us to a higher level in the Lord, or will it be a fire that burns up the chaff in our lives that we haven't been willing to surrender on our own? The choice is ours, but the fact is, that divine fire will come, whether we like it or not.

So today I urge you to willfully examine your heart. If you find that you have chaff that is destined to be burned, get rid of it yourself so that you can avoid the fire that burns up chaff — and prepare yourself to accept the holy fire that comes to purify and to take you higher in your walk with the Lord. *I know that this is the deepest desire of your heart!*

MY PRAYER FOR TODAY

Father, I thank You that Your love for me is so intense that You want to burn up the chaff in my life. Your highest will is for me to surrender these problem areas to You so I do not have to experience that chaff-burning fire. Instead I would experience the holy fire that comes to purify me and take me higher in my walk in the Spirit. So today, Holy Spirit, I ask You to help me examine my heart and willfully surrender those chaff-areas of my life that do not reflect Your character or Your purpose for my life. Open my heart to Your holy, purifying fire, oh God, that I may be cleansed to ascend into the high places of Your glory!

I pray this in Jesus' name!

MY CONFESSION FOR TODAY

I purpose in my heart to respond humbly to the dealing of God so that His fire that kindles upon me will ignite me into a burning flame for His glory. Daily I choose to walk before the Lord in a way that His holy fire will purify and take me to a higher level in Him. I know that the fire of God will burn up the chaff of self-willed works and ways that I wasn't willing to surrender on my own. The choice is mine, and I choose to yield to the refining fire because I know that, whether I like it or not, divine fire will come. And when its fires try the metal of my life, I want all that remains of me through the flames to be found before Him as pure gold.

I declare this by faith in Jesus name!

QUESTIONS FOR YOU TO CONSIDER

1. Have you ever had a time when the fire of God came to burn "chaff" out of your life? Can you describe what that experience was like? When did that happen? Is it something that you are going through right now?
2. The holy purifying fire of God comes to make us ready for higher realms of God's glory. Have you experienced that type of divine fire? Have you ever been in a church service where it felt like the holy, purifying, sanctifying fire of God fell upon the congregation?
3. When you think of Jesus' eyes being "as" a flame of fire, what does that mean to you?

NOVEMBER 13

The Similarity Between Pastors and Stars

And he had in his right hand seven stars....
The seven stars are the angels [messengers]
of the seven churches....
— Revelation 1:16,20

Did you know that Jesus symbolically likened pastors to "stars?" *That's right* — that's what the Bible tells us in Revelation 1:16 and 20. Why did Christ liken pastors to "stars," and what does this tell us about pastors? If you have a pastor, I think you'll really enjoy reading this *Sparkling Gem*. I believe this discussion today will deepen your appreciation and esteem for the gift God placed in your life when He gave you your pastor. And I pray it will fuel your desire to consistently pray for your pastor so his light shines strong and burns long for Jesus Christ!

The word "stars" comes from the Greek word *asteras,* which simply means *stars* — the same word we would use to describe the *stars* in the universe. The meaning of these stars is found in Revelation 1:20, where Jesus explained, "...The seven stars are the *angels* of the seven churches...." The word "angels" is from the Greek word *angelos,* which, in this case, refers to human *messengers.* Specifically, it referred to the *pastors* of the churches Christ was addressing.

Why did Jesus use "stars" to describe the pastors He was addressing in the book of Revelation? What was the symbolic significance of this, and what does the scriptural use of this metaphor tell us about the ministry of a pastor?

Let's begin by pondering the following scientific facts about stars. Then we'll see how these facts relate to pastoral ministry and why Christ likened pastors to stars.

- Every star has a beginning and an end. After its birth, a star lives through several cycles of growth, but eventually it begins to cast off its outer layers in preparation for death. Thus, *there is no such thing as a permanent star.*
- The lifespan of a star is determined by the amount of fuel it has *at its core* and the rate at which it uses that fuel.
- Massive stars have shorter life spans because they experience *greater pressure* at their cores, which causes them to burn energy more rapidly.
- Smaller stars burn less brilliantly, but because they experience *less pressure* at their core than massive stars, the smaller stars usually burn longer.
- As is true with human beings, the behavior of young stars and older stars is very different by comparison. Younger stars are known to rotate rapidly and have high levels of "surface activity." As stars mature and grow older, they slow down and their surface activity begins to diminish.
- Although older stars rotate more slowly and have less surface activity, it is in their mature years that they produce the strongest and most stable light.
- Like human beings, no two stars are alike. Out of all the stars in the universe, each one is unique in its physical characteristics and size. Furthermore, each star gives off its own unique level of luminosity and hue based on surface temperatures. A star can be a diversity of colors — red, yellow, white, and blue — depending on a variety of factors.
- Although stars may cross the orbits of other stars, each star has a specific, predetermined orbit, from which it veers very little, even over a time span of thousands of years. This explains why the signs in the heavens haven't changed over the course of history.

Now let's consider how these scientific facts about stars help explain why Jesus symbolically and spiritually compares *pastors* to *stars.*

- Like the stars in the heavens, even the most bright and shining pastoral ministry is *temporary* and *fading*. Although a pastor may serve in one location for many years, there is no such thing as a permanent pastor. Eventually a time comes when his or her light begins to fade so a new "star" can be born. In time, each pastor begins to wind down and prepare for another pastor to take his or her place and become a guiding light for that church and community.
- The lifespan of a pastor's ministry may be short or long, depending on several factors. One key factor is the amount of *spiritual fuel* and endurance he has at his core, as well as the rate at which he expends that fuel in running his race.
- Often pastors of larger churches have ministries with shorter life spans because they experience such great pressure at their core, which can cause them to burn out more quickly. And although it may seem as if pastors with smaller congregations burn less brilliantly or have less impact, they may shine their light longer because they experience less pressure at the core. The amount of spiritual fuel resident within a pastor, his use of that fuel, and his ability to endure pressure at his core are all critical factors in determining the longevity of his ministry.
- Like massive stars, those pastors who have larger congregations run the risk of experiencing undue pressure *at their core* if they burn too quickly and furiously. Pastors who lead smaller congregations may not shine as brightly in terms of prominence or notoriety, but they may burn longer because they're not subjected to the incessant pressure at their core that pastors of larger churches experience. What transpires *at the core* of a pastor's life is what determines his or her *brevity* or *longevity* in the ministry.
- Like stars, younger pastors can be much more involved in "surface activity" and spin much faster in terms of a schedule. Constant movement and a fixation on what impresses the flesh is the fruit of some younger "stars" in the ministry. But as they grow older and more consistent in their walk with God, pastors often come to the conclusion that "surface activity" is not a mark of maturity.
- As a result, the strongest and best years of ministry for pastors usually occur as they grow more mature and come to know Jesus Christ in a deeper way. Pastors who survive the pressure at their core and use their Spirit-given fuel wisely find that their latter years of ministry are their strongest years, because they are able to provide a steady and stable source of light for their churches and communities.
- Like the stars in the universe, no two pastors are exactly alike. God calls some pastors to lead massive churches, others to lead medium-sized churches, and still others to lead smaller churches. Some pastors are called to be bright lights who are well known to the masses, whereas others are called to have less visibility in smaller churches or communities. Regardless of the size of their congregation or ministry, however, pastors are called to shine their light in a way that is consistent with their own unique calling.

- Like stars, each pastor will be different from every other pastor in his specific characteristics, luminosity, and hue. Each person has his own unique experiences to draw from and his own "spiritual temperature" in God. Pastors shine with different hues, yet all represent various facets of God's character.
- Just as stars have an appointed orbit, God has a predetermined course or an "orbit" for each pastor to follow. This would include the details that make a pastor's call to minister the Gospel distinct and unique, such as where he is called to serve, what culture he is called to impact, and which people he is called to minister to. Just as stars cross the paths of other stars, each pastor's course will cross the paths of other pastors so he can fellowship with and be influenced by them. Nevertheless, a pastor must be careful not to veer from his own divine call so his light can shine in the area or "orbit" God has ordained for *him*.

From the facts and symbolic comparisons we've read today, we can see there are many similarities between *pastors* and *stars*. It's an understatement to say that Christ knew these facts a long time before science knew them — that's why He used *stars* symbolically to describe pastoral ministry.

In light of what we've read in today's *Sparkling Gem*, let's commit to praying daily for our pastors: 1) that they become everything God intends them to be; 2) that they will possess a sustained supply of spiritual energy at their core and shine as God intended them to shine; and 3) that they'll be empowered to provide the necessary guiding light for their congregations and communities. Our prayers of faith will avail much, impacting for eternity not only our pastors' lives, but also every place and every person they are called to reach with the truth of the Gospel and the love of Jesus Christ!

MY PRAYER FOR TODAY

Heavenly Father, I thank You for what I have learned today about pastoral ministry. I specifically pray for my pastor — that he will have sufficient spiritual fuel in the core of his being for a long-lasting ministry; that my pastor's ministry will be more stable and strong the older he gets; that my pastor will take his unique role among all pastors; that he knows the "orbit" designed and laid out for his pastoral ministry; and that he will fulfill the divine destiny that You have planned for his life. I thank You for the way my pastor serves, and I ask You, Father, to bless him abundantly. Give him the wisdom, power, and strength that is needed for a long-term ministry that brings forth much fruit for the Kingdom of Heaven.

I pray this in Jesus' name!

MY CONFESSION FOR TODAY

Today I release my faith for my pastor. I specifically confess that my pastor has sufficient spiritual fuel in the core of his being for a long-lasting ministry; that my pastor's ministry will be stable and stronger the older he gets; that my pastor will take his unique role among all pastors; that my pastor knows the orbit designed for his pastoral ministry; and that he will fulfill the divine destiny that You have planned for his life. I confess that You, Father, give my pastor the wisdom, power, and strength that is needed for a long-term ministry that brings forth much fruit for the Kingdom of Heaven.

I declare this by faith in Jesus' name!

QUESTIONS FOR YOU TO CONSIDER

1. Did you learn something new today about pastoral ministry? Of everything you read, what stood out above all else? What specifically will you carry with you from this *Sparkling Gem*?
2. Not only does Jesus refer to pastors as stars, but also as angels. Have you ever considered how your pastor is a God-sent angel to your church? What does this mean to you? What do you think of the Bible using this analogy to depict your pastor's ministry?
3. Do you regularly pray for your pastor? If the answer is no, maybe today would be a good day to add him or her to your prayer list and to begin regularly praying for your pastor to have the wisdom and strength to lead the church and give light to the community.

NOVEMBER 14

Moving On in Life at the Right Time

And he [Paul] went into the synagogue,
and spake boldly for the space
of three months, disputing and persuading
the things concerning the kingdom
of God. But when divers were hardened,
and believed not, but spake evil
of that way before the multitude,
he departed from them, and separated the disciples,
disputing daily in the school of one Tyrannus.
— Acts 19:8,9

One of the most difficult moments in life is when you realize one season has ended, and the time is right for you to move on to the next season. Perhaps *you* are in such a season now — when you are realizing it's time for you to move on from where you are to the next period of your life. As you will see in today's *Sparkling Gem*, this could possibly be the beginning of one of the most glorious times in your life. Let's look at the life of the apostle Paul for an example of this kind of life transition.

When Paul's ministry first began in Ephesus, it started out very successfully in the synagogue, but eventually a time came when that season ended, and it was time for him to move on. Acts 19:8 says that Paul entered the synagogue and "...spake boldly for the space of three months, disputing and persuading the things concerning the kingdom of God."

Paul's manner was so compelling that many who heard him were convinced and won over by the message they heard him preach. Yet despite Paul's success with some of his listeners, he didn't have this same effect on all who heard him. When many Jews began converting to Jesus Christ, the hospitable atmosphere evaporated. Acts 19:9 says, "But when divers were hardened, and believed not, but spake evil of that way before the multitude, he departed from them...."

The phrase "spake evil" comes from the Greek word *kakologeo*, which is a compound of the words *kakos* and *logos*. The word *kakos* describes something *evil, harmful, injurious, malevolent, malicious, spiteful*, or *mean*. The word *logos* simply means *words*. But when the two words compounded, they form the word *kakologeo*, which describes *malicious words that are deliberately devised and spoken to produce harm, hurt, and injury*.

These *kakos* words spoken by unbelieving Jews were cleverly designed words and preplanned statements intended to damage Paul's reputation and ruin the impact of his message and ministry. Those hostile people were spewing out premeditated, sinister, and villainous allegations in hopes of shutting Paul down. And, unfortunately, they did it *publicly*! That is why the verse goes on to say they spoke these words "before the multitude." The word "multitude" probably refers to those in the synagogue, which explains why Paul made the decision to leave the synagogue at the end of that three-month period.

The opposition became so intense that Paul knew his effectiveness in the synagogue had ceased. Every time he tried to raise his voice to speak to the crowd, the opposition was so vocal, loud, and nasty that he was unable to successfully carry on his ministry. Paul had the maturity to recognize when he had lost his effectiveness and it was no longer profitable to debate with this audience. Had he stayed and fought longer or harder, it wouldn't have produced anything of lasting quality and may have created an even worse situation. He perceived that his season in the synagogue was coming to a close, and it was the right time for him to move on to the next season in his ministry.

Likewise, if we will listen to the Holy Spirit, He will show *us* when to speak and when to be quiet — when to stay and when to move on. We must learn to be sensitive to the voice of the Holy Spirit in every situation. Then we can know when we are to remain in the battle or when it is wiser for us to withdraw, break camp, and relocate to new territory where greater victories will be won. The Holy Spirit will lead us — *if* we will quiet our hearts and listen for His voice.

When Paul realized that the battle in the Ephesian synagogue was counter-productive and no longer worth the effort, the Bible tells us, "...He departed from them, and separated the disciples, disputing daily in the school of one Tyrannus" (Acts 19:9).

Every so often, occasions like this come to us in life — landmark moments when we must choose to make a break with where we are in order to move into the new place where God is calling us. Such moments can be difficult. However, just beyond our struggle is where we discover the greatest power of God. But once we are where God wants us and we surrender to the Holy Spirit, resurrection power is soon released in our lives. This is exactly what happened in Acts 19:9. It was only *after* Paul left the synagogue that God unleashed miracles in the city of Ephesus.

We don't know how Paul felt when he left the synagogue. He may have had high hopes initially that the positive response he first received from this Jewish community would last. As he gathered his disciples and walked away from the synagogue to begin afresh in a new place, it's possible that Paul felt heartbroken over the souls he had to leave behind. Perhaps he was tempted to feel discouraged or as if he had lost an important battle.

Regardless of how Paul may have felt, Acts 19:9 relates that he found an effective venue to continue preaching the Gospel as he "...disputed daily in the school of one Tyrannus." It looked as if an important door for the Gospel were closing, but God had already prepared another, more effective place for Paul and his group of disciples to meet.

The same thing happens in our lives as we seek to obey God's will. In moments when it looks like all is lost, we must remind ourselves that when a door closes, God is already behind the scenes, working to open another door. In Paul's case, the door God opened was a place the Bible calls "the school of one Tyrannus."

Paul's entire stay in Ephesus lasted approximately three years. But regarding the apostle's teaching ministry in the school of Tyrannus, Acts 19:10 states that Paul "...continued by the space of two years; so that all they which dwelt in Asia heard the word of the Lord Jesus, both Jews and Greeks."

The school of Tyrannus was located in the most prestigious areas of Ephesus — right in the central section of the city. Hour after hour, revelation and insight poured forth from the apostle for anyone who wished to listen. In fact, the verse goes on to say Paul's teaching became so well known that "all they which dwelt in Asia" heard of it.

Of course, it was humanly impossible for Paul to personally preach to "all they which dwelt in Asia." But Paul's influence in Ephesus grew as he taught every day during those two years in this central location. Those who heard Paul's teaching passed it along to others, and fellow team members were dispatched to start churches in other regions. As a result, the population of Asia was exposed to the Gospel in a very short period of time — a much greater result than if he had stayed in the synagogue, which provided the apostle a very limited audience. Although it seemed a great door had closed, it was actually the beginning of a glorious period in Paul's ministry.

Today I want to tell you that if you sense a door is closing or a season is ending, it may turn out to be one of the best things that has ever happened to you. It may not be comfortable to go through this change, and it may be one of the most difficult things you've ever done. But *if* you put your eyes on the Lord and trust in Him, you'll discover that He is working behind the scenes to prepare the next place for you.

Take that to heart today. Open your spiritual ears and listen to what the Holy Spirit is saying to you. He will show you when to stay and when to move on — when it is wiser to withdraw, break camp, and relocate to new territory where greater victories will be won. The Holy Spirit will lead you *if* you will quiet your heart and listen for His voice. One door may be closing, but another door is getting ready to open for you — and it could possibly be the most wonderful season of life you've ever known!

MY PRAYER FOR TODAY

Father, I needed this word today. I do feel that I'm beginning a new season in my life. Knowing how to move on has been the challenge for me. I ask You to give me wisdom to know what steps to take, discernment to know what to say and what not to say, and understanding as to how to do this in a manner pleasing to Jesus. For me to do this correctly, I need Your help and guidance. So, Holy Spirit, I open my spiritual ears to hear You, and I extend my hand for You to lead me through all the steps I need to take — until I land securely in the next place and the new season that You have ordained for my life.

I pray this in Jesus' name!

MY CONFESSION FOR TODAY

I confess that God, by His Spirit, is leading me into the next season of my life. Although it is difficult to leave the present season, I know and declare that God is opening a new door for me and that the next season will be the most wonderful time I have ever known in my life thus far. Because I lean upon the Holy Spirit and I follow His voice, He will show me what to say, what not to say, what steps to take, and how to transition from where I am to where I am headed. The Holy Spirit is speaking to me and leading me, and I will end up in the next God-ordained place for my life.

I declare this by faith in Jesus' name!

QUESTIONS FOR YOU TO CONSIDER

1. Do you sense that a door is closing in your life? Why do you think that is the case? How is it closing?
2. Can you see where you are headed? Paul didn't know where he was going to teach until he made the decision to leave the synagogue. Are you stepping out in faith before you have all the answers, as Paul was required to do?
3. Have you ever done anything like this before? Have you considered seeking counsel *before* you take this step just to make sure you're on the right course?

NOVEMBER 15

The Role of 'Handkerchiefs and Aprons' in Healing the Sick

So that from his [Paul's] body were brought
unto the sick *handkerchiefs* or *aprons*,
and the diseases departed from them,
and the evil spirits went out of them.
— Acts 19:12

As we saw in yesterday's *Sparkling Gem*, a time came when God instructed the apostle Paul that it was time for him to start his ministry in the local school of Tyrannus. Rather than fight the opposition in the synagogue — unbelieving Jews who were raising their voices against him — Paul had the wisdom to know it was time to withdraw, break camp, and relocate to new territory. Although it looked like a significant door was closing, another door was opening for him that would prove to be even more significant. And at the moment that new door swung open, it would initiate the most wonderful season of miracles Paul had ever known in his ministry!

That next season in Paul's life literally *overflowed* with the supernatural. Although God had performed a great number of miracles through Paul in different phases of the apostle's ministry, the miracles that occurred in Acts 19 were simply *spectacular*. During this new season in Paul's life, special miracles *exploded* in his ministry. God's power was even being released through articles of his clothing when they were laid upon the sick and those oppressed by evil spirits.

Acts 19:12 refers to this supernatural phenomenon: "So that from his body were brought unto the sick *handkerchiefs* or *aprons*, and the diseases departed from them, and the evil spirits went out of them." The Greek word for "handkerchief" is *soudarion*, a word used to describe *a garment that is wrapped about one's head*, such as the richly decorated head garments men in the Middle East wear today.

In the First Century, it was customary for wealthier, sophisticated men to wear beautifully patterned pieces of material around their heads, especially if temperatures were hot. The headdress provided protection from the sun, kept the head cool in hot weather, and soaked up sweat that would otherwise stream down the brow and face. The word "handkerchief" in all likelihood refers to such a headdress since that was the way this particular Greek word was most commonly used.

The word "apron" is *simikinthion* — and it depicts *a decorative garment worn around the waist for wealthy, educated, and sophisticated men*. Those who gathered near the School of Tyrannus — where Paul was conducting his ministry during this time — were sophisticated intellectuals who congregated to show off, to prove their wealth, to communicate new ideas and concepts, and to share new philosophical hypotheses with others of the same socioeconomic status.

The people who gathered in this section of the city were from the "upper crust" of society and dressed appropriately for their rank. In hot temperatures, the majority of these men wore stylish headdresses with brightly colored patterns and elegant wraps around their waists. This type of clothing was a *status symbol* for the rich and sophisticated. It is probable that Paul was likewise dressed suitably in an expensive headpiece with an elegant wrap tied about his waist.

Some have speculated these were workers' rags that Paul might have worn from laboring in the leather industry. However, such common worker's attire would be completely inappropriate for the prestigious corner of Ephesus where the School of Tyrannus was located. This view is very unlikely to be true. The facts seem to point to elegant clothes that Paul wore as he taught in one of the most prestigious schools in one of the most prestigious neighborhoods of Ephesus. This is my personal view, as I believe Paul would have been appropriately dressed for the audience he was trying to reach with his message. Few of those who were gathered would have had any interest in listening to a common worker in rags. This was simply unfitting for the vicinity near the School of Tyrannus.

But what *is* known about these garments — whatever kind of garments they were — is that they were *saturated* with the anointing of God! These articles of clothing, infused with divine power, were taken from Paul's body to be laid upon people too ill to make the journey to where the apostle was ministering. Although the text doesn't explicitly state the details, it seems logical to assume that these articles of clothing were cut into smaller pieces so they could be taken to larger numbers of sick, diseased, and demon-possessed people who lived throughout the city of Ephesus.

This is the only record of "prayer cloths" being used in the book of Acts, so there must be a logical reason as to why this particular manifestation of God's power happened in Ephesus. When people in Ephesus visited a pagan temple, it was common for them to "take home a piece of the power" by purchasing a fetish. They believed *objects* carried power.

So it seems that God met these pagans at the point of their faith. Because they believed that *objects* could transmit power, they believed that if they could take home a piece of Paul's clothing, they would "take home a piece of the power" that operated in his ministry. Consequently, it is probable that these pieces of clothing were cut into smaller pieces and shared among listeners, who took them home and laid them on the sick and diseased with outstanding results. *Many* were miraculously healed and delivered as evil spirits went out of them.

If Paul had remained in the synagogue — arguing and debating with people who opposed him — it is likely that this flow of divine power would have never manifested in his life. But after Paul took the big step of faith, withdrew from that environment, and stepped by faith into a new territory — *that's* when God unleashed levels of power that Paul had never seen or experienced theretofore. Even his clothes carried the anointing of God to the sick, diseased, and demon-possessed — and they were healed!

Just think what could happen if *you* moved into the next season of your life where God is calling you! You may not see the miraculous results yet, but you could be getting ready to move into the most miraculous season of your life. Just as Paul would never have dreamed God would use his clothes to transmit the anointing, it may be that God has things planned for you that are beyond your wildest imagination. He simply needs you to be in the right place at the right time — and that depends on your willingness *to follow* and *to obey*!

MY PRAYER FOR TODAY

Father, I ask You for the grace to step out of my comfort zone and into the place You have designed for me. I've been reluctant to let go of what is known and comfortable — but without faith, it is impossible to please You! I know that You are calling me onward and upward. I receive the courage I need to release the familiar and to step out by faith to enter the next season of my life. And, Father, just as Paul experienced miracles he had never known once he obeyed, I pray that my life will explode with miraculous answers to prayer as I step forward to obey what You are telling me to do.

I pray this in Jesus' name!

MY CONFESSION FOR TODAY

I confess I have the grace to step out of my comfort zone and into the place God has designed for me. I am not afraid to let go of what is known and comfortable, because I know that God is calling me onward and upward. He gives me courage to step out in faith to enter the next season of my life. Just as Paul experienced miracles he had never known once he obeyed, my life will explode with the miraculous as I step forward to obey what the Holy Spirit is telling me to do.

I declare this by faith in Jesus' name!

QUESTIONS FOR YOU TO CONSIDER

1. Have you ever known individuals whose lives literally exploded with miraculous results once they moved from where they were to where God wanted them to be? Who were those individuals? What kind of miraculous results did they see and experience once they got into the right place?
2. God worked unusual miracles through Paul — even saturating his clothing with His anointing so that His power to heal and deliver could be transferred onto the sick, diseased, and demon-possessed. What is the most unusual miracle you have ever heard of or observed in your life?
3. Since we're talking about God using articles of clothing to transmit the anointing, have you ever known someone who was healed as a result of a prayer cloth being laid upon him or her?

NOVEMBER 16

The Judgment Seat of Christ

...We shall all stand before the judgment seat of Christ.
— Romans 14:10

For we must all appear before the judgment seat of Christ;
that every one may receive the things done in his body,
according to that he hath done, whether it be good or bad.
— 2 Corinthians 5:10

The fact is that soon everything in this world will pass away. Only those things that were done for Jesus — in obedience to Him — will last for eternity. In light of this truth, it's imperative that we frequently examine our hearts to determine our real spiritual condition. If we find areas that need improvement, the Holy Spirit will help us correct those areas that are out of harmony with Him.

The Bible says that a day is coming when we will all stand before the Judgment Seat of Christ to give an account for what we've done with His Word and with His plan for our lives. Romans 14:10 says, "...For we shall all stand before the judgment seat of Christ." And Second Corinthians 5:10 says, "For we must all appear before the judgment seat of Christ; that every one may receive the things done in his body, according to that he hath done, whether it be good or bad."

It's important to understand that this is *not* the Great White Throne Judgment (*see* Revelation 20:11), before which unbelievers will stand and give account to God for their lack of faith. The Judgment Seat of Christ speaks of the moment in God's timeline when Christians will be rendered eternal rewards — or where they will discover that they have accumulated no eternal reward — according to their works in their lifetime.

The word "judgment seat" is a translation of the Greek word *bema*, a word that described *an official place where judgments and rewards were rendered to those who stood before an official judge.* Paul used this word to emphatically warn us that a time will come when each of us will stand before Christ, answer for what we have done, and be rewarded or *not rewarded* accordingly. The books will be opened and everything will be made known, including the motives of men's hearts (*see* 1 Corinthians 4:5).

Since a day is coming when the truth will be revealed, wouldn't it be better for you and me to take an honest look at ourselves *right now* so we can get things completely right in our hearts before that great day when we stand before Christ?

I've prepared the following questions to help you see areas of your spiritual life that may need attention. *These are questions I regularly ask myself to keep my own heart open and pliable in the hands of the Holy Spirit.* I pray they are as helpful to you as they are to me. They're not meant to be condemning. I share them with you only to help you determine if there are areas in which you need divine assistance and change. I know that I will give account one day for the way I truthfully answer the following basic questions — so for me, this is a meaningful starting point to help me regularly make sure my heart is right.

Prayerfully consider asking these questions for yourself, bringing them before the Lord so He can help you keep your heart aligned with His and walk in the light of His truth for your life.

- ***What do I give to God financially?***

  Does your giving show that the Kingdom of God and world missions are still your heartbeat — something you deeply value?

  Since actions really do speak louder than words, it would be a healthy exercise for all of us to look at our financial giving and see what our giving reveals about our priorities.

- ***What do my spending habits and my acquisition of personal possessions say about me and my character?***

  Do you spend money on possessions that you know should have been used in the expansion of the Gospel in places where its voice needs to be heard? If so, what changes do you need to make?

  We can all mislead ourselves to think we're more generous than we really are. But if God Himself gave His view of our spending habits, what would He say about us? Would He say that the propagation of the Gospel is the most important thing to us — or that our spending habits reveal that our own comforts are most important? We must be willing to allow Him to deal with us and then make changes as He lovingly touches those areas of our lives that need improvement.

- ***What am I doing with my time?***

  How you use your time is a great indicator of what you really deem as important. Do you spend time with God and His Word as a top priority in your life? Or do you somehow find time to watch television, go to the movies, or do other things you want to do while failing to find time to saturate your heart in the Word?

  A good question we could ask ourselves is this: *If God looked at our lives and measured what we love most by the things we give our time to, what would He say we loved the most in life?*

- ***Whom am I really serving with my talents?***

  An honest answer to this question will reveal the depth of your commitment to God and to the local church. Serving the Lord means that you have willingly given Him the final say about what you do with your time — and that you are willing to *make* time to serve in the local body He has set you in.

Is there anything you're laying down or sacrificing in order to walk in obedience and service to God? Are you willing to be inconvenienced to help someone else or to serve in the church — to jeopardize your own comforts and pleasures to further the cause of Christ and make a difference in the lives of others?

Words are easily spoken, but actions prove a person's sincerity. By looking at our lives — our talents, our gifts, and our time — would God say our actions prove we're devoted mostly to ourselves and our own needs and interests, or would He say we're truly living for the expansion of His Kingdom?

- ***What do I spend most of my time praying about?***

  What does your prayer life reveal about you? Do you only pray about yourself, or do you pray for the needs of others also? It's easy to think of your own needs and desires — because they're *your* needs, and no one knows them like you do. There's certainly nothing wrong with that. But how often do you focus on the needs of others when you pray? Does God hear you primarily praying for yourself, or does He hear you praying for other people too?

Would God say that your life reveals a willingness to pick up your cross to do what *He* asks you to? If God opened the books to reveal the sacrifices you've made in response to Him, would the records reveal that you care deeply about pleasing Him and living in obedience to His commands, both in His Word and His specific direction for your life?

I believe these questions, though basic, are a good starting point to examine ourselves to determine our spiritual gauge. If the needle points toward "empty" or even "half full," we need to spend time in the presence of God to be refilled and resupplied. None of us wants to look ashamedly into the eyes of Jesus on that great day — on what should be one of the most wonderful days in our eternal lives!

I want to encourage you to take time to think over the questions in this *Sparkling Gem* and let the Holy Spirit shine His light upon your life. Then through time in prayer and in God's Word, let Him tell you what action you need to take to bring correction and be fully refilled and resupplied!

MY PRAYER FOR TODAY

Father, since the day is coming when I will stand before the judgment seat of Christ to be rewarded or not rewarded according to my works, please help me take a serious look at my life now and evaluate where I need to make changes. On that glorious day, I do not want to look into Jesus' eyes while feeling regret and sadness — I want to look into His eyes, knowing that I did all He asked of me to fulfill His plan for my life. Holy Spirit, help me examine my heart and my actions to see what I need to change now. And Holy Spirit, I ask You to remind me continually that a day is coming when I will stand before Christ to answer for my life. Please keep me in remembrance of this so that I will live at all times with eternity at the forefront of my mind.

I pray this in Jesus' name!

MY CONFESSION FOR TODAY

I acknowledge that I live each day with an awareness that I will stand before the Judgment Seat of Christ one day. As a result, I take a serious look at my life regularly to see where I need to make changes. I am determined that I will look into His eyes on that glorious day without regrets, knowing that I did my best to fulfill His plan for my life. Hence, I will live in obedience and yieldedness to the direction of the Holy Spirit so that I can be ready for that great and notable day.

I declare this by faith in Jesus' name!

QUESTIONS FOR YOU TO CONSIDER

1. Have you ever thought about the day when you will stand before the Judgment Seat of Christ? In what ways would your life change if you stayed more aware of that fact throughout each day?
2. Have you ever heard a preacher or Bible teacher teach on this subject? If not, why do you think this subject has not had more attention when it deals with one of the most critical moments in our eternal existence?
3. We will *all* stand at the Judgment Seat of Christ. How does that thought personally impact your heart? Why does it affect you that way? What does your answer tell you about your own spiritual confidence and condition?

NOVEMBER 17

Ordering a Phone Call and Waiting for Three Days!

For through him we both [Jew and Gentile]
have access by one Spirit unto the Father.
— Ephesians 2:18

In today's technologically sophisticated, interconnected society, it's so easy to pick up the phone, call anywhere in the world, and make an immediate connection to whomever you are calling. But when my family first moved to the Soviet Union to follow God's call on our lives, placing an international phone call was quite a difficult task!

First of all, all international phone calls had to be "scheduled" and "ordered" in advance. In the city where we lived, it took three days to order a phone call to the United States. We would call the operator, tell her that we'd like to place a call to America, and give the number we wanted to call. The operator would respond, "Your call will come in three days" — however, she couldn't tell us what time the call would be placed — so on that third day, we didn't dare leave the house for any reason, because the call could come at any unknown minute.

If the call came through, and the number was busy, we couldn't simply say, "Can we try another number?" That call was our only chance! If the line was busy, we had to schedule another call and wait for another three days. The connections were so horrible that often we had to yell and scream for our voices to be heard — *if* we actually connected to the person we were calling. Furthermore, special agents were on the phone line with us, listening to our conversations in order to monitor what we were saying. They were so obviously listening in that once I asked the agent to get off the phone, and he answered by telling me it was his *job* to listen!

Connecting was so difficult in those days! Finally, someone suggested that we purchase a satellite phone with a gigantic antenna. I would dial the call on a huge black box, and Denise would hold a gigantic antenna and point it this way and that way toward the sky, trying to figure out its optimal position so we could get the best possible connection. The antenna was huge! Denise and I must have looked like quite the sight as we stood in the front yard with a giant, umbrella-shaped antenna and a huge satellite phone, trying to figure out how to best connect with our families in the United States!

I've often thought of those difficult days of poor communication during my morning prayer times — when all I have to do is open my heart, express my faith, and I am instantly and effortlessly connected to Heaven! There are no three days of waiting and no waving of a giant antenna trying to find the correct "channel" that connects me to Heaven. All it takes is a single moment of faith, and an instant connection is made. I call it "instant access" to the throne of God.

This "instant access" is referred to in Ephesians 2:18, where the apostle Paul wrote that through Christ we have "access" by the Holy Spirit unto the Father. Today I want to talk to you about this word "access."

The word "access" is the Greek word *prosagoge*. It is a Greek word that was used to describe individuals who had *free entrance, access*, or *unhindered approach* to a king's court. There was no need for pleading or begging and no waiting in long lines to be recognized. It was an *unhindered approach* at any time and any moment. This means that when you are in Christ Jesus, the Holy Spirit provides a way for you to *immediately connect* with the Father at any time!

I don't know the details of what you are facing today, but if you are in Christ Jesus, I can assuredly tell you that you have immediate access to the Father through the Spirit. Thank God, you don't have to order a heavenly phone call and wait for three days to get through to the throne.

You don't have to worry that your connection will be put off again and again. Your position in Christ guarantees you instant, immediate access to the Father at any time and at every moment!

MY PRAYER FOR TODAY

Father, I give glory, honor, and praise to You that through Jesus Christ, I have instant, unhindered access to Your throne. Because Your Spirit lives inside me, the door to Heaven is open above me and Your ears are attentive to hear and answer me. Furthermore, because my heart is an open door to you, this same connection gives You access through me to others. Holy Spirit, teach me how to live every moment in an active, engaged faith that pleases You and keeps me continually aware of my connection with You.

I pray this in Jesus' name!

MY CONFESSION FOR TODAY

I confess that my life is hidden with Christ in God. According to Ephesians 2:18, I have instant access to God through Christ Jesus. Furthermore, the Father has access through me to reach those around me because my heart is an open door to Him. I do not need to fear that God won't hear me. I thank my God that He always hears me! When I pray in faith, the Holy Spirit enables me immediately to connect with the Father to access His wisdom and His power with no delay!

I declare this by faith in Jesus' name!

QUESTIONS FOR YOU TO CONSIDER

1. Have you ever had moments when you "felt" like you weren't getting through to God in prayer? After reading today's *Sparkling Gem*, do you now understand that if you are in Christ, you have instant access to the Father, regardless of what you may be feeling?
2. How does the message you've read today affect you? Does it help give you assurance that God is listening and that you immediately connect to Him when you pray in faith?
3. Can you rest in the Lord when you pray — confidently assured that He is listening to you? Or have you been hampered in your thoughts without understanding that you have unrestricted access to the throne of God?

During my morning prayer times, all I have to do
is open my heart, express my faith,
and I am instantly and effortlessly
connected to Heaven!

NOVEMBER 18

My 'Rabies Shots' Ordeal

For where envying and strife is,
there is confusion and every evil work.
— James 3:16

During our early years in the former USSR, Denise and I were invited to minister at three European conferences in Austria, Switzerland, and Germany, and I decided to bring our sons to give them the experience of ministering in Europe. When the day finally arrived for our long-anticipated trip, things got a little hectic, to say the least. The clock was ticking, and it was time for us to depart to the airport so we wouldn't miss our flight. However, instead of getting ready, the boys were just poking around, and Denise hadn't even finished packing. I knew that if we didn't leave on time, we'd miss our flight. So in the midst of it all, I lost my temper and began to yell and threaten everyone to get downstairs immediately and pile in the car, or I was going to leave without them!

Our ministry administrator at that time had agreed to housesit for us while we were gone, and she had just arrived, bringing along her beautiful golden retriever who had never encountered our St. Bernard that lived outside in our yard. But that all changed in a moment's time! When I couldn't quite seem to get my family together to leave on time, I became furious that they were jeopardizing our flight — and in that angry moment, I threw open the front door to carry a few suitcases to the car. However, as I threw open that door, our administrator's golden retriever darted out the door ahead of me — and in a split second, the two dogs started attacking one another. I watched as our St. Bernard wrapped its jaws around the neck of the golden retriever and bit down. I thought, *Oh, great, not only are we going to be late for our flight, but our St. Bernard is also going to kill our administrator's golden retriever!*

I was already worked up into a frenzy over my family being late — and now we had a *very* ugly dogfight happening in our driveway. So in a moment when I was already angry, I jumped into the middle of the fray to try to pull the dogs apart from each other. But I stuck my right hand too close to the dogs' mouths, and my own dog bit me! I lifted my right hand to see how badly I had been bitten, and all I could see was blood pouring from the tip of my ring finger.

I pulled the dogs apart, rushed into the house, and quickly put my finger under water to wash away the blood so I could assess how badly I was bitten. Looking down in disbelief, I saw that the entire *tip* of my finger had been bitten off, and blood was pouring out like an open hydrant. My family was finally ready to go to the airport, but I told Denise, "Forget the airport, because now we're headed to the hospital!"

With my hand wrapped in blood-soaked towels, I was immediately admitted into the emergency room, and after examining me, the doctors on duty decided to check me into the hospital for a night. My family and I walked down the hallway to my assigned hospital room, which was a dismal affair in its own right. A single light bulb dangled precariously from a wire in the ceiling. The sink was barely bolted to the wall and looked like it could fall off at any moment. The wallpaper was peeling off the walls, and the windowpanes were cracked. And there I was — wounded, flustered, and wearing a tattered hospital gown for an overnight stay in this decrepit hospital. Denise graciously called the pastor in charge of the first conference to say we'd be a day late, while I waited for the chief physician to pay me a visit.

When the doctor in charge finally arrived, he asked me a question I didn't anticipate. "Mr. Renner," he said, "I understand that you were bitten by your own dog. Has your dog had rabies shots?" When I answered in the negative, the doctor replied, "Well, I regret to tell you that in this country, if you are bitten by a dog that has not had rabies shots, *you* must have rabies shots. That's the law of the land."

I lay in my hospital bed *speechless* as I realized that this doctor was preparing to give me the first of a series of rabies injections. He continued to say, "We used to give 30 of these shots in the stomach, but the French have come up with a strong new rabies vaccine that requires only seven injections — and we are going to give you your first injection right now."

After instructing me to turn over so they could give me an injection in my backside, the doctor casually said, "There's just one downside to this particular form of rabies vaccination. Once you start these injections, you have to take the following six injection right on schedule, or you will actually develop rabies!" I thought, *That's just great. If I'm a day late, I'll end up as a rabid preacher, foaming at the mouth!*

The next day, the nurse administered another rabies shot and then gave me a packet containing five more doses of the rabies vaccine along with a packet of syringes — and she firmly reminded me *not* to miss a single dose at the scheduled time or I would develop rabies.

Dismissed from the hospital, I went home to gather my family, and we flew to Europe where three conferences awaited us. At every conference I attended, I had to ask the pastor, "Excuse me, but do you have a nurse in your congregation who can give me a rabies injection?" I felt *horribly humiliated* by the entire ordeal.

However, I learned a big lesson from that experience. *Strife* throws open the door for the devil to attack in ways you never would have imagined. If I hadn't allowed strife and anger to get me all worked up that day, I never would have flung open the door to the house in such thoughtless anger. The guest's dog would have never run out before me, and the ugly dogfight would have never happened. That moment of rage and anger resulted in my getting bit and having to endure the debacle that followed.

And it only took *seconds* for things to get out of control that day! *Can you think of a time when strife caused a situation in your life to quickly spiral out of control?*

James wrote about the destructive potential of strife in James 3:16, saying, "For where envying and strife is, there is confusion and every evil work." According to this verse, whenever a concoction of such attitudes is allowed to exist, it opens the door for "confusion and every evil work."

The word "confusion" is the Greek word *akatastasia,* which originally described *thorn bushes* or *prickly plants*. Essentially, it calls to mind something that causes pain when someone becomes ensnared in it. Think of what an accurate description that is for the confusion caused by strife! It tells us that strife ensnares people and inevitably results in pain.

Eventually the word *akatastasia* developed to describe various situations that are filled with *disorder, disturbance,* or *trouble.* It portrayed such *chaotic confusion* that early authors occasionally used it in a political sense to depict *riots* and *anarchy*! Well, that's a pretty good description of what happened in our house that morning when I lost my temper! Things quickly spun out of control and turned *ugly*!

James goes on to say that such attitudes result in every "evil" work. The word "evil" is *phaulos,* which means *bad, foul,* or *vile*. In addition to James 3:16, the word *phaulos* is used in John 3:20 and John 5:29 to describe *evil behavior*, and in Titus 2:8, it simply denotes something *bad.* In fact, this Greek word *phaulos* is where we get the English word *foul* — rightly depicting a behavior or situation that is *appalling, atrocious, distasteful, sickening,* or, simply put, really *ugly*. James' usage of this word affirms that *bad attitudes* result in appalling *bad behavior* that often has hurtful consequences.

After losing the tip of my finger, I realized that I was personally responsible for the chaotic events of that day because I allowed an angry attitude to have a place in our home. God was gracious, and the end of my finger grew back. But my family resolved that from that day forward, we would have a "no strife" policy in our home. We learned the hard way that strife-filled attitudes can open the door to *painful, chaotic confusion* that results in hurtful consequences. It's far better to never allow strife to rear its ugly head than it is to give in to it like I did and later have to repair the damage left in its wake.

Today I urge you to listen carefully and heed what you've read in this *Sparkling Gem.* Make a "no strife" policy for your life, refusing to get into strife on any issue. By being vigilant in this matter, you can protect yourself and your family from ugly situations that would have detrimental and painful results.

MY PRAYER FOR TODAY

Father, I thank You for instructing me so vividly about the consequences of strife and the confusion that will ensue. I can remember moments in my own life when I allowed strife to escalate and produce chaos and confusion in a foul situation that should have never been permitted. Thank You for reminding me how important it is to submit to the Holy Spirit and to resist the attempt of my own flesh to control me or those around me by giving place to strife. In moments when I am tempted to fall into a rage about something, help me remember that such attitudes open the door for the devil's attack. Help me be controlled and vigilant about my attitudes so the devil cannot attack me and bring chaos into my life. Holy Spirit, I look to You for Your help!

I pray this in Jesus' name!

MY CONFESSION FOR TODAY

I confess that I do not allow strife to throw me into moments that result in chaotic events or ugly situations. Strife simply has no place in my life, and I refuse to be a participant in anything that even hints of it. From this moment onward, I operate with a "no strife" policy in my life. When I am tempted to get into anger or to yield to an ugly, strife-filled attitude, I will turn from it before it releases negative consequences in my life. The Holy Spirit is at work inside me, and I choose to cooperate with Him in order to prevent this from occurring in my life!

I declare this by faith in Jesus' name!

QUESTIONS FOR YOU TO CONSIDER

1. Can you think of a time when you allowed strife to open a door to an attack from the devil in your life, the lives of family members, your business, or your local church? How could you have prevented that situation before it had a chance to start?
2. I don't want you to dwell on the past, but I do want you to really learn from past mistakes when you allowed strife to gain a foothold in your life. What happened when strife entered into the picture? Can you identify why you allowed that door to swing open so the devil could find an entrance to attack your life?
3. As you regularly read your Bible and develop a prayer life, it will make you more sensitive to moments when your flesh is tempted to act ugly. What are you doing to develop your Bible reading and prayer time?

NOVEMBER 19

Allow God To Prepare You

But now hath God *set* the members
every one of them in the body,
as it hath pleased him.
— 1 Corinthians 12:18

When I look at my life, I see that God has always put me in the right place to prepare me for my next step in ministry. For example, before Denise and I began our teaching ministry many years ago, God placed me under a pastor who taught the Word with great depth and authority, pulling insight from the original Greek text of the New Testament. Over the course of several years, I worked under him as his assistant, and he disciplined me and taught me how to dedicate myself to the serious study of the Word. God used that Bible-rich environment to prepare Denise and me for our itinerant teaching ministry, and it continues to impact our ministry today.

When Denise and I began traveling and teaching all over America, we made dear friends with pastors across the country who would later support us when we moved to the USSR. At the time, we had no idea that those men and women of God and their congregations would become our financial lifeline when we later pursued the call of God overseas. But if we hadn't traveled and cultivated those relationships in those early years, we wouldn't have had the connections to support God's next assignment for our lives.

Being in the right place at the right time is vital to your preparation!

So what environment are you in? Are you where *God* placed you in the Body of Christ, or are you where *you* want to be? Remember, God knows what you need and is working a plan to fully develop the gifts He's placed in you, but you have to allow Him to place you in the environment He knows is best.

First Corinthians 12:18 says, "Now hath God *set* the members every one of them in the body, as it hath pleased him." This word "set" is a translation of a form of the Greek word *tithemi*, which means *to place, to arrange*, or *to position*. This tells us that God knows where we need to be and when we need to be there. He has a plan for us to be in specific places at specific times in life. And First Corinthians 12:18 say that God has a plan and a place for "every one" of us! The words "every one" in Greek include *every single believer, no one excluded*!

It might be that God has asked you to go somewhere and you think, *Lord, why in the world are You taking me there?* Just relax and stay in the flow of the Holy Spirit's leading each day. As you keep the ear of your spirit attentive to His voice, your steps will be ordered of the Lord (*see* Psalm 37:23).

Perhaps the Lord has told you that the place you're at right now is a step toward fulfilling your destiny but not your final destination. If that's the case, make sure you *stay put* until the Lord tells you to change direction. Your present position may be your personal training ground to prepare for the next season, helping you learn how to submit to authority and serve others.

Do you find it difficult to discern what direction the Holy Spirit is leading you? It may be that you're too busy. Or there may be so much mental noise and clutter that you can't easily hear what God is saying. Perhaps the influence of the people around you is hindering you from stepping out in a certain direction or from developing certain gifts. Or maybe you're too comfortable where you are, and your own complacency is keeping you from taking a step that requires stretching your faith and totally depending on God. Regardless of your situation, it's vital that you remain open to the place where *God* wants to position you. The right environment is a major key to finding and fulfilling His will for your life.

Don't be afraid to obey the Lord. He's not going to hurt you or mislead you. He's trying to equip you. If you are careful always to be where you know God is leading you to be at any given time, He will use your experience in the present season to prepare you for the next step of your calling.

I encourage you to allow God to prepare you to do His will. Be flexible and pliable. Allow His Word to dwell richly in your life, and submit yourself to the leaders He has placed over you. You will find that by doing so, God will bring you into the fullness of His will, and you will see your next assignment through to completion!

MY PRAYER FOR TODAY

Dear Father, as I walk through this time of transition, I know that You are preparing me for the next steps. I thank You, for I know that You are committed to preparing me for the next season of my life. You are helping me get ready by placing me with the right people in the right places to receive the training I need. Please help me yield to and follow Your leading. I fully trust You to order my steps according to what pleases You. My times are in Your hands, Father. Help me be flexible and pliable toward the work You are doing in me as You faithfully complete that which You have begun in me. I know that if I am obedient and follow Your voice, You will empower me to see and to fulfill the high calling You've placed on my life!

I pray this in Jesus' name!

MY CONFESSION FOR TODAY

I confess that I know the voice of my Good Shepherd and the voice of a stranger I will not follow. My heavenly Father is ordering and directing my steps so that I will walk with the wise and be wise. As He positions me to stand among the right people, with great ease He is directing my steps to receive the training I need so I can do what the Lord has called me to do. I do not falter; I do not fear. He who has called, equipped, and justified me is near to me and has clothed me with His very own self. Therefore, having done all to stand in this time of testing, I will pass every test and stand fully approved before Him!

I declare this by faith in Jesus' name!

QUESTIONS FOR YOU TO CONSIDER

1. Has there been a time in your life when God was preparing you for a future assignment that you didn't yet know about? When was that, and how did God use that time in your life to prepare you for the future?
2. Can you think of a time when God put you under someone's spiritual influence — or put you with a group of believers — and it was part of your training for what you were going to do later? When was that season of your life? In what way did their influence uniquely equip you for what God called you to do?

3. Are you in that place of training and preparation right now? As you look at where you are and what you are doing, can you see the hand of God guiding and leading you to get you ready for the next phase of your life?

NOVEMBER 20

It Takes Desire To Get to the Top!

This is a true saying, If a man *desire* the office
of a bishop, he desireth a good work.
— 1 Timothy 3:1

Today I want to talk to you about "desire" and what it takes to get to the top — *to be the best at anything you do.* This issue of "desire" is hugely important in all aspects of our lives. In fact, when the apostle Paul instructed Timothy on how to choose the top leaders for his church, he urged the young pastor to choose people who have this specific quality. He said, "This is a true saying, If a man *desire* the office of a bishop, he desireth a good work" (1 Timothy 3:1).

The word "desire" is the Greek word *orgidzo*, and it describes *a longing, a craving, an urge, a burning desire*, or *a yearning ambition* to achieve something. It portrays a person so fixed on the object of his desire that his whole being is stretched forward to take hold of that goal or object, and he will not be satisfied until he reaches and obtains it.

Paul held the qualification of "desire" above everything else on his list of requirements for leaders — and it takes only a few personal experiences with "desireless" people to clearly understand why he did this! However, to illustrate *the power of desire*, I would like to share a true story from my own life that took place many years ago.

I once saw a photograph that had been taken from the summit of one of Canada's tallest mountains. It was unquestionably the most beautiful photograph I had ever seen. In fact, it was such an amazing sight that I determined I wanted to take a trip to Canada and climb to the top of that mountain to see the view in real life!

Eventually my dream came to fruition, and I made arrangements to travel to Canada and join a mountaineering expedition up this mountain. Upon my arrival, I linked up with a group of men who would serve as my climbing partners and accompany me to the summit of this mountain. All of these other men were experienced climbers — I was not. They were all in superb physical conditions — I was not. I had no idea how difficult the journey was going to be, but I knew that I had enough *desire* to keep me going and get me to the top!

After some preparation, the expedition team began the difficult ascent. This route wasn't the most technical or dangerous path to follow with the help of a guide. But it could be extremely treacherous to a person unfamiliar with navigating rugged, glaciated landscapes, and it had claimed the lives of several people through the years. In fact, just days before our own climb, two professional climbers had made a tragic misstep on a patch of black ice along this very same route and had fallen several thousand feet to their deaths on the glacier below!

I huffed, puffed, and pushed my way to the top of that mountain. With each step, the weight of my backpack got heavier. I scrambled up steep inclines that led to even sharper inclines. Rocks tumbled under my feet. I fell. I rolled. I promised God again and again that I would never attempt to do such a stupid thing again if I could just get to the top of that mountain and then make it back down alive!

Finally, we made it to the summit, and I stood on the top of that mountain and looked out over the peaks of the Canadian Rockies. Spread out before me was a stunning panoramic view of hundreds of incredibly beautiful mountain peaks. The sky was so clear that I could see for a hundred miles. I could see peak after peak after peak. As the sun went down, I watched as orange, blue, and purple tones colored the sky. I'd seen sunsets in beautiful places all over the world, but this was gorgeous beyond words! Hard as it was to believe, the photograph I had seen paled in comparison to the real thing.

My exhaustion disappeared, and for a few minutes, I forgot about the hardships I had encountered to get to the summit. I had conquered that mountain! *I had really done it!* My heart was shouting, and I was filled with inexpressible joy.

However, my great victory was about to be interrupted in a big way by altitude sickness. A few hours later, my victorious celebration came to a screeching halt as I began to feel nausea and dizziness wash over me. It came fast and hard, wave after wave of nausea pounding against me until I was unable to stand. My eyes began to see black spots. My head seemed to spin round and round, and I started violently vomiting until I had nothing left in my stomach to throw up. Even then, my body still convulsed with dry heaves.

Dehydrated and weak, I didn't know how I could physically make it through the night. All night long my body wrenched with dry heaves, even though my stomach was empty. I cried. I pleaded for help. I prayed. It was a sickness like nothing I had ever experienced in my life.

The next morning I was still sick and so physically weak that I had to muster the energy to take a few steps. The problem was that we had to start the trip back down the slope to where we had begun the climb the day before. The other men didn't know how I was going to make it. But I was determined that the mountain wasn't going to conquer me! I was going to make it up *and down* that mountain successfully!

I took one small step down the mountain — then another small step and then another. Each step took such an effort that I had to work up the nerve to take each next small step.

The other men in our group knew the risks inherent in an expedition of this nature, and they'd assumed that I knew them too. However, I was uninformed and ill-prepared. If I had possessed the right knowledge, it wouldn't have made the climb easier, but at least I would have understood the potential risks and been better prepared to overcome them. My ignorance on this subject meant that I had to figure it all out on my own, and that is always the most difficult way to learn!

Why am I telling you this story? Because you, too, will run into many obstacles in life that no one prepared you to face. Most likely, people did not deliberately deny you the information. They may have assumed you already understood, or they may have wrongly believed that you were more prepared than you actually were. However, if you have the inward desire to achieve your goal:

- Any obstacle can be overcome.
- Any challenge can be conquered.
- Any mountain can be successfully climbed.

Paul stressed the importance of "desire" — *a yearning ambition to achieve a goal* — in First Timothy 3:1 because it is absolutely fundamental to achieving success in any arena of life. It is without a doubt the chief characteristic needed to survive the challenges of ministry and life while serving God with a pure heart.

If your level of "desire" is strong, it doesn't matter if you're ill-equipped or uninformed in certain areas. You *will* complete your assigned task because your inward determination and resolve will not let you give up!

Of course, First Timothy 3:1 is specifically talking about a person's desire to attain to a leadership position within the ministry. But that word "desire" could also pertain to anyone who desires to reach "...the mark for the prize of the high calling of God in Christ Jesus" (Philippians 3:14) for their own lives.

Each person's calling is different, and you are uniquely gifted to fill a specific role within the great plan of the Father. However, to truly realize your potential, you must possess a strong inner desire — *a desire that refuses to quit at all costs and continually presses forward to reach new heights.* This is the desire to be *all* God has destined and created you to be, and it will propel and sustain you even when the going gets tough and you feel like you can't take another step!

Today I urge you to pray the following prayer and make the subsequent confession of faith. Let it come from your heart, asking God to insert His mighty hand into your spirit to stir up the faith that resides there! Then let your faith lift you up and move you toward conquering any mountain that lies in your path. *Remember, if you've got enough desire, there is nothing that you cannot achieve!*

MY PRAYER FOR TODAY

Father, I ask You to stir up desire in my heart that is strong enough to make me yearn to be the best possible me and achieve all that I can achieve. I know that You expect me to perform to my fullest potential, but I admit that my desire needs an upgrade in order for me reach that highest level. You have given me the talents I need, and I have ideas that I've never taken the time to develop. Now I see that I need greater desire at work in my life. So today, Father, I ask the Holy Spirit to stir desire deeply inside me so that I'll never again be satisfied with mediocrity or the status quo!

I pray this in Jesus' name!

MY CONFESSION FOR TODAY

I confess that a strong, God-given desire propels me forward, energizes me, and compels me to be the best I can be at whatever I set my hand to do. I reject laziness; I reject any idea that just doing "what's required" is enough for me; and I put forth whatever effort is required to reach the top of the mountain God has set before my life. I intend to scale that mountain, shout the victory — and rejoice that God has done such a wonderful work in my life and granted me the desires of my heart!

I declare this by faith in Jesus' name!

QUESTIONS FOR YOU TO CONSIDER

1. After reading the Greek definition for "desire" at the beginning of this *Sparkling Gem*, would you say that desire is a force that is at work in you? If yes, how do you see it in your life? If no, why not?
2. Have you seen others who were super-talented and naturally gifted, yet failed to achieve something magnificent with their lives because they had no motivation or desire? Think about who those people are. Reflect on the decisions they have or haven't made and consider how they affected the outcome of their own lives. What can you learn to do and *not* to do from what you've observed in their lives?
3. If God were to say what He saw in your life, would He say that He sees desire at work, or would He say that you've been willing to lay low and just accept the status quo? What do you need to do or change in order for God to see that "desire" is propelling you toward a grand and glorious future?

To truly realize your potential,
you must possess a strong inner desire
that refuses to quit at all costs
and continually presses forward to reach new heights.

NOVEMBER 21

Do Not Budge From Your Post!

Preach the word;
be instant in season, out of season....
— 2 Timothy 4:2

After Paul's very long, detailed description in Second Timothy 3 of the things that would become more and more prevalent in the last of the last days, he made this charge to Timothy in Second Timothy 4:2, "Preach the word; *be instant in season, out of season....*"

The word "instant" is from the Greek word *ephistemi*, and it means *to stand at your post.* The word *ephistemi* is a *military* term. That's important because standing at your post entails *engaging in spiritual warfare.* I won't delve into a deep study of the subject of spiritual warfare here, but I will say that declaring the Word of God in faith is the highest level of spiritual warfare there is. That's why it's especially important for a preacher, or *any* believer who has God's Word planted deeply in his heart, to stand *and to keep on standing* at his post without moving an inch!

The declaration of God's Word from the pulpit is another form of spiritual warfare. The preaching and teaching of God's Word can have a life-changing, yoke-destroying effect on people's lives. When you proclaim the Gospel, it touches people who are in sin. The Word of God breaks down strongholds, releases His supernatural power, and transforms minds and lives.

That's why Satan is always after the pulpit. He attacks it not so much because of the individuals who stand in the pulpit, but rather because of what they declare from their position in Christ and the authority Jesus has delegated to them as ministers of the Gospel. The enemy wants to stop the light from going forth because of the high level of warfare that's effectively demonstrated when truth penetrates the human spirit and enlightens a person's mind.

There's power in the proclamation of the Gospel to snatch a person right out of a lifetime of bondage and plant his feet firmly on the right path, where there is light for his feet, freedom for his mind, strength and resolve for his will, and vision for a bright future. That's what God's Word can do, so it's no wonder that Satan tries to stop the preaching, teaching, and ministry of the Word! Mental, emotional, and spiritual strongholds are *demolished* when the Word of God is proclaimed!

Now you can better see why Paul would go to such great lengths to urge and admonish Timothy to "stay put" — to remain in his place of ministry, or *stay at his post.* It's obvious that he wouldn't exhort Timothy to stay put somewhere unless Timothy was being tempted *not* to stay put. Believers in the church of Ephesus were suffering intense persecution for their faith in Christ. But Paul said to Timothy, "*You* be instant" or, "Stay at your post! Don't leave the position where God placed you!"

Then Paul's next words — "in season, out of season" — give us further clues as to why remaining continually stationed where God places us is so important. The phrase "in season" was translated from the Greek word *eukairos*, which basically means *in good times.*

For those of us in the ministry, it's so much nicer to preach when everyone in the congregation is on our side and thinks we're great! When everything in the church or ministry is running smoothly with no challenges to distract us, those are good times! But when people in the church start gossiping about us and about each other; when newspapers are writing stories about us or a family member that are untrue; or when your well-being, or the well-being of your family, is threatened either financially or physically — those are not very good times.

That's why Paul said we need to stay at our posts *even* when things seem to be "out of season." That phrase was translated from the word *akairos*, and that prefix *a* puts a negative spin on *kairos*. It means *when things have changed and they are NOT so wonderful.* The whole phrase could be translated *"in good times and bad times!"*

What are you supposed to do when pleasant times begin to shift? What do you do when dark storm clouds begin to form in skies that just moments before were clear and blue? *You do the same thing you were doing before when times were good!* You remain at your post, refusing to budge!

In fact, Paul wrote previously in Second Timothy 3:14, "But *continue* thou in the things which thou hast learned and hast been assured of, knowing of whom thou hast learned them." In other words, Paul was telling Timothy, "Don't you budge! Don't move from the place where God has called you. *Stay put!*"

Paul wrote these words to Timothy, but through these Spirit-inspired writings, He is also saying to us: "Stay at your post and don't budge an inch! Stay there and do what God has told you to do when times are good — and if times turn bad, remain steady and unflinching." One thing is sure: If you'll remain faithful to the call and to the place where God has assigned you — *if you will decide to stay put and refuse to budge an inch* — He will empower you with inner strength that will enable you to see that divine assignment through to a glorious conclusion!

MY PRAYER FOR TODAY

Father, I hear You saying, "Stay at your post, and don't budge an inch! Stay there, and do what I have told you to do. Be faithful when times are good — and if times turn bad, remain steady and unflinching." I know that if I'll remain faithful to the call and to the place where You have assigned me, You will empower me with inner strength and sufficient grace that will enable me to see my calling through to a glorious conclusion! So, Holy Spirit, I receive Your fortitude to withstand the pressure to give up, give in, and throw in the towel. Strengthen me with the might I need inwardly to stay put and see my assignment through to completion!

I pray this in Jesus' name!

MY CONFESSION FOR TODAY

I confess that God strengthens me with His might to be faithful, steadfast, and persevering. When times are good or when times are tough, I am consistently constant. I stay put, no matter what. I will not be moved in my committed stance. The grace of God is teaching me how not to be provoked or lured to move away from my post. I keep my focus fastened on Jesus, and my roots grow down deep into Him. His stability keeps me grounded and enables me to be faithful to the call and to the place where God has planted me.

I declare this by faith in Jesus' name!

QUESTIONS FOR YOU TO CONSIDER

1. Where has God called you that requires you to have inner fortitude to "stay put"? Are you remaining faithful to stay in that place, regardless of whether the times are good or bad?
2. Can you think of a time when the conditions for what you were doing were nearly perfect, but then suddenly or slowly the atmosphere changed and it became more difficult? What did you do when things turned more difficult? Did you stay put or did you relinquish your God-given place to someone else?
3. What about right now? Are you in a good season or a difficult season? Are you allowing yourself to be filled and refilled with the Spirit so that you have the inner strength you need to finish to a grand and glorious conclusion, *regardless* of what it feels like right now?

NOVEMBER 22

You Are What You Are by the Grace of God!

But by the grace of God I am what I am....
— 1 Corinthians 15:10

When I was young, my father tried to encourage me to join in all kinds of sports along with the other young boys from church and school. He tried to motivate me to get interested in baseball, football, basketball, and even bowling. But there was a problem: I had absolutely no interest in any type of sport that had to do with any kind of a ball. It was all boring and monotonous to me. I gave it my best, but I just didn't have it "in me" to get involved in sports. My heart and my interest were simply not there.

God had made me to enjoy other things, like attending the orchestra, visiting museums, listening to classical music, and taking art lessons to develop my natural artistic talent. But those were not the kinds of things that young boys were "supposed" to be interested in, so I ardently pushed forward — trying to force myself to be interested in sports. But it was to no avail, because I just didn't have an interest in it.

The devil tormented me for years, telling me that there was something wrong with me because I was not like other boys and men who rapturously talked about and played sports. To be honest, sports disgusted me — and decades later, I still have no interest in sports, and I didn't produce any interest in my sons in sports. Even today, we are a "no sports" family. However, we love operas, classical music, art auctions, and other things of that nature. Each one of us is tuned into the world of the arts.

When I was a boy, I thought I was weird because of how I was made. But now that I live in Russia, where classical art, music, ballet, and arts of all sorts are a vital part of the culture, I understand that God created me *exactly* the way I needed to be for my assignment in the former USSR. Furthermore, He designed our sons' desires to align with this culture. In Russia, we are perfectly fitted for the world around us. God knew all of that when I was a young boy. At the time, I struggled with coming to terms with my disinterest in sports and the reason why I had such a profoundly deep love for the arts. But it was all a part of how God needed me to be "fitted" for where I would live the bulk of my adult life.

The truth is, many people secretly struggle with why they are the way they are. Some are deeply affected by their characteristics that others might perceive as shortcomings, whereas others have learned to overlook them. For some, the devil has used these feelings as a launching pad to tell them there is something wrong with them — and he has convinced many that they are indeed an aberration from what other people are like.

But I want to tell you that God fashioned you perfectly for His calling and gifting in your life. Your "fitting" may be different from what is considered normal in your neighborhood, but that does not mean something is wrong with you. It just means God has "fitted" you for something that your neighbors will probably never do! Let them enjoy who they are, and you need to learn to accept yourself and enjoy who God made you to be!

I don't know anyone else from my hometown who has a ministry in the heart of Moscow, Russia. The vast majority of people I grew up with and attended school with are living the American dream. But God knew that would not be my life, so He designed me for my own unique calling.

Thankfully, I had a mother who understood there was something different about me and encouraged me to pursue my interests. My father never understood when I was young, but as I grew older and the call of God on my life became more evident, he came to understand why I never fit the mold of other boys in our church and school. It took time for him to grasp it, but before he went to Heaven, my dad fully understood and encouraged me in who I am. *Amen!*

Have you ever felt like a misfit? If so, let me encourage you with a verse that I've spoken to myself over and over through the years. Especially in years when I struggled with my differences from others, I learned to lean on the truth of this verse. It is First Corinthians 15:10, where Paul says, "But by the grace of God I am what I am…."

When Paul wrote this verse, he was writing about how *different* he was from all the other apostles. They had walked with Jesus; he had not. His knowledge of Christ came from direct revelation, whereas the other apostles had walked with Jesus, heard His voice, felt His tender touch, and witnessed His earthly ministry. Paul, however, had been called into apostolic ministry by revelation, and this put him in a category that made him *different* from all the other apostles. They could all lay claim to an earthly experience with Christ that Paul could not claim.

Is it possible that Paul was tempted to feel inferior because his experience was different from theirs? I think the answer may be yes, because in First Corinthians 15:8 and 9, he wrote, "And last of all, he was seen of me also, as of one born out of due time. For I am least of the apostles that am not meet to be called an apostle…." Yet he was one of the mightiest apostles; he wrote more of the New Testament than anyone else; and he traveled to more of the Gentile world than any other apostle of that time. His education, his travels, his love of languages — it all perfectly outfitted Paul for the ministry God had entrusted to him.

When Paul wrote, "But by the grace of God I am what I am...," it was his recognition that everything that made him who he was uniquely prepared him to fulfill his purpose by the grace of God. So rather than focus on the fact that he was different from others, Paul continued by saying, "But by the grace of God I am what I am, and his grace which was bestowed upon me was not in vain; but I labored more abundantly than they all: yet not I, but the grace of God which was with me."

According to Paul, God's grace was bestowed on him, and it was not in "vain." The word "vain" is the Greek word *kenos*, and it describes something that is *empty*, *wasted*, or *void*. Paul declared that the grace of God, which poured mightily into his life, did not produce *hollow* results. Rather, he said, "I labored more abundantly than they all; yet not I, but the grace of God which was with me."

The word "labored" is the Greek word *kopiao*, which describes *labor and work of the most intense type*. The word "abundantly" comes from a form of the word *perissos*, and it is comparative, which means Paul was essentially saying, "Compared to the other apostles, I worked harder than any of them." But he went on to acknowledge that it was not he alone doing this strenuous, nonstop work; it was the grace of God that was at work within him. The word "grace" here is *charis*, which denotes the *empowering presence* of God.

Paul was indeed different than the other apostles. But he was mightily anointed and perfectly gifted and fitted for the call God had given him to reach the Gentile world. And although Paul had no earthly experience with Jesus like the other apostles did, he was no less an apostle. On the contrary, he was a mighty, world-changing force for the Gospel. But Paul had to come to a place where he surrendered his inadequate feelings and accepted that fact that he was what he was by the grace of God.

Today I want to tell you to stop badgering yourself if you are a little different from others. You may not have realized it, but if everyone was alike, it would be a pretty uninteresting world to live in. Your differences make you unique. God made you with certain characteristics and personality traits because you need them for the assignment He has planned for your life. So rather than struggle with yourself or put yourself down for being a little different from others, it's time for you to claim First Corinthians 15:10 and declare, "I AM WHAT I AM BY THE GRACE OF GOD!"

MY PRAYER FOR TODAY

Father, I ask You to help me really see and realize that the way You made me is not a mistake. You have fitted me exactly for the call that You have placed upon my life. Although I may be different from others around me, it is OKAY, because my call is different than that of my neighbors and friends. I confess that I've struggled with myself, but today I surrender it all — and I thank You that I am what I am by the grace of God. I ask You to help me understand it and receive it. With the help of Your grace, any self-imposed self-rejection I have lived under comes to an end. I receive Your grace; I accept who You have made me to be; and I confidently shine as a trophy of Your masterful making!

I pray this in Jesus' name!

MY CONFESSION FOR TODAY

I confess that I am made exactly as God intended for me to be made. He fitted with me thoughts, gifts, and talents that may be different from others, but they are essential for what God has called me to do. These differences will be precisely what is needed when I fully step forward into the plan that God has designed for me and my family. I have battered myself long enough — and starting today, I accept who I am and what the grace of God has made me to be!

I declare this by faith in Jesus' name!

QUESTIONS FOR YOU TO CONSIDER

1. Let's think about it: Haven't there been many people in the Bible who were fashioned differently from their contemporaries, but it was because God had a special call on their lives that required them to be different?
2. Who are some of those Bible characters? Take time to consider those who grew up differently from those around them with different gifts and different dreams because God had a special path for them to take in life.
3. Can you think of individuals outside of the Bible in secular realms who were seen as "different" from the time they were young, yet their differences contributed to their success in life? Who are some of those individuals?

NOVEMBER 23

Hold Your Position and Refuse To Move!

But *continue thou* in the things
which thou hast learned and hast been assured of,
knowing of whom thou hast learned them.
— 2 Timothy 3:14

One day, after reading Paul's prophecy concerning the changes that will characterize society in the last days (*see* 2 Timothy 3:1-13), I realized that a person could become very alarmed or concerned from these verses. However, the Holy Spirit didn't reveal these things to *scare* us; He showed them to *prepare* us. He provided us with the means to be overcomers, to continue in our callings and assignments, and to help bring others to a place of victory in Christ in the midst of great peril.

After Paul listed the characteristics of a last-days society, he provided specific instructions that tell us how to overcome any challenge we might face in these tumultuous times. His instructions are *especially* crucial today because they provide God's divine solution to all the dark, negative things that many believers will encounter head-on as we approach the end of the age. He wrote, "But *continue thou* in the things which thou hast learned and hast been assured of, knowing of whom thou hast learned them" (2 Timothy 3:14).

Paul wrote his second epistle to Timothy in the midst of a very difficult time in the young pastor's life. The church in Ephesus that Timothy pastored — once a thriving congregation and the largest church in that region of the world — was suffering tremendously at the hands of the Roman government. At the time, the cruel and demented emperor Nero had instigated a large-scale persecution against the Church, and believers in Timothy's city faced *very* intense hardships.

By writing to Timothy and the congregation of believers in Ephesus, Paul — under the inspiration of the Holy Spirit — also gave *us* instructions concerning the evil that will come upon the earth in the last of the last days. Paul began with a very sober word: "continue."

The word "continue" in Second Timothy 3:14 is a translation of the Greek word *meno*, which means to *habitually abide* or *stay put*. It describes *a decision from which the one abiding will not budge or move from his spot*. It's the same word that's used over and over in John 15, where Jesus said, "If ye abide in me, and my words abide in you, ye shall ask what ye will, and it shall be done unto you" (v. 7). Jesus was saying in essence, "If you *habitually reside* in Me, *refusing to budge and never moving out of Me* — and if My Word *habitually resides* in you, *never budging and never moving out of you* — you shall ask what you will, and it shall be done unto you."

This word *meno* describes a person making the decision, "This is my spot; I will not move!" That's what Paul was instructing us to do: to *continue*. Paul exhorted us to resolve that *regardless of what was happening around us*, we would not *change our position* where the Word and the will of God were concerned.

Paul continued, "But continue thou in the things which thou hast learned and hast been assured of, knowing of whom thou hast learned them. And that from a child thou hast known the holy scriptures, which are able to make thee wise unto salvation through faith which is in Christ Jesus" (2 Timothy 3:14,15).

I also want to point out the word "wise" in the phrase "…which are able to make thee *wise* unto salvation…." Paul was referring to the wisdom that is produced in a person's life who knows the "holy Scriptures." This word "wise" was translated from the word *sophos*, and it means *special enlightenment*. The Holy Scripture, the Word of God, is able to enlighten us and show us the way to salvation — absolute healing, wholeness, and the saving and delivering power of God — in *whatever* circumstances we're facing.

God's Word is God's power! Therefore, we can conclude that without God's Word in our hearts, we can't have God's power working in us. That's why I want to share with you the importance of the Scriptures in our lives, especially as we approach the time of Jesus' returning when the world around us will grow darker and darker.

So today I want to remind you — as you see society rapidly deteriorating all around you and changes coming so fast that you can hardly keep count of them, you need to "continue" in the Word of God. That means you need to *habitually abide* or *stay put* where the Word of God is concerned. Regardless of what the world says about what is right or wrong, *stay put* and *continue* in what you have learned from the Holy Scriptures — for they are able to make you "wise" — that is, they will fill you with the *discernment* and *enlightenment* that you need for victorious living in these perilous times!

MY PRAYER FOR TODAY

Lord, I recommit myself to the Word of God. Society is changing what it believes all the time, and it is drifting further and further away from the truths found in the Word of God. But according to Your commandment, I will "continue" in the teachings of the Holy Scriptures that have the power to make me "wise" for living in these times. Holy Spirit, I ask You to stir my heart with a new passion for the Word of God — that I would hunger and thirst for it continually — and then empower me not only to devour it but also to do it steadfastly. Teach me to draw my strength and nourishment from the Word of God in order to strengthen my spirit, soul, and body so that I will stand strong and victorious in these last days!

I pray this in Jesus' name!

MY CONFESSION FOR TODAY

I confess that I hunger and thirst for God's Word more than my necessary food and drink. I make a deliberate decision to abide in the Word of God and to allow it to abide in me. I will not budge from my position on the Word as final authority in all manner of life. Therefore, as the world and its practices grow darker and darker beneath the sway of the wicked one, the Word of God shall remain a lamp unto my feet and a sure guide to my path. I will not be moved when I see governmental legislation and even some church leaders make drastic shifts in defiance of God's Word. I will "stay put" and hold the course of my commitment to God's ways, as I continue to occupy until He comes!

I declare this by faith in Jesus' name!

QUESTIONS FOR YOU TO CONSIDER

1. Have you personally known times when the Word of God gave you strength and power to overcome challenges that were in your life? When was that time, and what exactly did you experience?
2. What does the word "continue" mean to you? Does it mean read and believe the Word once a month, once a week, or daily? What kind of consistency do you think Paul was talking about when he encouraged us to "continue" in the "holy Scriptures?"
3. Can you think of a time when the Word of God made you "wise" — that is, it gave you special discernment and enlightenment for a situation you were facing?

NOVEMBER 24

What Is Delaying the Coming of the Lord?

The Lord is not slack concerning his promise,
as some men count slackness; but is longsuffering
to us-ward, not willing that any should perish,
but that all should come to repentance.
— 2 Peter 3:9

At a time when it is so essential that we put forth our best efforts to reach the unreached, many churches and organizations are cutting back on their giving to foreign missions.

They are opting instead to develop their own local churches. There's certainly nothing wrong with that, but the emphasis on reaching the lost is very often diminished in favor of simply forming social communities for their congregations.

What happened to the days when we did BOTH?

It is clear that we need to support *home missions* in the United States, where multitudes have yet to hear the good news of the Gospel. But we must never stop ardently supporting *foreign missions* to reach the nations and ethnic groups that have never heard the name of Jesus. It isn't a matter of one or the other — we must give sacrificially in this last-days period to do *both*.

The sad truth is that we are living in a time when passion for the lost is waning. Many pulpits don't deliver messages about Heaven and hell — and they don't give invitations for the lost to be saved in their churches.

On top of that, there has been a steady decrease among churches in giving to foreign missions. Unfortunately, all of this is indicative of a radical change in beliefs, practices, and philosophy of overseas ministry at exactly the moment when foreign-missions support is needed more than ever.

If only churches would band together to support foreign-mission organizations! Added to the new communications technology of our day, that support would accelerate the time it would take to reach every nation and ethnic group of the earth as a precursor to Christ's return.

I certainly don't condemn churches that spend money on building projects because their existing facilities have been outgrown or are in need of renovation. Our own church in Moscow recently completed a major reconstruction process, so I understand the need. But I feel saddened when churches continue to buy "bigger and better" while at the same time overlooking souls for whom Christ died — *yet those same souls have never heard His name!*

Even with all our local building programs and church needs, foreign missions simply *must remain* at the top of our list of priorities as pastors and leaders.

I shudder to think of the moment when we will stand before Jesus and give account for what we did or did not do for those who'd never heard the Gospel message. Those believers who gave sacrificially will be elated to look into the Savior's loving eyes. But those who gave nothing to reach the lost will not stand well with the One who gave *His life* to reach them.

If you were to stand before Jesus today and give an account of how you used your money and personal efforts to reach the lost, how do you think you would fare in terms of eternal reward?

When the apostle Peter wrote about the last days, he said, "Knowing this first, that in the last days scoffers will come after their own lusts. And saying, Where is the promise of his coming? For all things continue as they were from the beginning of the creation" (2 Peter 3:3,4).

Indeed, there are many scoffers who mock those who believe that these are the last days or that there will be a rapture of the Church. These cynical "dissenters" argue that people have been talking about "the last days" for 2,000 years, yet nothing has changed during that time. They allege that it's all a fantasy.

The word "scoffers" means *those who scoff and make fun of something through mockery.* This group is very prevalent today. They say, "If Christ was going to come, He would have come by now. This 'rapture' business is simply *fantasy.* The world hasn't really changed as you claim. We simply have better news coverage, so we're more *aware* of the darkness and tragedy in the world." Many in this group are bold to assert that the heralding of Christ's soon return is based on ancient texts that have no relevance to today and no basis in reality.

Peter predicted a day when scoffers would come — *before* Jesus returns — and rise up to mock people (*like me!*) who teach others what God says regarding the end times.

But what these mockers don't understand is that the last days started on the Day of Pentecost when the Holy Spirit was poured out (*see* Acts 2:16-18). For 2,000 years, we have been living in what is theologically called *the last days.* That may seem like a long time to us, but Second Peter 3:8 says, "...Beloved, be not ignorant of this one thing, that one day is with the Lord as a thousand years, and a thousand years as one day."

Theologically, this 2,000-year period called "the last days" has only been two days on God's prophetic calendar! But why has God taken so long to wrap up this period and move to the next prophetic phase on His calendar? The next verse, Second Peter 3:9, answers that question: "The Lord is not slack concerning His promise, as some count slackness; but is longsuffering to us-ward, not willing that any should perish, but that all should come to repentance."

The word "slack" is a form of the word *bruduno,* which means to be *tardy, slow, delayed,* or *late* in time. By using this word, the Holy Spirit tells us that God is not slow regarding the promises He has made. He made them, and He will fulfill them — but He is "longsuffering" for the sake of those who still need to come to repentance. The Rapture will occur the *instant* the last person who will repent is saved. Then we will be miraculously transformed and translated to meet the Lord in the air (*see* 1 Thessalonians 4:17).

The word "longsuffering" is from the Greek word *makrothumia,* a compound of the word *makros* and *thumia.* The word *makros* means *long* — and the word *thumia* describes *great patience. The New Linguistic and Exegetical Key to the Greek New Testament* says, "It is the Spirit who *could* take revenge, but who *utterly refuses* to do so. The delay of God's punishment rests on God's long-suffering...."[14]

In other words, God is exceedingly patient with those who are unsaved, and He is willing to wait for the redemption of that *one last person* who will repent. That is the longsuffering of God — and the reason why God has waited and waited and waited. But as we conclude these *last of the* last days, that one unsaved person will repent and come to Christ. When that occurs, this age will close and we will be removed from the earth. The Tribulation will commence in that split second.

[14] Cleon L. Rogers Jr. and Cleon L. Rogers III, *The New Linguistic and Exegetical Key to the Greek New Testament* (Grand Rapids, MI: Zondervan, 1998), p. 588.

Second Peter 3:9 says, "God is not slack concerning his promise, as some men count slackness...." This refers to the scoffers who say the Rapture and prophetic events that lie before us will never take place. *But God is not slack!* In other words, He is not tardy, delayed, or slow in fulfilling His promise. His heart of love is simply holding out for the last soul to be saved.

Verse 9 goes on to say that God is "...not willing that any should perish...." Although it's true that all will obviously not be saved, He is waiting for the Gospel to reach the "four corners" of the earth and for that last person who will turn to Him and be saved. This shows just how *long* is the longsuffering of God!

You see, God knows what hell is, and He doesn't want anyone to go there — which is why we *must* be serious and committed about taking the saving message of Jesus to the world now, at the end of this age. We must win as many as possible to Christ because that door is still open for the lost to be saved — to be brought into glorious fellowship with God, to avoid hell, and to make Heaven their eternal home.

In the end of these last days, it is imperative that we stay sensitive to the leading of the Holy Spirit, always ready to open our hearts and witness to people. God is waiting for that last person who will repent to enter His Kingdom — and then the Rapture of the Church will occur. In light of all the end-time events that are occurring right now, it is possible that this could happen at any moment.

Today I want to encourage you to be sensitive to the Holy Spirit as you share Christ with others. Stay open and obedient to every nudge to witness. And every time you share Jesus with someone, do it with the anticipation that with each person won to Christ, we are coming closer and closer to the wrap-up of this age!

MY PRAYER FOR TODAY

Father, thank You for helping me see as You see. Thank You for giving me Your heart for those who are lost and headed for hell. More and more, I sense Your compassion and Your longing that every person would receive the free gift of salvation as we approach the end of this age. Help me stay sensitive and obedient to Your Spirit so that I never miss an opportunity to share the Good News of Jesus with a heart that is ready to receive.

I pray this in Jesus' name!

MY CONFESSION FOR TODAY

I confess that I am regularly spending time with my Heavenly Father and becoming more and more sensitive to what is important to Him. The Father loved people so much that He gave His only Son to die on the Cross to redeem them. He doesn't want even one person to be lost and eternally separated from Him. More and more, the desires of my Father's heart are becoming the desires of my heart. Therefore, I live every day endeavoring to stay sensitive to the leading of the Holy Spirit. And every day He gives me divine opportunities to share the life-changing Gospel of Jesus Christ with those I encounter whose hearts are ready to receive.

I declare this by faith in Jesus' name!

QUESTIONS FOR YOU TO CONSIDER

1. Do you live each day with an awareness that one day you will stand before Jesus and give an account for what He has asked you to do regarding reaching the lost?
2. When is the last time you obeyed the leading of the Holy Spirit to share Jesus with someone? What was the outcome of your obedience?
3. Can you think of a time when you sensed the Holy Spirit asking you to witness to someone — but you held back? Since a person's eternal destiny is at stake in that kind of situation, what can you do today to make sure you are ready to obey the next time you sense the Holy Spirit leading you to share the Good News of Jesus with someone?

NOVEMBER 25

Why Did Jesus Promise a White Stone?

...To him that overcometh
will I give...*a white stone*....
— Revelation 2:17

For years, I carried a small white stone in my pocket. In times when I felt discouraged, I would reach into my pocket to touch that stone and remind myself that Jesus promised a "white stone" to those who overcome. Of course, a stone has no magical powers, but that little stone reminded me of what the Lord said when He promised a "white stone" in Revelation 2:17 to those who overcome.

So what is the significance of the "white stone" that Jesus promised?

Let's delve into the Greek language and history today to see what we can find about how "white stones" were used at the time this was written by John on the isle of Patmos and why Christ promised a "white stone" to those who overcome.

In the original text of Revelation 2:17, the wording in the phrase "a white stone" is ordered differently in Greek. The Greek wording actually reads *"psiephon leuken."* The word *psiephon* refers to a *stone* or *pebble*, and *leuken* means *white*. So rather than "a white stone," it should be literally translated, "A stone, a *white* one." This lays a particular emphasis on the color of the stone, so we must examine the primary way "white stones" were used in early New Testament times.

When a Roman trial concluded, and it was time for a panel of judges to vote for the defendant's innocence or guilt, the judges registered their votes by casting a black or white stone into an urn. A black stone symbolized a vote for guilt, and a white stone denoted a vote for innocence. When all the votes had been cast, the stones were emptied from the urn and counted one by one. If there were more black stones, it meant the judges had found the defendant *guilty*; if there were more white stones, it meant they had found the individual to be *not guilty*.[15]

Therefore, when Christ offered "a stone, a *white* one" to overcomers — placing a definite emphasis on the word *white* — it meant: *"I have reviewed all the evidence, and I have judged you not guilty!"*

Jesus' message to that church, and to us today, was that regardless of *who they had been* or *what they had done* before they came to Christ, what mattered now was *who they had become* in Christ. Viewing them in light of His blood, Jesus had cast "a stone, a *white* one" in their direction, affirming their full acquittal and complete release from their past sinful lives and memories.

Therefore, when the devil — or any person, for that matter — tries to throw a stone of judgment against us by mentally tormenting us about past actions we've already been forgiven for, we may boldly answer, "Christ has already cast His vote. He has found me NOT GUILTY!" Regardless of any actions we may have committed in the past, Jesus' blood has purged our conscience from dead works to serve the living God (*see* Hebrews 9:14).

There was another way the ancient Greeks also used white and black stones for vote-casting. One of the greatest privileges in Greek society was to vote about civic issues in a public election. In these elections, people used white and black stones to cast their votes, similar to the way such stones were used in legal trials.[16] Votes were customarily registered by casting a black or white pebble into large vases that were set up throughout the city at designated locations. When the time for voting had concluded, the pebbles were separated into white and black piles and then counted. A white stone represented a person voting *in favor of* some issue, whereas a black stone represented a person was voting *against* it.

Thus, when Christ promised "a stone, a *white* one" to the believers who overcame, He was not only announcing freedom, forgiveness, and acquittal from a past sinful life, but He was also telling them: *"My vote is for you. I am putting My full support behind you."*

How powerful this is when we realize what the "white stone" means in Revelation 2:17. It declares that Christ has found us not guilty and that He is putting His full support behind you and me. *Christ is voting for us!*

---

[15] Ovid, *Metamorphoses*, XV. 41.

[16] Charles Dexter Cleveland, *A Compendium of Grecian Antiquities* (Boston: Hilliard, Gray, Little, and Wilkins, 1831), p. 68.

Years ago, I actually preached on this subject in the city of Moscow — then we distributed white stones to the whole congregation. I urged people to carry them in their pockets or purses as a reminder that if they were washed in the blood of Christ, Jesus has found them *not guilty*. And regardless of what the devil tries to tell them, Christ's blood has freed them from the past, and they are free! Furthermore, I encouraged them when life seemed to be getting tough to let that white stone remind them that if no one else was voting for them, *Christ* was voting for them and, therefore, they were going to make it!

Today I want to tell *you* that if you have been forgiven and washed in the precious blood of Christ, you are forgiven — *period*. The devil may try to hassle you in your mind and torment you with past memories that God Himself doesn't remember. But just realize that Christ reviewed all the evidence, and since His blood was applied to your life, He has found you completely blameless and free from shame.

Furthermore, if it doesn't feel at the moment like anyone else is for you, just remember that Christ Himself has cast His vote for you. Romans 8:31 tells us, "...If God be for us, who can be against us?" My friend, if Jesus has cast His vote for you — and He has! — you can throw off all despair and start rejoicing, because the one vote that *really* matters has been cast in your favor!

MY PRAYER FOR TODAY

Father, I thank You for the blood of Jesus Christ, which has cleansed me from all sinful actions of the past. Although I admittedly did wrong in the past, it is not held against me, because the blood of Christ has made me free. You have officially declared me clean. I stand before You as a born-again individual, free from the offenses of my past. A white stone has been cast in my favor. I am cleansed and free, and You are voting for me and my success!

I pray this in Jesus' name!

MY CONFESSION FOR TODAY

I confess that I refuse to wallow in condemnation over my past sins that even God Himself doesn't remember. Instead, I focus my attention on the blood of Jesus as I remember all He has done for me. When the devil — or anyone, for that matter — tries to throw a stone of judgment against me by mentally tormenting me about past actions that I've already been forgiven for, I boldly answer: "Christ has reviewed all the evidence and already cast His vote. He has found me innocent!" I toss aside any garments of despair, and I put on the garment of praise because Jesus' blood has purged my conscience from dead works to serve the living God. Since God is for me, who can be against me? Jesus has cast His vote of a white stone in my favor — and that is the only vote that matters!

I declare this by faith in Jesus' name!

QUESTIONS FOR YOU TO CONSIDER

1. When the devil tries to assault your mind and drag you into memories of the past, how do you resist him? Do you allow him to attack you, or do you stand

up to those allegations that no longer have any application concerning who you are today? How do you resist the devil in such circumstances?

2. When you think of Christ casting a "white stone" in your favor — a favorable vote for you — how does that affect you?
3. In light of Christ casting a white stone in your favor, don't you think it's time for you to stop submitting to the devil's actions of throwing stones of accusation at you — or at others?

NOVEMBER 26

A Simple Command That Will Require Your Strictest Obedience

Let us therefore follow after the things
which make for peace, and things
wherewith one may edify another.
— Romans 14:19

There are so many opportunities for distrust and lack of peace in this world that we as believers must make it our aim to follow after things that make for peace. In fact, this was the commandment that the apostle Paul gave to the Romans when he addressed them in Romans 14:19. What you are about to read applies to friendships, church congregations, churches in the same community, marriages, sibling relationships, and so on.

The verse says, "Let us therefore follow after the things which make for peace, and things wherewith one may edify another." Today I want us to dissect this verse and see exactly what the Holy Spirit is urging us to do. The fact that the verse begins with "let us therefore" tells us that this is a commandment that is issued to *every one of us* in every part of the Christian community and that Paul expected us to heed his words. It is not a suggestion; it is a divinely inspired commandment.

The word "follow" is the Greek word *dioko*, a word that we've seen many times as we've studied *Sparkling Gems 2*. It is an often-used word in the New Testament; hence, this tells us how important it is that we understand it and obey its command to us. The word *dioko* had two primary meanings — and to understand this word, you need to understand the way that it was used in both senses.

First, as we've seen before, it was a hunting term that depicted a hunter who was following his game. He wasn't haphazardly "hoping" that an animal would walk by him, but instead he was committed to getting into the territory where his game was located. He was determined to follow the animal's scent and its tracks on the ground, to watch for broken branches indicating the presence of the animal and the direction it was headed, and so on. That hunter was absolutely committed to following that animal — and to watching for all the signs necessary to track it — until he captured his trophy.

Furthermore, the Greek word for "follow," *dioko*, is a participle, which means it should be understood to mean *habitually follow*. In other words, this hunter is bound and determined that he will *not* stop his pursuit until he comes home with a bagged animal!

Second, the word *dioko* is also frequently translated *to persecute*. The deliberateness contained in this word tells us that persecution is not accidental or haphazard. It is done very deliberately. Just as a hunter follows the tracks and scent of an animal, one who persecutes another does so deliberately. He seeks where the subject of his persecution lives, whom he talks to, where he fellowships, and so forth. After ascertaining vital information about his subject, he then begins *on purpose* to implement a strategy to rendezvous with his subject in order to entrap him. It is deliberate, planned, and executed with meticulous detail. This mean persecution is not a chance happening; it is *intentional.*

I could tell many stories of believers who were persecuted in parts of the world where the Gospel was once not accepted — and where the Gospel is still not welcome. Persecution against believers is well planned, thought-out, and deliberate. The word *dioko* describes just this exactly. It involves a well-executed plan to entrap the one whom the perpetrator wishes to punish or persecute.

That is the word that Paul uses when he admonishes us to "follow" after the things that make for peace. He was telling us to be proactive in achieving peace. He was urging us to develop a plan that can be executed. Sitting and hoping for it will never get the job done. There must be a Spirit-inspired plan that is followed explicitly — and the seeker must be committed to *habitually follow* that plan until peace is finally captured. Just as a hunter persistently follows after his prey, or just as a persecutor consistently and deliberately follows after the one he seeks to persecute, we must be *that* committed to do the things that make for peace.

But Paul tells us that we are to follow after "the things" that make for peace. The words "the things" are a translation of the little word *ta*, which seems so small, but it's *huge* in what it embraces. The meaning of this tiny word includes *many things* that could contribute to peace. For example, it could include:

- Asking for forgiveness.
- Admitting you were wrong.
- Acknowledging that you were wrong in the role you played in a matter.

The word "peace" is the word *eirene* — an old Greek word that indisputably describes *a time of peace as a replacement for war*. It has been translated *tranquility* or *harmony*. It gives the idea that although there was a time of strife, conflict, and war — to obtain this "peace," weapons and long-held disagreements must now be laid aside; peace negotiations must be discussed and implemented; and peace must usurp the conflicts that have long waged between two or more warring factions.

This is not a suggestion. It is Paul's inspired command. We must seek this *eirene* and follow ardently after it until we obtain it in our relationships.

Furthermore, Paul told us that we are to follow after "...things wherewith one may edify another." Instead of using weapons to injure one another or to put others down, Paul commands us to make it our professional objective to "edify" one another. This is so totally contrary to distrust, suspicion, and war. But this is what the Holy Spirit wants to achieve between us!

The word "edify" is the Greek word *oikodome*, a compound of the words *oikos* and *domos*. The word *oikos* describes *a house* — fully built and complete — while the word *domos* describes the *engineering* and *building process* by which that house was constructed. In order to build a house correctly — one that will stand for many years and serve its occupants well — first, a plan must be developed. Once all parts of the blueprint are designed, only then can the building process transpire, and it must be done according to the plan that has been devised!

This means that building a house is a very thoughtful endeavor. By God's grace, Denise and I have constructed several buildings in the history of our ministry. Every one of them has started with a plan and an architect and engineer who put everything on paper. Then everything must be followed according to the plan if the building is to be constructed correctly. Exact obedience and adherence to the plan is essential. Carefulness is obligatory if one wants to do what's right and achieve and obtain the best possible outcome.

Paul used this word *oikodome* — translated "edify" — to describe how we must build our relationships with each other in the Christian community. There is no room for sloppy, last-minute thinking about how to construct relationships that need to last for generations. It takes serious prayer and consideration, taking into account the various views of the different contributors — and once the plan is finalized, it must be followed carefully and considerately.

When we constructed our church building in Moscow, we followed the plans exactly. When we were finished, the building looked exactly as the plans had projected. If we had deviated and gone another way, we would have produced a different-looking building and, worse, one that was structurally unsound. But because we carefully obeyed the architect and engineers, their digital image looks identical to the actual building we constructed.

In the same way, if we lay down our weapons of war and suspicions of each other — and ardently follow after peace with each other, doing the things that make for peace and edification — we will build exactly what the Holy Spirit wants to build between us. We must seek the Holy Spirit for His plan of construction or reconstruction. There is no doubt that the Holy Spirit knows *exactly* how to bring about peace. He knows what we need to do to "edify," or to build properly, when constructing relationships in the Body of Christ.

If you have been through a war with a fellow believer, a nearby church, another pastor, or so on, God's Word in Romans 14:19 commands you to lay down your weapons and do the things that make for peace, restoration, and edification.

Rather than tear each other down, the Holy Spirit — who is the Chief Architect and Engineer — wants to show us a plan for construction that will build strong relationships for years to come.

Are you ready to receive His plan? If you're willing to lay down your weapons, repent for wrong attitudes, and come to His table to hear what He has to say, the Holy Spirit is ready to impart a plan that will work *if* you will not deviate from it.

This is the will of God according to Romans 14:19, so why not get started today? Great things lie ahead of those who will obey this verse, *and that includes you!*

MY PRAYER FOR TODAY

Father, I now have a clearer understanding of the enemy's well-planned attacks to incite Christians to wage war among ourselves and ultimately fall prey to his divisive tactics. I ask You to help me apply a more meticulous approach to pursue peace and to preserve it. Father, I receive Your specific wisdom in this very intentional endeavor. I can no longer allow any room for sloppy, last-minute thinking about how to construct relationships that need to last for generations. Thank You for strengthening each member of Your Body internally so that externally we can build the Christian community by prayer and with peace, love, and serious consideration of the high priority that we edify one another so that the world may truly know we are Yours by our love.

I pray this in Jesus' name!

MY CONFESSION FOR TODAY

I confess that I engage an intentional pursuit of those things that make peace. I see to it that my words, attitudes, and actions edify and build others up rather than injure or put them down. I obey the Lord's command to make it my premeditated objective to edify others. Therefore, I give no place to the devil by allowing distrust, suspicion, or contempt to spring up and manifest in my life. I choose to follow the great plan of the Chief Architect, the Holy Spirit, and I refuse to deviate from it so He can build us into the glorious design the Father envisioned before the foundations of the world!

I declare this by faith in Jesus' name!

QUESTIONS FOR YOU TO CONSIDER

1. Have you ever witnessed a battle between two believers or between congregations? It isn't a pretty sight, is it? It is certainly not God's will. After reading today's *Sparkling Gem*, what should the participants in such conflicts do to make it right before God?

2. Are you in conflict with another believer? Is it really worth all the pain and blame? Don't you hear God telling you to lay down your distrust and learn to build and edify one another? It may be difficult to do, but isn't that exactly what Romans 14:19 tells you to do?
3. I'm not suggesting that you do something God hasn't required of me and other leaders over the years. But I'm here to testify that the peace obtained by following His plan for peace is so much better than the grief caused by strife and internal discord. Are you going to pull up to the table and let the Holy Spirit give you a plan to turn things around in the relationship(s) you find difficult?

NOVEMBER 27

Where Are We in Time?

...What shall be the sign of thy coming,
and of the end of the world?
— Matthew 24:3

Today I want to talk to you about "where" we are in time in reference to the return of Jesus and the end of the age. Many seem to have an inner knowing that we are getting very close to the end, so let's look at Matthew 24:3 to see what Jesus Himself had to say about His return and the end of the age.

Nearly 2,000 years ago, Jesus' disciples took an opportunity to ask Him a very pointed question about the last days. They specifically asked the Lord, "...What shall be the sign of thy coming, and of the end of the world?" (Matthew 24:3).

Let's make one thing clear as we get started. The word "world" in this phrase does not refer to the end of the world itself — because the world will never end; it will be *changed* (*see* 2 Peter 3:12,13). The word used here was translated from the Greek word *aionos*, which refers to *an age*. Thus, the disciples were actually interested in knowing when *this present age* would come to a close. The *New King James Version* states it correctly: "...What will be the sign of Your coming, and of the end of the age?"

This word "end" in Greek is the word *suntelos* and it describes the *completion*, *conclusion*, *closure*, *culmination*, *ending*, *finish*, *sum-up*, or the ultimate *wrap-up* of a thing. The disciples wanted to know what the sign would be that this current age was experiencing its final *wrap-up*.

The word "sign" is a translation of the Greek word *semeion*. It was used to describe an *authenticating mark* or a *guarantee*. It could have been used to *authenticate* that a document was real or that an object was genuine. In other words, *semeion* indicated *the absolute proof, reality*, or *genuineness* of a thing.

An example of *semeion* could be *signs* placed outside a city limits as indicators to help travelers *authenticate* exactly where they were at the moment. This means the disciples were asking Jesus what sign should be taken as an *authenticating mark* or *guarantee* — an *absolute, genuine proof* — that His coming was imminent and that the end of the age was nigh.

Because I live in a suburb of Moscow, I'll use my daily travels to this enormous city as an example of the point I want you to understand.

No matter what direction I approach Moscow from, I can see *signs* on the road that are strategically placed to let travelers know they're headed toward the city limits. The closer I get to Russia's capital city, the closer together the signs appear so that I can know how far I have remaining on my journey before I cross the border into this immense region. The signs validate and alert me to the fact that I am approaching my destination.

The nearer I get to this city, the environment around me also starts to change. For example, on my route into Moscow from my home, I see a lot of Russia's countryside along the way. The road I travel winds among beautiful spruce and fir trees. But the closer I get to this metropolitan center, the scenery begins to change. I see industry, multifamily housing, and high-rise buildings, and the roads become denser with traffic.

At first, these changes are subtle and barely noticeable. But the nearer I get to my destination, the more obvious and vast the changes in the scenery become. As I reach the very outskirts of the city, the changes appear almost abruptly. Change, change, change — *rapid change* — is what I encounter as I travel from just outside Moscow to just inside the city.

When I finally reach the city limits, I see a huge sign that reads MOSCOW. That sign separates the outskirts from the city itself, and the moment I drive past it, the sign *authenticates* that I have entered new territory. I'm no longer *traveling toward* Moscow — I *have entered* the city and arrived at my destination.

When I'm driving from the countryside toward Moscow, without *signs* telling me where I'm headed, I could think I'm just somewhere out in the country. In other words, I would know only intellectually that this immense city was somewhere out in front of me — just as we know that Jesus' return will occur at some time out in front of us.

Of course, travelers could understand when they're about to approach the city limits of Moscow based on their Global Positioning System, their rate of speed, and traffic conditions. But under normal circumstances, they wouldn't know that their arrival was imminent without *signs*.

As we approach Christ's return and the end of this present age, we will likewise see visible changes all around us that appear almost abruptly. I actually believe that we're no longer *approaching* the last part of the last days; rather, we have *crossed the border*, and we are *already there*.

When did the "last days" begin? In biblical terms, the "last days" officially began on the Day of Pentecost. Peter announced in Acts 2:17 and 18 that the last days of this age were officially initiated when the Holy Spirit was poured out. So for the last approximate 2,000 years, we have been living in "the last days" on God's prophetic calendar. We are now living in the final stages of this period.

Let me use the example of a football game to illustrate this point. When the players return to the field just after halftime, play begins in the second half, or the last half, of the game. That would be an example of the beginning of the end. But when the game is winding down in the last half to the last minutes and seconds of the fourth quarter, that very vividly describes a wrap-up — the very end of the game.

I personally believe that this perfectly depicts where we are in history. We've been playing this last-days game for about 2,000 years. But now it's the fourth quarter, and the game is winding down to the last "minutes and seconds" before Jesus comes and the game is wrapped up.

As we head into the very last moments of the last days, you and I are on this end-times team as members of the Body of Christ. God, who summons each generation to live on this planet, has called you and me for such a time as this (*see* Isaiah 41:4; Esther 4:14). And with that calling, a divine role has been assigned to each one of us. It has never been more important to discover that role, get in our place, and apply ourselves to it *spirit, soul, and body* with all the strength and enthusiasm we can muster.

As believers, we must be fully engaged and not sidelined or relegated to "sitting on the bench" in these last moments of the last days. If we will honor the transforming Cross of Christ and His Word, we can be confident we'll be positioned to participate in this last, greatest move of God's Spirit the world has ever seen!

Are you ready?

This is a time to set our hearts to seek God and get prepared for the last moments of this age that Jesus prophesied about. The fact is that we are *privileged* to be personal witnesses of the time that the Old Testament prophets, Jesus, Paul, John, and Peter all prophesied would come! We are truly a chosen generation as we experience the wrap-up of the age and wait for the soon return of Christ!

MY PRAYER FOR TODAY

Father, I ask You to help me do all I can to prepare my heart for the soon return of Jesus. Times are changing — and I'm thankful to know what Jesus had to say about the end of the age in Matthew 24:3. Help me comprehend the significance of the fact that I've been chosen to be a part of a very special generation. Help me find my role, get in my place, and do all I can to help advance the Gospel and its message before the age ends and Jesus returns. And especially help me to reach my family, friends, acquaintances, and coworkers with the message that the Cross has the power to save them, forgive them, and transform their lives!

I pray this in Jesus' name!

MY CONFESSION FOR TODAY

I confess that I am blessed to be a part of the wrap-up of the age before the return of Jesus Christ. It is no accident that I am alive at this time. God made me for such a time as this — and I will step into my place, fulfill my role, and do all I can to shine the light of the Gospel to those who are sitting in darkness. God will use me to remove the blinders that are on the eyes of unbelievers and bring them into the Kingdom of His dear Son!

I declare this by faith in Jesus' name!

QUESTIONS FOR YOU TO CONSIDER

1. What signs do you see that make you think we are living in the very closing days of the last days? Can you make a list and back it up with scriptural references?
2. If you don't think we're living in the last part of the last days, how have you come to that conclusion?
3. If you believe we *are* living at the very end of the age, as many believe, what specific actions do you need to take to tell others about the saving message of Jesus? Has the Lord put certain unsaved people on your heart as your personal assignment to faithfully lift up in prayer until they come to the saving knowledge of Jesus Christ? Who are those individuals?

NOVEMBER 28

Sitting in Front of 40 Sunlamps for 8 Hours!

Be careful for nothing: but in every thing by prayer
and supplication with thanksgiving
let your request be made known unto God.
And the peace of God, which passeth all understanding,
shall keep your hearts and minds through Christ Jesus.
— Philippians 4:6,7

When our TV ministry first began in the former USSR, we needed low-hanging, directional lights for our studio. Our staff was inexperienced, but they were all we had, so I sent them out to search for lights we could use to illuminate the studio where we were going to be filming our TV programs. With great delight, they returned with 40 big lights that they were sure would work to light up the studio. For a week, the staff members carefully hung the lights in place and tested them. After being satisfied that the lights were exactly what we needed, they said, "OK, now we can begin to film new TV programs!"

I was excited that the studio was so well lit and that the low-hanging lights looked so professional. But our studio had no air-conditioning, which made the room very hot. To stay cool, I wore a dress shirt, tie, and suit jacket from the waist up — and from the waist down, I wore shorts and put each leg into a big bucket of cool water in an effort to cool down while we were filming. Even with my legs submerged in that water, sweat would pour from my brow, and I would have to wipe my forehead the whole time we filmed. However, on this particular day, it felt *especially* hot — much hotter than usual.

After two hours of non-stop filming under those 40 lights, I felt very hot, so I took my legs out of the buckets, untied my tie, unbuttoned my top shirt, and went outside to get some fresh air. When I walked into the edit suite where the producers were working, they were trying to adjust the colors on the camera, because my skin looked so red on the monitors. They twisted this knob and that knob, trying to get the color to look right. They were so focused on what they were looking at on the monitors that they never actually looked at me! Eventually I heard them say, "We think we've got it fixed. So, Rick, why don't you head back into the studio, and let's film more programs."

Once I resumed filming, I didn't stop again until I had filmed a total of eight hours of TV programs that day. It was a personal record for the most TV programs I had ever filmed in a single day.

But this time when I walked out of the studio, the producers looked at me to congratulate me for completing such a successful day. When they saw me, they gasped. It was at that moment they realized the 40 lights they were so proud of — that I had been sitting in front of for eight hours — were *sunlamps*! My face was severely burned and red beyond imagination. Try to imagine what you would look like if you sat in front of 40 sunlamps for eight hours! To make matters worse, I had been sitting in shorts with my legs in two buckets of water, and the radiation from those lamps literally scorched my legs. But the worst of all was what happened to my eyes — I could hardly see because my eyes were so burned. And every time I blinked, it felt like shredded pieces of glass were being dragged across my eyes.

At that time, pharmaceutical products were scarce in the former Soviet Union, so there were no medications or ointments to put on my burnt body. Instead, a local doctor recommended that I be *covered in sour cream* and that I then be *tightly wrapped in plastic*, like Saran Wrap, to keep the moisture trapped around my body! So I lay on the couch as Denise and her helpers literally doused me from head to toe in sour cream, and then had me roll over and over so the plastic would tightly stretch around me. My arms were trapped under the plastic; my legs were bound; I was immovable. I remember telling Denise that I felt like a huge enchilada!

Hour by hour, the pain increased all over my face and legs — every place that had been exposed to the 40 sunlamps. I cried because of the horrible pain in my eyes every time I blinked. We called a doctor in the United States who warned that it was *possible* I would wake up blind the next morning because I had spent eight straight hours looking directly into 40 sunlamps. Fear tried to grip my heart. Denise lovingly stayed right at my side the entire night to comfort me because of the pain that wracked my body. The pain in my eyes was especially horrific. Denise comforted me and reassured me that I would be able to see and that, by the grace of God, we *were* going to get through this horrific ordeal!

That night I shuddered with pain every time I blinked, and fear kept trying to sink its talons into my mind. So to fight against that fear, I decided to meditate on Philippians 4:6,7. When the pain raged through my eyes, I would quote this verse and focus on the promise of God instead of my excruciating condition. I probably quietly spoke that passage to myself hundreds of times that night as I released all my faith that my eyes would be all right, regardless of the pain that tormented me throughout that seemingly endless night.

The first verse of this passage, Philippians 4:6, tells us not to worry about anything. It reads, "Be careful for nothing: but in everything by prayer and supplication with thanksgiving let your request be made known unto God." Honestly, it took all of my determination that night not to worry about my eyes.

But the verse commands us to present our supplications and requests to God with thanksgiving and to leave worry behind. So that night I cried out to God and made my request known, asking for my eyesight. Hour after hour, I expressed thanksgiving to the Lord and did my best to praise Him from a grateful, thankful heart in spite of the pain. Denise prayed with me and helped me keep giving thanks to God through the night.

I wish that I could tell you that night was my last experience with sour cream and plastic, but the doctor recommended that I continue this treatment over the course of a few more days. As I lay trapped in that plastic during those long days — smelling like sour cream and suffering from tremendous pain all over my eyes, face, hands, and legs — I especially focused on God's promise in Philippians 4:7. This verse specifically held me in peace during that difficult time, and it has done so again and again throughout the years as I've continued to walk with Jesus. Verse 7 says, "And the peace of God, which passeth all understanding, shall keep your hearts and minds through Christ Jesus."

The word "peace" is the Greek word *eirene* — a powerful, often-used word in the New Testament that describes *tranquility experienced after the cessation of war*. It conveys the idea that the conflict is over; the war is finished; victory is achieved; and it is time for *tranquility* and *rest*. I had already expressed my supplications and thanksgiving to God, so it was time for me to rest in the fact that the battle for my sight was won. Since I had fulfilled the conditions of verse 7, I *rested* and allowed *tranquility* to come over me, and that tranquility ministered "peace" to my soul when I desperately needed it.

As I experienced this peace of God, it spoke to me far louder than the pain. Inwardly I knew that the battle for my eyes was over and that they were going to be all right. And just as verse 7 promises, "the peace that passeth understanding" began to "keep" my heart and mind.

The word "passeth" is a form of the word *huperecho*, which denotes something that is *superior* or *surpassing*. Because nothing compares to it, it is in a category of its very own. Furthermore, because this Greek word is a participle, we know that the peace of God expresses itself in us *continuously*. Thus, when I claimed peace in my situation, it began to continuously work in my heart and soul.

The word "understanding" is a translation of the Greek phrase *panta noun*, which literally means *all understanding*. It encompasses *everything* connected to the mind or reason. God's peace surpasses *all* reasoning, *all* understanding, and *all* thoughts that enter and work through the mind. This means that even though my mind screamed *pain*, God's peace surpassed its vehement voice and enabled me to hear His healing words.

Paul concludes verse 7 by saying "...The peace of God, which passeth all understanding, shall *keep your hearts and minds through Christ Jesus*." The word "keep" is the Greek word *phroureo*, which means *to guard*. However, it specifically referred to soldiers whose mission was to *stand guard* at the gate of a city to decide who was permitted inside. They had the power to decide who entered and who was restricted from entering the city. The word "heart" is *kardia*, which describes *the center of a person from which thoughts and affections flow*, and "mind" is *noema*, the Greek word for *thoughts*.

When you take this entire picture conveyed in verse 7 into consideration, we see that the peace of God stands like a guard at the entrance to our hearts, affections, and thoughts. If we allow peace to work, it will say "yes" to healthy, positive thoughts that want to enter those "gates" to our lives. But if something negative, detrimental, or destructive wants to enter our hearts, affections, and thoughts, the peace of God acts as a guard to *block* it from gaining access inside us. Thus, the peace of God acts as a *sentinel* of our hearts and minds.

As I recovered from my 8-hour encounter with 40 sunlamps, scary, fear-filled thoughts tried to enter my heart and mind. But when I claimed Philippians 4:6 and 7, the peace of God stood at the door to my heart and mind and refused to allow negativity and fear to enter my heart, The peace of God — the *guard* to my heart and mind — threw open the gates for a positive, healing influence. As a result, I recovered completely.

If you find yourself in a difficult position, and fearful thoughts try to enter your mind and emotions to create havoc, be quick to apply Philippians 4:6,7 to your situation. Very simply, do the three requirements laid out in verse 6:

1. Refuse to worry.
2. Let your requests be made known unto God by prayer and supplication.
3. Express thanksgiving — because heartfelt thankfulness is a powerful force to lift you up!

As you fulfill these conditions, God will go to work to perform His promise in verse 7.

1. The peace of God will go to work for you, producing supernatural *tranquility* and *rest* for your soul.
2. That peace will *surpass* any other thoughts that are trying to make you fearful.

3. That peace will act as a *guard* to prevent wrong thoughts from entering your heart, mind, and emotions — and it will throw open the door for positive, faith-filled thoughts to find entrance to your mind as well!

Philippians 4:6,7 is a very powerful passage of Scripture. If you'll fulfill the conditions of verse 6, God will be faithful to fulfill His promise to you in verse 7. So if you need a measure of peace in your life, you can assuredly know that God is anxiously waiting to fulfill His promises to you and to all those whose lives you touch. Just allow the grace of God to touch you today, and watch how He strengthens you as you shake off the chains of anxious, negative thinking!

MY PRAYER FOR TODAY

Father, I thank You for Philippians 4:6,7. Starting today, I ask You to help me fulfill the conditions in verse 6. And as I do, I expect You by faith to start performing the promise in verse 7 on my behalf. I thank You that Your peace will bring tranquility and rest to my soul and serve as a sentinel to prohibit detrimental, damaging, and negative thoughts from entering my heart. Jesus fought the battle for me; the war is won; and now it's time for peace to express its full power in me!

I pray this in Jesus' name!

MY CONFESSION FOR TODAY

I boldly confess that I refuse to worry as I let my requests be made known unto God. I give God thanks for working in my life. As a result, I will experience the peace of God, and it will work for me to produce supernatural tranquility and rest for my soul. That peace will surpass any thoughts, which are trying to make me fearful. That peace will act as a guard to keep wrong thoughts from entering my heart — and it will throw open the door for positive, faith-filled thoughts to find entrance instead.

I declare this by faith in Jesus' name!

QUESTIONS FOR YOU TO CONSIDER

1. Can you remember a moment in your life when fearful thoughts assailed your heart and mind, but after prayer, the peace of God brought tranquility and rest to your soul?
2. Do you know any individuals who are struggling and need the encouragement found in this *Sparkling Gem*? If you really care about them, why not share it with them and let it strengthen them for the fight they are in?
3. Does peace or anxiety rule you? If you tend to be tossed about by anxiety, I want to tell you *emphatically* that the peace of God is the best medication for the soul. Ask God today to let His peace that passes understanding go to work in your heart, mind, and emotions!

NOVEMBER 29

The Woman Who Refused To Leave!

Jesus said unto him, If thou canst believe,
all things are possible to him that believeth.
— Mark 9:23

When our TV program was broadcast on Channel One in Belarus, *every* home in the *entire* nation had the ability to watch it. The proof of how many people watched our program was the mountains of mail we received every week from Belarus. The impact we had was simply phenomenal.

So at the urging of a pastor in Minsk, the capital of Belarus, we took the train to that city and held a three-day meeting for our television viewers. People came from all over Belarus, to the point that the auditorium could not hold everyone who tried to get into the meeting. It blessed us to see such a response to the Gospel message delivered through our TV program.

However, the first night of the meeting was a real struggle because they gave me an interpreter who knew almost no English. All night he and I wrestled back and forth on the stage, trying to understand each other, and I knew that the crowd was missing what God wanted to say to them. When the meeting was over, I was exasperated and exhausted. I didn't want to talk to anyone, and I didn't want to pray for anyone. I just wanted to go home to our hotel and forget about what a disastrous evening that first meeting had been.

Yet there was a little lady who I could not shake off. She kept following me and saying, "Lay your hands on my ear, and my hearing will be restored." To be honest, I was so discouraged from the evening that I didn't want to pray. But she adamantly insisted, "Lay your hands on me, and I'll be healed."

The woman followed and *followed* me until finally, I asked an usher to remove her. I just wasn't in the mood for praying and really didn't believe anything would *happen* if I prayed for her that night. As they dragged her away, she kept yelling, "Just lay your hands on me, and I'll be healed. Did you hear me? Just lay your hands on me, and I'll be healed." I watched as the ushers removed her, and I did not pray for her.

Before we left the auditorium that night, the pastor and I had a serious talk about how to choose interpreters, and I pleaded with him to get me an interpreter for the next night who knew English. By the time our talk concluded, it was very dark outside. We carefully made our way down the steps to the car, when suddenly a familiar voice called out from the shadows: "Lay your hands on me, and I'll be healed!"

Although I felt absolutely nothing, I quickly turned to the deaf woman in that pitch darkness. Out of exasperation, I placed my hands on each side of her head, and commanded her ears to be opened. To my surprise, she started weeping and cried, "My ear has been opened! I can hear! I told you that if you would just lay your hands on me, I would be healed, and that is exactly what has happened!" She came back to the meeting the next night and publicly testified that her deaf ear had been completely healed as I laid hands on her the previous night. It remains one of the most remarkable miracles I've ever witnessed in my ministry — because I know it had nothing to do with me. *It had to do entirely with that woman and with what she believed!*

This woman in Minsk reminds me of the words that Jesus spoke in Mark 9:23. In that verse, Jesus addressed a father who had a son who was inflicted with a dumb and deaf spirit. The father cried out for Jesus to help his son. And "Jesus said unto him, If thou canst believe, all things are possible to him that believeth" (Mark 9:23). What a promise Jesus made to this father and to all who dare to believe! According to this verse, "all things are possible" to them who believe!

"All things" in Greek is *panta*, an all-inclusive word that throws off all limitations and blows the door open for *anything* to happen to a person who believes. The word "possible" is the word *dunata*, a form of the word *dunamis*, which is a well-known and often-used word that carries the idea of *power*, *strength*, and *ability*. This word was even used to depict *the strength of a whole army*. Thus, when a person believes, it opens the door for power, strength, and ability to work — and that power is so mighty, it is like the full force of an entire army that is moved to operate on your behalf. How would you like the full force of an army to be at your disposal? *That's what happens when you believe!*

But wait, there's more that you must see in this verse. It concludes by saying all things are possible "to him that believeth." In Greek, the tense means that all things are possible to the one who *is believing*. This is not a promise to one who *used to* believe or to one who *once* believed in the past. It is a guarantee to the one who is *presently believing* for something to happen. If a person will get in faith and stay in faith, Jesus says that absolutely *anything* can happen. For the believing one, *anything and everything* is possible!

That leads me back to the woman in Minsk. She came to that meeting *believing* that if I would touch her, she would be healed. She was so filled with faith that when I didn't cooperate with her, it didn't move her faith at all. She simply refused to leave the facility until I touched her and she received her healing. And what happened? *Exactly what she believed.* I touched her, and the power of God moved *according to her faith* — and within seconds, she was weeping because her hearing had been instantly restored. It had nothing to do with me and everything to do with her and what she believed. What she believed is precisely what she received. It came to her exactly as she had said: *"Lay your hands on me, and I'll be healed."*

This woman was determined that neither she nor I would leave that facility without my laying hands on her and her hearing being restored. To be honest, I didn't even pray when I touched her. I simply lay my hands on her, as she demanded, and spoke to the ear to be opened — and the power of God moved liked a mighty army in response to her faith and opened her ear! Her miracle had everything to do with what *she* believed.

- ➢ What about you and your faith?
- ➢ What do *you* believe?

If you are believing *right now*, you are in a position for the ability of God to move against your problem and bring you the result you seek. If you are in faith and *staying* in faith, it's only a matter of time until things will begin to change. That's a promise that Jesus made to you, to me, and to anyone who will believe! *So let's get our faith in gear and determine to STAY in faith! As we make that rock-solid commitment, we'll begin to experience the truth that anything really is possible to the one who believes and releases his or her faith!*

MY PRAYER FOR TODAY

Father, I realize that I have let some things slip regarding my walk of faith. Lord, I repent for being so carnal that I was moved by what I saw and what I felt. I commit afresh not to be provoked by circumstances that are subject to change. By Your grace, from this moment onward, I will be moved to take action only on the Word and by the Spirit of God. Thank You for strengthening my resolve to make a quality, lasting decision to step it up and get my faith in gear! You empower me by Your Spirit to stay consistent with my intake of the Word of God so my faith can remain fresh, current, and active and I can be strong in spirit to receive what I need.

I pray this in Jesus' name!

MY CONFESSION FOR TODAY

I confess that my faith is alive and well and that I remain "in faith" to receive what I need! I keep my fellowship with the Lord intimate, fresh, and vibrant by spending time in His Word and in prayer daily. I keep myself in the love of God, and as a result, my faith does not fail. I give my attention to God's words and His desired end results; therefore, the Lord Himself keeps my thoughts in agreement with His will. I speak and act in agreement with God's words; therefore, I walk in and release the peace, wisdom, and supernatural ability of God everywhere I go. According to Jesus' promise in Mark 9:23, anything and everything is possible to me!

I declare this by faith in Jesus' name!

QUESTIONS FOR YOU TO CONSIDER

1. What do you think about the tenacious attitude of the woman in Minsk and the fact that she would not leave the facility until she received her hearing? Do you see that her healing had nothing to do with me, but everything to do with what she believed? Are you as persistent as she was to receive from God?
2. What exactly are you standing on the Word of God and exercising your faith to believe for right now? *Are you unwilling to be denied?*
3. Would God say that your faith is presently being released? Did the words that were once burning and alive in your heart now only flicker as a fact that you

vaguely recall but no longer act upon? Or would He say that you have grown old in your confession and that your faith needs to be rekindled? If your faith needs to be rekindled, what are you going to do to make that happen?

NOVEMBER 30

Not Ashamed of the Gospel of Christ

For I am not ashamed of the Gospel of Christ:
for it is the power of God unto salvation
to every one that believeth….
— Romans 1:16

In the early days of our TV ministry, there was a national journalist who literally despised me because I taught the Bible on television. An avowed atheist, he often took advantage of his deep dislike for me by printing stories of my preaching in the national newspaper. In each of these news stories, he likened my preaching about Jesus and His parables to fairytales, and he particularly delighted in calling me "the Pinocchio preacher." For years, he had taken every advantage possible to attack me and to deal a blow to the Gospel message.

One day I was flying from Riga to Moscow, and — lo and behold — who was seated on the plane directly across the aisle from me but this journalist who treated me with so much disdain! This man was *filled* with antagonism and hatred toward the Gospel, and he badgered me the entire flight. But regardless of how hard he tried to pick a fight with me, the peace of God ruled in my heart, and I responded to him in the love of Christ — which I think made him even angrier. He was traveling with a group of like-minded journalists, and he actually stood up on the plane and announced: "Hey, look who we're flying with — *the Pinocchio preacher*!"

The companions of this journalist all joined in with him, laughing and mocking me. The more hard liquor they drank, the greater the velocity of their insults thrown my way across the aisle. The flight attendant became embarrassed and apologized to me for their behavior, but there was nothing she could do to stop them once they started. They were doing their best to humiliate and embarrass me in front of the other passengers in our section of the plane.

Have you ever found yourself in a position where you were mocked because of your faith? It isn't an enjoyable experience, but if you've ever endured such persecution, please know that you are not alone.

On that flight as I suffered the brunt of those men's words for several hours, I made up my mind to grab hold of and meditate on Romans 1:16. In that verse, Paul says, "For I am not ashamed of the Gospel of Christ: for it is the power of God unto salvation to every one that believeth...."

The apostle Paul faced hostile reactions to the Gospel in both the pagan and Jewish worlds. There were times when he was not only poked fun at, but he was physically abused by those whose hearts were filled with antagonism toward him. When Paul said, "I am not ashamed of the Gospel of Christ," he used the Greek word *epaischunomai* — translated as "ashamed" in this verse, which is a compound of *epi* and *aischunomai*. The word *epi* means *for*, and *aischunomai* means to be *confounded* or *embarrassed*. Literally, Paul declared that he did not find the Gospel a reason for *embarrassment*. In modern language, Paul did not find the Gospel a reason to feel awkward, self-conscious, or humiliated.

On the contrary, Paul said, "I am not ashamed of the Gospel of Christ, for it is *the power of God* unto salvation to them that believe." Paul knew that for those who believed, the Gospel unleashed the power of God! The word "power" is the Greek word *dunamis*, a word that generally denoted *the strength of a whole army*. Paul was in fact declaring that when faith is mixed with the Gospel *and declared*, it releases divine energy equal to the fighting force of an entire army!

A faith that is active releases this power for those who are "believing" — that is, for those whose faith is engaged. Based on the usage of *dunamis* throughout history, it clearly means that this power of God is like a host of troops placed at the disposal of anyone who has his faith forward-directed and actively working. *Why would anyone be ashamed of such power?*

I may have *looked* like one singular man sitting in that section of a plane with many people arrayed against me, mocking me. But inside me, there was an entire "army" of divine strength and power at work — and that's true for *anyone* who believes! The power that was in operation that day was far greater than those who were poking fun at me. And it was that *dunamis* power that enabled me to love them in spite of their ugly behavior.

When I find myself in a difficult situation because of the hurtful actions of people or because life is sometimes tough and I'm tempted to feel isolated and alone, I often stop to meditate on the *dunamis* power of God that is at work within me. There is a mighty reservoir of divine power residing in me every moment of every day, and that means I never face a truly isolated moment. God has placed a "full army" of *dunamis* power at my disposal!

This is true for you too. If you feel isolated, alone, and solitary — and it seems like you're facing troubles with no one at your side — let me remind you that God's *dunamis* power is inside you and is continually available to you if you will engage your faith.

I saw that atheist reporter again years later, and he was still hostile toward the Gospel. I felt sorry for him, for the very thing he hated and resisted had the power to completely alter his life, change his disposition, and deliver him from a horrible eternal fate. But as before, his heart was hard like stone, and he wanted nothing to do with the Gospel or with "the Pinocchio preacher."

Today I want to encourage you that when your faith is forward-directed, it throws open the door for a whole army of divine power to work on your behalf. The Holy Spirit dwells within you. He is the very source of *dunamis*, and He is just waiting to unleash that power on your behalf! All He needs is for you to be in a state of "believing." It will throw open the door for that *dunamis* power to flow through you and strengthen you against any opposition or obstacle you could ever face!

MY PRAYER FOR TODAY

Father, I thank You for the Person of that the Holy Spirit who resides within me. I acknowledge that His presence within me has imparted to me dunamis power — the strength of an entire army. Therefore, with confident assurance I boldly proclaim: the Greater One in me is mightier than any force that opposes me in this world! Father, I ask You to forgive me for times when I've retreated and acted in shame about the Gospel. I know I should have engaged my faith and released a flood of divine energy to empower me and overwhelm the enemy. So from this moment on, I make a firm decision that I will not be ashamed of the Gospel of Christ, but I will allow its strengthening might to flow through me, no matter what opposition or obstacle I face!

I pray this in Jesus' name!

MY CONFESSION FOR TODAY

I declare that there is a whole army of divine power at my disposal because the Holy Spirit indwells me. I believe the Gospel and its claim; therefore, I am strong and courageous knowing that divine signs of God's presence and approval are manifest in my life. I am not confounded, confused, or embarrassed when others poke fun at my faith. I don't shrink back or cringe in terror or intimidation. Instead, I simply draw from the supply of the Holy Spirit within me, engage my faith, and let His power strengthen me for what I am confronting at that moment. It is absolutely true that greater is He who is in me than He that is in the world! This dunamis power in me lifts me above any foe around me, and as I continually activate God's power by faith, I am an overcomer over every challenge that I'll ever face in this life!

I declare this by faith in Jesus' name!

QUESTIONS FOR YOU TO CONSIDER

1. Can you think of a time when you felt bullied or made fun of because of your faith? How did you respond when that event occurred in your life?
2. Now that you know the *dunamis* power of God is at your disposal, what will you do differently the next time you're challenged in your faith?
3. After your salvation, when were you filled with the Holy Spirit? What was that experience like when you received His supernatural enabling power?

DECEMBER 1

Are You Preparing for the Christmas Holidays?

Wherefore, beloved, seeing that ye look for such things,
be diligent that ye may be found of him in peace,
without spot, and blameless.
— 2 Peter 3:14

This is the time of the year when many people decorate their houses and dress things up for the Christmas season. People elaborately decorate the interior of their homes, sometimes even with multiple Christmas trees for different rooms, each tree adorned in a different style. They line the exterior of their homes, trees, and shrubs in colorful, flashing lights. People are so committed to this tradition, in fact, that many begin decorating a few days before Thanksgiving Day and then keep the decorations up until just after the New Year.

When I was a young boy, my family always had a Christmas tree, but we didn't hang exterior lights on our house, trees, or shrubs. Yet each year my parents would pile all of us Renner kids into the car, and we'd drive around the neighborhood the week prior to Christmas to see how other people had decorated their homes. Then we'd drive across our city to a particular shopping mall to gaze at the beautifully illuminated trees. The sight was so beautiful that it looked nearly magical. It was a special family moment in our holiday festivities that we really enjoyed and looked forward to each year.

That was decades ago. Today people are more elaborate than ever before in the way they decorate their homes for the Christmas season. It can take many hours, a lot of manpower, and large amounts of money for people to adorn their homes the way many do today. The effect is beautiful and truly changes a neighborhood into a spectacular sight during this special time of year.

I appreciate the time and effort people put into celebrating at Christmastime. It is something I really miss, living in Russia, because Russians do not decorate for the Christmas season. However, regardless of how beautiful and ornate Christmas decorations are, they are all seasonal and temporary. The decorations go up, and then they are taken down, put away in boxes, and stored until the next Christmas season rolls around.

No condemnation is implied in this question, but when I see the manpower, time, and money people put into celebrating Christmas, I often wonder, *While people are putting so much manpower, time, and money into decorating their Christmas trees and homes to celebrate Christ's first coming, I wonder what kind of effort they are putting forth to prepare for His NEXT coming?*

In Second Peter 3, the apostle Peter wrote an entire section of Scripture about how to be prepared for Jesus' return — a task that requires an entirely different level of dedication than it takes to put up decorations for a short-lived Christmas season. Preparing for Christ's return requires a *lifelong commitment.* In Second Peter 3:14, Peter wrote, "Wherefore, beloved, seeing that ye look for such things [referring to the coming of the Lord], be diligent that ye may be found of him in peace, without spot, and blameless."

First, Peter pled with us to "look" for the next coming of the Lord. The word "look" is from a Greek word that means *to earnestly wait for with sincere and unrelenting conviction.* In other words, we must have a constant awareness that the Lord could return at any moment. Christ's coming for the Church should be such a reality in our hearts that we constantly wait for it with a conviction that *consumes us* and *keeps us on our toes,* so to speak.

Verse 14 says we need to be "diligent" in waiting for the Lord to come. The word "diligent" is the Greek word *spoudadzo,* which gives the sense of *constant readiness* and *diligence.* It means *to work hard*; *to give it your best shot*; *to give it effort*; or *to commit yourself to it entirely and constantly.* In other words, this kind of preparation is not seasonal or on-and-off according to the whims of emotions. It is a *firm commitment* to constantly *be ready* for the coming of Christ.

When I say "diligent," I'm talking about a perpetual attitude that is conscientious and persistent and that never lets go of constantly preparing for Christ's return for His saints. It is a conviction that one must never stop being ready and prepared for that grand moment. It is "decorating" one's life with godly traits *every* day of the year!

Christ is coming back for His Church! If Christmastime reminds us of anything, it should be that since He came once, He *will* come again. Therefore, we must be constantly on guard and in a state of preparation so that He will find us fully "spiritually decorated" upon His arrival. He longs to find us "...in peace, without spot, and blameless" (2 Peter 3:14). If we would diligently and constantly work on adorning our spiritual lives with the same effort and dedication we put forth naturally to decorate our homes for Christmas, Christ would find us in splendid condition when He returns!

So I want to ask you today — what are you doing to make sure your spiritual life is fully decorated with life, godliness, purity, and spiritual power when Christ returns? If He were to come today, would He find you adorned with these godly attributes or lacking them? As you spend manpower, time, and money to decorate your physical house, it would be prudent for you to ask yourself if Christ would find these other vital qualities in your life when He returns for His Church. Forgive me for being so blunt, but are you putting as much into your heart and spiritual condition as you are putting into your physical decorations? *That's something for you to think about today.*

MY PRAYER FOR TODAY

Father, I ask You to help me look truthfully at my own spiritual condition to determine if I am doing all I should to prepare for the coming of the Lord. There is no doubt that He is coming — and He is coming soon. But am I living in a way that will bring Him pleasure when He comes? This is a hard question to ask and pray, but I feel the need to be honest with myself and with You about it today, Lord. Speak to my heart, Holy Spirit, and reveal to me the areas where I need to put forth more effort into my spiritual life. I ask You to strengthen me with might in my inner man to be courageous, persistent, and diligent until it is done.

I pray this in Jesus' name!

MY CONFESSION FOR TODAY

I confess that how I adorn and decorate my life with godliness and holiness is more important than how I physically decorate my house for Christmastime. I want to be found pleasing to the Lord when He comes. Therefore, to get myself ready for His coming — and to stay prepared for His coming — is the chief goal of my life. Whatever changes I need to make, I am willing to make. Whatever God is calling me to lay aside, I am willing to lay aside. More than anything else, I want to be a vessel that is found pleasing to Jesus when He comes for His Church. Lord, if there is any hint of anything in me that is unwilling to yield to this as my chief desire, I declare that it's moving out and being replaced by an unrelenting desire to be pleasing to You as the chief desire of my life.

I declare this by faith in Jesus' name!

QUESTIONS FOR YOU TO CONSIDER

1. Jesus' first coming is, of course, worth celebrating, for it was the beginning of deliverance and salvation for the world. But in addition to decorating the interior and exterior of your home, what are you doing to prepare your heart for the soon coming of Jesus for His Church?
2. Do you live with a daily awareness that Christ will soon return? Does the condition of your heart, your mind, and your soul reflect that the blessed hope of eternity consistently influences how you choose to live? What changes do you need to make in your spiritual life?
3. What are you doing to help others get their lives in order to be prepared to meet the Lord in peace? Do you regularly reach out to share the Gospel with people who need to know Christ as their Savior?

What are you doing to make sure your spiritual life is fully decorated with life, godliness, purity, and spiritual power when Christ returns?

DECEMBER 2

What To Do When Someone You Know Is Struggling and Needs Help

We then that are strong ought to bear
the infirmities of the weak, and
not to please ourselves.
— Romans 15:1

From time to time, we have all known individuals who wrestled with a problem or personal challenge, and we witnessed them struggle and inwardly fight for survival. In fact, you may know someone who fits this very description right now. Especially as we approach a holiday season, feelings of loneliness, isolation, and hopelessness can become even more pronounced. So what should you and I do to help people who are struggling and need support? What kind of support can we give to them to help them make it through Christmastime?

In Romans 15:1, Paul says, "We then that are strong ought to bear the infirmities of the weak, and not to please ourselves." According to this verse, there are some of us who are stronger than others, and those of us who are stronger need to reach out to help those who are struggling!

Take a little time to ask yourself this question today: *Is there someone I know who needs a little extra encouragement and strength that I could provide along the way?*

In fact, Romans 15:1 says we "ought" to do this for those who are weak. The word "ought" is the Greek word *opheilo*, and it means *to be morally obligated* or *to do something as an obligation.* In other words, we are obligated to do this for others. After all the ways people have helped us in our times of need, we are spiritually and morally obligated to do the same for others.

But for whom are we to do this? This verse says we are to do this for those who are feeling overwhelmed with personal "infirmities." The word "infirmities" is *asthenema,* and it describes *those who are weak, powerless, or struggling in some way, whether physically or emotionally.* The word "weak" is *adunatos*, which depicts *those who are depleted of power due to something they have experienced or gone through that has rendered them weak.*

Take a moment to ponder the following questions. When you see people struggle:

- Do you come a little closer to check on them?
- Have you invited them to dinner, especially if they are feeling very alone?

- Could you possibly include that person in your holiday celebration so they conquer their feeling of isolation and feel included in someone else's life?
- If you know someone who has experienced loss or grief of some kind, such as the loss of a relationship due to death or hardship, what can you do to help that person know that he or she is going to make it through this difficult season?

I personally ask myself these questions during the Christmas season. Our ministry receives so many letters from people who struggle during the holidays. Christmastime can and should be a time of rejoicing, but it can also invoke painful memories of what has been lost through the passage of time. Rather than be consumed with your own celebrations and events, God's Word encourages us "not to please ourselves," but to reach out to those who are disempowered and suffering from painful circumstances. If you are strong, you have an obligation to reach out to those who are weak and hurt.

So this Christmastime, have you considered those who have suffered loss or stress due to hardships in their lives? What can you do to bring strength and friendship to those who have lost so much this year? This is your opportunity to be a source of strength to those who are in need. You may not know exactly what to say or to do, but perhaps your mere presence and friendship can bring them to a place of hope.

I encourage you to look beyond yourself and see what you can do for someone else this holiday season! If you'll look to the Holy Spirit, He will show you how to be a source of power and strength to those who are in need. He is faithful to strengthen the weak and give power to the lowly — and He may very well choose *you* to be the vehicle that He uses to reach them with His love!

MY PRAYER FOR TODAY

Heavenly Father, in the midst of this season when many are happy and joyfully celebrating Your gift of love to mankind, I realize that this is also a time of year when some people feel a profound sense of loss or sadness. Father, I ask You to let me be a hand of help to those who are in need. Help me bring encouragement to those who feel loss, who are disempowered, or who feel like they are struggling beyond their natural capacity to overcome. I know that You want to use me to reach them. I surrender myself as an instrument You can use to bring strength to the weak, hope to the hopeless, and support to those who need it the most. According to Romans 15:1, I commit to being a source of power and support to those who are in need.

I pray this in Jesus' name!

MY CONFESSION FOR TODAY

I confess that I look beyond my own needs to see the needs of others. I am not self-consumed, but I am concerned about those about me who are suffering in all sorts of ways. The Holy Spirit uses me as I surrender to His sanctifying power so I can effectively undergird those who feel weak, especially in this holiday season. The Holy Spirit opens my eyes so I can see and feel what they see and feel and help them through their current struggle!

I pray this in Jesus' name!

QUESTIONS FOR YOU TO CONSIDER

1. Do you know someone that needs extra-special care and support during this Christmas season? What can you do to reach out to them in a special way?
2. Loneliness is a powerful force. Can you think of individuals who may be experiencing loneliness this year and who need someone to reach out to them, comfort them, or befriend them in their time of need?
3. There are many people who feel extra pressures when the holiday season comes. Have you looked around you to see who is struggling and who needs some emotional support? What can you do to help strengthen them in a time that could be especially troubling or emotionally difficult?

DECEMBER 3

The Attraction of Something Special

And Jesus went about all Galilee, teaching in their synagogues,
and preaching the gospel of the kingdom,
and healing all manner of sickness and all manner of disease among the people.
And his fame went throughout all Syria;
and they brought unto him all sick people
that were taken with divers diseases
and torments, and those which were possessed with devils,
and those which were lunatic,
and those that had the palsy; and he healed them all.
And there followed him great multitudes of people....
— Matthew 4:23-25

People come to Jesus in a myriad of ways. In the verses above, they were attracted to His miracles, signs, and wonders. People are still attracted to Christ's miraculous power today, but sometimes the catalyst that brings a person to a saving knowledge of Jesus Christ is far smaller and more subtle.

An example of this "saving influence" is how my mother came to know Jesus as her Savior as a young girl. Her catalyst was a gift of candy. My mother (whose maiden name was Erlita Miller) was eight years old at the time. A neighbor knew young Erlita was unsaved, so she invited her to attend the local Baptist church. That Christmas season, Erlita's Sunday school teacher invited her to the church's Christmas service — with the enticement of a satchel of candy that would be given to each child who attended that particular service.

A satchel of candy might not sound like much today, but when my mother was eight years old, World War II was an ongoing reality, and sugar, among other commodities, was scarce. This made candy a *very* rare treat. When Erlita heard that candy was going to be given to each child who attended the service, she asked her mother for permission to go. Not only did her mother say yes, but she even accompanied her to that event. That night Erlita not only received her small satchel of candy, but she also heard the Gospel explained for the first time. Later that same night at home, Erlita bowed down on her knees and surrendered her life to Jesus Christ. *This amazing miracle all started with the lure of a small satchel of candy!*

In the day in which Jesus lived, one thing that was a truly scarce commodity was the power *to heal*. Even if doctors could diagnose a medical condition, they didn't have the medications to heal it. So when the news of Jesus and His healing power began to spread across the region, Matthew 4:24 says that a great "fame" of Him traveled throughout all those regions.

The word "fame" is the Greek word *akoe*, which is the Greek word for the human *ear*. In this case, it describes a *rumor* or something that is *repeated* or *heard by those who were listening*. The people who were really profoundly listening were those who needed a healing touch. The reports and "rumors" of the supernatural healing power of God were big news and served as a drawing card that beckoned people with all types of sicknesses and diseases. As a result of this news, people came from all over the surrounding regions, and multitudes experienced Jesus' healing and delivering power. Then *more news* about Him spread *further and further* until the entire region was abuzz with "news" about Jesus and His healing power!

It wasn't healing power that attracted my mother when she was eight years old. She didn't need healing power. But that satchel of candy was a major attraction and a huge "rumor" in her neighborhood — which attracted scores of children and young people to a Christmas service at church, where they heard the message of Jesus.

It took something as simple as a gift of candy to bring my mother to the feet of Jesus — and so much fruit has resulted from my mother's salvation! Little did she know that she would have a little boy who would grow up and impact the Russian nation with the Word and the power of God. The legacy she provided as a deeply committed Christian — to her children, her grandchildren, and her *great*-grandchildren — will speak for all eternity.

And to think that it all started with a neighbor's invitation to attend her church — and a Sunday School teacher's follow-up offer of a gift of candy given out at a Christmas service. It amazes me when I think of what that little satchel of candy has done to reach millions of people for Christ over the ensuing decades!

What are you doing this year to attract people to the message of Jesus Christ? Don't deprecate yourself as insignificant or minimize your efforts as being small and unnoticeable. You have no idea who someone may turn out to be later in life. You don't realize how your seemingly small touch of God's love may result in magnificent eternal fruit. Every person is important — and it's our job to take the "fame" of Jesus to as many people as possible and to draw them to His saving power, especially at Christmastime!

MY PRAYER FOR TODAY

Father, I thank You for the encouragement I've received today. I have discounted myself as being too insignificant to make a large impact in Your Kingdom. But today I see that I could make a huge and eternal impact with something as small as a satchel of candy! Rather than look at what I can't do, help me look around to see what I have and what I could do that would make a difference in bringing others to Christ, especially during this Christmas season.

I pray this in Jesus' name!

MY CONFESSION FOR TODAY

I confess that I am an instrument that God will use to touch others with the Good News of Jesus Christ. I have judged myself as being small and insignificant for too long. From this moment forward, I make the decision to look around me to see what I have to offer others that will cause the love of Jesus and His name to become a reality to them. I am not insignificant or too minor to be used by God in a big way. God wants to use me to reach people — even those who will themselves later impact multitudes for the Kingdom of God!

I declare this by faith in Jesus' name!

QUESTIONS FOR YOU TO CONSIDER

1. When you think of people who are lost and without Christ, what can you do this year to pique their interest in knowing Christ? What creative ways can you think of to bring them to a place where they can hear the true Christmas message?
2. What memories do you have from Christmastime that attracted you to the saving message of Jesus Christ?
3. Maybe it wasn't candy that attracted you to Jesus, but was there something the Holy Spirit used to grab your attention and bring you to Jesus? What person, place, or thing did the Lord use to bring you to that moment of repentance and salvation?

The legacy my mother provided as a deeply committed Christian — to her children, her grandchildren, and her great-grandchildren — will speak for all eternity.

DECEMBER 4

My Personal Memories of Candy Canes at Christmastime

Go ye therefore, and teach all nations,
baptizing them in the name of the Father,
and of the Son, and of the Holy Ghost.
— Matthew 28:19

Just as there are many ways to preach the Gospel, there is a diverse array of effective methods and strategies used to attract people to a place where they can hear the Good News of Jesus Christ. I told you yesterday how my mother was saved after attending a church service where candy was given to children and young people. I also remember our pastor promising 12-inch-long and 1-inch-thick peppermint candy-cane sticks to every child and youth who attended the annual special Christmas service at our church. The goal was to preach the Gospel, but the bait to get all of those people there was a huge candy-cane stick!

All of us kids in the church were so excited for that service when those 12-by-1-inch-thick candy canes would be distributed. In today's society, this is probably not viewed the special treat that it was many decades ago. Today candy is available in overabundance. But when I was a young boy, it was still a real treat and something we looked forward to with great anticipation.

That particular service was always held on a Sunday night, and I can remember all the pews being packed with young children and youth. They had all come to the Christmas service — awaiting the moment when those huge, striped peppermint candy canes would be unpacked from big boxes and passed down the pews to each child and youth who eagerly awaited them. We weren't allowed to open them in church, but as soon as the service was over and we were outside the building, we all raced to peel off the plastic covering on that striped candy cane to take our first lick!

I was a little different than the other kids in my approach. I barely pulled the plastic off the very top of my candy cane, exposing only the tip. And I was so excited to have that candy that I'd put mine in the freezer each year so it would last as long as possible. Once a day, I'd run to the freezer, take it out, and take a single fresh lick — then I'd wrap it back up and put it back into the freezer. I did my best to prolong this wonderful experience for as long as possible! One year I almost made my candy cane last until the next Christmas!

I also remember that each year at the special Christmas service, our pastor's wife played Christmas carols on an antique pump organ that they assembled in the middle of our church platform. She played that old organ while our pastor led the church in singing Christmas carols. These songs always preceded the distribution of candy canes. Then the pastor would preach about the birth of Jesus — *the real reason for Christmas* — and give an altar call for people to come forward to surrender their lives to Jesus. Each year we would see a generous number of people walk the aisles to make that eternal decision. Only after that were the candy canes distributed. The candy was a big deal to the kids in the pews — but in truth, it was "bait" to attract lots of unsaved people to that service to hear the Good News of Jesus.

Those children and youth were attracted to church with the promise of a candy-cane stick, but they ended up in the family of God because the candy came with an opportunity to hear the Gospel message. As a result, the church grew, and Sunday school increased. But most importantly, people were born into the Kingdom of God — all because they came for the promised candy canes!

In Matthew 28:19, Jesus commanded us, "Go ye therefore, and teach all nations, baptizing them in the name of the Father, and of the Son, and of the Holy Ghost." The word "go" is the Greek word *poreuthentes*, a Greek word that portrays us *being constantly on the go* to make disciples of all men — and, of course, to ultimately baptize them "...in the name of the Father, and of the Son, and of the Holy Ghost." It is interesting that this verse doesn't mention any specific techniques that we are to use in our pursuit of "going" to reach them. There are *many* ways to attract the lost to the best news in the whole world — *the news that Jesus saves*!

It's possible for a person to be saved through a Gospel tract, a TV program, a personal testimony, or even through the offer of a peppermint candy cane. Carrying on this candy-cane tradition from my own childhood, our church in Russia offers packages of beautifully wrapped candy to children and youth each year at Russian Christmas — and it has the same effect today in Russia that it had on me as a small boy. And what is this effect? Not only do we see *hundreds of children* receive Christ as their Savior, but their parents, who are sitting in the adult service in the main auditorium, hear a Christmas message that is especially designed for them. Many of the parents who come are unsaved prior to attending our special Christmas services — and each year, our altar is filled with adults who come forward to repent and commit their lives to the Lord.

We must be serious about finding a way to bring the Good News to the lost. Jesus told us to be on the "go"— to be constantly in motion, trying to find ways to bring this glorious news to those who are in need.

So I want to ask you, what are you or your church doing this Christmas to attract people of all ages to the Gospel's good news? Are you on the "go" as Jesus commanded us to be?

MY PRAYER FOR TODAY

Father, I ask You to help me be creative in the ways I introduce the message of Jesus to those who are unsaved. Help me think "outside the box" and plan new and creative ways to present this eternal message. I know people who need salvation, but I need to think of new ways to present the message to them. Lord, You are the ultimate creative force in the universe, so I ask You to release Your creativity in me and help me as I take this greatest message of all to those I love and am praying for to receive Christ.

I pray this in Jesus' name!

MY CONFESSION FOR TODAY

I confess that I am filled with the power of the Holy Spirit, and He empowers me with strength and creative ideas on how to present the message of Jesus Christ to my family, friends, and acquaintances. I have no excuse to say I am lacking ideas, because the greatest source of ideas lives inside me. So, Holy Spirit, I open myself to You — and I ask you to unleash Your creative flow to show me how to be on the "go" to take this saving message to those who are in need of it.

I declare this by faith in Jesus' name!

QUESTIONS FOR YOU TO CONSIDER

1. Like my mother, I was attracted to church at a very young age by the lure of candy. Have you thought about what you could offer children or young people that would make them attend a service where they will hear the saving message of Jesus Christ?
2. Which individuals in your life are unsaved — whether children or adults — and need to hear the truth of the Gospel? What are you doing this year to make sure that each of these precious people knows the real message of the season?
3. Who is on your prayer list to receive salvation this Christmas season? Have you made a prayer list of people who need to repent and surrender to Christ? Can you think of anything more wonderful that you could do than to pray for them to come to Jesus this year?

DECEMBER 5

Purposefully Making Christ the Focus of the Christmas Season

Set your affection on things above,
not on things on the earth.
— Colossians 3:2

It is so easy to be distracted at Christmastime by the anticipation of gifts and holiday festivities. That is why it is so important that you follow Paul's instruction in Colossians 3:2 and purposefully "set your affection on things above, not on things on the earth" during the Christmas season. I'll elaborate a bit more on this verse in just a moment, but first I want to tell you how my mother helped me as a young boy to focus my attention on the true meaning of Christmas.

Each year at Christmastime, my parents loaded my sisters and me into the car, and we drove to one of many Christmas tree "lots" in our city. We walked back and forth among the rows of trees, trying to select the tree that was just "perfect" for our family. Once we chose a tree, Dad purchased it, tied it to the top of the car, drove it home, and set it in our living room. Then we gleefully decorated it with silver tinsel, lights, strings of popcorn, Christmas bulbs of all sorts, and then we topped it off by putting a red and silver aluminum lighted star on the very peak of the tree. Doing this every year was a major event in the Renner household.

I'd sit and look at the lights and decorations literally for hours at a time. So to keep my focus fixed on Christ and not fixated on the Christmas tree, my mother came up with a brilliant idea — she encouraged me each year to make a manger scene out of construction paper. First, I pulled out my big box of crayons and colorfully drew a little barn, filled with animals, shepherds, wise men, Joseph, Mary, Jesus, and an angel sitting on top of the roof of the barn. Then using my little scissors, I carefully cut it out. Right where "hoped-for" gifts would eventually sit under the tree, I'd use dried ice cream sticks and glue to concoct a support structure that would make my little Christmas scene stand upright under the tree.

For me, this was the most important element of our Christmas tree. Instead of focusing on the bulbs and lights, I'd lie on my stomach in front of the tree and look at my "work of art" that displayed the scene of that miraculous night when Jesus was born. By encouraging me to do this, my mother purposely helped me to keep the right focus at Christmastime and not dwell on Christmas tree ornaments or gifts. With her encouragement, Jesus' birth — and the characters and scene around His birth — became the "center" for my little heart and imagination, and the tree became secondary. My focus shifted to the scene that sat right under the Christmas tree, where I could lie on the floor and imagine what Jesus' birth must have been like.

I learned a big lesson from my mother at that early age. She taught me to do whatever is necessary to set my thoughts on things above and not on things of the earth (*see* Colossians 3:2). The word "set" in this verse is the present imperative active form of the Greek word *phroneo*, which means *to think*. However, the tense used here conveys a commandment to actively, purposefully, and deliberately *think* about something. In this case, we are commanded to actively think about things above, not on things of the earth.

Rather than focus on that Christmas tree, I needed to lift my thoughts and purposefully think about Jesus and what His birth meant to me. The word *phroneo* in Colossians 3:2 depicts a practical pursuit of lifting one's thinking from things below — from being fixated on things below to becoming fixated on things above, or those things that are more connected with Heaven and the divine.

So I want to ask you: What are you purposefully doing this year to make Christ the "center" of your Christmas season for yourself and those around you? Are you focused and fixated more on the natural part of the season, or have you purposefully lifted your thoughts to Christ and the real message of the season? Today I want to encourage you to think of ways to elevate your thoughts — to set your mind on Jesus, seated at the right hand of the Father. After all, He is the *real* reason for the season. *You can do it, and you can help others do it too!*

MY PRAYER FOR TODAY

Father, I ask You to help me purposefully and deliberately lift my thoughts to a higher realm than where they've been in past holidays. Yes, the season is joyful and full of festivities, but help me remember that it is Your commandment that my thoughts go to a higher place than short-lived, seasonal experiences. I will meditate on what really matters at this time of the year, and I will grow spiritually as a result!

I pray this in Jesus' name!

MY CONFESSION FOR TODAY

I confess that I am not fixated on low-level, temporal concerns that won't even matter a year from now. I refuse to allow myself to become swamped in festivities, holiday events, and the giving and receiving of gifts. Instead, I choose to meditate on the real reason for the season. This year I lift my thoughts to a higher realm, and as a result, this will be the best Christmas season I've experienced in my life thus far!

I declare this by faith in Jesus' name!

QUESTIONS FOR YOU TO CONSIDER

1. People often get so caught up in the purchasing and giving of gifts or in holiday activities that the real message of Christmas gets sidetracked in the midst of it all. What are you purposefully doing this year to make sure that Jesus remains the very center of your Christmas experience?
2. If you have children, grandchildren, or other children who are close to you, what can you do to help them focus on the real story of Christmas this year?
3. Christmas is a time when we celebrate God's gift of love — Jesus Christ — by giving gifts to others. Some of life's most precious gifts don't cost any money at all; they cost only the sacrifice of ourselves. In what ways can you give to others that will represent the true meaning of Christmas in their lives? Do you give to people who don't know you or who can't reciprocate by giving back to you?

What are you purposefully doing this year
to make Christ the "center"
of your Christmas season
for yourself and those around you?

DECEMBER 6

Staying Connected to Christ!

As ye have therefore received Christ Jesus the Lord,
so walk ye in him: rooted and built up in Him....
— Colossians 2:6,7

After my family would purchase our Christmas tree and bring it home each year, we'd face the same challenge every other family did — that is, how to get the tree to stand straight and to stay green for as long as possible. Because the tree had been cut from its roots, it had no nourishing life source to keep it vibrant, so something had to be done to keep it looking fresh and green.

Like millions of other fathers, my dad purchased a tree stand for our big fir tree. It was a red metal bowl with four green legs connected to a round metal ring at the top, and it had four bolts that went through the metal ring.

The round ring at the top could be adjusted to fit the width of the tree trunk, and my dad would insert the tree through the metal ring and center it so that the tree stood upright. Next, dad would tighten those four bolts into the tree from four directions so it would stand firmly and straight. Once he decided exactly where to set the tree in the living room, he'd set it in its place and pour water into the basin of the tree stand so the tree would have a water source to keep it looking lush and green. Every day or so, we had to refill that basin because the tree kept soaking up the water. If we forgot to do it, the tree would begin to dry up and the needles would become brittle and start turning brown.

Our beloved Christmas tree was basically a dead tree that we artificially kept looking beautiful by pouring water into the basin. Because it had been chopped from its roots, it had no natural source to keep it alive. Thank God, we as believers are not like Christmas trees, which are chopped off at the roots, fragile, and artificially kept alive. We are rooted in Christ and firmly established in Him. We are told in Colossians 2:6 and 7, "As ye have therefore received Christ Jesus the Lord, so walk ye in him: Rooted and built up in Him...."

Unlike chopped-off Christmas trees, we believers are "rooted" in Christ, and we are "built up" in Him. The word "rooted" is the Greek word *erridzomeno*, the perfect passive participle of *ridzoo*. The word *ridzoo* means *to be firmly rooted* or *fixed into place*, like a tree that is deeply rooted and therefore immovable. It points to a past completed action, performed at the moment of repentance, with continuing results of salvation. The words "built up" in Him are from the Greek word *epoikodomoumenoi*, the present passive participle of *epoikodomeo*. This word depicts *something that grows upward and is built on a strong, solid foundation* — just like a tree's root structure that holds the tree firmly in place and provides the tree with a constant stream of nourishment.

Today people purchase artificial trees as well, and although these decorations are beautiful, they are utterly lifeless. They are repackaged year after year into boxes and then pulled out each Christmas season, looking just as they looked during the previous Christmas season.

This isn't the way it is for us who are in Christ. God doesn't want us just to *look* like Christians, "artificial" and "packaged" but dull in our hearts toward Him. And He doesn't want us to live "brittle and dry" as though we've been cut off from Him as our source of life. That's why we must maintain our connection to Him, continually drawing our nourishment and life from Him. To that end, God commands us to focus on rooting ourselves deeply in Him so we can then be "built up" in Him. This can only happen as we regularly commune with the Lord in the Word and in prayer, allowing Him to refresh us continually with the waters of His Spirit that we need to stay alive and vibrant.

So in the midst of the busy Christmas season, don't forget the most important thing of all — taking time to stop and honestly evaluate your walk with the Lord. Ask yourself today: *What steps am I taking to stay connected to my root Source so I can keep receiving a fresh, daily infilling of the Holy Spirit?*

MY PRAYER FOR TODAY

Father, I refuse to be beautiful but lifeless, having a form of godliness but denying the power that only comes through a vital connection with my Life Source, Jesus Christ. Holy Spirit, I ask You to reveal to me how I can let my roots grow down deeper into Him in every way. Please help me remain deeply connected to Jesus by hearing, receiving, loving, and obeying His Word so my roots will grow down deep into Him. And as I become more deeply rooted in Christ, I thank You for helping me flourish and remain vibrant in every season of life.

I pray this in Jesus' name!

MY CONFESSION FOR TODAY

I confess that I put my roots deep into Christ and that His presence fills me with everything I need to be refilled and "reflourished" so I keep growing outward and upward as a Christian. I ask You, Holy Spirit, to assist me in remaining rooted and built up in Jesus Christ. I refuse to allow any event in life to cause me to behave as if I've been cut off from my roots in Christ Jesus. With my root structure based firmly in Him, I will continue to flourish as a growing Christian!

I declare this by faith in Jesus' name!

QUESTIONS FOR YOU TO CONSIDER

1. How are you sending your roots deeper and deeper into Christ? Are you drawing your strength and resources from being rooted in Him?
2. What is the evidence that manifests in your life that you are rooted and grounded in Christ?

3. How can you tell if a believer is no longer drawing his or her life support from being rooted in Christ? What are specific indicators?

DECEMBER 7

Carefully Selecting Gifts To Bless — An Act of Love

...Let each esteem other better than themselves.
— Philippians 2:3

Buying Christmas gifts for people when I was a child was one of my absolute favorite moments of the year. I cherished the privilege of giving, which had been taught to me by my parents. As I have spent time remembering my childhood Christmas experiences, one prominent memory that stands out in my mind is the first year my parents gave me money to spend on other family members for Christmas. That shift changed from what I would *receive* to what I could *give* to others.

With great seriousness, my father gave me $2 and instructed me that it was my budget to purchase gifts for the entire family. Ronda was older, so she got $5 for her Christmas shopping spree. Since the family included Daddy, Mother, Ronda, and Lori, it meant I had about 50 cents for each gift. Of course, it seems like a small amount of money by today's standards, but when I was a boy, that was a substantial amount of money for my parents to give a small boy. Lori was too young to receive a Christmas budget, so it was up to Ronda and me to buy gifts for the family.

To start the process, Ronda and I went to Woolworth's department store and to TG&Y to make Christmas purchases with our "gargantuan" budgets. I wondered what I could buy for each member of the family with the budget that had been given to me. Dad had stressed the value of money, and his words had imparted such a seriousness in me that I held that money like it was holy. Even more, Dad impressed on me the need to purchase something that people needed and that they would appreciate.

So Ronda and I walked those shopping aisles seriously, contemplating what we should purchase with our budgets. I remember that first year, I bought mother a comb and a compact, a fish for dad's aquarium, a small tube of lipstick for Ronda, and a doll brush for Lori. To my little mind, those seemed like real "needs" for each member of the family. And after all those expenditures were purchased, I still had a few cents left over — just enough to put a few cents into a gum machine to get a big, round piece of bubble gum!

I was so proud of the purchases that I had made. I carefully wrapped them to the best of my abilities, and then I placed them under the tree next to my homemade manger scene. I eagerly waited for Christmas morning when the family would unwrap the gifts I had carefully selected for them.

Yet on Christmas morning when we started ripping the wrapping off the boxes with our names written on them, I was *overwhelmed* with the gifts Daddy and Mother had bought for us. That year they bought me a fabulous *robot* that walked when I inserted the antenna into its head. Having gotten an idea of what items cost as I carefully spent my $2, I had a "wake-up" call when I looked at that robot. I realized that Dad and Mom's gifts had really *cost* them something compared to the miniscule gifts Ronda and I had purchased for everyone else. That's when it dawned on me that they had really gone out of their way and sacrificed for us. I knew they had needs, but they had denied themselves to purchase those gifts for us. For the first time, I understood the concept of making a sacrifice for others.

That event impacted my life. Now almost every year when it's time for us to purchase Christmas gifts for people I love, I recall that early realization — and how my parents demonstrated to us that it is better to esteem others over ourselves (*see* Philippians 2:3). My parents denied themselves and sacrificed to purchase those gifts. They understood that although Philippians 2:3 is not a Christmas verse, the principle certainly applies to Christmas as well.

Thinking of *others* before we focus on taking care of our own needs and wants is how we're supposed to live every day of the year. And certainly that is true for the Christmas season!

The word "esteem" is the Greek word *hegeomai*, which means *to count, to consider, to regard,* or *to deem.* The word "other" is *allelous*, and it means *others — those besides yourself.* The word "better" is *huperecho*, a compound of *huper* and *echo*. The word *huper* means *significantly higher*, and the word *echo* means *to hold.* When compounded, the new word means *to deliberately hold someone in a very high regard.* It carries the idea of having a *superior view* of a person — a feeling so fervent that it would definitely affect the way you deal with him or her. You would treat that person with the *greatest care* and the *highest treatment.* In fact, you would treat that individual better than yourself! Since money is a great revealer of the truth, it means even your use of money to benefit that person may reveal how highly you esteem him or her.

Mother needed new clothes; Dad really wanted a fishing boat; we needed new carpet and a new divan; and the list goes on and on. But when it came to Christmas, they showed how highly they loved and esteemed their children by denying themselves the things they needed so they could bless Ronda, Lori, and me.

This Christmas is your opportunity to esteem others better than yourself. Most of what you "think" you need can be delayed. Meanwhile, this holiday is your chance to really show your love to those who are dear to you. So rather than think of yourself this Christmas, put aside your own needs, and focus on the needs and desires of others. Not only will it deal with selfishness in you, but it will also teach those around you the great lesson of making sacrifices for others!

MY PRAYER FOR TODAY

Father, I see now that money is a great revealer of my heart and how I use it to bless others reveals the level of my esteem for them. I thank You for this encouragement. Instead of selfishly spending all my money on my own needs, I will pay attention to my opportunities to demonstrate selflessness for the sake of others. And help me remember that Jesus gave the greatest gift of all when He could have called 12 legions of angels to deliver Himself in the Garden of Gethsemane, but He surrendered to the arresting forces and gave his life so we could receive salvation. How I thank God that Jesus esteemed us better than Himself!

I pray this in Jesus' name!

MY CONFESSION FOR TODAY

I confess that because the love of God rules my thoughts and actions, I deliberately live more focused on other's needs than on my own needs, wants, and desires. The law of sowing and reaping works, and I am fully confident that as I sow into the needs and desires of others before I take care of my own desires, God will be faithful to multiply it back to me and will meet my needs in a far greater way than I could ever imagine!

I declare this by faith in Jesus' name!

QUESTIONS FOR YOU TO CONSIDER

1. Do you have memories of shopping for others on a very limited budget, but it gave you such joy to know that you could give to someone else that you loved so much?
2. Even now, do you find joy in giving to others at Christmastime? What kind of joy does it give you to deny yourself and to spend your money on others instead of spending it on yourself?
3. Christ gave Himself. He was the perfect Gift. But it cost Him everything to redeem us and to esteem us higher than Himself. When you think about the sacrifice Christ made to impart His life to us, how does it impact you?

Rather than think of yourself this Christmas, put aside your own needs, and focus on the needs and desires of others.

DECEMBER 8

Our Annual Trip to Woolworth's Department Store and to TG&Y

"In every thing give thanks: for this is the
will of God in Christ Jesus concerning you."
— 1 Thessalonians 5:18

As I told you yesterday, I didn't have much money to spend on Christmas when I was young, but I was so *thankful* for what my parents gave me to buy presents for other people. My first Christmas allowance for family gifts was $2 — which worked out to 50 cents per person!

When the day came for me and my older sister to do our Christmas shopping, we wandered the aisles of Woolworth's department store and TG&Y to try to find the perfect gifts for our father, mother, and siblings, and we had to fit our purchases into our "gigantic" budgets! I walked through the aisles with pad and pencil in hand so I could add up the amount of items I had placed in my cart, and I was overwhelmed with how much money it took to buy nice gifts!

It made me appreciate the gifts that were given to me, and it taught me to value money. It taught me to seriously think before I put items into the cart and went to the cash register to pay the bill. I learned to think about the amount of money that had been given to me, and how I needed to be thankful and steward it the best that I could.

This lesson has been repeated multiple times in my life, as I am sure it has been repeated in your life too. When presented with choices and a limited budget, you are required to work within the resources you have been given. Unless you have a special gift of faith that enables you to believe for more cash, then you must learn to operate in the amount of cash that has been afforded to you.

God has been amazingly faithful to support Denise and me and our ministry with the finances that we need to reach our part of the world with the Gospel. But we've had moments when we had to say "No, we cannot do this right now. This is too big of a stretch. It would be better for us to operate in the budget that we have and wait until later to take this door of opportunity." We are so thankful for our ministry partners whom God has used to further our work, but we know that it would be incorrect to overburden them when they are already sacrificing an amazing amount. Most projects are not so urgent that they cannot wait — and most of the time, opportunities will still be available later.

I learned this lesson when Ronda and I were walking those store aisles. We saw many things we wanted to buy that were beyond the budget my parents had graciously given to us. In those cases, rather than complain or moan about it, we learned to be *thankful* for what we could do. We picked up many items that we laid right back down, because they did not fit into the budget we had been given!

In First Thessalonians 5:18, the apostle Paul says, "In every thing give thanks: for this is the will of God in Christ Jesus concerning you." Notice it says "in everything"— the Greek words *en panti*, which is an all-inclusive phrase that means *in every circumstance*. This even includes all manner of disappointments, such as not being able to do what we'd like to do or not being able to purchase or attain what we really want. In those moments, we are to be thankful anyway.

The phrase "give thanks" is translated from the present imperative active of the Greek word *eucharisteo*. This is a compound of *eu*, meaning *an inner feeling of being overwhelmed with gratification*, and *charis*, which is the Greek word for *grace*. When compounded and used in this context, the new word is a commandment to have *a graceful, thankful attitude* — and to keep it up! It is just the opposite of complaining, moaning, and grumbling. Paul wrote, "...*This* is the will of God in Christ Jesus concerning you."

Paul left no room for doubt. We are to have gracious and thankful attitudes, regardless of the situation we find ourselves in. Perhaps we wish for more, but the truth is, we don't have more at present, and groaning won't change it. So *being thankful* for what we do have is God's commandment to us! And when we have a thankful attitude, we put ourselves in a position where God can continue to open new doors and bring us into higher levels of blessing!

So today I want to ask you:

- Does gracefulness and gratitude rule your life?
- Are you thankful for what you have, or do you find yourself often complaining in different situations of life?
- Even when it seems that what you have is short of what you need, are you able to maintain a thankful attitude for what God *has* provided for you?

These are important questions to ask yourself, so I urge you to let these questions sink deep into your heart and mind today. Let the Holy Spirit speak to you about your own level of contentment and of thankfulness for what you have right now.

This is a lesson I learned early in life, and I am so glad my parents and the Holy Spirit taught it to me. It's such a blessing to live life this way — being truly thankful for whatever I have and for whatever I am able to do, even as I continue to believe God for the fullness of provision that He desires for me!

MY PRAYER FOR TODAY

Father, I confess that I have moments when I am tempted to moan and complain that I don't have more than I currently have to spend on myself and on others. Especially during this Christmas season, I am facing the frustration of wishing I could do more than I can do. I repent for the times when I've yielded to emotions stemming from ingratitude. I ask You to help me always be grateful for what I have rather than to focus on what I don't have. Let me never forget the gifts I can give — such as lovingkindness, thoughtfulness, and investments of time and attention. These are gifts that are not held in our hands, but they leave the lingering fragrance of Your goodness long after this season is past.

I pray this in Jesus' name!

MY CONFESSION FOR TODAY

I confess that I am a grateful and thankful person. In moments when ingratitude and an unthankful attitude try to rule me, I reject it and deliberately adopt the posture of a grateful heart. Not only am I blessed and thankful for what I can give to others, but I am also thankful for what I receive. Everything is an act of grace; therefore, I choose to have a grateful attitude for anything I am able to give or receive!

I declare this by faith in Jesus' name!

QUESTIONS FOR YOU TO CONSIDER

1. If God were to conduct a review of your life, would He say that you have a thankful attitude in most situations? What kind of a score would He give you for maintaining a grateful heart?
2. Have you had times when you wanted to do something, but lacked the resources to do it? What did you do in that situation? Did you lay it aside, or did you avoid your conscience and charge it to credit, which later became a struggle for you?
3. If you had waited for that item you charged, would it have still been available later? Is it possible that God wanted to give it to you with no credit charge? Think it over, and be honest with yourself, because God already knows the truth.

DECEMBER 9

Divorce and Holidays

...He hath sent me to heal the brokenhearted....
— Luke 4:18

Although Christmastime was a joyous time for our family, Christmas Day itself reminded me about the pain of broken families. My grandfather had been married four times; two of my grandmothers had been married twice; a great-grandmother had been married five times; an uncle had been married three times; and the list seemed to go on and on. I had six grandmothers and three grandfathers — some natural, others added by divorce and remarriage.

I always felt this brokenness at Christmastime because Dad and Mom faithfully took us to visit every single faction of our multiple family branches. We'd spend a little time with one set of grandparents, then the next, then go on to the next, and then we'd start on visiting our various grandmothers. In a certain way, Christmas Day felt a bit like geriatric ministry as we spent most of the afternoon trying to see and honor all the old people in our family who had been married various times.

Those Christmas afternoon "tours" each year were difficult for our family in that they brought up painful memories for those old enough to remember. This particular childhood memory of Christmastime always makes me pray for people who are from broken homes and are confronted with this brokenness during the holidays. It's just a fact that holidays are not always easy to celebrate for people who have fragmented families.

However, I have a scripture I want to share with you — one that I believe will encourage you during this holiday season if you are confronted by painful memories or brokenness. In Luke 4:18, Jesus said, "The Spirit of the Lord is upon me, because he hath anointed me to preach the gospel to the poor; he hath sent me to heal the brokenhearted…."

I want to particularly look at the word "brokenhearted" in this verse. It is from the Greek word *tethrasamenous*, the perfect passive participle of *thrauo,* and it depicts *a person who has been shattered or fractured by life*. It is the picture of those whose lives have been continually split up and fragmented. It well describes the situation that I saw in my family when I was growing up. If you are from a divided family, this word could describe you and the shattered emotions you may deal with as an aftermath of the broken relationships you've experienced.

But Jesus said that He came to "heal" the brokenhearted! The word "heal" is the Greek word *aphiesi*, which means to *set free* or *to loosen* from the detrimental effects of a shattered life. In the *King James Version*, it is translated to "heal," but the Greek speaks of a *release* from the destructive effects of brokenness. In other words, although there is every reason to experience and feel brokenness, the anointing that is on Jesus is more than enough to release you from its adverse effects. Even though you were once broken by life, the anointing of the Holy Spirit has the power to *restore* and *release* you from this captivity that has held you in emotional bondage.

I can say that although our family was filled with the brokenness of failed relationships, God's powerful presence was enough to restore those failed covenants. There was no hate that I can remember, and people who were once at odds with each other were congenial toward each other as we fellowshipped during the holiday season. It was a true miracle of God's grace. It didn't fix the relationships and put them back in their original order, but the grace of God made them peaceable.

If you have been through the experience of failed relationships and broken families, I want to tell you that the anointing of Jesus is sufficient to release you from the pain of that experience. It may not happen overnight, but with the grace of God working in you — and you cooperating with His grace — He can restore what the enemy meant for destruction. Today I encourage you to throw open your arms and receive the grace of God that empowers and restores. It's yours for the taking — and if you are in a difficult family relationship, you need it!

MY PRAYER FOR TODAY

Father, my family grapples with the aftereffects of different situations that have caused fracturing of relationships. I have felt pain and cried many tears over the brokenness in my family. Yet I can also see Your faithfulness to me and to each one of us through the years. No matter who may fail, forsake, or disappoint us, You have always kept Your Word to intervene and lift us up. Today as I read about the anointing of Jesus that comes to release us from feelings of hurt and brokenness, I am greatly encouraged. I throw open my arms to receive His healing and delivering power! Although things can never be as they once were — or perhaps never were but should have been — I ask that the peace of God and the anointing of God release me and my family members from the pain that has hurt each one of us so badly in different ways as a result of these failed relationships.

I pray this in Jesus' name!

MY CONFESSION FOR TODAY

I confess that I am not an emotional slave to the dysfunctional ordeals my family has been through over the years. Although there may have been times when I felt trapped by the pain of hurt and misunderstanding, the anointing of God has set me free and I am now liberated from these past wounds and inner hurts. I am not shattered, fractured, or inwardly torn to pieces. Regardless of what the enemy tried to do, I am whole, free, and full of love for every member of my family!

I declare this by faith in Jesus' name!

QUESTIONS FOR YOU TO CONSIDER

1. Do you find yourself in a fractured family situation? How has this affected your holiday season each year?
2. Have you experienced the healing power of Jesus' love as it invades those broken places within you and your loved ones to set you free? Can you recall a time when the Lord has ministered His love to you in a special way during the Christmas season?
3. Has God placed love and restoration in your heart for those broken relationships within your family? Are you ready and willing to allow the love of God to work through you as you yield to His leadership through all the challenges attached to the holidays?

DECEMBER 10

One Christmas When God's Power Sustained Us in a Very Special Way

Blessed be God…
who comforteth us in all our tribulation, that we may be able
to comfort them which are in any trouble, by the comfort
wherewith we ourselves are comforted of God.
— 2 Corinthians 1:3,4

I was a university freshman when my Grandmother Renner was hospitalized over the Christmas holiday with a heart condition and my wonderful Grandpa Renner — a man who had a strong impact on my life — was home alone for several weeks. Everyone in our family noticed that he had begun to act oddly during those weeks, but we simply attributed it to the medication he was taking for severe arthritis. He seemed to be thinking irrationally a lot, lost in the fog of his imagination while he was home alone and Grandma was in the hospital.

One day while I was home on holiday break, my father called me and said, "Grandpa doesn't answer the phone, and he hasn't been to the hospital to see Grandma today. She's worried about him, and it's not normal that no one has heard from him. Would you please meet me at your grandparents' house so we can make sure that everything is all right?"

Without going into the details, I'll tell you that everything was *not* all right. The house was locked, and since Grandpa was nowhere to be seen, we ventured into his beloved garage to see if he was doing something in there. It was there that we discovered that my grandpa had taken his life. I'll never forget that moment, and the great grief that overwhelmed my father. However, in that moment, the Holy Spirit filled me with a tangible sense of His power so I could be a supernatural support to my father in that moment of intense grief and shock.

Dad stayed with Grandpa's body and asked me to call our pastor. Within minutes, our pastor rang the doorbell to announce his arrival. Not long after that, medical workers arrived in an ambulance to examine my grandpa's body and transport him to the morgue. As if that day had not already been difficult enough, Dad and I then had to go to the hospital to break the sorrowful news to Grandma. When we told her, she and Dad simply held each other and cried — a sight I shall never forget as long as I live.

That next year, we all dreaded Christmas *because* we knew that it would remind us of the previous year's tragedy, and we knew that we would feel the absence of Grandpa and potentially live through the pain of those emotions all over again.

However, God was with us in a mighty and faithful way that Christmas season. His grace was simply upon us — comforting us and helping us move forward with no great, crushing grief. It was truly miraculous to see how God worked to help us through what could have been a very difficult time.

When I think of that heart-wrenching moment, my thoughts go to Second Corinthians 1:3 and 4, where Paul wrote, "Blessed be God, even the Father of our Lord Jesus Christ, the Father of mercies, and the God of all comfort; Who comforteth us in all our tribulation, that we may be able to comfort them which are in any trouble, by the comfort wherewith we ourselves are comforted of God."

In verse 3, Paul called God the Father of "mercies." This is the Greek word *oiktirmos*, which describes *compassion*, *lament*, or *sorrow*. It tells us that God completely understands and identifies with the suffering soul. The word "comfort" is *paraklesis*, which describes the *encouragement*, *consolation*, and *comfort* that one provides to another who is undergoing bereavement, hardship, or suffering. It is encouragement in a time of desperate need. When these words are used together, they tell us that God Himself comes to the assistance of those who are suffering difficulty, whether physical or emotional.

In verse 4, Paul continued, "Who comforteth us in all our tribulation, that we may be able to comfort them which are in any trouble, by the comfort wherewith we ourselves are comforted of God."

The word "tribulation" in Greek is *thlipsis*, and it depicts *a crushing pressure* — far beyond what the normal human being could undergo or survive. It tells us that when Paul wrote these words, he was suffering immensely. But God "comforted" him — that is, God stood by Paul and gave him the strength he needed to go through the trial successfully. As a result, Paul was able to "...comfort them which are in any trouble."

Perhaps there is nothing more powerful than a personal testimony, and Paul could testify that God had sustained him through a crushing period of his life. He had been "comforted by God" — *God stepped forward to personally sustain and encourage Paul and assure him that he would make it through the end of his trial.*

This is precisely what my family experienced when Grandpa Renner took his life. At the time, it felt crushing, debilitating, and so very painful. However, God stepped forward to personally strengthen us through that crushing ordeal. As a result, we are able to tell others that, regardless of what they might face or have to deal with in life, God will be with them and will sustain them to the end! *He is the God of all comfort, and He is faithful to help us through each and every trial!*

MY PRAYER FOR TODAY

God, I thank You that Your presence is constantly available when I go through hardship and trials. When it seems that emotions will overwhelm me, You are there — sustaining me and giving me the power I need to overcome each hardship. Just as you sustained the apostle Paul, you will sustain me — regardless of what I am facing in my life. You will step forward as my personal Helper to strengthen and assist me in my time of need. I am so thankful for this, and I praise You for it today!

I pray this in Jesus' name!

MY CONFESSION FOR TODAY

I confess that I am more than a conqueror through Jesus Christ! On my own, I would suffer endless loss, but because Jesus lives BIG inside me, I have the power to overcome every single obstacle that I face in life. There may be some events that I thought I would never face, but God's power has stood at my side and has strengthened me to make it to victory. God has ordained victory for my future. I latch hold of it and refuse to let go until I've experienced the total victory that Jesus Christ has planned for my life!

I declare this by faith in Jesus' name!

QUESTIONS FOR YOU TO CONSIDER

1. We all confront difficult situations in life. However, the power of God is present to sustain us and carry us to victory. Can you think of a moment that would have been devastating, but God's power carried you to victory?
2. Can you think of a time when you know that you would have crumbled if the Lord had not stood by and sustained you? What was that situation? How did the Lord help you? What did you learn about His goodness in the midst of it all?
3. If you know someone who is going through a crushing experience right now, what would you encourage them to do? How would you exhort them to open up to the empowering presence of God to carry them through to victory?

DECEMBER 11

Shaking the Gifts!

For ye have need of patience….
— Hebrews 10:36

Oh, how I looked forward to Christmas morning as a young boy, when we would finally be able to open all the gifts under the Christmas tree! Day by day, Daddy and Mother would gradually add gifts, and the pile of presents would grow higher and higher. I'd always wonder, *Did they get me what I really wanted? What is inside those beautifully wrapped boxes?*

As the Christmas gifts begin to stack up around the base of the Christmas tree, I'd feel a strong temptation to vigorously shake the boxes up and down to try to figure out what was inside. I remember Daddy telling me to stop and to put them back in their places under the tree. That urge to shake the gifts and "guess" their contents was too great a temptation to resist! In fact, all three of us siblings — Ronda, Lori, and I — got in trouble multiple times each year for giving in to that temptation! It would only be a short time before we'd be allowed to open those gifts, but the desire to figure out what was inside them was almost too much for us to control. Maybe you can relate to this as you remember back to *your* childhood!

One year, Ronda even coaxed me to get up after everyone was asleep and join her in secretly unwrapping all the gifts to find out what they were. Once we examined all the presents, we carefully rewrapped each gift so we wouldn't get caught and get in trouble. To our misfortune, we weren't that good at rewrapping, so Daddy and Mother figured out what we had done — and we got in trouble anyway! Even worse, it took all the fun out of Christmas morning because we already knew what was in every gift box. And the saddest part was that it really took the joy out of the event for our parents, who were so disappointed that they missed the thrill of seeing us surprised as we discovered what was in each wrapped gift.

Patience is something that everyone struggles with in life. Whether it's a child who wants a gift immediately, a teenager who wants a car, a wife who wants a new dress, or a husband who wants a new car or fishing boat — in some respect, everyone has to learn the lesson of patience.

In Hebrews 10:36, the Bible says, "For ye have need of patience, that, after ye have done the will of God, ye might receive the promise." We know that the Bible is full of promises that are part of our inheritance in Christ. Every one of those promises is a "gift" to unwrap. But if you've walked any length of time with the Lord, you know that there is sometimes a period of waiting between the "believing" that a particular gift from Heaven is yours and the "unwrapping" of that gift!

Perhaps there is a particular promise that you have released your faith to receive, and it seems that the manifestation of that promise keeps being delayed again and again. Maybe that promise even involves God's good plan for your life and the fulfillment of the very reason He put you on this earth. To you, the Bible says, "For ye have need of *patience*...."

The word "patience" is the Greek word *hupomeno*, a compound of *hupo* and *meno*. The word *hupo* means *to firmly stand by a thing*, and the word *meno* means *to resolutely stay in one spot with no intention to move for any reason*. When compounded, they form the word *hupomeno*, which is the *resolute decision* that you *will* receive what you desire and that you will not be moved by any situation until you receive it. It is to be *immovable* until the thing prayed for is manifested.

Inherent in this word *hupomeno* is the implication that situations will arise in life that will try to move you off your targeted goal. But with *hupomeno* working inside you, you have the ability to outlast *any* competition or obstacle and stay on course until you've fully done the will of God — and at long last, you receive the coveted prize of your faith.

Spiritually speaking, if you've asked the Father for a specific thing that He has already promised you in His Word, there is no need for you to go about "shaking boxes" to see if He has given you what you've released your faith to receive. In fact, "shaking the gift" to figure out what is in it should alert you that you're still not fully in faith about your request!

You have to find what God has said about the matter in His Word and get it settled in your heart. That promise is sitting "wrapped under the tree," and it already has your name on it!

So whenever you're feeling impatient about God's timing, don't start trying to figure out in your mind what's in the box before He's ready for you to open it. Trust the Lord that He has His best in store for you. If you've asked in faith, God will do what you've asked Him to do in Jesus' name. The timing may be a little different than what you anticipated, but you can rest assured that God *will* come through for you — because *He is faithful* and He *cannot* lie (*see* Titus 1:2).

Your part is to obey God, believe His Word, let *hupomeno* work inside you, and enter into the *rest* of faith (*see* Hebrews 4:3). As you do, *it will only be a matter of time* until you receive exactly what the Father has desired to give you all along. *That* is the promise of Hebrews 10:36!

MY PRAYER FOR TODAY

Father, I repent for my impatience as I wait for the fulfillment of what I've asked You to do for me. In a certain sense, I've been "shaking the gifts" and not trusting that You would do what You said You would do. Waiting a little longer won't hurt me. In fact, it will help me develop my character and learn patience. For this, I say thank You. And for my impatience, I ask You to forgive me and to help me keep growing in this aspect of my life.

I pray this in Jesus' name!

MY CONFESSION FOR TODAY

I confess that patience is a strong force in my life. As I walk with Christ and learn to trust in Him ever more dearly, the attribute of patience is growing stronger and stronger in me. I don't have to mistrust the Lord or check Him out to see if He is really doing what I asked. If I have asked for something in faith, it's only a matter of time until what I've prayed for comes to pass!

I declare this by faith in Jesus' name!

QUESTIONS FOR YOU TO CONSIDER

1. Spiritually speaking, did you ever "shake the boxes" to see if God had done what He has promised to do for you? Is it possible that you haven't fully trusted Him and have tried to figure out what He is doing in your own natural reasoning?
2. How are you doing in the "patience realm" of your life? Do your actions reveal a need for growth in this area?
3. Think about how much pleasure it gives God when you ask Him to do something and then simply trust Him to do it. Are you giving God this pleasure, or are you disappointing Him by continually checking to see if He is going to be faithful?

DECEMBER 12

The Year I Threw My Gift Back at My Grandparents and Told Them To Keep It!

For the wrath of man worketh
not the righteousness of God.
— James 1:20

I remember well a particular Christmas memory that isn't very pleasant. I was about five years old, and I threw a horrible fit of anger because I was so upset with the gift that my Grandfather Miller and Grandma Jo gave me.

As I said in the December 9 *Gem*, our family had many divorced relatives. In order not to show favoritism to any one side of the family, my parents tried to visit every single part of the family each Christmas afternoon. It made for a busy afternoon driving from house to house — and one house we stopped at was my Grandfather Miller's and his fourth wife, whom we called Grandma Jo.

To be honest, none of us Renner kids liked Grandma Jo very much. She seemed old, wrinkled, and cranky — and when we were in their home, we had to sit on the couch like little statues, and we even got rebuked if we touched the coffee table in the middle of the room. Oh, how I loathed going to their home because we couldn't move an inch the whole time we were there! However, Grandfather Miller was our real grandfather, and although Jo wasn't my mother's real mother, she was married to him. So we were bound to visit her whenever we saw our grandfather.

As I noted previously, one year when I was about five years old, I had sat still on the couch for so long that I just about couldn't take it any longer. My patience was running out, and Grandma Jo was about to get the best of me. The only thing that kept me together was the thought that if we paid the painful price of motionless silence a little longer, eventually my sisters, Ronda and Lori, and I would receive Christmas gifts!

Finally, the moment came when Grandfather and Grandma Jo presented their gifts to us. I was so excited to see what kind of toy I would receive as a "reward" for enduring Jo's impatience with us. But when I opened the package, it was a *shirt*! After sitting immobile on that couch for what seemed like *forever*, waiting and waiting to see what kind of toy I was going to receive, they gave me a *shirt*! I got so mad that, as my mother tells it, I threw the shirt at my grandparents and angrily told them to keep it. Of course, my parents were very embarrassed, and I received a strong correction that I *still* remember to this day!

This story brings to mind James 1:20, which says, "For the wrath of man worketh not the righteousness of God." The word "wrath" is precisely what I expressed that Christmas afternoon when I threw that shirt back in the faces of my grandparents. It is the Greek word *orges*, and it depicts an *angry impulse* that grows out of proportion and is most often directed toward a person or persons. It is an explosive outbreak of anger — an outrageous, hostile display that usually results in someone's feelings getting hurt. It is the picture of a person losing control of his emotions. This loss of control may be accompanied with ranting and raving or violent actions — just like when I threw the shirt back at my grandparents and rudely yelled, "Just keep it!"

James says that this type of behavior "worketh not" the righteousness of God." The word "worketh" is *ergadzomai*, which means this type of wrathful behavior does not *produce* the righteous type of behavior God desires — which in my case would have sounded something like this: "It's a beautiful shirt. Thank you so much." But the whole day had been a difficult one for this young boy. Sitting motionless on the divan for hours, anticipating a toy as recompense for enduring the moment and then opening the box and seeing only a shirt — I just let my emotions go and exploded.

Before we left the house that day, I was taken into a bedroom, corrected for my behavior, and told to apologize and thank my grandparents for the beautiful shirt. It was difficult for me to do at the time, but I obeyed my parents. By the way, the next Christmas they gave me a marvelous toy that I kept for years and may even still have in storage!

I tell this story because we all are tempted to express displeasure when we are deeply disappointed, but violent explosions don't produce the godly behavior God desires of us. Whenever we are feeling upset or disappointed and are tempted to just "let loose" and explode, we should find a place to retreat and be alone with God so we can process those negative emotions in His presence. He is always ready and available to stabilize us and help us bring our emotions back under control.

So I encourage you to make a conscious decision today to yield to the working of God's Spirit in your life on a daily basis. As you do, you'll find that your self-control grows as you draw more and more on *His* strength within you. And the next situation you encounter where your emotions are tested, you'll find it easier to hold yourself steady on the inside and to respond in a way that brings pleasure and glory to Jesus!

MY PRAYER FOR TODAY

Dear Father, I confess that I've had moments when I've exploded, lost my temper, and said things that I later regretted. I ask You to forgive me — and I ask You to help me learn how to submit my emotions to the control of the Holy Spirit. Whether it's me, my family members, or my friends who are acting in ugly ways, help me realize that such behavior is irrational. Thank You for Your grace to help us upgrade our emotional responses to the various situations in life we encounter each day.

I pray this in Jesus' name!

MY CONFESSION FOR TODAY

I confess that my emotions and reactions are controlled by the Holy Spirit. When my flesh tries to act up, the Spirit of God inside me helps me regain control and bring my flesh into subjection to the Word of God and the behavior of Christ. My mind, my emotions, my reactions, my mouth — they are all tools to be used by the Holy Spirit, and I will NOT use them in explosive ways that could damage and hurt the people whom I love and respect.

I declare this by faith in Jesus' name!

QUESTIONS FOR YOU TO CONSIDER

1. Have you ever been disappointed by something you received, because you were expecting something different? How did you respond?
2. In moments when you've shown "wrath" because of a disappointment, were you later embarrassed and sorry that you acted so badly in that moment?
3. If you have listened to the Holy Spirit, I am sure that He has tried to calm you down so you wouldn't react in wrath and anger on different occasions. Can you name a time when you listened to Him instead of getting angry, and you were thankful that you avoided an ugly scene?

DECEMBER 13

Finding Time To Uplift and Encourage With Christmas Carols

Speaking to yourselves in psalms and hymns
and spiritual songs, singing and making melody
in your heart to the Lord.
— Ephesians 5:19

Somehow in the midst of the busy holiday schedule, the youth group I attended as a teenager managed to find time to sing Christmas carols in our church's local neighborhood. We'd bundle up to stay warm, and then we would walk from house to house to sing to people who stood on their porches to listen.

I'm not sure it's still customary as it once was many years ago for people to walk from house to house to sing Christmas carols, but it remains a precious memory in my life from my younger years. We'd sing with all our hearts, trying to bring joy to people during the Christmas season. And of course, we saw it as a method of evangelism because we were singing songs about the birth of Jesus Christ. Afterward we'd invite people to come to church for the Christmas service.

Several years ago, Denise's mother was living in an assisted-living complex and drawing near the end of her life. It was the Christmas season, and she was feeling very lonely. One night an entire family knocked on her door and asked if they could come into her little living room to sing Christmas carols to her. Her eyes lit up, she sat upright in her recliner, and joyfully welcomed them in. As the carolers sang, she joined in with them, singing with all the might she could muster. When the carolers finished, they hugged and prayed for her. Denise's mother talked about that event for several weeks afterward because it had brought such intense joy into her solitary life.

Paul talks about the importance of songs and hymns in Ephesians 5:19, and although it is not specifically a Christmas verse, it certainly could apply to the Christmas holidays. It reads, "Speaking to yourselves in psalms and hymns and spiritual songs, singing and making melody in your heart to the Lord." The word "psalms" is the Greek word *psalmos*, and it refers *to singing songs of praise*. It depicts singing psalms with a stringed instrument, such as a guitar or something similar. The word "hymns" is *humnos*, and it refers to *sacred compositions* whose primary goal is to give glory and honor to God.

There's just something about singing songs that glorify the Lord that releases joy and takes people to a higher level. Those who are depressed or lonely are uplifted when they hear and sing these kinds of songs.

So today I want to make a holiday suggestion to you: Why not put together a Christmas carol group this year and revive this old-time tradition? You need not walk from home to home. You could choose specific homes where difficulty and sadness prevailed for a time. Just knock on the door or ring the doorbell, and when those who live there answer the door, pour out your heart as you sing about Jesus to them. It may be just what they need to lift them up from the sadness and depression they are feeling. And you might even ask them to join you as you make your way to the next house!

What an easy and thoughtful way to make a big difference in someone's life this Christmas season!

MY PRAYER FOR TODAY

Father, I appreciate what I've read today about ministering in music and Christmas carols at this time of the year. Help me not to focus on my own needs and problems but to take a day or two to focus on people who are living lonely and solitary. If possible, help me gather a group of people who will join with me to creatively bring the praise and glory of God to people who need a lift!

I pray this in Jesus' name!

MY CONFESSION FOR TODAY

I confess that I have a voice to glorify the Lord and that this holiday season, I am going to use it to bring emotional encouragement and spiritual exhortation to people who need a lift from the cares of life. I may not be the best singer, but I can sing with others. I choose to obey Ephesians 5:19 and speak and sing to one another in psalms, hymns, and spiritual songs this Christmas season. God will join me with a group of praisers with like-minded hearts, and together we'll become a "musical troupe" to bring joy to people who need encouragement!

I declare this by faith in Jesus' name!

QUESTIONS FOR YOU TO CONSIDER

1. How long has it been since you went Christmas caroling? What did it do for your own soul to know that you went out of the way to be a blessing to someone in this way?
2. How long has it been since someone came to your door to sing Christmas carols to you or to your family? How would it affect you?
3. Who do you know that is lonely, depressed, feeling solitary, and could use some special encouragement at this time of the year? Why not put together a group of carolers, wrap up and stay warm, and go have fun singing carols to that person?

DECEMBER 14

The Sears Christmas Catalog

Now the works of the flesh are.... lasciviousness....
— Galatians 5:19

Several months before the Christmas season began, my Grandpa and Grandma Renner would receive a Sears Christmas catalog in the mail. When that catalog arrived, we three Renner kids could hardly wait to see what Sears was offering for Christmas. The experience was made even more enticing when my parents took us to the Sears department store, and we'd walk floor to floor to personally inspect the products to see if they were as wonderful as they appeared in the catalog.

Ronda, Lori, and I would pore over the pages of that catalog. It was huge — filled with clothes, camping gear, and gifts of all sorts. Of course, since we were kids, we were especially drawn to the multiple pages filled with images of wonderful toys. I knew I couldn't have them all, but I'd dream about getting certain toys for my Christmas gifts. In fact, that is where I found my robot that walked when the antenna was placed into its head. Oh, at Christmastime, there was just nothing as exciting as a Sears Christmas catalog! (Maybe you're of the generation that can relate to that memory!)

When we went to the store to peruse the products, Ronda looked at clothes; I looked at toys; Lori looked at dolls; Mother looked at washing machines; and Dad looked at tools. Each of us were attracted to different things.

I would have to say that one word summed it up for us — *greed*. Even though I knew it wasn't possible, I wanted the BB gun, the Indian Fort with all of its little plastic Indians and cowboys, and the 2-foot-high rocket; Lori wanted the Barbie dollhouse and all of the accessories that went with it; and Ronda wanted a whole new wardrobe of clothes every year. We vigorously flipped through those catalog pages, looking at this thing, that thing, and this other thing — and *greed* just about ate us up! What was worse, we knew we couldn't have it all! So we struggled with a dilemma each Christmas season: How did we choose what we wanted out of all the marvelous things that were offered on those pages?

Even at our young age, *greed* was already working in us — a characteristic the Bible calls a "work of the flesh." Galatians 5:19 says, "Now the works of the flesh are…[among others] lasciviousness…."

As Paul listed the works of the flesh in the book of Galatians, he mentioned "lasciviousness." This strange word comes from the Greek word *aselgeia*. This Greek word describes *excess*, but it primarily refers to the *excessive consumption of food* or *wild, undisciplined living*. In fact, it refers to the wild, undisciplined desire for anything — and that's why it is often translated as the word *greed*. It's the desire for *more and more — never satisfied*.

Although the three of us were young, that work of the flesh had already reared its ugly head. Daddy and Mother had to reel us in and teach us to be more disciplined in our thinking. They taught us to be more selective about what we wanted, because they were not rich enough to buy everything we thought should go on our lists!

As a young boy, I started the process of learning to repent for being materialistic. All of the works of the flesh can be forgiven — but before forgiveness comes, sin must be acknowledged. My parents helped me understand that having everything one wants is not a reality of life and is not even good for us. I came to recognize the desire to have more and more of whatever I wanted as sin — so I repented and confessed, and I was cleansed. And I learned one more important point: When greed is removed, *thankfulness* for anything you receive takes over!

If you have fallen into any aspect of this work of the flesh, ask the Holy Spirit to open your eyes to see this sin as He sees it. Once you get a revelation of *His* perspective, you won't want to be the same! You'll understand the grossness of sin in God's sight, and you will want to be changed!

Just confess your sin, and God will forgive you so you can move on with your life *free* (*see* 1 John 1:9). Pray for God's mighty grace to be upon you to forgive you. Dear friend, God is with you, and He wants to change your life. Open your heart, and let the Holy Spirit be your Helper. He wants to help you live continually cleansed, set free, and morally strong and stable. *With His help, you can do it!*

There was nothing wrong with dreaming about what we saw in the Sears Christmas Catalog — and there is nothing wrong with our dreaming about upgrading every part of our lives. But when desire becomes *greed,* it is sin, and we must ask forgiveness for it. God is always standing by as our personal Helper to guide us through this very important process!

MY PRAYER FOR TODAY

Father, I ask You to forgive me for wanting everything all at one time. I didn't realize this was greed trying to get a foothold in my life. Help me know how to dream without falling headlong into greed at the same time. As I set my sights toward things on the earth, help me to recognize which desires are pure and inspired by You and which are just my own carnal lusts or worldly desires. I truly want to please You, Lord, so I ask You to help me conform my thoughts to Your will.

I pray this in Jesus' name!

MY CONFESSION FOR TODAY

I confess that I am moderate in the way I live and in the things I desire to obtain. I refuse to allow greediness to rule me. I live by the law of the Spirit of life in Christ Jesus that works mightily in me. His love in me enables me to focus on what others need more than what I want for myself. I am thankful for this work of Christ that helps me to esteem others more highly than myself.

I declare this by faith in Jesus' name!

QUESTIONS FOR YOU TO CONSIDER

1. Can you think of a time when greed consumed your life — and you could think of nothing more than what additional worldly possessions you could add to your life?
2. What broke the power of greediness in your life? What instigated the big change?
3. If you were advising someone today who is consumed with worldly possessions, what advice would you give them to walk free from this dominating control?

There is nothing wrong with our dreaming about upgrading every part of our lives. But when desire becomes greed, it is sin, and we must ask forgiveness for it.

DECEMBER 15

Christmas Lunch

And let us consider one another to provoke
unto love and good works.
— Hebrews 10:24

Different families have different traditions regarding how they spend Christmas Day. As for my family, once all the gifts were opened and things were cleaned up around our own house, we always headed next to Grandpa and Grandma Renner's house, where another Christmas tree with gifts awaited us. Grandma Renner had one of those cameras with huge flashbulbs, and after each photo, we all had to wait while she replaced four burned-out bulbs with fresh ones. She had to repeat that process every time a photo was taken.

After gifts were opened, we all knew it was just a short time before we'd sit down to have Christmas lunch. There we all were — Daddy, Mother, Ronda, Lori, myself, Grandpa, Grandma, and Grandmother Faulkner (my great-grandmother and mother of Grandmother Renner, a woman who had been married five times). I can even tell you the seating arrangement at the table, because it never changed from year to year. I was always seated next to Grandmother Faulkner, who had milky-like cataracts that slipped around both of her eyes and were rather horrid to look at.

The talk at the table could go from positive to negative in a very short period of time. My father was the moderator, and if things swung in a negative direction, he would say "Enough of that!"

The food was amazing. We had turkey, ham, baked green beans in bacon sauce, corn on the cob, sweet potatoes, regular potatoes and gravy, biscuits — and all of that was just starters — to be followed by an array of desserts that covered one end of the table to the other end. The Christmas lunch would literally last for hours. It was a tradition that became very important in the Renner household. All of it was prepared by multiple hands — and before we ate it, we always joined hands and thanked God for another wonderful year.

When I think of those Christmas meals, my mind always goes to Hebrews 10:24, which says, "And let us consider one another to provoke unto love and good works." The word "consider" is the Greek word *katanoeo*, a compound of *kata* and *neoeo*. The word *kata* means *down*, and *neoeo* means to *think*. When compounded, they form a new word that means *to deeply reflect*, *to consider*, or *to think deeply about*. The word "provoke" is the Greek word *paroxusmos*, which negatively means to *irritate*, but positively means to *stimulate*. In this case, it is used in a positive sense to *stimulate* each other unto love and good works. When all of these words are used together, it is the image of a person or a group of people who are actively pondering how to stimulate each other to love and do good works.

That's what happened at our Christmas dinner each year. With Dad as the moderator, he grabbed hold of any conversation that swung in a negative direction and swung it back in a positive direction. This demonstrated to me the power that one person can have in making sure a conversation is positive and Christ-filled. My dad taught that to me through example, because without his input, the conversation would have swung in a very negative, nasty direction. But he would not allow it. He purposely kept the conversation on track, and he made sure that kind things were said about every person who was mentioned at that Christmas meal. Dad encouraged me to always say kind things about others — even when I had opportunity to say something nasty or uncomplimentary. He simply wouldn't allow it.

As you get ready for your own Christmas dinner with your family this year, make the decision that you'll make kind remarks about every person who is mentioned. Christmas isn't a time for gossip or unkind remarks. It's a time to express thankfulness for all that God has done through various individuals. And if you can't easily think of something good to say about someone, maybe the best route is just to keep your mouth shut. Sometimes that's the greatest wisdom of all!

MY PRAYER FOR TODAY

Father, this year when we gather around the Christmas table, I ask You to set a watch over my lips and a guard over my mouth. I make the decision now that my words will glorify You and bless and edify others. If the conversation turns negative and those around me begin to talk about various individuals, help me to be bold and courageous enough to lovingly say, "Enough of that" — and then shift the conversation toward the positive. I refuse to be negative and give way to sarcasm. The carnal mind enjoys that, and so does the devil because it gives him an opportunity to interject his lies. But I thank You, Holy Spirit, that You are my Counselor, and with Your help, my heart deeply ponders and guides what my mouth speaks before I ever say a word.

I pray this in Jesus' name!

MY CONFESSION FOR TODAY

I confess that I am a source that provokes others to love and to good works! My mouth is a life-spring of good works that encourages others to do what God would have them to do. I do NOT speak critical words, nor am I a source of negative talk. When my family or friends are together as a group, I see myself as a moderator who keeps the conversation on course. I will influence the group to speak of things that are praiseworthy and of a good report. I am a positive force, and because of me, others are stimulated to love and to good works!

I declare this by faith in Jesus' name!

QUESTIONS FOR YOU TO CONSIDER

1. Can you remember specific negative conversations you've participated in and how they led to nowhere positive? In light of those memories, what are you going to do at this Christmas meal to keep things headed in a positive direction?
2. The fact is that all is not well with everyone we know. However, if we will make the effort, we'll be able to think of something good to say about everyone. Have you given serious contemplation about what you are going to be saying about people this year at your Christmas meal?
3. You may have someone in your family who isn't well liked by other family members. Have you prayed for that person and asked God to help you find something positive to say about him or her as you learn to see that family member through *His* eyes?

DECEMBER 16

Holiday Fellowship

And they...breaking bread from house to house,
did eat their meat with gladness
and singleness of heart.
— Acts 2:46

Another holiday tradition my family followed at Christmastime was to gather at close friends' houses on the Sunday nights leading up to Christmas. For about a month, each week we'd gather at a different house after the Sunday evening church service — and we'd fellowship for hours after the service. People would gather to play board games and other types of games. We also prayed together and sang songs around the piano. These memories formed the foundation of my understanding of the way fellowship should exist in the local church. Those adults and their children were important to me, and I loved them like they were part of my own family.

As a participant in those Sunday night fellowship times, my dad would often buy large sacks of uncooked peanuts, which he would then pour into cake tins and cook in the oven until they were toasted and piping hot. When they were done, he'd pull those baking tins out of the oven and carry them into the main room of the house, where he had spread newspapers over the floor. He'd pour the peanuts out onto the paper, and we would all begin the process of cracking open those warm peanuts. Piles of empty shells would soon fill the newspapers as we gobbled up the peanuts one by one!

On one Sunday night, someone would bring tacos; the next Sunday, someone would bring desserts. Each Sunday night, we waited to see what special treats we'd share from house to house. What a joy it was to meet in various homes each week in that month before Christmas. The truth is, our group of friends did this all year long — but in the month of December, we *really* spent time fellowshipping within our circle of Christian friends.

When I think of it, I am reminded of the Early Church and how they were committed to fellowshipping with each other. Acts 2:46 says, "And they [the believers]… breaking bread from house to house, did eat their meat with gladness and singleness of heart."

Let's look at this verse today and see what we can learn about the Christian fellowship that occurred in the Early Church and what God desires for us today. You're about to discover that Christian fellowship has always been built around food, even in the Early Church!

This verse says that they were "breaking bread from house to house." Don't let the words "breaking bread" mislead you into thinking this was a ritual Communion service. The words "breaking bread" was translated from a Greek phrase used to denote *sharing a wonderful meal and a time of fellowship and relaxation with friends*. It was such a common phrase that even heathens used it when they wanted to experience a time of fellowship with others.

The *King James Version* says these times of fellowship occurred "from house to house," but the Greek simply says in *private houses*. These fellowship events were simply the sharing of food with other friends in Christ — similar to the Sunday night tradition we had among our Christian friends when I was growing up. It is certainly possible that they rotated from house to house, as we did, but the Greek language actually only states that they experienced these times of fellowship in *private houses*.

And what did they do there in those private houses where their fellowship occurred? They "did eat…" (Acts 2:46). What a role food has had in the fellowship of the saints both then and now!

The words "did eat" are from the word *metalambano* — a word that means *to fully partake of*. The grammar used here means there was a lot of eating connected with this rich fellowship! It even tells us *what* they ate! It says they "did eat their meat." Meat, of course, was not a part of an official Communion service, but it *was* a key ingredient in a regular meal! These early believers were eating *meals* in private homes as a key part of their rich fellowship with one another.

And notice it says they "…did eat their meat with gladness and singleness of heart." The phrase "gladness and singleness" of heart is from the Greek word *apheloteti*, which refers to *generosity*. In other words, they left the complications of life outside the door. They enjoyed each other fully once inside those private homes, where generous portions of food and fellowship took place among a house full of believers! *Ah* — this is *exactly* what it was like on the Sunday nights leading up to Christmas when I was a young boy!

As you approach this year's holiday season, why not consider having a houseful of people from your church over for a generous evening of food, fun, and fellowship? These times build relationships and make your union stronger. It doesn't have to be an eight-course meal. Just throw some peanuts in the oven and bake them until they are ready — or have tacos, chili, or something inexpensive and easy to make. The food helps pull everyone together, but in the end, it's really not about the quality of the food. *It's about fellowship!*

From the beginning of the Church Age to the last of these last days, God's people have been getting together to strengthen their relationships, to share the love of Christ, and to enjoy one another in "private houses" — outside of a church setting. If you've never opened your own home for such an event, maybe this is the year for you to step out by faith and invite a small *or large* group of people over for an evening of fellowship. And who knows what the Lord will do among you? It may turn out to be a life-changing event for some in the group. *Is this your year to step out in faith and throw open the door to your home?*

MY PRAYER FOR TODAY

Father, I thank You for the fellowship that exists in the Body of Christ. Because of fellowship, we are made stronger. Fellowship with close friends and family — and the Holy Spirit — makes us stronger and gives us a sound foundation of relationships in the Body of Christ! Help me to use my home to help build stronger relationships in the Christian community to whom I belong!

I pray this in Jesus' name!

MY CONFESSION FOR TODAY

I confess that I am a stronger Christian because of my fellowship with other believers over the years. Their fellowship has strengthened me, encouraged me, and taken me to a higher level in my walk with Christ. When I fellowship with other believers, it becomes an opportunity for iron to sharpen iron as we grow in Him together and allow the love of God to bring out the best in one another. I readily acknowledge that I need Christian fellowship, and I cherish it as a treasured gift in my life.

I declare this by faith in Jesus' name!

QUESTIONS FOR YOU TO CONSIDER

1. Have you considered the effect that Christian fellowship has on making you stronger as a believer?
2. If you've ever lacked Christian fellowship, how did that void affect your life?
3. What can you do to encourage more Christian fellowship in your life and to reinforce your Christian walk? I encourage you to make a list and really think it through.

DECEMBER 17

Grandmother Bagley and Her Special Christmas Offerings

And he said, Of a truth I say unto you,
that this poor widow hath cast in more than they all.
— Luke 21:3

Grandmother Bagley was a very beloved grandmother in our array of six different grandmothers — and she was a true genetic grandmother. She was a very simple woman who had a lot of faith. She had lost several husbands and children due to sickness, and although she was a financially poor woman, she was rich in faith. When I visited her house, she always made the most wonderful lunches. But when I asked for seconds, she was quick to remind me that I needed to be satisfied with what she had fed me because she didn't have enough for seconds.

One thing I'll never forget about Grandmother Bagley was her commitment and devotion to give offerings to Oral Roberts Ministries. I can still visualize her writing the name "ORAL ROBERTS," filling out the address on her envelope, and then inserting a one-dollar-bill into the envelope. She would hold it to her heart, pray over it, and put it out in the mailbox for the postman to collect it. When I saw this happen, I always knew I was beholding a very holy moment in the life of my Grandmother Bagley, for this was a huge sum of money for her to sow into that ministry.

Oh, how I loved Grandmother Bagley! She was kind, precious, and generous to others who were in need. She had suffered so much in life — the loss of her husbands and children — that she had a deep-seated compassion for people who were hurting in some way. However, when I saw her put money into that envelope, I knew she was truly sacrificing and giving what she could give by faith. It affected me deeply.

Every time I think of Grandmother Bagley, my mind goes to Luke 21:1-4, where Jesus said, "And He [Jesus] looked up, and saw the rich men casting their gifts into the treasury. And he saw also a certain poor widow casting in thither two mites. And he said, Of a truth I say unto you, that this poor widow hath cast in more than they all: For all these have of their abundance cast in unto the offerings of God: but she of her penury hath cast in all the living that she had."

It is, first of all, amazing to me that Jesus was standing near enough that He could see what people were giving in their offerings! Suddenly He saw a "certain poor widow." The word "poor" is the Greek word *penichros*, which would depict someone who is *abjectly poor*. Jesus saw her place "two mites" into the offering box. A "mite" is from the Greek word *lepton*, the plural version of *lepta*, affirming that she placed *two mites* into the offering. It was the smallest, least valuable bronze coin in the currency of that day.

Yet in verse 3, Jesus was so impressed with the enormity of this widow's faith and the size of her gift compared to what she financially had to give that He stopped everyone and drew attention to what this woman had done. He described this *very* poor woman, who had barely enough to survive, as one who put into the offering "more than they all." The Greek here is comparative, and it indicates that all of the other wealthy people's accumulated gifts did not equal what this poor widow put into the offering of God.

Then in verse 4, Jesus explained, "For all these [rich people] have of their abundance cast in unto the offerings of God: but she of her penury hath cast in all the living that she had."

Jesus said the rich had given of their "abundance." This is the Greek word *perisseuo*, and it describes *excess*. In other words, it didn't touch their real fortune; it was just a small tip that they put into the treasury. But the poor widow woman gave of her "penury" — the Greek word *husterema*, which refers to *the last bit of money she possessed*. It took no faith for the rich to give of their excess, but it took great faith for this poor widow to cast into the offering box all that she had. She was fully entrusting herself to the care of God in the belief that He would supernaturally meet her ongoing physical needs. Even though the amount the woman gave was smaller, the faith required to give it was larger.

Every year at Christmastime when we receive special offerings for our church in Moscow, I see Grandmother Bagley in my mind's eye. Just like this poor widow woman Jesus described in Luke 21:1-4, my grandmother gave nearly all she had at Christmastime to support the Oral Roberts Evangelistic Association. It was a monumental act of her faith as she placed that special offering into the envelope, licked the seal, pressed it shut, and then held it to her heart in prayer.

When Grandmother Bagley left that envelope for the postman to pick up, she was sowing her best seed into that ministry. And just as Jesus watched the poor widow woman, He was watching my grandmother — as He watches all those who sacrificially give with faith. This is something that really gets Jesus' attention!

I don't know what your financial situation is like this Christmas season, but I urge you to give an offering into the work of God's Kingdom that will cause Jesus to stop and take note. It's not the amount; it's the faith required to give the amount that causes Jesus to stop and pay special attention. *Pray about it, and see what the Holy Spirit would put into your heart to give during this holiday season to help impact people's lives for eternity!*

MY PRAYER FOR TODAY

Father, so often I've given of my excess and never really dipped into an amount that could cost me to use my faith. I am corrected today, and I will change. Today I make a deliberate decision to exercise my faith in a greater way by choosing not to refrain from giving even when my offering is small. Like the widow's mite, my offering will please and honor Jesus because it is a gift from my heart that requires more faith than if it were merely a token from a surplus supply. Without faith it is impossible to please You, Father. And I seek to please You above all else. Holy Spirit, help me to know how much to stretch my faith, how much to give, and where to sow my seed so it will make a difference. I am sincerely asking for and receiving Your wisdom in this matter.

I pray this in Jesus' name!

MY CONFESSION FOR TODAY

I confess that from this moment onward, I will not casually give offerings out of my excess. Rather, I will dip deeper and truly give sacrificially to the Lord. I thought I was doing what was right, but I am convicted by what I have read today. I am going to make a change in my manner of giving. I am going to give on a level that requires more faith on my part. I affirm this day that whether I am giving of my time, my talent, or my finances, faith and love will be evident by the manner in which I give.

I declare this by faith in Jesus' name!

QUESTIONS FOR YOU TO CONSIDER

1. Can you think of someone who gives sacrificial gifts, especially at Christmastime? Who is that person, and how has his or her giving affected you?
2. Can you think of someone who struggles financially but continues to faithfully give his or her tithes and offerings to the Lord?
3. Did you have a friend or family member in your life like my Grandmother Bagley who deeply impacted you with their faithful giving? If so, who was that person? Would you consider taking a moment, if it's still possible, to thank this individual for his or her faithfulness to the work of God?

DECEMBER 18

Reading the Christmas Story

...Continue thou in the things
which thou hast learned and hast been assured of,
knowing of whom thou hast learned them;
and that from a child thou hast known the holy scriptures,
which are able to make thee wise unto salvation
through faith which is in Christ Jesus.
— 2 Timothy 3:14,15

When my sisters and I were young, Dad would take time on Christmas morning to read the Christmas story to our family. He'd sit in his recliner in the corner of the living room near the Christmas tree, and he'd call for us to come near where we could hear. Mother, Ronda, Lori, and I would gather around as Dad opened his *King James Bible* to the familiar Christmas passage in Luke. If we were really attentive and Dad thought he still had our attention, he would take extra time to turn to Matthew's account of the three wise men who came to worship Jesus as a young child. *I especially loved it when he told us the story of the three wise men!*

Although Dad did not continue this family tradition throughout my growing-up years, the years that he did make that a part of our Christmas morning impacted me personally as a young boy. I remember how his voice carried such authority as he read those sections of Scripture to us.

Do you read this story at Christmastime? Or do you and your family members simply dive into gifts and food and let the most important moment of the day slip by? *I encourage you not to miss this great opportunity to put Jesus in the center of your Christmas by reading the story of His birth to your family!*

In Second Timothy 3:14 and 15, Paul told Timothy, "...Continue thou in the things which thou hast learned and hast been assured of, knowing of whom thou hast learned them; and that from a child thou hast known the holy scriptures, which are able to make thee wise unto salvation through faith which is in Christ Jesus."

How I wish my father had continued that family tradition, because the story of Christmas is truly the center of what the holiday is all about. In those moments when Dad read the Word to us on Christmas mornings, he was aflame with the Spirit. Over the years, however, that flame started gradually burning dimmer and dimmer. Dad always faithfully took us to church and taught us to put the Lord first in our lives, but that bright flame I remember burning in his heart when I was a young boy grew to a simmer over a number of years, and eventually he stopped reading the Christmas story to us at Christmastime. Thankfully, later in my father's life, that flame for the things of God began to burn again.

When the apostle Paul wrote to Timothy, he stated that he had heard the Holy Scriptures since childhood — and that they were able to make him "wise" unto salvation. This word "wise" is the Greek word *sophos*, and it denotes *special wisdom* or *special insight*. It clearly means that even a child can have special insight into the Word of God if his parents or parental authority pours it into him at an early stage.

I'm so thankful that my mother consistently taught the Bible to me. In fact, my earliest memories are when mother would lie at my side each night with a big picture Bible and instill those Bible stories into me. As a result of that continual imparting of scriptural truth into my young heart, I began to receive spiritual insight at a very early age. Just as Paul told Timothy, it made me "wise" — the Greek word *sophos* — or especially enlightened. I was so full of insight, in fact, that I was able to walk the aisle and surrender my heart to Jesus at the age of five and truly comprehend what I was doing.

The Word of God is powerful, and if you have younger children or grandchildren, this Christmas I urge you to make the telling of the Christmas story the main theme of your day's celebration. It won't hurt the kids to wait a few more minutes before they dive into the gifts. And telling this story will remind them what this day is all about. As Scripture promises, it will bring *wisdom* and *special insight* to everyone who listens! *Can you think of any better gift to give to your children on Christmas Day?*

MY PRAYER FOR TODAY

Father, this is a simple, yet powerful Sparkling Gem that I've read today. It is something I can implement in my family starting this year. Holy Spirit, give me the courage and boldness to tell my family that we're starting with God's Word first — and then we'll dive into the gifts and presents. I ask You, Holy Spirit, to honor this commitment to bring special wisdom and insight to my children — and to us — as a result of giving the Word of God first place in our Christmas Day.

I pray this in Jesus' name!

MY CONFESSION FOR TODAY

I confess that this year will mark a Christmas that's very different than those we've experienced in previous years. This year we are starting a new tradition with eternal significance — one that we'll continue year after year. We will begin our Christmas morning with the reading of the Christmas story together as a family. This will teach us all patience, and it will put the most important element of Christmas — Jesus — right in the center of the day as just as He ought to be. And as a result, we will all grow in wisdom and insight regarding the significance of that special day, for the One whose birth we are celebrating has been made unto us wisdom!

I declare this by faith in Jesus' name!

QUESTIONS FOR YOU TO CONSIDER

1. Does your family gather together on Christmas morning to read the story of Jesus' miraculous birth from the gospels (*see* Matthew 1,2; Luke 1,2)? If not, why not make a plan to do so?
2. If you have children, why not let them ask questions about what you are reading? It will invigorate the conversation and make it much more interactive. You will be surprised by some of their thoughts and insights!
3. Did anyone take the time to read the Christmas story to you when you were a child? If not, how do you think it might have impacted you if that had been part of your Christmas Day experience?

A child can have special insight into the Word of God if his parents pour it into him at an early stage.

DECEMBER 19

Christmas Morning at Our House Today!

...Continue thou in the things which thou hast learned and
hast been assured of, knowing of whom thou hast learned them;
and that from a child thou hast known the holy scriptures,
which are able to make thee wise unto salvation
through faith which is in Christ Jesus.
— 2 Timothy 3:14,15

When Denise and I began our family, we made a decision that we would open no gifts on Christmas morning until we had *first* read the Christmas story in its entirety to our sons. The impact my father made on me by following this practice for a few years during my childhood never left me. I pledged that when I became a father, my own family would read the Christmas story before a single gift was opened.

Although our sons were eager to open gifts, they understood the rules — and those rules meant that we were going to place God's Word *first* before opening gifts. Knowing that this was the plan, *and that nothing was going to alter it,* actually helped our children listen attentively. Not only did we carefully read the Christmas story to them, we also involved them in the conversation. Sometimes we devoted *a full hour* to this discussion before we even moved toward the Christmas tree. The Word of God — and reading as a family about the *real* reason for Christmas — reigned supreme above everything else. And guess what? As we discussed Herod, the wise men, the angels, the guiding star, and so forth, this biblical story became a favorite highlight of Christmas and a cherished memory for our sons.

Each year as I'd read from the Bible, I'd ask our sons questions, and the boys would raise their hands, eager to give the answers. It became like a holiday game. As result, our sons became soundly educated in the Christmas story and the many interesting facts surrounding this momentous event that even most adults don't know.

Unlike my father who started a tradition but didn't continue it, we *continued* in it. Now our sons are adults with their own children, and Denise and I have allowed our sons to take the prominent role in reading the Christmas story. Even today, no one would think to violate this holy tradition in our family. *How could we open gifts before putting God's Word first?* To put Him first and continue this handed-down custom is the most wonderful part of our Christmas experience!

Traditions are something that must be started and maintained. The apostle Paul told Timothy, "...*Continue* thou in the things which thou hast learned and hast been assured of, knowing of whom thou hast learned them; and that from a child thou hast known the holy scriptures...."

Let's look at the word "continue" for a moment. It was translated from the Greek word *meno*, which means *to abide* or *to stay*. But when it becomes the present active imperative voice, as it appears here, it means it is a *command that is to be actively followed and never broken*. It describes *a constant and continual habit*. This word *meno* could be used to describe my own daily Bible reading, for example. I am firmly committed to never breaking this *constant* and *continual* habit. It is my daily *tradition*, *custom*, *ritual*, or *practice* — one that I abide in and refuse to violate.

Today I want to encourage you with the seed of an idea: Please consider starting an unbreakable, *once-a-year* tradition of setting gifts aside momentarily to read the Christmas story with your children or grandchildren — or with whomever you share your Christmas morning — *before* opening those gifts. It will take discipline for you to do this, and you'll have to stress to your children or grandchildren that this is a new tradition that you're beginning this year. Then plan on *continuing* the tradition year after year from this point forward.

I can tell you with assurance that this new tradition will add richness and depth to your Christmas experience. And as those portions of Scripture become interwoven in the fabric of your Christmas memories over the years, the eternal truth found within the words will get planted deeper and deeper in your hearts. More and more, you and your family will be able to better comprehend the magnitude of the miracle we all celebrate at Christmastime — *when the Word became flesh and dwelt among us*!

MY PRAYER FOR TODAY

Father, I realize that continual, godly habits build stability into a life and a family. Today's Sparkling Gem is a practical example of how traditions can help cultivate godly character through the good habit of placing God's Word first before natural enjoyment. I can see the benefits of starting and continuing this wonderful tradition for my family. Help me be a voice of loving influence in getting this Christmas tradition started and then to help sustain it through the years with my family. I pray that all of us who share our Christmas mornings together — no matter how young or how old — will grow in our knowledge of the Lord Jesus Christ because we have made the commitment to start this tradition!

I pray this in Jesus' name!

MY CONFESSION FOR TODAY

This Christmas I will start a new tradition with my family and my loved ones. BEFORE anything else on Christmas, we will begin the day by reading the Christmas story from the Bible. I am confident that the Holy Spirit will help us make this a happy and joyful time in the Word of God as a family. Afterward, we'll enjoy the rest of our Christmas festivities together. But from this year on, we will begin our Christmas Day focused on the reason we are even celebrating this holiday in the first place!

I declare this by faith in Jesus' name!

QUESTIONS FOR YOU TO CONSIDER

1. How will you get started with this new tradition? It's easy to do. Just make an announcement that you're going to read the Christmas story before you open gifts. Have everyone bring their Bibles into the room where your Christmas tree and gifts are (or whatever room you choose), gather together, and let members of the family read different verses of the story so that everyone feels like he or she is a part of what is happening.
2. As you're reading, be sure to stop and ask, "What does this mean to you?" Let your family members know that you're not rushing — that you're going to soak in this most important story. You'll be amazed at what different family members, especially your children or grandchildren, will come up with in what they ask and what they answer! Why not read through the Christmas story in advance for yourself and write down a few questions that would be good to ask your family members? Did you learn anything new as you did this?
3. Once you're finished reading the Christmas story, I encourage you to join hands and pray together — and thank your Heavenly Father that He sent Jesus into the world to redeem us from our sins. Then tear into those gifts! Consider writing down your memories from this first experience of your new lifelong tradition.

DECEMBER 20

Now We Read the Christmas Story to Our Grandchildren — in Russian!

And ye shall teach them your children,
speaking of them when thou sittest in thine house,
and when thou walkest by the way, and when thou
liest down, and when thou risest up.
— Deuteronomy 11:19

Decades have passed, but we Renners are still reading the Christmas story as a family tradition *before* we open gifts. Every Christmas, our immediate family members come to our home in Moscow, where all the grandchildren excitedly wait to open their presents. But just as our sons had to wait until the Christmas story was first read and discussed, we have continued this family tradition — only now the whole event takes place in the Russian language, since that has become the primary language of the Renner households in Russia!

We read the Christmas story from Matthew and Luke — *all in Russian* — and then our ever-growing group of grandchildren interacts and joins the conversation about what we just read about the birth of Jesus. As questions are asked, the older ones eagerly lift their hands to be acknowledged, and they each participate in a wonderful discussion about Jesus and all the events that surrounded His miraculous birth. One hand shoots up into the air — *then the next and the next* as our grandchildren compete to give the right answers to questions, such as:

- ➢ Where did the wise men come from?
- ➢ Why was Herod so paranoid about Jesus being born?
- ➢ How old was Mary when she became pregnant?
- ➢ How did she become pregnant?
- ➢ What was the job of a carpenter?

The list of questions goes on and on. And if any child *dare* approach the gifts before this conversation is concluded, they are quickly corrected by the other grandchildren, who have come to love this as their favorite part of Christmas Day!

In fact, this family tradition has become so interesting that no one gets in a hurry to move on to the time of opening gifts. The children realize that the gifts will still be there regardless of how much time our story takes. We have so much fun talking about the Gospel message that no one ever becomes anxious about opening the gifts. The big event of our Christmas morning is *the story of Christmas* and the fun challenge of trying to out-answer everyone else with the correct responses to the questions that are asked!

Deuteronomy 11:19 says, "And ye shall teach them your children, speaking of them [God's words] when thou sitteth in thine house, and when thou walkest by the way, and when thou liest down, and when thou risest up."

In the Greek version of the Old Testament, called the Septuagint, the word "teach" is the Greek plural form of the word *didasko*. This word emphatically means that parents have the responsibility to teach their children how to live by God's law and ordinances and to have a working knowledge of His Word. According to this verse, parents are to take every opportunity to teach their children. Deuteronomy 11:19 says we're to speak God's Word when they rise, when they walk by the way, when they lie down, and when they rise again. One of the foremost responsibilities of parents is to impart the teaching and traditions of the Word of God to their children.

People often ask what Denise and I did to raise such godly sons — and, now, godly grandchildren. The answer is that we took Deuteronomy 11:19 very seriously. Denise and I didn't hold a daily Bible study with our sons — but in the process of living life, we pointed out creation and the Creator, the love of God, His plan of redemption, and so on. We constantly and habitually reminded our children of God Almighty and His goodness in our lives. And we applied this same principle on Christmas Day.

What a wonderful day to speak truth to your children or grandchildren — to make the Word of God the highest priority of the day on Christmas morning. The impact and the memories will last a lifetime as you make it a fun and meaningful time together — and then move on to open presents, partake of special foods, and enjoy precious time with family for the rest of the day.

I've taken three days to exhort you on this subject because I believe it is such a serious tradition for a Christian family to build into their lives. If you do not already have such a tradition, today I want to encourage you to think about what kind of Christmas customs you can establish for your family to practice on this important holiday!

MY PRAYER FOR TODAY

Father, I continue to be stirred by this exhortation on the importance of deliberate traditions and habits to place God's Word first on a daily basis. Teach me how to make practical applications of Deuteronomy 11:19 every day in every area of my life beyond this holiday season. I ask You to show me how to start new traditions for our family that can be passed down to ensuing generations. I also ask You to help our family really think through what kind of Christian tradition we can start and continue year by year to keep You and Your Word the focal point of all that we do. Once we get started, give us the strength of will to keep it up perpetually and pass it on to other generations. Most of all, we want not only a Christian tradition but also a daily lifestyle that will honor Christ and bring Him glory!

I pray this in Jesus' name!

MY CONFESSION FOR TODAY

I confess that I create deliberate habits to bring God's Word into my daily life and the lives of those around me. This year I'm going to seriously consider what kind of Christian traditions I can begin in my family and will move forward to initiate a godly heritage in my home. There's no better time to start than now, so I plan to get started this Christmas season!

I declare this by faith in Jesus' name!

QUESTIONS FOR YOU TO CONSIDER

1. What other kind of Christian traditions have you heard of that people practice with their families?
2. Have you ever considered taking Communion as a part of your Christmas Day events? When would you do it, and how would you talk to your family about this sacrament of Communion?
3. Once you start a tradition, you want to make sure it is one that you can continue year by year, so really think this through before you get started. Why not write it down and discuss it with your spouse — or, if you're single, with another

relative or close friend? It's important not to make a big announcement to your children that you don't follow through with each year.

DECEMBER 21

Christmas Cleanup!

Let all things be done decently and in order.
— 1 Corinthians 14:40

My precious daddy was a *fanatic* when it came to order and cleanliness. He couldn't bear the thought of wrapping paper scattered around the house on Christmas Day after all the gifts had been opened. So on the day before Christmas each year, he would start organizing a way to quickly collect paper wrapping, ribbons, and other trash so that it wouldn't lie strewn around the living room on Christmas Day.

Sure enough, my dad's plan always worked. When Christmas Day came, the wrapping paper and ribbons were collected just as quickly as they were removed from the gifts. There was never any evidence that there had been a mess in our living room. Instead of waiting till the last present was unwrapped, Dad made sure that room *remained* as clean as it was when we began opening gifts.

My father was *committed* when it came to cleanliness and order every day of the year! Our yard was always mowed on time, and the curbs, driveway, and sidewalks were perfectly edged. The flowerbeds looked orderly, and our bushes were always neatly trimmed. Because we had a dog, it was my daily duty to walk the yard to look for dog excrement and remove it. So with my hand-shovel and garbage sack, I'd walk back and forth across the back yard to make sure it was spotless before Dad's truck pulled into the driveway at 5:00 p.m. each weekday. As soon as my dad stepped out of his vehicle, the first thing he'd do was walk through the yard to see if I had done my job and to see how well I'd done it.

That's just the way it was at our house — inside and out. And it was good because it taught me so much about staying on top of situations before they spun out of control. It's usually better to be ahead of a problem than to have a pile of various "messes" to clean up later on.

This reminds me of a Bible verse about doing things "decently and in order." It's not a Christmas verse, but it has application to every area of life every day of the year. It is First Corinthians 14:40, which says, "Let all things be done decently and in order." This verse is actually talking about the right and wrong way to conduct a worship service, but it contains a principle that I wish to expound on in today's *Sparkling Gem.*

The word "decently" is from the Greek word *euschemonos.* Besides this verse, the word *euschemonos* is found only two other times in the New Testament — in Romans 13:13 and First Thessalonians 4:12. In both of these places, it is translated *to do something honestly* or *to walk honestly.* It carries the notion of something that is done *properly* as opposed to *improperly.*

The word "order" is the Greek word *taksis.* It carries the idea of *something done in a fitting way* or *something done according to order.* The Jewish historian Josephus used the word *taksis* when he recorded the *orderly way* in which the Roman army erected their camps — indicating their camps were *orderly, organized,* and *well-planned.* The commanders didn't engage in last-minute planning. Their camps were not hastily thrown together. Rather, they were set up in an *organized* and *thoughtful* manner.

Josephus also used the word *taksis* to describe the way the Essene Jews behaved so respectfully of others. These Jews would wait until others were finished speaking before they'd take their turn and speak out. In Josephus' depiction of this behavior among the Essenes, he used the word *taksis* to portray people who were *respectful, deferential, courteous, accommodating, well-mannered,* and *polite.*

Do you see how this verse could be applied to many situations in life? It could be interpreted, "*Let everything be done in a fitting and proper manner that is organized, well-planned, respectful, well-mannered, and polite.*"

My father regularly quoted this verse — usually out of context — but it ensured that things were done "decently and in order" in our house. Our home, and any event held in our home, was *orderly, organized,* and *well-planned.* We didn't know anything about last-minute planning. Rather, things were done in an *organized* and *thoughtful* manner because our father believed it showed *respect, courtesy,* and *politeness* to everyone present.

I'm so thankful that this lesson was passed from my Grandfather Renner to my father and then to me and to my sons. Now I even see our grandchildren carrying on the same "decently and in order" tradition. Even now, before even the second gift is opened on Christmas Day, the trash remaining from the first gift has already been picked up and discarded. We have fun in a trash-free, orderly environment!

Whether on Christmas Day or *any* day, when things get out of control, it leaves room for confusion and often anger later on when others don't join in the task of cleaning up. If you've never tried it, why not institute the "decent and in order" approach! Have some fun in a trash-free, orderly environment. It will make your day so much more enjoyable when you don't have strife over who is going to clean up a mess!

MY PRAYER FOR TODAY

Father, I accept the challenge to keep things decent and in order as we celebrate and have fun together. There's no reason to let piles of trash build up and make it really hard for someone to clean up later in the day. Show me every opportunity to demonstrate kindness and consideration and to help my family do likewise so that no one gets their feelings hurt because they feel left alone in the task of bringing order back to the house. Lord, help me to set the standard, and to set the rules. And help us do things in a way that makes it a joyful day for everyone involved!

I pray this in Jesus' name!

MY CONFESSION FOR TODAY

I confess that I am going to lead my family in keeping things decent and in order this Christmas season. Rather than let the house go and allow stacks of trash and piles of messes to build up that could later cause strife, I will rid my house of the problem before it ever gets started. I'll set the example and ask others to help me keep the house looking nice before it descends into a mess that looks horrible. This sounds simple, and it IS simple. With God's help, this year we're going to keep things looking decent and orderly around our house!

I declare this by faith in Jesus' name!

QUESTIONS FOR YOU TO CONSIDER

1. What has been your Christmas experience in years past? Has the devil used trash to create strife and turmoil at the end of a wonderful holiday event?
2. Why not simply make the announcement that this year you're going to be doing things differently to keep things clean and orderly as the day goes by? Have everyone participate. Put plastic trash sacks around the room, and inform everyone that as soon as a gift is opened, the wrapping, ribbons, and filler are to be put into the trash bag *before* the next gift can be opened. It will bring such order to your day!
3. You have most likely experienced the difference between a chaotic, disorderly environment and one in which a sense of order and peace pervades. How would you describe the different ways both types of environments affect you?

DECEMBER 22

Denise's Birthday

And be ye kind one to another....
— Ephesians 4:32

During the Christmas season each year, I always feel a little sorry for Denise. I always felt the same way about my father when he was alive on the earth.

Let me explain. Denise was born on December 22, and my father was born on December 25 — which, of course, is Christmas Day. Like it or not, their birthdays played "second fiddle" to Christmas. With all the other holiday celebrations that were always happening during that time of year, their birthdays often passed unceremoniously. Today my father is in Heaven — but Denise, thankfully, is very much still here, and she loves to have her birthday celebrated.

I've always tried faithfully to do something to make Denise's birthday memorable, but the fact that her special day is three days before Christmas makes it challenging to include additional party events into our schedule. I never remember anything special happening for my father's birthday except an acknowledgment on Christmas Day that it was his birthday. Mother gave him a gift, a birthday kiss, and that was about it. Dad and Mom were focused on making sure that we kids had a wonderful Christmas Day, so Dad's birthday became sort of sidelined along the way.

Actually, for anyone born in December, it's a challenge to have a meaningful birthday celebration. Efforts are put in so many other directions: church-wide events, smaller Sunday school parties, special Christmas outreaches to the lost, school activities — and, of course, decorating the house for the holidays, shopping for last-minute gifts, and lots of special cooking for the family. All of these activities can interfere with people whose birthdays are in December. There's so much to do during the holiday season that it can throw people into a tailspin to add multiple birthday celebrations on top of it all.

Our Renner family has multiple December birthdays to celebrate each year (including my dear mother earlier in the month!), and trying to keep up with them in the midst of everything else can present a challenge. But Denise's birthday is very important to her, probably because her special day was "overlooked" when she was younger for all the reasons I just named. So on December 22, or as close to December 22 as possible, I try to take the immediate family to dinner for the *sole* purpose of celebrating Denise!

We live in Moscow, which is geographically huge and statistically has some of the worst traffic in the world in the month of December. Getting our family together for any event in December is a big deal. When I'm able to get us all together under one roof — in the same room breathing the same air — Denise sees the effort it took for us to all get together, and it puts a smile on her face and joy in her heart.

Most often we're able to pull off this departure from all the bustle and stir of holiday activities. But there have been years when we haven't been so successful. But whether we're able to pull it off or not, there is one thing I always do that means the world to Denise. It seems simple, but it means everything to her. *What is it?* I buy her a birthday card and write her a special note. And if birthday cards in Russia are not to be found, I actually *make* her a card with my own pencil and colored pens, and then I write her a heartfelt note. I think the notes that I create myself mean more to her than the ones I buy, because she knows I really put my heart and a lot of thought into it.

Why do I put so much effort into making sure Denise feels especially honored on her birthday? Because I desire to show kindness to my wife and even to grow in the demonstration of my kindness toward her. Ephesians 4:32 says, "And be ye kind one to another...."

The words "be ye" are a translation of the word *ginesthe*, the present imperative middle voice of *ginomai*. Used in this way, it means *be ye constantly becoming*. It depicts a devotion to becoming something more than one presently is. Hence, it presents the image of one who is in the constant process of becoming "kinder." The word "kind" is the Greek word *chrestos*, and it depicts something that is *useful*, *good*, *worthy*, or *benevolent*. Paul listed it in Galatians 5:22 as a "fruit" that the Holy Spirit produces in our lives.

This tells us that when the Holy Spirit is working in us, He is constantly working to change us, to transform us, to mature us, and to make us kind — that is, *useful*, *good*, *worthy*, or *benevolent*. We start where we are, but by allowing the Holy Spirit to work in us, He causes us to progressively demonstrate kindness more and more to others.

It may sound minor, but sometimes an act of kindness or tender attention is just what someone needs on his or her birthday. Your flesh might say, "There's no time for that this year; life is too busy." But the kindness of the Holy Spirit in me causes me to say, *If it's important to my loved one, I'll do my best to make it important to me.*

Becoming "kind" is not something you arrive at overnight. It takes a commitment — almost akin to *an obsession* — to be more like Christ, who definitely would give care and attention to someone on a day that is important to him or her. So rather than say, "It's an inconvenient time for me to give my attention to this," we need to say, "Holy Spirit, show me how to show kindness and to act in a way that is worthy of You. What would You have me do? That's what *I* want to do on this person's special day!"

If you will take this approach and "be ye kind," whether it concerns someone's birthday or simply the way you interact with others in life, you will never go wrong!

MY PRAYER FOR TODAY

Father, I'm embarrassed by how often I have failed simply to "be kind" toward others — especially those closest to me. I feel almost silly that I've overlooked it or counted it as unimportant. Help me start where I am and, day by day, become more focused on the special needs and special days in other people's lives. I know this is what You would do, so help me to be more like You!

I pray this prayer in Jesus' name!

MY CONFESSION FOR TODAY

I confess that God never overlooks any detail about our lives. He is Love, and He goes out of His way to show honor and esteem so others will know they are valued. I am determined to be thoughtful of others. I confess that I will work harder on this than I've ever worked on it before, and I will show care and kindness to people who have special days in the month of December.

I declare this by faith in Jesus' name!

QUESTIONS FOR YOU TO CONSIDER

1. Do you know anyone whose birthday falls in the month of December? Who is that person? Have you ever considered how overlooked that person may feel because of all the other events that are going on in the same month?
2. Even if it's simple, what can you do solely for that person to show that you're thinking of him or her at this time? A birthday celebration doesn't have to be a monumental event every year. Even a small but meaningful act of recognition would be deeply appreciated.
3. How long has it been since you personally created a birthday card for someone you love? It's easy to buy a card, but to sit down and create one and write a note in it shows great love and care. Have you ever considered doing this for someone for his or her birthday?

DECEMBER 23

Holiday Confusion and the One Constant That Remains

But made himself of no reputation,
and took upon him the form of a servant,
and was made in the likeness of men.
— Philippians 2:7

Today I want to give you a little insight into what it's like to live in two worlds — the *Western* world and the *Eastern* world. When you live in the West, Christmas is celebrated on December 25. But in Russia and in the former countries of the USSR, religious holidays typically fall two weeks later than the western celebrations.

For example, Russian Christmas is celebrated on January 7 — two weeks *after* Christmas is finished in the West. So while the western world is putting away its decorations, Russian Christmas hasn't even started. In fact, if December 25 falls on a weekday, that date is nothing more than a regular workday in Russia. So while the western world is celebrating Christmas, we — that is, our family and our church in Moscow — are mostly going about a normal workday with no special festivities.

You might wonder how all this "confusion" began. As you probably know, the entire world once operated according to the Julian calendar — but in 1582, the world switched to the Gregorian calendar. Secular Russia changed to the new Gregorian calendar with the rest of the world.

However, the Orthodox Church — because the new calendar was Catholic-based — rejected it and decided to stay with the old Julian calendar. As a result, Russia has two calendars: a secular calendar (Gregorian) and a religious calendar (Julian), the latter of which is honored by the Russian Orthodox Church. Believe me when I tell you this can create *holiday confusion*!

That means when people are done celebrating Christmas in the United States and western Europe, and they're getting ready for the New Year's celebration, Russia is still 14 days away from Christmas. Then when the West is done with their New Year's celebration, and everyone moves past January 1 on the calendar, Russia also has a *second* New Year also *14 days later*, according to the Russian Orthodox calendar. Furthermore, when western Easter is done and decorations are being put away, Russia is just preparing for its festivities, for Russian Easter is *also* typically two weeks later than this holiday on the western calendar.

Do you see what I mean by my phrase *"holiday confusion"*?

Let me give you an example of how this affects our personal lives. Having grown up in America, Denise and I are accustomed to celebrating Christmas on December 25. That is a very strongly ingrained tradition in us. But our sons and their families, having grown up in Russia, are accustomed to celebrating Christmas 14 days later on January 7. In fact, they are so acclimated to life in Russia that they don't recognize December 25 as Christmas. To them, it's not a holiday; it's just another day.

That puts Denise and me in quite a dilemma: *How do we celebrate Christmas?* We often end up looking strangely at each other on December 25, feeling that something is seriously missing or out of sync! Since our sons and their families celebrate Christmas on January 7, along with the rest of the Russian people, it leaves Denise and me to figure out what to do by ourselves on December 25. Sometimes it's very lonely, so we have to get creative about what to do.

One year, Denise and I bought tickets to the circus so we'd have something to do on December 25 while most Russians were engaged in a normal workday. Another year, Denise and I went to the ballet. Still another year, we invited friends over for a special dinner on December 25. It was not Christmas to them, but they joined us to honor our invitation.

Of course, when January 7 rolls around — the traditional date for Christmas in Russia — everyone here in Moscow is finally ready to celebrate this holiday! But while our Moscow office is closed for the Christmas holidays, the Tulsa office is open because Christmas has already been celebrated in the West. (And by the same token, while our Tulsa office is closed for the Christmas holidays, the Moscow office is brimming with activity and the daily work of the ministry. Consequently, whether in Moscow or Tulsa — no matter who's celebrating their Christmas around the world — Denise and I are still very much engaged in the everyday work of the ministry!)

I know this probably sounds confusing. Trying to make sense of it and work around these various dates can be very convoluted. Although we've lived in Russia for decades, we *still* have to work hard to navigate this holiday confusion.

But regardless of the date on which Christmas is celebrated, the fact remains that *Jesus was born*! Whether that momentous event is celebrated on December 25 or January 7 — *or some other date* — Jesus' birth is what is most important. In Philippians 2:6 and 7, Paul wrote, "Who, being in the form of God, thought it not robbery to be equal with God: but made himself of no reputation, and took upon him the form of a servant, and was made in the likeness of men."

Let me talk to you about these miraculous verses. Paul began by describing the preexistence of Jesus before He came to the earth as a man. Paul said, "Who, being in the form of God...." The word "being" is a translation of the Greek word *huparcho*, a compound of the words *hupo* and *arche*. In this case, the word *hupo* means *from*, and the word *arche* means *first, original*, or *ancient*. When they become the word *huparcho*, it depicts *something that has always existed.*

By using this key word that means *to eternally exist*, Paul was declaring that Jesus had no beginning, but rather had always existed. This also explains Jesus' statement when He declared, "...Before Abraham was, *I am*" (John 8:58). Thus, Philippians 2:6 could be translated, *"Who, eternally existing in the form of God...."* In other words, Jesus' human birth in Bethlehem was not His *beginning*, but merely His *manifestation to mankind*, a brief appearance in His eternal existence.

Paul wrote that Jesus always existed in the "form" of God. The word "form" is the Greek word *morphe*. This word describes *an outward form*, which means that in Jesus' preexistence, He looked just like God. He was not just a component of God, nor a symbol of God. In reality, He *was* God. And as the eternal God Himself, Jesus possessed the very shape and outward appearance of God — a form that includes great splendor, glory, power, and a Presence so strong that no flesh can endure it.

God existed in glory more wonderful than the human mind can comprehend and more powerful than human flesh can endure. Yet He desired to come to earth to purchase redemption for man. Therefore, God had no choice but to "reclothe" Himself in a manner that could be tolerated by man. This is why He "...made himself of no reputation, and took upon him the form of a servant, and was made in the likeness of men."

This is the true story of Christmas — minus the confusion!

The phrase "made himself of no reputation" comes from the Greek word *kenos*, which means *to make empty*, *to evacuate*, *to vacate*, *to deprive*, *to divest*, or *to relinquish*. Because it was impossible for God to appear to man as God, He had to change His outward form. The only way He could make this limited appearance as a man was to willfully, deliberately, and temporarily let go of all the attributes we usually think of when we consider the characteristics of God. For 33 years on this earth, God divested Himself of all His heavenly glory and "...took upon him the form of a servant..." (Philippians 2:7).

The phrase "took upon him" perfectly describes that marvelous moment when God reached out to lay hold of human flesh and take it upon Himself so that He might appear as a man on the earth. The words "took upon him" are from the Greek word *lambano*, which means *to take*, *to seize*, *to catch*, *to latch on to*, *to clutch*, or *to grasp*. This word lets us know that God literally reached out from His eternal existence into the material world He had created — and took human flesh upon Himself in "the form of a servant."

Not only did God become man, but a "servant." This word "servant" is from the Greek word *doulos*, which refers to *a slave*. Paul used this word to picture the vast difference between Jesus' preexistent state and His earthly life.

Paul goes on to say that Jesus "...was made in the likeness of men." The phrase "was made" is the Greek word *ginomai*, which means *to become*, indicating that this was not Jesus' original form but it *became* His new form. This clearly describes the miracle that occurred when God *became* a man. Jesus had always existed in the form of God, not the form of man. But taking upon Himself human flesh, He was formed in the womb of the Virgin Mary and *became* a man.

God literally took upon Himself the "likeness" of a man. The word "likeness" is the Greek word *homoioma*, which refers to *a form* or *resemblance*. This refers not only to Jesus' being made in the *visible* likeness of men, but also in the *human* likeness of men. In other words, when Jesus appeared on this earth, He came in the actual form of a man and was just like man in every way.

Jesus was so completely made in the "likeness" of men that Hebrews 4:15 declares He was even tempted in every way that men are tempted. It says, "For we have not an high priest which cannot be touched with the feeling of our infirmities; but was in all points tempted like as we are, yet without sin."

So we see that when God the Father sent His Son into the world, Jesus left His heavenly home and took upon Himself human flesh. And because of this great exchange, He has stood in our place; He has felt what we feel. Even today, He is touched with the feelings of our infirmities, and He intercedes for us with great compassion as our High Priest.

At this time of the year — whether we celebrate on December 25 or January 7 or some other day — we are prone to think of Jesus as a little baby in a manger in a Bethlehem stable. Certainly this is true, but we should never forget that His birth in Bethlehem was *not* Jesus' beginning. It was merely the moment of His brief appearance in His eternal existence.

Out of His deep love for you and me, Jesus was willing to leave His majestic realms of glory to enter the realm of humanity. Shedding all His visible attributes that were too much for man's flesh to endure, He dressed Himself in the clothing of a human being and was manifested in the flesh. That little Baby in Bethlehem was the eternal, ever-existent God Almighty, who came to us in human flesh so that He could dwell among men and purchase our salvation. He was and is the only "constant" in a world that is chaotic and confused!

MY PRAYER FOR TODAY

Father, I thank You that regardless of what day it happened — Jesus took on the form of a servant and was made in the likeness of men. He stooped to the level of His creation and died the death of a Cross, all because He loved me and wanted me to become a part of His eternal family. Help me not to get stuck on "what" day it actually happened, but rather to rejoice in the fact that it did happen! Because Jesus came to earth in the form of a man and died for me, today I am a child of God. For this, I can say thank You for the greatest gift. I am so glad I am redeemed!

I pray this in Jesus' name!

MY CONFESSION FOR TODAY

I understand that the exact day on which Jesus' birth occurred is not so important — but what is important is that He put aside His glorious attributes and took on the form of a human being and a servant, and humbled Himself to die the death of a Cross. Because of the price He paid, I have been permanently saved and set free. For this, I declare my thankfulness at Christmastime!

I declare this by faith in Jesus' name!

QUESTIONS FOR YOU TO CONSIDER

1. Have you ever thought about two different sides of the world celebrating Christ's birth at two different times on the calendar? Can you name someone who celebrates Christmas on a different day than December 25?
2. When you think of Jesus' birth and the fact that He laid aside His glorious appearance as God to take on the form of a man, how does this affect you? If you were to describe it to someone else, what would you say?
3. What is most meaningful to you about the celebration of Christmas?

DECEMBER 24

Christmas Eve — Traditions and Relationships

If there be therefore any consolation in Christ, if any comfort of love,
if any fellowship of the Spirit, if any bowels and mercies, fulfill
ye my joy, that ye be likeminded, having the same love,
being of one accord, of one mind.
— Philippians 2:1

One of our Renner holiday traditions when I was young was visiting some close, lifelong friends to our family on Christmas Eve. It was a Christmas tradition to gather with this family every Christmas Eve at their home until the Pope finished giving his annual Christmas message on television. Then we said our farewells to everyone for the evening.

I never understood why we waited for the Pope, seeing that we were such staunch Baptists. But that message from the Pope was the signal to the Renner family that Christmas Eve was coming to a close. After that speech, we piled into the car to head home, go bed, and eagerly wait to wake up the next morning so we could gleefully open our gifts.

When I think of those Christmas memories, I think of friends, family, and entire evenings of fellowship shared at our close friends' home. I can remember those moments like they just happened last week. They were tender moments shared with our Christian friends — singing Christmas carols, fellowshipping around church events, and thanking God we knew the Lord and enjoyed fellowship with others in Christ.

I can remember driving home on Christmas Eve from our friends' home and passing a bar along the way that looked like it was packed with people. I felt so sad for people who went to a bar on such a special night. They obviously did not know Christ. This left such sadness in my heart — and such thankfulness that my parents had led me to Christ at an early age.

Christmas Eve was a special night when our family gathered with God's people and fellowshipped around His Word. All of this was a part of what Christmas Eve meant to me. This makes me think of Philippians 2:1, which says, "If there be therefore any consolation in Christ, if any comfort of love, if any fellowship of the Spirit, if any bowels and mercies, fulfill ye my joy, that ye be likeminded, having the same love, being of one accord, of one mind."

This verse speaks of the "fellowship" of the Spirit — that is definitely what we enjoyed with our friends each Christmas Eve. The word "fellowship" is the Greek word *koinonia*, which describes something that is *mutually shared*. We *mutually shared* our common church membership; we *mutually shared* our faith in Christ; and we *mutually shared* our joy of the holiday and of our special night together. From beginning to end, Christmas Eve with the Renners and their close family friends was a night of *koinonia* and one of the greatest memories of my life.

I encourage you to find a way to share Christmas Eve with people who are close to you. Let it be a time when you mutually rejoice and spend time together. It is such a special night, so don't let it slip by with you being alone. There are others out there, like you, who are longing to spend time with someone on that special evening!

MY PRAYER FOR TODAY

Father, I thank You for the fellowship of the Spirit that we have with other Christians who mutually share faith with us. What a fellowship, what a joy, and what a blessing — to build years of fellowship and Christian traditions with other believers. I ask You to help me start thinking about how to build Christian traditions for myself and my own family, especially in moments like Christmas Eve. I am so thankful for fellow believers who share the same hope I possess. I'm so grateful we can spend cherished times together in our mutual love for the Lord and for each other.

I pray this in Jesus' name!

MY CONFESSION FOR TODAY

I confess that I will work on building traditional Christian events for myself and my family in order to deepen the true significance of this beautiful season. God has given me friends that I can spend those moments with — and if I haven't developed those friends yet, I declare by faith that I'm going to step out of my comfort zone and begin to connect with other Christian believers. I need this, my family needs this — and I will look for ways to do it.

I declare this by faith in Jesus' name!

QUESTIONS FOR YOU TO CONSIDER

1. Do you have a Christmas Eve tradition? If so, what is it and how long have you been doing it?
2. Do you spend time with other believers — or with family — on Christmas Eve? What do you do? How do you spend that time together to make it really meaningful?
3. Do you open Christmas gifts on Christmas Eve or Christmas morning? Different families have different traditions — what are your traditions?

DECEMBER 25

The Real Gift That Keeps On Giving!

...Seek ye first the Kingdom of God, and his righteousness;
and all these things shall be added unto you.
— Matthew 6:33

"*Merry Christmas!*"

Those were the first words we heard on Christmas Day when we were children. We were awakened when Dad would turn on the floodlights attached to his Kodak camera, and all three Renner kids would crawl out of bed in our pajamas, rubbing our eyes in the bright lights that were glaring down on us as Dad filmed practically every movement of the Christmas morning for us.

Today we still have those films that Dad took of all three of us as we scampered from our beds into the living room to begin the process of opening gifts. Those films are now decades old, and I am thankful for the thoughtfulness of my father to film those precious memories, which otherwise would have been completely lost. Now that they've been transferred to a digital format, we can enjoy them for years to come. Dad is in Heaven, but these are his treasures that he left for the rest of us to watch and enjoy.

Every so often, we watch those films and remember our childhood Christmases and the gifts that Daddy and Mother gave us. The greatest gift my parents ever gave me on Christmas was a study Bible — a very nice, leather-lined study Bible. I was so *proud* of it! They hit it right on the target when they gave me that Bible, as my heart was *aflame* to know more about God's Word at that time in my life. I still have that Bible today. Dad wrote his favorite Bible verse right in the front of the inside cover. There, in Dad's handwriting, it says, "...Seek ye first the kingdom of God, and his righteousness; and all these things shall be added unto you" (Matthew 6:33).

Dad would quote this verse to us kids all the time. He wrote it in birthday cards, in letters that he occasionally wrote to us when we were at the university — and, of course, in the front covers of *every* Bible he ever gave to each of us. He really believed this verse, and he wanted to embed it in our souls.

Dad quoted Matthew 6:33 so often, and wrote it to us so many times, that one day I decided to pick up my Greek New Testament and look at the word "seek" to see what it means. It is the present imperative active form of the Greek word *zeteo*, and it depicts *a constant attitude to actively and constantly seek for a thing.*

Furthermore, *zeteo* is a *command.* Jesus was literally commanding us to actively and constantly be seeking after the Kingdom of God. Jesus promised that if we did, everything else we needed in life would be supplied to us. No wonder Dad wanted to get that verse into our hearts! He knew that if we got this right, everything else would be okay in our lives.

So I want to ask you: Are you obeying Jesus' command to habitually, constantly seek the Kingdom of God? Are you *on-again, off-again* in your spiritual passion, or would Jesus say you are consistent in your seeking of Him and His Kingdom? All those other things you need to be supplied for life *will* come if you'll place Jesus first and never stop seeking the purposes of His Kingdom. *Jesus truly is the Gift that keeps on giving!*

This is Jesus' promise to you — and these are my words of encouragement to you on this Christmas Day!

MY PRAYER FOR TODAY

Father, I don't want to be on-again, off-again in my pursuit of You. But as You command, I want to be habitual and constant in the way I seek You and Your Kingdom. There are many other things I need in life, but You promised that if I seek Your Kingdom first, all these other things will eventually be added unto me. So today I ask You to help me focus on the Kingdom of God and to keep my focus there for as long as I live on this earth!

I pray this in Jesus' name!

MY CONFESSION FOR TODAY

I confess that nothing in the world is more important to me than seeking the Kingdom of God and His righteousness. God's Word promises that if I'll remain focused and constant in seeking God's Kingdom and His righteousness first, before anything else, He'll make sure every other need is met in my life. So I confess by faith that starting today — and for every day following this new commitment — I am going to make God's Word, His Kingdom, and His righteousness the chief priority in my life.

I declare this by faith in Jesus' name!

QUESTIONS FOR YOU TO CONSIDER

1. What do you do on a practical basis to seek the Kingdom of God above everything else in your life? For example, do you start your day out by reading the Bible and praying? That might be a good way for you to start this important commitment if you're not already doing it.
2. I start my day with a cup of coffee and my Bible in a secluded part of our house, where I read the Word as the highest priority of my day. I suggest that you consider doing this. Would you be willing to give this schedule a try?
3. Do you have any other ideas about how you can make the Kingdom of God and His righteousness the first priority in your life? Why don't you think it over and see what the Lord shows you that would work best?

Are you on-again, off-again
in your spiritual passion,
or would Jesus say you are consistent
in your seeking of Him and His Kingdom?

DECEMBER 26

Eating Leftovers!

...Therefore every scribe which is instructed
unto the kingdom of heaven
is like unto a man that is an householder,
which bringeth forth out of his treasure things new and old.
— Matthew 13:52

Are leftovers a part of *your* after-Christmas holiday tradition? After you read today's *Sparkling Gem*, you may never look at leftovers the same way again!

When I was young, we always enjoyed a smorgasbord of leftovers each year after Christmas — which included turkey sandwiches smeared with lots of mayonnaise, warmed-up meatloaf spread with ketchup, and mashed potatoes covered with melted butter. Of course, we also had an array of leftover biscuits, cake, pie, and other desserts to choose from that hadn't been consumed on Christmas Day.

The truth is, we had *all kinds* of leftovers the day after Christmas — and we sometimes had them for *days* after Christmas! But we eventually got tired of eating the same old thing, and it became time to clean out the refrigerator and start eating something fresh and new.

Oh, how my mother prepared for Christmas Day! When I was young, I didn't appreciate all the food she prepared each year for Christmas; I simply *consumed* it. But now that our own family has grown so large — and I see what it takes to feed a small multitude — I have such gratitude for all the cooking my mother did for us when we were younger. And I'm so thankful to Denise and our daughters-in-law for the luscious meals *they* prepare for our Christmas celebrations. Even my son Paul jumps into the fray, smoking a lamb that is given to us by a church member each year at Christmas.

It takes time and effort to feed people — and to feed them food prepared from both old recipes and new recipes makes eating more interesting. Most everyone appreciates eating food prepared from old, tried-and-true recipes as well as trying foods that are new.

This makes me think of Matthew 13:52, where Jesus said, "...Therefore every scribe which is instructed unto the kingdom of heaven is like unto a man that is an householder, which bringeth forth out of his treasure things new and old."

Notice that in this verse, a scribe — or a teacher — is pictured as "bringing forth of out of his treasure things new and old." The word "new" is from the Greek word *kaina*, and it refers to something absolutely *new* and *previously untried*. The word "old" is *palaia*, and it refers to that which *is old* and *has existed for a long time*. Although this verse is talking about teachers bringing forth new revelation versus old revelation, I like the example of leftovers and new recipes to further make this point.

There are some teachings, like good leftovers, that are always tasty and enjoyable — and a common staple around the dinner table. But there also comes a time when you want to eat something new. The good news is that the Kingdom of Heaven is full of wonderful *established* teaching — and it is also overabounding with *new*, fabulous teaching that you've never heard or tried before. A good teacher — like a good food-preparer — will bring out *new* and *old* recipes for a family to enjoy! Good "leftovers" are always enjoyable, but your spiritual taste buds will eventually cry out to eat something new!

I know from personal experience that as we give our attention to the Word of God, the Holy Spirit adds new insights to the old ones and causes our understanding of God and His Word to be marvelously expanded. I relate well to the scribe described in Matthew 13:52. Many of the Greek word studies you read in this book are old to me; yet so many of them are *brand new*. Often I think that I have unearthed every gem that can possibly be found in a particular verse of the New Testament. But then I study that same verse again, and the Holy Spirit wonderfully *opens my eyes* and *illuminates my mind* to show me truths that I previously didn't see!

So let's keep our minds and eyes open for the Holy Spirit to provide not only great leftovers, but also new teachings that we haven't learned yet. Let us remain hungry for new teachings and new revelation from the Word of God that we've never attained to before. The old, familiar truths of Scripture are always healthy and good, but there is a cry in the spirit of man to know more, to attain more, and to taste new levels of the Lord's goodness. So let's enjoy the leftovers, but let's also press forward to attain new truths in the spiritual feast the Lord has waiting for us. We must never forget Psalm 34:8, which says, "O taste and see that the Lord is good…"!

MY PRAYER FOR TODAY

Lord, I am hungry for fresh revelation of the Word of God. How could I be anything but thankful for the foundational truths that I've already received, yet my spirit is crying out to know You better and to receive revelatory truths that unveil aspects of Your character and Your ways yet unknown to me. I ask You to help those who teach me to be like a good scribe, knowing when to emphasize the old and when to introduce the new. Then You will equip them to bring forth new truths that my spirit is crying to hear and to know.

I pray this in Jesus' name!

MY CONFESSION FOR TODAY

I boldly confess that I am grateful for every teaching I've ever received and that each one has added to the foundation of my life. But I am hungry for more of the Lord. I want more of His Word, more of His revelation. I want to learn new things, based on the teaching of the Bible, that will feed my spirit in a way I've never been fed before. I thank God for my pastor and for those teachers who teach me — but I purpose to keep an open ear and an open heart so I can also receive fresh heavenly revelation from the Spirit of God to feed to my spirit!

I declare this by faith in Jesus' name!

QUESTIONS FOR YOU TO CONSIDER

1. What is the primary source of spiritual teaching for your life? Do you hear the same thing over and over again, or do you find that you are growing in your knowledge of the Word of God?
2. Who is the primary person God uses to feed you spiritual food — whether leftover food you've heard before or new teaching that is new to your ears? That person works very hard to prepare spiritual meals for you. Have you taken time to thank that minister for the spiritual meals he or she prepares for you?
3. As I grow older in the Lord, I have realized the great impact people have had on my spiritual life when I was younger. I have felt the responsibility to communicate with them and thank them for the impartation they made in my life. Who are the people who have imparted spiritual truth into *your* life? Have you ever thanked them for all the time, prayer, work, and diligent effort they invested to spiritually feed you?

DECEMBER 27

Being Thankful!

In every thing give thanks:
for this is the will of God
in Christ Jesus concerning you.
— 1 Thessalonians 5:18

Isn't it amazing how quickly the excitement of new possessions can wear off? Within days of getting all those gifts at Christmas as a young boy, I was already dreaming of what I would receive for my birthday — which was *a full seven months away*! All those items I saw in the Sears catalog that I didn't get for Christmas were so fresh in my mind that I nearly ignored the toys I had received as I longed for the next round of gifts.

But the Bible tells us to be *thankful*! In First Thessalonians 5:18, Paul wrote, "In everything give thanks: for this is the will of God concerning you." My parents had to teach me to be thankful. Sometimes they had to literally sit down with me, explain the cost of gifts, the sacrifices that were made to purchase them, and the importance of not being greedy. God blessed me with such wonderful parents who took the time to teach and instruct me on the most basic and elementary principles of life.

As a mature adult, the concept of "thankfulness" is deeply ingrained into my being because my parents so deeply planted it in my character. There is nothing I have that I did not receive, and I am thankful for everything God has sent into my life and for every partner who has helped us fulfill our heavenly mission. I have so much to be grateful for!

In First Thessalonians 5:18, we are instructed to be thankful "in *everything*." This phrase in the Greek language is *en panti*, and it means *in every detail*, even *in the smallest way*. One expositor has translated it to read, "In every circumstance, be thankful...."

The word "thankful" is the present imperative active tense of *eucharisteo*, a compound of *eu* and *charis*. The word *eu* denotes *good* or *well* and always denotes *a good inner disposition* or *a good feeling* about something. The word *charis* is the Greek word for *grace*. When compounded, the new word paints the picture of one who is so *grateful* that he has *an outpouring of overwhelmingly good feelings* about everything. Regardless of what is happening — or not happening — he has decided to be *thankful*.

Let's be honest. Perhaps things could be better than they are in your life right now. However, you probably will admit that they are not as bad as they could be! The truth is, you have *a lot* to be thankful about — even about the smallest details of your life.

Years ago I made a decision that when anyone asks me how I'm doing, I would answer by simply saying, "THANKFUL!"

Thankfulness is a choice. You and I must turn our eyes *toward* the good in our lives and *away* from the foul things that try to hold our focus — and *choose* to be grateful. It's not that we're hiding our heads in the sand concerning those bad things; we're simply obeying the Lord as we focus on what is good, and we display an attitude of thanksgiving "*in everything*." Paul said, "In every thing give thanks: for this is the will of God in Christ Jesus concerning you" (1 Thessalonians 5:18). Could Paul's words be any clearer? God wants you and me to be thankful — not resentful, not forgetful, but *thankful*. Really, if we consider all the terrible things that could have come about in our lives but *didn't*, we can find a lot of reasons to be grateful. God has spared you and me from so much — and it is His will that we maintain a consistent, thankful attitude for the goodness He has shown us.

So I encourage you to make the decision today to put away all the bad memories of the past and start purposefully focusing on the good things God has done in your life. Even if you think life has been tough, I assure you that it has not been as tough as it could have been. God has been good to you. The best thing you can do when someone asks you how you're doing is to respond, "I'm *thankful*!" Keep this attitude of thankfulness coming out of your mouth at all times, and speak it with conviction. I promise you, that one practice alone will change the way you see life!

MY PRAYER FOR TODAY

Heavenly Father, I've been through rough times, but the truth is, those times could have been a lot rougher. When I consider what You have brought me through — and the place of peace and rest You've brought me into — I can only say THANK YOU. Please forgive me for often quickly forgetting the good things You have done for me, and help me cultivate this attitude of thankfulness in my heart, for this is Your will in Christ Jesus concerning me!

I pray this in Jesus' name!

MY CONFESSION FOR TODAY

I declare that I have a lot to be thankful for. Yes, it's true that there are things I need and desire, but compared to where I used to be and how I experienced lack, I am living in the land of superabundance. I will not be forgetful of the good things God has done for me. I purpose to keep a grateful attitude for all the things He has done and is doing for me, both great and small. And when others ask me how I'm doing, I will confidently answer them, "THANKFUL!"

I declare this by faith in Jesus' name!

QUESTIONS FOR YOU TO CONSIDER

1. I challenge you to pray this prayer: "Heavenly Father, when I consider all that You have done for me, to be honest, there have been times when I've been a real ingrate — complaining about this, that, and the other thing, forgetting all the good things You have performed in my life. Honestly, if it hadn't been for Your grace, I cannot imagine what my life would have become. Lord, I ask You to help me to make a list of all the ways that You have been good to me. I will post it in a place where I am regularly reminded of it to help me maintain an attitude of thankfulness." *Now make that list!*
2. If you have a tendency to display a lack of thankfulness, it's time for you to reprogram your brain — that is, to renew your mind — to be grateful for all the good things God has done for you. How are you going to start the process of renewing your mind to recognizing more of God's goodness in your life?
3. Have you ever met a person who is truly *thankful* for all he has in his life? How does his attitude of thankfulness affect you? Does it have a positive impact on you and make you wish you could be different?

Put away all the bad memories of the past and start purposefully focusing on the good things God has done in your life.

DECEMBER 28

Getting Ready for a New Year

If we confess our sins, he is faithful and just
to forgive us our sins,
and to cleanse us from all unrighteousness.
— 1 John 1:9

I have spent the whole month of December recalling personal experiences surrounding Christmas from my childhood and exhorting you in the Word of God from those personal memories. But now it's time to take inventory of this past year: what you accomplished that you promised yourself you would do — and what you *didn't* accomplish. As you take inventory, you may find that you've made some progress but are still "in process" on some of the things you had promised you'd do this year. And, honestly, you may find that you need to ask God for forgiveness for not responding to things the Holy Spirit had prompted you earlier to change during this year.

Each year at a meeting that kicks off our New Year's holiday, our Moscow team gathers for a wonderful afternoon celebration together, where we rejoice over the victories of the past year and share our vision for the upcoming year. Over the years, we also developed a tradition of handing out paper and envelopes — and we ask people to write down what they want God to do in their lives in the upcoming year. We've done this for so many years that everyone now comes prepared for what he or she is going to write on that piece of paper.

After the team members write down their goals, they insert that piece of paper into the envelope. I stand before all of our employees with my hands laid on those envelopes, and as a group, we pray over them. Afterward, all the envelopes are placed in a "safe" where they are not touched for a year — until the next New Year's team celebration.

When we all gather the following year to celebrate, we take the envelopes out of the safe and redistribute them to those whose names are written on them. People quickly tear them open to see if they fulfilled what they believed God had told them to do a year earlier — or if they had fallen short of those goals. Often we hear praise reports of fulfilled victories; at other times people recognize that they are still in the process of fulfilling what they had written down. Some have to conclude that they wrote down hopes and dreams that were yet to be fulfilled.

I'll be honest and tell you that for years, I wrote on my concealed piece of paper the goal of building a permanent home for our Moscow church. Year after year, I wrote it again, again, and again — never giving up on my confident expectation and my faith that God would enable us to actually own a permanent property for our church.

Like everyone else on our team, each year when envelopes are redistributed, Denise and I receive ours and open them to read what we wrote the year before. After the year-end celebration is finished, Denise and I have often gone to dinner by ourselves, where we share what we wrote down the previous year. Then we share with each other what was accomplished; what is in the process of being fulfilled; or even at times what we totally failed to do. It is a time when we hold ourselves accountable to the Lord and to each other. Sometimes it's been a time of rejoicing. Other years we've repented for failing in major areas that God had dealt with us about. If we had a major victory — if something we wrote down the year before came to pass — we are certain to rejoice and give thanks to God!

This time of personal inventory has become very important to us, not only as a married couple, but also as a ministry. It is a time of accountability before the Lord for us all.

This leads me to ask you about your past 12 months. Have you fulfilled the promises you made to yourself and to the Lord when this year started?

If you're looking back on a year that holds some victories, rejoice and share it with someone else! But if you have utterly failed at reaching specific targets that God put on your heart, I suggest that you immediately put First John 1:9 into operation, which says, "If we confess our sins, he is faithful and just to forgive us our sin and to cleanse us from all unrighteousness." What a powerful verse to release us from condemnation of failure or non-performance!

The word "confess" is the Greek word *homologia*, and it means *to say the same thing as God says*. In other words, rather than debate with God about where you have failed, *it's time for you to get into agreement with God about your shortcomings*. And when your confession is heartfelt, the Bible says that God is faithful and just to forgive you. The word "forgive" is the Greek word *aphiemi,* and it means *to release, to let go*, or *to totally dismiss*. In other words, if you've made a real heartfelt confession about where you have blown it, God promises that He won't hold it against you. In fact, He'll release you from it and send that failure as far away as the east is from the west (*see* Psalm 103:12). Not only will He forgive you and dismiss your failure, He'll start with you all over again to win that victory you missed this past year!

Never forget that God is on your side, and He wants to see you victorious and burden-free! He just needs your heart agreement — a true acknowledgement of any failure or sin. The moment He has that, He will dismiss that failure or sin from you and release the resurrection power of Christ to help you achieve what He has put in your heart to accomplish!

MY PRAYER FOR TODAY

Father, I admit that I've failed to fulfill some of the things You definitely told me to do in the past year. I confess it, I admit it, and I walk free of it. You do not hold it against me, because I am making a heartfelt confession about it. In fact, You take my failure and remove it from me as far as the west is from the east! And Your resurrection power helps me pick up right where I am to start anew and to gain those victories that belong to You and that You long to impart to me! I thank You, too, for helping me reset the start button to gain new victories in these areas of my life.

I pray this in Jesus' name!

MY CONFESSION FOR TODAY

I confess that God's mercies over me are new each day. Therefore, each day is a brand-new opportunity to forget those things which are behind me as I press toward the prize of God's calling that is drawing my attention to focus more and more upon Him. As I prepare my heart and mind to evaluate this past year, while giving attention to what God desires of me for the next year, I consider my ways and evaluate myself in the light of God's Word. I trust in the Lord to reveal to me throughout the coming year how to stay on track with His plan for me. I receive fresh grace to do whatever it takes to discipline my body and mind, and to order my days so I don't waste precious time. I am diligent and I am faithful; therefore, I abound with blessing and I live free of regrets!

I declare this by faith in Jesus' name!

QUESTIONS FOR YOU TO CONSIDER

1. Have you made a spiritual inventory to see how well you did at keeping the commitments you made to the Lord at the beginning of this year? Perhaps it would be helpful for you to take the time to do this so you can be honest with God about where you did well and where you could have done better.
2. Denise and I help each other at this time of the year to see how well we fared on our spiritual commitments. Whom do you have who can help you honestly look at your commitments and help hold you accountable?
3. What other steps do you need to take to put the past behind you and to get ready for the new year?

DECEMBER 29

Spiritual Hoarders!

...I have suffered the loss of all things, and
do count them but dung, that I may win Christ.
— Philippians 3:8

I had always heard of *house-hoarders* — that is, people who hoarded belongings until they had so much "stuff" in their houses that they had to walk on top of it all or forge little trails to get through the maze. I even watched a TV program about hoarders, and I was horrified that anyone could live with so much garbage in his or her home.

Watching this hoarding experience on TV was mind-boggling to me. But then a relative needed help moving from her home to a new house. When I walked into the old house, I was *stunned* by what I saw. It was exactly what I had seen on the television program, if not worse. There were piles, piles, and *more piles* of goods that still had original tags on them, plus ceramic items that were stacked high on shelves. The wallpaper was falling off the walls, and there was a huge nest of mud daubers living in the corner of the living room! The only way to get from one part of the house to the next was to walk a tiny little corridor that had been left between the mounds of trash that had accumulated over the years. If I hadn't seen it with my own eyes, I would never have believed that a human being could live in such squalor.

The outside of this relative's house was no better. Rather than throw away old magazines, she had stacked them high, one on top of another — and they were rotting into a "wall" of magazines that surrounded part of her property like a barricade. It was truly beyond anything I had ever witnessed.

Hoarding. That's exactly what this dear relative had been doing — just like the hoarders I'd seen on TV. Only now it was *my* job to remove it all so that the house could be put on the market. Honestly, it would have been easier to bulldoze the house and start all over than to try to get the old one back into shape. *I had never seen anything like it.*

Some people's spiritual lives are like that. Rather than deal with issues and keep their lives clean and clear, the spiritual rubbish just keeps building up, deeper and deeper, until it seems almost impossible for them to clean up and put themselves back into working order. They have so many piles of unforgiveness, bitterness, and other forms of spiritual garbage that they can barely make it from one room to the next in their "house."

When people hoard — or refuse to let go of — things like fear, doubt, jealousy, bitterness, and envy, their spiritual lives become a mess! Their lives can eventually be compared to those houses we see on TV in which the wallpaper is falling off the walls, the electricity doesn't work right, the sink in the kitchen is a slimy, wretched mess, and rodents and all kinds of other pests live in the midst — *right along with the person who lives there with them*!

When I saw this unbelievable mess at our relative's home — something I truly thought only existed in fantasy TV programs — I was speechless. There is no way a person can be healthy in his or her mind and emotions, and think that way of living is acceptable. It brought my mind to Philippians 3:8, where Paul uses the word "dung" to describe his life before Christ. He says, "…I have suffered the loss of all things, and do count them but dung, that I may win Christ."

The word "dung" is the word *skubalon*, and it is the word for *refuse*. To be more pointed, it refers to things like *a half-eaten corpse, filth, lumps of manure or human excrement,* or *food thrown away from the table* and then left lying around, piled up on the floor as it rots. *Skubalon* would be a sickening sight that would tend to make one want to *vomit.*

When I saw how our relative was living in such chaos and squalor, I realized that it is impossible to live a normal life under such wretched circumstances. And when Paul used the word *skubalon*, which depicts this very type of scene, he was admitting that all he had done before he came to Christ was nothing more than a *skubalon* pile of rubbish; it was spiritual defilement. That may sound harsh to say, but that is precisely the word that the apostle Paul used to describe his life before He came to Christ. In the end — after Paul came to a saving knowledge of Jesus — he recognized that his entire life until that time had all been rubbish, with nothing worth saving. But after Paul came to Christ, he was set free from the spiritual garbage of his past and his life was cleansed and set apart to be used of the Lord.

As we approach the end of the year, I want to ask you: Are you living in spiritual squalor — or are you abiding in a lifestyle that gives glory to Jesus Christ? Many people pile up grief, resentment, bitterness, and other things that block their ability to function normally for the Lord. What about you? Are things as they ought to be in your spiritual life? *It's something for you to really think about today!*

MY PRAYER FOR TODAY

Father, I confess that there is spiritual trash in my life — and I've just tolerated it and let it grow deeper and deeper. Help me recognize it for what it is and begin the process of removing it from my life. You can't use me as You wish if I'm surrounded by piles of squalor. So I ask You to help me, Holy Spirit, as I start the cleanup process so I can function freely and clearly when You have a job for me to do!

I pray this prayer in Jesus' name!

MY CONFESSION FOR TODAY

I confess that I've been a spiritual hoarder — letting things build up in my life that hindered my effectiveness. I repent before the Lord for letting this buildup of spiritual refuse take hold in my life. If I'm going to be used mightily of Him, I have to keep my heart and soul clean, so today I commit to making this a serious endeavor in my life.

I declare this by faith in Jesus' name!

QUESTIONS FOR YOU TO CONSIDER

1. Can you think of areas where you've allowed yourself to hoard attitudes that are unproductive to your spiritual life? If yes, what are you going to do to start changing this mess in your life?
2. To be honest, when hoarding has already begun, it takes a very serious commitment to bring things back into order. Are you willing to make the kind of commitment that is required to bring order back into your spiritual life? God will help you, but you must turn and commit your way to Him.
3. What is the area in your life that gives you the most trouble in discarding spiritual "refuse" that isn't good for you? Can you name it?

DECEMBER 30

What Does the Holy Spirit Want You To Do Before This Year Ends?

Being confident of this very thing, that he which
hath begun a good work in you will perform
it until the day of Jesus Christ.
— Philippians 1:6

I have no doubt that there are a few things I need to wrap up before the year ends. It has been a good year — very productive and full of good fruits. I am so thankful for this — yet I know there are still some things that the Holy Spirit wants to accomplish in my life before the clock strikes midnight and a new year begins. The new year is just two days away — so it means I must intensely focus on what the Holy Spirit desires to get done before this year ends.

Just as has been true every year, this past year has been a year of both challenges and victory. But I want the year to end in total victory by allowing the Spirit of God to inwardly finish what He has started in me at the first of this year. Philippians 1:6 says, "Being *confident* of this very thing, that he which hath begun a good work in you *will perform it* until the day of Jesus Christ."

The word "confident" is the Greek word *peitho,* and it means *to be sure, to be certain,* and *to have absolute conviction.* I don't know about you, but the Holy Spirit has been working fervently in my heart all year, and I have *absolute conviction* that He is going to finish what He started. Do you have that same conviction concerning your own life?

What does the Holy Spirit want to accomplish in *your* life in the next two days? You might say, "Two days is too short a period of time!" But nothing is impossible when the Holy Spirit has a willing vessel who is willing to cooperate with Him. If you are willing, the Holy Spirit can accomplish anything in you — *even* in two days before the year ends. Then you can start the new year fresh and ready for what God wants to do in the next year, with nothing trailing behind you from the year before. Don't let yourself drag anything negative from this year into next year! The Holy Spirit's power is available to do a fresh, quick work of grace in your life. He wants to set you free and get you ready for a brand-new start!

In the first seven devotionals in this book (January 1-7) I challenged you with certain goals the Holy Spirit may want you to focus on in the ensuing 12 months. I want to encourage you to skim those seven days and see if you have allowed the Spirit of God to do what He wanted to do in those areas of your life. If not, this is a good time to seek forgiveness and cleansing — and to move into the new year with a fresh sense of faith and courage to allow the Holy Spirit to do the work He desires to do in you in the coming 12 months.

I'll honestly tell you that one of my goals for *this* year was to finish and publish the book you hold in your hands. It required a great level of commitment and fortitude to accomplish this goal. But I knew it was the will of God, so I set my heart to accomplish it. And with the Holy Spirit's help, it has been done according to the plan.

Knowing God's plan — and operating according to that — is so essential for living effectively for Him. If you don't know the Lord's will for the next year of your life, the Holy Spirit wants to help you know it, so ask Him to show you. As I've already noted, the Holy Spirit will work fervently in you to finish what He has started. Philippians 1:6 assures us that this is true: "Being confident of this very thing, that he which hath begun a good work in you will perform it until the day of Jesus Christ."

Just stop a moment to consider that promise! God *begins* the good work in you, and then He *performs* it. From start to finish, it's *His* grace that enables you to accomplish what you need to do before the clock strikes midnight on December 31. So don't say it's too late, because it's *never* too late to address those issues the Holy Spirit has been talking to you about. If nothing else, get started in this new calendar year — and His power will help you quickly get the victory.

I am praying for you today. God has wonderful things in store for you. He simply needs your cooperation, and His supernatural power will quickly do what otherwise would take a long time to do. *So throw open your arms and say, "Holy Spirit, I am ready to cooperate with You! Do quickly in my life what only You can do, and show me what my part is so I can do what You want me to do!"*

MY PRAYER FOR TODAY

Father, the race for this year is almost over, but it's not too late for me to come out a winner by faith in every area of my life. I surrender every obstacle that has hindered me as a result of my own thoughts and actions. I ask You to supernaturally quicken me so I can achieve the goals You desire to perform in me. I am absolutely convinced that You will perform this work in me and that You'll keep doing it until the day of Jesus Christ!

I pray this in Jesus' name!

MY CONFESSION FOR TODAY

I confess that God's power is working inside me — and He will quickly do those things He has wanted to accomplish in my life this past year. My wrong choices may have hindered them from being done earlier. But right now, I choose to cooperate with the will and the power of God to see His plan for me accelerated and accomplished because of my obedience. According to Philippians 1:6, I am absolutely sure and completely persuaded that God is doing His work in me!

I declare this by faith in Jesus' name!

QUESTIONS FOR YOU TO CONSIDER

1. What internal changes do you need to wrap up before the clock strikes midnight on December 31? The Holy Spirit can quickly do what you could never do on your own. Why not write down the changes you desire to make *today* and release your faith for a quick work to be done?
2. Do you have relationships that need to be mended and healed before the end of this year? If so, you know that restoration is possible through the power of the Holy Spirit. Ask Him to help you to know how to approach that person, how to apologize, and how to make amends. He will show you what to do.
3. Do you owe a debt to someone that you should have taken care of this year but failed to do so? Has that unpaid debt grieved you and hurt the person to whom you owe the debt? Why don't you humble yourself, make a phone call, sincerely apologize, and get on the path toward making things right with that person?

DECEMBER 31

One Year Ends and a New Year Begins

...forgetting those things which are behind,
and reaching forth unto the things which are before....
— Philippians 3:13

Well, today one year is closing, and another year is about to begin. Is your year ending the way you prayed it would? Or do you need to make alterations in your heart *quickly* to get back on track with what God wants to do in your life so you can start the next year right?

Many times as I've come close to the end of a calendar year, I've wondered if I was going to accomplish everything I sensed the Lord instructing me to do in that year. But if it's too late to do what you should have done this year, it's time for you to *forget* those things that are behind and to reach forth unto the things that are before you (*see* Philippians 3:13). The word "forget" in this verse is the Greek word *epilanthanomai*, which depicts something that is *done with*, *accomplished*, and *no longer an issue* before you. The word "behind" is the word *opiso*, which describes something that no longer has relevance in your life. It is *old*, *antiquated*, *outdated*, and *no longer applicable*.

Rather than focus on things of the past that no longer have relevance in your life, it's time for you to "reach forth" unto those things that are before you. The words "reach forth" are translated from the Greek word *epikteinomai*, and it pictures a runner in a race — running with every ounce of strength he can muster to get around that final bend in the stadium one last time and finish as the winner! His whole body and eyes are fastened on that goal as he leans forward and runs with all his might to break through that finish line.

Today is your last day to make wrongs right and to do things that you know you ought to do. This year is closing in a mere matter of minutes or hours. But before you is a glorious new beginning! The Holy Spirit wants to divinely energize you to run your race in the new year with your eyes and your whole being fixed on the goal. It may be challenging, but if you'll surrender to the Holy Spirit's control, He'll take you where you never could have gone by yourself!

When you lay your head on your pillow tonight and say farewell to this year, make sure that you also welcome the new year with faith, confidence, and commitment that in this new year you will accomplish every dream, goal, and desire that God has put in your heart to accomplish over the next 12 months!

MY PRAYER FOR TODAY

Heavenly Father, this has been an awesome year in which You have taught me so much. My heart is overflowing with thankfulness for every challenge You've helped me overcome and for every lesson You've taught me that has helped mold me more to the image of Jesus Christ. I am simply filled with gratitude that You have done so much in my heart during this year — and I believe that the next year will be even richer and fuller than the one I am presently completing. As I reach the finish line of this year, I forget what is behind me, and I reach for what is ahead. For all of this, I give You thanks!

I pray this in Jesus' name!

MY CONFESSION FOR TODAY

I boldly declare that the year before me will be the best year I've ever known in my life thus far. The Holy Spirit is energizing me — and He will help me run my race better than I've ever run it before. I say no distractions or obstacles will stop me — and that I will run until I reach the finish line! Jesus has already laid out the race before me — I only need to jump up, give it my best shot with the Spirit's power, and finish everything God wants me to achieve in this new year!

I declare this by faith in Jesus' name!

QUESTIONS FOR YOU TO CONSIDER

1. Is it too late — have you run out of time to do what you were supposed to do? What could you have done differently to produce a more fruitful outcome? Write down what you should have done and what you could have done better to achieve your goals and dreams. Then repent and forget the guilt of it. The past is over, irrelevant, and *no longer an issue* before you. Ask the Lord to help

you accomplish old responsibilities in a new way by the grace and mercy that are freshly available to you today!

2. Before you is a glorious new beginning! Have you consulted the Holy Spirit to find out what He wants you to know about the race set before you in the new year? If you make the decision now to yield to the Holy Spirit's direction at every turn, He will take you where you never could have gone by yourself!
3. Have you written down the ways you want to use your faith to be a bigger blessing to the Kingdom of God in the coming year? In what way can you better serve your pastor and your church? What are the steps you need to take to be a stronger spiritual influence for God in the lives of your family and friends? What do you need to do to be a brighter light and better representative of Christ to the lost? When you lay your head on your pillow tonight, say farewell to this year, and welcome the new year with faith, confidence, and a commitment to glorify God as never before.

Today is your last day to make wrongs right
and to do things that you know you ought to do.
But before you is a glorious new beginning!
The Holy Spirit wants to divinely energize you
to run your race in the new year
with your eyes and your whole being fixed on the goal.
It may be challenging, but if you'll surrender
to the Holy Spirit's control, He'll take you
where you never could have gone by yourself!

INDEX OF GREEK WORDS USED IN

SPARKLING GEMS FROM THE GREEK 2

ENGLISH INDEX

A

a moment (*homou*) 1009
abide (*meno*) 137, 197, 219, 333, 336, 621, 950, 1115, 1135, 1062, 1063
abounded (*pleonadzo*) 369
abounds (*perisseuo*) 369, 1130
about (*peri*) 93, 301
above (*huper*) 289, 463, 826, 1105
above (*huperano*) 431, 432
abstain (*apecho*) 44, 677
abundance (*perisseuo*) 953, 1130
abundantly (*perissos*) 1060
access (*prosagoge*) 1044
according (*kata*) 723
adultery (*moichalis*) 579
adversaries (*antikeimenoi*) 298
affection (*phileo*) 581
affectionately desirous (*homeiromai*) 749, 750
affliction (*thlipsis*) 608, 611
afraid (*deilos*) 190
after (*epi*) 330
against (*anti*) 152
against (*epi*) 159
against (*kata*) 730, 829
agree (*sumphoneo*) 518, 834
alive (*zoontas*) 647
all (*pan*) 640, 660, 995
all (*panta*) 995
all (*panton*) 38, 93
all (*pas*) 431, 432
all things (*panta*) 640, 1084
alongside (*para*) 22, 123, 238, 374, 401, 537, 538, 540
always (*aei*) 89
always (*pantote*) 93, 176
among yourselves (*eis allelous*) 58
angels (*angelos*) 1030
anger (*thumeo*) 909
anger (*thumos*) 695
anointed (*chrio*) 250
answer (*apologia*) 89
appearance (*eidos*) 44
apron (*simikinthion*) 1037
arm (*agkale*) 355
around (*peri*) 166, 889
ashamed (*aischunomai*) 1087
ashamed (*epaischunomai*) 1087
ask (*aiteo*) 85, 90, 179, 508
authority (*huperarche*) 615
away (*apo*) 73, 395, 497, 625

B

babbler (*spermologos*) 416
back (*apo*) 56, 89
baptize (*baptidzo*) 365
be ready always (*etoimoi aei*) 89
be thou (*ginou*) 211
be touched with (*sumpatheo*) 292
be ye (*ginomai*) 1143
bear up (*kartereo*) 156
because (*hoti*) 362
before (*pro*) 198
beginning (*arche*) 439
beheld (*anatheoreo*) 409
behind (*opiso*) 3, 1165
believeth (*pistis*) 358
beloved (*agapao*) 428, 758
berate (*oneinidzo*) 182
beseech (*parakaleo*) 374
better (*huperecho*) 1105
blameless (*anepilemptos*) 159
blasphemers (*blasphemeo*) 463
blasphemy (*blasphemia*) 1001
blinded (*tuphloo*) 295
blow (*pneuma*) 867

C

D

denied (*arneo*) 686
departed (*apallasso*) 115
departed (*aperchomai*) 809
desire (*euche*) 156, 1066
desire (*orgidzo*) 1052
desire (*potheo*) 492
despised (*kataphroneo*) 333, 339
despisers of those that are good (*aphiloagathos*) 476
determined (*horidzo*) 843
devil (*diabolos*) 643, 644
devotion to family (*storgos*) 471, 484
devotions (*sebo*) 410
did eat (*metalambano*) 1127
diligent (*spoudadzo*) 1090
diligently seek (*ekzeteo*) 445
direct (*kateuthuno*) 168, 169
diseased (*astheneo*) 363
diseases (*nosos*) 114
disobedient (*aithpees*) 464
dispense (*nemoo*) 77, 78
dispute (*dielegeto*) 404
disputings (*dialogismos*) 958
doctrine (*didaskalia*) 26
doing (*poieo*) 49
doing good (*euergeteo*) 719, 720
dominions (*kuriotes*) 432
door (*thura*) 298
double-minded (*dipsychos*) 235
double-tongued (*dilogos*) 738
doubt (*diakrinomai*) 508
down (*kata*) 168, 223, 237, 238, 273, 333, 339, 402, 506, 586, 672, 723, 1124
due (*idios*) 49
dung (*skubalon*) 1161, 1162
dwell (*katoikeo*) 506
dwelleth (*katoikidzo*) 586
dwelleth (*oikeo*) 148, 506

E

earth (*ostrakinos*) 61
earthen vessels (*ostrakinos*) 108, 257, 596
edify (*oikodome*) 1073
edifying (*oikodomeo*) 195, 489, 1073
effectual (*energes*) 298
effectual working (*energeia*) 634
elect (*eklektos*) 427,428
end (*suntelos*) 1075
endure (*anecho*) 877
endured (*hupomeno*) 333, 336
enjoyable (*arestos*) 815
enmity (*echthra*) 582
entangle (*pagideuo*) 998
entered (*eiserchomai*) 101
enthusiastic (*zao*) 246
entrance (*eisodon*) 742
envy (*phthonos*) 591
escape (*ekbasis*) 308, 521
established (*bebaios*) 249
established (*keimai*) 198
established (*steridzo*) 662, 663
esteem (*hegeomai*) 1105
even (*de*) 901
ever (*pantote*) 57
every (*panta*) 162
every (*panti*) 660, 698
every joint (*aphe*) 633
every man (*hekastos*) 73, 893, 894, 948
every man (*panti*) 89
every part (*en metros*) 634
everything (*ta*) 995
everywhere (*pantachou*) 290
evil (*kakos*) 48, 56, 779, 942, 1034
evil (*phaulos*) 1048
evil (*poneros*) 45, 115, 922, 923
evil for evil (*kakon anti kakou*) 57
examine (*peiradzo*) 656
example (*hupogrammos*) 326, 330
exceeding (*huperballo*) 344, 345

exceeding fierce (*chalepos*) 453, 454
exceedingly sorrowful (*perilupeo*) 166
exhort (*parakaleo*) 238, 760

F

faint (*ekluo*) 50
faithful (*pistis*) 81
faithful (*pistoi*) 19, 384
faithful (*pistos*) 81, 145, 211
false (*pseudos*) 850
false accusers (*diabolos*) 473
fame (*akoe*) 1095
fatherless (*orphanos*) 608
fear (*deilos*) 407
fear (*phobos*) 930
fell (*pipto*) 770
fellowship (*koinonia*) 1149
fierce (*anemeros*) 476
fight (*agonidzo*) 184
fight (*polemos*) 665, 730
filth of the world (*perikatharma*) 889
find (*eurisko*) 81, 145, 689, 690, 767
finish (*apartismos*) 840
finish (*teleo*) 495
fire (*pur*) 246
fire (*puri*) 224
first (*prota*) 801
first works (*prota erga*) 801
fitly joined together (*sunarmologeo*) 633
flattering words (*kolakeia*) 745
fled (*ekpheugo*) 928
flee (*pheugete*) 651
flee (*pheugo*) 135, 928
flow (*rheo*) 527
follow (*dioko*) 57, 523 , 1071, 1072
follow (*epakoloutheo*) 330
foolishly (*euphrosune*) 515
for (*epi*) 1087
forbearing (*anechomai*) 389
foreigner (*xenos*) 484
forget (*epilanthanomai*) 1165
forgetting (*epilanthano*) 2, 3
forgive (*aphiemi*) 203, 334, 637, 806, 1159
forgiving (*charis*) 389
form (*morphe*) 900, 1146
forsaking (*egkataleipontes*) 238
foundation (*themelios*) 216, 220, 285
frankincense (*libanos*) 266
friendship (*philia*) 581
from (*apo*) 44
from (*ek*) 601
from heaven (*ek tou ourano*) 601
full proof (*plerophoreo*) 992

G

gave heed (*prosecho*) 1010
gentle (*nemeros*) 476
gift (*charisma*) 662, 894
give (*didomi*) 56, 152, 181
give thanks (*eucharistos*) 176, 1108
giveth (*didontos*) 181, 182
giving of thanks (*eucharistos*) 614
gladly received (*apodechomai*) 273
gladness and singleness (*apheloteti*) 1127
glorify (*doxadzo*) 576
glory (*kauchaomai*) 226
go (*erchomai*) 101
go (*poreuthentes*) 1098
go on (*phero*) 286
god (*theos*) 486, 867
godly manner (*kata theon*) 131
gods (*damonia*) 407
gold (*chrusos*) 61, 68, 104, 105
good (*agathos*) 57, 720
good (*eu*) 93, 157, 176, 1066, 1156
good (*kalos*) 184, 672, 821
good pleasure (*eudokia*) 957
goodness (*agathusune*) 720
grace (*charis*) 93, 157, 176, 662, 894,
1108, 1060, 1066, 1156
gratification (*eu*) 1108

great (*mega*) 344
great (*megale*) 60, 61, 298
great (*polloo*) 680
great (*polus*) 362
greatness (*megethos*) 344, 345
grieve (*lupete*) 583, 584, 995
grievous (*lupe*) 15
guard (*phroureo*) 1081
guide (*odega*) 572

H

hand (*cheira*) 515
handkerchief (*soudarion*) 1037
hast not (*ouk*) 685
hate (*miseo*) 240
hay (*chortos*) 69, 72
he did (*poieo*) 362
heady (*propetes*) 479
heal (*aphiesi*) 1110
healing (*iaomai*) 873, 874
heap (*episoreuo*) 879
hearts (*kardias*) 168, 1081
heathen (*ethnos*) 850
help in time of need (*boetheia*) 690
helpeth (*sunantilambano*) 911, 916
highminded (*typhoo*) 481
hold (*echo*) 672, 1010, 1105
hold fast (*katecho*) 672
holiness (*hagias*) 524
holy (*hagios*) 428
holy (*hosios*) 855
holy (*nosios*) 468
honorable (*timao*) 68
honourable (*kalos*) 943
house (*oikos*) 60, 77, 144, 506, 705, 706
humble (*tapeinos*) 388, 694
humbled (*tapeinoo*) 901
humbleness of mind (*tapeinophrosune*) 694
hymns (*humnos*) 1120

I

I can do (*ischuos*) 640, 641
I have (*echo*) 788
I say (*lego*) 427
I will come (*erchomai*) 803
if (*ei*) 37
ignorance (*agnosis*) 289
impart (*metadidomi*) 492, 662, 750
in (*en*) 48, 346, 634, 680, 779
in everything (*en panti*) 1108, 1156
in season (*eukairos*) 1057
increase (*auxano*) 141, 618, 860
infirmities (*asthenema*) 1092
infirmities (*asthenia*) 911
injurious (*hubristes*) 1002
inspiration (*theopneustos*) 867
instant (*ephistemi*) 875, 1056
instruction (*paideia*) 27
intercessions (*huperentugchano*) 614, 912, 915
into (*eis*) 101, 742
into (*en*) 640
intreat (*parakaleo*) 123

J

joint (*armos*) 633
journey (*poreuomai*) 115
joyful (*chara*) 15
judged (*krino*) 560, 570
judgment seat (*bema*) 1040
just (*dikaios*) 27

K

keep (*phulasso*) 448
kind (*chrestos*) 628, 1143
kindness (*chrestotes*) 693
know (*ginosko*) 453, 925
know (*oida*) 310, 581, 1021
knowledge (*gnosis*) 289

L

labored (*kopiao*) 1060
labour (*kopos*) 162, 163, 649, 758, 882, 1060
lack (*leipo*) 178, 238
lasciviousness (*aselgeia*) 1122
last (*eschatos*) 456, 457
lay down (*tithemi*) 216
leads (*ago*) 269
leaving (*aphiemi*) 286, 789
led (*ago*) 372, 450, 548
liberally (*haplos*) 182
likeness (*homoioma*) 1147
live peaceably (*eireneuo*) 37
long (*epipotheo*) 492
long (*makros*) 695, 909
longsuffering (*makrothumia*) 695, 909
loosen (*luo*) 50
lord (*kurios*) 930
loseth (*apollumi*) 767, 768
loss (*zemia*) 223
lost (*appololos*) 319
love (*agape*) 428, 429, 788, 936, 937
love for family (*philostorgos*) 484
love for humanity (*philanthropia*) 484
love for strangers (*philoxenos*) 484
love of money (*philaguria*) 484
love of wisdom (*philosophia*) 484
lovers of God (*philotheoi*) 486
lovers of pleasure (*philodonos*) 483, 484
lovers of their own selves (*philautos*) 459, 460
lusteth (*epipothei*) 588, 589
lying (*pseudos*) 511

M

mammon (*mamonas*) 19, 384
manifest (*phaneros*) 73
mankind (*anthropos*) 484
market (*agora*) 304, 414
marketplace (*agoridzo*) 726
meekness (*prautes*) 694
men (*anthropon*) 38
mercies (*oiktirmos*) 691, 692, 693, 1113
midst (*meso*) 813, 1021
might (*dunamis*) 163, 432
might (*ischuos*) 784
mighty (*biaias*) 602
mind (*nous*) 277, 278, 290, 295, 637, 729
mind (*phronos*) 694
minds (*noema*) 295, 1081
minister (*diakoneo*) 894
minister (*diakonia*) 886
minister (*diakonos*) 783
miracles (*dunamis*) 111
miracles (*semeion*) 362
mite (*lepton*) 1129
mock (*empaidzo*) 840
mocked (*echidna*) 424
money (*arguros*) 460, 484
more than (*mallon*) 486
much more abound (*huperperisseo*) 369
much trembling (*en tromos polloo*) 680
multitude (*ochlos*) 362
must (*dei*) 381
my faith (*ten pisten mou*) 686

N

new (*kaina*) 1153
night (*nuktos*) 381
no need of you (*chreian sou ouk*) 504
nomos (*law*) 78, 144, 705
not laying again (*kataballo*) 285
now I (*echometha*) 942
nurse (*trophos*) 755

O

obsolete (*lanthano*) 2
obtain (*lambano*) 689
of (*para*) 179
of a different kind (*heteros*) 939

offscouring (*peripsema*) 890
on (*epi*) 187, 660
one accord (*homothumadon*) 1009
oneself (*autos*) 460
order (*taksis*) 1140
other (*allelous*) 1105
other doctrine (*heterodidaskalos*) 939
ought (*dei*) 912, 1005
ought (*opheilo*) 1092
ought (*ti*) 378
out (*ek*) 7, 50, 115, 238, 308, 427, 436, 445, 521, 601, 928
out (*ex*) 304, 726
out of season (*akairos*) 876
overcometh (*nikao*) 772, 773, 903

P

part (*metro*) 634
passeth (*huperecho*) 1080
passion (*thumos*) 1009
patience (*hupomene*) 137
patience (*hupomeno*) 115, 116, 197, 621, 950, 951, 977, 978, 979
peace (*eirene*) 37, 1072, 1073, 1080
perceive (*theoreo*) 406
perceived (*ginosko*) 998
perfect (*telios*) 162
perfection (*teleiotes*) 286
perform (*epiteleo*) 495
perform (*epiteleoo*) 963
perilous (*chalepos*) 453, 454, 831
perils (*kindunos*) 850
persecutor (*dioko*) 1001
persuade (*peitho*) 464
petition (*aitema*) 85
phren (*mind*) 187
phroneo (*set*) 187, 1100
place (*tithemi*) 22, 220, 285, 497, 1050
place (*topos*) 643
plague (*mastigos*) 683, 684
plant (*phuton*) 141
planted (*phuteuo*) 141
please (*euarestesai*) 815
pleasing (*aresko*) 742
pleasure (*dokia*) 957
pleasure (*hedonos*) 485
pollutions (*alisgema*) 677
poor (*penichros*) 1129
possible (*dunata*) 358
possible (*dunaton*) 37, 1084
power (*dunamis*) 34, 173, 344, 345, 358, 640, 945, 981, 1087
power (*endunamoo*) 640, 641
power (*kratos*) 346
powers (*exousias*) 432
pray (*eratao*) 533, 534
prayer (*proseuche*) 156, 613, 1065, 1066
precious stones (*lithous timious*) 68
prepared (*etoimadzo*) 40
present (*paristemi*) 375
present (*paron*) 15
prevailed (*ischuos*) 927
pricked (*katanusso*) 273
prince (*archon*) 823
prince (*ho archon*) 569
principalities (*arche*) 432
principles (*arches*) 285
profitable (*opheilo*) 26
proud (*huperephanos*) 463
prove (*dokimadzo*) 668, 669
psalms (*psalmos*) 1120
puncture (*nusso*) 273
pure (*kathara*) 608, 889
put off (*apotithemi*) 497, 498
put on (*enduo*) 501, 936

Q

quarrel (*mamphe*) 390
quicken (*zoopoieo*) 897
quiet (*isuchadzo*) 605

R

race (*agona*) 197
reach forth (*epikteinomai*) 1166
reaching forth (*epekteino*) 7
ready (*etoimos*) 89
rebuke (*epitimao*) 637
receive (*lambano*) 159, 894
reckon (*logidzomai*) 205, 647
recompense (*antapodidomi*) 152
reconciled (*diallassomai*) 378
redeem (*exagoridzo*) 304, 726, 857
religion (*threskeia*) 608
remember (*mneia*) 398, 792, 795
remembrance (*hupomimnesko*) 557
remorse (*metamelomai*) 277, 281, 282
render (*apodidomi*) 56
repeating (*ana*) 246
repent (*metanoeo*) 131, 277, 281, 290, 316, 637, 729, 798
report (*marturia*) 821
reproof (*elegmos*) 26
reprove (*elegcho*) 268, 269, 270, 563, 566
required (*zeteo*) 77, 78, 82, 1151
resist (*antitasso*) 387
rest (*anesis*) 30, 128
rest (*sabbatismos*) 100
return (*apo*) 152
revealed (*apokalupsis*) 41, 395, 624, 625
revealed (*apokalupto*) 73
reviled (*loidoreo*) 334
reward (*misthos*) 220
rich (*plousios*) 865
riches (*ploutos*) 393
righteous (*dikaios*) 152
righteousness (*dikaiosune*) 27
road (*odon*) 742
robbers (*listes*) 850
rooted (*erridzomeno*) 1102
ruler (*basileuo*) 11, 823
run (*trechos*) 197
rushing (*pheromones*) 602

S

salt (*halas*) 228
save (*sodzo*) 319
saw (*theoreo*) 401, 867, 409
seal (*sphragidzo*) 598, 599
season (*kairos*) 49, 876
see (*oida*) 1021, 1022
seed (*sperm*) 416
seek (*zeteo*) 186, 319, 445, 1151
seemeth (*dokeo*) 15
sent (*pempo*) 381
sent forth (*apostello*) 886
sentence (*krino*) 703
separate (*asphortidzo*) 97
separated (*aphoridzo*) 53
serpent (*ophis*) 708
servant (*doulos*) 1147
serve (*douleuo*) 278
set before (*prokeimenon*) 198
setter forth (*katanggelos*) 420
shall reap (*therismos*) 49
shame (*aischune*) 333, 334, 339
sharp (*xusmos*) 401
show (*anagello*) 574
sick (*astheneo*) 114
signs (*semeion*) 977, 1075, 1076
silver (*arguros*) 61, 68
sinner (*hamartolos*) 316
sitteth down (*kathidzo*) 840
slave (*doulos*) 402, 900
slave market (*agoridzo*) 304
smallest detail (*ti*) 660, 994
solitary (*ermos*) 810
sorrowful (*lupeo*) 165, 166
sorrows (*oodin*) 439
sorry (*lupeo*) 130, 131
soul (*psyche*) 166
sound (*echos*) 601
sound (*hugiaino*) 879
spake evil (*kakologeo*) 1034
special (*tugchano*) 111

speech (*logos*) 443
stagger (*diakrino*) 235
stand (*en*) 34, 784
standeth (*istemi*) 795
stars (*asteras*) 1030
steadfast (*hedrios*) 882
steps (*ichnos*) 330
steward (*oikonomos*) 77, 78, 144, 705
stir up (*anadzoopureoo*) 246
stir up (*zoos*) 246
stirred (*paroxuneto*) 401
stone (*lithos*) 68, 216, 220, 285, 785
straight (*orthos*) 27
straight path (*euthus*) 168
straightway (*eutheos*) 355
strange (*xenos*) 420
strange things (*znidzo*) 421
strengtheneth (*endunamounti*) 640
strengthening (*enischuo*) 784
striving (*agonidzo*) 163
struggle (*agonidzo*) 451
stubble (*kalame*) 69, 72
study (*philotimeomai*) 604, 605
submit (*hupotasso*) 387
suddenly (*aphno*) 601
suffered (*pascho*) 325
superstitious (*deisidaimonia*) 407
supplications (*deisis*) 613
supply (*epichoregeo*) 633, 634
supply (*pleroo*) 393
swerved (*astocheo*) 940
sword (*machaira*) 322
sword (*rhomphia*) 731

T

take heed (*blepo*) 795
teach (*didasko*) 555, 1137
teaching (*didaskalos*) 939
temperance (*egkrateia*) 346
temperance (*enkrateia*) 346, 347
temple (*naos*) 311, 312, 594
temptation (*peirasmos*) 307
testify (*martureo*) 561
thankful (*charistos*) 466, 467, 468
thankful (*eucharisteo*) 1156
thankful (*eucharistos*) 1156
thanks (*eucharistos*) 93
thanksgiving (*eucharistia*) 157, 1066
there came (*ginomai*) 601
things above (*ta ano*) 187
think (*phroneo*) 333, 339, 826
think highly (*huperphroneo*) 826
thinketh (*dokeo*) 795
thoroughly furnished (*exartidzo*) 869, 870
thought (*merimnao*) 763, 764
through (*dia*) 224, 643
time (*kairos*) 304, 726, 878
to (*pros*) 156
to be manifested (*phanos*) 463
to call (*kaleo*) 123, 238, 374, 436, 540, 853
to do (*poieo*) 801, 897, 942, 994
to follow (*akoloutheo*) 330
to love (*phileo*) 459, 460, 484
to make a sound (*phoneo*) 518
to plant (*phuteuo*) 618
to see (*orao*) 289
to stretch out (*teino*) 7
to throw (*ballo*) 285, 344, 643
to turn (*meta*) 290
took upon him (*lambano*) 900
transform (*metaschimatidzo*) 990
treaty (*spondos*) 472
trembling (*tromos*) 680
tribulation (*thlipsis*) 153, 1112, 1113, 1115
tried (*peiradzo*) 717
troubled (*taresso*) 190, 263
troubled (*thlipsis*) 30
trucebreakers (*aspondos*) 472
true (*alethinos*) 19, 384
truth (*alethes*) 546
truth (*alethosi*) 511
try (*dokimadzo*) 74, 118, 119
turned (*epistrepho*) 278
turning (*epi*) 2

U

undefiled (*amiantos*) 608
under (*hupo*) 137, 197, 333, 336, 387, 621, 950
under (*hupotasso*) 434
understanding (*panta noun*) 1081
unholy (*anosios*) 467, 468
unmoveable (*ametakinetos*) 882
unprofitable (*achreios*) 954
unrighteous (*adikia*) 19, 384
unthankful (*acharistos*) 466, 467, 468
unto (*archi*) 212
unto (*mechri*) 901
unto thee (*soi*) 803
up (*ana*) 355
upbraideth not (*me oneididzontos*) 182
upon (*epi*) 7, 220

V

vain (*kenos*) 649, 883, 899, 1060
veil (*kalupsis*) 73, 395, 624
very heavy (*ademoneo*) 165
vessels (*skeuos*) 61
vexed (*basinadzo*) 481
visit (*episkeptomai*) 608

W

walk (*basis*) 308, 521
walk (*pateo*) 301
walk (*peripateo*) 301, 302
was made (*ginomai*) 1147
watch (*gregoreo*) 157, 1066
watered (*potidzo*) 141, 618
waters (*potamos*) 850
wave (*kludunai*) 508
we have (*echomen*) 596
weak (*adunatos*) 1092
weak (*astheneo*) 443
weary (*egkakeo*) 48
well (*eu*) 815
well (*kalos*) 49
went out (*ekporeuomai*) 115, 116
wept (*dakruo*) 263
what (*ti*) 912
whatsoever (*ti ean*) 994
whence (*pothen*) 795
whenever (*epan*) 27
white (*leuken*) 1068
white stone (*psiephon leuken*) 1068
wholly given to idols (*kateidoolos*) 402
widows (*chera*) 611
wilderness (*heremia*) 850
willing (*eudokeo*) 750
wind (*pnoe*) 602
winked (*hupereidon*) 289, 290
wisdom (*sophos*) 178, 484, 711, 1063
wise (*sophia*) 302
wise (*sophos*) 64, 1132
with (*sum*) 518
with God (*para*) 152
without (*exouthen*) 821
without ceasing (*adialeiptos*) 698
without natural affection (*astorgos*) 471
witness (*martus*) 753
wood (*zulina*) 61
wood (*zulos*) 69, 72
word (*rhema*) 323, 660
word (*rhemati*) 660
words (*logos*) 89, 416, 633, 995, 1034
worketh (*ergadzomai*) 1118
working (*energeo*) 163
works (*erga*) 801
works (*ergadzomai*) 381
works (*ergos*) 73, 381
world (*kosmos*) 569
wrath (*orges*) 1118
wrought (*poieo*) 111

Y

yesterday (*exthes*) 630

GREEK INDEX

A

apo (*return*) 152
apodechomai (*gladly received*) 273
apodeixsis (*demonstration*) 173
apodidomi (*render*) 56
apokalupsis (*revealed*) 41, 395, 624, 625
apokalupto (*revealed*) 73
apollumi (*loseth*) 767, 768
apologia (*answer*) 89
apostello (*sent forth*) 886
apotithemi (*put off*) 497, 498
appololos (*lost*) 319
arche (*beginning*) 439
arche (*principalities*) 432
arches (*principles*) 285
archi (*unto*) 212
archon (*prince*) 823
aresko (*pleasing*) 742
arestos (*enjoyable*) 815
arguros (*money*) 460, 484
arguros (*silver*) 61, 68
armos (*joint*) 633
arneo (*denied*) 686
aselgeia (*lasciviousness*) 1122
asphortidzo (*separate*) 97
aspondos (*trucebreakers*) 472
asteras (*stars*) 1030
asthenema (*infirmities*) 1092
astheneo (*diseased*) 363
astheneo (*sick*) 114
astheneo (*weak*) 443
asthenia (*infirmities*) 911
astocheo (*swerved*) 940
astorgos (*without natural affection*) 471
autos (*oneself*) 460
auxano (*increase*) 141, 618, 860

B

ballo (*to throw*) 285, 344, 643
baptidzo (*baptize*) 365
basileuo (*ruler*) 11, 823
basinadzo (*vexed*) 481
basis (*walk*) 308, 521
bebaios (*established*) 249
bema (*judgment seat*) 1040
biaias (*mighty*) 602
blasphemeo (*blasphemers*) 463
blasphemia (*blasphemy*) 1001
blepo (*take heed*) 795
boetheia (*help in time of need*) 690

C

chalepos (*exceeding fierce*) 453, 454
chalepos (*perilous*) 453, 454, 831
chalkolibanos (*bronze*) 265, 266
chalkos (*bronze*) 266
chara (*joyful*) 15
charis (*forgiving*) 389
charis (*grace*) 93, 157, 176, 662, 894, 1108, 1060, 1066, 1156
charisma (*gift*) 662, 894
charistos (*thankful*) 466, 467, 468
cheira (*hand*) 515
chera (*widows*) 611
chortos (*hay*) 69, 72
chreian sou ouk (*no need of you*) 504
chrestos (*kind*) 628, 1143
chrestotes (*kindness*) 693
chrio (*anointed*) 250
chrusos (*gold*) 61, 68, 104, 105

D

daimonian (*demons*) 420, 928
dakruo (*wept*) 263
damonia (*gods*) 407
de (*even*) 901
dei (*must*) 381
dei (*ought*) 912, 1005
deilos (*afraid*) 190
deilos (*fear*) 407
deisidaimonia (*superstitious*) 407

deisis (*supplications*) 613
dia (*through*) 224, 643
diabolos (*devil*) 643, 644
diabolos (*false accusers*) 473
diakoneo (*minister*) 894
diakonia (*minister*) 886
diakonos (*minister*) 783
diakrino (*stagger*) 235
diakrinomai (*doubt*) 508
diallassomai (*reconciled*) 378
dialogismos (*disputings*) 958
didaskalia (*doctrine*) 26
didaskalos (*teaching*) 939
didasko (*teach*) 555, 1137
didomi (*give*) 56, 152, 181
didontos (*giveth*) 181, 182
dielegeto (*dispute*) 404
dikaios (*just*) 27
dikaios (*righteous*) 152
dikaiosune (*righteousness*) 27
dilogos (*double-tongued*) 738
dioko (*follow*) 57, 523, 1071, 1072
dioko (*persecutor*) 1001
dokeo (*seemeth*) 15
dokeo (*thinketh*) 795
dokia (*pleasure*) 957
dokimadzo (*prove*) 668, 669
dokimadzo (*try*) 74, 118, 119
douleuo (*serve*) 278
doulos (*servant*) 1147
doulos (*slave*) 402, 900
doxadzo (*glorify*) 576
dunamis (*might*) 163, 432
dunamis (*miracles*) 111
dunamis (*power*) 34, 173, 344, 345, 358, 640, 945, 981, 1087
dunata (*possible*) 358
dunaton (*possible*) 37, 1084
dusphemeo (*defamed*) 122

E

echidna (*mocked*) 424
echo (*hold*) 672, 1010, 1105
echo (*I have*) 788
echomen (*we have*) 596
echometha (*now I*) 942
echos (*sound*) 601
echthra (*enmity*) 582
egkakeo (*weary*) 48
egkataleipontes (*forsaking*) 238
egkrateia (*temperance*) 346
ei (*if*) 37
eidos (*appearance*) 44
eirene (*peace*) 37, 1072, 1073, 1080
eireneuo (*live peaceably*) 37
eis (*into*) 101, 742
eis allelous (*among yourselves*) 58
eiserchomai (*entered*) 101
eisodon (*entrance*) 742
ek (*from*) 601
ek (*out*) 7, 50, 115, 238, 308, 427, 436, 445, 521, 601, 928
ek tou ourano (*from heaven*) 601
ekbasis (*escape*) 308, 521
ekklesia (*church*) 436,437
eklektos (*elect*) 427,428
ekluo (*faint*) 50
ekpheugo (*fled*) 928
ekporeuomai (*went out*) 115, 116
ekzeteo (*diligently seek*) 445
elegcho (*reprove*) 268, 269, 270, 563, 566
elegmos (*reproof*) 26
empaidzo (*mock*) 840
en (*in*) 48, 346, 634, 680, 779
en (*into*) 640
en (*stand*) 34, 784
en humin (*shall be in you*) 553
en metro (*every part*) 634
en panti (*in everything*) 1108, 1156
en tromos polloo (*much trembling*) 680

G

genos (*countrymen*) 850
ginomai (*be ye*) 1143
ginomai (*there came*) 601
ginomai (*was made*) 1147
ginosko (*know*) 453, 925
ginosko (*perceived*) 998
ginou (*be thou*) 211
gnosis (*knowledge*) 289
gregoreo (*watch*) 157, 1066

H

hagias (*holiness*) 524
hagios (*holy*) 428
halas (*salt*) 228
hamartolos (*sinner*) 316
haplos (*liberally*) 182
hedonos (*pleasure*) 485
hedrios (*steadfast*) 882
hegeomai (*esteem*) 1105
hekastos (*every man*) 73, 893, 894, 948
hemera (*day*) 381
heremia (*wilderness*) 850
heterodidaskalos (*other doctrine*) 939
heteros (*of a different kind*) 939
ho archon (*prince*) 569
homeiromai (*affectionately desirous*) 749, 750
homoioma (*likeness*) 1147
homologia (*confess*) 1159
homothumadon (*one accord*) 1009
homou (*a moment*) 1009
horidzo (*determined*) 843
hosios (*holy*) 855
hoti (*because*) 362
hubristes (*injurious*) 1002
hugiaino (*sound*) 879
humnos (*hymns*) 1120
huper (*above*) 289, 463, 826, 1105
huperano (*above*) 431, 432
huperarche (*authority*) 615
huperballo (*exceeding*) 344, 345
huperecho (*better*) 1105
huperecho (*passeth*) 1080
hupereidon (*winked*) 289, 290
huperentugchano (*intercessions*) 614, 912, 915
huperephanos (*proud*) 463
huperperisseuo (*much more abound*) 369
huperphroneo (*think highly*) 826
hupo (*by*) 1115
hupo (*under*) 137, 197, 333, 336, 387, 621, 950
hupogrammos (*example*) 326, 330
hupomene (*patience*) 137
hupomeno (*endured*) 333, 336
hupomeno (*patience*) 115, 116,197, 621, 950, 951, 977, 978, 979
hupomimnesko (*remembrance*) 557
hupotasso (*submit*) 387
hupotasso (*under*) 434
hustereo (*come behind*) 226

I

iaomai (*healing*) 873, 874
ichnos (*steps*) 330
idios (*due*) 49
ischuos (*I can do*) 640, 641
ischuos (*might*) 784
ischuos (*prevailed*) 927
istemi (*standeth*) 795
isuchadzo (*quiet*) 605

K

kaina (*new*) 1153
kaio (*burn*) 223
kairos (*season*) 49, 876
kairos (*time*) 304, 726, 878
kakologeo (*spake evil*) 1034

kakon anti kakou (*evil for evil*) 57
kakos (*evil*) 48, 56, 779, 942, 1034
kalame (*stubble*) 69, 72
kaleo (*to call*) 123, 238, 374, 436, 540, 853
kalos (*good*) 184, 672, 821
kalos (*honourable*) 943
kalos (*well*) 49
kalupsis (*veil*) 73, 395, 624
kardias (*hearts*) 168, 1081
kartereo (*bear up*) 156
kata (*according*) 723
kata (*against*) 730, 829
kata (*down*) 168, 223, 237, 238, 273, 333, 339, 402, 506, 586, 672, 723, 1124
kata theon (*godly manner*) 131
kataballo (*not laying again*) 285
katakaio (*burned*) 223
katanggelos (*setter forth*) 420
katanusso (*pricked*) 273
katapauo (*cease*) 102
kataphroneo (*despised*) 333, 339
katecho (*hold fast*) 672
kateidoolos (*wholly given to idols*) 402
kateuthuno (*direct*) 168, 169
kathairo (*cleanse*) 889
kathara (*pure*) 608, 889
kathidzo (*sitteth down*) 840
katoikeo (*dwell*) 506
katoikidzo (*dwelleth*) 586
kauchaomai (*glory*) 226
keimai (*established*) 198
kenos (*vain*) 649, 883, 899, 1060
kindunos (*perils*) 850
kludunai (*wave*) 508
koinonia (*fellowship*) 1149
kolakeia (*flattering words*) 745
kollaoo (*clave*) 425
kopiao (*labored*) 1060
kopos (*labour*) 162, 163, 649, 758, 882, 1060
kosmos (*world*) 569
kradzo (*crying*) 551
kratos (*power*) 346
krino (*judged*) 560, 570
krino (*sentence*) 703
kurios (*lord*) 930
kuriotes (*dominions*) 432

L

lambano (*obtain*) 689
lambano (*receive*) 159, 894
lambano (*took upon him*) 900
lanthano (*obsolete*) 2
lego (*I say*) 427
leipo (*lack*) 178, 238
lepton (*mite*) 1129
leuken (*white*) 1068
libanos (*frankincense*) 266
listes (*robbers*) 850
lithos (*stone*) 68, 216, 220, 285, 785
lithous timious (*precious stones*) 68
logidzomai (*reckon*) 205, 647
logos (*communication*) 194
logos (*speech*) 443
logos (*words*) 89, 416, 633, 995, 1034
loidoreo (*reviled*) 334
luchnia (*candlestick*) 259, 260
luchnos (*candle*) 256
luchnos (*candlesticks*) 108
luo (*loosen*) 50
lupe (*grievous*) 15
lupeo (*sorrowful*) 165, 166
lupeo (*sorry*) 130, 131
lupete (*grieve*) 583, 584, 995

M

machaira (*sword*) 322
makros (*long*) 695, 909
makrothumia (*longsuffering*) 695, 909
mallon (*more than*) 486

mamonas (*mammon*) 19, 384
mamphe (*quarrel*) 390
martureo (*testify*) 561
marturia (*report*) 821
marturomai (*charged*) 760
martus (*witness*) 753
mastigos (*plague*) 683, 684
me oneididzontos (*upbraideth not*) 182
mechri (*unto*) 901
mega (*great*) 344
megale (*great*) 60, 61, 298
megethos (*greatness*) 344, 345
meno (*abide*) 137, 197, 219, 333, 336, 621, 950, 1115, 1135, 1062, 1063
merimnao (*thought*) 763, 764
meso (*midst*) 813, 1021
meta (*change*) 277, 637, 729
meta (*to turn*) 290
metadidomi (*impart*) 492, 662, 750
metalambano (*did eat*) 1127
metamelomai (*remorse*) 277, 281, 282
metanoeo (*repent*) 131, 277, 281, 290, 316, 637, 729, 798
metaschimatidzo (*transform*) 990
metro (*part*) 634
miseo (*hate*) 241 240
misthos (*reward*) 220
mneia (*remember*) 398, 792, 795
modios (*bushel*) 257
moichalis (*adultery*) 579
morphe (*form*) 900, 1146

N

naos (*temple*) 311, 312, 594
nekros (*dead*) 205, 646
nemeros (*gentle*) 476
nemoo (*dispense*) 77, 78
nikao (*overcometh*) 772, 773, 903
noema (*minds*) 295, 1081
nomos (*law*) 78, 144, 705
nosios (*holy*) 468
nosos (*diseases*) 114
nous (*mind*) 277, 278, 290, 295, 637, 729
nuktos (*night*) 381
nusso (*puncture*) 273

O

ochlos (*multitude*) 362
odega (*guide*) 572
odon (*road*) 742
oida (*know*) 310, 581, 1021
oida (*see*) 1021, 1022
oikeo (*dwelleth*) 148, 506
oikodome (*edify*) 1073
oikodomeo (*build*) 220
oikodomeo (*edifying*) 195, 489, 1073
oikonomos (*steward*) 77, 78, 144, 705
oikos (*house*) 60, 77, 144, 506, 705, 706
oiktirmos (*mercies*) 691, 692, 693, 1113
oneinidzo (*berate*) 182
oodin (*sorrows*) 439
opheilo (*bound*) 176
opheilo (*ought*) 1092
opheilo (*profitable*) 26
ophis (*serpent*) 708
opiso (*behind*) 3, 1165
orao (*to see*) 289
orges (*wrath*) 1118
orgidzo (*desire*) 1052
orphanos (*comfortless*) 530, 533
orphanos (*fatherless*) 608
orthos (*straight*) 27
ostrakinos (*earth*) 61
ostrakinos (*earthen vessels*) 108, 257, 596
ouk (*hast not*) 685

P

pagideuo (*entangle*) 998
paideia (*chastening*) 14

paideia (*instruction*) 27
pais (*child*) 27
pan (*all*) 640, 660, 995
panta (*all things*) 640, 1084
panta (*all*) 995
panta (*every*) 162
panta noun (*understanding*) 1081
pantachou (*everywhere*) 290
panti (*every man*) 89
panti (*every*) 660, 698
panton (*all*) 38, 93
pantote (*always*) 93, 176
pantote (*ever*) 57
para (*alongside*) 22, 123, 238, 374, 401, 537, 538, 540
para (*of*) 179
para (*with God*) 152
paradidomi (*committed*) 334
parakaleo (*beseech*) 374
parakaleo (*exhorting*) 238, 760
parakaleo (*intreat*) 123
paraklesis (*comfort*) 489, 1113
parakletos (*comforter*) 537, 538, 540, 543, 553
paramutheomai (*comforted*) 760
parangello (*command*) 290
parathou (*commit*) 22
paristemi (*present*) 375
paron (*present*) 15
parousia tou somatos (*bodily presence*) 443
paroxuneto (*stirred*) 401
parresia (*bold*) 192, 688
pas (*all*) 431, 432
pascho (*suffered*) 325
pateo (*walk*) 301
peiradzo (*examine*) 656
peiradzo (*tried*) 717
peirasmos (*temptation*) 307
peitho (*confident*) 192, 495, 963, 1163
peitho (*persuade*) 464
pempo (*sent*) 381
penichros (*poor*) 1129
peri (*about*) 93, 301
peri (*around*) 166, 889
perikatharma (*filth of the world*) 889
perilupeo (*exceedingly sorrowful*) 166
peripateo (*walk*) 301, 302
peripsema (*offscouring*) 890
perisseuo (*abounds*) 369
perisseuo (*abundance*) 953, 1130
perissos (*abundantly*) 1060
phaneros (*manifest*) 73
phanos (*to be manifested*) 463
phaulos (*evil*) 1048
phero (*carried*) 602
phero (*go on*) 286
pheromones (*rushing*) 602
pheugete (*flee*) 651
pheugo (*flee*) 135, 928
philadelphos (*brotherly love*) 484
philanthropia (*love for humanity*) 484
philarguria (*love of money*) 484
philarguros (*covetous*) 460
philautos (*lovers of their own selves*) 459, 460
phileo (*affection*) 581
phileo (*to love*) 459, 460, 484
philia (*friendship*) 581
philodonos (*lovers of pleasure*) 483, 484, 485
philosophia (*love of wisdom*) 484
philostorgos (*love for family*) 484
philotheoi (*lovers of God*) 486
philotimeomai (*study*) 604, 605
philoxenos (*love for strangers*) 484
phobos (*fear*) 930
phoneo (*to make a sound*) 518
phren (*mind*) 187
phroneo (*set*) 187, 1100
phroneo (*think*) 333, 339, 826
phronos (*mind*) 694
phroureo (*guard*) 1081
phthonos (*envy*) 591

R

S

T

X

Z

SCRIPTURE INDEX

KEY:

Bold font = main text
Regular font = secondary reference

BIBLIOGRAPHY

Alford, Henry. *Greek Testament Critical Exegetical Commentary*. Volume IV. Boston: Lee & Shepard, 1878.

Bacon, David Francis. *Lives of the Apostles of Jesus Christ*. New Haven: L. H. Young, 1836.

Barclay, William. *The Letters to the Corinthians*. Philadelphia: Westminster Press, 1975.

Barnes, Albert. *Notes on the Bible*. London: Blackie & Son, 1884-85. Reprinted by Baker Books, 1996.

Cleveland, Charles Dexter. *A Compendium of Grecian Antiquities*. Boston: Hilliard, Gray, Little, and Wilkins, 1831.

Elliott, Charlotte. "Just As I Am." *The Christian Remembrancer Pocket Book Poetry*, 1835.

Josephus, Flavius. *Antiquities of the Jews*. IV.VI.2.

Ovid. *Metamorphoses*. XV. 41.

Philo. *De Vita Moysis*. I.48.

Renner, Denise. *Redeemed From Shame*. Tulsa, OK: Harrison House, 2004.

Rogers, Cleon L., Jr. and Cleon L. Rogers III, *The New Linguistic and Exegetical Key to the Greek New Testament*. Grand Rapids. MI: Zondervan Publishing House, 1998.

Stearns Davis, William. *A Day in Old Athens: A Picture of Athenian Life*. Needham Heights. MA: Allyn & Bacon, 1914.

Vegetius Renatus, Publius Flavius. *Concerning Military Matters (De Re Militari)*. Book I.

Verbrugge, Verlyn D. *New International Dictionary of New Testament Theology: Abridged Edition*. Grand Rapids, MI: Zondervan Publishing House, 2000.

STUDY REFERENCE BOOK LIST

1. *How To Use New Testament Greek Study Aids* by Walter Jerry Clark (Loizeaux Brothers).
2. *Strong's Exhaustive Concordance of the Bible* by James H. Strong.
3. *The Interlinear Greek-English New Testament* by George Ricker Berry (Baker Book House).
4. *The Englishman's Greek Concordance of the New Testament* by George Wigram (Hendrickson).
5. *New Thayer's Greek-English Lexicon of the New Testament* by Joseph Thayer (Hendrickson).
6. *The Expanded Vine's Expository Dictionary of New Testament Words* by W. E. Vine (Bethany).
7. *New International Dictionary of New Testament Theology* (DNTT); Colin Brown, ed. (Zondervan).
8. *Theological Dictionary of the New Testament* (TDNT) by Geoffrey Bromiley; Gephard Kittle, ed. (Eerdmans).
9. *The New Analytical Greek Lexicon*; Wesley Perschbacher, ed. (Hendrickson).
10. *The Linguistic Key to the Greek New Testament* by Fritz Rienecker and Cleon Rogers (Zondervan).
11. *Word Studies in the Greek New Testament* by Kenneth Wuest, 4 Volumes (Eerdmans).
12. *New Testament Words* by William Barclay (Westminster Press).
13. *Word Meanings* by Ralph Earle (Hendrickson).
14. *International Critical Commentary Series* by J. A. Emerton, C. E. B. Cranfield, and G. N. Stanton, eds. (T. & T. Clark International).
15. *Vincent's Word Studies of the New Testament* by Marvin R. Vincent, 4 Volumes (Hendrickson).
16. *New International Dictionary of New Testament Theology* by Verlyn D. Verbrugge (Zondervan).

ABOUT THE AUTHOR

RICK RENNER is a highly respected Bible teacher and leader in the international Christian community. Rick is the author of a long list of books, including the bestsellers *Dressed To Kill* and *Sparkling Gems From the Greek 1* and *2*, which have sold millions of copies in multiple languages worldwide. Rick's understanding of the Greek language and biblical history opens up the Scriptures in a unique way that enables readers to gain wisdom and insight while learning something brand new from the Word of God.

Rick is the founding pastor of the Moscow Good News Church. He also founded Media Mir, the first Christian television network in the former USSR that broadcasts the Gospel to countless Russian-speaking viewers around the world via multiple satellites and the Internet. He is the founder and president of RENNER Ministries, based in Tulsa, Oklahoma, and host to his TV program that is seen around the world in multiple languages. Rick leads this amazing work with his wife and lifelong ministry partner, Denise, along with the help of their sons and committed leadership team.

CONTACT RENNER MINISTRIES

For further information
about RENNER Ministries, please contact
the RENNER Ministries office nearest you
or visit the ministry website at
www.renner.org.

ALL USA CORRESPONDENCE:
RENNER Ministries
P. O. Box 702040
Tulsa, OK 74170-2040
(918) 496-3213
Or 1-800-RICK-593
Email: renner@renner.org
Website: www.renner.org

MOSCOW OFFICE:
RENNER Ministries
P. O. Box 789
101000, Russia, Moscow
+7 (495) 727-14-67
Email: blagayavestonline@ignc.org
Website: www.ignc.org

RIGA OFFICE:
RENNER Ministries
Unijas 99
Riga LV-1084, Latvia
+371 67802150
Email: info@goodnews.lv

KIEV OFFICE:
RENNER Ministries
P. O. Box 300
01001, Ukraine, Kiev
+38 (044) 451-8315
Email: blagayavestonline@ignc.org

OXFORD OFFICE:
RENNER Ministries
Box 7, 266 Banbury Road
Oxford OX2 7DL, England
+44 (0) 1865 355509
Email: europe@renner.org

BOOKS BY RICK RENNER

Chosen by God
Dream Thieves*
Dressed To Kill*
The Holy Spirit and You*
How To Keep Your Head on Straight in a World Gone Crazy
How To Receive Answers From Heaven!*
Insights to Successful Leadership
Life in the Combat Zone*
A Light in Darkness, Volume One,
  Seven Messages to the Seven Churches series
The Love Test*
No Room for Compromise, Volume Two,
  Seven Messages to the Seven Churches series
Paid in Full*
The Point of No Return*
Repentance*
Signs You'll See Just Before Jesus Comes*
Sparkling Gems From the Greek Daily Devotional 1*
Sparkling Gems From the Greek Daily Devotional 2*
Spiritual Weapons To Defeat the Enemy*
Ten Guidelines To Help You Achieve Your Long-Awaited Promotion!*
Turn Your God-Given Dreams Into Reality*
Why We Need the Gifts of the Spirit*
The Will of God — The Key to Your Success*
You Can Get Over It*

*Digital version available for Kindle, Nook, and iBook.
Note: Books by Rick Renner are available for purchase at:
www.renner.org

SPARKLING GEMS FROM THE GREEK 1

365 Greek Word Studies for Every Day of the Year
To Sharpen Your Understanding of God's Word

1,048 pages
(Hardback)

Rick Renner's ***Sparkling Gems From the Greek 1*** has quickly gained widespread recognition for its unique illumination of the New Testament through more than 1,000 Greek word studies in a 365-day devotional format. Today *Sparkling Gems 1* remains a beloved resource that has spiritually strengthened believers worldwide. As many have testified, the wealth of truths within its pages never grows old. Year after year, *Sparkling Gems 1* continues to deepen readers' understanding of the Bible.

WHO STOLE CINDERELLA?

The Art of 'Happily Ever After'

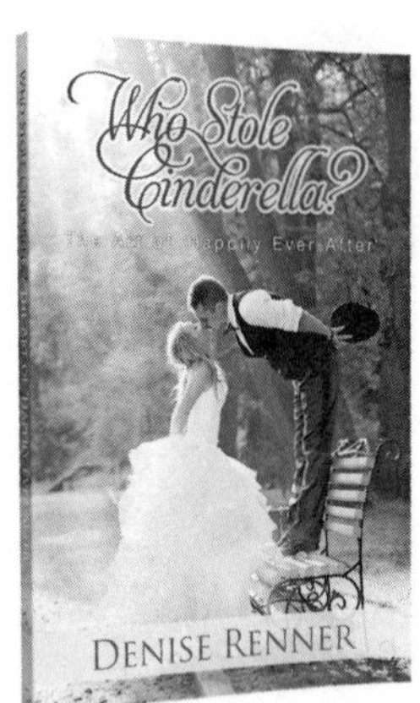

192 pages
(Paperback)

In ***Who Stole Cinderella?***, Denise Renner shows why "happily ever after" is not a gift for a selected few, but rather an art that anyone can master who is willing to learn. With genuine warmth and candor, Denise recounts the journey of her own struggles in marriage and the unique insights she learned along the way to attaining emotional health and happiness. Your life will be enriched by the biblical wisdom Denise imparts and the originality with which she sheds light on your path to *happily ever after* and shows you right where to begin again if you've lost your way.

Even if the clock shows "past midnight" in your marriage, don't give up on your dream of experiencing a happy ending. Cinderella and Prince Charming are not lost — they just need to be rediscovered *God's way*!

To order, visit us online at: **www.renner.org**
Book Resellers: Contact Harrison House at 800-722-6774
or visit **www.HarrisonHouse.com** for quantity discounts.

A LIGHT IN DARKNESS

VOLUME ONE

Step into the world of the First Century Church as Rick Renner creates a panoramic experience of unsurpassed detail to transport you into the ancient lands of the seven churches of Asia. Within the context of this fascinating — and, at times, shocking — historical backdrop, Rick outlines the challenges that early believers faced in taking the Gospel to a pagan world. After presenting a riveting account of the apostle John's vision of the exalted Christ, Rick leads you through an in-depth study of Jesus' messages to the churches of Ephesus and Smyrna — profoundly relevant and urgent messages for the daunting challenges of the Church today.

This volume contains:

- In-depth scriptural teaching that makes the New Testament come alive.
- A more than 800-page beautifully designed, full-color hardback book — filled with photos shot on location, plus photos of classic artwork, artifacts, *and much more.*
- A comprehensive, completely indexed reference book.

This volume will speak to generations to come. An authoritative "encyclopedia" of knowledge, this book is a definitive go-to resource for any student of the Bible, and a classic must-have for Christians everywhere.

NO ROOM FOR COMPROMISE

VOLUME TWO

No Room for Compromise: Jesus' Message to Today's Church is Volume Two of the *Seven Messages to the Seven Churches* series. It presents an engaging exploration of the pagan culture surrounding the First Century Church, with an emphasis on the city of Pergamum. In this volume, Rick highlights Jesus' message to the church there when the exalted Christ appeared to the apostle John on the island of Patmos.

Providing superb photographs, many of which were shot on location in Turkey, Rick guides readers through a fascinating, detailed explanation of Jesus' message to the Pergamene church as Rick prophetically declares the critical significance of this message to the Church in these last days before Jesus returns. Rick also takes readers through a revealing overview of the first three centuries AD in which the infant Church grew amidst severe opposition — demonstrating that darkness can never overcome the light, life, and power that Jesus Christ offers all those who believe.

This comprehensive, completely indexed reference book includes:

- In-depth scriptural teaching that makes the New Testament come alive
- Over 400 pages, including 330 beautifully designed, full-color pages
- Nearly 400 images of historical sites, classic artwork, artifacts, and more

DRESSED TO KILL

A Biblical Approach to Spiritual Warfare and Armor

Rick Renner's ***Dressed To Kill*** is considered by many to be a true classic on the subject of spiritual warfare. This book, which has sold hundreds of thousands of copies, is a curriculum staple in Bible schools worldwide. In this beautiful volume, you will find:

- 504 pages of text with 16 pages of full-color illustrations
- An exacting guide to the purpose and function of each piece of ancient Roman armor
- Questions in each chapter to guide you into deeper study

In this book, Rick uses Paul's inspired description of Roman armor to explain the significance of our *spiritual* armor not only to withstand the onslaughts of the enemy, but also to overturn the tendencies of the carnal mind. Furthermore, Rick delivers a clear, scriptural presentation on the biblical definition of spiritual warfare — what it is and what it is *not.*

Armed with the knowledge of who you are in Christ, you will be dangerous to the works of darkness, unflinching in the face of conflict, and equipped to take the offensive and gain mastery over any opposition from your spiritual foe. You don't have to accept defeat anymore once you are *dressed to kill*!

LIFE IN THE COMBAT ZONE

How To Survive, Thrive, and Overcome in the Midst of Difficult Situations

The battle lines are drawn. A collision course is set. In the coming battle, will you rush to the front lines or shrink from the conflict? Although the risk is great, the rewards for engaging in the fight are sure.

In ***Life in the Combat Zone***, author Rick Renner encourages you to *fight* like a Roman soldier, *train* like a Greek athlete, and *work* like a farmer — all to become that unwavering warrior who hears God's voice, surrenders to His call, and willingly enters the combat zone poised to win.

Spiritual conflicts are unavoidable. There are no shortcuts to victory, but there *can* be an inevitable outcome. Rick will help you discover the key qualities you'll need to withstand the heat of the battle so you can emerge triumphant and receive the victor's crown.

THE WILL OF GOD — THE KEY TO YOUR SUCCESS

Positioning Yourself To Live in God's Supernatural Power, Provision, and Protection

A faith-filled adventure awaits you as you step out to do what God is beckoning you to do. It may seem daunting at first, but once the journey begins, you'll never regret that you left your comfort zone to follow His leading! But as you step out in faith, it's essential that you stay on track with God's plan if you want to experience His power, protection, and supernatural provision.

Rick writes: "If you are seeking to know the will of God for your life, I believe this is a book that you will find very helpful in your journey of faith. It is important for you to understand that *knowing* the will of God and actually being *in* it are two very different things. Many know God's will, but they struggle to comply with what He has revealed about the path He has ordained for them to walk in."

Get ready for an eye-opening undertaking as Rick delves into the journey of the apostle Paul and other key Bible characters as they sought to walk out God's will for their lives. In their fascinating journeys, Rick reveals vital lessons to help you in your own pursuit to fully align with God's will for your life — which is the key to your success!

THE HOLY SPIRIT AND YOU!

Working Together as Heaven's 'Dynamic Duo'

There is a *secret place.* A *partnership of power.* A *place of peace.* A *wellspring of living water* that enriches your life. This hidden fortress is accessed when your spirit is in constant fellowship with the Holy Spirit. Together you are truly a dynamic duo!

The Holy Spirit dwells within you, and His purpose in your life includes equipping you with exactly *what* you need, *when* you need it. If He drops a thought into your mind to do something, it will work if you'll obey it.

The Holy Spirit was the key to Jesus' ministerial success. And He is God's gift to you for *your* life's journey!

To order, visit us online at: **www.renner.org**
Book Resellers: Contact Harrison House at 800-722-6774
or visit **www.HarrisonHouse.com** for quantity discounts.

CHOSEN BY GOD

GOD HAS CHOSEN *YOU* FOR A DIVINE ASSIGNMENT — WILL YOU DARE TO FULFILL IT?

Rick's book ***Chosen by God*** will help you overcome your limited thinking about following God's plan for your life. Rest assured, God has a plan! And He will thoroughly prepare you to fulfill it if you'll say yes with all your heart and stir yourself to pursue it. God is calling you to do something significant in the earth for Him. What's holding you back? This book will thrill you with the possibilities that await because you are *chosen by God*!

SIGNS YOU'LL SEE JUST BEFORE JESUS COMES

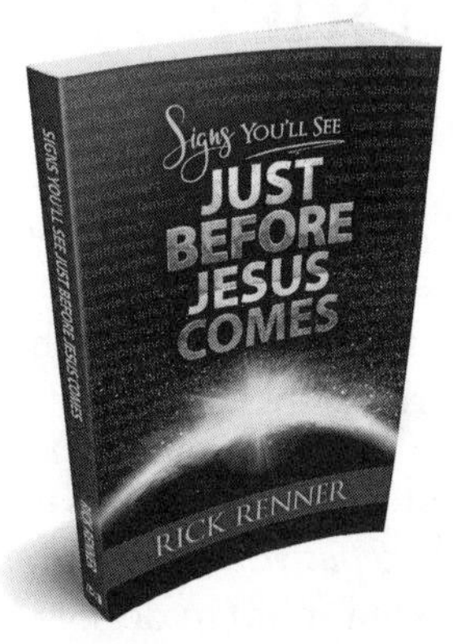

As we advance toward the golden moment of Christ's return for His Church, there are signs on the road we're traveling to let us know where we are in time. Jesus Himself foretold the types of events that will surely take place as we watch for His return.

In his book ***Signs You'll See Just Before Jesus Comes***, Rick Renner explores the signs in Matthew 24:3-12, expounding on each one from the Greek text with his unique style of teaching. Each chapter is written to prepare and embolden a last-days generation of believers, not send them running for the hills!

The signs on the road are appearing closer together. We are on the precipice of something new. Soon we'll see the final sign at the edge of our destination as we enter the territory of the last days, hours, and minutes *just before Jesus comes.*

HOW TO KEEP YOUR HEAD ON STRAIGHT IN A WORLD GONE CRAZY

400 page
(Paperback)

The world is changing. In fact, it's more than changing — it has *gone crazy.*

We are living in a world where faith is questioned and sin is welcomed — where people seem to have lost their minds about what is right and wrong. It seems truth has been turned *upside down.*

In Rick Renner's new book ***How To Keep Your Head on Straight in a World Gone Crazy***, he reveals the disastrous consequences of a society in spiritual and moral collapse. In this book, you'll discover what Christians need to be doing to stay out of the chaos and remain anchored to truth. You'll learn how to stay sensitive to the Holy Spirit, discern right and wrong teaching, how to be grounded in prayer, and how to be spiritually prepared for living in victory in these last days.

Leading ministers from around the world are calling this book essential for every believer. Topics include:

- Contending for the Faith in the Last Days
- How To Pray for Leaders Who Are in Error
- How To Judge if a Teaching Is Good or Bad
- Seducing Spirits and Doctrines of Demons
- How To Be a Good Minister of Jesus Christ

To order, visit us online at: **www.renner.org**
Book Resellers: Contact Harrison House at 800-722-6774
or visit **www.HarrisonHouse.com** for quantity discounts.

Harrison House

The Harrison House Vision

Proclaiming the truth and the power
of the Gospel of Jesus Christ with excellence.
Challenging Christians
to live victoriously,
grow spiritually,
know God intimately.

STUDY NOTES

STUDY NOTES

STUDY NOTES

STUDY NOTES

STUDY NOTES

STUDY NOTES

STUDY NOTES

STUDY NOTES

STUDY NOTES

STUDY NOTES

STUDY NOTES

STUDY NOTES

STUDY NOTES

STUDY NOTES

STUDY NOTES

STUDY NOTES

STUDY NOTES

STUDY NOTES

STUDY NOTES